INTRODUCTION TO PSYCHOLOGY

EIGHTH EDITION

RITA L. ATKINSON

RICHARD C. ATKINSON
University of California, San Diego

ERNEST R. HILGARD
Stanford University

HARCOURT BRACE JOVANOVICH, PUBLISHERS
San Diego   New York   Chicago   Washington, D.C.   Atlanta
London   Sydney   Toronto

ISBN: 0-15-543677-5

Library of Congress Catalog Card Number: 82-82436

Printed in the United States of America

ACKNOWLEDGMENTS AND COPYRIGHTS

COVER: Painting by Alexei Jawlensky, "Sounds of Winter" 1927,
courtesy The Blue Four Galka Scheyer Collection, Norton Simon
Museum, Pasadena, California.

New technical art: Jeanne Mulderig

Text, figure, and picture credits appear on pages 681–86, which constitute a continuation of the copyright page.

INTRODUCTION TO
PSYCHOLOGY

EIGHTH EDITION

PREFACE

There is an old story concerning a peasant woman whose shawl kept unraveling at one end, and who kept knitting on an equivalent amount at the other end. After all the material had changed, was it the same shawl? A similar question may be asked of a textbook going into its eighth edition, with each edition thoroughly revised. Is it still the same textbook? The reply in each case is a conditional "yes," because both shawl and book serve the same purposes today that they served in the past. There is continuity in the midst of change. The purpose of this book has always been to introduce contemporary psychology to the beginning student, in full recognition that between editions both psychology and students change. As a simple measure of the amount of change that occurs in psychology, we note that about 40 percent of the references are new to this edition.

Students take introductory psychology for a variety of reasons, but few of them are motivated by the desire to know what psychologists are doing. Most students are concerned with what is relevant to their lives and their futures and with the problems confronting society. As in previous editions, we have attempted to write for the student but in a manner that will satisfy the critical psychologist as well. Our goal has been to be responsive to student interests without sacrificing scientific rigor or scholarship.

To accomplish this goal, we have relied on consultation and feedback from three sources—students, instructors, and specialists in various areas of psychology. To make certain our subject matter was readily comprehensible to students and pertinent to the human issues with which they are concerned, we asked a number of students to comment on each section of the manuscript in terms of interest value, clarity, and level of difficulty. Their responses were helpful and enlightening.

Several college instructors who specialize in teaching the introductory course read the manuscript as it evolved, commenting on its suitability for their students and on any problems they foresaw in teaching the material to beginning psychology students. We also benefited from the many comments and suggestions we received from users of previous editions.

To keep abreast of developments in psychological theory and research, we asked experts to review each chapter. Typically, several specialists commented on each chapter in the early stages of revision and in its final form. By such consultation, we sought to ensure that the material represents accurately the current state of knowledge in psychology.

We have tried to cover contemporary psychology in a textbook of reasonable length. But each instructor must design his or her course according to course objectives, type of students, and available time. Even if all chapters are not assigned, students will at least have them for reference. For a short course, we believe that it is better to treat fewer chapters fully than to cover the entire text. Two possible 14-chapter courses are proposed below—one for a course with an experimental–biological emphasis; the other for a course with a personal–social emphasis. These outlines only illustrate possible combinations, however.

CHAPTER	EXPERIMENTAL–BIOLOGICAL EMPHASIS	PERSONAL–SOCIAL EMPHASIS
Nature of Psychology	1	1
Neurobiological Basis of Psychology	2	—
Psychological Development	3	3
Sensory Processes	4	—
Perception	5	5
States of Consciousness	6	6
Learning	7	7
Memory	8	8
Language and Thought	9	—
Basic Drives and Motives	10	—
Motivation and Emotion	—	11
Mental Abilities and Their Measurement	12	12
Personality and Its Assessment	13	13
Conflict and Stress	14	14
Abnormal Psychology	—	15
Methods of Therapy	—	16
Individual Social Behavior	17	17
Social Influence	—	18

The order of chapters can be changed. For example, some instructors feel that student interest can be better aroused by beginning the course with material on personality, abnormal, and social psychology while leaving more experimental topics such as memory, perception, and physiological psychology until later. The authors have tried this approach but have not found it satisfactory. Beginning with the more personally relevant and intriguing topics may get the course off to a fast start, but it often gives the students a distorted idea of what psychology is about. In addition, many students are ill prepared for, and disgruntled by, the more difficult experimental material when it is sprung on them later in the course. Our preferred approach is to cover the chapter on developmental psychology early in the course, thereby exposing students to a range of provocative topics in psychology. Then we turn to the more technical areas like perception, memory, and motivation, and end the course with personality, abnormal, and social psychology. But each instructor must choose the order of topics he or she finds congenial; the book has been written so that a variety of arrangements is possible.

The many decisions that must be made in teaching the introductory psychology course are discussed in the *Instructor's Handbook*. Instructors are urged to obtain a copy of this handbook, which is useful for both beginning and experienced instructors, as well as for teaching assistants. As further instructional aids, we have again provided a thoroughly revised *Study Guide* for students and an expanded set of test items.

We are again pleased to include the contributions of our former colleagues at Stanford University, Edward E. Smith and Daryl J. Bem. Professor Smith, who is now at Bolt, Beranek, and Newman, Inc., and Harvard University, was responsible for Chapter 8 (Memory) and Chapter 9 (Language and Thought). Professor Bem, now at Cornell University, has reorganized his two chapters on social psychology. Chapter 17 (Individual Social Behavior) is concerned with how people process social information; Chapter 18 (Social Influence) focuses on group and environmental influences on behavior. These chapters, from two outstanding scientists and teachers, add immeasurably to the quality of this book.

Among the individuals acknowledged on pages ix–xii, we owe special thanks to John Foley, University of California, Santa Barbara, for his contributions to Chapters 4 and 5, and to Edmund Fantino, University of California, San Diego, for his contributions to Chapter 7.

RITA L. ATKINSON
RICHARD C. ATKINSON
ERNEST R. HILGARD

ACKNOWLEDGMENTS

Over the years we have been helped immeasurably by countless people who have shared with us their scholarly and pedagogical expertise. It is impossible to thank them all individually, but they have our continuing gratitude.

A number of professors teaching introductory psychology offered us invaluable chapter-by-chapter comments on the seventh edition as inputs for our planning of the eighth edition:

Douglas W. Atwood, Southeast Missouri State University

Raymond Baird, University of Texas—San Antonio

Elizabeth Barton, Southeast Missouri State University

Don E. Batten, Lewis and Clark College

Raymond M. Bragiel, Franklin College

Martin Brown, Montclair State College

David Burrows, Skidmore College

William H. Calhoun, University of Tennessee at Knoxville

Nicholas J. Cavoti, Washington and Jefferson College

André Cedras, Macomb County Community College

James P. Chaplin, St. Michael's College

R.J. Christman, Utica College

Robert A. Cicerone, Montclair State College

Lowell W. Coutant, Eastern Oregon State College

Donna F. Cruse, Oregon State University

Suzanne Davis, Westfield State College

Peter J. Donovick, State University of New York, Binghamton

Donald D. Dorfman, University of Iowa

Vern Dorschner, Brainerd Community College

Karen G. Duffy, State University of New York, Geneseo

Janis L. Dunlap, Tulane University

Louis L. Elloie, Jr., San Diego Mesa College

V.P. Estes, Jr., San Antonio College

Frank T. Etscorn, New Mexico Institute of Mining and Technology

Philippe Falkenberg, Wake Forest University

Michael S. Fanselow, Rensselaer Polytechnic Institute

Karen B. Feniello, Washington and Jefferson College

Edna Fiedler, St. Mary's University

Helen L. Field, Holyoke Community College

William F. Ford, Bucks County Community College

David Gerbing, Baylor University

L.I. Gerstman, Erie Community College

Zulfiqar H. Gilani, William Paterson College

Seymour Giniger, Baruch College, City University of New York

Carlos Goldberg, Indiana University—Purdue University at Indianapolis

Charles Graessle, Olivet College

Judith Green, William Paterson College

R. Lee Greene, Grossmont College

Larry Gregory, New Mexico State University

Andrew Harver, Ohio University

John C. Hay, University of Wisconsin–Milwaukee

M.A. Hering, Henry Ford Community College; University of Michigan—Dearborn; Wayne County Community College

Steve Hinkle, Miami University

Morton Hoffman, Metropolitan State College

W.G. Hughes, U.S. Naval Academy

George Janzen, Ferris State College

Michael C. Kaufman, City Colleges of Chicago—Richard J. Daley College

John P. Keith, Clark County Community College

Khalil Akhtar Khavari, University of Wisconsin—Milwaukee

Richard K. Kimball, Muhlenberg College

David W. King, Howard Payne University

Melvyn B. King, State University of New York at Cortland

David L. Kohfeld, Southern Illinois University at Edwardsville

Ronald L. Koteskey, Asbury College

Kenneth Kotovsky, Community College of Allegheny County

Shari Kuchenbecker, Chapman College

Hella Lange, Normandale Community College

Michael R. Leippe, St. Norbert College

Keith J. Lindsay, Angelo State University

Emma Lou Linn, St. Edwards University

Thomas F. Lohr, Muhlenberg College

Lola Lopes, University of Wisconsin—Madison

Katherine A. Loveland, Rice University

Geula Lowenberg, University of Wisconsin—Parkside

Frances Lucas, Albion College

Gary A. Lucas, Indiana University

Ruth G. Lyell, San José State University

H.L. Madison, University of Wisconsin—Milwaukee

William A. Mahler, Ferris State College

Steven F. Maier, University of Colorado at Boulder

Theodore Maiser, Muhlenberg College

Richard G. Marriott, Lamar University

Dorothy L. Mattson, Lakewood Community College

Loren K. McBride, Willamette University

Michael McBride, Gonzaga University

Warren McClintock, West Hills College

Rick McNeese, Sam Houston State University

Ken Merrifield, Grand Canyon College

Ralph R. Miller, State University of New York at Binghamton

Rowland S. Miller, Sam Houston State University

James C. Mitchell, Kansas State University

Alberto Montare, William Paterson College

Maribel Montgomery, Linn-Benton Community College

James R. Moore, Prairie State College

Gerald Moverman, Community College of Rhode Island

Jeffrey Nagelbush, Ferris State College

Gary B. Nallan, Benedictine College

William Newman, Lehigh University

Teri L. Nicoll-Johnson, Modesto Junior College

Patricia Owen, Southeast Missouri State University

Joseph J. Palladino, St. Francis College

Edward J. Pavur, Jr., University of New Orleans

Thomas P. Petzel, Loyola University

Richard Pisacreta, Ferris State College

Terry Pruitt, David Lipscomb College

G. Ray Reglin, Mid-America Nazarene College

D.B. Reutener, Smith College

Samuel Roll, University of New Mexico

Douglas A. Ross, Indiana University of Pennsylvania

Stephen Royce, University of Portland

Timothy Schallert, University of Texas at Austin

Lowell Schipper, Bowling Green State University

David J. Schneider, University of Texas at San Antonio

Alan Searleman, St. Lawrence University

P. Selkow, William Paterson College

Alice Sheppard, Eastern Oregon State College

Charlotte Simon, Montgomery College

Lora S. Simon, Holyoke Community College

William P. Smotherman, Oregon State University

George R. Soika, University of Wisconsin—Oshkosh

K.W. Steere, Manchester Community College

Gwendolyn Stevens, Southeast Missouri State University

Dee Stroub, Truckee Meadows Community College

Robert Sturgeon, Abilene Christian University

Elizabeth V. Swenson, John Carroll University

Anthony J. Testa, Community College of Rhode Island

Stephen Truhon, Valparaiso University

Barbara Tversky, Stanford University

Vern Tyler, Western Washington University

Martha H. Tyson, University of Houston—Downtown College

William S. Verplanck, University of Tennessee—Knoxville

David Volckmann, Whittier College

Phyllis A. Walrad, Macomb County Community College

Wilson J. Walthall, Jr., University of Wyoming

Malcolm W. Watson, Brandeis University

Chris Wickers, University of Illinois

Kipling D. Williams, Drake University

Elaine Hauff Wilson, Minneapolis Community College

Larry Wise, Mt. Hood Community College

Steven Zecker, Hamilton College

Shea Zellweger, Mount Vernon College

Claire Zimmerman, Wellesley College

Rudolph L. Zlody, Holy Cross College

Critical and technical reviews of various aspects of the book (in some cases, chapters; in others, parts or sections) were generously provided by the following people:

Lynn L. Atkinson, Medical College of Virginia

Albert Bandura, Stanford University

Ellen S. Berscheid, University of Minnesota

Thomas J. Bouchard, Jr., University of Minnesota

Gordon H. Bower, Stanford University

Robert M. Boynton, University of California, San Diego

Nancy S. Breland, Trenton State College

Rae Carlson, Rutgers University

Eve V. Clark, Stanford University

Herbert H. Clark, Stanford University

Frank Costin, University of Illinois at Urbana—Champaign

Ian N. Creese, University of California, San Diego

Gerald C. Davison, University of Southern California

David M. Drucker, Medical College of Virginia

Edmund Fantino, University of California, San Diego

John Foley, University of California, Santa Barbara

Merrill F. Garrett, Massachusetts Institute of Technology

Kenneth J. Gergen, Swarthmore College

Richard Griggs, University of Florida

Ronald Growney, University of Connecticut

Patrick R. Harrison, U.S. Naval Academy

Steven A. Hillyard, University of California, San Diego

Keith W. Jacobs, Loyola University in New Orleans

Walter Kintsch, University of Colorado

Ellen M. Markman, Stanford University

Gerald Murch, Portland State University

Ulric Neisser, Cornell University

Leon H. Rappoport, Kansas State University

Joseph Rychlak, Purdue University

Sandra Scarr, Yale University

Evalyn Segal, San Diego State University

Jerome L. Singer, Yale University

Richard L. Solomon, University of Pennsylvania

Albert J. Stunkard, University of Pennsylvania

Carl E. Thoresen, Stanford University

Barbara Tversky, Stanford University

Richard A. Weinberg, University of Minnesota

Christopher D. Wickens, University of Illinois at Urbana—Champaign

Jeffrey Wine, Stanford University

CONTENTS

Part one

PSYCHOLOGY AS A SCIENTIFIC AND HUMAN ENDEAVOR

Part two

BIOLOGICAL
AND DEVELOPMENTAL PROCESSES

Part three

PERCEPTION
AND CONSCIOUSNESS

6 STATES OF CONSCIOUSNESS   164

Part four
LEARNING, REMEMBERING, AND THINKING

7 LEARNING   192

8 MEMORY   220

by Edward E. Smith
Bolt, Beranek, and Newman, Inc., and Harvard University

9 LANGUAGE AND THOUGHT   252

by Edward E. Smith
Bolt, Beranek, and Newman, Inc., and Harvard University

Part five
MOTIVATION AND EMOTION

Part six
PERSONALITY AND INDIVIDUALITY

Part seven

CONFLICT, ADJUSTMENT, AND MENTAL HEALTH

Part eight
SOCIAL BEHAVIOR

INTRODUCTION TO
PSYCHOLOGY

EIGHTH EDITION

Part one
PSYCHOLOGY AS A SCIENTIFIC AND HUMAN ENDEAVOR

1 / Nature of Psychology

1
NATURE
OF PSYCHOLOGY

Psychology touches almost every aspect of our lives. As society has become more complex, psychology has assumed an increasingly important role in solving human problems. Psychologists are concerned with an astonishing variety of problems. Some are of broad concern. What child-rearing methods produce happy and effective adults? How can mental illness be prevented? What can be done to eliminate race prejudice? What family and social conditions contribute to alienation, aggression, and crime?

Other problems are more specific. What is the best treatment for smoking or obesity? Can men care for infants as ably as women? To what extent are political surveys self-fulfilling prophecies? How should the instruments in an air-traffic control tower be arranged to minimize controller errors? How can one help a terminally ill person achieve a peaceful death? How effective is psychotherapy in the treatment of alcoholism? Can memory be improved by the use of drugs that facilitate neural transmission? Psychologists are working on these and many other questions.

Psychology also affects our lives through its influence on laws and public policy. Laws concerning discrimination, capital punishment, pornography, sexual behavior, and the conditions under which individuals may be held legally responsible for their actions are influenced by psychological theories and research. For example, laws pertaining to sexual deviancy have changed markedly in the past 30 years as research has shown that many sexual acts previously classed as perversions are "normal" in the sense that most people engage in them.

The effect of TV violence on children is of concern to parents and psychologists. Only after studies provided evidence of the harmful effects of such programs has it been possible to modify TV programming policies. More brutal TV fare is gradually being replaced with shows of other kinds. Some follow the model of *Sesame Street* and *The Electric Company*, which represent concerted efforts by psychologists and educators to make learning interesting, fun, and effective.

Because psychology affects so many aspects of our lives, it is important, even for those who do not intend to specialize in the field, to know something about its basic facts and research methods. An introductory course in psychology should give you a better understanding of why people behave as they do and should provide insights into your own attitudes and reactions. It should also help you evaluate the many claims made in the name of psychology. Everyone has seen headlines like these:

- Experiences during infancy determine adult intelligence
- New drug discovered to improve memory
- Anxiety controlled by self-regulation of brain waves
- Proof of mental telepathy found
- Psychologist devises method for curing impotency
- Violent crimes related to defective genes
- Emotional stability and family size closely related
- Homosexuality linked to parental attitudes

How can you judge the validity of such claims? In part, by knowing what psychological facts have been firmly established and by being familiar with the kind of evidence necessary to give credence to a new "discovery." This book reviews the current state of knowledge in psychology. It also examines the nature of research—how a psychologist formulates a hypothesis and designs a procedure to prove or disprove it.

Psychology is a young science compared to other scientific disciplines, and recent years have seen a virtual explosion in psychological research. As a result, psychological theories and concepts continue to change and evolve. For this reason, it is difficult to give a precise definition of psychology. Basically, psychologists are interested in finding out why people act as they do. But there are different ways of explaining human actions. Before we provide a formal definition of psychology, it will be useful to consider some alternative approaches to psychological phenomena.

APPROACHES TO PSYCHOLOGY

Any action a person takes can be explained from several different points of view. Suppose, for example, you walk across the street. This act can be described as the firing of the nerves that activate the muscles that move the legs that transport you across the street. It can also be described without reference to anything within the body: the green light is a stimulus to which you respond by crossing the street. Or your action might be explained in terms of its purpose or goal: you plan to visit a friend, and crossing the street is one of many acts involved in carrying out the plan.

Just as there are different ways of describing such a simple act as crossing the street, there are also different approaches to psychology. Many approaches are possible, but the five presented here provide an insight into the major conceptions of modern psychology. Because these diverse viewpoints will appear throughout the book, we will provide only a brief description of some main points.

One should bear in mind that these approaches are not mutually exclusive; rather, they tend to focus on different aspects of a complex problem. There is no "right" or "wrong" approach to the study of psychology. Most psychologists take an eclectic viewpoint, using a synthesis of several approaches in explaining psychological phenomena.

Neurobiological approach

The human brain, with its 12 billion nerve cells and almost infinite number of interconnections, may well be the most complex structure in the universe. In principle, all psychological events are represented in some manner by the activity of the brain and nervous system. One approach to the study of human beings attempts to relate behavior to events taking place inside the body, particularly within the brain and nervous system. This approach seeks to specify the neurobiological processes that underlie behavior and mental events. For example, a psychologist studying learning from the neurobiological approach is interested in changes that take place in the nervous system as the result of learning a new task. Perception can be studied by recording the activity of nerve cells in the brain as the eye is exposed to various visual displays.

Recent discoveries have made it dramatically clear that there is an intimate relationship between the brain's activity and behavior and experience. Emotional reactions, such as fear and rage, can be produced in animals by mild electrical stimulation of specific areas deep in the brain. Electrical stimulation of certain areas in the human brain will produce sensations of pleasure and pain and even vivid memories of past events (see Figure 1-1).

Because of the complexity of the brain and the fact that live human brains are seldom available for study, tremendous gaps exist in our knowledge of neural functioning. A psychological conception of ourselves based solely on neurobiology would be inadequate indeed. For this reason, other methods are used to investigate psychological phenomena. In many instances, it is more practical to study antecedent conditions and their consequences without worrying about what goes on inside the organism.

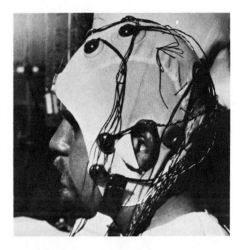

Figure 1-1
A Brain Wired for Pleasure
Microelectrodes implanted in specific areas deep in the brain of this young man produce a sensation of pleasure when stimulated by a mild current. He had previously been driven to the brink of suicide by spells of deep depression. When the wired cap is attached to the microelectrodes, the man can produce pleasurable sensations by pressing a button on a control box. Brain stimulation studies with microelectrodes in animals are helping psychologists understand emotion-producing centers of the brain. Diagnostic procedures with humans, such as the one depicted here, are employed only in extreme cases, when other methods have failed to relieve suffering.

Behavioral approach

A person eats breakfast, rides a bicycle, talks, blushes, laughs, and cries. All these are forms of *behavior*, those activities of an organism that can be observed. With the behavioral approach, a psychologist studies individuals by looking at their *behavior* rather than at their internal workings. The view that behavior should be the sole subject matter of psychology was first advanced by the American psychologist John B. Watson in the early 1900s. Before that, psychology had been defined as the study of mental experiences, and its data were largely self-observations in the form of *introspection*.

Introspection refers to an individual's careful observing and recording of his or her own perceptions and feelings. It ranges from reporting immediate sensory impressions to the onset of a stimulus (for example, the flash of a light) to the long-term probing of emotional experiences (for example, during psychotherapy). As unlike as these "introspections" may seem, they have in common a *private* quality that distinguishes them from observations in other fields of science. Any qualified scientist can replicate an observation in the natural sciences, whereas the introspective observation can be reported by only one observer.

Watson felt that introspection was a futile approach. He argued that if psychology were to be a science, its data must be observable and measurable.

B.F. Skinner

Only you can introspect about your perceptions and feelings, but others can observe your behavior. Watson maintained that only by studying what people do—their behavior—is an objective science of psychology possible.

Behaviorism, as Watson's position came to be called, helped shape the course of psychology during the first half of this century, and its outgrowth, stimulus-response psychology, is still influential, particularly because of the work of Harvard psychologist B.F. Skinner. *Stimulus-response psychology* (or S-R psychology for short) studies the stimuli that elicit behavioral responses, the rewards and punishments that maintain these responses, and the modifications of behavior obtained by changing the patterns of rewards and punishments (Skinner, 1981).[1]

Stimulus-response psychology is *not* concerned with what goes on inside the organism, and for this reason, it has sometimes been called the "black box" approach. The activities of the nervous system inside the box, so to speak, are ignored or blocked from view. S-R psychologists maintain that a science of psychology can be based strictly on what goes into the box and what comes out, without worrying about what takes place inside. Thus, a theory of learning can be developed by observing how learned behavior varies with environmental conditions—for example, what patterns of reward and punishment lead to the fastest learning with the fewest errors. The theory need not specify the changes that learning produces in the nervous system in order to be useful. In science and engineering, such an approach to the study of mechanical systems is referred to as an *input-output analysis.*

A strict S-R approach does not consider the individual's *conscious experiences.* Conscious experiences are simply those events the experiencing person is aware of. You may be aware of the various thoughts that go through your mind as you solve a difficult problem. You know what it feels like to be angry or frightened or excited. An observer may judge from your actions which emotion you are experiencing, but the conscious process—the actual awareness of the emotion—is yours alone. A psychologist can record what a person *says* about his or her conscious experiences (the verbal report) and from this objective data make *inferences* about the person's mental activity. But, by and large, S-R psychologists have not chosen to study the mental processes that intervene between the stimulus and the response.

Today, few psychologists would regard themselves as strict behaviorists. Nevertheless, many modern developments in psychology have evolved from the work of behaviorists.

Cognitive approach

Cognitive psychologists argue that we are not passive receptors of stimuli; the mind actively processes the information it receives and transforms it into new forms and categories (see Figure 1-2). What you are looking at on this page is an arrangement of ink particles. At least, that is the physical stimulus. But the sensory input to the visual system is a pattern of light rays reflected from the page to the eye. These inputs initiate neural processes that transmit information to the brain and eventually result in seeing, reading, and (perhaps) remembering. Numerous transformations occur between the stimulus and your ex-

---

[1]Throughout this book the reader will find references, cited by author and date, that document or expand the statements made here. Detailed publishing information on these studies appears in the reference list at the end of the book. The reference list also serves as an index to the pages on which the citations appear.

perience of reading. These include not only transformations of the light rays into some kind of visual image, but also processes which compare that image with others stored in memory.

Cognition refers to the mental processes of perception, memory, and information processing by which the individual acquires knowledge, solves problems, and plans for the future. *Cognitive psychology* is the scientific study of cognition. Its goal is to conduct experiments and develop theories that explain how mental processes are organized and function. But explanation requires that the theories make predictions about observable events, namely behavior. As we shall see, one can theorize about cognitive processes and how they work without resorting to neurobiological explanations.

The cognitive approach to the study of psychology developed partly in reaction to the narrowness of the S-R view. To conceive of human actions solely in terms of stimulus input and response output may be adequate for the study of simple forms of behavior, but this approach neglects too many interesting areas of human functioning. People can think, plan, make decisions on the basis of remembered information, and selectively choose among stimuli that require attention.

In its origin, behaviorism rejected the subjective study of "mental life" in order to make psychology a science. It provided a valuable service by making psychologists aware of the need for objectivity and measurement. Cognitive psychology represents an attempt to investigate mental processes once again, but—as later chapters will show—in an objective and scientific manner.

An analogy has been made between the strict S-R approach and a telephone switchboard: the stimulus goes in, and after a series of cross connections and circuits through the brain, the response comes out. Cognitive psychology can be considered analogous to a modern computer—or to what in its most general sense is called an "information processing system." Incoming information is processed in various ways: selected, compared, and combined with other information already in memory, transformed, rearranged, and so on. The response output depends on these internal processes and their state at that moment.

Kenneth Craik, a British psychologist and one of the early advocates of cognitive psychology, proposed that the brain is like a computer capable of modeling or paralleling external events. "If," he said, "the organism carries a 'small-scale model' of external reality and of its own possible actions within its head, it is able to try out various alternatives, conclude which is the best of them, react to future situations before they arise, utilize the knowledge of past events in dealing with the future, and in every way to react in a much fuller, safer and more competent manner to the emergencies which face it" (Craik, 1943). The notion of a "mental model of reality" is central to a cognitive approach to psychology.

Psychoanalytic approach

The psychoanalytic conception of human behavior was developed by Sigmund Freud in Europe at about the same time that behaviorism was evolving in the United States. Unlike the ideas discussed thus far, psychoanalytic concepts are based on extensive case studies of individual patients rather than on experimental studies. Psychoanalytic ideas have had a profound influence on psychological thinking.

The basic assumption of Freud's theory is that much of our behavior stems from processes that are unconscious. By *unconscious processes* Freud meant

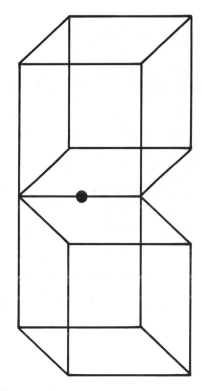

Figure 1-2
Perception as an Active Process
We continually extract patterns from objects we see, trying to match them with something meaningful. Stare at the dot in the center between the cubes to establish for yourself the fluctuating nature of perception. Your brain performs all sorts of transformations, seeking the different patterns inherent in the cubes.

Sigmund Freud

thoughts, fears, and wishes a person is unaware of but which nevertheless influence behavior. He believed that many of the impulses that are forbidden or punished by parents and society during childhood are derived from *innate instincts*. Because each of us is born with these impulses, they exert a pervasive influence that must be dealt with in some manner. Forbidding them merely drives them out of awareness into the unconscious, where they remain to affect behavior. According to Freud, unconscious impulses find expression in dreams, slips of speech, mannerisms, and symptoms of mental illness as well as through such socially approved behavior as artistic or literary activity.

Most psychologists do not completely accept Freud's view of the unconscious. They would probably agree that individuals are not fully aware of some aspects of their personality. But they prefer to speak of degrees of awareness rather than assume that a sharp distinction exists between conscious and unconscious thoughts.

Freud's theories of personality and the psychoanalytic method for treating mental disturbances will be discussed in later chapters. Freud believed that all of our actions have a cause but that the cause is often some unconscious motive rather than the rational reason we may give for our behavior. Freud's view of human nature was essentially negative. We are driven by the same basic instincts as animals (primarily sex and aggression) and are continually struggling against a society that stresses the control of these impulses. Because Freud believed that aggression was a basic instinct, he was pessimistic about the possibility of people ever living together peacefully.

Phenomenological approach

The phenomenological approach focuses on *subjective experience*. It is concerned with the individual's personal view of the world and interpretation of events—the individual's *phenomenology*. This approach seeks to understand events, or phenomena, as they are experienced by the individual and to do so without imposing any preconceptions or theoretical ideas. Phenomenological psychologists believe that we can learn more about human nature by studying how people view themselves and their world than we can by observing their actions. Two people might behave quite differently in response to the same situation; only by asking how each interprets the situation can we fully understand their behavior.

In its emphasis on internal mental processes rather than behavior, the phenomenological approach is similar to the cognitive approach. There is a major difference, however, in the kinds of problems studied and in the scientific rigor of the methods used to study them. Cognitive psychologists are concerned primarily with how individuals perceive events and code, categorize, and represent information in memory. They seek to identify variables that influence perception and memory and to develop a theory of how the mind works so as to predict behavior. Phenomenological psychologists, in contrast, are more concerned with understanding the inner life and experiences of individuals than with developing theories or predicting behavior. They are interested, for example, in a person's self-concept, feelings of self-esteem, and self-awareness.

Phenomenological psychologists tend to reject the notion that behavior is controlled by unconscious impulses (psychoanalytic theories) or by external stimuli (behaviorism). They prefer to believe that we are not "acted on" by forces beyond our control but instead are "actors" capable of controlling our own destiny. We are the builders of our own lives because each of us is a *free*

Encounter group participants "feeling space" in an attempt to expand sensory awareness.

agent—free to make choices and set goals and, thus, accountable for our life choices. This is the issue of *free will* versus *determinism*. The ideas of phenomenological psychologists on this issue are similar to those expressed by such existential philosophers as Kierkegaard, Sartre, and Camus.

Some phenomenological theories are also called *humanistic* because they emphasize those qualities that distinguish people from animals—in addition to free will, primarily the drive toward *self-actualization*. According to humanistic theories, an individual's principal motivational force is a tendency toward growth and self-actualization. All of us have a basic need to develop our potential to the fullest, to progress beyond where we are now. Although we may be blocked by environmental and social obstacles, our natural tendency is toward actualization, or realization, of our potential (Royce and Mos, 1981).

With its emphasis on developing one's potential, humanistic psychology has been closely associated with encounter groups and various types of "consciousness-expanding" and mystical experiences. It is more aligned with literature and the humanities than with science. In fact, some humanists reject scientific psychology, claiming that its methods can contribute nothing worthwhile to an understanding of human nature.

As a warning that psychology needs to focus its attention on solving problems relevant to human welfare rather than studying isolated bits of behavior in the laboratory, the humanistic view makes a valuable point. But to assume that the difficult problems in today's highly complicated society can be solved by discarding all that we have learned about scientific methods of investigation is fallacious indeed. To quote one psychologist concerned with this issue, "We can no more afford a psychology that is humanistic at the expense of being scientific than we can afford one that is 'scientific' at the expense of human relevance" (Smith, 1973).

Application of different approaches

The details of each of these different psychological conceptions will become clearer as we encounter them in subsequent chapters. Any aspect of psychology may be approached from several viewpoints. For example, in studying aggression, the physiological psychologist would be interested in investigating

Viewpoints in Psychology

The analysis of psychological phenomena can be approached from several viewpoints. Each offers a somewhat different explanation of why individuals act as they do, and each makes a contribution to our conception of the total person. The Greek letter psi, ψ, is sometimes used as an abbreviation for psychology.

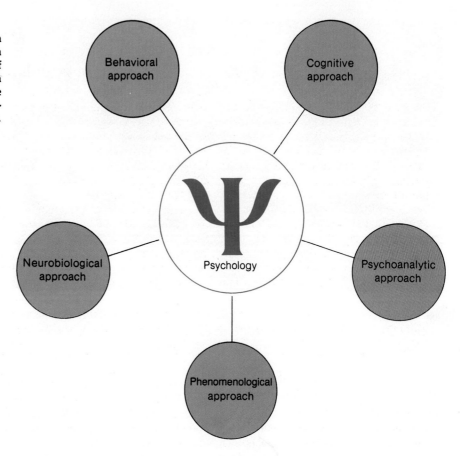

the brain mechanisms responsible for such behavior. As we shall see in Chapter 11, aggressive behavior in animals can be controlled by electrical and chemical stimulation of specific areas in the brain. A behavioral psychologist might be interested in determining the kinds of learning experiences that make one person more aggressive than another. He or she might also study the specific stimuli that provoke hostile acts in a particular situation. A cognitive psychologist might focus on how individuals represent certain events in their minds (in terms of anger-arousing characteristics) and how these mental representations can be modified by providing the person with different types of information. A psychoanalyst might want to find out what childhood experiences foster the control of aggression or its channeling into socially acceptable forms. The humanistic psychologist might focus on those aspects of an individual's life situation that promote aggression by blocking progress toward self-actualization.

Each approach suggests a somewhat different way to modify or change an individual's behavior. For example, the physiological psychologist would look for a drug or some other biological means, such as surgery, for controlling aggression. The behaviorist would try to modify the environmental conditions to provide new learning experiences that reward nonaggressive behavior. Cognitive psychologists would use an approach similar to that of the behaviorists, although they might focus more on the individual's mental processes and strategies for decision making in anger-arousing situations. The psychoanalyst might probe the individual's unconscious to discover why the hostility is di-

Developmental and Interactive Explanations

We have discussed five conceptual approaches to the study of psychology. Cutting across these five approaches are two modes of explanation that will recur as we look at various topics throughout the book. One of them is *developmental;* the other, *interactive.* A developmental explanation stresses the historical roots of present behavior; it focuses on the individual's genetic endowment, cultural environment, and past learning experiences. An interactive explanation deals with the current influences that together act on the individual to arouse or control behavior; these include motives and needs that are currently active, the stimuli that are perceived, and the possibilities for action that are available.

Suppose, for example, you ask why Greg started a fist fight with a classmate. A developmental explanation of this behavior might include the following facts: his inherited size and strength made it easy for him as a toddler to get his way by aggressive actions; his parents never punished him for fighting; the classmate unconsciously reminds Greg of his own

[2]Critical discussions are introduced from time to time to point out controversial issues or to treat a topic in more detail. They may be omitted at the discretion of the instructor.

older brother with whom he has a long-standing rivalry. An interactive explanation might point to these facts: it was a hot day; the school bus had been late; Greg was reprimanded by the teacher for his tardiness; and, to top it off, he had forgotten his lunchbag.

The two modes of explanation, developmental and interactive, belong together because development always provides the potential that is capitalized on in the present. If Greg's background had not included factors that predisposed him to act aggressively, he might have responded differently in the current frustrating situation; for example, he might have withdrawn to a corner and sulked instead of fighting with his classmate. At some points in the text, we will find that explanations of behavior are largely developmental; at other points, interactive explanations are stressed. But one explanation never excludes the other.

Psychoanalysis, with its emphasis on early childhood experiences, favors developmental explanations. Behaviorism, which stresses learning, is also largely a developmental psychology. In contrast, phenomenological theories and some cognitive theories are primarily interactive because they focus on the individual's current perception and interpretation of events. But all psychological theories must be concerned with present influences on behavior as well as residues from the past.

It is important to keep both modes of explanation in mind in order to avoid explaining too much according to the past or too much according to the present. For example, if we discover that teen-age boys with alcoholic fathers are more apt to get in trouble with the law than boys whose fathers are not alcoholics, we should not be tempted to adopt the developmental explanation that a particular boy is delinquent *because* he has an alcoholic father. His delinquency reflects the fact that he is having problems *at the present time*—in relation to specific temptations, friends, lack of other opportunities, and so on.

It is the current problems that must be understood if they are to be corrected. Yet it may help us in the long run to deal with juvenile crime if we know the kind of early history that contributes to delinquency as well as the kinds of neighborhoods and social problems that encourage delinquent behavior. It is not illogical to accept both a developmental and an interactive explanation simultaneously.

rected toward certain people or situations and then try to redirect it into more acceptable channels. A humanistic psychologist might be concerned with helping the individual explore his or her feelings and express them openly in an attempt to improve interpersonal relationships. A broader goal for some humanistic psychologists is to change those aspects of society that foster competition and aggression rather than cooperation.

In making these distinctions, we have overstated the case. Although some psychologists might consider themselves strict behaviorists and others might hold a firm psychoanalytic view, most are fairly eclectic. They feel free to select from several approaches the concepts that seem most appropriate for the problem with which they are working. Put another way, all of these approaches have something important to say about human nature, and few psychologists would insist that only one of them contained the "whole truth."

SCOPE OF CONTEMPORARY PSYCHOLOGY

Definition of psychology

Throughout its brief history, psychology has been defined in many different ways.[3] The early psychologists defined their field as "the study of mental activity." With the development of behaviorism at the beginning of this century and its concern for studying only those phenomena that could be objectively measured, psychology was redefined as "the study of behavior." This definition usually included the investigation of animal as well as human behavior on the assumptions that (1) information from experiments with animals could be generalized to the human organism and (2) animal behavior was of

Table 1-1
Changing Definitions of Psychology

Psychology is the Science of Mental Life, both of its phenomena and of their conditions. . . . The phenomena are such things as we call feelings, desires, cognitions, reasonings, decisions, and the like.

William James, 1890

Psychology has to investigate that which we call internal experience—our own sensations and feelings, our thoughts and volition—in contradistinction to the objects of external experience, which form the subject matter of natural science.

Wilhelm Wundt, 1892

All consciousness everywhere, normal or abnormal, human or animal, is the subject matter which the psychologist attempts to describe or explain; and no definition of his science is wholly acceptable which designates more or less than just this.

James Angell, 1910

For the behaviorist, psychology is that division of natural science which takes human behavior—the doings and sayings, both learned and unlearned—as its subject matter.

John B. Watson, 1919

As a provisional definition of psychology, we may say that its problem is the scientific study of the behavior of living creatures in their contact with the outer world.

Kurt Koffka, 1925

Conceived broadly, psychology seeks to discover the general laws which explain the behavior of living organisms. It attempts to identify, describe, and classify the several types of activity of which the animal, human or other, is capable.

Arthur Gates, 1931

Today, psychology is most commonly defined as "the science of behavior." Interestingly enough, however, the meaning of "behavior" has itself expanded so that it now takes in a good bit of what was formerly dealt with as experience . . . such private (subjective) processes as thinking are now dealt with as "internal behavior."

Norman Munn, 1951

Psychology is usually defined as the scientific study of behavior. Its subject matter includes behavioral processes that are observable, such as gestures, speech, and physiological changes, and processes that can only be inferred as thoughts and dreams.

Kenneth Clark and George Miller, 1970

Psychology is the scientific analysis of human mental processes and memory structures in order to understand human behavior.

Richard Mayer, 1981

[3]A brief history of psychology is presented in Appendix I. One can gain a better understanding of contemporary psychology by viewing it in its historical context.

interest in its own right. From the 1930s through the 1960s, most psychology textbooks used this definition. The cycle has come around again with the development of cognitive and phenomenological psychology; most current definitions of psychology include references to both behavior and mental processes (see Table 1-1).

For our purposes, we will define psychology as *the scientific study of behavior and mental processes*. This definition reflects psychology's concern with an objective study of observable behavior. It also recognizes the importance of understanding mental processes that cannot be directly observed but must be inferred from behavioral and neurobiological data. But we need not dwell on a definition. From a practical viewpoint, we can get a better idea of what psychology *is* from looking at what psychologists *do*.

Fields of psychology

About half the people who have advanced degrees in psychology work in colleges and universities, although teaching is not always their primary activity. They may devote much of their time to research or counseling. Others work in the public schools, in hospitals or clinics, in research institutes, in government agencies, or in business and industry. Yet others are in private practice and offer their services to the public for a fee; they represent a relatively small but growing fraction of the field. Table 1-2A gives an estimate of the proportion of psychologists engaged in different specialized fields; Table 1-2B gives proportions in terms of employment settings—that is, where psychologists work.

We now turn to a description of some of the fields of specialization in psychology.

EXPERIMENTAL AND PHYSIOLOGICAL PSYCHOLOGY The term "experimental" is really a misnomer because psychologists in other areas of specialization carry out experiments too. But this category usually consists of those psychologists who use experimental methods to study how people react to sensory stimuli, perceive the world, learn and remember, respond emotionally, and are motivated to action, whether by hunger or the desire to succeed in life. *Experimental psychologists* also work with animals. Sometimes they attempt to relate animal and human behavior; sometimes they study animals in order to compare the behavior of different species (*comparative psychology*). Whatever their interest, experimental psychologists are concerned with developing precise methods of measurement and control.

An area of research closely related to both experimental psychology and biology is physiological psychology. *Physiological psychologists* (also called *neuropsychologists*) seek to discover the relationship between biological processes and behavior. How do sex hormones influence behavior? What area of the brain controls speech? How do drugs like marijuana and LSD affect personality and memory? Two areas of interdisciplinary research are the *neurosciences* (concerned with the relationship between brain function and behavior) and *psychopharmacology* (the study of drugs and behavior).

DEVELOPMENTAL, SOCIAL, AND PERSONALITY PSYCHOLOGY The categories of developmental psychology, social psychology, and personality psychology overlap. *Developmental psychologists* are concerned with human growth and the factors that shape behavior from birth to old age. They might study a specific ability, such as how language develops and changes in the growing child, or a particular period of life, such as infancy, the preschool years, or adolescence.

Table 1-2A
Field of Specialization
The percentage of individuals holding a doctorate degree in psychology and their primary field of specialization (After Stapp and Fulcher, 1981)

FIELD	PERCENTAGE
Experimental and physiological	6.9
Developmental, personality, and social	10.4
Clinical, counseling, and school	60.5
Engineering, industrial, and organizational	6.3
Educational	5.4
Other	10.5
	100.0

Table 1-2B
Employment Setting
The percentage of individuals holding a doctorate degree in psychology and their principal employment setting (After Stapp and Fulcher, 1981)

SETTING	PERCENTAGE
Academic setting (university, medical school, college, other)	43.1
Schools and school systems	4.6
Clinics, hospitals, community mental health centers, and counseling centers	23.9
Private practice	14.7
Business, government, research organizations, industry	13.0
Other	.7
	100.0

Because human development takes place in the context of other persons—parents, siblings, playmates, and school companions—a large part of development is social. *Social psychologists* are interested in the ways that interactions with other people influence attitudes and behavior. They are concerned also with the behavior of groups. Social psychologists are perhaps best known for their work in public opinion surveys and in market research. Surveys are now widely used by newspapers, magazines, radio and TV networks and government agencies such as the Bureau of the Census.

Social psychologists investigate such topics as propaganda and persuasion, conformity, and intergroup conflict. A significant part of their research effort is directed toward identifying the factors that contribute to prejudice and to aggression.

To the extent that personality is a developmental and social product, the province of personality psychology overlaps both of the other categories. *Personality psychologists* focus on differences between individuals. They are interested in ways of classifying individuals for practical purposes as well as in studying each individual's unique qualities.

CLINICAL AND COUNSELING PSYCHOLOGY   The greatest number of psychologists are engaged in clinical psychology, the application of psychological principles to the diagnosis and treatment of emotional and behavioral problems: mental illness, juvenile delinquency, criminal behavior, drug addiction, mental retardation, marital and family conflict, and other less serious adjustment problems. *Clinical psychologists* may work in mental hospitals, juvenile courts or probation offices, mental health clinics, institutions for the mentally retarded, prisons, or university medical schools. They may also practice privately, often in association with other professionals; their affiliations with the medical profession, especially psychiatry, are close.

Counseling psychologists serve many of the same functions as clinical psychologists, although they usually deal with less serious problems. They often work with high school or university students, providing help with problems of social adjustment and vocational and educational goals. Together, clinical and counseling psychologists account for about 55 percent of all psychologists in the United States.

A youngster discusses some problems with a clinical psychologist.

SCHOOL AND EDUCATIONAL PSYCHOLOGY The elementary and secondary schools provide a wide range of opportunities for psychologists. Because the beginnings of serious emotional problems often appear in the early grades, many elementary schools employ psychologists whose training combines courses in child development, education, and clinical psychology. These *school psychologists* work with individual children to evaluate learning and emotional problems; administering and interpreting intelligence, achievement, and personality tests is part of their job. In consultation with parents and teachers, they plan ways of helping the child both in the classroom and in the home. They also provide a valuable resource for teachers, offering suggestions for coping with classroom problems.

Educational psychologists are specialists in learning and teaching. They may work in the schools but more often are employed by a university's school of education, where they do research on teaching methods and help train teachers and school psychologists.

A school psychologist administering a test

INDUSTRIAL AND ENGINEERING PSYCHOLOGY *Industrial psychologists* (sometimes called *organizational psychologists*) may work for a particular company or as consultants for a number of business organizations. They are concerned with such problems as selecting people most suitable for a particular job, developing job training programs, and participating in management decisions that involve the morale and welfare of employees.

Engineering psychologists seek to make the relationship between people and machines as satisfactory as possible—to design machines so that human errors are minimized. For example, engineering psychologists were involved in developing space capsules in which astronauts could live and function efficiently. Designing underwater habitats for oceanographic research and developing artificial limbs and other prosthetic devices for handicapped individuals are other examples of their work.

Along with social psychologists and engineering psychologists, there is a group of psychologists concerned with environmental issues: problems of noise, air and water pollution, overcrowding, and the psychologically optimal design of working and living areas. The term for this area of research is *environmental psychology*.

EMERGING SPECIALITIES In addition to the areas mentioned, there are other, new career possibilities in psychology. *Forensic psychologists* work within the legal, judicial, and correctional systems in a variety of ways—for example, consulting with police departments and probation officers to increase their understanding of the human problems with which they must deal, working with prison inmates and their families, participating in decisions about whether an accused person is mentally competent to stand trial, and preparing psychological reports to help judges decide on the most appropriate course of action for a convicted criminal.

Psychologists who specialize in *computer science* may plan the design and data analysis of large-scale experiments and surveys that require the kind of complex calculations that can only be done with a computer. Or they may work in the field of *artificial intelligence,* developing computers and robots that can perform intellectual tasks considered characteristic of human thought (see Chapter 9).

Because of their expertise in experimental design—the procedures for gathering and analyzing data—psychologists also work in the area of *evaluation research*. Many of the federal and local programs designed to solve social problems involve large expenditures of money and personnel. Consequently, it is essential to determine whether such programs—aimed, for example, at establishing early education for underprivileged children, preventing drug abuse among high school students, or providing job training for unemployed youths—are effective. Psychologists are involved in the evaluation of public programs in such areas as education, health, and employment.

Behavioral and social sciences

The study of human behavior must go beyond what happens to an isolated individual and consider the institutional arrangements in which individuals live: the family, the community, and the larger society. Because these arrangements are much too varied to be understood from any single standpoint, a number of fields of inquiry have developed: anthropology, economics, linguistics, political science, sociology, and other specialties. Taken together, these are known as the *behavioral* and *social sciences*. The term "social science" used to be the more inclusive one, with behavioral science restricted to those fields that focused on individual behavior (psychology, anthropology, and linguistics). As all fields have grown to appreciate that individual and social behavior cannot be understood one without the other, the terms "behavioral science" and "social science" have come to be used somewhat interchangeably.

A subfield of psychology like social psychology would tend to be viewed as part of the social sciences because it focuses on social phenomena. Physiological psychology, on the other hand, would be thought of as a behavioral science because it studies the biological basis of the behavior of individual organisms. Educational psychology, when studying how an individual child learns to read or do arithmetic, would be labeled as a behavioral science; but in its study of group interactions in the classroom, it would be a social science. Thus, psychology may be referred to as a behavioral science when the discussion emphasizes the individual and as a social science when the emphasis is on groups of individuals in interaction.

RESEARCH METHODS

The aim of science is to provide new and useful information in the form of verifiable data: data obtained under conditions such that other qualified people can repeat the observations and obtain the same results. This task calls for orderliness and precision in investigating relationships and in communicating them to others. The scientific ideal is not always achieved, but as a science becomes better established, it rests on an increasing number of relationships that are taken for granted because they have been validated so often.

Experimental method

The experimental method can be used outside the laboratory as well as inside. Thus, it is possible in an experiment to investigate the effects of different psychotherapeutic methods by trying these methods out on separate but similar groups of emotionally disturbed individuals. The experimental method is a matter of logic, not of location. Even so, most experiments take place in special laboratories, chiefly because the control of conditions commonly requires special facilities, computers, and other instruments.

The distinguishing characteristic of a laboratory is that it is a place where the experimenter can carefully control conditions and take measurements in

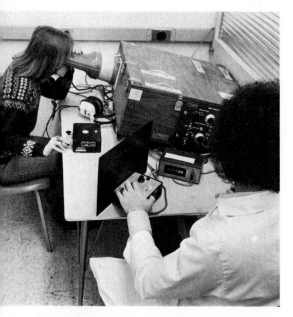

A psychologist determines how much of a briefly presented display a subject can perceive and accurately report.

order to discover *relationships among variables.* A *variable* is something that can occur with different values. For example, in an experiment seeking to discover the relationship between learning ability and age, both learning ability and age can have different values. To the extent that learning ability changes systematically with increasing age, we can discover an orderly relationship between these two variables.

The ability to exercise precise control over variables distinguishes the experimental method from other methods of observation. If the experimenter seeks to discover whether learning ability depends on the amount of sleep a person has had, the amount of sleep can be controlled by arranging to have several groups of subjects spend the night in the laboratory. Two groups might be allowed to go to sleep at 11:00 P.M. and 1:00 A.M., respectively, and a third group might be kept awake until 4:00 A.M. By waking all the subjects at the same time and giving each the same learning task, the experimenter can determine whether the subjects with more sleep master the task more quickly than those with less sleep.

In this study, the different amounts of sleep are the antecedent conditions; the learning performances are the results of these conditions. We call the antecedent condition the *independent variable* because it is independent of what the subject does. The variable affected by changes in the antecedent conditions is called the *dependent variable;* in psychological research, the dependent variable is usually some measure of the subject's behavior. The phrase *is a function of* is used to express the dependency of one variable on another. Thus, for the experiment above, we could say that the subjects' ability to learn a new task is a function of the amount of sleep they had.

An experiment concerned with the effect of marijuana on memory may make the distinction between independent and dependent variables clearer. Subjects were randomly assigned to four groups. When subjects arrived at the laboratory, they were given an oral dose of marijuana in a "brownie cookie." All subjects were given the same type of cookie and the same instructions. But the dosage level of the marijuana was different for each group: 5, 10, 15, or 20 milligrams of THC, the active ingredient in marijuana.

After consuming the marijuana, a subject was required to memorize several lists of unrelated words. One week later, the subject was brought back to the laboratory and asked to recall as many words as possible. Figure 1-3 shows the percentage of words recalled for each of the four groups. Note that recall decreases as a function of the amount of marijuana taken at the time the subject studied the lists.

The experimenters had worked out a careful plan before bringing the subjects to the laboratory. Except for the dosage of marijuana, they held all conditions constant: the general setting for the experiment, the instructions to the subjects, the material to be memorized, the time allowed for memorization, and the conditions under which recall was tested. The only factor permitted to vary across the four groups was the dosage of marijuana—the *independent variable.* The *dependent variable* was the amount of material recalled one week later. The marijuana dosage was measured in milligrams of THC; memory was measured by the percentage of words recalled. The experimenters could plot the relationship between the independent and dependent variables as shown in Figure 1-3. Finally, the experimenters used enough subjects (20 per group) to justify expecting similar results if the experiment was repeated with a different sample of subjects. The letter N is generally used to denote the number of subjects in each group; in this study, $N = 20$.

The degree of control possible in the laboratory makes a laboratory experi-

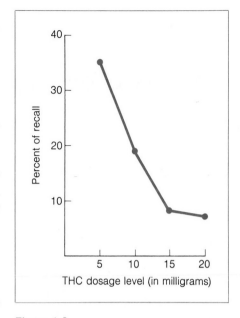

Figure 1-3
Marijuana and Memory
Subjects memorized word lists after taking varying dosages of THC (the active ingredient in marijuana). Recall tests administered a week later measured how much of the memorized material was retained. The figure shows the relationship between dosage level (independent variable) and recall score (dependent variable). (After Darley and others, 1973)

Figure 1-4
Baboons Observed
in Their Natural Habitat
Such naturalistic studies tell more about social behavior than strictly experimental studies can. For example, grooming behavior, as shown in the picture, is a common form of social contact among baboons in the wild.

ment the preferred method when it is appropriate. Precision instruments are usually necessary to control the presentations of stimuli and to obtain exact measures of behavior. The experimenter may need to produce colors of known wavelengths in vision studies or sounds of known frequency in audition studies. It may be necessary to expose a visual display for a precisely timed fraction of a second in a memory experiment. With precision instruments, time can be measured in thousandths of a second, and physiological activity can be studied by means of very slight electrical currents amplified from the brain. Thus, the psychological laboratory has audiometers, photometers, oscilloscopes, electronic timers, electroencephalographs, and computers.

It is not essential that all psychological problems be brought into the laboratory for study. Some sciences, such as geology and astronomy, are experimental only to a very limited extent. Now that we have seen the value of the laboratory approach, we turn to other methods used in psychological investigations.

Observational method

The early stages of a science necessitate exploration to become familiar with the relationships that later will be the object of more precise study. Careful observation of animal and human behavior is the starting point of psychology. Observation of primates in their native environment may tell us things about their social organization that will help us conduct our laboratory investigations (see Figure 1-4). Study of preliterate tribes reveals the ranges of variation in human institutions, which would go unrecognized if we confined our study to men and women of our own culture. Motion pictures of newborn babies reveal the details of movement patterns shortly after birth and the types of stimuli to which babies are responsive.

In making observations of naturally occurring behavior, however, there is a risk that interpretive anecdotes may be substituted for objective descriptions. We may be tempted, for example, to say that an animal known to have been without food for a long time is "looking for food" when all we observe is heightened activity. Investigators must be trained to observe and record accurately to avoid projecting their own wishes or biases into what they report.

Observational methods have also been brought into the laboratory. In their extensive study of the physiological aspects of human sexuality, Masters and Johnson (1966) developed techniques that permitted direct observation of sexual responses in the laboratory. The intimate nature of the research required careful planning to devise procedures for making the subjects feel at ease in the laboratory and to develop appropriate methods for observing and recording their responses. The data included (1) observations of behavior, (2) recordings of physiological changes, and (3) responses to questions asked about the subject's sensations before, during, and after sexual stimulation.

Masters and Johnson would be the first to agree that human sexuality has many dimensions in addition to the biological one. But, as they point out, we need to know the basic anatomical and physiological facts of sexual response before we can understand the psychological aspects. Their research has shown that some of the psychological hypotheses regarding sex (for example, the nature of the female orgasm and factors that contribute to sexual adequacy) are based on false biological assumptions. We will return to this topic in a later chapter.

Survey method

Some problems that are difficult to study by direct observation may be studied through the use of questionnaires or interviews. For example, prior to the Masters and Johnson research on sexual response, most of the information on how people behave sexually (as opposed to how laws, religion, or society said they should behave) came from extensive surveys conducted by the late Alfred Kinsey and his associates some 30 years ago. Information from thousands of individual interviews was analyzed to form the basis of *Sexual Behavior in the Human Male* (Kinsey and others, 1948) and *Sexual Behavior in the Human Female* (Kinsey and others, 1953).

Surveys have also been used to obtain information on political opinions, consumer preferences, health care needs, and many other topics. The Gallup poll and the United States Census are probably the most familiar surveys. An adequate survey requires a carefully pretested questionnaire, interviewers trained in its use, a sample of people carefully selected to ensure they are representative of the population to be studied, and appropriate methods of data analysis, so that the results can be properly interpreted.

"How would you like me to answer that question? As a member of my ethnic group, educational class, income group, or religious category?"

Drawing by D. Fradon © 1969 *The New Yorker Magazine*, Inc.

Test method

The test is an important research instrument in contemporary psychology. It is used to measure all kinds of abilities, interests, attitudes, and accomplishments. Tests enable the psychologist to obtain large quantities of data from people with minimal disturbance of their daily routines and without elaborate laboratory equipment. A test essentially presents a uniform situation to a group of people who vary in aspects relevant to the situation (such as intelligence, manual dexterity, anxiety, and perceptual skills). An analysis of the results then relates variations in test scores to variations among people.

The construction of tests and their use are not simple matters. They require many steps in item preparation, scaling, and establishing norms. Later chapters will explore the problems of testing in some detail.

Case histories

Scientific biographies, known as case histories, are important sources of data for psychologists studying individuals. There can, of course, be case histories of institutions or groups of people as well.

Most case histories are prepared by *reconstructing the biography* of a person on the basis of remembered events and records. Reconstruction is necessary because the individual's earlier history often does not become a matter of interest until that person develops some sort of problem; at such time, knowledge of the past is important to comprehension of present behavior. The retrospective method may result in distortions of events or oversights, but it is often the only method available.

Case histories may also be based on a *longitudinal study*. This type of study follows an individual or group of individuals over an extended period of time, with observations made at periodic intervals. The advantage of a longitudinal study is that it does not depend on the memories of those interviewed at a later date.

MEASUREMENT IN PSYCHOLOGY

Whatever methods psychologists use, sooner or later they find it necessary to make statements about *amounts*, or *quantities*. Variables have to be assessed in an objective manner so that investigations can be repeated and verified by others. Occasionally a variable can be sorted into *classes*, or *categories*, as when boys and girls are separated for the study of sex differences. Sometimes the variables are subject to ordinary *physical measurement:* for example, hours of sleep deprivation, dosage level of a drug, or time required to press a brake pedal when a light flashes. Sometimes variables have to *scaled* in a manner that places them in some sort of order. For example, in rating a patient's feelings of insecurity, a psychotherapist might use a five-point scale ranging from never through rarely, sometimes, often, and always. Usually, for purposes of precise communication, *numbers* are assigned to variables. The term *measurement* is used when a procedure is specified for assigning numbers to different levels, amounts, or sizes of some variable.[4]

Experimental design

An investigator must plan all the details of an experiment. This includes specifying equipment and measuring instruments, the procedure to be used in collecting data, and how the data will be analyzed. The expression *experimental design* is used to describe the steps that must be planned before an experiment is conducted. Part of the experimental design is to specify how measurements are to be made.

The simplest experimental designs are those in which the investigator manipulates one variable (the *independent variable*) and studies its effects on another variable (the *dependent variable*). The ideal is to hold everything constant except the independent variable so that at the end of the experiment a statement like this can be made: "With everything else constant, when X is increased, Y also increases." Or, in other cases, "When X is increased, Y decreases." Almost any content can fit into this kind of statement as is indicated by the following examples: (1) "When the dosage of THC is increased, the recall of memorized material decreases"; (2) "The more early stimulation children receive, the better their ability to learn as adults"; (3) "When the physical frequency of a tone is increased, the perceived pitch increases"; or (4) "The more prolonged stress one is under, the greater the likelihood of ulcers."

Sometimes an experiment focuses only on the influence of a single condition, which can be either present or absent. (Such a condition is an independent variable with two values, one representing its presence, the other its absence.) In this case, the experimental design calls for an *experimental group* with the condition present and a *control group* with the condition absent. The results of such an experiment are presented in Figure 1-5. Inspecting the figure, we see that the experimental group, which received computer-assisted learning, scored higher on reading achievement tests than the control group, which did not receive such instruction.

Limiting an investigation to the effects of only one independent variable is too restrictive for some problems. It may be necessary to study how several independent variables interact to produce an effect on one or even several

"I'm suffering a real identity crisis . . . I keep getting assigned to the control group."

---

[4]This discussion is designed to give the reader a general introduction to the problems of measurement and statistics in order to facilitate understanding of the tables and charts in later chapters. A more thorough discussion of statistics is provided in Appendix II.

dependent variables. Studies involving the simultaneous manipulation of several variables are called *multivariate experiments* and are frequently used in psychological research. The experimental design of such studies can be quite complicated, but sometimes the questions being asked can be answered only through a multivariate experiment.

Interpreting statistical statements

Because descriptions of the results of psychological studies usually include statistical statements, it is well to be familiar with the most common of these so that the reports will appear less baffling.

The most common statistic is the *mean*. The mean is simply the technical term for an arithmetic average; it is the sum of a set of scores divided by the number of scores. In studies involving an experimental and control group, there are two means to be compared: a mean for the scores of the subjects in the experimental group and a mean for the scores of the subjects in the control group. The difference between these two means is, of course, what interests us. If the difference is large, we may accept it at face value. But what if the difference is small? What if our measures are subject to random error? What if a few extreme cases are producing the difference?

Statisticians have solved these problems by developing tests of the *significance of a difference*. A psychologist who says that the difference between the experimental and the control group is "statistically significant" means that a statistical test has been applied to the data and that the observed difference is trustworthy. The psychologist is not commenting on the practical significance of the results but is telling us that the statistical test indicates that the difference observed is extremely likely to occur again if the experiment is repeated. Many chance factors can influence the results of an experiment. By using statistical tests, psychologists can judge the likelihood that the observed difference is, in fact, due to the effect of the independent variable rather than an unlucky accident of chance factors.

Correlation as an alternative to experimentation

Sometimes an experimental approach to a problem is not possible. For example, the researcher interested in the human brain is not free to remove portions surgically, as can be done with lower animals. But when brain damage occurs through disease or injury, we can study how parts of the human brain are related to behavior. For instance, by keeping records on patients with accidental damage in a particular area of the brain, a relationship may be found between the extent of the damage and the amount of loss in language ability. A controlled study that experimentally manipulates brain damage has not been conducted, but important information has been obtained. This method of investigating relationships between variables is known as *correlation*. Results of correlational studies can be summarized using the *coefficient of correlation*, usually symbolized by the lower-case letter *r*. The correlation coefficient is an estimate of the degree to which two variables are related. It is a number between 0 and 1. No relationship is indicated by 0; a perfect relationship, by 1. As *r* goes from 0 to 1, the strength of the relationship increases.

COEFFICIENT OF CORRELATION   The nature of a correlation coefficient can be made clearer by examining a graphic presentation of data from an actual study. In this study, subjects were tested for their susceptibility to hypnosis and were given a score; a low score indicated minimal susceptibility whereas a high

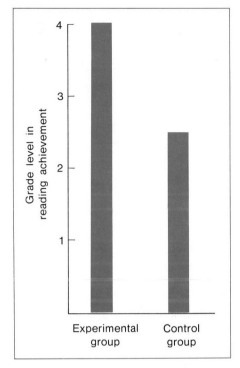

Figure 1-5
Experimental and Control Groups
Each day, grade-school children in the experimental group participated in a computer-assisted learning (CAL) program in reading. The computer was programmed to present different types of materials and instructions to each student, depending on the difficulty a student was having at any point in the reading curriculum. CAL has the advantage of working with each student in a highly individualized way, concentrating on those areas in which the student is having the most difficulty. The control group had no supplementary CAL in reading. At the end of the third grade, all students in both groups were given a standardized reading test. It was administered by testers who had no knowledge of which students had received CAL and which had not. As the figure indicates, students in the experimental group scored higher on the test than students in the control group, suggesting that CAL had been beneficial. In this experiment, the independent variable is the presence or absence of CAL; the dependent variable is the student's score on the reading test. (After Atkinson, 1976)

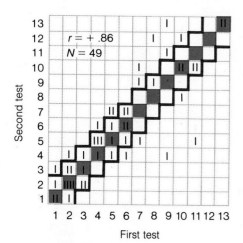

Figure 1-6
A Scatter Diagram
Illustrating Correlation

Each tally indicates the scores of one subject on two separate tests of hypnotic susceptibility. Tallies in the colored area indicate identical scores on both tests; those between the solid lines indicate a difference of no more than one point between the two scores. The correlation of $r = +.86$ means that the performances were fairly consistent on the two days. There were 49 subjects in this study; thus, $N = 49$. (After Hilgard, 1961)

score indicated that they were easily hypnotized. Several weeks later, they were tested again and given a new susceptibility score. The study was concerned with how effectively one can predict hypnotizability on one occasion from performance on a prior occasion. Each tally in Figure 1-6 represents the results for one subject on the two tests. For example, note that two subjects made scores of 1 on both test days (the two tallies in the box to the lower left), and two subjects made scores of 13 on both days (box to upper right). One subject (see lower right portion of diagram) made a score of 11 on the first test but only 5 on the second test. And so on.

If all subjects had exactly the same score on both tests, all of the tallies would have fallen in the diagonal squares (in color), and the coefficient of correlation would have been $r = 1$. Enough tallies fall to either side, however, so that in this study the correlation was $r = .86$. A correlation of .86 indicates that the first test of hypnotizability is a very good, but not perfect, predictor of hypnotizability on a later occasion. The numerical method for calculating a correlation coefficient is described in Appendix II; at this point, we will set forth some rules of thumb that will help you interpret correlation coefficients when they are encountered in later chapters.

A correlation can be either + or −. The sign of the correlation indicates whether the two variables are positively or negatively correlated. The sign of a correlation is arbitrary. For example, if the number of times a student is absent from class correlates − .40 with the final course grade, then the correlation between number of classes attended and the course grade would be + .40. The strength of the relationship is the same, but the sign indicates whether we are looking at classes missed or classes attended.

The strength of the relationship between two variables is specified by the value of r. As r goes from 0 to 1, the degree of the relationship increases. Let us consider a few examples of correlation coefficients:

- A correlation coefficient of about .75 between grades in the first year of college and the grades in the second year.
- A correlation of about .70 between scores on an intelligence test given at age 7 and a retest of intelligence at age 18.
- A correlation of about .50 between the height of a parent and the adult height of the child.
- A correlation of about .40 between scholastic aptitude tests given in high school and grades in college.
- A correlation of about .30 between scores on paper-and-pencil personality inventories and judgments by psychological experts of individuals in a social setting.

In psychological research, a correlation coefficient of .60 or more is judged to be quite high. Correlations in the range from .20 to .60 are of practical and theoretical value and useful in making predictions. Correlations between 0 and .20 must be judged with caution and are only minimally useful in making predictions. One should be suspicious of investigators who make strong claims that are based on correlation coefficients in this lower range.

CAUSE-AND-EFFECT RELATIONSHIPS Before concluding this section, we should emphasize an important distinction between experimental and correlational studies. In an experimental study, one variable (the independent variable) is systematically manipulated to determine its effect on some other variable (the dependent variable). Similar *cause-and-effect relationships* cannot be inferred from correlational studies. The fallacy of interpreting correlations as implying cause and effect can be illustrated with a few examples. The softness of the asphalt in the streets of a city may correlate with the number of sunstroke cases, but this does not mean that soft asphalt gives off some kind of poison that sends people to hospitals. We understand the cause in this example—a hot sun both softens the asphalt and produces sunstroke. Another common example is the high positive correlation obtained for the number of storks seen nesting in French villages and the number of childbirths recorded in the same communities. We shall leave it to the reader's ingenuity to figure out possible reasons for such a correlation without postulating a cause-and-effect relationship between storks and babies. These examples provide sufficient warning against giving a causal interpretation to a correlation. When two variables are correlated, variation in one may *possibly* be the cause of variation in the other, but in the absence of experimental evidence, no such conclusion is justified.

OVERVIEW OF THE BOOK

Psychologists today are in the process of investigating thousands of different problems ranging from microelectrode studies of how individual brain cells change during learning to studies of the effects of population density and overcrowding on social behavior. Deciding how to classify these investigations topically and how to present the topics in the most meaningful order is difficult. In older sciences, such as physics and chemistry, where facts and theories are fairly well established, most introductory textbooks arrange their topics in approximately the same order—starting with basic concepts and proceeding to the more complex. In a science as young as psychology, however, where theories are still very preliminary and so much remains unknown, the natural order of topics is not always clear.

If you examine a number of introductory psychology texts, you will find considerable variation in the grouping and ordering of topics. Should we know how people perceive the world around them in order to understand how they learn new things? Or does learning determine how we perceive our environment? Should we discuss what motivates a person to action so that we can understand his or her personality? Or can motivation be better understood if we look first at the way personality develops over the course of a lifetime? Despite such unresolved questions, we have tried to arrange the topics in this book so that the understanding of the issues in each chapter will provide a background for the study of problems in the next.

To understand how people interact with their environment, we need to know something about their biological equipment. In Part Two ("Biological and Developmental Processes"), the first chapter describes how the nervous and endocrine systems function to integrate and control behavior. Since behavior also depends on the interaction between inherited characteristics and environmental conditions, this chapter includes, in addition, a discussion of genetic influences on behavior.

The second chapter in Part Two provides an overview of the individual's psychological development from infancy through adolescence and adulthood. By noting how abilities, attitudes, and personality develop and the problems that must be faced at different stages of life, we can appreciate more fully the kinds of questions to which psychology seeks answers.

We know the world around us through our senses. To understand how individuals react to their world, we should know how the sense organs mediate the sensations of light, sound, touch, and taste; how the organism interprets and reacts to patterns of stimuli; and the characteristics of human consciousness under both normal and altered states of awareness. These are the topics of Part Three ("Perception and Consciousness").

Part Four ("Learning, Remembering, and Thinking") is concerned with the processes by which we acquire skills and knowledge, remember them, and use them for purposes of communication, problem solving, and thinking.

Part Five ("Motivation and Emotion") deals with the forces that energize and direct behavior; these include biological needs as well as psychological motives and emotions.

The ways in which individuals differ from one another, both in personal characteristics and abilities, is the substance of Part Six ("Personality and Individuality"). Coping with stress and the development and treatment of abnormal behavior provide the topics for Part Seven ("Conflict, Adjustment, and Mental Health").

Part Eight ("Social Behavior") is concerned with our social interactions: how we influence others and are influenced by them, and how we function in groups.

Summary

1   The study of psychology can be approached from several viewpoints. The *neurobiological approach* attempts to relate our actions to events taking place inside the body, particularly in the brain and nervous system. The *behavioral approach* focuses on those external activities of the organism that can be observed and measured. *Cognitive psychology* is concerned with the way the brain actively processes incoming information by transforming it internally in various ways. The *psychoanalytic approach* emphasizes unconscious motives stemming from sexual and aggressive impulses repressed in childhood. *Phenomenological* and *humanistic* approaches focus on the person's subjective experiences, freedom of choice, and motivation toward self-actualization. A particular area of psychological investigation can be approached from several of these viewpoints.

2   *Psychology* is defined as the *scientific study of behavior and mental processes.* Its numerous areas of specialization include experimental and physiological psychology; developmental, social, and personality psychology; clinical and counseling psychology; school and educational psychology; industrial and engineering psychology. Psychology is one of the *behavioral,* or *social, sciences.*

3   When applicable, the *experimental method* is preferred for studying problems because it seeks to control all *variables,* except the ones being studied. The *independent variable* is the one manipulated by the experimenter; the *dependent variable* (usually some measure of the subject's behavior) is affected by changes in the independent variable.

4   Other methods for investigating psychological problems include the *observational method,* the *survey method,* the *test method,* and *case histories.*

5   *Measurement* involves specifying a procedure for assigning *numbers* to different levels, amounts, or sizes of a variable. The expression *experimental design* is used to describe the array of procedures (including measurement procedures) to be followed in conducting an experiment. In the simplest experimental designs, the experimenter manipulates one variable (the independent variable) and observes its effect on another variable (the dependent variable).

6   In many experiments, the independent variable is something that is either present or absent. In this case, the experimental design includes an *experimental group* (with the condition present) and a *control group* (with the condition absent). If the difference in *means* between the experimental and control groups is *statistically significant*, we know that the experimental condition had a reliable effect; that is, if the study was repeated, a similar difference in means would be observed.

7   Another approach to research is by way of *correlation*. If an independent variable cannot be experimentally manipulated, it is still possible to observe how two variables are related. One can make many observations of the two variables as they occur by chance in nature and then use the data to determine how one variable changes as the other changes. Cause-and-effect conclusions cannot be drawn for a correlational study, but such studies are extremely important particularly when experiments are not possible.

8   The *correlation coefficient*, r, is a useful way of describing the degree of relationship between two variables. It is a number between 0 and 1. No relationship is indicated by 0; a perfect relation, by 1. As r goes from 0 to 1, the strength of the relationship increases. The correlation coefficient can be positive or negative depending on whether one variable increases with another ($+$) or one variable decreases as the other increases ($-$). The sign of the correlation does not affect the strength of the relationship.

Further Reading

The topical interests and theories of any contemporary science can often be understood best according to their history. Several useful books are Murphy and Kovach, *Historical introduction to modern psychology* (3rd ed., 1972); Watson, *The great psychologists: From Aristotle to Freud* (1978); Wertheimer, *A brief history of psychology* (2nd ed., 1979); and Schultz, *A history of modern psychology* (3rd ed., 1981). A brief history of psychology is presented in Appendix I to this book.

The various conceptual approaches to psychology are discussed in Hall and Lindzey, *Theories of personality* (3rd ed 1978): Anderson, *Cognitive psychology and its implications* (1980); Royce and Mos (eds.), *Humanistic psychology: Concepts and criticisms* (1981); Bower and Hilgard, *Theories of learning* (5th ed., 1981); and Mayer, *The promise of cognitive psychology* (1981). The methods of psychological research are presented in Wood, *Fundamentals of psychological research* (2nd ed., 1977); Johnson and Solso, *An introduction to experimental design in psychology: A case approach* (2nd ed., 1978); Meyers and Grossen, *Behavioral research: Theory, procedure, and design* (2nd ed., 1978); and Ray and Ravizza, *Methods toward a science of behavior and experience* (1981). A simple but elegant introduction to basic concepts in statistics is Phillips, *Statistical thinking: A structural approach* (2nd ed., 1982).

Appendix III to this book lists some of the major journals of psychology and a description of the types of articles they publish. These journals are available in most college and university libraries. Current issues of the journals generally can be found on racks in an open section of the library. An excellent overview of psychology can be gained by spending some time perusing recent issues of these journals.

The *Annual review of psychology*, published in book form each year, selects 15 to 20 areas of psychology for a review of recent literature; these reviews provide a useful access to the world literature in psychology. The National Academy of Sciences presents an assessment of the significance and social utility of research in the behavioral and social sciences in Adams, Smelser, and Treiman (eds.), *Behavioral and social science research: A national resource* (1982).

To find out more about career opportunities in psychology and the training required to become a psychologist, write to the American Psychological Association (1200 Seventeenth Street N.W., Washington, D.C. 20036) for a copy of their booklet, *A career in psychology*.

Part two
BIOLOGICAL AND DEVELOPMENTAL PROCESSES

2
NEUROBIOLOGICAL BASIS
OF PSYCHOLOGY

B ehavior, from blinking an eyelid to playing tennis or solving a mathematical
equation, depends on the integration of numerous processes within the
body. This integration is provided by the nervous system with the help of the
endocrine system.

Consider, for example, all the processes that must coordinate effectively for
you to stop your car at a red light. First of all, you must see the light; this means
that the light must impinge on one of your sense organs, your eye. Neural
impulses from your eye are relayed to your brain, where various features of the
stimulus are analyzed and compared with information about past events stored
in your memory. (You recognize that a red light in a certain context means
"stop.") The process of moving your foot to the brake pedal and pressing it is
initiated by the motor areas of the brain that control the muscles of your leg and
foot. In order to send the proper signals to these muscles, the brain must know
where your foot is as well as where you want it to go. The brain must maintain
some sort of register of the position of body parts relative to one another, which
is used to plan directed movements. You do not stop the car with one sudden
movement of your leg, however. A specialized part of your brain receives
continual *feedback* from leg and foot muscles so that you are aware of how much
pressure is being exerted and can alter your movements accordingly. At the
same time, your eyes and some of your other body senses tell you how quickly
the car is stopping. If the light turned red as you were speeding toward the
intersection, some of your endocrine glands would also be activated, leading to
increased heart rate, more rapid respiration, and other metabolic changes associated with fear; these processes would speed your reactions in an emergency.
Your stopping at a red light may seem quick and automatic, but it involves
numerous complex messages and adjustments. The information for these activities is transmitted by large networks of nerve cells, or neurons.

Many aspects of human behavior and mental functioning cannot be fully
understood without some knowledge of the underlying biological processes.
Our nervous system, sense organs, muscles, and glands enable us to be aware

of and adjust to our environment. Our perception of events depends on how our sense organs detect stimuli and how our brain interprets information coming from the senses. Much of our behavior is motivated by such needs as hunger, thirst, and the avoidance of fatigue or pain. Our ability to use language, to think, and to solve problems depends on a brain structure that is incredibly complex. Indeed, many physiological psychologists believe that specific patterns of electrical and chemical events in the brain are the very basis of our most intricate thought processes.

Some of the research relating psychological events to biological processes will be discussed when we talk, for example, about perception or motivation and emotion. This chapter provides a brief overview of the nervous system. Students with a background in biology will find most of the material familiar.

BASIC UNITS OF THE NERVOUS SYSTEM

The human brain is composed of 12 billion or more specialized cells called *neurons,* the basic units of the nervous system. It is important to understand neurons, for they undoubtedly hold the secrets of learning and mental functioning. We know their role in the transmission and coordination of nerve impulses, and we know how some types of neural circuits work; but we are just beginning to unravel their more complex functioning in learning, emotion, and thought.

Neurons and nerves

Although neurons differ markedly in size and appearance, depending on the specialized job they perform, they have certain common characteristics (see Figure 2-1). Projecting from the *cell body* are a number of short branches called *dendrites* (from the Greek word *dendron,* meaning "tree"). The dendrites and the membrane covering the cell body receive messages from adjacent neurons. These messages are in turn transmitted to other neurons (or to muscles and glands) by a long, slender tubelike extension of the cell called an *axon.* If an axon is stimulated in its center, it will conduct impulses in either direction (that is, toward the cell body or away from it). However, nervous impulses can cross the junctions between neurons, called *synapses,* only in one direction—from the axon of one neuron to the cell body or dendrites of another neuron. A synapse is not a direct connection; there is a slight physical separation across which the impulse is transmitted by means of chemicals contained in the *terminal buttons* at the end of the axon. The axons from a great many neurons (perhaps 1,000) may synapse upon the dendrites and cell body of a single neuron (see Figure 2-2).

Although all neurons have these general features, they vary greatly in size and shape. A neuron in the spinal cord may have an axon 2 to 3 feet long, running from the tip of the spine to the big toe; a neuron in the brain may cover only a few thousandths of an inch with all its parts (see Figure 2-3, page 34).

There are three types of neurons. *Sensory neurons* (also called *afferent neurons*) transmit impulses received by *receptors* to the central nervous system. The receptors are specialized cells in the sense organs, muscles, skin, and joints that

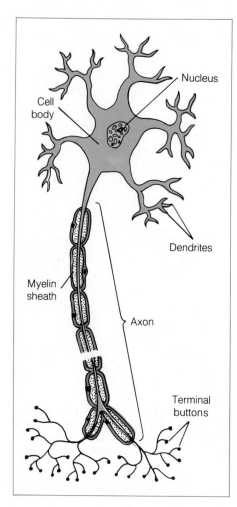

Figure 2-1
Neuron

An idealized diagram of a neuron. Stimulation of the dendrites or the cell body activates an electrochemical nerve impulse that travels along the axon to the terminal buttons. The myelin sheath covers the axons of some, but not all, neurons; it helps to increase the speed of nerve impulse conduction.

detect physical or chemical changes and translate these events into impulses that travel along the sensory neurons. *Motor neurons* (also called *efferent neurons*) carry outgoing signals from the brain or spinal cord to the effector organs, namely the muscles and glands. *Interneurons* (also called *associative neurons*) receive the signals from the sensory neurons and send impulses to other interneurons or to motor neurons. Interneurons are found only in the brain and spinal cord.

A *nerve* is a bundle of elongated axons belonging to hundreds or thousands of neurons. A single nerve may contain axons from both afferent and efferent neurons. Closely interwoven among the neurons are a large number of *glial cells* (from the Greek word *glia,* meaning "glue"). The glial cells help to hold the neurons in place and provide them with nutrients.

Axonal conduction

The movement of a neural impulse along an axon is quite different from the flow of electric current through a wire. Electricity travels at the speed of light (186,300 miles per second), whereas a nerve impulse in the human body may travel at anywhere from 2 to 200 miles per hour, depending on the diameter of the axon and other factors. The analogy of a firework fuse has sometimes been used: when a fuse is lighted, one part of the fuse lights the next part, the impulse being regenerated along the way. However, the details of neural transmission are much more complex than this. The process is *electrochemical.* The thin membrane that holds together the protoplasm of the cell is not equally permeable to the different types of electrically charged ions that normally float in the protoplasm of the cell and in the liquid surrounding the cell. In its resting state, the cell membrane keeps out positively charged sodium ions (Na^+) and allows in potassium ions (K^+) and chloride ions (Cl^-). As a result, there is a small electrical potential, or voltage difference, across the membrane. The inside of a nerve cell is more negative than the outside; this is its *resting potential.*

When the axon is stimulated, the electrical potential across the membrane is reduced at the point of stimulation. If the reduction in potential is large enough, the permeability of the cell membrane suddenly changes, allowing the sodium ions to enter the cell. This process is called *depolarization;* now the outside of the cell membrane becomes *negative* with respect to the inside. This change affects the adjacent portion of the axon, causing its membrane to depolarize and thereby permit the inflow of sodium ions. This process, repeating itself down the length of the axon, is the nerve impulse. The nerve impulse is also known as the *action potential,* in contrast to the resting potential. Because the nerve impulse is generated anew at each stage along the axon, it does not diminish in size during transmission.

The axons of most neurons are covered by a thin fatty sheath, the *myelin sheath,* which serves to insulate them; such fibers are known as *myelinated* fibers. If the myelin sheath were continuous, it would prevent conduction; but it is interrupted approximately every 2 millimeters by junctions called *nodes,* where the myelin is very thin or absent. Because conduction jumps along the axon from node to node, it is much more rapid in myelinated fibers than in nonmyelinated fibers. The myelin sheath was a late development in evolution and is characteristic of the nervous systems of higher animals. The fact that the formation of the myelin sheaths in many regions of the brain is not completed until some time after birth suggests that the maturation of the infant's sensory and motor abilities is related to the gradual process of myelination.

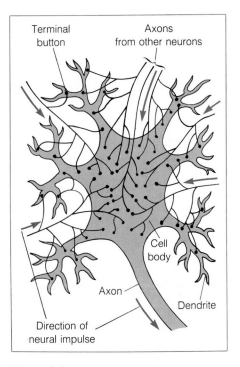

Figure 2-2
Synapses at the Cell Body
of a Neuron
Many different axons, each of which branches repeatedly, synapse on the dendrites and cell body of a single neuron. Each branch of an axon ends in a swelling called a terminal button, which contains the chemical that is released and transmits the nerve impulse across the synapse to the dendrites or cell body of the next cell.

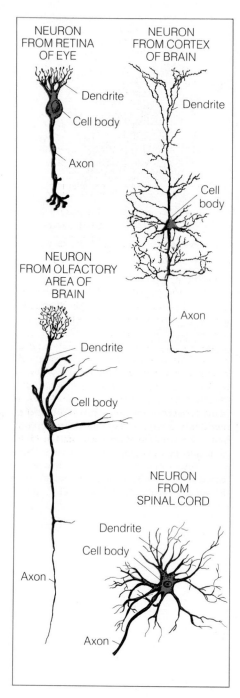

Figure 2-3
Shapes and Relative Sizes of Neurons
The axon on a neuron from the spinal cord may be several feet long.

Synaptic transmission

The synaptic junction between neurons is of tremendous importance because it is there that nerve cells transfer signals. A single neuron discharges, or "fires," when the stimulation reaching it via multiple synapses exceeds a certain threshold level. Because its axon does not transmit prior to this, the neuron is said to follow an *all-or-none* principle of action. The neuron fires in a single, brief burst and is then temporarily inactive (in what is called a *refractory phase*) for a few thousandths of a second. During the refractory phase, the cell returns to its resting potential. The size of the action potential is constant, and once started, it travels down the axon to the synapses. But whether the neuron fires or not depends on *graded potentials* (potentials that are not all-or-none) in the dendrites and cell body. These graded potentials are induced by stimulation from other neurons across the synapses, and their size varies with the amount and kind of incoming activity. When the sum of the graded potentials becomes sufficiently large, enough depolarization is generated to trigger the all-or-none action potential. If the graded potentials do not reach the discharge threshold of the action potential, no activity is transmitted down the axon.

Since the action potential is all-or-none, how is information about stimulus intensity conveyed? The answer is that a strong stimulus will (1) cause the individual neuron to fire more frequently and (2) fire more neurons than a weaker stimulus. For example, the neurons that are responding to the stretching of a muscle will fire at a rate proportional to the amount of stretch; the greater the stretch, the more neurons will fire.

NEUROTRANSMITTERS   As we have said, neurons do not connect directly at a synapse; there is a slight gap across which the signal must be transmitted (see Figure 2-4). Although in a few areas of the nervous system the electrical activity in one neuron can stimulate another neuron directly, in the vast majority of cases, a chemical serves as the transmitter agent. When a neural impulse reaches the end of the axon, a chemical—called a *neurotransmitter*—is released into the synaptic gap. The neurotransmitter binds to specific receptors on the membrane of the receiving cell and changes its permeability in the direction of depolarization. If depolarization becomes large enough to exceed threshold, the cell fires an all-or-none action potential down its axon to influence other neurons.

This process occurs at an *excitatory synapse*. But there are also *inhibitory synapses* that work in an analogous but opposite manner. The neurotransmitter released at an inhibitory synapse produces a shift in the cell membrane potential of the receiving neuron that is *opposite* in direction to the action potential; that is, at an inhibitory synapse, the neurotransmitter tends to keep the membrane potential of the receiving cell *below* threshold. During this brief period, it is considerably more difficult for excitatory synapses to fire the neuron. Remember that any one neuron receives synapses from many other neurons. Some of these synapses may be excitatory and some inhibitory. The constant interplay of excitation and inhibition determines the likelihood that a given neuron will fire an all-or-none action potential at any given moment.

A number of neurotransmitters have been definitely identified, and many others probably exist. Acetylcholine (ACh) is the chemical transmitter at every synapse where a nerve axon terminates at a skeletal muscle fiber and hence is responsible for muscle contraction. Certain drugs that block the release of ACh from the terminal buttons can cause fatal muscular paralysis. For example, *botulinus toxin*, which forms from bacteria in improperly canned foods, can cause death when the muscles for breathing become paralyzed. *Curare*, a poison once used by South American Indians to tip their arrows, occupies the ACh receptor sites in the receiving cell, thus preventing ACh from acting and resulting in temporary paralysis. Death from curare, too, occurs because of paralysis of the muscles for breathing. But if the victim is artificially respirated until the effects of the drug wear off, there is no permanent damage. Some nerve gases developed for warfare cause paralysis by destroying an enzyme that normally inactivates ACh once a nerve has fired. This produces a buildup of ACh so that normal synaptic transmission is impossible.

Some mood-altering drugs (such as chlorpromazine and LSD) create their effects by changing activity at the synapses. Chlorpromazine, a drug used to treat schizophrenia, blocks the receptors for the neurotransmitter dopamine and thus allows fewer messages to get through. LSD is similar in chemical structure to the neurotransmitter serotonin, which affects emotions. Evidence shows that LSD accumulates in certain brain cells, where it may act like serotonin and overstimulate the cells.

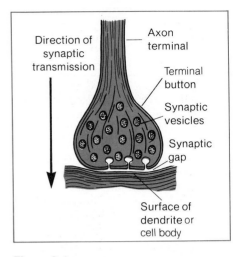

Figure 2-4
Synaptic Junction
When a nerve impulse reaches the end of an axon, it stimulates the synaptic vesicles to discharge a chemical neurotransmitter into the synaptic gap. The neurotransmitter molecules combine with receptor molecules in the membrane of the receiving cell in a lock-and-key type of action. The combination of molecules changes the membrane permeability of the receiving cell, making it either more likely to fire (excitatory synapse) or less likely to fire (inhibitory synapse). Any given neuron will have only one type of neurotransmitter in all of its synaptic vesicles.

ORGANIZATION
OF THE NERVOUS SYSTEM

All parts of the nervous system are interrelated. However, for purposes of anatomical discussion, the nervous system can be separated into the following divisions and subdivisions:

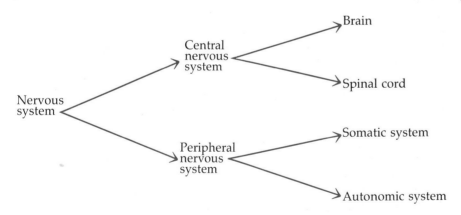

The *central nervous system* includes all the neurons in the brain and spinal cord, and it contains the majority of the body's neurons. The *peripheral nervous system* consists of the nerves connecting the brain and spinal cord to the other parts of the body. The peripheral nervous system is further subdivided into the *somatic system* and the *autonomic system.*

The sensory nerves of the somatic system transmit information about external stimulation from the skin, muscles, and joints to the central nervous system; they make us aware of pain, pressure, and temperature variations. The motor nerves of the somatic system carry impulses from the central nervous system to the muscles of the body, where they initiate action. All the muscles we use

When the electrical impulse reaches the end of an axon, *neurotransmitter molecules* are released that cross the synapse and combine with *receptor molecules* in the membrane of the target neuron. The neurotransmitter and receptor molecules fit together in the same way as one piece of a jigsaw puzzle fits another or as a key fits a lock. The *lock-and-key* action of the two molecules changes the electrical properties of the target cell, causing it to fire or preventing it from firing.

To serve its function, every key requires a lock and every neurotransmitter requires a receptor. Many commonly used drugs—from tranquilizers such as Valium to street drugs like angel dust—interact with receptor molecules in very much the same way as neurotransmitters. Molecules of these drugs are shaped enough like those of the neurotransmitters to work as if they were keys to the lock of receptor molecules.

A good example is the *opiates*, a class of psychoactive drugs that includes heroin and morphine. In molecular shape, the opiates resemble a group of neurotransmitters in the brain called *opiate peptides*. The discovery that there are naturally occurring peptides in the brain

that mimic opiates has led to speculation about a chemical control system in the body to cope with stress and pain. Individuals who appear indifferent to pain may have an unusual ability to increase the production of these natural painkillers when they are needed. Research with one of the opiate peptides, *enkephalin*, has helped explain why a painkiller like morphine can be addictive. Under normal conditions, enkephalin occupies a certain number of opiate receptors. Morphine relieves pain by binding to receptors that are left unfilled. Too much morphine can cause a drop in enkephalin production, leaving opiate receptors unfilled. The body then requires more morphine to fill the unoccupied receptors and to reduce pain. When morphine is discontinued, the opiate receptors are left unfilled, causing painful withdrawal symptoms.

Psychoactive drugs are those agents that influence mental functions. As with opiates, the other psychoactive drugs can be understood in relation to their effects on the various neurotransmitter systems. Most drug actions on the nervous system occur at synapses. Different drugs can have different actions at

the same synapse. One drug might prevent the release of a neurotransmitter, and another might occupy the receptor site so that the normal neurotransmitter is blocked out. Table 2-1 lists some of the psychoactive drugs and relates them to the neurotransmitters they are thought to influence. The drug action will either increase or decrease the effectiveness of neural transmission at the synapse; the + and − signs in the table indicate whether the drug listed increases or decreases efficiency.

Listed in the table are the antipsychotic agents *chlorpromazine* and *reserpine*, which have proved effective in treating schizophrenia (a mental illness to be discussed in Chapter 15). Both drugs act on norepinephrine and dopamine systems, but their antipsychotic action is primarily due to their effect on the neurotransmitter dopamine. It appears that chlorpromazine blocks dopamine receptors, whereas reserpine reduces dopamine levels by destroying storage vesicles in the terminal buttons of the axon. The effectiveness of these drugs in treating schizophrenia has led to the *dopamine hypothesis*, which postulates that schizophrenia is due to an ex-

in making voluntary movements, as well as involuntary adjustments in posture and balance, are controlled by these nerves.

The nerves of the autonomic system run to and from the internal organs, regulating such processes as respiration, heart rate, and digestion. The autonomic system, which plays a major role in emotion, will be discussed later in this chapter.

The nerve fibers running from various parts of the body to and from the brain are gathered together in the *spinal cord,* where they are protected by the bony spinal vertebrae. Some of the simplest stimulus-response reflexes are carried out at the level of the spinal cord. One example is the knee jerk, the extension of the leg in response to a tap on the tendon that runs in front of the knee cap. Frequently a doctor uses this test to determine the efficiency of the spinal reflexes. The natural function of this reflex is to ensure that the leg will extend when the knee is bent by the force of gravity so that the organism remains standing. When the knee tendon is tapped, the attached muscle

Psychoactive Drugs and Neurotransmitters

cess of dopamine activity in critical cell groups within the brain. The key evidence for the hypothesis is that all known antipsychotic agents block the transmission of impulses by dopamine molecules. Also, *amphetamines*, which can cause a schizophrenic-like state in normal individuals, appears to enhance dopamine activity. The dopamine hypothesis has wide support, but as of yet, efforts to demonstrate an actual increase in dopamine concentrations in schizophrenics as compared with normals have not been successful.

Research on the relationship between psychoactive drugs and neurotransmitters has increased our understanding of how these drugs work. Other avenues of research have demonstrated that human memory can be temporarily enhanced by drugs that affect cholinergic activity (the activity of neurons that use ACh as a neurotransmitter). But due to the complexity of the cholinergic system, drugs that permanently enhance memory are still a long way off (Davis and Mohs, 1982). Many psychological problems will become clearer as we discover more about the intricacies of neural communication.

Table 2-1
Psychoactive Agents and Neurotransmitters

Listed are the neurotransmitter systems upon which various drugs are thought to act. The drug action will either be to increase (+) or decrease (−) the efficiency of transmission at the synaptic junction. (After Kolb and Whishaw, 1980)

DRUG	NEUROTRANSMITTER	ACTION
Sedative-hypnotics		
Barbiturates	Norepinephrine	−
Benzodiazepines	Norepinephrine	−
Alcohol	Norepinephrine	−
Stimulants		
Amphetamines	Norepinephrine	+
Cocaine	Norepinephrine	+
Desipramine	Norepinephrine	+
Imipramine	Serotonin	+
Antipsychotic agents		
Chlorpromazine	Dopamine	−
Reserpine	Dopamine, norepinephrine	−
Opiates		
Heroin, morphine	Opiate peptides, such as endorphins and enkephalins	+
Psychedelics		
Atropine	Acetylcholine	−
Muscarine	Acetylcholine	+
Mescaline, cannabis	Norepinephrine	+
LSD, psilocybin	Serotonin	+ or −
	Norepinephrine	+

stretches, and a message from sensory cells embedded in the muscle is transmitted through sensory neurons to the spinal cord. There the sensory neurons synapse directly with motor neurons, which transmit impulses back to the same muscle, causing it to contract and the leg to extend.

Although this response can occur solely in the spinal cord without any assistance from the brain, it normally is modulated by messages from the higher nervous centers. If you grip your hands just before the knee is tapped, the extension movement is exaggerated. Or if you consciously want to inhibit the reflex just before the doctor taps the tendon, you can do so. The basic mechanism is built into the spinal cord, but it can be modified by higher brain centers.

The simplest reflex may involve only sensory and motor neurons, but most reflexes also involve one or more *interneurons* in the spinal cord, which mediate between incoming and outgoing neurons. Figure 2-5 (on next page) shows a basic three-neuron reflex arc.

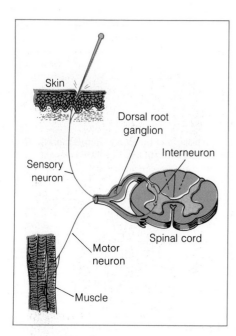

Figure 2-5
Three-Neuron Reflex Arc
Diagram illustrates how nerve impulses from a sense organ in the skin reach a skeletal muscle by a three-neuron arc within the spinal cord. Awareness of this automatic reflex occurs because impulses also reach the cerebral hemisphere by way of an ascending tract. The H-shaped portion is gray matter at the center of the spinal cord, consisting largely of cell bodies and their interconnections.

HIERARCHICAL STRUCTURE OF THE BRAIN

Some brain structures are clearly demarcated; others gradually merge into each other, and this leads to debate about their exact boundaries and the functions they control. For our purposes, it will be helpful to think of the human brain as composed of three concentric layers that developed at different stages in evolution: (1) a primitive *central core;* (2) the *limbic system,* which evolved upon this core at a later stage of evolution; and (3) the *cerebral hemispheres* (together known as the *cerebrum*) responsible for higher mental processes. Figure 2-6 shows how these layers fit together. The three concentric layers may be compared with the more detailed cross section of the human brain in Figure 2-7.

Central core

The central core includes most of the brain stem. The first slight enlargement of the spinal cord as it enters the skull is the *medulla,* a narrow structure (about $1\frac{1}{2}$ inches long) that controls breathing and some reflexes that help the organism maintain an upright posture. At this point, also, the major nerve tracts coming up from the spinal cord and descending from the brain cross over so that the right side of the brain is connected to the left side of the body, and the left side of the brain, to the right side of the body. We will have more to say about the significance of this crossover later.

CEREBELLUM   Attached to the rear of the brain stem, slightly above the medulla, is a convoluted structure, the *cerebellum.* The cerebellum is concerned primarily with the coordination of movement, and its structure is much the same in lower vertebrates (such as snakes and fish) as in humans. Specific movements may be initiated at higher levels, but their smooth coordination depends on the cerebellum. The cerebellum regulates muscle tone and orchestrates the intricate movements of a fish swimming, a bird flying, or a human being playing a musical instrument. Damage to the cerebellum results in jerky, uncoordinated movements; often the person can no longer perform simple movements (such as walking) automatically but must concentrate on each component of the total action.

THALAMUS AND HYPOTHALAMUS   Located just above the brain stem inside the cerebral hemispheres are two egg-shaped groups of nerve cell nuclei that make up the *thalamus.* One region of the thalamus acts as a relay station and directs incoming information to the cerebrum from the sense receptors for vision, hearing, touch, and taste. Another region of the thalamus plays an important role in the control of sleep and wakefulness and is considered part of the reticular system.

The *hypothalamus* is a much smaller structure, located just below the thalamus. Despite its size, the hypothalamus plays an extremely important role in many aspects of motivation. Centers in the hypothalamus govern eating, drinking, and sexual behavior. The hypothalamus regulates endocrine activity and maintains *homeostasis.* Homeostasis refers to the general level of functioning characteristic of the healthy organism, such as normal body temperature, heart rate, and blood pressure. Under stress, the usual equilibrium is disturbed, and processes are set into motion to correct the disequilibrium and return the body to its normal level of functioning. For example, if we are too warm, we perspire; and if we are too cool, we shiver. Both of these processes tend to restore normal temperature and are controlled by the hypothalamus. The hypothalamus contains control mechanisms that detect changes in body systems and correct the imbalance.

The hypothalamus also plays an important role in emotion. We noted in Chapter 1 that mild electrical stimulation of certain areas in the hypothalamus produces feelings of pleasure, while stimulation in adjacent regions produces sensations that appear to be unpleasant or painful. By its influence on the pituitary gland, which lies just below it (see Figure 2-7), the hypothalamus controls hormonal reactions to fear and stress.

RETICULAR SYSTEM A network of neural circuits that extends from the lower brain stem up to the thalamus, traversing through some of the other central core structures, is the *reticular* ("network") *system*. The reticular system plays an important role in controlling our state of arousal or awareness. When an electric current of a certain voltage is sent through electrodes implanted in the reticular system of a cat or dog, the animal goes to sleep; stimulation by a current with a more rapidly changing wave form awakens the sleeping animal. If lesions are made in the reticular system, the animal often becomes permanently stuporous or goes into a coma.

The reticular system may also play a role in our ability to focus our attention. All of the sense receptors have nerve fibers that feed into the reticular system; and the system appears to act as a filter, allowing some of the sensory

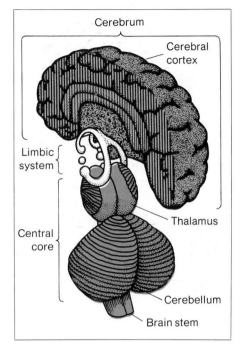

Figure 2-6
Three Concentric Layers
of the Human Brain
The central core and the limbic system are shown in their entirety, but the left cerebral hemisphere has been removed. The cerebellum of the central core controls balance and muscular coordination; the thalamus serves as a switchboard for messages coming from the sense organs; the hypothalamus (not shown but located below the thalamus) regulates endocrine activity and such life-maintaining processes as metabolism and temperature control. The limbic system is concerned with actions that satisfy basic needs and with emotion. The cerebral cortex, an outer layer of cells covering the cerebrum, is the center of higher mental processes, where sensations are registered, voluntary actions initiated, decisions made, and plans formulated.

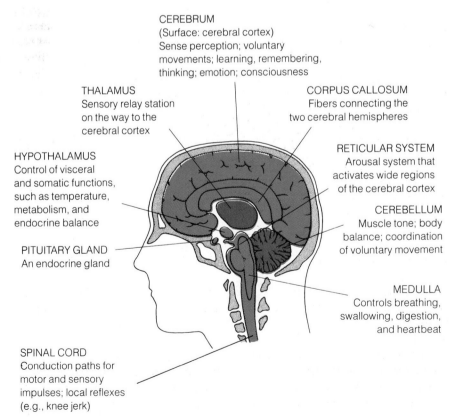

CEREBRUM
(Surface: cerebral cortex)
Sense perception; voluntary
movements; learning, remembering,
thinking; emotion; consciousness

THALAMUS
Sensory relay station
on the way to the
cerebral cortex

CORPUS CALLOSUM
Fibers connecting the
two cerebral hemispheres

HYPOTHALAMUS
Control of visceral
and somatic functions,
such as temperature,
metabolism, and
endocrine balance

RETICULAR SYSTEM
Arousal system that
activates wide regions
of the cerebral cortex

PITUITARY GLAND
An endocrine gland

CEREBELLUM
Muscle tone; body
balance; coordination
of voluntary movement

MEDULLA
Controls breathing,
swallowing, digestion,
and heartbeat

SPINAL CORD
Conduction paths for
motor and sensory
impulses; local reflexes
(e.g., knee jerk)

Figure 2-7
The Human Brain
This schematic drawing shows the main subdivisions of the human central nervous system and their functions. (Only the upper portion of the spinal cord, which is also part of the central nervous system, is shown.)

messages to pass to the cerebral cortex (to conscious awareness) while blocking others. Thus, in a moment of intense concentration, you may be unaware of the noises around you or a pain that was previously quite noticeable.

Limbic system

Around the central core of the brain, lying along the innermost edge of the cerebral hemispheres, are a number of structures that together are called the *limbic system*. From an evolutionary view, the limbic system is more recent than the central core; it is fully developed only in mammals. This system is closely interconnected with the hypothalamus and appears to impose additional controls over some of the "instinctive" behaviors regulated by the hypothalamus and brain stem. Animals that have only rudimentary limbic systems (for example, fish and reptiles) carry out activities such as feeding, attacking, fleeing from danger, and mating by means of very stereotyped behaviors. In mammals, the limbic system seems to inhibit some of the instinctive patterns, allowing the organism to be more flexible and adaptive to changes in the environment.

One part of the limbic system, the *hippocampus,* plays a special role in memory. Individuals with damage to this area are apparently unable to store new information in memory. They can remember skills and information learned prior to the injury but cannot remember anything new.

The limbic system is also involved in emotional behavior. Monkeys with lesions in some regions of the limbic system show rage reactions at the slightest provocation, suggesting that the destroyed area was exerting an inhibiting influence. Monkeys with lesions in other areas of the limbic system no longer express aggressive behavior and show no hostility, even when attacked. They simply ignore the attacker and act as if nothing had happened.

Treating the brain as three concentric structures—the central core, the limbic system, and the cerebrum—must not lead us to think of these interrelated structures as independent. We might use the analogy of a bank of interrelated computers. Each has specialized functions, but they still work together to produce the most effective result. Similarly, the analysis of information coming from the senses requires one kind of computation and decision process (for which the cerebrum is well adapted) differing from that which controls a reflexive sequence of activities (the limbic system). The finer adjustments of the muscles (as in writing or playing a musical instrument) require another kind of control system, in this case mediated by the cerebellum. All these activities are ordered into complex systems that maintain the integrity of the organism.

Both playing (left) and fighting (right) appear to be controlled by the limbic system.

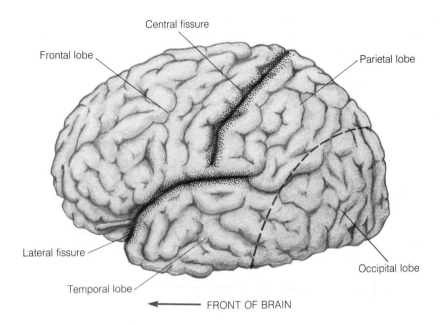

Central fissure

Frontal lobe

Parietal lobe

Lateral fissure

Occipital lobe

Temporal lobe

← FRONT OF BRAIN

Figure 2-8
The Four Lobes of the Left Cortex
The central fissure and lateral fissure are landmarks separating the lobes of the cortex.

CEREBRAL CORTEX

Structure of the cerebral cortex

The cerebrum is more highly developed in human beings than in any other organism. The *cerebral cortex* is the layer of nerve cell bodies about 3 millimeters thick covering the cerebrum; in Latin, *cortex* means "bark." The cortical layer of a preserved brain appears gray because it consists largely of nerve cell bodies and unmyelinated fibers—hence, the term "gray matter." The inside of the cerebrum, beneath the cortex, is composed mostly of myelinated axons and appears white. It is in the cerebral cortex that our more complex mental activities take place.

The cerebral cortex of a lower mammal, such as the rat, is small and relatively smooth. As we ascend the phylogenetic scale to the higher mammals, the amount of cortex relative to the amount of total brain tissue increases accordingly, and the cortex becomes progressively more wrinkled and convoluted, so that its actual surface area is far greater than it would be if it were a smooth covering over the surface of the cerebrum. There is a general correlation between the cortical development of a species, its position on the phylogenetic scale, and the complexity of its behavior.

All of the sensory systems (for example, vision, audition, and touch) project information to specific areas of the cortex. The movements of body parts (motor responses) are controlled by another area of the cortex. The rest of the cortex, which is neither sensory nor motor, consists of association areas. These areas are concerned with more complex aspects of behavior—memory, thought, and language—and occupy the largest area of the human cortex.

Before discussing some of these areas, we need a few landmarks to use in describing areas of the *cerebral hemispheres.* The two hemispheres are basically symmetrical with a deep division between them, running from front to rear. So, our first classification is the division into *right* and *left hemispheres.* Each hemisphere is divided into four *lobes:* the *frontal, parietal, occipital,* and *temporal.* The divisions between these lobes are shown in Figure 2-8. The frontal lobe is separated from the parietal lobe by the *central fissure,* running from near the top of the head sideways to the ears. The division between the parietal lobe and the occipital lobe is less clear-cut; for our purpose, it suffices to know that the parietal lobe is at the top of the brain behind the central fissure and that the occipital lobe is at the rear of the brain. The temporal lobe is demarcated by a deep fissure at the side of the brain, the *lateral fissure.*

Cortical areas and their functions

MOTOR AREA   The *motor area* (or *motor cortex*) controls the voluntary movements of the body; it lies just in front of the central fissure (see Figure 2-9). Electrical stimulation at certain spots on the motor cortex produces movement of specific body parts; when these same spots are injured, movement is impaired. The body is represented on the motor cortex in approximately upside-down form. For example, movements of the toes are mediated near the top of the head, whereas tongue and mouth movements are mediated near the bottom of the motor area. Movements on the right side of the body are governed by the motor cortex of the left hemisphere; movements on the left side, by the right hemisphere.

SOMATOSENSORY AREA   In the parietal lobe, separated from the motor area by the central fissure, lies an area that if stimulated electrically produces a sensory experience somewhere on the opposite side of the body. It is as though a part of the body were being touched or moved. This is called the *somatosensory* (body-sense) *area* (or *somatosensory cortex*). Heat, cold, touch, pain, and the sense of body movement are all represented here. The lower extremities of the body are represented high on the area of the opposite hemisphere; the face, low on the area of the opposite hemisphere.

Most of the nerve fibers in the pathways that radiate to and from the somatosensory and motor areas cross to the opposite side of the body. Thus, the sensory impulses from the right side of the body go to the left somatosensory cortex, and the muscles of the right foot and hand are controlled by the left motor cortex. The motor and somatosensory cortex on each side of the brain is concerned mainly with the opposite side of the body.

Figure 2-9
Localization of Function
in the Left Cortex
Much of the cortex is involved in generating movements and in analyzing sensory inputs. These areas (which include motor, somatosensory, visual, auditory, and olfactory areas) are present on both sides of the brain and in all species that have a well-developed cortex. Other areas are more narrowly specialized, often found on only one side of the brain, and present only in human beings. For example, Broca's area and Wernicke's area are involved in the production and understanding of language, and the angular gyrus is involved in matching language in a visual and auditory mode; these functions exist only on the left side of the human brain. The right side of the human brain, not shown in this figure, has its own specialized functions, including the analysis of complex visual scenes and some aspects of music perception.

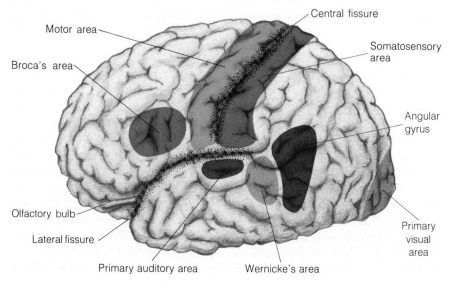

It seems to be a general rule that the amount of somatosensory or motor cortex associated with a particular part of the body is directly related to its sensitivity and use. Among four-footed mammals, the dog has only a small amount of cortical tissue representing the forepaws, whereas the raccoon (which makes extensive use of its forepaws in exploring and manipulating its environment) has a much larger representative cortical area, including regions for the separate fingers of the forepaw (Welker, Johnson, and Pubols, 1964). The rat, which learns a great deal about its environment by means of its sensitive whiskers, has a separate cortical area for each whisker (Van der Loos and Woolsey, 1973).

VISUAL AREA   At the back of each occipital lobe is an area of the cortex important in vision, known as the *visual area*. Figure 2-10 shows the optic nerve fibers and neural pathways leading from each eye to the visual cortex. Notice that some of the fibers go from the right eye to the right cerebral hemisphere and from the left eye to the left hemisphere, whereas other fibers cross over at a junction called the *optic chiasma* and go to the opposite hemisphere. Fibers from the right sides of both eyes go to the right hemisphere of the brain, and fibers from the left sides of both eyes go to the left hemisphere. Consequently, damage to the visual area of one hemisphere (say, the left) will result in blind fields in the left sides of *both* eyes causing a loss of vision to the right side of the environment. This fact is sometimes helpful in pinpointing the location of a brain tumor or injury.

When the visual area of a human being is stimulated electrically during the course of brain surgery, the patient (who is under local anesthetic) reports seeing flashes or spots of light. This phenomenon forms the basis for research that may in time provide "artificial vision" for blind people. An array of electrodes is implanted in the visual area of the blind subject. When different groups of these electrodes are stimulated electrically, the blind subject experiences patterns of visual sensations. These sensations are a crude approximation of real sight, but further research may provide a device that will enable blind persons to perceive objects and to read (Dobelle and others, 1976).

AUDITORY AREA   The *auditory area* is found on the surface of the temporal lobe at the side of each hemisphere and is involved in the analysis of the more complex aspects of auditory signals. It is particularly concerned with the patterning of sound in time, as in human speech. There is some spatial mapping in the auditory area, one part being sensitive to high tones and a different part sensitive to low tones. Both ears are represented in the auditory areas on both sides; however, the connections to the contralateral side are stronger.

ASSOCIATION AREAS   The many large areas of the cerebral cortex that are not directly concerned with sensory or motor processes are called *association areas*.

The *frontal association areas* (those parts of the frontal lobes anterior to the motor area) appear to play an important role in the thought processes required for problem solving. In monkeys, for example, lesions in the frontal lobes destroy the ability to solve a delayed-response problem. In this kind of problem, food is placed in one of two cups while the monkey watches, and the cups are covered with identical objects. An opaque screen is then placed between the monkey and the cups; after a specified time (from 5 to 60 seconds), the screen is removed, and the monkey is allowed to choose one of the cups. Normal monkeys can "remember" the correct cup after delays of several minutes, but monkeys with frontal lobe lesions cannot solve the problem if the delay is more

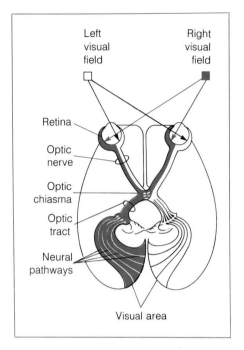

Figure 2-10
Visual Pathways
Light waves from objects in the right visual field fall on the left half of each retina; light waves from the left visual field fall on the right half of each retina. The optic nerve bundles from each eye meet at the optic chiasma, where the nerve fibers from the inner, or nasal, half of the retina cross over and go to opposite sides of the brain. Thus, stimuli falling on the right side of each retina are transmitted to the occipital cortex of the right cerebral hemisphere, and stimuli impinging on the left side of each retina are transmitted to the left cerebral hemisphere. In terms of the visual field, this means that objects in the right visual field are projected to the left cerebral hemisphere, whereas objects in the left visual field are projected to the right hemisphere.

than a second or so. This delayed-response deficit following brain lesions is unique to the frontal cortex; it does not occur if lesions are made in other cortical regions (French and Harlow, 1962).

Human beings who have suffered damage to the frontal association areas can perform many intellectual tasks normally, including delayed-response problems. Their ability to use language probably enables them to remember the correct response. They do have difficulty, however, when it is necessary to shift frequently from one strategy to another while working on a problem (Milner, 1964).

The *posterior association areas* are located among the various primary sensory areas and appear to consist of subareas, each serving a particular sense. For example, the lower portion of the temporal lobe is related to visual perception. Lesions in this area produce deficits in the ability to recognize and discriminate different forms. The lesion does not cause loss of visual acuity as would a lesion in the primary visual area of the occipital lobe; the individual "sees" the forms (and can trace the outline) but cannot identify the shape or distinguish it from a different form. In contrast, the association areas of the parietal lobe are important for locating objects in sensory space and for maintaining internal "maps" of the environment.

A DIVIDED BRAIN

So far we have treated the cerebral hemispheres as if they were identical, save for the fact that the left hemisphere controls the right side of the body and the right hemisphere controls the left. And, indeed, to the naked eye, the two halves of the human brain do look like mirror images of each other. But closer examination reveals certain asymmetries; when brains are carefully measured during autopsies, one hemisphere, usually the left, is almost always larger than the other.

As early as 1861, the French anthropologist Paul Broca examined the brain of a patient with speech loss and found damage in an area of the left hemisphere just above the lateral fissure in the frontal lobe. This region, known as *Broca's area* and shown in Figure 2-9, is involved in the production of speech sounds. Destruction of the equivalent region in the right hemisphere usually does not result in speech impairment. The brain areas involved in understanding speech and in the ability to write and understand written words are also usually located in the left hemisphere. Thus, a person who suffers a stroke that damages the left hemisphere is more likely to show language impairment than one whose damage is confined to the right hemisphere. This is usually true for right-handed individuals because their left hemisphere is almost always dominant. (Remember that the left hemisphere controls the motor functions of the right side of the body.) Some left-handed people have speech centers located in the right hemisphere or divided between the two, but the majority have language functions in the left hemisphere (the same as right-handed individuals).

Although the left hemisphere's role in language has been known for some time, only recently has it been possible to investigate what each hemisphere can do on its own. In the normal individual, the brain functions as an integrated whole; information in one hemisphere is immediately transferred to the other by way of a broad band of connecting nerve fibers called the *corpus callosum.* This connecting bridge can cause a problem in some forms of epilepsy, because a seizure starting in one hemisphere may cross over and trigger a massive discharge of neurons in the other. In an effort to prevent such generalized seizures in some severe epileptics, neurosurgeons have surgically severed the corpus callosum. The operation has generally proved successful and results in a significant decrease in seizures. In addition, there appear to be no undesirable aftereffects; the patients seem to function in everyday life as well as individuals whose hemispheres are still connected. It took some very special tests to demonstrate how mental functions are affected by separating the two hemispheres. A little more background information is needed to understand the experiments we are about to describe.

We have seen that the motor nerves cross over as they leave the brain, so that the left cerebral hemisphere controls the right side of the body and the right hemisphere controls the left. We noted also that the area for the production of speech (Broca's area) is located in the left hemisphere. When the eyes are fixated directly ahead, images to the left of the fixation point go through both eyes to the right side of the brain and images to the right of the fixation point go to the left side of the brain (see Figure 2-11). Thus, each hemisphere has a view of that half of the visual field in which "its" hand normally functions; that is, the left hemisphere sees the right hand in the right visual field. In the normal brain, stimuli entering one hemisphere are rapidly communicated, by way of the corpus callosum, to the other, so that our brain functions as a unit. We will see what happens when the corpus callosum is severed—called a *split brain*—so that the two hemispheres cannot communicate.

Experiments with split-brain subjects

Roger Sperry pioneered research in this field and was awarded the Nobel Prize in 1981 for his research. In one of Sperry's test situations, a male subject who has undergone a split-brain operation is seated in front of a screen that hides his hands from view (see Figure 2-12A). His gaze is fixed at a spot on the center of the screen and the word *nut* is flashed very briefly (for one-tenth of a second) on the left side of the screen. Remember that this visual image goes to the right side of the brain, which controls the left side of the body. With his left hand, the subject can easily pick up the nut from a pile of objects hidden from view. But he cannot tell the experimenter what word flashed on the screen because speech is controlled by the left hemisphere and the visual image of *nut* was not transmitted to the left side. When questioned, the split-brain subject seems unaware of what his left hand is doing. Since the sensory input from the left hand goes to the right hemisphere, the left hemisphere receives no information about what the left hand is feeling or doing. All information is fed back to the right hemisphere, which received the original visual input of the word *nut*.

It is important that the word be flashed on the screen for no more than one-tenth of a second. If it remains longer, the subject can move his eyes so that the word is also projected to the left hemisphere. If the split-brain subject can move his eyes freely, information goes to both cerebral hemispheres; this is one reason why the deficiencies caused by severing the corpus callosum are not readily apparent in a person's daily activities.

Further experiments demonstrate that the split-brain subject can only communicate through speech what is going on in the left hemisphere. Figure 2-12B shows another test situation. The word *hatband* is flashed on the screen so that *hat* goes to the right hemisphere and *band* to the left. When asked what word he saw, the subject replies, "band." When asked what kind of band, he makes

Figure 2-11
Sensory Inputs to the Two Hemispheres
With the eyes fixated straight ahead, stimuli
to the left of the fixation point go to the right
cerebral hemisphere and stimuli to the right
go to the left hemisphere. The left hemisphere controls movements of the right hand
and the right hemisphere controls the left
hand. Hearing is largely crossed in its input,
but some sound representation goes to the
hemisphere on the same side as the ear. Olfac-
tion is received on the same side as the nos-
tril. The left hemisphere is dominant for most
people; it controls written and spoken language and mathematical calculations. The minor right hemisphere can understand only
simple language. Its main ability seems to
involve spatial construction and pattern
sense.

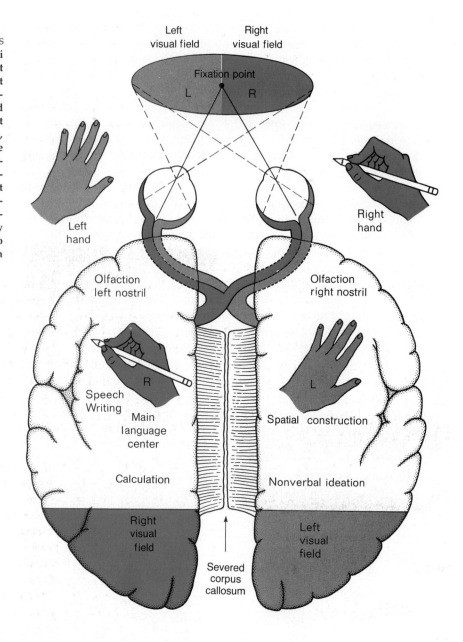

all sorts of guesses—"rubber band," "rock band," "band of robbers," and so
forth—and only hits on "hatband" by chance. Tests with other word combinations (such as *keycase* and *suitcase*), split so that half is projected to each hemisphere, show similar results. What is perceived by the right hemisphere does
not transfer to the conscious awareness of the left hemisphere. With the corpus
callosum severed, each hemisphere seems oblivious of the experiences of the
other.

If the split-brain subject is blindfolded and a familiar object (such as a
comb, toothbrush, or keycase) is placed in his left hand, he appears to know
what it is; for example, he can demonstrate its use by appropriate gestures. But
he cannot express his knowledge in speech. If asked what is going on while he
is manipulating the object, he has no idea. This is true as long as any sensory

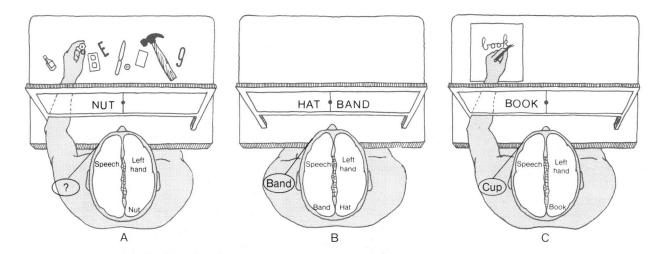

input from the object to the left (talking) hemisphere is blocked. But if the subject's right hand inadvertently touches the object or if it makes a characteristic sound (like the jingling of a keycase), the speaking hemisphere immediately gives the right answer.

Although the right hemisphere cannot speak, it does have some linguistic capabilities. It recognized the meaning of the word *nut,* as we saw in our first example, and it can write a little. In the experiment illustrated in Figure 2-12C, a split-brain subject is first shown a list of common objects such as cup, knife, book, and glass. This list is displayed long enough for the words to be projected to both hemispheres. Next, the list is removed and one of the words (for example, *book*) is flashed briefly on the left side of the screen so that it goes to the right hemisphere. If the subject is asked to write what he saw, his left hand will begin writing the word *book.* If asked what his left hand has written, he has no idea and will guess at any of the words on the original list. The subject knows he has written something because he feels the writing movements through his body. But because there is no communication between the right hemisphere that saw and wrote the word and the left hemisphere that controls speech, the subject cannot tell you what he wrote.

Figure 2-12
Testing the Abilities
of the Two Hemispheres
A. The split-brain subject correctly retrieves an object by touch with the left hand when its name is flashed to the right hemisphere, but he cannot name the object or describe what he has done. B. The word *hatband* is flashed so that *hat* goes to the right cerebral hemisphere and *band* goes to the left hemisphere. The subject reports that he sees the word *band* but has no idea what kind of band. C. A list of common objects (including *book* and *cup*) is initially shown to both hemispheres. One word from the list (*book*) is then projected to the right hemisphere. When given the command to do so, the left hand begins writing the word *book,* but when questioned the subject does not know what his left hand has written and guesses "cup." (After Sperry, 1970; and Nebes and Sperry, 1971)

Hemispheric specialization

Studies with split-brain subjects have made clear the striking differences between the functions of the two hemispheres. The left hemisphere governs our ability to express ourselves in language. It can perform many complicated logical and analytic activities and is skilled in mathematical computations. The right hemisphere can comprehend very simple language. It can respond to simple nouns by selecting objects such as a nut or comb, and it can even respond to associations of these objects. For example, if the right hemisphere is asked to retrieve from a group of objects the one used "for lighting fires," it will instruct the left hand to select a match. But it cannot comprehend more abstract linguistic forms. If the right hemisphere is presented with such simple commands as "wink," "nod," "shake head," or "smile," it seldom responds. The right hemisphere can add simple two-digit numbers but can do little beyond this in the way of calculation.

The right hemisphere appears to have a highly developed spatial and pattern sense. It is superior to the left hemisphere in constructing geometric

A great deal of our information about brain mechanisms for language comes from observations of patients suffering from brain damage. The damage may be due to tumors, penetrating head wounds, or the rupture of blood vessels. The term *aphasia* is used to describe language deficits caused by brain damage.

As already noted, Broca observed in the 1860s that damage to a specific area on the side of the left frontal lobe was linked to a speech disorder called *expressive aphasia*. Individuals with damage in Broca's area have difficulty enunciating words correctly and speak in a slow and labored way. Their speech often makes sense, but it includes only key words. Nouns are generally expressed in the singular; and adjectives, adverbs, articles, and conjunctions are apt to be omitted. However, these individuals have no difficulty understanding either spoken or written language.

In 1874, Carl Wernicke, a German investigator, reported that damage to another site in the cortex (also in the left hemisphere but in the temporal lobe) was linked to a language disorder called *receptive aphasia*. People with damage in Wernicke's area are not able to comprehend words; they can hear words, but they do not know their meaning. They can produce strings of words without difficulty and with proper articulation, but there are errors in word usage and

their speech tends to be meaningless.

Based on an analysis of these defects, Wernicke developed a model for language production and understanding. Although the model is 100 years old, its general features still appear to be correct. In recent years, Norman Geschwind has built on them and developed the theory known as the *Wernicke–Geschwind model*. A schematic overview of the model is presented here. According to the model, Broca's area is assumed to store "articulatory codes" that specify the sequence of muscle actions required to pronounce a word. When these codes are transferred to the motor cortex, they activate the muscles of the lips, tongue, and larynx in the proper sequence and produce a spoken word.

Wernicke's area, on the other hand, is where "auditory codes" and the meanings of words are stored. If a word is to be spoken, its auditory code must be activated in Wernicke's area and transmitted by a bundle of nerves to Broca's area, where it activates the corresponding articulatory code. The articulatory code in turn is transmitted to the motor cortex for the production of the spoken word.

If a word spoken by someone else is to be understood, it must be transmitted from the auditory cortex to Wernicke's area, where the spoken form of the word is matched to its auditory code,

which in turn activates the word's meaning. When a written word is presented, it is first registered in the visual cortex and then relayed to the angular gyrus, which associates the visual form of the word with its auditory code in Wernicke's area; once the word's auditory code has been found, so has its meaning. Thus, the meanings of words are stored along with their acoustical codes in Wernicke's area. Broca's area stores articulatory codes, and the angular gyrus matches the written form of a word to its auditory code; neither of these two areas, however, stores information about word meaning. The meaning of a word is retrieved only when its acoustical code is activated in Wernicke's area.

The model explains many of the language deficits shown by aphasics. Damage restricted to Broca's area disrupts speech production but has little effect on the comprehension of spoken or written language. Damage to Wernicke's area disrupts all aspects of language comprehension, but the individual can still articulate words properly (even though the output is meaningless) since Broca's area is intact. The model also predicts that individuals with damage in the angular gyrus will not be able to read but will have no problem in comprehending speech or in speaking. Finally, if damage is restricted to the audi-

and perspective drawings (see Figure 2-13). It can assemble colored blocks to match a complex design much more effectively than the left hemisphere. When split-brain subjects are asked to use their right hand to assemble the blocks according to a picture design, they make numerous mistakes. Sometimes they have trouble keeping their left hand from automatically correcting the mistakes being made by the right hand.

Studies with normal individuals tend to confirm the different specializations of the two hemispheres. For example, verbal information (such as words) can be identified faster and more accurately when flashed briefly to the left hemisphere (that is, in the right visual field) than to the right hemisphere. And *electroencephalogram* (EEG) studies indicate that electrical activity from the left hemisphere increases during a verbal task, whereas during a spatial task,

Language and the Brain

Wernicke–Geschwind Model

The left panel illustrates the sequence of events when a spoken word is presented and the individual repeats the word in spoken form. Neural impulses from the ear are sent to the primary auditory area, but the word cannot be understood until the signal is next transmitted to Wernicke's area. In Wernicke's area, the word's acoustical code is retrieved and

transmitted via a bundle of nerve fibers to Broca's area. In Broca's area, an articulatory code for the word is activated, which in turn directs the motor cortex. The motor cortex drives the lips, tongue, and larynx to produce the spoken word.

The right panel describes the case where a written word is presented and the individual is to speak the word. The visual

input to the eye is first transmitted to the primary visual cortex and then relayed to the angular gyrus. The angular gyrus associates the visual form of the word with the related acoustical code in Wernicke's area. Once the acoustical code is retrieved and the meaning of the word is established, speaking the word is accomplished through the same sequence of events as before.

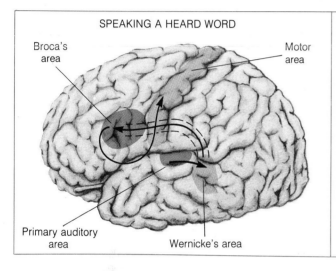

SPEAKING A HEARD WORD

Broca's area — Motor area — Primary auditory area — Wernicke's area

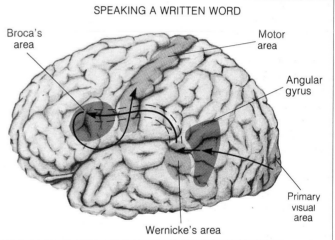

SPEAKING A WRITTEN WORD

Broca's area — Motor area — Angular gyrus — Primary visual area — Wernicke's area

tory cortex, a person will be able to read and to speak normally; but he or she will not be able to comprehend spoken speech.

Still, there are some research findings that the Wernicke–Geschwind model does not adequately explain. For

example, when the language areas of the brain are electrically stimulated in the course of a neurosurgical operation, both receptive and expressive functions may be disrupted at a single site. This suggests that some brain areas may share common mechanisms for produc-

ing and understanding speech (Calvin and Ojemann, 1980). We are still a long way from a comprehensive model of language function, but there can be no doubt that some aspects of language function are highly localized in the brain (Geschwind, 1979).

EEG activity increases in the right hemisphere (Ornstein, 1977).

Thus, a range of evidence indicates that the two hemispheres operate in quite different ways. The left hemisphere controls speech, reading, writing, and arithmetic. It operates in a logical, analytical mode, focuses on details, and perceives in terms of individual features rather than holistic patterns. The right hemisphere, on the other hand, plays a special role in musical and artistic abilities, in imagery and dreaming, and in the perception of complex geometric patterns. Its perceptions are holistic, and it is particularly effective on tasks that require the visualization of relationships. The right hemisphere also shows more emotion and impulsiveness than its companion.

Some researchers have speculated that individual differences in *cognitive style* are related to individual differences in the relative efficiency of the two

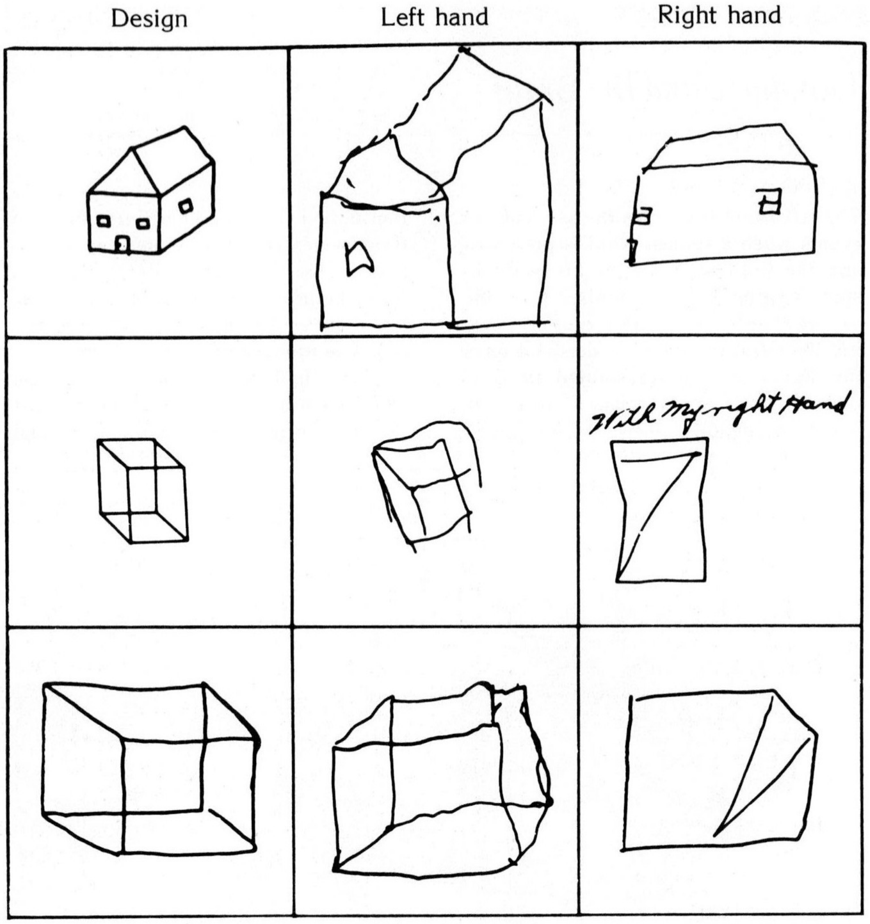

Figure 2-13
Spatial Drawing by Split-Brain Subject
The left hand, guided by the right hemisphere, can copy three-dimensional designs (although somewhat crudely because the subject is right-handed). The right hand, guided by the dominant left hemisphere, is unable to reproduce the geometric designs (although it can write words with ease). (After Gazzaniga, 1970)

hemispheres. Thus, individuals who are very logical, analytical, and verbal would have highly efficient left hemisphere functions, whereas those who are unusually holistic, musical, intuitive, and impulsive would have a balance in favor of the right hemisphere. The notion of a differential balance in hemispheric functioning to explain individual differences in cognitive style is an attractive idea, though as yet it is based more on speculation than direct empirical evidence.

Because of the left hemisphere's special role in language, it has sometimes been called the *major* (or *dominant*) hemisphere, and the right has been called the *minor* (or *nondominant*) hemisphere. These terms, however, are disappearing from the literature as more and more research has shown the right hemisphere to be critical (dominant) in an increasing number of functions. The current view is that neither hemisphere is dominant but that each is specialized for a variety of important functions. (Sperry, 1982).

AUTONOMIC NERVOUS SYSTEM

We noted earlier that the peripheral nervous system consists of two divisions. The somatic system controls the skeletal muscles and receives information from the skin, muscles, and various sensory receptors. The autonomic system con-

PARASYMPATHETIC
DIVISION

SYMPATHETIC
DIVISION

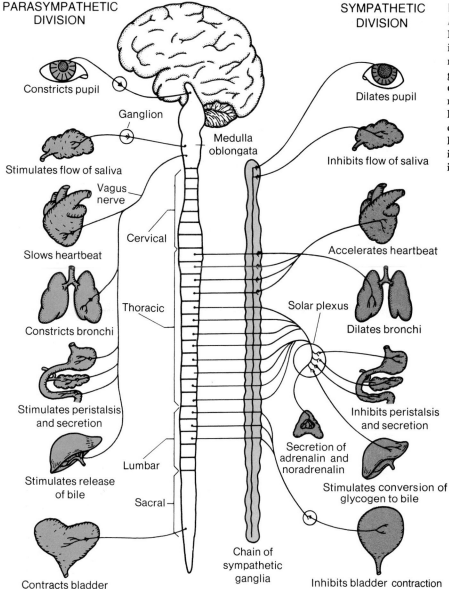

Constricts pupil

Ganglion

Stimulates flow of saliva

Vagus
nerve

Cervical

Slows heartbeat

Thoracic

Constricts bronchi

Stimulates peristalsis
and secretion

Stimulates release
of bile

Lumbar

Sacral

Contracts bladder

Medulla
oblongata

Solar plexus

Chain of
sympathetic
ganglia

Dilates pupil

Inhibits flow of saliva

Accelerates heartbeat

Dilates bronchi

Inhibits peristalsis
and secretion

Secretion of
adrenalin and
noradrenalin

Stimulates conversion of
glycogen to bile

Inhibits bladder contraction

Figure 2-14
Autonomic Nervous System
Neurons of the sympathetic division originate in the thoracic and lumbar regions of the spinal cord; they form synaptic junctions with ganglia lying just outside the cord. Neurons of the parasympathetic division exit from the medulla region of the brain stem and from the lower (sacral) end of the spinal cord; they connect with ganglia near the organs stimulated. Most, but not all, internal organs are innervated by both divisions, which function in opposition to each other.

trols the glands and the smooth muscles, which include the heart, the blood vessels, and the lining of the stomach and intestines. These muscles are called "smooth" because that is how they look when examined under a microscope. (Skeletal muscles, in contrast, have a striated appearance.) The autonomic nervous system derives its name from the fact that many of the activities it controls are autonomous, or self-regulating—such as digestion and circulation, which continue even when a person is asleep or unconscious.

The autonomic nervous system has two divisions—the *sympathetic* and the *parasympathetic*—which are often antagonistic in their actions. Figure 2-14 shows the contrasting effects of the two systems on various organs. For example, the parasympathetic system constricts the pupil of the eye, stimulates the flow of saliva, and slows heart rate; the sympathetic system has the opposite effect in each case. The normal state of the body, somewhere between extreme excitement and vegetative placidity, is maintained by the balance between these two systems.

The sympathetic division tends to act as a unit. During emotional excitement, it simultaneously speeds up the heart, dilates the arteries of the skeletal muscles and heart, constricts the arteries of the skin and digestive organs, and causes perspiration. It also activates certain endocrine glands to secrete hormones that further increase arousal.

Unlike the sympathetic system, the parasympathetic division tends to affect one organ at a time. If the sympathetic system is thought of as dominant during violent and excited activity, the parasympathetic system may be thought of as dominant during quiescence. It participates in digestion and, in general, maintains the functions that conserve and protect bodily resources.

As noted above, the sympathetic and parasympathetic systems are usually antagonistic to one another, but there are some exceptions to this principle. For example, the sympathetic system is dominant during fear and excitement; however, a not uncommon parasympathetic symptom during extreme fear is the involuntary discharge of the bladder or bowels. Another example is the complete sex act in the male, which requires erection (parasympathetic) followed by ejaculation (sympathetic). Thus, although the two systems are often antagonistic, they interact in complex ways.

ENDOCRINE SYSTEM

Many of the body's reactions that result from activity of the autonomic nervous system are produced by the action of that system on the endocrine glands (see Figure 2-15). The endocrine glands secrete *hormones* that are carried throughout the body by the bloodstream. These chemicals are as essential as the nervous system to the integration of the organism's activities and to the maintenance of *homeostasis*. Some endocrine glands are controlled by the nervous system, whereas others respond to the internal state of the body.

One of the major endocrine glands, the *pituitary*, is partly an outgrowth of the brain and is joined to it just below the hypothalamus (refer back to Figure 2-7). The pituitary gland is directly under the control of the hypothalamus and thereby under the control of other brain centers via the hypothalamus. The pituitary gland has been called the "master gland" because it produces the largest number of different hormones and controls the secretion of several other endocrine glands. One of the pituitary hormones has the crucial job of controlling body growth. Too little of this hormone can create a dwarf, while oversecretion can produce a giant. A number of other hormones released by the pituitary trigger the action of other endocrine glands such as the thyroid, the sex glands, and the outer layer of the adrenal gland. Courtship, mating, and reproductive behavior in many animals is based on a complex interaction between the activity of the nervous system and the influence of the pituitary on the sex glands.

The *adrenal glands* play an important role in determining an individual's mood, level of energy, and ability to cope with stress. Each adrenal gland has two parts, an inner core and an outer layer. The inner core secretes *epinephrine* (also known as *adrenalin*) and *norepinephrine* (*noradrenalin*). Epinephrine acts in a number of ways to prepare the organism for an emergency; it often works in conjunction with the sympathetic division of the autonomic nervous system.

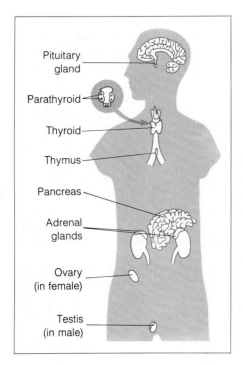

Figure 2-15
Some of the Endocrine Glands
Hormones secreted by the endocrine glands are as essential as the nervous system to the integration of the organism's activity. The endocrine system and nervous system, however, differ in the speed with which they can act. A nerve impulse can travel through the organism in a few hundredths of a second. Seconds, or even minutes, may be required for an endocrine gland to produce an effect; the hormone, once released, must travel to its target site via the bloodstream—a much slower process.

Epinephrine, for example, acts on the smooth muscles and the sweat glands in a way similar to that of the sympathetic system. It causes constriction of the blood vessels in the stomach and intestines and makes the heart beat faster (as anyone who has ever had a shot of adrenalin knows). It also acts on the reticular system, which excites the sympathetic system and in turn stimulates the adrenals to secrete more epinephrine. Hence, a closed circuit is formed to maintain emotional arousal. Such a closed system is one reason why it takes a while for strong emotional excitement to subside even after the disturbing cause has been removed.

Norepinephrine also prepares the organism for emergency action. When it reaches the pituitary in its travels through the bloodstream, it stimulates the pituitary to release a hormone that acts on the outer layer of the adrenal glands; this hormone, in turn, stimulates the liver to increase the blood-sugar level so the body has energy for quick action.

The hormones of the endocrine system and the neurotransmitters of the nervous system have similar functions; they both carry *messages* between cells of the body. A neurotransmitter carries messages between adjacent neurons. In contrast, a hormone may travel a long distance through the body and act in various ways on cells of various types. The basic similarity between these chemical messengers despite their differences is shown by the fact that some molecules serve both functions. Epinephrine, for example, acts as a neurotransmitter when released by a neuron and as a hormone when released by the adrenal gland.

GENETIC INFLUENCES ON BEHAVIOR

To understand the biological foundations of psychology, we need to know something about hereditary influences. The field of *behavior genetics* (also called *psychogenetics*) combines the methods of genetics and psychology to study the inheritance of behavioral characteristics. We know that many physical characteristics—such as height, bone structure, and hair and eye color—are inherited. Behavioral geneticists are interested in the degree to which psychological characteristics—such as ability, temperament, and emotional stability—are transmitted from parent to offspring.

All psychological characteristics depend on the *interaction* between heredity and environment. The old heredity versus environment question is no longer meaningful. Instead, researchers ask how heredity limits the individual's potential and to what degree favorable or unfavorable environmental conditions can modify the inherited potential.

Chromosomes and genes

The hereditary units we receive from our parents and transmit to our offspring are carried by structures, known as *chromosomes,* that are found in the nucleus of each cell in the body. Most body cells contain 46 chromosomes. At conception, the human being receives 23 chromosomes from the father's sperm and 23 chromosomes from the mother's ovum. These 46 chromosomes form 23 pairs, which are duplicated each time the cells divide (see Figure 2-16).

Each chromosome is composed of many individual hereditary units called *genes.* A gene is a segment of DNA (*deoxyribonucleic acid*), which is the actual carrier of genetic information. The DNA molecule looks like a twisted ladder

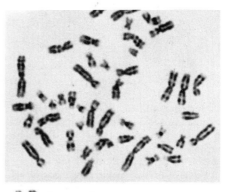

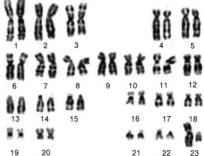

Figure 2-16
Chromosomes
The upper panel is a photo (enlarged about 1,500 times) of the 46 chromosomes of a normal human male. In the lower panel, the chromosomes are arranged in the appropriate pairs. A human female would have the same pairs 1 through 22, but pair 23 would be XX rather than XY. Each chromosome appears double here because the preparation was made at a stage during mitosis, in which each chromosome has duplicated itself and is about to split apart.

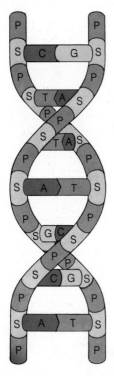

Figure 2-17
Structure of the DNA Molecule
Each strand of the molecule is made up of an alternating sequence of sugar (S) and phosphate (P); the rungs of the "twisted" ladder are made up of four bases (A,G,T,C). The double nature of the helix and the restriction on base pairings make possible the self-replication of DNA. In the process of cell division, the two strands of the DNA molecule come apart with the base pairs separating; one member of each base pair remains attached to each strand. Each strand then forms a new complementary strand using excess bases available in the cell; an A attached to a strand will attract a T and so forth. By this process, two identical molecules of DNA come to exist where there was previously one.

or a double-stranded helix, as shown in Figure 2-17. (A helix is a spiral.) All DNA has the same chemical composition. It consists of a simple sugar (deoxyribose), phosphate, and four bases: adenine, guanine, thymine, and cytosine (A,G,T,C). The two strands of the DNA molecule are composed of phosphate and sugar, and the strands are held apart by pairs of bases. Due to the structural properties of these bases, A always pairs with T and G always pairs with C. The bases can occur in any sequence along a strand, and these sequences constitute the genetic code. The fact that many different arrangements of bases are possible is what gives DNA the ability to express many different genetic messages. The same four bases specify the characteristics of every living organism and, depending on their arrangement, determine whether a given creature turns out to be a bird or a lion, a fish or a Michelangelo.

Genes, like chromosomes, occur in pairs. One gene of each pair comes from the sperm chromosomes and one gene from the ovum chromosomes. Thus, a child receives only half of each parent's total genes. The total number of genes in each human chromosome is around 1,000—perhaps higher. Because the number of genes is so high, it is extremely unlikely that two human beings would have the same heredity, even if they were siblings. One exception is *identical twins*, who, because they developed from the same fertilized egg, have exactly the same genes.

An important attribute of some genes is *dominance* or *recessiveness*. The genes determining eye color, for example, act in a pattern of dominance and recessiveness. When both members of a gene pair are dominant, the individual manifests the form of the trait specified by these dominant genes. When one gene is dominant and the other recessive, the dominant gene again determines the form of the trait. Only if the genes contributed by both parents are recessive is the recessive form of the trait expressed. Blue eyes are recessive. Thus, a blue-eyed child may have two blue-eyed parents, or one blue-eyed parent and one brown-eyed parent who carries a recessive gene for blue eyes, or two brown-eyed parents, each of whom carries a recessive gene for blue eyes. A brown-eyed child, in contrast, never has two blue-eyed parents.

Some of the characteristics that are carried by recessive genes are baldness, albinism, hemophilia, and a susceptibility to poison ivy. Not all gene pairs follow the dominant-recessive pattern, and—as we shall see later—most human characteristics are determined by many genes acting together rather than by a single gene pair.

SEX-LINKED GENES Male and female chromosomes appear the same when examined under the microscope, except for pair number 23. Pair 23 determines the sex of the individual and carries genes for certain traits that are called sex-linked. A normal female has two similar-looking chromosomes in pair 23, called X chromosomes. A normal male has one X chromosome in pair 23 and one that looks slightly different, called a Y chromosome (see Figure 2-16). Thus, the normal female chromosome pair 23 is represented by the symbol XX, and the normal male pair, by XY.

When most body cells reproduce, the resulting cells have the same number of chromosomes (46) as the parent cell. However, when sperm and egg cells reproduce, the chromosome pairs separate and half go to each new cell. Thus, egg and sperm cells have only 23 chromosomes. Each egg cell has an X chromosome, and each sperm cell has either an X or a Y chromosome. If an X-type sperm is the first to enter an egg cell, the fertilized ovum will have an XX chromosome pair, and the child will be a female. If a Y-type sperm fertilizes the egg, the twenty-third chromosome will be of the XY type, and the child will be a male. The female inherits one X chromosome from the mother, one from the father; the male inherits his X chromosome from the mother, his Y chromosome from the father. Thus, it is the father's chromosome contribution that determines a child's sex.

The X chromosome may carry either dominant or recessive genes; the Y chromosome carries a few genes dominant for male sexual characteristics but otherwise seems to carry only recessive genes. Thus, most recessive characteristics carried by a man's X chromosome (received from his mother) will be expressed since they are not blocked by dominant genes. For example, colorblindness is a recessive sex-linked characteristic. A man will be colorblind if he inherits a colorblind gene on the X chromosome he receives from his mother. Females are less often colorblind, because a colorblind female has to have both a colorblind father and a mother who is either colorblind or carries a recessive gene for colorblindness. A number of genetically determined disorders are linked to abnormalities of, or recessive genes carried by, the twenty-third chromosome pair. These are called sex-linked disorders.

CHROMOSOMAL ABNORMALITIES   On rare occasions, a female may be born with only one X chromosome instead of the usual XX. Females with this condition (known as *Turner's syndrome*) fail to develop sexually at puberty. Although usually of normal intelligence, they show some specific cognitive defects: they do poorly in arithmetic and on tests of visual form perception and spatial organization.

Sometimes when the twenty-third chromosome fails to divide properly, the developing organism ends up with an extra X or Y chromosome. An individual with an XXY twenty-third chromosome is physically a male, with penis and testicles, but with marked feminine characteristics. His breasts are enlarged and his testes are small and do not produce sperm. This condition (known as *Klinefelter's syndrome*) is surprisingly common—about 1 in every 400 births.

Another sex chromosome abnormality in males has received considerable publicity. Men with an extra Y chromosome (type XYY) are taller than average and are reported to be unusually aggressive. Early studies suggested that the incidence of XYY males among prison inmates—particularly those convicted of violent crimes—was much higher than in the population at large. Newspaper accounts exaggerated these findings, portraying the XYY male as an individual genetically predisposed toward aggression and violence. Several XYY men were even acquitted of criminal charges on the grounds that they were helpless victims of their inheritance and, thus, could not be held responsible for their acts.

More recent studies question whether there is a link between the presence of an extra Y chromosome and aggression. They find that XYY males in the general population are no more aggressive than normal males (Owen, 1972; Hook, 1973). Nevertheless, survey data indicate that males with this genetic makeup *are* more likely than normal males to be inmates of prisons or mental hospitals. We do not know why this is so; at this point, little is known about the effects of the XYY chromosomal type on personality and behavior.

"You can't talk to that crowd
—they've all got extra Y chromosomes."

Genetic studies of behavior

A few disorders result from chromosomal abnormalities, and some traits are determined by single genes. But most human characteristics are determined by many genes; they are *polygenic*. Traits such as intelligence, height, and emo-

A sex-influenced gene seems to be related to the relative length of the index finger as compared to the other fingers. A gene that causes the index finger to be shorter than the fourth finger appears to be dominant in males and recessive in females. The male index finger, on the left, is shorter than the fourth finger, but the female index finger on the right is longer than the fourth finger. (Courtesy A. M. Winchester)

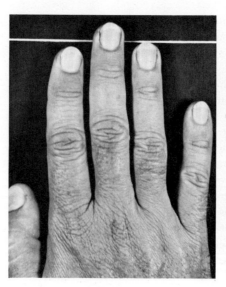
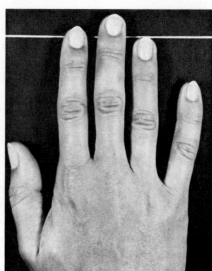

tionality do not fall into distinct categories but show continuous variation. Most people are neither dull nor bright; intelligence is distributed over a broad range with most individuals located near the middle. Sometimes a specific genetic defect can result in mental retardation, but in most instances, a person's intellectual potential is determined by a large number of genes that influence the factors underlying different abilities. And, of course, what happens to this genetic potential depends on environmental conditions.

SELECTIVE BREEDING   One method of studying the heritability of traits in animals is by selective breeding. Animals that are high or low in a certain trait are mated with each other. For example, to study the inheritance of learning ability in rats, the females that do poorly in learning to run a maze are mated with males that do poorly; the females that do well are mated with the males that do well. The offspring of these matings are tested on the same maze. On the basis of performance, the brightest are mated with the brightest and the dullest with the dullest. (To ensure that environmental conditions are kept constant, the offspring of "dull" mothers are sometimes given to "bright" mothers to raise so that genetic endowment rather than adequacy of maternal care is being tested.) After a few rodent generations, a "bright" and a "dull" strain of rats can be produced (see Figure 2-18).

Selective breeding has been used to show the inheritance of a number of behavioral characteristics. For example, dogs have been bred to be excitable or lethargic; chickens, to be aggressive and sexually active; fruit flies, to be more or less drawn to light; and mice, to be more or less attracted to alcohol.

If a trait is influenced by heredity, it should be possible to change it by selective breeding. If selective breeding does not alter a trait, we assume that trait is primarily dependent on environmental factors and is not differentially influenced by the genes.

TWIN STUDIES   Since carefully controlled breeding experiments cannot be carried out with human beings, we must look instead at similarities in behavior among individuals who are related. Family histories often show that certain traits run in families. The problem is that families are not only linked genetically but also share the same environment. Thus, if musical talent runs in the family, is it because of genetic potential or the importance parents place on music and musical training? Do children of alcoholics become alcoholics because of genetic tendencies or environmental conditions? In an effort to overcome this problem, psychologists have turned to twin studies.

Identical twins develop from a single fertilized egg and thus share the same heredity. (They are called *monozygotic* since they come from a single zygote, or fertilized ovum.) Fraternal twins develop from different egg cells and are no more alike genetically than are ordinary siblings. (They are called *dizygotic*, or two-egged.) Studies comparing identical and fraternal twins help to sort out the influence of environment and heredity. Identical twins are found to be more similar in intelligence than fraternal twins, even when they are separated at birth and reared in different homes (see Chapter 12). Identical twins are also more similar than fraternal twins in some personality characteristics and in susceptibility to the mental disorder of *schizophrenia* (see Chapter 15). Twin studies have proved to be a useful method of investigating genetic influences on human behavior.

Environmental influences on gene action

The hereditary potential with which an individual enters the world is very much influenced by the environment that she or he encounters. This interaction will be made clear in the following chapters. At this point, two examples will suffice to illustrate the point. The tendency to develop diabetes is hereditary, although the exact method of transmission is unknown. Diabetes is manifested as an elevation of the blood-sugar level. The assumption is that the genes determine the production of insulin, which in turn affects the metabolism of carbohydrates and, hence, the level of sugar in the blood. But people who carry the genetic potential for diabetes do not always develop the disease. A study of identical twins (one or the other of whom had diabetes) found that in 15 percent of the pairs, only one twin developed the disease. The unafflicted twin clearly carried the genes for diabetes but apparently was spared because his or her diet made fewer demands for carbohydrate metabolism. Thus, diabetes is caused by neither heredity nor environment alone but by the interaction of the two.

A similar situation is found in the mental illness called *schizophrenia*. As we shall see in Chapter 15, substantial evidence indicates a heredity component to the disorder. If one identical twin is schizophrenic, chances are high that the other twin will exhibit some signs of mental disturbance. But whether the other twin develops the full-blown disease will depend on a number of environmental factors. The genes may predispose, but the environment shapes the outcome.

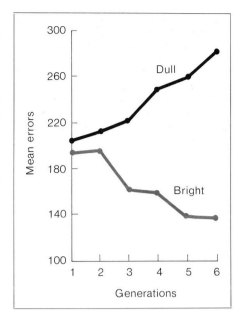

Figure 2-18
Inheritance of Maze Learning in Rats
Mean error scores of "bright" and "dull" rats selectively bred for maze-running ability. (After Thompson, 1954)

Summary

1 The nervous system is composed of cells called *neurons*, which receive stimulation by way of their *dendrites* and *cell bodies* and transmit impulses via their *axons. Afferent neurons* carry messages from the sense *receptors* to the brain and spinal cord; *efferent neurons* transmit signals from the brain and spinal cord to the muscles and glands. Axon fibers group together to form *nerves.*

2 Two aspects of the transmission of the nerve impulse are important: conduction along axon fibers and transmission across the synaptic junction between neurons. Axonal conduction is via the *action potential,* an electrochemical process involving the interchange of sodium and potassium ions through the cell

membrane. Chemical intermediaries, called *neurotransmitters,* pass the impulse from one neuron to the next across a *synapse.* The neurotransmitters are released from axon terminals and act on the dendrites and cell body of the receiving neuron to change its membrane permeability either toward the firing threshold (at an *excitatory synapse*) or away from the threshold (at an *inhibitory synapse*). The combination of excitatory and inhibitory inputs to its many synapses determines whether a neuron will fire.

3 The nervous system is divided into the *central nervous system* (the brain and spinal cord) and the *peripheral nervous system* (the nerves leading from the brain and spinal cord to other parts of the body). Subdivisions of the peripheral nervous system are the *somatic system* (which carries messages to and from the sense receptors, muscles, and the body surface) and the *autonomic system* (which connects with the internal organs and glands).

4 The human brain is composed of three concentric layers: a *central core,* the *limbic system,* and the *cerebrum.*

a The central core includes the *medulla,* responsible for respiration and postural reflexes; the *cerebellum,* concerned with motor coordination; the *thalamus,* a relay station for incoming sensory information; and the *hypothalamus,* important in emotion and in maintaining homeostasis. The *reticular system,* which crosses through several of the above structures, controls the organism's state of wakefulness and arousal.

b The *limbic system* controls some of the "instinctive" activities (feeding, attacking, fleeing from danger, mating) regulated by the hypothalamus; it also plays an important role in emotion and memory.

c The *cerebrum* is divided into two *cerebral hemispheres.* The convoluted surface of these hemispheres, the *cerebral cortex,* controls discrimination, decision making, learning, and thinking—the "higher mental processes." Certain areas of the cortex represent centers for specific sensory inputs or for control of specific movements. The remainder of the cortex consists of *association areas.*

5 When the *corpus callosum* (the band of nerve fibers connecting the two cerebral hemispheres) is severed, significant differences in the functioning of the two cerebral hemispheres can be observed. The left hemisphere is skilled in language and mathematical abilities. The right hemisphere can understand some language but cannot communicate through speech; it has a highly developed spatial and pattern sense.

6 The *autonomic nervous system* is made up of two parts, a *sympathetic* and a *parasympathetic* division. Because its fibers mediate the action of the smooth muscles and of the glands, the autonomic system is particularly important in emotional reactions. The sympathetic division is usually active during excitement and the parasympathetic during quiescent states.

7 The *endocrine glands* secrete hormones into the bloodstream that are important for emotional and motivational behavior and for some aspects of personality. They are an essential partner to the nervous system in integrating behavior, and their action is closely tied to the activity of the hypothalamus and the autonomic nervous system.

8 An individual's hereditary potential, transmitted by the *chromosomes* and *genes,* influences psychological as well as physical characteristics. Genes are composed chiefly of *DNA molecules,* which are the actual carriers of genetic information. Some genes are *dominant,* some *recessive,* and some *sex-linked.* Most human characteristics are *polygenic*—that is, determined by many sets of genes.

9   *Selective breeding* (mating animals that are high in a certain or low in a certain trait) is one method of studying the influence of heredity. Another method for sorting out the effects of environment and heredity is *twin studies*, in which the characteristics of identical, or *monozygotic*, twins (who share the same heredity) are compared with those of fraternal, or *dizygotic*, twins (who are no more alike genetically than ordinary siblings).

10 All behavior depends on the *interaction* between heredity and environment; the genes set the limits of the individual's potential, but what happens to this potential depends on the environment.

Further Reading

Good introductions to physiological psychology are Kolb and Whishaw, *Fundamentals of human neuropsychology* (1980); Brown and Wallace, *Physiological psychology* (1980); Cotman and McGaugh, *Behavioral neuroscience: An introduction* (1980); Carlson, *Physiology of behavior* (2nd ed., 1981); and Rosenzwieg and Leiman, *Physiological psychology* (1982).

A survey of genetic influences on behavior is provided by Fuller and Thompson, *Foundations of behavior genetics* (1978); and Plomin, DeFries, and McClearn, *Behavioral genetics: A primer* (1980). For a survey of research on the function of the two cerebral hemispheres, see Springer and Deutsch, *Left brain, right brain* (1981).

3
PSYCHOLOGICAL DEVELOPMENT

Of all mammals, human beings are the most immature at birth and require the longest period of development before they are capable of all the activities and skills characteristic of their species. In general, the higher on the phylogenetic scale the organism is, the more complex its nervous system and the longer the time required to reach maturity. For example, the lemur, a primitive primate, can move about on its own shortly after birth and is soon able to eat adult food and fend for itself. The newborn monkey is dependent for several months; the infant baboon remains with its mother for several years. The human offspring, in contrast, is dependent for many years and requires a long period of learning and interaction with others before becoming self-sufficient.

Adult behavior and personality characteristics are influenced by events that occur during the early years of life. The saying "the child is father of the man" reflects this continuity between childhood and adulthood. Thus, to understand the psychological processes of human adults—their perceptions, patterns of thinking, motives, emotions, conflicts, and ways of coping with conflicts—we need to know how these processes originate and change over time.

Psychologists often study the average or "typical" rate of development. At what age does the average child begin to speak? How rapidly does vocabulary increase with age? Such data, in addition to having intrinsic interest, are important in solving problems of education.

Developmental psychologists are concerned also with how certain behaviors develop and why they appear when they do. Why do most children not walk or utter their first word until they are about a year old? What behaviors precede these accomplishments? Can normal development be accelerated? What factors produce abnormal development, such as mental illness or retardation?

From a practical standpoint, knowing how early experiences mold an individual may make us wiser in the way we raise our children. Many problems that

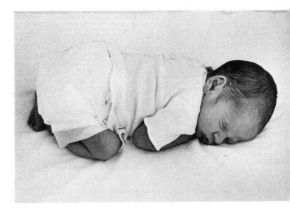

The human infant is helpless at birth.

confront society—aggression, alienation, suicide, and mental illness—could perhaps be averted if we better understood how parental behavior and attitudes affect children, how some of these problems originate, and how they might be dealt with at an early age.

In this chapter, we discuss several general principles of development as well as some behavior and attitude changes that occur as the individual matures from infancy to adulthood. Our purpose is to provide an overview of psychological development. The development of certain specific abilities, such as language and perception, will be considered later in the chapters devoted to these topics.

FACTORS GOVERNING DEVELOPMENT

Human development is determined by a continuous interaction between heredity and environment. At the moment of conception, a remarkable number of personal characteristics are already determined by the genetic structure of the fertilized ovum. Our genes program our growing cells so that we develop into a person rather than a fish, a bird, or a monkey. They decide our skin and hair color, general body size, sex, and (to some extent) our intellectual abilities and emotional temperament. The *biological predispositions* present at birth interact with the *experiences* encountered in the course of growing up to determine individual development.

Our experiences depend on the specific culture, social group, and family in which we are raised. Cultures differ in their methods of child-rearing. For example, among the Utku Eskimos of Hudson Bay, aggression is regarded as an undesirable characteristic. When the child is about 2 or 3 years old, Utku parents begin to discourage expressions of anger and aggression by means of the "silent treatment"—that is, by ignoring the child whenever such behaviors occur. This method seems to be fairly effective; Utku children over 4 or 5 years of age rarely exhibit aggressive behavior (Briggs, 1970). In the United States, the amount of aggression a child shows depends partly on the social group and partly on the family in which the child is raised. Children from very poor families tend, *on the average,* to be more aggressive than children from middle- or upper-class homes (Langner, Gersten, and Eisenberg, 1977). But a child's tendency to fight or show other forms of aggression also depends on the particular family in which he or she is raised—the kind of behavior modeled by the parents and the way they reward or punish aggressive acts. In short, a child is exposed to many different conditions. Some are shared with other children in the culture, some are common to the child's social group, and some are unique to his or her family.

The question of whether heredity ("nature") or environment ("nurture") is more important in determining the course of human development has long been a topic of debate. But it seems clear that the two are inseparable. The development of the newborn infant depends on the interaction between biological predispositions and the experiences provided by the environment. For example, almost all human infants are born with the ability to learn a spoken language; other species are not. In the normal course of development, human beings learn to speak. But they are not able to talk before they have attained a certain level of neurological development—no infant less than a year old speaks in sentences. Children raised in an environment where people talk to them and

"Grantz is charting his life based on genetic vs. environmental factors."

reward them for making speechlike sounds will talk earlier than children without such attention. For example, children raised in middle-class American homes begin to speak at about 1 year of age. Children raised in San Marcos, a remote village in Guatemala, who experience little verbal interaction with adults, do not utter their first words until they are over 2 years old (Kagan, 1979). The language children speak, of course, will be that of their own culture. Thus, learning to speak has both biological and environmental components. Most aspects of human development are similar in that the result depends on the interaction between biological predispositions and environmental experiences.

Maturation

Genetic determinants are expressed through the process of *maturation*. Maturation refers to innately determined sequences of growth or bodily changes that are *relatively* independent of environmental events. We say "relatively" because such changes occur over a wide range of environmental conditions; however, if the environment is decidedly atypical or inadequate in some way, maturational processes will be affected. Although maturation is most apparent during childhood, it continues into adult life. Some of the changes that occur at adolescence, as well as some of the changes that occur with aging (the appearance of gray hair, for instance), are regulated by a biologically determined time schedule.

Maturation is demonstrated clearly by fetal development. The human fetus develops within the mother's body according to a fairly fixed time schedule, and fetal behavior (such as turning and kicking) also follows an orderly sequence that depends on the stage of growth. Premature infants who are kept alive in an incubator develop at much the same rate as infants who remain in the uterus full term. The regularity of development before birth illustrates what we mean by maturation. However, if the uterine environment is seriously abnormal in some way, maturational processes can be disrupted. For example, if the mother contracts German measles during the first three months of pregnancy (when the basic organ systems are developing according to an innately programmed schedule), the infant may be born deaf, blind, or brain damaged—the type of defect depending on which organ system was in a critical stage of development at the time of infection. Maternal malnutrition, alcohol, smoking, and certain drugs are among the other environmental factors that can affect the normal maturation of the fetus.

Motor development after birth—using the hands and fingers, standing, walking—also follows a regular sequence. For example, such activities as rolling over, crawling, and pulling up to a standing position occur in the same order in most children. Unless we believe that all parents subject their offspring to the same training regime (an unlikely possibility), we must assume that growth processes determine the order of behavior. As Figure 3-1 shows, not all children go through the sequence at the same rate; some infants are four or five months ahead of others in standing alone or walking. But the *order* in which they go from one stage to the next is generally the same in all infants.

Because the child's mastery of the movements necessary for sitting, standing, walking, and using hands and fingers follows such an orderly sequence and because children in all cultures accomplish these skills at *roughly* the same age, motor development appears to be primarily a maturational process little influenced by the environment in which the child is reared.

Figure 3-1
Babies Develop at Diffferent Rates
Although development is orderly, some infants reach each stage ahead of others. The left end of the bar indicates the age by which 25 percent of infants have achieved the stated performance, whereas the right end gives the age by which 90 percent have accomplished the behavior. The vertical mark on each bar gives the age by which 50 percent have achieved it. (After Frankenburg and Dodds, 1967)

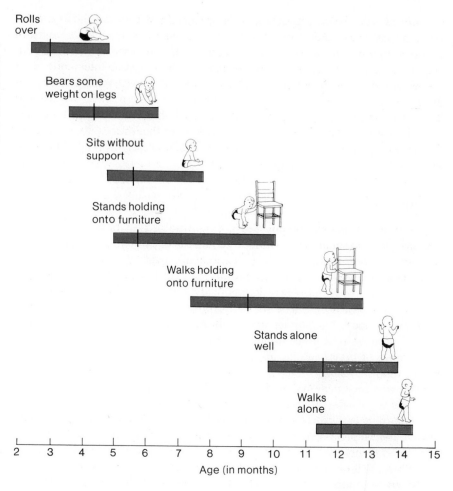

Sequences and stages in development

Many behaviors follow a natural sequence of development. Infants reach for an object before they are able to pick it up. We learn to walk before we run; we learn to speak words before sentences; we learn to count by rote before we understand the concept of numbers. Sequences in development usually proceed from simple behaviors to those that are more differentiated and complex. For example, newborn infants can clasp and unclasp their fingers and wave their arms about, occasionally managing to connect the thumb with the mouth. As infants mature, these simple actions become differentiated into more complex behaviors: patting an object, grasping it, picking it up, moving it toward the mouth, or throwing it.

Psychologists generally agree that there are orderly sequences in development that depend on the maturation of the organism as it interacts with its environment. In explaining developmental sequences, some psychologists prefer to interpret them as a *continuous process*, in which biological factors interplay with learning to produce a smooth and continuous change in behavior. Other psychologists agree on the sequential character of development but are less impressed by the continuity of the process and see it more as a series of steps. For this reason, they have introduced the concept of *stages*.

We identify broad stages when we divide the life span into successive periods of infancy, childhood, adolescence, and adulthood. Parents use the term *stage* when they refer to their 2-year-old as going through a "negative stage" (saying "no" to every request) or their adolescent as being in a "rebellious stage" (challenging parental authority). When psychologists refer to developmental stages, they have a more precise concept in mind: the concept of stages implies that (1) behaviors at a given stage are organized around a *dominant theme*, (2) behaviors at one stage are *qualitatively different* from behaviors that appear at earlier or later stages, and (3) all children go through the same stages *in the same order*. Environmental factors may speed up or slow down development, but the order of stages is invariant; a child cannot achieve a later stage without going through an earlier one.

Later in this chapter, we will look at several stage theories: one focuses on stages of cognitive development; another, on stages of moral development; and the third, on stages of social development. Although some psychologists believe that stage theories are a useful way of describing development, others believe that development is better interpreted as a continuous process of acquiring new behaviors through experience. They do not accept the qualitative shifts in behavior that stage theories imply. We will examine the evidence for both viewpoints as we go along.

EARLY YEARS

Newborn infants appear to be helpless creatures who spend most of their time sleeping, feeding, or crying. However, new experimental techniques tell us that they are much more responsive to their environment than was previously supposed. For example, infants as young as 1 or 2 days old can discriminate differences in taste. They much prefer sweet-tasting liquids to those that are salty, bitter, or bland, and they can even discriminate degrees of sweetness. Infants normally suck in bursts (short groups of sucks) with rest pauses in between. When a sweet fluid is delivered through the nipple, they engage in more sucks per minute, suck more deeply, and take fewer rest pauses than they do with plain water or less sweet fluids. As the sugar concentration doubles, there is a doubling of tongue pressure on the nipple (Nowlis and Kessen, 1976). It is a little disconcerting to find that even infants have a "sweet tooth"! Given the choice between human breast milk and a sweeter formula of cow's milk, however, infants clearly prefer the breast milk (MacFarlane, 1977).

A newborn's sense of smell has been tested by presenting different smells on cotton swabs and noting head turning as well as changes in heart rate and respiration (see Figure 3-2). When a sweet smell is presented, infants turn their heads toward it, and their heart rates and respiration slow down—presumably a measure of interest and attention. A sour or acid smell causes infants to turn their heads away, and heart rates and respiration accelerate, indicating distress. Infants are able to discriminate even subtle differences in smells. After only a few days of nursing experience, an infant will consistently turn his or her head toward a pad saturated with its mother's milk in preference to one saturated with another mother's milk (MacFarlane, 1977). The innate ability to distinguish among smells has a clear adaptive value—helping the infant to avoid noxious substances.

The sucking response has also been used to test hearing. A normal infant

Motor development in twins
Rolling over at 5 months (top); crawling at 7 months (middle); sitting up at 9 months (bottom).

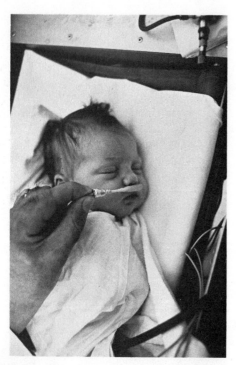

Figure 3-2
Testing the Newborn's Sense of Smell
Head turning and measures of heart rate and respiration are used to determine a 2-day-old infant's reaction to various odors.

will stop sucking and pause to listen to a new sound. After a few repetitions, the infant will no longer pay attention; if a slightly different sound is introduced, the infant will pause to attend again.

Newborn infants appear to find human voices more interesting than other sounds, and by 1 week of age they can pick out mother's voice from a group of female voices. At 2 weeks, infants seem to recognize that the mother's face and voice are part of a unit. For example, they show signs of distress when the mother appears and speaks to them in the voice of a stranger (by means of a recording) or when a strange female speaks in the mother's voice (Carpenter, 1973).

Vision is probably the least developed sense at birth. Newborn infants can follow a moving object with their eyes shortly after birth, and they can perceive the general contours of objects. However, their visual acuity is poor; they do not see objects clearly until about 2 to 4 months of age.

As early as the first weeks of life, infants show individual differences in activity level, responsiveness to changes in their environment, and general mood (see Chapter 13). One infant might cry very little, have periods of alert and quiet wakefulness, nurse easily, and endure diapering or bathing without much fuss. Another might be extremely fussy, spending most of its waking moments crying. Parents will find caring for the latter infant very frustrating and will tend to blame themselves for the infant's difficulties.

The traditional view has been that parents shape their children's behavior. But research with newborns makes it increasingly clear that the influence is reciprocal. The infant's behavior also shapes the parent's response. An infant who is easily soothed, who snuggles and stops crying when picked up, increases the mother's feelings of competency and attachment. One who stiffens and continues crying, despite all efforts to comfort, makes the mother feel inadequate and rejected. The more responsive an infant is to the stimulation provided by the parent (snuggling and quieting when held, attending alertly when talked to or played with), the easier it is to establish a loving bond between parent and child.

Early experience and infant development

The development from an alert but fairly helpless newborn to a walking and talking 2-year-old progresses at an astonishing rate. Indeed, changes occur more rapidly during the first two years of life than at any other period, except for the nine months before birth. As we noted earlier, the achievement of such physical skills as sitting, reaching for objects, crawling, and walking depends on the maturation of the muscles, nervous system, and other body parts. All babies achieve these skills without any special training. But psychologists have long been interested in whether environmental conditions can accelerate or retard maturational processes.

Although no special training is required for a child to walk at the appropriate time, a certain amount of environmental stimulation appears to be necessary. Children raised in institutions who are handled infrequently and given little opportunity to move about will sit, stand, and walk much later than normal. One study of an orphanage in Iran found that only 42 percent of the children were able to sit alone at 2 years, and only 15 percent could walk alone at age 4 (Dennis, 1960). Contrast these percentages with the norms given for home-reared children in Figure 3-1 (on page 64). It should be emphasized that this particular orphanage provided a more impoverished environment than most. The caregivers were low in intelligence and had little education. They provided for the physical needs of the children but made no effort to play with or talk to them. Infants remained in their cribs all day except when being fed or changed. Older children were placed in a playpen for part of the day, but there were few toys or other objects to play with.

To determine whether increased stimulation and the opportunity to move about improves the development of motor skills, two psychologists tested 30 of the Iranian orphan infants on a scale measuring various aspects of infant development and then divided them into two groups. One group remained in their cribs as before. The other babies were taken to a playroom for an hour each day, propped into a sitting position, and allowed to play with a variety of toys and objects. When the two groups were tested again a month later, the infants in the experimental group showed a marked gain in development compared with those who had remained in their cribs. Although motor development is largely dependent on maturation, the experiences of being able to move about freely and reach for interesting objects are necessary.

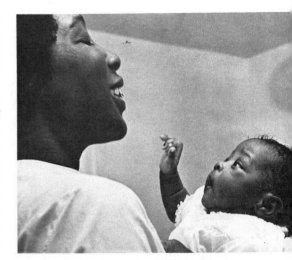

To cite another example, an infant's ability to reach for and successfully grasp an object develops in clearly specified maturational steps. A month-old infant lying on his or her back will stare at an attractive object held above but make no attempt to reach for it. By 2 months, the baby swipes at it accurately but with a closed fist. By 4 months, the baby alternates glances between his or her raised open hand and the object, gradually narrowing the gap. By 5 months, the baby can accurately reach for the object and grasp it.

Although this sequence is the same for all infants, because it depends on the maturation of visual and motor skills and the ability to coordinate the two, stimulation can accelerate the rate of development. Infants who are provided with colorful mobiles hanging above their cribs succeed in visually directed reaching several months earlier than infants who have nothing interesting to look at (White, 1971).

Early experience and later development

How permanent are the effects of early stimulation or deprivation? As far as motor skills are concerned, early experiences probably do not have a lasting effect. Children from the Iranian orphanage who were adopted before the age of 2 quickly attained, and thereafter maintained, normal development (Dennis, 1973).

Infants in an isolated Indian village in Guatemala are kept inside the family's windowless hut for the first year of life in the belief that sunshine and air will cause sickness. They have little opportunity to crawl about, and their parents seldom play with them. When these children are allowed to leave the hut, they are behind American children in physical skills. But they catch up, and by the age of 3 are as well-coordinated as other children (Kagan and Klein, 1973).

In other areas of development—language ability, intellectual skills, and emotional development—the effects of early deprivation appear to be more lasting. Children whose learning opportunities are restricted during the first two or three years of life—who are not talked to, read to, or encouraged to explore their environment—are seriously behind in language and intellectual skills by the time they enter school and may never catch up.[1]

---

[1]See Chapter 12 for a discussion of Headstart programs for culturally disadvantaged children.

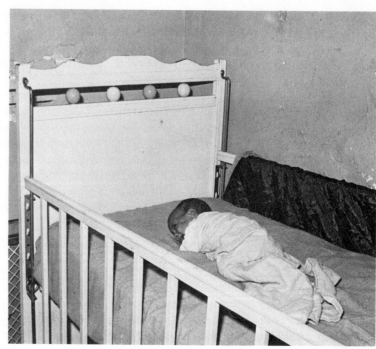

Stimulating and restricted
early environments
To some degree, an infant's rate of development is dependent on the environment.

The importance of a stimulating environment in the early years for later intellectual development is illustrated by a classic study by Skeels and Dye (1939). A group of orphaned children whose development at about 2 years of age was so retarded that they were not considered adoptable was transferred to an institution for the mentally retarded. In this institution, in contrast to the overcrowded orphanage, each child was placed in the care of an older, mildly retarded girl who served as a surrogate mother, spending great amounts of time playing with, talking to, and informally training the child. In addition, the living quarters were spacious and well equipped with toys. As soon as the children could walk, they began to attend a nursery school where additional play materials and stimulation were provided. After a period of four years, this experimental group showed an average gain in intelligence of 32 IQ points; a control group (matched in age and intelligence) that remained in the orphanage showed a loss of 21 points. A follow-up study over 20 years later found the experimental group to be still superior to the control group (Skeels, 1966). Most of the experimental group had completed high school (one third had gone to college), were self-supporting, and had married and produced children of normal intelligence. Most of the control group, on the other hand, had not progressed beyond third grade and either remained institutionalized or did not earn enough to be self-supporting.

Although the number of subjects in this study was small and the possibility of some innate intellectual differences between the experimental and control groups cannot be completely ruled out, the results are sufficiently impressive to indicate the importance of a stimulating early environment for later intellectual development.

As we shall see later in this chapter, the lack of a close and caring relationship with an adult during the early years can have a profound effect on subsequent emotional and social development.

COGNITIVE DEVELOPMENT

As adults, we take many aspects of our world for granted. We know, for example, that our arm is part of our body and that the table it is resting on is not. We recognize our hat as the same object whether it is lying on the table or on the closet shelf. We know that if we leave the house to walk across the street, we have to turn around to get back home. We know that a lead ball weighs more than a plastic one, and we adjust our muscles accordingly when we pick up one or the other. But these facts, taken for granted by adults, are a matter of learning for infants. From their encounters with objects and people, children learn to make sense of their world. They proceed with remarkable speed from the elementary knowledge gained by manipulating objects to the kind of abstract thinking characteristic of adults.

Although most parents are aware of the intellectual changes that accompany their children's physical growth, they would have difficulty describing the nature of these changes. The Swiss psychologist Jean Piaget (1896–1980) made the most intensive study of children's cognitive development. After many years of careful observation, Piaget developed a theory of how children's abilities to think and reason about their world progress through a series of distinct stages as they mature (see Table 3-1).

Sensorimotor stage

Noting the close interplay between motor activity and perception in infants, Piaget designated the first two years as a *sensorimotor stage*. During this period, infants are busy discovering the relationships between their actions and the consequences of these actions. They learn, for example, how far they have to reach to grasp an object, what happens when they push their food dish over the edge of the table, and that their hand is part of their body and the crib rail is not. Through countless "experiments," infants begin to develop a concept of themselves as separate from the external world. An important discovery during this stage is the concept of *object permanence:* an awareness that an object continues to exist even when it is not present to the senses. If a cloth is placed over a toy for which an 8-month-old is reaching, the infant immediately stops and appears to lose interest. The baby seems neither surprised nor upset, makes no attempt to search for the toy, and acts as if it had ceased to exist (see Figure 3-3). In contrast, a 10-month-old will actively search for an object that has been hidden under a cloth or behind a screen. The older baby seems to realize that the object exists even though it is out of sight. He or she has attained the concept of object permanence. But even at this age, search is limited. If the infant has had repeated success in retrieving a toy hidden in one place, he or she will continue to look for it in that spot even after watching an adult conceal it in a new location. The baby repeats the action that produced the toy earlier, rather than looking for it where it was last seen. Not until about 1 year of age will a child consistently look for an object where it was last seen to disappear regardless of what has happened on previous trials.

Preoperational stage

By about 1½ to 2 years of age, children have begun to use language. Words, as symbols, can represent things or groups of things. And one object can repre-

Figure 3-3
Object Permanence
When the toy is hidden by a screen, the infant acts as if it no longer exists. The infant does not yet have the concept of object permanence.

Table 3-1
Piaget's Stages of Intellectual
Development
The ages given are averages. They may vary considerably depending on intelligence, cultural background, and socioeconomic factors; but the order of progression is assumed to be the same for all children. Piaget has described more detailed phases within each stage; only a very general characterization of each stage is given here.

	STAGE	CHARACTERIZATION
1	Sensorimotor (birth–2 years)	Differentiates self from objects Recognizes self as agent of action and begins to act intentionally: for example, pulls a string to set a mobile in motion or shakes a rattle to make a noise Achieves object permanence: realizes that things continue to exist even when no longer present to the senses
2	Preoperational (2–7 years)	Learns to use language and to represent objects by images and words Thinking is still egocentric: has difficulty taking the viewpoint of others Classifies objects by a single feature: for example, groups all the red blocks together regardless of shape or all the square blocks regardless of color
3	Concrete operational (7–12 years)	Can think logically about objects and events Achieves conservation of number (age 7), mass (age 7), and weight (age 9) Classifies objects according to several features and can order them in series along a single dimension, such as size
4	Formal operational (12 years and up)	Can think logically about abstract propositions and test hypotheses systematically Becomes concerned with the hypothetical, the future, and ideological problems

sent (symbolize) another. Thus, in play a 3-year-old may treat a stick as if it were a horse and ride it around the room; a block of wood can become a car; one doll can become a mother and the other a baby.

Although 3- and 4-year-olds can think in symbolic terms, their words and images are not yet organized in a very logical way. Piaget calls the 2-to-7-years stage of cognitive development *preoperational*, because the child does not yet comprehend certain rules or *operations*. An operation is a mental routine for transposing information, and it is reversible; every operation has its logical opposite. Cutting a circle into four equal pie-shaped wedges is an operation because we can reverse the procedure and put the pieces back to form a whole. The rule that we square the number 3 to get 9 is an operation because we can reverse the operation and take the square root of 9 to get 3. In the preoperational stage of cognitive development, a child's understanding of such rules is absent or weak. Piaget illustrates this deficit by some experiments on the development of what he calls *conservation*.

As adults, we take conservation principles for granted: the amount (mass) of a substance is not changed when its shape is changed or when it is divided into parts; the total weight of a set of objects will remain the same no matter how they are packaged together; and liquids do not change in amount when they are poured from a container of one shape to a container of another shape. For children, however, attainment of these concepts is an aspect of intellectual growth that requires several years.

In a study of the conservation of mass, a child is given some clay to make into a ball equal to another ball of the same material; the child declares them to be "the same." Now, leaving one for reference, the experimenter rolls the other

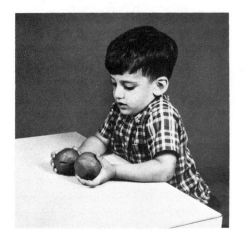  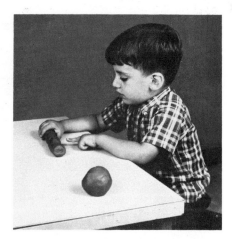

into a long sausage shape while the child watches. The child can plainly see that no clay has been added or subtracted. In this situation, children about 4 years old no longer consider the two objects to contain the same amount of clay: the longer one contains more, they say (see Figure 3-4). Not until the age of 7 do the majority of children reach the stage where the clay in the longer object is perceived to be equal in amount to that in the reference ball.

The same kind of experiment can be used to study the conservation of weight. For example, children who know that equal things will balance on a scale (they can test this with the two balls to begin with) are asked whether the sausage-shaped form will keep the scale arm balanced as did the original ball. Conservation of weight is a more difficult concept than conservation of mass, and it comes a year or so later in development.

One reason that children younger than 7 have difficulty with conservation concepts is that their thinking is still dominated by visual impressions. A change in the appearance of the clay mass means more to them than less obvious qualities, such as weight. The young child's reliance on visual impressions is made clear by an experiment on the conservation of number. If a row of black checkers is matched one for one against an equal row of red checkers, the 5- or 6-year-old will say there are the same number of each. If the black checkers are brought closer together to form a cluster, the 5-year-old says there are now more red ones—even though no checkers have been removed (see Figure 3-5). The visual impression of a long row of red checkers overrides the numerical equality that was obvious when the black checkers appeared in a matching row. In contrast, 7-year-olds assume that if the number of objects was equal before, it must remain equal. At this age, numerical equality is more significant than visual impression.

Operational stages

Between the ages of 7 and 12, the *concrete operational stage*, children master the various conservation concepts and begin to perform still other logical manipulations. For example, they can order objects on the basis of a dimension, such as height or weight. They can also form a mental representation of a series of actions. Five-year-olds can find their way to a friend's house but cannot direct you there or trace the route with paper and pencil. They can find the way because they know they have to turn at certain places, but they have no overall picture of the route. In contrast, 8-year-olds can readily draw a map of the route.

Figure 3-4
Concept of Conservation
A 4-year-old acknowledges that the two balls of clay are the same size. But when one ball is rolled into a long thin shape, he says that it has more clay. Not until he is several years older will he state that the two different shapes contain the same amount of clay.

Figure 3-5
Conservation of Number
When the two rows of seven checkers are evenly spaced, most children report that they contain the same amount. When one row is then clustered into a smaller space, children under 6 or 7 will say the original row contains more.

Piaget calls this period the concrete operational stage: although children are using abstract terms, they are doing so only in relation to concrete objects. Not until the final stage of cognitive development, the *formal operational stage,* which begins around age 11 or 12, are youngsters able to reason in purely symbolic terms.

In one test for formal operational thinking, the subject tries to discover what determines the amount of time that a pendulum will swing back and forth (its period of oscillation). The subject is presented with a length of string suspended from a hook and several weights than can be attached to the lower end. He or she can vary the length of the string, change the attached weight, and alter the height from which the bob is released.

Children still in the concrete operational stage will experiment changing some of the variables but not in a systematic way. Adolescents of even average ability will set up a series of hypotheses and proceed to test them systematically. They reason that if a particular variable (weight) affects the period of oscillation, the effect will appear only if they change one variable and hold all others constant. If this variable seems to have no effect on the time of swing, they rule it out and try another. Considering all the possibilities—working out the consequences for each hypothesis and confirming or denying these consequences—is the essence of what Piaget calls formal operational thought.

This ability to conceive of possibilities beyond what is present in reality—to think of alternatives to the way things are—permeates adolescent thinking and is tied in with adolescents' tendency to be concerned with philosophical and ideological problems and to question the way in which adults run the world.

Non-stage approaches

Piaget's theory provides a broad overview of cognitive development. It is the most comprehensive theory to date and has influenced much of the research on the way children think about the world and solve problems. Most studies support Piaget's observations on the sequences in cognitive development, although the ages at which children reach the different levels vary considerably, depending on such factors as intelligence and experiences. For example, children from middle-class homes develop concepts of conservation earlier than children from poor families.

Some critics believe that Piaget underestimated the abilities of preschool children. For example, if test conditions are carefully arranged in conservation experiments so that the children's responses do not depend on their language ability (their understanding of what the experimenter means by "more" or "longer"), then even 3- and 4-year-olds show some awareness of number conservation; they can distinguish between the number of items in a set and the way these items are spatially arranged (Gelman and Gallistel, 1978).

This and similar studies suggest that the quality of a child's thinking does not change dramatically from one stage to the next. Transition between stages of intellectual growth is gradual, involving a consolidation of earlier skills so that they become automatic. Consider conservation of liquid. If the task is simplified in various ways (for example, by drawing the child's attention to both the height and the width of the containers), preschoolers are able to conserve. A 7- or 8-year-old, in contrast, hardly needs to glance at the containers. He or she *knows* that the quantity of liquid remains the same regardless of the shape of the container into which it is poured.

Instead of focusing on stages, some psychologists view cognitive development as a gradual increase in knowledge and in mastery of skills. One important cognitive skill is remembering. Many of the differences in performance between an older and younger child may be due to differences in their ability to remember (Case, 1982). The younger child may be unable to acquire certain concepts (such as conservation) because to do so would require holding more items of information in mind simultaneously than the child's current memory capacity permits.

Preschool children perform poorly on tests of memory compared to school-age children. With increasing age, their performance improves. For example, if children hear a list of 15 simple words and are then asked to recall them, a 6-year-old will recall about four words; a 9-year-old, five words; an 11-year-old, seven words (Yussen and Berman, 1981).

The poorer performance of the younger children may be due to a limited memory capacity—a capacity that increases as they mature physically. But it seems more likely that what changes with age is the ability to use various strategies to improve memory. For example, children learn to rehearse information (to repeat it to themselves several times), to organize lists of words into meaningful categories and memorize them accordingly, and to use a variety of cues to aid memory (see Chapter 8).

PERSONALITY AND SOCIAL DEVELOPMENT

Our first social contacts are with the person who cares for us in early infancy, usually the mother. The manner in which the caregiver responds to the infant's needs—patiently with warmth and concern or brusquely with little sensitivity to discomfort—will influence the child's attitudes toward other people. Some psychologists believe that a person's basic feelings of trust in others are determined by experiences during the first years of life (Bowlby, 1973; Erikson, 1963, 1976).

Early social behavior

By 2 months of age, the average child will smile at the sight of the mother's face. Most mothers, delighted with this response, will go to great lengths to encourage repetition. Indeed, the infant's ability to smile at such an early age may play an important role in strengthening the mother-child bond. The first smiles tell the caregiver that the infant "recognizes (loves) me"—which is not true in any personal sense as yet—and encourages the caregiver to be even more affectionate and stimulating in response. The infant smiles and coos at the mother; she pats, smiles, and vocalizes in return, thereby stimulating an even more enthusiastic response from her infant. Each reinforces social responses in the other.

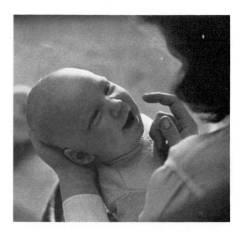

Infants all over the world begin to smile at about the same age, whether raised in a remote African village or a middle-class American home. This suggests that maturation is more important in determining the onset of smiling than conditions of rearing. The fact that blind babies smile at about the same age as sighted infants (in response to their parents' voices rather than faces) adds support to this conclusion (Eibl-Eibesfeldt, 1970).

By their third or fourth month, infants show that they recognize and prefer familiar members of the household—by smiling or cooing more when seeing their faces or hearing their voices—but they are still fairly receptive to strangers.

At about 8 months, however, this indiscriminate acceptance changes. The infant begins to show wariness or actual distress at the approach of a stranger (even while being held by the mother) and, at the same time, to protest strongly when left by the parent in an unfamiliar setting or with an unfamiliar person. Parents are often disconcerted to find that their formerly gregarious infant, who had always welcomed happily the attentions of a babysitter, now cries inconsolably when they prepare to leave—and for some time afterward.

"Stranger shyness" increases dramatically from about 8 months of age until the end of the first year (see Stevens, 1971; Bronson, 1972). Distress over separation from the parent—a distinct but related phenomenon—reaches a peak between 14 to 18 months and then gradually declines. By the time they are 3 years old, most children are secure enough in their parents' absence to be able to interact comfortably with other children and adults.

The waxing and waning of separation fears appears to be only slightly influenced by conditions of child rearing. The same general pattern has been found among American children raised entirely at home and those attending a day-care center, Israeli infants raised in a kibbutz, Indian children living in a Guatemalan Village, and Bushmen children living in the Kalahari Desert (Kagan, 1979).

How do we explain these fears? Two factors seem to be important in both their onset and their decline. First is the growth of memory capacity. Beginning at about 8 months, an infant is able to form a mental image of people or situations. Called a *schema* (plural, *schemata*), this image can be stored in memory and then retrieved for comparison with the present situation. Thus, a 1-year-old can wake up from a nap, confront an unfamiliar face, and realize that the mother's more familiar one is not present; this realization may generate feelings of uncertainty. In the months ahead, increased memory competence will be accompanied by an ability to anticipate the future. As the child's memory for past instances of separation and return improves, the child becomes better able to anticipate the return of the absent parent and both uncertainty and distress decline.

The second factor is the growth of autonomy. One-year-olds are still highly dependent on care from adults, but children of 2 or 3 can head for the snack plate or toy shelf on their own. Also, they can use language to communicate their wants and feelings. Thus, dependency on caregivers in general and on familiar caregivers in particular decreases, and the issue of the parent's presence becomes less central for the child.

Attachment

The infant's tendency to seek closeness to particular people and to feel more secure in their presence is called *attachment*. The young of other species show attachment to their mother in different ways. Infant monkeys cling to their mother's chest as she moves about; puppies climb over each other in their attempts to reach the warm belly of their mother; ducklings and baby chicks follow their mother about, making sounds to which she responds and going to her when they are frightened. These early, unlearned responses to the mother have a clear adaptive value: preventing the organism from wandering away from the source of care and getting lost.

Psychologists at first theorized that attachment to the mother developed because she, as a source of food, satisfied one of the infant's most basic needs. But some facts did not fit. For example, ducklings and baby chicks feed themselves from birth, yet they still follow their mothers about and spend a great deal of time in contact with them. The comfort they derive from the mother's presence cannot come from her role in feeding. A series of well-known experiments with monkeys showed that there was more to mother-infant attachment than nutritional needs.

ATTACHMENT IN MONKEYS Infant monkeys were separated from their mothers shortly after birth and placed with two artificial "mothers" constructed of wire mesh with wooden heads; the torso of one mother was bare wire; the other was covered with foam rubber and terry cloth, making it more cuddly and easy to cling to (see Figure 3-6). Either mother could be equipped to provide milk by means of a bottle attached to its chest.

The experiment sought to determine whether the mother that was always the source of food would be the one to which the young monkey would cling. The results were clear-cut; no matter which mother provided food, the infant monkey spent its time clinging to the terry-cloth, cuddly mother. This purely passive but soft-contact mother was a source of security. For example, the obvious fear of the infant monkey placed in a strange environment was allayed if the infant could make contact with the cloth mother. While holding on to the cloth mother with one hand or foot, the monkey was willing to explore objects that were otherwise too terrifying to approach. Similar responses can be observed in 1- to 2-year-old children who are willing to explore strange territory as long as their mother is close by.

Further studies revealed some additional features that infant monkeys seek in their mothers. They prefer an artificial mother that rocks to an immobile one, and they prefer a warm mother to a cold one. Given a cloth mother and a wire mother of the same temperature, the infant monkeys always preferred the cloth mother. But if the wire mother was heated, the newborns chose it over a cool cloth mother for the first 2 weeks of life. After that, the infant monkeys spent more and more time with the cloth mother.

The infant monkey's attachment to its mother is thus an innate response to certain stimuli provided by her. Warmth, rocking, and food are important, but *contact comfort*—the opportunity to cling to and rub against something soft—seems to be the most important attribute for monkeys.

Although contact with a cuddly, artificial mother provides an important aspect of "mothering," it is not enough for satisfactory development. Infant monkeys raised with artificial mothers and isolated from other monkeys during the first six months of life showed various types of bizarre behavior in adulthood. They rarely engaged in normal interaction with other monkeys later on (either cowering in fear or showing abnormally aggressive behavior), and their sexual responses were inappropriate. When female monkeys that had been deprived of early social contact were successfully mated (after considerable effort), they made very poor mothers, tending to neglect or abuse their infants. For monkeys, interaction with other members of their species during the first six months of life appears to be crucial for normal social development.

ATTACHMENT IN HUMAN INFANTS Although we should be careful in generalizing from experimental work on monkeys to human development, there is evidence that the human infant's attachment to the mother (or person providing most of the initial care) serves the same important functions: it provides the security necessary for the child to explore his or her environment, and it forms the basis for interpersonal relationships in later years. Young children are much more willing to investigate strange surroundings when mother is nearby. The failure to form an attachment to one or a few primary persons in the early years has been related to an inability to develop close personal relationships in adulthood (Bowlby, 1973; Ainsworth and others, 1978).

Figure 3-6
A Monkey's Response
to an Artificial Mother
Although fed via the wire mother, the infant spends more time with the terry-cloth mother. The terry-cloth mother provides security and a safe base from which to explore strange objects.

A series of studies designed to investigate attachment in young children has revealed some interesting differences in the quality of the mother-child relationship. The laboratory setup, called the "Strange Situation," involves the following episodes:

1   The mother brings the child into the experimental room, places the child on a small chair surrounded by toys, and then goes to sit at the opposite end of the room.
2   After a few minutes, a stranger enters the room, sits quietly for a while, and then attempts to engage the child in play with a toy.
3   The mother leaves the room, leaving her handbag on her chair as a sign that she will return.
4   The mother returns and engages the child in play while the stranger slips out.
5   The mother leaves again and the child is left alone for 3 minutes.
6   The stranger returns.
7   The mother returns.

The child is observed through a one-way mirror during the entire sequence, and any number of different measures can be recorded: child's activity level and play involvement, crying or other distress signs, proximity to and attempts to gain attention of mother, proximity to and willingness to interact with the stranger, and so on.

Studies of 1-year-olds placed in the Strange Situation found that some of the most significant individual differences showed up in the baby's reaction to the mother when she returned. Most of the babies were uneasy during the mother's absence, whether left with the stranger or completely alone; signs of distress ranged from fussing and visually searching for the mother to loud crying. On the mother's return, more than half of the babies immediately sought close contact with her and showed a need for closeness for a while thereafter. But some babies conspicuously ignored the mother on her return; and some displayed seemingly ambivalent behavior—for example, they would cry to be picked up and then squirm angrily to get down.

Observation of the same babies in the home revealed that those babies who sought contact with the mother on reunion were much more secure (cried less often, were more responsive to their mother's verbal commands, and were less upset by their mother's coming and going) than babies who were either avoidant or ambivalent on reunion in the Strange Situation.

The investigators concluded, on the basis of these and other data, that all babies become attached to the mother by the time they are 1 year old, but the quality of the attachment differs depending on the mother's responsiveness to the baby's needs. Most babies show *secure attachment*, but some show *insecure attachment*. The avoidant or ambivalent behavior shown by insecurely attached babies on reunion with the mother is assumed to be a defense against the anxiety occasioned by a mother who cannot be depended on. It is a mild form of the more extreme kind of detachment observed in young children who have had to endure long separations from the parents. Such children often appear indifferent to their parents when they are first reunited with them (Ainsworth, 1979).

Insecure attachment is associated with insensitive or unresponsive mothering during the first year of life. The mothers of babies who show insecure attachment tend to respond more on the basis of their own wishes or moods than to signals from the baby. For example, they will respond to the baby's cries for attention when they feel like cuddling the baby but will ignore such cries at other times (Stayton, 1973). Mothers of infants who are securely attached are more responsive to their infants' needs, provide more social stimulation (talking to and playing with the infant), and express more affection (Clarke-Stewart, 1973).

ATTACHMENT AND LATER DEVELOPMENT   There is mounting evidence that the pattern of early attachment influences the way an infant copes with new experiences during the next few years. For example, in one study, 2-year-olds were given a series of problems requiring the use of tools; some of the problems were within the child's capacity, whereas others were quite difficult. Those toddlers who had been rated as securely attached (at 12 months of age) approached the problems with enthusiasm and persistence. When they encountered difficulties, they seldom cried or became angry but sought help from the adults who were present. Those who had been rated earlier as insecurely attached behaved quite differently. They became easily frustrated and angry, seldom asked for help, tended to ignore or reject directions from the adults, and quickly gave up trying to solve the problems (Matas, Arend, and Sroufe, 1978).

Another study looked at the social behavior of nursery-school children (age 3½ years) whose attachment relationships had been assessed at 15 months of age. The children rated earlier as securely attached tended to be the social leaders; they were active in initiating and participating in activities and were sought out by the other children. Their teachers rated them as forceful, self-directed, and eager to learn. The insecurely attached children tended to be socially withdrawn and hesitant about participating in activities. Their teachers rated them as less curious about new things and less forceful in pursuing their goals. These differences were not related to intelligence (Waters, Wippman, and Sroufe, 1979).

These studies suggest that children who are securely attached by the time they enter their second year of life are better equipped to cope with new experiences and relationships. However, we cannot be certain that the quality of children's early attachments is directly responsible for their later competence in problem solving and social skills. Mothers who are responsive to their children's needs in infancy probably continue to provide effective "mothering" during early childhood, encouraging autonomy and efforts to cope with new experiences yet ready with help when needed. Thus, the child's competency and social skills at age 3½ may reflect the current state of the parent-child relationship rather than the relationship that existed two years earlier.

In addition, as we stressed earlier, part of the responsibility may lie with the child. A "difficult" child may find it hard to cope with new tasks and to form relationships, despite receiving quite adequate parenting. At this point, we can say only that it seems likely that early patterns of parent-child attachment do influence later development.

Although an infant's primary attachment is to the person who provides most of the early care, other familiar persons are a source of security, too. Studies of the Strange Situation using the father indicate that infants react to his presence or absence in ways similar to those described for mothers, although attachment to the father seems to develop more slowly (Kotelchuk, 1976). For example, 1-year-olds usually cry and stop playing when mother leaves them alone; such responses to the father's departure do not appear (on the average) until 15 months. In addition, the 1-year-old infant usually protests the mother's departure more vigorously than the father's and clings to her somewhat longer on reunion. These differences lessen with age (see Figure 3-7).

Children whose fathers are actively involved as caregivers tend to be less disturbed when left alone with a stranger than children from families where

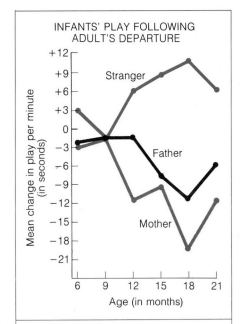

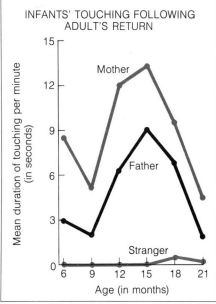

Figure 3-7
Age Changes in Infants' Responses
Children (6 to 21 months) were observed in the Strange Situation with either their mothers, fathers, or a stranger. When the adult left briefly, the child's reaction depended on who had left. When either mother or father left, the child's play was disrupted, although such responses to father's departure appeared at a later age. When the stranger left, the child played more actively, apparently feeling more comfortable alone than with a stranger. The return of either parent was followed by a period of touching or clinging, although the child clung somewhat longer to the mother on reunion.

More and more women today are working outside of the home. There are some five million working mothers in the United States with children under 5 years of age, and the number appears to be increasing. In view of the research on infant attachment and on the benefits of a stimulating environment during the early years, it is important to consider how this trend will affect future generations.

Working mothers provide a variety of arrangements for their children's care. The majority leave their preschoolers at home to be cared for by a sitter or a relative while they work. The rest leave their young ones at day-care centers. Clearly, the effects of maternal employment on the child's development depend, to a large extent, on the quality of the substitute care. Research has focused on two broad areas: (1) the general effects on children of having a working, versus a full-time, mother; (2) the effects of group versus individual child care.

Having a working mother appears to benefit girls more than it does boys. Daughters of working mothers tend to be more independent, better adjusted socially, and more likely to do well academically and aspire to a career than daughters of mothers who are not employed (see Gold, Andres, and Glorieux, 1979; Birnbaum, 1975; Hoffman, 1980). Sons of working mothers are also more independent and better adjusted socially than sons of nonworking mothers. But they do not do as well in school or on tests of cognitive ability (Brown, 1970; Banducci, 1967). How do we explain these findings? There are a number of possibilities. It may be that the loss of intellectual stimulation when the mother works has an adverse effect on both boys and girls.

Chinese infants in a factory nursery
The infants' mothers, working nearby, will nurse them during breaks in the work shift.

But the daughter's loss may be offset by other benefits, such as increased independence and the model of an achieving and competent mother. Little boys who have a full-time mother during the preschool years tend to be more intellectually able as adolescents (but also more conforming, inhibited, and fearful). The nonworking mother may be so immersed in her role that she encourages dependency and has difficulty letting her son develop mature behavior.

Group care for infants and very young children is a novel and somewhat disconcerting idea for many American parents, but communal child rearing has a longer history in some other countries such as China, Russia, and Israel. In China, for example, mothers can leave their infants in a nursery at their place of

work as soon as the infants are 2 months old. The mothers go to the nursery at intervals to nurse the infants. By the age of 2 or 3 years, most infants are dropped off at day-care centers near home in the morning and picked up by their parents after they return from work in the evening.

On the collective farms, or *kibbutzim*, of Israel the children are cared for from early infancy by professional caregivers, called *metapelets*, in houses separate from those of the parents. Practices differ somewhat from one kibbutz to another, but the following arrangement is typical. During the first year of life, the mother provides the major portion of the feeding and care of her infant, although the infant is housed in the communal nursery. After the first

Working Mothers: The Effect on Children's Development

year, the mother works full time and the parents see their child mainly during the evening and on Saturdays.

Information about the effects of communal care on children's development in China and Russia is limited, but there have been a number of studies of kibbutz children. For example, one study found that kibbutz children were equal in physical and mental skills to Israeli children raised in private homes, and both groups were superior to Israeli children reared in orphanages (Kohen-Raz, 1968). Because earlier studies had shown that children raised in orphanages were retarded in social and intellectual development, those responsible for setting up the kibbutz child-care centers were especially concerned with providing a warm relationship with a mother-substitute as well as sufficient intellectual stimulation. Consequently, the metapelets receive special training in all areas of child development.

Because they spend more time with their peers, kibbutz-raised children develop some social characteristics earlier than children raised at home. For example, they develop a feeling of group concern and identification while very young; they also acquire early the ability to understand how another child feels (Rabkin and Rabkin, 1969; Nahir and Yussen, 1977).

Interestingly enough, being separated from the mother for most of the day does not appear to weaken the mother-child attachment. When kibbutz children were observed in the Strange Situation at age 2½, they were just as concerned over separation from the mother as were American children raised at home (Maccoby and Feldman, 1972). When kibbutz children were left with mother and a stranger, they ap-

peared more secure than when left with the metapelet and a stranger—as evidenced by the amount of time they spent playing (Fox, 1975). Similar results have been found when day-care children in the United States are compared with home-reared children. There seems to be little difference between the two groups either in the amount of protest shown when left by the mother in an unfamiliar room or in the tendency to seek closeness to the mother when tired or upset (Kagan, Kearsley, and Zelago, 1978).

Any attempt to evaluate the effects of home care versus group care obviously depends on the quality of the child-care facility and the nature of the home. For example, the earlier statement that sons of working mothers do not do as well academically as sons of nonworking mothers is true for boys from middle-class homes. Boys from very low-income families, in contrast, score *higher* on tests of cognitive ability when the mother works. A number of factors probably contribute to this differential effect of maternal employment, but an important one is the mother's role as a teacher. Middle-class mothers are better educated than lower-class mothers; they are more effective teachers and a greater source of intellectual stimulation for their children (Goldberg, 1978). Thus, maternal employment may take more away from the middle-class child than from the lower-class. If the lower-class child is provided with a more intellectually stimulating environment in the mother's absence (for example, in a well-run day-care center with trained teachers), we would expect improvement in academic skills.

Many day-care centers are run by trained personnel in charge of small groups of children with a concerted ef-

Nursery in an Israeli kibbutz
Kibbutz-raised children spend more time with their peers, encouraging them to develop feelings of group concern and identification at an early age.

fort made to provide each child with emotional support and training in social and academic skills; some, on the other hand, provide for little beyond the child's physical needs. Since experiences during the preschool years form the basis for later development, children who spend most of their working hours under conditions that are not very stimulating lose a great deal. In view of the fact that mothers of young children are working in increasing numbers (roughly 45 percent of married and 60 percent of single mothers with preschool children are employed), the provision of adequate and affordable child care is an important social issue.

mother provides most of the care; and the period during which they strongly protest separation from either parent is apt to be shorter (Kotelchuk, 1976). Thus, having more than one caregiver seems to help the child cope with the stress of separation.

Interaction with peers

Although a close relationship with a warm and responsive adult is essential for a child's emotional development, interaction with other children plays an important role, too.

As we saw before, infant monkeys that are raised with only their mothers and have no opportunity to play with other young monkeys do not develop normal patterns of behavior. When introduced to other monkeys later on, they may be abnormally fearful of contact—screaming in fright at the approach of another monkey—or overly aggressive; they also show inappropriate sexual responses (Suomi, 1977).

In the normal course of development, an infant monkey spends the first eight weeks of life exclusively with its mother. From then on, the young monkey spends more and more time swinging, chasing, and wrestling with its age-mates. From these early play activities, the young monkey learns to enjoy physical contact, to control aggression, and to develop the grasping and mounting responses that will lead to adult sexual behavior.

Human children also learn many of their social skills in interaction with each other. They learn to give and take, to share in cooperative ventures, to enjoy each other's actions, and to understand how another person feels. Peers become models to imitate as well as important dispensers of rewards and punishments. By watching the actions of peers, children may learn a new skill (how to build a bridge with blocks) or the consequences of certain behaviors (aggression gets other children into trouble).

A number of experiments have shown the influence of peer models on children's behavior. For example, 4- and 5-year-olds who watched one of their classmates being very generous in sharing some prizes were much more generous when their turn came to share than children who had not watched the

Interaction with other children plays an important role in the emotional development of the child.

generous model (Hartup and Coates, 1967). As we will see in Chapter 11, if a child watches a model being rewarded for certain behaviors, the child is more likely to imitate those behaviors than if she or he sees the model being punished.

The way other children respond to a child's behavior is an important modifying influence. For example, selfishness that was accepted by doting parents may not be tolerated by the child's peers. Children reinforce certain actions in their playmates—by approval and attention—and punish others.

Moral thought and behavior

Understanding the values that govern behavior in one's society and regulating one's own behavior accordingly are important parts of development. Children's concepts of right and wrong change in interesting ways as they grow older. Most 5-year-olds say that it is wrong to lie, or steal, or injure another person. But their comprehension of these statements changes with age. Only gradually do they begin to understand what kinds of statements are lies, how borrowing differs from stealing, or that injuring someone intentionally evokes greater blame than accidental injury.

Children's ability to make judgments about moral issues is related to their cognitive development. Older children are more capable of handling abstract concepts and making inferences about social relationships than younger children. Although maturing cognitive abilities play a role in the development of a child's sense of right and wrong, other factors (the models provided by parents and peers, for example) are equally important. And children's moral *behavior* (their ability to inhibit actions that are disapproved by society and to be concerned about the welfare of others) depends on much more than an understanding of moral problems.

STAGES OF MORAL JUDGMENT   How reasoning about moral issues changes with age has been the subject of intensive research by Kohlberg (1969, 1973). Influenced by Piaget's theory of cognitive development and his work on moral reasoning (*The Moral Judgment of the Child*, 1932), Kohlberg sought to determine whether there are universal stages in the development of moral judgments. He presented stories such as the following to children and adults of various ages and cultural backgrounds.

> In Europe, a lady was dying because she was very sick. There was one drug that the doctors said might save her. This medicine was discovered by a man living in the same town. It cost him $200 to make it, but he charged $2,000 for just a little of it. The sick lady's husband, Heinz, tried to borrow enough money to buy the drug. He went to everyone he knew to borrow the money. But he could borrow only half of what he needed. He told the man who made the drug that his wife was dying, and asked him to sell the medicine cheaper or let him pay later. But the man said, "No, I made the drug and I'm going to make money from it." So Heinz broke into the store and stole the drug.

The subject is asked, "Should Heinz have done that? Was it actually wrong or right? Why?" By analyzing the answers to a series of stories of this type—each portraying a moral dilemma—Kohlberg arrived at six developmental stages of moral judgment grouped into three broad levels (see Table 3-2). The answers are scored as belonging to a certain stage not on the basis of whether the action is judged right or wrong but on the reasons given for the decision. For example,

Table 3-2
Stages of Moral Reasoning
Kohlberg believes that moral judgment develops with age according to the following stages. (After Kohlberg, 1969)

LEVELS AND STAGES	ILLUSTRATIVE BEHAVIOR
Level I Preconventional morality	
Stage 1 Punishment orientation	Obeys rules to avoid punishment
Stage 2 Reward orientation	Conforms to obtain rewards, to have favors returned
Level II Conventional morality	
Stage 3 Good-boy/good-girl orientation	Conforms to avoid disapproval of others
Stage 4 Authority orientation	Upholds laws and social rules to avoid censure of authorities and feelings of guilt about not "doing one's duty"
Level III Postconventional morality	
Stage 5 Social contract orientation	Actions guided by principles commonly agreed on as essential to the public welfare; principles upheld to retain respect of peers and, thus, self-respect
Stage 6 Ethical principle orientation	Actions guided by self-chosen ethical principles (that usually value justice, dignity, and equality); principles upheld to avoid self-condemnation

agreeing that Heinz should have stolen the drug because "If you let your wife die, you'll get in trouble" or condemning him for his actions because "If you steal the drug, you'll be caught and sent to jail" are both scored at Stage 1. In both instances, the man's actions are evaluated as right or wrong on the basis of anticipated punishment.

Kohlberg's studies indicate that the moral judgments of children who are 7 years old and younger are predominantly at Level I—actions are evaluated in terms of whether they avoid punishment or lead to rewards. By age 13, a majority of the moral dilemmas are resolved at Level II—actions are evaluated in terms of maintaining a good image in the eyes of other people. This is the level of conventional morality. In the first stage at this level (Stage 3), one seeks approval by being "nice"; this orientation expands in the next stage (Stage 4) to include "doing one's duty," showing respect for authority, and conforming to the social order in which one is raised.

According to Kohlberg, many individuals never progress beyond Level II. He sees the stages of moral development as closely tied to Piaget's stages of cognitive development, and only those who have achieved the later stages of formal operational thought are capable of the kind of abstract thinking necessary for postconventional morality at Level III. The highest stage of moral development (Level III, Stage 6) requires formulating abstract ethical principles and upholding them to avoid self-condemnation. Kohlberg reports that fewer than 10 percent of his subjects over age 16 show the kind of "clear-principled" Stage-6 thinking exemplified by the following response of a 16-year-old to Heinz's dilemma: "By the law of society he was wrong but by the law of nature or of God the druggist was wrong and the husband was justified. Human life is above financial gain. Regardless of who was dying, if it was a total stranger, man has a duty to save him from dying" (Kohlberg, 1969, p. 244).

Kohlberg views children as "moral philosophers" who develop moral standards of their own; these standards do not necessarily come from parents or peers but emerge from the cognitive interaction of children with their social environment. Movement from one stage to the next involves an internal cognitive reorganization rather than a simple acquisition of the moral concepts prevalent in their culture (Kohlberg, 1973).

Other psychologists disagree, pointing out that the development of a conscience, a sense of right and wrong, is not simply a function of maturing cognitive abilities; children's identification with their parents and the way in which they are rewarded or punished for behavior in specific situations will influence their moral views. So also will the moral standards espoused by the children's peers and by characters on television and in books. Studies have shown that moral judgments can be modified by exposure to models; when children watch adults who are reinforced for expressing a moral viewpoint based on principles different from their own, they may change their judgments up or down a level (Bandura and McDonald, 1963).

Thus, although there are obviously *age trends* in the way children think about moral issues, these may be explained more simply by looking at what parents teach and reinforce in children at different ages than by proposing a set sequence of stages. Very young children may need the threat of punishment to keep them from doing something wrong ("If you hit your little sister, I will put you to bed *right now*"). As children mature in their ability to understand language, social sanctions become more effective ("If you hit your little sister, I will be very angry; good children don't hurt other people").

Researchers using stories much simpler than Kohlberg's and posing moral dilemmas more relevant to a child's daily experiences have found that children as young as 4 or 5 years (whom Kohlberg would place in the preconventional stage) have some awareness of important moral principles. Consider, for example, the question of *intention:*

> David was playing with his dog. He bumped against the table and knocked his mother's tea set to the floor, and the teapot and all the cups broke into many pieces. Eric was angry at his mother. He threw one of her teacups to the floor, breaking it in many pieces. Which boy was naughtier?

Most 3-year-olds focus on the amount of damage and judge that David was naughtier. Children of 4 or 5 years, however, begin to consider intentions as well as consequences in evaluating the "badness" of an act. With increasing age, consequences (damage) become less important than motives (intent) when children judge how much punishment the culprit should receive (Leon, 1977; Surber, 1977).

Children as young as 4 also show an ability to integrate the concepts of need and achievement in allocating rewards. Children 4–8 years old were asked to play Santa Claus and divide a fixed number of toys between two boys in a fair manner. Each of the boys was described by two pieces of information: how hard he worked (indicated by a picture showing how many dishes he had washed for his mother) and his need (indicated by a picture showing how many toys he already had). According to Piaget (1932), the younger children should give greater weight to the objective information about achievement and less weight to the more subjective factor of need. However, the data showed essentially the same pattern for all age groups; the children considered need as important as achievement in deciding on a fair distribution of the toys (Anderson and Butzin, 1978).

The above studies indicate that even preschoolers recognize some important moral principles when presented with situations they can understand. This is not to deny, of course, that ways of thinking about moral issues change with age.

MORAL BEHAVIOR   How well does *moral reasoning*—as measured by responses to moral dilemmas—correlate with *moral behavior?* Are youngsters who show advanced moral judgment more likely to resist temptation or behave unselfishly than those less advanced? There is clearly some relationship between moral thought and moral action. For example, juvenile delinquents show lower levels of moral judgment than law-abiding youngsters of the same age and intelligence (Kohlberg, 1969). And people who attain higher moral levels on Kohlberg's dilemmas are more likely than low scorers to offer help to a person in distress (Huston and Korte, 1976). But, in general, research relating Kohlberg's levels to behavior in specific situations—for example, whether a child will cheat on a test or behave unselfishly—have found low correlations (Mischel and Mischel, 1976).

Often we know how we *should* act but may not do so when our own self-interest is involved. For example, children's judgment of "fairness" tended to be more mature in a hypothetical situation (how should candy bars be distributed among workers in a group) than their reasoning when the situation became real. Those who had suggested giving the most candy to the person who produced the most when the situation was hypothetical were apt to say that everyone should share equally when it came to dividing the candy among their own work group, particularly if they had been among the less productive workers. Some who had earlier advocated an equal division demanded the largest share in the real situation (Damon, 1977).

Moral conduct depends on a number of factors in addition to the ability to reason about moral dilemmas. Two important factors are the ability to consider the long-range consequences of one's actions (rather than the immediate gain) and to control one's behavior. Equally important is the ability to empathize with other people—that is, to be able to put oneself in someone else's place. Understanding what another person is feeling motivates us to help.

Child-rearing practices and later behavior

Methods of child rearing vary considerably from country to country and from one social group to another. Even within middle-class homes in the United States, attitudes have tended to fluctuate in cycles on such matters as toilet training, feeding schedules, bottle versus breast feeding, and permissiveness versus firm control.

During the first third of this century, child-rearing practices were fairly strict. Parents were advised not to spoil their babies by picking them up every time they cried, to feed them according to a fixed schedule (whether hungry or not), and to toilet train within the first year. Thumb-sucking and handling the genitals were to be vigorously discouraged. This quite rigid approach was partly the result of the influence of behaviorism; the goal was to build "good" habits and extinguish "bad" ones—and the earlier the parents started, the better. The following quotation from John B. Watson, the father of behaviorism, carries to a ridiculous extreme the notion of a controlled, objective, unemotional way of handling children.

There is a sensible way of treating children. Treat them as though they were young adults. Dress them, bathe them with care and circumspection. Let your behavior always be objective and kindly firm. Never hug and kiss them, never let them sit on your lap. If you must, kiss them once on the forehead when they say goodnight. Shake hands with them in the morning. Give them a pat on the head if they have made an extraordinarily good job of a difficult task. Try it out.

> In a week's time you will find how easy it is to be perfectly objective with your child and at the same time kindly. You will be utterly ashamed of the mawkish, sentimental way you have been handling it. (Watson, 1928)

It is doubtful that many parents followed such a rigid program, but this was the advice of the "experts" at the time.

During the 1940s, the trend shifted toward more permissive and flexible child-care methods. Views on child development were being influenced by psychoanalytic theory, which stressed the importance of the child's emotional security and the damage that might result from harsh control of natural impulses. Under the guidance of Dr. Benjamin Spock, parents were advised to follow their own inclinations and adopt flexible schedules that fit both the child's and their own needs. Toilet training should be delayed until the child was old enough to understand its purpose (not before the middle of the second year), and neither thumb-sucking nor genital-touching was to be considered a matter of great concern.

Now the pendulum appears to be swinging back. Parents today seem to feel that permissiveness is not the answer. Their approach to child rearing includes a moderate degree of control, firm discipline, and even punishment when necessary.

That children flourish under a variety of rearing methods is a tribute to their adaptability and probably an indication that specific methods are less important than the basic attitude of the parents.

Attempts to relate specific child-rearing techniques—type of feeding schedule, age of weaning or toilet training—to later personality characteristics have not been very successful. The inconsistent results obtained probably are due to several factors. For one thing, parents' reports of how they handled their children may be fairly inaccurate, particularly when memory for the children's early days is required. Parents tend to report what they *think they should do* in handling their offspring rather than what they actually do. There are also numerous ways of applying any specific child-rearing method. For example, two children may be toilet-trained at the same early age; one mother is firm but patient, whereas the other is firm and impatient, expressing disappointment when the child fails. Both mothers toilet train their children "early," but they communicate quite different attitudes to the child.

Although specific techniques may not be very predictive of later personality traits, we do have some evidence of the kind of parent-child relationships that produce competent and self-confident youngsters. In a series of studies, 3- and 4-year-old children were observed at home and in nursery school and rated on five measures of competency: (1) self-control, (2) the tendency to approach new or unexpected situations with curiosity and enthusiasm, (3) vitality, (4) self-reliance, and (5) the ability to express warmth toward playmates. On the basis of ratings on these characteristics, three groups of children were selected for further study. Children in Group I were the most mature and competent, scoring high on all five characteristics. Group II children were moderately self-reliant and self-controlled but rather apprehensive in new situations and not much interested in interacting with other children. Group III children were the most immature; they were much less self-reliant and self-controlled than the children in the other two groups, highly dependent on adults for help, and apt to retreat from new situations.

The investigator next looked at the child-rearing practices of all the parents by interviewing them and by observing how they interacted with their children in the home. The investigator focused on four dimensions of the parent-child

In both single-parent and two-parent families, a warm, nurturing environment encourages childen to be self-reliant and self-confident.

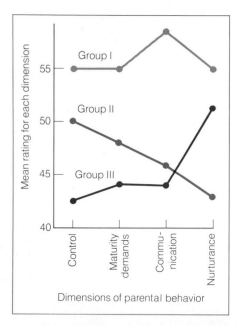

Figure 3-8
Parental Behavior as Related
to Child Behavior
Nursery school children were evaluated in terms of competency and maturity; Group I are the most competent children; Group III are the most immature and dependent. The figure shows how the parents of each group were rated on four dimensions: control of the child's activities, pressure demands for mature behavior, clarity of parent-child communication, and nurturance or warmth. (After Baumrind, 1967)

relationship: (1) *control*—how much the parents tried to influence the child's activities and modify the expression of dependent or aggressive behavior in line with their own standards; (2) *maturity demands*—the amount of pressure on the child to perform at his or her level of ability; (3) *clarity of parent-child communication*—how well the parents explained their reasons when they wanted the child to obey and the extent to which they took the child's opinions and feelings into consideration; (4) *parental nurturance*—the warmth and compassion the parents showed toward the child and their pleasure in his or her accomplishments.

As Figure 3-8 shows, the parents of the mature and competent children (Group I) are high on all four dimensions. They are warm, loving, and communicate well with their children. Although they respect their children's opinions, they are generally firm and clear about the behavior they consider appropriate. The parents of the children who were moderately self-controlled and self-reliant but somewhat withdrawn and distrustful (Group II) tend to be fairly controlling but not very warm and affectionate toward their children or concerned with their opinions. The parents of the most immature children (Group III) are affectionate toward their children but not very controlling, demanding, or communicative. These parents tend to be ineffective and disorganized in running their households and lax in setting guidelines for behavior and in disciplining or rewarding their children.

In subsequent studies, the investigator proceeded in the reverse direction, selecting parents who fit the above descriptions and then looking at the behaviors of their preschool children. Although the results are too detailed to describe here, we can draw some general conclusions. Parents who are fairly firm and consistent in their expectations of how their children should behave but who are also warm and affectionate and respect their children's opinions tend to produce competent and self-reliant preschoolers. When the parents are very controlling and more concerned with their own needs than with those of their children, their offspring may be fairly self-controlled but not very secure or confident in their approach to new situations or other people. Very permissive parents, who neither reward responsible behavior nor discourage immature behavior, produce youngsters with the least self-reliance and self-control. In summary, competence and self-confidence in young children seem best fostered by a warm and nurturant home where parents reward responsible behavior but also encourage independent actions and decision making (Baumrind, 1972).

IDENTIFICATION

As children develop, they acquire many attitudes and behavior patterns that are similar to those of their parents. Sometimes the resemblance between a youngster and a parent in such characteristics as manner of walking, gestures, and voice inflection is striking. The child is said to *identify* with the parent.

The concept of identification comes from psychoanalysis and played an important role in Freud's theorizing. In psychoanalytic theory, identification refers to the unconscious process by which an individual takes on the characteristics (attitudes, patterns of behavior, emotions) of another person. Young children, by duplicating the attitudes and attributes of their parents, come to feel that they have absorbed some of the parent's strength and adequacy.

Identification, according to the psychoanalytic view, is more than the imitation of parental behavior; the child responds as if he or she *were* the parent.

Thus, a young girl who identifies with her mother feels proud when her mother receives an award or honor—as if she herself had been the recipient. She feels sad when her mother suffers a disappointment. Through the process of identification, the child acquires the diverse behaviors involved in developing self-control, a conscience, and the appropriate sex role. For example, Freud believed that the child's conscience is formed by incorporating parental standards of conduct so that the child acts in accordance with these standards even when the parent is absent and experiences guilt when he or she violates them.

Some psychologists question the psychoanalytic view of identification as an unconscious, unitary process. They point out that not all children identify with their parents in all respects. A girl, for example, may emulate her mother's social skills and sense of humor but not her moral values. They view identification as a form of learning; children imitate certain parental behaviors because they are rewarded for doing so. Siblings, peers, teachers, and TV heroes are other models who serve as sources of imitation or identification. According to this view, identification is a continuous process in which new responses are acquired as a result of both direct and vicarious experiences with parents and other models.

Most psychologists—regardless of how they define it—view identification as the basic process in the socialization of children. By modeling themselves after the important people in their environment, children acquire the attitudes and behaviors expected of adults in their society. Parents, because they are children's earliest and most frequent associates, serve as the primary source of identification. The parent of the same sex usually serves as the model for sex-typed behavior.

Sex roles

All cultures define approved ways in which men and women are expected to behave. Certain personality characteristics, work tasks, and activities are considered appropriate for males and others appropriate for females. The definitions of sex-appropriate behavior vary from culture to culture and may change over time within a culture. Certainly, our view of appropriate masculine and feminine behavior today is radically different from what it was 50 years ago. Women are no longer expected to be dependent, submissive, and noncompetitive; men are not criticized for enjoying such domestic activities as cooking and child care or for expressing artistic and tender feelings. Standards of dress and appearance have also become much more unisex—indeed, from a distance it is often difficult to determine whether the individual with medium-length hair, wearing jeans, is male or female. In the areas of education, work, and athletics, earlier sex-role differentiations have been breaking down. Nevertheless, within any culture the roles of men and women and the behavior expected of them still differ.

SEX TYPING *Sex typing* refers to the acquisition of those characteristics and behaviors that one's culture considers appropriate for females or males. Sex typing must be distinguished from *sex-role identity*, which is the degree to which one regards oneself as female or male. A girl may have a firm acceptance of herself as female and still not adopt all of the behaviors that her culture considers feminine nor avoid all behaviors labeled masculine. A boy may identify with an artistic and sensitive father whose behavior does not fit the cultural masculine stereotype; the boy may be secure in his masculine identify, yet his behavior will not be strongly sex-typed.

A child identifies with the parent

Both boys and girls believe that girls
like to play with dolls
like to help mother
talk a lot
never hit
say "I need some help"
will grow up to be a nurse or a teacher

Both boys and girls believe that boys
like to play with cars
like to help father
like to build things
say "I can hit you"
will grow up to be boss

Table 3-3
Sex-Role Stereotypes in Young Children
Two- and 3-year olds were introduced to a male and female paper doll, Michael and Lisa, and then played a game in which they were asked to identify the doll that said or did certain things. For example, when the experimenter said "I like to play with dolls" and showed a sketch portraying dolls and a doll house, the child placed one of the two paper dolls in the picture. The children's choices for a number of such statements were tabulated. Many items were not sex typed. For example, neither boys nor girls believe that one sex more than the other is smart, runs fast, likes to play outside, says "I can't do it." And on some items, boys and girls disagreed. For example, girls (but not boys) believe that boys like to fight, are mean, say "I did it wrong." And boys (but not girls) believe that girls cry sometimes, say "you hurt my feelings," say "you're not letting me have a turn." The items listed in the table are the sex-role stereotypes on which both boys and girls agreed. (After Kuhn, Nash, and Brucken, 1978)

Despite the current trend toward equality of the sexes, sex-role stereotypes are still very prevalent in our culture. By *sex-role stereotypes* we mean the belief that an individual should behave in certain ways or show certain characteristics because that person is male or female. For example, it is difficult to distinguish newborn males from females provided their diapers are on. Yet adults, viewing newborn infants through the window of a hospital nursery, believe that they can detect differences. Infants thought to be boys are described as robust, strong, and large-featured; girls are seen as delicate, fine-featured, and "soft" (Luria and Rubin, 1974). To cite another example, college students viewed a videotape of a 9-month-old infant's responses to a variety of situations. Some students were led to believe that the infant was a boy, and others that the infant was a girl. When the infant showed a strong reaction to a jack-in-the-box, the reaction was more often labeled *anger* if the child was thought to be a boy and *fear* when the infant was thought to be a girl (Condry and Condry, 1976).

Children themselves show some knowledge of sex-role stereotypes as early as 2 years of age (see Table 3-3). And by 3 years, they begin to show sex-typed behavior in their choice of toys and play activities. But boys are more likely than girls to prefer sex-typed toys; at this age, many girls show a preference for "masculine" toys and games. As they grow older, both boys and girls make a larger number of sex-typed choices, but boys consistently make more of them than girls do (see Figure 3-9). Other studies also indicate that boys are more strongly sex-typed than girls.

How do we account for these differences? For one thing, there is an unfortunate tendency for both sexes to view "masculine" activities as superior to "feminine" ones. And in our culture, the taboos against feminine behavior for boys are stronger than those against masculine behavior for girls. Conforming to the masculine stereotype seems to be largely a matter of avoiding any behavior regarded as "sissyish." Four and 5-year-old boys are more likely to experiment with feminine toys and activities (such as dolls, a lipstick and mirror, hair ribbons) when no one is watching than when an adult or another boy is present. For girls, the presence of an observer makes little difference in their choice of play activities (Kobasigawa, Arakaki, and Awiguni, 1966; Hartup and Moore, 1963). These findings suggest that young boys are interested in feminine activities but have learned to expect negative reactions for showing such interests.

CAUSES OF SEX-TYPED BEHAVIOR   Parents clearly play a major role in sex typing. They serve as the child's first models of feminine and masculine behavior. Their attitudes toward their own sex roles and the way they interact with each other will influence the child's views. In addition, parents shape sex-typed behavior directly in numerous ways: by the toys they provide, the activities they encourage, and their responses to behaviors considered appropriate or inappropriate for the child's sex. From infancy on, most parents dress boys and girls differently and provide them with different toys. When they are old enough to be given household chores, girls are usually assigned such tasks as caring for younger children and helping with cleaning and food preparation. Boys are usually asked to do things outside the house, such as raking leaves or shoveling snow. Parents tend to emphasize independence, competition, and achievement in raising boys; girls are expected to be trustworthy, sensitive, and concerned with the welfare of others (Block, 1980).

Fathers appear to be more concerned with sex-typed behavior than mothers, particularly in the case of boys. They tend to react negatively (interfering with the child's play or expressing disapproval) when their sons play with "feminine" toys, whereas mothers do not. Fathers are less concerned when their daughters engage in "masculine" play, but they still show more disapproval than mothers (Langlois and Downs, 1980).

Once children enter nursery school or kindergarten, their peers serve as models for imitation and also exert pressure toward sex-typed behavior. Parents who consciously seek to raise their children without the traditional sex-role stereotypes (by encouraging the child to engage in a wide range of activities without labeling any activity as masculine or feminine) are often dismayed to find their efforts undermined by peer pressure. Again, boys tend to experience more pressure than girls. Girls seem to have no objection to other girls playing with boys' toys or engaging in masculine activities. Boys, on the other hand, do criticize other boys when they see them engaged in girls' activities. They are quick to call another boy a sissy if he plays with dolls, cries when he is hurt, or shows tender concern toward a younger child in distress (Langlois and Downs, 1980).

In addition to parental and peer influences, children's books and television programs play an important part in promoting sex-role stereotypes. Until recently, most children's books portrayed boys in active, problem-solving roles. They were the characters who displayed courage and heroism, persevered in the face of difficulty, constructed things, and achieved goals. Girls were usually much more passive. Female story-book characters were apt to display fear and avoidance of dangerous situations, give up easily and ask for help, and watch while someone else achieves a goal. Similar differences have been noted in the sex roles portrayed in children's TV programs (Sternglanz and Serbin, 1974).

Attempts to modify children's sex-role stereotypes by exposing them to television programs in which the stereotypes are reversed (for example, the girls win in athletic events or construct a club house, or a girl is elected president) have shown some success (Davidson, Yasuna, and Tower, 1979). But television exposure cannot counteract real-life experiences. For example, when 5- and 6-year-olds were shown films where the usual sex-typed occupations were reversed (the doctors were women and the nurses were men), they tended to relabel the occupations of the characters; when questioned about the films afterwards and shown pictures of the actors, they were apt to identify the female actor as the nurse and the male as the doctor. Having a mother who worked outside the home and being exposed to female physicians and male nurses in real life increased the likelihood that the child would accept the less conventional roles (Cordua, McGraw, and Drabman, 1979).

Factors influencing identification

Many personal qualities are not strongly sex typed. For example, enthusiasm, sense of humor, friendliness, and integrity are characteristics shared by men and women. A child may learn such traits from *either* parent without violating the cultural sex roles. When college students were interviewed about their behavioral similarities to their parents in temperament and interests, a fourth of the men believed that they resembled their mothers in these respects and a similar proportion of girls thought they resembled their fathers; many reported resemblances to both parents (J. Hilgard, 1970).

Experiments give us some clues as to the kinds of variables that influence identification. Several studies have shown that adults who are warm and nurturant are more likely to be imitated than those who are not. Boys who score high on masculinity tests tend to have warmer, more affectionate relationships with their fathers than boys who score low. Girls

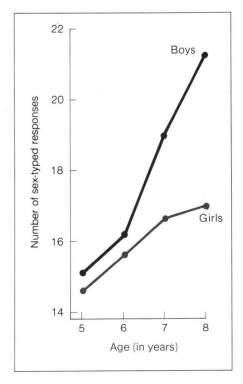

Figure 3-9
Sex Typing in Young Children
Children were given a choice between two toys, one "masculine" (such as a dump truck or set of tools) and one "feminine" (such as a doll carriage or set of dishes). The number of sex-typed responses increases with age for both boys and girls. Note that boys consistently make more of these responses than girls do, although the difference is very small at ages 5 and 6. (After DeLucia, 1963)

"Girls are more fluent verbally; boys are better at math." "Girls can memorize well, but boys are superior in abstract thinking." "Girls tend to be passive and to seek approval; boys are aggressive and independent." You have probably heard these and other claims about psychological differences between the sexes. What is the evidence? Do males and females differ consistently in abilities and personality traits? And, if so, are these differences the result of biology or of social learning? A careful review of more than 2,000 books and research articles concludes that many common assumptions about sex differences are myths with no foundation in fact; but there appear to be some real and interesting psychological differences betwen males and females (Maccoby and Jacklin, 1974).

Tests of overall intelligence show no consistent sex differences—in part because the tests are designed not to. In constructing intelligence tests, care is taken either to eliminate items on which the sexes are found to differ or to balance items on which females have an advantage with those that give males an advantage. Tests of specific intellectual abilities, however, do show some sex differences. These differences, which are absent or negligible during childhood, begin to appear in early adolescence. For example, beginning at about 10 or 11 years of age, girls *on the average* outscore boys on many measures of *verbal ability*—vocabulary size, comprehension of difficult written material, and verbal fluency.

Although adolescent males may lag behind in verbal skills, they tend *on the average* to be superior to females on tests of *visual-spatial ability*. Visual-spatial skills are used in such tasks as conceptualizing how an object in space would look from a different perspective, aiming at a target, reading a map, or finding a simple geometric form embedded in a more complex figure (see Figure 3-10). The mathematical skills of boys also appear to increase faster than those of girls after age 13, but the differences are not as consistent as those for spatial ability. Girls are about equal to boys when mathematical problems are given in verbal form; boys excel in dealing with numbers or geometric forms.

In talking about sex differences in verbal and spatial abilities, two points should be stressed. First, the differences, although consistent over studies, are *small* (Hyde, 1981). Second, it is important to remember that we are referring to *average* differences over large groups of youngsters; some girls are bet-

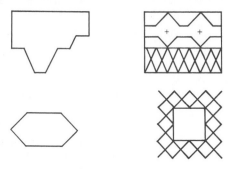

Figure 3-10
Embedded-Figures Test
The subject must identify the simple figure on the left within the more complex one on the right.

ter at spatial tasks than most boys, and some boys are more verbally fluent than most girls.

Because sex differences in these abilities do not emerge until adolescence, it seems reasonable to conclude that they reflect differences in training and social expectations. After all, girls are usually encouraged to develop interests in poetry, literature, and drama; boys are expected to be more concerned with science, engineering, and mechanics. This is undoubtedly part of the story, but it is also possible that some sex differences in ability may be based on biological differences that do not appear until the nervous system reaches a certain level of maturation—namely, puberty.

There is evidence that the timing of sexual maturity is related to specific abilities. For example, in a study of youngsters aged 10–16 years, late maturers were found to be better at visual-spatial tasks than early maturers, regardless of sex; and the older the youngster at the onset of puberty, the better his or her performance on spatial, relative to verbal, tasks (Waber, 1977). Another study of 6,000 adolescents (ages 12–18) found that girls who matured late matched or outscored their male age-mates on tests of mathematical ability. And early maturing boys had better verbal skills than late maturers (Carlsmith, Dornbusch, and Gross, 1983). Thus, early maturation appears to favor verbal skills and late maturation, spatial and mathematical abilities. Since females, on the average, mature earlier than males, rate of physical maturation may be an important determiner of sex differences in ability.

who are rated as quite feminine also have a warmer, closer relationship with their mothers than girls evaluated as less feminine (Mussen and Rutherford, 1963).

The adult's power in controlling the child's environment also affects the tendency to identify. When the mother is dominant, girls tend to identify much more with her than with the father, and boys may have difficulty developing the masculine sex role. In father-dominant homes, girls are more

Sex Differences in Behavior

The connection between maturity and specific skills is uncertain. It may be related to *lateralization*, or specialization, of the brain. As the brain develops, the two cerebral hemispheres become increasingly specialized for different abilities: the left hemisphere for verbal skills and the right for spatial and geometric abilities (see Chapter 2). There is some evidence that males and females differ as to which hemisphere develops more rapidly (the left among girls and the right among boys) as well as in degree of brain lateralization: women's verbal and spatial abilities seem to be more evenly divided between the two hemispheres than men's (Witelson, 1976). For example, a man whose left hemisphere is damaged (by a stroke or other injury) usually shows a more severe loss of verbal ability than a woman with a similar injury.

Whether these differences in brain organization are innate or the result of experience is not clear. Perhaps boys and girls spend more time practicing the skills they are expected to have and hence develop those skills and the associated hemisphere more quickly. But even if sex differences are present at birth, treating boys and girls differently will affect how their skills develop.

In terms of personality traits, most studies have found surprisingly few differences between the sexes, particularly during the early years. Little girls are *not* more dependent than little boys, as is commonly believed, nor are they more sociable. Toddlers of both sexes seek to be close to their parents, especially when they are under stress, and they seem equally willing to leave their par-

ents to explore a new environment (Maccoby and Jacklin, 1974). Differences in sociability show up only to the extent that boys during the elementary grades tend to play in "gangs," whereas girls are more apt to get together in groups of two or three.

The one area in which observed sex differences are consistent with popular beliefs is aggression. Boys *are* more aggressive than girls, starting at about age 2 or 3. Although there appear to be no differences in activity level, boys are much more prone than girls to engage in "rough and tumble" play—pushing, pulling, hitting, chasing, and wrestling with each other (DiPietro, 1981). This is true in a wide range of settings and for almost every culture that has been studied. Boys are not only more physically aggressive than girls but also more verbally aggressive; they are more likely than girls to exchange verbal taunts and insults—often as a prelude to physical aggression.

Clearly, social learning has much to do with the expression of aggression. Many parents believe that a boy should be able to fight for his rights, and a boy has all kinds of aggressive models (in books, television, and movies) to show him how. Girls, on the other hand, are expected to get their way by more subtle means. In view of such social conditioning, it seems reasonable to assume that girls have the same potential for aggression as boys but inhibit its expression for fear of punishment. Some psychologists believe that this is the case (Feshbach and Feshbach, 1973). Others believe that although social expectations and role models influence the expres-

sion of aggression, females are by their biological nature less aggressive (Maccoby and Jacklin, 1974). They point to the fact that girls show less aggression in their fantasies than boys. If girls are suppressing hostile impulses because of fear of punishment, such impulses might be expected to occur in fantasy or in "safe" situations. But even in an experimental situation where aggression is expected and encouraged—the subject is instructed to administer electric shocks to a "learner" whenever the learner makes a mistake—males tend to administer longer and stronger shocks to their victims than females (Titley and Viney, 1969). These findings do not suggest that females have "bottled-up" aggression waiting for a safe outlet.

In their survey of sex differences, Maccoby and Jacklin discovered that males and females are alike in more respects than is commonly supposed. Among the differences found, some may be the result of social learning and others may reflect biological predispositions. But even those differences that have a biological base can be modified by learning. For example, girls, who initially score lower than boys on tests of visual-spatial ability can equal the boys' scores with a little practice. And certainly girls can be taught to be more aggressive (if necessary), and boys can learn to modify their aggressive responses.

In rearing their young, societies can accentuate what they believe to be innate differences, or they can choose to encourage in both sexes the characteristics most useful for their particular society.

similar to their fathers than in mother-dominant homes, but they still identify to a large degree with the mother. For girls, the mother's warmth and self-confidence seem to be more important than her powerfulness (Hetherington and Frankie, 1967).

A third factor that influences identification is the perception of similarities between the child and the model. To the extent that a child has some objective basis for perceiving himself or herself as similar to the parent, the child will

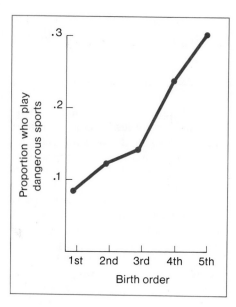

Figure 3-11
Birth Order and Participation
in Dangerous Sports
**The graph shows the proportion of male un-
dergraduates who play dangerous sports
(football, rugby, soccer) in relation to their
birth order. Note that the first-born is less
likely to engage in a dangerous sport than
later-borns. The study found no relationship
between birth order and participation in non-
dangerous sports, such as baseball or crew.
(After Nisbett, 1968)**

tend to identify with that parent. A girl who is tall and large-boned with facial
features similar to those of her father may have more difficulty identifying with
her petite mother than a younger sister who is similar to the mother in build.

To the extent that both parents are seen as nurturant, powerful, and competent, the child will identify with both, although the stronger identification
generally will be with the parent of the same sex.

Identification with siblings

Although parents are the primary identification figures, siblings play an important role, too. The sex of the other siblings influences the child's interests
and behavior; girls with older brothers are likely to be more masculine (tomboyish) and competitive than girls with older sisters. Similarly, boys with older
sisters tend to be less aggressive than boys with older brothers.

First-born or only children occupy a unique position in the family for
several reasons. Parents have more time and attention to devote to their first
child and are apt to be more cautious, indulgent, and protective. The first-born
does not have to compete with older siblings; and for a while, he or she has
only adult models to copy and adult standards of conduct to emulate, whereas
later-borns have siblings with whom to identify.

Research indicates that these factors do have an effect. First-born or only
children are more likely to score at the upper extremes on intelligence tests, do
well in college, and achieve eminence. Among finalists for the National Merit
Scholarship from two-children families, there are twice as many first-borns as
second-borns. Among finalists from three-child families, there are as many
first-borns as second- and third-borns combined (Nichols, 1968). First-born or
only children have also been found to be more conscientious, cooperative, and
cautious than later-born children (Altus, 1966); as Figure 3-11 shows, they are
also less likely to engage in dangerous sports. We should stress the fact that
these are only *trends*; many famous achievers were later-born children (Benjamin Franklin, for example, was the fifteenth of 17 children), and many
first-born children do not possess any of the characteristics just noted.

The more conscientious and cooperative nature of first-borns probably
reflects an attempt to maintain their "privileged" status with the parents in the
face of possible displacement by the newly arrived sibling. The later-born may
feel less competent than the older sibling (not realizing that his or her inade-
quacies are a function of age) and may try to excel in other ways—for example,
by being more physically daring.

Although competition with younger siblings may partially account for the
higher achievement of first borns, it does not explain the equally high achievement of only children. The most likely explanation is that parents have more
time and energy to devote to an only child and, thus, may provide a richer,
more stimulating environment. As the family becomes larger, the parents may
pay increasingly less attention to each child. It may be, too, that first-borns and
only children identify more strongly with their parents than later-borns do.

ADOLESCENCE

Adolescence refers to the period of transition from childhood to adulthood. Its
age limits are not clearly specified, but it extends roughly from age 12 to the late
teens, when physical growth is nearly complete. During this period, the young

person develops to sexual maturity, establishes an identity as an individual apart from the family, and faces the task of deciding how to earn a living.

A few generations ago, adolescence as we know it today was nonexistent. Many teen-agers worked 14 hours a day and moved from childhood into the responsibilities of adulthood with little time for transition. With a decrease in the need for unskilled workers and an increase in the length of apprenticeship required to enter a profession, the interval between physical maturity and adult status has lengthened. Such symbols of maturity as financial independence from parents and completion of school are accomplished at later ages. Young people are not given many adult privileges until late in their teens; in most states, they cannot work full time, sign legal documents, drink alcoholic beverages, marry, or vote.

A gradual transition to adult status has some advantages. It gives the young person a longer period in which to develop skills and prepare for the future, but it tends to produce a period of conflict and vacillation between dependence and independence. It is difficult to feel completely self-sufficient while living at home or receiving financial support from one's parents.

Sexual development

At the onset of adolescence, most youngsters experience a period of very rapid physical growth (the *adolescent growth spurt*) accompanied by the gradual development of reproductive organs and *secondary sex characteristics* (breast development in girls, beard growth in boys, and the appearance of pubic hair in both sexes). These changes occur over a period of about two years and culminate in *puberty*, marked by menstruation in girls and by the appearance of live sperm cells in the urine of boys.

There is wide variation in the ages at which puberty is reached. Some girls menstruate as early as 11, others as late as 17—the average age is 12 years 9 months. Boys show a similar range in the ages at which they reach sexual maturity; but on the average, boys experience their growth spurt and mature two years later than girls (see Figure 3-12). Boys and girls average the same height and weight until about 11, when the girls suddenly spurt ahead in both dimensions. Girls maintain this difference for about two years, at which point the boys forge ahead and remain there for the rest of their lives. This difference in rate of physical development is striking in seventh- or eighth-grade classrooms, where quite mature young women can be observed seated alongside immature boys.

Although girls on the average mature earlier than boys, there are large individual differences. Some girls will mature *later* than some boys. Numerous studies have investigated whether there are personality differences between early- and late-maturing children. How does a late-maturing boy feel when he is shorter than most of his classmates? How does an early-maturing girl feel when she towers over most of the boys in her class?

Late-maturing boys face a particularly difficult adjustment because of the importance of strength and physical prowess in their peer activities. During the period when they are shorter and less sturdy than their classmates, they may lose out on practice of game skills and may never catch up with the early maturers, who take the lead in physical activities. Studies indicate that boys who mature late tend to be less popular than their classmates, have poorer self-concepts, and engage in more immature attention-seeking behavior. They feel rejected and dominated by their peers. The early maturers, on the other

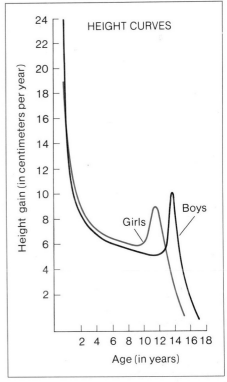

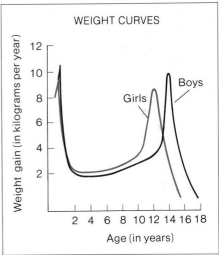

Figure 3-12
Annual Gains in Height and Weight
The period of most rapid growth comes earlier for girls than for boys. (After Tanner, Whitehouse, and Takaishi, 1966)

hand, tend to be more self-confident and independent. A few of these personality differences between early and late maturers persist into adulthood, long after the physical differences have disappeared (Mussen and Jones, 1958).

The effects of rate of maturation on personality are less striking for girls. Some early-maturing girls may be at a disadvantage because they are more grown-up than their peers in the late elementary grades; but by the junior high-school years, the early maturers tend to have more prestige among classmates and to take leadership in school activities. At this stage, the late-maturing girls, like the boys, may have less adequate self-concepts and poorer relations with their parents and peers (Weatherly, 1964).

Sexual standards and behavior

The last 20 years have witnessed an almost revolutionary change in attitudes toward sexual activity. Views regarding premarital sex, homosexuality, extramarital sex, and specific sexual acts are probably more open and permissive today than they have been at any time in recent history. Young people are exposed to sexual stimuli in magazines, television, and the movies to a greater extent than ever before. Satisfactory birth control methods and the availability of abortions have lessened fear of pregnancy. All of these changes give the newly matured individual more freedom today. These changes may produce more conflict, too, since guidelines for "appropriate" behavior are less clear than they were in the past. In some families, the divergence between adolescent and parental standards of sexual morality may be great.

Have more permissive attitudes toward sex been accompanied by changes in actual behavior? At first, some experts maintained that young people were simply being more open about activities their predecessors carried on in secret. But the data indicate definite changes in adolescent sexual behavior. A nationwide survey of 13- to 19-year-olds in 1973 found that 59 percent of the boys and 45 percent of the girls had experienced sexual intercourse—most of them before age 16 (Sorensen, 1973). A 1976 survey found that 55 percent of the 19-year-old females interviewed had experienced sex (Zelnik and Kantner, 1977).

Although strictly comparable data from earlier periods are not available, the studies conducted by Alfred Kinsey about 35 years ago found that less than 20 percent of the females and about 40 percent of the males reported experiencing sexual intercourse by the time they were 20 years old. Today's adolescents are engaging in sexual activity at an earlier age than their parents did. The change is most dramatic for girls, who are now almost as likely as boys to have intercourse while still in their teens (see Table 3-4).

The change in sex standards does not seem to be in the direction of greater promiscuity. Although some of the boys said they had experienced intercourse with several partners, most of the girls reported they had limited their sexual relations to one boy with whom they were "in love" at the time. These young people feel that sex is a part of love and of intimate relationships and that it need not necessarily be restricted to the context of marriage.

Search for identity

A major task confronting the adolescent is to develop a sense of individual *identity*—to find answers to the questions "Who am I?" and "Where am I going?" The search for personal identity involves deciding what is important or worth doing and formulating standards of conduct for evaluating one's own

STUDY AND YEAR	PERCENTAGE REPORTING SEXUAL INTERCOURSE
Kinsey and others (1938–1949)	18%
Sorensen (1973)	45
Zelnik and Kantner (1976)	55

Table 3-4
Premarital Intercourse
Among Teen-age Females
The table gives the percentage of 19-year-old, unmarried females who reported having experienced sexual intercourse. The period of data collection is given below each study. This and other evidence indicate a marked increase in premarital sexual experience over the past 50 years.

behavior as well as the behavior of others. It also involves feelings about self-worth and competence.

Adolescents' sense of identity develops gradually out of the various identifications of childhood. Young children's values and moral standards are largely those of their parents; their feelings of self-esteem stem primarily from the parents' view of them. As youngsters move into the wider world of high school, the values of the peer group become increasingly important, as do the appraisals of teachers and other adults. Adolescents try to synthesize these values and appraisals into a consistent picture. To the extent that parents, teachers, and peers project consistent values, the search for identity becomes easier.

When parental views and values differ markedly from those of peers and other important figures, the possibility for conflict is great and the adolescent may experience what has been called *role confusion*: the adolescent tries one role after another and has difficulty synthesizing the different roles into a single identity. As one teen-age girl put it:

> I'm fairly prim and proper at home because my parents have firm views about how a young girl should behave. At school, I toe the line too, although I don't hesitate to express my opinions. When I'm with my girl friends, I relax and act fairly silly; I'm usually the first to suggest smoking pot or doing something crazy. On a date, I tend to act helpless and docile. Who am I really?

In a simple society where identification models are few and social roles are limited, the task of forming an identity is relatively easy. In a society as complex and rapidly changing as ours, it is a difficult and lengthy task for many adolescents. They are faced with an almost infinite array of possibilities in terms of how to behave and what to do in life.

One way of approaching the identity problem is to try various roles and ways of behaving. Many experts believe that adolescence should be a period of role experimentation in which the youngster can explore different ideologies and interests. They are concerned that today's academic competition and career pressures are depriving many adolescents of the opportunity to explore. As a result, some are "dropping out" temporarily to have time to think about what they want to do in life and to experiment with various identities. Youth movements, both political and religious, often provide temporary commitments to an alternative life style; they give the young person a group to identify with and time to formulate a more permanent set of beliefs.

The search for identity can be resolved in a number of ways. Some young people, after a period of experimentation and soul searching, commit themselves to a life goal and proceed toward it. For some, the "identity crisis" may not occur at all; these are adolescents who accept their parents' values without question and who proceed toward adult roles that are consistent with their parents' views. In a sense, their identity "crystallized" early in life.

Still other young people adopt a *deviant identity*—one that is at odds with the values of the society. For example, a young man who has been pressured all his life to go to law school and then join the family firm may rebel and decide to become a bum. Some ghetto adolescents, rather than risk failure in attempting to rise above their social conditions, may adopt a deviant identity and take pride in being "nothing."

Other adolescents may go through a prolonged period of identity confusion and have great difficulty "finding themselves." In some cases, an identity definition may ultimately be worked out after much trial and error. In

During adolescence, the values of the peer group become increasingly important and young people establish individual identities apart from their families.

others, the person may never have a strong sense of personal identity even as an adult. This is the individual who never develops any commitments or loyalties.

A study of college students who were in a state of identity confusion found that many of them were dissatisfied with their parents' way of life yet could not get very involved in fashioning one of their own. In the words of one subject:

> Let's say I'm a Psych. major. I have no idea what I will do with it. I try not to plan more than a week in advance. My parents would like me to settle down and get married. That seems pretty far off right now. Mother would love it if I stayed right at home. . . . I have plans to go to Africa this summer, go to Europe by myself next fall. After that, I don't know (Waterman and Waterman, 1974).

This same study found that a large proportion of college freshmen were still struggling with problems of identity formation, but by the senior year, many had been resolved.

An individual's personal identity, once formed, is not necessarily static. People can acquire new interests, ideas, and skills during their adult years that may change their sense of who they are. Married women, for example, often find a new sense of identity as their child-rearing duties diminish and they have time to develop new interests or pursue a career.

DEVELOPMENT AS A LIFELONG PROCESS

Development does not end with the attainment of physical maturity. It is a continuous process extending from birth through adulthood to old age. Bodily changes occur throughout life, affecting the individual's attitudes, cognitive processes, and behavior. The kinds of problems people must cope with change throughout the life span, too.

Erik Erikson has proposed a series of eight stages to characterize development from the cradle to the grave. He calls them *psychosocial stages* because he believes that the psychological development of individuals depends on the social relations established at various points in life. At each stage, there are special problems or "crises" to be confronted. Erikson's stages of psychosocial development are shown in Table 3-5. Although these stages are not based on scientific evidence, they call attention to the kinds of problems people encounter during life.

We touched on some of these problems earlier in the chapter. We noted that the infant's feelings of trust in other people depend to a large extent on the way early needs are handled by the mother. During the second year of life (when children begin to move about on their own), they want to explore, investigate, and do things for themselves. To the extent that parents encourage such activities, children begin to develop a sense of independence or autonomy. They learn to control some of their impulses and to feel pride in their accomplishments. Overprotection—restricting what the child is permitted to do—or ridiculing unsuccessful attempts may cause the child to doubt his or her abilities.

During the preschool years (ages 3 through 5), children progress from simple self-control to an ability to initiate activities and carry them out. Again, parental attitudes—encouraging or discouraging—can make children feel inadequate (or guilty, if they initiate an activity that the adult views as shameful).

During the elementary-school years, children learn the skills valued by

STAGES	PSYCHOSOCIAL CRISES	SIGNIFICANT SOCIAL RELATIONSHIPS	FAVORABLE OUTCOME
1 First year of life	Trust versus mistrust	Mother or mother substitute	Trust and optimism
2 Second year	Autonomy versus doubt	Parents	Sense of self-control and adequacy
3 Third through fifth years	Initiative versus guilt	Basic family	Purpose and direction; ability to initiate one's own activities
4 Sixth year to puberty	Industry versus inferiority	Neighborhood; school	Competence in intellectual, social, and physical skills
5 Adolescence	Identity versus confusion	Peer groups and outgroups; models of leadership	An integrated image of oneself as a unique person
6 Early adulthood	Intimacy versus isolation	Partners in friendship and sex; competition, cooperation	Ability to form close and lasting relationships; to make career commitments
7 Middle adulthood	Generativity versus self-absorption	Divided labor and shared household	Concern for family, society, and future generations
8 The aging years	Integrity versus despair	"Mankind"; "My Kind"	A sense of fulfillment and satisfaction with one's life; willingness to face death

Table 3-5
Stages of Psychosocial Development
Problems in relating to other people change with age. Erikson defines eight major life stages in terms of the psychosocial problems, or crises, that must be resolved. (After Erikson, 1963)

society. These include not only reading and writing, but also physical skills and the ability to share responsibility and get along with other people. To the extent that efforts in these areas are successful, children develop feelings of competence; unsuccessful efforts result in feelings of inferiority.

Finding one's personal identity, as we noted in the last section, is the major psychosocial crisis of adolescence.

Early adulthood

During the early adult years, people commit themselves to an occupation, and many will marry or form other types of intimate relationships. Intimacy means an ability to care about others and to share experiences with them. People who cannot commit themselves to a loving relationship—because they fear being hurt or are unable to share—risk being isolated. Studies indicate that an intimate relationship with a supportive partner contributes significantly to a person's emotional and physical health. People who have someone to share their ideas, feelings, and problems with are happier and healthier than those who do not (see Traupmann and Hatfield, 1981).

Approximately 95 percent of Americans do marry, and most of them do so during the early adult years. Individuals tend to look for marriage partners whose ethnic, social, and religious backgrounds match their own. Contrary to popular opinion, women appear to be *less* romantic in their approach to mate selection than men. Men tend to fall in love more quickly than women and to be satisfied with the qualities of their prospective mate. Women, on the other hand, are more practical and cautious in deciding whom to marry (Rubin, 1973).

This finding is not surprising when we consider that marriage traditionally requires a greater change in life style for women than for men. A married man

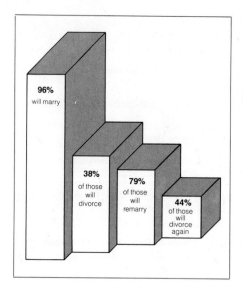

Figure 3-13
The Marriage Odds
Percentages are for U.S. adults during the early 1980s.

usually continues in his career, whereas a woman may be required to give up the relative independence of single life for the demands and responsibilities of wife and mother. There are some egalitarian marriages in which family and financial responsibilities are shared and the careers of both partners are given equal consideration. However, for most women, the person she marries determines where and how well she lives, as well as what her role in life will be.

Once married, both partners must learn to adapt to new demands and responsibilities. The arrival of children requires even greater adjustment. That such adjustments are not easy in a society as complex as ours is indicated by the high divorce rate. More than 38 percent of all *first* marriages in the United States end in divorce. Taking into account remarriages and divorces, about 40 percent of *all* marriages end in divorce (see Figure 3-13).

Much debate centers on whether happy marriages are based on similarity of interests and temperament ("like attracts like") or on the fact that the two partners complement each other ("opposites attract"). There are studies that support each viewpoint, so no conclusive answer can be given.

It is clear that many different patterns of marital relations function satisfactorily. They seem to share the following elements: (1) mutual respect—each partner finds some important quality or ability to respect in the other (and the greater the number of areas of respect, the more satisfactory the marriage); (2) tolerance—the ability to accept one another's shortcomings; and (3) the ability to agree on common goals and work toward them.

Middle adulthood

For many people, the middle years of adulthood (roughly ages 40–65) are the most productive period. Men in their forties are usually at the peak of their careers. Women have less responsibility at home now that the children are growing up and can devote more time to career or civic activities. This is the age group that essentially runs society, in terms of both power and responsibility.

What Erikson means by *generativity* in middle adulthood is a concern with guiding and providing for the next generation. Feelings of satisfaction at this stage in life come from helping your teen-age children become adults, providing for others who need help, and seeing your contributions to society as valuable. Feelings of despair may come from the realization that you have not achieved the goals set as a young adult or that what you are doing is not important.

As people approach their fifties, their view of the life span tends to change. Instead of looking at life in terms of time-since-birth, as younger people do, they begin to think in terms of years-left-to-live. Having faced the aging or death of their parents, they begin to realize the inevitability of their own death. At this point, many people restructure their lives in terms of priorities, deciding what is important to do in the years remaining. A man who has spent his years building a successful company may leave it to return to school. A woman who has raised her family may develop a new career or become active in politics. A couple may leave their jobs in the city to purchase a small farm.

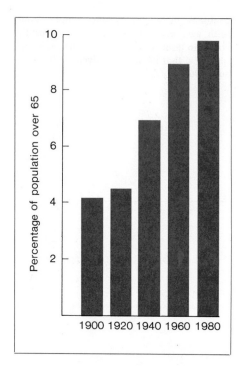

Figure 3-14
The Aged in the United States
The percentage of the total population aged 65 or over has more than doubled in the last half-century, though the trend shows signs of slackening. (United States Bureau of the Census)

The aging years

The years after 65 bring new problems. Declining physical strength limits the older person's activities; a debilitating illness can make the individual feel demoralizingly helpless. Retirement, which brings idle hours to be filled, may

An elderly woman volunteers at a day-care center; an elderly man returns to school. Active involvement in community life can bring satisfaction after retirement.

lessen feelings of worth and self-esteem. The death of a spouse, siblings, and friends can make life unbearably lonely, particularly for those whose children live far away. Since the proportion of older people in the population is progressively increasing (see Figure 3-14), such problems require renewed attention and research. Retirement villages and programs that actively involve older people in community life—as teacher aids, library assistants, guards at school crossings—have proved to be a step in the right direction. But much more needs to be done.

Despite the obvious problems of aging, a study of 70- to 79-year-olds suggests that growing old is not so bad: 75 percent reported that they were satisfied with their lives after retirement. Most were fairly active and not lonely, and few showed signs of senility or mental illness (Neugarten, 1971).

Erikson's last psychosocial crisis, *integrity versus despair,* is concerned with the way a person faces the end of life. Old age is a time of reflection—of looking back on the events of a lifetime. To the extent that an individual has successfully coped with the problems posed at each of the earlier stages of life, he or she has a sense of wholeness and integrity—of a life well lived. If the elderly person looks back on life with regret, seeing it as a series of missed opportunities and failures, the final years will be ones of despair.

Summary

1 Human development involves a *continuous interaction* between *heredity* (biological predispositions determined by the individual's genes) and *environment* (the experiences encountered while growing up in a particular family and culture). Genetic determinants express themselves through the process of *maturation*: innately determined sequences of growth or bodily changes that are relatively independent of the environment. Motor development, for example, is largely a maturational process because all children master skills such as crawling, standing, and walking in the same sequence and at roughly the same age.

2 Development proceeds in *orderly sequences* from simple behaviors to those that are more differentiated and complex. An unresolved question, however, is whether development should be viewed as a *continuous process* of acquiring new behaviors through experience or a series of successive *stages* that are qualitatively different from each other.

3   Although the development of physical skills depends largely on maturation, restricted environments can delay motor development, and increased stimulation can accelerate it. Although early deprivation or stimulation do not appear to have a lasting effect on motor skills, development in other areas—language, intelligence, personality—may be permanently affected by early experiences.

4   Piaget's theory describes stages in *cognitive*, or *intellectual, growth*, proceeding from the *sensorimotor stage* (where an important discovery is *object permanence*), through the *preoperational stage* (symbols begin to be used), and the *concrete operational stage* (*conservation concepts* develop), to the *formal operational stage* (hypotheses are tested systematically in problem solving).

5   Early social attachments form the basis for close interpersonal relations in adulthood. Insensitive mothering or repeated separations may undermine the child's trust and produce *insecure attachment*. Children who are *securely attached* are better able to cope with new experiences and relate to others. Interactions with siblings and peers are also important for normal development.

6   Children's concepts of right and wrong change as they mature. Younger children tend to evaluate moral actions in terms of anticipated *rewards* and *punishments*; with increasing age, *avoiding disapproval* and *conforming* to social norms become important. In the highest stage of moral reasoning, actions are evaluated in terms of one's own ethical principles. *Moral behavior* depends on a number of factors in addition to the ability to reason about moral issues.

7   Although no consistent relationships have been found between specific child-rearing techniques and later personality traits, a child's competency and self-confidence are best fostered by a warm and nurturant home where parents reward responsible behavior but also encourage independent actions and decision making.

8   Children acquire the attitudes and behaviors expected by society—self-control, a conscience, and the appropriate sex role—largely through the process of *identification*. *Sex typing*, the tendency to view certain activities as appropriate only for one sex, develops through parental and cultural influences. Children are most apt to identify with adults who are warm, nurturant, and powerful, and whom they view as similar to themselves in some way.

9   The age at which adolescents reach *puberty*, or sexual maturity, varies greatly, although girls, on the average, mature two years earlier than boys. Late maturers of either sex tend to have poorer self-concepts than early maturers. Survey data indicate that adolescents today are experiencing sexual intercourse at an earlier age than did their parents.

10 In their search for personal *identity*, adolescents try to synthesize the values and views of people important to them (parents, teachers, and peers) into a cohesive self-picture. When these values are not consistent, adolescents may experience *role confusion*: trying out one social role after another before finding a sense of individual identity.

11 Development is a life-long process: individuals change both physically and psychologically, and they encounter new adjustment problems throughout life. Erikson's *psychosocial stages* describe problems, or crises, in social relations that must be confronted at various points in life. These range from "trust versus mistrust" during the first year of life, through "intimacy versus isolation" in early adulthood, to "integrity versus despair" as individuals face death.

Comprehensive textbooks on child development include Elkind and Weiner, *Development of the Child* (1978); Gardner, *Developmental psychology: An introduction* (1978); and Mussen, Conger, and Kagan, *Child development and personality* (5th ed., 1982). *Child development: An introduction* (1976) by Biehler includes some interesting background material in the form of "on the spot" visits to the laboratories of well-known child psychologists (past and present) as they investigate and theorize about children's behavior.

Development in infancy (2nd ed., 1981) by Bower describes current research in infant perception and cognition. A two-volume overview of the major theories and research in child development may be found in Mussen (ed.), *Manual of child psychology* (4th ed., 1983).

Cognitive development (1977) by Flavell presents a thorough introduction to this topic. For a brief introduction to Piaget, see Phillips, *Piaget's theory: A primer* (1981).

The problems of adolescence are dealt with in Conger, *Adolescence and youth: Psychological development in a changing world* (2nd ed., 1977); and Jersild, Brook, and Brook, *The psychology of adolescence* (3rd ed., 1978). For the later years, see Kennedy, *Human development: The adult years and aging* (1978); and Poon (ed.), *Aging in the 1980s* (1980).

The handbook of developmental psychology (1982) edited by Wolman covers many topics from infancy to old age.

Part three
PERCEPTION AND CONSCIOUSNESS

4
SENSORY PROCESSES

All information about the world comes to us by way of our senses. They warn us of impending danger and furnish the information we need to interpret events and anticipate the future. They also provide pleasure and pain. How do we distinguish colors, interpret the rhythm of music, or judge the temperature of something we touch? These are fundamental psychological questions.

To understand perception, we need to know something of how the sensory mechanisms are constructed and how they mediate sensations of light, sound, touch, and taste. But perception involves more than the discrimination of simple stimuli, for the human organism interprets and reacts to *patterns* of stimuli. To do this, it must be able to extract information from the changing array of stimulation provided by the environment. In this chapter, we consider the role of the specific sense organs in perceiving. In the next chapter, we discuss the perception of complex objects and events.

There are two different but closely related approaches to the study of sensory processes: basic research and applied research. Basic research attempts to discover what aspects of the environment the sense organs respond to, how they register this information, and how it is conveyed to the brain. Such knowledge is sought with no concern for specific applications; it is a first step in understanding the higher-order cognitive processes.

As our technology becomes increasingly complex, it depends more and more on accurate perceptual discriminations by human beings. Here is the need for applied research. The radar operator in a control tower must distinguish the visual blips on the radar screen that indicate the approach of aircraft. The sonar operator must discriminate between the echoes returning from a school of fish and those from a submarine. The pilot must monitor an elaborate panel of instruments and make necessary adjustments. The astronaut must make countless complex discriminations under conditions of weightlessness and acceleration that alter normal functioning. Through applied research on sensory processes, scientists seek to determine our ability to discriminate and interpret

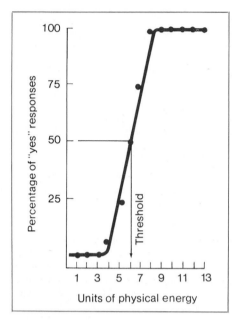

Figure 4-1
Psychometric Function
Plotted on the ordinate is the percentage of times the subject responds, "Yes, I detect the stimulus"; on the abscissa is the measure of the physical energy of the stimulus. Psychometric functions can be obtained for any sensory modality.

sensory stimuli so that our capabilities can be matched to the task requirements. Both the basic and the applied approach have contributed to our understanding of sensory phenomena.

THRESHOLDS

Absolute threshold

A certain minimum stimulation of any sense organ is required before there will be a sensory experience. A spot of light in a dark room must reach some measurable intensity before it can be distinguished from darkness. A sound emitted in an otherwise soundproof room must reach a certain intensity level before it can be heard. The minimum physical energy necessary to activate a given sensory system is known as the *absolute threshold*. The absolute threshold can be determined by presenting a subject with a stimulus of given intensity and asking whether it is detectable; on the next trial, a different stimulus intensity is used, and so on, through a range of intensities. The term "absolute threshold" is somewhat inappropriate, however, because the investigator does not arrive at a *single* intensity value below which the stimulus is never detected and above which it is always detected. We find, instead, a range of intensities over which the physical energy of the stimulus gradually moves from having no effect to having a partial effect (sometimes detected and sometimes not) to having a complete effect.

This region of partial effect is illustrated in Figure 4-1. The curve in the figure is called a *psychometric function*. It plots the percentage of times the subject says, "Yes, I detect a stimulus," against a measure of the physical energy of the stimulus. In this example, the subject almost never reports the presence of a stimulus below an energy level of 3 units and almost always reports one above 9 units. In the figure, the frequency of reporting the presence of a stimulus gradually increases between 3 and 9 units.

Obviously, when performance can be characterized by a psychometric function, the definition of a threshold must be somewhat arbitrary. For various reasons, psychologists have agreed to define the *absolute threshold* as that value at which the stimulus is detected 50 percent of the time. Thus, for the data displayed in Figure 4-1, the absolute threshold is 6 units.

Table 4-1 lists some estimates of absolute thresholds for various senses in terms that are readily familiar. Of course, the absolute threshold varies considerably from one individual to the next. The threshold for a particular individual will also vary from time to time, depending on the person's physical condition and motivational state.

Table 4-1
Absolute Thresholds
Approximate values of absolute thresholds for various sense modalities. (After Galanter, 1962)

SENSE	THRESHOLD
Vision	A candle flame seen at 30 miles on a dark, clear night
Hearing	The tick of a watch at 20 feet under quiet conditions
Taste	One teaspoon of sugar in 2 gallons of water
Smell	One drop of perfume diffused into the entire volume of six rooms
Touch	The wing of a fly falling on your cheek from a distance of 1 centimeter

Difference threshold

Just as there must be a certain minimum amount of stimulation before we can perceive a stimulus, so there must be a certain magnitude of difference between two stimuli before we can distinguish one from the other. The minimum amount of stimulation necessary to tell two stimuli apart is known as the *difference threshold*. Two red lights must differ in wavelength by some finite amount before they can be discriminated from each other; two tones must differ in intensity by a measurable amount before one can be heard as louder than the other. Thus, thresholds are identified at the transitions between no experience and some experience (the absolute threshold) and between no difference and some difference (the difference threshold).

Like the absolute threshold, the difference threshold is defined statistically. It is the amount of change along some stimulus dimension that is necessary for a subject to detect a difference between two stimuli in 50 percent of the trials. Psychologists frequently use the term *just noticeable difference (jnd)* to refer to this amount of change.

Difference thresholds for the intensity or magnitude of a stimulus increase with stimulus magnitude. This was pointed out by Ernst Weber over a century ago. He proposed that the difference threshold tends to be a constant fraction of the stimulus magnitude. To illustrate, let us estimate the difference threshold for a subject judging weights. If the subject is given a 100-gram weight, we note that the *jnd* is 2 grams; that is, the 100-gram weight must be compared to a weight of 102 grams in order for the subject to detect a difference in 50 percent of the trials. If the subject is given a 200-gram weight, the *jnd* is 4 grams. For a 400-gram weight, the *jnd* is 8 grams; for an 800-gram weight, the *jnd* is 16 grams. Note that the ratio of *jnd* to the weight being judged is constant:

$$\frac{2}{100} = \frac{4}{200} = \frac{8}{400} = \frac{16}{800} = .02$$

This relationship is known as *Weber's law*. Stated mathematically, if I is the amount of stimulation taken as a referent, and ΔI is the increase in stimulation necessary for a *jnd*, then

$$\frac{\Delta I}{I} = k$$

where k is a constant that does not depend on I. The quantity k is called *Weber's constant*. In our example, $k = .02$.

Weber's law does not hold perfectly; nevertheless, it is a good first approximation to the manner in which the difference threshold increases with stimulus intensity. Table 4-2 presents values of Weber's constant for various senses. The tremendous range in values reflects the fact that some sensory systems are much more responsive to change than others.

We can see approximations of Weber's law operating in our everyday experience. For example, consider the brightness of a three-way light bulb (50-100-150 watts): the change in brightness from 50 to 100 watts is very noticeable, that from 100 to 150 much less so. A 10-minute increase in air-travel time from Los Angeles to San Francisco may be detected as a just noticeable difference, but a similar increase in travel time from San Francisco to London is not. An increase of five dollars in the cost of a skirt is quite noticeable, whereas a similar increase in the cost of a new car is of little concern.

Why does the difference threshold increase with intensity? Soon after

SENSE	WEBER'S CONSTANT
Pitch of a tone	.003
Visual brightness	.017
Lifted weights	.020
Loudness of a tone	.100
Pressure on skin surface	.140
Taste for saline solution	.200

Table 4-2
Weber's Constant
Approximate values of Weber's constant for various sensory discriminations. The smaller the number, the smaller the amount of additional stimulation needed to produce a *jnd*. (Data are approximate from various determinations.)

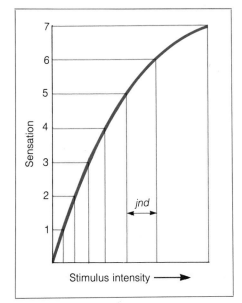

Figure 4-2
Fechner's Law
If Weber's law is correct and each *jnd* corresponds to a constant increase in sensation, sensation increases as a logarithmic function of stimulus intensity.

The problems that confront researchers trying to establish thresholds can be illustrated by the following experiment. Suppose we wanted to determine the likelihood that a subject will detect a particular weak auditory signal. An experiment could be set up involving a series of trials, each initiated with a warning light followed by the auditory signal. The subject would be asked to indicate on each trial whether she or he heard the signal. Suppose that on 100 such trials the subject reported hearing the signal 62 times. How should this result be interpreted? On each trial, precisely the same signal is presented, and the responses presumably tell us something about the subject's ability to detect it. But if the subject knows the same tone will be presented on each trial, what prevents him or her from always saying yes? Obviously nothing, but we assume that the subject is honest and is trying to do as good a job as possible. The task of detecting very weak signals is difficult, however, and even a conscientious subject will often be uncertain whether to respond yes or no on a given trial. Further, motives and expectations can influence our judgments; even the most reliable subject may unconsciously tend toward yes answers to impress the experimenter with his or her ability.

To deal with this problem, we can introduce *catch trials*, on which there are no signals, to see what the subject will do. The following results are typical of a subject's performance in an experiment involving several hundred trials, 10 percent of which are randomly selected as catch trials.

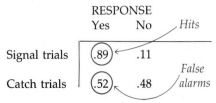

Each entry in the table represents the proportion of times the subject answered yes or no when the signal was or was not presented. For example, in 89 percent of the trials on which a signal was presented, the subject said, "Yes, there was a signal." We refer to these correct responses as *hits*. When the subject says "yes, there was a signal" on a trial when the signal was not presented, the response is called a *false alarm.* In the example, the probability of a hit was .89 and the probability of a false alarm was .52.

How can we interpret the fact that the subject falsely reported hearing the signal on 52 percent of the catch trials? We might conclude that the subject is careless or inattentive except for the fact that these results are typical of data obtained with dedicated, highly trained subjects. Even under the best conditions, subjects make false alarms. The answer to the question of how to interpret false alarms appears when some additional observations are made. Sup-

pose that the subject is tested on several days with the same signal but with the percentage of catch trials varied from day to day. Results from such an experiment, in which the number of catch trials ranged from 10 percent to 90 percent, are given in the table in Figure 4-3. These data show that hits and false alarms both change as the proportion of catch trials is manipulated. As the proportion of catch trials increases, the subject becomes aware of this fact (either consciously or unconsciously) and biases his or her judgments in favor of more "no" responses. Put another way, the subject's *expectation* of a large number of catch trials inhibits "yes" responses, which leads to a decrease in both hits and false alarms.

Obviously, there is no fixed probability that the subject will detect a given intensity signal; the probability varies as the proportion of catch trials is manipulated. At first glance, this is a discouraging picture, and we may question whether a simple measure can be devised to describe the subject's sensitivity level for a particular signal. Fortunately, recent developments have provided a clever answer. It requires plotting the hit and false alarm probabilities, as is done in the left-hand graph in Figure 4-3. Note, for example, that the point farthest to the right is for data obtained when 10 percent of the trials were catch trials; referring to the table, we see the hit rate plotted on the ordinate is .89 and the false alarm rate on the abscissa is .52.

Weber proposed his law, Fechner (1860) offered an explanation. Fechner's hypothesis was that the response of sensory systems (he called it *sensation*) does not increase in proportion to stimulus intensity. Instead, sensation increases more and more slowly as intensity increases, as shown in Figure 4-2 on page 107. Fechner assumed that the difference threshold corresponds to a constant change in sensation, so that sensation can be measured by counting successive *jnd*'s. If this is the case and Weber's law holds, sensation is proportional to the logarithm of stimulus intensity. This logarithmic relationship, illustrated

ROC Curves

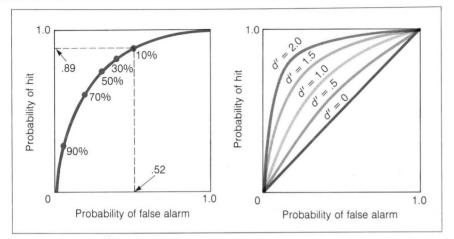

Percentage of catch trials	Probability of a hit	Probability of a false alarm
10	.89	.52
30	.83	.41
50	.76	.32
70	.62	.19
90	.28	.04

Figure 4-3
Plotting ROC Curves from Data
The table presents data on the relationship between hits and false alarms as the percentage of catch trials is increased. The left-hand figure plots these same data in the form of an ROC curve. The right-hand figure presents ROC curves for several different values of _d′_. The more intense is the signal, the higher the value of _d′_; the _d′_ value for the data in the table is 1.18.

When all five points are plotted, an orderly picture emerges. The points fall on a symmetric bow-shaped curve. If we ran still other experiments with the same signal but different percentages of catch trials, the hit and false alarm probabilities would differ from those in the table but would fall somewhere on the curve. This curve is called the _receiver-operating-characteristic curve_—or more simply, the _ROC curve_. The term "ROC" describes the fact that the curve measures the operating, or sensitivity, characteristics of a person receiving signals.

The points that are plotted in the left-hand figure are for a fixed signal intensity. When the signal is more intense, it is more detectable and the ROC curve arches higher; when the signal is weaker, the ROC curve is closer to the diagonal line. Thus, the degree of bowedness of the ROC curve is determined by the intensity of the signal. The measure used to define the bowedness of the ROC curve is called _d′_. The right-hand graph in Figure 4-3 gives ROC curves for values of _d′_ ranging from 0 to 2.

Thus, hit and false alarm rates can be converted into a _d′_ value that is a psychological dimension measuring the subject's sensitivity level for a particular signal. Manipulating the percentage of catch trials (or any of a number of other variables) will affect hits and false alarms for a fixed signal, but the proportions will always fall on an ROC curve defined by a particular _d′_ value.

Theoretical work based on this method for measuring sensitivity is called _signal detectability theory_ (Green and Birdsall, 1978). Even in a simple task like signal detection, performance is not just a function of the signal intensity but depends on the experience, motives, and expectations of the subject. Signal detectability theory permits us to separate these factors and obtain a relatively pure measure of the sensory process. This measure, _d′_, characterizes the sensory capacities of a subject, independent of nonsensory variables that influence his or her judgments. These developments have led to a change in the way the absolute threshold is defined. In modern research, it is common to define the threshold as the stimulus value at which _d′_ has a particular value, such as 1.

in Figure 4-2, is known as _Fechner's law_. Like Weber's law, Fechner's law is only an approximation; modern researchers have proposed many variations on it to fit a wide variety of experiments. Nevertheless, logarithmic equations relating sensory experience to the intensity of the physical stimulus have proved extremely helpful in designing telephones, video displays, tape recorders, and other types of communication equipment. They tell the designer how intense a signal must be in order to be perceived accurately under varying conditions.

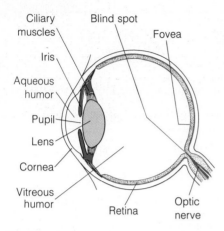

Figure 4-4
Top View of Right Eye
A light ray entering the eye on its way to the retina passes through the following parts: *cornea*—a tough transparent membrane; *aqueous humor*—a watery fluid; *lens*—a transparent body whose shape can be changed by the ciliary muscles, thereby focusing near or distant objects on the retina; and *vitreous humor*—a transparent jelly filling the interior of the eye. The amount of light entering the eye is regulated by the size of the *pupil*, a small hole in the front of the eye formed by the *iris*. The iris consists of a ring of muscles that can contract or expand, thereby controlling pupil size. The iris gives the eyes their characteristic color.

An Object as an Array of Points
Each point on an object sends light rays in *all* directions, but only some of these rays actually enter the eye. Light rays from the same point on an object pass through different places on the lens. If the eye is to see the object, these different rays have to come together (converge) at a single point on the retina. For each point on an object, there will be matching points on the retinal image. Note that the retinal image is inverted and is much smaller than the actual object. This figure shows only two rays of light from a point at the top of the arrow and two from a point at the bottom. Remember that light rays go in every direction from each point on the object. The two lines in our figure are a schematic way of showing boundaries on the collection of rays from a point on the object that enter the eye and converge to a single point on the retina.

VISUAL SENSE

Each sense organ responds to a particular type of physical energy. The eye is sensitive to that portion of the electromagnetic spectrum that we call visible light. It is convenient to think of electromagnetic energy as traveling in waves, with wavelengths (the distance from one crest of a wave to the next) varying tremendously from the shortest cosmic rays (4 trillionths of a centimeter) to long radio waves that may measure many miles. The wavelengths that human beings perceive as light extend from about 380 nanometers (nm) to about 780 nm. Since a nanometer is one billionth of a meter, it is clear that visible energy is but a very small section of the total electromagnetic spectrum.

More than 300 years ago, Sir Isaac Newton discovered that sunlight passing through a prism breaks into a band of varicolored light (called a *spectrum*), such as we see in a rainbow. The different colors are produced by different wavelengths. The longest visible wavelengths evoke a sensation of red, and increasingly shorter wavelengths are experienced as orange, yellow, green, blue, and violet. The prism spreads out the light waves by bending the short wavelengths more than the long ones (see Figure 4-8).

Visual experience may occur by stimulation other than light waves. Pressure on the eyeball or electrical stimulation of certain areas of the brain will produce the sensation of light. These observations indicate that the experience of light is produced in the visual system. The visible portion of the electromagnetic spectrum is called *light* because it is what usually produces sensation in the visual system.

Visual system

The main parts of the human eye are shown in Figure 4-4. Light enters the eye through the transparent *cornea*. The amount of light entering the eye is regulated by the diameter of the *pupil;* the *lens* then focuses the light on the sensitive surface, the *retina*. The lens of the eye works in roughly the same way as a camera lens, which focuses images of objects at various distances on the film as it moves toward or away from the plane of the film. Constriction and dilation of the pupil are controlled by the autonomic nervous system (Chapter 2): the parasympathetic division controls the change in pupil size as a function of change in illumination (just as we increase the shutter opening of a camera to admit more light on a dark day and decrease the opening under bright condi-

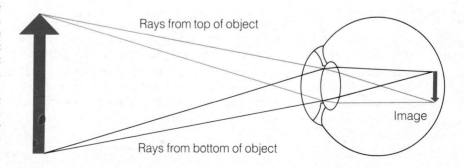

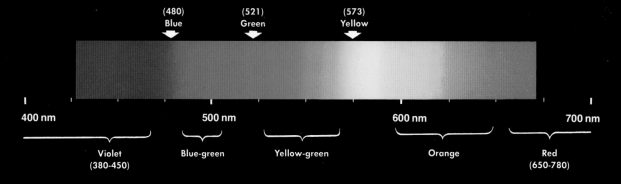

(480) Blue

(521) Green

(573) Yellow

400 nm   500 nm   600 nm   700 nm

Violet (380-450)   Blue-green   Yellow-green   Orange   Red (650-780)

Figure 4-8
Solar Spectrum
The colors are in the order of the rainbow, as they are seen when sunlight is sent through a prism. The numbers give the wavelength of the various colors in nanometers (nm); a nanometer is one billionth of a meter.

Figure 4-9
A Color Circle Showing Complementary Colors
The colors opposite each other, if in proper proportions, will mix on a color wheel to yield the neutral gray at the center. Wavelengths are indicated around the circle in nanometers (nm). Note that the spectral colors lie in their natural order on the circle, but their spacing is not uniform by wavelength. The circle also includes the nonspectral reds and purples.

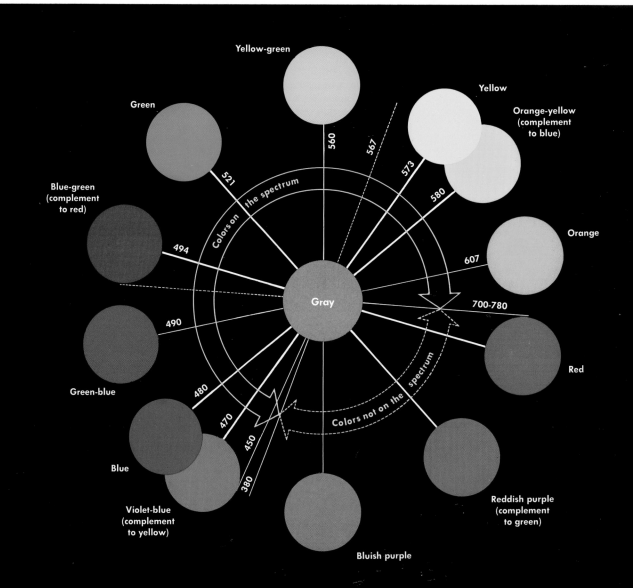

Yellow-green

Green

Yellow

Blue-green (complement to red)

Orange-yellow (complement to blue)

560
567
521
573
580

Colors on the spectrum

494

Orange

607

Gray

700-780

490

480
470
450
380

Green-blue

Red

Colors not on the spectrum

Blue

Violet-blue (complement to yellow)

Bluish purple

Reddish purple (complement to green)

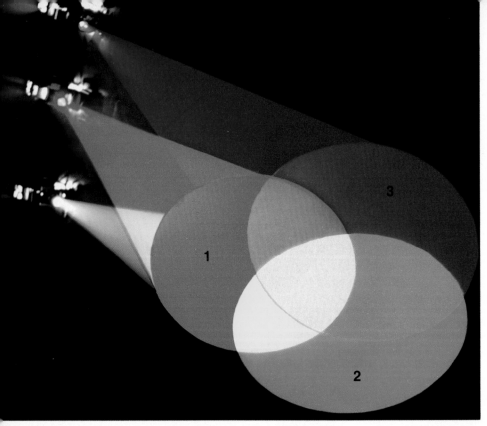

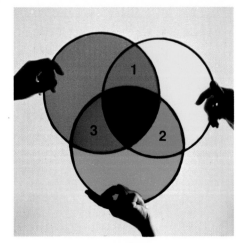

Figure 4-10
Additive and Subtractive Color Mixtures
Additive color mixture (illustrated by the figure at the left) takes place when lights are mixed. Red and green lights combine to give yellow, green and bluish purple to give blue, and so on. The three colors overlap in the center to give white. Mixture of any two of the colors produces the complement of the third, as shown in the triangular portions.

Subtractive color mixture (illustrated by the figure at the right) takes place when pigments are mixed or when light is transmitted through colored filters placed one over another. Usually, blue-green and yellow will mix to give green, and complementary colors will reduce to black, as in the example given. Unlike an additive mixture, we cannot always tell from the color of the components what color will result. For example, blue and green will commonly yield blue-green by subtractive mixture; but with some filters, they may yield red. Note that in the photograph to the right, the numbered triangular portions are the original complementary colors used in the additive mixture, but here they appear as a result of subtractive mixture.

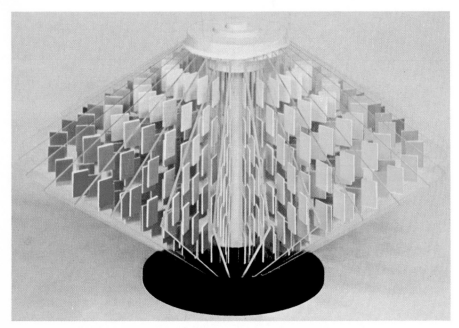

Figure 4-11
Color Solid
The three dimensions of color can be represented on a double cone: hue is represented by points on the circumference; saturation, by points along the radius; and brightness, by points on the vertical axis. A vertical slice taken from the color solid will show differences in saturation and brightness of a single hue.

Figure 4-12
Purkinje Shift
The Purkinje shift illustrates the difference between rod and cone vision. In daylight or normal conditions of illumination, the two flowers above are seen with cone vision and are equally visible, the red appearing brighter than the blue. If you look at them in very dim light, however, the red flower will no longer be visible. If the light is dim enough, only rod vision will be involved. You can hasten the effect by staring at the center of the red flower. This causes the red to fall on the area of the retina with increased density of cones and the blue to fall on the area with greater density of rods.

Figure 4-13
Tests for Colorblindness
Two plates used in colorblindness tests. In the left plate, individuals with certain kinds of red-green blindness see only the number 5; others see only the 7; still others, no number at all. Those with normal vision see 57. Similarly, in the right plate, people with normal vision see the number 15, whereas those with red-green blindness see no number at all.

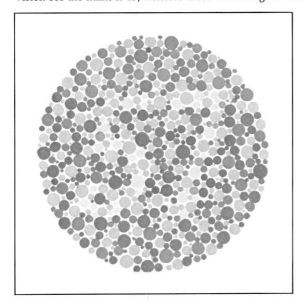
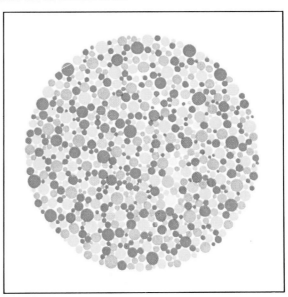

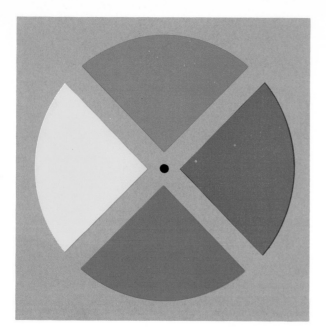

Figure 4-14
Negative Afterimages
Look steadily for about a minute at the dot in the center of the colors; then transfer your gaze to the dot in the gray field on the right. You should see patches that are the complementary colors of the original—the blue, red, green, and yellow will be replaced by yellow, green, red, and blue.

Negative afterimages are also illustrated in this contemporary work of art by Jasper Johns. Stare at the dot in the middle of the upper square for about a minute and then shift your eyes to the dot in the middle of the white field. (*Targets,* litho from nine stones and two aluminum plates, 1967–1968)

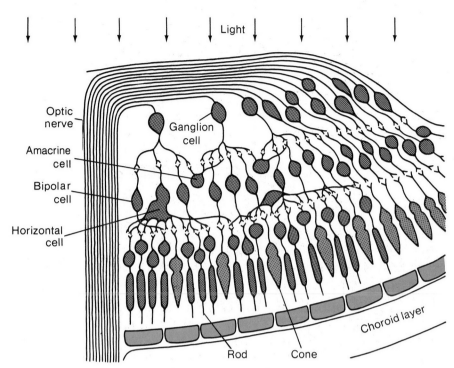

Light

Optic nerve

Ganglion cell

Amacrine cell

Bipolar cell

Horizontal cell

Choroid layer

Rod   Cone

Figure 4-5
Layers of the Retina
Shown here are the main layers of the retina: rods and cones, bipolar cells, and ganglion cells. The bipolar cells receive signals from one or more rods or cones and transmit them to the nerve fibers, whose cell bodies are shown as the ganglion cells. Integration across the retina is accomplished by horizontal cells that connect rods and cones and by amacrine cells at the ganglion cell level.

tions). The sympathetic division also controls pupil size. It dilates the pupil under conditions of strong emotion, either pleasant or unpleasant. Even conditions of mild emotional arousal will result in systematic changes in pupil size.

The retina, the light-sensitive surface at the back of the eye, has three main layers: (1) the *rods* and *cones*—the photosensitive cells (or photoreceptors) that convert light energy into neural signals; (2) the *bipolar cells,* which make synaptic connections with the rods and cones; and (3) the *ganglion cells,* the fibers of which form the *optic nerve* (see Figure 4-5). Strangely enough, the rods and cones form the *rear* layer of the retina. The light waves not only must pass through the lens and liquids that fill the eyeball (none of which is a perfect transmitter of light) but also must penetrate the network of blood vessels and the bipolar and ganglion cells that lie on the inside of the eye before reaching the photoreceptors. Note the "direction of light" arrows at the top of Figure 4-5.

If you stare at a homogeneous field, such as a blue sky, you can see the movement of blood through the retinal blood vessels that lie in front of the rods and cones. The blood vessel walls can be seen as pairs of narrow lines in the periphery of our vision, and the disk-shaped objects that appear to move between these lines are the red blood cells flowing through the vessels.

The most sensitive portion of the eye (in normal daylight vision) is a part of the retina called the *fovea.* Not far from the fovea is an insensitive area, called the *blind spot,* where the nerve fibers from the ganglion cells of the retina come together to form the optic nerve. Although we are not normally aware of the blind spot, its existence is easy to demonstrate. (Follow the instructions in Figure 4-6 on page 112.)

RODS AND CONES   The retinal cells of special interest are the photoreceptors; the cylindrical rods and the more bulbous cones. The cones, active only in daylight vision, permit us to see both *achromatic colors* (white, black, and

Figure 4-6
Locating the Blind Spot
A. With your right eye closed, stare at the cross in the upper right-hand corner. Move the book back and forth at about one foot from the eye. When the black circle on the left disappears, it is projected onto the blind spot. B. Without moving the book and with your right eye still closed, stare at the cross in the lower right-hand corner. When the white space falls in the blind spot, the black line appears to be continuous. This phenomenon helps us to understand why we are not ordinarily aware of the blind spot. In effect, the brain "fills in" parts of the visual field to which we are not sensitive.

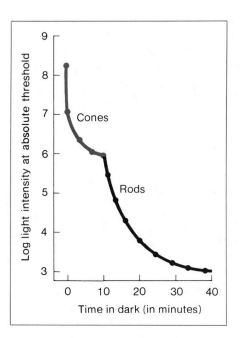

Figure 4-7
Course of Dark Adaptation
Subjects look at a bright light until the retina has become light adapted. When the subjects are then placed in darkness, they become increasingly sensitive to fainter test flashes as the retina gradually becomes dark adapted. The curve shows the minimum light intensity for the test flash to be seen. The color data points indicate at which points the color of the test flash was clearly visible; the black data points indicate when the test flash appeared colorless. Note the sharp break in the curve at about 10 minutes, which is called the *rod–cone break.* By changing the color of the light flash or the area of the retina tested, it can be shown that the first part of the curve describes adaptation of the cones and the second, adaptation of the rods.

the intermediate grays) and *chromatic colors* (red, green, blue, yellow). The rods function mainly under reduced illumination (at twilight or night) and permit us to see only achromatic colors. The two types of photoreceptors differ in much the same way that color film differs from black and white film. Black and white film (rods) is more sensitive than color film and can produce a picture even under conditions of dim illumination. Color film (cones) requires much more intense light to produce an image.

More than 6 million cones and 100 million rods are distributed, somewhat unevenly, throughout the retina. The center of the fovea contains only cones—some 50,000 of them packed in an area smaller than a square millimeter. The area outside the fovea contains both rods and cones, with the cones decreasing in number from the center of the retina to the periphery.

It would be a mistake to think of the visual pathway from eye to brain as a bundle of individual wires, each running from a photoreceptor in the retina to the visual cortex. In general, many receptors synapse with a single bipolar cell and many bipolars with a single ganglion cell. This convergence is much greater in the periphery than in the fovea. The lower degree of convergence in the fovea is the main reason why our ability to see detail (*visual resolution*) is much greater in the fovea than in the periphery. The great convergence in the periphery makes this region very low in visual resolution. Consequently, we must look directly at something in order to image it on the fovea, if we want to see it clearly. The periphery, on the other hand, with its more sensitive rods and its high degree of convergence, is best for detecting dim spots of light.

DARK ADAPTATION Most motorists find driving at dusk hazardous. This is because the transition from day to night vision takes place gradually as daylight diminishes. At twilight, both cones and rods are operating but neither with full effectiveness. A sudden change from conditions of light to dark, or vice versa, makes vision difficult for a different reason. It takes a minute or two for the eye to adjust to a change from dim light to brightness and even longer to adjust to a change from bright light to darkness. We have all experienced the difficulty of finding our way to an empty seat right after entering a dark theater. After a few minutes, our eyes become accustomed to the dark, and we are able to see people around us even though the lighting has not changed. We have undergone *dark adaptation.*

The course of dark adaptation provides further evidence for the difference in action between rods and cones (see Figure 4-7). The first part of the curve shows that the cones become increasingly sensitive to fainter lights, but after 5 minutes in the dark, their sensitivity has increased as much as it will. The rods, however, continue to adapt and do not reach their maximum sensitivity for about a half-hour.

The dark-adapted eye is much more sensitive to light with wavelengths in the blue-green region than to the longer wavelengths in the red region (see Figure 4-12). This difference has an important practical implication for the individual who must work in a darkened room or shift quickly from conditions of light to dark, such as a photographer or a ship's navigator on night duty. Wearing red goggles (or working in a room illuminated by red light) greatly reduces the time required for dark adaptation. Since red light stimulates the cones but not the rods, the rods remain in a state of dark adaptation. Under conditions of red light, the person can see well enough to work and still be almost completely dark-adapted when it becomes necessary to go into the dark.

Color vision

COLOR MIXTURE For the human subject, the color spectrum fades into invisibility at the extreme ends, red and violet (see Figure 4-8).[1] Some vivid colors that we see are not in the spectrum at all. They do not correspond to any single wavelength of light but are produced by mixing lights of different wavelengths. These are the nonspectral purples, which are a mixture of red and blue. Another nonspectral color is a red that looks like the "purest" red to most observers but is actually a particular mixture of wavelengths.

An interesting relationship exists among colors. If the spectral colors are wrapped around the circumference of a circle, allowing room between the red and violet ends of the spectrum for the nonspectral purples and reds, the colors opposite each other on the circle will be *complementary*. If lights of these colors are mixed in proper proportions, they disappear into a neutral gray. Figure 4-9 presents such a *color circle;* the main complementary pairs are blue-yellow and red-green.

Those familiar with painting may argue that yellow and blue are not complementaries because those pigments when mixed become green, not gray. However, we are discussing mixing *lights,* not pigments. The principles of mixture in the two cases are not contradictory. The mixture of lights is an *additive* mixture, whereas the mixture of pigments is a *subtractive* mixture—due to the way in which pigments selectively absorb different wavelengths of light. Light is the source of all color, and pigments are simply reflectors and absorbers of light. They achieve their color by absorbing certain parts of the spectrum and reflecting the parts that remain. For example, the pigment in the chlorophyll of plants absorbs most of the violet, blue, and red wavelengths of light; the green that remains is reflected back to the eye, so we see most vegetation as various shades of green. Black pigment absorbs all wavelengths and reflects very little light. White pigment reflects equally all the colors of light but in much greater amounts than black pigment. For more information on additive and subtractive color, see Figure 4-10.

Three widely spaced colors on the color circle can be combined by additive mixture to match *almost* any color of light. The colors used to demonstrate this are usually a red, a green, and a blue. The hue of a light is determined by its wavelength composition. Thus, colors between red and green on the color circle can be produced by additively mixing a pure red and pure green; the exact color obtained will depend on the respective energy levels of the red and green light sources. Similarly, colors between green and blue on the color circle can be obtained by their additive mixtures, and the same holds for blue and red.

[1]A useful mnemonic for remembering the order of colors on the spectrum is the name "ROY G. BIV," formed from the first letters of the colors: red, orange, yellow, green, blue, indigo, and violet.

One of the earliest theories of color vision—proposed by the English physicist Thomas Young in 1802 and modified by the German physiologist Hermann von Helmholtz a half-century later—was based on the fact that three colors are sufficient to produce all the colors in the spectrum. The *Young–Helmholtz theory* proposes three different kinds of color receptors, designated red, green, and blue. Each receptor is maximally sensitive to a different wavelength but broadly tuned so that a particular wavelength will stimulate more than one type of receptor. All colors are produced by the combined stimulation of these receptors. Yellow is produced when red and green receptors are stimulated simultaneously. White is produced when all three receptors are stimulated simultaneously. The modern form of the Young–Helmholtz theory attempts to link three kinds of cones (each containing a different photosensitive pigment) with the three colors.

However, the Young–Helmholtz theory has not been able to explain some of the facts of colorblindness and color appearance. If yellow is produced by activity in red and green receptors, how is it that a person with red-green colorblindness has no difficulty seeing yellow? Another color theory, formulated by Ewald Hering in 1870, attempted to solve this problem. Hering felt that the Young–Helmholtz theory did not adequately reflect visual experience. He based his theory of color vision on the phenomenology of color experience rather than on the facts of color mixture and argued that yellow is as basic a color as red, blue, or green. It does not appear to be a mixture of other colors, as orange appears to be a mixture of red and yellow or purple appears to be a mixture of red and blue.

Hering was impressed with the facts of *afterimages*, by the appearance of red-green and blue-yellow as pairs in so many circumstances. He proposed that there were three types of receptors: one receptor responding to degrees of brightness, the black-white continuum, and two color receptors, one providing the basis for red-green perception and the other for blue-yellow. Each receptor was assumed to function in two ways. One color of the pair was produced when the receptor was in a building-up phase (*anabolic*), and the other appeared when the receptor was in a tearing-down phase (*catabolic*). The two phases cannot occur at the same time in a given receptor; when a yellow-blue receptor is stimulated, it responds with either yellow or blue. It cannot react both ways simultaneously. That is why, according to the theory, we never see a red-green or a blue-yellow, whereas it is possible to see a reddish blue or greenish yellow. When stimulation is withdrawn, as in the negative afterimage experiment, the contrasting color appears because the anabolic-catabolic process is reversed. When we look at a blue circle and then transfer our gaze to a white sheet of paper, a yellow circle appears when the catabolic process takes over (see Figure 4-14). Hering's theory has become known as the *opponent-process theory*. In its modern form, this theory assumes that the opponent processes take place not in the receptors but in coding mechanisms closer to the brain in the visual system.

Recent developments suggest that both theories may be partially correct. If special procedures are used, it is possible to direct different wavelengths of light through single cones in the human retina and analyze their responses by means of a computer. Three kinds of light-sensitive pigments in the cones have been identified using this technique. One type is primarily sensitive to wavelengths in the blue band, one is sensitive to green, and the third is sensitive to yellow. Although the third cone type had its peak sensitivity at 577 nm (which is yellow), it was also sensitive to the longer wavelengths (up to 650 nm) of the yellowish-red part of the spectrum. To the extent that they confirm the existence of three types of cones, these measurements appear to support the assumptions of the Young–Helmholtz theory.

At the same time, recordings taken from single cells using microelectrodes (a procedure described on page 119) give evidence of an "on" and "off" type of process in ganglion cells and in cells of the lateral geniculate body—that portion of the thalamus where visual impulses are relayed to the visual cortex. Some cells respond with a burst of impulses when stimulated by short wavelengths but are inhibited (respond as "off" cells) during illumination with long wavelengths, showing a burst of firing when stimulation ceases. Other cells are active when stimulated by long wavelengths and inhibited by short wavelengths. These results indicate an *opponent process* operating not in the cones themselves, but farther along in the pathway from the eye to the brain.

At this point of scientific development, it appears that color vision is at least a two-stage process: the retina contains three cone pigments that respond differentially to lights of different wavelength; these responses are encoded into two-color, opponent signals by cells farther along in the visual system for transmission to the higher visual centers. Modern theories of color vision include these two stages. It is interesting that two theories, those of Hering and Young–Helmholtz, proposed over a century ago, have had to wait until recent technological developments could provide verification of their propositions.

With additive mixing, almost the entire color circle can be produced with just three colors.

Color television provides a common example of additive color mixture. Examination of the television screen with a magnifying glass will reveal that there are tiny dots of only three colors (red, green, and blue). Addition occurs because the dots are so close together that the eye cannot separate them, so their retinal images overlap.

PSYCHOLOGICAL DIMENSIONS OF COLOR   How do you describe a color? Light waves can be described physically through the measurement of wavelengths and amplitude (the height of the wave). But when we try to describe what we see, we must resort to three psychological dimensions: hue, brightness, and saturation. *Hue* refers to what we ordinarily think of as the "name" of the color—for example, red, green, and so forth. The circumference of the color circle provides the scale along which the hues can be placed in order.

Another dimension of color is *brightness.* The physical basis of brightness is primarily the energy of the light source, which corresponds to the amplitude of the wave. But brightness also depends to some extent on wavelength. Yellow, for example, appears somewhat brighter than red and blue wavelengths, even when all three have equal amplitudes.

The third dimension is *saturation.* Saturation refers to the colorfulness of light, where white corresponds to the total absence of color. Highly saturated colors appear to contain no white. Unsaturated colors appear pale or whitish. Saturation is determined primarily by how spread-out the wavelengths are. A color consisting of a wide range of wavelengths appears unsaturated; a single wavelength appears highly saturated.

The relationship between hue, brightness, and saturation will become clearer if we look at the *color solid* (see Figure 4-11), which represents all three simultaneously. The dimension of hue is represented by points on the circumference; saturation, by points along the radius, going from a pure or highly saturated color on the outside to a gray or unsaturated color in the center; and brightness, by points along the vertical axis, going toward black at the bottom and white at the top. On any vertical half-slice taken through the center of the solid, all the colors are the same hue but vary in brightness and saturation.

COLORBLINDNESS   To understand colorblindness, we may think of the normal visual system as consisting of three subsystems: light-dark, yellow-blue, and red-green. All other combinations can be derived from these. Colorblindness results from a deficiency in one or two of these systems, the light-dark system remaining intact if the person can see at all. The person with normal vision is called a *trichromat.* The person who lacks one system but has use of the other two is called a *dichromat* and is partially colorblind. Finally, the person with only the light-dark system is a *monochromat* and is totally colorblind.

By far the most common form of colorblindness is red-green blindness, with the blue-yellow and light-dark systems intact. Total colorblindness—in which the person sees merely black, white, and gray—is extremely rare; yellow-blue blindness, in which red-green discrimination is preserved, is rarer still.

Many colorblind persons are unaware of their defect because they are able to make such skillful use of their remaining color discrimination, combining it with the learned colors and color names of familiar objects. Because our color vocabulary is not clear for unsaturated colors, the colorblind person can make some mistakes on these troublesome colors without being noticed.

A person with red-green colorblindness can still distinguish a traffic signal by the brightness and position of the light.

There are many tests available for the detection of colorblindness. They usually require the subject to read a figure composed of colored dots on a background of other colored dots (see Figure 4-13). The colors are chosen to confuse subjects who have the various forms of color deficiency.

NEGATIVE AFTERIMAGES   If you stare at a *red* circle and then look at a plain gray surface, you are likely to see a *green* circle on it; that is, you experience a negative afterimage. It is called a negative afterimage because green is the complementary color of red on the color circle. Not all afterimages are in the complementary color, however. After staring at a very bright light, you are likely to see a whole succession of colors, but seeing the complementary color is very common. Afterimages are illustrated in Figure 4-14. The phenomena of color mixing, colorblindness, and negative afterimages have played an important role in theorizing about color vision.

PATTERN VISION

Visual resolution

The problem that most often brings people to an eye specialist is difficulty in seeing patterns such as road signs or printed words. The capacity to see patterns is called *visual resolution.* Normally, resolution is measured by having a person look at a chart on which the patterns become progressively smaller, such as that shown in Figure 4-15. This kind of test allows the eye specialist to determine a threshold for the minimum size of detail that the tested person can detect; it assesses visual acuity by comparing the performance of the person being tested with the performance of a normal observer.

Most difficulties in visual resolution result from a failure of the eye to focus images on the retina. In the normal eye, the lens changes shape to form a sharp image of the object being viewed regardless of its distance. This adjustment is called *accommodation.* For some people, the lens will focus *near* objects but not far objects. These people have poor acuity for far objects but good acuity for near objects; they are said to be *near-sighted. Farsighted* people have good acuity for far objects but not for near. Both problems can be corrected with eyeglasses. As we get older, the lens loses its flexibility and becomes fixed at its farthest focus. This is why most people need reading glasses after they reach middle age.

We may wonder could we produce superacuity if we made the image much sharper than the image in the normal eye? The answer is no, because resolution is limited not only by the focusing capacity of the eye but also by the ability of the visual pathways to transmit patterns. It turns out that the limit imposed by the visual pathway is about the same as that imposed by the structure of the normal eye.

Recently, a new approach to pattern detection has been introduced. Instead of decreasing the size of a pattern until it can no longer be resolved, the pattern is held fixed in size, but the difference in intensity between the lightest and darkest regions (contrast) is varied until the pattern is just detectable. The contrast at which the pattern is just detectable is called the *contrast threshold.* The stimuli used in studying contrast thresholds have frequently been patterns of light and dark stripes called *gratings* (see Figure 4-16). In a typical experiment, several gratings of different stripe widths are selected. One of these gratings is

Figure 4-15
Snellen Scale

A typical test for measuring visual acuity uses the Snellen Scale. An acuity of 20/20 means that a person is able to read a row of letters at a distance of 20 feet that a normal observer can also read at 20 feet. An acuity of 20/40 means that the person is able to read letters at 20 feet that are large enough for a normal person to read at 40 feet; that is, visual acuity is less than normal. An example of better than normal acuity is 20/10, which means that the person can read at 20 feet what a normal person can only read at 10 feet. Thus, visual acuity is measured relative to the performance of a normal observer.

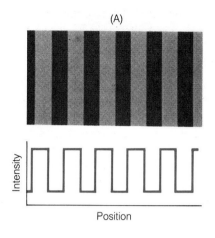

(A)

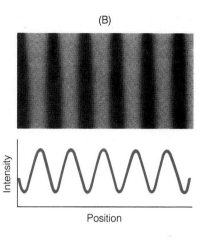

(B)

Figure 4-16
Gratings
The stripe pattern on the left is a square-wave grating; plotted below it is a curve giving intensity as a function of location. The pattern on the right is called a sine-wave grating because its intensity is a sinusoidal function of location. Different gratings can be constructed by varying *frequency* (number of cycles) and *contrast* (difference in intensity between the lightest and darkest parts of the pattern). (After Cornsweet, 1970)

presented at a time, and its contrast is varied to find the contrast threshold. For very narrow stripes, the contrast threshold is high. As the stripes get broader, the contrast threshold decreases. For still broader stripes, the threshold increases again. This variation in threshold with stripe width is illustrated in Figure 4-17. As stripes are made progressively broader, we approach a condition in which the entire retina is uniformly illuminated. It is very difficult to detect intensity differences in such uniform fields. The visual system is designed to detect changes over space.

A similar phenomenon occurs in the detection of flickering lights. If the flicker rate becomes very high, we cease to see any flicker. It is also true that if the flicker is very slow, it becomes difficult to detect. Thus, perceptual systems are designed to detect change over time as well as space. A dramatic illustration of this is what happens in *stabilized vision*. Even when we are trying to look steadily at a single point, our eyes are always moving slightly. This means that

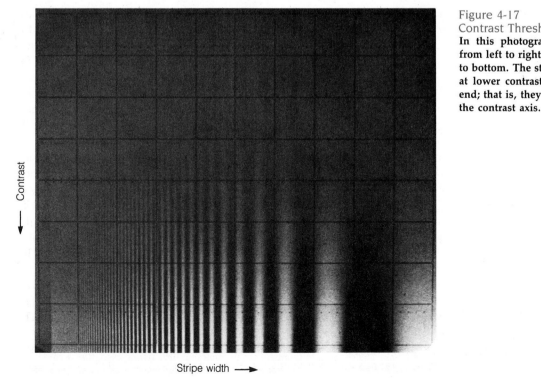

Stripe width ⟶

Figure 4-17
Contrast Threshold and Stripe Width
In this photograph, stripe width increases from left to right; contrast increases from top to bottom. The stripes in the middle are seen at lower contrasts than the stripes at either end; that is, they are visible farther down on the contrast axis.

Figure 4-18
Stabilized Image
A device to demonstrate that without movement of the eye in relation to a scene, the
scene disappears. A tiny projector mounted
on a contact lens is worn over the subject's
cornea. With each movement of the eyeball,
the lens and projector also move so that the
projected image always falls on the same area
of the retina. After a few seconds, the image
will fade and then disappear.

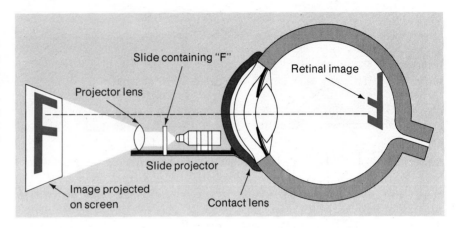

the image is always moving over the receptors. When this movement is eliminated, the visual world disappears within a few seconds. It takes delicate
equipment to stabilize a retinal image completely (see Figure 4-18), but approximate stabilization will fade a blurry image, as demonstrated by Figure 4-19.
These phenomena appear to be a consequence of the way visual neurons
respond to patterned stimuli.

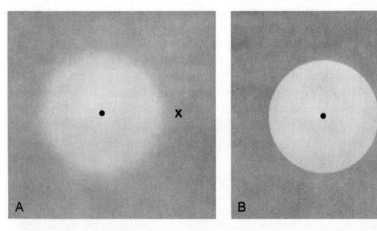

Figure 4-19
Fading of a Nearly Stabilized Image
With one eye closed, stare at the dot in the middle of A. You will notice that the blurred,
light-colored disk soon fades and disappears. Close the seeing eye for a few seconds and
then open it; the disk will reappear and then fade again. If you stare at the dot until the
disk fades and then shift your gaze to the ×, you will find that the disk reappears, and it will
reappear each time you shift your eyes between the dot and the ×.
    If you try doing the same thing with B, the disk will not disappear. Although you think
you are staring at the dot steadily, your eyes are constantly making little oscillating
movements. These minute oscillations, which we are unaware of even though they occur
continually, cause light from the stimulus to strike different retinal receptors from one
moment to the next. When you are looking at the edge of something and your eye shifts
from one side of the edge to the other, the receptors perceive a change in intensity. The
intensity changes that occur with eye oscillations allow the receptors to continue firing at
a high rate, and the disk remains visible. The same thing happens when you stare at the
dot in A; but because the gradient of intensity of the blurred disk is more gradual, the eye
movements produce a smaller change in intensity on the receptors viewing the edge of the
blurred disk. The changes in intensity are so small that little neural excitation occurs in the
receptors, and the disk fades. Closing and opening your eye causes marked changes in
intensity and so does moving your eye to stare at the ×. (After Cornsweet, 1970)

Neural processing of patterns

When an image is projected on the eye, certain neural events are initiated in the retina. These neural events can be thought of as messages sent from the eye to the brain via the visual pathways. Just how do neural events at the level of the retina get coded into messages that are understandable to the brain? Experiments recording neural activity in a single cell of the visual cortex of the brain have helped explain the process.

SINGLE CELL RECORDING A typical *single cell recording* experiment is illustrated in Figure 4-20. An animal (in this case a monkey, but other animals have been studied including human patients undergoing brain surgery) is placed in a restraining device that holds its head in a fixed position; the animal is partially anesthetized so that it is possible to control accurately where its eyes look. Facing the animal is a screen on which various stimuli can be projected. A microelectrode is inserted into a selected area of the visual cortex through a small hole drilled in the animal's skull. The electrode (a thin wire insulated except at its tip) is positioned so that it will pick up electrical changes occurring in a single brain cell while the animal's eyes are being stimulated. These tiny electrical changes are amplified and input to an oscilloscope, which converts the electrical currents into a moving picture displayed on a television-like screen. An active neuron emits a series of impulses that appear on the oscilloscope screen as vertical spikes. If a cell is responding strongly, a fast train of spikes is seen on the oscilloscope; if the cell is not responding, only an occasional spike will be seen. During the experiment, the microelectrode can be moved to test different neurons in the visual cortex.

Unlike cells in the retina, most cells in the visual cortex do not respond when the eye is stimulated by large or diffuse spots of light. Instead, these cortical cells are highly specific in terms of the stimuli to which they react. Further, each cortical cell will respond only to a stimulus that falls on a limited patch of the retina; the area of the retina associated with a given cortical cell is called the cell's *receptive field*. Different cells in the visual cortex have different receptive fields. Since the animal's head and eyes are fixed in position, the receptive field of a given cortical cell can be mapped on the projection screen as a stimulus is moved about (see Figure 4-20).

FEATURE DETECTORS Hubel and Wiesel (1968) were pioneers in single-cell recording studies of the brain and shared the Nobel Prize in 1981 for their research. They identified several types of cells in the visual cortex that could be differentiated by the visual features to which they respond. Some they called *simple cells,* others *complex cells,* and yet others *hypercomplex cells.* These names reflect the degree of perceptual abstraction performed by each type of cell.

Simple cells become active when the eye is exposed to a line stimulus, such as a thin bar of light or a straight boundary between a light and dark region. Whether a particular simple cell responds depends on the orientation of the bar of light and its location in the animal's visual field. A bar shown vertically on the screen may activate a given cortical cell (see Figure 4-21), whereas the same cell will not respond (though others will respond) if the bar is moved appreciably out of the vertical or displaced to one side or the other. A simple cell responds only to a bar or a straight edge with a specific orientation; further, that stimulus must fall on a limited region of the retina.

A complex cell also fires to a line segment with a particular orientation (for example, at a 45° angle), but its receptive field tends to be much larger than that of a simple cell. Moreover, complex cells respond with sustained firing as the line segment moves across the receptive field, as long as the line segment maintains its proper orientation.

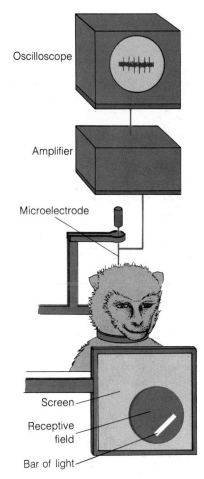

Figure 4-20
Recording Cortical Activity

A partially anesthetized monkey is placed in a device that holds its head in a fixed position. A moving bar of light, which varies in direction and speed, is projected onto the screen. A microelectrode implanted in the visual cortex of the monkey monitors activity from a single neuron, and this activity is amplified and displayed on an oscilloscope.

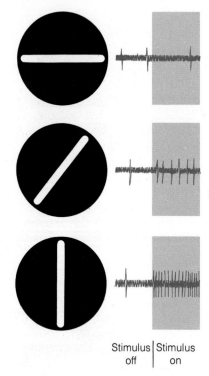

Stimulus | Stimulus
off | on

Figure 4-21
Feature Detectors
The response of a single cell in the visual cortex to a bar of light. When there is no stimulus, only an occasional spike is seen on the oscilloscope. But when the stimulus is turned on, the cell may or may not fire depending on the orientation of the light bar. For this cell, there is no response to a horizontal bar, a slight response to a bar at 45°, and a very fast train of spikes to a vertical light bar.

As the name suggests, hypercomplex cells are responsible for a yet higher level of abstraction. These cells are active if the stimulus line is in a particular orientation—but the line must be of a specific length. Thus, hypercomplex cells not only code for the orientation of a line segment but also fire most actively in response to a bar of light whose corners and ends are well defined.

Since these cells are tuned to specific features of a stimulus, they are often called *feature detectors*. Recently, a dispute has arisen as to what feature these cells detect. Hubel and Wiesel got a large response to light and dark bars and characterized the cells as bar detectors. Other researchers, however, have shown that many of these cells are more sensitive to gratings consisting of several dark and light stripes than to single bars. This suggests that the cells might better be considered to be spatial frequency detectors (DeValois and DeValois, 1980).

The work on single cell recording has greatly increased our knowledge of how the brain can analyze and extract features from a visual display. More research is needed in this area, but it is likely that there are still other cells in the visual cortex that respond to specific patterns, such as curves and angles. There is also some evidence for the existence of cells so finely tuned that they respond only to particular shapes of objects. Since anything we see can be approximated by a series of line segments at angles to each other, it may well be that these feature-detector cells are the building blocks from which a pattern recognition system is formed.

Pattern recognition

Can the notion of feature detectors be used to explain how we recognize complicated pictorial scenes? This question represents an active area of research in psychology, particularly among cognitive psychologists, who have used the concept of feature detectors as a cornerstone for their theories. The work in psychology has its counterpart in computer science. Computer scientists are interested in building systems that can analyze pictorial images into forms of information that can be understood by computers. Sophisticated examples of the type of system that computer scientists want to build are robots, equipped with TV cameras, that can move about in the world and react to their environment. Efforts to build computer systems that have the capability of image processing have much in common with psychological theories of perception. In fact, there is an active interplay between the two fields, and each is profiting from the research of the other.

Work in this area, whether by psychologists or computer scientists, is generally referred to by the title *models for pattern recognition*. Most such models assume a set of feature detectors as the basic components of a pattern recognition system.

Pattern recognition models tend to be very complicated, but we can gain an understanding of what they are like by examining one very simple model for recognizing hand-printed letters of the alphabet (Selfridge and Neisser, 1960). The model has been implemented on a computer and used with success in recognizing letters printed by different people and under different conditions. Although we would not claim that the model simulates the actual processes that a human uses in recognizing letters, it suggests how the perceptual system might work.

Recognizing hand-printed letters is not a trivial task when one considers the tremendous variations in width, height, slant, and so forth that may occur from one printing to the next. The model assumes that letters can be described in terms of a *feature list*. For example, the letter *H* consists of two lines that are more vertical than horizontal and one line that is more horizontal than vertical; it also has a concavity (open space) at the top and at the bottom. These features taken together specify the letter *H*, but any of these features alone would not be enough to specify it.

A feature list is stored in the computer's memory for each letter in the alphabet. When a test letter is presented, its features are extracted and compared with each of the feature lists in memory until a match occurs. To illustrate the process, we will consider a highly simplified program to distinguish among the letters A, H, V, and Y. With such a small set of letters, the pattern recognition process can rely on the presence or absence of just three features: a concavity at the top of the letter, a crossbar, and a vertical line. When a test letter is presented, the computer first asks: "Is there a concavity at the top?" If the answer is "no," the test letter is classified as an A. If "yes," the computer would next ask: "Is there a crossbar?" If "yes," the letter is H. If "no," the next question would be: "Is there a vertical line?" If "yes," the letter is Y; if "no," the letter is V. The scheme for checking features is illustrated in Figure 4-22. It is called a *sorting tree*; as we move through the tree, we sort inputs into appropriate output categories.

This program is extremely simple. Far more complex ones are now in operation that are accurate in discriminating both hand-printed and hand-written letters. Although most of these programs are still in an experimental stage, several have reached technological maturity. The postal service, for example, has installed Zip Code readers that can discriminate hand-printed or typed digits. These elaborate programs are based on the same principle as simpler ones: a set of feature detectors is used in conjunction with a sorting tree to identify complex patterns.

The human perceptual system may operate in a similar manner. Stored in your memory might be a feature list for "Aunt Sara"; it would include the width of her mouth, the slant of her nose, the color of her eyes, and so forth. When you encounter someone, the feature detectors are activated, and if the extracted features match the list in your memory for Aunt Sara, you know who it is. Another term for a feature list is *schema* (plural *schemata*). A subject has a schema of a stimulus stored in memory and recognizes the stimulus when the features extracted from it match the schema for that stimulus.

The process of extracting features from a stimulus and trying to match them with a feature list or schema stored in memory is called *encoding*; that is, we are trying to form a code from the stimulus input that will allow us to locate information previously stored in our memory about the stimulus. The notion of encoding is central to developments in cognitive psychology and will be encountered elsewhere in this book.

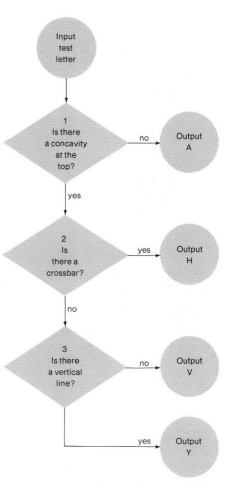

Figure 4-22
Sorting Tree
This pattern recognition program employs three test features to categorize the hand-printed letters A, H, V, and Y. The tests are applied in order, with each outcome determining the next step. Each diamond indicates a decision point that requires a yes or no answer.

AUDITORY SENSE

Auditory system

Whereas the eye responds to electromagnetic energy, the ear is sensitive to mechanical energy—to *pressure changes* among the molecules in the atmosphere. A vibrating object, such as a tuning fork, causes successive waves of compression and expansion among the air molecules surrounding it. The sound waves generated by the vibration of molecules (in air, water, or some

Figure 4-23
Cross Section of the Ear
This drawing shows the general structure of the ear. For the detailed structure of the cochlea, see Figure 4-24.

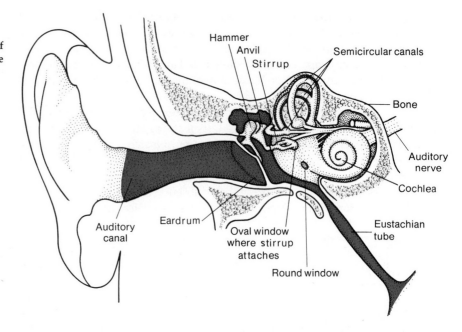

Figure 4-24
The Cochlea
The figure to the lower right is a cross section through the snail-shaped cochlea, a coiled tube, which is shown here on the left as if it were uncoiled. Vibrations cause the stirrup to move the oval window, resulting in waves in the fluid that fills the cochlear canal. The pressure wave in the fluid sets up a traveling wave in the basilar membrane, stimulating the receptors in the organ of Corti, which are connected to the auditory nerve. The round window permits the pressure wave to leave the cochlea.

other medium) are the stimuli for hearing. Unlike light, sound must travel through a medium; a ringing bell suspended in a vacuum jar cannot be heard when the air is pumped out.

The *external ear* connects with the *auditory canal* leading to the *eardrum*—a movable diaphragm activated by sound waves entering the ear (see Figure 4-23). On the inner side of the eardrum is a cavity housing the bony transmitters of the *middle ear* (three small bones called the *hammer*, *anvil*, and *stirrup*). The hammer is attached firmly to the eardrum and the stirrup to another membrane, the *oval window*. The oval window conducts the sounds to the *cochlea*, the

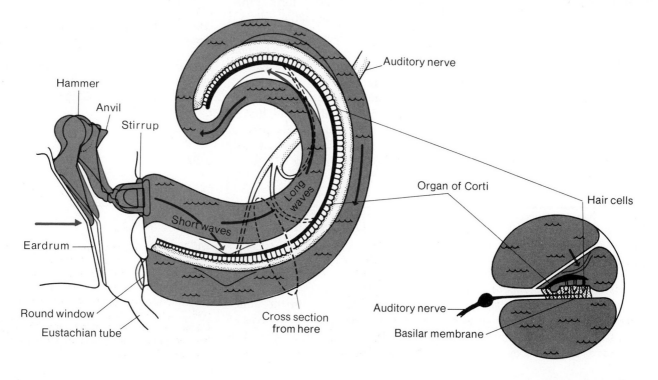

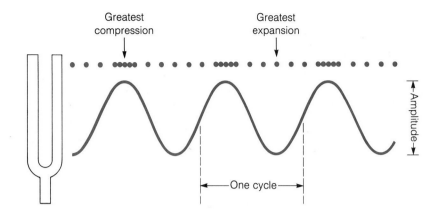

Figure 4-25
Pure Tone
As the tuning fork vibrates, it produces successive waves of compression and expansion of the air. If the tuning fork makes 100 vibrations per second, it produces a sound wave with 100 compressions per second (that is, 100 Hz). A sound in which the pressure variation corresponds to a sine wave is called a *pure tone*. The wave form for any sound (no matter how complex) can be decomposed into a series of different sine waves with appropriate amplitudes. When the sine waves are added together, the result is the original wave form.

auditory portion of the *inner ear*. Because the oval window is much smaller than the eardrum, small movements at the eardrum are condensed into a magnified pressure on the oval window.

Pressure at the oval window sets into motion the fluid inside the cochlea (see Figure 4-24). Pressure changes in the fluid displace the *basilar membrane* in the cochlea, on which the *organ of Corti* rests. This displacement stimulates receptors in the *hair cells* of the organ of Corti, which are connected with the auditory nerve. The pathways of the auditory nerve travel to both cerebral hemispheres, terminating in the temporal lobes. Thus, destruction of one temporal lobe will not cause complete deafness in either ear.

Pitch and loudness

A sound in which the pressure variation corresponds to a sine wave is illustrated in Figure 4-25. Such a sound is called a *pure tone*. The cycles of the wave represent the successive compression and expansion of the air as the sound wave moves along. The two main characteristics of such a wave are its frequency and its amplitude. *Frequency* is measured in the number of vibrations per second; that is, the number of times per second that the complete cycle of the sound wave is repeated. The unit Hertz (abbreviated Hz) is used to denote

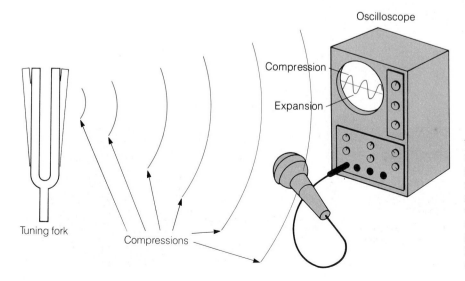

Viewing a Sound Signal
Using an oscilloscope, we can produce pictures of sound waves. Vibrations of the air molecules in a sound wave are picked up by a microphone. These movements are converted by the microphone into an electric current. The oscilloscope changes the current into a moving picture on a screen. The oscilloscope picture is a graph of how pressure changes with time.

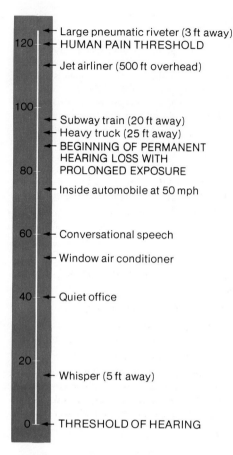

120 — Large pneumatic riveter (3 ft away)
    — HUMAN PAIN THRESHOLD

    — Jet airliner (500 ft overhead)

100 —

    — Subway train (20 ft away)
    — Heavy truck (25 ft away)
    — BEGINNING OF PERMANENT
       HEARING LOSS WITH
80 —   PROLONGED EXPOSURE

    — Inside automobile at 50 mph

60 — Conversational speech

    — Window air conditioner

40 — Quiet office

20 —

    — Whisper (5 ft away)

0 — THRESHOLD OF HEARING

Figure 4-26
Decibel Scale
The loudness of various common sounds scaled in decibels. The takeoff blast of the *Saturn V* moon rocket measured at the launching pad is approximately 180 db. For laboratory rats, prolonged exposure to 150 db causes death.

cycles per second; that is, one cycle per second is 1 Hz. Amplitude refers to the amount of compression and expansion of air, as represented by the height of the wave from base to crest.

The frequency of a sound wave is primarily responsible for what we experience as *pitch*. However, the pitch of a tone can be somewhat affected by intensity. So, even pitch is not simply related to a single physical attribute of the stimulus. Similarly, loudness is most strongly related to the amplitude of the sound wave, or intensity of the sound. However, a low-frequency sound wave having the same amplitude as a high-frequency sound wave may not sound equally loud.

Human beings can hear frequencies that range from about 20 to 20,000 Hz. A familiar reference on this range is provided by the piano, which produces frequencies from roughly 27 to 4,200 Hz. Species do not all hear the same range of frequencies; for example, dog-calling whistles make use of tones that are too high in frequency for humans to hear.

We all know the difference between a loud and a soft sound, but assigning scale values to intensity is not so easy. Scientists from the Bell Telephone Laboratories have formulated a convenient unit for converting the physical pressures at the eardrum into an understandable scale. The unit is called a *decibel* (one tenth of a *bel*, named in honor of Alexander Graham Bell, and abbreviated db). A rough idea of what the decibel measures is provided by the scale of familiar sounds shown in Figure 4-26. At about 120 db, sound intensity becomes painful; the loudness of normal conversation is at about 60 db. Exposure to sound intensities of 90 db or above for extended periods can result in permanent deafness. Some rock musicians, for example, have suffered serious hearing loss. Airport runway crews and pneumatic drill operators wear ear mufflers to guard against possible damage.

The absolute threshold for hearing varies with the frequency of the stimulus (see Figure 4-27). Zero decibels is arbitrarily set as the absolute threshold for hearing a 1,000 Hz tone. Tones in the range of 800 to 6,000 Hz require less than 10 db to reach threshold, whereas tones less than 100 Hz or greater than 15,000 Hz require 40 db or more to reach threshold.

Rock bands can generate sounds at 120 db or more, causing permanent hearing loss.

Complex sounds

Just as the colors we see are seldom pure hues produced by a single wavelength of light, so the sounds we hear are seldom pure tones represented by a sound wave of a single frequency. For example, striking middle C on the piano not only produces a *fundamental tone* of 262 Hz, but it also produces *overtones*, which are multiples of that frequency. The overtones occur because while the piano wire vibrates as a whole, producing the fundamental tone, it also vibrates in halves, thirds, quarters, fifths, and so on, with each partial vibration producing its own frequency.

A sound consisting of a fundamental tone plus overtones has a dominant pitch that corresponds to the pitch of the fundamental. The pitches corresponding to the overtones are usually not heard, although the lower ones can be heard if we listen carefully.

This raises a question. Why do the same notes sound different on the piano and the trumpet? The sounds of one musical instrument differ from those of another in the number of overtones produced. They also differ because the construction of the instrument enhances certain overtones—parts of the instrument vibrate in step (resonate) with some overtones more than with others. The perceptual quality associated with a particular overtone pattern is called *timbre*. It is the timbre of a tone that tells us whether it is being produced by a piano or a clarinet. If all overtones are eliminated by the use of sound filters, it is impossible to determine what instrument is being played. Instead of the regular sound wave pictured in Figure 4-25, a tone from a musical instrument has a complex wave form, preserving only the peaks and troughs that define the fundamental pitch; the high and low points are the same, but the wave is jagged or irregular rather than smooth (see Figure 4-28).

An important phenomenon of pitch perception is that when a sound consists only of overtones of some fundamental, the fundamental being absent, the dominant pitch that a person hears still corresponds to the fundamental. This is called the pitch of the *missing fundamental*. It has played an important role in theoretical controversies about pitch perception.

If we compare the psychological dimensions of color with those of tone, the following correspondences hold approximately:

$$\text{Hue} \longleftrightarrow \text{Pitch}$$
$$\text{Brightness} \longleftrightarrow \text{Loudness}$$
$$\text{Saturation} \longleftrightarrow \text{Timbre}$$

Hue and pitch are functions of wave frequency; brightness and loudness are functions of amplitude; saturation and timbre are results of mixture. But these are only analogies and are limited, as all analogies are.

What happens when two tones are sounded together? There is nothing in audition analogous to color mixture. Mixtures of different tones never sound exactly alike. If two pure tones are sufficiently separated in frequency, the pitches of both will be heard simultaneously as a chord. When they are close together, the individual pitches will not be heard, and the sound will tend to be dissonant (unpleasant). The main factor determining how consonant (pleasant) musical notes are when played together is the spacing of their overtones (Roederer, 1975). Cultural factors also play a role in determining what sounds consonant.

A *noise* is a sound composed of many frequencies not in harmonious relation to one another. Acoustical experts sometimes speak of *white noise* when referring to a noise composed of all frequencies in the sound spectrum at

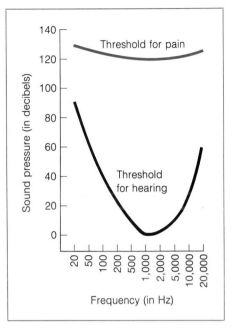

Figure 4-27
Threshold for Hearing
The top curve is the threshold for pain. The convex curve below is the threshold for hearing. The threshold for hearing takes on its minimal value at roughly 1,000 Hz. (Data are approximate from various determinations.)

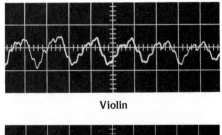

Violin

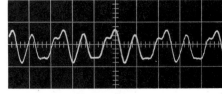

Clarinet

Figure 4-28
Comparable Musical Notes
Oscilloscope pictures of the same note played on two different instruments

As we have noted, sound waves traveling through the fluid of the cochlea displace the basilar membrane, thus activating the hair cells of the organ of Corti, which are connected to fibers of the auditory nerve. But how does a structure as small as the organ of Corti (less than the size of a pea in a human being) enable us to differentiate thousands of different tones? What are the mechanisms that provide for discriminations in pitch and loudness?

Loudness appears to be determined by the total number of nerve fibers firing and by the activation of certain high threshold fibers—that is, nerve fibers that require considerable bending of the hair cells in order to be stimulated. Pitch is a more complicated matter. Historically, the two major theories of pitch discrimination have been the place theory and the frequency theory. The *place theory* assumes that the frequency of a tone is indicated by the region of the basilar membrane that is maximally displaced by the sound wave. Von Békésy tested this theory in a series of experiments for which he was awarded the Nobel Prize in 1961. He cut tiny holes in the cochlea of guinea pigs and observed the basilar membrane with a microscope as the ear was being stimulated by tones of different frequencies. He discovered that high frequency tones maximally displaced the narrow end of the basilar membrane near the oval window; tones of intermediate frequency caused displacement farther toward the other end of the basilar membrane. (These actions of short and longer waves are illustrated in Figure 4-24). Unfortunately for the

consistency of the theory, however, low tones displaced the membrane in roughly the same way as intermediate tones (Lewis and others, 1982).

Moreover, even in the range of frequencies where the portion of the basilar membrane that is displaced (called the *displacement envelope*) does differ for different frequencies, the displacement envelopes are so similar as to make this a doubtful basis for our ability to discriminate very small differences in frequency—that is, differences of about 1 Hz. Further, the place theory has provided no satisfactory explanation for the fact that we hear the missing fundamental pitch when its overtones are sounded.

This leads us to the *frequency theory*, which (in its simplest form) assumes that the cochlea acts like a microphone and the auditory nerve like a telephone wire. According to this theory, pitch is determined by the frequency of impulses traveling up the auditory nerve. The greater the frequency is, the higher the pitch. Studies have shown that for tones of up to 4,000 Hz, the electrical response of the auditory nerve does track the frequency of the tone. Thus, a tone of 1,000 Hz produces 1,000 evoked responses per second in the nerve; a tone of 2,000 Hz produces 2,000 responses; and so on.

Individual neurons can respond at almost 1,000 times a second. The auditory nerve as a whole is able to follow the wave form because different neurons respond on different cycles. It is not a matter of their rigidly taking turns; rather each cell has a certain probability

of firing on each cycle of the sound wave. Sometimes it will fire on two successive cycles, and sometimes not fire for several cycles (Green, 1976).

As with theories of color vision, an ultimate explanation of pitch discrimination will probably include some aspects of both theories. Both the *place* of excitation on the basilar membrane and the *frequency* of nerve response appear to be involved in transmitting information about the frequency of a tone. Place seems to be important for high frequencies (above 4,000 Hz), whereas synchronous discharge in nerve fibers is important for the lower frequencies.

Additional coding of auditory information takes place in the auditory pathways closer to the brain and in the auditory cortex itself. An auditory nerve fiber makes synaptic connections with at least four other neurons on its way to the auditory cortex. At each of these levels, neurons can be found that fire at the onset of a tone, or decrease their firing when a tone is turned on, or discharge continuously to a maintained tone, or discharge only when a sound is presented to both ears. In addition, as we ascend from the auditory nerve to the auditory cortex, the range of frequencies to which a particular cell will respond becomes increasingly narrow. Thus, coding of the auditory input becomes more precise as the information progresses from the ear to the cortex. A general theory of hearing will also have to take into account neural codes based on different types of response patterns at each synaptic level of the auditory system (Zwislocki, 1981).

roughly the same energy level, or loudness. White noise is analogous to white light, which is composed of all frequencies in the light spectrum. The sound of an empty TV channel or a bathroom shower approximates the sound of white noise.

A noise with energy concentrated in certain frequency bands may have a characteristic pitch. For example, we may use the musical term "bass" to characterize the sound of a drum, even though a drum is more noisy than tonal.

OTHER SENSES

Senses other than vision and audition are important for survival, but they lack the richness of patterning and organization that have led us to call sight and hearing the "higher senses." Our symbolic experiences are expressed largely in visual and auditory terms. Our spoken language is to be *heard;* our written language is to be *seen.* Musical notation permits music to be read or played on an instrument. Except for Braille (the raised form of printing that permits the blind to read), we do not have any comparable symbolic coding of odors, tastes, or touches.

Smell

From an evolutionary viewpoint, smell is one of the most primitive and most important of the senses. The sense organ for smell has a position of prominence in the head appropriate to a sense intended to guide behavior. Smell has a more direct route to the brain than any other sense. The receptors high in the nose, in the *olfactory epithelium* of each nasal cavity, are connected without synapse directly to the olfactory bulbs of the brain, which lie just below the frontal lobes. The olfactory bulbs are in turn connected with the olfactory cortex on the inside of the temporal lobes. In fish, the olfactory cortex makes up almost all of the cerebral hemispheres; in dogs, about one third; in humans, about one twentieth. These differences in cortical representation correspond to differences in sensitivity among these species. For this reason, both the U.S. Postal Service and the Bureau of Customs have dogs trained to check unopened packages for heroin and marijuana, and specially trained police dogs can sniff out hidden explosives.

Insects and some higher animals use their sense of smell as a means of communication. They secrete chemicals, known as *pheromones,* that float through the air to attract other members of the species. For example, female moths release a pheromone so powerful that males are drawn to a single female from a distance of several miles. It is clear that the male moth responds only to the pheromone and not to the sight of the female; the male will be attracted to a female in a wire container, even though she is blocked from view, but not to a female clearly visible in a glass cage from which the scent of the pheromone cannot escape.

Pheromones represent one of the most primitive forms of communication. There is some evidence to suggest that a vestigial form of pheromone may influence human behavior. For example, chemicals that are sex-attractant pheromones for monkeys have been identified in the vaginal secretions of women (Michael, Bonsall, and Warner, 1974). We also know that women have a lower absolute threshold for certain musklike odors than men and that this threshold varies with the menstrual cycle, reaching its most sensitive level near the time of ovulation (Vierling and Rock, 1967). The sex pheromones secreted by the males of several mammalian species have a musklike odor. It may be that the human female's sensitivity to these substances is related to a human male sex pheromone that at some point in our evolutionary history played a role in human reproductive behavior. Such a process may still be at work for human beings, although in a greatly attenuated form. The presence of so many men's colognes with a musklike odor is suggestive in this regard.

A dog at work for the Postal Service

Experts evaluating subtle differences in the taste of coffee

Taste

The primary taste qualities are *sweet, sour, salty,* and *bitter.* Other taste experiences are composed of mixtures of these qualities. Smell, texture, temperature, and sometimes pain (judging from the pleasure some diners derive from highly spiced food) all contribute to the sensations we experience when we taste a food. When we drink a cup of coffee, we enjoy its aroma and its warmth through senses other than taste; the taste sense provides only for the sweet, sour, salty, or bitter components.

The taste receptors are found in the *taste buds,* on the edges and toward the back of the tongue; a few are located elsewhere in the soft palate, the pharynx, and the larynx. It is known that the number of taste buds decreases with age; so older people are less sensitive to taste than children. Some taste buds at the tip of the tongue react only to sweet, salty, or sour; others react to some or all of these in combination. In general, sensitivity to sweet is greatest at the tip of the tongue, to salty on the tip and the sides, to sour on the sides, and to bitter on the back.

Each of the approximately 10,000 taste buds in the human adult has 15 to 20 taste cells arranged in budlike form on its tip, much like the segments of an orange. These taste cells are continuously reproducing themselves at the rate of a complete turnover for each taste bud every seven days. Consequently, the taste cells you kill when you scald your tongue with hot coffee provide no cause for concern; they are quickly replenished. Recordings from microelectrodes implanted in single cells show that even the individual cells vary in their response to the four basic taste stimuli; that is, some cells may respond only to sugar and salt, whereas others on the same taste bud may respond only to salt and acids, and so forth.

Measurement of impulses from the taste nerve fibers and behavioral evidence show that other animals differ from humans in the receptivity of their taste buds. Cats and chickens, for example, appear to have no taste receptors that respond to sweet, whereas dogs, rats, pigs, and most other vertebrates do. This helps explain the observation by pet owners that dogs are usually fond of desserts, whereas cats generally ignore them (Dethier, 1978).

Skin senses

The familiar sense of touch is not a single sense but includes at least four: *pressure, pain, warm,* and *cold*—all felt through distinct kinds of sensitive spots on the skin surface. All other skin sensations that we commonly describe—such as itch; tickle; quick, pricking pain; or dull, long-lasting pain—are variations of these four basic sensations. An itching sensation, for example, can be produced by stimulating pain spots with a gentle, repeated needle prick; tickle is experienced when adjacent pressure spots on the skin are touched lightly in rapid succession.

The precise receptors for the various skin sensations have been the subject of much study and dispute. At one time, scientists identified a number of quite different nerve-end structures in the skin, each of which was thought to be the specific receptor for one of the four sensations. Subsequent studies, however, failed to substantiate such claims: when investigators "mapped" cold, warm, pressure, and pain spots on their own skin, excised the underlying tissue, and examined it microscopically, there was no consistent relationship between the type of sensation experienced and the type of underlying nerve-end structure. Only two things can be stated with some degree of certainty:

This electronic system enables a blind woman to "see" by skin sensation. The TV camera on her right converts the image of the telephone into the pattern of dots shown on the TV monitor behind her. Then hundreds of tiny cones vibrate against her back, allowing her to feel the dot pattern (shown here by fluorescent paint) and perceive the image of the phone.

1   Nerve fibers at the base of hair follicles serve as receptors for light pressure (but they are not the only such receptors, since the lips—which are hairless—are quite sensitive to pressure).
2   Free nerve-endings that terminate in the epidermis are involved in pain reception.

If there are only warm and cold sensitive spots on the skin's surface, how can we experience the feeling of hot? The answer is that hot results from the *simultaneous* stimulation of warm and cold spots. This is demonstrated with a device that allows two streams of water to be passed through intertwined coils (see Figure 4-29). If cold water passes through both coils, they of course feel cold when grasped with one hand. If warm water passes through both, they feel warm. But when cold water circulates through one set of coils and warm water through the other, the coils feel *hot*. Although this is not the way the experience of "hot" is usually produced, it is the way the receptors respond. Cold spots have two thresholds. They respond to stimuli of low temperature, do not respond to stimuli of intermediate temperature, but respond again to stimuli of high temperature. High temperatures, then, activate *both* warm and cold spots, and the felt experience of hot depends on this simultaneous effect.

Kinesthesis and equilibratory senses

Our ordinary vocabulary lacks a word for the sensory system that informs us of the position and movement of parts of the body. In technical language, it is *kinesthesis:* the muscle, tendon, and joint sense. Sense organs in the joints and tendons detect position and movement; sense organs in the muscles serve to modulate muscle contraction or expansion automatically but give little information that we are directly aware of.

Without kinesthesis, we would have great difficulty in maintaining posture and in walking, climbing, and controlling voluntary movements such as reaching, grasping, and manipulating. Whenever we act, we first make somewhat tentative movements and then adjust them according to their environmental effects. If an object turns out to be heavier than expected, we brace ourselves and lift with greater effort. If we slip or stumble as we walk, we promptly make corrective movements. The kinesthetic sense gives us a feedback from the environment that keeps telling us how things are going. We take this sense for granted until a foot "goes to sleep," and we realize how strange it is to walk without any information about the foot's contact with the floor.

Cooperating with kinesthesis are the *equilibratory senses*, which deal with total body position in relation to gravity and with motion of the body as a whole. The relation of bodily parts to one another is the responsibility of kinesthesis; the orientation of the body in space is the responsibility of the equilibratory senses.

The sense organs for equilibrium, located in the inner ear, are a series of cavities extending from the cochlea. There are two systems: the *semicircular canals* and the *vestibular sacs.*

The three semicircular canals, each roughly perpendicular to the others, lie in three planes, so that bodily rotation in any one of the planes will have maximum effect on one of the canals and rotation at any angle to the planes will affect more than one. The canals are filled with a fluid that moves when the head rotates and exerts pressure on hair cells similar to those of the organ of Corti. Displacement of these hair cells by the movement of the fluid stimulates a nonauditory branch of the auditory nerve. When rotation is slow and of

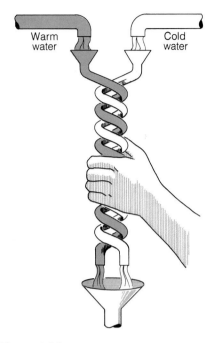

Figure 4-29
Hot as a Simultaneous Stimulation
of Warm and Cold Spots
When cold water (0–5°C) is circulated through one coil and warm water (40–44°C) through another intertwining coil, the subject experiences a hot, burning sensation on grasping the coils. This experiment demonstrates that the sensation of hot is produced by the simultaneous stimulation of warm and cold spots in the skin.

moderate amount, the chief consequence is information that we are moving. When it is more extreme, we experience dizziness and nausea.

The vestibular sacs, located between the base of the semicircular canals and the cochlea, provide for our perception of bodily position when the body is at rest. They respond to the tilt or position of the head and do not require motion to be stimulated. The receptors, again, are hair cells that protrude into a gelatinous mass containing small crystals called *otoliths* (literally, "ear stones"). The normal pressure of the otoliths on the hair cells gives us the sense of upright position, and any distortion tells us that the head is tilted.

The equilibratory senses also signal accelerated motion in a straight line, but sometimes they produce illusions that distort the true path of motion. These illusions occur in flying due to changes in speed and the banking and climbing of the plane. For example, when a plane is increasing its speed gradually, a blindfolded subject may feel sure that the plane is climbing; if its speed is decreasing gradually, the subject may feel equally sure that it is diving. Thus, under conditions of poor visibility, pilots do better to trust their instruments than their equilibratory senses.

Summary

1   All sense experiences have an *absolute threshold* and *difference thresholds* (*jnd's*). A *psychometric function* expresses the likelihood of detecting a stimulus as its intensity is gradually increased. According to *Weber's law,* difference thresholds tend to be a constant fraction of the stimulus intensity.

2   The eye receives light waves by way of the *cornea, pupil, lens,* and *retina.* The actual receptors are the *rods* and *cones* of the retina. The cones, scattered throughout the retina but concentrated in the *fovea,* are receptors both for black and white and for hue (*chromatic* colors). The rods, in the periphery of the eye, allow us to see only black and white (the *achromatic* colors), and function mainly under reduced illumination. In night vision, only the rods function.

3   The distinctive roles of the rods and cones can be inferred from *dark adaptation,* in which the cones reach their maximum sensitivity in 5 to 10 minutes, while the rods continue to become increasingly sensitive for about 30 minutes.

4   The chromatic colors can be arranged on a color circle (following the order of wavelengths) with space allowed for the nonspectral purples and reds. When properly spaced, the colors opposite each other are *complementaries.* When complementary colors are mixed as lights (*additive* mixture), they cancel each other and result in a neutral gray. Three lights (red, green, and blue) are enough to produce the range of hues by additive mixture. The chief dimensions of color are *hue, brightness,* and *saturation.*

5   The normal vision system consists of three subsystems: light-dark, yellow-blue, and red-green. A colorblind individual is deficient in either the red-green or yellow-blue system (a *dichromat*) or both (a *monochromat*). *Negative afterimages* emphasize the pairing of colors, for the withdrawal of stimulation of one hue usually produces the complementary hue.

6   *Visual resolution* refers to the ability to see patterns. Most difficulties in resolution can be corrected by eyeglasses. The visual system is well adapted to detect changes in stimulation over space and time. *Stabilized retinal images* rapidly disappear.

7   Research on the electrical responses of individual neurons in the visual system shows cortical cells to be tuned to bars and edges (or gratings) of various sizes and orientations. These neurons are called *feature detectors.* They are thought to be the basic components of a pattern recognition system, in which patterns are identified through comparison with *feature lists* or *schemata* stored in memory.

8   The auditory apparatus consists of the *external ear*, leading by way of the auditory canal to the *eardrum*, which is next to the *middle ear.* The bones of the middle ear transmit the sound waves to the *oval window*, leading to the *inner ear.* The *cochlea* houses the receptors of the inner ear—sensitive *hair cells* in the *organ of Corti*, which is located on the *basilar membrane.* Wave motion in the fluid of the inner ear bends the hairs on these hair cells, which in turn activate the auditory nerve.

9   The chief dimensions of auditory experience are *pitch*, determined by the *frequency* of vibration of the sound waves, and *loudness*, determined by the *amplitude* of these waves. The absolute threshold for hearing depends on the frequency of the tone; very low- or very high-frequency tones must be more intense than tones in the middle range of frequencies to be heard.

10 Most tones are not pure; that is, they are not composed of only a single frequency. Musical instruments may be differentiated by the *timbre* of their tones, a quality that depends on the patterns of *overtones* that the instruments produce. Complex sounds composed of many frequencies not in harmonious relation to one another are called *noise.*

11 The other senses, important as they are, do not enter as much into our symbolic behavior; so they are thought of as "lower senses." They include *smell, taste,* the four *skin senses* (pressure, pain, warm, cold), *kinesthesis* (muscle, tendon, and joint sense), and the *equilibratory senses.*

Further Reading

For a general introduction to the various senses, see Lindsay and Norman, *Human information processing* (2nd ed., 1977). Also see Rock, *An introduction to perception* (1975); Coren, Porac, and Ward, *Sensation and perception* (1978); Kaufman, *Perception* (1979); Goldstein, *Sensation and perception* (1980); and Schiffman, *Sensation and perception* (2nd ed., 1982).

Experimental psychology (3rd ed., 1971), edited by Kling and Riggs, is a useful reference book, with a number of chapters on sensory psychology. The multiple-volume *Handbook of perception* (1975–1979), edited by Carterette and Friedman, covers most aspects of the sensory processes.

5
PERCEPTION

We live in a world of objects and people—a world that bombards our senses with stimuli. Only under the most unusual circumstances are we aware of a single stimulus, such as a point of light, a pure tone, or a regular pattern of black and white stripes. Instead, we see a three-dimensional world of light and color and hear words, music, and other complex sounds. We react to elaborate patterns of stimuli, usually with little awareness of their individual parts. *Perception* is the process by which we organize and interpret these patterns of stimuli in the environment.

In Chapter 4, we were concerned with simple stimuli traditionally classified under the heading of "sensation." In most cases, the psychological characteristics of such stimuli are determined by their physical characteristics in a direct and relatively uncomplicated way. Brightness depends primarily on intensity, hue on wavelength, pitch on frequency, and so on. The perceptual phenomena considered in this chapter are more complex. At one time, the distinction between sensation and perception had great theoretical importance, with perception viewed as a process of combining sensations. Today, the dividing line between sensory experiences and perceptual ones is much less clear, and it seems best to view such experiences as lying along a continuum.

Unlike simple sensory events, which can often be explained by peripheral events in the sensory systems, perceptual phenomena are thought to depend on higher-level processes. Thus, the study of perception is closely related to the study of cognitive processes such as memory and thinking, discussed in later chapters.

DISTANCE PERCEPTION

Distance perception was a puzzle to early perceptual theorists because they tended to think of what an individual perceives, called the *percept*, as corresponding to the retinal image, which is two-dimensional. Gradually, it was discovered that a visual stimulus also has characteristics that are related to its distance from the observer. These are called *distance cues*. Some of them are present only when a scene is viewed with both eyes (binocular cues); others are present in the stimulus to each eye (monocular cues). Distance perception is complicated by the fact that it depends on a large number of cues.

Binocular cues

Many aspects of vision can be studied by considering phenomena that are registered with one eye only. Individuals with vision in only one eye have most of the visual experiences of individuals using two eyes. They see colors, forms, and space relationships, including three-dimensional configurations. We might suppose that two eyes have evolved merely to provide a spare in case of injury, just as there are two kidneys, although one is enough.

People with vision in both eyes, however, do have advantages over those with vision in one eye. Their total visual field is larger (so that more can be seen at once), and they have the benefit of stereoscopic vision. In *stereoscopic vision*, the two eyes cooperate so that we have a much more precise sense of depth and distance. The device called a *stereoscope* can be used to demonstrate that the cooperation of the two eyes does produce an experience of depth and distance. A card showing two normal photographs, each taken from a slightly different angle, is inserted into the stereoscope. The two photographs, presented one before each eye, combine to form a picture with depth very different from that of a single photograph. The depth appears real, as though the objects pictured have been set up on a stage in three dimensions.

Stereoscopic experience differs from the experience of the third dimension in single, flat pictures because of *binocular disparity*. Since our eyes are separated in our head, the left eye does not get exactly the same view as the right eye; the stereoscopic effect results from the combination of these slightly different pictures into one view. You can easily demonstrate binocular disparity for yourself. With one eye closed, hold a pencil about a foot in front of you and line it up with some vertical edge on the opposite wall. Open that eye and close the other. The pencil will appear to have moved a considerable distance from its original alignment. If you line up the pencil with both eyes open and then close each eye alternately, you can determine which is your dominant eye; if the pencil shifts when you close the right eye, your right eye is dominant (which is usually the case with right-handed individuals).

The facts of stereoscopic vision are clear enough, but just how the process works is not so clear. Because of the way in which the nerve fibers from the eyes are separated in passing to the brain (see Figure 2-10 on page 43), the combination cannot take place in the eyes. Information from the two eyes must somehow be combined in the brain, probably at the level of the visual cortex.

Monocular cues

Although two eyes help us to perceive depth and distance, we are by no means restricted to binocular effects for depth and distance perception. Closing one eye causes the loss of some precision, but there is much left to go on. Artists are able to give depth to a picture because they make use of the many *monocular cues* that tell us the distance of objects.

Figure 5-1 illustrates four types of cues that are used in depth perception.

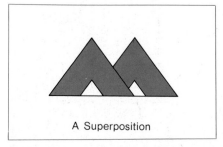

A Superposition

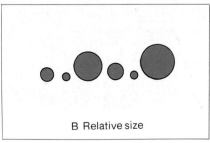

B Relative size

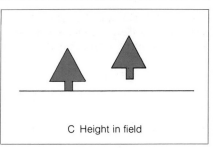

C Height in field

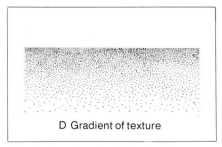

D Gradient of texture

Figure 5-1
Monocular Distance Cues
Because these distance cues do not depend on stereoscopic vision, artists can employ them to give depth to drawings of three-dimensional scenes.

Figure 5-2
Deliberate Misuse of Depth Cues
Engraving entitled *Satire on False Perspective* after William Hogarth (1754). At first glance, the picture appears sensible, but
closer inspection indicates that the scene could not appear as
depicted. Note the many ways in which the artist has misused
depth cues to achieve unusual effects.

Figure 5-3
Paradox of Depth
Engraving by the Dutch artist M.C. Escher, *Waterfall* (1961). The
artist's "false use" of depth cues makes the water appear to move
uphill through a series of "level" channels. This is Escher's solution to the energy crisis.

If one object appears to cut off the view of another, we usually perceive the first
object as nearer (see Figure 5-1A). If there is an array of like objects of different
sizes, the smaller ones are perceived as being in the distance. Even a series of
scattered circles of different sizes may be viewed as spheres of the same size at
varying distances (see Figure 5-1B). Another monocular-depth cue is height in
the visual field. As we look along a flat plane, objects farther away are higher
in our field of view, so that we can create the impression of distance between
objects of the same size by placing them at different heights (see Figure 5-1C).
Even for irregular surfaces, such as a rocky desert or the waving surface of the
ocean, there is a gradient of texture with distance, so that the "grain" becomes
finer as distance becomes greater (see Figure 5-1D).

Just as artists can indicate depth in a picture, so can they distort distance
cues. In the engraving in Figure 5-2, various cues for depth perception have
been deliberately misused to produce an absurd figure. Another example is
Figure 5-3, in which the water at the top of the waterfall is supplied from the
bottom through a series of "level" channels.

The more distance cues that are present, the more precise and accurate distance perception becomes. Little is known about the process by which the visual system integrates the various cues to produce a percept of distance, although some progress is being made (Foley, 1978).

MOTION PERCEPTION

Previously it was thought that motion was perceived when the image of an object moves across the retina successively stimulating different receptors. This cannot be the whole story, however, because the eyes are constantly in motion, as they must be to keep the image from fading (see page 118); yet these eye movements do not generally produce the sensation of object movement.

Gibson (1968) has proposed that the cues for motion perception are present in the environment. We see an object in motion because as it moves it successively covers and uncovers portions of the immobile background. Also, we see objects in motion as changing in space; we see new portions while other portions disappear from view. Thus, it does not matter whether our eyes track the moving object or fixate on the background. Both cases will produce a sensation of object movement. An interesting special case occurs when the entire visual field is in motion. Such a situation produces ambiguous cues that can lead to a false perception. Thus, it is difficult to tell whether your car is rolling backward or is stationary when a truck or bus beside you (which fills the window of your car) pulls forward.

Gibson's theory gives a good account of motion perception in well-illuminated environments, but it does not explain our ability to perceive the motion of a point of light in a completely dark room. It appears that the perceptual system must receive information about the movement of the eyes as they track the point of light and that motion perception depends on this type of information as well as on environmental cues.

Apparent motion

It is also possible to perceive motion without a moving pattern of stimulation. An example of this kind of apparent motion, familiar to us as the basis for motion-picture films, is known as *stroboscopic motion*. This illusion of motion is created when separate stimuli, not in motion, are presented in succession.

When we watch a movie, the screen is actually dark for about half the time. This is because motion pictures are a series of still photographs (frames), each slightly different from the preceding one. The frames are projected one after another onto the screen and each is followed by a brief period of darkness. When the frames are presented rapidly, the pictures blend into smooth motion. However, the speed at which the frames are presented is critical for the experience of motion. In the early days of motion pictures, the frame rate was 16 per second, whereas today the rate is typically 24 per second. This is the reason why very old films appear jerky and disjointed.[1]

A simpler form of stroboscopic motion, known as the *phi phenomenon*, has been studied extensively in the laboratory. One arrangement is diagrammed in

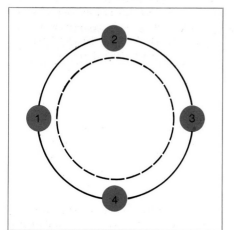

Figure 5-4
Stroboscopic Motion
In a dark room, if one of these four lights blinks on and off, followed shortly by another, there is the illusion of a single light moving from the first position to the second. When all four lights flash on and off in rapid sequence, it appears that a single light is traveling in a circle, but the perceived size of the circle is smaller (indicated by the dashed lines) than would be the case if the lights were actually rotating.

[1]Even at the rate of 24 frames per second, we would detect some flicker in the image. Modern projectors, however, repeat each frame two or three times in quick succession, so that although only 24 *different* frames are on the screen each second, a total of 48 or 72 frames appears in that time.

Figure 5-4. The four lights can be turned on and off in any order. When one light blinks on and off, followed shortly by another, there is the illusion of a single light moving in a straight line from the position of the first to the position of the second. The apparent movement is seen as occurring through the empty space between the two lights. When the four lights flash on and off in a clockwise sequence, you see a rotating circle. However, the apparent diameter of the circle is less than that of a circle that would actually pass through the four lights. Whatever "attracts" the light to the position of the next light operates also to "attract" it toward the center of the circle, thereby making the circle smaller. The two tendencies result in a compromise: a circle too small to pass through the actual position of the lights.

Even though the motion is illusory, we perceive the same structure we would perceive if the motion were real. For example, in Figure 5-5A, the perceived motion is through an arc in the plane of the paper; in Figure 5-5B, the motion is seen in the third dimension, with the figure turning over as it moves from left to right.

Real motion

Examples of apparent motion demonstrate that the perception of motion does not depend *solely* on real physical movement of stimuli in the environment. We can see apparent motion when there is no real motion at all. The perception of real motion is even more complex; it depends on the relationships between objects within the visual field and the interpretation we place on these relationships. Whenever there is movement, the perceptual system must decide what is moving and what is stationary with respect to some frame of reference.

Experiments have shown that when the only information we have about movement is visual, we tend to assume that large objects are stationary and smaller objects are moving. This can be illustrated by viewing a spot of light placed in the center of a luminous rectangular frame. In a dark room, all that will be seen is the spot of light and the frame. If the frame is moved while the spot remains stationary, the subject will perceive the spot as moving. Regardless of which is moved, the spot or the frame, the subject will report that it is the spot that is moving against the background. We experience this type of *induced movement* when we view the moon through a thin cover of moving clouds. In a clear sky, the moon appears to be stationary. When framed by the moving clouds, the moon appears to race across the sky while the clouds appear stationary.

When we are walking or running, the decision about what aspect of our

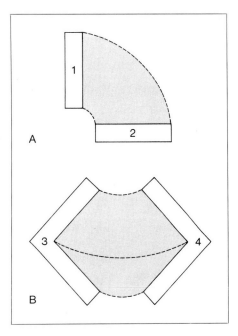

Figure 5-5
Special Cases of Stroboscopic Movement
If a light is flashed on and off behind opening 1 in a screen and a moment later behind opening 2, it looks to an observer as though a single bar of light were moving in an arc between the two positions in the plane of the paper. If a light is flashed on and off behind opening 3 and an instant later behind 4, the motion is seen in the third dimension, as if the figure were flipping over as it moves, like the page of a book being turned.

Illusions of movement are a special problem for astronauts operating in unfamiliar environments.

surroundings is moving is less of a problem because sensations from our limbs inform us of our motion along the ground. When we are moving in a car or plane, our principal source of information is visual. Under these conditions, we are more susceptible to illusions of induced movement. We are not always certain whether it is our car that is moving or the one next to us. Illusions of this kind are so frequent in air travel (particularly during night flights when it is difficult to establish a frame of reference) that pilots learn to trust their instruments rather than their perceptions. Astronauts faced an even greater problem when attempting to land a spacecraft on the moon. In the unfamiliar conditions of space, the size, distance, and velocity of objects may be misjudged when evaluated on the basis of perceptual experiences on earth.

THE WHOLE PERCEPT

When we put together a jigsaw puzzle, the colors and sizes of the many individual pieces look different from the way they look when the puzzle is completed. A detail of an oil painting may appear to be a meaningless collection of daubs of paint. The total impression from organized stimuli has properties not predictable from the parts in isolation.

The theoretical significance of the organization of stimuli in producing a perceptual experience was recognized early by proponents of *Gestalt psychology*, a school of psychology that developed in Germany early in the twentieth century. *Gestalt* is a German word that has no exact English translation, though "form," "configuration," or "pattern" comes close. The word helps to emphasize that the whole affects the way in which the parts are perceived; perception acts to draw the sensory data together into a holistic pattern, or *Gestalt*. For this reason, it is sometimes said that "the whole is different from the sum of its parts"—a favorite principle of Gestalt psychologists.

Max Wertheimer, one of the leaders of the Gestalt school, used stroboscopic motion to illustrate this principle. The experience of motion produced

On the right, is the painting *La Parade* by the French artist Georges Seurat. An enlargement of one part of the picture (shown above) illustrates how it is composed of separate daubs of paint. The total impression is more than the sum of its parts.

by a series of still pictures viewed in quick succession is not present in the pictures individually, he pointed out. Instead, it arises from the relation between them.

Over the years, a large number of perceptual phenomena have been shown to illustrate this Gestalt principle. Most of these phenomena fall into one of three classes: perceptual organization, perceptual constancy, and perceptual illusion.

Perceptual organization

The Gestalt psychologists discovered a number of perceptual phenomena concerned with how one part of a stimulus appears in relation to another. They referred to these as instances of *perceptual organization* and went on to propose a number of laws to explain them. One example of a Gestalt assumption about perceptual organization is the *law of simplicity:* the percept corresponds to the simplest possible interpretation of the stimulus. Among the phenomena of perceptual organization are figure-and-ground effects and perceptual grouping.

FIGURE AND GROUND Geometrical patterns are always perceived as figures against a background and thus appear to have contours and boundaries, just as objects do. Organizing stimuli into *figure* and *ground* is basic to stimulus patterning. Patterns do not have to contain identifiable objects to be structured as figure and ground. Patterns of black and white and many wallpaper designs are perceived as figure-ground relationships, even though the figure and ground may reverse from one moment to the next. In Figure 5-6, note that the part you see as *figure* seems more solid and well defined and appears in front of the background, even though you know it is printed on the surface of the page. You seem to look through the spaces in and around the figure to a uniform background, whether the background is the light or dark color. Figure 5-8 shows somewhat different kinds of reversible figure-ground effects.

We can perceive figure-ground relationships through senses other than vision. For example, we may hear the song of a bird against the background of outdoor noises or the melody played by a violin against the harmonies of the rest of the orchestra. Some of the factors that determine what is perceived as figure against ground will be considered later in the discussion of selective attention.

PERCEPTUAL GROUPING Even simple patterns of lines and dots fall into ordered relationships when we look at them. In the top part of Figure 5-7, we tend to see three *pairs* of lines, with an *extra* line at the right. But notice that we could have seen three pairs beginning at the right with an extra line at the left. The slight modification in the lines in the lower part of the figure causes us to do just that. This tendency to *structure* what we see is very compelling; what we see in figures seems to be forced on us by the patterns of stimulation. The properties of wholes affect the ways in which parts are perceived. This illustrates the idea of Gestalt psychology that the whole is different from the sum of its parts.

Perceptual constancies

If you look around the room and ask yourself what you see, the answer is likely to be "a room full of objects" or "a room full of people and objects." Or you may pick out specific people or objects. But you are not likely to report that you see

Figure 5-6
Reversible Figure and Ground
The reversible goblet is a demonstration of a figure-ground reversal. Note that either the light portion (the goblet) or the dark portion (two profiles) can be perceived as a figure against a background.

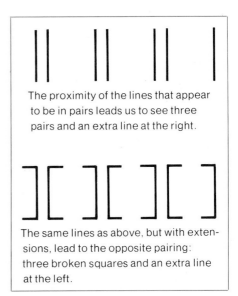

The proximity of the lines that appear to be in pairs leads us to see three pairs and an extra line at the right.

The same lines as above, but with extensions, lead to the opposite pairing: three broken squares and an extra line at the left.

Figure 5-7
Patterning and Perceptual Grouping

Figure 5-8
The Slave Market with Disappearing Bust of Voltaire
In the center of this painting by Salvador Dali is a reversible figure. Two nuns standing in an archway reverse to form a bust of Voltaire.

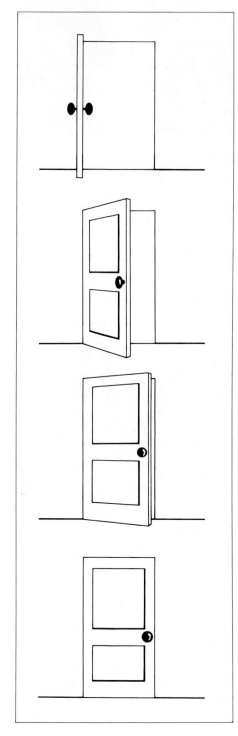

Shape Constancy
The various retinal images from an opening door are quite different, and yet we perceive a rectangular door.

a mosaic of light and shadow. We tend to perceive *things* rather than the *sensory features* that describe them. Detached sensory features ("blueness," "square-ness," or "softness") can be perceived, but they are usually perceived as the qualities of objects. You are aware of the blue flowers or the square box or the soft pillow—not "blueness," "squareness," or "softness."

Our perceptual experiences are not isolated; they build a world of identifiable things. Objects endure; so we meet the same object over and over. We usually perceive a familiar object as permanent and stable regardless of light conditions, the position from which we see it, or its distance from us. The tendency to see a familiar object as having a consistent shade (white to black) regardless of the light conditions is called *lightness constancy,* and the tendency to see its color as stable is called *color constancy.* The tendency to see an object's shape as unchanging regardless of the viewing angle is called *shape constancy.* The tendency to see an object as the same size regardless of distance is called *size constancy.* Finally, the tendency to see an object retaining its position in space when we move about is known as *location constancy.* The word *constancy* is an exaggeration, but it dramatizes our relatively stable perceptions of objects.

LIGHTNESS AND COLOR CONSTANCY   Black velvet looks just as black to us in sunlight as in shadow, even though it reflects more light in the sunlight. We refer to this fact as *lightness constancy.* Although the effect holds under ordinary circumstances, a change in the surroundings can destroy it. Attach the black velvet to a white board and throw a bright light on both, and the velvet still looks black. But now place an opaque screen between you and the velvet, with a small opening in the screen so that you can see only a small patch of the velvet (see Figure 5-9). This screen (called a *reduction screen*) reduces what you see to the actual light reflected from the velvet, independent of the surroundings. Now the velvet looks white because the light that reaches your eye through the reduction screen is brighter than the screen itself. When we perceive objects in natural settings, several objects are usually visible. Lightness constancy depends on the relations among the intensities of light reflected from the different objects.

Color constancy shows a similar dependence on the presence of a heterogeneous field. It fails when only a single-colored region is seen. For example, if you look at a ripe tomato through a tube that obscures the surroundings and the nature of the object, the tomato will appear blue or green or some other color, depending on the wavelengths of light reflected from it. If we recognize what something is, our memory for its color contributes to color constancy. Even under optimal conditions, color constancy can be far from perfect. Shoppers sometimes learn this the hard way by picking colors under store lighting conditions only to discover later that their purchases do not look the same at home. Color constancy is not completely understood, but a major influence is the relation between the light reflected from an object and the light reflected from surrounding surfaces.

SHAPE AND SIZE CONSTANCY   When a door swings toward us, its shape (projected on the retina) goes through a series of changes. The door's rectangular shape becomes a trapezoid, with the edge toward us looking wider than the hinged edge; then the trapezoid grows thinner, until all that is projected on the retina is a vertical line the thickness of the door. We can readily distinguish these changes, but our psychological experience is of an unchanging door swinging on its hinges. The fact that the door's shape does not seem to change is an example of *shape constancy*.

As an object is moved farther away, we tend to see it as more or less unchanging in size. This is referred to as *size constancy*. Hold a quarter a foot in front of your eyes and then move it out to arm's length. Does it appear to get smaller? Not noticeably so. Yet the retinal image of the quarter when it is 12 inches away is twice the size of the retinal image of the quarter when it is 24 inches from the eye (see Figure 5-10). We certainly do not perceive it as becoming half its size as we move it to arm's length.

Like the other constancies, size constancy is not perfect. Very distant objects appear to be smaller than the same objects close up, as anyone who has looked down from an airplane in flight knows. For near objects, constancy becomes imperfect as distance cues are eliminated. For example, the moving

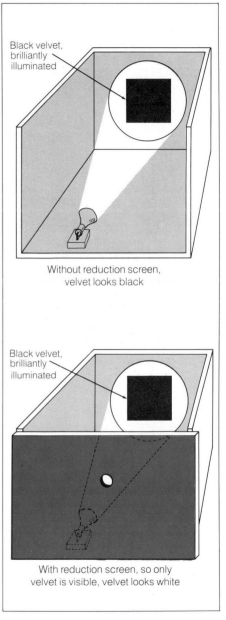

Without reduction screen, velvet looks black

With reduction screen, so only velvet is visible, velvet looks white

Figure 5-9
Effects of Surroundings on Lightness Constancy
Even though the square of velvet is brilliantly illuminated, it still looks black, provided the illuminated white background is also visible. However, when only the velvet is visible through the reduction screen, it looks white, even though the illumination on it is the same.

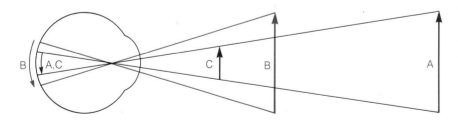

Figure 5-10
Object Size and Retinal Image
This figure illustrates the geometric relationship between the physical size of an object and the size of its projection on the retina. Arrow A and arrow B represent objects of the same size, but one is twice as far from the eye's lens as the other. As a result, the image projected on the retina by A is approximately half as large as that projected by B. The object represented by arrow C is smaller than A but closer to the eye; note that arrows A and C produce retinal images of the same size.

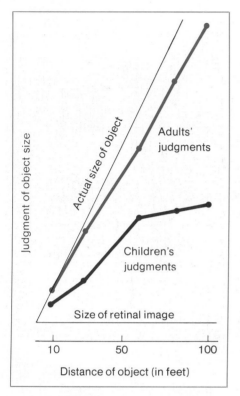

Figure 5-11
Size Perception and Age
Adults and 8-year-old children viewed objects at distances ranging from 10 to 100 feet. The physical sizes of the objects were adjusted at the various distances so that the image projected on the retina was always the same size. The horizontal line indicates the size of the retinal image (which is constant for all distances), and the diagonal line indicates the size of the physical object (which increases with distance). Note that adults make fairly accurate size judgments no matter how distant the object. The judgments of children, however, appear to be increasingly influenced by the size of the retinal image as the object is placed farther away. (Zeigler and Leibowitz, 1957)

quarter described above appears to change more in size if it is viewed with only one eye than it does when binocular distance cues are present. The fewer distance cues we have, the more likely we are to underestimate the size of a distant object. In the absence of distance cues, there is some constancy for familiar objects, but familiarity alone will not produce perfect constancy.

Size constancy develops as the result of experience. Figure 5-11 shows the results of an experiment comparing the performance of 8-year-olds and adults in judging the size of objects (of constant retinal image size) at different distances. At a distance of 10 feet, both children and adults make accurate size judgments. As distance increases, the children judge the size of the object to increase somewhat, but at a much lower rate than the physical size of the object does. The adults' judgments of size, on the other hand, remain quite accurate as distance increases.

The effect of limited experience on the development of size constancy is further illustrated by an incident concerning a Pygmy who was taken for the first time from his home in the forest (where distance viewing is naturally obstructed by trees and foliage) into open country. When he spotted a herd of buffalo grazing several miles away, he thought they were "insects." He refused to believe that they were buffalo and actually larger in size than the forest buffalo with which he was familiar. As he approached the animals, he became alarmed because they appeared to be growing in size; he suspected that he was the victim of some sort of magic. Later, when he saw a boat with several men in it sailing some distance from the shore, he perceived it as a scrap of wood floating on the water. Just as a small child's limited experience causes errors in perceptions, the Pygmy's inexperience with distance viewing created similar misperceptions (Turnbull, 1961).

LOCATION CONSTANCY   Despite the fact that a myriad of changing impressions strike the retina as we move, we perceive objects in a setting that remains essentially fixed—*location constancy*. We take location constancy for granted, but unusual conditions show that it, too, depends on past experience.

Experiments that use special glasses to rearrange the visual environment demonstrate the role of learning in location constancy. In a classic study conducted more than 85 years ago, Stratton fitted himself with lenses that not only inverted the visual field, so that he saw the world upside down, but also reversed it, so that objects perceived on the left were actually on the right, and vice versa. Stratton reports that at first the world seemed to lose its stability:

> When I moved my head or body so that my sight swept over the scene, the movement was not felt to be solely in the observer, as in normal vision, but was referred both to the observer and to objects beyond. . . . I did not feel as if I were visually ranging over a set of motionless objects, but the whole field of things swept and swung before my eyes. (Stratton, 1897, p. 342)

After a few days, he began to regain some location constancy, and the swirling sensation decreased. Another sign of restored location constancy was that he was again able to hear a fire crackle in the fireplace where he saw it, a harmony of location that at first he had lost because only his eyes—and not his ears—were perceiving in reverse. Although the distortion provided by the lenses made even the simplest task difficult, Stratton adjusted as the experiment progressed. He bumped into objects less frequently and was able to perform such tasks as washing and eating, which initially had been very difficult. When he finally removed the glasses, he again needed time to adjust before he regained his old visual-motor habits. Since then, similar experiments have been conducted with comparable results. Human subjects show a remarkable ability to regain location constancy in a visually rearranged world (Welch, 1978).

Perceptual illusions

An *illusion* is a percept that is erroneous in that it differs from the state of affairs described by physical science with the aid of its measuring instruments. Some illusions, such as the break we see in a stick where it enters water or the distorted images we see in fun-house mirrors, are *physical:* they are due to distortion in the stimulus reaching our receptors. Other illusions are *perceptual* in that they arise in our perceptual systems. These are the illusions that are of interest in psychology.

Geometrical illusions constitute one very large class of illusions that has received considerable attention. These are line drawings in which some aspect is perceptually distorted. Some illusions are based on relative size (see Figure 5-12A). Others may be understood if we suppose the figures to be projected in the third dimension (see Figures 5-12B through E and 5-13). If the horizontal lines in B were actually drawn on the surface of a solid double cone or if those in C were placed on a system of wires meeting at the horizon, they would have

Figure 5-13
Perspective and the Ponzo Illusion
The two rectangles superimposed on the photograph are precisely the same size. However, because we know that the railroad ties are all the same length, the rectangle that is farther away is unconsciously enlarged. In fact, if the rectangles were real objects lying between the tracks, we would correctly judge the more distant one to be larger.

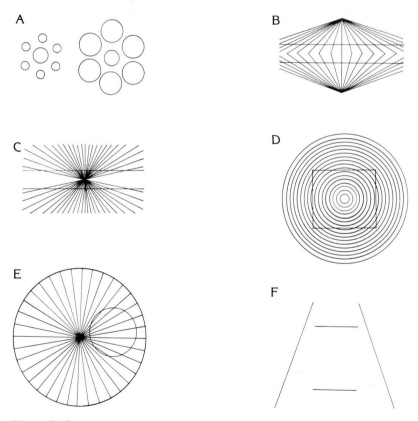

Figure 5-12
Some Geometrical Illusions
A is an illusion based on relative size. The center circles are the same size, but the one to the left looks larger. B, C, D, E are illusions based on intersecting lines. The horizontal lines in B and C are parallel. The inscribed figures in D and E are perfectly symmetrical. F is the Ponzo illusion. The two horizontal lines are the same length, but the upper one appears longer.

Figure 5-14
Emmert's Experiment
Hold the book at normal reading distance under good light. Fixate the cross in the center of the figure for about 1 minute. Then look at a distant wall. You will see an afterimage of the two circles that appears larger than the stimulus. Then look at a piece of paper held close to your face. Now the afterimage will appear smaller than the stimulus. If the afterimage fades, blinking can sometimes restore it.

Early writers on perception, such as Bishop Berkeley, who published an essay on the subject in 1709, held that perception consists of experiencing many sensations simultaneously while at the same time remembering other sensations that had previously been associated with these. Constancies and illusions, however, show that the percept is very different from the sum of sensations evoked by each of its parts. Unlike some of the simpler phenomena discussed in Chapter 4, the perception of size, shape, and location (whether veridical or illusory) depends on at least two stimulus variables and often more. Understanding these more complex phenomena requires us to specify (1) how the percept is related to the stimulus variables that influence it, and (2) what goes on in the head to bring about the percept. Current work on the first issue (the relationship between stimulus variables and percept) may best be illustrated by considering size perception.

Two variables that have long been recognized as important in size perception are the size of the retinal image and perceived distance. Emmert (1881) was able to separate the effects of these variables by studying the perceived size of afterimages. An afterimage is produced by fatiguing the visual cells in one area of the retina (by staring fixedly at an object). The fatigued area of the retina remains fixed in size, but the perceived size of the afterimage varies, depending on the distance of the surface one looks at. Thus, the afterimage seems larger when one looks at a distant background and smaller against a nearby background. Emmert's experiment is easy to do (see Figure 5-14). Perform the experiment before reading on.

On the basis of observations like this, Emmert proposed that the perceived size of an afterimage is proportional to its distance (Emmert's law). Later this was generalized into the *size-distance invariance principle*, which states that the ratio of perceived size, S', to perceived distance, D', is equal to the visual angle. The principle is illustrated in Figure 5-15.

The principle may be described in equation form as follows:

$$\frac{S'}{D'} = \theta \quad \text{or} \quad S' = \theta \times D'$$

The principle explains size constancy in the following way. When the distance to an object increases, its visual angle decreases. But if distance cues are present, perceived distance will increase. Thus, the product of $\theta \times D'$ will remain approximately constant and so will perceived size.

The size-distance invariance principle seems to be fundamental to understanding a number of illusions of size. A good example is the moon illusion. This refers to the observation that the moon near the horizon looks about 50 percent larger than the moon at the zenith, even though both subtend the same visual angle. The perceived distance of the horizon is judged to be farther than the zenith by approximately the same amount.

Although the size-distance invariance principle can explain many phenomena of perceived size, it does not explain all. For example, some people report that the horizon moon looks larger *and nearer* than the zenith moon. According to the principle, when it looks larger, it should look farther away. Similarly, geometrical illusion figures are not usually perceived as having depth even though they contain distance cues. The distance cues appear to influence perceived size without producing a corresponding effect on perceived distance.

Understanding Constancy and Illusion

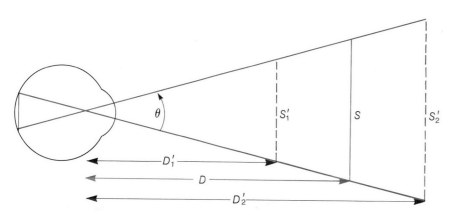

Figure 5-15
Size-Distance Invariance Principle
The angle θ is called the visual angle. It is proportional to the retinal image size. Suppose the object's true size is S and its true distance is D. If the observer believes that the object is at D_1', its perceived size will be S_1'. If the observer believes that the object is at D_2', its perceived size will be S_2'.

Other invariance principles have been proposed to explain constancies and illusions of shapes, lightness and color, and location. The approach shows a great deal of promise, but it is likely that invariances in relations among more than two variables will be needed to account for many of these percepts.

Let us now consider the second part of the problem of understanding constancies and illusions—what goes on in the perceiver's head so that a particular relation among variables gives rise to a particular percept. Helmholtz, whose theory of color vision was discussed in Chapter 4, proposed that the percept is arrived at by a process of inference from the sensations evoked by the different variables. In the case of size perception, this means that the perceiver senses the retinal image size and the distance and from the two infers the object's size. It is as if the perceiver inserts the values of D' and θ in the above equation and solves for S'. Since perception usually happens very fast and perceivers have no awareness of either the original sen-

sations or the process of inference, Helmholtz referred to *unconscious inference* from unnoticed sensations.

Without taking issue with Helmholtz's analysis, it is possible to imagine biological bases for this process of inference. Given the discovery of feature detectors (see pages 119–20), it is natural to ask if there might be higher-level detectors tuned not to individual features but to relations among features. Although this idea has much appeal, little progress has been made thus far in discovering the kinds of invariance detectors needed to explain the constancies. An encouraging exception is the constancy of location during eye movement. Recording in an area of the brain that mediates responses to visual stimuli (the superior colliculus), Robinson and Wurtz (1976) found cells that respond when a bar is moved across the retina, but not when the retina moves across the bar. It would appear that the cells may be sensitive to the relationship between an image-movement signal and an eye-movement signal.

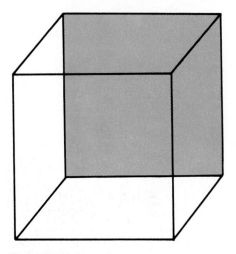

Figure 5-16
Necker Cube

An illusion devised in 1832 by the Swiss naturalist L.A. Necker. Note that the tinted surface can appear as either the front or the rear surface of a transparent cube.

to be curved to be seen as parallel. But because we tend to view these figures as though they were three-dimensional scenes drawn in perspective, we see the parallel lines as curved. Similarly, the backgrounds in illusions D and E can be viewed as three-dimensional (either concave or convex), thereby distorting the square and circle superimposed on them.

Figure 5-12F, the Ponzo illusion, can be better understood if we look at the photograph in Figure 5-13. The illusion in Figure 5-12F can be thought of as a flat projection of three-dimensional space, with the vertical lines converging in the distance, as in the picture of the railroad tracks. We know from experience that the distant railroad ties are the same size as the near ones, even though the retinal image they give is much smaller. If real objects were lying between the tracks, the one represented by the upper, colored rectangle in the picture would be correctly perceived as more distant and larger.

The fact that the Ponzo illusion becomes greater from childhood to adulthood suggests that the illusion depends on learning to use perspective cues in two-dimensional drawings (Parrish, Lundy, and Leibowitz, 1968).

COGNITIVE PROCESSES IN PERCEPTION

Figure 5-16 shows a classic reversible figure—the Necker cube. As you study the figure, your perception of it will change. You will find that the tinted surface sometimes appears as the front of the figure and sometimes as the back. Once you have seen the cube change perspective, it will jump back and forth between the two perspectives without any effort on your part. In fact, you will probably find it impossible to maintain a steady percept of only one aspect.

Active nature of perception

PERCEPTUAL HYPOTHESES   Reversible figures like the Necker cube indicate that our perceptions are not a static mirroring of visual stimuli. Perceiving can be thought of as a search for the best interpretation of sensory information, based on our knowledge of objects. Cognitive psychologists, building on some of the earlier ideas of the Gestaltists, argue that the percept is a *hypothesis* suggested by the sensory data. The pattern of the Necker cube contains no clue as to which of two alternative hypotheses is correct, so the perceptual system entertains, or tests, first one and then the other hypothesis and never settles on an answer. The problem arises because the Necker cube is a three-dimensional object represented on a two-dimensional surface. If we were to see it in three-dimensional form, there would be many cues to tell us which hypothesis to choose (Gregory, 1970, 1981).

The notion of *hypothesis testing* emphasizes the active nature of perception. The perceptual system does not passively receive inputs but searches for the percept that is most consistent with the sensory data. In most situations, there is only one reasonable interpretation of the sensory data, and the search for the correct percept proceeds so quickly and automatically that we are unaware of it. Only under unusual conditions, as when we view ambiguous figures, does the hypothesis-testing nature of perception become apparent.

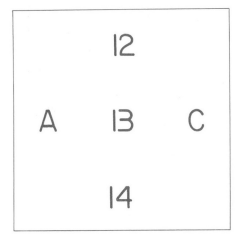

Figure 5-17
Effect of Context on Perception

The figure in the center is ambiguous, and the way we see it depends on whether we look from left to right or from top to bottom.

CONTEXT AND EXPERIENCE   The hypotheses tested and the percepts formed depend not only on the features of the object but also on the *context* within which the object is viewed. Figure 5-17 illustrates the role of context in perception. The center of the figure can be seen as either the letter B or the number 13, depending on the context in which it appears. Similarly, *past experience* influences the perceptual hypotheses we form when we see something for the first time. Look at the ambiguous drawing of the young woman/old woman in Figure 5-18. On first viewing, about 65 percent of the people report seeing an attractive young woman and 35 percent see an old woman. But if we first show a group of subjects a set of unambiguous pictures all depicting young women and then show them the ambiguous picture, they almost always see it as a young woman. The reverse can be demonstrated by first showing subjects a set of pictures all showing old women. Textbooks on perception are filled with examples demonstrating that the same stimulus can give rise to different percepts, depending on the context in which it is observed and the past experience of the observer.

Analysis-by-synthesis

A theory that views perception as an active, hypothesis-testing process—influenced by context and past experience—has been called *analysis-by-synthesis* (Neisser, 1976). According to this theory, the perceiver uses *features* of the object, its context, and past experiences to make a "best guess" about what is seen. The term "analysis-by-synthesis" implies that the perceiver "analyzes" the object into features and then uses these features to "synthesize" (or construct) a percept that best fits all of the information—the sensory input, the context, and past experience.

Analysis-by-synthesis assumes that the observer has stored in memory a *schema* for each of the stimuli that he or she has experienced in the past. The notion of a schema was encountered in Chapters 3 and 4 (see pages 74 and 121); for this discussion it can be regarded as a list of features stored in a person's memory that characterize a given stimulus. When a stimulus is encountered, a two-stage process is activated (see Figure 5-19). First, a hypothesis—or guess—is made about the identity of the stimulus, based on the context in which it is presented and the past experiences and expectations of the observer. The observer then retrieves from memory the schema associated with the "guessed" stimulus.

In the second stage, the observer extracts features from the presented stimulus and tries to match them with the schema retrieved from memory. If a match occurs, the process is over and the stimulus has been recognized. If a match does not occur, the observer makes a new guess and starts the process again. This cycle continues until a schema is retrieved that matches the features of the presented stimulus, confirming the hypothesis being evaluated.

The theory of analysis-by-synthesis views perception as an *active cognitive process* of checking one hypothesis after another until one is found that matches with reality. This view is very different from *static* approaches proposing that physical features are extracted in a mechanistic way from the stimulus input—independent of context—and only then processed for recognition. Some aspects of perception may proceed in a mechanistic fashion, but when dealing with complicated percepts, a hypothesis-testing approach seems necessary.

What we perceive is not a bundle of physical features impacting on the sensory system but things that have *meaning* for us. When the schema for a stimulus input is retrieved from memory, the stimulus takes on a fuller meaning. That meaning is based on our memory for the stimulus, which associates it with past events and experiences. The meaning of a stimulus is not in the stimulus itself but is provided by the perceiver.

Figure 5-18
Ambiguous Stimulus
An ambiguous drawing that can be seen either as a pretty young woman or as an unattractive old woman.

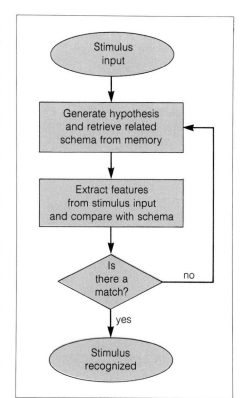

Figure 5-19
Analysis-By-Synthesis
The recognition of a stimulus can be seen as an active process of generating and testing hypotheses.

Attention

Although many different stimuli reach us at the same time, we are sharply limited in what we are able to perceive in any one moment. What we do perceive depends not only on the stimuli but also on cognitive processes that reflect our interests, goals, and expectations at that moment. This perceptual focusing is called *attention*.

As you sit reading, stop for a moment, close your eyes, and attend to the various stimuli affecting you. Notice, for example, the tightness of your left shoe, the pressure of clothing on your shoulders, the sounds coming from outside the room. We are constantly bombarded by stimuli to which we do not attend. In fact, our brains would be hopelessly overloaded if we had to attend to every stimulus present in our environment. Somehow, our brains select those stimuli that are pertinent and ignore the others, until a change in a particular stimulus makes it important for us to notice it.

SELECTIVE ATTENTION   There is evidence, however, that even when we are not actively attending to certain stimuli, they still register at least momentarily in our perceptual system—although we may not recognize them. Consider what takes place during a cocktail party. Out of the complex mixture of sounds generated by the many voices, you are able to listen to one voice. Although you may think you are not attending to the other voices, let someone in the far corner of the room mention your name, and you are immediately aware of it. Apparently the nervous system monitors the other voices for relevant stimuli without your being aware of such activity.

The cocktail party situation raises two interesting questions: (1) How are we able to focus attention on one conversation out of the many that surround us? (2) How much do we register of the conversations to which we are not attending?

Some of the cues that enable us to concentrate on one voice in a babel of many are the direction of sound, lip movements of the speaker, and the particular voice characteristics of the speaker (whether the voice is male or female, its speed, and its intonation). Even if all these cues are eliminated (by recording two messages spoken by the same speaker and playing them simultaneously), it is still possible to distinguish the messages. The task is a difficult one that requires intense concentration, but most subjects can separate the two messages, apparently by relying on the grammatical and semantic content of the spoken material for cues. In the absence of appropriate grammatical cues, however, the task of separating two simultaneous messages by the same speaker becomes impossible.

Information about how much we register from conversations to which we are not attending is provided by an experimental situation similar to the cocktail party. Two different spoken messages are presented to the subject by means of earphones, one to the right ear and the other to the left. The subject has no difficulty in listening to either message at will; he or she can reject the unwanted one or switch attention back and forth from one speech to the other. If asked to repeat aloud the speech presented to one ear, the subject can do it fairly well even though the message is continuous. The subject's words are slightly delayed behind those of the message being repeated, and the voice tends to have a monotonous noninflective quality. At the end of the passage, the subject may have little idea of what it was all about, particularly if the material is difficult. What about the message to which the subject was not attending? How much information is assimilated via the unattended ear? The subject usually can recall nothing of the verbal content of the unattended message. The subject is aware of certain general characteristics, whether the message was speech or a pure tone, whether the voice was male or female, and whether his or her own name was mentioned in the message.

If the subject is interrupted while repeating the message to the attending ear and asked quickly what was just presented to the other ear, there does appear to be some temporary memory for the message not attended to. This is similar to the situation in which someone to whom you are not listening asks you a question; your immediate response is "What did you say?"—but before the question is repeated, you suddenly realize what was asked.

DETERMINERS OF STIMULUS SELECTION   Studies of this kind have led to the conclusion that the nervous system must have some kind of register where incoming sensory information is temporarily stored in a rather crude and un-analyzed form. Of all the stimuli that bombard our senses, only those that our higher mental processes tell us are relevant at the moment will be selected for attention. Some sort of attention mechanism selects for further processing those sensory inputs that seem most important or pertinent. Certain sensory inputs (such as the sound of one's name) can be expected to have consistently high levels of pertinence but most will fluctuate, depending on ongoing events. (Norman, 1976).

What factors determine which of many competing stimuli will be selected for attention? Some physical characteristics of the stimulus are important: *intensity, size, contrast*, and *movement*. Certain internal variables, such as motives, expectations, and interests also determine which stimulus attracts attention. The naturalist hears sounds in the woods that the ordinary picnicker misses. A mother hears her baby's cry above the conversation in a room full of people. These two illustrations represent abiding interests. Sometimes momentary interest controls attention. When you leaf through a book looking for a particular diagram, only pages with illustrations cause you to hesitate. Physical states such as hunger and emotional states, especially mood, may also affect attention. When we are in a hostile mood, we notice personal comments that we might not pay attention to when we are in a more friendly mood.

External factors as well as internal variables (such as motives and interests) determine which stimuli will attract our attention.

PHYSIOLOGICAL CORRELATES OF ATTENTION When a stimulus attracts our attention, we usually perform certain body movements that enhance reception. If it is a visual stimulus, we turn our head and eyes so that the image falls on the fovea. Our pupils dilate momentarily to allow more light to enter the eye, and the lens muscles work to bring the image clearly into focus. If the stimulus is a faint auditory signal, we may cup our hands behind our ears or turn one ear in the direction of the sound, keeping the rest of our body very still so as to enhance reception. These body movements are accompanied by certain physiological changes. The physiological reactions that occur in response to stimulus changes in the environment form such a consistent pattern that they have been called the *orienting reflex*, and they have been studied extensively by psychologists.

The orienting reflex occurs in both humans and animals in response to even minimal changes in the stimulus environment. In addition to the body movements just mentioned, it includes dilation of the blood vessels in the head, constriction of the peripheral blood vessels, certain changes in the gross electrical responses of the brain (EEG), and changes in muscle tone, heart rate, and respiration. These responses serve two functions: (1) they facilitate the reception of stimulation, and (2) they prepare the organism for a quick response in case action is needed. We can see why such a reflex is valuable for self-preservation.

The facilitating effect of the orienting reflex on sensory reception can be demonstrated in the laboratory. The arousal of the reflex by a loud tone increases visual sensitivity, making it possible for the subject to see a light that was too faint to be detected earlier. The orienting reflex habituates over time, however. With repeated presentation of the sound, the reflex gradually diminishes; the visual threshold returns to its original level, and the same light intensity no longer evokes a response. Any change in the tone, or the introduction of a new stimulus, will reactivate the orienting reflex to its original strength (Sokolov, 1976).

EYE MOVEMENTS AND READING

Fixations and saccades

When we watch the eyes of an individual inspecting a picture or object, it is evident that they are not stationary but engaged in a scanning process. Scanning is not a smooth, continuous motion, however. Rather, the eyes are still for a brief period, then jump to another position, are still for another brief period, then jump again, are still again, and so on. The periods during which the eyes are still are called *fixations,* and the quick, almost instantaneous movements between fixations are called *saccades* ("saccade" is French for "jump"). There are a number of techniques for tracking eye movements. The simplest method is to monitor the eyes with a TV camera in such a way that what the eye is gazing at is reflected onto the cornea of the eye; thus superimposed on the TV picture of the eye is a reflected picture of the object being inspected. From such a superimposed image, the point on the object where the eye is fixated can be accurately determined. This procedure provides an unobtrusive method for monitoring eye movements, and the TV tape can be replayed at a slow speed to measure the duration of each fixation.

As noted in the previous chapter, the fovea has the best resolution, and visual acuity diminishes rapidly as we move to the periphery of the retina. The eye movements used in scanning a picture ensure that different parts of the

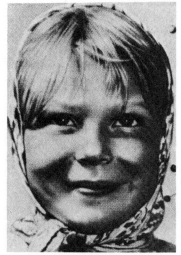

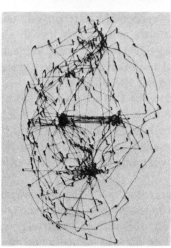

Eye Movements in Perception
Below the picture of the young girl is a record of the eye movements made by a subject inspecting the picture for 3 minutes. Note that most of the eye fixations are directed at the most visually informative areas. (After Yarbus, 1967)

picture will fall on the fovea so that all its details can be seen. Further, research suggests that perception can occur only during the fixation period and not during the saccadic movement. Thus, the process of executing a series of eye fixations is like assembling a picture from a set of snapshots—with each snapshot in sharp focus in its center area.

Reading

Reading is a complex skill, and like all skills, it improves in both precision and speed with practice. Monitoring eye movements during reading tells us a great deal about the process. As we read a line of print, our eyes move from one fixation point to the next in left to right order; occasionally our eyes will move backwards, or *regress*, to reread something, but for a good reader such regressions are infrequent. The rate at which we read depends on the difficulty of the material and on our intentions. If the text is difficult, we may fixate on almost every word, but skimming the material may require only one or two fixations per sentence.

Figure 5-20 presents some eye movement data from an experiment by Just and Carpenter (1980). Their subjects read a series of passages concerned with fairly difficult scientific material; the figure presents the protocol of one subject reading two sentences from such a passage. Consecutive fixations on the same word have been aggregated into units called *gazes*. Above the words in the figure, the gazes have been numbered in sequence and the duration of each gaze is indicated. Duration is recorded in milliseconds (1000 msec to a second).

Note, first of all, that almost every word is fixated. The words that are not fixated tend to be short function words like *of*, *a*, and *the*. This is typically the case when a reader is encountering new text materials that are fairly difficult to comprehend. When a good reader is given familiar material or simple texts like children's stories, he or she may average several words per eye fixation. Similarly, readers may make even fewer eye fixations if they are intentionally skimming the material just to get its gist.

Further inspection of Figure 5-20 indicates that the duration of fixations varies considerably from word to word. For example, in this protocol the word *flywheel* was fixated for over a second on each of its two appearances; no other word was inspected for so long. Longer fixations are due to longer processing times for words that are unfamiliar to the reader or have special thematic importance. Fixations at the end of a sentence also tend to be longer, indicating that the reader is taking time to integrate information from the whole sentence.

The data on eye movements presented here typify the normal adult reader. Of course, individuals differ in their reading speeds, but the differences are not primarily due to differences in the number of fixations a reader makes. Most words are fixated by all readers if the material is new and reasonably difficult. Systematic research on reading in general and eye movements in particular

1	2	3	4	5	6	7	8	9	1	2		
1566	267	400	83	267	617	767	450	450	400	616		
Flywheels	are	one	of the	oldest	mechanical	devices	known	to	man.	Every	internal-	

3	5	4	6	7	8	9	10	11	12	13
517	684	250	317	617	1116	367	467	483	450	383
combustion	engine	contains	a	small	flywheel	that	converts	the jerky	motion	of	the	pistons	into the

14	15	16	17	18	19	20	21
284	383	317	283	533	50	366	566
smooth	flow	of	energy	that	powers	the	drive	shaft.

Figure 5-20
Eye Fixations in Reading
Eye fixations of a college student reading a scientific passage. A gaze is the total time spent fixating a word or group of words. Gazes within each sentence are sequentially numbered above the fixated words with the durations in milliseconds indicated below the sequence number. Note that there is only one regress—namely, from fixation 4 to 5 in the second sentence. (After Just and Carpenter, 1980)

A number of theories of reading have been proposed in recent years. All of them are fairly complicated, requiring a familiarity not only with ideas about perception but also with ideas about memory and language, which will be presented later (Chapters 8 and 9). Nevertheless, it will prove instructive to outline at least one such theory of reading. Some terms will be used in our discussion that are not fully explained, but the gist of the work should be evident.

The theory to be discussed originated with Just and Carpenter (1980) and is principally concerned with explaining eye-movement data of the sort presented in Figure 5-20. The components of the theory are schematically presented in Figure 5-21; on the left side of the figure is a column of boxes representing the sequence of processes executed by the reader as each word of a text is encountered. The reader's knowledge (including knowledge about spelling, grammar, and the meaning of words) is stored in the reader's *long-term memory*—represented by the large box on the right. The middle box, *short-term memory*, is a temporary storage device and serves to mediate between long-term memory and the execution of the various reading processes. Two key assumptions of the theory are (1) that the reader processes each content word of a

text as it is encountered and (2) that the eyes remain fixated on a word as long as it is being processed.

Let us begin our analysis of the theory by considering the boxes on the left. As indicated in the top box, the reading process begins when the eyes move to a new word in the text. Immediately, a process is initiated to extract a list of physical features from the appearance of the printed word (page 121). This feature list then serves as a code for finding the mental representation of the word in the reader's long-term memory (that is, for gaining access to that part of long-term memory where information about words is stored, called the *lexicon*). Lexical access activates the word in long-term memory that, in turn, provides information about the word's meaning and its relationship to other words in the sentence. As a sentence is read, a mental representation of its meaning is being formed in short-term memory. The fifth box in the column indicates that as each word is encountered its content must be integrated with that evolving mental representation in short-term memory. Finally, the bottom box refers to a step that occurs only at the end of a sentence; additional time is required at this point to clarify ambiguities that were not resolved while the sentence was being read and to com-

plete the reader's mental representation of the meaning of the sentence.

The theory makes assumptions about how each of these processes works and the time required to execute it. For example, it is assumed that the time required for encoding and lexical access is a function of the word's frequency of use in the English language. Given these assumptions, we can then predict eye-movement data of the sort shown in Figure 5-20. The predictions of the theory are in excellent agreement with actual data, and consequently we can have some confidence in the validity of the theory's assumptions.

The assumption that the reader processes each content word of a text as it is encountered is quite different from the view that a group of words (or even a whole phrase) is processed as a unit. Not too many years ago, it was believed that readers did in fact process words in *parallel* (as groups) rather than *serially* (one at a time). This misunderstanding was based on some early research on eye movements in reading; the research proved to be misleading because the equipment for measuring eye movements in those days was cumbersome and it was difficult to make observations except under constrained and artificial conditions. Educators were greatly influenced by the early eye-movement re-

dates back to the turn of the century, but only in the last decade have psychologists been able to formulate theories of reading that are sophisticated enough to explain eye movements and how material is comprehended as it is read. This field of research is alive with important new work, and much progress can be anticipated in the years ahead.

Speed reading

As noted above, when we skim a text, we make fewer eye fixations than when we read carefully. This observation is the basis for many speed-reading courses that claim to increase both reading speed and comprehension; the idea behind these courses is to train readers to make fewer eye fixations and take in several

Theories of Reading

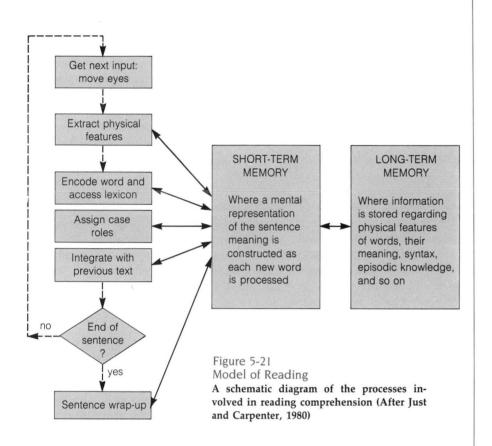

Figure 5-21
Model of Reading
A schematic diagram of the processes involved in reading comprehension (After Just and Carpenter, 1980)

search, and unfortunately some features of the reading curricula used in schools today—as well as in speed-reading courses—still reflect that fact. Current psychological research on the reading process has important implications that should guide the development of improved curricula for reading instruction.

words or a whole phrase in each fixation. Some groups even argue that one can register a whole line of printed text in a single fixation and thus read straight from the top to the bottom of a page rather than from left to right on each line. Student readers are told to imagine a line down the center of the page and to move their eyes along that imaginary line, registering a whole line of print with each eye fixation. The instructor may suggest that they move the tip of a finger slowly down the center of the page at the same time, as a guide.

A common training exercise in speed-reading courses involves projecting short sentences on a screen for a very brief exposure (a flash of one fourth of a second or less). The student attempts to register the sentence and read it aloud. If the exposures of sentences are well spaced, the student can learn to perceive a sentence of four or more words with practice; however, if the ex-

posures occur rapidly, each new sentence will blank out the last one. This exercise bears little resemblance to actual reading, in which the eyes move without delay from one fixation point to the next.

Many claims have been made about speed-reading courses, but the claims tend not to hold up when evaluated under carefully controlled conditions (Carver, 1981). Nevertheless, people who have taken speed-reading courses often are convinced that they have substantially improved their reading skills, and in a sense, they may be right. By rapidly skimming material to pick out key words and main ideas, the reader can acquire a great deal of information and in some cases infer much of what the author of the text is trying to communicate. In fact, some reading materials contain so little new information that skimming is all they require. However, if the text presents new and challenging material, there is no evidence that speed reading is effective. Under these conditions, the reader must fixate almost word by word to comprehend the material.

Do these findings suggest that there is no way of improving reading skills? On the contrary, we do know that the more reading a person does the more his or her reading skills improve, particularly for younger children. But attempts to force oneself to read at a faster rate only reduce comprehension, and such forced practice does not lead to an improvement in reading skills.

What, then, are we to make of the claims for speed-reading courses? Some courses claim that they can increase reading speed threefold or more without a loss in comprehension; this claim cannot be substantiated. On the other hand, some courses do teach what might be called techniques for skimming, and there are occasions when skimming is useful. For example, before reading a chapter in a textbook, it is a good strategy to skim the material in order to identify key topics and gain a general impression of the chapter's organization. The information gained by skimming helps to frame a context within which to read the material more carefully. Also, skimming can help readers decide what materials are worth reading in detail. Given what we now know about the reading process, courses for teaching skimming can be designed that would be more effective than those developed to teach speed reading.

ROLE OF LEARNING IN PERCEPTION

The phenomena of distance and movement perception, perceptual organization, and the various perceptual constancies are easily and convincingly demonstrated, so that by now there is general agreement over what is perceived. Disagreements remain, however, over how to *explain* what happens. One of the traditional questions about visual perception has been whether our abilities to perceive the environment are learned or innate—the familiar nature-nurture problem. Its investigation with relation to perception goes back to the philosophers of the seventeenth and eighteenth centuries.

One group, the *nativists* (including Descartes and Kant), argued that we are born with the ability to perceive the way we do. In contrast, the *empiricists* (including Berkeley and Locke) maintained that we learn our ways of perceiving through experience with objects in the world about us. As noted earlier in this chapter, contemporary psychologists believe that a fruitful integration of these two viewpoints is possible. No one today really doubts that practice and experience influence perception. The question is to what extent is perceptual capacity inborn and to what extent is it acquired as a function of experience. There are several areas of research that yield information on the role of learning in perception.

Restored vision

In the year 1690, Locke quoted a letter he received from a colleague that posed the following problem:

> Suppose a man *born* blind, and now adult, taught by his *touch* to distinguish between a cube and a sphere of the same metal, and nighly of the same bigness, so as to tell, when he felt one and the other, which is the cube, which the sphere. Suppose that the cube and the sphere placed on a table, and the blind man be made to see . . . [could he] now distinguish and tell which is the globe, which the cube?

Locke, supporting the empiricist viewpoint, concluded that he could not.

A partial answer to this question is provided by studies of individuals who were blind from birth with cataracts on both eyes and whose vision was restored by surgery when they were adults (Senden, 1960). When the eye bandages were removed for the first time, the patients were confused by the bewildering array of visual stimuli. They were, however, able to distinguish figure from ground (apparently perceiving figure-ground relationships in much the same way as normally sighted people do), to fixate and scan figures, and to follow moving figures with their eyes. These abilities then appear to be innate. Patients could not identify by sight objects familiar by touch—such as faces, knives, and keys. They could not distinguish a triangle from a square without counting the number of corners or tracing the outline with a finger. They also could not tell which of two uneven sticks was longer without feeling them, although they might report that the two sticks looked somehow different. It took several weeks of training for such patients to learn to identify simple objects by sight; and even after identification had been learned in a specific situation, the patients showed little evidence of generalization to other situations. A white triangle might not be recognized when viewed with colored light or when turned upside down. The poor performance cannot be attributed to difficulty in discriminating colors; the restored-vision patients could distinguish between colors (although they did not at first know which name to attach to which color) long before they could distinguish between shapes.

Studies of previously blind adults indicate that some visual capacity exists in people who have had no visual experience. The inconsistencies in the data, however, do not allow us to conclude much more than this (Gregory, 1977). Nor is it likely that this kind of study will ever provide a definitive answer to the nature-nurture problem in perception. The reason is that it is doubtful that the perception of an adult with just-restored vision is much like that of an infant. On the one hand, the adult's visual system may have deteriorated from years of disuse. On the other hand, they have a great deal of knowledge, which allows them to take maximum advantage of whatever information their visual system does pick up. Adults have also learned to rely on other senses.

Selective rearing

Another approach, which offers an opportunity for experimental control, is to study the effects of selective rearing in animals. *Selective rearing* means rearing under conditions in which each animal receives only specific kinds of visual stimulation. Just as with humans, however, if only adult visual systems are studied, we cannot know whether visual stimulation simply maintains systems present at birth or facilitates their development. Fortunately, in kittens it has been possible to study single cells in the visual cortex prior to visual experience. Much to empiricists' surprise, newborn kittens prove to have receptive fields very much like adult cats (page 119). Their cells are tuned to bars of various sizes and orientations and come in the same three types—simple, complex, and hypercomplex—that are found in the adult (Hubel and Wiesel, 1962). The only difference that has been found is that cells in the adult are somewhat more sharply tuned than those in the newborn. This result is extremely important because it shows that the "wiring" of these cells is innately determined. Given this baseline, studies of animals that have been selectively reared become easier to interpret.

Investigators who reared infant chimpanzees in total darkness until they were 16 months old found that the animals had serious perceptual deficiencies when they were tested on their first exposure to light. It was discovered later that these chimpanzees had suffered neuronal deterioration in various parts of the visual system. Apparently a certain amount of light stimulation is necessary to maintain the visual system. Without any light stimulation, nerve cells in the retina and the visual cortex begin to atrophy. This fact is interesting in itself, but it does not tell us much about the role of learning in perceptual development.

Later studies made use of translucent goggles. Though the animals received light stimulation with these goggles, it was diffuse and unpatterned. Studies with monkeys, chimpanzees, and kittens wearing translucent goggles from birth to anywhere from 1 to 3 months old show that although some simple perceptual abilities were unimpaired, more complex visual activity was seriously affected. The visually deprived animals did almost as well as normal animals in distinguishing differences in color, brightness, and size. But they could not follow a moving object with their eyes or discriminate forms (a circle from a square) (Riesen, 1965).

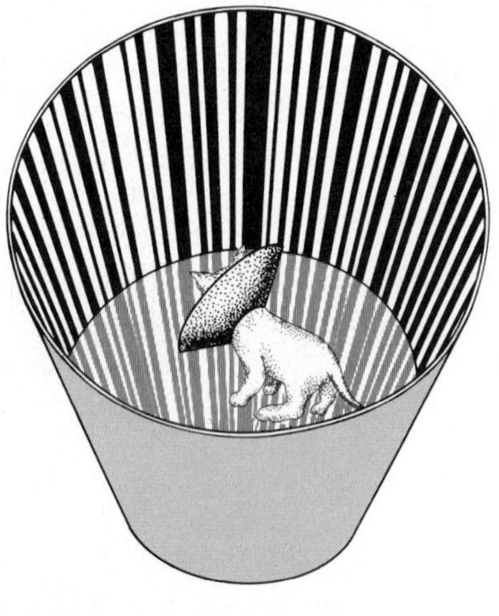

Kittens have also been reared with exposure only to vertical stripes or only to horizontal stripes. This was accomplished by placing the kitten in a striped tube with a ruff around its neck that prevented head tilting and sight of its own body (see Figure 5-22). After five months of this, the kittens acted as if they were blind to objects in the orientation to which they had not been exposed. Recording from single cortical cells in kittens that had seen only horizontal stripes showed a greatly reduced number of cells tuned to verticals; kittens that had seen only vertical stripes had few cells that responded to horizontals. It is not clear whether cells initially tuned to the nonexposed orientation have their tuning changed to conform to the environment or simply become unresponsive. In any case, it appears that an animal deprived of stimulation in one orientation loses acuity for contours in that orientation.

Similar effects may occur for humans. Euro-Canadians raised in a "carpentered" environment with its vertical and horizontal contours (straight sidewalks and rectangular buildings) were tested against Cree Indians from a more diverse environment. The Cree life style, for example, alternates between a summer cook tent and a winter lodge—both structures have line contours of virtually all orientations. Visual acuity was tested by presenting parallel lines in various orientations; the subject had to judge whether the lines were fused or separated. The Euro-Canadians exhibited a higher acuity for vertical and horizontal orientations than for diagonal orientations. The Crees, however, showed no differences; they were equally good at all orientations. There is no evidence

Figure 5-22
Controlled Visual Environment
Kittens were housed from birth in a completely dark room. At the age of 2 weeks, they were placed in a special apparatus for about 5 hours each day. The kittens stood on a clear glass platform inside a brightly illuminated tall cylinder. The entire surface of the cylinder was covered with black and white stripes. For some animals, the stripes were vertical and for others horizontal. The kitten could not see its own body, for it wore a wide black collar. This routine was stopped when the kittens were 5 months old, and thereafter lived in a normal environment. The early visual experience affected the development of the brain, and there were profound perceptual consequences. (After Blakemore and Cooper, 1970)

An environment of diagonal lines
A Cree Indian summer cook tent, or *meech-wop,* **at Wemindji, a small Indian village on the east coast of James Bay, Quebec. These structures, along with the Cree winter lodges, or** *matoocan,* **have contours in virtually all orientations.**

to suggest genetically determined differences in the visual system of the two groups. Rather, the acuity of the Crees may be the result of their visual experience (Annis and Frost, 1973).

Perception in infants

If human infants could tell us what their world looks like, many of our questions concerning the development of perception might be answered. Since they cannot, experimenters have had to stretch their ingenuity to try to measure the visual abilities of infants.

A number of indices have been used to assess infants' ability to discriminate stimuli. The simplest of these is *the preferential looking technique.* Infants strongly prefer looking at patterns rather than uniform surfaces. If an infant is presented with a choice between a uniform surface and a pattern, a threshold for seeing the pattern can be determined by making the pattern progressively more difficult to see until the infant no longer looks at it more than the uniform surface (Fantz, Ordy, and Vdelf, 1962). This technique has been used to show that infants can see patterns at least as early as 1 month of age. Initially their acuity is much less than adults, but it increases rapidly, reaching adult levels at about 6 months of age.

Several investigators have studied the infant's perception of height (a special case of depth perception), using the "visual cliff" shown in Figure 5-23. They have tested human and various animal infants in attempts to determine whether the ability to perceive and avoid a brink is innate or must be learned by the experience of falling off and getting hurt. Most parents, mindful of the caution they exercise to keep their offspring from falling out of the crib or down the stairs, would assume that the ability to appreciate height is something the child must learn. But observation of human infants' susceptibility to such accidents does not tell us whether they are unable to discriminate depth or can indeed respond to depth cues but lack the motor control to keep from falling.

Gibson and Walk (1960) tested the response of infants, ranging in age from 6 to 14 months, when placed on the center board of the visual cliff. The mother called to the child from the cliff side and from the shallow side successively. Almost all the infants crawled off onto the shallow side but refused to crawl onto the deep side. Since the infants could not be tested until they were old

Figure 5-23
The "Visual Cliff"

Infants and young animals show an ability to perceive depth as soon as they can move about. The visual cliff consists of two surfaces, both displaying the same pattern, which were covered by a sheet of thick glass. One surface is directly under the glass; the other is dropped several feet. When placed on the center board (the area between the deep and the shallow sides), the infant refuses to cross to the deep side but will readily move off the board onto the shallow side. (After Gibson and Walk, 1960)

A young goat cautiously approaching the deep side of a visual cliff

enough to crawl, the experiment does not prove that depth perception is present at birth. The results of studies with other organisms, however, indicate that depth perception is present at least as soon as the animal is able to move about. Chickens tested when less than 24 hours old never made a mistake by stepping off onto the deep side. Goats and lambs placed on the center board as soon as they could stand (some only 1 day old) always chose the shallow side. When placed on the deep side, such animals characteristically froze in a state of immobility.

There is evidence for a number of other perceptual capacities early in life. These include the ability to discriminate color, visual direction, and size. An infant only 10 minutes old will consistently turn his or her eyes in the direction of a clicking sound. There is also evidence for perceptual constancies in the first months of life (Bower, 1981). These findings suggest that more of perceptual capacity is innate than was previously realized. However, they also show that experience has a large role as well, particularly during the critical first year of life.

EXTRASENSORY PERCEPTION

Is it possible for us to acquire information about the world in ways that do not involve sense organ stimulation? The answer to this question is the source of a continuing controversy within psychology over the status of *extrasensory perception* (ESP). Although some psychologists believe that the evidence for the existence of certain forms of ESP is now incontrovertible, most remain unconvinced.

Three kinds of ESP are said to exist, and ESP itself belongs to a larger class of phenomena called *parapsychological phenomena*. These phenomena may be described as follows:

1 Extrasensory perception (ESP).
   a. Telepathy, or thought transference from one person to another.
   b. Clairvoyance, or the perception of objects or events not influencing the senses (such as stating the number and suit of a playing card that is in a sealed envelope).
   c. Precognition, or the perception of a future event.
2 Psychokinesis (PK), or mentally manipulating objects without touching them (for example, "willing" that a particular number come up in the throw of dice).

ESP *experiments*

Experimenters investigating parapsychological phenomena work in accordance with the usual rules of science and generally disavow any connection between their work and spiritualism, supernaturalism, and other occult doctrines. Yet the phenomena with which they deal are so extraordinary and so similar to superstitious beliefs that many scientists reject even the legitimacy of their inquiries. Such a priori judgments are out of place in science; the real question is whether the empirical evidence is acceptable by ordinary scientific standards. Many psychologists who are not convinced are nevertheless ready to accept evidence that they find satisfactory. For example, the possibility of some sort of influence from one brain to another, other than by way of the sense organs, would not be inconceivable within the present framework of science. Some of the other phenomena, such as precognition, are more difficult to find believable; but if the experiments were reproducible, previous beliefs would have to yield to the facts.

Much of the early research on ESP was done by Rhine (1942) using a card "guessing" procedure. The typical ESP pack consists of 25 cards with five different symbols—so that by guessing alone, the person being tested should average five hits per pack (see Figure 5-24). Even very successful subjects seldom score as many as seven hits on a regular basis, but they may score above five often enough to meet accepted standards for statistical significance. In the typical experiment, the cards are shuffled and placed out of the subject's view; the subject then identifies the cards one at a time. If the experimenter, or "sender," looks at each card before the subject responds, the study is concerned with telepathy. If the experimenter does not look at the card (it is face down on the pack), the study is concerned with clairvoyance.

The card-guessing procedure may seem artificial and not conducive to good psychic performance, but it has several advantages: (1) the experiment can be carefully controlled, so that there is no possibility of cheating; (2) the experiment can be repeated with the same subject at different times, or with different groups of subjects; and (3) the statistical significance of an experimental outcome (number of correct matches) can be evaluated using standard statistical techniques.

The kind of evidence used in support of the nonchance nature of the findings is illustrated by the successive runs of one "sensitive" subject, Mrs. Gloria Stewart, who was studied in England over a long period (see Table 5-1). If the evidence is viewed in the same way as that from any other experiment, it is clear that Mrs. Stewart responded above chance on the telepathy trials but not on the clairvoyance ones. These results meet certain objections about card arrangements sometimes voiced against such experiments; her chance performance on the clairvoyance trials shows that above-chance scores are not an inevitable result possibly related to the method of shuffling the cards.

Figure 5-24
ESP Cards
Each card in the ESP pack bears one of five symbols (cross, wave, circle, star, rectangle). There are five of each in a pack of 25 cards.

YEAR OF SUCCESSIVE BLOCKS OF 200 TRIALS	HITS PER 200 TRIALS (EXPECTED = 40)	
	Telepathy Trials	Clairvoyance Trials
1945	65	51
	58	42
	62	29
	58	47
	60	38
1947	54	35
	55	36
	65	31
1948	39	38
	56	43
1949	49	40
	51	37
	33	42
Total hits	707	509
Expected hits (20% of 2,600)	520	520
Difference	+187	−11
Hits per 25 trials	6.8	4.9

Table 5-1
ESP Results
Results of telepathy and clairvoyance trials with one subject studied over a long period (After Soal and Bateman, 1954)

Skepticism about ESP

One of the chief reasons for skepticism about ESP is that no method has been found for reliably demonstrating the phenomena. Procedures that produce significant results for one experimenter do not do so for another. Even the same experimenter testing the same individuals over a period of time may obtain significant results on one occasion and yet be unable to repeat the results later. Lack of replicability is a serious problem. In other scientific fields, an experimental finding is not considered established until the experiment has been repeated by several researchers with comparable results. Until ESP experiments can be shown to be replicable, the authenticity of the phenomena is open to question.

A second complaint about ESP research is that the results do not vary systematically with the introduction of different experimental manipulations. This objection, however, is not entirely fair. Some results are reported where subjects are more successful on early trials than later ones, and there is evidence that subjects with a favorable attitude to ESP produce positive results, whereas an unfavorable attitude leads to below-chance scores. It has also been reported that the emotional states of the sender and receiver are important; when the sender is emotionally aroused and the receiver is reclining in a relaxed state, ESP is maximal. Finally, there are a number of studies that find ESP to be better when the receiver is dreaming or in a hypnotic state rather than in a normal, walking state. For a review of these studies, see Wolman and others (1977).

Empirical findings that meet ordinary statistical standards are offered in support of ESP and PK. Why, then, do the results not become a part of established psychological science? The arguments used against ESP and PK can be summarized as follows:

1   Many claims of extraordinary phenomena in the past have been shown to be fraudulent.
2   Many apparently decisive experiments have been found to have methodological flaws.
3   Improved experimental methods have failed to yield larger and/or more reliable effects than crude methods.
4   There is a general lack of consistency in the phenomena, without which formal theorizing cannot replace the current vague speculations about what may be taking place.

These criticisms are not decisive. It is desirable to keep an open mind about issues that permit empirical demonstration. At the same time, it should be clear that the reservations of the majority of psychologists are based on more than stubborn prejudice. For critiques of recent work in parapsychology, see Hansel (1980) and Marks and Kammann (1980).

In the following discussion, we will expand on the objections that psychologists have to the ESP and PK experiments and to *psi*, the special ability attributed to the "sensitive" subject.

General Skepticism About Extraordinary Phenomena Throughout history, there have always been reports of strange happenings, ghosts, poltergeists (noisy spirits who throw things), and dreams foretelling the future. The continuing appearance of these stories does not make them true. The much publicized Israeli "psychic" Uri Geller is an example. Geller claims that he is able to read people's minds, "magically" cause metal objects to bend, and perform a number of other supernatural feats. Some scientists who have observed Geller's performances are convinced of his psychic powers. On several occasions, however, Geller has been caught—even filmed—in acts of deception, and his tricks exposed (Randi, 1978). Despite this evidence, some believers continue to maintain that Geller's psychic powers are genuine and that he resorts to deception only on occasion.

This case is not unique. Almost every year, strong claims are made for the powers of some newly discovered psychic. Careful examination reveals that the individual is using trickery and that the psychic feats can be duplicated by a skilled magician. Yet some researchers in parapsychology are so messianic about their field that they either do not see through the obvious trickery or they conclude that though the individuals may occasionally cheat, they still have paranormal powers. When those most convinced about ESP are also con-

vinced about already disproved phenomena, their testimony carries less weight than it would if they were more critical.

Failure of Improved Methods to Increase the Yield In most scientific fields, the assay from the ore becomes richer as the experimental methods become more refined. But the reverse trend is found in ESP experiments; it is almost a truism in research in the fields of telepathy and clairvoyance that the poorer the conditions, the better the results. In the early days of Rhine's experiments at Duke University, subjects who had high ESP scores were rather common. As the experiments became better controlled, however, the number of high-scoring subjects diminished. A similar decrease in significant results with improved experimental control has been found in PK studies (Hyman, 1977).

Lack of Consistency in the Phenomena Sensitive subjects in Rhine's experiments appear to be equally successful at clairvoyance and telepathy, but subjects in a British laboratory appear to be good at telepathy and not at clairvoyance. Other peculiarities emerge. In a famous series of experiments in England, one subject gave no evidence of either telepathy or clairvoyance when scored in the usual way against the target card. Instead, he was shown to be successful in *precognition telepathy*—that is, in guessing what was going to be on the experimenter's mind on the next trial (Soal and Bateman, 1954). Why, the skeptic asks, does the direct telepathy fail with this subject in favor of something far more mysterious than the telepathic success of Mrs. Stewart?

Because *psi* ability appears to lack consistency, explanations of it can be produced with the greatest of freedom. It need not be affected in any ordinary way by space or time, so that success over great distances is accepted as a sign of its extraordinary power rather than as a reason to search for artifacts. Similarly, the precognition experiments are merely evidence to the ESP proponents that it is as easy to read what is *about* to be on someone else's mind as what is on it now. The PK effects, which require the subject to produce a certain outcome in dice rolling by mental effort ("mind over matter"), are said to occur without any transfer of physical energy—thus presumably violating the physical principle of energy conservation. But in any experimental work, *some* aspects of time and space have to be respected. Unless some restraint is shown, we might invent any number of hypotheses: the subject was perceiving the cards in reverse order, in a place-skipping order, and so on. With an unlimited number of hypotheses, no test is possible (Diaconis, 1978).

Believers in *psi* are impatient with these kinds of criticism. They say that more is asked of them than of other experimenters. And, in fact, we do ask more of them. To demonstrate something highly implausible requires better evidence than to demonstrate something plausible. Supporting evidence for the plausible finding comes from many directions, whereas the implausible finding must hang on a slender thread of evidence until systematic relationships are found that tie it firmly to what is known.

Summary

1 *Perception* refers to phenomena in which the relation between stimulus and experience is more complex than for the phenomena considered under *sensation*. Perceptual phenomena are thought to depend on higher-level processes.

2 Distance perception depends on a large number of stimulus variables called *distance cues*. The principal binocular cue is *binocular disparity*. Monocular cues include *superposition, relative size, height in field,* and *gradient of texture.*

3 Early theories of motion perception assumed that the cues for movement were the successive stimulation of rods and cones as the image of an object moved across the retina. It is now known that motion perception is more complicated than this and depends on environmental cues. *Stroboscopic motion* is a phenomenon in which an object is perceived to move without actually moving.

4 The *Gestalt psychologists* emphasized the principle that the whole percept is different from the sum of the percepts produced by each of its parts. A number of phenomena of perceptual organization, constancy, and illusion illustrate this principle.

5 *Perceptual organization* refers to the dependence of the percept on the relations among the parts of the stimulus configuration. Examples are *figure-ground phenomena* and *perceptual grouping*.

6 *Perceptual constancy* refers to the tendency for objects to appear the same in spite of changes in the stimuli reaching our receptors. Under normal conditions, the perceived *lightness, color, shape, size,* and *location* of objects remain approximately constant. Constancy is rarely perfect and depends on how we interpret information reaching the sense organs.

7 An *illusion* is a percept that is erroneous. A distinction is made between *physical illusions*, which have external causes, and *perceptual illusions*, which arise in the perceptual system. *Geometrical illusions* are perceptual illusions that appear in line drawings.

8 From a cognitive viewpoint, a percept is a hypothesis suggested by the sensory data. *Hypothesis testing* emphasizes the active nature of perception and depends on *context* and *past experience*. *Analysis-by-synthesis* is a theory of perception based on the concept of hypothesis testing.

9 Perception is *selective*. At any moment in time, we *attend* to only part of the influx of sensory stimulation. Stimuli to which we are not actively attending may be registered temporarily in the nervous system, allowing us to transfer our attention to them if they seem pertinent. Factors that favor attention to one stimulus in preference to another reside in the stimulus' physical properties (intensity, size, contrast, and movement) and in the perceiver's needs, expectancies, and momentary interests.

10 The *orienting reflex* is a pattern of physiological reactions that correlates with attention. These reactions facilitate the reception of stimuli and prepare the organism for action.

11 In normal vision, the eyes make an abrupt movement called a *saccade* every few milliseconds. These movements bring different parts of a scene onto the high-resolution fovea where fine detail can be seen.

12 Eye movements during reading are an important source of information about the reading process. Modern theories of reading usually analyze reading into a sequence of processes that are applied to each word as it is encountered in the text.

13 The question of to what extent perceptual capacity is innate and to what extent it depends on experience has long been a subject of controversy. *Selective rearing* experiments with animals show that particular kinds of stimulation are necessary for the development of a normal visual system. Human infants have been

shown to have considerable perceptual capacity as early as they can be tested and to improve rapidly in the first months of life.

14 *Extrasensory perception* (ESP) in its various forms (telepathy, clairvoyance, precognition) and *psychokinesis* (PK) are areas of controversy in psychology. There are many reasons for reserving judgment on these phenomena, but an a priori condemnation of the experiments is not justified. The experiments raise interesting issues about the criteria by which scientific credibility is established.

Further Reading

Textbooks covering the topics dealt with in this chapter are Coren, Porac, and Ward, *Sensation and perception* (1978); Hochberg, *Perception* (2nd ed., 1978); Kaufman, *Perception* (1979); and Schiffman, *Sensation and perception* (2nd ed., 1982).

Problems of attention, perceptual coding, pattern recognition, and visual search are discussed in Norman, *Memory and attention: An introduction to human information processing* (2nd ed., 1976); Boden, *Artificial intelligence and natural man* (1977); Wickelgren, *Cognitive psychology* (1979); Anderson, *Cognitive psychology and its implications* (1980), and Spoehr and Lehmkuhle, *Visual information processing* (1982).

For a review of extrasensory perception, see Wolman, Dale, Schmeidler, and Ullman (eds.), *Handbook of parapsychology* (1977); and Marks and Kammann, *The psychology of the psychic* (1980).

6
STATES OF
CONSCIOUSNESS

As you read these words, are you awake or dreaming? Hardly anyone is confused by this question. We all know the difference between an ordinary state of wakefulness and the experience of dreaming. We also recognize a variety of other states of consciousness including those induced by drugs like alcohol and marijuana.

A person's state of consciousness is changing all the time. At this moment, your attention may be focused on this book; in a few minutes, you may be sunk in reverie. To most psychologists, an *altered state of consciousness* exists whenever there is a change from an ordinary pattern of mental functioning to a state that *seems* different to the person experiencing the change (Tart, 1975). Although this is not a very precise definition, it reflects the fact that states of consciousness are personal and thereby subjective. Altered states of consciousness can vary from the distraction of a vivid daydream to the confusion and perceptual distortion of drug intoxication. In this chapter, we will look at some states of consciousness that are experienced by everyone (sleep and dreams, for instance) as well as some that result from special circumstances (meditation, hypnosis, and the use of drugs).

CONSCIOUSNESS

Many topics discussed in other chapters have a direct bearing on the study of consciousness. In asking how we interpret sensory information (Chapters 4 and 5), how we store and recover memories (Chapter 8), and how we think and solve problems (Chapter 9), psychologists are essentially asking questions about consciousness.

But what is consciousness? The word is most often used as a collective term for an individual's perceptions, thoughts, feelings, and memories that are active at a given moment. In this sense, consciousness is synonymous with awareness. However, as we will see, consciousness also includes perceptions and thoughts of which the individual may be only dimly aware until his or her attention is drawn to them. Hence, there are degrees of awareness within consciousness.

The early psychologists equated "consciousness" with "mind." In fact, they defined psychology as "the study of mind and consciousness" (see Table 1-1, page 14) and used the introspective method to study consciousness. As we noted in Chapter 1, both introspection as a method and consciousness as a topic for investigation fell from favor with the rise of behaviorism in the early 1900s. John Watson, the founder of behaviorism, and his followers believed that if psychology were to become a science its data must be objective and measurable. Behavior could be publicly observed and various responses could be objectively measured. In contrast, an individual's private experiences, as revealed through introspection, could not be observed by others or objectively measured.

During the last 20 years, the increasingly cognitive orientation of many psychologists, together with other developments, has revived interest in consciousness. A strict behaviorist insistence on observable behavior now seems too confining, and many researchers would hesitate to say that subjectivity and science are totally incompatible. The definition of "altered states of consciousness," offered above, illustrates the new acceptability of subjective experience.

The historical reasons for these changes are complex (see Appendix I). In addition to developments within psychology as a professional field, they include the prevailing spirit of the 1960s, which favored enlarging the boundaries of personal awareness, and the wave of public interest in phenomenological psychology that occurred during the same period.

Passive and active modes of consciousness

A preliminary distinction can be drawn between two modes of consciousness that characterize ordinary wakefulness: *passive consciousness*, in which the attitude is one of receptivity to what is going on at the moment, and *active consciousness*, in which the focus is on initiative and seeking, on planning and future possibilities (Deikman, 1971).

Receiving information from the environment is the main function of the body's sensory systems. Sensory experience blends in complex ways with memories, fantasies, and dreams—all of which may be represented in passive consciousness. In addition to providing knowledge, sensory stimulation is the basis for esthetic satisfaction. The counterculture of the 1960s emphasized passive modes of consciousness, assigning great value to sensitivity for the present moment and to detachment from all concern for either past or future. Some of these ideas are based on Eastern religious practices, such as yoga, in which individuality is given up through merging with an object of meditation, producing a state of tranquility or bliss.

Receptivity or sensitivity is only part of consciousness. Active planning is a major part of mental life, whether the plan is simple and readily completed ("I'll mail this letter at the corner box") or long range ("I'm going to become a lawyer"). Events that have not yet occurred can be represented in consciousness as future possibilities and alternative scenarios envisioned, choices made, and appropriate activities initiated. For example, the creative artist, scientist, or inventor uses active consciousness to do the hard work needed to turn a creative idea into a product. Active consciousness plays its role as the person looks ahead, tests the product against an ideal, and presses on against discouragement.

Two models of consciousness: passive receptivity to one's environment versus active concentration on a task

Of course, the distinction between the active and passive modes is not sharp. Thinking goes on in both modes, and in both, the flow of thoughts is within or very near awareness.

Processes at the fringes of awareness

In the competition for attention, some objects or events have an advantage over others because of inherent qualities like intensity, surprise, or change. Other stimuli have an advantage for reasons that reflect the perceiver's interests or preoccupations. Whatever the cause, these stimuli capture the perceiver's focal attention, which like a flashlight penetrating the dark brings them to the center of awareness. But much goes on at the fringes of awareness.

Many stimuli that are not consciously perceived are registered somehow. For example, you may not be aware of hearing a clock strike the hour. After a few strokes, you become alert; then you can go back and count the strokes that you did not know you heard. Another example of peripheral attention was considered in Chapter 5 in the example of the cocktail party phenomenon: you are talking to someone in a crowded room, ignoring the noise around you, when the distant sound of your own name suddenly catches your attention. A considerable body of research indicates that we are able to register stimuli we do not know we perceive.

Interests or momentary preoccupations prepare our attentive processes so that predictions can be made about the advantages that one stimulus will have over another (of equal physical potency) in commanding attention. These preparatory processes need not be in consciousness at the time of the response. Conscious preparation can occur in advance. For example, if you know that you will be asked to respond to a word with its opposite, you will make preparations to do so. When the stimulus word appears, your response may be quite automatic. To "up" you say "down"; to "right," you say "left." No describable thoughts intervene between the stimulus and the response; all of your thinking has been done in advance. Various labels, including *mental sets* and *preattentive processes,* have been attached to preparatory adjustments for later conscious experiences. Such processes are on the very edges of consciousness.

Freud and the unconscious

Memories that are available for recall constitute a repository of experiences. These memories consist of both "public" information shared with other members of a culture and private information based on an individual's own experiences. The retrievability of these memories places them within the domain of consciousness.

According to the psychoanalytic theories of Freud and his followers, other memories exist that are not retrievable or retrievable only with great difficulty. Psychoanalytic theory assigns these memories to the *unconscious.* For emotional or motivational reasons, Freud said, some conscious memories and wishes may be *repressed*—that is, diverted to the unconscious, where they remain active although lost to recall. In some instances, repression may divert unacceptable thoughts to the unconscious before they ever become conscious. The unconscious is believed to be responsible for dreams, mannerisms, slips of the tongue, even symptoms of illness. Carl Jung, an early disciple who broke with Freud, expanded Freud's notion of the unconscious to include a *collective unconscious,* which is said to be inherited and shared by all individuals. One source of Jung's theory is the presence in diverse cultures of certain closely related myths with many common symbols for creation, birth, and other important life events. Just as Freud used the individual dream as evidence for the personal unconscious, Jung treated the myth as a "dream of the people" and evidence for the collective unconscious. The views of Freud and Jung are controversial, but the kinds of evidence to which they point pose important problems for psychological interpretation.

DAYDREAMS

"A penny for your thoughts, hon."
Drawing by Corem; ©1980 *The New Yorker Magazine*, Inc.

In the well-known story by James Thurber (1942), a mild-mannered man named Walter Mitty entertains himself with a series of elaborate fantasies in which he is a fearless and powerful figure. Although most people do not achieve Walter Mitty's flights of fancy, almost all of us spend some time each day absorbed in our own thoughts and images—creating and planning, thinking through problems, reliving past events, or just letting our minds drift. We call this state of consciousness *daydreaming*. For some of us, daydreaming consumes many hours of the day; for others, it is less absorbing.

Although the systematic study of daydreaming is only a few decades old, psychologists have learned much about the nature of daydreams and the functions they serve. These researchers do not view daydreaming as a bad habit or a sign of emotional disturbance. Daydreaming, they argue, is a normal state of consciousness characterized by a shift in attention. Instead of focusing on the physical or mental task at hand, the daydreamer's attention turns to thoughts and images based in memory.

For most people most of the time, daydreams are pleasant fantasies about the future. Many people also have anxious daydreams in which fleeting worries distract them from what they are doing. A third pattern is the guilty or angry daydream, in which a frequent theme is fear of failure (Singer, 1975).

Why people daydream is still an open question. Research suggests several possible reasons. Since our minds are rarely empty, daydreaming may simply reflect normal, ongoing consciousness. Researchers have found, for example, that even when people are well paid, they tend to fall into reverie when doing dull and repetitive tasks (Antrobus, Greenberg, and Singer, 1966). While daydreaming, people may be tapping into a stream of thoughts that they are able to ignore when concentrating on a task. Or daydreaming may be a creative way to relieve boredom or a way to work out unsolved problems and unresolved feelings.

SLEEP AND DREAMS

Sleep seems the opposite of wakefulness, yet the two states have much in common. We think when we sleep, as dreams show, although the thinking in dreams departs in various ways from the thinking we do while awake. We form memories while sleeping, as we know from the fact that we remember dreams. Sleep is not entirely quiescent: some people walk in their sleep. People who are asleep are not entirely insensitive to the environment: parents can be awakened by their baby's cry. Nor is sleep entirely planless: some people can decide to wake at a given time and do so. A good deal is now known about this most familiar altered state of consciousness.

Sleep

Many aspects of sleep have interested investigators. Researchers have looked at normal rhythms of waking and sleeping, the depth of sleep at different periods of the night, and individual and environmental factors that affect sleep. The physiological concomitants of sleep are also of interest.

SLEEP SCHEDULES   Newborn babies tend to alternate frequently between sleeping and waking. Much to the relief of parents, a rhythm of two naps a day and a longer sleep at night is eventually established. An infant's total sleeping time drops from 16 hours per day to 13 hours per day within the first six months of life. Most adults average about 7½ hours of sleep per night, but this time varies greatly. Some people manage on as little as 3 hours of sleep per night (Jones and Oswald, 1968), and there are occasional reports of people who get by on less. One elderly woman averaged only 45 minutes of sleep per night (Meddis, Pearson, and Langford, 1973). Sleep patterns vary from person to person. We all know "larks" who go to bed early and rise early and "owls" who go to bed late and rise late (Webb, 1975).

Humans share with other mammals a biological clock known as the *circadian rhythm* that closely follows the night-and-day periodicity of the world we live in. In conditions in which a person has no way to mark the passing of day and night, the cycle tends to have a natural period of 25 hours. The cause of this departure from a 24-hour cycle is a matter of speculation. In any case, exposure to the normal environment of light and dark modifies the natural rhythm in favor of a 24-hour period (Aschoff, 1965).

A blind person may have a natural rhythm that departs from the 24-hour cycle, and this rhythm may prove very resistant to change. In one carefully studied case, a young professional man, blind since birth, had a circadian rhythm of 24.9 hours. As a consequence, he was completely out of phase with the night-day cycle about every two weeks. The only way he could stay in phase and meet the requirements of his professional life was to take heavy doses of stimulants and sedatives to counteract the rhythmical changes during the different phases of his cycle. Careful efforts to modify his sleep cycle by monitoring and controlling his sleep in a sleep laboratory did not prove successful (Miles, Raynal, and Wilson, 1977).

Circadian rhythms cause the jet lag that bothers many airline passengers. Their difficulty in adapting to the new time cycle often persists for several days. In one study of American students who traveled from the United States to Germany, performance on a task of manual dexterity showed a marked change in proficiency with time of day. At home, the high point came around 3 P.M., whereas during the first day in Germany, the high point came in the middle of the night (Figure 6-1). The students who traveled from the United States to Germany took 12 days to recover from the outbound flight and 10 days to recover from the homeward flight. Apparently, it is easier to return to an old cycle than to adjust to a new one (Klein, Wegmann, and Hunt, 1972). Related experiments indicate that jet lag is due to interference with the normal circadian rhythm rather than to loss of sleep (Webb, Agnew, and Williams, 1971).

DEPTH OF SLEEP   Some people are readily aroused from sleep; others are hard to awaken. Research begun in the 1930s (Loomis, Harvey, and Hobart, 1937) has produced sensitive techniques for measuring the depth of sleep as well as for determining when dreams are occurring (Dement and Kleitman, 1957). This research uses devices that measure (1) electrical changes on the

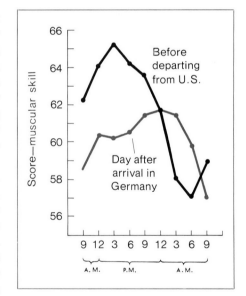

Figure 6-1
Change in Circadian Rhythm
After Travel to a New Time Zone
Average results for eight subjects flying from the United States to Germany, with a 6-hour time difference. The black line represents the scores on a test taken more than three days prior to departure; the red line represents corresponding scores on the day after arrival in Germany. (After Klein, Wegmann, and Hunt, 1972)

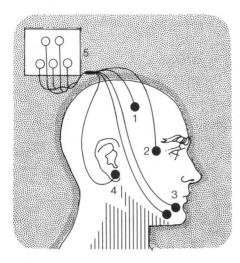

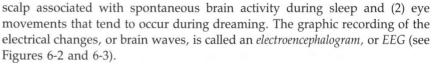

scalp associated with spontaneous brain activity during sleep and (2) eye movements that tend to occur during dreaming. The graphic recording of the electrical changes, or brain waves, is called an *electroencephalogram*, or *EEG* (see Figures 6-2 and 6-3).

Analysis of the patterns of brain waves suggests that sleep involves five stages—four depths of sleep, and a fifth stage, known as rapid-eye-movement sleep, in which dreams commonly occur. When a person who is awake closes his or her eyes and relaxes, the brain waves characteristically show a regular pattern of 8 to 13 vibrations (Hz, or Hertz) per second; these are known as *alpha waves*. As the individual drifts into Stage 1 sleep, the brain waves become less regular and are reduced in amplitude with little or no alpha. Stage 2 is characterized by the appearance of *spindles*—short runs of rhythmical responses of 13 to 16 Hz, slightly more rapid than alpha—and occasional rises and falls in the amplitude of the whole EEG. The still deeper Stages 3 and 4 are characterized by slow waves (known as *delta waves*). The sleeper is hard to awaken during these stages. However, someone who is deeply asleep may be aroused by something personal, such as a familiar name, whereas a more impersonal disturbance, such as a loud sound, may be ignored.

After an adult has been asleep for an hour or so, another change occurs. The EEG pattern of Stage 1 reappears, but the subject does not wake. Instead, rapid eye movements appear on the record. This stage is known as *REM sleep*; other stages are known as *non-REM* (or *NREM*). When aroused from the REM stage, the subject commonly reports a dream. Even though sleep at this stage is relatively light, the sleeper is as difficult to arouse as from Stage 2.

The stages alternate throughout the night. The exact pattern varies from person to person and with age. Newborn infants spend about half their sleeping time in REM sleep. This proportion drops to 20 or 25 percent of sleeping time by the age of 5 and then remains fairly constant until old age, when it drops to 18 percent or less. For people of all ages, the deeper stages (3 and 4) tend to disappear in the second half of the night as REM becomes more prominent (see Figure 6-4 on page 172).

INSOMNIA AND SLEEP DISORDERS   Most people have good voluntary control over the decision to sleep or stay awake, though some have more control than others. For example, a study of college students found that 20 percent of the sample could nap at will; another 40 percent could nap if they had lost sleep recently; and the final 40 percent never napped (Evans and others, 1977).

Nighttime insomnia affects fewer people but troubles them more. In a large survey of adults, 6 percent of the males and 14 percent of the females complained that they often or fairly often had great difficulty falling asleep or staying asleep throughout the night (Kripke and Simons, 1976). One researcher who treated 141 insomniacs found that medical or psychological problems accounted for most sleep disturbances. About one patient in six had severe medical reasons for insomnia, two patients in six had serious psychological disturbances, and the rest had either mild psychological problems or learned behavior patterns that interfered with sleep (Hauri, 1976).

A perplexing feature of insomnia is that people seem to overestimate their sleep loss. One study that monitored the sleep of people who identified themselves as insomniacs found that only about half of them were actually awake as much as 30 minutes during the night (Carskadon, Mitler, and Dement, 1974). The problem may be that light or restless sleep sometimes feels like wakefulness or that some people remember only time spent awake and think they have not slept because they have no memory of doing so.

Figure 6-2
Arrangement of Electrodes for Recording the Electrophysiology of Sleep
The diagram shows the way in which electrodes are attached to the subject's head and face in a typical sleep experiment. Electrodes on the scalp (1) record the patterns of brain waves. Electrodes near the subject's eyes (2) record eye movements. Electrodes on the chin (3) record tension and electrical activity in the muscles. A neutral electrode on the ear (4) completes the circuit through amplifiers (5) that produce graphical records of the various patterns (see Figure 6-3).

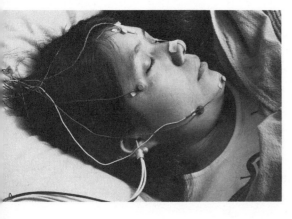

Two relatively rare but severe disorders of sleep, narcolepsy and apnea, are characterized by a lack of voluntary control over the onset of sleep. A person with *narcolepsy* may fall asleep while writing a letter, driving a car, or carrying on a conversation. If the student falls asleep while a professor is lecturing, that is perfectly normal, but if the professor falls asleep while lecturing, that may be narcolepsy. In a study of 190 patients who complained that they could not stay awake in the daytime, 65 percent were diagnosed as having narcolepsy (Dement, 1976). Usually, the sudden, brief periods of sleep in narcolepsy are accompanied by muscular relaxation; the person may simply nod or may collapse. However, some narcoleptics are able to continue automatic behavior that they later forget, such as driving a car satisfactorily for some miles.

In *sleep apnea,* the individual stops breathing while asleep (either because the windpipe closes or because the brain centers that control respiration are not functioning properly). People with apnea must awaken repeatedly throughout the night in order to breathe, although they are unaware of doing so. For these people, daytime sleepiness is a function of nighttime sleep deprivation. Sleep apnea is common among older individuals; it is estimated that one third of those over 65 suffer from this disorder (Ancoli-Israel, 1981). Sleeping pills, which make arousal more difficult, lengthen periods of apnea (during which the brain is deprived of oxygen) and in some cases may prove fatal.

Apnea and narcolepsy show that complex voluntary and involuntary control systems are involved in sleep.

SLEEP DEPRIVATION The need for sleep seems so important that total sleep deprivation lasting several nights might be expected to have serious consequences. Numerous studies have shown, however, that the only consistent effects of sleep deprivation are drowsiness, a desire to sleep, and a tendency to fall asleep easily (Dement, 1976). Subjects kept awake for 50 hours or more show nothing more noticeable than "transient inattentions, confusions, or misperceptions" (Webb, 1975). Even sleepless periods exceeding four days produce little in the way of severely disturbed behavior. In one study in which a subject was kept awake for 264 hours (11 days and nights), there were no unusually deviant responses (Gulevich, Dement, and Johnson, 1966). Intellectual activities like answering short test questions seem unaffected by several nights of sleep deprivation.

If sleep deprivation has no serious consequences, what about dream deprivation? This question has been investigated by depriving subjects of REM sleep. Dement (1960) woke his subjects at the onset of every REM period. He found that after five nights there was a *rebound effect*, with an abnormal amount of time spent in REM sleep during the recovery night. Control tests were run by awakening subjects an equal number of times during NREM sleep; no rebound of REM was found. Dement's findings have been confirmed by many others. Researchers had hoped that REM deprivation would provide clues to the function of REM sleep, but answers have not been forthcoming, although the search has continued. Some minor effects of REM deprivation on memory have been reported; however, memory disturbances are also found after deprivation of NREM sleep (McGaugh, Jensen, and Martinez, 1979).

Dreams

Dreaming is an alteration in consciousness in which remembered images and fantasies are temporarily confused with external reality. Investigators do not

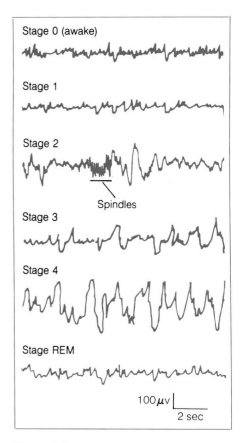

Figure 6-3
Electrophysiological Activity
During Sleep
The figure presents EEG recordings during wakefulness and during the five stages of sleep. Note the similarity of the EEG records for Stage 1 and Stage REM; these two stages do not differ in EEG activity, but Stage REM is accompanied by rapid eye movements whereas Stage 1 is not. Note the spindles that occur during Stage 2 and the irregularity that characterizes Stages 3 and 4 (the deeper stages of sleep). The calibration for the EEG record is given at the bottom; its amplitude is in microvolts (μv), and time is in seconds.

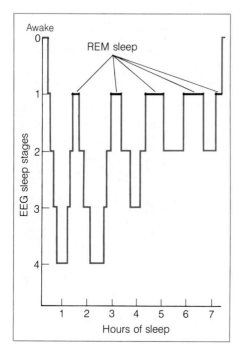

Figure 6-4
Succession of Sleep Stages
The graph provides an example of the sequence and duration of sleep stages during a
typical night. The subject started in Stage 0
(awake) and then went successively through
Stages 1 to 4 during the first hour. He then
moved back through Stages 3 and 2 to the
REM stage. The REM stage is like Stage 1 in
terms of its EEG pattern, but it is accompanied by rapid eye movements. The width of
each horizontal line segment indicates the duration of the corresponding stage of sleep.
There are large individual differences from
subject to subject. However, the general pattern is to proceed through the first four stages
during the initial hour of sleep before REM
occurs. The deeper Stages 3 and 4 tend to
disappear in the second half of the night as
REM becomes more prominent. (After Cartwright, 1978)

yet understand why people dream at all, much less why they dream what they do. However, modern methods of study have answered a great many questions about dreaming.

DOES EVERYONE DREAM? Although many people do not recall their dreams in the morning, REM-sleep evidence suggests that nonrecallers do as much dreaming as recallers (Goodenough and others, 1959). Several hypotheses have been proposed to account for differences in dream recall. One possibility is that nonrecallers simply have more difficulty than recallers in remembering their dreams. (Lewis and others, 1966). Another hypothesis suggests that some people awaken relatively easily in the midst of REM sleep and thus recall more dreams than those who sleep more soundly (Webb and Kersey, 1967). The most generally accepted model for dream recall supports the idea that what happens on awakening is the crucial factor. According to this hypothesis, unless a distraction-free waking period occurs shortly after dreaming, the memory of the dream is not consolidated (Koulack and Goodenough, 1976).

HOW LONG DO DREAMS LAST? Some dreams seem almost instantaneous. The alarm clock rings, and we awaken to complex memories of a fire breaking out and fire engines arriving with their sirens blasting. Because the alarm is still ringing, we assume that the sound must have produced the dream. Research suggests, however, that a ringing alarm clock or other sound merely reinstates a complete scene from earlier memories or dreams. This experience has its parallel during wakefulness when a single cue may tap a rich memory that takes some time to tell. The length of a typical dream can be inferred from a REM study in which subjects were awakened and asked to act out what they had been dreaming (Dement and Wolpert, 1958). The time it took them to pantomime the dream was almost the same as the length of the REM sleep period, suggesting that the incidents in dreams commonly last about as long as they would in real life. Although the short dream instigated by a sound or other outside stimulus is not typical of most people's dream life, it does occur frequently (Arkin and Antrobus, 1978).

DO PEOPLE KNOW WHEN THEY ARE DREAMING? Surprisingly, the answer to this question is "sometimes yes." People can be taught to recognize that they are dreaming, and their awareness does not interfere with the dream's spontaneous flow. For example, subjects have been trained to close an open switch when they noticed that they were dreaming (Salamy, 1970).

People who have *lucid dreams* are aware of dreaming and typically report doing "experiments" within their dreams to prove that the events are not those of ordinary waking reality. A Dutch physician, van Eeden (1913), was one of the first to give an accurate account of initiating actions within a lucid dream to prove that events were not occurring normally. In a later report, Brown (1936) described a standard experiment in which he jumped and suspended himself in the air. If he did this successfully, he knew he was dreaming. Both Brown and van Eeden report an occasional "false awakening" within a dream. For example, in one of Brown's dreams, having discovered that he was dreaming, he decided to call a taxicab as an indication of his control over events. He reached into his pocket to see if he had some change to pay the driver and thought that he woke up. He then found the coins scattered about the bed. At this point, he really awoke and found himself lying in a different position and, of course, without any coins. One of the authors of this textbook (E.R.H.) has occasionally experienced such dreams and has tested his state of consciousness by the voluntary act (within the dream) of flying above the ground.

CAN PEOPLE CONTROL THE CONTENT OF THEIR DREAMS?   Psychologists have demonstrated that some control of dream content is possible by making suggestions to subjects in the presleep period and then analyzing the content of the dreams that follow. In a carefully designed study of an *implicit predream suggestion,* reseachers tested the effect of wearing red goggles prior to sleep. Although no actual suggestion was made and the subjects did not understand the purpose of the experiment, many subjects reported that their visual dream worlds were tinted (Roffwarg and others, 1978). In a study of the effect of an *overt predream suggestion,* subjects were asked to try to dream about a personality characteristic that they wished they had. Most of the subjects had at least one dream in which the intended trait could be recognized (Cartwright, 1974).

Post-hypnotic predream suggestion is another way of influencing dream content. In one extensive study using this method, detailed dream narratives were suggested to highly responsive hypnotic subjects. After the suggestion, the subject slept until roused from REM sleep. Some of the resulting dreams reflected the thematic aspects of the suggestion without including many of the specific elements, whereas other dreams reflected specific elements of the suggestion (Tart and Dick, 1970).

WHEN DO SLEEPTALKING AND SLEEPWALKING TAKE PLACE?   Careful laboratory studies of sleeptalkers and sleepwalkers have shown that most of this behavior takes place during NREM sleep. In one study of 13 subjects who averaged 3.9 speeches per night, researchers found that 75 to 80 percent of the talking took place during NREM sleep (Arkin and others, 1970). This finding does not mean that all sleeptalking is independent of dreams. Dreaming is not limited to REM sleep, as was thought when REM was first discovered, although dreams that take place during REM sleep are more likely to be recalled than are NREM dreams (Herman, Ellman, and Roffwarg, 1978). Sleepwalking can occur at any stage of sleep. Subjects usually forget what they did while sleepwalking, and the dreams they report bear no resemblance to what they did while walking about (Jacobson and Kales, 1967).

Taken together, these findings suggest that the study of dreams and their manipulation may be a way of learning more about various mental processes.

"Greetings. You are now entering the Rapid Eye Movement phase of your sleep cycle."

Drawing by Ed Fisher. Reprinted by permission of the *Chicago Tribune.* New York News Syndicate.

Dream theories

One of the earliest and most comprehensive attempts to explain the content of dreams without reference to the supernatural was Freud's theory that dreams are mental products that can be understood and interpreted. In his book on dreams, Freud (1900) presented his controversial notion that dreams are a disguised attempt at *wish fulfillment.* By this he meant that the dream touches on wishes or needs that the individual finds unacceptable and *represses* (or banishes) from consciousness. These wishes then appear in symbolic form as the *latent content* of the dream. Freud used the metaphor of a "censor" to explain the conversion of latent dream content to *manifest content* (the characters and events that make up the actual narrative of the dream). In effect, Freud said, the censor protects the sleeper, enabling him or her to express warded-off impulses while avoiding the frightening intensity of the unconscious wish that is being expressed. However, sometimes the "dream work," as Freud called it, fails, and anxiety wakens the dreamer (Freud, 1933).

Freud's followers, whether they broke with him or remained generally faithful to his views, have modified the theory in many ways. Even so, a dream

Does Spontaneous Neural Activity Cause Dreams?

With the development of electrophysiological measures of sleep and the discovery of REM as an indicator of dreaming, some researchers turned their attention from psychological to physiological hypotheses about the origins of dreams.

A physiological theory of how dreams originate has been developed by two investigators (Hobson and McCarley, 1977), who have taken the position that dreams are the result of spontaneous activation of neurons in the pons, a portion of the brain that lies close to the cerebellum. They challenged the notion that dreams reflect the emotional concerns of the sleeper, arguing that physiological activation during dreams is "motivationally neutral." According to their hypothesis, brain waves that start in the pons spread to the forebrain, which synthesizes the impulses into a dream. They support this hypothesis with evidence from an analysis of 104 dreams recorded after awakening subjects from REM sleep. They note a predominance in these dreams of references to (1) movements of the lower extremities, which would be expected if dreams originate in the pons and (2) auditory sensations, which would be expected if the forebrain is activated in REM sleep (McCarley and Hoffman, 1981).

Their hypothesis has created considerable controversy. Opponents cite the large body of experimental evidence that dreams can be influenced by specific kinds of predream stimulation (see the accompanying text). They also argue that the Hobson–McCarley hypothesis is incomplete and uses one oversimplified explanation to account for information that can be adequately explained in other ways (LaBruzza, 1978). Finally, the theory does not take into account available contradictory neurophysiological evidence. The correspondence between activity in the pons and dreaming is not as close as would be required by the hypothesis (Vogel, 1978).

Clearly, this theory of neural activation ignores too much that has been established about dreams and dreaming to be acceptable. The neurophysiological study of dreams has much to teach us, but it seems doubtful that the origin of dreams can ever be fully explained by a theory that rejects the idea of a meaningful relationship between an individual's dream thoughts and psychological experience. Spontaneous neural activity may influence the content of some dreams, but the dreamer's anxieties, conflicts, and daily preoccupations probably play a more important role.

research psychologist, deeply involved in the laboratory study of dreams by psychophysiological methods, has this to say about Freud's influence:

> Freud's genius is best attested to by the fact, on the one hand, that subsequent empirical research rarely has been conducted without some direct influence of his views, and, on the other hand, that dream theory since 1900 has been, by and large, but a series of variations of Freud's early themes. (Foulkes, 1978, p. 127)

The cognitive side of dreaming—its role in problem solving and thinking—has been increasingly recognized (see Foulkes, 1978; French and Fromm, 1963; Hall, 1966). Although cognitive psychologists reject many of Freud's ideas, they also note that his theory has cognitive aspects. In fact, Freud's emphasis on thought transformations through free association goes far beyond the oversimplified popular notion that all the transformations in dreams can be explained as wish fulfillment.

MEDITATION

In *meditation,* a desired state of consciousness is reached by performing certain rituals or exercises.

Traditional forms of meditation

Traditional forms of meditation follow the practices of *yoga,* a system of thought based on the Hindu religion, or *Zen,* which is derived from Chinese and

Meditation

Japanese Buddhism. Two common techniques are (1) an *opening-up* meditation in which the subject clears his or her mind for receiving new experiences and (2) a concentrative meditation in which the benefits are obtained through actively attending to some object, word, or idea (Naranjo and Ornstein, 1977). The following is a representative statement of opening-up meditation:

> This approach begins with the resolve to do nothing, to think nothing, to make no effort of one's own, to relax completely and let go of one's mind and body . . . stepping out of the stream of ever-changing ideas and feelings which your mind is in, watch the onrush of the stream. Refuse to be submerged in the current. Changing the metaphor, it may be said, watch your ideas, feelings, and wishes fly across the firmament like a flock of birds. Let them fly freely. Just keep a watch. Don't let the birds carry you off into the clouds. (Chauduri, 1965, pp. 30–31)

Below is a corresponding statement used in an experimental study of concentrative meditation:

> The purpose of these sessions is to learn about concentration. Your aim is to concentrate on the blue vase. By concentration I do not mean analyzing the different parts of the vase, but rather, trying to see the vase as it exists in itself, without any connections to other things. Exclude all other thoughts or feelings or sounds or body sensations. (Deikman, 1963, p. 330)

After a few sessions of concentrative meditation, subjects typically report a number of effects including: (1) an altered, more intense perception of the vase; (2) some time-shortening, particularly in retrospect; (3) conflicting perceptions, as if the vase fills the visual field and does not fill it, or agitation that is at once disturbing and pleasurable; (4) decreasing effectiveness of external stimuli (less distraction and eventually less conscious registration); and (5) an impression of the meditative state as pleasant, valuable, and rewarding.

Experimental studies of meditation, which are necessarily of short duration, provide only limited insight into the alterations of consciousness that can be achieved when meditative practice and training extend over many years. In his study of the *Matramudra,* a centuries-old Tibetan Buddhist text, Brown (1977) has described the complex training required to master the technique. He has also shown that cognitive changes can be expected at different meditative levels. (In this type of meditation, five levels succeed each other until a thoughtless, perceptionless, selfless state known as concentrative *samdhi* is reached.)

Meditation for relaxation

A somewhat commercialized and secularized form of meditation has been widely promoted in the United States and elsewhere under the name of Transcendental Meditation or TM (Forem, 1973). The technique, which is simple, is learned from a qualified teacher. This person gives the novice meditator a *mantra* (a special sound) and instructions on how to repeat it over and over to produce the deep rest and awareness characteristic of TM.

A similar state of relaxation can be produced without the mystical associations of TM. Developed by Benson and his colleagues, the technique includes the following steps:

1   Sit quietly in a comfortable position and close your eyes.
2   Deeply relax all your muscles, beginning at your feet and progressing to your face. Keep them deeply relaxed.

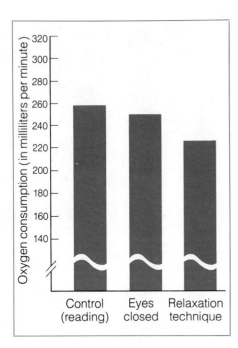

Figure 6-5
Effect of Relaxation Technique
on Oxygen Consumption
Subjects in this experiment consumed significantly less oxygen when they were meditating for relaxation than when they were reading or sitting quietly with their eyes closed. (After Benson and others, 1977)

3   Breathe through your nose. Become aware of your breathing. As you breathe out, say the word "one" silently to yourself. For example, breathe in . . . out, "one"; in . . . out, "one"; and so on. Continue for 20 minutes. You may open your eyes to check the time, but do not use an alarm. When you finish, sit quietly for several minutes at first with closed eyes and later with opened eyes.

4   Do not worry about whether you are successful in achieving a deep level of relaxation. Maintain a passive attitude and permit relaxation to occur at its own pace. Expect other thoughts. When these distracting thoughts occur, ignore them by thinking "oh well" and continue repeating "one." With practice, the response should come with little effort.

5   Practice the technique once or twice daily but not within 2 hours after any meal, since the digestive processes seem to interfere with the subjective changes. (Benson and others, 1977, p. 442)

During this kind of meditation, subjects consume less oxygen, eliminate less carbon dioxide, and breathe more slowly than during comparable periods when they are reading or sitting with their eyes closed (see Figure 6-5). They report feelings quite similar to those generated by other meditative practices: peace of mind, a feeling of being at peace with the world, and a sense of well-being. Benson's success with this relatively simple method should not be taken to suggest that he has captured the essence of the Eastern traditions. There is much to be learned from authentic meditative forms.

PSYCHOACTIVE DRUGS

Since ancient times, drugs have been used for their psychological effects—to stimulate or relax, to bring on sleep or prevent it, to enhance ordinary perceptions, or to produce hallucinations. Drugs that have psychological effects are called *psychoactive*. They include not only "street drugs" such as heroin and marijuana but also tranquilizers and other drugs used to treat mental disorders (discussed in Chapter 16) as well as more familiar drugs such as alcohol, tobacco, and coffee.

From this large and varied group of substances, we have chosen six for discussion here: alcohol, heroin, amphetamines, cocaine, LSD, and marijuana. All have been used by large numbers of people for their presumably pleasant effects—although all can have unwanted effects as well. These drugs will come up again in Chapter 15 when we consider drug dependence as a personal and social problem; here, the focus is on the changes they produce in mood and state of consciousness.

Depressants

ALCOHOL   In small quantities, alcohol appears to increase people's energy and make them feel lively and sociable. In reality, alcohol is a central nervous system depressant, not a stimulant. The feeling of stimulation comes from its ability to relax some of the ordinary restraints on social behavior. At concentrations of .03 to .05 percent in the blood, alcohol produces lightheadedness, relaxation, and release of inhibitions. People say things they might not ordinarily say; they tend to become more sociable and sometimes show off. Self-confidence may increase, whereas motor reactions begin to slow (a pair of effects that does much to account for the danger of driving after drinking).

At a concentration of .1 percent (say, after three cocktails or three bottles of beer), sensory and motor functions become noticeably impaired. Speech becomes slurred; there may be difficulty coordinating arm and leg movements. Some people tend to become angry and aggressive, whereas others grow silent and morose. The drinker is seriously incapacitated at a level of .2 percent, and a level above .4 percent may cause death. Intoxication usually is legally defined as a concentration of blood alcohol of .10 to .15 percent.

Among the less pleasant effects of alcohol intoxication are "blackouts," a loss of memory for what happened when the person was drunk. Often, however, these memories return when the individual becomes intoxicated again (Overton, 1972). This sequence reflects what is called *state-dependent learning:* something that is learned in state A can be recalled again only in state A; in state B, it is forgotten. Drugs like alcohol that characteristically produce state-dependent learning are classified as dissociative drugs (Ho, Chute, and Richards, 1977).

Hallucinations, or imaginary experiences with perceptual reality, are also associated with excessive use of alcohol. In *delirium tremens* (DTs), the hallucinations are usually visual and often take the form of snakes, turkey gobblers, or other frightening animals. The condition occurs at the cessation of a long period of heavy drinking. Other symptoms include extreme agitation and hyperactivity. Delirium tremens is serious and may cause death. In *alcoholic hallucinosis,* the hallucinations are usually auditory. The patient may hear voices while under the influence of alcohol but is otherwise not disoriented. The symptoms correspond in some respects to those of schizophrenia (see Chapter 15), and there may be underlying personality problems that produce the condition. Auditory hallucinations produced by alcohol and other drugs are relatively rare; visual hallucinations are more common (Zikmund, 1972).

"Hey, what is this stuff? It makes everything I think seem profound."

Drawing by W. Miller; © 1978 *The New Yorker Magazine,* Inc.

HEROIN Opium and its derivatives, collectively known as *opiates,* are drugs that diminish physical sensation and the capacity to respond to stimuli by depressing the central nervous system. (These drugs are commonly called "narcotics," but "opiates" is the more accurate term; the word "narcotics," as used by law-enforcement officials and by the public, is not well defined and covers a variety of illegal drugs.) Opiates are medically useful for their pain-killing properties. Their ability to alter mood and reduce anxiety has led to widespread illegal, nonmedical consumption. Opium, which is the air-dried juice of the opium poppy, contains a number of chemical substances including morphine and codeine. Codeine is relatively mild in its effects; morphine is stronger; and heroin, derived from morphine, is even more potent. When administered by the same method, pure heroin is about three times as potent as morphine. Street heroin contains many impurities and therefore is less powerful by weight than morphine.

Like all human motives, the reasons people use heroin are complex. At first, heroin produces a sense of well-being. Experienced adult users report a special "thrill," or "rush," within a minute or two after an intravenous injection. Some describe this sensation as intensely pleasurable, similar to an orgasm. Young people who sniff heroin report that they forget everything that troubles them (Chein and others, 1964). Following this, the user feels "fixed," or gratified, with no awareness of hunger, pain, or sexual urges. She or he may "go on the nod," alternately waking and drowsing while comfortably watching television or reading a book. Unlike the alcoholic, the heroin user can readily produce skilled responses to agility and intellectual tests and seldom becomes aggressive or assaultive. The changes in consciousness produced by heroin are not very striking; there are no exciting visual experiences or feelings of being transported elsewhere. Apparently, it is the changes in mood or self-confidence and the sensation of reduced anxiety that prompt people to *start* using this dangerous drug. However, even a brief period of heroin usage can create physical dependence so that the individual experiences highly unpleasant symptoms when the drug is withdrawn (see Chapter 16 for a discussion of tolerance and addiction). Thus, the motivation to *continue* using the drug stems from the need to avoid pain and discomfort.

Stimulants

AMPHETAMINES In contrast to depressants, stimulants are drugs that increase arousal. Amphetamines are powerful stimulants, sold under such trade names as Methedrine, Dexedrine, and Benzedrine and known colloquially as "speed," "uppers," or "Bennies." The immediate effects of consuming such drugs are an increase in alertness and wakefulness and a decrease in feelings of fatigue and boredom. Strenuous activities that require effort and endurance may become easier when amphetamines are taken (Weiss and Laties, 1962). As with other drugs, the ability of amphetamines to alter mood and increase self-confidence is the principal motivation for their use. People also use them to stay awake and to lose weight. Since increasingly large doses are needed as the user continues to take the drug and since high doses can produce dangerous side effects, the drugs should be used with caution.

Low doses that are taken for limited periods to overcome fatigue (as during nighttime driving) seem to be relatively safe, although some users show impaired judgment or post-amphetamine depression (Tinklenberg, 1972). When sustained use results in gradually increasing doses, the user may become inappropriately suspicious or hostile or have persecutory delusions (Snyder, 1973). Large intravenous doses commonly produce an immediate pleasant experience, termed a "flash" or "rush"; this sensation is followed by irritability and discomfort, which can be overcome only by additional injection. The sequence is repeated every few hours over a period of days, ending in a "crash," a deep sleep followed by a period of lethargy and depression. The amphetamine abuser may seek relief from this discomfort by turning to alcohol or heroin.

COCAINE Like other stimulants, cocaine, or "coke," a substance obtained from dried leaves of the coca plant, increases energy and self-confidence and decreases fatigue and appetite. In the early part of the century, cocaine was widely used and easy to obtain. Its use then declined, but recently its popularity has been increasing among middle-class people, even though it is now illegal. The study of the specific psychological effects of cocaine has been neglected by modern researchers, despite the existence of one of the earliest careful studies of the psychopharmacological effects of the drug by Sigmund Freud (1885; reproduced in Freud, 1974). His account of his own use of cocaine was at first highly favorable to the drug and encouraged its use. He noted:

> the exhilaration and lasting euphoria, which in no way differs from the normal euphoria of the healthy person. . . . You perceive an increase of self-control and possess more vitality and capacity for work. . . . In other words, you are simply normal, and it is so hard to believe that you are under the influence of any drug. . . . Long intensive mental or physical work is performed without any fatigue. . . . This result is enjoyed without any of the unpleasant after-effects that follow exhilaration brought about by alcohol. . . . Absolutely no craving for the further use of cocaine appears after the first or even repeated taking of the drug; one feels rather a curious aversion to it. (Freud, 1974, p. 9)

Freud soon withdrew this unreserved support, however, for he treated a friend with cocaine and the results were disastrous. The friend developed a severe addiction, demanded larger dosages of the drug than Freud ever recommended, and was debilitated until his death.

Recent investigations have looked at both the size of the dose and the mode of administration—that is, sniffing or intravenous injection. One study found that sniffing produces immediate acute effects, described as "highs," which peak in 10 minutes and (except in the case of large doses) disappear within 30 minutes. Intravenous injections add "speeding" effects (the sense of high-energy levels) and reduce hunger; no specific effects on the user's strength can be detected (Resnick, Kestenbaum, and Schwartz, 1977). Small doses taken by either method, produce generally pleasant effects, although some depressed persons describe unpleasant reactions. Large doses produce unpleasantly rapid heart rates and severe loss of appetite.

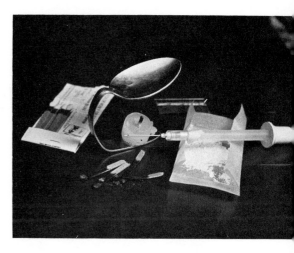

Because the reactions to cocaine and amphetamines are almost indistinguishable, some cocaine sold on the street is adulterated with amphetamines, which are cheaper and more readily available than cocaine but also more dangerous at usual doses. Either type of drug can cause acute paranoia that is indistinguishable from paranoid schizophrenia.

Hallucinogens

Drugs whose main effect is to change perceptual experience are called *hallucinogens*, or *psychedelics*. The stronger hallucinogens, such as LSD, quite commonly produce dramatic perceptual changes, including hallucinations. Marijuana ordinarily causes much milder perceptual alterations.

Some hallucinogenic drugs are derived from plants—for example, mescaline from cactus and psilocybin from mushrooms. Others are synthesized in the laboratory—for example, LSD (lysergic acid diethylamide), DMT (dimethyltriptamine), and DOM (dimethoxy-methyl-amphetamine—also known as STP, for "serenity-tranquility-peace"). Psychedelics differ in the duration of their acute action. The effects of DMT last only for an hour, whereas LSD and mescaline last from 8 to 12 hours.

LSD Although LSD, or "acid," was once the most popular psychedelic drug, the widespread knowledge that its effects are highly individual and unpredictable has reduced its use. Some users have vivid hallucinations of colors and sounds, whereas others have mystical or semireligious experiences. Anyone can have an adverse reaction (or "bad trip"), even those who have had many pleasant LSD experiences. The disturbances are often severe enough to cause the user to seek the help of a psychiatrist or clinical psychologist.

Another adverse LSD reaction is the "flashback," which may occur days, weeks, or months after the last use of the drug. The individual may experience illusions or hallucinations similar to those experienced when using the drug. Since LSD is almost completely eliminated from the body within 24 hours after it is taken, the flashback is probably some sort of restoration of memories of the prior experience (Stanton, Mintz, and Franklin, 1976).

More threatening to the LSD user is the loss of reality orientation that can occur during mystical states associated with the drug. This alteration in consciousness can lead to highly irrational and disoriented behavior and, occasionally, to a panic state in which the victim feels that he or she cannot control what the body is doing or thinking. There have been reports of people jumping from high places to their death when in this state.

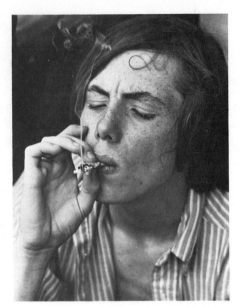

MARIJUANA   The most popular of all the illicit drugs, marijuana (*cannabis*), commonly known as "pot" or "grass," is derived from the hemp plant. Users smoke or eat the leaves to induce a relaxed state of heightened perceptiveness. In recent decades many young people in the United States have used marijuana for its intoxicating effects as other generations used alcohol. The legal restrictions today appear to be no more likely to inhibit its use than were those outlawing alcohol during Prohibition.

The active ingredient in marijuana is THC (tetrahydrocannabinol). Taken orally in small doses (5 to 10 milligrams), THC produces a mild "high"; larger doses (30 to 70 milligrams) produce severe and longer-lasting reactions that resemble those of more strongly hallucinogenic drugs. As with alcohol, the reaction often has two stages: a period of stimulation and euphoria, followed by a period of tranquility and, with higher doses, sleep.

The effects on consciousness of marijuana use have been studied by Tart (1971). He interviewed 150 subjects, all of whom had used marijuana at least a dozen times prior to the study and most of whom used it once a week or more during the months of the study. The subjects reported many sensory and perceptual changes: a general euphoria and sense of well-being, some distortions of space and time, changes in social perception and experience, and a number of out-of-body experiences. Characteristic responses are summarized in Table 6-1.

Many experimental studies on the effects of marijuana have been confounded by the subjects' lack of experience with the drug or by their simultaneous use of other drugs. One study in which these factors were carefully controlled found few measurable effects of prolonged use (Schaeffer, Andrysiak, and Ungerleider, 1981). The subjects were 10 persons, all Caucasians

Table 6-1
Characteristic Effects of Marijuana
The hallucinogenic quality of marijuana can be seen in the frequent reports of altered perceptions and enhanced sensory experiences by experimental subjects. The effects enclosed in parentheses are less common. (After Tart, 1971, p. 245)

LEVEL OF MARIJUANA INTOXICATION	REPORTED EFFECTS
Mild	Less noisy at parties than when "tipsy" or drunk New, subtle quality to sounds
Fair	Taste sensations have new qualities Easy to get to sleep at bedtime Enjoy eating a lot (Hard to play ordinary social games) (Less need to feel in control of things) (Invariably feel good from turning on) (Understand words of songs better)
Fair to strong	Time passes more slowly Distance in walking changed More childlike, open to experience Physically relaxed (See patterns in normally ambiguous material) (Difficult to read) (Touch more exciting, sensual) (Greater spatial separation between musical instruments) (Visual imagery more intense)
Strong	(Easily sidetracked)
Strong to very strong	(Forget start of conversation)

born and raised in the United States, who are members of a religious sect that uses marijuana, in the form of ganja, as part of their religious sacrament. Members of the sect abstain from alcohol and other psychoactive drugs and eat little meat. The subjects had used between 2 and 4 ounces of ganja-tobacco mixture each day, for a mean duration of 7.4 years, and their urine specimens indicated the presence of large amounts of cannabis. Nevertheless, their intelligence levels were unimpaired; they performed adequately on other cognitive measures; and they showed no signs of poor health. (However, the long-range effect that smoking may have on these subjects' lungs remains to be determined.)

In concluding this discussion, several points regarding the use of drugs and their effects on consciousness are worth noting. First, drugs produce a wide range of subjective experiences. Considerable variation is found in the responses of many people to a particular drug and in the responses of one person to many drugs. Some drug-induced experiences are highly pleasurable, whereas others are frightening. Second, objective changes in behavior, such as the reduction of fatigue or the instigation of aggression, are also highly variable and depend on dosage. Third, the social setting in which the drug is taken may influence the user's experiences and behavior. Finally, the fact that the results of drug use may endure—and reappear as flashbacks—suggests that the influences of drugs on brain processes may in some instances be profound.

HYPNOSIS

Of all states of altered consciousness, none raises more questions than the *hypnotic condition*, which can be described as a highly responsive state induced in a subject by a hypnotist. Once associated with the bizarre and occult, hypnosis has now become the subject of rigorous scientific investigation. As in all fields of psychological investigation, uncertainties remain, but by now many facts have been established.

The hypnotic experience

In hypnosis, a willing and cooperative subject (the only kind that can be hypnotized under most circumstances) relinquishes some control over his or her behavior to the hypnotist and accepts some reality distortion. The hypnotist uses a variety of methods to induce this condition. For example, the subject may be asked to concentrate all thoughts on a small target (such as a thumbtack on the wall) while gradually becoming relaxed. A suggestion of sleepiness may be made because, like sleep, hypnosis is a relaxed state in which a person is out of touch with ordinary environmental demands. But sleep is only a metaphor. The subject is told that he or she will not really go to sleep but will continue to listen to the hypnotist.

The same state can be induced by methods other than relaxation. A hyperalert hypnotic trance is characterized by increased tension and alertness, and the trance-induction procedure is an active one. For example, in one study, subjects riding a stationary laboratory bicycle while receiving suggestions of strength and alertness felt less than normal fatigue and were as responsive to hypnotic suggestions as conventionally relaxed subjects (Banyai and Hilgard, 1976). This result denies the common equation of hypnosis with relaxation but is consistent with the trance-induction methods of sects like the whirling dervishes.

Involuntary movement of the arms or paralysis of movement may be produced readily by hypnotic suggestion.

Modern hypnotists do not use authoritarian commands. Indeed, with a little training, subjects can hypnotize themslves (Ruch, 1975). The subject enters the hypnotic state when the conditions are right; the hypnotist merely helps set these conditions. The following changes are characteristic of the hypnotized state.

1   *Planfulness ceases.*   A deeply hypnotized subject does not like to initiate activity and would rather wait for the hypnotist to suggest what to do.
2   *Attention is redistributed and becomes more selective than usual.*   A subject who is told to listen only to the hypnotist's voice will ignore any other voices in the room.
3   *Enriched fantasy is readily evoked.*   A subject may find herself or himself enjoying experiences at a place distant in time and space.
4   *Reality testing is reduced and reality distortion accepted.*   A subject may uncritically accept hallucinated experiences (for example, conversing with a hallucinated person believed to be sitting in an empty chair) and will not check to determine whether the experience is real.
5   *Suggestibility is increased.*   A subject must accept suggestions in order to be hypnotized at all, but whether suggestibility is increased under hypnosis is a matter of some dispute. Careful studies do find some increase in suggestibility following hypnotic induction, although less than is commonly supposed (Ruch, Morgan, and Hilgard, 1973).
6   *Post-hypnotic amnesia is often present.*   When instructed to do so, a highly responsive hypnotic subject will forget all or most of what transpired during the hypnotic session. When a prearranged release signal is given, the memories are restored.

Responsiveness to suggestions is typical of relatively superficial levels of hypnosis. When highly responsive subjects are encouraged to go deeper into hypnosis, they eventually reach a state in which they are unresponsive to the hypnotist's suggestions (except when a prearranged signal returns them to a level at which they can communicate). This state may be similar to a mystical experience. People who have been deeply hypnotized describe a sense of mind-body separation, a feeling of oneness with the universe, an impression of gaining knowledge of a kind that cannot be communicated (Tart, 1979).

Not all subjects are equally responsive to hypnotic procedures (Figure 6-6). Responsiveness seems to have both learned and genetic components. The capacity to set ordinary reality aside and become deeply absorbed in reading a book, watching a play, listening to music, or enjoying nature is an important predictor of hypnotizability (J.R. Hilgard, 1979). This is probably a learned capacity, developed in early childhood through experiences with parents rich in imagination. Evidence that native ability is also involved comes from two kinds of studies: comparisons of changes in hypnotizability over time and comparisons of hypnotizability in twins.

One test-retest study demonstrated that responsiveness is a fairly stable trait (Morgan, Johnson, and Hilgard, 1974). Subjects who were tested as undergraduates and retested 10 years later achieved scores on a measure of hypnotizability that showed a correlation of .60 between the two tests. Stronger support for a hereditary component comes from studies of twins. For example, when identical (monozygotic) twins were compared with fraternal (dizygotic) twins, there was a significant difference between the groups. The identical twins achieved more similar hypnotizability scores than did the fraternal twins (Morgan, 1973).

A variety of behaviors and experiences can result from suggestions given

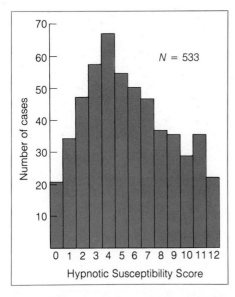

Figure 6-6
Individual Differences in Hypnotizability
After using a standard procedure designed to induce hypnosis, 12 test suggestions from the Stanford Hypnotic Susceptibility Scale were given, testing the appearance of hypnotic responses such as those described in the text. (Examples are being unable to bend one's arm or separate interlocked fingers when the hypnotist suggests these possibilities.) The response is scored as present or absent, and the present or "passed" responses are totaled to yield a score ranging from 0 for the totally unresponsive to 12 for the most responsive. As with other psychological measurements, most subjects fall in the middle ranges with a few very high and a few very low. (After Hilgard, 1965)

to a hypnotized subject. The person's motor control may be affected; new memories may be lost or old ones reexperienced; and current perceptions may be radically altered.

CONTROL OF MOVEMENT   Many hypnotic subjects respond to direct suggestion with involuntary movement. For example, if a person stands with arms outstretched and hands facing each other and the suggestion is made that the hands are attracted to one another, the hands will soon begin to move, and the subject will feel that they are propelled by some force that she or he is not generating. Direct suggestion can initiate movement, and it can also inhibit movement. If a suggestible subject is told that an arm is stiff (like a bar of iron or an arm in a splint) and then is asked to bend the arm, it will not bend or more effort than usual will be needed to make it bend. This response is less common than is suggested movement.

Subjects who have been roused from hypnosis may respond with movement to a prearranged signal from the hypnotist. This is called a post-hypnotic response. Even if the suggestion has been forgotten, the subject will feel a compulsion to carry out the behavior. Subjects may try to justify such behavior as rational, even though the urge to perfom it is impulsive. For example, a young man searching for a rational explanation of why he opened a window when the hypnotist took off his glasses (the prearranged signal) remarked that the room felt a little stuffy.

POST-HYPNOTIC AMNESIA   At the suggestion of the hypnotist, events occurring during hypnosis may be "forgotten" until a signal from the hypnotist enables the subject to recall them. This is called *post-hypnotic amnesia*. Subjects differ widely in their susceptibility to post-hypnotic amnesia, as Figure 6-7 shows. The items to be recalled in this study were 10 actions the subjects performed while hypnotized. A few subjects forgot none or only one or two items; most subjects forgot four or five items. However, a sizable number of subjects forgot all 10 items. This type of bimodal distribution, showing two distinct groups of subjects, has been found in many studies of post-hypnotic amnesia (Cooper,1979). The group of subjects with the lower scores is larger and presumably represents the average hypnotic responders; the smaller group of high scorers have been described as hypnotic virtuosos. Differences in recall between the two groups following post-hypnotic suggestion do not appear to be related to differences in memory capacity; once the amnesia is canceled at a prearranged signal from the hypnotist, highly amnesic subjects remember as many items as those who are less amnesic (Nace, Orne, and Hammer, 1974). It has been suggested that hypnosis temporarily interferes with the person's ability to search for a particular item in memory but does not affect actual memory storage (Kihlstrom and Evans, 1979).

Current research in post-hypnotic amnesia is related more directly to cognitive psychology's interest in memory retrieval. Lists of words are learned during hypnosis and the effect of suggested amnesia on subsequent recall is studied (Kihlstrom, 1980). This research promises to provide some interesting leads about how information is stored and organized in memory (see Chapter 8).

AGE REGRESSION   In response to hypnotic suggestion, some individuals are able to relive episodes from earlier periods of life, such as a birthday at age 10. To some subjects, the episode seems to be pictured as if it were on a TV screen; the subjects are conscious of being present and viewing the event but do not feel as if they are producing it. In another type of regression, subjects

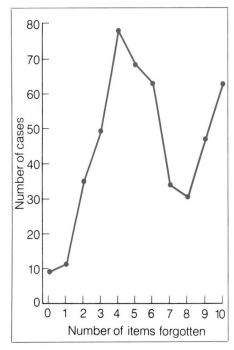

Figure 6-7
Distribution of Post-Hypnotic Amnesia
Subjects performed 10 actions while hypnotized and were then given post-hypnotic amnesia instructions. When asked what occurred during hypnosis, subjects varied in the number of actions they failed to recall; the level of forgetting for a given subject ranged from 0 to 10 items. The experiment involved 491 subjects, and the graph plots the number of subjects at each level of forgetting. The plot shows a bimodal distribution for post-hypnotic amnesia with peaks at 4 and 10 items forgotten. (After Cooper, 1979)

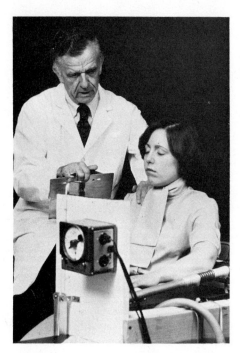

Pain under hypnosis

Previously, when her hand was in the ice water, the subject felt no pain following suggestions of hypnotic anaesthesia. By placing a hand on her shoulder, however, Dr. Hilgard can tap a "hidden observer" that reports pain that the subject had felt at some level.

feel as if they are having the experiences. They may describe the clothing they are wearing, run a hand through their hair and describe its "length," or recognize their elementary-school classmates. The hypnotist may be incorporated in the illusion, perhaps as a visitor to the school.

Occasionally a childhood language, no longer available, emerges during suggested regression. For example, an American-born boy whose parents were Japanese and who had spoken Japanese at an early age but forgotten it began speaking it fluently again while under hypnosis (Fromm, 1970).

POSITIVE AND NEGATIVE HALLUCINATIONS   Some hypnotic experiences require a higher level of hypnotic talent than others. For example, the vivid and convincing perceptual distortions of hallucinations are relatively rare. Two types of suggested hallucinations have been documented: *positive hallucinations*, in which the subject sees an object or hears a voice that is not actually present, and *negative hallucinations*, in which the subject does not perceive something that would normally be perceived. Many hallucinations have both positive and negative components. For example, in order not to see a person sitting in a chair (a negative hallucination), a subject must see the parts of the chair that would ordinarily be blocked from view (a positive hallucination).

Hallucinations can also occur as the result of post-hypnotic suggestion. For example, subjects may be told that on arousal from the hypnotic state, they will find themselves holding a rabbit that wants to be petted and that the rabbit will ask, "What time is it?" Seeing and petting the rabbit seem natural to most of the subjects. But when they find themselves giving the correct time of day, they are surprised and try to provide an explanation for the behavior: "Did I hear someone ask the time? It's funny, it seemed to be the rabbit asking, but rabbits can't talk!" is a typical response.

Negative hallucinations can be used effectively to control pain. In many cases, pain is completely eliminated by hypnosis, even though its source—a severe burn or a bone fracture—continues. The failure to perceive something (pain) that would normally be perceived qualifies this response as a negative hallucination. The pain reduction need not be complete in order for hypnosis to be useful in giving relief. Pain reduction of as little as 20 percent can make the patient's life tolerable. Experimental studies on the relief of pain have shown that the amount of pain reduction is closely related to the degree of measured hypnotizability (Hilgard and Hilgard, 1975). Pain reduction through hypnosis is useful in dentistry, obstetrics, and surgery, especially when chemical anesthetics are ill-advised because of the patient's condition.

Theories of hypnosis

Experts have been arguing about what hypnosis is and how it works since the late 1700s, when Franz Mesmer claimed that it was caused by "animal magnetism." A hundred years later, the French neurologist Charcot suggested that hypnosis is a sign of hysteria and classified it as a neurological disturbance. His views were opposed by Bernheim, a physician who argued that hypnosis is the result of suggestion and insisted that normal people can be hypnotized. Although Bernheim won the argument, hypnosis remained a source of controversy.

Pavlov, famed for his work on conditioned reflexes, believed that hypnosis is a form of sleep, from which, in fact, its name derives. His theory has been largely discredited by (1) physiological studies that show a difference between the EEG in sleep and in hypnosis and (2) demonstrations of alert hypnosis.

CRITICAL DISCUSSION

The "Hidden Observer" in Hypnosis

The neodissociation theory of hypnosis originated with Hilgard's (1977) observation that in many hypnotized subjects, a part of the mind that is not within awareness seems to be watching the subject's experience as a whole. His finding has been described as follows:

The circumstances of Hilgard's discovery of a doubled train of thought in hypnosis were suitably dramatic. He was giving a classroom demonstration of hypnosis using an experienced subject who, as it happened, was blind. Hilgard induced deafness, telling him that he would be able to hear when a hand was put on his shoulder. Cut off from what was going on around him, he became bored and began to think of other things. Hilgard showed the class how unresponsive he was to noise or speech, but then the question arose as to whether he was as unresponsive as he seemed. In a quiet voice, Hilgard asked the subject whether, though he was hypnotically deaf, there might be "some part of him" that could hear; if so, would he raise a forefinger? To the surprise of everyone—including the hypnotized subject—the finger rose.

At this, the subject wanted to know what was going on. Hilgard put a hand on his shoulder so he could hear, promised to explain later, but in the meantime asked the subject what he remembered. What he remembered was that everything had become still, that he was bored and had begun thinking about a problem in statistics. Then he felt his forefinger rise, and he wanted to know why.

Hilgard then asked for a report from "that part of you that listened to me before and made your finger rise," while instructing the hypnotized subject that he would not be able to hear what he himself said. It turned out that this second part of the subject's awareness had heard all that went on and was able to report it. Hilgard found a suitable metaphor to describe this detached witness—the hidden observer. (Hebb, 1982, p. 53)

Thus, the hidden-observer metaphor refers to a mental structure that monitors everything that happens, including events that the hypnotized subject is not consciously aware of perceiving at the time.

The presence of the hidden observer has been demonstrated in many experiments. In studies on pain relief, subjects are able to describe how the pain feels, using automatic writing or speaking, at the same time that their conscious system accepts and responds to the hypnotist's suggestion of pain relief. In other studies using automatic writing, hypnotized subjects have written messages of which they were unaware while their focal attention was directed to another task, such as reading aloud or naming the colors on a display chart (Knox, Crutchfield, and Hilgard, 1975). Hilgard and his colleagues have compared these phenomena to everyday experiences in which an individual divides attention between two tasks, such as driving and conversing at the same time or making a speech and simultaneously evaluating his or her performance as an orator.

Hidden-observer experiments, although replicated in many laboratories and clinics, have been criticized on methodological grounds. Skeptics argue that implied demands for compliance may have produced the results (see, for example, Spanos and Hewitt, 1980). In a careful experiment designed to determine the role of compliance, researchers have shown that it is possible to distinguish the responses of the truly hypnotized from the merely compliant. They asked subjects of proven low hypnotizability to simulate hypnosis while highly responsive subjects behaved naturally. The group to which a subject belonged was not known by the experimenter. The simulators did conform to the implied demands as they would be expected to do, but their reports of the subjective experiences differed significantly from those individuals who were actually hypnotized (Hilgard and others, 1978).

An important but unresolved problem is why some highly responsive hypnotized subjects do not have access to a hidden observer. One difference between the two groups has been reported. Subjects *without* a hidden observer are more "compliant" to age-regression suggestions—that is, they report feeling like children again—whereas those *with* a hidden observer invariably report a persistent duality of awareness. During age regression, they see themselves simultaneously as adult observers and as children. This division between an active participant and an observer is spontaneous and not suggested by the hypnotist (Laurence, 1980).

These are complex matters, not to be simply explained or lightly dismissed. They have implications not only for theories of hypnosis but for our view of consciousness more generally.

Nevertheless, the tie between hypnosis and relaxation is still prominent (Edmonston, 1981).

A psychoanalytic theory suggests that hypnosis is a state of partial regression in which the subject lacks the controls present in mature waking consciousness and therefore acts impulsively and engages in fantasy produciton (Gill, 1972). A theory based on the dramatic nature of many hypnotic behaviors emphasizes a kind of involuntary role enactment as a response to social demands. This theory does *not* imply that the subject is playacting in a deliberate attempt to fool the hypnotist; it assumes that the subject becomes so deeply involved in a role that actions take place without conscious intent (Coe and Sarbin, 1977).

Another theorist believes that hypnosis is goal-directed fantasy. With a collaborator, he has developed a measurement scale based on this concept, known as the Creative Imagination Scale (Barber and Wilson, 1977). A theory, similar to a nineteenth-century interpretation by Pierre Janet, treats hypnosis as a *dissociative phenomenon,* in which some aspects of mental functioning are separated from other aspects. A modified form of this theory, called a *neo-dissociation theory* (Hilgard, 1977), suggests that under hypnosis a kind of split in consciousness occurs (see the accompanying critical discussion).

Competing theories of hypnosis were argued more vehemently a decade or so ago than they are today. With the facts and relationships now better understood at an empirical level, differences between explanations fade in importance. Each theory calls attention to some significant features of hypnosis, and as new data become available, differences are being resolved (see Hilgard, 1973; Sheehan and Perry, 1976; Spanos and Barber, 1974).

UNFOUNDED CLAIMS FOR THE MIND

No discussion of consciousness is complete without considering some esoteric and mystical claims about the mind that have attracted widespread interest in recent years (Ornstein, 1977; Tart, 1975). Whether they are associated with respected ancient religious and philosophical traditions or with more theatrical excursions into the occult, these beliefs ordinarily lie outside the province of a naturalistic psychology. When the claims are tangible, however, psychologists may examine them using ordinary scientific criteria (see the discussion of ESP, Chapter 5).

Mind over body

A person's attitudes and expectations can control what happens to bodily processes. For centuries, experienced yogis have demonstrated remarkable control over processes that are ordinarily involuntary (Wenger and Bagchi, 1961). Until recently, it was assumed that such control resulted only from long and disciplined exercise. It now appears that similar, although less striking, effects can be achieved through *biofeedback* training, which is described in Chapters 7 and 14.

Simple practice, too, can lead to remarkable voluntary control over the body, as any skilled acrobatic performance shows. Even a trick like wiggling one's ears, which is beyond the capacity of most people, can be learned with patient practice. There need be no appeal to religion or otherworldly powers for evidence of the mind's power over the body.

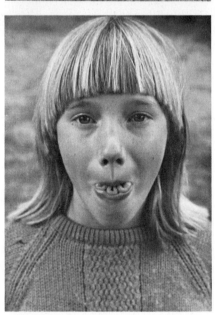

Voluntary muscular control
Not all people are able to groove their tongues, but this young woman is able to form up to three grooves when she wishes. (Courtesy of A.J. Hilgard)

Another illustration of mind over body is firewalking, a religious ceremony carried out in many parts of the world. Even children in some cultures can walk barefoot over hot coals without injuring their feet. (Occasionally, a participant is seriously burned, but believers explain the injury as a consequence of the victim's having annoyed a responsible "spirit.") Surprisingly, firewalking can also be explained without resorting to otherworldly powers. After careful experimentation, a physicist has shown that if the person walks rapidly over the coals, perspiration protects the feet (Walker, 1977). To show his confidence in his own theory, he put his finger into a vessel of molten lead and withdrew it without injury. He was also successful in walking across a bed of coals, and a student in his class joined him without mishap. (On a later occasion, he caught some embers between his toes and ended up with a few blisters.)

Yet evidence for mental control over bodily functions should not be used to support such hoaxes as "psychic surgery," practiced in some parts of the Philippines. Without the use of a knife, the healer appears to open the skin, remove organic matter, and close the wound without a scar. The trick involved has been exposed; still the belief dies hard (Nolen, 1974).

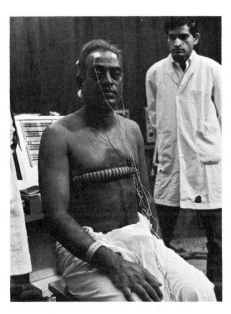

Control of vital functions
Ramanand Yogi has transducers attached for the study of EEGs, heart rate, and breathing as he prepares to reduce his oxygen needs while sealed in an airtight box. (From Calder, 1971)

Mind over matter

A young magician, Uri Geller, became famous in the United States and Great Britain by claiming paranormal (even supernatural) power. Geller managed to convince a number of scientists and even a few magicians (who are often better at detecting tricks than scientists) that his paranormal abilities were genuine (see, Panati, 1976). Among his claims were the abilities to bend keys and repair broken watches without touching them.

To make broken watches operate, Geller instructed participants to hold "broken" watches in their hands and to think, "Work! Work! Work!" The watches often started but not because of his power. Skeptics point out that most watches brought to a jeweler for repair are not actually broken; holding the watch for a few minutes and handling it to free the working parts will often start it running. In a test of the "Geller effect," six jewelers were asked to try to start broken watches by using the holding-and-handling method before opening the watch to inspect it. Of more than 100 watches brought in during one week, 57 percent started working. In one of Geller's stage performances, he was given 12 watches on stage; 4 started. Out of 17 watches that members of the audience held, 3 started. This yields 7 of 29 (24 percent), which is less success than that achieved by the jewelers (Marks and Kammann, 1977).

Reincarnation

Psychic researchers have long searched for tangible evidence of survival after death (Gould, 1977). Related to these efforts is a revived interest in *reincarnation*, the belief that life continues after death as the spirit of the dead person is reborn in the body of another person (Stevenson, 1977).

Instances in which individuals report experiences of prior lives while hypnotized have been cited as evidence of reincarnation. One case was a young American housewife, who under hypnosis described vividly her previous life in Ireland under the name of Bridey Murphy (Bernstein, 1956). A widely publicized account described the matter as a hoax (Gardner, 1975), but the precise refutation was questionable on the basis of later evidence (Wilson, 1982). Hence, some unresolved questions remain. Nevertheless, the case is not convincing as evidence for reincarnation.

It is easy under hypnosis to produce fantasies of the birth experience or of an earlier life, and such evidence need not be taken seriously. One of the authors (E.R.H.) has been able to assign prior lives to hypnotizable subjects. These subjects produce quite satisfactory evidence of having lived at the time and place they were assigned. They have even given believable accounts when (on separate occasions) they were assigned prior lives in two different places at the same previous time. Clearly, under hypnosis, fantasy is interpreted as reality.

The desire to experience mysterious happenings is very great. The role of psychology is not necessarily to contradict occult beliefs but to understand why they have originated and why they persist.

Summary

1 A person's perceptions, thoughts, and feelings at any moment in time constitute that person's *consciousness*. An *altered state of consciousness* is said to exist when mental functioning seems changed or out of the ordinary to the person experiencing the state. Some states, such as daydreaming, are not dramatically different from ordinary consciousness; others are characterized by hallucinations or distortions of objective reality.

2 Two basic modes of consciousness may be distinguished: a *passive, receptive mode* and an *active, goal-directed mode*. Thinking goes on within or near awareness in both modes. Objects or events that capture the person's attention are at the center of awareness, but stimuli of which we are only dimly aware may also register in consciousness. Accessible memories, which are available for recall, are also on the fringes of consciousness.

3 According to psychoanalytic theory, other memories are repressed and become part of the *unconscious*, from which they are retrieved with difficulty. They and the motives associated with them remain active in the unconscious, however, and are responsible for dreams, mannerisms, slips of speech, and even symptoms of illness. Carl Jung, an early disciple of Freud, broke with Freud and modified the theory to include a collective unconscious.

4 In *daydreaming*, a person's attention shifts from the task at hand to more internal matters, often fantasies of past and future incidents. Daydreaming has a relaxed, drifting quality that is usually experienced as pleasant.

5 *Sleep*, an altered state of consciousness that everyone experiences, is of interest because of the rhythms evident in sleep schedules and in the depth of sleep, studied with the aid of the *electroencephalogram* (EEG). Patterns of brain waves show four stages (depths) of sleep, and also a fifth stage characterized by *rapid eye movements* (REMs). These stages alternate throughout the night. Dreams occur more often during REM sleep than during non-REM (NREM) sleep.

6 The most influential theory of dreams was proposed by Sigmund Freud in 1900. It attributes psychological causes to dreams, distinguishing between the *manifest* and *latent content* of dreams and stating that dreams are wishes in disguise.

7 *Meditation* represents an effort to alter consciousness by following planned rituals or exercises such as those of yoga or Zen. Simple exercises combining concentration and relaxation can help novices experience meditative states.

8 *Psychoactive drugs* have long been used for their psychological effects. They include *depressants*, such as alcohol and heroin; *stimulants*, such as amphetamines and cocaine; and *hallucinogens*, such as LSD and marijuana.

Each drug alters consciousness in characteristic ways, depending on dosage, individual differences among users (including personal history), and the surroundings in which the drug is taken.

9   *Hypnosis* is a responsive state in which attention is usually focused on the hypnotist and the hypnotist's suggestions. Some people are more readily hypnotized than others, though most people show some susceptibility. Self-hypnosis can be learned by those who are responsive to hypnosis induced by others.

10 Characteristic hypnotic responses include enhanced or diminished *control over movements*, the distortion of memory through *post-hypnotic amnesia, age regression*, and positive and negative *hallucinations*. The reduction of pain, as a variety of negative hallucination, is one of the beneficial uses of hypnosis in the treatment of burns and in obstetrics, dentistry, and surgery.

11 Theories of hypnosis have long been a source of controversy, with each explaining some aspect of hypnotic behavior but none explaining all. With better agreement on the empirical facts, the theories are gradually becoming supplementary rather than antagonistic.

12 A great deal of control can be exercised over bodily processes without resorting to belief in occult agencies or paranormal processes. Some "miraculous" processes, such as firewalking, can be explained according to ordinary physical principles. Psychology as a natural science is committed to an open-minded testing of claims that are unusual or surprising, but it has an obligation to remain critical.

Further Reading

Several books deal in general with the problems of consciousness and its alterations, such as Tart (ed.), *States of consciousness* (1975); Ornstein, *The psychology of consciousness* (2nd ed., 1977); and Pope and Singer (eds.), *The stream of consciousness* (1978). Problems of divided consciousness—including discussions of possession states, fugues, multiple personalities, and other manifestations in and outside of hypnosis—are treated in Hilgard, *Divided consciousness* (1977).

The literature of sleep and dreams continues to expand. Useful books are Webb, *Sleep: the gentle tyrant* (1975); Arkin, Antrobus, and Ellman (eds.), *The mind in sleep* (1978); Cartwright, *A primer on sleep and dreaming* (1978); and Drucker-Colin, Shkurovich, and Sterman (eds.), *The functions of sleep* (1979).

On meditative practices, see Goleman, *The varieties of meditative experience* (1977); or Naranjo and Ornstein, *On the psychology of meditation* (1977). On meditation for relaxing, see Benson, *The relaxation response* (1975).

Amphetamines and cocaine are treated in Ellinwood and Kilbey (eds.), *Cocaine and other stimulants* (1977); and in Peterson and Stillman (eds.), *Cocaine: 1977* (1977). The collection of Freud's early papers in Byck (ed.), *Cocaine papers* (1974) is of more than historical interest. On hallucinogens, see Siegel and West, *Hallucinations: Behavior, experience, and theory* (1975).

There are a number of books on hypnosis. Treatments that include methods, theories, and experimental results are E.R. Hilgard, *The experience of hypnosis* (1968); Fromm and Shor (eds.), *Hypnosis: Developments in research and new perspectives* (2nd ed., 1979); and J.R. Hilgard, *Personality and hypnosis* (2nd ed., 1979).

There are many books on miraculous and paranormal experiences, but few of them have scientific merit. A serious effort to collect a variety of viewpoints, primarily of those who are committed to their beliefs, has been made by Wolman and others (eds.), *Handbook of parapsychology* (1977). This includes, in addition to the more usual problems of parapsychology, two chapters on life after death. The best recent critiques of pseudoscientific claims are Gardner, *Science: Good, bad, and bogus* (1981); and Wilson, *All in the mind* (1982).

Part four
LEARNING, REMEMBERING, AND THINKING

7
LEARNING

Learning is basic to understanding behavior. The psychological study of learning embraces much more than the learning of a new job or an academic subject; it also bears upon the fundamental problems of emotional development, motivation, social behavior, and personality. We have already discussed many instances of learning—how, for example, children learn to perceive the world around them, to identify with the appropriate sex, and to control their behavior according to adult standards. In this part of the book, we turn to a systematic study of learning. In this chapter, we examine several simple forms of learning that can be studied in the laboratory and that provide a basis for understanding more complicated phenomena. In Chapter 8, we deal with memory, an essential element of learning. And in Chapter 9, we discuss learning as it relates to language and thought.

How do organisms learn? There is no simple reply to that question, but we can begin our discussion by examining *associative learning*. Making a new association or connection between two events is the most basic form of learning. Psychologists distinguish between two forms of associative learning: *classical conditioning* and *operant conditioning*. In classical conditioning, an organism learns that two *stimuli* tend to go together. For example, a baby learns that the sight of a breast (one stimulus) is associated with the taste of milk (another stimulus). In operant conditioning, an organism learns that some *response* it makes leads to a particular *consequence*. For example, a baby learns that taking a nipple to his or her mouth (the response) brings milk (the consequence).

We begin this chapter with a consideration of classical and operant conditioning. But there is more to learning than associating one event with another. In later sections of the chapter, we turn to more complex forms of learning, which involve interpreting present perceptions in the light of past information to reason our way through unfamiliar routes. These more complicated processes, called *cognitive learning,* are a prelude to our study of human memory and language in the next two chapters.

Ivan Pavlov (center) with assistants in his laboratory

CLASSICAL CONDITIONING

The study of *classical conditioning* began with a series of experiments conducted by the Russian Nobel Prize winner Ivan Pavlov at the turn of the century. While studying digestion, Pavlov noticed that a dog began to salivate at the mere sight of a food dish. Any dog salivates when food is placed in its mouth. But this dog had learned to associate the sight of the dish with the taste of food. Pavlov decided to see whether a dog could be taught to associate food with other things, such as a light or a tone.

Pavlov's experiments

A dog is prepared for Pavlov's experiment by having a minor operation performed on its cheek so that part of the salivary gland is exposed to the surface. A capsule is attached to the cheek to measure salivary flow. The dog is brought to a soundproof laboratory on several occasions and is placed in a harness on a table. The preliminary training is needed so the animal will stand quietly in the harness once the actual experiment begins. The laboratory is so arranged that meat powder can be delivered to a pan in front of the dog by remote control. Salivation is recorded automatically. The experimenter can view the animal through a one-way glass panel, but the dog is alone is the laboratory, isolated from extraneous sights and noises (see Figure 7-1).

A light is turned on. The dog may move a bit, but it does not salivate. After a few seconds, meat powder is delivered; the dog is hungry and eats. The recording device registers copious salivation. The procedure is repeated a number of times. Then the experimenter turns on the light but does not deliver any meat powder. The dog salivates nonetheless. It has learned to associate the light with food.

Pavlov called this a *conditioned response* (CR). The dog has been taught, or conditioned, to associate the light with food and to respond to it by salivating. Naturally, a dog salivates when it tastes meat. This is an *unconditioned response*

Figure 7-1
Classical-Conditioning Apparatus
Arrangements used by Pavlov in classical salivary conditioning. During a typical experiment, a light (the conditioned stimulus) appears in the window and meat powder (the unconditioned stimulus) is delivered automatically to the food bowl. (After Yerkes and Margulis, 1909)

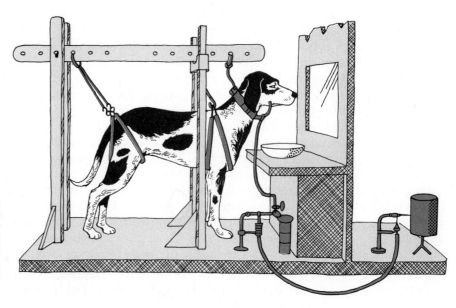

(UR); no learning is involved. By the same token, meat is an *unconditioned stimulus* (US). It automatically makes the dog salivate. Again, no learning is involved. Ordinarily a light would not produce this response, however. Only when the dog has learned that the light signals food does it salivate to the light. Hence, the light is a *conditioned stimulus* (CS) that acquires its power to elicit salivation through association. Pavlov's experiment is diagramed in Figure 7-2.

Acquisition and extinction

Because classical conditioning represents an extremely simple form of learning, many psychologists regard it as an appropriate starting point for an investigation of learning. We will now consider some of the laws that characterize classical conditioning.

ACQUISITION   Each paired presentation of the conditioned stimulus (CS) and the unconditioned stimulus (US) is called a *trial,* and the period during which the organism is learning the association between the two stimuli is the *acquisition* stage of conditioning. The time interval between the presentation of the conditioned and unconditioned stimuli may be varied. Again, let us use Pavlov's experiment as an example. In *simultaneous conditioning,* the light (CS) is turned on as the meat (US) is presented and is left on until the dog salivates (the response). In *delayed conditioning,* the light (CS) is turned on several seconds or more before the meat (US) is presented and again is left on until the response occurs. In *trace conditioning,* the light (CS) is turned on first and then turned off before the meat (US) is presented so that only a "memory trace" of the light, or CS, remains to be conditioned. These three situations are illustrated in Figure 7-3.

In delayed and trace conditioning, the experimenter knows that the organism has made the new association if the response (salivating) occurs before the unconditioned stimulus (meat) has been presented. With simultaneous conditioning, the experimenter has to use test trials in which the unconditioned stimulus (meat) is withheld to determine if the organism has made the new association; if salivation occurs when the conditioned stimulus (light) is presented alone, we know that conditioning has occurred.

Repeated pairings of the conditioned stimulus (light) and the unconditioned stimulus (meat) strengthen, or *reinforce,* the association between the two. Figure 7-4 (left-hand curve) illustrates the gradual strengthening of the conditioned response over a series of acquisition trials, using a trace-conditioning procedure.

EXTINCTION   If the conditioned behavior is not reinforced (if the unconditioned stimulus is omitted repeatedly), the conditioned response gradually diminishes. Repetition of the conditioned stimulus without reinforcement (turning on the light without offering meat) is called *extinction.* Its effect on the animal's performance is shown by the right-hand curve in Figure 7-4.

Examples of classical conditioning

A wide variety of responses, including some we would not ordinarily consider learnable, have been successfully conditioned in both animal and human subjects. In one study, an insulin reaction was conditioned in rats (Sawrey, Conger, and Turrell, 1956). Insulin, a hormone that controls the blood-sugar level, is often used in treating diabetics. An overdose of insulin causes a severe

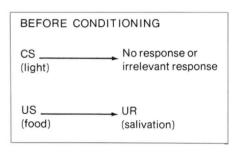

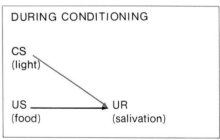

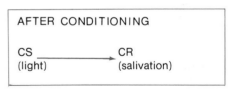

Figure 7-2
Diagram of Classical Conditioning
The association between the unconditioned stimulus and the unconditioned response exists at the start of the experiment and does not have to be learned. The association between the conditioned stimulus and the conditioned response is learned. It arises through the pairing of the conditioned and unconditioned stimuli followed by the unconditioned response. The conditioned response resembles the unconditioned one but generally differs in some details.

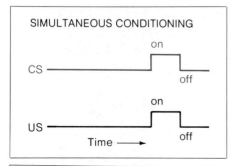

SIMULTANEOUS CONDITIONING

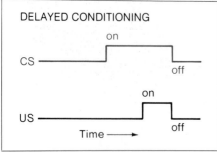

DELAYED CONDITIONING

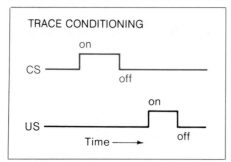

TRACE CONDITIONING

Figure 7-3
Temporal Relations in Conditioning
Delayed conditioning is most effective when the CS precedes the US by approximately one-half second. Simultaneous conditioning is somewhat less effective, and both delayed and trace conditioning become progressively poorer as the CS-US interval increases. It used to be thought that little if any learning occurs when the US precedes the CS (called *backward conditioning*), but recent evidence suggests that under certain conditions backward conditioning may be readily demonstrated.

physiological reaction known as *insulin shock,* which is often acompanied by unconsciousness. In the experiment, the rats were exposed to a bright light and at the same time were injected with an overdose of insulin. The bright light and the hypodermic needle served as the conditioned stimuli; the insulin injection, which elicited shock, was the unconditioned stimulus. After several pairings of the CS and US, a saline solution (which has no physiological effect) was substituted for the insulin. The animals continued to show a shock reaction almost indistinguishable from the reaction produced by insulin. The shock reaction had become a conditioned response.

In this experiment, the conditioned response is not a single, easily measured response such as salivation but the complex pattern of physiological and muscular responses that constitutes insulin shock. A more quantitative physiological measure of conditioning was obtained in the following experiment using human subjects. Exposure of the human body to cold automatically results in vasoconstriction, the constriction of the small blood vessels close to the body surface—a response that keeps the body warm. Although we are not consciously aware of this response, it can be conditioned. A buzzer (CS) is sounded as the subject's left hand is immersed in a container of ice water (US). Since vasoconstriction of the left hand automatically results in some constriction of the blood vessels in the right hand, the degree of vasoconstriction can be measured by using a special instrument placed on the subject's right hand. After a number of paired presentations of the buzzer and water immersion, vasoconstriction occurs in response to the buzzer alone (Menzies, 1937).

Classical conditioning has also been used to study learning in 5- to 7-day-old human newborns (see Figure 7-5). When a puff of air is blown on the eye, the natural response is to blink. If a tone is sounded immediately before

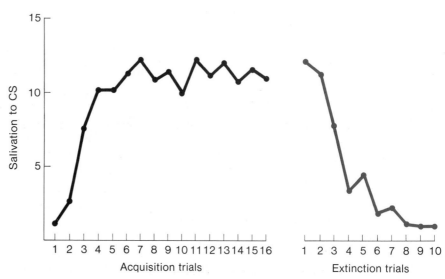

Figure 7-4
Acquisition and Extinction of a Conditioned Response
The curve in the panel on the left depicts the acquisition phase of an experiment using the trace-conditioning procedure. Drops of salivation in response to the conditioned stimulus (prior to the onset of the US) are plotted on the vertical axis; the number of trials, on the horizontal axis. The CR gradually increases over trials and approaches an asymptotic level of about 11 to 12 drops of saliva. After 16 acquisition trials, the experimenter switched to extinction; the results are presented in the panel at the right. Note that the CR gradually decreases when reinforcement is omitted. (After Pavlov, 1927)

the air puff, the newborn soon learns to associate the tone with the air puff and blinks on hearing the tone alone. This procedure is useful for studying learning in very young infants.

In laboratory studies of classical conditioning with humans and animals, the response usually follows the stimulus immediately, as in the air puff/blink sequence just described. However, not all unconditioned responses occur immediately—as *taste aversion studies* demonstrate. In these experiments, a novel-tasting solution (CS) is given to the animal along with an illness-producing drug (US) that has a delayed action (the drug induces a severe intestinal illness several hours later). As a consequence of this pairing, the animal develops a strong aversion to the flavor of the solution and will make every effort to avoid it. A human who becomes ill after eating a particular food (say, lobster) for the first time is also likely to develop an aversion to that food. Interestingly, no aversion develops toward familiar foods eaten at the same time or towards people or events present during the interval between the meal and the illness.

In the laboratory, aversions have been conditioned in a single trial and may occur even when there is a 5- to 10-hour delay between the taste of the solution and the illness. Conditioning will not occur with longer delay intervals, however, or if a light or tone is used as the CS rather than a flavored solution. Some believe that an innate biological relationship between taste and illness is critical in determining the readiness with which conditioning occurs—a fact that has adaptive significance for animals in the wild (Garcia, McGowan, and Green, 1972).

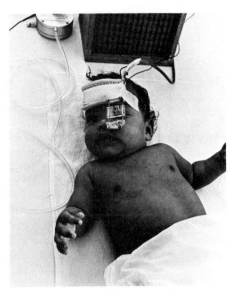

Figure 7-5
Eye-Blink Conditioning with Newborns
The CS is a tone, and the US is a mild puff of air. The response is an eye-blink that is soon conditioned to the onset of the tone. (Courtesy of Lewis Lipsitt)

Generalization and discrimination

GENERALIZATION When a conditioned response has been acquired to a particular stimulus, other similar stimuli will evoke the response. A dog that learns to salivate to the sound of a tuning fork producing a tone of middle C will also salivate to higher or lower tones without further conditioning. The more nearly alike the new stimuli are to the original, the more likely they are to evoke the conditioned response. This principle, called *generalization,* accounts for our ability to react to novel situations insofar as they are similar to familiar ones.

A study using the galvanic skin response (GSR) illustrates generalization. The GSR is an easily measured change in the electrical activity of the skin that occurs during emotional stress. A mild electric shock will elicit the GSR. In the experiment, a pure tone of a specified pitch served as the CS; shock served as the US. After the GSR had been conditioned to the tone, the subject was tested with tones of higher and lower pitches. Figure 7-6 shows the results, plotted in terms of the amplitude of the GSR versus test tones of varying pitches. The high point of the curve represents the amplitude of the GSR to the original tone. The points to the left show the GSR amplitudes to tones lower than the CS; the points to the right, the amplitudes to tones higher than the CS. As you can see, the GSR amplitude decreases as the tones become progressively more dissimilar to the original tone. This plotted relationship is called the *gradient of generalization.*

Stimulus generalization need not be confined to a single sense. For example, with human subjects, a GSR conditioned to the sound of a bell may also appear (although in a lesser amount) at the sight of a bell or the sound of the word *bell.* Conditioning a response to the meaning of a word is called *semantic conditioning.* A Russian psychologist (Volkova, 1953) provided an interesting

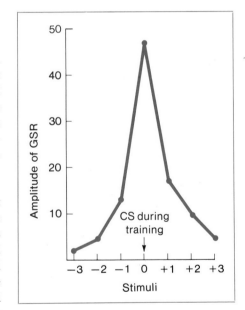

Figure 7-6
Gradient of Generalization
Stimulus 0 denotes the tone to which the galvanic skin response (GSR) was originally conditioned. Stimuli +1, +2, and +3 represent test tones of increasingly higher pitch; stimuli −1, −2, and −3 represent tones of lower pitch. Note that the amount of generalization decreases as the difference between the test tone and the training tone increases. (After Hovland, 1937)

Two quite different theoretical explanations of classical conditioning have been offered. They have their origins in the *cognitive* and *behavioral* approaches to psychology, discussed in Chapter 1.

The cognitive viewpoint assumes that in classical conditioning the organism observes (over a series of trials) that the CS and US occur together and stores this information in memory. When the CS is presented at some later time, the information is retrieved from memory, and the organism makes the CR in *expectation* of the US. The organism is viewed as an information processing system that stores information about stimuli it experiences. Later, when confronted with the CS, it retrieves the relevant information from memory and acts in an appropriate way; namely, it has learned to expect food and accordingly begins to salivate.

The behavioral viewpoint is more mechanistic: it emphasizes the automatic nature of learning. Traditional behaviorists adopted Pavlov's assumption that *temporal contiguity* of the CS and US (that is, closeness in time) is essential for

conditioning. According to this view, the association between the two stimuli is formed because of temporal contiguity. Once formed, the association is strengthened automatically by repeated pairings of the CS and US.

Thus, for the traditional behaviorist, learning depends on the contiguity of CS and US; for the cognitivist, learning depends on an expectancy that when CS occurs US will follow. Recent research suggests a theory of classical conditioning that integrates features of both approaches. This integrated view states that having the CS and US occur with little time between them (temporal contiguity) is a necessary but *not* sufficient requirement for the formation of an association. Temporal contiguity is effective for conditioning only if the CS also has informational value. Specifically, conditioning will take place if, and only if, the CS reliably predicts the occurrence of the US. In other words, there must be a higher probability that the US will occur when the CS has been presented than when it has not.

This view can be illustrated with an

experiment by Rescorla (1968), who held the probability of the US constant in the presence of the CS across several experimental groups. For all groups of rats, the probability that the US (shock) would follow the CS (tone) was .4. What Rescorla varied across groups was the probability of shock occurring in the *absence* of the CS (that is, on trials when the tone did not occur). Each group, therefore, received the same number of temporally contiguous pairings of tone and shock. Manipulating the occurrence of shock in the absence of tone caused the predictive relationship between the tone and the shock to vary across groups. In the group where shocks never occurred in the absence of the tone (all shocks were predicted by tones) rapid conditioning resulted. However, when shocks occurred with a probability of .4 in the absence of the tone (that is, shocks were as likely to occur when the tone had *not* been presented as when it had), no conditioning resulted. For the various experimental groups, the strength of the conditioned response was directly related to

"Perhaps, Dr. Pavlov, he could be taught to seal envelopes."

example of semantic conditioning and generalization. Volkova used a modification of Pavlov's conditioning experiment with young children. The US was cranberry puree delivered to the child's mouth via a chute; the response was salivation. The CS was the Russian word for "good" pronounced aloud by the experimenter. After conditioning had been established, the experimenter tested for generalization by reciting some Russian sentences that could be construed as communicating something "good" and some that could not. Volkova found that children would salivate to sentences like "The pioneer helps his comrade" and "Leningrad is a wonderful city," but not to ones like "The pupil was rude to the teacher" and "My friend is seriously ill."

DISCRIMINATION   A process complementary to generalization is *discrimination*. Whereas generalization is reaction to similarities, discrimination is reaction to differences. Conditioned discrimination is brought about through selective reinforcement and extinction, as shown in Figure 7-7.

Theoretical Interpretations of Classical Conditioning

Table 7-1
Rescorla's Experiment

The table presents a schematic representation of two groups from Rescorla's study. For each group, the events for 16 trials are presented. Note that on some trials CS occurs and is followed by US (CS + US), on other trials CS or US occurs alone, and on other trials neither CS nor US occurs. The boxes to the far right give a count of these trial outcomes for the two groups. The number of CS + US trials is identical for both groups, as is the number of trials on which only the CS occurs. But the two groups differ in the number of trials on which US occurred alone (never in Group A and as frequently as any other type of trial in Group B). Thus, the experimenter established for Group A a situation where the tone was a useful (but not perfect) predictor that shock would follow shortly, whereas for Group B the tone was of no value in predicting subsequent shock. A conditioned response to CS developed readily for Group A but did not develop at all for Group B.

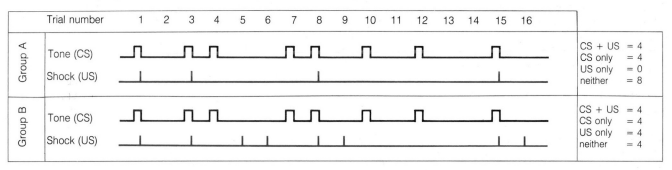

the predictive value of CS in signaling the occurrence of US (see Table 7-1). Subsequent experiments support the conclusion that the predictive relation between CS and US is more important than either temporal contiguity or the frequency with which they are paired (see Rescorla, 1972, 1975; Fantino and Logan, 1979).

These experiments challenge the traditional behavioral view that conditioning is a mechanistic process dependent solely on temporal contiguity between the CS and US. Temporal contiguity is a necessary requirement, but it is not sufficient; conditioning will not occur if the CS does not acquire predictive value. Thus, in even as simple a type of learning as classical conditioning, expectancies play a role and cognitive factors cannot be overlooked.

In the experiment illustrated, two clearly different tones, CS_1 and CS_2, served as the discriminative stimuli. One or the other of the two tones was presented on each trial. The first tone (CS_1) was followed by a mild electric shock; the second (CS_2) was not. Initially, subjects made the conditioned response (in this case, the GSR) to both tones. During the course of the experiment, however, the amplitude of the conditioned response to CS_1 gradually increased while the amplitude of the response to CS_2 decreased. Thus, by the process of differential reinforcement, the subjects were conditioned to discriminate between the two tones.

Generalization and discrimination appear in everyday behavior. The young child who has been frightened by a snapping dog may understandably respond with fear to all dogs (generalization). Eventually, through differential reinforcement and extinction, the range of fearful stimuli narrows to include only dogs that behave in a threatening way.

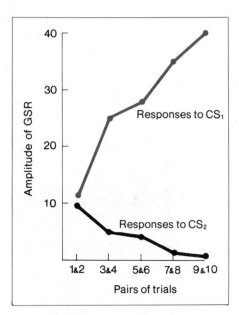

Figure 7-7
Conditioned Discrimination
The discriminative stimuli were two tones of clearly different pitch (CS$_1$ = 700 Hz and CS$_2$ = 3500 Hz). The unconditioned stimulus, an electric shock, applied to the left forefinger, occurred only on trials when CS$_1$ was presented. The strength of the conditioned response, in this case the GSR, gradually increased following CS$_1$ and extinguished following CS$_2$. (After Baer and Fuhrer, 1968)

OPERANT CONDITIONING

In Pavlov's experiment, the conditioned response typically resembles the normal response to the unconditioned stimulus; salivation, for example, is a dog's normal response to food. But when you teach a dog a trick, you cannot use classical conditioning. What unconditioned stimuli would make the animal sit up or roll over? So you get the dog to do the trick as best you can and *afterward* reward it with either approval or food.

To describe this kind of conditioning, B.F. Skinner introduced the concept of *operant conditioning*. To understand operant conditioning, we need to distinguish betwen what Skinner called respondent and operant behavior. *Respondent behavior* is a direct response to a stimulus, as in the unconditioned responses of classical conditioning: the flow of saliva in response to food in the mouth, the constriction of the pupil in response to a flash of light on the eye, the knee jerk in response to a tap on the patellar tendon. In contrast, *operant behavior* is controlled by its consequences. Initially, it simply happens; that is, it appears to be spontaneous rather than a response to a specific stimulus. For example, alone in a crib, a baby may kick and twist and coo spontaneously in response to nothing in particular. When left alone in a room, a dog may pad back and forth, sniff, perhaps pick up a ball, drop it, and play with it. Neither is responding to stimuli in the outside world. They are *operating* on that world. Once the behavior occurs, however, the likelihood it will be repeated depends on the nature of its consequences. Thus, you are less likely to return to a restaurant after eating a dismal meal there but more likely to take a second psychology class if you enjoyed the first one.

Skinner's experiments

To demonstrate operant conditioning in the laboratory, a hungry rat is placed in a box like the one shown in Figure 7-8, which is called a "Skinner box." The inside of the Skinner box is bare except for a protruding bar with a food dish beneath it. A small light above the bar can be turned on at the experimenter's discretion.

Left alone in the box, the rat moves about exploring. Occasionally it inspects the bar and presses it. The rate at which it first presses the bar is the baseline level of bar-pressing. After establishing the baseline level, the experimenter activates a food magazine located outside the Skinner box. Now, every time the rat presses the bar, a small food pellet is released down a chute into the food dish. The rat eats and soon presses the bar again. The food *reinforces* bar-pressing, and the rate of pressing increases dramatically. If the food magazine is disconnected so that pressing the bar no longer delivers food, the rate of bar-pressing will diminish. That is, the operant response undergoes *extinction* with nonreinforcement just as a classical-conditioned response does.

The experimenter can set up a *discrimination* by presenting food if the bar is pressed while the light is on but not if the light is off. This selective reinforcement conditions the rat to press the bar only in the presence of the light. In this example, the light serves as a *discriminative stimulus* that controls the response.

With this illustration before us, we are ready to consider the definition of operant behavior. As indicated above, the behavior "operates" on the environment—the rat's pressing the bar *produces* or *gains access* to the food. In

Figure 7-8
Apparatus for Operant Conditioning
The photo shows the interior arrangement of the box used in the operant conditioning of a rat. This box has been named a "Skinner box" after its developer.

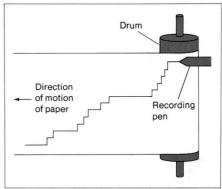

classical conditioning, the animal is passive; it merely waits for stimuli. In operant conditioning, the animal is active; its own behavior brings on important consequences.

Thus, *operant conditioning* increases the likelihood of a response by following its occurrence with a *reinforcer*.[1] Usually the reinforcer is something that can satisfy a basic drive (like food to satisfy hunger or water to satisfy thirst), but as we will see later, it need not be.

MEASURES OF OPERANT STRENGTH   Because the bar is always present in the Skinner box, the rat can respond to it as frequently or infrequently as it chooses. Hence, *rate of response* is a useful measure of operant strength. The more frequently the response occurs during a given interval of time, the greater the operant strength.

The rate of response in operant conditioning is usually portrayed by a *cumulative curve* (Figure 7-9). The bar of the Skinner box is attached to a recording pen, which rests on a slowly moving strip of paper. Each time the animal presses the bar, the pen steps up a fixed distance and then continues on its horizontal path. Because the paper moves at a fixed rate, the slope of the

Figure 7-9
Cumulative Recorder
The axis of the drum is fixed, and as the drum rotates, the recording paper moves from right to left under the head of a writing pen. The pen is rigged so that it can only move upward, never downward. Each time the animal makes a response, the pen steps up a fixed amount. When no responses are being made, the pen moves in a straight line across the paper. Thus, the height of each step is the same, but the length of the horizontal line varies as a function of the time between responses. Since the paper is moving at a fixed rate, the slope of the cumulative curve indicates the response rate. When the animal is responding at a high rate, the slope of the cumulative curve will be quite steep; when the animal is responding very slowly, there will be hardly any slope at all.

---

[1]The term *reinforcement* is used to refer both to the presentation of a reinforcer and to the *effect* of the reinforcer—that is, to the increase in the likelihood of the reinforced response.

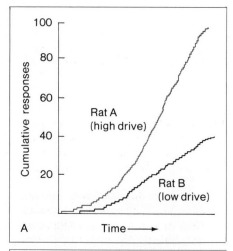

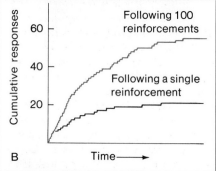

Figure 7-10
A. Cumulative Curves During Acquisition
This figure shows a comparison of the cumulative response curves for two rats during acquisition of a bar-pressing response. Rat A had been deprived of food for 30 hours and rat B for 10 hours prior to the experiment. This difference in the drive level of the two rats is reflected in the rate of responding.
B. Cumulative Curves During Extinction
Curves of extinction of operant responses in a rat are plotted following a single reinforcement and following 100 reinforcements. The plot shows the cumulative number of bar-pressing responses; every response raises the height of the curve, and the curve levels off when responses cease.

cumulative curve is a measure of response rate. A horizontal line indicates that the animal is not responding; a steep curve indicates a fast response rate. Figure 7-10A presents cumulative curves for two rats during acquisition of a bar-pressing response. Rat A had been deprived of food for 30 hours and rat B for 10 hours. The hungrier rat responded much more rapidly.

Another measure of operant strength is the *total number of responses during extinction*. As Figure 7-10B shows, a single reinforcement can produce considerable strength according to this measure.

PARTIAL REINFORCEMENT   Operant conditioning shows a high degree of orderliness. Experiments with *partial reinforcement*—when the behavior is reinforced only a fraction of the time it occurs—demonstrate this.

In a typical experiment, a pigeon learns to peck at a lighted disk mounted on a wall to obtain a small quantity of grain as reinforcement. Once this conditioned operant is established, the pigeon will continue to peck at a high rate, even if it receives only occasional reinforcement. The pigeon, whose remarkably regular pecking is illustrated in Figure 7-11, was rewarded with food on the average of once every 5 minutes (12 times an hour), yet it pecked at the disk some 6,000 times per hour.

Extinction following the acquisition of a response on partial reinforcement is slow—*much* slower, in fact, than extinction following the acquisition of a response on continuous reinforcement. This phenomenon, known as the *partial-reinforcement effect*, occurs because there is less difference between the new and old situations (between extinction and acquisition) when reinforcement is discontinued following partial reinforcement. A broken slot machine may maintain hundreds of coin insertions by the gambler accustomed to infrequent payoffs. When a food machine fails to operate, however, no more than one extra coin insertion is likely to occur since vending machines operate on continuous-reinforcement schedules.

The partial-reinforcement effect has far-reaching practical implications. For example, a parent who *occasionally* reinforces its child's temper tantrums by giving in to the child is ensuring more potent and more persistent tantrums than the parent who *always* gives in. The child with a history of partial reinforcement of tantrums will emit them with remarkable persistence even when the parent attempts to extinguish the tantrums by ignoring them. What the parent should have been doing all along, of course, is reinforcing the child's appropriate behaviors, not the tantrums.

Conditioned reinforcement

Pavlov noted that once a dog has learned to respond to a conditioned stimulus in a highly dependable way, the conditioned stimulus itself can be used to

Figure 7-11
Partial Reinforcement
The curves record one pigeon's pecking responses, which were reinforced irregularly but at an average interval of 5 minutes. The reinforcements are represented by horizontal dashes. Each of the sloping lines represents 1,000 responses—the pen resets after each 1,000.

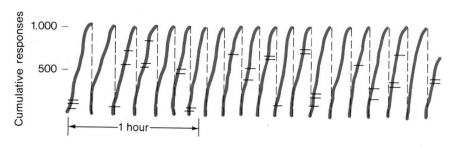

Partial reinforcement procedures are of particular interest because they represent the type of reinforcement regime under which most organisms operate in nature. In addition, on partial reinforcement schedules, an animal's response rate tends to be extremely sensitive to changes in the environment. These procedures thus provide a natural barometer for assessing the effects of radiation, drugs, fatigue, and other variables on performance. In the early exploration of space, scientists frequently housed rats, pigeons, and other animals in the space capsule and placed them on a partial reinforcement schedule. By observing changes in reponse rate during actual flight, they were able to determine the effects of acceleration, weightlessness, and the like on performance.

Many different reinforcement schedules have been studied, but most can be categorized according to two dimensions: (1) the period between successive reinforcements is determined either by the number of intervening nonreinforced responses or by elapsed time, and (2) the periods between successive reinforcements are either regular or irregular. Accordingly, four basic reinforcement schedules can be defined.

FIXED RATIO (FR) On this schedule, reinforcement occurs after a fixed number of responses; if it occurs every 20 responses, for example, the ratio of reponses to reinforcers is 20 to 1.

FIXED INTERVAL (FI) Reinforcement follows the first response emitted after a fixed time period measured from the last reinforcement. For example, on a fixed-interval schedule of 1 minute, no further reinforcement will occur following a reinforced response until 1 minute has passed; once it has elapsed, the first response made will be reinforced.

VARIABLE RATIO (VR) Like the fixed-ratio schedule, reinforcement oc-

curs after a specified number of responses. But for this schedule, the number of responses intervening between reinforcements varies from one reinforcement to the next. For example, a 20-to-1 variable-ratio schedule might be produced by requiring that the number of intervening responses be randomly selected from 0 to 40, with an average of 20.

VARIABLE INTERVAL (VI) In this schedule, reinforcement occurs after a specified period of time that varies from one reinforcement to the next. A simple variable-interval schedule of 1 minute might be generated by randomly setting the time period between reinforcements in a range of values from 0 to 120 seconds; this schedule yields an average time period of 1 minute, but a given interval can range anywhere from 0 seconds to 2 minutes.

These four reinforcement schedules produce characteristic modes of responding. On an FI schedule, the animal's pattern of responding suggests that it is keeping careful track of time. Immediately after a reinforcement, its rate of responding drops to near 0 and then increases at an accelerating pace as the end of the interval approaches. As Fantino and Logan (1979) note, some reinforcers are naturally programmed on FI schedules. In the wild, for example, food may be available only at certain places and times, such as water holes that attract small animals at dusk or flowers that secrete nectar at dawn. Under these circumstances, the organism's investigation of these food locations may show an FI pattern comparable to those observed in the laboratory. Houston (1981) suggests that "mail-checking behavior" also "resembles behavior under the control of an FI schedule. If we know that the mail arrives [around] noon, we do not begin to look for it at 8

A.M. As noon approaches, we begin to look, listen, and check the mailbox. After the delivery arrives, there is very little chance that we will check again until the next day."

On VI schedules, the response rate does not fluctuate as much between reinforcement as it does on FI schedules. This is to be expected; since there are no cues indicating when the interval will terminate, the animal responds at a fairly steady rate and receives reinforcement promptly whenever it becomes available. Houston (1981) notes: "Some types of still fishermen may well operate under a VI schedule. They drop their lines in and wait. They do not know when the fish will bite, if at all, but they check their lines regularly and steadily."

In contrast to the interval schedules, both the fixed- and variable-ratio schedules tend to produce extremely rapid rates of responding. Thus, it is not surprising that ratio schedules are popular in industry and in gambling houses. An example of an FR schedule is a wage paid on a *piecework* system. VR schedules, ideally suited for generating high rates of uninterrupted responding, are used by gambling houses in slot machines.

If the ratio (fixed or variable) is small, responding begins immediately after a reinforcement; when the ratio is moderate, there may be a brief pause after each reinforcement followed by a steady burst of responding. When the ratio is large, there may be a long pause after each reinforcement; especially on fixed-ratio schedules, responding may cease altogether. Except for such extreme cases, however, the animal responds on ratio schedules as though it knows that the next reinforcement depends on its making a certain number of responses, and it bursts forth with them at as fast a rate as possible.

The training of Shamu, the whale at Sea World, San Diego, was based on the shaping of operant responses.

reinforce new behavior. Suppose the animal has learned to salivate to a tone as a conditioned stimulus. If a flashing light is then presented with only the tone, the flashing light will come to elicit the conditioned response. The tone has become a *conditioned reinforcer*.

The introduction of a minor variation in the typical operant-conditioning situation will illustrate how conditioned reinforcement works. When a rat in a Skinner box presses a lever, a tone comes on momentarily, followed shortly by delivery of a food pellet. After the animal has been conditioned in this way, extinction is begun, so that when the rat presses the lever neither the tone nor the food appears. In time, the animal virtually ceases to press the lever. Now the tone is connected again but without food. When the animal discovers that pressing the lever turns on the tone, the rate of pressing markedly increases, overcoming the extinction, even though no food follows. The tone has acquired reinforcing qualities of its own—it has become a conditioned reinforcer.

Conditioned reinforcers get their power through association with a *primary reinforcer:* something that satisfies a basic drive, as food satisfies hunger or water satisfies thirst. But how is this association established? It was once thought that the value of a conditioned reinforcer depended simply on the number of times it had been paired with a primary reinforcer. In discussing classical conditioning, we noted that conditioning seems to depend less on the number of pairings than on the predictive power of the CS—that is, on how useful the CS is in predicting the occurrence of the US.

A similar picture has emerged with respect to conditioned reinforcement. The pairing of a stimulus with a primary reinforcer provides only a weak source of conditioned reinforcing strength (Rose and Fantino, 1978). Instead the conditioned reinforcing value of a stimulus depends on how valuable the stimulus has been to the animal as a predictor of the availability of the primary reinforcer. A stimulus that reliably signals that a primary reinforcer will soon follow quickly becomes a strong conditioned reinforcer; a stimulus that is less reliable, even though it is frequently paired with a primary reinforcer, will become a weaker conditioned reinforcer (Fantino, 1977).

Conditioned reinforcement greatly increases the range of possible conditioning. If everything we learned had to be followed by a primary reinforcer, the occasions for learning would be very much restricted. A verbal promise of food can reinforce behavior that would otherwise require food; mere praise (without promise of a primary reinforcer) itself becomes reinforcing.

Shaping behavior

In classical conditioning, a conditioned stimulus (the light in Pavlov's experiment) becomes a substitute for an unconditioned stimulus (the meat powder). This process, however, does not permit *novelty* to occur in behavior—the learning of totally new responses. In contrast, operant conditioning plays an important role in the development of novel behavior.

The experimenter can induce novel behavior by taking advantage of natural variations in a subject's actions. To train a dog to press a buzzer with its nose, for example, the experimenter can give a food reinforcer each time the animal approaches the area of the buzzer, requiring it to move closer and closer to the desired spot for each reinforcer until finally the dog's nose is touching the buzzer. This technique of reinforcing only the responses that meet the experimenter's specifications and extinguishing all others is called *shaping* the animal's behavior.

Pigeon carrier

Search and Rescue by Pigeons

Pigeons have been used by the Coast Guard in searching for victims lost at sea. The pigeons are trained, using shaping methods, to spot the color orange—the international color of lifejackets. Three pigeons are strapped into a plexiglass chamber attached to the underside of a helicopter. The chamber is divided into thirds so that each bird faces a different direction. When a pigeon spots an orange object, or any other object, it pecks a key that buzzes the pilot. The pilot then heads in the direction indicated by which bird responded. Pigeons are better suited than people for the task of spotting distant objects at sea. They can stare over the water for a long time without suffering eye fatigue, have excellent color vision, and can focus on a 60–80° area whereas a person can only focus on a 2–3° area. (After Simmons, 1981)

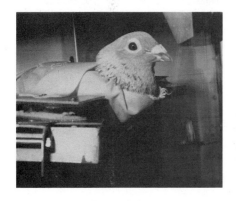

Pigeon sitting

Pigeon signaling

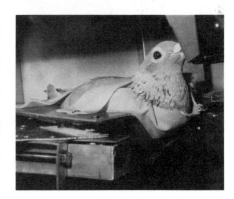

Pigeon rewarded

Animals can be taught elaborate tricks and behavior routines by means of shaping. For example, two psychologists and their staff have trained thousands of animals of many species for TV shows, commercials, and county fairs. One popular show featured a pig called "Priscilla, the Fastidious Pig." Priscilla turned on the TV set, ate breakfast at a table, picked up dirty clothes and put them in a hamper, vacuumed the floor, picked out her favorite food (from among foods competing with that of her sponsor!), and took part in a quiz program, answering questions from the audience by flashing lights indicating "Yes" or "No." She was not an unusually bright pig; in fact, because pigs grow so fast, a new "Priscilla" was trained every three to five months. The ingenuity was not the pig's but the experimenters', who used operant conditioning and shaped the behavior to produce the desired result (Breland and Breland, 1966). Pigeons have been trained by the shaping of operant responses to locate persons lost at sea; porpoises have been trained to retrieve underwater equipment.

The phenomenon of *autoshaping* provides an example of behavior that appears to be determined by principles of both operant and classical conditioning. A hungry pigeon, never before an experimental subject, is placed in

Figure 7-12
Water and Food Autoshaped Responses
The two photographs show the autoshaped responses of a pigeon at the moment of key contact. The top response is to a key paired with food, whereas the bottom response is to a key paired with water. The pigeon's beak movements are clearly different in the two situations. The top photo resembles a pigeon eating whereas the bottom photo resembles a pigeon drinking. The pigeon appears to "eat" the key when working for food and "drink" the key when working for water. (After Jenkins and Moore, 1973)

a chamber. A key in the chamber is lit repeatedly once every minute for about 6 seconds. When the light is turned off (by the automated apparatus), a bit of food is provided. The key then remains unlit for 54 seconds, turns on again, and so on. Note that food is delivered independent of the pigeon's behavior toward the key; that is, food occurs whether or not the pigeon pecks the key. Nonetheless, after a few trials, the pigeon begins to peck the key as soon as it is lit.

The procedure is called "autoshaping" because it does not require an active observing experimenter. (*Auto* means "self.") Since the initial demonstration of autoshaping (Brown and Jenkins, 1968), literally hundreds of experiments have sought to understand the phenomenon. It is believed that classical conditioning is involved since—by virtue of repeated pairings with food—the key light becomes a conditioned stimulus (CS) for the response to food (pecking, the UR). Once the first peck occurs to the lit key, it produces food almost immediately, as in an operant-conditioning experiment. Hence, it is likely that autoshaped responding is maintained by operant as well as by classical conditioning.

It seems that by pairing the key light with food, the light comes to substitute for food and the pigeon responds to the light in a manner similar to the way it responds to food. Photographs of a pigeon's autoshaped pecks support this notion (see Figure 7-12). When the beak hits the key, it is positioned as if seizing food when food is the reinforcer but *not* when water is the reinforcer. Thus, stimuli paired with food come to elicit the same response as the food itself, as in classical conditioning (Schwartz and Gamzu, 1977).

Operant conditioning of human behavior

In the following study, college students were unaware that an experiment was being conducted. The experimenter carried on what appeared to be an informal conversation with the subject but actually behaved according to a plan. The experimenter determined in advance to reinforce all statements of opinion the subject made, such as sentences beginning "I think," "I believe," "It seems to me," and the like. The *reinforcer* was the experimenter's saying "You're right," "I agree," or "That's so" after each statement of opinion. Extinction was carried out in another portion of the experiment by mere nonreinforcement—silence—following a statement of opinion (Verplanck, 1955).

During the period when verbal reinforcement was given, statements of opinion increased markedly in frequency; during extinction, they decreased. The experimenter controlled verbal behavior in this situation in much the same way that a rat's bar-presses in a Skinner box are controlled. In studies of this kind, subjects may begin to realize that the experimenter is manipulating their behavior. There is evidence, however, that in many cases the subjects are not consciously aware of what the experimenter is doing and learning still occurs (Rosenfeld and Baer, 1969).

When we discuss psychotherapy (Chapter 16), we will see other evidence that reinforcement can be highly effective in modifying human behavior. However, the possibility of adverse effects must be recognized. In a study by Lepper, Greene, and Nisbett (1973), two groups of preschool children were asked to draw pictures with special felt-tipped pens—an activity that initially held intrinsic interest. In the Expect Award group, subjects agreed to engage in this activity to obtain a reinforcement (a "Good Player Award" adorned with a gold seal and red ribbon). Subjects in the No Award group neither expected nor received the reward but otherwise duplicated the experiences of the other subjects. Several weeks later, when observed unobtrusively in their classrooms, Expected Award subjects showed less interest in drawing than the No Award subjects. The provision of rewards turned "play" (that is, an activity engaged in for its own sake) into "work" (an activity engaged in only when extrinsic incentives are present).

A distinction must be made between the effectiveness of extrinsic rewards in the acquisition of behavior and their role in the maintenance of frequently occurring behavior. Extrinsic rewards have proved extremely useful in instituting and maintaining a host of desirable behaviors, for example, study behavior in problem school children or language acquisition in retardates. Once these behaviors are acquired, they tend to lead naturally to reinforcing events such as social approval and, more generally, to increase the child's control of the environment. Thus, extrinsic rewards may be phased out following acquisition of the desired behavior. The study just cited, involving preschool children, suggests that providing additional extrinsic rewards may actually disrupt behavior that is already well maintained. We should not, however, lose sight of the important role extrinsic rewards may have played in the acquisition of that behavior.

Operant conditioning of autonomic responses

Classical conditioning has traditionally been viewed as a "lower" form of involuntary learning, involving glandular and visceral responses; operant conditioning has been viewed as a "higher" form of voluntary learning, involving responses of the skeletal muscles. Until recently, some psychologists believed that responses mediated by the autonomic nervous system could be learned only by classical conditioning, whereas responses mediated by the central nervous system could be acquired only operantly. This assumption has been challenged by a series of studies indicating that both autonomic and skeletal responses can be conditioned by either classical or operant procedures (Kimmel, 1974; Miller, 1974; Hearst, 1975).

The operant conditioning of autonomic responses has important implications for psychologically based illnesses, discussed in Chapter 14. A child's fear of attending school may lead to certain autonomic symptoms, like an upset stomach or a headache. If the child is given permission to skip school, those autonomic responses are reinforced—and will increase in frequency. Thus, a pattern is set whereby a response (upset stomach) is followed by reinforcement (staying home). Through operant conditioning, the child "learns" to be sick in order to avoid an unpleasant situation.

The practical implications of operant conditioning of autonomic responses are important. Human subjects have been trained by operant methods to control such autonomic responses as heart rate, blood pressure, and the secretion of stomach acids that may produce ulcers. To control blood pressure, for example, the individual watches a machine that provides continuous visual feedback about blood pressure. Whenever the blood pressure falls below a specified level, a light flashes. The subject tries to analyze whatever he or she is thinking or doing when the blood pressure is low and to repeat that thought or emotion so as to keep it low. This type of procedure is called *biofeedback* training: the subject is given information (feedback) about some aspect of his or her physiological state and reinforced for altering that state.

The medical applications of such research are obvious. It would be better

Animals have been taught very complex responses by means of shaping techniques. At the Yerkes Primate Research Center in Atlanta, a chimpanzee named Lana has learned to answer questions and make requests by pressing symbols on a computer console. At bottom is an example of how the experiment works. A researcher outside the room asked Lana a question by pressing the symbols on the console for the words "What name of this" and also holding up a candy. The chimp answered by pressing symbols for "M & M name of this." Chapter 9 will provide additional examples of how chimpanzees have been taught to communicate with humans.

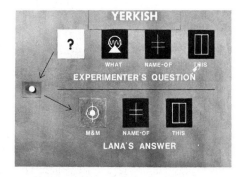

for people with high blood pressure to learn to control it themselves than to depend on medications that are only partially successful and may have undesirable side effects. Research on voluntary control of autonomic responses is still in the pioneer stage. The results so far indicate that biofeedback procedures are effective. They have been used successfully in treating several types of cardiovascular disorders, with the best results obtained for high blood pressure. Biofeedback for blood flow in the forehead has also proved effective in the treatment of migraine headaches (Tarler-Benlolo, 1978).

CONCEPT OF REINFORCEMENT

In our discussion of classical conditioning, we used the term *reinforcement* to refer to the paired presentation of the unconditioned stimulus and the conditioned stimulus. In operant conditioning, reinforcement refers to the occurrence of an event, such as giving food or water, following the desired response. Although the reinforcement is different in the two situations, the result in both cases is an increase in the likelihood of the desired response. We can therefore define *reinforcement* as any event that increases the probability of a response.

We distinguish between positive and negative reinforcers. A *positive reinforcer* is a stimulus that when presented following a response, increases the probability of the response; food and water qualify as positive reinforcers for appropriately deprived organisms. A *negative reinforcer* is a stimulus that when removed following a response, increases the probability of the response; electric shock and painful noise qualify as negative reinforcers if they can be turned off when the desired response is made.

The term *reward* is sometimes used as a synonym for positive reinforcement. *Punishment*, however, is not the same as negative reinforcement. The effect of reinforcers, whether positive or negative, is to strengthen the preceding response. Punishment has the opposite effect: it decreases the probability of a response. If an animal is given an electric shock after every bar-press, thus weakening the response, bar-pressing is said to have been punished.

Premack's principle

Although we have discussed reinforcers as stimuli whose presentation strengthens the preceding response, Premack (1959) has suggested that reinforcers may be thought of more usefully as *responses* (or *activities*). In Premack's view, it is not the food pellet itself (a stimulus) that reinforces lever-pressing but the eating of the pellet (an activity). Moreover, any activity an organism performs can reinforce (strengthen) any other activity the organism typically engages in less frequently. For example, Premack offered children the choice of operating a pinball machine or eating candy. Children who preferred eating candy would increase their rate of operating the pinball machine if playing the machine led to eating candy. In other words, eating candy reinforced playing the pinball machine. For children who preferred playing pinball, however, the reverse was true: they increased their intake of candy only if this increased the chance to play pinball.

From this pioneer experiment, Premack developed a powerful conception of reinforcement that can be conveyed in two statements: (1) for any organism, a reinforcement hierarchy exists in which reinforcers at the top of the hierarchy are those activities engaged in with greatest likelihood, given the opportunity; (2) for a given organism, any activity in the hierarchy may be reinforced (made

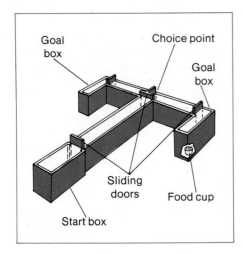

Figure 7-13
T-Maze
A maze used in the study of simple choice learning. Plexiglass covers on the start box and goal boxes are hinged so that a rat can be easily placed in or removed from the apparatus. The sliding doors (which usually are operated by a system of strings and pulleys from above) prevent the animal from retracing its path once it has made a choice. Note that the goal boxes are arranged so that the rat cannot see the food cup from the choice point.

more likely) by any activity above it and may itself reinforce any activity below it. This second statement is *Premack's principle*. It expresses a technique that has long been applied by parents who require a child to do homework before going out to play rather than letting the child play first provided he or she agrees to do the homework later.

Application of Premack's principle has had success in the classroom as well as in the home environment. The writing ability of pupils, for example, has been enhanced by allowing them the opportunity to play after successful completion of a writing assignment. Even 3-year-old nursery school children have responded well to use of the principle. For these students, activities high on their reinforcement hierarchies included screaming, working jigsaw puzzles, and running around the room. These reinforcing activities were made permissible if desired behavior first occurred. For example, the behavior of sitting quietly while attending to the blackboard was followed occasionally by the sounding of a bell and the instruction "run and scream." The subjects indeed leaped to their feet and raced around the room screaming. After a few days, virtually perfect control of classroom behavior was achieved (Homme and others, 1963).

Is the reinforcement hierarchy stable or does it change with changes in the organism's motivational state? Although eating candy did not reinforce pinball playing in those children who preferred pinball playing, Premack found that when the children became sufficiently hungry the reinforcement relation reversed: eating candy came to reinforce pinball playing. Similar results have been found in more extensive studies with rats: a thirsty rat will run in order to drink whereas a long-idle rat will drink for the chance to run in a running wheel (Premack, 1962). Thus, when an organism is deprived of the chance to engage in a naturally occurring activity, that activity will become, at least momentarily, a more potent reinforcer, since it will reinforce responses that typically are above it on that organism's reinforcement hierarchy.

Amount and delay of reinforcement

Psychologists have systematically investigated the effect of a number of reinforcement variables on the course of learning. Not surprisingly, the *amount of reinforcement* has been found to be important. Within limits, the greater the amount of reinforcement, the more rapid the rate of learning. This relationship is illustrated in an experiment using a T-maze (Figure 7-13). After a rat was placed in the start box, it ran to the *choice point*, where it had to decide between a right and a left turn to reach food placed in one of the goal boxes. In this experiment, there were three groups of rats, each of which received a different amount of food for a correct turn. The results are shown in Figure 7-14A. Note that the group with the largest amount of reinforcement learned at the fastest rate; the other two groups learned more slowly.

The *delay of reinforcement* is another important variable. A common assumption has been that in training animals or young children it is most effective to reward or punish the organism immediately after it responds. A spanking given by a parent when he or she returns home from work is less effective (other things being equal) in reducing a child's aggressive behavior than punishment delivered immediately following the act.

The effectiveness of immediate reinforcement in a laboratory learning situation is demonstrated by the following experiment. The apparatus used was a T-maze with goal boxes equipped with food dispensers that could be set to delay the presentation of food pellets. One group of rats received its food

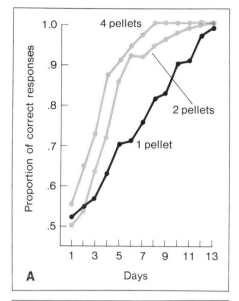

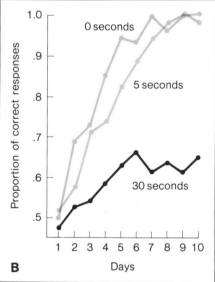

Figure 7-14
A. Amount of Reinforcement

Rats learned to run a T-maze without error more quickly for a large reward than for a small one. The groups were distinguished by the number of food pellets a rat received when it entered the correct goal box. Each rat ran four trials per day. The curves start at about .5; since there are only two choices, the animal should make the correct turn 50 percent of the time by chance alone. (After Clayton, 1964)

B. Delay of Reinforcement

For these three groups of rats, the time interval between entering the correct goal box and receiving a pellet of food varied. The curves show that immediate reinforcement is more effective than reinforcement after a delay. (Unpublished data from R.C. Atkinson)

Threat of punishment as a controller of behavior

immediately upon entering the correct goal box, another group was fed following a 5-second delay, and food for a third group was delayed 30 seconds. Figure 7-14B shows the learning curves for the three groups. The 0-second group and the 5-second group both reached near-perfect scores by the ninth day, but the 0-second group learned at a faster rate. The 30-second-delay group was markedly inferior and never achieved a very high level of performance.

Role of punishment in learning

Folklore suggests that punishment is an effective way of controlling behavior. "Spare the rod and spoil the child" is not an isolated epigram. Fines and imprisonment are forms of social control that are sanctioned by all governments. For many years, arguments have continued over the relative advantages and disadvantages of benevolent treatment (rewarding good behavior) and stern treatment (punishing errors).

Punishment has several significant disadvantages. First, its effects are not as predictable as the results of reward. Reward says, "Repeat what you have done"; punishment says, "Stop it!" but fails to give an alternative. As a result, an even less desirable response may be substituted for the punished one. Second, the byproducts of punishment may be unfortunate. Punishment often leads to dislike of the punishing person (parent, teacher, or employer) and to a dislike of the situation (home, school, or office) in which the punishment occurred. Finally, an extreme or painful event used as a punisher may elicit aggressive behavior that is more serious than the original undesirable behavior.

These cautions do not mean that punishment should never be employed. It can effectively eliminate an undesirable response if the available alternative responses are rewarded. Rats that have learned to take the shorter of two paths in a maze to reach food will quickly switch to the longer path if they are shocked in the shorter one. The temporary suppression produced by punishment provides the opportunity for the rat to learn to take the longer path. Punishment was an effective means of redirecting behavior.

Punishment can also be effective when we merely want the learner to respond to a signal to avoid punishment. For example, people learn to come inside when they hear thunder or to seek shade to avoid sunburn. Avoiding a threatened punishment can be rewarding. The police officer is less often a punishing person than a symbol of *threatened* punishment.

Finally, punishment may be informative. A child who gets a shock from an electrical appliance may learn which connections are safe, which hazardous. A teacher's corrections on a student's paper can be regarded as punishing; but they are also informative and can provide an occasion for learning. Informative punishment can redirect behavior so that the new behavior can be rewarded.

Parents often wonder how and how much they should punish their children. In practice, most resort to some kinds of deprivations at times, if not to the actual inflicting of pain. The most effective use of punishment is the informative one, so that the child will know what is and is not allowed. Children occasionally "test the limits" to see what degree of unpermitted behavior they can get by with. When they do, it seems advisable to use discipline that is firm but not harsh and to administer it promptly and consistently. Nagging a child to conform may be less humane in the end than an immediate spanking. A child who is threatened with a vague and postponed punishment ("What kind of person do you think you will grow up to be?") may learn less and suffer more than one who pays a consistent penalty for infringement but afterward is welcomed back into the family circle.

Brain Stimulation and Reinforcement

Some 30 years ago, James Olds made the startling discovery that electrical stimulation of certain regions of the brain can be reinforcing. Olds was investigating the rat's brain by means of microelectrodes. These tiny electrodes can be implanted permanently in specific brain areas without interfering with the rat's health or normal activity. When connected with the electrical source, they can supply stimulation of varying intensities. An electrode was implanted accidentally in an area near the hypothalamus, and Olds delivered a very mild current through the electrodes. He found that the animal repeatedly returned to the place where it had been when stimulated. Further stimulations at the same cage location caused the animal to spend most of its time there. Later, Olds found that other animals with electrodes implanted in the same brain region learned to press a bar in a Skinner box to produce their own electrical stimulation (see Figure 7-15). These animals pressed the bar at a phenomenal rate: a not unusual record would show an average of over 2,000 responses an hour for 15 or 20 hours, until the animal finally collapsed from exhaustion.

Since the initial brain stimulation discovery, experiments with microelectrodes implanted in many different areas of the brain and brain stem have been carried out, using rats, cats, and monkeys in a wide variety of tasks. The reinforcing effects of stimulation in certain areas (primarily the hypothalamus) are powerful: hungry rats will endure a more painful shock while crossing an electric grid to obtain brain stimulation than they will to obtain food. When given a choice between food and electric brain stimulation in a T-maze, extremely hungry rats will choose the path leading to stimulation. On the other hand, stimulation of some areas of the brain stem serves as a *punisher.* When the electrodes were moved to these different brain areas, rats that previously pressed

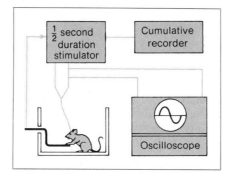

Figure 7-15
Brain Stimulation

The animal's bar-press delivers a 60-cycle current for one-half second, after which the animal must release the bar and press again for more current. The animal's response rate is recorded on the cumulative recorder, and the delivery of the current is monitored by means of the oscilloscope. Rats respond with rates up to 100 bar-presses per minute with electrodes in the medial-forebrain region of the hypothalamus.

the bar at a rapid rate to receive stimulation suddenly stopped responding and avoided the bar entirely. Apparently the new stimulation was unpleasant. And other animals have learned various responses to terminate stimulation in these areas—for example, pressing a lever to turn *off* the current, an example of *negative reinforcement.* Much progress has been made in mapping out the neutral, punishing, and reinforcing areas of the brain (Carr and Coons, 1982).

Psychologists are not yet agreed on the significance of brain-stimulation studies. It would be nice to think that these studies map the anatomical location of reinforcement: that when we stimulate one brain-stem area in a rat, for example, the sensations are similar to those experienced when the animal is reinforced with food, and that the sensations in another area are similar to reinforcement with water. Unfortunately, the rat cannot describe its sensations.

What data we have on human subjects come from patients with abnormal conditions (such as epilepsy or the intractable pain of terminal cancer), so the results cannot be readily generalized to normal individuals. These patients report relief from pain and anxiety and feeling "wonderful," "happy," and "drunk" following stimulation of certain areas of the limbic system. Those whose brains were stimulated 1,000 times per hour were content to do nothing else for 6 hours, the maximum period allowed (Campbell, 1973).

In some respects, learning with brain stimulation as reinforcement does not follow the same rules as learning with food or other external rewards. The extinction of a bar-press response that has been reinforced with brain stimulation is much more rapid than extinction following termination of a food or water reward. If the current is turned off, the animal's responses stop quite abruptly, but it will start responding again at a rapid rate if given one or two stimulations. In addition, although partial reinforcement can be used quite effectively with food or water reinforcement, it is far less effective with brain stimulation. These and other data suggest that brain stimulation may operate differently from other reinforcers; it seems to create a temporary sensation that does not increase in strength with deprivation. However, brain stimulation can be linked to natural needs. For example, if electrodes are placed in the "feeding centers" of the hypothalamus, food deprivation will increase the rate of bar-pressing for electrical stimulation. Rats will also bar-press for tiny injections of norepinephrine into these same brain areas. The release of the neurotransmitter norepinephrine into this part of the brain is associated with the presentation of food. Thus, electrical stimulation may be reinforcing because it stimulates the release of a neurotransmitter that normally signals food (Olds and Fobes, 1981).

COGNITIVE LEARNING

The kinds of phenomena that we have considered thus far all stress associative learning. In studying more complex forms of learning, attention must be given to the role of *cognitive processes*; that is, how the learner perceives, organizes, and rehearses information in an effort to master a new topic.

Psychologists identified with the cognitive viewpoint argue that learning, particularly in humans, cannot be satisfactorily explained in terms of conditioned associations. They propose that the learner forms a *cognitive structure* in memory, which preserves and organizes information about the various events that occur in a learning situation. When a test is made to determine how much has been learned, the subject takes the stimulus (the question) and scans it against memory to determine an appropriate action. What she or he does depends on the cognitive structure retrieved from memory and on the context in which the test occurs. Thus, the subject's response varies with the nature of the test situation and with the subject's memory for prior events. It is not simply a reflexive response to a stimulus but rather depends on underlying cognitive processes.

Insight experiments

Partly in protest against too much study of learning through conditioning, Wolfgang Köhler performed a series of experiments designed to determine chimpanzees' ability to solve complex problems. Although conducted over 50 years ago, these experiments are still dramatic illustrations of cognitive learning. At some point in working on a problem, the chimpanzees appeared to grasp the problem's inner relationships through *insight*; that is, they solved the problem not by trial and error but by perceiving the relationships essential to solution. The following experiment by Köhler is typical.

> Sultan [Köhler's most intelligent chimpanzee] is squatting at the bars but cannot reach the fruit which lies outside by means of his only available short stick. A longer stick is deposited outside the bars, about two meters on one side of the object and parallel with the grating. It cannot be grasped with the hand, but it can be pulled within reach by means of the small stick. [See Figure 7-16 for an illustration of a similar multiple-stick problem.] Sultan tries to reach the fruit with the smaller of the two sticks. Not succeeding, he tears at a piece of wire that projects from the netting of his cage, but that too, is in vain. Then he gazes about him (there are always in the course of these tests some long pauses, during which the animals scrutinize the whole visible area). He suddenly picks up the little stick once more, goes up to the bars directly opposite to the long stick, scratches it towards him with the "auxiliary," seizes it, and goes with it to the point opposite the objective (the fruit), which he secures. From the moment that his eyes fall upon the long stick, his procedure forms one consecutive whole, without hiatus, and although the angling of the bigger stick by means of the smaller is an action that could be complete and distinct in itself, yet observation shows that it follows, quite suddenly, on an interval of hesitation and doubt—staring about—which undoubtedly has a relation to the final objective, and is immediately merged in the final action of the attainment of the end goal. (Köhler, 1925, pp. 174–75)

Another celebrated example of insight, also based on Sultan's exploits, is shown in the series of photographs on the next page. Here, the bananas are out of reach; but by stacking boxes, Sultan was able to garner them. Although some

Figure 7-16
A Chimpanzee Solving a Multiple-Stick Problem
Using the shorter sticks, the chimpanzee pulls in a stick long enough to reach the piece of fruit. It has learned to solve this problem by understanding the relationship between the sticks and the piece of fruit—an example of insight.

psychologists have argued that complex problem solving such as that shown by Sultan is restricted to higher primates, Epstein (1981) has demonstrated comparable insight in the pigeon. Epstein's study shows how complex behavior may emerge "spontaneously" after the relevant component behaviors have been trained.

Epstein trained pigeons to peck at a banana that was out of reach in order to obtain pigeon food. As in Sultan's box-and-banana problem, the pigeon was trained to move a box beneath the banana, hop on the box, and peck the banana. Epstein accomplished this by shaping two component behaviors in the pigeon, neither of which the pigeon normally does: (1) climbing on an object to reach another one and (2) pushing objects around. First, he trained the pigeon to peck at a free-standing box, moving it toward a stimulus on the floor of the chamber. Next, the pigeon was shaped to climb on a box beneath a toy banana and to peck the banana to obtain grain. Now came the problem. The banana was raised out of reach in one corner of the chamber, while the box was placed in another corner. Would the pigeon utilize its new behaviors to restructure this novel situation and obtain food? The pigeon "looked around" for a while and then moved into action. It pecked at the box, moving it under the banana, then hopped on the box, and pecked the banana. One pigeon accomplished this in just 39 seconds! Although other pigeons took longer—one required 24 minutes—all six pigeons tested displayed the "insightful" solution.

Control studies show that both the climbing and pushing behaviors must be taught before the problem can be solved. In Epstein's words: "We are thus constructing a plausible account of the emergence of 'insightful' behavior entirely in terms of known environmental histories." Thus, this demonstration not only shows that the pigeon is capable of complex problem-solving behavior but demonstrates that insightful behavior can be facilitated by conditioning of necessary component behaviors.

Cognitive structures

An early advocate of a cognitive interpretation of learning was Edward C. Tolman, whose research dealt with the problem of rats learning their way through very complex mazes (Tolman, 1932). In Tolman's view, a rat running through a maze was not learning a sequence of right and left turns but rather developing a *cognitive map*—a mental picture of the layout of the maze. Thus, if a familiar path was blocked, the animal adopted another route based on the spatial relations represented in its cognitive map.

LATENT LEARNING   Experiments on latent learning support the concept of cognitive structures. *Latent learning*, broadly conceived, refers to any learning that is not demonstrated by behavior at the time of the learning. Typically, such learning goes on in the absence of reward. When an appropriate reward appears, there is a sudden use of what has been previously learned.

In one latent learning experiment, three groups of rats were run daily in the maze diagrammed in Figure 7-17. One group was given a food reinforcer when it reached the goal box at the end of the maze. A second group was allowed to explore the maze, but when the rats reached the goal box, they were removed with no reinforcement. A third group was treated in the same way as the second group (no food) for the first 10 days and then treated like the first group (given food) for the remaining 7 days. As we can see in Figure 7-17, all groups learned something in that they made fewer errors each day in reaching the goal box. But the reinforced group clearly learned more rapidly than the

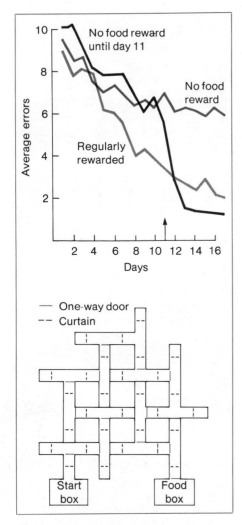

Figure 7-17
Latent Learning in Rats
Note that after the reward is introduced on the eleventh day, the rats represented by the black line perform as well as, and even a little better than, those regularly rewarded (gray line). Beneath the graph is a diagram of the maze used in this study. (After Tolman and Honzik, 1930)

two nonreinforced groups. However, on the eleventh day, when food was introduced for the third group, it was soon performing as well as the reinforced group. Evidently the rats in the third group were learning something about the maze prior to the time that they were rewarded. Tolman would claim that the rats were developing a cognitive map of the maze in the absence of specific rewards. When reward was introduced later, that map permitted the animals to reach a high level of performance almost immediately. Thus, learning, even for a rat, is not a "stamping in" of specific responses because they are followed by reinforcement; rather, it is the forming of a cognitive structure, which occurs even in the absence of reinforcement.

COGNITIVE MAPS AND SCHEMATA   A cognitive map is another example of what psychologists refer to more generally as a schema. We have encountered this term before. In Chapter 3 (page 74), the term was used in describing how infants form mental images of people and situations and thus learn to distinguish the familiar from the strange. In Chapters 4 and 5 (pages 121 and 147), schema was synonymous with the term "feature list"—a set of stimulus characteristics stored in memory that the perceptual system matches with incoming stimuli to determine whether a person or object has been seen before. And the term will be used in later chapters, particularly in our discussion of memory, language, and social behavior. There is no generally agreed upon definition of schema. Some psychologists use the term to designate specific theoretical ideas about mental events; others use it in a very broad sense. However used, the term refers to cognitive structures stored in memory that are abstract representations of events, objects, and relationships in the real world. It is a key ingredient of cognitive approaches to psychological phenomena.

ASSOCIATIVE VERSUS COGNITIVE LEARNING   As noted at several points in this chapter, there has been a good deal of controversy among psychologists about how to explain learning. One approach views learning as the formation of conditioned associations; the other emphasizes the cognitive nature of the process. For our purposes, it is possible to view associative learning and cog-

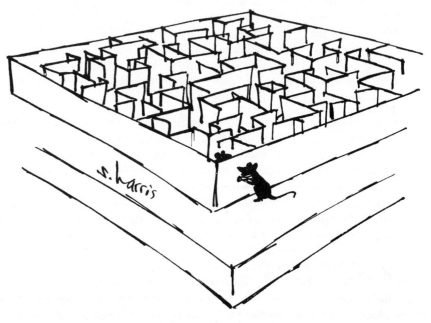

"Psst—want a map?"

nitive learning as complementary; neither in itself provides a complete explanation, but each helps to explain some features of learning that the other neglects or explains with greater difficulty.

Examples of learning can be graded on a scale with the most automatic kind of learning (explained most easily as associations) at one end and the most insightful and rational kind (explained most easily according to cognitive principles) at the other. Those habits learned by classical conditioning, without conscious awareness, would be at one extreme of the scale. Perhaps learning to salivate when we see a delicious meal or becoming anxious when we encounter a dangerous situation would be examples of such conditioning. Toward the middle of the scale would be tasks learned with full awareness but still somewhat automatically, such as a foreign language vocabulary or a motor skill like swimming. At the other end of the scale are tasks that require reasoning about many facts in complex relationships, such as mastering the content of a difficult textbook. Most learning would probably fall between the extremes of the scale, reflecting a mixture of associative and cognitive learning.

From this perspective, learning may or may not involve conscious awareness, depending on the complexity of the specific task. If the mastery of the task requires conscious attention, introspective reports by the learner should reveal something about the nature and details of the learning process. If the task, however, does not require conscious attention, learning will be mediated by automatic processes not open to introspection (Kellogg, 1982).

COMPUTER-ASSISTED LEARNING

For centuries, teachers have stood in front of classrooms and dispensed words of wisdom. Students passed or failed depending on how much of the knowledge they could recall at the time of an examination. This form of instruction has obvious limitations when compared to a tutorial arrangement—a one-to-one instructional relationship between the student and teacher. But the cost of tutorial education makes it impractical on a large-scale basis. In the 1950s, an effort was made to approximate some aspects of tutorial instruction in the form of a *teaching machine*. The work was guided by B.F. Skinner, the same person who played a key role in research on operant conditioning. Skinner felt that many of the ideas developed in the laboratory study of animal learning could be applied to the task of improving instruction.

An example of an early teaching machine is shown in Figure 7-18. The basic idea is to present information to the student in a series of frames. Each frame contains a new item of information and also poses a question that the student must answer. After writing the answer (usually a word or brief phrase), the student turns a knob that uncovers the correct answer and exposes the next instructional frame. In this way, the student goes step-by-step through the course, gradually being introduced to more difficult materials—being tested and immediately reinforced at each step.

Individualized instruction

With the advent of computers, it became evident that teaching devices could be developed that would be far more flexible and responsive to the student than the Skinner-type teaching machine. As yet, the use of computers in

Figure 7-18
An Early Teaching Machine
A statement with a fill-in blank is presented in the window at the left of the machine. The student writes an answer in the space on the right-hand side. After being shown the correct response, the student turns a knob on the left to proceed to the next item.

Figure 7-19
Computer-Assisted Learning
Shown here is an individual student's station. A first-grade student is learning word meanings as part of a course in reading. The microfilm display is on the left, and the cathode ray tube (TV-like screen) is on the right side. (After Atkinson, 1976)

business, science, and engineering far exceeds applications in education. However, if potentials are properly realized, the nature of education will be radically changed by the computer during our lifetime. The most important feature of computerized instruction is that it permits a high degree of *individualization;* students can proceed at their own pace, following a path through the curriculum best suited to their particular interests and talents.

Figure 7-19 displays one of the student terminals of a computer-assisted learning (CAL) system. Located at each student's station is a cathode ray tube, a microfilm display device, earphones, and a typewriter keyboard. Each device is under computer control. The computer sends out instructions to the terminal to display a particular image on the microfilm projector and to write a message of text or construct a geometric figure on a cathode ray tube; simultaneously, it sends an auditory message. The student sees the visual display, hears the auditory message, and then may be required to respond—either by operating the typewriter keyboard or by touching the surface of the cathode ray tube with an electronic pencil. This response is fed back to the computer and evaluated.

If the student's response is correct, the computer moves on to the next instructional item; if incorrect, the computer diagnoses the type of error made and branches to appropriate remedial material. A complete record for each student is stored in the computer and is updated with each new response. The record is checked by the computer to evaluate the student's progress and to determine any particular difficulties. A student making exceptionally good progress may be moved ahead in the lesson sequence or branched out to special materials designed to enrich his or her understanding of the curriculum. A student having difficulties may be branched back to review earlier materials or to a special remedial sequence. In a very real sense, the CAL system simulates the human tutorial process.

Although CAL has had only limited development, research suggests that it will have wide application in the future. For example, CAL programs designed to teach reading in the early grades have proved remarkably successful.

Children receiving computer-based instruction made significant gains over comparable groups taught by traditional classroom methods (Atkinson, 1976). Computer-based instruction has also been used at the college level and in industry with great success (Sleeman and Brown, 1982; Suppes, 1981).

Instructional programs

The essence of instruction, whether in the classroom or under computer control, lies in the arrangement of the material to be learned. A body of material arranged to be readily mastered is called an *instructional program.* Instructional programs for CAL tend to be quite complex. They incorporate an estimate of the student's current state of knowledge and use that information to make moment-by-moment decisions about what to teach next. Figure 7-20 illustrates the process:

1 An estimate of the current state of the student's knowledge is matched against the curriculum to identify gaps between what is already known and what is eventually to be mastered.
2 An instructional sequence is chosen with the intent of remedying some limited set of gaps in the student's knowledge.
3 Instruction is given, a few questions are asked, and the computer records the student's responses.
4 The response information is used to infer what has been learned and to update the program's estimate of the student's current state of knowledge. The process is cyclical and repeats these four steps until the course has been mastered.

It is not possible to prescribe a definite set of rules for developing a successful CAL program. The development of a good program is still very much an art in the same sense as writing a good textbook or preparing an effective lecture. Because the work is elusive, pilot tests of CAL programs are carried out. Pilot testing ordinarily consists of trying the CAL program on a group of students, revising it to take care of the difficulties they experience, trying it on a second group, revising it again, and so on, until the program works well. This process of successive revisions of a program is important. It focuses attention on the individual learning process and helps the programmer isolate and analyze the parts of the program that cause particular difficulties.

From a psychological viewpoint, what makes a CAL program effective? At least three factors seem to be particularly important.

1 *Active participation.* The learner is actively interacting with the curriculum materials by responding, practicing, and being tested at each step. The old adage "learning by doing" is well exemplified, in contrast to the passive learning that takes place during a lecture.
2 *Information feedback.* The learner finds out with minimal delay whether the response is correct; thus, an error can be corrected immediately. Immediate feedback has been shown to be important in a range of tasks—from operant conditioning with animals (in which immediate reinforcement produces faster learning) to learning with human subjects (in which immediate knowledge of results provides similar benefits).
3 *Individualization of instruction.* The learner moves ahead at his or her own rate. The rapid learner can progress quickly through the material, whereas the slower learner can move less rapidly (often being diverted to a remedial program) until the basic concepts have been mastered. Branching allows the learners to move through the material on a path designed to fit their aptitudes and abilities.

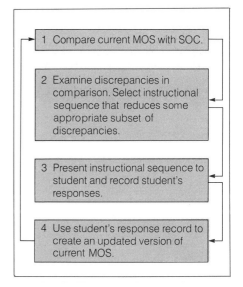

Figure 7-20
Diagram of an Instructional Program
MOS (model of student) is a theoretical representation of the student's current knowledge of the subject matter being taught. SOC (structure of curriculum) is the logical structure of the subject matter being taught. The computer is programmed to compare MOS with SOC and determine what should be taught next.

The diagram boxes read:
1 Compare current MOS with SOC.
2 Examine discrepancies in comparison. Select instructional sequence that reduces some appropriate subset of discrepancies.
3 Present instructional sequence to student and record student's responses.
4 Use student's response record to create an updated version of current MOS.

It should be recognized that self-paced instruction has been utilized effectively even when computers have not been available. For example, self-paced instruction has increased the rate of learning in children when the completion of a unit is reinforced with *tokens* (conditioned reinforcers that may be exchanged later for treats or privileges). The computer, however, maximizes the opportunity for active participation and swift feedback. Moreover, computers can provide extremely salient reinforcers for correct answers—such as vivid graphic displays—which are particularly effective in motivating children.

Summary

1 Two forms of *associative learning* are *classical conditioning* and *operant conditioning*. In classical conditioning, the organism learns that two stimuli tend to go together, whereas in operant conditioning it learns that some response it makes leads to a particular consequence.

2 Pavlov's experiments in classical conditioning demonstrated several principles useful in understanding associative learning. These include *reinforcement, acquisition, extinction, generalization,* and *discrimination.*

3 Skinner's experiments in operant conditioning extended conditioning principles to responses that are not elicited by an unconditioned stimulus. *Operant behavior* acts on the environment to produce or gain access to reinforcers, and it is strengthened by reinforcement. Rate of responding is a useful measure of *operant strength.*

4 Partial reinforcement illustrates the orderliness of operant behavior; once a particular response has been established, it can be sustained by occasional reinforcement. Extinction occurs much more slowly after partial reinforcement than after continuous reinforcement (the *partial-reinforcement effect*).

5 *Conditioned reinforcement,* the fact that a stimulus associated with a reinforcer acquires reinforcing properties, increases the possible range of conditioning, and explains the reward value of such incentives as social approval and money.

6 In *shaping*, behavior is modified by reinforcing variations in the subject's behavior that lead to a desired response and extinguishing those that do not. Thus, operant conditioning can account for the learning of novel behavior. Experiments have shown that some autonomic responses such as blood pressure can be modified through operant conditioning.

7 *Reinforcement* refers to any event that increases the probability of a response. According to *Premack's principle,* activities that are engaged in more frequently reinforce activities engaged in less frequently. *Amount* and *delay* of reinforcement are important variables that affect learning. *Punishment* refers to an event that decreases the probability of a response.

8 Some psychologists warn against an overemphasis on research concerned with associative learning. They stress instead situations in which understanding is a prominent component of the learning process and have introduced the concept of *cognitive structures.* Recent experiments suggest that even pigeons are capable of *insight* into problem-solving relationships, given the proper training.

9 *Latent learning* experiments illustrate how the concept of a *cognitive map* or *schema* (an example of a cognitive structure) can be used to explain learning that is not demonstrated in behavior immediately.

10   *Computer-assisted learning* is proving to be a valuable aid to learning. Some of the features of CAL that make it effective are as follows: active participation by the learner, immediate feedback, and the rate and path through the learning materials being adjusted to individual differences.

Further Reading

Pavlov's *Conditioned reflexes* (1927) is the classic work on classical conditioning. Skinner's *The behavior of organisms* (1938) is the corresponding statement on operant conditioning. Cognitive theories also have their classics: Köhler's *The mentality of apes* (1925) describes the famous insight experiments with chimpanzees; Tolman's *Purposive behavior in animals and men* (1932) is the major statement of his cognitive position. The principal points of view toward learning, presented in their historical settings, are summarized in Bower and Hilgard, *Theories of learning* (5th ed., 1981).

For a general introduction to learning, there are a number of textbooks, such as Hintzman, *The psychology of learning and memory* (1978); Fantino and Logan, *The experimental analysis of behavior: A biological perspective* (1979); Houston, *Fundamentals of learning and memory* (2nd ed., 1981); and Norman, *Learning and memory* (1982).

At the advanced level, the six-volume Estes (ed.), *Handbook of learning and cognitive processes* (1975–1979) covers most aspects of learning and conditioning; and Honig and Staddon (eds.), *Handbook of operant behavior* (1977) provides a comprehensive treatment of operant conditioning.

8
MEMORY

All learning implies memory. If we remembered nothing from our experiences we could learn nothing. Life would consist of momentary experiences that had little relation to one another. We could not even carry on a simple conversation. To communicate, you must remember the thoughts you want to express as well as what has just been said to you. Without memory you could not even reflect upon yourself, for the very notion of a self depends on a sense of continuity that only memory can bring. In short, when we think of what it means to be human we must acknowledge the centrality of memory.

DISTINCTIONS ABOUT MEMORY

Psychologists find it useful to make two basic distinctions about memory. The first concerns three stages of memory—encoding, storage, and retrieval. The second deals with two types of memory—short-term and long-term.

Three stages of memory

Suppose one morning you are introduced to a student and told her name is Barbara Cohn. That afternoon you see her again and say something like, "You're Barbara Cohn. We met this morning." Clearly you have remembered her name. But what exactly did you do?

Your minor memory feat can be broken into three stages (see Figure 8-1). First, when you were introduced, you somehow deposited Barbara Cohn's name into memory. This is the *encoding stage*. You transformed a physical phenomenon (sound waves) that corresponds to her spoken name into the kind of code that memory accepts, and you placed that code in memory. Second, you retained, or stored, the name during the time between the two meetings. This is the *storage stage*. And, third, you recovered the name from storage at the time of your second meeting. This is the *retrieval stage*.

Memory can fail at any of these three stages. Had you been unable to recall

221

Figure 8-1
Three Stages of Memory
Modern theories of memory attribute forgetting to a failure at one or more of these stages.

Barbara's name at the second meeting, this could have reflected a failure in encoding, storage, or retrieval. Current research on memory is aimed at specifying the operations that occur at each stage in different situations and explaining how these operations can go awry and result in memory failure.

Two types of memory

Do the three stages of memory operate in the same way in all memory situations? Research suggests that they do not. Memory seems to differ between those situations that require us to store material for a matter of seconds and those that require us to store material for longer intervals—from minutes to years. The former situations are said to tap *short-term memory*, whereas the latter reflect *long-term memory*.

We can illustrate this distinction by amending our story about meeting Barbara Cohn. Suppose that during the first meeting, as soon as you had heard her name, a friend came up and you said, "Doug, have you met Barbara Cohn?" In this case, remembering Barbara's name would be an example of short-term memory. You retrieved the name after only a second or so. Remembering her name at the time of your second meeting would be an example of long-term memory, for now retrieval would take place hours after the name was encoded.

When we recall a name immediately after encountering it, retrieval seems effortless, as if the name were still active, still in our consciousness. But when we try to recall the same name hours later, retrieval is often difficult, as the name is no longer conscious. This contrast between short- and long-term memory is similar to the contrast between conscious knowledge and the subconscious knowledge we have but are not currently thinking about. We can think of memory as a vast body of knowledge, only a small part of which can ever be active at any moment. The rest is passive. Short-term memory corresponds to the active part, long-term memory to the passive.

The next two sections of this chapter consider short- and long-term memory in some detail—mainly the nature of encoding, storage, and retrieval stages in each. Then after exploring how long-term memory may be improved, we will examine the relation between the two types of memory. In the last section, we focus on memory for more complex material, with an emphasis on how one embellishes what is put into memory.

SHORT-TERM MEMORY

Even in situations where you must remember information for only a few seconds and the information may still be active, memory includes three stages.

Encoding

To encode information into short-term memory, you must attend to it. Since we are selective about what we attend to (see Chapter 5), our short-term memory will contain only what has been selected. This means that much of what we are exposed to never even enters short-term memory and, of course, will not be available for later retrieval. Indeed, many difficulties labeled "memory problems" are really lapses in attention. For example, if you bought some groceries and someone asked you later for the color of the clerk's eyes, you might well be unable to answer because you had not paid attention to them in the first place.

When information is attended to, it is encoded into short-term memory. As mentioned earlier, encoding means not only that information is deposited in memory but also that it is deposited in a certain form, or code. For instance, when you look up a phone number and retain it until you have dialed it, in what code do you store the digits? Is the code visual—a mental picture of the digits? Or is the code acoustic—the sound of the names of the digits? Or is the code partly semantic (based on meaning)—some meaningful association we might have to the digits? Research indicates that we can use any of these possibilities to encode information into short-term memory. However, we seem to favor an acoustic code when we are trying to keep the information active by *rehearsing* it—that is, by repeating it over and over in our minds. Rehearsal is a particularly popular strategy when the information consists of verbal items such as digits, letters, or words. So in trying to remember a phone number, we are most likely to encode the number as the sounds of the digit names and to rehearse these sounds to ourselves until we have dialed the number.

In one experiment showing evidence for an acoustic code, subjects were shown a list of six consonants (for example, RLBKSJ). The letters were removed, and subjects had to write all six letters in order. Although the entire procedure took only a second or two, subjects occasionally made errors. When they did, the incorrect letter tended to be similar in sound to the correct one. Thus, for the list above, a subject might have written RLTKSJ, replacing the *B* with the similar sounding *T* (Conrad, 1964). This finding supports the idea that the subjects encoded each letter acoustically (for example, "bee" for *B*), sometimes lost part of this code (only the "ee" part of the sound remained), and then responded with a letter ("tee") that was consistent with the remaining part of the code.

When we do use a visual code for verbal materials, it often fades quickly and is soon dominated by the acoustic code. To illustrate, after looking at the address 5 OAK CREEK DRIVE, you may have a visual code of it for a second or so. This code would preserve visual details, such as the fact that the address was written in upper-case letters. After a couple of seconds, though, all that would remain would be the sound of the address—the acoustic code—and this code would not preserve information about the case of the letters. (The experiment in Figure 8-2 demonstrates the fading of the visual code.)

This dominance of the acoustic code may apply mainly to verbal materials. Recent research suggests that when a person must store nonverbal items (such as pictures that are difficult to describe and therefore difficult to rehearse acoustically), the visual code may become more important. A few people, most of them children, are able to encode pictures in fine photographic detail. Codes linked to other senses, such as touch and smell, can also be used to encode short-term memories. The pungent odor of sour milk, for example, seems to stay with us for a few seconds after we experience it.

Storage

Perhaps the most striking fact about short-term memory is that it has a very limited capacity. On the average, the limit is seven items, give or take two

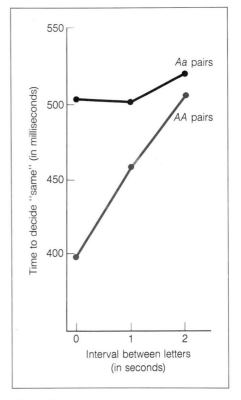

Figure 8-2
Fading of Visual Code
in Short-Term Memory
On each trial, subjects were shown two letters in succession; the interval between the letters varied from 0 to 2 seconds. Subjects had to determine whether the second letter had the same name as the first. In the sample trials shown below, the two letters have the same name.

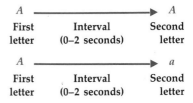

When the interval between the letters was roughly a second, the visual code for the first letter should not yet have faded. Consequently, subjects could make a direct visual comparison between letters. This kind of comparison will work for pairs like *AA*. But pairs like *Aa* can only be determined to have the same name by comparing their names acoustically. So we might expect *AA* decisions to be made faster than *Aa* decisions. When the interval between the letters is about 2 seconds, however, the visual code has faded and only the sounds of the letters remain in short-term memory. Now decisions about *AA* and *Aa* should take the same amount of time because both must be based on acoustic codes. (After Posner and Keele, 1967)

Although most of us occasionally retain a visual memory of something we have seen, such memories usually seem vague and lacking in detail. Some people, however, are able to hold in their short-term memory visual images that are almost photographic in clarity. They can look briefly at a picture and, when it is removed, still "see" its image located somewhere in space before their eyes. They can maintain the image for as long as several minutes, scan it, and describe it in far more detail than is usually possible. Such people are said to have a "photographic memory," or, to use the psychologist's term, *eidetic imagery.*

Eidetic imagery is quite rare. Studies with children indicate that only about 5 percent report visual images that last for more than a half-minute and possess sharp detail. The existing evidence suggests that there are even fewer individuals who have eidetic images after adolescence. In a typical procedure for investigating eidetic imagery, the experimenter places a richly detailed picture against a gray easel, gives the child 30 seconds to look at it, removes the picture, and then asks the child to describe what he or she can still see on the easel. Most children either report seeing nothing or describe fleeting afterimages

Figure 8-3
Testing for Eidetic Images
This test picture was shown for 30 seconds to elementary school children. After removal of the picture one boy saw in his eidetic image "about 14" stripes in the cat's tail. The painting, by Marjorie Torrey, appears in Lewis Carroll's *Alice in Wonderland*, abridged by Josette Frank.

of the picture. But some report images that are vivid and prolonged—that is, true eidetic images. When questioned, they can provide a wealth of detail, such as the number of stripes on a cat's tail (see Figure 8-3) or the number of buttons on a jacket. Such children seem to be reading the details directly from their eidetic image (Haber, 1969).

Studies with eidetic children indicate that a viewing time of 3 to 5 seconds is necessary to produce an image. The children report that when they do not look at the picture long enough, they do not have an image of parts of it, although they may remember what those parts contain. Exaggerated eye blinking or looking away from the easel usually makes the image disappear.

Other evidence indicates that eidetic imagery is truly visual in nature. For example, when an eidetic child tries to transfer the image onto another surface other than the gray easel, it disappears. At the same time, the eidetic image is not an exact photographic reproduction. The image usually contains additions, omissions, and distortions of the stimulus picture. The aspects of the picture that are most interesting to the child are the ones that tend to be reproduced in greatest detail in the eidetic image.

(7 ± 2). Some people store as few as five items; others can hold onto as many as nine. It may seem strange to give such an exact number to cover all people when it is clear that individuals differ greatly in their memory abilities. These differences, however, are primarily due to long-term memory. For short-term memory, most normal adults have a capacity of 7 ± 2. This constancy has been known since the earliest days of experimental psychology. Ebbinghaus, who began the experimental study of memory in 1885, reported results showing his own limit was seven items. Some 70 years later, Miller (1956) was so struck by the constancy that he referred to it as the "magic number seven."

Psychologists determined this number by showing subjects various sequences of unrelated items (digits, letters, or words) and asking them to recall the items in order. The items are presented rapidly, and the subject does not have time to relate them to information in long-term memory; thus, the number of items recalled reflects only the storage capacity for short-term memory. On the initial trials, subjects have to recall just a few items (say, four or five), which they can easily do. Then the number increases until the experimenter determines the maximum number a subject can recall in perfect order. The maximum (almost always between five and nine) is the subject's *memory span*. This task is so simple that you can easily try it yourself. The next time you come across a list of names (a directory in a business or university building, for example), read through the list once and then see how many names you can recall in order. It will probably be between five and nine.

Given this fixed capacity, it is tempting to think of short-term memory as a sort of mental box with roughly seven slots. Each item entering short-term memory goes into its own slot. So long as the number of items does not exceed the number of slots, we can recall the items perfectly. Though this "box" view cannot be taken literally, it does suggest a cause of forgetting in short-term memory: when all the slots are filled and a new item enters, one of the old ones must go. The new item displaces an old one.

The principle of *displacement* explains how an item is lost from short-term memory (see Figure 8-4). Suppose your short-term memory is empty. An item enters. Let us say you have been introduced to Barbara Cohn (remember her?), and the name Cohn enters your short-term memory. Others are introduced soon after, and the list of names in short-term memory grows. Finally, the limit of your memory span is reached. Then each new item that enters short-term memory has some chance of displacing Cohn. After one new item, there has been only one chance to displace Cohn; after two new items, there have been two chances, and so on. The likelihood that Cohn will be lost from short-term memory increases steadily with the number of items that have followed it. Eventually, Cohn will go.

Displacement has been demonstrated experimentally many times. In one study, subjects were given a list of 13 digits. After the last digit in the list, a probe digit was presented (it is called a *probe* because subjects must use it to

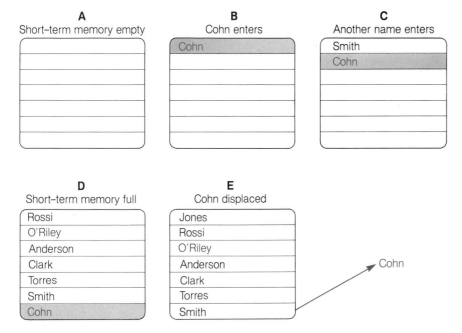

Figure 8-4
Displacement Principle
Due to the limited capacity of short-term memory, the addition of a new item can result in the loss of an old one.

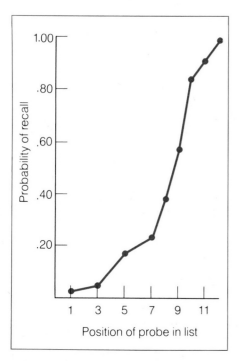

Figure 8-5
Recall as a Function of Probe Position
When probes are drawn from the end of the list, few items have followed the one to be recalled, and the probability of recall is high. When probes are drawn from the beginning of the list, many items have followed the one to be recalled, and the probability of recall is low. (After Waugh and Norman, 1965)

"probe" their memory). The probe was always identical to one of the digits in the list. The subjects' task was to report the digit that had followed the probe in the list. For example, given the list 3, 9, 1, 6, 9, 7, 5, 3, 8, 2, 5, 6, 4 and the probe 2, subjects should report 5. (The probe always occurred just once in the list.) When the probe is drawn from the end of the list the item following it should still be in short-term memory and very likely to be recalled. When the probe is from the beginning of the list, however, many items have followed the one to be recalled. Most likely it has been displaced and should not be recalled. For probes drawn from the middle of the list, the chances of displacement should be intermediate and so should the chance of recall. Figure 8-5 shows that the data from this experiment support the principle of displacement. The more items that intervene between the occurrence of a particular digit and the attempt to recall it, the less the chance of recall.

It appears, then, that information at the forefront of our memory must soon give way to newer information. There is one major exception, though: items that are rehearsed are not readily displaced. (In experiments that try to demonstrate displacement, subjects are typically discouraged from rehearsing.) Why should rehearsing information protect it from displacement? One possibility is that we cannot encode new items at the same time we are rehearsing old ones. In other words, rehearsal may prevent displacement by preventing the encoding of new items.

Displacement may not be the only cause of short-term forgetting. Information may simply decay with time, regardless of whether new information follows (Reitman, 1974). That is, we may think of the stored information as a trace that fades with time, much as a color photograph fades as the years pass. To the extent that decay causes forgetting, we can see another way that rehearsal benefits memory. Rehearsing an item that has partly faded may bring it to full strength again.

Retrieval

Let us think of the contents of short-term memory as being available to consciousness. Intuition suggests that access to this information is immediate. You do not have to "dig for it"; it is right there. Retrieval, then, should not depend on the number of items in consciousness. But in this case intuition is wrong.

We now have evidence suggesting that retrieval requires a search of short-term memory, in which the items are examined one at a time. This serial search takes place at a very fast rate—so fast in fact that we are not aware of it. Most of the evidence for such a search comes from a type of experiment introduced by Sternberg (1966). On each trial of the experiment, a subject is shown a set of digits, called the *memory list*, that he or she must temporarily hold in short-term memory; it is easy for the subject to maintain the information in short-term memory because each memory list contains less than seven digits. The memory list is then removed from view, and a probe digit is presented several seconds later. The subject must decide whether the probe was on the memory list. For example, if the memory list is 3, 6, 1 and the probe is 6, the subject should respond "yes"; given the same memory list and a probe of 2, the subject should respond "no." Since the memory list has been removed by the time the probe is presented, the probe must be compared with the encoded representation of the list in short-term memory.

Subjects rarely make an error on this task; what is of interest is the speed at which the subject makes the decision. The *decision time* is the elapsed time between the onset of the probe and the subject's press of a "yes" or a "no" button to indicate whether the probe was or was not on the memory list. The decision times are extremely fast and must be measured with equipment that permits accuracy in milliseconds (thousandths of a second). In a typical experiment, the subject is tested over several hundred trials. On each trial, a new memory list is presented that can vary in length from one to seven items. Thus, over the course of the experiment, a researcher can examine decision time as a function of the number of items that the subject must search through in short-term memory.

Figure 8-6 presents data from such an experiment, indicating that decision time increases directly with the length of the memory list. What is remarkable about these decision times is that they fall along a straight line. This means that each additional item in short-term memory adds a fixed amount of time to the search process—approximately 40 milliseconds (40 thousandths of a second). The subject, of course, is not aware of such brief time intervals, but the data clearly indicate that decision time increases with the amount of information that must be searched through in short-term memory.

The search process is composed of three *stages*. In the first stage, the subject encodes the probe stimulus into a form that can be compared with the items stored in short-term memory. In the second stage, the subject compares the code serially against each item in short-term memory: to check one item takes 40 milliseconds; two items, 80 milliseconds; three items, 120 milliseconds; and so forth. In the third stage, the subject initiates a response that results in the press of the "yes" or the "no" button. Decision time, then, is the sum of the times taken to complete each of the three stages. Together, the first and third stages, which do not depend on the number of items in short-term memory, take about 400 milliseconds. The time required to complete the second stage is 40 milliseconds multiplied by the length of the memory list. Thus, decison time in milliseconds equals

$$400 + 40x$$

where x is the number of items in short-term memory. This equation gives a good account of the data in Figure 8-6 and suggests that the search of short-term memory involves a *serial process* in which the probe is compared sequentially to each item on the memory list.

The same results are found when the items are letters, words, tones, or pictures of peoples' faces. Adding an extra item usually adds about 40 thousandths of a second to retrieval time, although faces of people seem to take slightly longer to evaluate than verbal items (Sternberg, 1969). Similar results are obtained with groups as varied as patients diagnosed as schizophrenic, college students under the influence of marijuana, and people from preliterate societies. Thus, for all individuals, retrieval from short-term memory seems to require a search.

Short-term memory and thought

Researchers believe that short-term memory may play an important role in conscious thought. When consciously trying to solve a problem, we seem to be using the same capacity needed to store a list of numbers. To see this, try to solve even a simple arithmetic problem (8 × 15) while remembering a phone number (745-1739). The result is confusion and interference; the two activities compete for the same mental resources. This kind of competition for a limited

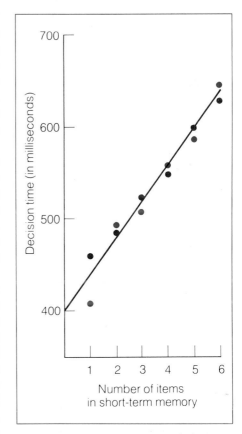

Figure 8-6
Retrieval as a Search Process
Decision times increase in direct proportion to the number of items in short-term memory. Colored circles represent "yes" responses; black circles, "no" responses. The times for both types of decision fall along a straight line. (After Sternberg, 1966)

Serial Versus Parallel Processes

Figure 8-6 suggests a retrieval process in which the probe is compared serially to each item in short-term memory. But other interpretations are possible. In particular, some have argued that the comparisons are actually done in parallel. That is, the subject compares the probe to all memory items simultaneously, responding "yes" as soon as a match is found and "no" when none of the comparisons yields a match. At first, this idea seems incompatible with the finding that decision times increase with the number of comparisons to be made. For it would seem that if all the comparisons are made at once it should take no longer to do multiple comparisons than to do one. However, even when things are done in parallel, the time to do all of them may increase with the number that have to be done.

We can use a horse race as an analogy. While all the horses run the race together (in parallel), the time for the last horse to cross the finish line generally increases with the number of horses in the race. As the number of horses increases, the chances that slower horses will be included in the race also increase, and then we will have to wait until the slowest of them crosses the finish line. Thus, several things are happening in parallel, yet the time for the whole process to finish increases with the number of things to be done.

Let us apply this horse-race logic to retrieval from short-term memory. Now we are considering the time for mental operations (comparisons) to run their course. The more operations to be performed, the more likely it is that one of them will be unduly slow. This means that decision time will, in general, increase with the number of items in short-term memory. But will such an increase be of the straight-line form shown in Figure 8-6? The answer, based on a mathematical analysis, is probably not (Sternberg, 1966).

There is, however, another way that parallel comparisons can increase decision times. To use another analogy, suppose you are searching for a bomb in a two-room apartment. You have the assistance of two experts from the bomb squad. If you know which room the bomb is in, you can send both experts there, and they should find it relatively quickly. But if you do not know which room the bomb is in, you will probably send one expert to each room. They will be searching in parallel, but clearly the time to find the bomb is likely to increase. For the efficiency with which each room is searched must decrease with fewer searchers. That is, with limited resources (two experts), a parallel search of the two rooms requires a division of labor that results in less efficient individual searches.

This reasoning transfers nicely to retrieval from short-term memory. Just as our physical resources can be limited, so can our mental resources. We may have only a fixed capacity for retrieval; and when an item is added to short-term memory, the total capacity must be further divided among the simultaneous comparisons. This decrease in capacity per comparison results in lowered efficiency for each comparison. And the less efficient a comparison, the longer it takes to execute. This line of reasoning clearly leads us to expect an increase in decision time as the number of items in memory increases. With suitable mathematical assumptions about how the capacity is divided, the expected increases can be shown to fall on a straight line (Townsend, 1971). This alternative explanation of the straight line in Figure 8-6 involves parallel rather than serial processing.

The parallel process just described is called a *limited-capacity* process. This kind of process may be quite widespread in mental life. It can be used to describe how we divide our attention among multiple inputs or perhaps even to describe how we divide our thinking capacity among various ideas. It fits with our intuition that we can engage in more than one mental activity at a time—but only at the cost of lower efficiency per activity.

short-term memory capacity has been demonstrated in the laboratory (Baddeley and Hitch, 1974).

When reading for understanding, often we must consciously relate new words or sentences to some prior material in the text. If this relating of new to old occurs in short-term memory, people who have more short-term capacity should be better at reading comprehension. There is some evidence for this prediction (Daneman and Carpenter, 1981). Other experiments show that the readability of a text depends partly on the likelihood that relevant connecting material is still in short-term memory (see Miller and Kintsch, 1980).

Short-term memory also seems to be involved in the kind of everyday thinking we do about other people. In research on personality, for example, when subjects are asked to form an impression of someone on the basis of one meeting, they tend to describe the person in terms of roughly 7 ± 2 traits (Mischel, 1968). It is as if the capacity of short-term memory, 7 ± 2, places a limit on the number of ideas or impressions we can entertain at one time.

Chunking

In the preceding discussion, we considered only short-term memory, for our goal was to isolate this kind of memory so we could best understand it. But in life, often both short- and long-term memory play a role in the same situation. One particularly important interaction between short- and long-term memory is the phenomenon of *chunking,* which can occur in memory-span tasks.

Recall that in a memory-span task, subjects can repeat a sequence of verbal items in perfect order as long as the number of items is 7 ± 2. So you would probably be unable to repeat the sequence SRUOYYLERECNIS since it contains 14 letters. Should you ever notice, however, that these letters spell the familiar phrase "SINCERELY YOURS" in reverse order, your memory-span task would become easier. By using your knowledge that these letters spell "SINCERELY YOURS" backwards, you have decreased the number of items that must be held in short-term memory from 14 to two. But where did this spelling knowledge come from? From long-term memory, of course, where knowledge about words is stored.

Thus, you can use long-term memory to recode new material into larger meaningful units and then store those units in short-term memory. Such units are called *chunks,* and the capacity of short-term memory is best expressed as 7 ± 2 chunks (Miller, 1956).

The notion of chunks has some important implications. If short-term memory could hold only seven letters, it could not retain even a simple sentence. Fortunately, though, letters can be grouped into word chunks, and word chunks themselves can be grouped into phrase chunks. This enables us to hold in short-term memory as much as the last few sentences we have heard—a capacity critical for understanding written and spoken communications. Language provides a natural chunking device, since it groups letters and words into larger meaningful units.

Sometimes we can chunk letters without forming words. This occurs when the letters stand for some meaningful (but nonword) unit. The letter string IB-MFB-ITVU-SA is hard to recall because it contains more than seven chunks. But suppose the spacing is changed so that the string is IBM-FBI-TV-USA. Each letter group is now a familiar unit. The result is four chunks and a string that is easy to remember (Bower and Springston, 1970). Chunking can occur with numbers as well. The string 149-2177-619-83 is beyond our capacity, but 1492-1776-1983 is well within it. In both examples, the regrouped strings contain familar units in long-term memory. The general principle seems to be that we can boost our short-term memory by regrouping sequences of letters and digits into units that can be found in long-term memory.

LONG-TERM MEMORY

Long-term memory involves information that has been retained for intervals as brief as a few minutes (a point made earlier in a conversation) or as long as a lifetime (an adult's childhood memories). In experiments on long-term memory, psychologists generally have studied forgetting over intervals of minutes, hours, or weeks, but a few studies have involved years or even decades.

Encoding

For verbal materials, the dominant long-term memory code is neither acoustic nor visual; instead, it seems to be based on the meanings of the items. If you memorize a long list of words and try to recall them several minutes later, you will undoubtedly make errors. Many of the erroneous words will be similar in meaning to the correct items. For example, if "quick" is on the original list, you may mistakenly recall "fast" instead (Kintsch and Buschke, 1969). Encoding items in terms of their meaning is particularly striking when the items are sentences. A few minutes after hearing a sentence, most of what is left in memory is its meaning. Suppose you heard the sentence "The author sent the committee a long letter." Two minutes later you could not tell whether you had heard that sentence or one that has the same meaning: "A long letter was sent to the committee by the author" (Sachs, 1967). Encoding for long-term memory, then, tends to maintain meaning.

Often the items we have to remember are meaningful but the connections between them are not. In such cases, memory can be improved by thinking up a real or artificial link between the items. For example, people learning to read music must remember that the five lines in printed music are referred to as EGBDF; although the symbols themselves are meaningful (they refer to notes on a keyboard), their order seems arbitrary. What many learners do is convert the symbols into the sentence "Every Good Boy Does Fine"; the first letter of each word names each symbol and the relations between the words in the sentence supply a meaningful connection between the symbols.

Numerous experiments have shown that adding meaningful connections is a powerful memory aid. In one study, subjects were asked to memorize a long list of word pairs so that on a later test when given the first term of a pair (the *stimulus*), they could supply the second term (the *response*). If "horse–table" was one pair to be memorized, subjects had to respond "table" when later tested with the stimulus term "horse." The relationship between the terms in each pair was meaningless. One group of subjects was instructed to memorize each pair by thinking of a sentence that used both terms. For example, for the "horse–table" pair, they might think of the sentence "The horse kicked the table." Each sentence thus related the items in a meaningful way. A second group, the control group, was left to its own devices to learn the list. The group instructed to think of sentences recalled about 75 percent of the word pairs, whereas the control group recalled only 35 percent (Bower, 1972).

Making sentences out of unrelated letters or words is not the only means of adding meaningful connections to verbal materials. Another way is to use imagery. In a variation of the experiment just described, the first group was instructed to memorize each pair by forming a visual image that related the two words—for example, an image of a horse jumping over a table. In this experiment, too, the first group recalled roughly twice as much as the control group. Thus, using either images or sentences to add meaningful connections leads to an improvement in memory.

Although meaning may be the dominant way of coding verbal material in long-term memory, we sometimes code other aspects as well. We can, for

example, memorize poems and recite them word for word. In such cases, we have coded not only the meaning of the poem but the words themselves. We can also use an acoustic code in long-term memory. When you get a phone call and the other party says "Hello," you often recognize the voice. To do this, you must have coded the sound of that person's voice in long-term memory. Tastes and smells are also coded in long-term memory. Thus, coding in long-term memory is like that in short-term memory: we have a preferred code for verbal material—meaning for long-term memory, acoustic for short-term memory—but other codes can be used as well.

Coding by meaning, however, seems to result in the best memory. And the more deeply or elaborately one encodes the meaning, the better memory will be. Thus, if you have to remember a point made in a textbook, you will recall it better if you concentrate on its meaning rather than on the exact words involved. And the more deeply and thoroughly you mull over its meaning, the better you will recall it.

An experiment performed by Craik (1977) illustrates these points. Subjects were shown words one at a time and asked if the word could fit into a particular sentence, where the sentence was either short or long. For example, if the word was "watch," the short sentence might be "He dropped the _____" and the long sentence might be "The glass shattered into pieces because he dropped the _____." With long sentences, subjects had to elaborate the word's meaning more to make sure it fit the sentence. When subjects were later tested on their memory for the words, they recognized more words associated with long sentences than with short ones. The more subjects had to elaborate the meaning of a word, the better they remembered it.

Elaborating meaning seems to work by adding extra retrieval possibilities. In the above experiment, subjects who determined that "watch" fit in the long sentence might have encoded it in the following form:

(1) He dropped the watch

(2) Glass of watch shattered into pieces

That is, subjects might have encoded the sentence as two phrases with connections between them. If so, when later given the memory test, subjects could have retrieved the word "watch" from either phrase (1) or (2). In contrast, subjects who determined that "watch" fit in the short sentence would have only phrase (1) encoded in memory. Thus, the more that subjects had to elaborate the meaning of the critical word, the more retrieval paths to the critical word they created; and the more paths to the word, the more likely it was to be retrieved (Anderson and Reder, 1979).

Our ability to remember material as complex as a chapter in a textbook also benefits from elaboration. This ability has been demonstrated in an experiment where subjects had to read part of a text so that they could later answer questions about it from memory. Prior to reading the text, one group of subjects was given a set of advance questions (different from the memory questions they would later be asked). These subjects were to find answers to the advance questions while reading the text. Trying to find these answers should have led the subjects to elaborate on parts of the text. A second, or control, group of subjects studied the text without any advance questions. When both groups were later given the memory questions, the first group got more correct than the control group. Again, an experimental technique that fostered elaboration enhanced memory (Frase, 1975; Anderson, 1980).

Storage and retrieval

When we deal with long-term memory, we must consider storage and retrieval together. Many cases of forgetting from long-term memory seem to result from a loss of access to the information rather than from a loss of the information itself. That is, poor memory may reflect a retrieval failure rather than a storage failure. (Note that this is unlike short-term memory, where forgetting results from exceeding storage capacity, whereas retrieval is thought to be virtually error-free.) Trying to retrieve an item from long-term memory is analogous to trying to find a book in a large library. Failure to find the book (an item) does not necessarily mean it is not there; you may be looking in the wrong place, or it may simply be misfiled and therefore inaccessible.

Common experience provides much evidence for this view. Everyone has been unable to recall a fact, only to have it come to mind later. How many times have you taken an exam and not been able to recall a specific name or date, only to remember it after the exam? Another example is the "tip-of-the-tongue" experience, in which a particular word or name lies tantalizingly outside our ability to recall it (Brown and McNeill, 1966). We may feel quite tormented until a search of memory (dredging up and then discarding words that are close but not quite right) finally retrieves the correct word. A more striking example of retrieval failure is that some people under hypnosis feel they can recover memories of early childhood that are otherwise unavailable. Similar experiences occur in psychotherapy. Although we lack firm experimental evidence for some of these observations, they at least suggest that some seemingly forgotten memories are not lost. They are just difficult to get at and require the right kind of *retrieval cue* (anything that can help us retrieve a memory).

For stronger evidence that retrieval failures can cause forgetting, we consider the following experiment. Subjects were asked to memorize a long list of words. Some of the words named specific animals, like "dog" and "cat"; some named specific fruit, like "apple" and "orange," and so on (see Table 8-1). At the time of recall, the subjects were divided into two groups. One group was supplied with retrieval cues like "animal," "fruit," and so on; the control group was not. The group given the retrieval cues recalled more words than the control group. In a subsequent test, when both groups were given the retrieval cues, they recalled the same number of words. Hence, the initial difference in recall between the two groups must have been due to retrieval failures.

Thus, the better the retrieval cues, the better our memory. This principle explains why we usually do better on a recognition test of memory than on a recall test. In a recognition test, we are asked if we have seen a particular item before (for example, "Was Harry Smith one of the people you met at the party?"). The test item itself is an excellent retrieval cue for our memory of that item. In contrast, in a recall test, we have to produce the memorized items with minimal retrieval cues (for example, "Recall the names of everyone you met at the party."). Since the retrieval cues in a recognition test are generally more useful than those in a recall test, recognition tests usually show better memory performance than recall tests (Tulving, 1974).

Are retrieval failures the only cause of forgetting? It is difficult to say. How

William James Writing in 1890 on the Tip-of-the-Tongue Experience

"**Suppose we try to recall a forgotten name. The state of our consciousness is peculiar. There is a gap therein; but no mere gap. It is a gap that is intensely active. A sort of wraith of the name is in it, beckoning us in a given direction, making us at moments tingle with the sense of our closeness and then letting us sink back without the longed-for term. If wrong names are proposed to us, this singularly definite gap acts immediately so as to negate them. They do not fit into its mold. And the gap of one word does not feel like the gap of another, all empty of content as both might seem necessarily to be when described as gaps.**" (James, 1890)

LIST TO BE MEMORIZED		
dog	cotton	oil
cat	wool	gas
horse	silk	coal
cow	rayon	wood
apple	blue	doctor
orange	red	lawyer
pear	green	teacher
banana	yellow	dentist
chair	knife	football
table	spoon	baseball
bed	fork	basketball
sofa	pan	tennis
knife	hammer	shirt
gun	saw	socks
rifle	nails	pants
bomb	screwdriver	shoes

RETRIEVAL CUES		
animals	cloth	fuels
fruit	color	professions
furniture	utensils	sports
weapons	tools	clothing

Table 8-1
Examples from a Study
of Retrieval Failures
Subjects not given the retrieval cues recall fewer words from the memorized list than other subjects who did have the cues. This finding shows that problems at the retrieval stage of long-term memory are responsible for some memory failures. (After Tulving and Pearlstone, 1966)

can we tell whether a person has totally forgotten something or has not yet found the right retrieval cue—the one that leads to the target memory? On the other hand, it seems unlikely that everything ever learned is still there in memory waiting for the right cue. Some information may actually be lost from storage, perhaps due to some form of displacement by subsequent information or to decay with time.

Whether or not retrieval failures are the only cause of forgetting from long-term memory, they are certainly a major cause. Thus, it is essential to know what factors increase and decrease retrieval. In the rest of this section, we will discuss such factors.

Organization and context

Research has identified two factors that increase the chances of successful retrieval: (1) organizing the information in storage and (2) ensuring that the context in which we retrieve information is similar to the context in which we encoded it.

The more we organize the material we store, the easier it is to retrieve. For example, suppose you were at a meeting where you met various professionals—doctors, lawyers, teachers, and journalists. When you later tried to recall their names, you would do better if you organized your recall by profession: Who were the doctors I met? Who were the lawyers? And so forth. A list of names or words is far easier to recall when we can sort the words into categories and then recall the words on a category-by-category basis.

The following experiment illustrates the use of categories in organizing recall. The subjects were asked to memorize four separate lists of words. For some subjects, the words in a list were arranged in the form of a hierarchical

Figure 8-7
Hierarchical Organization
to Improve Retrieval
Trees like this are constructed according to the following rule: all items below a node are included in the class labeled by that node; for example, the items "bronze," "steel," and "brass" are included in the class labeled "alloys." (After Bower and others, 1969)

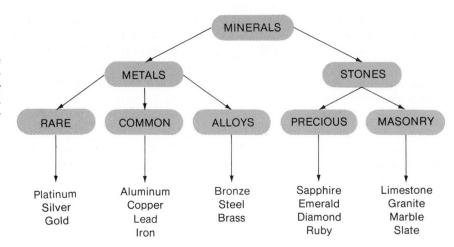

tree, much like the example shown in Figure 8-7. For the other subjects, the words were arranged randomly. When tested later, subjects recalled 65 percent of the words presented in the hierarchical organization but only 19 percent of the same words presented in random arrangements. Studies like this leave little doubt that retrieval is best when the material is highly organized.

Why does hierarchical organization improve memory? Probably because retrieval from long-term memory requires some kind of search process, and hierarchical organization makes this search more efficient. In the preceding experiment, for example, subjects who had the words hierarchically organized, as in Figure 8-7, might have searched long-term memory as follows: first, they found a high-level cluster, like "metals"; from that high-level cluster, they then searched for a low-level cluster like "common metals"; and then they searched that low-level cluster for specific words ("aluminum," "copper," "lead," "iron"); and so on. By operating in this way, at no point would subjects have to search a large set: there are only two high-level clusters, never more than three low-level clusters connected to a high-level one, and never more than four specific words in a low-level cluster. Thus, hierarchical organization allows us to divide a "big" search into a sequence of "little" ones. And with a "little" search, there is less chance we will bog down by continuing to turn up the same specific words again and again, which is exactly what seems to happen when we search material that is not organized (Raaijmakers and Shiffrin, 1981). This same principle—divide the search into manageable parts so that we do not keep retrieving the same items—may lay behind many beneficial effects of organization on memory.

It is also easier to retrieve a particular episode if you are in the same context in which that episode occurred (Estes, 1972). For example, it is a good bet that your ability to retrieve the names of your classmates in the first and second grade would improve were you to walk through the corridors of your elementary school. Similarly, your ability to retrieve, say, an emotional moment with your parents would be greater if you were back in the place where the incident occurred than if you were somewhere else. Perhaps it is for this reason that when we visit a place we once lived, we are sometimes overcome with a torrent of memories about our earlier life. Thus, the context in which an event was encoded is itself one of the most powerful retrieval cues possible. There is a mass of experimental evidence to support this (see Figure 8-8 for a representative study).

Context is not always something external to the memorizer, like a physical location or a specific face. What is happening inside of us when we encode information—our internal state—is also part of the context. To take an extreme example, if we experience some event while under the influence of a particular drug, like alcohol or marijuana, perhaps we can best retrieve it when we are again in that drug-induced state. In such cases, memory would be partly dependent on the internal state during learning—what is called *state-dependent learning* (see Chapter 6). There has been a good deal of research on state-dependent learning, and even though the evidence is controversial, it suggests that memory does indeed improve when our internal state during retrieval matches that during encoding (see Eich and others, 1975).

Interference

There are also factors that decrease retrieval, particularly the factor of interference. If we associate different items to the same cue, when we try to use that cue to retrieve one of the items (the target item), the other items will come to mind and interfere with our recovery of the target. For example, if your friend Dan moves and you finally learn his new phone number, you will find it difficult to retrieve the old number. Why? You are using the cue "Dan's phone number" to retrieve the old number, but instead this cue activates the new number that interferes with recovery of the old one. Or suppose that your reserved space in a parking garage, which you have used for a year, is changed. You may initially find it difficult to retrieve from memory your new parking location. Why? You are trying to learn to associate your new location to the cue "my parking place," but this cue retrieves the old location, which interferes with the learning of the new one. In both examples, the power of retrieval cues ("Dan's phone number" or "my parking place") to activate particular target items decreases with the number of other items associated with those cues. The

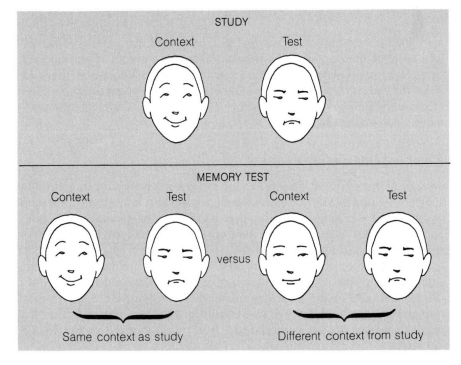

Figure 8-8
Effects of Context on Retrieval
In an experiment to demonstrate how context affects retrieval, subjects first studied pairs of faces like the one at the top. (Since only the right-hand face was ever tested, it was the test face, whereas the left-hand one was the context face.) Later, in a memory test, subjects were again shown pairs of faces and asked whether the test face (the one on the right) was one they had previously studied. In some cases, the context face was the same one that appeared in the original pair; in other cases, it was not. Subjects made more accurate decisions when the context face was the same. (After Watkins, Ho, and Tulving, 1976)

more items associated with a cue, the more overloaded it becomes and the less well it can retrieve.

In one experiment demonstrating interference, subjects first learned to associate various facts with names of professions (such as doctor, lawyer). For example, they learned that:

1   The banker was asked to address the crowd.
2   The banker broke the bottle.
3   The banker did not delay the trip.
4   The lawyer realized the seam was split.
5   The lawyer painted an old barn.

The occupational names "banker" and "lawyer" were the retrieval cues here. Since "banker" was associated with three facts, whereas "lawyer" was associated with just two, "banker" should have been less useful in retrieving any one of its associated facts than "lawyer" was. When subjects were later given a recognition test, they in fact took longer to recognize the facts learned about the banker than those learned about the lawyer. In this study, then, interference slowed the speed of retrieval. Many other experiments show that interference can lead to a complete retrieval failure if the target items are very weak or the interference is very strong (Anderson, 1980).

If we had no way to counteract it, interference would soon overwhelm us. The preceding experiment indicates that the more facts we learn about a topic, the more difficult it is to retrieve any one of them, which suggests that it should be impossible to ever retain very much about a topic. There is, however, a way to offset interference: if we organize the various facts about a topic, they will no longer interfere with one another. This has been demonstrated in a variation of the experiment just described. Whenever three facts had to be learned about an occupation, they were organized. For example,

1   The banker was asked to christen the ship.
2   The banker broke the bottle.
3   The banker did not delay the trip.

Only the first sentence was changed, so it integrated the other two "banker" facts with the theme of christening a ship. When later given a recognition test, subjects in this experiment took no longer to recognize one of the three facts about the banker than one of the two about the lawyer. Organization has offset interference (Smith, Adams, and Schorr, 1978). To memorize a large amount of information about a topic, then, we must organize the facts.

Emotional factors in forgetting

So far, we have treated retrieval as if it were a mechanical operation. What about emotional factors? Don't we sometimes fail to retrieve material because of its emotional content? There has been a great deal of research on this question. The results suggest that emotion can influence retrieval from long-term memory in at least four distinct ways.

The simplest notion is that we tend to think about emotionally charged situations, negative as well as positive, more than we think about neutral ones. We rehearse and organize exciting memories more than we do their blander counterparts. For example, you may usually forget where you saw this or that movie. However, if a fire breaks out while you are in a theater, you will describe the setting over and over to friends, thereby rehearsing and organizing it. Since we know that rehearsal and organization can improve retrieval from long-term memory, it is not surprising that many researchers have found better memory for emotional than for unemotional situations (Rapaport, 1942).

In some cases, however, negative emotions hinder retrieval. An experience that most students have at one time or another illustrates this.

> You are taking an exam about which you are not very confident. You can barely understand the initial question let alone answer it. Signs of panic appear. Although the second question really isn't hard, the anxiety triggered by the previous question spreads to this one. By the time you look at the third question, it wouldn't matter if it just asked for your name. There's no way you can answer it. You're in a complete panic.

"And then I say to myself, 'If I really wanted to talk to her, why do I keep forgetting to dial 1 first?' "

Drawing by Modell; © 1981 *The New Yorker Magazine*, Inc.

What is happening to memory here? Failure to deal with the first question produced some anxiety. Anxiety is often accompanied by extraneous thoughts, like "I'm going to flunk out," or "Everybody will know how stupid I am." These thoughts then interfere with any attempt to retrieve the information relevant to the question, and that may be why memory fails so utterly. According to this view, anxiety does not directly cause memory failure. Rather, it causes, or is associated with, extraneous thoughts, and these thoughts cause memory failure by interfering with retrieval (Holmes, 1974).

A third way that emotion can affect memory is by *context effects*. As mentioned earlier, memory is best when the context at retrieval matches that at encoding. Since our emotional state during learning is part of the context, if we feel sad when we learn some material, we can best retrieve that material when we feel sad again. Such an emotional-context effect has been demonstrated in the laboratory. Subjects agreed to keep diaries for a week, recording daily every emotional incident that occurred and noting whether it was pleasant or unpleasant. One week after they handed in their diaries, subjects returned to the laboratory and were hypnotized (they had been preselected to be highly hypnotizable). Half the subjects were put in a pleasant mood, and the other half were put in an unpleasant mood. All were asked to recall the incidents recorded in their diaries. For subjects in a pleasant mood, most of the incidents they recalled had been rated as pleasant when experienced; for subjects in an unpleasant mood at retrieval, most of the incidents recalled had been rated as unpleasant when experienced. As expected, recall was best when the dominant emotion during retrieval matched that during encoding (Bower, 1981).

We have now considered three means by which emotion can influence memory, improving or hindering retrieval. All three rely on principles already discussed—rehearsal, interference, and context effects. The fourth view of emotion and memory—Freud's theory of the unconscious—brings up new principles. Freud proposed that some emotional experiences in childhood are so traumatic that to allow them to enter consciousness many years later would cause the individual to be totally overwhelmed by anxiety. (This was not the case in the example of the exam, where the anxiety was tolerable to consciousness.) Such traumatic experiences, as well as later ones associated with them, are said to be stored in the unconscious, or *repressed*. They can be retrieved when some of the emotion associated with them is defused, usually by therapeutic means. Repression, therefore, represents the ultimate retrieval failure: access to the target memories is actively blocked. This notion of active blocking makes the repression hypothesis qualitatively different from the views

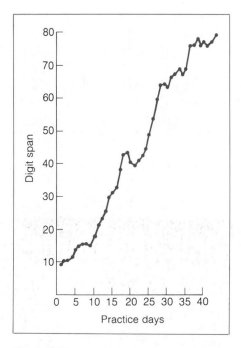

Figure 8-9
Number of Digits Recalled by SF
This subject greatly increased his memory span for digits by devising a recoding system using chunking and hierarchical organization. Total practice time was about 215 hours. (After Ericsson, Chase, and Faloon, 1980)

Figure 8-10
A Mnemonic System
The method of loci aids memory by associating items (here, entries on a shopping list) with an ordered sequence of places.

we considered earlier. (For a fuller discussion of Freud's theory, see Chapter 14.)

Repression is such a striking phenomenon that we would of course like to study it in the laboratory. But this has proved difficult to do, although many attempts have been made. To induce repression in the laboratory, the experimenter must have the subject experience something extremely traumatic. Ethical considerations prohibit this. Nevertheless, the idea of repression continues to fascinate those who study memory, even in the absence of firm experimental support.

IMPROVING MEMORY

Having considered the basics of short- and long-term memory, we are ready to tackle the question of improving memory. First, we will consider how to increase the short-term memory span; then we will turn to a variety of methods for improving long-term memory. These methods work by increasing the efficiency of encoding, of retrieval, or of both.

Chunking and memory span

For most of us, the capacity of short-term memory cannot be increased beyond 7 ± 2 chunks. However, we can enlarge the size of a chunk and thereby increase the number of items in our memory span. We demonstrated this point earlier: given the string 149-2177-619-83, we can recall all 12 digits if we recode the string into 1492-1776-1983 and then store just these three chunks in short-term memory. Although recoding digits into familar dates works nicely in this example, it will not work with most digit strings since we know only a limited number of dates. But if a recoding system could be developed that worked with virtually *any* string, then short-term memory span could be dramatically improved.

Recently, there has been an in-depth study of a particular subject who discovered such a general-purpose recoding system and used it to increase his memory span from seven to 79 digits (see Figure 8-9). The subject, referred to as SF, had average memory abilities and average intelligence for a college student. For a year and a half, he engaged in a memory-span task for about 3 to 5 hours each week. During this extensive practice, SF, a good long-distance runner, devised the strategy of recoding digits into running times. For example, SF would recode 3492 as "3:49.2—near world-record time for the mile," which for him was a single chunk. Since SF was familiar with many running times—that is, had them stored in long-term memory—he could readily chunk most sets of four digits. In those cases where he could not (3771 cannot be a running time because the second digit is too large), SF recoded the four digits into a familiar date.

Use of the above recoding systems enabled SF to increase his memory span from seven to 28 digits (since each of SF's seven chunks contains four digits). But how did SF build to 79 digits? By hierarchically organizing the running times. Thus, one chunk in SF's short-term memory might have pointed to three running times; at the time of recall, SF would go from this chunk to the first running time and emit its four digits, then move to the second running time in the chunk and emit its digits, and so on. This chunk was therefore worth 12 digits. Now we can see how SF could achieve his remarkable span of nearly 80 digits, the largest ever documented in the psychological literature. And it was due to increasing the *size* of a chunk (by relating the items to information in long-term memory), not to increasing the *number of* chunks that short-term memory can hold. For when SF was switched from digits to letters, his memory span want back to seven—that is, seven letters (Ericsson, Chase, and Faloon, 1980).

The above research is among the first major projects to deal with improvement in a short-term memory task. In contrast, there has long been interest in how to improve long-term memory, which is the focus of the rest of this section. We will look first at how material can be encoded more efficiently and then consider how retrieval itself may be improved.

Imagery and encoding

We mentioned earlier that recall for a word pair improved greatly when the two words were connected by an image. When we link the terms "horse" and "table" by an image, we may establish a meaningful connection between them. Imagery, then, seems to connect things in memory. And this is the main principle behind many *mnemonic* (memory-aiding) systems.

One famous mnemonic system is called the *method of loci* (*loci* is Latin for "places"). The method works especially well with an ordered sequence of arbitrary items, like unrelated words. The first step is to commit to memory an ordered sequence of places, say the locations you would come upon in a slow walk through your house. You enter through the front door, come into a hallway, move next to the bookcase in the living room, then to the television in the living room, then to the curtains at the window, and so on. Once you can easily take this mental walk, you are ready to memorize as many unrelated words as there are locations on your walk. You form an image that relates the first word to the first location, another image that relates the second word to the second location, and so on. If the words are items on a shopping list— "bread," "eggs," "beer," "milk," and "bacon"—you might imagine a slice of bread nailed to your front door, an egg hanging from the light cord in the hallway, a can of beer in the bookcase, a milk commercial playing on your television, and curtains made from giant strips of bacon (see Figure 8-10). Once you have memorized the items this way, you can easily recall them in order by simply taking your mental walk again. Each location will retrieve an image, and each image will retrieve a word. The method clearly works and is a favorite among those who perform memory feats professionally.

Imagery is also used in the *key-word method* of learning a foreign vocabulary. For example, suppose you had to learn that the Spanish word *caballo* means "horse." The key-word method has two steps. The first is to find a part of the foreign word that sounds like an English word. Since *caballo* is pronounced "cob-eye-yo," "eye" could serve as the key word. The next step is to form an image that connects the key word and the English equivalent—say, a horse kicking a giant eye (see Figure 8-11). This should establish a meaningful connection between the Spanish and English words. To recall the meaning of *caballo*, you would first retrieve "eye" and then the stored image that links it to "horse." Note that the key-word method can also be used to link English words to Spanish words. If you want to recall the Spanish word for *horse*, you would first retrieve the image involving a horse, thereby obtaining the key word "eye" that serves as a retrieval cue for *caballo*. The key-word method may sound complicated, but studies have shown that it facilitates learning a foreign language (Atkinson, 1975; Pressley, Levin, and Delaney, 1982).

CABALLO → eye → HORSE

PATO → pot → DUCK

Figure 8-11
Foreign Language Learning
Mental images can be used to associate spoken Spanish words with corresponding English terms.

SPANISH	KEY WORD	ENGLISH
caballo	[eye]	horse
charco	[charcoal]	puddle
muleta	[mule]	crutch
clavo	[claw]	nail
lagartija	[log]	lizard
cebolla	[boy]	onion
payaso	[pie]	clown
hiio	[eel]	thread
tenaza	[tennis]	pliars
jabon	[bone]	soap
carpa	[carp]	tent
pato	[pot]	duck

Key-Word Method
Examples of key words used to link Spanish words to their English translation. For example, when the Spanish word *muleta* is pronounced, part of it sounds like the English word "mule." Thus, "mule" could be used as the key word and linked to the English translation by forming an image of a mule standing erect on a crutch.

"When you're young, it comes naturally, but when you get a little older, you have to rely on mnemonics."

Elaboration and encoding

We have seen that the more we elaborate items, the more we will remember. In other words, the more connections we establish between items, the larger the number of retrieval possibilities. The practical implications of these findings are straightforward. If you want to remember something, expand on its meaning. To illustrate, suppose you read a newspaper article about an epidemic in Boston that health officials are trying to contain. To expand on this, you could ask yourself questions about the *causes* and *consequences* of the epidemic: Was the disease carried by a person or an animal? Was the disease transmitted through the water supply? To contain the epidemic, will officials go so far as to stop outsiders from visiting the city? How long is the epidemic likely to last? Questions about the causes and consequences of an event are particularly effective elaborations because each question sets up a meaningful connection to the event.

Context and retrieval

Since context is a powerful retrieval cue, we can improve our memory by restoring the context in which the learning took place. If your psychology lecture always meets in one room, your memory for the lecture material will be best when you are in that room, for then the context of the room is a retrieval cue for the lecture material. This has direct educational implications. Students will do better on exams when they are tested in their habitual classroom and when the proctor is their instructor than when these factors are changed (Abernathy, 1940).

Most often, though, when we have to remember something, we cannot physically return to the context in which we learned it. If you want to remember the name of a particular high-school classmate and it does not come immediately to mind, you are not about to go back to your high school just to recall it. In these situations, however, you can try to re-create the context mentally. To retrieve the long-forgotten name, you might think of different classes, clubs, and other activities that you were in during high school and see if any of these bring to mind the name you are seeking. When subjects in an actual experiment used these techiques, they were often able to recall the names of high-school classmates that they were sure were truly forgotten (Williams and Hollan, 1981).

Another illustration of mentally re-creating context is this one, adapted from Norman (1976). Suppose someone asked you, "What were you doing at 1 P.M. on the third Monday of October two years ago? "Ridiculous," you might say. "No one can remember things like that." But re-creating the context can lead to surprising results:

> Well, two years ago, I was a senior in high school; let me see, October—that's fall semester. Now what courses did I take that semester? Oh yes, chemistry. That's it—I had a chemistry lab every afternoon; that's where I was at 1:00 P.M. on the third Monday of October two years ago.

In this example, mentally restoring the context seems to have done the trick. However, we cannot be sure you actually remembered being in chemistry lab. Perhaps you inferred that you must have been there. Either way, though, you may come up with the right answer.

Organization and retrieval

We know that organization improves retrieval, presumably by making memory search more efficient. This principle can be put to great practical use. We seem to be capable of storing and retrieving a massive amount of information if only we organize it.

Some experiments have investigated organizational devices that can be used to learn many unrelated items. In one study, subjects memorized lists of unrelated words by organizing the words into a series of stories. Later, when tested for 12 such lists (a total of 120 words), subjects recalled more than 90 percent of the words (Bower and Clark, 1969). This appears to be a truly remarkable memory feat, but anyone can easily do it.

At this point, you might concede that psychologists have devised some ingenious techniques for organizing lists of unrelated items. But, you argue, what you have to remember are not lists of unrelated items but stories you were told, lectures, and readings like the present chapter. Isn't this kind of material already organized and doesn't this mean that the previously mentioned techniques are of limited value? Yes and no. Yes, this chapter is more than a list of unrelated words, but—and this is the critical point—there is always a problem of organization with any material that is long, including this chapter. Later you may be able to recall that imagery aids learning, but this may not bring to mind anything about, say, acoustic coding in short-term memory. The two topics do not seem to be intimately related. There is, however, a relation between the topics—both deal with encoding phenomena. The best way to see that relationship is to note the headings and subheadings in the chapter, for these show how the material in the chapter is organized. A most effective way to study is to keep this organization in mind. You might, for example, try to capture part of this chapter's organization by sketching a hierarchical tree like the one below. Then you can use such a hierarchy to guide your memory search whenever you have to retrieve information about this chapter. It may be even more helpful, though, to make your own hierarchical outline of the chapter. Memory seems to benefit most when the organizing is done by the rememberers themselves.

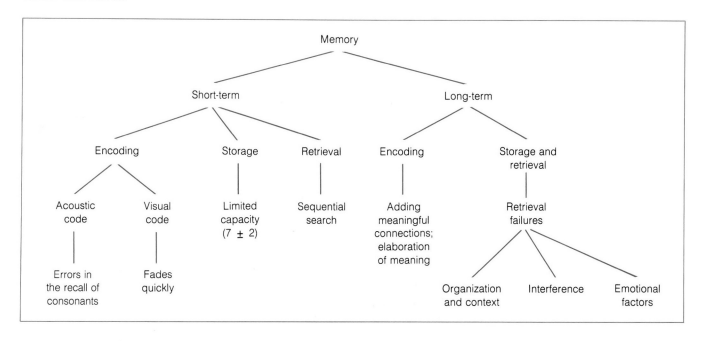

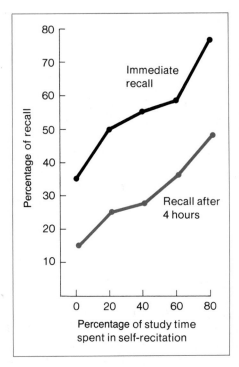

Figure 8-12
Practicing Retrieval
Recall can be improved by spending a large proportion of study time attempting retrieval rather than in silent study. Results are shown for tests given immediately and 4 hours after completing study. (After Gates, 1917)

Practicing retrieval

Another way to improve retrieval is to practice it—that is, to ask yourself questions about what you are trying to learn. Suppose you have 2 hours in which to study an assignment that can be read in 30 minutes. Reading and rereading the assignment four times is likely to be much less effective than reading it once and asking yourself questions about it. You can then reread selected parts to clear up points that were difficult to retrieve the first time around, perhaps elaborating these points so that they become particularly well connected to each other and to the rest of the assignment. Attempting retrieval is an efficient use of study time. This was demonstrated long ago by experiments using unrelated items as well as material like that actually learned in courses (see Figure 8-12).

PQ4R *method*

Thus far in this section, we have considered particular principles of memory—for example, the principle that organization aids memory search—and then shown their implications for improving memory. In establishing the practical application of memory principles, we can also go in the opposite direction. We can start with some well-known techniques for improving memory and show how they are based on principles of memory.

One of the best known techniques for improving memory, called the *PQ4R method*, is intended to improve a student's ability to study and remember material presented in a textbook (Thomas and Robinson, 1972). The method takes its name from the first letters of its six stages: (1) Preview, (2) Questions, (3) Read, (4) Reflect, (5) Recite, and (6) Review. In the first stage, students preview the material, such as a chapter, to get an idea of its major topics and sections. This kind of preview probably induces students to organize the chapter, perhaps even leading to the rudiments of a hierarchical organization like that shown on the preceding page. As we have repeatedly noted, organizing material aids one's ability to retrieve it.

The second and third stages—Questions and Read—form a package. In the Questions stage, students are to make up questions about each section, whereas in the Read stage, they are to read the section with an eye for answering those questions. For example, if you were applying these two stages to the present section of this chapter, you might look at the headings and make up questions like "How much can the short-term memory span be increased?" or "What exactly is the PQ4R method?" Then you would read the section and try to determine answers to your questions (for example, "One person was able to increase his short-term memory span to 79 digits"). These two stages almost certainly induce students to elaborate the material while encoding it.

In the fourth, or Reflect stage, students are told to reflect on the text while reading, thinking of examples, and making connections to other things they know. Again, elaboration seems to be the key principle. Elaboration may also play some role in the fifth and sixth stages, Recite and Review. Recite occurs after finishing a section, whereas Review occurs after finishing an entire chapter. For both stages, students are to try to recall the main facts in what they have read and try again to answer the questions they made up. In addition to prompting elaboration, these stages offer practice at retrieval, which we know to be beneficial to memory.

In summary, the PQ4R method relies on three basic principles for improving memory: organizing the material, elaborating the material, and practicing retrieval. Most of the study methods proposed by educators and other experts are based on these same principles.

RELATIONSHIP BETWEEN SHORT- AND LONG-TERM MEMORY

At the outset of this chapter, we suggested that short- and long-term memory might operate by different laws, and we have therefore treated them separately. In this section, we survey the evidence that they constitute separate memory stores and consider how the two are integrated into one working system.

Evidence for two kinds of memory

In discussing the stages of short- and long-term memory, we discover a number of differences between the two types of memory. First, the encoding stage favors an acoustic code in short-term memory (at least for situations that require rehearsal), but one based on meaning in long-term memory. Second, the storage capacity of short-term memory is limited to 7 ± 2 chunks, whereas the capacity of long-term memory seems unlimited for all practical purposes. And, third, retrieval from short-term memory is thought to be more or less error-free (if it is there, you can find it), whereas retrieval from long-term memory appears to be error-prone and a major cause of forgetting. Thus, there is evidence that the two memory stores show differences at all three stages—encoding, storage, and retrieval.

Clinical studies of the effects of brain injury are a second source of evidence that there are two memories. People who suffer a concussion or severe injury to the head often exhibit the symptom of *retrograde amnesia,* which means that they have no memory for the events that immediately preceded the injury, although their memory for earlier events may be intact. Why does the injury have such a devastating effect on recent memory but none on earlier memories? The answer seems to be that the brain injury affected only short-term memory and not long-term memory. The clinical facts on retrograde amnesia therefore support the idea of two different memories.

Retrograde amnesia has also been studied in animals. An animal first learns a task—for example, turning left in a maze. It is then subjected to electroconvulsive shock, which produces temporary unconsciousness, as with concussion. Later the animal is tested again on the maze to see if it has retained the original learned response. If the time between the original learning and the shock is brief, the learned response should still be in short-term memory. The shock should erase the memory, and the animal should remember little on the final test. If the interval between the learning and the shock is relatively long, however, the learned response should be in long-term memory. The shock should not affect it, and the animal should remember a lot on the final test. Several experiments have obtained this pattern of results (see Cotman and McGaugh, 1980).

Another kind of memory symptom that has been observed clinically is *anterograde amnesia.* It occurs, for example, in patients who have undergone surgery for relief of epileptic seizures. These patients, from whom part of the hippocampus (an area deep in the brain's temporal lobes) has been removed, seem incapable of learning new material. They have no trouble remembering

"On the contrary, I can't recall a thing from fifty years ago, but I remember exactly what I had for lunch yesterday."

skills and information learned before the operation, so their ability to retrieve information from long-term memory is intact. They can also hold onto a few verbal items if they are allowed to rehearse them continuously, so their short-term memory seems in working condition. What they have trouble doing is encoding new information into long-term memory. For example, several months after surgery, one patient's family moved to a house a few blocks from their old one, on the same street. A year later, the patient still could not remember his new address, although he recalled the old one perfectly, nor could he find his way to his new home. He could not remember where things he continually used were kept, and he would read the same magazines over and over without recognizing the contents (Milner, 1966). This, too, suggests that short- and long-term memory are separate systems.

Dual-memory theory

Given the evidence for two kinds of memory, the question arises: How are they related? A number of theories have been advanced. We will present one such theory to illustrate the basic ideas involved (Atkinson and Shiffrin, 1971, 1977).

This theory assumes that information we have attended to enters short-term memory, where it can be either maintained by rehearsal or lost by displacement (see Figure 8-13). Long-term memory is considered to have virtually unlimited capacity but to be vulnerable to retrieval failures. In addition, in order for information to be encoded into long-term memory, it must be transferred there from short-term memory. This is the critical assumption that relates the two memories. In its strongest form, it means that we can learn something (encode it in long-term memory) only by first processing it in short-term memory.

What about the transfer processes themselves? Some could involve the strategies we talked about earlier for adding meaningful connections to long-term memory. Relating two words by an image or by a linking sentence may be two ways to transfer them from short- to long-term memory. Another transfer strategy would be rehearsal. As the diagram in Figure 8-13 suggests, rehearsing an item not only maintains it in short-term memory but also causes it to be transferred to long-term memory.

This *dual-memory theory* not only brings together many of the findings we have covered but also provides a way of classifying severe memory disturbances. We have already noted that retrograde amnesia may reflect a disruption of short-term memory. We can now see that the memory disturbances caused by removal of the hippocampus may be manifestations of a breakdown of the transfer processes that relate short- and long-term memory. And, of

Figure 8-13
Dual-Memory Theory
Incoming items enter the memory system through short-term memory. Once in short-term memory, an item can be maintained there by rehearsal. As an item is rehearsed, information about it is transferred to long-term memory. Once rehearsal of an item is terminated, the item soon will be displaced by a new incoming item and thus lost from short-term memory. (After Atkinson and Shiffrin, 1971)

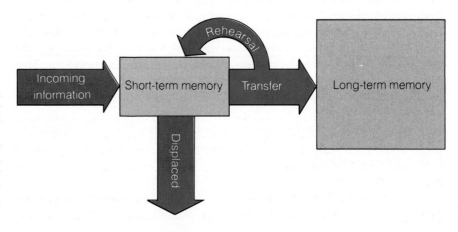

course, there is the classical type of amnesia, where individuals forget many of the personal memories that contribute to their sense of identity, such as their name, address, and family ties. Clearly, this is a disturbance in long-term memory. Furthermore, the fact that such amnesic victims can recover missing memories indicates that the loss was of access or retrieval, which again fits the notion of a long-term memory disturbance.

FREE-RECALL EVIDENCE   Some of the best known support for the dual-memory theory comes from experiments on *free recall*. In a free-recall experiment, subjects first see a list of, say, 20 or 40 unrelated words; the words on the list are presented one at a time. After all the words have been presented, subjects must immediately recall them in any order (hence the designation *free*). The results from such an experiment are shown in Figure 8-14A. The chance of correctly recalling a word is graphed as a function of the word's position on the list. The part of the curve to the left of the graph is for the first few words presented, whereas the part to the right is for the last few words presented.

The dual-memory theory assumes that at the time of recall the last few words presented are likely to be still in short-term memory, whereas the remaining words are in long-term memory. Thus, we would expect recall of the last few words to be high, since items in short-term memory can easily be retrieved. Figure 8-14A shows this is the case. But recall for the first words presented is also quite good. Why is this? Dual-memory theory has an answer. When the first words were presented, they were entered into short-term memory and rehearsed. Since there was little else in short-term memory, they were rehearsed often and were therefore likely to be transferred to long-term memory. As more items were presented, short-term memory quickly filled up and opportunities for rehearsal and transfer to long-term memory decreased to a low level. So, only the first few items presented enjoyed the extra opportunity of transfer, and that is why they are later recalled so well from long-term memory.

Varying the procedure of the free-recall experiment can produce results that tend to confirm the preceding analysis. Suppose that after the list is presented but before subjects try to recall it, they do arithmetic problems for 30 seconds. Doing arithmetic requires short-term memory capacity and should therefore displace many of the list words that are in short-term memory (the last words presented). Figure 8-14B shows that, as expected, the last few words were displaced.

The rate at which the words are presented should also affect recall. A slower rate of presentation—for instance, a word every 2 seconds instead of every second—should allow more time for rehearsal and, hence, for transfer to long-term memory. The slower rate should therefore boost recall for those words that have to be retrieved from long-term memory—that is, all words but the last few. The results of this variation, shown in Figure 8-14C, again conform to predictions. The slower rate improved recall for all words but the last few. The dual-memory theory offers a detailed account of the free-recall data shown in the three panels of Figure 8-14.

ALTERNATIVE VIEWPOINTS   Although the dual memory theory has successfully accounted for a wide range of memory phenomena, it is not without problems (see, for example, Bjork and Whitten, 1974). In recent years, some of these problems have become more evident, and alternatives to the theory are being developed.

One major problem concerns rehearsal. The dual-memory theory assumes that rehearsal can transfer information to permanent memory. That is, simply

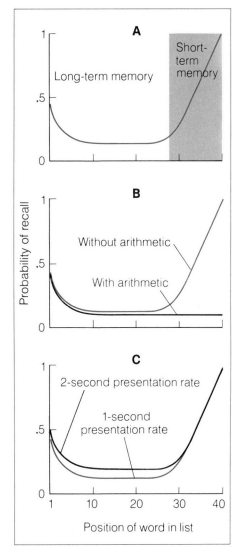

Figure 8-14
Curves of Free-Recall Experiments
Probability of recall varies with an item's position in a list, with the probability being highest for the last five or so positions, next highest for the first few positions, and lowest for the intermediate positions. Recall of the last few items is based on short-term memory, whereas recall of the remaining items is based on long-term memory (A). If an arithmetic task occurs between presentation and free recall, only recall from short-term memory is reduced (B). Slower presentation of items results in better recall from long-term memory (C). (After Murdock, 1962; and Glanzer, 1972)

repeating words to yourself, with no attempt to organize or relate them to other memories, should increase your long-term recall. But conflicting results—experiments that show more rehearsal increases long-term recall (Nelson, 1977) and experiments that show it does not (Craik and Watkins, 1973)—indicate that rehearsal is a more complicated phenomenon than we previously thought.

Another problem is that the dual-memory theory is incomplete. For example, it has little to say about why multiple meaningful connections between items should increase recall, yet this phenomenon has been demonstrated experimentally many times. Some critics of the dual-memory theory have emphasized this particular deficiency and have tried to develop an alternative approach, called *depth-of-processing*. The general idea of this approach is that an item entering the memory system is analyzed in stages. The early stages analyze perceptual properties of the item, such as visual or acoustic properties. Later stages analyze its meaning, including the categories it fits into and its connections to other items in memory. Each level of processing leaves a residue, or trace, in memory. The deeper the level of processing, the stronger the trace and the more durable the memory. According to this view, forgetting is relatively rapid in short-term memory studies because the items have been analyzed only to a relatively shallow acoustic (or visual) level. Similarly, persistence in long-term memory is attributed to deeper processing of the items, particularly to analyzing the items' meanings (Craik and Lockhart, 1972). The difference between short- and long-term memory, then, is seen as a difference in degree, not in kind.

Depth of processing offers an interesting alternative to dual-memory theory. Whether a processing depth theory by itself can account for all memory phenomena or whether its insights should be incorporated into an expanded version of dual-memory theory is still an open question (Craik, 1979).

CONSTRUCTIVE MEMORY

Throughout this chapter, we have considered research using simple verbal materials (lists of unrelated words, for instance) and also research using more complex materials (sentences, textbook chapters). We did this because many principles apply equally to simple and complex materials. However, some principles seem to apply only to memory for complex, meaningful materials. The most important of these principles is that memory can be *constructive*.

When we hear a sentence or story, we often take it as an incomplete description of a real event and use our general knowledge about how the world works to *construct* a more complete description of the event. How do we do this? By adding to the sentences and stories thoughts that are likely to follow from them. Thus, on hearing "Mike broke a bottle in a barroom brawl," we are likely to infer that it was a beer or whiskey bottle, not a milk or pop bottle. We add this inference to our memory of the sentence itself. Our total memory, then, goes beyond the original information given. We fill in the original information by using our general knowledge about what goes with what—for example, beer bottles go with bars.

Simple inferences

There is strong evidence that when we read a sentence we draw *inferences* from it and store the inferences along with the sentence. In one study (Bransford, Barclay, and Franks, 1972), subjects studied sentences like:

1 *Three turtles sat on a log and a fish swam beneath it.*

Now, if the fish swam beneath the log, it must have swum beneath the turtles. If subjects made this inference, it would become part of their memory for that sentence. Later subjects thought that they had seen sentence 2:

2 *Three turtles sat on a log and a fish swam beneath them.*

Sentence 2 is such a natural inference from sentence 1 that subjects had difficulty telling which of the two they actually saw.

The inference in the above study was necessarily true. If turtles are on a log and something goes beneath the log, the basic spatial facts of the world dictate that that something went beneath the turtles as well. But other studies show that people will draw inferences and make them part of their memory even when the inference is not necessarily true. Consider the following sentence:

3 *To fix the birdhouse, John pounded the nail.*

When hearing this, many subjects infer that John used a hammer. This is hardly a necessary inference (John could have used a mallet or even his shoe). Later, subjects who have drawn this inference have trouble remembering whether they actually saw sentence 3 or the following one:

4 *To fix the birdhouse, John hammered the nail.*

Again, there is an inability to distinguish between what was actually presented and what was added to the sentence.

Inferences can also affect memory for visual scenes, as illustrated by the following experiment. Subjects were shown a film of a traffic accident and soon after asked questions about their memory of the accident. One question about the speed of the vehicles was asked in two different ways. Some subjects were asked, "How fast were the cars going when they smashed into each other?" whereas others were asked, "How fast were the cars going when they hit each other?" Subjects asked the "smashed" question might infer that the accident was a very destructive one, perhaps more destructive than they actually remembered. These subjects might use this inference to alter their memory of the accident to make it more destructive (see Figure 8-15). Subjects asked the "hit" question, however, should be less likely to do this, since "hit" implies a less severe accident than "smashed" does.

This line of reasoning was supported by the results of a memory test given to the subjects a week later. In this test, subjects were asked, "Did you see any broken glass?" There was no broken glass in the film of the accident, but subjects who had been asked the "smashed" question were more likely to say mistakenly there had been glass than subjects who had been asked the "hit" question. Presumably the "smashed" question had led to a reconstruction of the memory for the accident, and the reconstructed memory contained details, like broken glass, that were never actually part of the accident. Such results have important implications for eye-witness identification in our legal system. A question phrased in a particular way ("smashed" rather than "hit") can alter the very memory an attorney is trying to probe (Loftus, 1980).

Stereotypes

Another means by which we fill in, or construct, memories is through the use of social *stereotypes*. A stereotype is a packet of knowledge about the person-

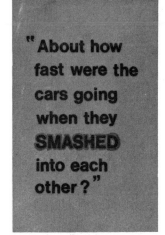

Figure 8-15
Reconstructing a Memory of an Accident
The picture at the top represents the subject's original memory for the accident. Then comes the "smashed" question, which leads the subject to draw inferences about the destructiveness of the accident. These inferences are used to reconstruct the original memory so that it now looks more like the picture on the bottom. (After Loftus and Loftus, 1975)

ality traits or physical attributes that we assume to be true of a whole class of people. We may, for example, have a stereotype of the typical German (intelligent, meticulous, serious), or of the typical Italian (artistic, carefree, fun-loving). These descriptions rarely apply to many people in the class and can often be misleading guides for social interaction. Our concern here, however, is not with the effects of stereotypes on social interaction (see Chapter 17 for a discussion of this) but with the effect of stereotypes on memory.

When presented with information about a person, we sometimes stereotype that person (for example, "He's your typical Italian") and then combine the information presented with that in our stereotype. Our memory of the person is thus partly constructed from the stereotype. To the extent that our stereotype does not fit the person, our recall can be terribly distorted. Hunter, a British psychologist, provides a first-hand account of such a distortion.

> In the week beginning 23 October, I encountered in the university, a male student of very conspicuously Scandinavian appearance. I recall being very forcibly impressed by the man's nordic, Viking-like appearance—his fair hair, his blue eyes, and long bones. On several occasions, I recalled his appearance in connection with a Scandinavian correspondence I was then conducting and thought of him as the "perfect Viking," visualizing him at the helm of a long-ship crossing the North Sea in quest of adventure. When I again saw the man on 23 November, I did not recognize him, and he had to introduce himself. It was not that I had forgotten what he looked like but that his appearance, as I recalled it, had become grossly distorted. He was very different from my recollection of him. His hair was darker, his eyes less blue, his build less muscular, and he was wearing spectacles (as he always does). (After Hunter, 1974)

Clearly, Hunter's memory of the student was severely distorted. His stereotype of Scandinavians seems to have so overwhelmed any information he actually encoded about the student's appearance that the result was a highly constructed memory. It bore so little resemblance to the student that it could not even serve as a basis for recognition.

Stereotypes can also work retroactively on recognition. We may first hear a relatively neutral description about a person, later find out this person belongs to a particular category, and then use our stereotype of that category to add to our memory of the original description. In a study demonstrating this, subjects first read a narrative about events in the life of a woman named Betty K. The narrative followed Betty K's life from birth to early adulthood and contained facts about her social life, like "Although she never had a steady boyfriend in high school, she did go out on dates." After reading the story, subjects were given additional facts about Betty K that would lead to stereotyping her. One group of subjects was told that Betty later adopted a lesbian life style. A second group was told that she later married. Apparently the first group fit Betty to their stereotype of lesbians, whereas the second group fit her to their stereotype of married women. Such stereotyping affected subsequent recognition about the original narrative. Subjects told about Betty's later lesbian activities were more likely to remember that "she never had a steady boyfriend" than that "she did go out on dates." Subjects told about Betty's later marriage did the reverse. Both groups may have reconstructed their memory of the original narrative to make it fit their stereotypes, or used their stereotypes to answer questions when they could not remember the original narrative (Snyder and Uranowitz, 1978; Bellezza and Bower, 1981).

Thus, memory for people seems to be particularly susceptible to construction. Our memory is a compromise between "what is" and "what we think should be."

Schemata

As explained in Chapter 7, psychologists use the term *schema* (plural, *schemata*) to refer to the notion of a cognitive structure in memory that is an abstract representation of an object or event in the real world. The process of perception can be regarded as a search for the schema in memory that is most consistent with the incoming sensory information. Thinking and perceiving in these ways, called *schematic processing*, permits us to filter, organize, and process large amounts of information swiftly and economically. Instead of having to perceive and remember all the details of each new object or event, we can simply note that it is like a schema already in memory and encode and remember only its most distinctive features.

The notion of a schema can be used to describe not only our knowledge about particular objects and events but also more general packets of knowledge. For example, most adults have a schema for how to drive a car ("sit behind the wheel, insert the ignition key, turn the key while pressing the gas pedal," and so on) and a schema for how to eat in a restaurant ("enter the restaurant, find a table, get a menu from the waiter, order food," and so on). Everyone but small children would have schemata for how to find the way home from various locations.

Stereotypes, as described above, can be regarded as a special class of schemata. Stereotypes are another name for those schemata that characterize identifiable groups of individuals (for example, Jews, women, homosexuals). Just as stereotypes influence how we perceive particular people, schemata influence the way we perceive and remember events and experiences.

Bartlett (1932) was perhaps the first psychologist to study systematically the effect of schemata on memory. He suggested that memory distortions can occur when we attempt to fit stories into schemata, distortions much like those that occur when we fit people into stereotypes. Research has confirmed Bartlett's suggestion. For example, after reading a brief story about a character going to a restaurant, subjects are likely to recall statements about the character eating and paying for a meal even when those actions were not mentioned in the story (Bower, Black, and Turner, 1979).

On the other hand, schemata can sometimes help memory. For example, some stories we read may be difficult to comprehend and remember unless we can fit them into their appropriate schemata. To illustrate this, read the following paragraph, and then try to recall it.

"Whatever he is, he certainly looks the part."

Drawing by Mulligan; © 1977 *The New Yorker Magazine*, Inc.

> The procedure is actually quite simple. First you arrange things into different groups. Of course, one pile may be sufficient, depending on how much there is to do. If you have to go somewhere else due to lack of facilities, that is the next step; otherwise you are pretty well set. It is important not to overdo things. That is, it is better to do too few things at once than too many. In the short run, this may not seem important but complications can easily arise. A mistake can be expensive as well. At first the whole procedure will seem complicated. Soon, however, it will become just another facet of life. It is difficult to foresee any end to the necessity for this task in the immediate future, but then one never can tell. After the procedure is completed, one arranges the materials into different groups again. Then they can be put into their appropriate places. Eventually they will be used once more and the whole cycle will then have to be repeated. However, that is part of life. (After Bransford and Johnson, 1973)

In reading the paragraph, you no doubt experienced some difficulty in trying to understand exactly what it was all about. Consequently, your recall of it was probably relatively poor. But given the hint that the paragraph describes "washing clothes," you can now use your schema for washing clothes to interpret all the cryptic parts of the passage. Your memory for the paragraph, if you reread it, should now be quite good. Schemata, then, can help or hurt.

Schemata seem to work their effects during both the encoding and retrieval stages of long-term memory. If a particular schema is active when we read a story, we tend to encode mainly those facts that are related to that schema. We can illustrate with the following simple story.

1   Steve and Edgar went to a restaurant.
2   Steve ordered lobster, and Edgar ordered spaghetti.
3   Steve and Edgar talked about business.

Assuming that sentence 1 activates our restaurant schema, we are more likely to encode sentence 2 than 3 because sentence 2 is more related to the schema. In later recalling this story, if we could remember that it had to do with eating at a restaurant, we could use our restaurant schema to search our memory: for example, was there anything in the story about ordering a meal? So schemata affect retrieval by guiding search processes (Anderson and Pichert, 1978).

Situations where memory is heavily constructive seem a far cry from the many simpler situations we covered earlier. Take, for example, the memory for a list of unrelated words; here memory processes appear more to *preserve* the input than to *construct* something new. However, there is even a constructive aspect to this simple situation, for techniques like using imagery add something meaningful to the input. Similarly, when we read a paragraph like the one about washing clothes, we must still preserve some of its specifics if we are to recall it correctly in detail. Thus, the two aspects of memory—to preserve and to construct—may always be present, although their relative emphasis may depend on the exact situation.

Summary

1   There are three stages of memory: *encoding, storage,* and *retrieval*. Encoding refers to the transformation of physical information into the kind of code that memory can accept; storage is the retention of the encoded information; and retrieval refers to the process by which information is recovered from memory when it is needed. The three stages may operate differently in situations that require us to store material for a matter of seconds—*short-term memory*—than in situations that require us to store material for longer intervals—*long-term memory*.

2   Information in short-term memory tends to be encoded *acoustically*, although other codes, such as a *visual code*, can be used.

3   The most striking fact about short-term memory is that its storage capacity is limited to 7 ± 2 items, or *chunks*. When this limit is reached, a new item can enter short-term memory only by displacing an old one. Items that have not been displaced can be retrieved by a search process that examines each item in turn.

4   In *chunking*, information in long-term memory is used to recode incoming material into large, meaningful units (chunks) that then are stored in short-term memory.

5   Information in long-term memory is usually encoded in terms of its *meaning*. If the items to be remembered are meaningful but the connections between them are not, memory can be improved by adding meaningful connections. The more one elaborates the meaning, the better memory will be.

6 Many cases of forgetting in long-term memory are due to *retrieval failures* (the information is there, but cannot be found). Retrieval failures are less likely when the items in storage are *organized* and when the *context* at retrieval is similar to that at learning. Retrieval failures are more likely when there is *interference* from items associated with the same retrieval cue and when *emotional factors* disrupt the usual retrieval processes.

7 Although we cannot increase the capacity of short-term memory, we can use recoding schemes to enlarge the size of a chunk and thereby increase the memory span. Long-term memory can be improved at either the encoding or retrieval stage. One way to improve encoding is to use imagery, which is the basic principle underlying mnemonic systems, like the *method of loci* and the *key-word method*. Another way to improve encoding is to elaborate the meaning of the items. The best ways to improve retrieval are to organize the material (hierarchical organization may be the best), attempt to restore the learning context at the time of retrieval, and practice retrieving information while learning it.

8 The *dual-memory theory* assumes that information is transferred from short-term to long-term memory, often by the process of *rehearsal*. The theory offers an explanation of several memory disorders. *Retrograde amnesia*, a loss of memory for events immediately preceding a head injury, is thought to be due to a disruption of short-term memory; *anterograde amnesia*, an inability to learn new information after removal of the hippocampus, is assumed to be caused by a breakdown of the transfer process between short-term and long-term memory.

9 The dual-memory theory also accounts for the results of experiments on *free recall*: items at the end of a list are remembered well because they are still in short-term memory, whereas items at the beginning of a list are remembered well because they are rehearsed more often. However, findings concerning rehearsal and the value of meaningful connections suggest the theory is incomplete. Another approach, called *depth-of-processing*, assumes that items are analyzed to various levels and that deeper levels of analysis lead to better memories.

10 Memory for complex materials, such as stories, is often *constructive*. For example, we may use our general knowledge of the world to construct a more complete memory of a story or an event. Construction involves adding simple *inferences* to the material presented or fitting the material into *stereotypes* and other kinds of *schemata*.

Further Reading

There are several introductory books on memory that are readable and up-to-date: Glass, Holyoak, and Santa, *Cognition* (1979); Klatzky, *Human memory: Structures and processes*, 2nd ed. (1979); Solso, *Cognitive psychology* (1979); Loftus, *Memory* (1980); Anderson, *Cognitive psychology and its implications* (1980); and Norman, *Learning and memory* (1982).

For an advanced treatment of theoretical issues in memory, see Anderson and Bower, *Human associative memory* (1973); Kintsch, *The representation of meaning in memory* (1974); Anderson, *Language, memory, and thought* (1976); and the six-volume *Handbook of learning and cognitive processes* edited by Estes (1975–1979).

For a review of research on the biological bases of memory and learning, see Bower and Hilgard, *Theories of learning*, 5th ed. (1981).

9
LANGUAGE AND THOUGHT

Perhaps the greatest accomplishment of our species is our ability to have complex thoughts and communicate them through language. Thinking includes a wide range of mental activities. We think as we daydream while waiting for class to begin. We think as we decide what groceries we need, plan a vacation, write a letter, or worry about a sick friend. Often, we can put our thoughts into words and communicate them to someone else.

Thinking requires the ability to imagine or represent objects and events that are not physically present. Thus, whenever we refer to an object that is not present (as in, "Let's get a sandwich") or to an activity that is not now going on (as in, "They played tennis") we must represent these objects and activities to ourselves. And whenever we communicate, we must transmit these representations to others.

To understand how we represent objects and actions to ourselves, we will first explore concepts because they are the building blocks of representation and thought. The second section of the chapter is concerned with how we express concepts and combinations of concepts in language. The third section deals with how children acquire language and whether other species can also learn it. The fourth section considers representations that lie outside of language—namely, visual images—and the role they play in thinking. Finally, the fifth section deals with how we organize our representations and thoughts when we try to solve complex problems.

CONCEPTS

The world is full of so many different objects that if we treated each one as distinct, we would soon be overwhelmed. For example, if we had to refer to every different object we encountered by a different name our vocabulary would have to be gigantic—so gigantic that communication would be impossible (we probably would not remember most of the words). Fortunately, we do not treat each object as unique but as an instance of a class or concept. Thus, many different objects are seen as instances of the concept *apple*, many others as instances of the concept *chair*, and so on. By treating many different objects as if they were roughly the same or the same with respect to certain properties, we reduce the complexity of the world to manageable proportions.

To have a concept is to know the properties common to all or most instances of the concept. Thus, our concept of *apple* consists of properties shared by most apples—that they are edible, have seeds, grow on trees, are round, have distinctive colors, and so on. Knowledge of these common properties has an enormous impact on how we deal with the objects around us. Having perceived some visible properties of an object—something round and red on a tree—we assign it to the concept of *apple*. This allows us to infer properties that are not visible—for instance, that it has seeds and is edible. Concepts, then, enable us to go beyond the information we perceive. This ability is fundamental to thought.

Often we do not have to perceive the properties of an object or a person to know much about it. If you are introduced to a doctor you immediately know he or she has a medical degree, extensive knowledge about disease, and experience with patients. You do not have to see any of these properties directly; you can infer them indirectly from the concept of *doctor*. Concepts, then, allow us to apply what we already know—the common properties of a doctor or an apple—to people and objects we encounter for the first time.

We also have concepts of activities, such as *eating;* of states, such as *being old;* and of abstract things, such as *truth, justice,* or even the number *two.* In each case, we know something about the properties common to members of the concept. Widely used concepts like these generally are associated with a one-word name: "apple," "doctor," "eating," "old," "truth," and so forth. This allows us to communicate quickly about things that occur frequently. Such concepts are the major concern of this section.

Classical and probabilistic concepts

We have talked about the common properties of a concept as if every property in a concept were true of every possible instance. Although some concepts, called *classical,* are like this, other concepts, called *probabilistic,* are not. An example of a classical concept is a *bachelor;* every instance of this concept must have the properties of being adult, male, and unmarried. If someone described an adult as a *married bachelor,* you would probably think that person did not really understand the concept of bachelor. An example of a probabilistic concept is *bird.* Even though most people's concept of bird includes the properties of flying and chirping, not all birds fly (ostriches and penguins do not) and not all birds chirp (ducks, crows, and chickens do not). So, if someone talked about a *nonflying bird,* you would find it perfectly acceptable. Most of our everyday concepts seem to be probabilistic (Smith and Medin,1981).

For probabilistic concepts, some instances will have more of the concept's properties than other instances. Among birds, for example, a robin will have the property of flying, whereas an ostrich will not. And the more properties of a concept that an instance has, the more typical people consider that instance to be of the concept. Thus, people rate a robin as more typical of *bird* than an ostrich, they rate red apples as more typical than green ones of *apple* (since red seems to be a property of the concept *apple*), and so on. Not only do people judge one instance of a concept to be more typical than the other, they also classify the more typical one faster. The question "Is a robin a bird?" produces an immediate "yes"; "Is a chicken a bird?" takes longer. In addition to being classified faster, typical instances are more accessible in memory than less typical ones; when asked to list all the birds they can think of, people produce robin before ostrich (Rosch, 1978).

Concepts about people are usually probabilistic and may contain numerous properties that are not true of all instances. Consider the concept *computer scientist*. Some properties—such as *knows how to program a computer*—are usually true of all members of the concept; others—such as *has a need for order and clarity*—are at best only characteristic of some members. Yet, if you were given a brief description of a person and told only that he or she had a need for order, you would be far more likely to think that the person was in computer science than, say, in education or social work. When we make such decisions, we are essentially dealing in stereotypes (Kahneman, Slovic, and Tversky, 1982).

Typicality has important implications for mental life.When we think of a concept, we are likely to think of a typical instance of it. Consider an example. Away from home, you feel ill and think about seeing a doctor. You cannot be thinking of a specific doctor (you do not know one there) but rather must be dealing with the concept *doctor*. Your concept fits some doctors (probably those who are middle-aged and male) better than others. Why? Because most doctors you have seen, either directly or through the media, have been middle-aged males. These properties have become part of your concept. If Doctor Jones turns out to be young and female, you will be surprised. Our thoughts and expectations, then, are biased in important ways. Since they are based on experience, however, presumably they can be changed by experience. As more and more women become doctors, our concepts of doctors should change.

Hierarchies of concepts

In addition to knowing the properties of concepts, we also know how they are related to one another. For example, apples are members—or a subset—of a larger category, fruit; robins are a subset of birds, which in turn are a subset of animals. These two types of knowledge—properties of a concept and relationships between concepts—are represented in Figure 9-1 as a hierarchy. An experiment by Collins and Quillian (1969) suggests how we might use this hierarchy to answer questions. Subjects are presented with such statements as "A robin is a bird" or "A robin is an animal." They must decide whether each

Figure 9-1
Hierarchy of Concepts
Words in capital letters represent concepts; lower-case words depict properties of these concepts. The black lines show relationships between concepts and the colored lines connect properties and concepts.

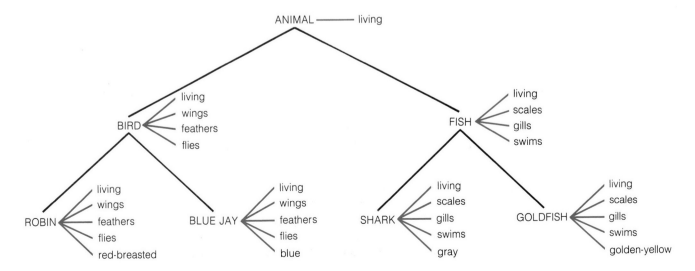

statement is true, as in the preceding examples, or false, as in "A daisy is a tree." With sentences this simple, errors are rare. Collins and Quillian were mainly interested in how quickly subjects made decisions. If the subjects referred to a hierarchy, they would search for a path that links the concepts. When presented with "A robin is a bird," for example, a subject would enter the hierarchy at *robin* and look for a path to the concept *bird*. A glance at Figure 9-1 shows that the path between robin and bird is only one link long. In the sentence, "A robin is an animal," there are two links between the concepts, so it should take more time to find the connecting path. The results confirmed this idea. Decision time increased with the distance between the concepts in the hierarchy.

As the hierarchy in Figure 9-1 makes clear, an object can be classified at different levels. The same object is at once a robin, a bird, and an animal. However, for any particular culture or subculture, one level is the basic or preferred one for classification. For many city dwellers, *bird* would be at the basic level; these people probably would be faster at classifying something as a *bird* than as a *robin* and would be more likely to call it a *bird* than a *robin*. For people from rural areas, the basic level would move down to *robin*. What determines which level is basic? The answer seems to be that the basic level is the one that has the most *distinctive* properties. In Figure 9-1, *bird* has several properties that are distinctive in that they are not shared by other kinds of animals (for example, wings and feathers are not properties of fish). *Robin*, as shown in this hierarchy, has fewer distinctive properties; most of a robin's properties are shared by a bluejay. However, *robin* also has properties distinguishing it from *bluejay* that are not shown in the figure, such as "migrates" and "sings." These properties would be familiar to people living in rural areas. As we learn more about a conceptual domain, then, we shift (downward) the level at which we prefer to operate (Mervis and Rosch, 1981).

Acquiring concepts

How someone learns a concept depends on the nature of the concept. People often acquire classical concepts such as *bachelor*, in which every property applies to every instance, by hypothesizing what the critical properties are and then testing their hypothesis. In learning probabilistic concepts such as *bird*, in which one or more properties do not apply to every instance, people sometimes use hypothesis testing. However, they can also acquire a probabilistic concept by identifying its most typical instances.

HYPOTHESIS TESTING The best evidence for hypothesis testing comes from experiments in which adults learn new classical concepts. The subjects may be shown a series of geometric forms that vary in shape, color, and size (see Figure 9-2). The experimenter has decided that every instance of a newly invented concept, TEP, is a large, red form. The subject's task is to discover the properties of TEP. Forms are presented one at a time. Subjects first guess whether each is a TEP, and the experimenter tells them whether they are correct. This allows subjects to generate hypotheses about which dimensions are relevant—for example, the color red. When they come across a figure that fits their hypothesis but not the experimenter's definition—say, a small, red figure—they abandon their current hypothesis and generate a new one (large, red figures). The more properties the concept has, the longer it takes to learn the concept. A concept that is defined by large, red, and square is harder to spot than one defined only by large and red. Similarly, the more dimensions

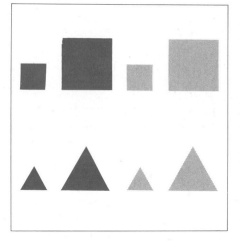

Figure 9-2
Hypothesis Testing of Concepts
Geometric forms like these are used to study how adults learn new concepts. For example, the experimenter may arbitrarily decide that the concept TEP is a large, red form. In this case, two of the forms are TEPs and six are non-TEPs. In the experiment, each of these eight forms is presented, and the subject guesses whether the form is a TEP or a non-TEP; then the experimenter provides the correct answer. The experimenter keeps cycling through the eight forms in random order until the subject classifies every form correctly. The number of errors made in mastering the concept is a measure of its difficulty.

there are that are potentially relevant, the longer it takes to come up with the right hypothesis. If there are four potentially relevant dimensions—size, color, shape, and orientation (figure upright or tilted)—it should take longer to learn the concept than if there are just three such dimensions (Bourne, Dominowsky, and Loftus, 1979).

Consider a naturalistic example of hypothesis testing. A club in town selects members on the basis of criteria it refuses to make public. Essentially, the club is a concept you want to acquire; the criteria are its properties. You know that a white male ski instructor who is a devotee of astrology is a member; an Asian female lawyer who scoffs at astrology was refused. You thus have at least four potentially relevent dimensions—race, sex, profession, and belief in astrology. Which of these are used in selecting club members? You may start with the hypothesis that it is an all-male club. If you find it has female members, you give up your initial hypothesis and generate another. Eventually, you zero in on the correct criteria (properties) of the club (concept). You will almost certainly take longer the more criteria the club uses to define membership and the more dimensions that are potentially relevant.

BIASES IN HYPOTHESIS TESTING   It may sound as if acquiring concepts is an inherently rational process, something like a chemist's deciding whether a sample is a member of a well-known chemical category. However, all sorts of biases creep in. Perhaps the most prevalent is our tendency to emphasize cases that support our hypothesis and to downplay those that refute it. To illustrate, suppose that on meeting a young woman, you hit on the hypothesis that she is an introvert (here, you would be using hypothesis testing with a probabilistic concept). You may well ask her questions that tend to confirm your hypothesis, like "Do you enjoy taking walks alone?" or "Do you spend a lot of time at the library?" Positive answers will make you very confident that she is an introvert. But you probably will not ask her questions that might disprove your hypothesis, like "Do you enjoy going to parties?" A positive answer here would not fit with her being an introvert. In short, you selectively seek evidence to support your hypothesis and fail to ask the critical questions that might disprove it (Snyder and Swann, 1978).

Another demonstration of biases in hypothesis testing appears in Figure 9-3. Subjects were given the four cards shown. Each had a letter on one side and a digit on the other. The subjects had to decide which two cards to turn over to determine whether the following hypothesis was correct: "If a card has a vowel on one side, it has an even number on the other side." This hypothesis essentially describes a relationship between letter and number concepts.

Most subjects wisely turned over the card with the vowel "E." If it had an even number on the other side, the hypothesis was supported; if it had an odd number on the other side the hypothesis was refuted. But most subjects also turned over the card with the even number "2." ("E" and "7" are the correct cards to turn over.) The number "2" card provided no information; for even if it had a consonant on the other side, the hypothesis would not be refuted (look at the hypothesis). Nevertheless, finding a vowel on the other side seems to support the hypothesis. Most subjects failed to turn over the card with the odd number "7." A vowel on the other side would have refuted the hypothesis. However, the "7" card offered no potential for supporting the hypothesis and so was left unturned.

LEARNING BY EXEMPLARS   Although hypothesis testing seems to be the major strategy for acquiring classical concepts, other strategies come into play in acquiring probabilistic concepts, especially when the learner is a child. Often

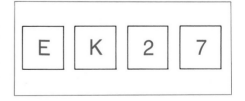

Figure 9-3
Biases in Hypothesis Testing
Which two cards should be turned over to test the hypothesis: "If a card has a vowel on one side, it has an even number on the other side"? (After Wason and Johnson–Laird, 1972)

Throughout our discussion of concepts and the rest of this chapter, we assume that words reflect already existing concepts and perceptions. We assume that language is designed to express thought and therefore that the structure of language reflects the structure of thought. However, it is possible that the relationship between language and thought is the other way around. Rather than thought determining language, it may be that language determines thought. This is essentially the *linguistic relativity hypothesis* proposed by Whorf (1956). Whorf argued that the kinds of concepts and perceptions we can have are affected by the particular language or languages we speak. Therefore, people who speak different languages perceive the world in different ways. This is called the linguistic relativity hypothesis because it proposes that thought depends on (is relative to) the language used to convey it. It is a provocative idea and has caused much debate among psychologists, linguists, and anthropologists.

Much of the evidence cited in favor of the hypothesis is based on vocabulary differences. For example, English has only one word for snow, whereas Eskimo has four. Consequently, speakers of Eskimo may perceive differences in snow that speakers of English cannot. Similarly, English has only one word for rice, whereas Garo, a language spoken in Burma, has different words for rice husked and unhusked, cooked and uncooked, and for various other kinds and conditions of rice. Again, the Garo may perceive differences that are lost on speakers of other languages.

Do these observations constitute strong evidence for the linguistic relativity hypothesis? Critics of the hypothesis argue that they do not (for example, Clark and Clark, 1977; Slobin, 1979). According to the critics, language may embody distinctions that are important to a culture, but it does not create those distinctions, nor does it limit its speakers' perceptions to them. English speakers may have the same capacity for perceiving variations in snow as Eskimo speakers, but since such variations are more important in Eskimo cultures than in Anglo cultures, one language assigns different words to the variations whereas the other does not. The best evidence for this view is the development of jargons and technical terminology. For example, American skiers talk of "powder" and "corn," not just "snow." This growth in vocabulary may be accompanied by changes in perception—Eskimos and skiers are more likely to notice variations in snow than Hawaiians—but the critical point is that such changes do not depend on the language spoken. If anything, the language seems to depend on the changes.

The linguistic relativity hypothesis has fared no better when it comes to explaining cultural variations in color terms. At one time, many linguists believed that languages differed widely in how they divided the color spectrum and that this led to differences in the perception of colors. Recent research indicates just the opposite. Of particular importance is the work of two anthropologists, Berlin and Kay (1969). They

what children learn about a concept are its most typical instances or *exemplars;* any item that is sufficiently similar to one of the learned exemplars will also be classified as an instance of the concept. To illustrate, consider a young child's concept of furniture. It might consist of just the most typical instances—say, table and chair. The child could use the exemplar strategy to classify many other instances of the concept, such as desk and sofa, because they are so similar to the learned exemplars. But the child may not correctly classify instances of the concept that look different from the learned exemplars, such as lamp and bookshelf. When learning is based on exemplars, typical instances will fare well, but atypical ones may not even be included in the concept (Mervis and Pani, 1981).

Combining concepts

As noted earlier, concepts are the building blocks of thought. Some simple thoughts, such as *Lorri is an accountant,* seem to include only a single concept. Most of our thoughts, however, are more complex and include some combinations of concepts. To illustrate, the thought *Lorri is a young accountant* combines the concepts of *young* and *accountant,* and *accountants file forms* combines the concepts of *accountants, file,* and *forms.* Are there any guidelines for combining

Linguistic Relativity Hypothesis

studied the *basic color terms* of many languages. Basic color terms are simple, nonmetaphoric words that are used to describe the colors of many different objects. Berlin and Kay found striking commonalities in such terms across languages. For one, every language takes its basic color terms from a restricted set of 11 names. In English these are "black," "white," "red," "yellow," "green," "blue," "brown," "purple," "pink," "gray," and "orange." No matter what color terms a language has, they inevitably correspond to some subset of the above. Furthermore, if a language uses fewer than 11 terms, the basic terms chosen are not arbitrary. If a language has only two terms (none has fewer), they correspond to "black" and "white"; if it has three, they correspond to "black," "white," and "red"; if it has six, they correspond to these three plus "yellow," "green," and "blue." Thus, the ordering of basic color terms seems to be universal rather than varying from language to language, as the linguistic relativity hypothesis might suggest.

In addition, people whose languages use corresponding basic color terms agree on what particular color best represents a color term. Suppose two different languages have terms corresponding to "red." When speakers of these languages are asked to pick the best example of red from an array of colors, they make the same choice. Even though their boundaries for what they would call red may differ, their idea of a good red, a quintessential red, is the same. Their perceptions are identical though their vocabularies are different. Further work by Rosch (1974) suggests that the Dani, whose language has only two basic color terms, perceive color variations in exactly the same way as people whose language has all 11. The perception of color gives little support to the linguistic relativity hypothesis.

We should not dismiss the hypothesis too quickly, however. Few language domains have been investigated in the same detail as color terms, and perhaps support for the hypothesis will yet be found in other domains (for example, whether a language codes a particular thing or event by a noun or a verb). Also, even though little support has been found for its major claims, the linguistic relativity hypothesis calls attention to an important point. In learning to make fine discriminations in a particular field, it is helpful to have a vocabulary that expresses these discriminations. As we gain expertise in a field—be it skiing, psychology, or whatever—we enlarge our vocabulary for distinctions in that field. Jargons help us to think about and communicate these distinctions. Can you imagine the practice of medicine without a specialized vocabulary for anatomical parts? Although a distinction must exist in someone's mind before a term can be made up to embody it, the importance of that embodiment should not be underestimated. Without the term, the distinction could not be easily talked about. Although sometimes annoying and pretentious, the jargon of a field plays an important cognitive role.

concepts, such that some combinations are to be preferred over others? Such guidelines have been studied for certain kinds of thoughts, called *propositions*, that can be expressed in sentences.

PROPOSITIONS To illustrate a proposition, consider the sentence "The accountant moved home." It asserts something, *moved home*, about a particular person, *the accountant.* Many simple sentences are like this. Thus, "Susan likes vegetables" asserts *likes vegetables* about *Susan.* In these examples, the assertion (for example, *likes vegetables*) is called the *predicate;* the person is called the *subject.* A *proposition,* then, consists of a subject plus a predicate. To put it another way, when we combine concepts into a proposition, some concepts must play the role of a subject whereas others play the role of a predicate. Each of the above sentences expresses exactly one proposition. Not all sentences are this simple, though. Consider "Susan likes vegetables, and Eve likes fruit." Here we again have *Susan* as a subject and *likes vegetables* as a predicate. But there is a second proposition with *Eve* as a subject and *likes fruit* as a predicate. Hence, this sentence expresses two propositions. All sentences, no matter how complex, can be broken down into propositions.

We have made a distinction between a sentence and the proposition it expresses because the same proposition can be expressed by different sentences. To illustrate, *The accountant filed the form* can be expressed by "The accountant filed the form," "The form was filed by the accountant," "It was the accountant who filed the form," and "The form is what the accountant filed." Intuitively, we feel all these sentences express the same thought; analyzing the sentences into propositions makes this clear.

Do propositions really correspond to thoughts? A good deal of evidence suggests they do. People take longer to read a sentence expressing two propositions than to read one expressing a single proposition, even when the sentences contain an identical number of words (Kintsch, 1974). Thus, in reading sentences, people extract the thoughts or propositions from them. The more thoughts or propositions there are, the longer it takes.

By viewing thoughts as propositions, we learn something about how concepts can combine into a simple thought or proposition: some concepts take the role of subject, which is often a person or object, whereas others take the role of predicate, which is often an attribute, state, or activity. We also learn something about how simple thoughts, or single propositions, can be combined into complex ones, or multiple propositions. The easiest way to combine propositions or thoughts is by simply joining them—for example, "Mitchell works and Barbara plays." A more complex way of combining propositions is to attach an entire proposition to part of another. In the sentence "Dave lifted the heavy television," we have two propositions: *Dave lifted the television* and *The television is heavy*. The second proposition is attached to part of the predicate (*lifted the television*) of the first. Perhaps the most complex way to combine propositions or thoughts is to insert one into the other. For example, "Herb's winning the fight was a surprise" contains two propositions. The first is *Herb won the fight*. This proposition—*Herb's winning*—then serves as the subject of the second proposition, where *was a surprise* serves as the predicate. Thus, the first proposition has been *embedded* into the second, and such embedding enables us to form very complex thoughts (Clark and Clark, 1977).

IMAGERY If thought were restricted to propositions expressed in sentences, we would have to deny thought to animals, to pre-verbal children, and even to adults with language disorders. Yet clearly all these beings can think. So there must be other forms of thought, other ways of representing knowledge to ourselves. One of these is visual imagery, which has been much explored recently.

The way concepts are represented as well as the way they combine are different in visual images than in propositions. Some of the major differences stem from the fact that propositions are abstract whereas images are concrete. A proposition is abstract in two senses: (1) it can as readily represent a whole class as a particular instance (for example, the proposition *dogs bark* seems no more complex than *Fido barks*); and (2) it cannot be identified with one particular manifestation or sentence (the same material expressed in a different sentence corresponds to the same proposition). In contrast, an image is concrete in that (1) it is much more useful for representing a particular instance than a class (for example, it is much easier to image a specific dog than all dogs in general), and (2) an image of an object can be identified with a particular manifestation or view of that object (the same material pictured differently corresponds to a different image). Another difference has to do with how concepts are combined. An image does not divide neatly into a subject and a predicate in the way a proposition does. Images do not contain such discrete components; rather all concepts in an image are integrated into one perceptual pattern (Kosslyn, 1980).

This list of differences can easily be extended, but it suffices to point out that images offer a different way of thinking than do propositions expressed in sentences. These two ways of thinking will figure centrally in the rest of this chapter. In the next two sections, we focus on language, which is used to communicate propositions. Then, we will return to imagery.

LANGUAGE AND COMMUNICATION

Every human society has a language. This is a remarkable fact, given how drastically societies differ from one another. The universality of language suggests that it may be an indispensable tool for humans. We have already noted that one function of this "tool" is to represent propositional thoughts; the other function, of course, is to communicate such thoughts. Communication requires not only that we put propositions into sentences but also that we get them out (that is, that we understand sentences).

Breaking sentences into thoughts

How do we extract propositions from sentences? Although there is no complete answer to this question, part of the procedure seems to go as follows.

We break a sentence into phrases in such a way that each phrase corresponds to the subject of a proposition, the predicate of a proposition, or an entire proposition. For example, we break a simple sentence such as "Lorri is an accountant" into two phrases: "Lorri" (the subject) and "is an accountant" (the predicate). The situation becomes more interesting with more complex sentences. Consider "Serious scholars read books." Intuition says the sentence divides into two phrases: "serious scholars" and "read books" (see Figure 9-4). Since the first centers on a noun ("scholars"), it is called a *noun phrase;* the second is called a *verb phrase.* If we focus on the noun phrase, "serious scholars," we see it expresses the entire proposition *scholars are serious.* The verb phrase, "read books," expresses only part of another proposition, *scholars read books.* Thus, in this example, the noun phrase expresses an entire proposition, whereas the verb phrase expresses only part—the predicate—of a proposition.

Breaking a sentence into noun and verb phrases may help greatly in getting at the propositions or thoughts behind it. There is evidence that people do this soon after hearing a sentence. In one study, subjects listened to sentences like "the poor girl stole a warm coat," where "the poor girl" is the noun phrase and "stole a warm coat" is the verb phrase. Immediately after each sentence, they were given a probe word from the sentence and asked to say the word that came after it. People responded faster when the probe and the response words came from the same phrase ("poor girl") than when they came

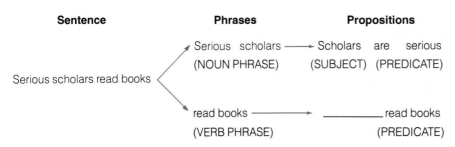

Sentence	Phrases	Propositions
Serious scholars read books	Serious scholars (NOUN PHRASE)	Scholars are serious (SUBJECT) (PREDICATE)
	read books (VERB PHRASE)	_____ read books (PREDICATE)

Figure 9-4
Phrases and Propositions
The first step in extracting the propositions from a complex sentence is to break the sentence into phrases.

from different phrases ("girl stole"). Apparently once a sentence is broken into phrases, each phrase is held in memory as a unit; and when the probe and response are from the same phrase, only one unit has to be retrieved (Wilkes and Kennedy, 1969).

Although using phrases to extract propositions works well with many sentences, this strategy runs into problems when the phrases of a sentence can be interpreted in two very different ways. Take the sentence "They are cooking apples." One interpretation is that some people are cooking apples; the other is that these are apples that normally get cooked. The need to choose one or the other interpretation makes such sentences more difficult to read and understand, although typically a reader or listener is unaware of having made any choice (MacKay, 1966).

Using speech

We have seen how a listener can get from a sentence to the thought or proposition it expresses. But we do not hear sentences already broken down into words. Rather we hear an almost continuous stream of sound. For a fuller understanding of communication, we must consider how we produce and interpret speech sounds.

PHONEMES In speaking, we use the lips, tongue, mouth, and vocal cords to produce a variety of physical sounds. Not all of these sounds are perceived as different, however. What we perceive are the 40 or so *phonemes*, or categories of speech sounds, that are used in English. For example, the sound corresponding to the first letter in "boy" is a phoneme symbolized as /b/. We have a great ability to discriminate different sounds that correspond to different phonemes. However, we are very poor at discriminating different sounds that correspond to the same phoneme—for example, the sound of the first letter in "pin" and the sound of the second letter in "spin" (Liberman and others, 1967). They are the same phoneme, /p/, and they sound the same to us even though they have different physical characteristics. The /p/ in "pin" is accompanied by a small puff of air, but the /p/ in "spin" is not (try holding your hand a short distance from your mouth as you say the two words).

Every language has a different set of phonemes, which is one reason we often have difficulty learning to pronounce foreign words. Another language may use speech sounds that never appear in ours. It may take us a while even to hear the new phonemes, let alone produce them. Or another language may not make a distinction between two sounds that our language treats as two phonemes. For example, in Japanese the English sounds corresponding to *r* and *l* (/r/ and /l/) are treated as the same phoneme.

When phonemes are combined in the right way, they form words. Each language has its own rules about which phonemes can follow others. In English, for example, /b/ cannot follow /p/ at the beginning of a word (try pronouncing "pbet"). Such rules show their influence when we speak and listen. For example, we have no difficulty pronouncing the plurals of nonsense words we have never heard before. Consider "zuk," and "zug." The plural of "zuk" is formed in accordance with a simple rule by adding the phoneme /s/, as in "hiss." In English, however, /s/ cannot follow *g* at the end of a word, so to form the plural of "zug," we must use another rule—one that adds the phoneme /z/, as in "fuzz." We may not be aware of these differences in forming plurals, but we have no difficulty producing them. It is as if we "know" the rules for

We can go further in analyzing sentences than just saying they can be divided into noun and verb phrases. Noun and verb phrases can themselves be further broken into smaller units.

Consider again the sentence "The poor girl stole a warm coat." We already know it divides into the noun phrase "the poor girl," and the verb phrase "stole a warm coat." The diagram below shows how we can divide each of these phrases. Intuition suggests the verb phrase may be broken into two units: the verb, "stole," and the rest of the phrase, "a warm coat." But the second unit is really another noun phrase. So, a verb phrase may be broken into a verb plus a noun phrase. In this case, the verb cannot be decomposed any further,

for it is a single word; but the noun phrase can be. It consists of a *determiner* ("a" or "the" are determiners), followed by an adjective ("warm"), followed by a noun ("coat"). Noun phrases that have this particular set of units, determiner + adjective + noun, are common in English. The initial noun phrase of the sentence, "The poor girl," also is made up of a determiner ("the"), followed by an adjective ("poor"), followed by a noun ("girl").

This is an example of a *syntactic analysis* of a sentence. Such analysis is a common tool of linguists and of psychologists who study language. It has revealed some basic facts about the structure of our language. Almost every English sentence must contain a noun

phrase and a verb phrase, and only certain kinds of noun and verb phrases are possible. For example, although a noun phrase can consist of an adjective followed by a noun ("poor girl"), it cannot consist of an adverb followed by a noun ("poorly girl") or of a noun followed by an adjective ("girl poor"). Other languages have different rules for noun phrases. In French, for example, most adjectives follow the noun. In any language, then, there are constraints on what a noun or verb phrase can contain, and these constraints are part of what we know when we know a language and, therefore, part of what we must learn when we learn a language.

Does a detailed syntactic analysis offer any new insights into how we extract propositions from sentences? It seems that it does. Having divided a noun phrase into the adjective "poor" and the noun "girl," we can see that *girl* is the subject of a proposition that has *is poor* as its predicate. More generally, whenever we have an adjective modifying a noun, we have a proposition with the noun as subject and the adjective as predicate. Every time we add an adjective to a sentence, we add another proposition; consequently, we increase the time needed to read and understand the sentence (Kintsch, 1974).

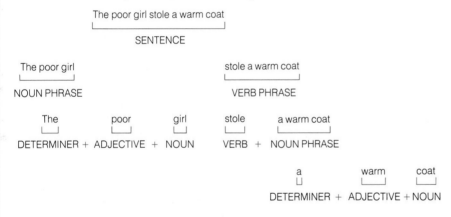

combining phonemes even though we are unaware of the rules—as if we are conforming to rules we cannot verbalize.

How do children learn about phonemes and their rules of combination? Children appear to come into the world preset to learn and discriminate phonemes. One-month-old infants, like adults, can easily discriminate between sounds corresponding to different phonemes, and infants quickly learn which phonemes are relevant to their language (Eimas and others, 1971). However, it takes several years for children to learn how phonemes can be combined to form words. When children first begin to talk, occasionally they produce "impossible" words, like "dlumber" for "lumber." They do not yet know that /l/ cannot follow /d/ at the beginning of a word. By age 4, children seem to have learned a good deal about phoneme combinations. Children of about 4 years of age were asked to say which of two made-up sequences of speech sounds would make a better name for a toy. One sequence was consistent with rules for combining phonemes (for example, "klek"), whereas the other was not (for example, "lkel"). Most chose the name that conformed to the rules (Messer, 1967).

Mastering the rules for combining phonemes amounts to learning how to pronounce words. Children may know how a word should be pronounced, even though they cannot say it themselves.

> A child asked if he could come along on a trip to the "mewwy-go-wound." An older child, teasing him about his pronounciation, said "David wants to go on the mewwy-go-wound." "No," said David firmly, "you don't say it wight." (Maccoby and Bee, 1965)

MORPHEMES A *morpheme* is the smallest linguistic unit that carries meaning. Most morphemes are themselves words, such as "time." Others are suffixes, such as "ly," or prefixes, such as "un," which are added onto words to form more complex ones, such as "timely" or "untimely." Many complex words are really just simple words with a host of prefixes and suffixes tagged onto them. An extreme case is "antidisestablishmentarianism," which breaks into "anti" + "dis" + "establish" + "ment" + "ary" + "an" + "ism" (a total of seven morphemes).

Every language has rules about how prefixes or suffixes are combined with words. For example, the suffix "er" is regularly added to many verbs to form nouns that refer to people who habitually perform the action described by the verb, as in "speak"—"speaker" and "paint"—"painter." Do we actually use these rules, or something like them, in speaking and listening? Our slips of the tongue suggest we do. For example, a speaker who intended to say, "McGovern favors busting pushers," uttered instead, "McGovern favors pushing busters" (Garrett, 1975). The morphemes "bust" and "push" were interchanged, whereas the morphemes "ing" and "er + s" stayed in their correct positions. This implies that the morphemes were treated as separate units.

Levels of language

We can summarize language in terms of different levels (see Figure 9-5). At the highest level are sentence units, including phrases and sentences, which can be related to thoughts. The next level is that of basic-meaning units, including morphemes and words. The lowest level contains speech sounds. These adjacent levels are closely related to one another. The phrases of a sentence are built from words and morphemes, whereas the words and morphemes are themselves constructed from phonemes. Since sentences can be related to thoughts, we can see that language is a system for relating thoughts to speech by basic-meaning and sentence units (Chomsky, 1965).

Note that at the lowest level, there are a limited number of units, only about 40 phonemes for any language. But rules for combining these phonemes make it possible to produce and understand thousands of words (a vocabulary of 20,000–30,000 words is not unusual for an adult). Similarly, rules for combining words make it possible to produce and understand millions of sentences (if not an infinite number of them). Its leveled nature thus gives language the power to express a virtually unlimited number of thoughts.

Figure 9-5 also suggests that understanding a sentence is the inverse of producing a sentence. To produce a sentence, we start with a thought or

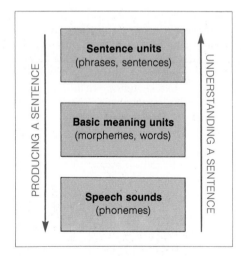

Figure 9-5
Levels of Language
Phonemes are at one level of language; morphemes and words constitute a second level. Sentences and phrases make up a third level. Since sentence units can be related to thoughts, language is a system for relating thought to speech sounds. The production of a sentence involves mainly top-down processing, whereas understanding a sentence involves mainly bottom-up processing.

proposition, translate it into the phrases and words of a sentence, and finally translate these words into speech sounds. We work from the top level down to the bottom level (*top-down processing*). To understand a sentence, however, we move in the opposite direction—from the bottom level to the top. We hear speech sounds, use them to construct the words and phrases of a sentence, and finally extract the propositions from the sentence units (*bottom-up processing*).

Although this analysis captures some of what goes on in sentence production and understanding, it is oversimplified and therefore incomplete. For one thing, understanding a sentence must be more than the simple inverse of producing it. There are many sentences we can understand but not produce (for example, sentences spoken in a foreign language that we have some familiarity with). Second, in understanding a sentence, sometimes after getting just a few words, we may jump to what we think the entire sentence means (the propositions behind it) and then use our guess about the propositions to help in understanding the rest of the sentence. In such cases, understanding involves going from the top level down as well as from the bottom level up. To illustrate, suppose that in a conversation about eating in a restaurant, someone said "The food was so bad that I complained to the manager." Immediately after hearing the word "bad" you might hypothesize that the rest of the sentence will express a thought about complaining to someone on the staff. In this case, you could use your stored knowledge about eating in restaurants (what we called the restaurant schema in Chapter 8) to guide sentence understanding. Such schema guidance is very common, which means that language and memory are intertwined in understanding conversations and stories (Adams and Collins, 1980; Schank, 1982).

DEVELOPMENT OF LANGUAGE

Our discussion of language should indicate the enormity of the task confronting children. They must master all levels of language—not only the proper pronunciations but also the infinite number of ways words can be combined into sentences to express thoughts. The wonder is that virtually all children in all cultures accomplish so much of this in a mere four to five years. What is perhaps even more amazing is that all children, no matter what their culture, seem to go through the same sequence of development. At age 1, a few isolated words appear; at about age 2, the child speaks two- and three-word sentences; at 3, sentences become more grammatical; and at 4, the child sounds much like an adult (Gleitman, 1981).

We have already considered the acquisition of phonemes and their rules of combination. In this section, we first consider how children learn to associate words to concepts. Then we focus (1) on how children learn to combine words into phrases and sentences and (2) on other issues in language development.

Words and concepts

At the age of about 1, children begin to name things. One-year-olds already know much about the world—they probably have concepts for parents, household pets, food, toys, and body parts before they know the names for them. What they are doing when they begin to speak is relating these concepts to words that adults use. This does not happen all at once. A 3-year-old girl may already have concepts of different colors and know that certain words are color names but not know which name goes with which color. When asked to name a blue color, she may say "red" (Miller and Johnson-Laird, 1976).

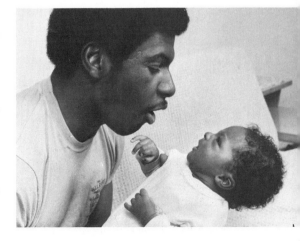

To learn which word goes with which concept, children look at what is happening around them when a word is used and take the important aspects of the situation as the meaning of the word. They are essentially creating hypotheses—for example, "Mommy said 'Fang' when she pointed to my pet, so 'Fang' means my pet." Children's hypotheses, however, may not be accurate. Sometimes they focus on something totally irrelevant.

> A mother said sternly to her child: "Young man, you did that on purpose." When later asked what "on purpose" meant, the boy replied: "It means you're looking at me." (E.E. Maccoby)

Children often pick out only one or two properties of a concept when a whole cluster of properties is relevant. A 2-year-old boy might hear "doggie" spoken in the presence of the family dog, focus on the fact that it has four legs and moves, and hypothesize these two features define "doggie." He then applies the term to cats and cows, which also have four legs and move. He *overextends* the meaning of "doggie" to other animals. Overextensions decrease as the child adds more properties to the word's meaning—for example, sound (barks), size (relatively small), and texture (furry). This restricts his use of "doggie." At the same time, he is learning more about cats (they meow) and cows (they moo and have horns). Thus, the meanings of these three animal terms become increasingly differentiated (Clark, 1973a).

By 3 or 4 years of age, the child's overextensions are less obvious, but closely related concepts can still lead to confusion. When told to place one toy below another on a staircase, the child may place it above the other instead. It is as if the child knows "above" and "below" have some properties in common (both refer to the same kind of spatial relationship) but she or he does not know how they differ and so associates both with the concept of *above*. Why "above" rather than "below"? Perhaps the concept *above* is the simpler one. Or perhaps the child is using a strategy that roughly says, "When you have to place an object but you are unsure of where, try the topmost part of the surface" (Clark, 1973b).

From primitive to complex sentences

At about 1½ to 2½ years, the next stage of language acquisition begins. Children start to combine single words into two-word utterances, such as "There cow" (*There's the cow*), "Jimmy bike" (*That's Jimmy's bike*), "Towel bed" (*The towel's on the bed*). Their utterances reflect an appreciation of the roles of agent, object, and location. Children know, for example, that people and animals can play the role of agents of actions, moving on their own as well as moving other objects. Other things (blocks, tables, and cribs) do not have this power, and play the role of objects. Still other things play the role of places, in that they are not moveable but can hold or receive objects (Braine, 1976).

There is a *telegraphic* quality about two-word speech. The child leaves out articles ("a," "an," "the"), auxiliary verbs (such as "is" in the phrase "is all gone"), and prepositions and puts in only those words that carry the most important meaning. Despite their brevity, these utterances express most of the basic functions of language, such as locating objects and describing events and actions (see Table 9-1).

Children progress rapidly from two-word utterances to more complex sentences that express propositions more clearly. Thus, "Daddy hat" may become "Daddy wear hat" and finally "Daddy is wearing a hat." Such expan-

FUNCTION OF UTTERANCE	LANGUAGE			
	ENGLISH	GERMAN	RUSSIAN	SAMOAN
Locate, name	there book that car see doggie	buch da [book there] gukuk wauwau [see doggie]	Tosya tam [Tosya there]	Keith lea [Keith there]
Demand, desire	more milk give candy want gum	mehr milch [more milk] bitte apfel [please apple]	yeshchë moloko [more milk] day chasy [give watch]	mai pepe [give doll] fia moe [want sleep]
Negate	no wet no wash not hungry allgone milk	nicht blasen [not blow] kaffee nein [coffee no]	vody net [water no] gus' tyu-tyu [goose gone]	le 'ai [not eat] uma mea [allgone thing]
Describe event, action, or situation	Bambi go mail come hit ball block fall baby highchair	puppe kommt [doll comes] tiktak hängt [clock hangs] sofa sitzen [sofa sit]	mama prua [mama walk] papa bay-bay [papa sleep] korka upala [crust fell]	pa'u pepe [fall doll] tapale 'oe [hit you] tu'u lalo [put down]
Indicate possession	my shoe mama dress	mein ball [my ball] mama hat [mama's hat]	mami chashka [mama's cup] pup moya [navel my]	lole a'u [candy my] polo 'oe [ball your]
Modify, qualify	pretty dress big boat	milch heiss [milk hot] armer wauwau [poor dog]	mama khoroshaya [mama good] papa bol'shoy [papa big]	fa'ali'i pepe [headstrong baby]
Question	where ball	wo ball [where ball]	gde papa [where papa]	fea Punafu [where Punafu]

sions of the verb phrase appear to be the first truly complex constructions that occur in children's speech. The next step is the use of conjunctions, like "and" and "so," to form compound sentences: "You play with the doll *and* I play with the block." The sequence of development is remarkably similar for all children.

At about the same time, children learn to use certain morphemes that are critical for making sentences grammatical. Important *grammatical morphemes* include the suffixes "ing" (added to verbs to form the progressive—"kicking"), "ed" (added to regular verbs to form the past—"kicked"), "s" (added to nouns to form the plural—"boys"—and added to verbs in the present tense for the third person singular—"The boy kicks"). Brown (1973) traced the acquisition of such morphemes by three children. He found that all three children learned in a specific order: "ing" before "ed" and the plural "s" before the third-person "s." What determines this order? Brown argued that some morphemes express simpler thoughts than others, and the simpler the thought, the earlier children acquire it. The plural "s" involves only the concept of number, whereas third-person "s" involves the concepts of both number and time. Thus, the plural "s" is acquired before the third-person "s."

In summary, children progress from one-word utterances to two-word

Table 9-1
Functions of Two-Word Sentences in Children's Speech
Children's earliest sentences in many languages serve the same basic functions. (After Slobin, 1971)

"telegrams." Then they begin to elaborate their nouns and verb phrases, adding conjunctions and acquiring the appropriate grammatical morphemes. The increasing complexity of children's language seems to mirror the increasing complexity of the thoughts they can entertain.

Learning processes

Perhaps the most interesting question is, *how* do children learn to utter sentences? Three possible answers are imitation, conditioning, and hypothesis testing. In discussing how concepts are acquired and how they are associated with words, we emphasized hypothesis testing. This process seems to be critical in many other aspects of language learning as well.

IMITATION   Common sense suggests that children learn to speak by imitation, or mimicking, adults. However, there is a good deal of evidence to the contrary. Young children constantly say things they never heard an adult say, such as, "All gone milk." Even when children at the two-word stage try to imitate longer adult sentences (for example, "Mr. Miller will try"), they produce their usual telegraphic utterances ("Miller try"). In addition, the mistakes children make (for example, "Daddy taked me") show they are tryng to apply something like rules, not simply trying to copy adults (Ervin–Tripp, 1964).

Imitation, though, may play a part in learning new words. When a parent points to a phone and says "phone," the child may repeat the name, and this helps the child learn the word "phone." However, not all children imitate their elders, and those who do may only imitate a word when they already know its meaning (Bloom, Hood, and Lightbown, 1974).

CONDITIONING   A second possibility is that children acquire language through conditioning. Adults may reward (positively reinforce) children when they produce a grammatical sentence and stop or reprimand them (negatively reinforce) when they make mistakes. For this to work, parents would have to respond to every detail in a child's speech. However, Brown, Cazden, and Bellugi (1969) found that parents did not pay attention to how the child said something so long as it was comprehensible. Rare attempts to correct a child (and hence apply conditioning) are often futile.

> CHILD: Nobody don't like me.
> MOTHER: No, say, "nobody likes me."
> CHILD: Nobody don't like me.
> MOTHER: No, now listen carefully; say "nobody likes me."
> CHILD: Oh! Nobody don't LIKES me. (McNeill, 1966)

HYPOTHESIS TESTING   The problem with imitation and reinforcement is that they focus on specific utterances (one can only imitate or reinforce something specific). However, children often appear to learn something general, such as a rule; that is, children seem to form a hypothesis about some aspect of language, test it, and hold on to it if it works.

Consider the morpheme "ed." As a general rule, you add "ed" to the present tense of verbs to form the past (as in "cook"—"cooked"). However, many common verbs are irregular and do not follow this rule (like "go"—"went" and "take"—"took"). These irregular verbs tend to be the ones children use first. So, at an early point, children use the past tense of some irregular verbs correctly. Then they learn the past tense for some regular verbs and discover the hypothesis: add "ed" to the present tense to form the past.

"Darling! Justin verbalized!"

This hypothesis leads them to add the "ed" ending to all verbs, including the irregular ones. They say things like "Annie goed home" and "Harry taked the book," which they never heard or said before. Eventually, children learn that some verbs are irregular, and they stop overgeneralizing their use of "ed." But whereas before they probably thought of "go" and "went" as separate words, they now understand them as different forms of the same word.

GENERATING HYPOTHESES   How do children generate these hypotheses? Recent studies suggest there are a small number of *operating principles* that children everywhere use as a guide to forming hypotheses. One is to pay attention to the ends of words; another is to look for prefixes and suffixes that indicate a change in meaning. A child armed with these two principles is likely to hit the hypothesis that "ed" at the end of verbs signals the past tense, since "ed" is a word ending associated with a change in meaning. A third operating principle is to avoid exceptions, which explains why children initially generalize their "ed"-equals-past-tense hypothesis to irregular verbs. Some of these principles appear in Table 9-2, and they seem to hold for some 40 languages studied by Slobin (1971).

Operating principles give the child a rough guide to analyzing adults' utterances. Adults and older children contribute to some aspects of the learning process by simplifying their speech when talking to youngsters. When speaking to a 2-year-old, we tend to use sentences that are half the usual length and speak at half the normal rate. We also avoid complex constructions (Sachs, Brown, and Salerno, 1976). So adults essentially provide young children with a special dialect, *motherese,* which is simpler than ordinary talk. There is some evidence that motherese makes it easier for children to find the right hypothesis about the meanings of grammatical morphemes, which play such a central role in language (Gleitman, 1981).

Is *language innate*?

Children do not generate hypotheses about language at random. They never seem to consider certain kinds of hypotheses—for example, that the meaning of a word is determined by its number of syllables. Also, children seem to form the same hypotheses regardless of the specific utterances to which they are exposed. These observations suggest that children come into the world genetically programmed to look at language in certain ways—that operating principles may be part of our biological heritage (Fodor, Bever, and Garrett, 1974).

There is substantial evidence for this view. A main difference between innate and learned behavior is that, given a few critical cues, innate behavior emerges more or less automatically. The organism does not have to learn each and every step through observation and imitation. This *seems* to be true of language. Children progress from simple to complex sentences, acquiring new grammatical constructions in a predictable order, despite large variations in how often adults around them use these constructions. The pattern is much the same for all children. However, the fixed sequences of language development may depend on the orderly development of perceptual and motor skills. If language development simply reflects the development of other skills, it would not be considered innate.

Another aspect of innate behavior is that it often depends on exposure to the right cues at a critical time period; the behavior may not be learnable after this critical period even with intensive instruction. There is evidence for a *critical period* in language development, some of which comes from children

1 Look for systematic changes in the form of words.

2 Look for grammatical markers that clearly indicate changes in meaning.

3 Avoid exceptions.

4 Pay attention to the ends of words.

5 Pay attention to the order of words, prefixes, and suffixes.

6 Avoid interruption or rearrangement of constituents (that is, sentence units).

Table 9-2
Operating Principles Used by Young Children in Generating Hypotheses
Children from many countries seem to follow these principles in learning to talk and to understand speech. (After Slobin, 1971)

who wandered off or were abandoned as infants and were left to grow up in the wild. Some of these "wild children" were not exposed to any human language before the age of 14 or so, and subsequent attempts to teach them language ended in failure (Lenneberg, 1967).

Although such failures fit with the notion of a critical period for language development, they might have been due to a general mental retardation rather than to lack of a specific language ability, particularly in view of the nonhuman environment in which these children grew up. A more recent case, however, provides better evidence. A child, Genie, was 14 when she was discovered in California. Apparently, she had lived tied to a chair without ever being spoken to since the age of 20 months. Since Genie's discovery, she has been taught language by psychologists and linguists (Fromkin and others, 1974), but she has not become proficient. Although Genie has learned some of the basics— she uses many words and can combine them into simple phrases—there are many grammatical morphemes that she has not acquired, and she cannot combine phrases to form elaborate sentences. In this case, the crucial factor behind the lack of language development seems to be the relatively late age at which language learning began (Gleitman and Gleitman, 1981).

The cases of Genie and wild children suggest that, at a minimum, the critical cues for language development include a normal social environment. Do these cues also include access to language users who can serve as models? That is, would a child in a normal social environment acquire language even if deprived of models? A study by Feldman, Goldin-Meadow, and Gleitman (1978) suggests the answer may be yes. They studied six deaf children of parents with normal hearing, who had decided not to let the children learn any sign language. Before the children had acquired any instruction in lip reading and vocalization, indeed before they had acquired any knowledge of English, they began to use a system of gestures, called *home sign.* Initially, their home sign was a kind of simple pantomime, but eventually it took on the properties of a language (for example, it was organized at the levels of both individual signs and combinations of signs). In addition, these deaf children, who essentially made up their language, went through the same stages of development as normal hearing children. Thus, the deaf children initially gestured one sign at a time, then later put their pantomimes together into two- and three-word sentences. These striking results support the idea that language is partly innate and play havoc with the notion that language is just a matter of imitation.

Can another species learn human language?

Some experts believe that the ability to learn language is not only innate but also unique to the human species (for example, Chomsky, 1972). They acknowledge that other species have communication systems but argue that these are qualitively different from ours. In effect, they are arguing that the human species is qualitatively different from its evolutionary "relatives" in the animal kingdom.

Until about 1970, attempts to teach chimpanzees, our closest relatives, to *speak* had failed. The failures, however, may have been due to limitations in the chimps' vocal abilities, not their cognitive abilities. Successful attempts to teach chimps to communicate with their hands have refueled the controversy about the uniqueness of human language.

In one of the best-known studies, Gardner and Gardner (1972) taught a female chimpanzee, named Washoe, signs adapted from American Sign Language for the deaf. Training began when Washoe was about a year old and

"Although humans make sounds with their mouths and occasionally look at each other, there is no solid evidence that they actually communicate among themselves."

continued until age 5. During this time, Washoe's caretakers communicated with her only by means of sign language. They first taught her signs by shaping procedures, waiting for her to make a gesture that resembled a sign and reinforcing her. Later they found that Washoe could learn signs if they put her hands into the proper position and guided her through the desired movement. Ultimately, Washoe learned signs simply by observing and imitating (see Figure 9-6).

By age 4, Washoe could produce 130 different signs and understand even more. She could also generalize a sign from one situation to another. For example, she first learned the sign for *more* in connection with *more tickling* and then generalized it to indicate *more milk*. Washoe is not unique. Other chimps have acquired comparable vocabularies. Some of these studies used methods of manual communication other than sign language. Premack (1971) taught a chimp named Sarah to use plastic symbols as words and to communicate by manipulating these symbols. And Lana, a chimp studied by Rumbaugh (1977), communicates by means of a keyboard console. The console has about a hundred keys, each representing a different word, and Lana types her messages on the keyboard. In addition to studies with chimps, Patterson (1978, 1981) attempted to teach sign language to a gorilla named Koko, starting when Koko was 1 year old. At age 7, Koko had a vocabulary of about 375 signs.

Do these studies prove that another species—the apes—can learn human language? In tackling this question, we must keep in mind the distinction between different levels of language, particularly that between words and sentences. There seems to be little doubt that the apes' signs are the equivalents of our words and that the concepts these signs stand for are the equivalents of our concepts. But there are grave doubts that apes can learn to combine these signs in anything like the way we combine words into a sentence. Thus, not only can people combine the words "snake," "Eve," "killed," and "the" into the sentence "The snake killed Eve," but they can also combine the same words in a different order to produce a sentence with a different meaning, "Eve killed the snake." Although there is some evidence that apes can combine signs into something like a sentence, there is little evidence that they can alter the order of the signs to produce a different sentence (Slobin, 1979).

Even the evidence that apes can combine signs into a sentence has come under attack. In early work, researchers reported cases where an ape produced

Figure 9-6
Two of Washoe's Signs
Washoe signs "sweet" for lollipop (left) and "hat" for woolen cap (right).

Is human language qualitatively different from the communication systems of other species? In attempting to answer this question, researchers have employed a two-part strategy. First, they use what they know about various human languages to compose a list of properties common to all languages. Then they examine an animal communication system to see if it has those properties.

To illustrate, many linguists agree that all human languages have at least four things in common (Langacker, 1973). The first is *productivity*. As noted earlier in the text, human languages permit the combination of a relatively small number of phonemes into thousands of words and the combination of these words into a virtually unlimited number of sentences. Second, as we have already mentioned, human languages are structured at several levels. In particular, there is a clear distinction between the level of words and morphemes, where the elements have meaning, and the level of sounds, where the elements (phonemes) do not carry any meaning. (The phoneme /b/, for instance, does not mean anything by itself in any language). This *duality of structure,* as it is sometimes called, is related to a third property: the relationship between the sound of a word and the entities it refers to is arbitrary. *Arbitrary symbols* are obvious because different languages use different-sounding words to refer to the same objects. Finally, all languages make some use of *word order* to indicate variations in meaning. In English, for instance, "Jonah ate the whale" means something quite different from "The whale ate Jonah."

The question is whether any of these properties—productivity, duality of structure, arbitrary symbols, and word order—are present in animal communication systems. One system that has been studied intensively is that of the bees (von Frisch, 1974). When a worker bee goes hunting for nectar and returns to the hive, she performs an intricate dance that communicates the location of the nectar to the other bees (see Figure 9-7). The bee first traces a semicircle and runs along its diameter wagging her abdomen. She then traces a semicircle in the opposite direction. The most important aspect of the dance is the straight-line run along the diameter where the bee wags her abdomen from side to side. The direction of this line or waggle corresponds to the direction of the nectar from the hive, and the duration of the waggle corresponds to the distance from the hive.

The dance of the bees is fascinating, but does it have the features of human language? It is not nearly as productive. All the bee's messages are about the same thing: "There is nectar at x distance from here in y direction" (Langacker, 1973). In contrast, human language can be used to communicate almost any topic we can think of. There is no duality of structure in the dance of the bees. Everything—even a single waggle—adds meaning to the message. Bees do not use arbitrary symbols: different groups of bees are unlikely to have different "dance languages." Finally, bees do not generally vary the order of their "symbols" to produce messages with different meanings. In short, the dance of the the bees seems most unlike our kind of talk.

what seemed to be a meaningful sequence of signs, such as *Gimme flower* and *Washoe sorry* (Gardner and Gardner, 1972). As data have accumulated, it has become apparent that unlike human sentences, the utterances of an ape are often highly repetitive. Thus, *you me banana me banana you* is typical of the

Animal Communication

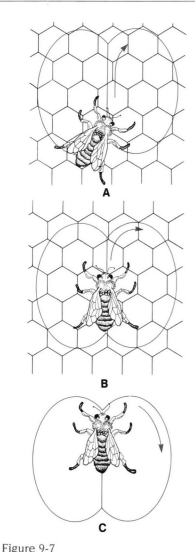

Figure 9-7
The Waggle Dance of the Bee
The direction of the straight-line part of the dance communicates the direction of the nectar source; the duration of this part of the dance communicates the distance of the nectar from the hive. (After von Frisch, 1974)

So, we have bested the lowly bee. What about the communication system of a species closer to us in the evolutionary scale—the chimpanzee? In nature, chimps use both vocalization and facial gestures to communicate. Their vocalizations are limited in number and refer to things critical to survival, such as "An attack is coming," "Food is here," and "Gather together." Their facial gestures are also limited and are primarily used to communicate dominance and emotion. Their total vocabulary is strikingly small in comparison to ours, and the productivity of their communication system is much lower. Again, there is no evidence for duality of structure, as every communication symbol carries meaning. Nor is there any hint of an arbitrary assignment of symbols. Rather the vocalizations and gestures are fixed patterns of behavior, and chimps everywhere use basically the same gestures to communicate the same things. Finally, chimps do not vary the order of their vocalizations or gestures to vary the meaning of their messages. Chimp communication, then, like bee communication, does not display the properties of human language.

This is by no means the last word on whether human language is unique. For one thing, we need to know more about the communication systems of other species. For another, the fact that chimpanzee communication is impoverished compared to our own does not mean chimps lack the capacity for a more productive system. Their system is adequate for their needs. To determine if chimps have the same capacity we do, we must look instead at the research aimed at teaching them our language.

signing chimps but would be most odd for a human child. These utterances are so repetitious that some researchers have claimed they are qualitatively different from human sentences (Seidenberg and Petitto, 1979). And in some cases when an ape utterance is less wordy and more like a sentence, the ape may simply be imitating the sequence of signs made by its human teacher. Thus, some of Washoe's most sentence-like utterances occurred when she was answering a question; for example, the teacher signed *Washoe eat?* and then Washoe signed *Washoe eat time.* Here, Washoe's combination of signs may have been a partial imitation of her teacher's combination, which is not how human children learn to combine words (Terrace and others, 1979).

No doubt, research and debate will continue on whether apes can learn our language. Perhaps novel training methods will enable apes to learn to string signs into sentences as we do. Alternatively, future research may support the conclusion that although apes can develop a humanlike vocabulary, they cannot readily learn to combine their signs in the systematic way we do. If this turns out to be the case, we will at last have evidence to support the age-old belief that language separates us from other species.

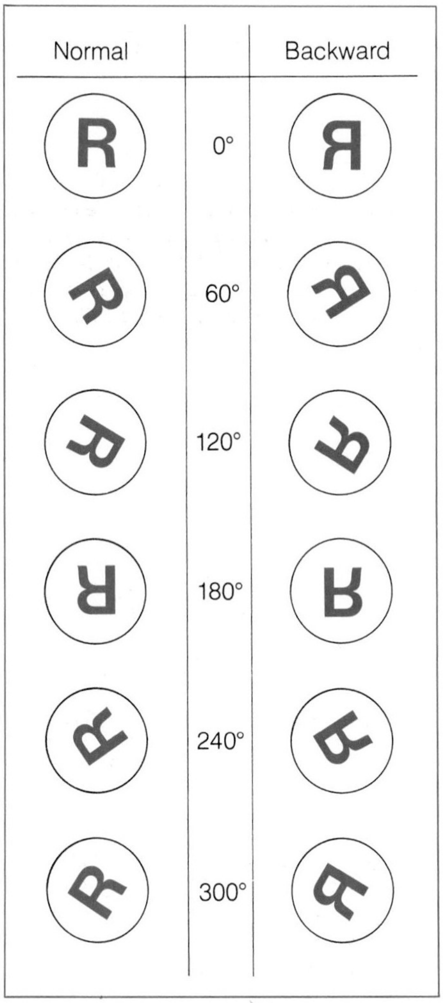

VISUAL THINKING

In the previous two sections, we have emphasized thoughts that take the form of propositions and can be expressed in language. But as we noted earlier, thoughts take other forms as well. In particular, some appear as visual images.

Examples of visual thinking

Many of us feel we do some of our thinking visually. Often it seems that we retrieve past perceptions, or parts of them, and then operate on them, sometimes in novel ways. For example, when asked *What shape are a German shepherd's ears?*, most people report that they form a visual image of a German shepherd's head and "look at" the ears to determine their shape. If asked *What new letter is formed when an uppercase N is rotated 90 degrees?*, people report first forming an image of an "N," then mentally "rotating" it 90 degrees and "looking at" it to determine its identity. And if asked *How many windows are there in your parents' living room?*, people report imagining the room, and then "scanning" their image while counting the windows (Kosslyn, 1980; Shepard and Cooper, 1982).

Though the above examples are only subjective impressions, they do suggest some important aspects of visual thinking. One is that our images of objects and places have visual detail: we see the German shepherd, the "N," or our parents' living room in our "mind's eye." Moreover, we may be capable of performing mental operations on these images that are analogous to the operations we carry out on real visual objects: we scan the image of our parents' room in much the same way we would scan a real room, and we rotate our image of the N similarly to the way we would rotate the real object. The experiments reported below try to provide objective evidence for the subjective impressions we have just described.

Experiments on visual thinking

Recent experiments have documented some aspects of visual thinking. In one study, subjects were presented first with pairs of names of states in the United States. They were asked to rate each pair according to the similarity of the states' shapes and then to put them in rank order with the most similar pair at the top and the least similar one at the bottom. With only the names of the

Figure 9-8
Study of Mental Rotation in Visual Thinking

Shown are examples of the letters presented to subjects in studies of mental rotation. On each presentation, subjects had to decide whether the letter was normal or backward. Numbers indicate deviations from the vertical in degrees. (After Cooper and Shepard, 1973)

states, subjects clearly had to rely on images. Then they were given pictures of the states and asked to repeat the task. These judgments were based on perceptions. The two rankings were virtually the same, suggesting that images have some of the visual detail of perceptions (Shepard and Chipman, 1970).

In an experiment on mental rotation, subjects saw the capital letter R on each trial. The letter was presented either normally, "R," or backward, "Я," in its usual vertical orientation or rotated various degrees (see Figure 9-8). The task was to decide if the letter was normal or backward. The more the letter had been rotated from its vertical orientation, the longer it took to make the decision (see Figure 9-9). This finding suggests that subjects made their decisions by mentally rotating the image of the letter until it was vertical and then checking whether it was normal or backward.

Studies of mental rotation suggest that people can manipulate images in their "mind's eye." Indeed, it is difficult to come up with a more natural way of telling whether a rotated letter is normal or backward. We cannot easily do it by describing the letter's appearance in propositions and manipulating the propositions. Mental rotation is thus the kind of task that fosters visual thinking, whereas other tasks may foster a verbal or propositional approach. We will return to this point in the final section.

The mental operations we perform on images appear to be analogous to those we perform on real visual objects. In another experiment, subjects studied the fictional map of an island, which contained seven critical locations. The map was removed, and subjects were asked to form an image of it and fixate a particular location (see Figure 9-10). Then the experimenter named another location; starting at the fixated location, the subjects were to scan their images until they found the named location and to push a button on "arrival" there. Subjects took longer to respond the greater the distance between the fixated location and the named one. For example, responses were longer when the fixated and named locations were on different sides of the island than when they were on the same side. Apparently, subjects were scanning their images in the same way they scan real objects.

Visual creativity

There are innumerable stories about scientists and artists producing their most creative work through visual thinking (see Shepard, 1978). Although not hard evidence, these stories are among the best indicators we have of the power of visual thinking. Surprisingly, visual thinking appears to be quite effective in highly abstract areas like mathematics and physics. Albert Einstein, for example, said he rarely thought in words; rather he worked out his conceptualizations in terms of "more or less clear images which can be 'voluntarily' reproduced and combined." Perhaps the most celebrated example is in chemistry. Friedrich Kekulé was trying to determine the molecular structure of benzene. One night he dreamed that a writhing, snakelike figure suddenly twisted into a closed loop, biting its own tail. The structure of the snake proved to be the structure of benzene. A dream image had provided the solution to a major scientific problem.

Visual images can also be a creative force for writers. Samual Coleridge's famous poem "Kubla Khan" came to him in its entirety as a prolonged visual image. Contemporary novelist Joan Didion says that her novels develop from visual images, images so detailed that she claims they sometimes direct the arrangement of the words in her sentences—the sort of thing you might expect to be affected by auditory rather than visual imagery.

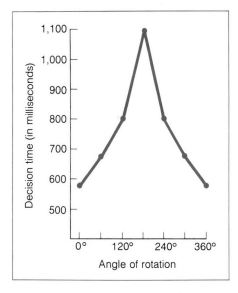

Figure 9-9
Decision Times in Mental Rotation Study
The time taken to decide whether a letter had normal or reversed orientation was greatest when the rotation was 180° so that the letter was upside down. Rotation was clockwise from upright (0°). (After Cooper and Shepard, 1973)

Figure 9-10
Scanning Mental Images
The subject scans the image of the island from south to north, looking for the named location. It appears as though the subject's mental image is like a real map and that it takes longer to scan across the mental image if the distance to be scanned is greater. (After Kosslyn, Ball, and Reiser, 1978)

PROBLEM SOLVING

For many people, the process of solving a complex problem epitomizes thinking itself. Although problem solving requires more than just transforming an image or stringing propositions together, representations still play a critical role.

Different representations

Being able to solve a problem often depends on whether we can come up with a useful representation of the problem. Sometimes a propositional or symbolic representation works best; at other times, a visual image is more effective. To illustrate, consider the following problem.

> One morning, exactly at sunrise, a monk began to climb a mountain. A narrow path, a foot or two wide, spiraled around the mountain to a temple at the summit. The monk ascended at varying rates, stopping many times along the way to rest. He reached the temple shortly before sunset. After several days at the temple, he began his journey back along the same path, starting at sunrise and again walking at variable speeds with many pauses along the way. His average speed descending was, of course, greater than his average climbing speed. Prove that there exists a particular spot along the path that the monk will occupy on both trips at precisely the same time of day. (Adams, 1974)

In trying to solve this problem, many people start with a symbolic representation. They try to write out a set of equations and soon confuse themselves. The problem is far easier to solve when it is represented visually. All you need do is visualize the upward journey of the monk superimposed on the downward journey. Imagine one monk starting at the bottom and the other at the top. No matter what their speed, at some time and at some point along the path the two monks will meet. Thus, there must be a spot along the path that the monk occupied on both trips at precisely the same time of day. (Note that the problem did not ask you where the spot was.)

There are also problems that can readily be solved by manipulating either propositions or images. We can illustrate with the following.

> Edgar is taller than Steve but shorter than Dan.
> Who's the shortest of the three men?

To solve this problem in terms of propositions, note that we can represent the first part of the problem as a proposition that has *Steve* as subject and *is shorter than Edgar* as predicate and represent the second part as a proposition with *Edgar* as subject and *is shorter than Dan* as predicate; we can then deduce that Steve is shorter than Dan, which makes Steve the shortest. To solve the problem by imagery, we might, for example, imagine the three men's heights as points on a line, like this

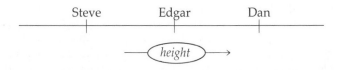

Then we can simply "read" the answer—Steve is shortest—directly from the image. Whether people prefer to represent problems like this as propositions or images remains a matter of debate (Clark, 1971; Huttenlocher and Higgins,

1971). And even problems that clearly call for one kind of representation (say, a propositional one) can be represented in several different ways.

Experts versus novices

Recent research indicates that experts represent problems in their area differently than novices do. Specifically, experts have many more representations stored in memory that they can bring to bear on a problem. A master chess player, for example, can look for 5 seconds at a complex board configuration of over 20 pieces and reproduce it perfectly; a novice in this situation can reproduce only the usual 7 ± 2 items (see Chapter 8). Experts can accomplish this memory feat because they have developed through years of practice representations of many possible board configurations; this permits them to encode a complex configuration in just a couple of chunks (Chase and Simon, 1973).

Another difference between experts and novices is that experts typically know several general rough-and-ready strategies, called *heuristics*, that can be applied to a variety of problems. An expert at solving mathematics problems, for example, might use the heuristic, "For a tough new problem, try to think of an analogous problem you can solve; then see if you can generalize this solution to the new problem." In trying to solve physics problems, experts at physics also invoke general heuristics before trying to generate specific equations, whereas novices, lacking these heuristics, typically start writing equations with no general plan in mind (Larkin and others, 1980).

Computer simulation

To study how people generate and use heuristics and plans, researchers often use the method of *computer simulation*. They first have people describe their own thought processes while solving a complex problem and then use these descriptions as a guide in programming a computer to solve that problem. Finally, the output of the computer can be compared to aspects of people's performance on the problem—particularly the heuristics and plans used—to see if they match. If they match, the computer program offers a theory of some aspects of problem solving.

Why use computers to learn about people? It turns out that there are some striking similarities between the kinds of mental operations we perform in solving a problem and the kinds of operations a computer performs in executing a program. People use various plans and heuristics to sort and organize information in arriving at a solution to a problem. So does a computer. We use information from memory stores as well as information from the environment. So does a computer. Thus, there are some basic similarities between human thinking and computer programs (see Figure 9-11).

One well-known computer program that emphasizes heuristics is called the *General Problem Solver*, or GPS (Newell and Simon, 1972). When GPS is fed specific information about a problem, it combines the information with heuristics to produce a program that can solve the problem. For example, if the problem is to play a game of chess, the rules of chess are combined with GPS's heuristics to yield a specific chess-playing program—and a good one at that.

GPS's major heuristic, called *subgoal analysis*, is one that many expert problem solvers use. The heuristic is based on two processes that follow each other in repeated cycles until the problem is either solved or abandoned as too difficult. The first is setting up appropriate subgoals. These subgoals are evaluated and a promising one selected for exploration. For example, a subgoal in chess is to put the opposing king in check. The second process is to identify any difference between a subgoal and the current state of affairs and then eliminate

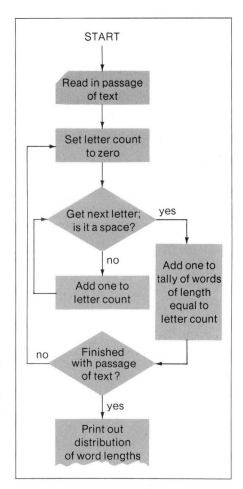

Figure 9-11
Flow Chart
A computer program is a detailed set of instructions, written in a language designed for the computer, that specifies every step the machine must take. To write a program, it is often first necessary to break the problem into its component parts and construct a flow chart, which shows how the components fit together. This figure is a flow chart for the problem of finding how many words in a particular text are one letter long, two letters long, and so on. The input to the program is a piece of text. The boxes represent operations to be performed; the diamonds represent decisions to be made. Once this flow chart is written, the programmer's next step is to translate each box and each diamond into more detailed instructions about how the operation or decision is to be made. This detailed set of instructions, which can contain thousands of steps, is the program.

or reduce this difference. If the opposing king is not in check, the computer runs through strategies for moving pieces to achieve that subgoal. If no piece can achieve this, the cycle continues with a smaller subgoal, perhaps getting one attacking piece out of the way of another. By constantly recycling these two processes, setting subgoals and reducing discrepancies, GPS approximates the step-by-step progress of human problem solving.

Computer simulation is not without its critics. Some argue that we do not yet know enough about human mental processes to evaluate the programs. How, for example, can we be sure that the computer memory resembles human memory? Other critics have challenged the analogy between computers and people: computers, they say, can only do what they have been programmed to do. However, it is quite possible that humans can also do only what heredity and past experience have "programmed" them to do. Another criticism is that the physical basis of human thought, the brain, is very different from the electrical circuitry of computers. Clearly, a brain and a computer differ physically, but they may be similar in how they are organized and how they function. How far one can trust the computer as a guide to human mental life is very much an open question.

At various points in this chapter on human thought and language, we raised questions about these abilities in nonhumans. We have discussed apes that talk or almost talk, and computers that think or almost think. These discussions and comparisons suggest that we can improve our understanding of human intelligence by comparing it with nonhuman intelligence, be it natural or of our own making.

Summary

1   To have a concept of something is to know its properties. For *classical* concepts, every property must be true of every instance; for *probabilistic* concepts, every property need be true of only some instances. Some instances of a probabilistic concept are considered *typical* because they have more of the concept's properties than others. The relationships between concepts can be represented as a *hierarchy* showing subsets (bird, fish) of larger categories (animal).

2   Adults often use hypothesis testing when acquiring new concepts, particularly classical ones. They are biased, however, to seek cases that confirm their hypothesis and to ignore those that might disprove it. Although children also use hypothesis testing, sometimes they acquire a probabilistic concept by learning its most typical instances (exemplars).

3   Concepts may be combined to form complex thoughts that can be expressed in sentences. Such thoughts take the form of *propositions*, with each proposition containing a *subject* (for example, *Susan*) and a *predicate* (for example, *likes fruit*). Two propositions can be combined in various ways—by joining them, by attaching one to part of the other, and by *embedding* one into the other. Concepts may also be represented and combined in the form of visual images.

4   In understanding language, we extract propositions from a sentence by breaking the sentence into phrases. Each phrase corresponds to the subject of a proposition, the predicate of a proposition, or an entire proposition.

5   The words of a sentence are built from units called *phonemes* and *morphemes*. A phoneme is a category of speech sounds; a morpheme is the smallest linguistic unit that carries meaning. Infants seem to come into the world preset to learn phonemes, but it takes children several years to learn the rules for combining phonemes into morphemes and words. Phonemes are at one level

of language; morphemes and words constitute a second level. Sentences and phrases make up a third level.

6   In learning which word goes with which concept, children form *hypotheses* about the crucial properties of a word's meaning. Children often select only a few properties when a whole cluster is relevant (for example, "doggie" means "has four legs and moves"); consequently, they *overextend* the meaning (for example, they use "doggie" to name cats and cows).

7   In learning how to produce sentences, children go through several stages. They begin with one-word utterances about agents, objects, and places, then move on to two-word *telegraphic speech,* and then elaborate their noun and verb phrases while acquiring the appropriate *grammatical morphemes.* All children seem to go through the same stages in the same order.

8   Children learn language mainly by testing hypotheses rather than by imitating adults' speech or by being reinforced for producing grammatical sentences. Children's hypotheses appear to be guided by a small set of *operating principles,* which call the children's attention to critical characteristics of utterances, such as word endings.

9   Some of our language-learning abilities seem to be innate; for instance, there is evidence that language can be learned only during a *critical period.* A controversial issue is whether language-learning abilities are unique to our species. Recent studies suggest that chimpanzees and gorillas can learn signs that are the equivalents of our words, but they have difficulty learning to combine these signs in the systematic way we do.

10   Not all thoughts are expressed in language; some are manifested as visual images. Such images contain the kind of visual detail found in perceptions. Also, the mental operations performed on images—such as scanning and rotation—are like the operations carried out on perceptions.

11   Some problems are easier to solve by using a propositional (symbolic) representation; at other times, a visual representation works best. Expert problem solvers differ from novices in that they have many more representations to bring to bear on the problem. Experts are also more likely to use *heuristics.* The heuristic called *subgoal analysis* is employed in a computer program (the General Problem Solver) that solves problems by setting up subgoals and reducing differences between a subgoal and the present state of affairs.

Further Reading

Introductions to the psychology of languge may be found in Glucksberg and Danks, *Experimental psycholinguistics* (1975); Clark and Clark, *Psychology and language* (1977); Foss and Hakes, *Psycholinguistics: An introduction to the psychology of language* (1978); Slobin, *Psycholinguistics* (2nd ed., 1979); and Miller, *Language and speech* (1981). For a more advanced treatment, particularly of issues related to Chomsky's theory of language and thought, see Chomsky, *Language and mind* (2nd ed., 1972); and Fodor, Bever, and Garrett, *The psychology of language* (1974). For an account of early language development, see Wanner and Gleitman (eds.), *Language acquisition: The state of the art* (1982). For an advanced treatment of visual imagery, see Kosslyn, *Image and mind* (1980).

There are also a number of books that attempt to provide an integrated account of language and memory, including Anderson, *Language, memory, and thought* (1976); Lindsay and Norman, *Human information processing* (2nd ed., 1977); Rumelhart, *An introduction to human information processing* (1977); and Schank, *Dynamic memory* (1982).

Computer-simulation models of thinking are discussed in Newell and Simon, *Human problem solving* (1972); Boden, *Artificial intelligence and natural man* (1977); and Barr and Feigenbaum (eds.), *The handbook of artificial intelligence* (1981).

Part Five
MOTIVATION AND EMOTION

10
BASIC DRIVES
AND MOTIVES

When we ask, "What *motivates* people to risk their lives to save another or to work long hours to achieve a particular goal?" we usually mean, "Why do people behave the way they do?" As it is popularly used, the term "motivation" refers to the *cause* or *why* of behavior. Used in this sense, motivation would cover all of psychology. Psychologists, however, confine the concept of motivation to those factors that *energize* behavior and give it *direction*. A motivated organism will engage in an activity more vigorously and more efficiently than an unmotivated one. In addition to energizing the organism, motivation tends to direct behavior (a hungry person is motivated to seek food and to eat; a thirsty person, to drink; a person in pain, to escape the painful stimulus).

Although many psychologists would concur with this definition of motivation, it is still a controversial concept. Some psychologists feel that motivation accounts only for the energizing aspects of behavior and that other mechanisms (namely, learning and cognition) account for the direction of behavior. Some even argue that a concept of motivation is unnecessary (Bolles, 1975). To help clarify this controversy, we will briefly describe how the concept of motivation developed and the various forms it has assumed since the beginning of this century. Then we will consider the basic biological needs that humans share with lower organisms. In the next chapter, we will discuss more complex human motives.

THEORETICAL APPROACHES TO MOTIVATION

The term "motivation" was not used until the beginning of the twentieth century. For hundreds of years, the predominant view of philosophers and theologians was that people were rational beings with intellects who freely chose goals and decided on courses of action. Reason determined what a person did; a concept of motivation was unnecessary. A person was free to choose, and choices were good or bad, depending on the individual's intelligence and education. It was assumed that the good choice, if known, would automatically be selected. According to this conception of the human being, called *rationalism,* a person is largely responsible for his or her own behavior.

Philosophers did not break away from the concept of rationalism until the seventeenth and eighteenth centuries. At this point, some philosophers began to take a more *mechanistic view* of behavior and suggested that actions arose from internal or external forces over which people had no control. In the seventeenth century, Hobbes held that no matter what reasons people gave for their conduct, the underlying causes of all behavior were the tendencies to seek pleasure and to avoid pain. This doctrine of *hedonism* still plays a major role in some motivation theories.

Instincts

The extreme of the mechanistic view is the theory of instincts. An *instinct* is an innate biological force that predisposes the organism to act in a certain way under appropriate circumstances. Animal behavior had long been attributed to instincts; animals were considered to have no soul or intellect and to be unable to reason. Darwin's theory that there was no sharp distinction betweeen humans and animals opened the door for the use of instinct theory to explain human behavior. The strongest advocate of instinct theory, the psychologist William McDougall, maintained that *all* our thoughts and behavior were the result of inherited instincts—compelling sources of conduct that could be modified by learning and experience. In his book *Social Psychology* (1908), McDougall mentioned the following instincts:

acquisition	pugnacity
construction	reproduction
curiosity	repulsion
flight	self-abasement
gregariousness	self-assertion

McDougall later expanded his list to 18 instincts, including some that related to specific bodily needs. By modifying and combining these instincts, he attempted to explain all human behavior.

Instinct theory was diametrically opposed to a rationalistic view of human beings. Instead of choosing goals and actions, a person was at the mercy of innate forces, which determined—or motivated—behavior.

Psychoanalytic theory also attributed behavior to powerful innate forces. Freud believed that two basic but unconscious energies were powerful motivational forces in determining behavior—the *life instincts* expressed in sexual behavior and the *death instincts* underlying aggressive acts (see Chapter 11). Both psychoanalytic theory and instinct theory influenced the change from a rationalistic conception of human beings to a motivational view, which saw behavior as the result of unconscious, irrational forces within the individual.

Needs and drives

It soon became clear that a great number of instincts would have to be postulated to account for the subtleties of human behavior. Such behaviors as rivalry, secretiveness, modesty, cleanliness, imitation, cruelty, sociability, and jealousy were identified as instincts. Eventually, almost any imaginable behavior could be termed an instinct. However, labeling a particular action "instinctive" did not really explain much about it except to imply that it might be inherited. To say that a man fought because he had a pugnacious instinct did not provide much more than a description of the behavior. It did not explain the behavior.

In addition, anthropologists noted that some instincts were not found in all cultures. Pugnacity, for example, was not typical of all primitive societies; in some societies, people had no need to fight.

During the 1920s, instinct theory was replaced by the concept of drives. A *drive* is an aroused state that results from some biological *need*, such as a need for food, water, sex, or avoidance of pain. This aroused condition motivates the organism to remedy the need. For example, lack of food produces certain chemical changes in the blood that in turn create a drive state. The organism attempts to reduce the drive by doing something (in this case, finding food) to satisfy the need. This is a *drive-reduction theory* of motivation.

Sometimes the terms "need" and "drive" are used interchangeably, but more often "need" refers to the physiological state of tissue deprivation and "drive" refers to the psychological consequences of a need. Need and drive are parallel but not identical. Drive does not necessarily become stronger as need becomes stronger. A starved organism may be so weakened by its need for food that drive (the motivation to find food) is weakened.

HOMEOSTASIS AND DRIVE THEORY   Basic to the drive concept is the principle of *homeostasis*—the body's tendency to maintain a constant internal environment. The healthy individual maintains a body temperature within the range of a few degrees. Slight deviations from normal temperature activate mechanisms that restore the normal condition. Exposure to cold constricts blood vessels on the body's surface to retain the warmth of the blood, and shivering produces heat. In warm weather, peripheral blood vessels dilate to permit heat to escape, and perspiration has a cooling effect.

Numerous biological states must be maintained within fairly narrow limits,

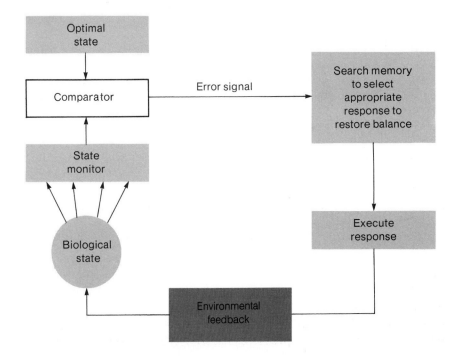

Figure 10-1
Motivational Control System
The state monitor continuously measures the internal condition of the organism. Whenever the comparator notes a difference between the state monitor and some optimal level, it emits an error signal. The error signal activates cognitive processes that select behaviors designed to restore the balance between the state monitor and the optimal state. These behaviors link the organism to its environment, producing feedback to the system that restores the imbalance between the optimal state and the current state. The system is organized to maintain the state monitor at a level nearly equal to the optimal level at all times.

The response patterns animals display in the care of their young provide a clear example of the type of behavior that has been called "instinctive." Building nests, removing the amniotic sac so the newborn can breathe, feeding the young, and retrieving them when they stray from the nest are all complex behavior patterns that animals exhibit without the opportunity to learn. A squirrel performs maternal duties in the same manner as all other mothers of its species, whether it is caring for the first litter or the fifth.

Interest in instinctive behavior, which declined during the early part of this century, has been revived by a group of European psychologists and zoologists who call themselves *ethologists*. These scientists study animals in their natural environment rather than in the laboratory, where the artificial surroundings often prevent behavior patterns from appearing in natural form (Lorenz, 1981).

Ethologists prefer the term *species-specific behavior* to the more controversial term "instinct." They study behavior that is specific to a certain species and that appears in the same form in all members of the species.

Imprinting—a concept introduced by ethologists—refers to a type of early learning that forms the basis for the young animal's attachment to its parents. A newly hatched duckling that has been incubated artificially without the presence of a mother duck will follow a human being, a wooden decoy, or almost any other moving object that it first sees after birth. Following a wooden decoy for as little as 10 minutes is enough to "imprint" the duckling on the decoy; the duckling will remain attached to this object, follow it even under adverse circumstances, and prefer it to a live duck. Imprinting occurs most readily 14 hours after hatching but can happen any time during the first two days of life. After this point, imprinting is difficult, probably because the duckling has acquired a fear of strange objects.

Imprinting has been found in a number of species—including dogs, sheep, and guinea pigs—but it is most clearly developed in birds that are able to walk or swim immediately after birth. An innate mechanism ensures that the young will follow and remain close to their mothers (normally the first moving object they see) rather than wander off into a perilous world.

Studies of mallard ducks have identified the stimuli that are important for imprinting in birds and indicate that the phenomenon begins even before birth. Ducklings begin to make sounds in their eggs a week before they break through the shells. Mallard mothers respond to these sounds with clucking signals, which increase in frequency about the time the ducklings hatch. Auditory stimuli before and after hatching, together with tactile stimulation in the nest after birth, thoroughly imprint

Imprinting in ducklings
The newly hatched duckling follows the model duck around a circular track. The duckling soon becomes imprinted on the model and will follow it in preference to a live duck of its own species. The more effort the duckling has to exert to follow the model (such as climbing a hurdle) the stronger the imprinting. (After Hess, 1958)

the ducklings on the female mallard in the nest. An unhatched duckling that hears a recording of a human voice saying "Come, come, come" instead of its mother's voice will imprint on a decoy that utters "Come, come, come" as easily as it will imprint on a decoy that

including the concentration of blood sugar, the levels of oxygen and carbon dioxide in the blood, and water balance in the cells. Various body mechanisms operate to keep these conditions stable. Sensors in the body detect changes from the optimal level and activate mechanisms that correct the imbalance. The principle is the same as a heater thermostat, which turns the heat on when the temperature falls below a certain level and off when the temperature rises.

Hunger and thirst can be viewed as homeostatic mechanisms because they initiate behavior that restores the balance of certain substances in the blood. Within the framework of homeostasis, a need is any physiological departure

Ethology and Species-Specific Behavior

utters normal mallard clucks. Ducklings that have been exposed to a mallard female's call prior to hatching are more likely to imprint on decoys that utter mallard clucks (Hess, 1972).

Ethologists have also developed the concept of a *releaser*—a particular environmental stimulus that sets off a species-specific behavior. In some young seagulls, a red or yellow spot on the mother's beak "releases" a pecking response, which causes the mother to regurgitate the food that the infant will

Austrian ethologist Konrad Lorenz demonstrates how young ducklings follow him instead of their mother because he was the first moving object they saw after they were hatched.

eat. Varying the color and shape of the spot on cardboard models and observing whether the young gull pecks at the "beak" make it possible to determine the characteristics of the releaser to which the bird responds.

Owl-like figures initiate mobbing behavior (a kind of feigned attack) by birds for which the owl is a natural enemy. The swollen abdomen of the female stickleback fish initiates courtship behavior by the male. The bowing and cooing behavior of the male ring dove releases the entire sequence of reproductive behavior in the female (nest-building, laying and incubating the eggs) and is responsible for the hormonal changes that accompany these activities (Lehrman, 1964).

The higher an animal is on the evolutionary scale, the fewer species-specific behaviors it exhibits and the more learning determines the actions it takes to satisfy its needs. But even humans have some built-in behavior patterns, including the rooting reflex of the human infant. Touching a nipple to the cheek of a newborn elicits head turning and simultaneous mouth opening. If the mouth contacts the nipple, it closes on the nipple and begins to suck. This behavior pattern is automatic and can occur even when the infant is sleeping. At about six months, the rooting reflex is superseded by voluntary behavior; the typical 6-month-old sees the nipple, reaches for it, and tries to bring it to his or her mouth.

from the optimal state; its psychological counterpart is drive. When the physiological imbalance is restored, drive is reduced and the motivated activity ceases. Many physiological imbalances are corrected automatically. The pancreas releases sugar stored in the liver to maintain the proper balance of sugar in the blood. But when automatic mechanisms can no longer maintain a balanced state, the organism becomes aroused (drive is activated) and is motivated to restore the balance. A person who experiences the symptoms of low blood-sugar level seeks food. Figure 10-1 (see page 285) schematically represents the type of control system that regulates such homeostatic mechanisms.

Psychologists have broadened the principle of homeostasis to include psychological as well as physiological imbalances. Any psychological imbalance will also motivate behavior designed to restore equilibrium. Thus, an anxious or fearful person will be motivated to do something to reduce the tension.

Incentives

During the 1950s, psychologists began to question the *drive-reduction theory* of motivation as an explanation of all types of behavior. It became apparent that the organism was not *pushed* into activity solely by internal drives; external stimuli, called *incentives,* also played an important part in arousing behavior. Motivation could be better understood as an interaction between stimuli in the environment and a particular physiological state of the organism.

Delicious-looking pastries in a bakery window may arouse the hunger drive of a person who is not hungry. In this case, the incentive (fresh pastries) activates rather than reduces hunger. A satiated animal will eat again if it sees another animal eating. In these instances, the motivation is not an internal drive but an external stimulus.

Furthermore, some evidence contradicted the homeostatic concept of drive as the organism's attempt to reduce tension and return to a quiescent state. Human beings often seek tension-arousing experiences, such as roller-coaster rides, car racing, white-water canoeing, or horror movies. These activities increase tension rather than reduce it.

More recent approaches to a theory of motivation have focused on the role of incentives—motivating objects or conditions in the environment. The organism approaches *positive incentives* and avoids *negative incentives.* To a thirsty animal, a positive incentive would be water; to a sexually aroused animal, a mate. An object or situation that has caused pain would be a negative incentive. An incentive arouses the organism and directs behavior toward or away from it.

The dual function of incentives can be demonstrated experimentally. A hungry rat will run through a maze to a goal box that it knows contains food; the positive incentive directs behavior. If it is given a small pellet of food at the start of the maze, the rat runs toward the goal box even faster; the incentive also arouses behavior. As in drive theory, arousal is an important aspect of motivation; here, however, arousal is evoked by an external incentive rather than by conditions of deprivation.

Now that we have considered various concepts of motivation, we will examine some specific motivational systems. All the concepts mentioned here are useful in explaining some aspects of behavior. Even instinct theory is being revitalized in the study of certain behavior patterns—although from a different viewpoint than at the beginning of this century.

HUNGER

Eating is influenced by social customs. Scene is the Great Hall of the People, Peking, on May Day eve.

Because it has been the subject of intensive research, hunger will be the first topic considered. Hunger can be a powerful motivator; people who have subsisted on semistarvation diets report that much of their thinking and dreaming concerns food and eating. The body needs an adequate supply of nutrients to function efficiently. Depletion of these nutrients activates homeostatic mechanisms to release food stored in the body; for example, the liver releases stored sugar into the bloodstream. Replenishment from body stores enables a person to continue to function even after missing several meals. When the body stores are diminished to a certain point, however, the automatic homeostatic mechanisms are no longer adequate and the entire organism becomes mobilized to seek food.

What internal signals tell the brain that the body's supply of nutrients is low and it must find food? The feelings most people describe as hunger—an empty or aching sensation in the stomach sometimes accompanied by a feeling of weakness—give us some clues, but there are other signals.

External stimuli can influence feelings of hunger and eating behavior. After a full meal, you may still want to eat a delicious dessert. In this case, your cue for hunger is not internal. The odor or sight of food can arouse hunger even when there is no physiological need.

Habits and social customs also influence eating behavior. You are accustomed to eating at certain times of the day and may suddenly feel hungry when you notice that it is noon. You may consume more when you have dinner with friends who eat voraciously than you do when you dine alone.

Eating behavior is influenced by a number of physiological, environmental, and social variables. Here, we will examine the physiological mechanisms that regulate food intake; we will consider the environmental and social factors that influence eating behavior when we discuss obesity in the next section.

Regulatory centers in the hypothalamus

Regulation of food intake is so crucial to the survival of the organism that nature has provided several homeostatic controls. If one or more sensory signals associated with eating is eliminated (smell, taste, or sensory information from the stomach), the organism is still able to regulate food intake. The control systems that regulate eating behavior are located in a region of the brain

Hunger can be aroused by external influences.

Figure 10-2
Hypothalamic Overeating
Lesions in the ventromedial hypothalamus (VMH) caused this rat to overeat and gain more than three times its normal weight.

called the *hypothalamus*—a small collection of cell nuclei at the base of the brain (see Figure 2-7) that is directly linked with other parts of the brain and with the pituitary gland. The hypothalamus also contains more blood vessels than any other area of the brain, so that it is readily influenced by the chemical state of the blood.

The development of precise instruments for exploring the brain has enabled researchers to specify two areas of the hypothalamus that influence food intake. The *lateral hypothalamus* (LH) initiates eating (it is a "start" or "feeding center"); the *ventromedial hypothalamus* (VMH) inhibits eating (it is a "stop" or "satiety center"). One way to study the function of a specific brain area is to stimulate the spot with a weak electric current. Stimulation of the LH causes a satiated animal to eat. Stimulation of the VMH inhibits eating; a weak current slows the animal's feeding behavior, and a stronger current will stop it entirely.

Another way to study the function of a brain area is to destroy cells and nerve fibers in the region and observe the animal's behavior when the area no longer exerts control. When tissue in the LH is destroyed, the animal refuses to eat or drink and will die unless it is fed and watered artificially. Damage to tissue in the VMH produces overeating and obesity in every species investigated—from rat and chicken to monkey and human (see Figure 10-2). People with tumors or injuries in the region of the hypothalamus may overeat (a condition called *hyperphagia*) and become obese.

Studies of this type demonstrate that the VMH area (satiety center) and the LH area (feeding center) act in opposite ways to regulate food intake. Moreover, two kinds of control systems appear to be integrated in the hypothalamus. One short-term control system is responsive to the immediate nutritive needs of the organism and tells the brain when to start and stop a meal. A second, long-term control system maintains a stable body weight over an extended time period regardless of how much the organism may eat in any one meal.

Short-term control of food intake

Investigators have identified three variables that influence hypothalamic control of immediate appetite: blood-sugar level, stomach fullness, and body temperature. A low sugar or glucose level in the blood makes the organism feel weak and hungry. Injections of insulin (which lower the blood-sugar level) increase food intake; injections of glucose (which raise the blood-sugar level) inhibit eating.

Studies indicate that the hypothalamus contains "glucoreceptors"—cells sensitive to the rate at which glucose passes through them. Glucoreceptors in the VMH and the LH respond differently to the glucose level in the blood. Microelectrodes have been implanted in the hypothalamus of dogs and cats to record neural activity in the VMH and LH before and after injections of glucose or insulin. After glucose injections, cells in the VMH (satiety center) became more active, whereas cells in the LH (feeding center) decreased in activity. The reverse results occurred after insulin injections. Cells monitored in other parts of the brain showed no changes (Anand, Sharma, and Dua, 1964; Oomura, 1975).

But digestion is a slow process. The organism stops eating long before the food it has consumed can be transformed into enough blood sugar to make up a deficit in the bloodstream. A more immediate signal—a full stomach—lets the brain know that the food is on its way. If food is injected directly into the stomach of a hungry animal (without passing through the mouth and throat), it eats much less than it would otherwise. If food is removed from a satiated animal's stomach (via a tube), the animal will eat enough to compensate for the food loss. Experiments suggest that cells in the VMH respond to the distension of the stomach and inhibit further eating (Deutsch, Young, and Kalogeris, 1978).

An empty stomach produces the periodic contractions of muscles in the stomach wall that we identify as "hunger pangs." This increased movement of the stomach wall activates cells in the LH. Therefore, an empty stomach signals the LH to initiate eating; a full stomach signals the VMH to stop eating.

A third short-term control mechanism of food intake is body temperature. Most animals and humans eat less in a warm environment than they do in a cold environment. Cooling the brain has a similar effect on food intake. The nature of these "thermoreceptors" in the brain is not clear, but evidence shows that the LH responds to decreased brain temperature and the VMH responds to increased brain temperature.

Thus, the LH responds to low blood-sugar level, increased motility of the stomach walls, and lowered brain temperature by initiating eating; conversely, the VMH responds to high blood-sugar level, stomach distension, and increased brain temperature by stopping eating. But these short-term mechanisms are subject to a long-term mechanism that attempts to stabilize body weight over time.

Long-term control of food intake

Most wild animals maintain about the same level of weight throughout their lifetimes, even though food may be plentiful one week and scarce the next. It is more difficult for human beings to maintain a constant weight because their eating behavior is strongly influenced by emotional and social factors. Even so, most people remain at approximately the same weight level from year to year. In addition to its short-term controls of food intake, the hypothalamus appears to regulate a delicate system that ensures that the organism's weight remains stable over time.

We noted that a rat with damage to the VMH overeats and becomes obese. Originally, this increase in appetite was attributed to the destruction of part of the short-term control system. But once the rat reaches a certain level of obesity (usually two or three times its normal weight), it no longer overeats. It reduces its food intake to slightly more than a normal level and maintains its new obese weight. If the animal's diet is restricted, it will decrease to its original normal weight; if it is allowed to eat freely again, it will overeat until it returns to its obese state. It appears that damage to the VMH disturbs the animal's long-term weight control system so that weight is regulated at a higher level.

If obese rats are force-fed until they become "super obese," they reduce their food intake until their weight returns to its "normal obese" level (see Figure 10-3). Some correlate of body weight must act on the VMH to influence food intake. Autopsies of animals with VMH lesions indicate that the influential factor may be the amount of free fatty acids in the bloodstream.

In contrast, rats with lesions in the LH refuse all food and water for some time after the operation and will die unless they are artificially fed. After several weeks, most of these rats will resume eating and drinking on their own, but they stabilize at a lower weight level, just as VMH-damaged rats stabilize at an obese level (Mitchel and Keesey, 1974). Again, this behavior indicates im-

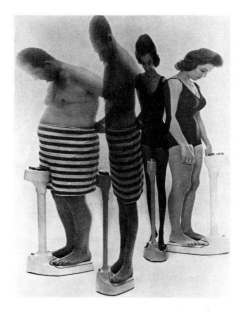

Figure 10-3
Effects of Forced Feeding and Starvation
on Body Weight of Rat with VMH Lesions
**Following VMH lesioning, the rat overeats
and gains weight until it stabilizes at a new,
obese level. Forced feeding or starvation alters the weight level only temporarily; the rat
returns to its stabilized level. (After Hoebel
and Teitelbaum, 1966)**

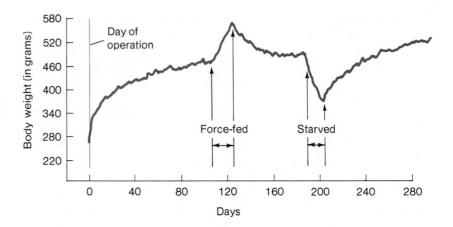

pairment of a long-term weight control system rather than simple decreased
appetite. Rats that are starved prior to LH lesioning do not refuse to eat after
the operation. In fact, many of them overeat, but only until their weight reaches
a new level—lower than their normal weight but higher than their starved,
preoperational weight (see Figure 10-4).

These findings indicate that the VMH and the LH have reciprocal effects
on the "set point" for body weight. Damage to the VMH raises the set point;
damage to the LH lowers it. If *both* areas are lesioned carefully so that an
equivalent amount of tissue is destroyed in each area, the animals do not
overeat or undereat but maintain their presurgery weight levels (Keesey and
Powley, 1975).

Although the hypothalamus plays a crucial role in the control of eating
behavior, other brain regions are also involved, including the limbic sytem and
certain nuclei in the brain stem where sensory neurons carrying information
about taste and smell converge. Thus, the hypothalamus may be more accurately described as a critical link between the higher and lower brain areas that
regulate eating behavior rather than as *the* area containing feeding and satiety
"centers."

Figure 10-4
Body Weight and
the Lateral Hypothalamus
**Prior to LH lesioning, one group of rats was
starved while the other group was allowed to
feed freely. Following surgery, the starved
animals increased their food intake and
gained weight and the freely fed group lost
weight. Both groups stabilized at the same
weight level. (After Powley and Keesey, 1970)**

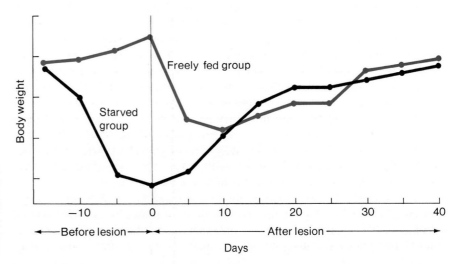

OBESITY

Obesity is a major health problem. Each year, people spend millions of dollars on special diets, drugs, and other treatments to lose weight. Most people are not very successful in losing weight; those who succeed in shedding pounds almost invariably regain them. These problems have stimulated much research on the origin and control of obesity.

A popular view is that obesity stems from unresolved emotional problems. Fat people were starved for love as children and food symbolizes "mother's love"; or overeating is a substitute for other satisfactions lacking in the individual's life. Although such explanations may be appropriate in some cases, the backgrounds of most overweight people are no more psychologically disturbed than those of normal-weight individuals. Fat people are often unhappy, but their distress is primarily a *result* rather than a cause of their obesity. In a society where thinness is equated with beauty, overweight people tend to be embarrassed by their appearance and ashamed of their supposed lack of control.

Thus far, research has failed to isolate a personality type that characterizes obese people. Rather than focusing on the individual's personality or emotional background, current studies of obesity are considering the situational factors that lead to overeating. What cues prompt a person to eat? How do obese people differ in their responses to these cues?

Factors that influence eating

RESPONSIVENESS TO FOOD CUES   The sight, aroma, and taste of food affect how much we eat and when we eat. Research suggests that obese individuals may be more responsive to these food cues than people of normal weight. One study examined the effects of taste on the eating behavior of underweight and overweight subjects. The subjects were allowed to eat as much vanilla ice cream as they wanted and then were asked to rate its quality. Some subjects were given a creamy, expensive vanilla ice cream; the others, a cheap vanilla ice cream with quinine added to make it slightly bitter. Figure 10-5 plots the subjects' ratings against the amount of ice cream eaten. Overweight subjects ate much more ice cream when they rated it "excellent" than they did when they rated it "bad." The ice-cream consumption of underweight subjects was less affected by taste; in fact, they ate somewhat more than the overweight subjects when the ice cream was rated "bad." Taste therefore appears to be particularly important to overweight subjects.

Obese individuals also seem to be highly responsive to the sight of food. When bright lights are focused on a dish of cashew nuts, overweight individuals eat twice as many nuts as they do when the lights are dimmed. People of normal weight eat about the same number of nuts regardless of how well they can see them (Ross, 1974). Even listening to a mouth-watering description of food prompts overweight individuals to eat much more than normal-weight individuals under the same conditions (Rodin, 1981).

Evidence from these and other studies indicates that the eating behavior of obese individuals is highly responsive to stimuli associated with food. But is this greater responsivity a *consequence* rather than a *cause* of being overweight? The question does not have a simple answer. There is substantial

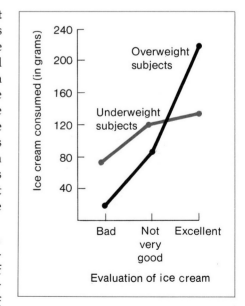

Figure 10-5
Taste and Obesity
The effects of food quality on the amount eaten by overweight and underweight subjects. The subjects rated the quality of ice cream and could eat as much as they desired. (After Nisbett, 1968b)

evidence, however, suggesting that responsivity plays a role in obesity; some individuals appear to be unusually sensitive to external cues that elicit eating (Rodin, 1981). Increased responsivity may also be influenced by an inherited component that can be identified at birth. In one study, infants who had two overweight parents showed a greater preference for sugar solutions and were generally more responsive to food cues than infants who had two normal-weight parents. Such findings suggest that the offspring of overweight parents are more likely to become obese than the offspring of normal-weight parents (Milstein, 1980).

EMOTIONAL AROUSAL   Overweight individuals often report that they tend to eat more when they are tense or anxious, and experiments suggest that this is true. Obese subjects eat more in a high-anxiety situation than in a low-anxiety situation; normal-weight subjects eat more in the low-anxiety situation (McKenna, 1972).

Any kind of emotional arousal seems to increase food intake in some obese people. In one study, overweight and normal-weight subjects saw four films during four different sessions. Three of the films aroused various emotions: one was distressing; one, amusing; one, sexually arousing. The fourth film was a boring travelogue. After viewing the films, the subjects were asked to taste and evaluate different kinds of crackers. The obese subjects ate significantly more crackers after viewing any of the arousing films than they did after seeing the travelogue. Normal-weight individuals ate the same amount of crackers regardless of which film they had seen (White, 1977).

CONSCIOUS RESTRAINT OF EATING   The studies we have examined suggest that obese people tend to be more responsive than normal-weight individuals to the taste and sight of food and other sensations aroused by food. They are also more apt to eat when emotionally aroused. But one variable we have not considered is that overweight individuals are more likely to be *dieting* than thin or normal-weight individuals, and some of their responsiveness to external cues may stem from this fact. People who are hungry all the time might be expected to pay more attention to food.

To better understand the effects of dieting, a questionnaire was developed that asked about diet and weight history (for example, "How often are you dieting?"; "What is the maximum amount of weight that you have ever lost in a month?") as well as concern with food and eating (for example, "Do you eat sensibly before others, yet make up for it when alone?"; "Do you have feelings of guilt after overeating?").

The results of the questionnaire showed that almost everyone—whether thin, plump, or fat—could be classified into one of two categories: people who consciously restrained their eating and people who did not. In addition, no matter what their actual weight, "restrained eaters" behaved more like obese individuals than "unrestrained eaters." For example, when normal-weight subjects were placed in an anxiety-producing situation, those categorized as restrained tended to increase their food intake (like the obese) whereas the unrestrained eaters tended to eat less (Herman and Polivy, 1980).

The control of the dieter is tenuous, however, and is vulnerable to external influences, as anyone who has repeatedly broken a diet knows. Dieting may actually increase the chances of overeating. In one study, restrained and un-restrained eaters (both of normal weight) were required to drink two milk-shakes, one milkshake, or none; they then sampled several flavors of ice cream and were encouraged to eat as much of the ice cream as they wanted. The more milkshakes the unrestrained eaters were required to drink, the less ice cream they consumed later. In contrast, the restrained eaters ate *more* ice cream after they had been preloaded with two milkshakes than they did after drinking one milkshake or none. Apparently, once the restrained eaters had overeaten through preloading, their control broke down completely (Herman and Mack, 1975).

A similar experiment with thin, normal, and obese subjects revealed that dieting was a more critical factor in predicting eating behavior than weight. The three weight groups did not differ significantly in the amount of ice cream they ate after being preloaded with two milkshakes or none. But when the data were analyzed for restrained versus unrestrained eaters regardless of weight, the differences were highly significant (see Figure 10-6). Nondieters (unrestrained subjects) ate much less after two milkshakes than after none, whereas dieters (restrained subjects) ate more.

In these experiments, the forced loading of milkshakes makes the subjects lose control of their eating behavior. Once restrained eaters lose control, they eat much more than unrestrained eaters do. Restrained eaters are continuously trying to inhibit their food intake; when they lose control (when their attempts to inhibit eating fail), motivation collapses and they begin overeating. Loss of inhibition is a key factor in influencing obesity, as illustrated by an experiment involving alcohol, which is well-known for its inhibition-releasing effects. The study indicated that alcohol increased food intake among restrained eaters but not among unrestrained eaters (Polivy and Herman, 1976). Anxiety and depression also tend to weaken self-control. And research indicates that restrained eaters eat more when they are anxious or depressed, whereas unrestrained eaters eat less (Herman and Polivy, 1980).

Exercise and eating

The body's level of energy expenditure is critical to weight control. Energy expenditure depends on two factors: (1) general activity level and exercise; and (2) the *basal metabolic rate*, or the energy required to maintain minimal body functions. Of the two, basal metabolism accounts for about two thirds of a normal-weight person's energy expenditure. For the overweight individual, however, energy expenditure is inhibited because the metabolic rate is lower in fat tissue than in lean tisssue. Thus, the individual's basal metabolic rate decreases as lean tissue is replaced by fat. Metabolic rate also decreases during periods of food deprivation; consequently, when an individual starts to diet, the basal metabolic rate decreases. Both of these factors work against the efforts of an overweight person to reduce.

Physical activity accounts for only about one third of a normal individual's energy expenditure, but it plays a more critical role in the amount of energy expended by an overweight person. Exercise, of course, burns off calories; the more an individual exercises, the more calories are burned off. But exercise also indirectly affects basal metabolism. If a person is sedentary, the metabolic mechanism fails to operate properly and produces a lower basal metabolic rate (Garrow, 1978). Lack of exercise sets up a vicious cycle: obesity makes physical exercise more difficult and less enjoyable, and inactivity results in fewer calories being burned off (directly through exercise and indirectly through a reduced basal metabolic rate). Thus, exercise is critical in weight loss—not only because it burns calories but also because it helps to regulate normal metabolic functioning (Thompson and others, 1982).

Our discussion indicates that obesity results from the interplay of genetic, metabolic, psychological, and environmental events. The importance of each of

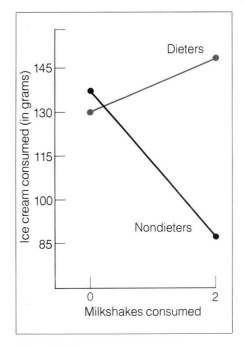

Figure 10-6
Restrained and Unrestrained Eaters
Subjects concerned with dieting consumed more ice cream after previously overindulging in milkshakes than subjects unconcerned about controlling their food intake, regardless of body weight. (After Hibscher and Herman, 1977)

these factors varies from individual to individual. Despite the complexity of the problem, weight control is possible in most cases. To diet successfully, overweight individuals must recognize that they tend to be unusually responsive to environmental cues that elicit eating and that anxiety or emotionally provocative situations tend to cause them to overeat. Being aware of these factors and guarding against their influence are important steps in gaining control of one's weight. Further, the role of exercise in weight control is more significant than folklore would suggest. Exercise burns calories and, equally important, ensures proper functioning of the metabolic process.

Behavior modification and weight control

To successfully control weight, the individual must become aware of the factors that lead to overeating and must try to establish a new set of eating and exercise habits. A study comparing methods for treating obesity illustrates this conclusion. For six months, obese individuals followed one of three treatment regimens: (1) behavior modification of eating and exercise habits, (2) drug therapy using an appetite suppressant (fenfluramine) and (3) a combination of behavior modification and drug therapy. Subjects in all three treatment groups were given information on exercise and extensive nutritional counseling, including a 1,000–1,200 calorie diet. There were two control groups. One control group consisted of subjects waiting to take part in the study, who received no treatment of any kind. The other control group consisted of subjects who saw a physician for traditional office treatment of weight problems, which involved the use of fenfluramine, a reducing diet, information on diet, advice, and encouragement.

Behavior modification, received by two of the three treatment groups, involved a program like the one described in Chapter 16 (see page 505). The

Are Some People Programmed to Be Fat?

Obesity runs in families; fat parents tend to have fat children. Except for a few cases that are clearly the result of hormonal disorders, no biological cause has been determined that predisposes people to obesity. However, the eating patterns of obese individuals and rats with VMH lesions are remarkably similar. Both eat more at a given meal and eat more rapidly than normal organisms, and both are highly responsive to food tastes. These similarities have led to the speculation that the hypothalamus of obese individuals sets a higher than normal baseline for fat tissue—that these individuals are "biologically programmed to be fat" (Nisbett, 1972).

Body fat is stored in special fat cells called *adipocytes*. Obese individuals differ from non-obese individuals both in the *size* and in the *number* of these fat cells. In one sample, obese subjects were found to have three times as many fat cells as normal subjects (Knittle and Hirsch, 1968). This is an important finding because the number of fat cells in an individual is set at an early age and remains relatively fixed throughout life. Overeating increases the size of a person's fat cells but not the number; starvation decreases the size of a person's fat cells but not the number. After weight loss, formerly obese individuals have the same number of fat cells, which will be filled up again if they start overeating. Individuals who have a large number of fat cells have a *higher baseline* of body fat than individuals who have fewer fat cells.

Heredity and early nutrition both probably play roles in determining an individual's number of fat cells, but the causal relationship is not clear. Some researchers believe that a person's fat-cell count is genetically fixed at birth. Others think that the number of fat cells is determined by nutrition during the early months of life; overfeeding an infant may stimulate the development of fat cells. In any event, evidence indicates that the individual's baseline of body fat is fairly well established by 2 years of age (Knittle, 1975). The hypothalamic centers maintain this baseline by regulating food intake to maintain fat stores at a certain set point or level.

We have seen that rats with damage to the VMH (satiety center) regulate their weight at a new, higher level and that rats with lesions in the LH (feeding center) regulate their weight at a new, lower level. It is possible, then, that the set points for obese and non-obese individuals of the same height and bone structure are different. If this is true, obesity for some individuals is their "normal" weight, which their hypothalamus tries to maintain. Attempts at weight reduction by such individuals would hold them below their biologically determined set point in a state of chronic deprivation; they would feel hungry all the time—just like a thin person on a starvation diet would feel.

Stunkard (1982) has theorized that appetite-suppressant drugs like fenfluramine act primarily to lower the set point and only secondarily to suppress appetite. His theory explains the findings on drug therapy for obesity discussed in the text—namely, the rapid regaining of body weight following the withdrawal of fenfluramine in contrast to the relative stability of weight loss achieved with behavior modification. The drug lowered the set point of patients, thereby facilitating weight loss; discontinuation of the drug caused the set point to return to its pretreatment level. The resulting biological pressure to gain weight until the higher set point is reached produced a greater weight gain in drug-therapy subjects than in subjects who lost weight without the aid of drugs. These ideas cast doubt on the effectiveness of appetite-suppressant medication in the treatment of obesity.

The *set-point theory* is intriguing but controversial. For example, according to the theory, increased sensitivity to food cues is a consequence rather than a cause of obesity. Extremely overweight people have eaten so much that they are at their set point. But many less obese individuals remain below their set point by dieting, and this deprivation increases their receptivity to stimuli associated with food. Thus, proponents of this theory argue that the longer obese individuals diet (the more weight they lose), the more sensitive they are to food cues. But experiments do not seem to confirm this prediction. Sensitivity to stimuli associated with food appears to remain relatively constant regardless of the amount of weight loss a person experiences (Rodin, 1981).

The set-point concept has generated considerable interest and research, but there are too many contrary findings for it to serve as a general theory of obesity. However, it may account for certain types of problems—particularly the individual who was moderately overweight as a child and remains moderately overweight throughout life. A higher than normal set point may be one reason for overconsumption, but there are undoubtedly others. Most overweight people, unlike the VMH-damaged rats, do not suddenly become obese. Their fat accumulates over a period of months or years—a kind of "creeping obesity" that results from gradually consuming more calories than the body expends in energy.

Table 10-1
Weight Loss Following
Different Treatments
Weight loss in pounds at the end of six months of treatment and at a follow-up one year later. Subjects in the two control groups were not available for the one-year followup. (After Craighead, Stunkard, and O'Brien, 1981)

	WEIGHT LOSS AFTER TREATMENT	WEIGHT LOSS AFTER ONE YEAR
Treatment groups		
Behavior-modification-only	24.0	19.8
Drug-therapy-only	31.9	13.9
Combined treatment	33.7	10.1
Control groups		
Waiting-list	2.9 (gain)	—
Physician office visits	13.2	—

subjects were taught to keep a daily record of their eating habits, to become aware of situations that prompted them to overeat, to change the stimulus conditions associated with their overeating, to reward themselves for appropriate eating behavior, and to develop a suitable exercise regimen.

Table 10-1 presents the results of the study. As might be expected, the subjects in all three treatment groups lost more weight than the subjects in the two control groups. At the end of treatment, the group combining behavior modification with drug therapy lost the most weight (33.7 pounds). The drug-therapy-only group did almost as well (31.9 pounds), but the behavior-modification-only group lost significantly less (24 pounds). However, during the year after treatment was discontinued, a striking reversal developed. The behavior-modification-only group regained far less weight than the other two groups; these subjects maintained an average weight loss of 19.8 pounds by the end of year, whereas the weight losses for the drug-therapy-only group and the combined treatment group were only 13.8 and 10.1 pounds, respectively.

What caused this reversal? An increased sense of "self-efficacy" may have been a factor. Subjects who received the behavior-modification-only treatment could attribute their weight loss to their own efforts, thereby strengthening their resolve to continue controlling their weight after the treatment was over. Subjects who received an appetite suppressant, on the other hand, probably attributed their weight loss to the medication and did not develop a sense of self-control; when the drug was withdrawn, releasing biological pressures to regain weight, their sense of self-efficacy was not strong enough to prevent them from returning to their old eating habits. The drug also decreased feelings of hunger, and subjects in the drug-therapy-only group and the combined treatment group may not have been prepared to cope with the increase in hunger that occurred when the medication was stopped.

This study demonstrates that short-term weight loss can be accomplished in a variety of ways. But the ability to keep weight off permanently depends on establishing self-control over eating habits and therefore over the total number of calories consumed.

SEX

Sex, another powerful motivator, differs in many respects from hunger. Unlike food, sex is not vital to the survival of the organism, but it is essential to the survival of the species. Eating reduces tissue deficits. With sex, however, there is no deficit; sexual behavior uses energy rather than restores it.

Sexual behavior depends on a combination of internal factors (hormones and brain mechanisms) and external factors (learned and unlearned environmental stimuli). We will look at the internal or physiological variables first; then we will discuss how external variables influence sexual behavior.

Biological basis of sexual behavior

The hormones that affect the development and functioning of the reproductive organs are controlled by the pituitary gland. In the female, pituitary hormones stimulate the ovaries to manufacture the sex hormones *estrogen* and *progesterone*. In the male, pituitary hormones stimulate the cells of the testes to manufacture and secrete a group of sex hormones called *androgens*, the most important of which is *testosterone*. The marked increase in the levels of these hormones at puberty produces changes in the primary and secondary sex characteristics during adolescence.

The degree of hormonal control over sexual behavior decreases from the lower to the higher vertebrates. Castration (removal of the testes) in the adult male rat or guinea pig results in the rapid decline and eventual disappearance of sexual activity. In male dogs, castration produces a more gradual decline of sexual activity, although some dogs with considerble sexual experience prior to castration do not decrease their sexual activity after castration. Most male primates show little or no decline in sexual activity following castration. In human males, the reaction to castration is complicated by emotional and social factors, but most studies show little or no diminution of sexual motivation.

In contrast, castration in a female (removal of the ovaries) usually results in the complete cessation of sexual activity in all animals from reptiles to monkeys. The castrated female immediately ceases to be receptive to the male and may vigorously resist any sexual advances. The only exception is the human female; although some women may be less interested in sex following menopause, most reports indicate that sexual motivation is not diminished by the cessation of ovarian functioning. In fact, some women show an increased interest in sex after menopause, possibly because they are no longer concerned about pregnancy.

Sex hormones are secreted fairly constantly from day to day in the male of most species, so that the level of sexual motivation derived from hormonal influence is relatively stable. In the female, however, hormones fluctuate cyclically with accompanying changes in fertility. During the first part of the cycle, while the egg is being prepared for fertilization, the ovaries secrete estrogen, which prepares the uterus for implantation and also tends to arouse sexual interest. After ovulation occurs, both progesterone and estrogen are secreted. Progesterone prepares the mammary glands for nursing and influences maternal behavior.

The *fertility* or *estrous cycle* (which varies from 36 days in the chimpanzee to 28 days in the human female to 5 days in the mouse) is accompanied by a consequent variation in sexual motivation in most species. Most female animals are receptive to sexual advances by a male only during the period of ovulation, when the estrogen level is at a maximum (when they are "in heat"). Among primates, however, sexual activity is less influenced by the estrous cycle; monkey, ape, and chimp females copulate during all phases of the cycle, although ovulation is still the period of most intense sexual activity. In the human female, sexual activity is more strongly influenced by social and emotional factors than by hormones.

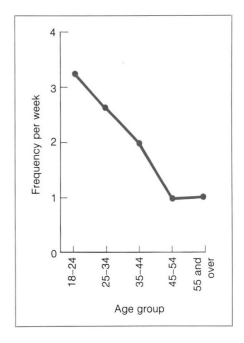

Frequency of marital intercourse
Estimates of the weekly frequency of sexual intercourse among married couples. The decline has both a biological and a psychological basis. With age, men take longer to ejaculate and require more time before they can perform again. In women, vaginal size and lubrication decrease noticeably after menopause, which may make intercourse uncomfortable. Psychological factors include work pressure and lack of free time due to career demands, fear of losing sexual potency, and boredom in marriage. However, there are large individual differences. Some couples experience virtually no decline over time; others decrease their sexual activities very early in the marriage. (After Hunt, 1974)

SEXUAL DIFFERENTIATION   In addition to influencing adult sexual behavior, hormones are even more important in determining our prenatal development as male or female. Until a human embryo is between 2 and 3 months old, only the cell chromosomes indicate whether it will develop into a boy or a girl. Up to this stage, both sexes are identical in appearance and have tissues that will eventually develop into testes or ovaries and a genital tubercle that will become either a penis or a clitoris.

Initial development is governed by a primitive sex gland, or *gonad*. If the embryo is genetically male (XY), the primitive gland develops into testes; if the embryo is genetically female (XX), ovaries will develop. Thus, the first step in sexual differentiation is genetically controlled. But once either testes or ovaries develop, they produce the hormones that determine the further development of the internal reproductive structures and the external genitals.

The basic blueprint appears to be female. If the embryonic sex glands do not produce enough male hormones (androgens), the newborn will have female genitals even though it is genetically a male (XY). The anatomical development of the female fetus apparently does not require female hormones, only the absence of male hormones.

In rare instances, when a hormonal imbalance occurs during pregnancy, the fetal reproductive system may fail to develop completely into a male or a female. Infants may be born with genitals that appear to be ambiguous (an external organ that could be described as a very large clitoris or a very small penis) or that conflict with the internal sex glands (ovaries and a penis). Such individuals are called *hermaphrodites*. Their development provides interesting information about the relative importance of biology and environment in determining sexual behavior.

In most cases, when a hermaphroditic infant is assigned the wrong sex label at birth—for example, an infant with ambiguous external genitalia who is called a "boy" but is later determined to be genetically female (XX) and to have ovaries—the assigned label and the sex role in which the individual is raised have a much greater influence on sexual identification than do the individual's genes and hormones. For example, two genetically female infants had ambiguous external genitals because their fetal sex glands had produced too much androgen. This metabolic error occurred too late in fetal development to affect the internal organs (they both had ovaries) but in time to change the appearance of the genitals. Both infants had surgery to correct their enlarged clitorises. One infant's genitals were "feminized," and she was raised as a girl; the other infant's genitals were modified to resemble a penis, and he was raised as a boy. Reports indicate that both children grew up secure in their respective sex roles. The girl was somewhat "tomboyish" but feminine in appearance. The boy was accepted as male by his peers and expressed a romantic interest in girls. Similar cases of matched pairs of hermaphrodites suggest that an individual's sexual identification is influenced more by the way a person is labeled and raised than by his or her hormones (Money, 1980).

NEURAL MECHANISMS   Neural control of sexual behavior is complex, and the mechanisms that influence sexual behavior vary considerably among different species. Some of the basic reflexes (such as erection, pelvic movements, and ejaculation in the male) are controlled at the level of the spinal cord and do not require control by the brain. Men whose spinal cord has been severed from the brain by injury (paraplegics) are still capable of these movements. However, much of the regulation of sexual arousal and more complex sexual behaviors takes place in the hypothalamus.

Electrical stimulation of the posterior hypothalamus of the rat produces not only copulation but the entire repertoire of sexual behavior. Male rats stimulated in that area do not mount indiscriminately but court the female by nibbling her ears and nipping the back of her neck until she responds. Intromission and ejaculation follow unless the electrical stimulation is terminated. Even a sexually satiated male rat will respond to electrical stimulation by pressing a bar to open a door leading to the female and will court and mate with her (Caggiula and Hoebel, 1966). The rat's behavior can be precisely controlled by implanting electrodes in both the lateral hypothalamus and the posterior hypothalamus and switching the current from one electrode to the other. With both food and a female available, the animal begins to copulate during posterior stimulation; when the current is switched to the lateral electrode, the male abandons the female and begins to eat. Resumption of posterior hypothalamic stimulation causes the rat to interrupt its meal and return to the female (Caggiula, 1967).

Role of experience

Experience has little influence on mating behavior in the lower mammals. Inexperienced rats will copulate as efficiently as experienced rats; sexual behavior is fairly specific and appears to be innate. However, experience and learning play increasingly important roles in sexual behavior in the progression from the lower to the higher mammals.

Young monkeys in their play with each other exhibit many of the postures required for later copulation. In wrestling with their peers, infant male monkeys display hindquarter grasping and thrusting responses that are components of adult sexual behavior. Infant female monkeys retreat when threatened by an aggressive male infant and stand steadfastly in a posture similar to the stance later required to support the weight of the male during copulation. These presexual responses appear as early as 60 days of age and become more frequent and refined as the monkey matures (see Figure 10-7). Their early appearance suggests that they are innate responses to specific stimuli; the modification and refinement of these responses through experience indicates that learning plays a role in the development of the adult sexual pattern.

Monkeys raised in partial isolation (in separate wire cages, where they can see other monkeys but have no contact with them) are usually unable to copulate at maturity. The male monkeys are able to perform the mechanics of sex: they masturbate to ejaculation at about the same frequency as normal monkeys. But when confronted with a sexually receptive female, they do not seem to know how to assume the correct posture for copulation. They are aroused but aimlessly grope the female or their own bodies (Harlow, 1971).

Monkeys raised without peer contact are usually atypical in all of their social reactions, not just in their sexual responses. As adults, they are unable to relate to other monkeys, exhibiting either fear and flight or extreme aggression. Harlow (1971) suggests that normal heterosexual behavior in primates depends on (1) the development of specific sexual responses, such as grasping the female and pelvis thrusting, (2) the influence of hormones, and (3) an affectional bond between two members of the opposite sex. The affectional bond is an outgrowth of interactions with the mother and with peers. Through these interactions, the young monkey learns to trust—to expose its more delicate parts without fear of harm; to accept and enjoy physical contact with another monkey; to develop the behavior pattern characteristic of its sex; and to be motivated to seek the company of other monkeys.

Figure 10-7
Infant Play and Adult Sexual Behavior
A. The first presexual step. B. Basic sexual posture. C. Inappropriate sexual response: male correct, female incorrect. D. Inappropriate sexual response: female correct, male incorrect.

Although we cannot generalize these findings with monkeys to the process of human sexual development, clinical observations of human infants suggest certain parallels. Human infants develop their first feelings of trust and affection through a warm and loving relationship with the mother (see Chapter 3). This basic trust is a prerequisite for satisfactory interactions with peers, and affectionate relationships with other youngsters of both sexes lay the groundwork for the intimacy required for heterosexual relationships among young adults.

CULTURAL INFLUENCES   In contrast with other primates, human sexual behavior is strongly determined by cultural influences. Every society places some restrictions on sexual behavior. Incest (sexual relations within the immediate family) is prohibited by almost all cultures. Other aspects of sexual behavior—sexual activity among children, homosexuality, masturbation, and premarital sex—are permitted in varying degrees by different societies. Among preliterate cultures studied by anthropologists, acceptable sexual activity varies widely. Some very permissive societies encourage autoerotic activities and sex

Sexual fantasies are a common form of sexual behavior. For most individuals, sexual fantasies begin soon after the onset of an active sex drive, typically at about the age of 13 for males and 15 for females. Initially, these fantasies are only vaguely sexual and do not involve particular sexual acts or partners. As the sex drive increases during adolescence, the fantasies become more detailed and involve specific partners (Storms, 1981).

Research on sexual fantasies has focused on their occurrence during masturbation. In the Kinsey study, 89 percent of the males reported that they fantasized on occasion while masturbating and 72 percent reported that they fantasized regularly when masturbating. For females, the percentages were somewhat lower; 64 percent had fantasized on some occasions, and 50 percent fantasized regularly. Today, these percentages undoubtedly would be higher.

A study of the fantasies people have while masturbating indicates that the most common theme involves intercourse with a loved person; 75 percent of the men and 80 percent of the women interviewed reported that they had such fantasies on some occasion while masturbating, and the percentages were

nearly the same for married and single individuals (Hunt, 1974). In addition to fantasies about intercourse with a loved person, a substantial percentage of the men and women surveyed indulged in more deviant types of sexual fantasies. Table 10-2 presents some of these fantasy themes and the percentage of individuals who reported having such fantasies on some occasions.

An inspection of the table indicates that men and women tend to differ in the frequency of reporting a particular fantasy theme. Men are more likely than women to fantasize about sex with a stranger, group sex, or forcing someone to have sex; women are more likely than men to fantasize about performing sexual acts they would not carry out in reality or about being overpowered and forced to have sex. For women, fantasies of being forced to have sex typically do not involve rape in the sense that the force is brutal or degrading; the force is psychological, and the experience is generally self-enhancing rather than humiliating. For example, such fantasies as yielding to sex with a banker who holds the family's house mortgage or being a harem slave forced to display her body to an admiring, all-powerful shiek allow a woman to think about engaging in sex

without assuming responsibility for her actions or feeling guilty about them.

Although men fantasize more often than women while masturbating, women fantasize as often or possibly more often than men during sexual intercourse (Sue, 1979; Hessellund, 1976). In this regard, an interesting observation is that the *duration* of physical stimulation required to reach orgasm while masturbating is the same for men and women. During intercourse, however, women typically respond more slowly, and this slower response time prevents many women from having an orgasm. Women may rely on fantasy to increase sexual arousal, thereby maximizing the likelihood of reaching climax during intercourse (Offir, 1982).

In a study of upper-middle class housewives, 65 percent reported frequent fantasies and an additional 28 percent reported occasional fantasies during intercourse. Only 7 percent reported that they never fantasized or thought about other sexual experiences during intercourse (Hariton, 1973). Two popular themes were being with another man (a past lover, a famous actor, a casual friend) and being overpowered and forced to surrender to an admiring but unidentified male. This study and others like it have provided no evidence that people who have sexual fantasies are psychologically disturbed or have less satisfactory marriages.

Sexual fantasies appear to be commonplace and add variety to sex. They illustrate the complicated interrelationship between the basic biological need and the cognitive overlay that together influence sexual behavior.

Table 10-2
Common Fantasy Themes
While Masturbating
Percentage of males and females who reported having a fantasy with a particular theme on some occasion while masturbating. Note the pattern of percentages is quite different for males and females. (After Hunt, 1974)

FANTASY THEMES	PERCENTAGE REPORTING FANTASY THEME	
	Male	Female
Intercourse with a loved person or acquaintance	75%	80%
Intercourse with a stranger	47%	21%
Sex with more than one person of opposite sex at the same time	33%	18%
Performing sexual acts that the individual would never carry out in reality	19%	28%
Forcing someone to have sex	13%	3%
Being forced to have sex	10%	19%
Having sex with someone of the same sex	7%	11%

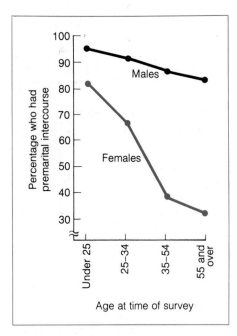

Figure 10-8
Premarital Intercourse
Percentage of married individuals who had premarital sexual intercourse as a function of age. *Age* refers to the individual's age at the time of the survey, not the age at which premarital sex occurred. Individuals over 55 at the time the survey was conducted were born before 1918; individuals under 25 were born after 1948. These data are based on a national sample of 1,400 individuals. (After Hunt, 1974)

play among children of both sexes and allow them to observe adult sexual activity. The Chewa of Africa, for example, believe that unless children exercise themselves sexually they will be unable to produce offspring later.

In contrast, very restrictive societies try to control preadolescent sexual behavior and keep children from learning about sexual matters. The Cuna of South America believe that children should be totally ignorant about sex until they are married; they do not even permit their children to watch animals give birth. And among the Ashanti of Africa, intercourse with a girl who has not undergone the puberty ceremony is punishable by death for both participants. Similar extreme attitudes are found toward other aspects of sexual behavior; homosexuality, for example, is viewed by some nonliterate societies as an essential part of growing up and by others as an offense punishable by death.

Until recently, the United States and most other Western countries would have been classified as sexually restrictive societies. Traditionally, the existence of prepubertal sexuality has been ignored or denied in Western society. Marital sex has been considered the only legitimate sexual outlet, and other forms of sexual expression (homosexual activities, premarital and extramarital sex) have been generally condemned and often prohibited by law. Of course, many members of these societies engaged in such activities but often with feelings of shame.

Attitudes toward sexual activities are more permissive today than they were 30 years ago. Premarital sex, for example, is more acceptable and occurs more frequently today than in the past. Among college-educated individuals interviewed in the 1940s, 27 percent of the women and 49 percent of the men had engaged in premarital sex by the age of 21 (Kinsey and others, 1948, 1953). Several surveys of college students in the 1970s report considerably higher incidences, ranging from 43 to 56 percent for females and from 58 to 82 percent for males (Packard, 1970; Hunt, 1974).

The change in attitude toward premarital sex has been greater among women. Figure 10-8 shows the results of a survey of premarital experience among married individuals of different ages. The difference between women born before 1918 and women born after 1948 is striking.

Although more and more women are engaging in premarital sex, men and women still differ in their attitudes toward sex before marriage. The majority of women who engage in premarital sex do so with only one or two partners with whom they are emotionally involved. Men, in contrast, are more likely to seek casual sex without emotional involvement; in one survey, the median number of premarital partners reported by males was six (Hunt, 1974).

When college students were asked to list their problems with "any aspect of sexual functioning," the concerns of males and females were quite different. Women most often expressed fears and insecurities:

> Fear of pregnancy
> Fear of rape
> Being conquered and of no further use
> Being rejected if they said no
> Masturbation (accepting it)
> Fear that their partners would be physically repulsed by them
> Fear of losing self-respect
> Fear of becoming too attached when the feeling was not mutual
> Guilt feelings about premarital sex
> Pressure to have sex even when they did not want to
> Fear of not satisfying their partner
> Embarrassment or concern over not being orgasmic

Men were more apt to list complaints about women rather than to express their own conflicts or worries:

Finding partners who were open to varying sexual experiences
Always having to be on the hunt
Not being able to have sexual relations when they wanted to
Women who tease, without wanting to engage in sexual activity
Women's refusal to take responsibility for their own sexuality
Women who used their sexual attractiveness in a manipulatory fashion
The excessive modesty of women (they wanted the lights off)
Passive women
Aggressive women
Necessity to say you loved the woman even if it was not true
Being expected to know all about sex
Inability to communicate feelings or needs during sex
(Tavris and Offir, 1977, p. 68)

These response differences reflect different attitudes—at least among males and females who are young and unmarried—about the relationship between sex and love. Women still tend to view sex as part of a loving relationship; men often consider sex and love to be separate experiences.

Attitudes toward extramarital sex and such sexual behaviors as masturbation and oral-genital stimulation have also become more permissive within the past 30 years. And homosexuality is viewed with greater tolerance now than it was 30 years ago, although there is no indication that the proportion of homosexual individuals is increasing. Thus, sexual behaviors are greatly influenced by the customs and values of society and may differ over time within the same society.

Homosexuality

The term *homosexual* can be applied to either a man or a woman, but female homosexuals are usually called *lesbians*. Most experts agree with Kinsey's view that homosexuality is not an "either-or matter"; sexual behavior falls on a continuum, with exclusively heterosexual and exclusively homosexual individuals at either end and various mixtures of sexual behavior in between. Most young boys engage in erotic play with other boys at some time during their childhood, and many men have one or more homosexual encounters later in life, although only about 4 percent become exclusively homosexual. Women are less apt than men to have sexual interactions with each other during childhood or a homosexual episode in later life, and only 1–2 percent are exclusively homosexual. Some individuals are *bisexual* and enjoy sexual relations with members of both sexes. And some married individuals may have homosexual encounters on the side.

Until recently, homosexuality was considered a "mental illness" or an abnormal perversion. Although many people still view homosexuality as unnatural, most psychologists and psychiatrists consider it to be a variant rather than a perversion of sexual expression and not, in itself, an indication or cause of mental illness.

Much remains to be learned about the causes of homosexuality. No reliable physical differences have been found that distinguish homosexuals from heterosexuals. Although some male homosexuals may be quite feminine and some female homosexuals may be quite masculine in appearance, this is often not the case. There is some indication that male homosexuals have lower levels of the hormone testosterone than heterosexual males, but there is no evidence that this is the cause of homosexuality. When male homosexuals are given additional hormones, their sex drive increases (also true for heterosexual men) but their sexual preferences do not change.

Results from a major study on homosexuality are summarized in Table 10-3. The study indicates a strong continuity between a person's childhood and adolescent sexual feelings and his or her adult sexual preference. Contrary to the popular notion that parents are somehow responsible for their children's homosexuality, the study reveals that parental influence was not a major factor in determining sexual preference. Sexual preference appears to depend on a complex pattern of feelings and reactions within the child that are not yet understood and cannot be traced to a single social or psychological cause.

Transsexualism

Transsexuals are people (usually males) who feel that they were born into the wrong body. They are not homosexuals in the usual sense. Most homosexuals are satisfied with their anatomy and think of themselves as appropriately male or female; they simply prefer members of their own sex. Transsexuals, in contrast, *think* of themselves as members of the opposite sex (often from early childhood) and may be so desperately unhappy with their physical appearance that they request hormonal and surgical treatment to change their genitals and secondary sex characteristics. Several thousand "sex-change" operations have been performed in the United States. For males, hormone treatments can enlarge the breasts, reduce beard growth, and make the figure more rounded; surgical procedures involve removing the testes and part of the penis and

Table 10-3
Variables Influencing Sexual Preference
Results are based on interviews conducted in 1969–1970 with approximately 1,500 homosexual men and women living in the San Francisco Bay area. The investigators analyzed the respondents' relationships with their parents and siblings while growing up, the degree to which the respondents conformed during childhood to the stereotypical concepts of what it means to be male or female, the respondents' relationships with peers and others outside the home, and the nature of their childhood and sexual experiences. Statistical analyses traced the relationship between such variables and adult sexual preference. (After Bell, Weinberg, and Hammersmith, 1981)

1 By the time both the boys and the girls reached adolescence, their sexual preference was likely to be determined, even though they might not yet have become very active sexually.

2 Among the respondents, homosexuality was indicated or reinforced by sexual feelings that typically occurred three years or so before their first "advanced" homosexual activity. These feelings, more than homosexual activities, appeared to play a crucial role in the development of adult homosexuality.

3 The homosexual men and women in the study were not particularly lacking in heterosexual experiences during their childhood and adolescent years. They were distinguishable from their heterosexual counterparts, however, in that they found such experiences ungratifying.

4 Among both the men and the women in the study, there was a powerful link between gender nonconformity as a child and the development of homosexuality.

5 The respondents' identification with their opposite-sex parents while growing up appeared to have had no significant impact on whether they turned out to be homosexual or heterosexual.

6 For both the men and the women in the study, poor relationships with fathers seemed to play a more important role in predisposing them to homosexuality than the quality of their relationships with their mothers.

7 Insofar as differences can be identified between male and female psychosexual development, gender nonconformity appeared to be somewhat more important for males and family relationships appeared to be more important for females in the development of sexual preference.

CRITICAL DISCUSSION

Homosexuality and Social Development

The course of sex-drive development for males and females is illustrated in the top part of Figure 10-9. The curves represent the cumulative percentage by age of individuals who have experienced the onset of the sex drive (as indicated by the appearance of sexual arousal, sexual fantasizing, and masturbation). The most dramatic increase in sex drive clearly occurs during adolescence. Although women experience puberty at an earlier average age than men, their sex-drive development begins later and progresses more slowly.

The bar graph at the bottom of Figure 10-9 indicates the approximate course of adolescent development from a *homosocial* environment to a *heterosocial* environment. Boys and girls tend to form separate homosocial groups from early childhood through preadolescence; during this period, individuals engage in social activities and form friendship bonds almost exclusively within same-sex peer groups. From age 15 on, most individuals continue some involvement in homosocial groups but spend an increasing amount of time in heterosocial relationships.

Storms (1981) has proposed that erotic orientation results from an interaction during early adolescence between sex-drive development and social development. Specifically, the onset of the sex drive during adolescence initiates the development of an erotic orientation, and the sexual stimuli in an individual's social environment at that time determine the direction of erotic orientation. According to this theory, an unusually early onset of the sex drive contributes to homosexuality, because the individual's environment at that time is primarily homosocial. It has been proposed that some individuals simply have stronger sex drives at an earlier age and therefore eroticize their homosocial experiences to a greater extent than others.

Storms' theory proposes that sexual preference in adulthood depends on the social environment that is present when the individual's sex drive comes into full force during adolescence. If the environment is primarily homosocial, the adult's sexual preference will tend to be homosexual; if heterosocial, the adult's sexual preference will tend to be heterosexual. This theory of sexual preference posits an interaction between the biological factors associated with the onset of sexual drive and the social and psychological factors involved in social development. The theory appears to explain many of the observations regarding homosexuality reported in Table 10-3.

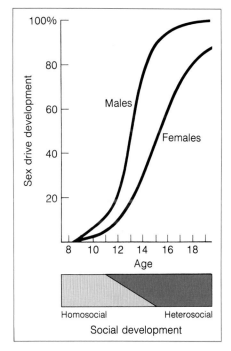

Figure 10-9
Sex Drive and Social Development
The curves in the top part of the figure give the cumulative percentages by age of individuals who have experienced the onset of the sex drive. The bar graph at the bottom indicates the approximate course of adolescent development from a homosocial to a heterosocial environment. (After Storms, 1981)

shaping the remaining tissue into a vagina and labia. For women, hormone treatments can increase beard growth, firm muscles, and deepen the voice; surgical procedures involve removing the ovaries and the uterus, reducing breast tissue, and, in some instances, constructing a penislike organ. Although a sex-change operation does not alter the individual's genetic sex or make reproduction possible, it can produce a remarkable change in the person's physical appearance.

Because sex-change surgery is so drastic, it is undertaken only after careful consideration. The individual is usually given counseling and hormone treatments and is required to live as a member of the opposite sex for a year or more prior to the operation. Expert opinion remains divided as to whether sex-change surgery results in better adjustment for transsexual individuals (Hunt and Hampson, 1980).

What explains transsexualism? An interesting speculation is that some cases of transsexualism may result from a prenatal hormonal error similar to the one producing hermaphrodites that occurs at a later stage of fetal development. If such an error were to occur after the formation of the external genitals but before the complete development of the brain mechanisms that influence sexual behavior, the individual's sense of sexual identity could be out of phase with his or her physical sex. This theory is only speculation, however. It seems reasonable to assume that both biological and social factors play a role in transsexualism (Money, 1980).

OTHER BASIC MOTIVES

Thirst

In order to survive, organisms must regulate their water intake as well as their food intake. An organism can subsist without food for weeks but cannot live without water for more than a few days.

An organism can replenish its water deficit in two ways—by drinking and by recovering water from the kidneys before it is excreted as urine. A water deficit motivates the organism to drink and also sets off a homeostatic mechanism by stimulating the release of the antidiuretic hormone (ADH) from the pituitary gland. ADH regulates the kidneys so that water is reabsorbed into the bloodstream and only very concentrated urine is formed. (After a night's sleep, you may notice that your urine is a darker color and has a stronger odor than it does at other times of the day; your body has recovered water from your kidneys to compensate for the fact that you have not consumed fluids while you were sleeping.) This homeostatic mechanism can maintain the body's water balance only to a certain point, however. When the water deficit is too great, thirst becomes intense and the organism is impelled to find water. What signals the organism that the body needs water?

A water deficit decreases the volume of both the blood and the fluids surrounding the body cells and increases the concentration of certain chemicals in these fluids (primarily sodium). When the body fluids surrounding the tissue cells become too concentrated, water passes from the cells by osmosis, leaving them dehydrated. Current theories postulate that two types of nerve cells in the brain control water intake: *osmoreceptors*, which are sensitive to the chemical concentration of the body fluids, and *volumetric receptors*, which are responsive to the total volume of the body fluids.

Although cellular dehydration occurs in all body cells, osmoreceptors (located in the hypothalamus just above the pituitary gland) respond specifically to dehydration, becoming slightly deformed or shriveled. This mechanical change triggers neural activity that stimulates the release of ADH from the pituitary gland. This hormone in turn signals the kidneys to reabsorb water from urine into the bloodstream, where it dilutes the chemical concentration of the blood and body fluids.

Loss of blood volume produces thirst even in the absence of cellular dehydration. An injured person who has lost a considerable amount of blood is extremely thirsty, although the chemical concentration of the remaining blood is unchanged. An individual engaged in vigorous activity loses salt through perspiration but still has the urge to drink a lot of water, which dilutes the salt concentration of the blood even more. There must be receptors that are sensitive to the total volume of blood and body fluids, regardless of their concentration.

Evidence indicates that *renin* (a substance secreted from the kidneys into the bloodstream) induces thirst in response to a decrease in the volume of blood and body fluids. Renin causes the blood vessels to constrict—a homeostatic device that prevents further blood loss. Renin also acts as an enzyme, converting one of the blood proteins, *angiotensinogen*, to angiotensin I. As blood passes through the lungs, angiotensin I is converted to angiotensin II, which acts on specific receptors in the hypothalamus to produce thirst. If angiotensin II is injected directly into the hypothalamus of animals, they drink copious amounts of water.

Our survey of research on thirst has been brief; nevertheless, some readers may be surprised that it received even this amount of coverage in a book on psychology. Because thirst is a drive that can be precisely manipulated in animals, it is ideal for experimental work. Many general principles and theories of motivation are based on animal research using thirst as a primary drive (Rolls and Rolls, 1982).

Avoidance of pain

The need to avoid tissue damage is essential to the survival of any organism. Even a weak pain stimulus may override other stimuli to control the direction of the organism's behavior. Pain will activate behaviors that reduce discomfort—removing a hand from a hot stove, taking off a shoe that pinches, swallowing an aspirin to relieve a headache.

The motivational aspects of pain depend on normal growth experiences. Dogs raised from birth with severely restricted sensory stimulation fail to show the normal avoidance reaction to painful stimuli; they do not respond to being pricked with a pin or having their tails stepped on and will repeatedly investigate a lighted match by putting their nose into the flame (Scott, 1968).

Some physiological conditions are aversive: they produce discomfort or pain and motivate the organism to take action to remedy the situation. Extremes of temperature, suffocation, the accumulation of excessive waste products in the body, and fatigue all activate the organism. Sometimes the physiological basis of a drive is acquired. Drug dependency provides an example. Initially, an individual has no physiological need for heroin, but continued use of the drug creates an imperative need for it and all of the individual's actions become determined by this need. Deprived of heroin, the individual becomes restless and develops symptoms of acute illness that can be relieved only by the drug.

Maternal behavior

In many species, care of the offspring is a more powerful determiner of behavior than hunger, thirst, or sex. For example, a mother rat will more frequently overcome barriers and suffer pain to reach its young than it will to obtain food when hungry or water when thirsty.

Maternal behavior among lower animals appears to depend on hormones as well as on environmental conditions. Virgin rats presented with rat pups for about a week will begin to build a nest, lick the pups, retrieve them, and finally hover in a nursing posture. If blood plasma from a mother rat that has just given birth is injected into a virgin rat, it will begin to exhibit maternal behavior in less than a day (Terkel and Rosenblatt, 1972). Maternal behavior patterns appear to be innately programmed in the rat's brain, and hormones serve to increase the excitability of these neural mechanisms. The hormonal effects depend on the balance between the female hormones (estrogen and progesterone) and prolactin from the anterior pituitary gland, which is involved in the production of milk.

Among primates, maternal behavior is largely influenced by experience and learning. Monkeys raised in isolation with cloth or wire mothers exhibit none of the normal maternal behaviors when they first become mothers (see Chapter 3). With subsequent pregnancies, however, they become more effective mothers.

Although a maternal instinct has been posited as universal among human females, the evidence does not support this belief. Some women abandon their newborn infants or even kill them, and battered children are more commonplace than many people realize. It is estimated that in the United States each year, over 1,000 children are killed by their parents and an additional 50,000 or more children are seriously beaten or tortured by parents, siblings, or other relatives. The parents involved in these cases generally received little or no love as children and frequently were beaten by their own parents. There is a parallel here between humans raised by inadequate parents and the monkeys that were raised by artificial mothers and subsequently became inadequate mothers themselves. In primates and in humans, experience far overrides whatever influence "maternal hormones" may have.

Curiosity and stimulus-seeking

Thus far, all of the motives discussed in this chapter have been affected by the physiological condition of the organism to some degree. As we noted earlier, the drive-reduction theory of motivation explains behavior as attempts to reduce drives created by bodily needs; the organism seeks to reduce the drive and return the body to its normal physiological state. This homeostatic model provides a useful conception of motives based on deprivation (hunger and thirst) and aversive stimulation (pain) but seems less appropriate as a description of sexual and maternal behavior.

According to drive-reduction theory, an organism that has satisfied its biological needs should be in a quiescent state. But the evidence indicates that

Young monkeys "monkeying"

both people and animals are motivated to *seek* stimulation—to actively explore their environment even when the activity satisfies no bodily need.

EXPLORATION AND MANIPULATION A form of exploratory activity is the manipulation or investigation of objects. We give babies rattles, crib gymnasiums, and other toys because we know they like to hold, shake, and pull them. Monkeys enjoy the same sort of activities; in fact, the word *monkey* used as a verb describes casual manipulation for whatever satisfaction it brings. A number of experiments have shown that monkeys do indeed like to "monkey." If various mechanical devices are placed in a monkey's cage, it will begin to take them apart, becoming more skilled with practice, without receiving any evident reward other than the satisfaction of manipulating them. If the monkey is fed each time it takes a puzzle apart, its behavior changes; it loses interest in manipulation and views the puzzle as a means of acquiring food (Harlow, Harlow, and Meyer, 1950).

Sometimes objects are manipulated for the purpose of *investigation*: the organism picks up the object, looks at it, tears it apart, and examines the parts, apparently attempting to discover more about it. Piaget has made a number of observations bearing on such responses in the early life of the human infant. Within the first few months of life, an infant learns to pull a string to activate a hanging rattle—a form of manipulation that might be considered merely entertaining. Between 5 and 7 months, the infant will remove a cloth from his or her face in anticipation of the peekaboo game. At 8–10 months, the infant begins to look for objects behind or beneath other objects; by 11 months, the infant begins to experiment with objects, varying their placement or position (Piaget, 1952). This kind of inquisitive or investigative behavior is typical of the growing child. We might call it *curiosity* or the individual's need to cope with his or her environment. In any event, this behavior seems to develop as a motive apart from any physiological needs of the organism.

NEED FOR SENSORY STIMULATION Exploration and manipulation provide new and changing sensory input. The need for such input has been demonstrated by studies in which sensory stimulation is markedly reduced. In the first study of this type, college students were paid to lie on a cot in a lighted, partially sound-deadened room. They wore translucent goggles so that they could see diffuse light but no shapes or patterns. Gloves and cardboard cuffs reduced tactile stimulation (see Figure 10-10). The hum of an exhaust fan and an air conditioner provided a constant masking noise. Brief "time outs" were allowed for meals and toilet needs, but otherwise the subjects remained in a condition of very restricted stimulation. After two or three days, most of the subjects refused to continue the experiment; the situation was sufficiently intolerable to negate even a large financial payment.

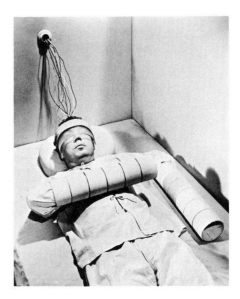

Some of the subjects began to experience visual hallucinations that varied from light flashes and geometric patterns to dreamlike scenes. They became disoriented in time and space, were unable to think clearly or concentrate for any length of time, and did poorly when given problems to solve. In short, the condition of *sensory deprivation* had a detrimental effect on functioning and produced symptoms not unlike those experienced by some mental patients (Heron, Doane, and Scott, 1956).

A number of similar studies have subsequently been conducted. In some studies, subjects lay immersed to the neck in a tub of warm water for several days in an attempt to reduce sensory stimulation further. Results have differed somewhat, depending on the procedure, but in most instances, the subjects

Figure 10-10
Sensory Deprivation Experiment
Cardboard cuffs and a translucent blindfold reduce stimulation.

soon became bored, restless, irritable, and emotionally upset. People require change in stimulation and react adversely to its absence (Zubek, 1969).

SENSATION SEEKING   Individuals have a need to seek variety in sensations and experiences and will take risks for the sake of such experiences. To measure this need, Zuckerman (1979) has developed a test called the *Sensation Seeking Scale*, abbreviated SSS. The scale includes a range of items designed to assess an individual's desire to engage in risky or adventurous activities, seek new kinds of sensory experiences, enjoy the excitement of social stimulation, and avoid boredom. Table 10-4 presents a sample of some of the items on the scale; you may want to answer them before reading further.

Research using the SSS has revealed large individual differences in sensation seeking (Carrol, Zuckerman, and Vogel, 1982). Moreover, sensation seeking appears to be a trait that is consistent across a variety of situations; individ-

Table 10-4
Sensation Seeking Scale
A sample of items from the SSS and a scoring procedure. Each item contains two choices. Choose the one that best describes your likes or feelings. If you do not like either choice, mark the choice you dislike the least. Do not leave any items blank. (Test items courtesy of Marvin Zuckerman)

1. A. I have no patience with dull or boring persons.
   B. I find something interesting in almost every person I talk to.
2. A. A good painting should shock or jolt the senses.
   B. A good painting should provide a feeling of peace and security.
3. A. People who ride motorcycles must have some kind of unconscious need to hurt themselves.
   B. I would like to drive or ride a motorcycle.
4. A. I would prefer living in an ideal society in which everyone is safe, secure, and happy.
   B. I would have preferred living in the unsettled days of history.
5. A. I sometimes like to do things that are a little frightening.
   B. A sensible person avoids dangerous activities.
6. A. I would not like to be hypnotized.
   B. I would like to be hypnotized.
7. A. The most important goal of life is to live to the fullest and experience as much as possible.
   B. The most important goal of life is to find peace and happiness.
8. A. I would like to try parachute jumping.
   B. I would never want to try jumping from a plane, with or without a parachute.
9. A. I enter cold water gradually, giving myself time to get used to it.
   B. I like to dive or jump right into the ocean or a cold pool.
10. A. When I go on a vacation, I prefer the comfort of a good room and bed.
    B. When I go on a vacation, I prefer the change of camping out.
11. A. I prefer people who are emotionally expressive even if they are a bit unstable.
    B. I prefer people who are calm and even-tempered.
12. A. I would prefer a job in one location.
    B. I would like a job that requires traveling.
13. A. I can't wait to get indoors on a cold day.
    B. I am invigorated by a brisk, cold day.
14. A. I get bored seeing the same faces.
    B. I like the comfortable familiarity of everyday friends.

Scoring:

Count one point for each of the following items that you have circled: 1A, 2A, 3B, 4B, 5A, 6B, 7A, 8A, 9B, 10B, 11A, 12B, 13B, 14A. Add your total for sensation seeking and compare it with the norms below:

0–3 Very low	6–9 Average	12–14 Very high
4–5 Low	10–11 High	

uals who report enjoying new experiences in one area of life tend to describe themselves as adventurous in other areas. High scores on the SSS have been found to be related to a number of behavioral characteristics: engaging in risky sports, occupations, or hobbies (parachuting, motorcycle riding, fire fighting, scuba salvage diving); seeking variety in sexual and drug experiences; behaving fearlessly in common phobic situations (heights, darkness, snakes); taking risks when gambling; and preferring exotic foods. Even when asked to describe their normal driving habits, high-sensation seekers report driving at faster speeds than low-sensation seekers (see Figure 10-11).

Variations in sensation seeking can influence the way in which individuals react to each other. High-sensation seekers may feel that low-sensation seekers are boring and lead restricted lives; conversely, low-sensation seekers may feel that high-sensation seekers are engaged in unproductive and foolhardy activities. These attitudes can be important in the choice of marital partners. There is a significant correlation between the SSS scores of husbands and wives; high-sensation seekers tend to marry highs, and low-sensation seekers tend to marry lows. Compatibility on this trait is a predictor of marital adjustment (Fisher, Zuckerman, and Neeb, 1981). If one partner has a very high SSS score and the other has a very low SSS score, the likelihood of marital disharmony increases; this is particularly true when the female partner's SSS score is high. The high-sensation seeker may find the low-sensation seeker uninteresting and confining. But why should this difference be more significant when the female is the high-sensation seeker? Perhaps there are more outlets for sensation seeking outside of marriage for the husband than for the wife. Perhaps the cultural expectation that the male should assume the leadership role in a marriage presents problems when the wife is more inclined to seek new experiences.

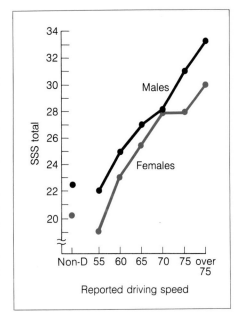

Figure 10-11
SSS Scores and Driving Speed
Subjects were asked at what speed they would usually drive on a highway if driving conditions were good and the posted speed limit was 55 mph. Results revealed a significant relationship between reported driving speed and SSS score. Nondrivers (Non-D) and those who drove at or below the speed limit had the lowest SSS scores; scores increased with each increment in driving speed. The sex difference observed in this study is generally the case; males typically score higher on the SSS than females. (After Zuckerman and Neeb, 1980).

CURRENT STATUS
OF MOTIVATIONAL CONCEPTS

Now that we have examined a number of motives, what can we say about the various theories of motivation described at the beginning of this chapter? No one theory provides a complete explanation of the full complexity of human behavior. Biological needs are powerful instigators of action because their satisfaction is essential to the survival of the organism and/or the survival of the species. We tend to be less aware of biological needs in our highly industrialized and affluent society, but the actions of people who do not know where to find their next scrap of food or how to protect themselves from the cold are dominated by biological needs. Other, more distinctly human motives—including motives related to our feelings of self-esteem and social motives concerned with our relationships with other people—become important only after our basic biological needs are satisfied.

In Chapter 11, we will consider some psychological motives that, as far as we know, are unrelated to biological needs and are acquired through experience—particularly the experience of living with other people. Originally, drive-reduction theorists attempted to explain *all* motivated acts as the result of biological needs. Thus, the motive to achieve was traced to the hunger drive and the motive to affiliate with others was based on the sex drive. But this approach has not added much to our understanding of complex human behavior.

Many psychologists have rejected the concepts of drive and homeostasis in favor of the concept of *arousal level*. The organism's state of arousal or activation can range from sleep and lethargy to alertness and intense excitement. Theoretically, there is an optimal level of arousal in terms of internal and external stimuli. Conditions that depart too severely from this optimal state in either direction incite the organism to act to restore the equilibrium. Arousal level can be affected by such internal drives as hunger and sex or by such external stimuli as the aroma of delicious food or the loud clang of a bell. The concept of an optimal level of arousal provides a fairly simple framework in which to view the results of experiments on exploration, manipulation, and sensory deprivation. Too little stimulation or boredom can motivate the organism just as much as too intense or dramatic a change in stimulation can. We seek novelty and complexity in our environment, but situations that are too strange or too complex arouse anxiety. We will say more about arousal level when we consider emotion in the next chapter.

Summary

1   Motivation refers to the factors that *energize* and *direct* behavior. Attempts to explain motivated acts have had various emphases:
    a   *Instinct theory* postulates innate predispositions to specific actions.
    b   *Drive-reduction theory* bases motivation on bodily *needs* that create a state of tension or *drive*; the organism then seeks to reduce the drive by doing something to satisfy the need. Biological needs prompt action because the body tends to maintain a constant internal environment, or *homeostasis*.
    c   *Incentive theory* emphasizes the importance of external conditions as a source of motivation. These conditions may be *positive incentives*, which the organism will approach, or *negative incentives*, which the organism will avoid. Incentives can arouse behavior as well as direct it.
2   Important brain areas in the regulation of food intake are the *lateral hypothalamus* (LH), or "feeding center," and the *ventromedial hypothalamus* (VMH), or "satiety center," which act reciprocally to maintain stable body weight. Both centers contain receptors that respond to stomach distension, glucose level in the blood, and body temperature to effect short-term control of eating.
3   Research on obesity suggests that overweight individuals may be more responsive than normal-weight individuals to external hunger cues, such as the taste and smell of food or the fact that it is mealtime. Overweight individuals also tend to eat more when they are emotionally aroused. Some of these differences may result from the fact that overweight people are usually dieting. The eating behavior of normal-weight individuals who are dieting and therefore classified as "restrained eaters" is similar to the eating behavior of obese people.
4   A comparison of methods for treating obesity suggests that an overweight individual can achieve a short-term weight loss in a variety of ways. However, the ability to keep weight off permanently depends on establishing self-control over eating habits and, in turn, over the total number of calories consumed. Behavior modification appears to be an effective method of gaining control over eating habits.
5   Sexual behavior in the lower animals is largely instinctive and is controlled by hormones that prime the organism to respond to stimuli emanating from animals of the opposite sex. The female hormones (*estrogen* and *progesterone*)

are secreted by the ovaries; the male hormones (*androgens*) are secreted by the testes. These hormones are also important in determining whether the fetus develops into a male or a female. The *posterior hypothalamus* appears to be the brain area most involved in sexual behavior.

6 Among human beings, hormones exert less influence on sexual behavior than either early experiences with parents and peers or cultural norms. Although attitudes toward sexual behavior are becoming increasingly permissive in Western society, men and women still differ in their views on sex. Sexual interactions with members of the same sex are common during childhood, but only a small percentage of people become exclusively *homosexual*. *Homosexuality* and *transsexualism* probably result from any of a number of psychological and social factors.

7 Other motives that are influenced by the physiological condition of the organism are *thirst, avoidance of pain,* and *maternal behavior*. In lower animals, maternal behavior appears to be controlled by innately programmed responses that are triggered by the changes in female hormones during pregnancy. In primates and human beings, however, experiences with parents play a major role in maternal behavior. Even the motivational aspects of pain depend to some extent on normal growth experiences.

8 *Curiosity*—the tendency to explore new environments and to investigate or manipulate interesting objects—seems to develop as a motive apart from any physiological needs of the organism. Research on *sensory deprivation* and *sensation seeking* demonstrates the importance of an individual's need for new and changing sensory input.

9 The concept of *arousal level* is central to current theories of motivation. Internal or external stimulation that produces too large a change from the optimal arousal level motivates the organism to do something to restore equilibrium.

Further Reading

Summaries of research and theory on motivation may be found in Bolles, *Theory of motivation* (2nd ed., 1975); Atkinson and Birch, *An introduction to motivation* (1978); Beck, *Motivation: Theories and principles* (1978); and Petri, *Motivation: Theory and research* (1981). A review of ethology is presented in Lorenz, *The foundations of ethology* (1981).

An interesting book that offers suggestions on the control of eating through behavior modification is Mahoney and Mahoney, *Permanent weight control* (1976). For a review of research on obesity, see Stunkard (ed.), *Obesity* (1980).

Research on sexuality is presented in Money and Musaph (eds.) *Handbook of sexology* (1977); Hyde, *Understanding human sexuality* (1979); and Offir, *Human sexuality* (1982).

11
MOTIVATION
AND EMOTION

Why does a scientist spend long hours at work in the laboratory, foregoing other activities and pleasures? Why does an athlete endure months of painful training in preparation for Olympic competition? Why does one person devote all efforts to amassing a fortune; another, to working with impoverished peoples in a remote and primitive region? Obviously, biological needs cannot begin to account for the diversity and complexity of human behavior.

It is true that an infant's early behavior is largely determined by basic biological needs: a child cries when hungry, cold, or in pain. But as the child grows, new motives appear that are learned by interacting with other people. We will call them *psychological motives* to distinguish them from motives based on physiological needs. Security, acceptance by and approval from those around us, feelings of self-worth and competency, and the search for new experiences are important psychological motives, although the way in which they are satisfied varies with each individual and culture. The distinction between biological and psychological motives is not a clear-cut one. In Chapter 10, we noted that biological motives can be aroused by external incentives and that learning to some extent determines the way such needs as hunger and sex are satisfied. Psychological motives are influenced *primarily* by the kind of society in which the individual is raised; they are only indirectly related to the physiological needs of the organism.

Abraham Maslow, a leader in the development of humanistic psychology (see Chapter 1), proposed an interesting way of classifying human motives. Maslow constructed a *hierarchy of needs*, ascending from the basic biological needs to the more complex psychological motives that become important only after the basic needs have been satisfied (see Figure 11-1). The needs at one level must be at least partially satisfied before those at the next level become important determiners of action. When food and safety are difficult to obtain, the satisfaction of those needs will dominate a person's actions and higher motives are of little significance. Only when basic needs can be satisfied easily will the individual have the time and energy to devote to aesthetic and intellectual

317

Figure 11-1
Maslow's Hierarchy of Needs
Needs that are low in the hierarchy must be at least partially satisfied before needs that are higher in the hierarchy become important sources of motivation. (After Maslow, 1954)

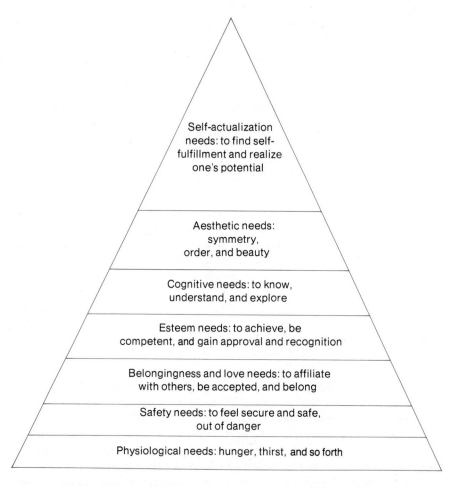

Self-actualization needs: to find self-fulfillment and realize one's potential

Aesthetic needs: symmetry, order, and beauty

Cognitive needs: to know, understand, and explore

Esteem needs: to achieve, be competent, and gain approval and recognition

Belongingness and love needs: to affiliate with others, be accepted, and belong

Safety needs: to feel secure and safe, out of danger

Physiological needs: hunger, thirst, and so forth

interests. Artistic and scientific endeavors do not flourish in societies where people must struggle for food, shelter, and safety.

Maslow's hierarchy provides an interesting way of looking at the relationships among human motives and the opportunities afforded by the environment. We will have more to say about Maslow's highest motive—*self-actualization*—when we discuss personality in Chapter 13.

Many theories have been proposed to explain human motivation, but as yet there is little consensus. In this chapter, we will concentrate on two theories that adopt very different views concerning human nature—*psychoanalytic theory* and *social learning theory*. We will then examine a specific area of motivated behavior—aggression—and explain aggressive behavior within the framework of each theory.

Motivation and emotion are closely related. Feelings determine our actions, and conversely, our behavior often determines how we feel. Later in the chapter, we will discuss the ways in which we experience and express emotions and how emotion influences our behavior.

THEORIES OF MOTIVATION

According to Freud's *psychoanalytic theory*, our actions are determined by inner forces and impulses that often operate at an unconscious level. In contrast, *social learning theory* maintains that our behavior is learned through interaction with and observation of the environment.

Psychoanalytic theory

Psychoanalysis, in addition to being a method for treating mental disorders (see Chapter 16), is also a theory of human motivation. Psychoanalytic theory began with the publication of Freud's *Interpretation of Dreams* (1900) and has evolved gradually. A complete exposition of psychoanalytic theory would require a lengthy discussion of its numerous changes. For our purposes, a broad outline of the theory will suffice.

INSTINCTUAL DRIVES   Freud believed that all behavior stems from two opposing groups of instincts: the *life instincts,* which enhance the individual's life and growth, and the *death instincts,* which push the individual toward destruction. The energy of the life instincts is *libido,* which revolves primarily around sexual activities. The death instincts can be directed inward in the form of suicide or other self-destructive behavior or outward in the form of aggression toward others. Freud therefore believed that sex and aggression were the two basic motives of human behavior. He was not unaware of the importance of physiological needs or of the influence of fear on behavior, but these factors played little part in his theory.

According to Freud, the forerunners of sexual and aggressive behavior are found early in a child's life. Sex is expressed in the pleasure derived from stimulating the sensitive regions of the body (see psychosexual stages of development, page 397); aggression is expressed in biting or hitting. When parents place taboos on both sex and aggression, the free expression of these motives becomes *repressed;* instead of finding full conscious expression, they remain active as *unconscious motives.* Sex is usually more severely repressed than aggression, but the expression of either motive may make the child anxious due to negative parental attitudes. Unconscious motives then find expression in disguised form. The concept of *unconscious motivation* is one of the cornerstones of psychoanalytic theory.

BEHAVIOR FROM WHICH UNCONSCIOUS MOTIVES ARE INFERRED   Although writers and philosophers had long recognized the existence of some unconscious controls over human conduct, Freud was the first to call attention to the powerful role unconscious motives play in human behavior. He specified several forms of behavior through which unconscious motives are expressed:

1   In dreams, we often express unconscious wishes and impulses.
2   Unconscious mannerisms and slips of speech may ''let the cat out of the bag'' and reveal hidden motives.
3   Symptoms of illness (particularly the symptoms of mental illnesses) often can be shown to serve the unconscious needs of the person.

Most psychologists have some reservations about Freud's theory of unconscious motivation. They agree that unconscious motives (or at least motives that are unclear to the person) may exist, but they prefer to think in terms of *degrees of awareness.* A person may be vaguely aware, for example, of the need to dominate others but may not realize the extent to which this need influences his or her behavior.

Interpreting dreams is difficult; very little is known about what the content of dreams supposedly symbolizes. Slips of speech may reveal unconscious

Vicarious learning

motives but just as often may point to motives the speaker is aware of but wishes to keep hidden. Think, for example, of the person who says to an unwelcome visitor, "I'm sad you came," when what was intended was, "I'm glad you came." We can acknowledge that often we may not be fully aware of why we behave the way we do without assuming that our motives are always unconscious.

Social learning theory

Social learning theory emphasizes the interaction between behavior and environment, focusing on behavior patterns that the individual develops to cope with the environment rather than on instinctual drives. We are not driven by internal forces, nor are we passive reactors to external stimulation. The type of behavior we exhibit partly determines the reward or punishment we receive, and this in turn influences our behavior.

Patterns of behavior can be acquired by direct experience or by observing the responses of others. Some responses may be successful; others may produce unfavorable results. Through this process of *differential reinforcement*, the person eventually selects the successful behavior patterns and discards the others.

Social learning theorists differ from strict behaviorists in that they stress the importance of *cognitive processes*. Because we can think and represent situations symbolically, we are able to foresee the probable consequences of our actions and alter our behavior accordingly. Our actions are governed to a large extent by *anticipated consequences*. We do not wait until we have experienced frostbite before we decide to wear warm gloves in freezing weather. Anticipated consequences (represented symbolically in a person's thoughts) can motivate behavior in much the same way actual consequences can.

VICARIOUS LEARNING   Social learning theory also stresses the importance of *vicarious learning*, or learning by observation. Many behavior patterns are learned by watching the behavior of others and observing what consequences it produces for them. Emotions can also be learned vicariously by watching the emotional responses of others as they undergo painful or pleasant experiences. A child who observes the pained expressions of an older sibling in the dentist's chair will probably be fearful when the time comes for his or her first dental appointment. Social learning theorists emphasize the role of *models* in transmitting both specific behaviors and emotional responses. And they have concentrated much of their research on discovering how modeled behavior is transmitted—what types of model are most effective and what factors determine whether the modeled behavior that is learned will actually be performed.

SELF-REGULATION   Another emphasis of social learning theory is the importance of *self-regulatory processes*. A specific behavior produces an external outcome, but it also produces a *self-evaluative reaction.* People set their own standards of conduct or performance and respond to their behavior in self-satisfied or self-critical ways, depending on how the behavior relates to their standards. Thus, reinforcement can be external or internal (self-evaluative). Sometimes these two sources of reinforcement coincide, and sometimes they are contradictory. A person may be rewarded socially or financially for behavior that is not acceptable according to his or her self-standards. Indeed, self-reproach is an important influence in motivating people to adhere to accepted standards of conduct in the face of opposing influences. For example, a person is tempted to cheat on an income tax return. The chances of getting caught (external punishment) may be slim and the financial gain may be substantial, but the anticipation of feelings of self-contempt prevent the individual from taking the action. The behavior is not in accord with self-standards.

External reinforcement is most effective when it is consistent with self-reinforcement—when society approves of actions that the individual values highly. An artist whose works are enthusiastically received by the public and the critics will probably be more motivated to work than an artist whose creative endeavors are appreciated by neither group. An individual must believe in his or her personal standards to persevere when external reinforcement is lacking.

Social learning theorists have been active in developing procedures that enable people to control their own behavior by self-reinforcement or self-punishment. Successful behavior-modification methods include the control of alcohol abuse and overeating by allowing individuals to reward themselves when they adhere to a certain regimen of drinking or eating (see Table 16-1).

We will explore both psychoanalytic theory and social learning theory further in Chapters 13 and 16 in conjunction with views on personality and the treatment of abnormal behavior, respectively. The contrast between these two theoretical approaches will be clearer if we explain one area of motivated behavior from the standpoint of each theory. Several motivational systems, such as the need for achievement or the need for affiliation, could be discussed, but some of the most interesting work has been done in the area of aggression. The need to understand what instigates aggression and how to control it is one of the most crucial problems facing society. In an age when powerful weapons are easily available, a single aggressive act can produce disastrous consequences.

MOTIVATIONAL FACTORS IN AGGRESSION

Aggression is usually defined as behavior that is intended to injure another person (physically or verbally) or to destroy property. The key word in this definition is *intent*. If someone accidentally steps on your toes in a crowded elevator and immediately apologizes, you are not likely to label the behavior aggressive. If someone walks up as you sit at your desk studying and stomps on your foot, you are apt to be outraged at such a blatantly aggressive act. But even intentionally aggressive acts can serve a goal other than that of inflicting injury. Power, wealth, and status are only a few of the ends that can be attained by aggressive means.

Some psychologists distinguish between *hostile aggression*, which is committed for the sole purpose of inflicting injury, and *instrumental aggression*, which is aimed at obtaining rewards other than the victim's suffering. Instrumental aggression includes fighting in self-defense, assaulting someone during a robbery, or fighting to prove one's power and dominance. But the distinction between hostile and instrumental aggression is not a clear-cut one. What appears to be a case of hostile aggression may serve other ends: a gang member who attacks an innocent passerby (on the surface, a case of hostile aggression) may be motivated by a need to gain status with the gang. A theory of aggression should account for both hostile and instrumental aggression.

Aggression as a drive

Freud viewed aggression as a basic instinct. The energy of the *death instincts* builds up within the organism until it must be discharged—either outwardly

Hostile or instrumental aggression?

in the form of overt aggression or inwardly in the form of self-destructive acts. Freud was pessimistic about the possibility of ever eliminating aggression; at best, its intensity could be modified by promoting positive emotional attachments between people and by providing substitute outlets (such as watching prizefights or engaging in sports).

Freud expressed his views on aggression in a letter written to Albert Einstein in 1932. Einstein, concerned with the efforts of the League of Nations to promote world peace, asked Freud for his opinions on why people engage in war. Is it possible, Einstein inquired, that human beings have a "lust for hatred and destruction?" Freud replied:

> You express astonishment at the fact that it is so easy to make men enthusiastic about a war and add your suspicion that there is something at work in them—an instinct for hatred and destruction—which goes halfway to meet the efforts of warmongers. I can only express my entire agreement. We believe in an instinct of that kind and have in fact been occupied during the last few years in studying its manifestations. The death instinct turns into the destructive instinct. It is directed outwards, onto objects. The living creature preserves its own life, so to say, by destroying an extraneous one (1963, p. 41).

Later theorists in the Freudian tradition rejected the idea that aggression was an innate drive or instinct and proposed that it was a frustration-produced drive. The *frustration-aggression hypothesis* assumes that thwarting a person's efforts to reach a goal induces an aggressive drive that in turn motivates behavior designed to injure the person or object causing the frustration (Dollard and others, 1939). The expression of aggression reduces the drive. Aggression is the dominant response to frustration, but other responses can occur if aggression has been punished in the past. By this formulation, aggression is not inborn. But since frustration is a fairly universal condition, aggression is still a drive that must find an outlet.

The idea of an aggressive drive is popular because we tend to view violence (particularly interpersonal violence) as a sudden, explosive, irrational type of behavior—as if some sort of aggressive energy had built up until it had to find an outlet. Newspaper and TV accounts of crimes tend to encourage this view. Some hideously brutal crimes have been committed by individuals who were reportedly very meek, quiet, and conforming until their outburst.

More often, however, the assailant's background is not as innocent as accounts would have us believe. In the 1960s, for example, a University of Texas student, positioned himself in the campus bell tower and shot as many people as he could until he was finally gunned down. Newspaper reports described him as a model American youth—a former altar boy and Eagle Scout. Sub-

A wild bull charges Dr. José Delgado, who is armed only with a cape and a radio transmitter (left photo). When he presses the transmitter, the bull abruptly stops his attack (right photo). The radio transmitter sends a mild current to electrodes implanted in specific areas of the bull's brain.

sequent investigation revealed, however, that his life was replete with aggressive acts, including assaults on his wife and others, a court-martial as a marine recruit for insubordination and fighting, and a passion for collecting firearms. With the exception of some psychotic individuals who may be driven to violent acts by delusional beliefs, most people who commit aggressive acts have a history of aggressive behavior.

BIOLOGICAL BASIS OF AGGRESSION Some evidence for a biologically based aggressive drive comes from studies showing that mild electrical stimulation of a specific region of the hypothalamus produces aggressive behavior in animals. When a cat's hypothalamus is stimulated via implanted electrodes, the animal hisses, its hair bristles, its pupils dilate, and it will strike at a rat or other objects placed in its cage. Stimulation of a different area of the hypothalamus produces quite different behavior: instead of exhibiting any of these "rage" responses, the cat coldly stalks and kills a rat.

Similar techniques have produced aggressive behavior in monkeys and rats. A laboratory-bred rat that has never killed a mouse or seen a wild rat killing one may live quite peacefully in the same cage with a mouse. But if the rat's hypothalamus is stimulated with certain neurochemicals, the animal will pounce on its mouse cage-mate and kill it with exactly the same response pattern exhibited by a wild rat (a hard bite to the neck that severs the spinal cord). It is as if the stimulation triggers an innate killing response that has previously remained dormant. Conversely, if a neurochemical blocker is injected into the same brain site in rats that spontaneously kill mice on sight, the rats become temporarily peaceful (Smith, King, and Hoebel, 1970).

In higher mammals, such instinctive aggressive patterns are controlled by the cortex and therefore are more influenced by experience. Monkeys living in groups establish a dominance hierarchy: one or two males become leaders, and the others assume various levels of subordination. When the hypothalamus of a dominant monkey is electrically stimulated, the monkey attacks subordinate males but not females. The same stimulation of a low-ranking monkey produces cowering and submissive behavior (see Figure 11-2). Thus, aggressive behavior is not automatically elicited by stimulation of the hypothalamus. The hypothalamus may send a message to the cortex indicating that its "aggression center" has been activated; but the cortex, in choosing the response it will initiate, considers what is going on in the environment and its memory of past experiences.

Like the lower animals, humans are equipped with neurological mechanisms that enable them to behave aggressively, but the activation of these mechanisms is under *cognitive control*. Some brain-damaged individuals may react aggressively to stimulation that normally would not instigate aggressive behavior; in these cases, cortical control is impaired. But in normal individuals, the frequency with which aggressive behavior is expressed, the forms it takes, and the situations in which it is displayed are determined largely by learning and social influences.

Aggression as a learned response

Social learning theory rejects the concept of aggression as an instinct or a frustration-produced drive and proposes that aggression is no different from any other learned response. Aggression can be learned through observation or imitation, and the more often it is reinforced, the more likely it is to occur. A person who is frustrated by a blocked goal or disturbed by some stressful event

Figure 11-2
Brain Stimulation and Aggression
A mild electrical current is delivered to electrodes implanted in the monkey's hypothalamus via remote radio control. The animal's response (attack or flight) depends on its position in the dominance hierarchy of the colony. (Courtesy Dr. José Delgado)

experiences unpleasant emotional arousal. The response that this emotional arousal elicits will differ, depending on the kinds of responses the individual has learned to use in coping with stressful situations. The frustrated individual may seek help from others, aggress, withdraw, try even harder to surmount the obstacle, or anesthetize him- or herself with drugs or alcohol. The response will be the one that has relieved frustration most successfully in the past. According to this view, frustration provokes aggression mainly in people who have learned to respond to aversive situations with aggressive attitudes and behavior (Bandura, 1977). Figure 11-3 shows how social learning theory differs from psychoanalytic theory and drive theory (the frustration-aggression hypothesis) in conceptualizing the motivational components of aggression.

In the social learning formulation, aversive experiences lead to emotional arousal. Frustration in the form of blocked goal seeking is one such experience, but there are others. Physical discomfort, for example, also increases emotional arousal and may lead to aggression if cues for eliciting aggressive behavior are present. In one study, subjects who were required to work on a task in a hot, stuffy room showed no more aggression than subjects who worked under cool conditions. However, after both groups observed an aggressive model, the overheated subjects became more aggressive than their comfortable counterparts (Baron and Lawton, 1972).

Even arousal that is *not* the result of unpleasant stimulation can increase aggression in the presence of aggression-provoking stimuli. For example, subjects who were aroused by vigorous physical exercise were more aggressive toward a person who had previously angered them than subjects who had not exercised. But aggression toward a person who had not angered the subjects did not increase after strenuous activity (Zillmann, Katcher, and Milavsky, 1972). Men who were sexually aroused by viewing erotic films were more aggressive toward someone who had previously annoyed them than men who had viewed nonarousing films. But subjects did not become more aggressive when there had been no prior annoyance (Zillmann and Sapolsky, 1977).

These studies lead to the conclusion that emotional arousal, regardless of

Figure 11-3
Motivational Determinants of Aggression
The diagram schematically represents the motivational determinants of aggression according to psychoanalytic theory, drive theory (the frustration-aggression hypothesis), and social learning theory. From the viewpoint of social learning theory, the emotional arousal caused by unpleasant experiences can lead to any number of different behaviors, depending on the behavior that has proved successful in the past. Cognitive factors, including knowledge of the results of past behavior and appraisal of the positive and negative incentives operating in the current situation, enable the individual to anticipate the consequences of his or her behavior and to act accordingly.

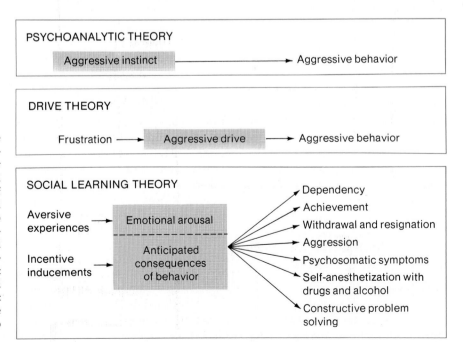

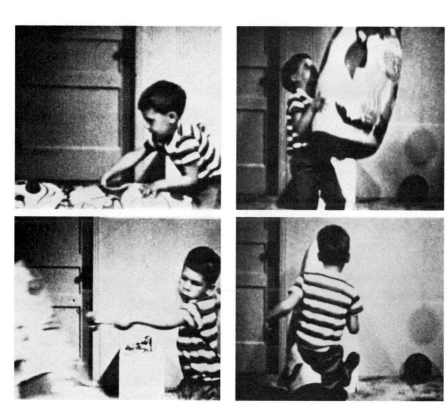

Figure 11-4
Children's Imitation of Adult Aggression
Nursery-school children observed an adult express various forms of aggressive behavior toward an inflated doll. After watching the adult, both boys and girls behaved aggressively toward the doll, performing many of the detailed acts of aggression the adult had displayed, including lifting and throwing the doll, striking it with a hammer, and kicking it.

the source, tends to increase aggression when aggression-eliciting stimuli are present. It may be that much of the violent behavior we observe in contemporary society is due to a combination of high arousal levels produced by the stresses of daily life and the widespread dissemination of stimuli that elicit aggression.

IMITATION OF AGGRESSION   A number of studies show that aggressive responses can be learned through imitation. Nursery-school children who observed an adult expressing various forms of aggressive behavior toward a large, inflated doll subsequently imitated many of the adult's actions, including unconventional and unusual aggressive behavior patterns (see Figure 11-4). The experiment was expanded to include two filmed versions of aggressive modeling (one showing an adult behaving aggressively toward the doll; the other showing a cartoon character displaying the same aggressive behavior). The results were equally striking. Children who watched either of the two films behaved as aggressively toward the doll as children who had observed a live model displaying aggression. Figure 11-5 measures aggressive behavior for each of the groups and for two control groups who observed no model or a nonaggressive model. Observation of either live or filmed models of aggression increases the likelihood of aggression.

REINFORCEMENT OF AGGRESSION   Children were more likely to express the aggressive responses they learned by watching aggressive models when they

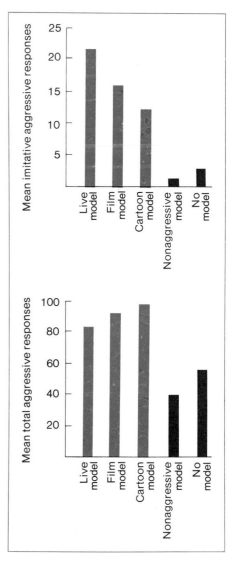

Figure 11-5
Imitation of Aggression
Observing aggressive models (either live or on film) greatly increases the amount of aggressive behavior children display compared to observing a nonaggressive model or no model at all. Note that observation of the live model results in the imitation of more specific aggressive acts, whereas observation of filmed (either real-life or cartoon) models instigates more aggressive responses of all kinds. (After Bandura, 1973)

Freud's view of aggression as an instinct can be related to the work of ethologists who study animal behavior in naturalistic settings. The view of some ethologists is that both humans and animals are innately aggressive, but animals have evolved mechanisms to control their aggressive impulses, whereas humans have not (Lorenz, 1966, 1981; Eibl–Eibesfeldt, 1970).

Predatory animals kill members of other species for food. But among their own species, animals fight mainly to protect their young and to compete for food, mates, and nesting sites. Fighting among members of the same species ensures that the strongest males will procreate, since they will be the winners in the competition for females. It also spaces the animals over the inhabited area so that each group establishes a specific "territory"; this enables the animals to make optimal use of available food resources.

According to Lorenz (1981), animals can safely enjoy these benefits of aggression because through the process of evolution, they have developed inhibitions that prevent them from destroying their own species. Many species exhibit ritualistic fighting behavior that appears to be largely innate (see Figure 11-6). They ward off combat by threatening displays. They fight according to a stylized pattern that seldom results in serious injury because the loser can display signals of submission that inhibit further aggression on the part of

Figure 11-6

Ritualistic Patterns of Fighting Behavior
The wildebeest bull defends its territory against a rival in a stylized challenge duel. These skirmishes, which may occur many times a day, seldom result in bloodshed. A. The two antagonists stand grazing head to head, taking each other's measure. B. Suddenly they drop to their knees in the eyeball-to-eyeball combat attitude. C. Pretending to sense danger, they raise their heads in mock alarm, apparently a means of easing tension. D. At this point, the challenge may be called off or may progress to a brief, horn-locked battle.

the victor; for example, a wolf lies down and exposes its throat.

But humans have developed powerful weapons that can cause instant death, often at a great distance. Perhaps if all combat had remained on a hand-to-hand or tooth-to-flesh level, without the benefit of even a rock or a club, we would have developed inhibitions that would prevent the destruction of our species.

Lorenz believes, as Freud did, that aggression is an innate instinct that must find some outlet. His prescription for a more peaceful society includes: safe outlets for aggression, such as engaging in competitive sports; broadening our view of "clan" and territory to include more people; and recognizing the stimuli that are "releasers" for aggression—a threatened in-group, a hated out-group, and the contagion of a group of angry people acting *en masse*.

were reinforced for such actions or when they observed aggressive models being reinforced. Aggressive responses can be learned through observation and reinforced by the consequences they produce. An observational study of nursery-school children shows the effects of reinforcement on aggression. Investigators observed the children for 10 weeks, recording instances of interpersonal aggression along with the events that immediately followed aggression—positive reinforcers (victim winced or cried), punishment (victim counterattacked), or neutral reactions (victim ignored the aggressor). For the

Humans as Aggressive Animals

Lorenz's views, although provocative, are highly speculative and have been criticized as lacking a substantial basis in empirical data. For example, many animals do not employ innate signals to stop attacks, and the stereotyped signals they do display have varying effects on the responses of their foes. Also, chimpanzees in their natural habitat have been observed engaging in group warfare; the males of one colony carried out a series of brutal attacks on the members of another social group, eventually killing all the males (Goodall, 1978).

In contrast to Lorenz's prescriptions, social learning theorists would stress minimizing the competitive and frustrating circumstances that lead to aggression and ensuring that aggressive behavior receives less reward than alternative forms of conduct.

Regardless of whether we focus on innate or learned aspects of aggression, studies of animals in their natural surroundings provide some valuable clues to the situations that trigger aggressive responses and the kinds of behaviors that inhibit or de-escalate them. For example, crowding increases fighting among many species, probably because it increases the competition for food and other resources. And aggressive behavior on the part of one animal is often contagious, exciting the other group members to behave aggressively.

Behaviors that appear to inhibit aggression include maintaining distance

Mutual grooming: a social response that inhibits aggression

from a potential foe (strong odors and loud vocalizations that permit animals to detect and withdraw from one another at a distance serve this purpose) and evoking a social response that is incompatible with aggression. One such response is mutual grooming—touching or fingering the fur or feathers of another animal. Many species appear to use this method to reduce the likelihood of aggression. Perhaps the most important factor in reducing aggression is familiarity. Many of the social rituals in which animals engage (such as sniffing and inspecting body parts and stereotyped greeting behaviors) familiarize them with each other's smell and appearance, which helps them to distinguish group members from strangers. When troops of primates divide and establish separate territories, the failure to perform such rituals may hasten the process by which familiar companions become aggression-arousing strangers. This may have happened in the case of the warfaring chimpanzees described earlier; originally, they all may have been part of the same colony.

children who showed the highest overall level of aggressive behavior, positive reinforcement was the most common reaction to their aggressive act. Passive children who were repeatedly victimized but who occasionally succeeded in stopping attacks by counteraggression gradually decreased their defensive behavior and began to initiate attacks of their own. Passive children whose counteraggression was unsuccessful remained submissive. Clearly, the *consequences* of aggression played an important role in shaping behavior (Patterson, Littman, and Bricker, 1967).

Aggressive expression as cathartic

Does the release of pent-up aggression decrease the person's need to aggress, or do such experiences actually increase the probability of future aggressive behavior? If aggression is a drive (either innate or frustration-produced), aggressive expression should be *cathartic*, resulting in a reduction in the intensity of aggressive feelings. But the evidence suggests that this is not the case (Geen and Quanty, 1977). Studies of children indicate that participation in aggressive activities either increases aggressive behavior or maintains it at the same level rather than reduces it. Experiments with adults have generally found similar results. When given repeated opportunities to shock another person (who cannot retaliate), college students become more and more punitive. And subjects who are angry become even more punitive on successive attacks than subjects who are not angry. If aggression were cathartic, the angry subjects should reduce their aggressive drive by acting aggressively and should become less punitive the more they aggress.

These studies are relevant to real-life instances in which assailants become progressively more brutal and "overkill," sometimes stabbing a victim as many as 50 times. Of course, other factors contribute to such cases, but there are indications that acting aggressively provides positive feedback that encourages more aggression.

Obviously, in some circumstances, the expression of aggression decreases its incidence. An aggressive threat may cause the antagonists to cease their provocative acts. Or behaving aggressively may arouse feelings of anxiety in the aggressors that inhibit further aggression, particularly if they observe the injurious consequences of their actions. But in these instances, the effect on aggressive behavior can be explained without concluding that an aggressive drive is being reduced.

VIEWING VIOLENCE   What effect does expressing aggression vicariously (through observing violence on television or in the movies) have on aggressive behavior? Is viewing violence cathartic, providing fantasy outlets for aggressive tension? Or does it elicit aggression in viewers by modeling violent behavior? We have already seen that children will imitate live or filmed aggressive behavior in an experimental setting. But how will they react in more natural settings? The amount of violence to which we are exposed through the media makes this an important question.

Some people in the TV industry claim that watching violence on television is beneficial; viewers discharge some of their own aggressive impulses through viewing, thereby reducing the likelihood that they will perform aggressive acts. Freud would probably have agreed with this claim; an instinct or drive theory of aggression assumes that aggression builds up until it is discharged by an aggressive act, either actual or vicarious. Social learning theorists, on the other hand, maintain that a state of arousal, or anger, can be reduced through behavior that is noninjurious as well as or better than it can be reduced through aggressive acts.

There have been several experimental studies in which children's viewing of television was controlled: one group watched violent cartoons for a specified amount of time each day; another group watched nonviolent cartoons for the same amount of time. The amount of aggression the children showed in their daily activities was carefully recorded. The children who watched violent cartoons became more aggressive in their interactions with their peers, whereas the children who viewed nonviolent cartoons showed no change in interpersonal aggressions (Steuer, Applefield, and Smith, 1971).

A number of correlational studies have shown a positive relationship between the amount of exposure to televised violence and the degree to which children use aggressive behavior to solve their interpersonal conflicts (Singer and Singer, 1981). Correlations, of course, do not imply causal relationships; it may be that children who are more aggressive prefer to watch violent TV programs. A longitudinal study that traced TV viewing habits over a 10-year period attempted to control for this possibility. More than 800 children were studied when they were between 8 and 9 years of age. Investigators collected information about each child's viewing time, the type of programs viewed, a number of family characteristics, and aggressiveness as rated by schoolmates. One of the major findings was that boys who preferred programs that contained a considerable amount of violence were much more aggressive in their interpersonal relationships than boys who preferred programs that contained little violence.

Ten years later, more than 400 of the original subjects (then aged 18 to 19) were interviewed concerning their preferred TV programs, given a test that measured delinquency tendencies, and rated by their peers as to the aggressiveness of their behavior. Figure 11-7 shows that high exposure to violence on television at age 9 is positively related to aggressiveness in boys at age 19. The correlation remains significant even when statistical methods are used to control for the degree of childhood aggressiveness, thereby reducing the possibility that the initial level of aggression determines both childhood viewing preferences and adult aggressiveness.

Interestingly, the results showed no consistent relationship between the TV viewing habits of girls and their aggressive behavior at either age. This agrees with the results of other studies indicating that girls tend to imitate aggressive behavior much less than boys do unless specifically reinforced for doing so. In our society, girls are seldom reinforced for behaving aggressively—quite the contrary. And since most of the aggressive roles on television are male, females are less likely to find aggressive models to imitate. However, the current increase in TV dramas starring aggressive heroines (for example, policewomen and female super-sleuths) may change these findings.

HOW VIEWING VIOLENCE AFFECTS SOCIAL BEHAVIOR   Although some psychologists question the extent to which television and movies actually influence people's behavior, the majority of studies point to the conclusion that viewing violence does increase interpersonal aggression, particularly in young children.[1] Exposure to filmed violence can elicit aggressive behavior in several ways.

1   *By teaching aggressive styles of conduct.*   We have already seen that children imitate the exact behavior of aggressive models. A number of cases have been reported of young children or teen-agers duplicating a violent act previously seen on television. In fact, in one instance, the parents of a victim took legal action against a TV network, claiming that a program shown during the hours when children were watching was responsible for a brutal attack on their 9-year-old daughter. The three youngsters responsible admitted that they had copied the method of assault shown on the program. Adult criminals, too, have improved their skills by adopting some ingenious methods demonstrated on television (Hendrick, 1977). And police departments report that a number

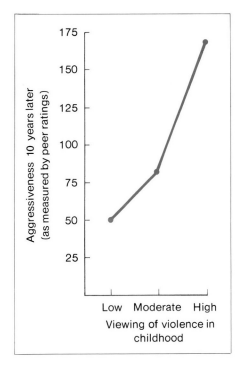

Figure 11-7
Relationship Between Childhood Viewing of Violent Television and Adult Aggression
Preference for viewing violent TV programs by boys at age 9 is positively correlated with aggressive behavior at age 19. (After Eron and others, 1972)

[1]A review of research on the effects of television on aggression and violence is available in a National Institute of Mental Health Report published in 1982 and titled *Television and behavior: Ten years of scientific progress and implications for the eighties.*

Children often imitate acts they see on television.

of violent crimes are the result of people trying to copy the plot of a TV show (Mankiewicz and Swerdlow, 1977).

2 *By increasing arousal.*   When children watch violent TV programs, they become much more emotionally aroused than they do when they watch nonviolent programs, as measured by a significant increase in their galvanic skin response, or GSR (Osborn and Endsley, 1971). The GSR is a rapid change in the electrical conductivity of the skin that occurs with emotional arousal; it results, in part, from changes in sweat-gland activity. We noted earlier that emotional arousal from various sources increases the probability of aggressive behavior if a person is already frustrated or annoyed.

3 *By desensitizing people to violence.*   Young children are emotionally aroused by viewing violence, but their physiological reactions decrease with repeated exposure to displays of violence. When 5- to 12-year-old boys were shown a violent boxing film, boys who had a history of extreme TV exposure (more than 40 hours per week) showed much less arousal (as measured by the GSR) than boys who watched television an average of only 4 hours a week (Cline, Croft, and Courrier, 1973). Other studies indicate that exposure to violence in the context of a TV drama decreases emotional responsiveness to real-life aggression in news films in both children and adults (Thomas and others, 1977). It is possible that the emotional blunting produced by continual exposure to filmed violence (both fictional and real) may affect our ability to empathize with a victim's suffering in real life and decrease our readiness to help.

4 *By reducing restraints on aggressive behavior.*   Most of us control our aggressive impulses. Although we may be angry and feel like injuring someone who has provoked or injured us, numerous restraints prevent us from doing so, including pangs of guilt, fear of retaliation, and the disapproval of others. Experiments indicate that observing another person behaving aggressively weakens these restraints (see Doob and Wood, 1972; Diener, 1976). When we observe others aggress with no undesirable effects, we are more apt to express our own hostility.

5 *By distorting views about conflict resolution.*   On the TV or movie screen, interpersonal conflicts are solved by physical aggression much more often than by any other means. The heroes (and even the heroines) do most of the killing. And watching the "good guys" triumph over the "bad guys" by violent means makes such behavior seem not only acceptable but also morally justified. Most of us realize that the dramas we watch on the screen bear only slight resemblance to what goes on in the real world. But young children do not have our degree of sophistication, and even adults may find their view of the world distorted by what they see on television.

Although TV violence does appear to increase aggressive behavior through some of the mechanisms just described, its effects probably differ for different children. A child who is very aggressive initially may become even more unrestrained and may learn new forms of aggressive behavior as a result of viewing violence. A child who is punished by parents or peers for imitating acts observed on television is apt to show a decrease in aggressiveness, although behavior that is prohibited in one setting may be displayed in another where there is less fear of punishment. Since programs that portray positive attitudes and cooperative behavior have been shown to *reduce* interpersonal aggression, the TV industry could perform a valuable public service by including more heroes and heroines who successfully overcome obstacles in a calm, firm, but nonviolent manner.

Clearly, many factors are involved in the instigation of aggression; conditions of poverty, overcrowding, the actions of authorities such as the police, and the values of one's cultural group are only a few. Some of these social influences will be considered in Chapter 18.

EMOTION

The discussion of aggression makes it clear that motivation and emotion are closely related. Anger is frequently an instigator of aggressive behavior, although such behavior can also occur in the absence of anger. Emotions can activate and direct behavior in the same way biological or psychological motives can. Emotions may also accompany motivated behavior; sex is not only a powerful motive but also a source of intense pleasure. Emotions can be a goal; we engage in certain activities because we know they will be pleasurable.

The nature of the relationship between motivation and emotion as well as the definition of emotion itself are unresolved issues in psychology. Most people would say that anger, fear, joy, and grief are emotions but would classify hunger, thirst, and fatigue as states of the organism that serve as motives. What is the difference? Why do we not call hunger an emotion?

There is no clear-cut distinction. The most common basis for differentiating between motivation and emotion assumes that emotions are usually aroused by external stimuli and that an emotional expression is directed toward the stimuli in the environment that arouse it. Motives, on the other hand, are more often aroused by internal stimuli and are "naturally" directed toward certain objects in the environment (for example, food, water, or a mate). However, this distinction does not hold in a number of instances. For example, an external incentive such as the sight or smell of delicious food can arouse hunger in the absence of internal hunger cues. And internal stimuli, such as those caused by severe food deprivation, can arouse emotion.

Most motivated behavior has some affective or emotional accompaniment, although we may be too preoccupied in our striving toward the goal to focus on our feelings at the time. When we talk about motivation, we usually focus on the goal-directed activity; in discussing emotion, our attention is drawn to the subjective, affective experiences that accompany the behavior. We are apt to be more aware of our emotions when efforts to achieve a goal are blocked (anger, despair) or when the goal is finally attained (pleasure, joy).

In the past, psychologists devoted considerable effort to trying to classify emotions. They attempted to find dimensions along which to scale such emotions as sorrow, disgust, surprise, jealousy, envy, and ecstasy. But such attempts have not proved very worthwhile. For our purposes, we will note that most emotions can be identified as *pleasant* (joy, love) or *unpleasant* (anger, fear). In addition, many emotional terms can be classified by *intensity*. Word pairs such as *displeasure–rage, pain–agony,* and *sadness–grief* convey differences of intensity. Some psychologists reserve the term *emotion* for the more intense states that are accompanied by widespread changes in body physiology and call the milder affective states *feelings*. But there are many intermediate states between mild experiences of pleasantness or unpleasantness and intense emotions. We will not attempt to pinpoint where "emotions" begin on the intensity scale; instead, we will concern ourselves with a variety of affective experiences.

Physiological responses in emotion

When we experience an intense emotion, such as fear or anger, we are aware of a number of bodily changes—rapid heartbeat and breathing, dryness of the throat and mouth, increased muscle tension, perspiration, trembling of the extremities, a "sinking feeling" in the stomach. Table 11-1 lists the symptoms

Table 11-1
Symptoms of Fear in Combat Flying
Based on reports of combat pilots during World War II. (After Shaffer, 1947)

DURING COMBAT MISSIONS DID YOU FEEL	OFTEN	SOMETIMES	TOTAL
A pounding heart and rapid pulse	30%	56%	86%
That your muscles were very tense	30	53	83
Easily irritated, angry, or "sore"	22	58	80
Dryness of the throat or mouth	30	50	80
"Nervous perspiration" or "cold sweat"	26	53	79
"Butterflies" in the stomach	23	53	76
A sense of unreality—that this could not be happening to you	20	49	69
A need to urinate very frequently	25	40	65
Trembling	11	53	64
Confused or rattled	3	50	53
Weak or faint	4	37	41
That right after a mission you were unable to remember the details of what had happened	5	34	39
Sick to the stomach	5	33	38
Unable to concentrate	3	32	35
That you had wet or soiled your pants	1	4	5

of fear reported by fliers during World War II and illustrates the complexity of the bodily changes that occur in an emotional state.

Most of the physiological changes that take place during emotional arousal result from activation of the sympathetic division of the autonomic nervous system as it prepares the body for emergency action (see pages 51–52). The *sympathetic system* is responsible for the following changes:

1   Blood pressure and heart rate increase.
2   Respiration becomes more rapid.
3   The pupils of the eyes dilate.
4   Perspiration increases while secretion of saliva and mucous decreases.
5   Blood-sugar level increases to provide more energy.
6   The blood clots more quickly in case of wounds.
7   Motility of the gastrointestinal tract decreases; blood is diverted from the stomach and intestines to the brain and skeletal muscles.
8   The hairs on the skin become erect, causing "goose pimples."

The sympathetic system gears the organism for energy output. As the emotion subsides, the *parasympathetic system*—the energy-conserving system—takes over and returns the organism to its normal state.

The kind of heightened physiological arousal we have described is characteristic of emotional states during which the organism must prepare for action—for example, to fight or flee. Some of the same responses may also occur during joyful excitement or sexual arousal. During emotions such as sorrow or grief, however, some bodily processes may be depressed, or slowed down.

Arousal and emotional intensity

Most of the time, we are fairly clear about the emotions we are experiencing; we know whether we are angry or frightened or merely excited. But our physiological responses under all three conditions are remarkably similar. Fear makes our heartbeat faster and our breath more rapid, but so does anger or the sight of a loved one. Our face may flush *or* pale when we are angry (depending on the individual), and the same response occurs when we are frightened. Although fairly accurate measures indicate when a person is emotionally aroused, research thus far has failed to reveal physiological patterns that are unique to different emotions. This is an important point. Despite a long history of research on the subject, investigators have *not* been able to identify patterns of physiological arousal that differ from one specific emotion to another.

Although bodily sensations may not be related to *specific* emotions, they do determine the *intensity* with which we experience emotions. The importance of bodily sensations is demonstrated by a study of the emotional life of individuals with spinal-cord injuries. When the spinal cord is severed, sensations below the point of injury are not communicated to the brain.

In one study, army veterans with spinal-cord injuries were divided into five groups, according to the level on the spinal cord at which the lesion occurred. In one group, the lesions were near the neck (at the cervical level), with only one branch of the parasympathetic nervous system intact and no innervation of the sympathetic system. In another group, the lesions were near the base of the spine (at the sacral level), with at least partial innervation of both sympathetic and parasympathetic nerves. The other three groups fell between these two extremes. The five groups represented a continuum of bodily sensation: the higher the lesion, the less the sensation.

Each subject was interviewed to determine his feelings in situations of fear, anger, grief, and sexual excitement. The subject was asked to recall an emotion-arousing incident prior to his injury and a comparable incident following the injury and to compare the intensity of emotional experience in each case. The data for states of fear and anger are shown in Figure 11-8. It is apparent that the higher the lesion (that is, the less the bodily sensation), the more emotionality decreased following injury. The same relationship was true for states of sexual excitement and grief. Deprivation of body sensation *does* result in a marked decrease in emotionality.

Comments by patients with the highest spinal-cord lesions suggested that they could act emotional when the situation called for it but that they did not really feel emotional. For example, "It's sort of a cold anger. Sometimes I act angry when I see some injustice. I yell and cuss and raise hell, because if you don't do it sometimes, I've learned people will take advantage of you; but it doesn't have the heat to it that it used to. It's a mental kind of anger." Or, "I say I am afraid, like when I'm going into a real stiff exam at school, but I don't really feel afraid, not all tense and shaky with the hollow feeling in my stomach, like I used to."

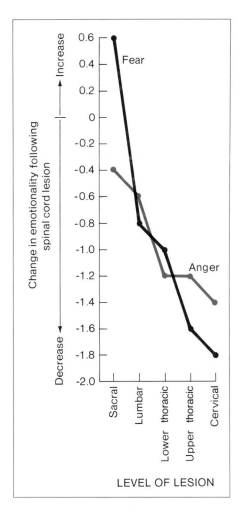

Figure 11-8
Relationship Between Spinal-Cord Lesions and Emotionality
Subjects with spinal-cord lesions compared the intensity of their emotional experiences before and after injury. Their reports were coded according to the degree of change: 0 indicates no change; a mild change (for example, "I feel it less, I guess") is scored −1 for a decrease or +1 for an increase; a strong change (for example, "I feel it a helluva lot less") is scored −2 or +2. Note that the higher the lesion the greater the decrease in emotionality following injury. (After Schachter, 1971 and adapted from Hohmann, 1962)

The theory underlying lie detection is that lying arouses emotional responses that can be measured. A machine called a *polygraph* (commonly known as a "lie detector") simultaneously measures several physiological responses known to accompany strong emotions. (The word "polygraph" means "many writings.") The measures most frequently recorded are changes in heart rate, blood pressure, respiration, and the galvanic skin response (GSR).

In operating a polygraph, the standard procedure is to make the first recording while the subject is relaxed; this recording will serve as a *baseline* for evaluating subsequent responses. The examiner then asks a series of carefully worded questions that the subject has been instructed to answer with a yes or a no response. "Critical" questions are interspersed among "neutral" questions, and sufficient time is allowed between questions for the measures to return to normal. Presumably, the subject's guilt is revealed by heightened physiological responses to the critical questions (Figure 11-9).

However, the use of the polygraph in detecting lies is not foolproof. An innocent subject may be very tense or may react emotionally to certain words in the questions and therefore appear to be lying when telling the truth. On the other hand, a practiced liar may show little emotional response when lying. And a knowledgeable subject may be able to "beat" the machine by thinking about something exciting or by tensing muscles during neutral questions, thereby creating a baseline comparable to reactions to the critical questions. The recording in Figure 11-9 shows the responses to an actual lie and a simulated lie. In this experiment, the subject picked a number and then tried to conceal its identify from the examiner. The

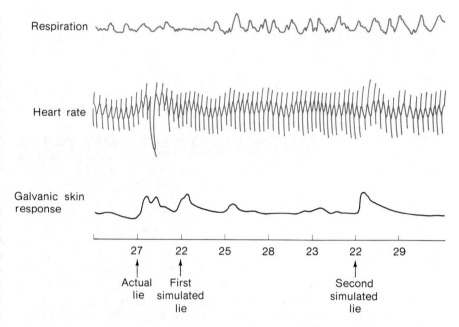

number was 27, and a marked change in heart rate and GSR can be seen when the subject denies number 27. The subject simulates lying to number 22 by tensing his toes, producing noticeable reactions in heart rate and GSR.

Because of these and other problems, most state and federal courts will not admit polygraph tests; those that do generally require that both sides agree to its introduction. Such tests are frequently used, however, in preliminary criminal investigations and by prospective employers hiring personnel for trusted positions.

Representatives of the American Polygraph Association have claimed an accuracy rate of 90 percent or better for polygraph tests conducted by a skilled operator. Critics consider the accuracy rate to be much lower. Lykken (1981), for example, asserts that the test is correct only about 65 percent of the time and is far more likely to be in error when

the person being tested is truthful. He argues that the polygraph detects not only the emotional arousal that accompanies lying but also the nervousness that an honest person experiences when strapped to the equipment. Nevertheless, many businesses believe that the benefits of these tests outweigh the risks, and their use is increasing rapidly in private industry. Their use in law enforcement is also increasing. The FBI, for example, administers several thousand polygraph tests per year, mostly to prove leads and verify specific facts—areas in which, experts agree, the polygraph is more useful. Tests given by the FBI to several government officials led to evidence of the Watergate cover-up. In criminal and private cases, anyone has the right to refuse a polygraph test. However, this is hardly a safeguard for someone whose refusal, for whatever reason, may endanger a career or job opportunity.

Lie Detection

Figure 11-9
Polygraph

The arm cuff measures blood pressure and heart rate, the pneumograph around the rib cage measures rate of breathing, and the finger electrodes measure GSR. The recording on the left shows the physiological responses of a subject as he lies and as he simulates lying. The respiratory trace (top line) shows that he held his breath as he prepared for the first simulation. He was able to produce sizable changes in heart rate and GSR at the second simulation. (After Kubis, 1962)

Another type of lie detector has been developed that measures certain changes in a person's voice that are undetectable to the human ear. All muscles, including those controlling the vocal cords, vibrate slightly when in use. This tremor, which is transmitted to the vocal cords, is suppressed by activity of the autonomic nervous system when a speaker is under stress. When a tape recording of a person's voice is played through a device called a *voice-stress analyzer* (at a speed four times slower than that at which it is recorded,) a visual representation of the voice can be produced on a strip of graph paper. The voice of a relaxed speaker resembles a series of waves (see the left-hand graph in Figure 11-10), which are produced by tremors of the vocal cords. When a speaker is under stress, the tremors are suppressed (see the right-hand graph in Figure 11-10).

The voice-stress analyzer is used in lie detection in essentially the same way as a polygraph; neutral questions are interspered with critical questions, and recordings of the subject's responses to both are compared. If answers to the critical questions produce the relaxed wave form, the person is probably telling the truth (as far as we know, vocal-cord tremors cannot be controlled voluntarily). A stressed wave form, on the other hand, indicates only that the individual is tense or anxious—not necessarily that he or she is lying.

The advantage of using the voice-stress analyzer rather than the polygraph is that the subject does not have to be hooked up to a lot of equipment. In fact, the subject does not even have to be present; the analyzer can work over the telephone, from radio or TV messages, or from tape recordings. Since people's voices can be analyzed without their knowledge, the potential for the unethical use of this instrument is a matter of considerable concern. A different concern is the question of the accuracy of the voice-stress analyzer. Some investigators claim that it is as accurate as the polygraph in distinguishing between the guilty and the innocent; others claim that it is no more accurate than chance. So far, few well-controlled studies have been conducted using the voice-stress analyzer; much more research is required to determine the relationship between voice changes and other physiological measures of emotion (Rice, 1978; Lykken, 1981).

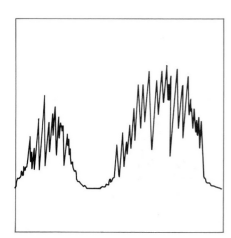
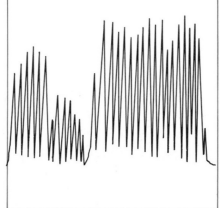

Figure 11-10
Effects of Stress on Voice Patterns
Graphic records of speech are produced by a voice-stress analyzer. The voice printout for a relaxed speaker resembles a series of waves, like the one shown on the left; the waves are produced by tiny tremors of the vocal cords. Under stress, the tremor is suppressed, producing a printout like the one on the right. (After Holden, 1975)

Emotional expression

FACIAL EXPRESSIONS DURING EMOTION   Sir Charles Darwin was intrigued with the expression of emotion in blind children and in animals. In *The Expression of Emotions in Man and Animals*, published in 1872, Darwin proposed an evolutionary theory of emotions. According to Darwin, many of the ways in which we express emotion are inherited patterns that originally had some survival value. For example, the expression of disgust or rejection is based on the organism's attempt to rid itself of something unpleasant that has been ingested. To quote Darwin:

> The term ''disgust,'' in its simplest sense, means something offensive to the taste. But as disgust also causes annoyance, it is generally accompanied by a frown, and often by gestures as if to push away or to guard oneself against the offensive object. Extreme disgust is expressed by movements around the mouth identical with those preparatory to the act of vomiting. The mouth is opened widely, with the upper lip strongly retracted. The partial closure of the eyelids, or the turning away of the eyes or of the whole body, are likewise highly expressive of disdain. These actions seem to declare that the despised person is not worth looking at, or is disagreeable to behold. Spitting seems an almost universal sign of contempt or disgust; and spitting obviously represents the rejection of anything offensive from the mouth.

Certain facial expressions do seem to have a universal meaning, regardless of the culture in which the individual is raised. When people from five different cultures (United States, Brazil, Chile, Argentina, and Japan) viewed photographs showing facial expressions of happiness, anger, sadness, disgust, fear, and surprise, they had little difficulty in identifying the emotions that each expression conveyed. Even members of remote, preliterate tribes that had had virtually no contact with Western cultures (the Fore and Dani tribes in New Guinea) were able to identify the facial expressions correctly. And American college students who viewed videotapes of emotions expressed by Fore natives identified the emotions accurately, although they sometimes confused fear and surprise (Ekman, 1982).

Some psychologists, impressed by the innate and universal nature of certain facial expressions, believe that they are as important in determining our subjective experience of emotion as are internal sensations of arousal; when we automatically react to a situation, messages to the brain from the muscles of the face tell us which of the basic emotions we are experiencing, while visceral sensations (which occur more slowly) signal the intensity of the emotion (Izard, 1977). This idea implies that if you make yourself smile and hold the smile for half a minute, you will begin to feel happier; if your scowl, you will feel tense and angry. Try it and see. Experiments in which subjects were instructed to manipulate their facial muscles (on the pretext that the effect of muscle movements on perception was being studied) have shown some degree of relationship between facial expression and feelings of emotion (Laird, 1974).

ROLE OF LEARNING IN EMOTIONAL EXPRESSION   Although some facial expressions and gestures may be innately associated with particular emotions, others are learned from specific cultures. One psychologist reviewed Chinese novels to determine how Chinese writers portray various human emotions. Many of the bodily changes in emotion (flushing, paling, cold perspiration, trembling, goose pimples) represent symptoms of emotion in Chinese fiction much as they do in Western writing. However, the Chinese have other, quite different ways of expressing emotion. The following quotations from Chinese novels would surely be misinterpreted by an American reader unfamiliar with the culture (Klineberg, 1938).

> *"They stretched out their tongues."*
> (They showed signs of surprise.)
>
> *"He clapped his hands."*
> (He was worried or disappointed.)
>
> *"He scratched his ears and cheeks."*
> (He was happy.)
> *"Her eyes grew round and opened wide."*
> (She became angry.)

Thus, superimposed on basic expressions of emotion, which appear to be universal, are conventional or stereotyped forms of expression—a kind of "language of emotion" recognized by others within a culture. Skilled actors are able to convey to their audiences any intended emotion by using facial expressions, tones of voice, and gestures in patterns the audience will recognize. In simulating emotion, those of us who are less skilled actors can convey our intent by exaggerating the conventional expressions: gritting our teeth and clenching our fists to indicate anger; turning down the corners of our mouth to look sad; raising our eyebrows to express doubt or disapproval.

THEORIES OF EMOTION

The James–Lange and Cannon–Bard theories

We tend to think that bodily changes that occur in response to stress are caused by emotion. But one of the earliest theories of emotion proposed that the perception of these physiological changes is the emotion. William James, a famous psychologist at Harvard during the late 1800s, believed that the important factor in our felt emotion is the feedback from the bodily changes that occur in response to a frightening or upsetting situation. He stated this theory in a form that seems to put the cart before the horse: "We are afraid because we run"; "we are angry because we strike." The Danish physiologist Carl Lange arrived at a similar proposal at about the same time, and accordingly the theory has come to be called the *James–Lange theory*.

We can think of instances when the recognition of emotion does follow bodily responses. If you stumble suddenly on the stairs, you automatically grab for the handrail before you have time to recognize a state of fear. After the crisis is over, your felt emotion includes the perception of a pounding heart, rapid breathing, and a feeling of weakness or trembling in the arms and legs. Because the feeling of fear follows the bodily responses, such a situation gives some plausibility to the James–Lange theory.

The major objections to the James–Lange theory came from Walter Cannon in the 1920s, who pointed out that (1) bodily changes do not seem to differ very much from one emotional state to another, despite the fact that we as individuals are usually fairly clear about which emotion we are experiencing; (2) the internal organs are relatively insensitive structures not well supplied with nerves, and internal changes occur too slowly to be a source of emotional feeling; (3) artificially inducing the bodily changes associated with an emotion (for example, injecting a drug such as epinephrine) does not produce the experience of the true emotion.

Figure 11-11
Two Theories of Emotion
Illustrated here is the sequence of events for two theories of emotion. According to the James–Lange theory, feedback to the brain from bodily responses produces the conscious experience of emotion. According to the Cannon–Bard theory, the emotional experience occurs as soon as the cortex receives the message from the thalamus; it does not depend on feedback from internal organs and skeletal responses.

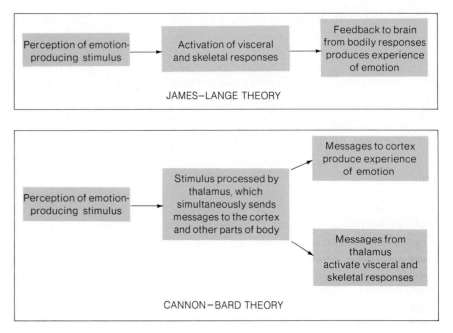

Cannon (1927) assigned the central role in emotion to the *thalamus,* which is part of the brain's central core (see page 38). Cannon suggested that the thalamus responded to an emotion-producing stimulus by sending impulses *simultaneously* to the cerebral cortex and to other parts of the body; emotional feelings were the result of the joint arousal of the cortex and the sympathetic nervous system. According to this theory—which was extended by Bard (1934) and is known as the *Cannon–Bard theory*—the bodily changes and the experience of emotion occur at the same time. Figure 11-11 illustrates the differences between the Cannon–Bard and James–Lange theories of emotion.

Subsequent investigation has made it clear that the *hypothalamus* and certain parts of the *limbic system,* rather than the thalamus, are the brain centers most directly involved in the integration of emotional responses. (We noted earlier that electrical stimulation of the hypothalamus elicits fear or anger in many animals.) Impulses from these areas are transmitted to nuclei in the brain stem that control the functioning of the autonomic nervous system. The autonomic nervous system acts directly on the muscles and internal organs to initiate some of the bodily changes characteristic of emotion and acts indirectly by stimulating the adrenal hormones to produce other bodily changes. Additional hormones, which play a crucial role in an individual's reaction to stress, are secreted by the pituitary gland on direct signal from the hypothalamus (see page 52).

In view of the complex interaction of neural and hormonal signals, it is difficult to determine whether the physiological responses precede or accompany the emotion. Emotion is *not* a momentary event, but an experience that takes place over time. An *emotional experience* may be initiated by external inputs to the sensory system; we see or hear the emotion-arousing stimuli. But the autonomic nervous system is activated almost immediately thereafter, so that feedback from bodily changes adds to the emotional experience. Thus, our conscious experience of emotion involves the *integration* of information about the physiological state of the body and information about the emotion-arousing situation. Both types of information tend to be continuous in time, and their integration determines the intensity and nature of our felt emotional state.

Within this conceptual framework, the time distinctions made by the James–Lange and Cannon–Bard theories are not too meaningful. On some occasions, such as when an individual is in sudden danger, the first signs of emotional experience may be preceded by autonomic activity (in which case, James and Lange are correct); on others, the awareness of an emotion clearly precedes autonomic activity (in which case, Cannon and Bard are correct). The felt emotional state is affected by a third source of data—*cognitive factors*. How an individual appraises the external situation is a cognitive process that influences emotion.

Cognitive theories of emotion

People are usually aware that something is going on internally when they are angry, excited, or afraid; but they cannot accurately perceive changes in their blood pressure or activity in their stomach. When people are asked to describe their emotions, they usually begin with the arousing circumstances—what angered, pleased, or frightened them—and then describe some of their bodily reactions and their difficulties in dealing with the situation. But they do not define the emotion primarily in terms of their internal feelings.

The individual's *appraisal* of the emotion-producing situation is an important determinant of his or her emotional response. Schachter (1971) believes that emotions are a function of the interaction of cognitive factors and a state of physiological arousal. His *cognitive–physiological theory of emotion* (see Figure 11-12) proposes that feedback to the brain from physiological activity initiates

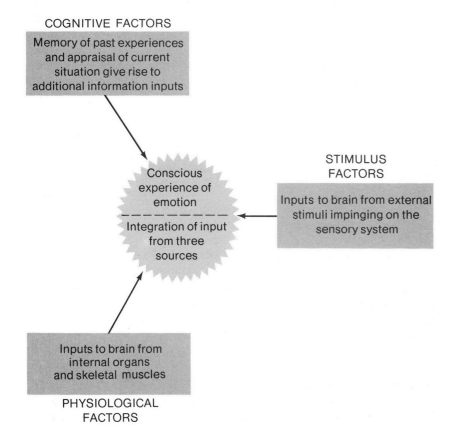

COGNITIVE FACTORS

Memory of past experiences and appraisal of current situation give rise to additional information inputs

Conscious experience of emotion

Integration of input from three sources

STIMULUS FACTORS

Inputs to brain from external stimuli impinging on the sensory system

Inputs to brain from internal organs and skeletal muscles

PHYSIOLOGICAL FACTORS

Figure 11-12
Emotion as Information Integration
The conscious experience of emotion involves the integration of information from three sources. Feedback to the brain from the internal organs and other body parts activated by the sympathetic nervous system gives rise to an undifferentiated state of arousal; but the emotion experienced is determined by the interpretation the subject assigns to the aroused state. Information stored in memory and the perception of what is taking place in the environment are used to interpret the current situation. This interpretation (based on cognitive and stimulus factors) interacts with feedback from bodily changes (physiological factors) to determine the emotional state.

A somewhat different approach to emotion that has attracted considerable attention in recent years is called the *opponent process theory* (Solomon and Corbit, 1974; Solomon, 1980). The theory assumes that the brain is organized to oppose or suppress emotional responses, whether they are pleasurable or aversive. If some event elicits an emotional state, the opposite emotional state (one that tends to cancel the first state) will be activated shortly thereafter. For simplicity, the first state is usually called State A and its opposite is called State B. (State B is essentially a slave process called forth whenever State A is active.) Each emotional state has an opposite emotional state; when one member of a pair is elicited, it triggers its opposite, which in time returns the system to its baseline:

Baseline → State A → State B → Baseline

This type of process is illustrated by reports on the emotional reactions typically experienced by parachutists in training (Epstein, 1967). During their first free fall (before the parachute opens), the response is one of fear. After landing, a trainee usually walks about with a stunned expression for a few minutes and then begins to smile and become very sociable. A feeling of great euphoria follows, which eventually fades to a baseline of normal behavior.

The temporal course of the emotional experience and its intensity are illustrated in Figure 11-13, which can be understood by looking at the left-hand panel of Figure 11-14. When the emotional stimulus is presented, it elicits an *a* process that gives rise to State A. Sometime after the *a* process is activated, the *b* process is aroused and functions to oppose and suppress the affective state generated by the *a* pro-

cess. At any moment, the *difference* between the magnitude of the *a* process and the magnitude of the *b* process specifies the manifest affective state. Thus, the difference between the *a* curve and the *b* curve specifies the experienced emotional state plotted in the top left-hand panel of Figure 11-14, which is the same curve plotted in Figure 11-13.

When an emotion-arousing stimulus is presented, an emotional response occurs that rises to a peak in a few seconds. As the stimulus exposure continues, the emotion recedes slightly from its peak and remains steady. This occurs because the *a* process is initially

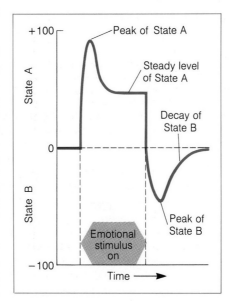

Figure 11-13
Temporal Dynamics
of an Affective Response
The standard pattern of an affective response produced by an emotion-arousing stimulus on its initial presentation. (After Solomon, 1980)

unopposed, giving rise to a peak level for State A. As the *b* process gradually becomes activated, it subtracts from the *a* process, thereby reducing the peak level for State A. Once the stimulus is removed, the opposite emotion is experienced. This happens because the *a* process disappears almost immediately but the *b* process recedes more slowly; thus, State B is experienced until the *b* process has run its course.

Now let us return to Figure 11-13 and interpret it in terms of these underlying opponent processes. Suppose we encounter a fear-arousing stimulus. The *a* process will be activated immediately, leading to an emotional peak for State A. Shortly after the onset of the stimulus, the *b* process will be aroused gradually and will subtract from the intensity of State A, but the person will still be in a state of fear. Once the fear-arousing stimulus is removed, the *a* process will disappear quickly but the *b* process will persist, giving rise to State B—a feeling of relief. This pattern of emotional response can be observed in our everyday life experiences but is often complicated by cultural factors and our efforts to suppress or control emotions. Nevertheless, in well-controlled laboratory situations, the temporal course of the emotional response presented in Figure 11-13 can be demonstrated.

The first time an emotion-arousing stimulus is experienced, the *b* process is fairly weak and slow to occur. But repeated experiences with the stimulus strengthen the *b* process, as indicated in the right-hand panel of Figure 11-14, until the *b* process is activated much more quickly and with much greater intensity. As a result, the manifest level for State A is reduced, and when the stimulus is removed, the intensity of State B is greatly amplified. The time

Opponent Processes in Emotion

course for an emotional response to a stimulus encountered many times is illustrated by the top curve in the right-hand panel of Figure 11-14. This pattern of events also has been verified by experimentation. Thus, the initial encounter with an emotion-arousing stimulus will lead to a strong State A experience followed by a mild State B experience. But after repeated experiences, the intensity of State A will be diminished, whereas the intensity of State B will be greatly amplified.

The effects of repeated exposures to an emotion-arousing stimulus can be illustrated by examining the emotional dynamics associated with the use of addictive substances. For example, the first few doses of an opiate produce a potent experience of pleasure called a "rush," which has been described as an intense type of sexual pleasure felt throughout the body. The rush is followed by a less intense state of euphoria. After the drug has worn off, the user lapses into an aversive state of craving called "withdrawal," which fades in time. This pattern conforms to the top left curve in Figure 11-14. The opiate produces a peak level for State A (the rush), followed by a decline in intensity (euphoria). When the drug dose loses its effect, State B (withdrawal) emerges and then gradually disappears.

If the drug doses are repeated frequently, the course of the emotional experience changes as predicted by the opponent process theory (see the right-hand panel of Figure 11-14). The rush is no longer experienced, and the feeling of euphoria is minimal or absent. The withdrawal syndrome becomes much more intense and its duration lengthens dramatically. Experienced drug users have mild "highs" followed by intense and extended "lows."

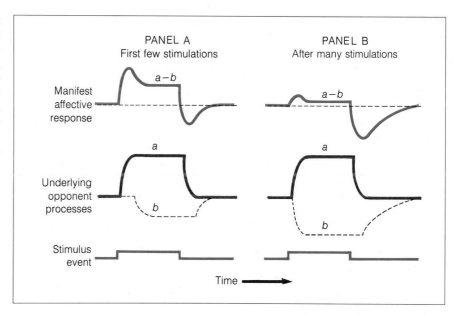

Figure 11-14
Opponent Processes in Emotion

The left-hand panel illustrates the affective response to the first few presentations of a stimulus; the right-hand panel illustrates the response after repeated presentations of the stimulus. The top curve in each panel is the manifest response produced by the interplay of the opponent processes; it is obtained by taking the difference between the underlying opponent processes *a* and *b* shown in the middle row of the figure (that is, subtracting the *b* curve from the *a* curve). The bottom row in the figure indicates the onset and offset of the emotion-arousing stimulus. Note that the *b* process has a shorter latency, an increased intensity, and a slower decay as the stimulus is presented repeatedly and becomes familiar. These changes in the *b* process explain why there is a change in the manifest emotional response as a stimulus is repeatedly experienced. (After Solomon, 1980)

Initially, addictive substances are taken because they produce pleasant effects. After repeated use, however, they are taken to counteract the unpleasant opponent process that persists from prior drug use. Thus, a vicious cycle is formed. The more often a drug is used, the more intense and longer lasting the opponent process becomes. To get rid of this unpleasant aftereffect, the drug user takes the drug again, further strengthening the opponent process.

An experienced drug user continues to use a drug to reduce the low that occurs after the previous dose rather than to produce the high originally associated with the substance. This cycle is not easily broken, as the high failure rates of most drug treatment programs indicate. The opponent process theory does not offer a prescription for the treatment of drug addiction, but it provides a useful framework within which to evaluate such programs (Solomon, 1980).

an undifferentiated state of arousal but that the felt emotion is determined by the "label" the person assigns to that aroused state. The assignment of a label is a *cognitive process;* individuals use information from past experiences and their perception of the present moment to interpret their feelings. This interpretation will determine the label they use to describe their emotional state.

A number of studies have tested Schachter's theory (see Schachter and Singer, 1962; Marshall, 1976; Maslach, 1979). The common feature of these studies involved giving subjects an injection of epinephrine, which typically causes an increase in heart and respiration rates, muscle tremors, and a "jittery" feeling (see page 52). The experimenter then manipulated the information the subject was given regarding the effects of epinephrine. Some subjects were told that the drug would produce a state of euphoria; other subjects were told that the drug would make them feel angry. After each subject was informed of the "effects" of the injection, he or she was left in a waiting room with a person who was ostensibly another subject but who was actually a confederate of the experimenter. Depending on whether the real subject had been told the drug produced a condition of euphoria or anger, the confederate acted euphoric (made paper airplanes, played "basketball" by throwing wads of paper into the wastebasket, and so on) or angry (complained about the experiment, resented the questionnaire that the subjects had to complete, and finally tore it up and stomped out of the room). Data from these experiments indicate that once a state of physiological arousal was induced (by the injection of epinephrine), subjects had a tendency to label their emotional state in accordance with the available information. If the information suggested that the injection would produce a feeling of euphoria, the subjects were somewhat more likely to feel euphoric; conversely, if they were told that the injection would make them feel angry, they were somewhat more likely to feel anger.

However, emotional experience is not as malleable as Schachter's theory suggests. According to the theory, the emotional label a person assigns to a state of arousal is determined *primarily* by the emotion being expressed by other people in the same situation. Although the physiologically aroused subjects in these various experiments accurately perceived the emotion being expressed by the confederate, they did not always use this emotion to explain or label their own state of arousal. Instead, the emotional interpretation appeared to be a complicated function of their past experiences and their current life situation; the mood of the confederate exerted only a minimal influence on the interpretation. Subjects in these experiments often interpreted physiological arousal more *negatively* than the actions of the confederate suggested. This is not surprising; when we experience strange symptoms in real life, we are more apt to suspect something is wrong with us than to assume we are happy.

The various experiments testing Schachter's theory demonstrate that cognitive factors influence emotion, but it would be a mistake to conclude that they *alone* determine which emotion will be experienced. As we noted earlier, there is no systematic evidence that different emotions are associated with different patterns of physiological arousal. However, this possibility cannot be ruled out and more sophisticated measurement procedures may in time establish such relationships. Moreover, as we have seen, specific facial expressions are associated with different emotions. In fact, Tomkins (1981) argues that certain types of stimuli activate innate structures in the brain, which represent primary emotions like fear, anger, and surprise; each of these brain structures is linked to a specific facial display. If different physiological arousal patterns and different facial expressions are innately associated with different emotions, it is hard to argue that an emotional experience is solely a function of cognitive factors. It is conceivable that under some circumstances and in the presence of some stimuli, the reaction of the organism is a highly differentiated physiological pattern and the experienced emotion is determined primarily by the specific characteristics of the physiological arousal. Under other circumstances, the organism's reaction may be an undifferentiated physiological pattern of arousal, in which case the experienced emotion will depend on the cognitive processes the individual brings into play to explain what has taken place.

Our discussion of theories of emotion leaves many unanswered questions. We cannot point to one theory that accounts for most of the facts; instead, we are faced with an array of theories, each correct to some degree but none comprehensive. This unsatisfactory situation is due, in large part, to the fact that emotions are difficult to study because of the complexity of the physiological responses involved and because the emotions that can be aroused in the laboratory do not compare in intensity with those experienced in real life. A clever experimenter may be able to arouse a moderate degree of anger in a subject, but ethical and practical constraints restrict the intensity of fear that can be induced during an experiment. Future advances in a theory of emotion will depend on the development of new methods and more powerful techniques for the study of emotion.[2]

OPTIMAL LEVEL OF AROUSAL

What role do emotions play in our lives? Are they beneficial? Do they help us to survive, or are they chiefly sources of disturbance and maladjustment? The answers to these questions depend on the intensity of the emotions involved. A mild level of emotional arousal tends to produce alertness and interest in the task at hand. When emotions become intense, however, whether they are pleasant or unpleasant, they usually result in some decrease in performance. The curve in Figure 11-15 represents the relationship between the level of emotional arousal and the effectiveness of performance. At very low levels of arousal (for example, at the point of waking up), the nervous system may not be functioning fully and sensory messages may not get through. Performance is optimal at moderate levels of arousal. At high levels of arousal, performance begins to decline, presumably because the central nervous system is responding to too many stimuli at once and the appropriate set of responses is prevented from dominating.

The optimum level of arousal and the shape of the curve differ for different tasks. A simple, well-learned habit would be much less susceptible to disruption by emotional arousal than a more complex response that depends on the integration of several thought processes. During a moment of intense fear, you would probably still be able to spell your name but your ability to play a good game of chess would be seriously impaired.

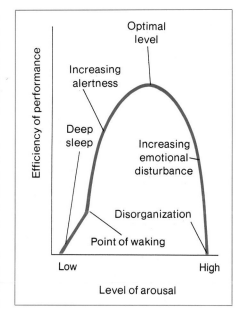

Figure 11-15
Emotional Arousal and Performance
The curve shows the hypothetical relationships between level of emotional arousal and efficiency of performance. The shape of the curve is probably somewhat different for different tasks or behaviors. (After Hebb, 1972)

[2]The cognitive theory of emotion proposed by Mandler (1980) goes beyond the scope of this book but deserves comment. In his view, the *interruption* (blocking or inhibiting) of ongoing thought processes or behavior sequences activates the autonomic nervous system; this is an innate response of the organism whenever some organized psychological process is interrupted. Thus, interruption leads to autonomic activity, which creates a state of general physiological arousal; this state of arousal in turn is given an emotional label based on a cognitive interpretation of the situation. The concept that activation of the autonomic nervous system is innately linked to any interruption of an ongoing psychological process is of adaptive value to an organism from an evolutionary viewpoint.

Individuals differ in the extent to which their behavior is disrupted by emotional arousal. Observations of people during crises, such as fires or sudden floods, suggest that about 15 percent show organized, effective behavior. The majority, about 70 percent, show various degrees of disorganization but are still able to function with some effectiveness. The remaining 15 percent are so disorganized that they are unable to function at all; they may race around screaming or exhibit aimless and completely inappropriate behavior (Tyhurst, 1951).

Sometimes emotions are not quickly discharged but continue to remain unresolved. Perhaps the situation that makes a person angry (for example, prolonged conflict with an employer) or fearful (for example, worry over the chronic illness of a loved one) continues for a long time. The state of heightened arousal that results can take its toll on the individual's ability to function efficiently. Sometimes continual emotional tension can impair physical health. The symptoms of a *psychosomatic illness* are physical, but the cause is primarily psychological. A number of different types of illnesses—including ulcers, asthma, migraine headaches, high blood pressure, and skin eruptions—are related to emotional stress. We will have more to say about psychosomatic disorders in Chapter 14. At this point, however, it should be noted that long-term emotional stress can impair a person's physical health as well as his or her mental efficiency.

Summary

1   In contrast to *biological motives, psychological motives* are determined primarily by learning. They appear at a later stage of development and become important after basic needs are satisfied.

2   Two quite different theoretical approaches to human motivation are illustrated by *psychoanalytic theory* and *social learning theory*.
    a   Freud's psychoanalytic theory emphasizes two basic drives: *sex* and *aggression*. These motives arise in infancy, but when parents forbid their expression, they are *repressed*. A repressed tendency remains active, however, as an *unconscious motive* and finds expression in indirect or symbolic ways.
    b   Social learning theory focuses on patterns of behavior that are *learned* in order to cope with the environment; learning may occur through direct reinforcement or *vicariously* through observing the consequences of behavior *modeled* by another person. *Cognitive processes* enable a person to foresee probable consequences and to alter behavior accordingly. *Self-reinforcement*, based on one's own standards of conduct, also provides an important motivational control.

3   Aggression, defined as behavior *intended* to injure another person or to destroy property, may be primarily *hostile* (aimed at inflicting injury) or *instrumental* (aimed at goals other than the victim's suffering). Freudian theorists view aggression as an *instinct* or a *frustration-produced drive;* social learning theorists propose that aggression is a *learned response* influenced by modeling and reinforcement.

4   In lower animals, aggression is controlled by neurological mechanisms centered in the hypothalamus. In human beings and other higher mammals, aggressive behavior is largely under cognitive control, determined by learning and social influences.

5   Evidence indicates that observing aggressive behavior, either live or filmed, tends to increase aggressiveness through one or more of the following pro-

cesses: teaching aggressive styles of conduct, increasing arousal, desensitizing people to violence, reducing restraints on aggressive behavior, or distorting views about conflict resolution.

6   The relationship between motivation and emotion, as well as a definition of emotion itself, are unresolved issues in psychology. A common but not entirely satisfactory basis for differentiating between the two assumes that emotions are aroused by external stimuli and that emotional responses are directed toward the stimuli in the environment that arouse them. Motives, on the other hand, are more often aroused by internal stimuli and are "naturally" directed toward specific objects in the environment like food, water, or a mate.

7   Intense emotions involve widespread physiological arousal that results from activation of the sympathetic division of the autonomic nervous system. Attempts to differentiate between emotions (such as fear and anger) on the basis of physiological response patterns have not been successful; however, this possibility cannot be ruled out and more sophisticated experimental procedures may in time establish such relationships.

8   Some facial expressions and gestures appear to be innately associated with particular emotions and have a universal meaning, regardless of the culture in which the individual is raised. But learning is involved in modifying emotional expression to conform to the patterns approved by a particular culture.

9   Theories of emotion are concerned with the role of physiological factors, stimulus factors, and cognitive factors as determiners of emotional experience. The *James–Lange theory* proposes that the pattern of physiological arousal is the principal determiner of emotion, whereas the *Cannon–Bard theory* argues that the input of the external stimulus directly to the brain determines emotion independent of feedback from internal organs. Modern theories, particularly the *cognitive–physiological theory*, emphasize the role of cognitive factors in emotion. Experiments in which subjects were injected with epinephrine show how cognitive processes influence the label the individual assigns to an emotional state.

10   Low levels of emotional arousal improve performance at a task, but intense arousal is usually disruptive. Continual emotional tension can result in *psychosomatic illness*.

Further Reading

For a general coverage of human motivation, see Bolles, *Theory of motivation* (2nd ed., 1975); Buck, *Human motivation and emotion* (1976); Petri, *Motivation: Theory and research* (1981); and Franken, *Human motivation* (1982).

The psychoanalytic theory of motivation is presented in two books by Freud: *Beyond the pleasure principle* (1920) and *New introductory lectures on psychoanalysis* (1933). For a social learning approach to motivation, see Bandura, *Social learning theory* (1977).

Books on aggression include Johnson, *Aggression in man and animals* (1972); Bandura, *Aggression: A social learning analysis* (1973); Montagu (ed.), *Learning non-aggression: The experience of non-literate societies* (1978); and Hamburg and Trudeau (eds.), *Biobehavioral aspects of aggression* (1981).

For an introduction to contemporary views on emotion, see Strongman, *The psychology of emotion* (2nd ed., 1978); and Plutchik, *Emotion: A psycho-evolutionary synthesis* (1980). For a more technical treatment, see Izard (ed.), *Emotion in personality and psychopathology* (1979); and Plutchik and Kellerman (eds.), *Theories of emotion* (1980). An interesting book on facial expressions and emotion is Ekman, *Emotion in the human face* (2nd ed., 1982). For a review and critical analysis of lie detection procedures, see Lykken, *A tremor in the blood: Uses and abuses of the lie detector* (1981).

Part Six
PERSONALITY AND INDIVIDUALITY

12
MENTAL ABILITIES AND THEIR MEASUREMENT

People vary widely in personality characteristics and mental abilities. In this chapter, we will look at individual differences in ability and at tests designed to measure these differences. We will then consider methods of assessing personality differences in Chapter 13. The features that make a test useful and trustworthy, however, are the same regardless of the test's purpose; the requirements for a good test, which are discussed in this chapter, apply equally to ability and personality tests.

The use of ability tests to assign schoolchildren to special classes, to admit students to college and professional schools, and to select individuals for jobs has become a topic of public debate and controversy. When ability tests were first developed around the turn of the century, they were hailed as an objective and impartial method of identifying talent and ensuring individual opportunity. Testing permitted people to be selected for jobs or advanced schooling on the basis of merit rather than family background, wealth, social class, or political influence. America—a democratic society with a large, heterogeneous population—was particularly enthusiastic about the use of tests to classify students and select employees. To cite one example, the Civil Service Examinations that thousands of people now take annually when applying for a variety of government jobs were initiated during the 1880s in an attempt to ensure that such jobs would be given to people who were qualified instead of to those who had gained favor by supporting the newly elected president.

Many people still view ability tests as the best available means of determining what people can do and of assigning them to jobs and professions. Others claim that such tests are narrow and restrictive; they do not measure the characteristics that are most important in determining how well a person will do in college or on the job—motivation, social skills, qualities of leadership— and they discriminate against minorities. As we examine mental testing, we will look at the evidence on both sides of this controversy.

TYPES OF ABILITY TESTS

By the time we finish high school, most of us have had some experience with ability tests. Driver's license examinations, grade-school tests of reading and math skills, the competency examinations required for graduation from many high schools, and tests that assess mastery of a particular course (typing, American history, chemistry, and so on) are all ability tests.

A *test* is essentially a sample of behavior taken at a given point in time. A distinction is often made between *achievement tests* (which are designed to measure accomplished skills and indicate what the person can do at present) and *aptitude tests* (which are designed to predict what a person can accomplish with training). But the distinction between these two types of tests is not clear-cut. All tests assess the individual's current status, whether the purpose of the test is to assess what has been learned or to predict future performance. Both kinds of tests often include similar types of questions and yield results that are highly correlated. Rather than considering aptitude and achievement tests as two distinct categories, it is more useful to think of them as falling along a continuum.

Aptitude versus achievement

Tests at the two ends of the aptitude–achievement continuum are distinguished from each other primarily in terms of purpose. For example, a test of knowledge of mechanical principles might be given on completion of a course in mechanics to measure the student's mastery of the course material—to provide a measure of *achievement*. A test with similar questions might be included in a battery of tests administered to select applicants for pilot training, since knowledge of mechanical principles has been found to be a good predictor of success in flying. The latter test would be considered a measure of *aptitude*, since its results are used to predict performance as a student pilot. Thus, whether the test is labeled an aptitude or an achievement test depends more on its purpose than on its content.

Tests at the two ends of the aptitude–achievement continuum can also be distinguished in terms of the *specificity of relevant prior experience*. At one end of the continuum are achievement tests designed to measure mastery of a fairly specific subject matter, such as music theory, European history, or the safe and legal operation of a motor vehicle. At the other extreme are aptitude tests that assume little more in terms of prior experience than the general experience of growing up in the United States. A musical aptitude test, for example, is intended to predict the degree to which a student will benefit from music lessons prior to any instruction. Thus, the Musical Aptitude Profile (Gordon, 1967) does not require any knowledge of musical techniques. It tests a person's ability to identify tones and rhythms that sound similar and to discriminate musical selections that are tastefully performed. However, although no specific experience is required, a person's ability to understand instructions given in English and his or her prior experience listening to music (Western versus Eastern music, for example) would undoubtedly influence the test results.

We will see later that performance on "intelligence" tests (aptitude tests designed to measure a person's general capacity for learning) does depend to some extent on prior experience, even though every attempt is made to devise questions that do not reflect the results of special training.

Somewhere between aptitude tests (which assume little in terms of relevant prior experience) and achievement tests (which measure the mastery of specific subject matter) are tests that measure both aptitude and achievement. An example is the Scholastic Aptitude Test (SAT) that is required for admission to many colleges. The SAT consists of a verbal section (see Table 12-1A), which measures vocabulary skills and the ability to understand what is read, and a mathematical section (see Table 12-1B), which tests the ability to solve problems requiring arithmetic reasoning, algebra, and geometry. Thus, although the test taps learned material (the verbal and quantitative skills that a person has acquired during 12 years of education), it attempts to avoid questions that depend on knowledge of particular topics and focuses on the ability to use acquired skills to solve newly posed problems.

VERBAL ITEMS

Antonyms (test extent of vocabulary)

1 Choose the word or phrase that is most nearly the *opposite* in meaning to the word in capital letters.

PARTISAN: A commoner   D ascetic
            B neutral   E pacifist
            C unifier

Analogies (test ability to see a relationship in a pair of words, to understand the ideas expressed in the relationship, and to recognize a similar or parallel relationship)

2 Select the lettered pair that *best* expresses a relationship similar to that expressed in the original pair.

FLURRY: BLIZZARD: A trickle: deluge   D spray: foam
                    B rapids: rock   E mountain: summit
                    C lightning: cloudburst

Sentence completion (test . . . ability to recognize the relationships among parts of a sentence)

3 Choose the word or set of words that *best* fits the meaning of the sentence as a whole.

Prominent psychologists believe that people act violently because they have been _____ to do so, not because they were born _____ :

    A forced—gregarious   D taught—aggressive
    B forbidden—complacent E inclined—belligerent
    C expected—innocent

Reading passages (test ability to comprehend a written passage)

Blocks of questions are presented following passages of roughly 400 to 500 words. Some questions ask about information that is directly stated in the passage, others require applications of the author's principles or opinions, still others ask for judgments (e.g., how well the author supports claims).

Table 12-1A
Scholastic Aptitude Test
A sample of items from the verbal section of the SAT. These items are of middle difficulty and are answered correctly by 50–60 percent of the test takers. The answers are as follows: 1—B, 2—A, 3—D. (After College Entrance Examination Board, 1978, 1979)

Table 12-1B
Scholastic Aptitude Test
A sample of items from the mathematical section of the SAT, also of middle difficulty. The answers are as follows: 1—C, 2—C, 3—B, 4—C. (College Entrance Examination Board, 1978, 1979)

MATHEMATICAL ITEMS

Regular items

Algebra:

1 If $x^3 = (2x)^2$ and $x \neq 0$, then $x =$

   A 1   D 6
   B 2   E 8
   C 4

Geometry:

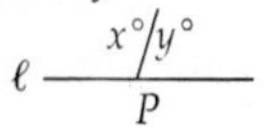

$$\ell \quad \overline{\quad \overset{x° \big/ y°}{} \quad}_{P}$$

Note: Figure is not drawn to scale.

2 If P is a point on line ℓ in the figure above and $x - y = 0$, then $y =$

   A 0   D 135
   B 45   E 180
   C 90

Quantitative comparison

Questions—each consists of two quantities, one in Column A and one in Column B. You are to compare the two quantities and on the answer sheet blacken space:

  A if the quantity in Column A is greater;
  B if the quantity in Column B is greater;
  C if the two quantities are equal;
  D if the relationship cannot be determined from the information given.

  Note: In certain questions, information concerning one or both of the quantities to be compared is centered above the two columns.

	Column A	**Column B**
Arithmetic:		
3	Number of minutes in 1 week	Number of seconds in 7 hours
Algebra:	$\dfrac{5}{x} = \dfrac{1}{3}$	
4	$\dfrac{3}{x}$	$\dfrac{1}{5}$

Generality versus specificity

Ability tests can also be distinguished along a general–specific continuum; that is, such tests vary in the broadness of their content. The Musical Aptitude Profile would be at the specific end of the continuum, as would a typing test, a driver's license examination, a test of mathematical ability, or a reading comprehension test. All of these tests measure fairly specific abilities. At the general end of the continuum would be high-school competency exams and scholastic aptitude tests (like the SAT)—which attempt to measure educational development in a number of areas—as well as most tests that are called "intelligence tests." An *intelligence test* is an aptitude test designed to predict performance over a range of abilities. Such tests usually do not contain items that can be answered by simple recall or the application of practiced skills. Instead they focus on items that require a mixture of the abilities to analyze, understand abstract concepts, and apply prior knowledge to the solution of new problems. Intelligence tests usually include an array of verbal, figurative, and quantitative

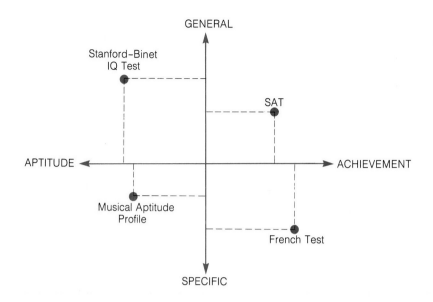

Two Dimensions That Describe Ability Tests
Any given test falls somewhere along an achievement–aptitude continuum and also along a general–specific continuum. For example, a French vocabulary test or a typing test that measures how many words a minute the subject can type accurately would fall toward the achievement end of the aptitude–achievement continuum and toward the specific end of the general–specific continuum. The Musical Aptitude Profile, which requires no prior musical knowledge and is designed to predict an individual's capacity to profit from music lessons, taps a fairly specific area of ability and also falls toward the aptitude end of the aptitude–achievement dimension. Most intelligence tests (such as the Stanford–Binet and Wechsler intelligence scales) are fairly general in that they sample a range of abilities and are designed to measure aptitude more than achievement of skills. Scholastic achievement tests, such as the SAT and ACT (American College Testing Program), are fairly general; they measure achievement in verbal and mathematical reasoning and comprehension but do not presume the mastery of certain courses.

tasks. Although the attempt to measure general intellectual ability in order to predict what an individual can accomplish with education or training is certainly worthwhile, the label "intelligence test" is unfortunate because it implies that people possess an innate capacity, called intelligence, that is fixed in amount and not influenced by education or experience. Later, we will see that many variables can influence a person's score on an intelligence test. In addition, although some individuals may be more able than others to accomplish a variety of tasks, abilities are not so consistent that a person who is above average at one task is above average at all tasks.

REQUIREMENTS FOR A GOOD TEST

In our society, much depends on test scores. In the elementary-school grades, children are often placed in instructional groups on the basis of their performances on tests of math and reading skills. Some high schools require students to pass minimum competency tests in order to graduate. Tests are part of the admissions procedure in many colleges and most professional and graduate schools. Most high-school students who are college-bound must take either the Scholastic Aptitude Test or a similar admission test, the American College Testing Program (ACT). Scores on these tests as well as high-school grades and other criteria determine who is admitted to the college. Applicants to law schools and medical schools must pass special admission tests—the Law School Admission Test (LSAT) and the Medical College Admission Test (MCAT); many graduate-school departments require students to pass the Graduate Record Exam (GRE). People applying to programs to be trained in most professions (dentistry, nursing, pharmacology, accounting, business administration, to name a few) must take special admission tests. And once such a program is completed, more tests must be passed to obtain a license to practice or a certificate of competency. Becoming certified or licensed in almost every trade or profession—as a plumber, beautician, physical therapist, doctor, clinical psychologist, or lawyer—requires the passage of a written examination. In addition, many industries and government agencies select job applicants and place or promote employees on the basis of test scores.

Since tests play such an important role in our lives, it is essential that they

High-school students taking the Scholastic Aptitude Test (SAT)

measure what they are intended to measure and that the scores accurately reflect the test taker's knowledge and skills. If a test is to be useful, its scores must be both *valid* and *reliable*.

Reliability

Test scores are *reliable* when they are reproducible and consistent. Tests may be unreliable for a number of reasons. Confusing or ambiguous test items may mean different things to a test taker at different times. Tests may be too short to sample the abilities being tested adequately, or scoring may be too subjective. If a test yields different results when it is administered on different occasions or scored by different people, it is unreliable. A simple analogy is a rubber yardstick. If we did not know how much it stretched each time we took a measurement, the results would be unreliable no matter how carefully we marked the measurement. Tests must be reliable if the results are to be used with confidence.

To evaluate reliability, two measures must be obtained for the same individual on the same test—by repeating the test, by giving the test in two different but equivalent forms, or by treating each half of the test separately. If each individual tested achieves roughly the same score on both measures, then the test is reliable. Of course, even for a reliable test, some differences are to be expected between the pair of scores due to chance and errors of measurement. Consequently, a statistical measure of the degree of relationship between the set of paired scores is needed. This degree of relationship is provided by the coefficient of correlation r (discussed in Chapter 1). The coefficient of correlation between paired scores for a group of individuals on a given test is a reliability coefficient. Well-constructed tests usually have a reliability coefficient of $r = .90$ or greater.

Validity

Tests are *valid* when they measure what they are intended to measure. A college examination in economics full of questions containing complex or tricky wording might be a test of a student's verbal ability rather than of the economics learned in the course. Such an examination might be reliable (a student would achieve about the same score on a retest), but it would not be a valid test of achievement for the course. Or a test of sense of humor might be made up of jokes that are hard to understand unless the test taker is very bright and well read. This test might be a *reliable* measure of something (perhaps intelligence or educational achievement) but still not be a *valid* test of humor.

To measure validity, we must also obtain two scores for each person: the test score and some other measure of the ability in question. This measure is called a *criterion*. Suppose that a test is designed to predict success in learning to type. To determine whether the test is valid, it is given to a group of individuals before they study typing. After completing the course, the students are tested on the number of words per minute they can type accurately. This is a measure of their success and serves as a criterion. A coefficient of correlation between the early test scores and the scores on the criterion can now be obtained. This correlation coefficient, known as a *validity coefficient*, tells something about the value of a given test for a given purpose. The higher the validity coefficient, the better the prediction that can be made from the test results.

Many tests, however, are intended to predict abilities that are more global and difficult to measure than typing skills. Scores on the Medical College Admission Test (MCAT), for example, are used (along with other information) to select medical students. If the purpose of the test is to predict success in medical school, a person's grade point average could be used as a criterion; correlating his or her MCAT score with the grade point average would be one way of validating the test. But if the MCAT is intended to predict success as a physician, the problem of validation becomes much more difficult. What criterion should be chosen—annual income, research achievements, contributions to community welfare, evaluation by patients or colleagues, number of malpractice suits? And even if the test administrators could agree on one of these criteria, it would probably be difficult to measure.

The validity of ability tests—how well they predict performance—will be discussed later. The important point to remember here is that the evaluation of a test's validity must take into account the intended uses of the test and the inferences to be made from its scores.

Uniform testing procedures

To a large extent, the reliability and validity of a test depend on the uniformity of the procedures followed in administering and scoring the test. In measuring ability, as in obtaining any scientific measurement, we attempt to control conditions in order to minimize the influence of extraneous variables. Thus, well-accepted ability tests contain clearly specified instructions, time limits (or lack of limits for untimed tests), and scoring methods. The explanations given by the examiner and the manner in which the examiner presents the test materials must be standard from one test administration to the next.

Of course, not all extraneous variables can be anticipated or controlled. The sex and race of the examiner, for example, will vary. These characteristics could influence a test taker's performance, as could the examiner's general demeanor (facial expression, tone of voice, and so on). Although such variables cannot be controlled, their influence should be taken into consideration in evaluating test results. Thus, if a black male child does poorly when tested by a white female examiner, the possibility that the child's motivation and anxiety levels would have been different with a black male examiner should be considered.

TESTS OF INTELLECTUAL ABILITY

Reliability, validity, and uniform testing procedures are essential requirements for any test—whether the test is designed to measure personality characteristics (to be discussed in Chapter 13), mastery of a specific subject matter, job skills, or the probability of succeeding in college or professional school. This chapter focuses primarily on tests that measure general intellectual ability. Such tests are often called "intelligence tests," but as we noted earlier, many psychologists consider that term inappropriate. There is no general agreement as to what constitutes intelligence, and intelligence cannot be considered apart from an individual's culture and experiences. During this discussion of intelligence tests, these qualifications should be kept in mind.

The first person to attempt to develop tests of intellectual ability, or intelligence, was Sir Francis Galton. A naturalist and mathematician, Galton was interested in individual differences. He believed that certain families were biologically superior—stronger and smarter—than others. Intelligence, Galton reasoned, was a question of exceptional perceptual-motor skills, which were

Alfred Binet with his daughters

passed from one generation to the next. Since all information is acquired through the senses, the more sensitive and accurate an individual's perceptual apparatus, the more intelligent the person. Galton administered a battery of tests (measuring such variables as head size, reaction time, visual acuity, memory for visual forms, breathing capacity, and strength of hand grip) to over 9,000 visitors at the London Exhibition in 1884. To his disappointment, he discovered that eminent British scientists could not be distinguished from ordinary citizens on the basis of their head size and that strength of grip was not particularly related to other measures of intelligence. Although his tests did not prove very useful, Galton did invent the correlation coefficient, which plays an important role in psychology.

The first tests that approximated contemporary intelligence tests were devised by the French psychologist Alfred Binet (1857–1911). In 1881, the French government passed a law making school attendance compulsory for all children. Previously, slow learners had usually been kept at home; now teachers had to cope with a wide range of individual differences. The government asked Binet to devise a test that would detect children who were too slow intellectually to benefit from a regular school curriculum.

Binet assumed that intelligence should be measured by tasks that required reasoning and problem-solving abilities rather than perceptual-motor skills. In collaboration with another French psychologist, Theodore Simon (1873–1961), Binet published a scale in 1905, which he revised in 1908 and again in 1911.

Binet's method: A mental-age scale

Binet reasoned that a slow or "dull" child was like a normal child but retarded in mental growth. On tests, the slow child would perform like a normal child of younger age. On the other hand, the mental abilities of a "bright" child were characteristic of older children. Binet devised a scale of *mental age* to measure intelligence in terms of the kinds of changes that are ordinarily associated with growing older. *Average mental-age* (MA) scores correspond to *chronological age* (CA), which is the age determined from the child's date of birth. A bright child's MA is above his or her CA; a slow child's MA is below his or her CA. The mental-age scale is easily interpreted by teachers and others who deal with children of differing mental abilities.

ITEM SELECTION Since intelligence tests are designed to measure brightness rather than the results of special training (that is, aptitude more than achievement), they should consist of items that do not assume any special training. There are two chief ways to select such items. One way is to choose *novel items*, which provide an untaught child with just as much chance to succeed as a child who has been taught at home or in school. Figure 12-1 illustrates a novel item; in this particular test, the child is asked to choose figures that are alike, on the assumption that the designs are unfamiliar to all children. The second way is to choose *familiar items*, on the assumption that all those for whom the test is designed have had the requisite prior experience to deal with the items. The following problem provides an example of a supposedly familiar item:

Mark F if the sentence is foolish; mark S if it is sensible.

S   F   Mrs. Smith has had no children, and I understand that the same was true of her mother.

Of course, this item is "fair" only for children who know the English language, who can read, and who understand all the words in the sentence. For such

Figure 12-1
Novel Items Used in Intelligence Tests
The following instructions accompany the test: *Mark every card to the right that matches the sample card on the left. You can rotate the sample card but not flip it over.* **(Cards 2, 3, and 6 are correct in the first line; cards 1, 3, and 5 are correct in the second line.)**

children, detection of the fallacy in the statement becomes a valid test of intellectual ability.

Many of the items on intelligence tests assume general knowledge and familiarity with the language of the test. But such assumptions can never be strictly met. The language spoken in one home is never exactly the same as that spoken in another; the available reading material and the stress on cognitive abilities also vary. Even the novel items test perceptual discriminations that may be acquired in one culture and not in another. Despite these difficulties, items can be chosen that work reasonably well. The items included in contemporary intelligence tests have survived in practice after many others have been tried and found defective. It should be remembered, however, that intelligence tests have been validated according to their success in predicting school performance within a particular culture.

CONTEMPORARY BINET TESTS The tests originally developed by Binet have undergone several revisions in this country. The best-known and most widely used revision, made by Lewis Terman at Stanford University in 1916, is commonly referred to as the Stanford–Binet test. This test was revised in 1937, 1960, and 1972.

In the Binet tests, an item is age-graded at the level at which a substantial majority of the children pass it. The present Stanford–Binet test assigns six items to each year; when passed, each item earns a score of two months of mental age. Some examples of items used at different age levels are given in Table 12-2. The Binet test items do not tap all of a child's skills, but they provide a fairly representative sample of what children at different ages can do.

Table 12-2
Examples of Items from
the Stanford–Binet Intelligence Scale

AGE	TASK
2	**Naming parts of the body.** Child is shown a large paper doll and asked to point to various parts of the body.
3	**Visual-motor skills.** Child is shown a bridge built of three blocks and asked to build one like it. Can copy a drawing of a circle.
4	**Opposite analogies.** Fills in the missing word when asked: "Brother is a boy; sister is a _____. "In daytime it is light; at night it is _____." **Reasoning.** Answers correctly when asked: "Why do we have houses?" "Why do we have books?"
5	**Vocabulary.** Defines words such as *ball*, *hat*, and *stove*. **Visual-motor skills.** Can copy a drawing of a square.
6	**Number concepts.** Is able to give the examiner nine blocks when asked to do so.
8	**Memory for stories.** Listens to a story and answers questions about it.
9	**Rhymes.** Answers correctly when asked: "Tell me the name of a color that rhymes with Fred." "Tell me a number that rhymes with free."
12	**Verbal absurdities.** Tells what is foolish about statements such as, "Bill Jones's feet are so big that he has to put his trousers on over his head."
14	**Inference.** Examiner folds a piece of paper a number of times, notching a corner with scissors each time. Subject is asked the rule for determining how many holes there will be when the paper is unfolded.
Adult (15 years and older)	**Differences.** Can describe the difference between "misery and poverty," "character and reputation." **Memory for reversed digits.** Can repeat six digits backwards (that is, in reverse order) after they are read aloud by the examiner.

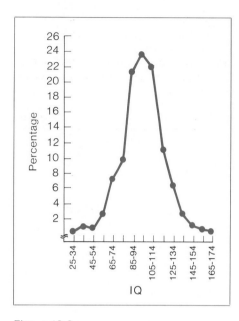

Figure 12-2
A Normal Distribution Curve of IQs
Distribution of Stanford–Binet IQs for 2,904 children and youths, ages 2 to 18. The slight bump on the left-hand tail represents those who are retarded as the result of specific genetic defects or birth injuries and are not part of the normal distribution. (After Terman and Merrill, 1937)

IQ	VERBAL DESCRIPTION	PERCENTAGE
Above 139	Very superior	1
120–139	Superior	11
110–119	High average	18
90–109	Average	46
80–89	Low average	15
70–79	Borderline	6
Below 70	Mentally retarded	3
		100

Table 12-3
Interpretation of IQs
The table presents the descriptive labels associated with IQ scores on the Stanford–Binet test. The far right-hand column lists the percentage of individuals in each category.

Intelligence quotient

Terman adopted a convenient index of intelligence suggested by the German psychologist William Stern (1871–1938). This index is the *intelligence quotient,* commonly known as the IQ. It expresses intelligence as a ratio of mental age (MA) to chronological age (CA):

$$IQ = \frac{MA}{CA} \times 100$$

The 100 is used as a multiplier so that the IQ will have a value of 100 when MA is equal to CA. If MA is lower than CA, then the IQ will be less than 100; if MA is higher than CA, then the IQ will be more than 100.

How is the IQ to be interpreted? The distribution of IQs approximates the form of curve found for many differences among individuals, such as differences in height; this bell-shaped *normal distribution curve* is shown in Figure 12-2. Most cases cluster around a midvalue on the normal curve; from there, the number gradually decreases to just a few cases at both extremes. The adjectives commonly used to describe various IQ levels are given in Table 12-3. In the 1960 and subsequent revisions of the Stanford–Binet test, the authors introduced a method of computing the IQ from tables. The meaning of an IQ remains essentially the same, but the tables allow the IQ at any age to be interpreted somewhat more exactly.

Tests with more than one scale

Tests following the pattern originated by Binet use an assortment of different items to test intelligence; a pass or a fail on one kind of item is scored the same as a pass or a fail on another. But those who are skilled in the use and scoring of the tests learn much more than the final IQ. They may note special strengths and weaknesses; a child may perform much better on a test of vocabulary, for example, than on a test that requires drawing geometric forms. These observations led to the conjecture that what is being measured is not one simple ability but a composite of abilities.

One way to obtain information on specific kinds of abilities, rather than a single mental-age score, is to separate the items into more than one group and to score the groups separately. The Wechsler Adult Intelligence Scale (described in Table 12-4) and the Wechsler Intelligence Scale for Children do this. The items on these tests are similar to the items in the Binet tests, but they are divided into two parts—a *verbal* scale and a *performance* scale—according to content. A *performance* item requires the manipulation or arrangement of blocks, beads, pictures, or other materials; both stimuli and responses are nonverbal. The separate scaling of the items within one test provides a clearer picture of the individual's intellectual strengths and weaknesses. For example, separate scores can indicate how well the person performs under pressure (some subtests are timed; others are not) or how verbal skills compare with the ability to manipulate nonverbal material. Figure 12-3 shows a test profile and how scores are summed to yield IQs. The subject who obtained these particular scores tends to do better on performance (nonverbal) tasks. Looking at the profile of scores, this 16-year-old does not appear to be doing as well scholastically as he could be; he scores lowest on subtests that are more closely related to "school learning" (information, arithmetic, and vocabulary). A discrepancy

TEST	DESCRIPTION
Verbal scale	
Information	Questions tap a general range of information; for example, "How many nickels make a dime?"
Comprehension	Tests practical information and ability to evaluate past experience; for example, "What is the advantage of keeping money in a bank?"
Arithmetic	Verbal problems testing arithmetic reasoning.
Similarities	Asks in what way certain objects or concepts (for example, *egg* and *seed*) are similar; measures abstract thinking.
Digit span	A series of digits presented auditorily (for example, 7-5-6-3-8) is repeated in a forward or backward direction; tests attention and rote memory.
Vocabulary	Tests word knowledge.
Performance scale	
Digit symbol	A timed coding task in which numbers must be associated with marks of various shapes; tests speed of learning and writing.
Picture completion	The missing part of an incompletely drawn picture must be discovered and named; tests visual alertness and visual memory.
Block design	Pictured designs must be copied with blocks; tests ability to perceive and analyze patterns.
Picture arrangement	A series of comic-strip pictures must be arranged in the right sequence to tell a story; tests understanding of social situations.
Object assembly	Puzzle pieces must be assembled to form a complete object; tests ability to deal with part–whole relationships.

Table 12-4
Tests Comprising the Wechsler Adult Intelligence Scale
The tests of the Wechsler Intelligence Scale for Children are similar with some modifications.

between verbal and performance scores prompts the examiner to look for specific learning problems, such as reading disabilities or language handicaps.

Both the Stanford–Binet and the Wechsler scales fit our requirements for trustworthy tests; that is, they show good reliability and validity. The Stanford–Binet scale has a reliability coefficient of about .90 on retest;[1] the WAIS has a retest reliability of .91. Both tests are fairly valid predictors of achievement in school; the correlation between IQ scores on these tests and school grades is approximately .40 to .60.

Group tests

The Stanford–Binet and the Wechsler scales are *individual ability tests*; that is, they are administered to a single individual by a specially trained tester. *Group*

---

[1]Reliability coefficients are based on fairly short test-retest intervals (usually less than a year). The reliability coefficients decrease when longer time periods elapse between the first and second tests. For example, the reliability for tests given 10 years apart is about .71.

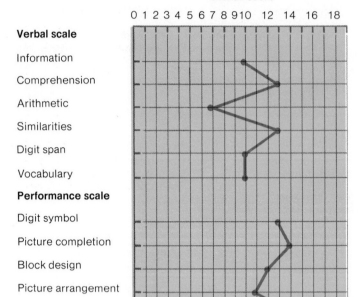

TEST		Scaled score
Information		10
Comprehension		13
Arithmetic		7
Similarities		13
Digit span		10
Vocabulary		10
Verbal score		63
Digit symbol		13
Picture completion		14
Block design		12
Picture arrangement		11
Object assembly		15
Performance score		65
Total score		128

VERBAL SCORE _63_ IQ _108_
PERFORMANCE SCORE _65_ IQ _121_
FULL SCALE SCORE _128_ IQ _115_

Figure 12-3
Profile for Wechsler Adult
Intelligence Scale (WAIS)
The table on the right shows the test scores for a 16-year-old male combined to yield verbal, performance, and full scale scores. The manual that accompanies the test provides tables (adjusted for age) for use in converting these scores into IQs. Note that the test taker's performance IQ is 13 points above his verbal IQ.

ability tests, in contrast, can be administered to a large number of people by a single examiner and are usually in pencil-and-paper form (see Figure 12-4). The advantages of an individual test over group tests are many. The tester can be certain the subject understands the questions, can evaluate the person's motivation (is the subject really trying?), and can gain additional clues to intellectual strengths and weaknesses by carefully observing the subject's approaches to different tasks. Group ability tests are useful, however, whenever large numbers of people have to be evaluated. For example, the armed services use a number of group tests that measure general intellectual ability and special skills to select men and women for special jobs, including pilots, navigators, electronic technicians, and computer programmers.

Other examples of group tests used to measure general ability are the SAT and the Professional and Administrative Career Examination (PACE), which was developed by the U.S. Civil Service Commission for use in selecting employees for government jobs.

PREDICTIVE VALIDITY OF TESTS

Tests of general ability, such as the Stanford–Binet and Wechsler Intelligence Scales, do predict achievement in school and do provide a measure of what most people think of as "brightness." When elementary-school teachers are asked to rank children in their classroom in terms of "brightness," correlations between the teacher's rankings and scores on intelligence tests range from .60 to .80 (Jensen, 1980). These correlations would probably be higher except for some interesting biases in judgment. For example, teachers tend to overrate the youngest children in their classroom and underrate the oldest; apparently, they base their judgments on mental age rather than on IQ, which expresses the relationship between mental age and chronological age. Teachers also tend to

SPACE PERCEPTION

Which of the four patterns would result when the box is unfolded?

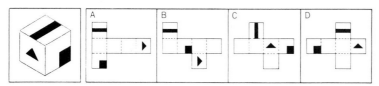

The D answer is correct.

MECHANICAL COMPREHENSION

Which bridge is the strongest?

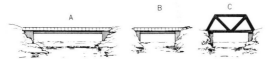

The C answer is correct.

WORD KNOWLEDGE

Stench most nearly means

A Puddle of slimy water
B Pile of debris.
C Foul odor.
D Dead animal.

Camaraderie most nearly means

A Interest in photography.
B Close friendship.
C Petty jealousies.
D Arts and crafts projects.

GENERAL INFORMATION

For which of the following taxes was it necessary to amend the US Constitution?

A Income.
B Sales.
C Liquor.
D Tobacco.

Picasso was a famous

A poet.
B painter.
C philosopher.
D soldier.

ARITHMETIC REASONING

It cost $0.50 per square yard to waterproof canvas. What will it cost to waterproof a canvas truck cover that is 15' x 24'?

A $6.67
B $18.00
C $20.00
D $180.00

The parcel post rate in the local zone is 18 cents for the first pound and 1½ cents for each additional pound. How many pounds can be sent in the local zone for $1.50?

A 88
B 89
C 100
D 225

Figure 12-4
Group Test
These are sample items from the Armed Services Vocational Aptitude Battery (ASVAB) — the basic recruit selection and placement test used by all military services since 1976.

overrate girls and underrate boys, probably due to a tendency to confuse conscientiousness and good manners with ability. In general, children who are sociable, eager, and self-confident—who volunteer for activities and raise their hands to recite—are viewed by their teachers and peers as brighter than children who are withdrawn and quiet, even though their test scores may be the same. In such instances, ability test scores provide a more accurate estimate of ability than the teacher's judgments.

Test scores and academic performance

Intelligence test scores correlate quite highly with measures of academic performance (grades, achievement test scores, continuation in school), at least during the elementary- and high-school years. Youngsters who achieve higher scores on tests like the Stanford–Binet and Wechsler Intelligence Scales get better grades, enjoy school more, and stay in school longer. But as students move up the educational ladder—from elementary school, to high school, to college, to graduate school—the correlations between intelligence test scores and measures of academic performance become progressively lower (see Table 12-5).

A person's performance on an ability test clearly is dependent on the culture in which she or he is raised. Obviously, this is true of verbal tests that require familiarity with a particular language. We would not expect a child from a home in which English is spoken as a second language to score as well on verbal items as a child whose parents speak only English. But even among children from English-speaking families, the vocabulary in a middle-class home may differ significantly from the vocabulary in a lower-class home. For example, consider the following item:

> Pick ONE WORD that does not belong with the others.
>
> cello   harp   drum
> violin   guitar

Most children from upper- or middle-class homes chose "drum," the intended correct answer. Children from lower-class homes commonly answered "cello," an unfamiliar word that they thought did not belong (Eells and others, 1951). Children from upper-class homes are more likely to be acquainted with cellos or at least to have heard the word than children from poorer homes.

Several tests have been developed that are based on black culture and language (see Williams, 1972; Boone and Adesso, 1974). The vocabulary and idioms used in these tests are more or less characteristic of "black English" and include items similar to the following:

> "Running a game" means:
> A writing a bad check
> B looking at something
> C directing a contest
> D getting what one wants

Those familiar with black English will recognize that D is the correct answer.

These tests emphasize the extent to which cultural factors can influence test scores; blacks score at least 20 IQ points higher than whites on such tests. But the test scores apparently bear little relationship to other measures of intelligence or achievement for members of either race (Matarazzo and Wiens, 1977).

Cultural experiences can also affect performance on nonverbal items. Numerical operations and mathematical concepts are taught primarily in school. And even items that presumably are unrelated to schooling (such as recognizing the missing element in a drawing of a common object or manipulating blocks to form a pattern) are not wholly independent of culture. For example, if children from poor families are shown a drawing of a comb with several teeth missing and asked to name the missing part (an item on the Wechsler Intelligence Scale), they may be puzzled; to them, a broken comb may be more common than a whole one (Hewitt and Massey, 1969).

In some nonliterate societies, drawings and pictures are rare. When Nigerian children were asked to manipulate colored blocks to form a design (a task included in several intelligence tests), they did quite well when the design to be copied was also made of blocks. But it was difficult for them to copy a design

EDUCATIONAL LEVEL	TYPICAL CORRELATIONS
Elementary School	.60–.70
High School	.50–.60
College	.40–.50
Graduate School	.30–.40

Table 12-5
Correlation Between IQ Scores and Academic Achievement

Table entries give the correlations typically observed between intelligence test scores and other measures of academic achievement (for example, grades, achievement test scores) at different levels of schooling. (After Jensen, 1980)

A number of factors contribute to the progressive decrease in the size of validity coefficients as schooling increases. We will see shortly that one of the most important factors is *selection*.

Thus far, we have talked about the relationship between academic performance and tests designed to measure general aptitude for learning (so-called "intelligence tests" that yield an IQ score). What about scholastic aptitude tests, like the SAT, that measure developed abilities and are designed to predict performance in college? The SAT has been given to millions of college applicants over many years, and numerous studies have correlated SAT scores with freshman grade point averages. The correlations vary from study to study, with a median correlation of about .38 for the verbal section of the SAT and .34 for the mathematics section (Linn, 1982).

These correlations underestimate to some extent the degree of relationship between test scores and college grades because the criterion data (grade point averages) are collected only for those individuals who actually attend college. If everyone who took the SAT attended college and their test scores were correlated with their freshman grades, the correlations would be much higher. The size of a correlation coefficient is affected by the amount of variability in the measures being correlated; in general, the more select the group is, the

Culture-Fair Tests

from a picture until the examiner demonstrated with the blocks (D'Andrade, 1967).

A number of attempts have been made to develop tests that are culture-fair (see Figure 12-5), but the results have not been promising. For one thing, the culture-fair tests do not predict scholastic performance (or, in some instances, performance on the job) as well as more conventional ability tests. This finding is not too surprising, since what is considered a good performance in school or on the job is also culture-dependent. Secondly, group differences on culture-fair tests are often as large as differences on the tests they have been designed to replace.

In principle, it is probably impossible to design a culture-fair test; an individual's performance will always be affected by his or her cultural background. The abilities that a society considers important are the ones it will take the trouble to test. If writing and quantitative skills are valued in a society, these skills will be viewed as predictive of success.

If social skills and the use of complex riddles in storytelling are valued (as they are among the Kpelle people of Liberia), these skills will be considered the important ones to test (Cole, 1981).

In the absence of satisfactory culture-fair tests, the best we can do at present is to recognize the cultural basis of our standard intelligence tests and interpret the scores with caution, always keeping in mind the individual's background—the language spoken in the home and the kinds of learning experiences provided.

Figure 12-5
Culture-Fair Test
Sample items from a test designed to be relatively independent of the culture in which one is raised. The test taker is to select one of the five items on the right that best completes the pattern on the left.

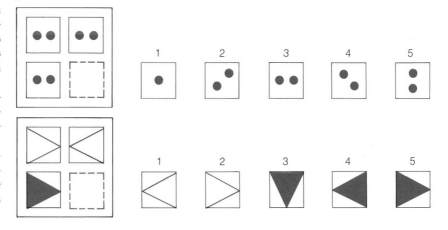

narrower the range of scores and the lower the correlation. College students are more capable than the population at large. If the entire college-age population were tested and attended college, the correlation between test scores and freshman grades would be higher still.

An example may help to explain why correlations are lower in a selected group. Before there were weight classifications in the sport of boxing, weight was a fairly good predictor of the outcome of a match. A 250-pound boxer could usually defeat a 150-pounder, regardless of differences in training; the correlation between weight and winning was quite high. However, once weight classifications were introduced so that boxers fought only boxers of similar weight (heavyweights versus heavyweights, lightweights versus lightweights, and so on), weight became a poor predictor of outcome (Fricke, 1975).

Although the effects of selection on correlations between SAT scores and grades are less extreme, they still can be substantial. For example, for colleges with freshman classes that show a wide range of scores on the verbal section of the SAT, the correlation between SAT-Verbal scores and freshman grade point averages is .44. For colleges with less variability, the correlation is .31 (Schrader, 1971). The more select or homogeneous the group is, the lower the correlation.

If correlations between SAT scores and freshman grades are "corrected" statistically to take into account the selective nature of the population, the resulting correlations are around .50. What does a correlation of this size mean in terms of predictability? A correlation of .50 indicates that the chances are 44 out of 100 that a student in the top fifth of the distribution of SAT scores will also be in the top fifth of the distribution of freshman grade point averages, whereas the chances that a student in the bottom fifth of the SAT scores will earn such grades are only 4 out of 100 (Schrader, 1965). With no knowledge of the test scores, the chances would, of course, be 20 out of 100. Thus, SAT scores improve prediction considerably, but it is also clear that the freshman grades of students with the same SAT scores will vary widely.

Group differences in test performance

Differences in *average* performance on ability tests are often found when certain subgroups of the population are studied. For example, children from middle- or upper-income families score higher, on the average, than children from poor families. Mean differences are found in performance on tests of general ability as well as on achievement tests, whether the group of children is defined in terms of parental occupation, education, or income (Speath, 1976).

Members of some minority groups—blacks, Hispanic Americans, American Indians—tend to score lower on ability tests than members of the white majority (see Coleman and others, 1966; Bock and Moore, 1982).

Males and females also score differently on some tests, depending on how the test was developed. Most intelligence tests (such as the Stanford–Binet and the Wechsler Intelligence Scales) have been constructed to minimize sex differences, either by deleting items showing large sex differences or by balancing items advantageous to females with items advantageous to males. One test of general ability that was not designed to eliminate sex differences (the Differential Aptitude Test) shows that high-school girls perform much better than boys on tests of clerical speed and accuracy and language usage, whereas boys perform much better than girls on tests of mechanical reasoning and spatial relationships (Linn, 1982). On the SAT, males and females score equally well on the verbal section, but males score higher on the mathematical section (Benbow and Stanley, 1980).

Two points should be emphasized whenever group differences in performance are discussed. First, these are only *average* differences; the size of the differences between subgroups is usually small compared to the variability within groups. Thus, some children from poor families will score higher than most children from upper-income families and, conversely, some wealthier children will score lower than most poor children. Second, as we will see later, group differences in average test scores cannot be viewed as evidence of innate differences in ability. They may reflect differences in a number of factors related to home environment and opportunities to learn. However, to the extent that group differences in average test scores reflect differences in the probability of success in school or on the job, they need to be understood.

Since most ability tests have been standardized on white, middle-class Americans, it has been argued that the tests are biased and do not fairly measure the performance of other groups. We will discuss some possible reasons for differences in test performance among racial, ethnic, and socio-economic groups later. But the existence of group differences does not mean that tests are not useful for predicting performance. Ability tests predict scho-

Coaching and Test Sophistication

Courses that claim to improve an applicant's score on admissions tests—such tests as the Scholastic Aptitude Test (SAT), the Law School Aptitude Test (LSAT), the Medical College Aptitude Test (MCAT), the Graduate Record Examination (GRE), and the Graduate Management Aptitude Test (GMAT)—are offered daily in the newspapers. Coaching for such tests has become a profitable business. The degree to which coaching can improve test scores is a controversial issue; if coaching does result in higher scores, applicants who can afford such courses have an advantage over those who cannot.

Being familiar with testing procedures is clearly helpful. An individual who has had prior experience in taking tests and who knows what to expect will be more self-confident than a person who has had limited test-taking experience. *Test sophistication* includes being familiar with separate answer sheets, considering *all* the answers in a multiple-choice item rather than picking the first one that seems right, not spending too much time on puzzling items, and spotting flaws in items that provide additional clues. It also helps to know when to guess. If there is no penalty for incorrect answers, it makes sense to always guess. On tests such as the SAT, where a wrong answer on a four-choice item is scored $-\frac{1}{4}$ (compared to 1 point for a correct answer and 0 for no response), it pays to guess if the answer can be narrowed to two or three possible alternatives.

Instruction in test-taking strategies and practice with sample test questions are included in most courses that prepare applicants for admissions tests. Commercially published practice booklets, available for the major admissions tests, can be used for a similar kind of "self-coaching." Familiarity with the test format, knowledge of test-taking strategies, and practice on sample test items do result in higher test scores, but the gain is substantial only for naive test takers (for example, recent immigrants or students from schools that require little testing). Students who have graduated from most American high schools, which provide substantial exposure to objective tests, probably would not benefit from spending more than a day on practice test items.

What about instruction in specific subjects? Admissions tests are designed to measure an individual's aptitude for a particular program of study, and test constructors try to avoid items on which performance can be raised by short-term drill or instruction in specialized topics. However, the verbal section of the SAT (and of other tests like the LSAT, MCAT, and GRE) relies heavily on vocabulary, and many of the problems in the quantitative section presume knowledge of high-school algebra and geometry. For individuals who feel deficient in the latter two subjects, a review would be worthwhile. Several studies have shown that coaching in mathematics raises scores on the quantitative section of the SAT for high-school students who are not currently studying math but is of little benefit for those enrolled in mathematics courses. Vocabulary flashcards and reading with the aid of a dictionary would be helpful in preparing for the verbal section.

Over the past 30 years, numerous studies have been conducted to determine the effects of coaching on SAT scores. The studies covered a variety of coaching methods and included commercial programs as well as programs offered to students in public and private high schools. The results vary markedly, depending on the length and type of program and the presence or absence of a control group. (Control groups are important because students who enroll in coaching courses are apt to differ from those who do not in a number of ways—especially in level of motivation—and it is difficult to evaluate their test-score gains without referring to a comparable group of students.)

A review of 11 studies with control groups estimated that coaching produces an average gain of 9–14 points on the SAT-Verbal and 13–15 points on the SAT-Quantitative (Messick and Jungeblut, 1981). Since SAT scores range from 200 to 800 points, gains of this size are not likely to affect admission decisions.

Several studies (without control groups) report much larger gains of 50–80 points on both sections of the SAT (Pallone, 1961; Marron, 1965). However, the subjects in these studies were enrolled in fairly intensive, long-term coaching programs of up to six months. The issue here is the difference between *education* and *coaching*. The SAT is designed to assess *developed* abilities. One year of high-school courses in English and algebra does increase SAT scores; it is not surprising that a six-month coaching course produces a similar effect.

What recommendations should be made regarding coaching for admissions tests? For purposes of equity, a brief course in test strategies plus practice on sample test items under examination conditions would help to equalize test sophistication among individuals with differing amounts of experience in taking objective tests. Reviews of vocabulary and of algebra and geometry skills would probably benefit individuals whose background in these areas is deficient. It is probably not worthwhile for people with a normal high-school education to spend much time and money on coaching courses.

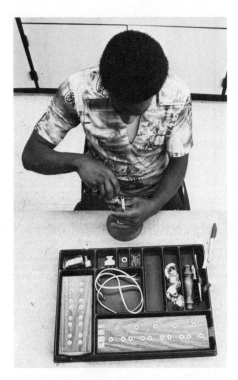

A mechanical aptitude test: assembling a lamp against time

lastic performance for minority students as well as they do for white students. For example, if black grade-school children are ranked according to scores on an intelligence test, the rankings predict school performance in mathematics and reading as well as they do for white children. And SAT scores predict college freshman grades for blacks and Mexican-Americans as well as they do for whites (Linn, 1982).

Saying that ability tests are not biased does not deny that society discriminates against minority groups. There is undoubtedly a bias in opportunity that results in lower scores on ability tests and lower scores on the criterion measure (grades, class standing, and so forth).

Using tests to predict performance

Although ability tests are useful in predicting academic performance, they are only one measure and should always be used in combination with other information. For example, senior-year high-school grades correlate about as highly with freshman grade point averages as SAT scores do. This fact raises some questions about the usefulness of admissions tests. However, it can be argued that college admission test scores provide an adjustment for the variability in the quality of education among different high schools (grades from one high school may not be equivalent to grades from another). Indeed, a combination of SAT scores and high-school grades does predict college grades better than either of these variables alone. The SAT multiple correlation for high-school grades plus test scores is about .59, compared to .50 for high-school grades alone (Schrader, 1971).

Ability tests can provide a reasonably good indication of whether a person can read and comprehend certain material or solve quantitative problems. But tests cannot assess an individual's social concerns, willingness to work, or interpersonal skills. Tests provide some basis for predicting academic success, but they do not indicate which students will become creative scientists or writers, talented teachers or lawyers, and outstanding medical researchers or physicians.

Scores on admissions tests provide one piece of information. They should be evaluated along with other measures (high-school grades, recommendations, special achievements) to predict an applicant's academic performance.

NATURE OF INTELLIGENCE

Some psychologists view intelligence as a general capacity for comprehension and reasoning that manifests itself in various ways. This was Binet's assumption. Although his test contained many different kinds of items (testing such abilities as memory span, arithmetic, and vocabulary), Binet noted that bright children tended to score higher than dull children on all of them. He assumed, therefore, that the different tasks sampled a basic ability or faculty:

> It seems to us that in intelligence there is a fundamental faculty, the alteration or the lack of which is of the utmost importance for practical life. This faculty is judgment, otherwise called good sense, practical sense, initiative, the faculty of adapting one's self to circumstances. To judge well, to comprehend well, to reason well, these are the essential activities of intelligence. (Binet and Simon, 1905)

Despite the diverse subscales that comprise his tests, David Wechsler, too, believes that "intelligence is the aggregate or global capacity of the individual to act purposefully, to think rationally, and to deal effectively with his environment" (Wechsler, 1958).

Factorial approach

Other psychologists question whether there is such a thing as "general intelligence." They believe that intelligence tests sample a number of mental abilities that are relatively *independent of one another*. One method of obtaining more precise information about the kinds of abilities that determine performance on intelligence tests is *factor analysis*. Factor analysis is a mathematical technique used to determine the minimum number of dimensions, or factors, that account for the observed relationships (correlations) among subjects' responses over a large number of different tests. The method is too intricate to describe in detail, but Table 12-6 (page 368) provides some understanding of factor analysis.

The originator of factor analysis, Charles Spearman, proposed that all individuals possess a general intelligence factor (called g) in varying amounts. A person could be described as generally bright or generally dull, depending on the amount of g he or she possessed. According to Spearman, the g factor is the major determinant of performance on intelligence test items. In addition, special factors, each called s, are specific to particular abilities or tests. For example, tests of arithmetic or spatial relationships would each tap a separate s. An individual's tested intelligence would reflect the amount of g plus the magnitude of the various s factors. Performance in mathematics would be a function of a person's general intelligence and mathematical aptitude.

A later investigator, Louis Thurstone (1938), objected to Spearman's emphasis on general intelligence. Thurstone felt that intelligence could be broken down into a number of primary abilities. To determine these abilities, he applied factor analysis to results from a large number of tests that employed many different types of items. One set of test items was designed to measure verbal comprehension; another, to measure arithmetical computation; and so on. Thurstone hoped to find a more definitive way of grouping intelligence test items than the rather crude method of item-sorting used in the Wechsler verbal and performance scales.

After intercorrelating the scores of all the tests (that is, correlating each subscore to every other subscore), Thurstone applied factor analysis to arrive at a set of basic factors. Test items that best represented each of the discovered factors were used to form new tests; these tests were then given to another group of subjects and the intercorrelations were reanalyzed. After a number of studies of this kind, Thurstone identified seven factors as the *primary abilities* revealed by intelligence tests: verbal comprehension, word fluency, number, space, memory, perceptual speed, and reasoning (see Table 12-7, page 369).

Thurstone devised a battery of tests, known as the *Test of Primary Mental Abilities*, to measure each of these abilities. This test is still widely used, but its predictive power is no greater than the predictability of tests of general intelligence, such as the Wechsler scales. Thurstone's hope of discovering the basic elements of intelligence through factor analysis was not fully realized for several reasons. His primary abilities are not completely independent; the significant intercorrelations among them provide some support for Spearman's concept of a general intelligence factor. In addition, the number of basic abili-

Table 12-6
The Method of Factor Analysis

What are the data that enter into factor analysis, and what are the major steps in the analysis? The data are simply scores on a variety of tests designed to measure various psychological contents or processes. Each of a large number of individuals obtains a score for each of a number of tests. All these scores can then be inter-correlated; that is, we know how the scores of many individuals on test 1 relate to their scores on test 2, and so on. These intercorrelationships yield a table of correlations known as a *correlation matrix*. An example of such a correlation matrix, based on only nine tests, is given below.

TESTS	2	3	4	5	6	7	8	9
1	.38	.55	.06	−.04	.05	.07	.05	.09
2		.36	.40	.28	.40	.11	.15	.13
3			.10	.01	.18	.13	.12	.10
4				.32	.60	.04	.06	.13
5					.35	.08	.13	.11
6						.01	.06	.07
7							.45	.32
8								.32

The three outlined clusters of correlations indicate that these are groups of tests with something in common not shared by other tests (that is, they show high correlations). The inadequacy of making such a judgment from a table of correlations of this kind is shown by noting the additional high correlations of test 2 with tests 4, 5, and 6, not included in the outlined clusters. We can use factor analysis to tell us more precisely what underlies these correlations. If the correlation matrix contains a number of statistically significant correlations and a number of near-zero correlations, it is apparent that some tests measure similar abilities of one kind and that others measure abilities of other kinds. The purpose of factor analysis is to be more precise about these underlying abilities.

Factor analysis then uses mathematical methods (assisted by high-speed computers) to compute the correlation of each of the tests with each of several possible underlying factors. Such correlations between test scores and factors are known as *factor loadings;* if a test correlates .05 on factor I, .10 on factor II, and .70 on factor III, it is most heavily "loaded" on factor III. For example, the nine tests with the above correlation matrix yield the *factor matrix* below.

TESTS	FACTORS I	II	III
1	.75	−.01	.08
2	.44	.48	.16
3	.72	.07	.15
4	.08	.76	.08
5	−.01	.49	−.01
6	.16	.73	.02
7	−.03	.04	.64
8	.02	.05	.66
9	−.01	.10	.47

The outlined loadings in the factor matrix show which tests are most highly correlated with each of the underlying factors. The clusters are the same as the clusters in the correlation matrix but are now assigned greater precision. The problem of test 2 remains because it is loaded almost equally on factor I and factor II; it is obviously not a "factor-pure" test. Having found the three factors that account for the inter-correlations of the nine tests, the factors can be interpreted by studying the content of the tests most highly weighted on each factor. The factor analysis itself is strictly a mathematical process, but the naming and interpretation of the factors depends on a psychological analysis.

ABILITY	DESCRIPTION
Verbal comprehension	The ability to understand the meaning of words; vocabulary tests represent this factor.
Word fluency	The ability to think of words rapidly, as in solving anagrams or thinking of words that rhyme.
Number	The ability to work with numbers and perform computations.
Space	The ability to visualize space-form relationships, as in recognizing the same figure presented in different orientations.
Memory	The ability to recall verbal stimuli, such as word pairs or sentences.
Perceptual speed	The ability to grasp visual details quickly and to see similarities and differences between pictured objects.
Reasoning	The ability to find a general rule on the basis of presented instances, as in determining how a number series is constructed after being presented with only a portion of that series.

Table 12-7
Thurstone's Primary Mental Abilities
Using factor analysis, Thurstone identified seven factors as the primary abilities revealed by intelligence tests. (After Thurstone and Thurstone, 1963)

ties identified by factor analysis depends on the nature of the test items. Other investigators using different test items have defined anywhere from 20 to 120 factors assumed to represent different intellectual abilities (Guilford, 1967; Ekstrom and others, 1976).

Componential approach

Until the 1960s, the measurement of intelligence was dominated by the factorial approach. However, the development of cognitive psychology over the past two decades has laid the groundwork for a reexamination of intelligence. This reexamination attempts to analyze and understand the underlying component processes responsible for the factors identified in the intercorrelation of test scores.

The *componential approach* is illustrated by the work of Sternberg (1981, 1982), who assumes that the test taker possesses a set of psychological processes, called *components*, that operate in an organized way to produce the responses observed on an intelligence test. There are a large number of components, all of which fall into one of the five classes given in Table 12-8. Sternberg selects a specific task from an intelligence test and uses it in an extensive series of experiments. The results of these experiments enable him to infer the components involved in the task; individual differences in performance are explained by assuming that some components work more efficiently for one individual than for another. For example, consider the following analogy problem:

lawyer : client : : doctor : (medicine, patient)

A series of experiments with problems of this sort led Sternberg to conclude that the critical component processes are *encoding* and *comparing*. The subject *encodes* the words by forming mental representations of them and then *compares* these representations to arrive at the answer. A mental representation of lawyer, for example, would include the features commonly associated with the word "lawyer" (college educated, versed in legal procedures, represents clients in court, etc.). The experimental evidence indicates that individuals who score high on analogy problems tend to spend more time encoding (forming more

Table 12-8
Components of Intelligence
Sternberg's scheme for classifying the many component processes operative in solving problems.

COMPONENTS	PROCESSES
Metacomponents	Higher-order control processes used for executive planning and decision making in problem solving.
Performance components	Processes that execute the plans and implement the decisions selected by metacomponents.
Acquisition components	Processes involved in learning new information.
Retention components	Processes involved in retrieving information previously stored in memory.
Transfer components	Processes involved in carrying over retained information from one situation to another.

elaborate mental representations of the words) and less time comparing representations than individuals who score low on such problems.

A factorial approach and a componential approach provide complementary interpretations of performance on intelligence tests. Factors such as Thurstone's primary mental abilities are useful in identifying broad areas of strengths and weaknesses. They may indicate that a person is very strong in word fluency and verbal comprehension but weak in reasoning. If additional testing is conducted, a component analysis can provide a diagnostic profile of the particular components responsible for the observed deficiency. A componential analysis may indicate a deficiency at the level of metacomponents (such as the choice of strategies used to attack the problem), or retention components (such as slow or inaccurate recall of relevant information), or transfer components (such as poor ability to transfer what has been learned about solving reasoning problems to new problem contexts.)

General characteristics of intelligence

A detailed understanding of Sternberg's approach to intelligence is beyond the scope of this book, but his work can be summarized here. The various components identified by Sternberg tend to be organized and to operate in clusters that can be labeled roughly as follows:

1   Ability to learn and profit from experience
2   Ability to think or reason abstractly
3   Ability to adapt to the vagaries of a changing and uncertain world
4   Ability to motivate oneself to accomplish expeditiously the tasks one needs to accomplish

These four general abilities are not unique to a componential analysis of intelligence; they are also found in most factor analyses of intelligence tests. Since research on intelligence—almost without regard to the theoretical approach used—identifies these four abilities, they can be regarded as necessary ingredients for a theory of intelligence.

Most intelligence tests in use today are effective in measuring the first two abilities on this list but are far less adequate in assessing the last two. Psychologists have tried to develop improved measures of the last two abilities (practical problem solving and motivation) with limited success. Our ability to measure intelligence with the type of tests in use today probably has reached a ceiling. New methods will have to be developed that more accurately assess motivation and practical problem-solving ability to improve significantly on present measures of intelligence. These new approaches will probably require a more adaptive testing situation than that provided by paper-and-pencil testing. Computer-controlled testing situations may provide the flexibility required, and research along these lines is underway. Computer-assisted instruction, discussed in Chapter 7, illustrates the type of environment for instructional purposes that can be developed for testing purposes.

Intelligence and creativity

Tests of general intelligence, such as the Binet and the Wechsler, correlate quite highly with achievement in school and, to a lesser extent, with intellectual achievements in later life. But they do not measure what some experts believe to be an essential aspect of intelligence—creative, or original, thinking.

Problem solving usually involves two phases—examining alternative solutions and choosing the one that seems most appropriate. The first phase—recalling possible solutions or inventing new ones—has been called *divergent thinking;* the individual's thoughts "diverge" along a number of different paths. The second phase—applying knowledge and the rules of logic to narrow the possibilities and "converge" on the most appropriate solution—has been called *convergent thinking* (Guilford and Hoepfner, 1971). In solving difficult problems, people often alternate between these two modes of thought; when initial solutions are discarded as inappropriate, additonal divergent thinking is necessary to conceive of new possibilities. Divergent thinking is more closely associated with originality and creativity.

Most intelligence tests emphasize convergent thinking; they present problems that have well-defined, correct answers. Thus, traditional intelligence tests may fail to identify individuals who excel in divergent thinking—who are skillful at producing new and original ideas. Attempts have been made to devise tests that measure divergent thinking. A sample test item might ask, "What uses can you think of for a brick?" The person who responds with many varied answers ("heat it to warm your bed," "as a weapon," "to hold the shelves of a bookcase") will score high on divergent thinking. Other examples of test items designed to measure divergent or creative thinking are given in Table 12-9 (page 372).

Two important questions concerning creativity tests must be asked. Do the abilities measured by creativity tests differ from the abilities measured by general intelligence tests? Do scores on these tests predict creative achievements in real life?

The abilities sampled by intelligence tests and creativity tests do appear to overlap considerably. For the population as a whole, scores on intelligence tests tend to be positively correlated with scores on creativity tests; that is, people with above-average IQs tend to achieve above-average scores on creativity tests. But beyond a certain level of intelligence (an IQ of about 120), there is little relationship between intelligence and creativity scores. Some individuals with very high IQs score low on creativity tests; some people with slightly above-average intelligence do extremely well on creativity tests. Thus, creativity appears to be independent of intelligence only at the upper end of the distribution.

These findings have led some experts to propose a "threshold model" of creativity. According to this model, a certain level of intelligence is necessary before an individual can make a creative contribution in his or her line of work

Table 12-9
Examples of Items Used in Tests of Creativity

---

1 Ingenuity (Flanagan, 1963)

A   A very rare windstorm destroyed the transmission tower of a TV station in a small town. The station was located in a town in a flat prairie with no tall buildings. Its former 300-foot tower enabled it to serve a large farming community, and the management wanted to restore service while a new tower was being erected. The problem was temporarily solved by using a ————— .

B   As part of a manufacturing process, the inside lip of a deep cup-shaped casting is machine threaded. The company found that metal chips produced by the threading operation were difficult to remove from the bottom of the casting without scratching the sides. A design engineer was able to solve this problem by having the operation performed ————— .

2 Unusual uses (Guilford, 1954)
Name as many uses as you can think of for:
A   a toothpick
B   a brick
C   a paper clip

3 Consequences (Guilford, 1954)
Imagine all of the things that might possibly happen if all national and local laws were suddenly abolished.

4 Fable endings (Getzels and Jackson, 1962)
Write three endings for the following fable: a moralistic, a humorous, and a sad ending.

THE MISCHIEVOUS DOG

A rascally dog used to run quietly to the heels of every passerby and bite them without warning. So his master was obliged to tie a bell around the cur's neck that he might give notice wherever he went. This the dog thought very fine indeed, and he went about tinkling it in pride all over town. But an old hound said. . . .

5 Product improvement (Torrance, 1966)
The subject is presented with a series of objects, such as children's toys or instruments used in his or her particular occupation, and asked to make suggestions for their improvement.

6 Pattern meanings (Wallach and Kogan, 1965)
The subject is shown a series of patterns of geometric forms (like the samples shown below) and asked to imagine all the things each pattern could be.

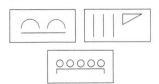

7 Remote associations (Mednick, 1962)
Find a fourth word which is associated with each of these three words:
A   rat—blue—cottage
B   out—dog—cat
C   wheel—electric—high
D   surprise—line—birthday

8 Word association (Getzels and Jackson, 1962)
Write as many meanings as you can for each of the following words:
A   duck
B   sack
C   pitch
D   fair

(discover a new scientific principle, invent a new mechanical device, write an outstanding poem or play). Beyond that threshold, creative achievement depends on other factors—the kind of fluency of ideas sampled by creativity tests as well as certain personality variables (Crockenburg, 1972). The intelligence threshold necessary for creative achievements is assumed to vary for different abilities. It probably requires a higher IQ to discover a new principle in theoretical physics or mathematics than to write an original short story.

We can only speculate on whether creativity tests predict actual creative achievements. As yet, few long-term studies have been conducted that relate scores on creativity tests to achievements in later life, but the results of some of these studies are pessimistic. For example, there seems to be little relationship between scores on tests of divergent thinking in the fifth or tenth grade and talented extracurricular accomplishments in leadership, drama, art, or science in high school (Kogan and Pankove, 1974). Creativity tests sample the individual's ability to provide novel responses, but originality is not the only component of creativity. To be creative, an idea or a product must be appropriate. A new theory must be in accord with the known facts; an invention must serve its purposes efficiently and economically; an artistic product must be aesthetically satisfying. Most creative discoveries require both convergent and divergent thinking—the abilities to envision new and unique solutions to a problem and to evaluate them in light of one's knowledge about the relevant facts.

Studies of scientists and artists who have made significant and original contributions in their fields suggest that such personality factors as independence of judgment, motivation to achieve, initiative, and a tolerance for ambiguity are important requirements for creative discoveries. Thus, creativity may not be a characteristic that can be measured accurately by a test.

GENETIC AND ENVIRONMENTAL INFLUENCES ON ABILITY

People differ in intellectual ability. How much of this difference is due to the particular genes we inherit and how much is due to the environment in which we are raised? The heredity-environment issue, which has been debated in regard to many aspects of human behavior, has focused primarily on the area of intelligence. Most experts agree that at least some aspects of intelligence are inherited, but opinions differ as to the relative contributions made by heredity and environment.

Genetic relationships and intelligence

Most of the evidence bearing on the inheritance of intelligence is derived from studies correlating IQs between persons of various degrees of genetic relationship. Table 12-10 summarizes the results of a large number of studies of this type. In general, the closer the genetic relationship, the more similar the tested intelligence. The average correlation between the IQs of parents and their natural children is .50; between parents and their adopted children, the correlation is about .25. Identical twins, because they develop from a single egg, share precisely the same heredity; the correlation between their IQs is very high—about .90. The IQs of fraternal twins (who develop from separate eggs and are no more alike genetically than ordinary siblings) have a correlation coefficient of about .55.

But although genetic determinants of intelligence are strong, the results shown in Table 12-10 indicate that environment is also important. Note that when siblings are reared in the same home environment, IQ similarity increases. Other studies have shown that the intellectual ability of adopted children is higher than would be predicted on the basis of their natural parents' ability (see Scarr and Weinberg, 1976). Environment does make a difference in intelligence.

It is possible to estimate what portion of the variability in test scores is due to environment and what portion is due to heredity from data similar to the data provided in Table 12-10. Several methods are used to make these estimates; the most common is to compare the variability of fraternal and identical twins on a given trait. To do this, two quantities are estimated: (1) the total variability due to both environment and heredity V_T, based on the differences between pairs of fraternal twins, and (2) the environmental variability alone V_E, based on the differences between pairs of identical twins. The difference between the two quantities is the variability due to genetic factors V_G. The heritability ratio, or simply *heritability* H, is the ratio between genetic variability and total variability:

$$H = \frac{V_G}{V_T}$$

In other words, heritability is the proportion of a trait's variation within a specified population that can be attributed to genetic differences.

RELATIONSHIP	CORRELATION
Monozygotic twins	
Reared together	.86
Reared apart	.72
Dizygotic twins	
Reared together	.60
Siblings	
Reared together	.47
Reared apart	.24
Parent/child	.40
Foster parent/child	.31
Cousins	.15

Table 12-10
Familial Studies of Intelligence
A summary of 111 studies identified in a survey of the world literature on familial resemblances in measured intelligence. The data represent average correlation coefficients for IQ test scores between persons of various relationships. In general, the pattern of correlations indicates that the higher the proportion of genes two family members have in common, the higher the average correlation between their IQs. (After Bouchard and McGue, 1981)

Quality of stimulation and emotional climate of the home are two factors that influence the development of an individual's intellectual potential.

Heritability ranges between 0 and 1. When identical twins resemble each other much more than fraternal twins on a given trait, H approaches 1. When the resemblance between identical twins is about the same as the resemblance between fraternal twins, H approaches 0.

There are a number of ways of estimating H other than comparing identical and fraternal twins. The theory that permits us to make such estimates is too lengthy to present here but is discussed in most genetics textbooks. For our purposes, it is sufficient to say that H measures the fraction of the observed variance in a population that is caused by differences in heredity. It is important to note that H refers to a population of individuals, not to a single individual. For example, height has an H of .90, which means that 90 percent of the variance in height observed in a population is due to genetic differences and 10 percent is due to environmental differences. (It does not mean that an individual who is 5 feet 10 inches tall grew to a height of 63 inches due to genetic factors and grew another 7 inches due to environmental factors.) In discussing intelligence, H is often misused to designate the fraction of an individual's intelligence that is due to heredity; the use of the term in this way is incorrect.

Heritability estimates for intelligence have ranged widely from one study to another. Some researchers have reported values as high as .87; others, values as low as .10. For the data presented in Table 12-10, the estimate of H is .74. The fact that heritability estimates vary so widely suggests that the research is plagued by a number of uncontrolled variables that are influencing the results in ways that cannot be specified. It must be kept in mind that heritability research is based not on well-controlled laboratory experiments but on field studies; often individual cases are observed where they can be found. Field studies are always subject to the influence of uncontrolled variables and are particularly suspect when different investigators report quite different conclusions.

Complicating the situation further is the fact that assumptions made in assessing heritability may not always be correct. In research on twins, for example, it is assumed that twins who are reared together experience roughly the same environment, whether they are fraternal or identical twins. But this may not be true. Identical twins look more alike than fraternal twins, and this fact alone may cause parents and others to treat them more alike than fraternal twins (for example, identical twins are more likely to be dressed in identical outfits than fraternal twins).

In the absence of better controlled studies than have been feasible until now, a reliable estimate of heritability is not possible. Heredity clearly has an effect on intelligence, but the degree of this effect is uncertain. It is probably less influential than some researchers have claimed (see Jensen, 1980) but not zero, as some critics of the research have claimed (Kamin, 1976). Most probably, intellectual ability is determined by a number of genes whose individual effects are small but cumulative. If as few as 5–10 pairs of genes are involved, the possible contributions would approximate a normal distribution of IQ scores and would allow for a wide range of intellectual ability, even within a single family (Bouchard, 1976).

Environmental influences

We can think of a person's genes as imposing a top and a bottom limit on intelligence, or establishing a *range* of intellectual ability. Environmental influences—what happens to the individual during the course of development—will determine where the person's IQ will fall within that range. In other words, genes do not specify behavior but establish a range of probable responses to the environment, called the *reaction range*. Figure 12-6 illustrates this concept; it shows hypothetical IQ reaction ranges for individuals of different genetic potential raised in deprived, average, and enriched environments. In each case, an enriched environment raises the individual's IQ score and a deprived one lowers it. But each type of individual has a specific reaction range; a person with the genetic potential for average or superior intelligence under normal environmental conditions (curves C and D) has a much larger reaction range than an individual who is retarded (curve B) or mentally defective (curve A). Presumably, the person with the superior potential (D) has the greatest capacity to utilize an enriched environment and would show the greatest decrease in IQ under deprived conditions. Several studies suggest that an adverse environment does have the greatest effect on children of above-average ability (see Weisman, 1966; Scarr–Salapatek, 1971).

The environmental conditions that determine how an individual's intellectual potential will develop include nutrition, health, quality of stimulation, emotional climate of the home, and type of feedback elicited by behavior. Given two children with the same genes, the child with the better prenatal and postnatal nutrition, the more intellectually stimulating and emotionally secure home, and the more appropriate rewards for academic accomplishments will attain the higher IQ score when tested in first grade. Studies have shown that IQ differences between children of low and high socioeconomic status become progressively greater between birth and entrance into school (Bayley, 1970), suggesting that environmental conditions accentuate whatever differences in intelligence are present at birth.

HEAD START PROGRAMS   Because children from underprivileged families tend to fall behind in cognitive development even before they enter school, efforts have been made to provide more intellectual stimulation for these children during their early years. In 1965, as part of President Johnson's "war on poverty," Congress authorized funds for a number of programs designed to provide learning experiences for 2- to 5-year-olds from poor homes. These

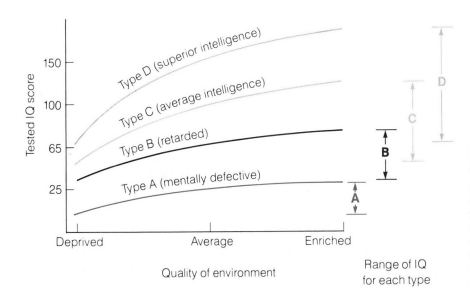

Figure 12-6
Effects of Different Environments on IQ
The curves represent hypothetical reaction ranges for four individuals who vary in inherited intellectual potential. For example, the individual labeled type D has an IQ of about 65 when raised in a deprived environment but an IQ of over 180 when raised in a maximally enriched environment. The vertical arrows to the right indicate the range of possible IQ scores for each type. (After Gottesman, 1963)

The debate over genetic contributions to intelligence has focused on the possibility of inherited racial differences in intelligence—specifically on the question of whether blacks are innately less intelligent than whites. In view of the heated controversy about this issue and its significance for social policy, it is important that we examine the available evidence.

On standard intelligence tests, black Americans as a group score 10–15 points lower than white Americans as a group. This fact is not debated; the controversy revolves around the interpretation of this difference. Some behavioral scientists and geneticists believe that the two groups differ in inherited ability (see Jensen, 1980). Others argue that black–white differences in average IQ can be attributed entirely to environmental differences between the two groups (see Kamin, 1976). Probably, the majority believes that genetic and environmental differences are so confounded that the question is unanswerable at present (Loehlin, Lindzey, and Spuhler, 1975). The issues involved are exceedingly complex; the best we can do here is to summarize a few of the main points.

1   Although blacks and whites may differ in physical appearance, they do not represent two distinct biological groups. In fact, differences in gene structures (where known) in most cases are greater *within* the races than between them.

2   Heritability is a population statistic (like infant mortality or birth rate); it depends on the environmental and genetic variation among a given group of people at a given time. Thus, although heritability ratios estimated for white populations indicate that variations in IQ are partly a function of heredity, such estimates do not permit us to make inferences about heritability ratios among black populations. More importantly, heritability estimates do not tell us anything about differences *between* populations. The heritability of a characteristic could be the same for two groups, even though the differences between them are caused entirely by environmental factors. For example, suppose the heritability of height is the same for two populations, A and B. If individuals in population A are raised on a starvation diet, they will be shorter, on the average, than individuals in population B. Variations in adult height within each group are still influenced by heredity (that is, undernourished individuals with tall parents will be taller than undernourished individuals with short parents), but the difference in average height between the two groups is clearly the result of environment. To summarize, heritability estimates do not permit us to draw conclusions about differences between populations.

3   Among black populations, there is some tendency for lightness of skin color (presumably an indication of the degrees of intermixture with whites) to correlate positively with IQ. But such correlations are very low (typically .15) and can be explained on the basis of environmental differences—a lighter skin color is associated with less discrimination and greater opportunity. A recent study found no relationship between degree of African ancestry (as estimated by skin color and blood type) and intellectual ability (Scarr and others, 1977).

4   A study of illegitimate children fathered by U.S. servicemen during the occupation of Germany after World War II found no overall difference in average IQ between chil-

programs, funded by Project Headstart, varied in approach. In some, special teachers visited the children at home several times a week to play with them. They engaged the children in such activities as building with blocks, looking at pictures, and naming colors, and taught them such concepts as big–little and rough–smooth. In brief, the teachers provided the kind of intellectual stimulation that children in upper-class homes usually receive from their parents. The visiting teacher also taught the mothers how to provide the same kinds of activities for their children. In other programs, the children attended special classes, where they interacted with teachers in similar play-learning activities. Some of these programs involved the parents; others did not.

In general, the results of these early education programs have been promising. Children who have participated in such programs score about 10 points

Race and Intelligence

dren whose fathers were black and those whose fathers were white. Since these children were all raised by German mothers of similar social status and were matched with children of the same age in the classroom, the results provide strong support for viewing environment as the major determinant of racial IQ differences (Eyferth, Brandt, and Wolfgang, 1960).

5 When black or interracial children (those with one black parent) are adopted before they are 1 year old and raised by white families with above-average incomes and educations, they score more than 15 IQ points higher than underprivileged black children reared by their biological families; the performance of the adopted children on school achievement tests is slightly above the national norms (Scarr and Weinberg, 1976).

The authors of this text believe that it is not possible to draw valid conclusions about innate racial differences in intelligence from the available evidence. Cultural and environmental differences between blacks and whites influence the development of cognitive abilities in complex ways, and no study has suc-

ceeded in estimating or eliminating these effects. So long as systematic differences remain in the conditions under which blacks and whites are raised (and so long as the effects of these differences cannot be reliably estimated), no valid conclusions can be drawn concerning innate differences in intelligence between the two races.

A postscript to this discussion of race and intelligence is provided by recent data indicating that the mean IQ in Japan has increased significantly over the past 80 years. On the performance scale of the Wechsler intelligence tests, Japanese born earlier in this century (1910–1945) have a mean IQ of 102–105. For Japanese born later (1946–1969), the mean IQ is 108–115 (Lynn, 1982). It is doubtful that an increase in IQ of this magnitude over a single generation can be accounted for by a change in the genetic structure of the population. Such environmental factors as improvements in health, nutrition, and the quality of early education provide the most likely explanations for the observed increase in IQ.

Changes of this magnitude in the tested intelligence of members of one race should caution us in drawing conclusions about innate racial differences in intelligence.

higher on the Stanford–Binet or WISC on entering school and tend to be more self-confident and socially competent than children who have not received special attention.

Follow-up studies indicate that early education programs produce some lasting academic and social benefits. For example, several studies have followed the progress through high school of disadvantaged children (primarily blacks) who participated in special preschool programs when they were 3 years old. By the age of 15, these students were more than a full grade ahead of a matched control group of students who had had no preschool experience. In addition, compared to the control group, the students with preschool experience (1) scored higher on tests of reading, arithmetic, and language usage, (2) were less apt to need special remedial classes, (3) exhibited less anti-social

Head Start programs provide preschool children with increased intellectual stimulation.

behavior, and (4) were more likely to hold after-school jobs (Palmer, 1976; Lazar, 1977; Hohmann, Banet, and Weikart, 1979).

Head Start programs have shown that early intellectual stimulation can have a significant impact on later school performance. The specific method used appears to be less important than parental involvement. Programs that actively involve the parents—interest them in their children's development and show them how to provide a more stimulating home environment—tend to produce the greatest gains.

The effect on intellectual performance of environmental changes more dramatic than Head Start is evidenced by studies of children living in Israeli kibbutzim. For some time, Israel has been faced with the problem of large differences in intellectual and educational background among Jews of different cultural ancestry. The average intellectual ability of Jews of European ancestry is generally considerably higher than that of Jews from Arabic countries. The average difference in IQ between the two groups is at least as large as the average difference between blacks and whites in this country. The exceptions to this observation are Israeli children who are raised on certain types of kibbutzim, where they do not reside with their parents but live in a children's house under the care of women specially trained in child rearing (see Chapter 3, page 78). Under these special conditions, the children's IQ scores tend to be unrelated to the country of parental origin. Children whose parents came from Arabic countries score as well as children whose parents came from Europe. Although individual differences in IQ scores still occur, the differences are not related to ancestry (Smilansky, 1974). Thus, we have some indication of the contribution an enriched environment can make toward helping children reach their intellectual potential.

ABILITY TESTS IN PERSPECTIVE

Despite their limitations, ability tests are one of the most widely used tools that psychology has developed. If these tests are to continue to be useful, however, they must be viewed realistically. They should not be overvalued as providing a fixed, unchangeable measure of what a person can do nor discarded because of their obvious shortcomings and replaced by other methods of evaluation that may be less valid.

One area of concern has been the use of ability tests to determine class placement in school. Children who achieve low scores may be assigned to a slower "track" or placed in a special class for "slow learners"; children who earn high scores may be placed in accelerated or "enriched" programs. Unless schools provide periodic reassessment and "slow learner" classes emphasize academic skills, a child's initial placement may well determine his or her academic future. Some youngsters who have the potential to succeed in college may be discouraged on the basis of early test scores from taking college preparatory courses. Both parents and teachers must realize that test scores—whether the test is called an intelligence or an achievement test—can only measure current performance. Questions on an intelligence test are less dependent on schooling but they do not measure innate capacity, and the test scores can change with changes in the environment.

The use of tests to classify school children is a controversial social issue because a disproportionately large number of minority and underprivileged children have been assigned to special classes for slow learners on the basis of their scores on group intelligence and achievement tests. Legal suits by parents have prompted a number of states to prohibit the use of group intelligence tests for purposes of classification (see Wigdor and Garner, 1982, pp. 110–16).

The issue is complicated. Ability tests (both intelligence and achievement) probably have been overused and misused in the schools. Teachers often do not know how to interpret test results and may draw sweeping conclusions about a child's ability on the basis of a single test score. More importantly, decisions about placement in special classes should be based on many factors— never on test scores alone. A child's medical and developmental history, social competency, and home environment are some of the variables that should be considered before the child is classified as a slow learner or retarded.

Ability tests can serve an important function when properly used. They help the teacher separate a large class of pupils of varying skills into homogeneous learning groups. (Children who are roughly at the same level in mastering reading or mathematical concepts can be taught together.)

Ability tests can also be used diagnostically to improve the educational opportunities for disadvantaged and minority children. A child who scores low on a group intelligence test (and such tests should be used only as initial screening devices) should be given a more intensive evaluation. Individual testing can help to reveal (1) whether the group test scores represent an accurate assessment of the child's current abilities, (2) the child's particular intellectual strengths and weaknesses, and (3) the best instructional program for improving his or her skills. Tests should be used to match instruction to individual needs, not to label a child.

A comparison of intelligence and achievement test scores often yields valuable information. For example, some children whose achievement test scores in math or reading are low may score quite high on an intelligence test. This discrepancy should alert the teacher to the possibility that the child's math and reading skills are not well developed and require special attention. This child may do quite well scholastically once his or her specific learning problems are remedied. Without the information from the intelligence test, such a child might be inappropriately placed in a slow-learner group.

Another point of concern is the type of talent measured by ability tests. As noted earlier, the SAT and other admissions tests have proved quite successful in predicting college grades. But when college admission officials place too much emphasis on test scores, they are apt to overlook students who may have an extraordinary talent in art, drama, or music. They may also overlook students who have aimed all of their energy and enthusiasm toward creative efforts in a specific area (for example, an award-winning science project or an innovative community program to help disadvantaged children). In any selection procedure, scores on intelligence and scholastic aptitude tests should be considered in conjunction with other information.

We must always question the validity of a test score for a particular individual or for a particular purpose, and we must continue to improve methods of assessment. But despite their limitations, ability tests are still the most effective aids we have for judging what job or class or type of training is most appropriate for a given individual. The alternatives are few. To rely entirely on subjective judgment would introduce the kinds of biases that such tests were designed to eliminate. To assign people at random to jobs or educational programs would benefit neither society nor the individual.

Summary

1   Ability tests range from *aptitude tests* (which are designed to predict what a person can accomplish with training) to *achievement tests* (which measure accomplished skills and indicate what the individual can do at present). Both tests may contain similar types of items, but they differ in their purposes and in the amount of *prior experience* they assume. Some ability tests measure very specific abilities; others cover a range of skills.

2   To be useful, tests must meet certain specifications. Studies of *reliability* tell us whether test scores are consistent over time. Studies of *validity* tell us how well a test measures what it is intended to measure—how well it predicts according to an acceptable criterion. *Uniform testing procedures* are necessary for a test to be reliable and valid.

3   The first successful intelligence tests were developed by the French psychologist Alfred Binet, who proposed the concept of *mental age*. A bright child's mental age is above his or her chronological age; a slow child's mental age is below his or her chronological age. The revision of the Binet scales (the Stanford–Binet) adopts the *intelligence quotient* (IQ) as an index of mental development. The IQ expresses intelligence as a ratio of mental age (MA) to chronological age (CA).

4   Two widely used ability tests, the Wechsler Adult Intelligence Scale (WAIS) and the Wechsler Intelligence Scale for Children (WISC), have both verbal and performance scales so that separate information can be obtained about each type of ability. The Stanford–Binet and the Wechsler scales are *individual tests* that are administered to a single individual by a specially trained tester. *Group ability tests* can be administered to a large number of people at one time.

5   Scores on ability tests correlate quite highly with what we think of as "brightness" and with measures of academic performance. But they do not measure motivation, leadership, and other characteristics that are important for success.

6   Both Binet and Wechsler assumed that intelligence was a *general capacity* for reasoning. Spearman proposed a general factor (g) plus specific abilities (each called s), which could be identified by the method of *factor analysis*. Thurstone used factor analysis to arrive at seven primary mental abilities he considered to be the basic elements of intelligence. The componential approach views intelligence in terms of psychological processes (such as *encoding* and *comparing*) that underlie intelligence test items.

7   Intelligence test items emphasize *convergent thinking;* creativity tests measure *divergent thinking*. Scores on creativity tests are independent of IQ only at the upper levels of intelligence, leading some experts to propose a *threshold model* to explain the relationship between intelligence and creative achievement. Most creative discoveries require both divergent and convergent thinking.

8   Studies correlating IQs between persons with varying degrees of genetic relationship show that heredity plays a role in intelligence. Estimates of *heritability* vary, however; such environmental factors as nutrition, intellectual stimulation, and the emotional climate of the home will influence where within the *reaction range* determined by heredity the person's IQ will fall.

9   Despite their limitations, ability tests are still the most objective method available for assessing individual capabilities. But test scores must always be considered in conjunction with other information.

For a general introduction to individual differences and psychological testing, see Vernon, *Intelligence: Heredity and environment* (1979); and Anastasi, *Psychological testing* (5th ed., 1982). More advanced treatments of these topics are Sternberg (ed.), *Handbook of human intelligence* (1982); and Wigdor and Garner (eds.), *Ability testing: Uses, consequences, and controversies* (1982).

A special issue of the journal *American Psychologist* is devoted to psychological testing. The issue, titled "Testing: Concepts, policy, practice, and research," *American Psychologist*, (October 1981, Vol. 36, No. 10), presents an excellent overview of many aspects of intelligence testing.

The genetics of intelligence is discussed in Plomin, DeFries, and McClearn, *Behavioral genetics: A primer* (1980). For a discussion of racial and social class differences in intelligence, see Scarr, *Race, social class, and individual differences in IQ* (1981).

13
PERSONALITY
AND ITS ASSESSMENT

As popularly used, the word "personality" has a number of meanings. When we say that someone has "a lot of personality," we are usually referring to that individual's social effectiveness and appeal. Courses advertised to "improve your personality" attempt to teach social skills and to enhance your appearance or manner of speaking in order to elicit favorable reactions from others. Sometimes we use the word "personality" to describe an individual's most striking characteristic. We may refer to someone as having an "aggressive personality" or a "shy personality."

When psychologists talk about personality, however, they are concerned primarily with *individual differences*—the characteristics that distinguish one individual from another. Psychologists do not agree on an exact definition of personality. But for our purposes, we will define personality as the *characteristic patterns of behavior and modes of thinking that determine a person's adjustment to the environment.*

The term *characteristic* in the definition implies some consistency in behavior—that people tend to act or think in certain ways in many different situations. For example, you can probably think of an acquaintance who seldom expresses anger, no matter what the provocation, and another who flies off the handle at the slightest irritation. Behavior is the result of interaction between personality characteristics and the social and physical conditions of the environment. But, as we will see later, personality theorists differ in the extent to which they believe behavior is *internally controlled* (determined by the personal characteristics of the individual and therefore fairly consistent) or *externally controlled* (determined by the particular situation in which the behavior occurs).

When we discuss behavior, we refer to the *public personality*—the "you" that others observe and listen to, the view of yourself that you present to the world. Your public personality includes expressive features and mannerisms (your speech patterns, the way you carry yourself), your general disposition (whether you are usually cheerful or grumpy), the way you react to threatening situations, the attitudes you express, and much more. You may behave differently in large social gatherings than you do in a small group of close friends, but the public side of your personality still can be observed by others and can be measured in various ways.

But there is also a private, hidden part of your personality. Your *private personality* includes the fantasies, thoughts, and experiences that you do not share with others. You may have had some special experiences you have never told anyone about, wishes that seem too childish or embarrassing to reveal, dreams and memories that remain yours alone. The stream of thoughts and memories that cycle through your mind as you wait for class to begin or stroll through the woods are part of your private personality. You may reveal some of these in a close, intimate relationship with another person, but generally they are yours alone.

Because the private personality is difficult to study, psychologists have tended to focus on the public personality, leaving the private personality for novelists and biographers to analyze and describe. However, psychologists have devised procedures for exploring the private personality through the study of fantasies and related methods.

SHAPING OF PERSONALITY

An infant is born with certain potentialities. Physical characteristics—such as eye and hair color, body build, and the shape of a person's nose—are essentially determined at the moment of conception. Intelligence and certain special abilities, such as musical and artistic talent, also depend to some extent on heredity. And there is increasing evidence that differences in emotional reactivity may be innate. A study of newborns found that reliable differences could be observed shortly after birth in such characteristics as activity level, attention span, adaptability to changes in the environment, and general mood. One infant might be characteristically active, easily distracted, and willing to accept new objects and people; another might be predominantly quiet, persistent in concentrating on an activity, and apprehensive of anything new. These original characteristics of temperament tended to persist in many of the children whose development was followed over a 20-year period (Thomas and Chess, 1977).

Parents respond differently to babies with different characteristics. In this way, a reciprocal process starts that may exaggerate some of the personality characteristics present at birth. For example, an infant who stops crying when picked up and snuggles closely is more pleasant to hold than one who stiffens, turns his or her head away, and continues to cry. Consequently, the "snuggler" is apt to be held more often than the "nonsnuggler"; the initial behavioral predispositions are reinforced by the responses of the parent.

The biological predispositions with which an individual is born are shaped by experiences encountered in the course of growing up. Some of these experiences are *common,* shared by most people growing up in a given culture or cultural subgroup; others are *unique* to the individual.

Biological influences

The fact that differences in mood and activity level can be observed so soon after birth suggests the influence of genetic factors. Research on the inheritance of personality characteristics has focused on the study of twins. As you may recall from our discussion of intelligence in Chapter 12, comparison of identical twins (who share the same heredity because they develop from a single egg) with fraternal twins (who are no more alike genetically than ordinary siblings) provides a basis for estimating heritability.

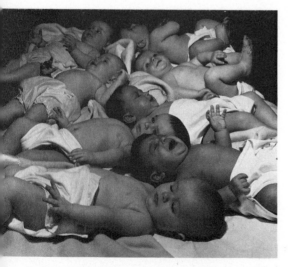

Infants react differently to the same environment.

	CORRELATIONS FOR BOYS		CORRELATIONS FOR GIRLS	
	IDENTICAL	FRATERNAL	IDENTICAL	FRATERNAL
Emotionality	.68	.00	.60	.05
Activity	.73	.18	.50	.00
Sociability	.65	.20	.58	.06

Table 13-1
Personality Similarities in Twins
In this study, 139 same-sex twins (average age, 55 months) were rated by their mothers on scales measuring three personality characteristics. Although identical twins may be treated more alike than fraternal twins (and therefore may have more similar environments), the size of these correlations suggests that genetic inheritance is an important determinant of personality. (After Buss and Plomin, 1975)

In one study, 139 same-sex twins (average age, 55 months) were rated by their mothers on a number of personality characteristics. Identical twins were judged to be much more alike in emotional reactivity, activity level, and sociability than fraternal twins (see Table 13-1). When personality tests are administered to adult twins, identical twins generally give more similar answers than fraternal twins (Loehlin and Nichols, 1976).

However, as we noted earlier, identical twins are often treated more alike than fraternal twins, and their personality similarities may result from a greater similarity in treatment. One way to circumvent this problem is to study identical twins who have been reared apart. A survey of studies comparing twins who were separated for part of their lives with twins who were reared together found no indication that being separated decreased personality similarity (Willerman, 1979). On the contrary, there is some indication that identical twins reared apart may be *more* alike than identical twins reared together. Presumably, twins reared together feel the need to develop separate or complementary identities. If one twin plays soccer, the other may decide to join the debate team; or if one excels at the piano, the other may turn to painting. Twins reared apart have no need to complement or to compete with each other and may be more apt to follow their natural inclinations.

Although twin studies suggest that some personality characteristics are inherited, there is no evidence that these characteristics are determined by specific genes. The similarities in body build and physiology shared by identical twins may account for their personality similarities.

BODY BUILD The idea that body build and personality characteristics are related is reflected in such popular stereotypes as "fat people are jolly" or "tall, skinny people who wear glasses are intellectuals." And this idea is far from new. Shakespeare has Julius Caesar say, "Let me have men about me that are fat; sleek-headed men, such as sleep o' nights. Yond Cassius has a lean and hungry look; he thinks too much: such men are dangerous. . . . Would he were fatter" (Shakespeare, *Julius Caesar*, Act I, Scene ii).

One early personality theory classified individuals into three categories on the basis of body build and related these body types to personality characteristics (Kretschmer, 1925; Sheldon, 1954). A short, plump person (*endomorph*) was said to be sociable, relaxed, and even-tempered; a tall, thin person (*ectomorph*) was characterized as restrained, self-conscious, and fond of solitude; a heavy-set, muscular individual (*mesomorph*) was described as noisy, aggressive, and physically active (see Figure 13-1).

However, attempts to relate body build to specific personality characteristics usually produce very low correlations, and most psychologists do not consider this classification useful. People's body weight and muscular strength change with age, diet, and exercise. You may know some short, plump individuals who are sociable and relaxed, but you probably also know some who are shy and withdrawn in social situations.

Figure 13-1
Body Types and Personality
These drawings illustrate a theory proposed
by Kretschmer (1925) that classified individuals into personality types on the basis of body
build. Research on this and related theories
has yielded little support for these ideas, and
most psychologists now doubt the usefulness
of such classifications.

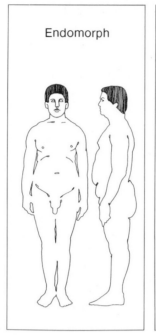

Endomorph

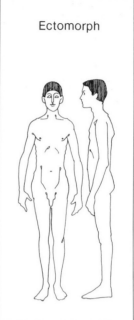

Ectomorph

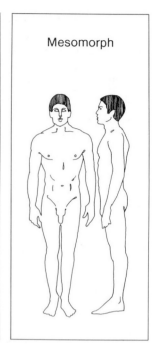

Mesomorph

Examples of low and high sensation seekers

On the other hand, there is little doubt that a person's physique has some
influence on personality—primarily through the limits it imposes on abilities
and the reactions it evokes from other people. For example, a girl with a short,
stocky build cannot realistically aspire to be a ballet dancer, fashion model, or
all-star basketball player; one who is over six feet tall probably will not become
an Olympic gymnast. Boys who are strong and muscular may be willing to risk
physical danger and to assert themselves; their weaker classmates may learn
early in life to avoid fights and to depend on intellectual abilities to get what
they want. Our physiques do not determine specific personality characteristics,
but they may shape our personalities by affecting how others treat us, the
nature of our interactions with others, and the kinds of situations we seek or
avoid.

BODY PHYSIOLOGY   In addition to differences in body build, people differ
in a number of physiological measures (for example, the size of their endocrine
glands, the reactivity of their autonomic nervous system, and the balance
among various neurotransmitters). Ultimately, we may find that some personality differences are related to physiological and biochemical differences. Current research is investigating some intriguing possibilities. One example is a
series of studies examining the physiological basis of a personality characteristic called "sensation seeking," or "thrill seeking." A person's desire for new
experiences and his or her willingness to take risks to achieve them can be
measured by a personality test (see page 312). Those who score high on the test
(the "sensation seekers") tend to have lower blood levels of an enzyme that
affects neural transmission in the brain than those who score low (Zuckerman,
1979). The enzyme (monoamine oxidase, or MAO) regulates the concentration
of two neurotransmitters that are believed to play an important role in emotional and motivated behavior.

The relationship is tentative for a number of reasons. MAO levels are
affected by a person's age and balance of sex hormones, and the level of MAO

in the blood may not accurately reflect the level in the brain. Nevertheless, the implications are intriguing: the stunt pilot and the chess player may differ in their body chemistry. And since MAO levels are heritable, sensation seeking may be a family trait.

There is no doubt that energy level and mood are influenced by complex physiological and biochemical processes. (Chapter 15 examines some biochemical theories of anxiety and depression.) At this point, however, it is difficult to separate cause and effect—to determine the extent to which such differences are part of our biological inheritance and the extent to which they stem from experiences encountered over the course of a lifetime.

Common experiences

All families in a given culture share certain common beliefs, customs, and values. While growing up, the child learns to behave in ways expected by the culture. One of these expectations has to do with *sex roles* (see Chapter 3). Most cultures expect different behaviors from males than from females. Sex roles may vary from culture to culture, but it is considered "natural" in any culture for boys and girls to have predictable differences in personality merely because they belong to one sex or the other.

A culture as complex as that of the United States contains numerous subcultures, each with its own views about such things as moral values, standards of cleanliness, style of dress, and definitions of success. The cultural subgroup exerts its influence on the developing personality. All boys are expected to exhibit certain personality characteristics (compared with girls), but a boy raised in an urban slum is expected to behave differently in some respects than a boy raised in a middle-class suburb.

Occupational stereotypes are changing.

Some roles, such as occupations, are of our own choosing. But such roles are also patterned by cultural dictates. Different behaviors are expected of doctors, truck drivers, rock stars, and opera singers. Occupational stereotypes have become much less rigid in recent years. The greatest change has been in sex roles: we are no longer surprised by female taxicab drivers, telephone repairpersons, or construction workers; or by male secretaries, nurses, or telephone operators. And styles of dress and appearance are more flexible: football players may have hair that curls below their helmets, doctors and lawyers may sport beards and beads, and opera stars may appear in blue jeans. Nevertheless, people tend to feel comfortable in an occupation if they behave as others in that occupation do.

To the extent that adult behavior conforms to social and occupational roles, it is predictable. Basically, we know how people will behave at a formal reception, a political demonstration, a football game, or a funeral.

Although cultural and subcultural pressures impose some personality similarities, individual personalities can never completely be predicted from a knowledge of the group in which a person is raised for two reasons: (1) the cultural impacts on the individual are not uniform because they are transmitted by parents and other people who may not all share the same values and practices, and (2) the individual has some experiences that are unique.

Unique experiences

Each person reacts in his or her own way to social pressures. As we noted earlier, personal differences in behavior may result from biological differences. They may also develop from the rewards and punishments the parents impose on the child's behavior and from the type of role models the parents provide. Even though they may not resemble their parents, children are influenced by them. The contrasting possibilities of these influences are described by two brothers in Sinclair Lewis' novel *Work of Art*. Each brother ascribes his personality to his home surroundings.

> My father [said Oral] was a sloppy, lazy, booze-hoisting old bum, and my mother didn't know much besides cooking, and she was too busy to give me much attention, and the kids I knew were a bunch of foul-mouthed loafers that used to hang around the hoboes up near the water tank, and I never had a chance to get any formal schooling, and I got thrown on my own as just a brat. So naturally I've become a sort of vagabond that can't be bored by thinking about his "debts" to a lot of little shopkeeping lice, and I suppose I'm inclined to be lazy, and not too scrupulous about the dames and the liquor. But my early rearing did have one swell result. Brought up so unconventionally, I'll always be an Anti-Puritan. I'll never deny the joys of the flesh and the sanctity of beauty.

> My father [said Myron] was pretty easy-going and always did like drinking and swapping stories with the boys, and my mother was hard-driven taking care of us, and I heard a lot of filth from the hoboes up near the water tank. Maybe just sort of as a reaction I've become almost too much of a crank about paying debts, and fussing over my work, and being scared of liquor and women. But my rearing did have one swell result. Just by way of contrast, it made me a good, sound, old-fashioned New English Puritan. (Lewis, 1934)

Although such divergent reactions to the same early environment are unlikely to occur in real life, individuals do respond differently to similar circumstances.

Beyond a unique biological inheritance and the specific ways in which the culture is transmitted, the individual is shaped by particular experiences. An illness accompanied by a long period of convalescence may create a fondness for being cared for and waited on that profoundly affects the personality. The death of a parent may disrupt the usual sex-role identifications. A traumatic accident, an opportunity to display heroism, leaving friends to move to another part of the country—countless personal experiences such as these influence development.

The individual's common and unique experiences interact with inherited potential to shape personality. How this occurs and how the resulting personality can best be described have been the subject of many theories. Most personality theories can be grouped into one of four classes: *trait, social learning, psychoanalytic,* or *phenomenological*. In the remainder of this chapter, we will briefly describe each of these theoretical approaches and provide examples of some of the methods used to assess personality. Personality cannot be studied scientifically unless there are satisfactory ways of measuring personality variables.

TRAIT APPROACH

The *trait approach* to personality attempts to isolate and describe the basic properties of the individual that direct behavior. This approach focuses on the public personality and is concerned more with personality description and prediction of behavior than with personality development. Trait theories assume that people vary on a number of personality *dimensions,* or *scales,* each of

Genetic Influences on Personality: Identical Twins Reared Apart

Identical twins, as we have already noted, tend to be more alike in personality characteristics than fraternal twins. Although this fact suggests the influence of heredity, it is difficult to separate the effects of environment and heredity. Because identical twins look alike, they may be treated more alike by their parents and by other people and therefore experience a more similar environment than fraternal twins.

An ideal situation for studying the effects of heredity on personality and behavior would be to separate identical twins at birth and raise them in radically different environments. Although humanitarian considerations prohibit a controlled experiment of this sort, a research project currently underway at the University of Minnesota comes close to fulfilling these conditions (Bouchard and others, 1981; Lykken, 1982). Experimenters located and brought to the laboratory for study 30 pairs of identical twins who were separated, on the average, at 6 weeks of age and reared by different families. The twins had not lived together since infancy nor met each other before they were in their teens. (In fact, some of the twins had never met until the study brought them together.)

The twins participated in lengthy interviews, during which they were asked questions about such topics as childhood experiences, fears, hobbies, musical tastes, social attitudes, and sexual interests. A variety of medical and psychological tests were also adminis-

tered. Analysis of the enormous amount of data collected will continue for several years, and at least 20 more sets of twins will be studied before conclusions are drawn. But the preliminary findings point to some startling similarities.

The twins with the most dramatically different backgrounds are 47-year-old Oskar Stohr and Jack Yufe. Born in Trinidad of a Jewish father and a German mother, they were separated shortly after birth. The mother took Oskar to Germany, where he was raised by his grandmother as a Catholic and a Nazi. Jack remained with his father, was raised as a Jew, and spent part of his youth on an Israeli kibbutz. Although the families never corresponded and the two brothers now lead quite different lives, remarkable similarities were evident when the pair met for the first time to participate in the study. Both men have mustaches and wear wire-rimmed glasses. Their mannerisms and temperaments are similar, and they share certain idiosyncracies: both like spicy foods and sweet liqueurs, are absentminded, flush the toilet before using it, and like to dip buttered toast in their coffee. Oskar tends to yell at his wife; Jack did also before he and his wife were separated.

Another pair of twins with fairly different backgrounds are now British housewives who were separated during World War II and raised by families of different socioeconomic status. Both twins, who never met before, startled

the experimenters by arriving for their interviews wearing seven rings on their fingers! Before we conclude that a fondness for rings is inherited, however, we should consider the more likely possibility that the twins inherited their pretty hands, thereby prompting their interest in rings. Despite the differences in their socioeconomic backgrounds, the twins showed striking similarities on many of the tests. Both performed about the same on ability tests, although the twin raised in the lower-class environment achieved a slightly higher score.

In the absence of carefully analyzed data, it is easy to be impressed by the personality similarities between twins and to ignore the differences. Nevertheless, the preliminary findings have surprised investigators, who note that the scores of the twins on many of the ability and personality tests were closer than would be expected if the same person took the test twice. Looking at the data obtained from all of the twin pairs, the greatest concordance is in ability test scores, brain-wave patterns, sociability, and what might be called "tempo" or "energy level."

Even when the results are tabulated, they may not be definitive because the sample will still be small. The discovery of personality *differences* between members of a twin pair may turn out to be more significant than the discovery of similarities. If identical twins are found to differ on some variable, we know that the variable is not genetically determined.

which represents a *trait*. Thus, we could rate an individual on a scale of intelligence, emotional stability, aggressiveness, and so on. To arrive at a global description of personality, we would need to know how the individual is rated on a number of dimensions.

A trait refers to any characteristic that differs from person to person in a relatively permanent and consistent way. When we informally describe ourselves and others with such adjectives as "aggressive," "cautious," "excitable," "intelligent," or "anxious," we are using trait terms. We abstract these terms from behavior. If we observe a man behaving aggressively on several occasions, we may describe him as an "aggressive individual." It is permissible to use "aggressiveness" as a trait term as long as we remember that the term is derived from *observations* of behavior. The danger lies in using the trait term to *explain* behavior. To say that a woman hit her roommate over the head because she has an aggressive trait explains nothing. We infer the trait from the behavior; we cannot turn around and use it as an explanation for behavior.

Psychologists working in the area of trait theory are concerned with (1) determining the basic traits that provide a meaningful description of personality and (2) finding ways to measure these traits.

Determining basic traits

The English language contains thousands of words that refer to characteristics of behavior. How do we reduce these to a manageable number of traits that are meaningful in describing personality? One approach uses *factor analysis* (see page 367). As we noted in Chapter 12, factor analysis is a complex statistical technique for reducing a large number of measures to a smaller number of independent dimensions.

For example, suppose you select a large number of words that describe personality characteristics and arrange them in pairs representing polar opposites (tidy–careless, calm–anxious, responsive–insensitive, cooperative–negativistic, and so on). You ask a group of people to rate their friends on each of these word pairs. Subjecting these ratings to factor analysis would yield a fairly small number of dimensions, or *factors,* that would account for most of the intercorrelations among the ratings. The five trait dimensions listed in Table 13-2 were found in one study of this kind.

The most extensive study of personality traits has been conducted by Raymond Cattell, who has collected data over three decades from questionnaires, personality tests, and observations of behavior in real-life situations. Cattell has identified 16 factors that he believes are the basic traits underlying

Table 13-2
Traits and Their Components
The table presents five traits identified in a study using factor analysis. The adjective pairs describe the two ends of the scales that comprise the dimension. (After Norman, 1963)

TRAIT DIMENSION	DESCRIPTIVE ADJECTIVE PAIRS
Extraversion	Talkative–Silent Open–Secretive Adventurous–Cautious
Agreeableness	Good-natured–Irritable Gentle–Headstrong Cooperative–Negativistic
Conscientiousness	Tidy–Careless Responsible–Undependable Persevering–Quitting
Emotional stability	Calm–Anxious Poised–Nervous Not hypochondriacal–Hypochondriacal
Culture	Artistically sensitive–Artistically insensitive Refined–Boorish Intellectual–Unreflective

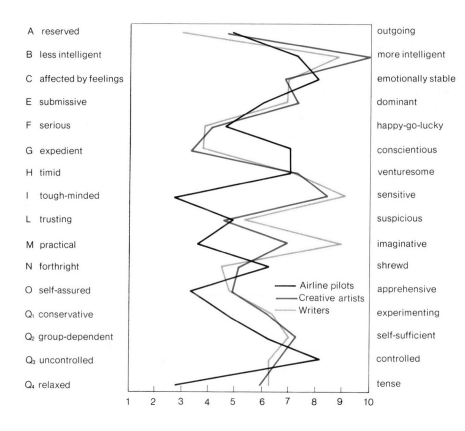

A reserved	outgoing
B less intelligent	more intelligent
C affected by feelings	emotionally stable
E submissive	dominant
F serious	happy-go-lucky
G expedient	conscientious
H timid	venturesome
I tough-minded	sensitive
L trusting	suspicious
M practical	imaginative
N forthright	shrewd
O self-assured	apprehensive
Q₁ conservative	experimenting
Q₂ group-dependent	self-sufficient
Q₃ uncontrolled	controlled
Q₄ relaxed	tense

— Airline pilots
— Creative artists
— Writers

1 2 3 4 5 6 7 8 9 10

Figure 13-2
Personality Profiles
The trait names represent the 16 personality factors obtained by factor analysis of a large number of ratings. The factors are assigned two names—one for a high score and another for a low score. Factors A–O were obtained from factor analyses of ratings of one person by another; the four Q factors were found only in data from self-ratings. A personality test based on the 16 factors measures the level of each factor, and the scores can be graphed as a profile—either for an individual or a group. The black profile shows the *average* scores for a group of airline pilots; the color profile, the average for a group of artists; and the gray profile, the average for a group of writers. Note that the writers and artists show similar traits that are somewhat different from the traits of the pilots. (After Cattell, 1973)

personality (see Figure 13-2). Each factor is given two names—one for a high score and another for a low score.

Cattell has devised a questionnaire to measure his 16 traits—the Sixteen Personality Factor Questionnaire (16 PF, for short). The yes or no answers to more than 100 questions are compiled to yield a score for each factor. For example, answering no to the question "Do you tend to keep in the background on social occasions?" would earn a point toward the "dominant" side of the E scale. By plotting an individual's test score for each factor, we arrive at a *personality profile*—a kind of shorthand description of the individual's personality. Cattell has studied diverse groups of people using the 16 PF. Figure 13-2 shows the average test scores for a group of airline pilots, a group of artists, and a group of writers. Comparing the personality profiles, we can see that artists and writers, as a group, differ significantly from pilots on a number of personality traits.

Evaluation of trait approach

Although the trait approach appears to be an objective, scientific way to study personality, some problems arise when this method is used. The personality factors found in a given study often depend on the type of data being analyzed (for example, self-ratings versus ratings of one person by another) and the specific factor-analytic technique used. Some investigators have identified as few as five factors as the basic dimensions of personality; others, as many as 20.

Despite the lack of agreement on the number of basic personality traits, some overlap does occur. Two dimensions found in most factor-analytic studies of personality are *introversion–extraversion* and *stability–instability*. Introversion–extraversion refers to the degree to which a person's basic orientation is turned inward toward the self or outward toward the external world. At the introversion end of the scale are individuals who are shy and prefer to work alone; they tend to withdraw into themselves, particularly in times of emotional stress or conflict. At the extraversion end are individuals who are sociable and prefer occupations that permit them to work directly with other people; in times of stress, they seek company. Stability–instability is a dimension of emotionality, with calm, well-adjusted, reliable individuals at the stable end and moody, anxious, temperamental, and unreliable individuals at the other.

A more important criticism of the trait approach, according to some personality theorists, is the possibility that behavior may vary widely from one situation to another. A young boy who obtains a high score on the "dominant" factor of the 16 PF may assume a dominant role with his schoolmates but not with his parents and teachers; even with his peers, he may behave aggressively on some occasions and docilely on others. As we will see later, tests designed to measure traits have not been as predictive as psychologists would like. In predicting behavior, we need to know how personal characteristics—tendencies to be sociable, aggressive, anxious, and so on—are influenced by particular environmental conditions. Research results indicate that the *interaction* between individual differences and situational variables is the most important factor.

SOCIAL LEARNING APPROACH

Trait theorists focus on *personal* determinants of behavior. They assume that traits predispose the individual to respond consistently in different situations. Situations have some impact: Tom does not respond as aggressively when an attractive waitress accidently spills a cup of coffee on him as he does when a truck driver cuts in front of him in congested traffic. But trait theorists assume that Tom will behave more aggressively in both situations than will Mike, who scores lower on the 16 PF scale measuring aggression.

Social learning theory, in contrast, emphasizes the importance of *environmental*, or *situational*, determinants of behavior. As we noted in Chapter 11, the social learning approach to motivation focuses on the patterns of behavior the individual learns in coping with the environment. For social learning theorists, behavior is the result of a continuous *interaction* between personal and environmental variables. Environmental conditions shape behavior through learning; a person's behavior, in turn, shapes the environment. Persons and situations influence each other reciprocally. To predict behavior, we need to know how the characteristics of the individual intereact with the characteristics of the situation.

Reinforcement and social learning

The effect of other people—the rewards and punishments they provide—is an important influence on an individual's behavior. According to social learning theory, individual differences in behavior result in large part from differences in the kinds of learning experiences encountered in the course of growing up. Some behavior patterns are learned through direct experience: the individual is rewarded or punished for behaving in a certain manner. But many responses are acquired without direct reinforcement, through *observational,* or *vicarious, learning* (see Chapter 11). People can learn by observing the actions of others and by noting the consequences of those actions. It would be a slow and inefficient process indeed if all of our behavior had to be learned through the direct reinforcement of our responses. According to social learning theorists, reinforcement is not *necessary* for learning, although it may *facilitate* learning by focusing the individual's attention in the appropriate direction.

Although reinforcement is not necessary for learning, it is crucial to the *performance* of learned behavior. A main assumption of social learning theory is that people behave in ways that are likely to produce reinforcement. A person's repertoire of learned behaviors is extensive; the particular action chosen in a specific situation depends on the expected outcome. Most adolescent girls know how to fight, having watched male classmates or TV characters aggress by hitting with the fist, kicking, and so on. But since this kind of behavior is seldom reinforced in girls, it is unlikely to occur except under unusual circumstances.

The reinforcement that controls the expression of learned behavior may be (1) *direct* (tangible rewards, social approval or disapproval, or alleviation of aversive conditions); (2) *vicarious* (observation of someone receiving reward or punishment for behavior similar to one's own); or (3) *self-administered* (evaluation of one's own performance with self-praise or reproach).

Social learning

Person—situation interaction

According to social learning theorists, a person's actions in a given situation depend on the specific characteristics of the situation, the individual's appraisal of the situation, and past reinforcement for behavior in similar situations (or observations of others in similar situations). People behave consistently insofar as the situations they encounter and the roles they are expected to play remain relatively stable.

Most social behaviors, however, are not uniformly rewarded across different settings. The individual learns to discriminate those contexts in which certain behavior is appropriate and those in which it is not. To the extent that a person is rewarded for the same response in many different situations, *generalization* takes place, ensuring that the same behavior will occur in a variety of settings. Thus, a boy whose father reinforces him for physical aggression at home as well as at school and at play will probably develop a personality that is pervasively aggressive. But, more often, aggressive responses are differentially rewarded, and learned *discriminations* determine the situations in which the individual will display aggression (for example, aggression is acceptable on the football field but not in the classroom).

PERSON VARIABLES   In predicting how a person will behave in a specific situation, social learning theorists emphasize the importance of individual differences in cognitive development and in social learning experiences rather than motivational traits (such as aggression or dependency). Some of the individual differences, or *person variables,* that interact with situational conditions to influence behavior are listed below.

1   *Competencies: What can you do?*   Competencies include intellectual abilities, social and physical skills, and other special abilities.

2 *Cognitive strategies: How do you see it?*   People differ in the way they selectively attend to information, encode (represent) events, and group them into meaningful categories. An event perceived by one person as "threatening" may be seen as "challenging" by another.

3 *Expectancies: What will happen?*   Expectations about the consequences of different behaviors will guide the individual's choice of behavior. If you cheat on an examination and are caught, what do you expect the consequences to be? If you tell your friend what you really think of her or him, what will happen to your relationship? Expectations about our own abilities will also influence behavior: we may anticipate the consequences of a certain behavior but fail to act because we are uncertain of our ability to execute the behavior.

4 *Subjective values: What is it worth?*   Individuals who have similar expectancies may choose to behave differently because they assign different values to the outcomes. Two students may expect a certain behavior to please their professor; however, this outcome is important to one student but is not important to the other.

5 *Self-regulatory systems and plans: How can you achieve it?*   People differ in the standards and rules they adopt for regulating their behavior (including self-imposed rewards for success or punishments for failure) as well as in their ability to make realistic plans for reaching a goal. (After Mischel, 1981)

All of these person variables interact with the conditions of a particular situation to determine what an individual will do in that situation.

SELF-GENERATED ENVIRONMENTS   But we are not simply passive reactors to situational conditions. The relationship between our behavior and the situations we encounter in life is reciprocal. Through their own actions, people produce the environmental conditions that affect their behavior. To use a simple experimental example, consider a rat in a Skinner box with an electrically charged grid for a floor. Shocks are scheduled to occur every minute, but the animal can forestall the shocks for 30 seconds by pressing a bar. The animals that learn the controlling behavior can create a punishment-free environment; the slow learners experience an unpleasant situation. Thus, the *potential environment* is the same for all animals, but the *actual environment* depends on their behavior (Bandura, 1977).

In the same way, a person who acts abrasively may often encounter a hostile social environment because his or her behavior elicits hostility from others. A friendly person who is skilled at making others feel comfortable will encounter a quite different environment. Situations are partly of our own devising.

Evaluation of social learning approach

Social learning theory, through its emphasis on specifying the environmental variables that elicit specific behaviors, has contributed in a major way to both clinical psychology and personality theory. It has led us to see human actions as reactions to specific environments and to focus on the way in which environments control our behavior and can be changed to modify behavior. As we will see in Chapter 16, the careful application of learning principles has proved successful in changing maladaptive behavior.

Social learning theorists have been criticized for overemphasizing the importance of situational influences on behavior and thus "losing the person" in personality psychology (Carlson, 1971). As we will see later, many personality theorists are unwilling to concede that personality has as little stability as social learning theory implies.

Environments can be self-generated.

PSYCHOANALYTIC APPROACH

Psychoanalytic theory approaches personality from a viewpoint that is quite different from either of the two theories discussed so far. Both trait and social learning theories focus on the public personality; they are concerned primarily with behavior. Psychoanalytic theories, in contrast, explore the private personality—the *unconscious* motives that direct behavior. Psychoanalytic theory is also concerned with the way in which personality develops.

Freud's theories, formulated during 50 years of treating emotionally disturbed persons, fill 24 volumes. The last, *Outline of Psychoanalysis*, was published in 1940, a year after his death. We can present only the barest outline of Freud's theory of personality here.

Freud compared the human mind to an iceberg. The small part that shows above the surface of the water represents *conscious experience*; the much larger mass below water level represents the *unconscious*—a storehouse of impulses, passions, and inaccessible memories that affect our thoughts and behavior. It was this unconscious portion of the mind that Freud sought to explore by the technique of *free association,* which requires the person to talk about everything that comes into his or her consciousness, no matter how ridiculous or trivial it might seem. By analyzing free associations, including the recall of dreams and early childhood memories, Freud sought to help his patients become aware of much that had been unconscious and thereby to discover the basic determinants of personality.

Personality structure

Freud believed that personality was composed of three major systems: the *id*, the *ego*, and the *supergeo*. Each system has its own functions, but the three interact to govern behavior.

THE ID   The *id* is the most primitive part of the personality, present in the newborn infant, from which the ego and the superego later develop. The id consists of the basic biological impulses (or drives): the need to eat, drink, eliminate wastes, avoid pain, and gain sexual pleasure. Freud believed that aggression was also a basic biological drive (see Chapter 11). The id seeks immediate gratification of these impulses. Like a young child, the id operates on the *pleasure principle:* it endeavors to avoid pain and obtain pleasure regardless of the external circumstances.

THE EGO   Children soon learn that their impulses cannot always be immediately gratified. Hunger must wait until someone provides food. The satisfaction of relieving bladder or bowel pressure must be delayed until the bathroom is reached. Certain impulses—hitting someone or playing with the genitals—may be punished. A new part of the personality, the *ego*, develops as the young child learns to consider the demands of reality. The ego obeys the *reality principle*: the gratification of impulses must be delayed until the appropriate environmental conditions are found. For example, taking the real world into consideration, the ego delays satisfaction of sexual impulses until conditions are appropriate. It is essentially the "executive" of the personality in that it decides what actions are appropriate and which id impulses will be satisfied in what manner. The ego mediates among the demands of the id, the realities of the world, and the demands of the superego.

"Very well, I'll introduce you. Ego, meet Id. Now get back to work."

THE SUPEREGO   The third part of the personality, the *superego*, is the internalized representation of the values and morals of society as taught to the child by the parents and others. It is essentially the individual's *conscience*. The superego judges whether an action is right or wrong. The id seeks pleasure, the ego tests reality, and the superego strives for perfection. The superego develops in response to parental rewards and punishments. It incorporates all the actions for which the child is punished or reprimanded as well as all the actions for which the child is rewarded.

Initially, parents control children's behavior directly by reward and punishment. Through the incorporation of parental standards into the superego, behavior is brought under self-control. Children no longer need anyone to tell them it is wrong to steal; their superego tells them. Violation of the superego's standards, or even the impulse to do so, produces anxiety over the loss of parental love. According to Freud, this anxiety is unconscious; the conscious emotion is guilt. If parental standards are overly rigid, the individual may be guilt-ridden and inhibit all aggressive or sexual impulses. In contrast, an individual who fails to incorporate any standards for acceptable social behavior will have few behavioral constraints and may engage in excessively self-indulgent or criminal behavior; such a person is considered to have a weak superego.

Sometimes the three components of personality are in opposition: the ego postpones the gratification that the id wants immediately, and the superego battles with both the id and the ego because behavior often falls short of the moral code it represents. But more often in the normal person, the three work together to produce integrated behavior.

ANXIETY AND DEFENSES AGAINST IT   Freud believed that the conflict between the id impulses (primarily sexual and aggressive instincts) and the restraining influences of the ego and the superego constitute the motivating source of much behavior. Because society condemns free expression of aggression and sexual behavior, such impulses cannot be expressed immediately and directly. Children learn early that they should not handle their genitals in public or hit their siblings. They eventually internalize parental restrictions on impulse satisfaction, thereby forming the superego. The more restraints a society (or its representatives, the parents) places on impulse expression, the greater the potential for conflict among the three parts of the personality.

The desires of the id are powerful forces that must be expressed in some way; prohibiting their expression does not abolish them. Individuals with an urge to do something for which they will be punished become anxious. One way of reducing anxiety is to express the impulse in disguised form, thereby avoiding punishment by society and condemnation by the superego. Aggressive impulses, for example, may be displaced to racing sports cars or to championing political causes.

Another method of reducing anxiety, called *repression*, is to push the impulse out of awareness into the unconscious. These methods of anxiety reduction, called *defense mechanisms*, are means of defending oneself against painful anxiety. They are never totally successful in relieving tension, and the residue may spill over in the form of nervousness or restlessness, which, as Freud pointed out, is the price we must pay for being civilized. Presumably, a society that placed no restrictions on free expression of the id's instincts would produce people who were completely free of anxiety or tension. But such a society would probably not survive; all societies must place some restrictions on behavior for the well-being of the group.

Defense mechanisms form the basis of Freud's theory of maladaptive behavior and will be examined more fully in Chapter 14. At this point, we will note only that people differ in the balance among their id, ego, and superego systems and in the defenses they use to deal with anxiety. The individual's approach to a problem situation reflects his or her manner of coping with the conflicting demands of the id, the ego, and the superego.

Personality development

Freud believed that the individual, during the first five years of life, progresses through several developmental stages that affect personality. Applying a broad definition of sexuality, he called these periods *psychosexual stages.* During each stage, the pleasure-seeking impulses of the id focus on a particular area of the body and on activities connected with that area.

Freud called the first year of life the *oral stage* of psychosexual development. During this period, infants derive pleasure from nursing and sucking; indeed, they will put their thumb or anything else they can reach into their mouth.

Toilet training is one of the child's first experiences with imposed control.

During the second year of life, the *anal stage,* children have their first experience with imposed control in the form of toilet training. Gratification is presumably derived from withholding or expelling feces.

In the *phallic stage,* from about age 3 to age 6, children begin to derive pleasure from fondling their genitals. They observe the differences between males and females and may direct their awakening sexual impulses toward the parent of the opposite sex.

A *latency period* follows the end of the phallic stage, during which children become less concerned with their bodies and turn their attention to the skills needed for coping with the environment.

The last stage, the *genital stage,* occurs during adolescence. Youngsters begin to turn their sexual interests toward others and to love in a more mature way.

Freud felt that special problems at any stage could arrest (or fixate) development and have a lasting effect on the individual's personality. The libido would remain attached to the activities appropriate for that stage. Thus, a person who was weaned very early and did not have enough sucking pleasure might become *fixated* at the oral stage. As an adult, this person may be excessively dependent on others and overly fond of such oral pleasures as eating, drinking, and smoking. Such a person is called an "oral" personality. The person fixated at the anal stage of psychosexual development may be abnormally concerned with cleanliness, orderliness, and saving and may tend to resist external pressure.

Modifications of Freud's theories

Later psychoanalysts felt that Freud placed too much emphasis on the instinctive and biological aspects of personality and failed to recognize that people are products of the society in which they live. The neo-Freudians—including Alfred Adler, Karen Horney, Erich Fromm, and Harry Stack Sullivan—considered personality to be shaped more by the people, society, and culture surrounding the individual than by biological needs. They placed less emphasis on the controlling power of the unconscious, believing that people are more rational in their planning and decisions than Freud had thought.

A current psychoanalytic approach stresses the role of the ego. According to this view, the ego develops independently of the id and performs other functions in addition to finding realistic ways of satisfying id impulses. These ego functions are (1) learning how to cope with the environment and (2) making sense of experience. Ego satisfactions include exploration, manipulation, and competency in performance. This approach ties the concept of the ego more closely to cognitive processes.

Evaluation of psychoanalytic approach

Psychoanalytic theory has had an enormous impact on psychological and philosophical conceptions of human nature. Freud's major contributions are his recognition that unconscious needs and conflicts motivate much of our behavior and his emphasis on the importance of early childhood experiences in personality development. His emphasis on sexual factors led to an awareness of their role in adjustment problems and paved the way for the scientific study of sexuality. But Freud made his observations during the Victorian period when sexual standards were very strict; so it is understandable that many of his patients' conflicts centered on their sexual desires. Today, feelings of guilt about sex are less frequent, but the incidence of mental illness remains about the same. Sexual conflicts are not the only cause of personality disturbances—and may not even be a major cause.

Some critics also point out that Freud's theory of personality is based almost entirely on his observations of emotionally disturbed individuals and may not be an appropriate description of the normal, healthy personality. In addition, many of Freud's ideas were decidedly "sexist." For example, his theory that female psychosexual development is shaped by "penis envy"—and the accompanying feelings of unworthiness due to the lack of such equipment—is certainly inadequate in view of our current awareness of the role that social factors play in gender identification (see Chodorow, 1978). It was probably not her brother's penis that a little girl during the Victorian era envied but his greater independence, power, and social status.

Although psychoanalysis has exerted a powerful influence on our thinking about human nature, it has been seriously questioned as a scientific theory. Freud's constructs are ambiguous and difficult to define. He does not specify, for example, what behaviors indicate that a child is fixated at the anal stage of psychosexual development and what behaviors indicate that he or she is not fixated. Research efforts to identify oral and anal personality types suggest that the parents' characteristic ways of handling the child (for example, continual demands for neatness and precision or attempts to make the child excessively dependent) have more influence on later personality than specific events that occur during particular psychosexual stages.

Psychoanalytic theory assumes that very different behaviors may be signs of the same underlying impulse or conflict. For example, a mother who feels resentful of her child may be punitive and abusive or she may deny her hostile impulses by becoming overly concerned and protective toward the child— what Freud would call a *reaction formation* (see Chapter 14). When very opposite behaviors are said to result from the same underlying motive, it is difficult to confirm the presence or absence of the motive. And, in turn, it is difficult to make theoretical predictions that can be empirically verified.

Most of the psychoanalysts who modified and expanded Freud's theories were concerned with concepts that would help them understand their patients; they had little or no training in theory construction or research methods. Recently, there has been a renewed interest in reformulating psychoanalytic theory in testable terms and subjecting the theory to rigorous evaluation. Research along these lines seems promising, as evidenced by the work of Silverman (1976), Fisher and Greenberg (1977), and others.

PHENOMENOLOGICAL APPROACH

The phenomenological approach to the study of personality includes a number of theories that differ in some respects but share a common emphasis on *subjective experience*—the individual's private view of the world. Phenomenological theories differ from the theories we have discussed so far in that they generally are not concerned with the person's motivational history or with predicting behavior. They focus instead on how the individual perceives and interprets events—on the individual's *phenomenology*.

In a sense, the phenomenological approach is a reaction against the psychoanalytic view that human beings are motivated by unconscious impulses. Rather than looking at objective measures of a situation or delving into childhood motives, phenomenologists focus on the individual's subjective view of what is taking place now.

Actions that seem puzzling to us as observers may become understandable when we know what the situation *means* to the individual. To cite an example, during a tennis tournament, one player suddenly starts shouting, protesting that her opponent is trying to unnerve her by deliberately delaying the game. To an observer, this reaction seems totally inappropriate; the other player has exhibited model court behavior. But the protester has experienced this particular opponent's delaying tactics in the past, and the slightest sign that such a tactic is about to recur is enough to infuriate her. From her viewpoint, her reactions are appropriate.

The phenomenological approach to personality includes theories that have been labeled "humanistic" (because they focus on the qualities that differentiate humans from animals—namely, self-direction and freedom of choice) and "self" theories (because they deal with the subjective, internal experiences that constitute a person's sense of being). Most phenomenological theories also emphasize the positive nature of human beings—their push toward growth and *self-actualization*. Some of the features of the phenomenological approach to personality will become clearer as we discuss the views of one of its leading spokesmen, Carl Rogers.

Self theory

Like Freud, Rogers developed his theory from his work with emotionally troubled people (Rogers, 1951, 1977). Rogers was impressed with what he saw as the individual's innate tendency to move in the direction of growth, maturity, and positive change. In his "nondirective," or "client-centered," therapy, Rogers assumes that every individual (given the proper circumstances) has the motivation and ability to change and that we are the best experts on ourselves. The therapist's role is to act as a sounding board while the individual explores and analyzes his or her problems. This approach differs from psychoanalytic therapy, during which the therapist "analyzes" the patient's history to determine the problem and devise a course of remedial action. (See Chapter 16 for a discussion of various approaches to psychotherapy.)

The most important concept in Rogers' theory of personality is the *self*. The

Carl Rogers writing on the phenomenological approach

" . . . the best vantage point for understanding behavior is from the internal frame of reference of the individual himself."

"The organism has one basic tendency and striving—to actualize, maintain, and enhance the experiencing organism."

"When the individual perceives and accepts into one consistent and integrated system all his sensory and visceral experiences, then he is necessarily more understanding of others and is more accepting of others as separate individuals." (Rogers, 1951)

self consists of all the ideas, perceptions, and values that characterize "I" or "me"; it includes the awareness of "what I am" and "what I can do." This perceived self, in turn, influences both the person's perception of the world and his or her behavior. An individual with a strong, positive self-concept views the world quite differently than a person with a weak self-concept does. The self-concept does not necessarily reflect reality; a person may be highly successful and respected but view himself or herself as a failure.

According to Rogers, the individual evaluates every experience in relation to this self-concept. People want to behave in ways that are consistent with their self-image; experiences and feelings that are not consistent are threatening and may be denied admittance to consciousness. This is essentially Freud's concept of repression, although Rogers feels that such repression is neither necessary nor permanent. (Freud would say that repression is inevitable and that some aspects of the individual's experiences always remain unconscious.)

The more areas of experience a person has to deny because they are inconsistent with his or her self-concept, the wider the gulf between the self and reality and the greater the potential for anxiety. An individual whose image is incongruent with personal feelings and experiences must defend himself or herself against the truth because the truth will result in anxiety. If the incongruence becomes too great, the defenses may break down, resulting in severe anxiety or other forms of emotional disturbance. The well-adjusted person, in contrast, has a self-concept that is consistent with thought, experience, and behavior; the self is not rigid but flexible and can change as it assimilates new experiences and ideas.

The other self in Rogers' theory is the *ideal self.* We all have a conception of the kind of person we would like to be. The closer the ideal self is to the real self, the more fulfilled and happy the individual becomes. A large discrepancy between the ideal and real selves results in an unhappy, dissatisfied person.

Thus, two kinds of incongruence can develop: one, between the self and the experiences of reality; the other, between the self and the ideal self. Rogers has some hypotheses about how these incongruences may develop.

Development of the self

Because the child's behavior is continuously being evaluated by parents and others (sometimes positively and sometimes negatively), the child soon learns to discriminate between thoughts and actions that are considered worthy and those that are not. The unworthy experiences are then excluded from the self-concept, even though they may be quite valid or natural experiences. For example, relieving physiological tension in the bowel or bladder is a pleasurable experience for the child. However, unless the child urinates or defecates privately and in the proper place, parents usually condemn such activities as "bad" or "naughty." To retain the parents' positive regard, the child must deny his or her own experience—that defecating or urinating provides satisfaction.

Feelings of competition and hostility toward a younger sibling who has usurped the center of attention are natural. But parents disapprove of hitting a baby brother or sister and usually punish such actions. Children must somehow integrate this experience into their self-image. They may decide they are bad and feel ashamed. They may decide their parents do not like them and feel rejected. Or they may deny their feelings and decide they do not want to hit

Sibling rivalry can arouse strong emotions.

the baby. Each of these attitudes contains a distortion of the truth. The third alternative is the easiest for children to accept; but in so doing, they deny their real feelings, which then become unconscious. The more people have to deny their own feelings and accept the values of others, the more uncomfortable they will feel about themselves.

Obviously, there must be certain restrictions on behavior. Household efficiency and sanitary considerations require some restraints on elimination of body waste; and children cannot be permitted to beat their siblings. Rogers suggests that the best approach is for the parents to recognize the child's feelings as valid while explaining their own feelings and the reasons for restraint.

Self-actualization

Rogers believes that the basic force motivating the human organism is self-actualization—"a tendency toward fulfillment, toward actualization, toward the maintenance and enhancement of the organism." A growing organism seeks to fulfill its potential within the limits of its heredity. A person may not always clearly perceive which actions lead to growth and which actions are regressive. But once the course is clear, the individual chooses to grow rather than to regress. Rogers does not deny that there are other needs, some of them biological; but he sees them as subservient to the organism's motivation to enhance and maintain itself.

The characteristics of "self-actualized" individuals—those who have developed their potentialities to the fullest—have been studied by Abraham Maslow. (In Chapter 11, we examined Maslow's hierarchy of human needs, progressing from basic physiological needs through psychological needs and culminating in the need for self-actualization.)

Maslow began his investigation in a somewhat unusual manner. He selected eminent historical figures whom he considered to be *self-actualizers*—men and women who had made extraordinary use of their potential. Included were such persons as Spinoza, Thomas Jefferson, Abraham Lincoln, William James, Jane Addams, Albert Einstein, and Eleanor Roosevelt. After studying their lives, Maslow arrived at a composite picture of a self-actualizer. The distinguishing characteristics of self-actualized persons are listed in Table 13-3, along with some of the behaviors that Maslow believed could lead to self-actualization.

Maslow extended his study to a population of college students. Selecting students who fit his definition of self-actualizers, Maslow found this group to be in the healthiest 1 percent of the population; these students showed no signs of maladjustment and were making effective use of their talents and capabilities (Maslow, 1970).

Many people experience transient moments of self-actualization, which Maslow calls *peak experiences*. A peak experience is an experience of *being* characterized by happiness and fulfillment—a temporary, nonstriving, non-self-centered state of perfection and goal attainment. Peak experiences may occur in different intensities and in various contexts: creative activities, appreciation of nature, intimate relationships with others, parental experiences, aesthetic perceptions, or athletic participation. After asking a large number of college students to describe any experience that came close to being a peak experience, Maslow attempted to summarize their responses. They spoke of wholeness, perfection, aliveness, uniqueness, effortlessness, self-sufficiency, and the values of beauty, goodness, and truth.

Albert Einstein

Eleanor Roosevelt

Table 13-3
Self-Actualization
Listed are the personal qualities that Maslow found to be characteristic of self-actualizers and the behaviors he considered important to the development of self-actualization. (After Maslow, 1967)

CHARACTERISTICS OF SELF-ACTUALIZERS

Perceive reality efficiently and are able to tolerate uncertainty

Accept themselves and others for what they are

Spontaneous in thought and behavior

Problem-centered rather than self-centered

Have a good sense of humor

Highly creative

Resistant to enculturation, although not purposely unconventional

Concerned for the welfare of humanity

Capable of deep appreciation of the basic experiences of life

Establish deep, satisfying interpersonal relationships with a few, rather than many, people

Able to look at life from an objective viewpoint

BEHAVIORS LEADING TO SELF-ACTUALIZATION

Experience life as a child does, with full absorption and concentration

Try something new rather than sticking to secure and safe ways

Listen to your own feelings in evaluating experiences rather than to the voice of tradition or authority or the majority

Be honest; avoid pretenses of "game playing"

Be prepared to be unpopular if your views do not coincide with those of most people

Assume responsibility

Work hard at whatever you decide to do

Try to identify your defenses and have the courage to give them up

Evaluation of phenomenological approach

By focusing on the individual's unique perception and interpretation of events, the phenomenological approach brings back the role of private experience to the study of personality. More than any other theory we have discussed, this approach concentrates on the whole, healthy person and emphasizes a positive, optimistic view of human nature.

The major criticism of the phenomenological approach is that it is difficult to validate its concepts. Self-actualization, for example, is not clearly defined, and the criteria Maslow used in selecting his self-actualized persons are vague. Someone else viewing the lives of the famous people Maslow studied might not find the characteristics listed in Table 13-3. And some of the characteristics might even be somewhat negatively related. For example, some individuals who were best known for their concern for human welfare did not have very satisfying interpersonal relationships with their spouses or children. Eleanor Roosevelt and Abraham Lincoln are two examples: they appear to have fulfilled their potential in some areas of life while neglecting other areas.

Phenomenologists do not always distinguish between the self as a causal agent (the *doer* of behavior) and the self-concept (the individual's attitudes and feelings about himself or herself) (Wylie, 1974). The self-concept certainly influences behavior, but the nature of this relationship is not clear. An individual may believe himself or herself to be honest and trustworthy but behave with varying degrees of honesty in different situations. And changes in personal beliefs and attitudes do not always result in changes in behavior. Often the reverse is true: people modify their beliefs to make them consistent with their behavior.

The way in which an individual perceives and interprets events is important to an understanding of personality. But a scientific study of personality also must investigate the *conditions* that influence the person's self-concept and that determine whether his or her potential will be realized.

PERSONALITY ASSESSMENT

In order to study personality—according to whatever theory—methods of assessing personality variables are necessary. We make informal appraisals of personality all the time. In selecting friends, sizing up potential co-workers, choosing candidates for political office, or deciding on a marriage partner, we make implicit predictions about future behavior. Sometimes our predictions are erroneous. First impressions may be distorted because we focus on one particular characteristic that we especially like or dislike and let it bias our perception of other aspects of the individual. This tendency to bias our judgment on the basis of one particular feature is known as the *halo effect*. Sometimes our first impression of a person is based on a *stereotype* of the characteristics believed to be typical of the group to which she or he belongs. And sometimes the person being appraised may be putting his or her "best foot forward." For these and other reasons, informal evaluations of others may be in error.

On many occasions, a more objective, unbiased assessment of personality is desirable. In selecting individuals for high-level positions, employers need to know something about their honesty, ability to handle stress, and so on. In helping students make vocational choices, counselors can offer wiser advice if they know something about a student's personality in addition to his or her school performance. Decisions about the kind of treatment that will be most beneficial to a mentally ill person or will help to rehabilitate a convicted felon require an objective assessment of the individual's personality. Personality assessment is also necessary for research purposes. Investigators who want to determine the relationship between anxiety and performance in school must have some way of objectively measuring anxiety as a personal trait. The many methods that have been used to assess personality can generally be classified under three headings: *observational methods, personality inventories,* and *projective techniques.*

Observational methods

Observations of an individual by a trained observer can take place in a natural setting (watching a child interact with classmates), in an experimental situation (observing a student try to complete a test deliberately designed to be too difficult to finish in the allotted time), or in the context of an interview. The interview differs from casual conversation in that it has a purpose—for example, to evaluate a job applicant, to determine whether a patient is suicidal, to estimate the extent of an individual's emotional problems, or to predict whether a prisoner is apt to violate parole. The interview may be *unstructured*, in which case the person interviewed largely determines what is discussed, although the interviewer usually elicits additional information through the skilled use of supplementary questions. Or the interview may be *structured*, following a standard pattern, much like a printed questionnaire, that assures all relevant topics are covered. The unstructured interview is used more frequently in a clinical or counseling situation; the structured interview is used more often with job applicants or research subjects when comparable data are required of all respondents.

The accuracy of the information obtained in an interview depends on a number of factors too lengthy to discuss here. But research on the interview process has made it clear that even slight changes in the behavior of the interviewer have a marked effect on what the person being interviewed says and does. For example, a simple nod of the interviewer's head at the right moment may encourage the person being interviewed to talk much more. If the interviewer increases the length of time that he or she speaks, the person being interviewed tends to do the same (Matarazzo and Wiens, 1972). As a means of measuring personality, the interview is subject to many sources of error and bias; the success of the technique depends on the skill and awareness of the interviewer.

RATING SCALES   Impressions gained from an interview or from observing behavior can be recorded in a standardized form by means of *rating scales*. A rating scale is a device for recording judgments about a personality trait. Some examples of rating scales appear in Table 13-4. Such scales give the observer a frame of reference within which to record impressions.

For the rating to be meaningful, the rater must (1) understand the scale, (2) be sufficiently acquainted with the person being rated to make meaningful judgments, and (3) avoid the halo effect. Unless the rater knows the person fairly well or the behavior being rated is very specific, ratings may be influenced by social stereotypes; that is, judgments may be based on how the rater *believes* a "suburban housewife," a "long-haired intellectual," or a "high-school athlete" acts and thinks rather than on the actual behavior of the subject being rated.

Despite such problems, descriptions of the same person provided by different raters in different situations often yield good agreement. In one study, for example, the aggressiveness of a group of schoolboys was rated by their peers and also by trained psychologists who watched them playing games in the schoolyard. There was close agreement between the two sets of ratings (Winder and Wiggins, 1964).

Personality inventories

Another method of personality assessment relies on the individual's self-observations. A *personality inventory* is essentially a questionnaire in which the person reports his or her reactions or feelings in certain situations. The personality inventory resembles a structured or standardized interview in that it asks the same questions of each person and the answers are usually given in a form that can be easily scored, often by a computer. A personality inventory may be designed to measure a single dimension of personality (such as anxiety level) or several personality traits simultaneously. The Sixteen Personality Factor Questionnaire (16 PF) discussed earlier in this chapter, for example, produces a personality profile showing the individual's scores on a number of different traits.

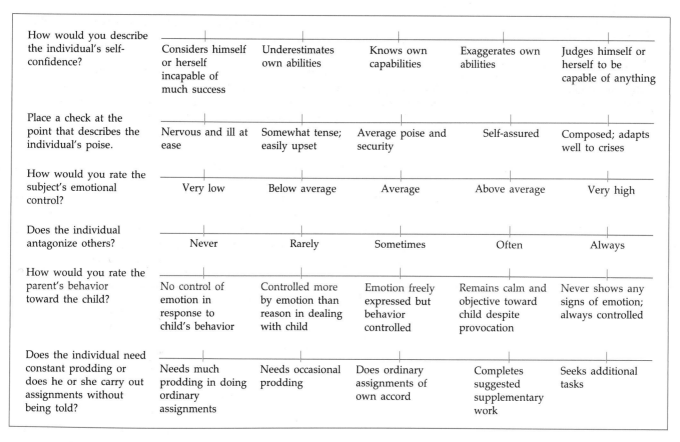

How would you describe the individual's self-confidence?	Considers himself or herself incapable of much success	Underestimates own abilities	Knows own capabilities	Exaggerates own abilities	Judges himself or herself to be capable of anything
Place a check at the point that describes the individual's poise.	Nervous and ill at ease	Somewhat tense; easily upset	Average poise and security	Self-assured	Composed; adapts well to crises
How would you rate the subject's emotional control?	Very low	Below average	Average	Above average	Very high
Does the individual antagonize others?	Never	Rarely	Sometimes	Often	Always
How would you rate the parent's behavior toward the child?	No control of emotion in response to child's behavior	Controlled more by emotion than reason in dealing with child	Emotion freely expressed but behavior controlled	Remains calm and objective toward child despite provocation	Never shows any signs of emotion; always controlled
Does the individual need constant prodding or does he or she carry out assignments without being told?	Needs much prodding in doing ordinary assignments	Needs occasional prodding	Does ordinary assignments of own accord	Completes suggested supplementary work	Seeks additional tasks

Table 13-4
Some Examples of Rating Scales

The 16 PF, as you may recall, is based on the statistical technique of *factor analysis.* Raymond Cattell used factor analysis to identify 16 basic personality traits. He then selected questions that best represented each trait and assembled them into a test that yielded scores on such personality characteristics as dominance, emotional stability, and self-control. A quite different method of test construction was used in the development of the Minnesota Multiphasic Personality Inventory (MMPI).

MINNESOTA MULTIPHASIC PERSONALITY INVENTORY The MMPI is composed of approximately 550 statements (about attitudes, emotional reactions, physical and psychological symptoms, and past experiences) to which the subject answers "true," "false," or "cannot say." Some sample test items are:

- I have never done anything dangerous for the thrill of it.
- I daydream very little.
- My mother or father often made me obey even when I thought it was unreasonable.
- At times my thoughts have raced ahead faster than I could speak them.

The responses are scored according to their correspondence to answers given by people with different kinds of psychological problems (see Table 13-5).

The MMPI was developed to aid clinicians in diagnosing personality disturbances. But instead of assuming specific personality traits and formulating questions to measure them, the test designers gave hundreds of test questions to groups of individuals; each group was known to differ from the norm on a particular criterion. Only those questions that discriminated between groups

Table 13-5
MMPI Scales

The first three scales are "validity" scales, which help to determine whether the person has answered the test items carefully and honestly. For example, the F (Frequency) scale measures the degree to which very infrequent or atypical answers are given. A high score on this scale usually indicates that the individual was careless or confused in responding. (However, high F scores often accompany high scores on the Schizophrenia scale, which measures bizarre thinking.) The remaining "clinical" scales were originally named for categories of psychiatric disorders, but interpretation now emphasizes personality attributes rather than diagnostic categories.

SCALE NAME	SCALE ABBREVIATION	INTERPRETATION OF HIGH SCORES
Lie	L	Denial of common frailties
Frequency	F	Invalidity of profile
Correction	K	Defensive, evasive
Hypochondriasis	Hs	Emphasis on physical complaints
Depression	D	Unhappy, depressed
Hysteria	Hy	Reacts to stress by denying problems
Psychopathic deviancy	Pd	Lack of social conformity; often in trouble with the law
Masculinity–femininity	Mf	Feminine orientation (males); masculine orientation (females)
Paranoia	Pa	Suspicious
Psychasthenia	Pt	Worried, anxious
Schizophrenia	Sc	Withdrawn, bizarre thinking
Hypomania	Ma	Impulsive, excitable
Social introversion–extraversion	Si	Introverted, shy

were retained to form the inventory. This technique is known as *empirical construction* because the test items bear an actual (empirical) relationship to the personality characteristic being measured. For example, to develop a scale of items that distinguish between paranoid and normal individuals, the same questions were given to two groups. The *criterion group* consisted of individuals who were hospitalized with the diagnosis of paranoia; the *control group,* of people who had never been diagnosed as having psychiatric problems but who were similar to the criterion group in age, sex, socioeconomic status, and other important variables. Questions that at face value might seem to distinguish normal from paranoid individuals (for example, "I think that most people would lie to get ahead") may or may not do so when put to an empirical test. In fact, patients diagnosed as paranoid were significantly *less* apt to respond "true" to this statement than normal individuals.

Since the MMPI is derived from differences between criterion and control groups, it does not really matter whether what the person says is true. What is important is the fact that she or he says it. If schizophrenics answer "true" and normal subjects answer "false" to the statement "My mother never loved me," their answers distinguish the two groups regardless of how their mothers actually behaved. This is one advantage of a test based on the method of empirical construction over a test based on a test constructor's assumption that certain answers indicate specific personality traits.

Although the MMPI scales were originally designed to identify people with serious personality disorders, they have been widely used in studying normal populations. Sufficient data have been collected to provide personality descriptions of people with different patterns of high and low scores on the various scales. A recent development is the use of a computer to score and interpret the test results (see Figure 13-3).

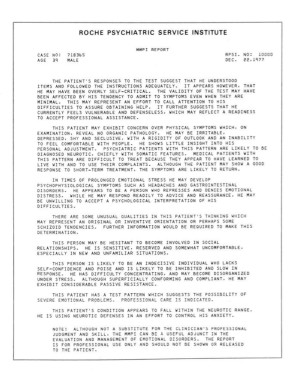

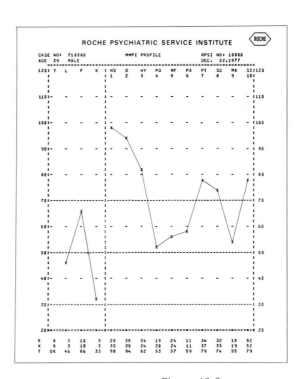

Figure 13-3
Computer Printout of an MMPI Profile with Interpretation

CALIFORNIA PSYCHOLOGICAL INVENTORY Another personality test based on the method of empirical construction is the *California Psychological Inventory* (CPI). The CPI uses some of the same quesions as the MMPI but is designed to measure more "normal" personality traits. The CPI scales measure such traits as dominance, sociability, self-acceptance, responsibility, and socialization. The comparison groups for some of the scales were obtained by asking groups of high-school and college students to nominate the classmates they would rate high or low on the trait in question. Thus, for the dominance scale, the criterion group consisted of students who were described by their peers as high in dominance (aggressive, confident, self-reliant) and the control group consisted of students who were described by their peers as low in dominance (retiring, lacking in self-confidence, inhibited). Items that revealed a statistically significant difference between the criterion and the control groups formed the dominance scale.

Several CPI scales measure traits that are related to academic achievement, and studies have correlated scores on these scales with college grades. One study, for example, found that students who scored high on the scale measuring "achievement via conformance" tended to do well in courses that rewarded conformity—courses in which fixed core material had to be learned and then regurgitated on objective tests. Students who scored high on the scale measuring "achievement via independence" tended to do well in courses that emphasized independent study and self-direction. The highest grade point averages were obtained by students who scored high on both scales (Domino, 1971).

Most personality inventories rely on the individual's ability to understand the questions and his or her willingness to answer them honestly. However, the "best" answer to many personality test items is fairly apparent, and individuals may try to bias their answers. If the test is given by a perspective employer, job applicants will clearly want to present themselves in the best light. If admission to a psychotherapy program depends on the test results,

"Rorschach! What's to become of you?"

applicants may bias their answers so that they appear to need help. Even if a person is trying to be accurate and objective, he or she may tend to give answers that are considered "socially desirable." It is difficult to answer yes to the MMPI question "I am certainly lacking in self-confidence," even though you may feel that way. Self-confidence is a desirable trait in our society; to be lacking in self-confidence is socially undesirable.

Another personality variable that influences test responses is the tendency of some people to acquiesce—to agree with the questions. For example, a person might answer yes to "I am a happy and carefree person" and to "I frequently have periods when I am extremely depressed." The test results would reflect something about the person's behavior—a tendency to agree with questions—but would tell us little about the individual's general mood. To counteract agreement tendencies, test constructors try (whenever possible) to reverse the wording of questions to provide yes and no versions of each item.

Various methods have been used to counteract deliberate falsifying and tendencies toward social desirability and acquiescence on personality inventories, but they have been only partially successful.

Projective techniques

Personality inventories strive for objectivity; they are easy to score and can be evaluated for reliability and validity. But their fixed structure—specific questions to which the individual must respond by selecting one of the answers presented—severely limits freedom of expression. *Projective tests*, in contrast, attempt to explore the private personality and allow the individual to become much more involved in the responses. A projective test presents an ambiguous stimulus to which the person may respond as she or he wishes. Theoretically, because the stimulus is ambiguous and does not demand a specific response, the individual *projects* his or her personality onto the stimulus. Projective tests tap the individual's imagination; through imaginative productions, it is assumed that the person reveals something about himself or herself. Two of the most widely used projective techniques are the Rorschach Test and the Thematic Apperception Test.

Figure 13-4
Rorschach Inkblot
This inkblot is one of the standardized blots used in the Rorschach Test. The subject is asked to tell what is seen in the blot; it may be viewed from any angle.

RORSCHACH TEST   The Rorschach Test, developed by the Swiss psychiatrist Hermann Rorschach in the 1920s, consists of a series of 10 cards, each displaying a rather complex inkblot like the one shown in Figure 13-4. Some of the blots are color; some are black and white. The subject is instructed to look at one card at a time and report everything the inkblot resembles. After the subject has finished the 10 cards, the examiner usually goes over each response, asking the subject to clarify some responses and to tell what features of the blot gave a particular impression.

The subject's responses may be scored in various ways. Three main categories are (1) *location* (whether the response involves the entire inkblot or some part of it; (2) *determinants* (whether the subject responds to the shape of the blot, its color, or differences in texture and shading); and (3) *content* (what the response represents). Most testers also score responses according to frequency of occurrence; for example, a response is "popular" if many people assign it to the same inkblot.

Several elaborate scoring systems have been devised based on these categories. But because these systems have proved to have a limited predictive value, many psychologists base their interpretations on an impressionistic evaluation of the response record as well as on the subject's general reaction to the test situation (for example, whether the individual is defensive, open, competitive, cooperative, and so on). Interpretation of the Rorschach requires more training and experience than interpretation of any of the other personality tests.

THEMATIC APPERCEPTION TEST   Another popular projective test—the Thematic Apperception Test (TAT)—was developed at Harvard University by Henry Murray in the 1930s. The subject is shown a series of as many as 20 ambiguous pictures of persons and scenes, similar to the one in Figure 13-5, and asked to make up a story about each. The subject is encouraged to give free rein to his or her imagination and to tell whatever story comes to mind. The test is intended to reveal basic themes that recur in a person's imaginative productions. *Apperception* is a readiness to perceive in certain ways based on prior individual experiences. People interpret ambiguous pictures according to their apperceptions and elaborate stories in terms of preferred plots or themes that reflect personal fantasies. If particular problems are bothering the subject, they may become evident in a number of the stories or in striking deviations from the usual theme in one or two stories. When shown a picture similar to the one in Figure 13-5, a 21-year-old male told the following story:

Figure 13-5
Thematic Apperception Test
This picture is similar to the pictures used on the Thematic Apperception Test. The pictures usually have elements of ambiguity so that the subject can "read into" them something from personal experience or fantasy.

> She has prepared this room for someone's arrival and is opening the door for a last general look over the room. She is probably expecting her son home. She tries to place everything as it was when he left. She seems like a very tyrannical character. She led her son's life for him and is going to take over again as soon as he gets back. This is merely the beginning of her rule, and the son is definitely cowed by this overbearing attitude of hers and will slip back into her well-ordered way of life. He will go through life plodding down the tracks she has laid down for him. All this represents her complete domination of his life until she dies.

Although the original picture shows only a woman standing in an open doorway looking into a room, the subject's readiness to talk about his relationship with his mother led to this story of a woman's domination of her son. Facts obtained later confirmed the clinician's interpretation that the story reflected the subject's own problems.

In analyzing responses to the TAT cards, the psychologist looks for recurrent themes that may reveal the individual's needs, motives, or characteristic way of handling interpersonal relationships.

PROBLEMS WITH PROJECTIVE TESTS   Many other projective tests have been devised. Some ask the subject to draw pictures of people, houses, trees, and so on. Others involve completing sentences that start with "I often wish . . . ," "My mother . . . ," or "I feel like quitting when they . . . ." In fact, any stimulus to which a person can respond in an individualistic way could be considered the basis for a projective test. But most projective tests have not been subjected to enough research to establish their usefulness in assessing personality.

The Rorschach test and the TAT, in contrast, have been intensively researched. The results, however, have not always been encouraging. Reliability of the Rorschach test has been generally poor because the interpretation of responses is too dependent on the clinician's judgment; the same test protocol may be evaluated quite differently by two trained examiners. And attempts to

Thematic Apperception Test

demonstrate the Rorschach's ability to predict behavior or discriminate between groups have met with limited success. Numerous efforts have been made to improve on Rorschach's method. For example, the Holtzman Inkblot Test presents the subject with 45 different inkblots and allows only one response per blot (Holtzman and others, 1961). It was hoped that this procedure would yield more reliable and valid scores; thus far, however, the results have been disappointing (Zubin, 1972).

The TAT has fared somewhat better. When specific scoring systems are used (for example, to measure achievement motives or aggressive themes), the interscorer reliability is fairly good. But the relationship of TAT scores to overt behavior is complex. Preoccupations are not necessarily acted on. A person who produces a number of stories with aggressive themes may not actually behave aggressively. The individual may be compensating for a need to inhibit aggressive tendencies by expressing such impulses in fantasy. When inhibitions about expressing aggression *and* strength of aggressive tendencies are estimated from the TAT stories, the relationship to behavior becomes more predictable. Among boys whose tests indicated they were not very inhibited, the correlation between amount of aggression in the TAT stories and overt aggression was .55. Among boys showing a high degree of inhibition, the correlation between the number of aggressive themes and overt aggression was −.50 (Olweus, 1969).

Defenders of the Rorschach test and the TAT point out that it is not fair to expect accurate predictions based on test responses alone; story themes or responses to inkblots are meaningful only when considered in light of additional information: the person's life history, other test data, and observations of behavior. The skilled clinician uses the results of projective tests to make tentative interpretations about the individual's personality and then verifies or discards them, depending on further information. The tests are helpful in suggesting possible areas of conflict to be explored.

CONSISTENCY OF PERSONALITY

In studying personality, psychologists try to discover regularities in behavior. An assumption basic to most personality theories is that people behave consistently from one situation to another and over time. Trait theories assume that certain basic personality traits characterize an individual over a variety of day-to-day situations and, to some extent, over the course of a lifetime. Thus, if an individual appears to behave honestly or conscientiously in several situations, we assume that we can predict how that person will act in a variety of situations and even how the person will behave a year from now. Psychoanalytic theory also assumes consistency; unresolved childhood conflicts (for example, centering on toilet training) lead to a cluster of personality characteristics (obstinancy, excessive cleanliness, and concern with details) that characterize a person throughout life.

In terms of our private personality, the feeling of consistency within our thoughts and behavior is essential to our well-being. The loss of a sense of consistency is characteristic of personality disorganization.

However, in many instances, research has failed to show as much personality consistency as either theories or our intuitions lead us to expect. The consistency of personality is an issue much debated among psychologists.

CRITICAL DISCUSSION

The Barnum Effect

There is no scientific evidence that the position of the stars and planets at the moment of a person's birth has any influence on personality. Yet astrology—the study of "how heavenly bodies influence the destinies of individuals"—is extremely popular. People buy books on astrology and avidly read their daily horoscope in the newspapers, accepting the personality characterizations and predictions as at least probabilities, if not facts. What reinforces their belief? The answer seems to be that the astrological descriptions are general enough to be true of almost anyone.

Studies have shown that people tend to view generalized descriptions as accurate summaries of their own personality. In one experiment, college students were given a personality inventory. A few days later, each student was handed a typed report in a sealed envelope and asked to rate the accuracy of the evaluation. Unknown to the subjects, all the personality descriptions were *identical*. Most students said they felt that the description fit them fairly well (Forer, 1949). A glance at some of the evaluative statements will show why:

- Under stressful circumstances, you occasionally experience some feelings of self-doubt.
- Although you have considerable affections for your parents, there have been times when you disagreed with them.
- Your sexual adjustment has presented problems for you.
- You have a tendency to be critical of yourself.
- At times, you are extraverted, affable, sociable, while at other times you are introverted, wary, reserved.

These statements resemble the kinds of statements found in astrological characterizations of personality based on the signs of the zodiac. Because such descriptions are true of many people, they create the illusion of accuracy when applied to the individual case. This phenomenon has been dubbed the "Barnum effect" in reference to the frequently quoted statement by the circus entrepreneur P.T. Barnum, "There's a sucker born every minute."

Several studies indicate that people are more likely to accept a personality description of themselves as accurate when they are told that the report is based on a projective test than when they are told that it is based on an interview or a personality inventory (Snyder, 1974). Apparently, a certain mystique is associated with projective tests—people believe they are revealing themselves in ways they do not quite understand. Interviews and personality inventories are more familiar techniques, and people assume that responses to them can be controlled consciously.

The popularity and acceptance of personality evaluations by astrologers, palmists, and readers of tea leaves or Tarot cards appear to stem from the mystical quality associated with the procedure and from the universality of the personality descriptions. In addition, some fortunetellers are quite skilled in picking up cues from the individual's appearance and reactions. The surprising accuracy of a small part of the personality description may predispose the subject to accept the total evaluation.

Consistency over time

Longitudinal studies of individuals indicate considerable consistency of personality characteristics. In one large-scale study, more than 100 subjects were followed over a 35-year period. They were first evaluated in junior high school by psychologists who rated each individual on a number of personality traits, using a standardized rating procedure. The same subjects were rated again in senior high school, in their mid-thirties, and in their mid-forties; each rating was conducted by a different group of judges. Over the three-year period from junior high school to senior high school, 58 percent of personality variables showed a significant positive correlation. Over the 30-year period from junior high school to the subjects' mid-forties, 31 percent of the items showed a significant correlation. Table 13-6 lists some of the personality characteristics that displayed the greatest consistency over time (Block, 1971, 1981).

This study indicates that trained observers looking at an individual find personality consistencies over time. In looking at *themselves*, people also tend to find personality consistencies over the years, at least once they reach adulthood. Scores on the California Psychological Inventory taken 10 years apart

CORRELATION JUNIOR HIGH TO SENIOR HIGH SCHOOL	CORRELATION SENIOR HIGH SCHOOL TO ADULTHOOD	ITEM RATED
Males		
.58	.53	Is a genuinely dependable and responsible person
.57	.59	Tends toward undercontrol of needs and impulses; unable to delay gratification
.50	.42	Is self-defeating
.35	.58	Enjoys aesthetic impressions; is aesthetically reactive
Females		
.50	.46	Basically submissive
.39	.43	Emphasizes being with others; gregarious
.48	.49	Tends to be rebellious and nonconforming
.45	.42	Is concerned with philosophical problems (for example, religion, values, the meaning of life)

Table 13-6
Consistency of Personality
The table lists some of the personality traits that showed the greatest consistency in ratings over the years from junior high school to adulthood. With correlations of this size, adult characteristics can be predicted fairly well from earlier ratings. (After Block, 1971)

(ages 30–40 in one group and 40–50 in another) showed consistency on many items (Block, 1977).

STABILITY AND CHANGE   Although some individuals exhibit fairly stable characteristics over a lifetime, others show quite dramatic changes in personality. In today's world of rapid social and technological change, many people are confronted with a conflict between maintaining their identity (remaining consistent) and realizing their full potential (exploring new roles and behavior). Personality development involves both constancy and change.

Although personality changes can occur at any time in life, they are most apt to take place during adolescence and early adulthood. Block's longitudinal study found marked individual differences in the degree of personality consistency over the age periods studied. Some individuals appeared to stabilize their personality quite early in life; others changed considerably over the years from high school to middle adulthood. In general, the "changers" were those whose adolescence was marked by conflict and tension, both within themselves and in relation to society and adult values. For example, male changers were described during their high-school years as insecure, vulnerable, lacking in direction, immature, and oriented toward the peer culture. Female changers were described as insecure and rebellious; they placed a high value on independence and viewed their parents as old-fashioned.

Nonchangers, in contrast, were relaxed, effective individuals who comfortably pursued culturally valued goals. They appeared to accept themselves and to assimilate traditional roles and the values of their culture. Male nonchangers were described as self-confident, mature, adaptable, and productive. Female nonchangers tended to have positive relationships with their parents and other adults; they were described as submissive, productive, and accepting of traditional sex roles. Thus, although there are undoubtedly many individual reasons for seeking change, we can draw a general conclusion that changers of both sexes found life a struggle and were impelled to change; for the nonchangers, life was a smoother process.

Consistency across situations

There is less evidence for personality consistency when we look at measures of behavior across different situations—for example, aggressive behavior at home and aggressive behavior at school. Except for intellectual and cognitive abilities, most personality characteristics show only modest consistency across situations. Studies of traits such as honesty, self-control, dependency, and aggression have usually found low correlations between measures of the trait in one situation and measures in another (Mischel, 1976). For example, studies show that the degree of honesty a child exhibits in one tempting situation (such as the chance to cheat on an examination) does not correlate very highly with the degree of honesty the child shows in response to a different kind of temptation (such as, stealing money or lying to save face with one's peers).

Attempts to relate responses on personality tests to behavior in real life also have been disappointing. Correlations between measures derived from personality inventories or projective techniques and independent measures of behavior are typically less than .30. Correlations of this size may be useful in determining a gross assessment of personality (for example, deciding whether a person is unfit for a sensitive diplomatic post) but would be of limited value in predicting specific behavior.

Social learning theorists point to the data showing low consistency of personality traits across situations as evidence that behavior is *situation-specific*—more dependent on the nature of the specific situation in which it occurs than on enduring traits or response tendencies in the person. They maintain that it is not very useful to characterize people in broad trait terms ("impulsive," "dependent," and so on) because individuals show so much variability and discrimination in their behavior. Whether a person acts "impulsively" depends to a great extent on the particular conditions she or he confronts.

According to social learning theorists, traits are more often in "the eye of the beholder" than in the person being observed; we tend to attribute more consistency to a person's behavior than actually exists. There are numerous reasons why we may do this. We will mention four:

1 Many personal qualities remain fairly constant—physical appearance, manner of speaking, expressive gestures, and so on. These constancies help to create an impression of personality consistency.
2 Our preconceived notions of how people behave may lead us to generalize beyond our actual observations. We may fill in the missing data according to our implicit personality theories of what traits and behaviors go together. Stereotypes of how a "homosexual," a "career woman," or an "athlete" behaves may cause us to attribute greater consistency to a person's actions than actual observations warrant.
3 Our presence can cause people to behave in certain ways. Thus, our acquaintances may appear to behave consistently because we are present as a stimulus during every observation we make. They may behave quite differently when we are not there.
4 Because the actions of another person are such a salient feature of any scene, we tend to overestimate the extent to which behavior is caused by personality characteristics and underestimate the importance of situational forces that may cause the person to act as he or she does. If we observe someone behaving aggressively, we assume that the person has an aggressive disposition and will behave similarly in other settings even though the situational factors may be quite different.

Personality theorists who believe that behavior is determined by enduring dispositions or motives (for example, trait and psychoanalytic theorists) maintain that personality is much more consistent than the cross-situational research indicates. They point to defects in the methodology of many personality studies and emphasize the need for (1) repeated observations, (2) considering individual differences in consistency, and (3) defining traits in more specific terms.

REPEATED OBSERVATIONS Most of the studies that find little cross-situational consistency are based on a small sample of behaviors. For example, such studies may correlate an individual's score on a scale measuring aggression with aggressive behavior in a laboratory experiment, or they may try to relate helpfulness in one situation (giving money to charity) with helpfulness in another (coming to the aid of a person in distress). Much greater consistency can be found when behavior is observed on a number of occasions. The advantage of repeated measures is shown by a study in which college students kept a daily log for several weeks. They were asked to note their most pleasant and unpleasant experiences each day, the emotions associated with each experience, their impulses to act (what they felt like doing in response to the situation), and their actual behavior.

When a subject's behavior or emotions on any two days were compared, the correlations were quite low (usually below .30). However, when the subject's behavior was averaged over a 14- or 28-day period, the correlations were much higher (often over .80). As the number of days in the sample increased, the reliability coefficients of the various measures (emotions, impulses, and behaviors) increased steadily (Epstein, 1977, 1979).

Other studies have shown similar results when behavior is observed over a period of time. For example, in a study by Leon (1977), observers followed people for four weeks and rated them on variables related to their sociability or their tendency to be impulsive. Although the correlations for any two days were quite low, the ratings averaged over the first 14 days correlated .81 with the ratings averaged over the second 14 days. Thus, it appears that we can find considerable cross-situational consistency in traits, given enough time. The practical implication is that if we wish to be accurate in our judgments about other people—in deciding whether they would be trustworthy business associates, reliable friends, or appropriate marriage partners—we need to observe them on a number of occasions. Too small a sample of behavior (a first impression) may prove inadequate. As one psychologist has noted:

> There is a considerable payoff, whether one is gambling for money or taking one's chances in interpersonal relationships, in being right most of the time. I considered the woman I was to marry to be a warm, considerate person. This does not mean I believed she would never get angry at me or would never misunderstand me. If her behavior were that invariant across situations, she would be rigid, a robot. It does mean that according to my assessment, her behavior, in general, would place her high on these attributes, high enough to make me willing to gamble my future happiness on my estimates, which fortunately were accurate. Note that in essence what was involved was being exposed to a sample of events from which a prediction was made of the average behavior in another sample of events. (Epstein, 1977, p. 84)

INDIVIDUAL DIFFERENCES IN CONSISTENCY Most of the research on personality traits assumes that every person can be described by every trait—that people differ from one another only in *how much* of the trait they possess. But although some people might be consistent on some traits, few people would be consistent on all traits. When we are asked to describe a friend, we pick a few traits that strike us as pertinent. When we are asked to describe another friend, we select a different set of traits. It may be that for any given individual, we should expect to find consistency only on those traits that are central to his or her personality.

In one study, college students were asked to rate their own cross-situational variability on a set of traits (Bem and Allen, 1974). Students who identified themselves as consistent on a particular trait tended to show much more consistency across different situations than students who identified themselves as variable on that trait. For example, students who said they were consistently friendly tended to show a fairly consistent level of friendliness on such measures as ratings by their parents and peers and direct observation in several settings (a cross-situational correlation of .57). Students who described themselves as variable in friendliness tended to be less consistent (a cross-situational correlation of .27).

If, as this study indicates, people do vary in their consistency on different traits, a random selection of subjects will contain some individuals who show consistency and some who show variability on a particular trait, such as honesty. An attempt to demonstrate cross-situational consistency with such a mixed group of subjects is bound to yield poor results.

Subsequent studies indicate that people who show behavioral consistency fall into two groups: those who are consistent across many dimensions of behavior (indeed, for them, consistency may be a trait) and those who are consistent on only one or two traits (for example, aggression or sociability). There is further evidence that both groups showing behavioral consistency are more attentive to and aware of their inner feelings than individuals who show little consistency (Underwood and Moore, 1981).

TRAITS TOO BROADLY DEFINED   Most personality inventories and rating scales define traits in fairly global terms. We may have to be more specific if we want to be accurate in predicting behavior. In the Bem and Allen study, for example, the investigators assumed that personal neatness was one component of the trait of conscientiousness. But the results showed that for most students the neatness of their rooms was *not* related to other measures of conscientiousness, such as completing homework assignments on time or arriving promptly for classes and appointments.

To take another example, in viewing aggression as a trait, we may want to distinguish between *verbal* and *physical* aggression. There is evidence that these two behaviors are not highly corrrelated. Youngsters who talk back to their teachers or insult their peers are often not the ones who start fights (Olweus, 1979).

Interaction of traits and situations

Thus far, our discussion makes it clear that to understand and predict behavior we need to know the characteristics of the individual *and* of the particular situation. It is not particularly useful to talk about general traits, such as hostility or anxiety, without considering environmental conditions. Two people may score high on a test designed to measure anxiety, but the situations in which they feel anxious may differ. One individual may become anxious in the face of physical danger (for example, when climbing a steep mountain); the other may feel anxious in interpersonal situations that are viewed as threatening to his or her self-esteem (for example, giving a speech or taking an examination).

Personality questionnaires designed to determine the kinds of situations that evoke anxious feelings have proved more successful in predicting actual behavior. For example, subjects whose scores indicated concern about physical danger reported much greater feelings of anxiety when placed in an experiment where they were threatened by the possibility of electric shock than subjects whost test scores indicated that their anxiety was associated with interpersonal situations (Endler and Okada, 1974). Subjects who scored high on interpersonal anxiety showed more stress just before an examination (being evaluated) than subjects who scored low (Endler, 1977).

In measuring traits, we need to examine individual differences (for example, stable tendencies to be anxious, hostile, or conscientious across different situations) in interaction with specific environmental conditions. Inner dispositions and external situations interact in complex ways. People respond to situations in light of their dispositions and beliefs, but they may also seek or avoid certain situations because of their personality characteristics. For example, an aggressive person who feels the need to dominate others might seek confrontation; a more submissive individual would try to avoid confrontation. In addition, as we noted earlier, behavior tends to shape environment. A person who acts in an abrasive manner is apt to encounter a more hostile social environment than someone who is more tactful and sensitive to the feelings of others.

TOWARD AN INTEGRATED VIEW OF PERSONALITY

We have looked at a number of different ways of conceptualizing personality. Each approach has dealt in some way with how individual characteristics develop and how they interact with environmental conditions to determine behavior. But what is the best perspective from which to view personality—to form a cohesive view of the individual person? Psychologists are attempting to answer this question. The field of personality psychology is in a state of flux and transition. Clearly, no simplified theory will suffice to explain personality, and the current trend is toward a synthesis of several influences.

In trying to weigh the relative importance of individual differences and environmental conditions in determining behavior, it is helpful to think of the situation as *providing information*—information that the person interprets and acts on according to his or her past experiences and abilities. Some situations are powerful. A red traffic light causes most drivers to stop; they know what it means, are motivated to obey it, and have the ability to stop when they see it. We would be fairly successful in predicting the number of individuals who would respond in the same way to a red traffic light. Other situations are weak. If an art teacher shows students a slide of an abstract painting and asks them to comment on its meaning, we would expect a variety of responses. The picture does not convey the same meaning to all the viewers, and there are no universal expectancies regarding the desired response. In weak situations, individual differences, rather than the stimulus, are the most important determinant of behavior.

Current research in personality places more emphasis on *cognitive processes* and attempts to balance them in conjunction with other aspects of personality. People differ in intellectual abilities, in the way they perceive events and code them in memory, and in the strategies they employ in solving problems.

Traditionally, intellectual abilities have been considered separately from personality, and although these topics are treated in different chapters of this book, they are actually closely interrelated. For example, studies indicate that the way in which people categorize objects and events is related to their personality characteristics. People whose categories are broad tend to be more open to experience and less rigid than individuals who restrict their categories to a narrower group of stimuli (see Block and others, 1981). Future research will probably broaden the definition of personality to include intellectual factors, particularly the variety of cognitive processes that an individual employs in solving problems and dealing with new situations.

Another area that is beginning to form an important part of personality theory has to do with social interactions. Other people are an important part of most situations, and behavior in social situations is a process of continuous reciprocal interaction. Your behavior determines how another person reacts, and his or her response in turn influences your behavior, ad infinitum. Prescribed social roles, the impressions we form of other people, and the qualities we attribute to them are all important influences on behavior. These social-psychological processes will be discussed in Chapters 17 and 18.

Summary

1   *Personality* refers to the characteristic patterns of behavior and modes of thinking that determine a person's adjustment to the environment. It includes a *public personality* that can be observed by others as well as a *private personality* that consists of thoughts and experiences seldom revealed.

2   Some personality characteristics (such as general mood and energy level) are influenced by inherited *biological factors*. Experiences common to the *culture* and the *subcultural group* (such as sex roles) and experiences that are unique to the individual interact with inborn predispositions to shape personality. The major theoretical approaches to an understanding of personality include *trait, social learning, psychoanalytic,* and *phenomonological* theories.

3   *Trait theories* assume that a personality can be described by its position on a number of *continuous dimensions,* or *scales,* each of which represents a trait. The method of *factor analysis* has been used to determine the basic traits. Two dimensions found fairly consistently in factor-analytic studies of personality are *introversion–extraversion* and *stability–instability.*

4   *Social learning theory* assumes that personality differences result from variations in learning experiences. Responses may be learned through *observation,* without reinforcement; but reinforcement is important in determining whether the learned responses will be *performed.* A person's behavior depends on the specific characteristics of the situation in interaction with the individual's appraisal of the situation and reinforcement history. People behave consistently insofar as the situations they encounter and the roles they are expected to play remain relatively stable.

5   *Psychoanalytic theory* assumes that much of human motivation is *unconscious* and must be inferred indirectly from behavior. Freud viewed personality as composed of three systems—the *id,* the *ego,* and the *superego*—which interact and sometimes conflict. The id operates on the *pleasure principle,* seeking immediate gratification of biological impulses. The ego obeys the *reality prin-*

ciple, postponing gratification until it can be achieved in socially acceptable ways. The superego (conscience) imposes *moral standards* on the individual.

6   The dynamic aspects of psychoanalytic theory assume that repressed id impulses cause *anxiety*, which can be reduced by *defense mechanisms*. The developmental aspects propose that some kinds of personality types (such as oral or anal) result from *fixation* (arrested development) at one of the *psychosexual stages*.

7   *Phenomenological theories* are concerned with the individual's *subjective experience*. They emphasize such humanistic qualities as *self-concept* and push toward growth, or *self-actualization*. For Rogers, the most important aspect of personality is the *congruence* between the *self* and *reality* and between the *self* and the *ideal self*. Rogers' basic motivating force, the innate tendency toward self-actualization, has been further studied by Maslow, who has examined the characteristics of self-actualizing persons.

8   Personality can be assessed by *observing* an individual in a natural setting or during an interview. The observers may record their impressions on a *rating scale*, taking care to avoid the *halo effect* and *stereotypes*. Self-observations can be reported by means of *personality inventories*, such as the Minnesota Multiphasic Personality Inventory (MMPI) and the California Psychological Inventory (CPI).

9   Less structured approaches to personality assessment are *projective tests*, such as the Rorschach and the Thematic Apperception Test (TAT). Because the test stimuli are ambiguous, it is assumed that the individual projects his or her personality onto the stimulus.

10 *Longitudinal studies* indicate that some personality characteristics are *consistent* over time, although some people stabilize their personality early in life and others change markedly from high school to middle adulthood. *Cross-situational studies* usually find low correlations between measures of a trait (such as honesty) in one situation and measures of a trait in another. Social learning theorists believe that this is because behavior is more dependent on the situation than on enduring traits. Trait and psychoanalytic theorists argue that by *repeated observations*, allowing for *individual differences in consistency*, and *defining traits in more specific terms*, higher cross-situational correlations can be found.

11 To understand behavior, we need to know how the characteristics of the individual *interact* with the characteristics of the situation. The situation provides information that the person interprets and acts on according to his or her past experiences and abilities.

Further Reading

General books on personality include Hall and Lindzey, *Theories of personality* (3rd ed., 1978); and Mischel, *Introduction to personality* (3rd ed., 1981); and Singer, *The human personality: An introductory textbook* (1983).

A synopsis of various personality theories may be found in Hjelle and Ziegler, *Personality theories: Basic assumptions, research, and applications* (2nd ed., 1981). A brief but well-written book emphasizing experimental studies is *Personality: The skein of behavior* (1976) by Geen.

For a social learning approach to personality, see Rotter, Chance, and Phares, *Applications of a social learning theory of personality* (1972); and Bandura, *Social learning theory* (1977). See also Mischel, *Introduction to personality* (3rd ed., 1981).

Freud's theories are presented in their most readable form in his *New introductory lectures on psychoanalysis* (1933). Another reference for psychoanalytical theories of personality is Holzman, *Psychoanalysis and psychopathology* (1970).

The phenomenological viewpoint is represented in Maddi and Costa, *Humanism in personology* (1972); and Keen, *A primer in phenomenological psychology* (1977). For Carl Rogers' views, see Rogers and Stevens, *Person to person: The problem of being human* (1967); and Rogers, *Carl Rogers on personal power* (1977). For Maslow's views, see Goble, *The third force: The psychology of Abraham Maslow* (1970).

The approach to studying traits in interaction with situations is represented in Magnusson and Endler (eds.), *Personality at the crossroads: Current issues in interactional psychology* (1977).

Cronbach, *Essentials of psychological testing* (3rd ed., 1970) has a number of chapters on personality appraisal, as does Weiner, *Clinical methods in psychology* (1976). Other books devoted to personality appraisal are Wiggins, *Personality and prediction: Principles of personality assessment* (1973); and Sundberg, *The assessment of persons* (1977).

Part seven
CONFLICT, ADJUSTMENT, AND MENTAL HEALTH

14
CONFLICT AND STRESS

No matter how resourceful we may be in coping with problems, the circumstances of life inevitably involve stress. Our motives are not always easily satisfied; obstacles must be overcome, choices made, and delays tolerated. Each of us develops characteristic ways of responding when our attempts to reach a goal are blocked. To a large extent, our responses to frustrating situations determine how adequately we adjust to life.

In the next three chapters, we will look at the ways in which people respond to frustration and stress, what happens when inadequate coping techniques pose a threat to adjustment, and the methods used to treat abnormal behavior. Because this area of psychology is not as firmly based on experimental data as some of the topics covered in previous chapters, the material will be more discursive, and case histories, rather than experiments, will be used at times to illustrate points.

FRUSTRATION

Frustration occurs when progress toward a desired goal is blocked or delayed. A wide range of obstacles, both external and internal, can interfere with an individual's efforts to reach a goal. The physical environment presents such obstacles as traffic jams, crowded lines at the supermarket, droughts that destroy agricultural crops, and noise that prevents concentration. The social environment presents obstacles in the form of restrictions imposed by other people, which may range from parental denials (Jane's parents insist that she is not old enough to have her own apartment) to broader problems of racial or sexual discrimination.

Sometimes the barriers to goal satisfaction stem from the individual's own limitations. Physical handicaps, lack of specific abilities, or inadequate self-control can prevent an individual from achieving a desired goal. Not everyone can become a skilled musician or pass the examinations necessary to become a physician or a lawyer. If an individual sets goals beyond his or her ability, frustration is apt to result.

Conflict

A major source of frustration is *conflict* between two opposing motives. When two motives conflict, the satisfaction of one leads to the frustration of the other. For example, a student may not be able to gain recognition as an outstanding athlete and still earn the grades required to enter law school. Even when only one motive is involved, conflict may arise if the goal can be approached in several different ways. For example, you can get an education at a number of colleges, but choosing which college to attend presents a conflict situation. Although the goal will eventually be reached, progress toward it is disrupted by the necessity of making a choice.

Sometimes conflict arises between a motive and a person's internal standards rather than between two external goals. An individual's sexual desires may conflict with his or her standards of acceptable social behavior. Achievement motives may conflict with individual standards of helpful and cooperative behavior; to succeed may require competing with—or even undermining—colleagues and associates. Conflicts between motives and internal standards often can be more difficult to resolve than conflicts between external goals.

Most conflicts involve goals that are simultaneously desirable and undesirable—both positive and negative. Candy is delicious but fattening. Going off for a weekend of skiing is fun, but losing study time can produce anxiety. A goal that is at once wanted and not wanted, liked and disliked, produces an *ambivalent attitude*. Ambivalent attitudes are very common. Adolescents have an ambivalent attitude toward independence: they wish to take charge of their own affairs but still want their parents to help them with difficult problems.

A person confronted with a goal that is at once attractive and dangerous may vacillate while trying to decide what to do. At a distance, the goal seems inviting, leading to approach reactions. But the sense of danger increases as the goal is approached, and the individual tends to withdraw as he or she nears the incentive. A shy teen-ager who wants to call to arrange a date is drawn to the telephone by the possibility of success, but anxiety about possible rebuff may mount as the phone is approached. The young person may make several false starts before either carrying through the plan or abandoning it. This type of conflict is called an *approach-avoidance conflict*.

Approach and avoidance

Studies of approach-avoidance conflicts indicate that the two motives operate somewhat differently. As you might expect, both approach and avoidance motives are strongest near the object. The closer you get to an attractive object, the stronger your tendency is to approach it; the closer you get to something unpleasant or fearful, the stronger your urge is to flee. But avoidance motives appear to drop off more rapidly with distance than approach motives do (see Figure 14-1). As you get farther away from a feared object, it seems much less frightening, but an attractive object is still appealing at a distance. This difference in the gradients of approach and avoidance helps explain why a person may be repeatedly drawn back into an old conflict situation. At a distance, the positive aspects seem more inviting than the negative aspects appear forbidding. Everyone knows of couples who go steady, break up, and make up, only to break up once more. Away from each other, their mutual attraction takes precedence because negative feelings are reduced; close to each other, the

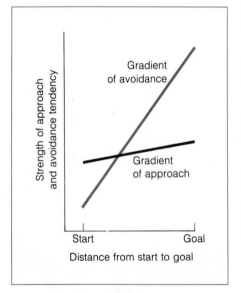

Figure 14-1
Gradients of Approach and Avoidance
When a goal is both desirable and undesirable (such as a place where a rat has been fed but also received an electric shock), it elicits both approach and avoidance responses. Both tendencies increase the closer the animal gets to the goal, but the tendency to avoid the goal rises more steeply than the tendency to approach it does. The slope of these gradients was determined by measuring how much effort animals exerted to reach food and how much effort they exerted to escape shock. At the point where the two gradients cross, the animals showed considerable vacillation.

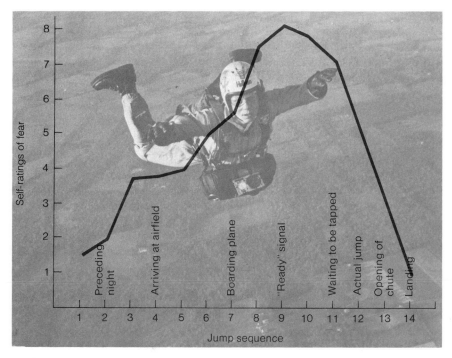

Figure 14-2
Reactions of Parachutists
Self-ratings by skydivers of feelings of avoidance (fear) at various times before and during their first parachute jump. (After Epstein and Fenz, 1965)

negative feelings drive them apart. Once the ambivalence of their attitudes is recognized, their attempts at reconciliation become understandable.

Studies of the reactions of skydivers to their first parachute jump show how negative feelings (fear of death or injury) become stronger as the moment of danger becomes more imminent (Figure 14-2). The day before the jump, positive feelings (the excitement and thrill of jumping) are predominant. But as the neophyte parachutist comes closer to the moment of jumping (arrives at the airfield, boards the plane, and waits for the ready signal), avoidance impulses increase rapidly, reaching a peak just before the signal is given. At this point, avoidance feelings far exceed approach tendencies, and the would-be parachutist might back down it if were possible to do so without embarrassment. (The individual now experiences what has been called an *avoidance-avoidance conflict*—having to choose between the two negative alternatives of jumping or losing face.) If the avoidance feelings had been this strong at some distance from the goal (the week before, for example, while the jump was being planned), the individual probably would not have gotten into such a conflict situation.

Interestingly enough, the peak of fear occurs not at the moment of greatest danger (in the free fall before the parachute opens) but at the point of final commitment, after which it would be difficult for the parachutist to change his or her mind. Once the decision is made, avoidance feelings begin to decrease.

The conflicts of real life are usually more complicated than our discussion implies. A conflict over drinking alcohol, for example, involves more than a choice between its short-term relaxing effects and its long-term destructive effects. The decision can be influenced by moral scruples, fear of losing self-control, need to feel more effective, search for companionship, or escape from responsibility.

Approach-avoidance conflict

In our society, the approach-avoidance conflicts that are most pervasive and difficult to resolve generally occur between the following motives:

1   *Independence versus dependence.* In times of stress, we may want to resort to the dependence characteristic of childhood—to have someone take care of us and solve our problems. But we are taught that the ability to stand on our own and assume responsibilities is a mark of maturity.
2   *Intimacy versus isolation.* The desire to be close to another person and to share our innermost thoughts and emotions may conflict with the fear of being hurt or rejected if we expose too much of ourselves.
3   *Cooperation versus competition.* In our society much emphasis is placed on competition and success. Competition begins in early childhood among siblings, continues through school, and culminates in business and professional rivalry. At the same time, we are urged to cooperate and help others. The concept of "team spirit" is as American as the success story. Such contradictory expectations can produce conflict.
4   *Impulse expression versus moral standards.* Impulses must be regulated to some degree in all societies. We noted in Chapter 3 that much of childhood learning involves internalizing the cultural restrictions placed on innate impulses. Sex and aggression are two areas in which our impulses most frequently conflict with moral standards, and violation of these standards may generate strong feelings of guilt.

These four areas present the greatest potential for serious conflict. As we will see in Chapter 15, failure to find a workable compromise may lead to serious psychological problems.

REACTIONS TO FRUSTRATION

Frustration—whether it is the result of environmental obstacles, personal limitations, or conflict—can produce a number of possible consequences. A classic experiment with young children illustrates some reactions to frustration (Barker, Dembo, and Lewin, 1941). The experiment will be described in the present tense as though we were observing it.

On the first day of the experiment, the children come one at a time into a room that contains several toys, all of which lack a part or expected accessory (a chair without a table, an ironing board without an iron, a dial unit without a telephone, a boat and other water toys without any water). Most of the children begin to play with the toys eagerly and happily, making up for the missing elements imaginatively. They use paper as water on which to sail the boat, or they use their fist for a telephone.

On the second day of the experiment, the children we observe behave quite differently. They seem unable to play constructively and cannot fit the toys into meaningful and satisfying activities. They play roughly with the toys, occasionally jumping on one and trying to break it. If they draw with the crayons, they scribble like younger children. They whine and nag at the adult who is present. One child lies on the floor, stares at the ceiling and recites nursery rhymes, as if in a trance.

What accounts for the differences in behavior? Is the second group suffering from some sort of emotional disturbance? Have some of these children been mistreated at home? Actually, the children in the first and second groups are the same, but the children in the second group are exhibiting symptoms of frustration, deliberately created in the following way.

On the second day, an opaque screen was removed, allowing the children to see that they were in a larger room containing not only the "half-toys" but also other more elaborate and attractive toys. This part of the room contained a table for the chair, an iron on the ironing board, a complete telephone, a pond of water for the boat. However, the children were separated from the more desirable toys by a wire screen. They were denied the "whole" toys and could use only the "half-toys." They were frustrated.

Why was the half-toy situation satisfying the first time and frustrating the second time? The answer is simple. *Goal-seeking behavior* was satisfied the first time as the children played happily with the available toys. The second time, they knew that more attractive toys existed and set a new goal. The first day, the goal was attainable; the second day, it was not. To play with the half-toys on the second day was to stop short of what seemed to be a richer experience, which was frustrating. Frustration is therefore a relative matter: a person may be quite satisfied with a life situation until confronted with a friend who has achieved more.

This experiment illustrates a number of immediate responses to frustration. In discussing some of these responses, we shall refer to additional details of the experiment and draw illustrations from other experiments and from the frustrating experiences of everyday life.

Aggression

Most of the children in the frustrating situation seemed restless and unhappy: they fidgeted, sighed, and complained. And many of them expressed feelings of anger: they kicked and hit the toys, often breaking them. (Only a few of the children did any kicking or hitting in the prefrustration stage of the experiment.)

Sometimes *aggression* is expressed directly against the individual or object that is the source of frustration. Some children attacked the wire barrier, trying to remove it or get around it. Aggression of this kind is not necessarily hostile; it may be a learned way of solving a problem. When one child takes a toy from another child, the second is likely to attack the first in an attempt to regain the toy. Adults usually express their aggression verbally rather than physically; they are more likely to exchange insults than blows.

Although the anger engendered by frustration may impel the individual to attack the obstacle, whether it is animate or inanimate, direct aggression is not always possible.

DISPLACED AGGRESSION In many instances, the frustrated individual cannot express aggression against the source of frustration. Sometimes the source is vague and intangible. The person does not know what to attack but feels angry and seeks *something* to attack. Sometimes the person responsible for the frustration is so powerful that an attack would be dangerous. When circumstances block direct attack on the cause of frustration, aggression may be *displaced*—the aggressive action may be directed toward an innocent person or object rather than toward the actual cause of the frustration. A person who is reprimanded at work may take out unexpressed resentment on his or her family. Susan's "blowup" at her roommate may be related to the poor grade Susan received on the midterm exam.

Prejudice against minority groups often contains an element of displaced

"Why can't you lead a life of quiet desperation like other people?"

aggression, or *scapegoating*. During periods of economic depression, when money and jobs are scarce, people are tempted to blame their troubles on some relatively powerless minority group. In the past, Nazis blamed Jews, farmers in the southern United States blamed blacks, Protestant laborers in Boston blamed Irish Catholics, California farm workers blamed Mexican illegal aliens, and so forth. As we will see in Chapter 17, many factors contribute to prejudice, but displaced aggression in response to frustration may be one of them—as the following experiment demonstrates.

Boys at a summer camp were required to participate in a lengthy and boring testing session that ran overtime so that they missed their weekly outing to the local movies. A survey of the boys' attitudes toward minority groups before and after the testing session showed a significant increase in unfriendly feelings after the testing session. The boys *displaced* their anger toward minorities rather than express it directly toward the administrators of the tests (Miller and Bugelski, 1948).

Apathy

One of the factors complicating the study of human behavior is the tendency of different individuals to respond to similar situations in a variety of ways. Although a common response to frustration is active aggression, the opposite response of indifference or withdrawal, called *apathy*, is not uncommon. We do not know why one person reacts with aggression and another with apathy to the same situation, but it seems likely that learning is an important factor. Reactions to frustration can be learned in much the same manner as other behaviors. Children who strike out angrily when frustrated and find that their needs are then satisfied (either through their own efforts or because a parent rushes to placate them) will probably resort to the same behavior the next time their motives are thwarted. Children whose aggressive outbursts are never successful—who find they have no power to satisfy their needs by means of their own actions—may resort to apathy and withdrawal when confronted with subsequent frustrating situations.

LEARNED HELPLESSNESS   Studies have shown that animals and people can learn to be helpless when faced with stressful situations. A dog placed in a shuttle box (an apparatus with two compartments separated by a barrier) quickly learns to jump to the opposite compartment to escape a mild electric shock delivered to its feet through a grid on the floor. If a light is turned on a few seconds before the grid is electrified, the dog can learn to avoid the shock entirely by jumping to the safe compartment on signal. However, if the dog has previously been placed in a situation in which shocks are unavoidable and inescapable—where nothing the animal does terminates the shock—then it is very difficult for the dog to learn the avoidance response later when it is appropriate. The animal simply sits and endures the shock, even though an easy jump to the opposite compartment would eliminate its discomfort. Some dogs never learn, even if the experimenter demonstrates the proper procedure by carrying them over the barrier. These dogs had previously learned that they were unable to avoid the shock and could not overcome this *learned helplessness* (Seligman, 1975).

Human subjects placed in experimental situations in which they are unable to control shock or loud noise make fewer escape responses, when escape is possible, than subjects who have not had a prior experience of helplessness (Thornton and Jacobs, 1971). In fact, many kinds of uncontrollable or

World War II prisoners in a Nazi concentration camp at the moment of liberation (Buchenwald, Germany; 1945)

CRITICAL DISCUSSION

Captivity: The Ultimate Frustration

Imagine yourself locked in a small, windowless cell with no one to talk to, no books or newspapers to read, and no paper or pencil with which to write. Months go by with no chance for you to breathe fresh air or see the sun or moon, grass, or trees. The sparse food your captors provide is of little nutritional value; you are constantly hungry. Injuries and illnesses go untreated, as do abscessed teeth; there is no medical or dental care. Your hands are often bound, or you may be chained to your bed for days on end.

It is difficult to conceive of many situations that would engender greater feelings of frustration, helplessness, and hopelessness. Yet many U.S. servicemen captured during the Vietnam Conflict endured this type of solitary confinement for months and, in some cases, for years. One factor that helped the Vietnam prisoners cope with captivity was their previous training in prison-survival techniques.

Studies of people confined as hostages, prisoners of war, or inmates of concentration camps indicate that apathy and depression are common reactions to frustrating and traumatic conditions from which there is no hope of escape. Faced with continual deprivation, torture, and threats of death, many prisoners become detached, emotionless, and indifferent to events taking place around them. Some may abandon any attempt to cope with the situation or continue living. Interviews with American servicemen released from prison camps after the Korean War showed that almost all experienced feelings of withdrawal and apathy at some time during their imprisonment. Some men gave up altogether; they curled up on their bunks and waited to die, making no effort to eat or take care of themselves. Two remedies seemed helpful in saving a man close to death—getting him on his feet and doing something, no matter how trivial, and getting him interested in some current or future project. In a sense, both remedies provided the individual with a goal toward which he could direct his efforts (Strassman, Thaler, and Schein, 1956).

Concern about the reactions of American prisoners during the Korean War led military officials to develop programs to prepare servicemen to cope with the frustrations of imprisonment. Reports from men imprisoned during the Vietnam Conflict indicated that their survival training was helpful. Knowing how to keep physically and mentally active, provide support for each other, and focus on ways to solve daily problems did much to combat apathy and feelings of helplessness. Returned POWs reported that the most helpful behaviors included *communication, thinking about the future,* and *physical exercise.* The least useful behaviors were *thinking about suicide, talking to oneself,* and *worrying about the family.*

Prison-camp rules forbidding communication were strictly enforced by the guards; to be caught talking to a fellow prisoner meant severe torture. However, the POWs developed some ingenious methods of communication, which they taught to each other. The sounds of finger tapping, coughing, spitting, and clearing the throat were used to convey messages. A prisoner could also communicate by dragging his sandals according to a code as he walked past another prisoner's cell. And a POW sweeping the prison compound could send a message to every prisoner in the area by moving his broom in a particular way (Richlin, 1977). Solving health problems (making toothpaste from crushed charcoal, toothpicks from bone or wire, and dental floss from blanket threads) was more helpful than worrying about families or rehashing past experiences.

Having some strategies for coping with the frustration and stress of imprisonment appears to have aided survival. Although American POWs were held captive in Vietnam more than twice as long (sometimes as long as eight years) as American POWs were held captive in Korea, POWs returned from imprisonment in Vietnam in better physical and emotional condition overall than the Korean War POWs and their mortality rate during captivity was much lower. Roughly 38 percent of all American servicemen imprisoned during the Korean War did not survive captivity; only about 15 percent of the American POWs in Vietnam died while imprisoned.

However, before concluding that survival training alone produced the differences in mortality rates, we should realize that the Korean and Vietnam POWs differed in other respects. In any scientific study, whether it is in the field or the laboratory, all variables must be considered. Most of the men captured during the Korean War were in the infantry; some were officers, but the majority were enlisted men. Most of the men imprisoned in North Vietnam were pilots; on the average, they were more mature at the time of capture (average age 31 years) and more highly educated than the Korean POWs. And due to the nature of pilot selection procedures, the Vietnam POWs were probably more emotionally stable and highly motivated than the average serviceman. Their maturity, emotional stability, and intellectual resources undoubtedly played a role in their ability to survive. Another factor that probably contributed to the lower survival rate of the Korean POWs was the extreme cold to which they were subjected, which helped to deplete their physical strength.

Thus, survival training was not the only variable affecting the ability of Vietnam POWs to endure imprisonment. However, such preparation does appear to help people cope with the stress of captivity, and the government now provides survival training for military and diplomatic personnel who have a high risk of capture.

Figure 14-3
A Case of Extreme Regression

The 17-year-old girl in the picture on the left found an old photograph of herself taken when she was 5 (center). She then cut her hair and tried to look as much as she could like the child in the photograph (right). She came from a very unstable home and showed her first signs of disturbance at age 4, when her parents began to quarrel violently. When the girl was 7, her mother refused sexual relations with the father; the girl, however, slept in her father's bed until she was 13. The mother, suspecting that her daughter was being incestuously seduced, obtained legal custody and moved with her to a separate home. The girl resented the separation from her father, quarreled with her mother, and became a disciplinary problem at school. On the girl's insistence, she and her mother visited the father after a three-year separation and found him living with a young girl. A violent scene ensued, and again the mother refused to let her daughter stay with the father. After this, the girl became sullen and withdrawn and would not attend school. In one of her destructive rampages through the house, she found the early picture of herself. She altered her appearance, became infantile and untidy, and no longer controlled her urine. She appeared to have regressed to a more desirable period in life that antedated conflicts and jealousies. (After Masserman, 1961, pp. 70–71, case of Dr. John Romano)

unsolvable events seem to impair the organism's ability to cope with subsequent problems.

In one study of learned helplessness, one group of subjects was given a series of solvable problems, the second group was given a series of unsolvable problems, and the third group was not given any problems. Later, all three groups were tested on an apparatus like the shuttle box in which they had to move their hand from one place to another to terminate a loud, unpleasant noise. Subjects who had been given solvable problems or no problems at all quickly learned the response that would terminate the noise. Subjects who had been given unsolvable problems made no attempt to learn the escape response and passively accepted the noise (Hiroto and Seligman, 1975). Helplessness in one situation apparently *generalizes* to other situations. We will have more to say about learned helplessness when we discuss depression in Chapter 15.

Regression

Regression is defined as a return to immature modes of behavior—to behavior characteristics of a younger age. In the toy experiment, observers rated the level of constructiveness of each child's play, first in the free-play situation and then in the frustrating situation. Most children showed a marked decrease in the constructiveness of their play: instead of drawing, they scribbled; instead of pretending to iron clothes, they knocked the ironing board down; instead of planning an imaginary trip with the toy cars and trucks, they pushed them around aimlessly.

Adults sometimes resort to immature forms of behavior when faced with frustrating situations. They may curse or yell or start a fist fight, or they may give up any attempt to cope and seek out someone to solve the problem for them. When attempts to solve a problem fail, a person understandably resorts to behaviors that have been successful in the past. A classic example is the 3-year-old who has been successfully toilet trained but begins bed-wetting again when a sibling is born; frustrated by being displaced as the sole object of parental affection, the child resorts to behavior that brought parental attention in the past. Under severe and prolonged stress, an adult may regress to infantile behavior (see Figure 14-3).

ANXIETY

We have discussed some observable reactions to frustration. To explain these reactions, as well as reactions to other forms of stress, psychologists have introduced the concept of *anxiety*. Any situation that threatens the well-being of the organism is assumed to produce a state of anxiety. Conflicts and other types of frustration are one source of anxiety. Threats of physical harm, threats to self-esteem, and pressure to perform beyond an individual's capabilities also produce anxiety. By anxiety, we mean the unpleasant emotion characterized by terms like "worry," "apprehension," "dread," and "fear" that we all experience at times in varying degrees. Since there is little agreement on a more precise definition for anxiety, we will not attempt to provide one.

Freud—one of the first to focus on the importance of anxiety—differentiated between *objective anxiety* and *neurotic anxiety*. Freud viewed objective anxiety as a realistic response to external danger, synonymous with *fear*. He believed that neurotic anxiety stems from an *unconscious* conflict within the individual; since the conflict is unconscious, the person is not aware of the reason for his or her anxiety. Many psychologists still find it meaningful to distinguish between fear and anxiety. However, since it is not clear that the two emotions can be differentiated—either on the basis of physiological responses or on the basis of the individual's descriptions of feelings—we will use the terms "anxiety" and "fear" interchangeably. Just as there are varying degrees of anxiety, ranging from mild apprehension to panic, there are probably varying degrees of awareness of the cause of an individual's discomfort. People who suffer from internal conflicts often have some idea of why they are anxious, even though they cannot specify all the factors involved clearly.

Theories of Anxiety

ANXIETY AS AN UNCONSCIOUS CONFLICT   Freud believed that neurotic anxiety was the result of an unconscious conflict between *id impulses* (mainly sexual and aggressive) and the constraints imposed by the *ego* and *superego* (see Chapter 13). Many id impulses pose a threat to the individual because they are contradictory to personal or social values. A young girl may not consciously acknowledge that she has strong hostile feelings toward her mother because these feelings conflict with her belief that a child should love her parents. If she acknowledged her true feelings, she would destroy her self-concept as a loving daughter and risk the loss of her mother's love and support. When she begins to feel angry toward her mother, the aroused anxiety serves as a *signal* of potential danger. The girl then engages in defensive maneuvers to exclude anxiety-producing impulses from her conscious awareness. These maneuvers, or *defense mechanisms*, form an important part of Freud's theory of neurotic behavior and will be discussed in the next section.

ANXIETY AS A LEARNED RESPONSE   Social learning theory focuses not on internal conflicts but on ways in which anxiety becomes associated with certain situations via learning. A little girl who is punished by her parents whenever she rebels against their wishes and attempts to assert herself eventually learns to associate the pain of punishment with assertive behavior. When she thinks about asserting her own wishes and defying her parents, she becomes anxious.

Sometimes fears learned in childhood are difficult to extinguish. If a child's first reaction is to avoid or escape the anxiety-producing situation, he or she may not be able to determine when the situation is no longer dangerous. The little girl who has been punished for assertive behavior may never learn that it is appropriate and rewarding for her to express her wishes in certain situations.

Studies with animals have shown how difficult it is to extinguish avoidance responses. An animal that has learned to jump the barrier in a shuttle box to avoid an electric shock may continue to jump into the opposite compartment indefinitely, even if no shock follows the warning signal after the first few trails. The animal never gives itself a chance to learn that the shock has been turned off.

Similarly, the child who has had a bad encounter with a dog and runs whenever he or she sees any other dog will not have the opportunity to discover that most dogs are friendly. Since running away from a dog is reinforcing (because the response reduces fear), the child is apt to continue this behavior. An adult may continue to avoid situations that produced anxiety in childhood because the individual never reappraises the threat or develops a method of coping with it.

ANXIETY AS LACK OF CONTROL   A third approach suggests that people experience anxiety whenever they encounter a situation that seems beyond their control. It might be a new situation that we somehow must organize and integrate into our view of the world and of ourselves. It might be an ambiguous situation—as many of our experiences are—that we must fit into our concept of how the world operates. The feeling of being helpless and not in control of what is happening seems central to most theories of anxiety. According to psychoanalytic theory, for example, anxiety arises when the ego is threatened by impulses it cannot control. According to social learning theory, people become anxious when they are confronted by painful stimuli that they can control only by avoidance. As we will see later, the degree of anxiety we experience in stressful situations is largely dependent on how much control we feel we have over the situation.

Coping with anxiety

Because anxiety is a very uncomfortable emotion, it cannot be tolerated for long. We are strongly motivated to do something to alleviate the discomfort. Over the course of a lifetime, each individual develops various methods of handling anxiety-producing situations and feelings of anxiety. There are two main ways of coping with anxiety. One focuses on the problem: the individual appraises the anxiety-producing situation and then does something to change or avoid it. The other focuses on the emotion; the person tries to reduce anxious feelings in various ways rather than attempt to deal directly with the anxiety-producing problem.

Suppose that you receive a warning that you are about to fail a course that is required for graduation. You might confer with the professor, devise a work schedule to fulfill the requirements, and then follow it. Or you might decide that you cannot fulfill the requirements in the time remaining and sign up to take the course again in summer school. Both of these actions are designed to

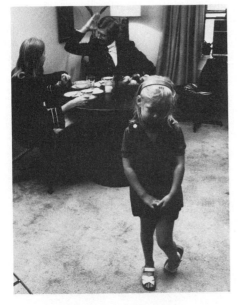

Helpless to control the situation

cope with the problem. On the other hand, you might try to reduce your anxiety about the failure warning by refusing to acknowledge the possibility of failing or by convincing yourself that a college degree is meaningless. Or you might deaden your anxiety with alcohol, tranquilizers, marijuana, or other drugs.

Each individual deals with stressful situations in his or her own unique way, often using a combination of emotion-focused and problem-focused strategies. In most instances, problem solving is probably the healthier approach. But not all problems have an easy solution. In such instances as the serious illness of a loved one or the dependency of an aging parent, individuals may need to defend themselves against anxiety as they try to handle the problem.

DEFENSE MECHANISMS

Some of the ways in which people reduce anxious feelings without addressing the problem have been employed so often that they have been given names. Freud used the term *defense mechanisms* to refer to unconscious processes that defend a person against anxiety by distorting reality in some way. These strategies do not alter the objective conditions of danger; they simply change the way the person perceives or thinks about it. Thus, all defense mechanisms involve an element of *self-deception*.

The word "mechanism" is not the most appropriate because it implies that some sort of mechanical device is involved. Freud was influenced by the nineteenth-century tendency to think of the human being as a complicated machine. Actually, we will be talking about the *strategies* that people learn to use to minimize anxiety in situations they cannot handle effectively. But since "defense mechanism" is still the most commonly applied term, we will continue to use it.

A number of defense mechanisms have been proposed; we will consider only a few of them here. In reading about defense mechanisms, the following precautions should be kept in mind.

1   Defense mechanisms are *hypothetical constructs* inferred from observations of the way people behave. They are useful ways of summarizing the psychological processes that we hypothesize are occurring in order to explain some observed behavior.
2   Labeling a person's behavior (for example, as projection, displacement, or reaction formation) may provide a useful description, but labels do not *explain* behavior. An explanation requires understanding what causes the person to rely on defense mechanisms when confronted with problems.
3   Used in moderation, defense mechanisms help us over the rough spots until we can deal more directly with the stressful situation. Defense mechanisms indicate personality maladjustment only when they become the dominant mode of responding to problems.

Denial

When an external reality is too unpleasant to face, an individual may deny that it exists. The parents of a fatally ill child may refuse to admit that anything is seriously wrong even though they are fully informed of the diagnosis and expected outcome. Because they cannot tolerate the pain that acknowledging reality would produce, they resort to the defense mechanism of *denial*, at least for a while. Less extreme forms of denial may be seen in individuals who consistently ignore criticism, fail to perceive that others are angry with them, or disregard all kinds of clues suggesting that a marriage partner is having an affair.

Sometimes, denying facts may be better than facing them. In a severe crisis, denial may give the person time to face the grim facts at a more gradual pace. For example, victims of a stroke or spinal-cord injury might give up altogether if they were fully aware of the seriousness of their conditions. Hope gives the individual the incentive to keep trying. Studies of patients with life-threatening illnesses suggest that many deny a fear of death or the possibility that they might die. Even witnessing the fatal cardiac arrest of another patient in the same room did not produce fear in most cardiac patients; they did not think it would happen to them (Hackett and Cassem, 1970).

Servicemen facing combat or the uncertainty of imprisonment report that denying the possibility of death helped them to function. In these situations, denial clearly has an adaptive value. On the other hand, the negative aspects of denial are evident in cases where people postpone seeking medical help—for example, women who deny that a lump in the breast may be cancerous and delay going to a physician.

Repression

The denial of reality is a defense against *external* threat; *repression* is a defense against *internal* threat. In repression, impulses or memories that are too threatening are excluded from action or conscious awareness. Freud believed that repression of certain childhood impulses is universal. For example, he maintained that all young boys have feelings of sexual attraction toward the mother and feelings of rivalry and hostility toward the father (the *Oedipus complex*); these impulses are repressed to avoid the painful consequences of acting on them. In later life, an individual may repress feelings and memories that would cause anxiety because they are inconsistent with his or her self-concept. Feelings of hostility toward a loved one and experiences of failure may be banished from memory.

Repression must be distinguished from *suppression*. Suppression is the process of deliberate self-control—of keeping impulses and desires in check (perhaps holding them privately while denying them publicly) or temporarily pushing aside painful memories in order to concentrate on a task. Individuals are aware of suppressed thoughts but are largely *unaware* of impulses or memories that are repressed.

Cases of *amnesia* illustrate some aspects of repression. In one instance, a man was found wandering the streets, unable to remember his name or where he had come from. By means of hypnosis and other techniques, it was possible to reconstruct his history and to restore most of his memory. Following an argument with his wife, he had gone on a drinking binge—completely out of keeping with his usual behavior—and subsequently suffered deep remorse. His amnesia was motivated by the desire to exclude the embarrassing experience from memory. He succeeded in forgetting all the events that might remind him of the binge, but the amnesia spread to the point that he completely lost his sense of personal identity. When his memories returned, he could recall events before the drinking episode as well as subsequent happenings, but he was unable to remember the period of which he was most ashamed.

Case histories such as this one and the inability of people to remember the details of catastrophic events (the horrors of combat, a fire, or an earthquake) lend support to Freud's idea that distressing memories and impulses may be forgotten or somehow kept from awareness. But repression has proved difficult to demonstrate in the laboratory (Holmes, 1974). Researchers cannot expose experimental subjects to events that produce intense anxiety. Nevertheless, there is evidence that momentary lapses of memory tend to be associated more with emotionally charged topics than with neutral ones and that people find it easier to remember neutral words than words that are emotionally arousing for them (Luborsky and Spence, 1978). It is possible that when emotionally charged words are about to be retrieved from memory, they trigger feelings of anxiety that may impede the use of appropriate retrieval cues (see Chapter 8).

Completely successful repression results in a total forgetting—a total absence of awareness of an unacceptable motive and the behavior resulting from such a motive. Usually, however, repression is not completely successful, and impulses find indirect expression. Some of the following defense mechanisms protect the individual from awareness of partially repressed impulses.

Rationalization

When the fox in Aesop's fable rejected the grapes he could not reach "because they were sour," he illustrated a defense mechanism known as *rationalization*. Rationalization does not mean "to act rationally"; it is the assignment of logical or socially desirable motives to what we do so that we *seem* to have acted rationally or properly. Rationalization serves two purposes: (1) it eases our disappointment when we fail to reach a goal ("I didn't want it anyway"), and (2) it provides us with acceptable motives for our behavior. If we act impulsively or on the basis of motives we do not wish to acknowledge even to ourselves, we rationalize what we have done to place our behavior in a more favorable light.

© 1975 United Features Syndicate

In the search for the "good" reason rather than the "true" reason, individuals make a number of excuses. These excuses are usually plausible; they simply do not tell the whole story. A few illustrations may serve to show how common rationalization is.

1   *Liking or disliking* as an excuse: "I wouldn't have gone to the party even if I had been invited. I don't like that crowd."
2   *Other people and circumstances* as an excuse: "My roommate failed to wake me"; "I had too many other things to do." Both statements may be true, but they are not the real reasons for the individual's failure to perform the behavior in question. Individuals who are really concerned set an alarm clock or find the time.
3   *Necessity* as an excuse: "I bought this new model because a lot of expensive repairs would have had to be made on the old car soon."

Although in these examples individuals are fooling themselves instead of others, people might consciously use these types of excuses to put themselves in a favorable light. More convincing evidence that rationalization may be unconsciously motivated is provided by the following experiment on posthypnotic suggestion.

A subject under hypnosis is told that when he wakes from the trance he will watch the hypnotist. When the hypnotist takes off his glasses, the subject will raise the window, but he will not remember that the hypnotist told him to do this. Aroused from the trance, the subject feels a little drowsy but presently circulates among the people in the room and carries on a normal conversation, furtively watching the hypnotist. When the hypnotist casually removes his glasses, the subject feels an impulse to open the window; he takes a step in that direction but hesitates. Unconsciously, he mobilizes his wishes to be a reasonable person; seeking a reason for his impulse to open the window, he says "Isn't it a little stuffy in here?" Having found the needed excuse, he opens the window and feels more comfortable (Hilgard, 1965).

Reaction formation

Sometimes individuals can conceal a motive from themselves by giving strong expression to the opposite motive. Such a tendency is called *reaction formation*. A mother who feels guilty about not wanting her child may become overindulgent and overprotective to assure the child of her love and to assure herself that she is a good mother. In one case, a mother who wished to do everything for her daughter could not understand why the child was so unappreciative. At great sacrifice, she had the daughter take expensive piano lessons and assisted her in the daily practice sessions. Although the mother thought she was being extremely kind, she was actually being very demanding—in fact, hostile. She was unaware of her own hostility, but when she was confronted with it, the mother admitted that she had hated piano lessons as a child. Under the conscious guise of being kind, she was unconsciously being cruel to her daughter. The daughter vaguely sensed what was going on and developed symptoms that required psychological treatment.

The involvement of some individuals in "anti" activities, such as censoring pornographic literature or preventing cruelty to animals, may be the result of reaction formation. The censoring individuals may actually be fascinated by pornographic literature. They wage a campaign against it to fight their fascination for it and to convince others of their own "purity." Some ardent antivivisectionists may fear their own tendency toward cruelty so deeply that they become sentimental about protecting animals from the implied cruelty of others.

The existence of reaction formation in some people does not mean that motives can never be taken at face value. Not all reformers are moved to action by veiled or hidden impulses. Real abuses need to be corrected, and concerned individuals will devote their efforts to such causes. But people who are defending themselves against their own unacceptable impulses often can be distinguished from socially concerned reformers by the excessive zeal with which they pursue their campaigns and by occasional slips that reveal their true motivation.

Projection

All of us have undesirable traits or qualities that we do not acknowledge, even to ourselves. One unconscious mechanism, *projection*, protects us from recognizing our own undesirable qualities by assigning them in exaggerated amounts to other people. Suppose you have a tendency to be critical of or unkind to other people but you would dislike yourself if you admitted this tendency. If you are convinced that the people around you are cruel or unkind, your harsh treatment of them is not based on *your* bad qualities—you are simply "giving them what they deserve." If you can assure yourself that everybody else cheats on college examinations, your unacknowledged tendency to take some academic shortcuts is not so bad. Projection is really a form of rationalization, but it is so pervasive in our culture that it merits discussion in its own right.

A classic experiment with fraternity members at a university illustrates projection. The members of each fraternity were asked to rate the other fraternity members on such undesirable traits as stinginess, obstinancy, and disorderliness. Each student was asked to rate himself as well. Of interest here are those students who possessed an undesirable trait to a high degree (indicated by how others rated them) but were unaware of possessing it (indicated by their rating of themselves). These individuals tended to assign that undesirable trait to other students to a far greater extent than did the rest of the students. The data are consistent with the idea of a projection mechanism (Sears, 1936).

A more recent study has shown that individuals who deny or repress their sexual impulses tend to project these impulses onto other people. They see others as more "lustful" than the reality of the situation warrants (Halpern, 1977).

Intellectualization

Intellectualization is an attempt to gain detachment from an emotionally threatening situation by dealing with it in abstract, intellectual terms. This kind of defense is frequently a necessity for people who must deal with life and death matters in their daily job. The doctor who is continually confronted with human suffering cannot afford to become emotionally involved with each patient; in fact, a certain amount of detachment may be essential for the doctor to function competently. In Chapter 11, we saw that intellectualization can lessen distress when a disturbing scene is viewed. This kind of intellectualization is a problem only when it becomes such a pervasive life style that individuals cut themselves off from all emotional experiences.

Displacement

The last defense mechanism we will consider fulfills its function (reduces anxiety) while partially gratifying the unacceptable motive. Through the mechanism of *displacement*, a motive that cannot be gratified in one form is directed into a new channel. An example of displacement was provided in our discussion of anger that could not be expressed toward the source of frustration and was redirected toward a less threatening or more readily available object.

Freud felt that displacement was the most satisfactory way of handling aggressive and sexual impulses. The basic drives cannot be changed, but the object toward which a drive is directed can be changed. For example, sexual impulses toward the parents cannot be safely gratified, but such impulses can be displaced toward a more suitable love object. Erotic impulses that cannot be expressed directly may be expressed indirectly in creative activities such as art, poetry, and music. Hostile impulses may find socially acceptable expression through participation in physical-contact sports.

It seems unlikely that displacement actually eliminates the frustrated impulses, but substitute activities do help to reduce tension when a basic drive is thwarted. For example, the activities of mothering, being mothered, or seeking companionship may help reduce the tension associated with unsatisfied sexual needs.

Defense mechanisms and adjustment

We all use defense mechanisms at times. The rationalization of failures that would otherwise cause us to despair or the partial justification of conduct that would otherwise make us despise ourselves sustains us until we can work out better solutions to our conflicts. Denial or repression may provide relief from anxiety until a way to solve a personal problem can be found.

Although they may provide temporary relief, defense mechanisms usually distort reality and thus prevent effective problem solving. A person who depends on defense mechanisms may never learn more effective ways of coping. For example, individuals who project their hostile feelings onto others may withdraw more and more from social contacts. By refusing to acknowledge the anger as their own, they never learn that most people are kind and that they can develop satisfactory interpersonal relationships.

The premedical student who is failing may be unable to admit that he or she lacks the interest and ability to handle the course work. A rationalization must therefore be found to account for failure. Getting sick will convert an academic problem into a health problem; getting into trouble with college officials will convert the problem into a disciplinary one. Defensiveness and denial of the realities of the situation prevent a more satisfactory solution, such as changing to an academic program more suited to the student's interests and abilities.

STRESS

Some stress is necessary for an individual to function normally. In Chapter 11, we noted that a mild level of emotional arousal produces alertness and interest in the task at hand. When life is peaceful and quiet for too long, people become bored and seek excitement; they go to a spy movie, engage in a game of tennis, or find stimulation in interacting with other people. Studies of sensory deprivation (see page 311) show that the absence of normal stimulation for more than a brief period of time is highly unpleasant and can have profound effects on behavior. The nervous system apparently needs a certain amount of stimulation to function properly. But stress that is too intense or prolonged can have destructive physiological and psychological effects.

We have already noted some of the psychological effects of stress in the discussion of the ways in which people react to frustration and the strategies they use to cope with stressful situations. If initial attempts at coping are unsuccessful, anxiety intensifies and the individual becomes more rigid in his or her efforts and less able to perceive alternative solutions to the problem. People have been trapped in flaming buildings because they persisted in pushing against exit doors that open inward; in their panic, they failed to consider the possibility of an alternative action.

In times of stress, people tend to resort to behavior patterns that have worked in the past. The cautious person may become even more cautious and withdraw entirely; the aggressive person may lose control and strike out heedlessly in all directions.

Physiological effects of stress

If the actions of the autonomic nervous system that prepare the individual for emergency (see pages 52–53) are prolonged, they can lead to such physical disorders as ulcers, high blood pressure, and heart disease. Severe stress

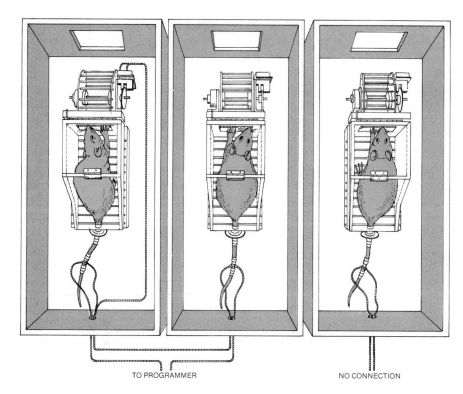

TO PROGRAMMER   NO CONNECTION

Figure 14-4
Ulcers in Rats
The rat on the left is the avoidance-escape subject; it can terminate the programmed shock by turning the wheel. Moreover, turning the wheel between shocks will postpone the shock. The rat in the center is electrically wired in series to the first rat, so that when the first rat receives a shock, the yoked rat simultaneously receives a shock of the same intensity and duration. The actions of the yoked rat do not affect the shock sequence. The electrodes on the tail of the control rat on the right are not connected, and this rat does not receive shocks at any time. At the end of the experimental session, gastric lesions are measured in each rat. (After Weiss, 1972)

(acting through the central nervous system to change hormonal balances) can also impair an individual's immune responses, decreasing the body's ability to fight invading bacteria and viruses. Indeed, it is estimated that emotional stress plays an important role in more than 50 percent of all medical problems.

Psychosomatic medicine—the study of the relationship between psychological variables and physical health—has become an increasingly important area of interdisciplinary research. The term "psychosomatic" is derived from the Greek words *psyche* ("mind") and *soma* ("body"). Allergies, migraine headaches, high blood pressure, heart disease, ulcers, and even acne are some illnesses believed to be related to emotional stress. Research on these disorders is too extensive to summarize here, but some studies demonstrating the relationship between psychological stress and two physical disorders—peptic ulcers and heart disease—will provide examples.

STRESS AND ULCERS A peptic ulcer is a lesion (a hole) in the lining of the stomach or duodenum that is produced by the excessive secretion of hydrochloric acid. In the process of digestion, hydrochloric acid interacts with various enzymes to break down food into components that can be utilized by the body. When hydrochloric acid is secreted in excessive amounts, it gradually erodes the mucus layer protecting the stomach wall, producing small lesions. A number of factors can cause an increased secretion of hydrochloric acid, and psychological stress appears to be one of them.

Animal studies have shown that, under certain conditions, stress can cause ulcers. In a series of experiments with rats, stress was produced by administering a mild electric shock to the tail. The rats, tested in sets of three, were placed in the apparatus shown in Figure 14-4. The rat in the left-hand chamber can terminate the programmed shocks by turning a wheel. Moreover, each shock is preceded by a warning signal; if the animal turns the wheel at the appropriate time, it can postpone the next shock. The rat in the middle compartment is "yoked" to the rat on the left so that it receives shocks of the same intensity and duration as the left-hand rat but can do nothing to control the shocks. The rat in the right-hand chamber is hooked up like the other two, but the electrodes are not connected so that it receives no shocks.

After the animals had participated in this procedure for some time, they were examined for ulcers. The rats who could do something to control the shocks showed much less ulceration than their helpless, yoked companions. The control animals, who received no shocks, showed little or no ulceration (Weiss, 1972).

This and similar experiments suggest that prolonged exposure to uncontrollable stress does contribute to the development of ulcers. Although we cannot generalize from animal to human subjects without further research, it seems likely that stress is one factor that leads to ulcers—particularly in individuals who are biologically predisposed to secrete a high level of hydrochloric acid. Air-traffic controllers, who work under intense pressure and must make instant decisions that affect the safety of hundreds of people, have the highest incidence of peptic ulcers in any profession and are more likely to develop high blood pressure and heart disease than the average person (Grayson, 1972).

STRESS AND HEART DISEASE   Stress also plays an important role in heart disease. One area of research has identified a behavior pattern, called "Type A," that appears to characterize people who have heart attacks (Friedman and Rosenman, 1974). Type A individuals are described as extremely competitive and achievement oriented; they have a sense of time urgency, find it difficult to relax, and become impatient and angry when confronted with delays or with people they view as incompetent. The assumption is that such individuals, although outwardly self-confident, are prey to constant feelings of self-doubt; they push themselves to accomplish more and more in less and less time. Pressure to achieve, combined with an underlying general hostility, are considered to be the characteristics most likely to contribute to heart disease. Some common Type A behavior characteristics are listed in Table 14-1. Type B individuals are defined as those who do *not* exhibit the characteristics listed for Type A individuals. Type B individuals are able to relax without feeling guilty and work without becoming agitated; they lack a sense of time urgency with its accompanying impatience. Angry and hostile feelings are not easily aroused in these individuals, and they show little need to display or discuss achievements.

Several long-range studies indicate that people who exhibit Type A behavior are much more likely to suffer a heart attack than Type B individuals (Rosenman and others, 1975; Haynes, Feinleib, and Kannel, 1980). How Type A behavior affects the cardiovascular system is still not clearly understood. The physiological effects of the kind of stress that Type A individuals experience may involve increased blood cholesterol levels, an enhanced tendency to blood-clot formation, elevated blood pressure, or increased secretion of the hormone norepinephrine, which can trigger abnormalities in heart rhythm. Such physiological changes have been observed in people undergoing temporary stress (such as pressure to meet deadlines) as well as in Type A individuals (Friedman, Thoresen, and Gill, 1981). A review of the research concluded that Type A behavior poses as significant a risk for heart disease as smoking, high blood pressure, or a high cholesterol level (Dembroski and others, 1981).

A current project aimed at modifying Type A behavior and involving more than 1,000 individuals who have experienced at least one heart attack reports considerable success (Thoresen, Telch, and Eagleston, 1981). Type A behavior

Meditating to reduce stress

Thinking of or doing two things at once

Scheduling more and more activities into less and less time

Failing to notice or be interested in the environment or things of beauty

Hurrying the speech of others

Becoming unduly irritated when forced to wait in line or when driving behind a car you think is moving too slowly

Believing that if you want something done well, you have to do it yourself

Gesticulating when you talk

Frequent knee jiggling or rapid tapping of your fingers

Explosive speech patterns or frequent use of obscenities

Making a fetish of always being on time

Having difficulty sitting and doing nothing

Playing nearly every game to win, even when playing with children

Measuring your own and others' success in terms of numbers (number of patients seen, articles written, etc.)

Lip clicking, head nodding, fist clenching, table pounding, or sucking in of air when speaking

Becoming impatient while watching others do things you think you can do better or faster

Rapid eye blinking or ticlike eyebrow lifting

Table 14-1
Type A Behavior Characteristics
Some behaviors that characterize people prone to coronary heart disease. (After Friedman and Rosenman, 1974)

is evaluated by means of videotaped interviews, which include a set series of questions. Two examples of questions are: "If there are five or ten persons waiting to eat at a restaurant, would you wait?" and "Would your 20-year-old self have been proud or disappointed in what you have accomplished and are at this time?" The interviewer notes not only the content of the answers but also the subject's behavior (such as tone and speed of voice, hand clenching, tics of eyebrows or mouth, and facial signs of hostility). The experimental subjects, working in small groups led by a psychiatrist or psychologist, are helped in various ways to modify their Type A behavior. For example, to reduce their sense of time urgency, individuals may be asked to practice standing in line (a situation Type As normally find extremely irritating) and to use the opportunity to reflect on things they do not normally have time to think about, or to people watch, or to strike up a conversation with a stranger. Treatment also includes learning to alter certain specific behaviors (such as interrupting the speech of others or talking or eating hurriedly), reevaluating basic beliefs (such as the notion that success depends on the quantity of work produced), and finding ways to make the home and work environment less stressful (such as encouraging spouses to reduce the number of unnecessary social engagements).

The two control groups in this study consist of Type A individuals who do *not* receive specific help in modifying their Type A behavior. One group meets regularly with a cardiologist, who provides information about diet, exercise, and medication; the other group receives the usual post-coronary medical care from their personal physicians. (Note that the experimental subjects also receive information on diet, exercise, and medication; subjects in the cardiologist-

Two techniques—*biofeedback* and *relaxation training*—show promise of helping people control their reactions to stress. In biofeedback training, individuals receive information (feedback) about some aspect of their physiological state and then attempt to alter that state. For example, in a procedure for learning to control tension headaches, electrodes are attached to the forehead, so that any movement in the forehead muscle can be electronically detected, amplified, and fed back to the person as an auditory signal. The signal, or tone, increases in pitch when the muscle contracts and decreases when it relaxes. By learning to control the pitch of the tone, the individual learns to keep the muscle relaxed. (Relaxation of the forehead muscle usually ensures relaxation of scalp and neck muscles also.) After four to eight weeks of biofeedback training, the subject learns to recognize the onset of tension and to reduce it without feedback from the machine (Tarler-Benlolo, 1978).

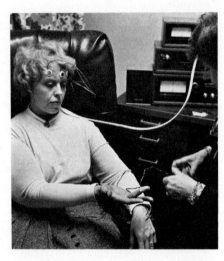

Biofeedback for headaches
The sensors measure forehead muscle contractions and finger temperature. Circulatory changes (indicated by finger temperature) play a role in some types of headaches.

Physiological processes that are controlled by the autonomic nervous system, such as heart rate and blood pressure, have traditionally been assumed to be automatic and not under voluntary control. However, experiments in the 1960s showed that rats could be operantly conditioned to raise or lower their heart rates (see DiCara and Miller, 1968). And subsequent laboratory studies have demonstrated that human subjects can also learn to modify both functions (see Figure 14-5). The results of these studies have led to the development of new procedures for treating patients who suffer from high blood pressure. One procedure is to show patients a graph of their blood pressure while it is being monitored and

led control group are given some information about psychological problems, such as anxiety and depression, but are not told how to cope with stress or to alter their life-style patterns.)

The most important dependent variable in this study is the occurrence of another heart attack. Preliminary data show that 3.4 percent of the experimental subjects have suffered a subsequent heart attack, compared to 5.6 percent of the individuals in the cardiologist-led control group. This difference is statistically significant. The recurrence rate for heart-attack victims treated by their personal physicians is about 7.8 percent. Clearly, learning to modify Type A behavior is beneficial to an individual's health.

An interesting finding is that general hostility may turn out to be the most

Biofeedback and Relaxation Training

to teach them techniques for relaxing various muscle groups. The patients are instructed to tense their muscles (for example, clench a fist or a tighten the abdomen), release the tension, and notice the difference in sensation. By starting with the feet and ankle muscles and progressing through the body to the muscles that control the neck and face, the patients learn to modify muscular tension. This combintion of biofeedback with relaxation training has lowered blood pressure in some individuals as effectively as treatment with anti-high blood pressure drugs (Tarler-Benlolo, 1978).

Treatment of stress-related illnesses with biofeedback and relaxation is still in the experimental stage, and it is too early to tell how useful such procedures will be. As is true of any new treatment, the enthusiasm of both clinicians and patients may produce a placebo effect: the belief that the procedures will work may play a role in their success.

Reviews of numerous studies using biofeedback and relaxation training to control headaches and hypertension conclude that the most important variable is *learning how to relax* (Runck, 1980). Some people may learn to relax faster when they receive biological feedback from tense muscles or blood pressure indicators. Others may learn to relax equally well when they receive

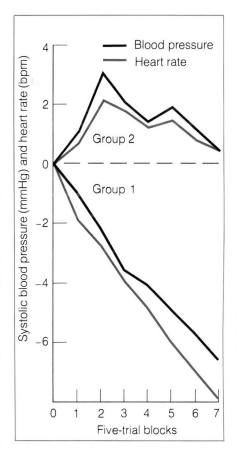

Figure 14-5
Operant Conditioning of Blood Pressure and Heart Rate
One group of male subjects received biofeedback (a light and a tone) whenever their blood pressure and heart rate decreased simultaneously (Group 1); the other group received the same feedback whenever their blood pressure and heart rate increased simultaneously (Group 2). Whenever a subject in either group produced 12 consecutive correct heart-rate/blood-pressure responses, he was reinforced with slides (landscapes and nude females) and a cash bonus. The subjects achieved significant simultaneous control of blood pressure and heart rate during a single conditioning session. The group reinforced for lowering both functions achieved increasingly more control over trials; the group reinforced for raising both functions was less consistent. (After Schwartz, 1975)

training in muscle relaxation without any specific biofeedback. How useful relaxation training is seems to depend on the individual. Some people who are not conscientious about taking drugs to relieve high blood pressure are more responsive to relaxation training; others who have learned to control their blood pressure through relaxation may eventually drop the procedure because they find it too time consuming. Interestingly, these people who benefit most from biofeedback-relaxation techniques are particularly responsive to stress, indicating that emotions play an important role in their illness.

significant predictor of heart disease—more important than competitiveness or time urgency. Individuals who suffered a subsequent heart attack, many of whom died, did not appear to differ from individuals who remained healthy in terms of many dimensions, including family background and overall measures of chronic stress, except for measures of hostility. When the videotaped interviews were scored for indications of hostility, individuals who experienced a second heart attack scored two or three times higher on measures of hostile behaviors than individuals who remained healthy, despite the fact that their total Type A scores were almost identical. Unfortunately, reducing underlying feelings of anger and hostility has turned out to be more difficult than modifying other aspects of Type A behavior.

Assuming that ways of handling stress are fixed fairly early in life—long before the symptoms of coronary heart disease appear—a current project is investigating how children and adolescents learn to cope with chronic stress (Thoresen, personal communication).

Factors influencing the severity of stress

The effects of stress—the intensity of the anxiety it arouses and the degree to which it disrupts the individual's ability to function—depend on a number of factors. These factors include some characteristics of the stress itself, the situation in which stress occurs, the individual's appraisal and evaluation of the stressful situation, and his or her resources for coping with it.

PREDICTABILITY   Being able to predict the occurrence of a stressful event— even if the individual cannot control it—usually reduces the severity of the stress. Laboratory experiments show that both human beings and animals prefer predictable aversive events to unpredictable ones. In one study, rats were given a choice between a signaled shock and an unsignaled shock. If the rat pressed a bar at the start of a series of shock trials, each shock was preceded by a warning tone; if the rat failed to press the bar, no warning tones sounded during that series of trials. All of the rats quickly learned to press the bar, showing a marked preference for predictable shock. In fact, rats prefer predictable shock even when it is much longer and more intense than unpredictable shock. With unpredictable shock, there is no "safe" period; with predictable shock, the animal can relax to some extent until the tone sounds to signal shock (Badia, Culbertson, and Harsh, 1973). Studies showing that people prefer immediate to delayed shock also indicate a preference for aversive events that are predictable.

CONTROL OVER DURATION   Having control over the duration of a stressful event also reduces the severity of the stress. In one study, subjects were shown color photographs of victims of violent deaths. The experimental group could terminate the viewing by pressing a button. The control subjects saw the same photographs for the time duration determined by the experimental group, but they could not terminate exposure. The experimental group showed much less anxiety (measured by the galvanic skin response, GSR) in response to the photographs than the group that had no control over the duration of viewing (Geer and Maisel, 1972).

In another study, two groups of subjects were exposed to a loud, extremely unpleasant noise. Subjects in one group were told that they could terminate the noise by pressing a button, but they were urged not to do so unless it was absolutely necessary. Subjects in the other group had no control over the noise. None of the subjects who had a control button actually pressed it, so the noise exposure was the same for both groups. Nevertheless, performance on subsequent problem-solving tasks was significantly worse for the group that had no control, indicating that they were more disturbed by the noise than the group that had the potential for control (Glass and Singer, 1972). The belief that we can control the duration of an aversive event appears to lessen anxiety, even if the control is never exercised or the belief is erroneous.

COGNITIVE EVALUATION   The same stressful event can be perceived quite differently by two people, depending on what the situation *means* to the individual. The objective facts of the situation are less important than the individual's appraisal of them. Physicians treating wounded soldiers in combat field stations are often amazed at the calm and unperturbed manner with which some men react to serious injuries—injuries that would cause civilian hospital patients to plead for painkillers. For the soldiers, wounds represent a reprieve from the ordeals and danger of combat. Similarly, the discomfort of childbirth is apt to be much less stressful for the woman who has been eagerly anticipating the birth of her child than for the woman who has no desire to be a mother.

An individual's perception of a stressful event also involves appraising the *degree* of threat. Situations that are perceived as threatening to survival (for example, a diagnosis of cancer) or to the individual's worth (for example, failure in a chosen occupation) impose a maximum of stress.

FEELINGS OF COMPETENCY   A person's confidence in his or her ability to handle a stressful situation is a major factor in determining the severity of the stress. Speaking before a large audience is a traumatic event for most people, but individuals who are experienced in public speaking have confidence in their ability and feel only minimal anxiety.

Emergencies are particularly stressful because our usual methods of coping do not work. Not knowing what to do can be demoralizing. People trained to deal with emergencies—such as police officers, fire fighters, or medical rescue squads—can act calmly and effectively because they know what to do, but the person who lacks such training may feel helpless. Since we tend to fall back on well-learned responses under stress, it is important that people who may have to deal with particular types of emergencies be taught a repertoire of responses to cope with various contingencies.

SOCIAL SUPPORTS   The emotional support and concern of other people can make stress more bearable. Divorce, the death of a loved one, or a serious illness is usually more devastating if an individual must face it alone. Sometimes, however, family and friends can increase the stress. Minimizing the seriousness of the problem or giving blind assurance that "everything will be all right" may produce more anxiety than failing to offer support at all. A study of graduate students facing crucial examinations suggests that spouses who are realistically supportive ("I'm worried, but I know you'll do the best you can") are more helpful than spouses who deny any possibility of failure ("I'm not worried; I'm sure you'll pass"). In the latter case, the student has to worry not only about failing the exam but also about losing respect in the eyes of the spouse (Mechanic, 1962).

Studies indicate that people with many social ties (marriage, close friends and relatives, church memberships and other group associations) tend to live longer and be less apt to succumb to stress-related illnesses than people who have few social supports (Cobb, 1976; Antonovsky, 1979).

Stress is easier to tolerate when the cause of the stress is shared with others. Community disasters (floods, earthquakes, tornadoes, wars) often seem to bring out the best in people (see Nilson and others, 1981). Individual anxieties and conflicts tend to be forgotten when people are working together against a common enemy or toward a common goal. During the intensive bombing of London in World War II, there was a marked decline in the number of people seeking help for emotional problems.

Measuring life stress

Any change in an individual's life—whether it is pleasant or unpleasant—requires some readjustment. Studies of personal histories suggest that physical and emotional disorders tend to cluster around periods of major change in a

Factors determining the severity of stressful events

Working together in times of disaster makes stress more bearable.

Table 14-2
Life Change Scale
This scale, also known as the Holmes and Rahe Social Readjustment Rating Scale, measures stress in terms of life changes. (After Holmes and Rahe, 1967)

LIFE EVENT	LIFE-CHANGE VALUE
Death of spouse	100
Divorce	73
Marital separation	65
Jail term	63
Death of close family member	63
Personal injury or illness	53
Marriage	50
Fired from job	47
Marital reconciliation	45
Retirement	45
Change in health of family member	44
Pregnancy	40
Sex difficulties	39
Gain of new family member	39
Business readjustment	39
Change in financial state	38
Death of close friend	37
Change to different line of work	36
Foreclosure of mortgage	30
Change in responsibilities at work	29
Son or daughter leaving home	29
Trouble with in-laws	29
Outstanding personal achievement	28
Wife begins or stops work	26
Begin or end school	26
Change in living conditions	25
Revision of personal habits	24
Trouble with boss	23
Change in residence	20
Change in school	20
Change in recreation	19
Change in church activities	19
Change in social activies	18
Change in sleeping habits	16
Change in eating habits	15
Vacation	13
Christmas	12
Minor legal violations	11

person's life. The scale in Table 14-2 was developed to measure stress in terms of life changes. The life events are ranked in order, from the most stressful (death of a spouse) to the least stressful (minor violations of the law). To arrive at this scale, the investigators examined thousands of interviews and medical histories to identify the kinds of events that people found stressful. Because marriage (a positive event, but one that requires a fair amount of readjustment) appeared to be a critical event for most people, it was placed in the middle of the scale and assigned an arbitrary value of 50. The investigators then asked approximately 400 men and women (of varying ages, backgrounds, and marital status) to compare marriage with a number of other life events. They were asked such questions as, "Does the event call for more or less readjustment than marriage?", and "Would the readjustment take shorter or longer to accomplish?" And they were asked to assign a point value to each event on the basis of their evaluation of its severity and the time required for adjustment.

These ratings were used to construct the scale in Table 14-2. The scale appears to be fairly universal in that minority groups in the United States and people in both underdeveloped and highly industrialized countries assigned similar ratings to stressful events.

STRESS AND ILLNESS The results of studies based on the Life Change Scale have revealed a consistent relationship between the number of stressful events in a person's life and that person's emotional and physical health. More than 50 percent of the people whose life-change units summed to between 200 and 300 in a single year exhibited health problems the following year; 79 percent of the people whose scores summed to over 300 became ill the following year.

The most stressful event on the scale is the death of a spouse—a loss that obviously requires a major readjustment in many aspects of life. In one study in Great Britain, 4,500 widowers were observed for six months after the deaths of their wives. These men exhibited high rates of illness and depression, and their mortality rate was 40 percent greater than the expected rate for their age (Parkes, Benjamin, and Fitzgerald, 1969).

To account for the findings relating life changes to illness, the authors of the Life Change Scale hypothesized that the more critical the changes an individual experiences, the greater effort the individual must expend to adapt; this effort presumably lowers the body's natural resistance to disease. Studies of animals show that stress can disrupt the organism's immune defenses in some instances (see Riley, 1981). However, the relationship between stress and illness in human beings probably involves a number of factors.

First, it is difficult to separate the effects of stress from such factors as diet, smoking, drinking, and other general health habits. Individuals who are trying to cope with the demands of a new and more difficult job may increase their alcohol intake, eat more snack foods, get less sleep, and fail to exercise. An increased susceptibility to illness in such a case is more likely to stem from these changes in health habits than from the direct action of stress on resistance to disease.

Second, people differ in their tendencies to focus on physical symptoms and to seek medical help. A respiratory infection or stomachache that one person ignores may send another person to a doctor. Individuals who are unhappy and discontented with their lives are more apt to focus on symptoms and to go to a doctor than people who are involved in activities they enjoy. Since the data for many life-change studies are derived from medical reports, the selective factor in help-seeking may be significant. Stress may be more important in triggering help-seeking behavior than in triggering actual illness.

Individual differences in help-seeking are even more pronounced when the discomfort is psychological rather than clearly physiological. One study compared students who went to a university counseling clinic with a random sample from the same general student population on a scale measuring symptoms of psychological distress. Although 54 percent of the students who sought counseling scored high on the scale, 22 percent of the random sample had equally high scores (Mechanic, 1975). Thus, a number of the students who did not seek help were as distressed as those students who did. In addition to degree of distress, many other factors determine whether or not an individual will seek help, including religious and social values, socioeconomic background, and attitudes toward self-sufficiency versus dependency.

STRESS-RESISTANT INDIVIDUALS   We noted in the last section that a person's cognitive evaluation of a situation is important in determining the severity of stress. Some events in the Life Change Scale (such as "change to different line of work" or "change in responsibilities at work") might be viewed as threatening by one individual but challenging by another.

Several investigators have been studying the personality characteristics that make people resistant to stress. In an initial study, more than 600 men who were executives or managers in the same company were given checklists and asked to describe all of the stressful life events and illnesses they had experienced in the past three years. (All the men were white, college graduates, aged 40–49, and married with two children.) Two groups were selected for comparison: the first group scored above average on both stress and illness; the second group scored equally high on stress but *below average* on illness. Members of both groups then filled out detailed personality questionnaires. Analysis of the results indicated that the high-stress/low-illness men differed from the men who became ill under stress on three major dimensions: they were more actively involved in their work and social lives, they were more oriented toward challenge and change, and they felt more in control of events in their lives (Kobasa, 1979).

Of course, it could be argued that these personality differences were the *result* rather than the *cause* of illness; for example, it is hard to be involved in work or social activity when a person is ill. The investigators therefore conducted a longitudinal study that considered the personality characteristics of business executives before they became ill and then monitored their life stress scores and the extent of their illnesses for a period of two years. The results showed that the executives whose attitudes toward life could be rated high on involvement, feelings of control, and positive responses to change remained much healthier than the men who scored low on these dimensions (Kobasa, Maddi, and Kahn, 1982). The most important factor appears to be attitude toward change. People who view change as a challenge—for example, the loss of a job viewed as an opportunity to find a new career rather than as a serious setback—are apt to experience less stress and to turn the situation to their advantage.

The personality characteristics of stress-resistant or *hardy* individuals have been summarized in capsule form by the terms *commitment, control,* and *challenge*. These characteristics are interrelated in numerous ways with the factors described earlier as determinants of the severity of stress (see page 444). For example, commitment to relationships with other people provides social support in times of stress. The sense of being in control of life events reflects feelings of competency and also influences the way in which stressful events are appraised. People who feel they are able to exert control over stressful situations (instead of feeling helpless) are more likely to take action to remedy the situation. Challenge also involves cognitive evaluation—the belief that change is normal in life and should be viewed as an opportunity for growth rather than a threat to security.

Stressful life events clearly play a role in illness. But they do so in interaction with biological factors (preexisting susceptibilities toward certain disorders), life habits that influence health, and the personality characteristics of the individual.

Summary

1   *Frustration* occurs when progress toward a goal is blocked or delayed. Environmental obstacles, social restrictions, and personal limitations all produce frustration; but one of the major sources of frustration is motivational conflicts.

2   When two motives conflict, the satisfaction of one leads to the blocking of the other. Most conflicts involve goals that are simultaneously positive and negative; the individual's attitude toward such goals is *ambivalent*.

3   Some immediate reactions to frustration are *aggression* (both direct and displaced), *apathy* (which may reflect learned helplessness), and *regression*. Individuals vary considerably in behavior when their goals are blocked.

4   Frustration and other forms of stress produce *anxiety*. Freud distinguished *objective anxiety* (fear of an external threat) from *neurotic anxiety* (the result of an internal, unconscious conflict). But here we have treated fear and anxiety synonymously. *Social learning theory* assumes that anxiety is a learned response to specific situations rather than the result of internal conflicts. A feeling of *helplessness* and *lack of control* is central to most theories of anxiety.

5   Individuals cope with anxiety by *focusing on the problem* (finding ways to change or avoid the anxiety-producing situation) or by *focusing on the emotion* (finding ways to reduce anxious feelings). *Defense mechanisms* are strategies that permit the individual to reduce feelings of anxiety without dealing with the problem.

6   Two basic defense mechanisms are (a) *denial*, when the person distorts external reality so that it seems less threatening, and (b) *repression*, when the individual attempts to keep painful impulses and emotions from conscious awareness. Other defense mechanisms that aid repression are *rationalization*, *reaction formation*, *projection*, *intellectualization*, and *displacement*.

7   Defense mechanisms may provide temporary relief from anxiety; but if used habitually, they prevent effective problem solving.

8   Prolonged stress can contribute to physical disorders, such as ulcers, high blood pressure, and heart disease. *Psychosomatic medicine* studies the relationship between emotional stress and health. The severity of stress depends on the *predictability* of the situation, the *potential for control*, the individual's *cognitive evaluation* and *feelings of competency*, and the presence of *social supports*.

9   Life changes can be stressful and can result in physical illness. Stress-resistant individuals tend to be *committed* to their work and social relationships, to feel in *control* of life events, and to view change as a *challenge*.

A classic account of defense mechanisms is given by A. Freud in *The ego and the mechanisms of defense* (rev. ed., 1967). An introductory treatment may be found in Coleman, *Abnormal psychology and modern life* (6th ed., 1980).

A wide range of papers on anxiety and ways of coping with it may be found in Spielberger (ed.), *Anxiety: Current trends in theory and research* (1972); and Coehlo, Hamburg, and Adams (eds.), *Coping and adaptation* (1974).

Interesting books on stress and health include Antonovsky, *Health, stress, and coping* (1979); and Elliott and Eisdorfer (eds.), *Stress and human health: Analysis and implications of research* (1982). Hamburg, Elliott, and Parrov (eds.), *Health and behavior: Frontiers of research in the biobehavioral sciences* (1982) presents the latest expert assessments of the relationship between behavior and many areas of health; it includes chapters on coping with stress, heart disease, alcoholism, and smoking.

Fear and courage (1978) by Rachman discusses the origins and treatment of human fears and includes data collected during conditions of war.

15
ABNORMAL PSYCHOLOGY

Most of us have periods when we feel anxious, depressed, unreasonably angry, or inadequate in dealing with life's complexities. Trying to lead a satisfying and meaningful life is not easy in an era of rapid social and technological change. Many of our traditional assumptions about work, religion, sex, marriage, and family are being questioned, and the social and religious values that gave our grandparents a sense of security no longer provide clear guidelines for behavior. A number of factors suggest that life today is more stressful than it was a century ago: the increased consumption of tranquilizers, sleeping pills, alcohol, and other drugs; the increase in violent crimes; increased attempts to find relief through meditation and various forms of therapy.

It is an unusual person who manages to get through life without periods of loneliness, self-doubt, and despair. When a representative sample of Americans were asked if they had ever felt they were going to have a nervous breakdown, one out of five answered yes (National Institute of Mental Health, 1970). But most people do not "break down"; they manage to cope with their problems and continue to function.

In this chapter, we will look at some individuals who have given up and can no longer manage on their own and some individuals who have developed self-destructive life styles. We will also consider a variety of ineffective ways of coping with the problems of living. The behaviors that we will discuss are classified as "abnormal," but, as we will see, the dividing line between "normal" and "abnormal" behavior is far from clear.

ABNORMAL BEHAVIOR

Defining abnormality

What do we mean by "abnormal" behavior? By what criteria do we distinguish it from "normal" behavior? There is no general agreement, but most attempts to describe abnormality are based on one or more of the following definitions.

DEVIATION FROM STATISTICAL NORMS The word *ab-normal* means "away from the norm." Many characteristics—such as height, weight, and intelligence—cover a range of values when measured over a population. Most people fall within the middle range of height; a few individuals are abnormally tall or abnormally short. One definition of abnormality is based on *statistical frequency:* "abnormal behavior" is statistically infrequent or deviant from the norm. But according to this definition, the person who is extremely intelligent or extremely happy would be classified as abnormal. Thus, in defining abnormal behavior, we must consider more than statistical frequency.

DEVIATION FROM SOCIAL NORMS Every society has certain standards, or norms, for acceptable behavior; behavior that deviates markedly from these norms is considered abnormal. Usually, but not always, such behavior is also statistically infrequent in that society. However, several problems arise when deviation from social norms is used as a criterion for defining abnormality.

Behavior that is considered normal by one society may be considered abnormal by another. For example, members of some African tribes do not consider it unusual to "hear voices" when no one is actually talking or to "see visions" when nothing is actually there, but such behaviors are considered abnormal in most societies. Another problem is that the concept of abnormality changes over time within the same society. Most Americans would have considered smoking marijuana or appearing nude at the beach abnormal behaviors 25 years ago. Today, such behaviors tend to be viewed as differences in life style rather than signs of abnormality.

Thus, ideas of normality and abnormality differ from one society to another and from time to time within the same society. Any definition of abnormality must include more than social compliance.

MALADAPTIVENESS OF BEHAVIOR Rather than defining abnormal behavior in terms of deviance from either statistical or societal norms, many social scientists believe that the most important criterion is how the behavior affects the well-being of the individual and/or the social group. According to this criterion, behavior is abnormal if it is *maladaptive*—if it has adverse effects on the individual or society. Some kinds of deviant behavior interfere with the welfare of the individual (a man who is so fearful of crowds that he cannot ride the bus to work; an alcoholic who drinks so heavily that he or she cannot keep a job; a woman who attempts suicide). Other forms of deviant behavior are harmful to society (an adolescent who has violent aggressive outbursts; a paranoid individual who plots to assassinate national leaders). If we use the criterion of maladaptiveness, all of these behaviors would be considered abnormal.

PERSONAL DISTRESS A fourth criterion considers abnormality in terms of the individual's subjective feelings of distress rather than the individual's behavior. Most, but not all, people diagnosed as "mentally ill" feel acutely miserable; they are anxious, depressed, or agitated and may suffer from insomnia, loss of appetite, and numerous aches and pains. Sometimes personal distress may be the only symptom of abnormality; the individual's behavior may appear normal to the casual observer.

None of these definitions provides a completely satisfactory description of abnormal behavior. In most instances, all four criteria—statistical frequency, social deviation, maladaptive behavior, and personal distress—are considered in diagnosing abnormality. The *legal* definition of abnormality, which declares a person *insane* largely on the basis of an inability to judge between right and wrong or to exert control over behavior, is less satisfactory for diagnostic purposes than any of these four criteria. It should be emphasized that *insanity* is a legal term and is not used by psychologists in discussing abnormality.

What is normality?

Normality is even more difficult to define than abnormality, particularly in a rapidly changing and complex society. Traditionally, psychologists have focused on the individual's *adjustment* to the environment and considered personality traits to be normal if they helped an individual to *adjust* to the world—to get along well with others and to find a place in society. Many psychologists now feel that the term "adjustment," if it is equated with conformity to what others do and think, carries too many negative connotations to describe the healthy personality. They focus on more positive attributes, such as individuality, creativity, and fulfillment of potential.

Maslow, for example, considered *self-actualization* to be the highest human motive. Most of his self-actualizing individuals (see Chapter 13) would be considered mentally healthy. However, few people are able to exploit their potential to the degree achieved by Maslow's self-actualizers (who include Martin Luther King, Jr., Pablo Casals, Adlai Stevenson, and Eleanor Roosevelt). Most of us lead fairly routine lives, restricted by the innumerable demands of daily existence, but we would not be considered maladjusted or mentally disturbed.

Despite a lack of consensus in defining the normal personality, most psychologists would agree that the following qualities indicate emotional well-being. These characteristics do not distinguish sharply between the "mentally healthy" and the "mentally ill"; they represent traits that the normal person possesses to a *greater degree* than the individual who is diagnosed as abnormal.

1   *Efficient perception of reality.*   Normal individuals are fairly realistic in appraising their reactions and capabilities and in interpreting what is going on in the world around them. They do not consistently misperceive what others say and do, and they do not consistently overevaluate their abilities and tackle more than they can accomplish or underestimate their abilities and shy away from difficult tasks.

2   *Self-knowledge.*   Well-adjusted people have some awareness of their own motives and feelings. Although none of us can fully understand our feelings or behavior, normal people do not hide important feelings and motives from themselves. They have more self-awareness than individuals who are diagnosed as "mentally ill."

3   *An ability to exercise voluntary control over behavior.*   Normal individuals feel fairly confident about their ability to control their behavior. Occasionally, they may act impulsively, but they are able to restrain sexual and aggressive urges when necessary. They may fail to conform to social norms, but the decision is voluntary rather than the result of uncontrollable impulses.

4   *Self-esteem and acceptance.*   Well-adjusted people have some appreciation of their own self-worth and feel accepted by those around them. They are comfortable with other people and are able to react spontaneously in social situations. At the same time, they do not feel obligated to subjugate their opinions to those of the group. Feelings of worthlessness, alienation, and lack of acceptance are prevalent among individuals who are diagnosed as abnormal.

5   *An ability to form affectionate relationships.*   Normal individuals are able to form close and satisfying relationships with other people. They are sensitive to the feelings of others and do not make excessive demands on others to gratify their own needs. Often, mentally disturbed people are so concerned with protecting their own security that they become extremely self-centered; preoccupied with

Detail of *Melancholia* by Edvard Munch

their own feelings and strivings, they seek affection but are unable to reciprocate. Sometimes they fear intimacy because their past relationships have been destructive.

6   *Productivity.*   Well-adjusted people are able to channel their abilities into productive activity. They are enthusiastic about life and do not need to drive themselves to meet the demands of the day. A chronic lack of energy and excessive susceptibility to fatigue are often symptoms of psychological tension resulting from unresolved problems.

It is argued that some people turn to creative work as an outlet for their unresolved conflicts. The artists van Gogh and Munch were probably seriously disturbed (judging from descriptions of their behavior), and one wonders if their creative powers would have been as great if they had been better adjusted emotionally. The question is debatable, but it is clear from accounts of the lives of these artists that their works were produced at great expense in the form of pain to themselves and those close to them. Although a few disturbed people manage to turn their troubles into advantages, most of them are unable to use their full creative abilities because their emotional problems inhibit productivity.

Classifying abnormal behavior

A broad range of behaviors has been classified as "abnormal." Some abnormal behaviors are acute and transitory, resulting from particularly stressful events; others are chronic and lifelong. Some abnormal behaviors result from disease or damage to the nervous system; others are the products of undesirable social environments and/or faulty learning experiences. And often these factors overlap and interact. Each person's behavior patterns and emotional problems are unique; no two individuals behave in exactly the same manner or share the same life experiences. However, enough similarities exist for mental health professionals to classify cases into categories.

A classification system has advantages and disadvantages. If the various types of abnormal behavior have different causes, we can hope to uncover them by grouping individuals according to similarities in behavior and then looking for other ways in which they may be similar. A diagnostic label also enables those who work with disturbed individuals to communicate information more clearly and concisely. The diagnosis of a *schizophrenic disorder* indicates quite a bit about a person's behavior. Knowing that an individual's symptoms are similar to those of other patients (whose progress followed a particular course or who benefited from a certain kind of treatment) is also helpful.

Disadvantages arise if we allow a diagnostic label to carry too much weight by overlooking the unique features of each case and expecting the person to conform to the classification or by forgetting that a label for maladaptive behavior is *not* an explanation of that behavior (it does not tell us how the behavior originated or what maintains it). It is also important to remember that we are labeling the individual's *behaviors* abnormal—*not* the individual. Thus, we speak of someone as having a schizophrenic disorder (which may or may not change over time) rather than saying that person is a "schizophrenic." Labels should be attached to the condition—not to the individual.

The classification of mental disorders used by most mental health professionals in this country is the *Diagnostic and Statistical Manual of Mental Disorders,* Third Edition (DSM-III, for short), which corresponds closely to the international system formulated by the World Health Organization. The major categories of mental disorders classified by DSM-III are listed in Table 15-1. Some of these disorders will be discussed in more detail later in the chapter.

DSM-III provides an extensive list of subcategories under each of these headings, as well as a description of the symptoms that must be present for the diagnosis to be applicable. The complete diagnosis for an individual is fairly comprehensive. It includes, in addition to the major diagnostic category, (1) a description of the individual's prominent personality characteristics and ways of coping with stress, (2) a list of any current physical disorders that may be relevant to understanding and treating the person, (3) documentation of stressful events that may have precipitated the disorder (such as divorce, death of a loved one), and (4) an evaluation of how well the individual has functioned socially and occupationally during the previous year. All of these variables are helpful in determining treatment and prognosis.

You have probably heard the terms "neurosis" and "psychosis" and may be wondering where they fit into the categories of mental disorders listed in Table 15-1 (pages 456–57). Traditionally, these terms denoted major diagnostic categories. *Neuroses* (plural of *neurosis*) included a group of disorders characterized by anxiety, personal unhappiness, and maladaptive behavior that were seldom serious enough to require hospitalization. The individual could usually function in society, although not at full capacity. *Psychoses* (plural of *psychosis*) included more serious mental disorders. The individual's behavior and thought processes were so disturbed that he or she was out of touch with reality, could not cope with the demands of daily life, and usually had to be hospitalized.

Neither neuroses nor psychoses appear as major categories in DSM-III. There are several reasons for this departure from earlier classification systems, but the main one concerns precision of diagnosis. Both categories were fairly broad and included a number of mental disorders with quite dissimilar symptoms. Consequently, mental health professionals did not always agree on the diagnosis for a particular case. DSM-III attempts to achieve greater consensus by grouping disorders according to very specific behavioral symptoms, without implying anything about their origins or treatment. The intention is to describe what clinical workers *observe* about individuals who have psychological problems in a way that ensures accurate communication among mental health professionals. Consequently, DSM-III includes many more categories than previous editions of the manual. Disorders that were formerly categorized as neuroses (because they were assumed to be ways of coping with internal conflicts) are now listed in DSM-III under three separate categories—anxiety disorders, somatoform disorders, and dissociative disorders.

Although "psychoses" is no longer a major category, DSM-III recognizes that people diagnosed as having schizophrenic and paranoid disorders, some affective disorders, and certain organic mental disorders exhibit *psychotic behavior*, at least at some point during their illness. The individual inaccurately evaluates his or her perceptions and thoughts and makes incorrect inferences about what is happening. The person may have *hallucinations* (false sensory experiences, such as hearing voices or seeing strange visions) and/or *delusions* (false beliefs, such as the individual's conviction that all of his or her thoughts are controlled by a powerful being from another planet).

These issues will become clearer as we look more closely at some of the mental disorders listed in Table 15-1. We should point out that "mental disorders" is a historical term that is not really applicable to many problems of living included in the classification. In the remainder of this chapter, we will examine anxiety disorders, affective disorders, schizophrenia, and one type of personality disorder, as well as alcoholism and drug dependence (both of which are classified as substance use disorders).

Sorrow by Vincent van Gogh. November 1882. Transfer lithograph. 15⅜'' × 11¾''. Collection, The Museum of Modern Art, New York

Table 15-1
Categories of Mental Disorders
Listed are the main diagnostic categories of the *Diagnostic and Statistical Manual of Mental Disorders*, Third Edition. Each category includes numerous subcategories. A few left-over categories ("not elsewhere classified") have been omitted from this table. (After American Psychiatric Association, 1980)

1 **Disorders first evident in infancy, childhood, or adolescence**

Includes mental retardation, hyperactivity, childhood anxieties, eating disorders (for example, anorexia), and other deviations from normal development.

2 **Organic mental disorders**

Covers disorders in which the psychological symptoms are directly related to injury to the brain or abnormality of its biochemical environment; may be the result of aging, degenerative diseases of the nervous system (for example, syphilis or Alzheimer's disease), or the ingestion of toxic substances (for example, lead poisoning or extreme alcoholism).

3 **Substance use disorders**

Includes excessive use of alcohol, barbiturates, amphetamines, cocaine, and other drugs that alter behavior. Marijuana and tobacco are also included in this category, which is causing considerable controversy.

4 **Schizophrenic disorders**

A group of disorders characterized by loss of contact with reality, marked disturbances of thought and perception, and bizarre behavior.

5 **Paranoid disorders**

Disorders characterized by excessive suspicions and hostility accompanied by feelings of being persecuted; reality contact in other areas is satisfactory.

6 **Affective disorders**

Disturbances of normal mood; the person may be extremely depressed, abnormally elated, or may alternate between periods of elation and depression.

7 **Anxiety disorders**

Includes disorders in which anxiety is the main symptom (generalized anxiety or panic disorders) or anxiety is experienced unless the individual avoids certain

ANXIETY DISORDERS

Most of us feel anxious and tense in the face of threatening or stressful situations. Such feelings are normal reactions to stress. Anxiety is considered abnormal only when it occurs in situations that most people can handle with little difficulty. *Anxiety disorders* include a group of disorders in which anxiety is either the main symptom (*generalized anxiety* and *panic disorders*) or anxiety is experienced when the individual attempts to control certain maladaptive behaviors (*phobic* and *obsessive-compulsive disorders*).

Generalized anxiety and panic disorders

A person who suffers from a *generalized anxiety disorder* lives each day in a state of high tension. She or he feels vaguely uneasy or apprehensive much of the time and tends to overreact to even mild stresses. An inability to relax, disturbed sleep, fatigue, headaches, dizziness, and rapid heart rate are some of the most common physical complaints. In addition, the individual continually worries about all kinds of potential problems and has difficulty concentrating or making decisions. When the individual finally makes a decision, it becomes feared situations (phobic disorders) or tries to resist performing certain rituals or thinking persistent thoughts (obsessive-compulsive disorders).

8 **Somatoform disorders**

The symptoms are physical, but no organic basis can be found and psychological factors appear to play the major role. Included are conversion disorders (for example, a woman who resents having to care for her invalid mother suddenly develops a paralyzed arm) and hypochondriasis (excessive preoccupation with health and fear of disease when there is no basis for concern).

9 **Dissociative disorders**

Temporary alterations in the functions of consciousness, memory, or identity due to emotional problems. Included are amnesia (the individual cannot recall anything about his or her history following a traumatic experience) and multiple personality (two or more independent personality systems existing within the same individual).

10 **Psychosexual disorders**

Includes problems of sexual identity (for example, transsexualism), sexual performance (for example, impotence, premature ejaculation, and frigidity), and sexual aim (for example, sexual interest in children). Homosexuality is considered a disorder only when the individual is unhappy with his or her sexual orientation and wishes to change it.

11 **Conditions not attributable to a mental disorder**

This category includes many of the problems for which people seek help, such as marital problems, parent-child difficulties, child abuse.

12 **Personality disorders**

Longstanding patterns of maladaptive behavior that constitute immature and inappropriate ways of coping with stress or solving problems. Antisocial personality disorder and narcissistic personality disorder are two examples.

the source of further worry ("Did I foresee all possible consequences?"; "Will disaster result?"). Some self-descriptions provided by people with chronically high levels of anxiety appear in Table 15-2 (page 458).

People who suffer generalized anxiety may also experience *panic attacks*— sudden episodes of acute and overwhelming apprehension or terror. During panic attacks, the individual feels certain that something dreadful is about to happen; this feeling is usually accompanied by such symptoms as heart palpitations, shortness of breath, perspiration, muscle tremors, faintness, and nausea. These symptoms result from excitation of the sympathetic division of the autonomic nervous system (see Chapter 2) and are the same reactions an individual may experience when extremely frightened.[1] During severe panic attacks, the person fears that he or she will die. The following personal account describes how terrifying such experiences can be:

I remember walking up the street, the moon was shining and suddenly everything around me seemed unfamiliar, as it would be in a dream. I felt panic

[1]Several physical conditions, such as overactivity of the thyroid gland, heart disease, withdrawal from drugs, hypoglycemia, and some endocrine disorders, can produce the same symptoms as an anxiety attack. Such possibilities should be ruled out before assuming that the symptoms are of psychological origin.

Table 15-2
Symptoms of Generalized Anxiety
The statements listed in the table are self-descriptions of individuals with chronically high levels of anxiety. (After Sarason and Sarason, 1980)

I am often bothered by the thumping of my heart.

Little annoyances get on my nerves and irritate me.

I often become suddenly scared for no good reason.

I worry continuously and that gets me down.

I frequently get spells of complete exhaustion and fatigue.

It is always hard for me to make up my mind.

I always seem to be dreading something.

I feel nervous and high strung all the time.

I often feel I cannot overcome my difficulties.

I feel constantly under strain.

rising inside me, but managed to push it away and carry on. I walked a quarter of a mile or so, with the panic getting worse every minute. . . . By now, I was sweating, yet trembling; my heart was pounding and my legs felt like jelly. . . . Terrified, I stood, not knowing what to do. The only bit of sanity left in me told me to get home. Somehow this I did very slowly, holding onto the fence in the road. I cannot remember the actual journey back, until I was going into the house, then I broke down and cried helplessly. . . . I did not go out again for a few days. When I did, it was with my mother and baby to my grandmother's a few miles away. I felt panicky there and couldn't cope with the baby. My cousin suggested we go to my Aunt's house, but I had another attack there. I was sure I was going to die. Following this, I was totally unable to go out alone, and even with someone else I had great difficulty. Not only did I get the panicky fainting spells, but I lived in constant fear of getting them. (Melville, 1977, pp. 1 and 14)

People who experience generalized anxiety and/or panic disorders usually have no clear idea why they are frightened. This kind of anxiety is sometimes called "free-floating" because it is not triggered by a particular stimulus or event but occurs in a variety of situations. It appears to be less a function of external events than of feelings and conflicts within the individual.

Phobias

In contrast to the vague apprehension of generalized anxiety disorders, the fears in phobic disorders are quite specific. Someone who responds with intense fear to a stimulus or situation that most people do not consider particularly dangerous is said to have a *phobia*. The individual usually realizes that his or her fear is irrational but still feels anxiety (ranging from strong uneasiness to panic) that can be alleviated only by avoiding the feared object or situation.

Most of us are afraid of something; snakes, high places, storms, doctors, sickness, injury, and death are the seven fears most commonly reported by adults (Agras, 1975). As you can see from Figure 15-1, the prevalence of specific fears changes with age. There appears to be a continuum between these common fears and phobias, making their distinctions somewhat arbitrary. However, a fear is usually not diagnosed as a phobic disorder unless it interferes considerably with the person's daily life. Examples of phobic disorders would be a woman whose fear of enclosed places prevents her from entering elevators (she has turned down several job offers because the offices were above the second floor) or a man whose fear of crowds prevents him from attending the theater or walking along congested sidewalks.

Some people may develop a specific phobia (fear of snakes or heights, for example) but be normal in other respects. In more serious cases, the individual's phobias are broad or numerous enough to interfere with many aspects of life and may be intertwined with obsessive or compulsive behavior (see Figure 15-2, page 460).

Among people seeking professional help, the most common phobia is a fairly broad one, called *agoraphobia*. (The Greek word *agora* means an assembly or marketplace.) People with this disorder fear being alone in an unfamiliar setting or being in a public place where escape might be difficult or help unavailable if they were suddenly incapacitated. The following incident in the life of a woman suffering from agoraphobia shows how distressful such fears may be.

The woman who lives next door is a very nice person and I like her. One day she asked me if I would drive over to a big shopping center that had recently opened about five miles from where we live. I didn't know how to tell her that there isn't a chance in the world that I'd go to that shopping center or any other place outside our neighborhood. She must have seen how upset I got, but I was shaking like a leaf even more inside. I imagined myself in the crowd, getting lost, or passing out. I was terrified by the openness of the shopping center and the crowds. I made an excuse this time, but I don't know what I'll say next time. Maybe I'll just have to let her in on my little bit of craziness. (Sarason and Sarason, 1980, p. 165)

Often, the individual has an earlier history of recurrent panic attacks and becomes reluctant to enter situations that may be associated with such attacks. Thus, agoraphobia overlaps with other anxiety disorders.

How do phobias develop? Learning theory provides a number of explanations. Some phobias may result from frightening experiences (developing a fear of flying after experiencing a near air disaster or a fear of dogs after being attacked by one). Once such a phobia develops, the individual may go to great lengths to avoid the feared situation and eliminate the possibility of reducing the fear.

Other phobias may be learned through observation. Fearful parents tend to produce children who share their fears. Although a tendency toward timidity could be inherited, it is more likely that parents provide a model for the child to imitate. A child who observes his or her parents react with fear to a number of situations may accept such reactions as normal.

Other phobias may develop because they are rewarded. "School phobias" produce an example. A school phobia in a young child is not usually a fear of school itself, but a fear of separation from the parents. A child who wants to stay close to his or her mother may invent various excuses (for example, a stomachache) to stay home. If the mother (who may also fear separation) gives in to the excuses, the child is rewarded with the comfort of staying home with her. Separation fears that are reinforced in childhood may develop into agoraphobia as a response to stress in later life. In one case, a man in his thirties whose job pressures were increasing developed a fear of leaving home to go to work or to crowded places, such as restaurants or stores. He had experienced a severe school phobia as a child, and his old fear of separation from a source of support (this time his wife) recurred when he was faced with stress (Agras, 1975).

But some phobias are difficult to trace to learning experiences. Many individuals with fears of air travel, snakes, heights, or germs report no unpleasant childhood experiences with these situations. Psychoanalytic theory assumes that phobias develop as a defense against impulses that the individual feels may become dangerous. For example, the student whose case is reported in Figure 15-2 could avoid the arousal of homosexual inpulses by staying in his room, away from other men, and by not using public toilets.

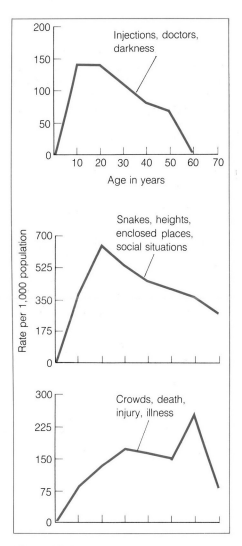

Figure 15-1
Fears Change with Age
The graphs show the prevalence of specific fears reported by people of different ages. Fears that follow the same general age pattern are represented together. For example, fears of injections, doctors, and darkness peak at about age 10 and decline thereafter. Fears of snakes, heights, enclosed places, and social situations reach a peak at age 20. Fears of crowds, death, injury, or illness become more prevalent later in life. (After Agras, Sylvester, and Oliveau, 1969)

Obsessive-compulsive disorders

Individuals with an *obsessive-compulsive disorder* feel compelled to think about things they would rather not think about or perform acts they do not wish to carry out. *Obsessions* are persistent intrusions of unwelcome thoughts or images. *Compulsions* are irresistible urges to carry out certain acts or rituals. Obses-

Figure 15-2
Phobias

An 18-year-old college freshman came for help at the student health center because each time he left his dormitory room and headed toward class, he experienced a feeling of panic. "It would get so bad at times that I thought I would collapse on the way to class. It was a frightening feeling, and I began to be afraid to leave the dorm." He could not understand these feelings because he was reasonably well pleased with his classes and professors. Even after he returned to the dormitory, he would be unable to face anyone for hours or to concentrate on his homework. But if he remained in or near his room, he felt reasonably comfortable.

During interviews with his therapist, the youth reported other fears, including become contaminated by syphilis and growing prematurely bald. Occasionally, these fears were sufficiently intense and persistent to cause him to scrub his hands, genitals, and

head compulsively until these parts became red and sometimes even bled. In addition, he touched doorknobs only reluctantly, never drank water from a public fountain, and only used the toilet in his home or dormitory. He realized that his fears were unfounded and exaggerated but also felt that many of his precautions and constant worrying were necessary to avoid even greater "mental anguish."

The student's past history revealed that he had serious concerns about his sexual identity and his adequacy as a male. When he was young, he had avoided playing with the other boys because he could not run as fast or hit a ball as far. His mother had strongly rewarded his tendency not to join others because she was convinced that he would get hurt if he participated in their "rough-housing." He was a late maturer and had spent a traumatic summer at camp about the time that most of his

peers were reaching puberty. Discovering that he was sexually underdeveloped in comparison to the other boys, he worried about his deficiency; he wondered whether he was destined to become a girl, and he feared that the other boys might attack him sexually.

Although his puberty made a belated appearance, he continued to worry about his masculine identity and even fantasized on occasion that he was a girl. At these times, he became extremely anxious and seriously considered suicide as a solution.

The therapist's immediate goal in treatment was to remove the student's irrational fear of leaving the dormitory, which was accomplished with the method of systematic desensitization [see page 500]. However, the phobias in this case were clearly part of a deep-rooted problem of sexual identity that would require extensive psychotherapy (Kleinmuntz, 1974, pp. 168–69).

sive thoughts may be linked with compulsive acts (for example, thoughts of lurking disease germs combined with the compulsion to wash eating utensils many times before using them).

At times, all of us have persistently recurring thoughts ("Did I leave the gas turned on?") and urges to perform ritualistic behavior (knocking on wood after boasting of good fortune). But when a person has an obsessive-compulsive disorder, such thoughts and urges occupy so much time that they seriously interfere with daily life. The individual recognizes that these thoughts and urges are irrational but feel unable to control them. Obsessive thoughts cover a variety of topics but most often are concerned with committing aggressive or sexual acts. A mother may have persistent thoughts of drowning her infant in the bathtub. A young man may have recurrent thoughts of exposing his genitals in public or shouting obscenities in church. The probability that these thoughts will be transformed into actions is slim. Nevertheless, individuals who experience such obsessive thoughts are horrified by them, cannot understand why they persist, and live in fear that they will perform these "dreadful" acts. Figure 15-3 reports the history of a young mother who was distressed by recurrent thoughts of murdering her two small children. The kind of prohibition her parents placed on any expression of negative feelings is fairly characteristic of the background of persons who develop obsessive-compulsive disorders. When normal feelings of anger must be suppressed or denied, they become an "alien" part of the personality and find expression only in indirect ways.

Compulsive acts range from mild kinds of superstitious behavior (such as not stepping on the cracks in sidewalks or arranging the material on a desk in a precise order before starting an assignment) to elaborate rituals like those described in Figure 15-4.

Most of us find comfort in certain familiar routines or rituals, particularly in times of stress. But people with obsessive-compulsive disorders become intensely anxious when they try to resist their compulsions and feel a release of tension once their acts are carried out.

Understanding anxiety disorders

We do not know why some people become chronically anxious, but their reactions seem to reflect feelings of inadequacy in the face of stresses they perceive as threatening. In Chapter 14, we discussed several theories of anxiety. Psychoanalytic theory assumes that the sources of anxiety are internal and unconscious. The person has repressed certain unacceptable or "dangerous" impulses—impulses that would endanger self-esteem or relationships with other people if they were expressed. In situations where these impulses (usually sexual or aggressive in nature) are likely to be aroused, the individual experiences intense anxiety. Because the source of anxiety is unconscious, the person does not know why he or she feels apprehensive.

From a psychoanalytic viewpoint, phobias are ways of coping with anxiety by displacing it onto an object or situation that can be avoided. Obsessions and compulsions also serve to protect the individual from recognizing the true

"Ronald is *extremely* compulsive."

Figure 15-3
Obsessive Thoughts

A 32-year-old mother of two small children sought help because she was distressed over obsessively intrusive and repugnant thoughts related to injuring or murdering her children. On infrequent occasions, her husband was also a "victim." These thoughts were so repugnant, made so little sense, and were so foreign to her conscious feelings that she had been afraid and embarrassed to seek help. She had kept this problem to herself for nearly two years, despite considerable psychological pain, tension, and turmoil. Finally, the steadily increasing difficulty had reached an intolerable level.

These thoughts that were so terribly disturbing to this patient really did not differ so greatly in quality from what every normal young woman may occasionally feel toward her children. Many less inhibited and more spontaneous young parents than this one might occa-

sionally say, "Oh, I feel just like throwing Johnny out of the window today! He makes me so mad!" Most mothers would not feel threatened by such a thought or feel very guilty about having had it and would probably forget it rather quickly. But this patient greatly feared and condemned such thoughts. To her, the thought was nearly as threatening and as guilt-provoking as the act.

Early in life, this woman had developed a defensive need to deny the presence of all negative feelings. To defend herself against the guilt occasioned by having such "terrible" thoughts, she endeavored to dissociate herself from them—to deny that they were her thoughts. "It's just awful words that pop into my head. . . . They have nothing at all to do with the way I feel. They couldn't be my thoughts at all. . . ."

The patient had been raised by an anxious and insecure mother who was

unable to permit herself or her children the slightest expression of negative feelings. The daughter soon realized that any feelings other than loving ones must be repressed or denied. The patient was the eldest of three siblings and had been assigned undue responsibility for their care. She felt deprived of her share of her parents' affection, was greatly resentful of her younger sister and brother, and fantasized about what it would be like if they were not around. Her occasional murderous fantasies about them were accompanied by tremendous guilt and anxiety. As a result, the fantasies and associated emotional feelings had been completely repressed from conscious awareness. These early conflicts were reactivated during her marriage when the needs of her husband and children seemed to take precedence over her own (Laughlin, 1967, pp. 324–25).

Figure 15-4
Compulsive Rituals

A 30-year-old woman had developed such an elaborate sequence of ritual acts that their consummation occupied most of her waking hours. She could not go to bed at night before she had checked each door and window three times to ensure that they were locked. The gas range and the pilot lights to the furnace and hot water heater also had to be checked to make certain that no gas was escaping. Bathing and dressing took up much of her time; she often took three or four showers in succession—scrubbing her body thoroughly with a special antibacterial cleanser each time—before she was convinced that she was clean enough to put on her clothes. She wore only clothing that could be washed, because she did not trust the dry cleaner to remove all possible germs, and each article had to be washed and rinsed three times before she would wear it. Similar hygienic procedures were involved whenever she prepared food; she scalded each dish and utensil with boiling water before and after using it and would not eat a meal unless she had prepared it herself.

This woman had always been unusually neat and clean, but her "security operations" had intensified over the years until they reached pathological proportions. At times, she realized the foolishness of her precautions, but she experienced intense anxiety whenever she attempted to cut short any of her procedures (Rita L. Atkinson, unpublished case report).

source of his or her anxiety. Obsessive thoughts are unacceptable impulses (hostility, destructiveness, inappropriate sexual urges) that have been repressed and somehow reappear in a disguised form. The individual feels that they are not a part of herself or himself and may commit compulsive acts to undo or atone for forbidden impulses. A mother who is obsessed with thoughts of murdering her infant may feel compelled to check many times during the night to assure herself that the child is well. Compulsive rituals also serve to keep threatening impulses out of the individual's conscious awareness; a person who is continually busy has little opportunity to think improper thoughts or commit improper actions.

According to social learning theories, anxiety is triggered less by internal conflicts than by specific external events. A person who suffers from generalized anxiety feels that he or she is not in control of so many life situations that anxious feelings are almost always present. Phobias are viewed as avoidance responses that may be learned directly (through a frightening experience) or vicariously (by observing fearful responses in others). Obsessive-compulsive behavior persists because it is associated somehow with a reduction of anxiety. For example, a person obsessed with fears of germs or contamination may find that hand-washing temporarily relieves such fears. Hand-washing therefore becomes associated with anxiety reduction and gradually becomes a ritual response whenever the person feels anxious.

Compulsive rituals also give the individual a feeling of order and control over a threatening world. Individuals who develop obsessive-compulsive disorders tend to be very cautious and perfectionistic (Steiner, 1972). In times of stress, they reduce anxiety by redoubling their efforts to be cautious, checking everything five or six times rather than twice. In addition, being continually preoccupied with endless rituals and tasks allows the individual to avoid more important issues (personal relationships, family or job problems) with which he or she feels unable to cope.

AFFECTIVE DISORDERS

Affective disorders are disturbances of *affect* or mood. The person may be severely depressed or manic (wildy elated) or may alternate between periods of depression and elation. These mood changes may be so extreme that the individual requires hospitalization.

Depression

Almost everyone gets depressed at times. Most of us have periods when we feel sad, lethargic, and not interested in any activities—even pleasurable ones. Depression is a normal response to many of life's stresses. Among the situations that most often precipitate depression are failure at school or on the job, the loss of a loved one, and the realization that illness or aging is depleting one's resources. Depression is considered abnormal only when it is out of proportion to the event and continues past the point at which most people begin to recover.

Hopelessness and dejection are two of the main characteristics of depression. The individual experiences an overwhelming inertia and is unable to make decisions, initiate activity, or take an interest in anything. He or she broods over feelings of inadequacy and worthlessness, has crying spells, and may contemplate suicide.

Sometimes depression is accompanied by anxiety—a sort of "agitated depression." The person feels exhausted and disinterested in life but at the same time is tense, restless, and unable to relax.

Manic episodes

People experiencing manic episodes behave in a way that appears, on the surface, to be the opposite of depression. During mild manic episodes (*hypomania*), the individual is energetic, enthusiastic, and full of self-confidence. She or he talks continually, rushes from one activity to another with little need of sleep, and makes grandiose plans but pays little attention to their practicality. Unlike the kind of joyful exuberance that characterizes normal elation, manic behavior has a driven quality and often expresses hostility more than elation.

People experiencing severe manic episodes (*mania*) behave somewhat like the popular concept of a "raving maniac." They are extremely excited and must be constantly active. They may pace about, sing, shout, or pound the walls for hours. They are angered by attempts to interfere with their activities and may become abusive. Impulses (including sexual ones) are immediately expressed in actions or words. These individuals are confused and disoriented and may experience delusions of great wealth, accomplishment, or power (see Figure 15-5).

Manic-depressive disorder

A few individuals may experience only manic episodes, but most people who have manic episodes also experience periods of depression. In some cases, a person alternates cyclically between manic and depressive episodes and often exhibits a period of normal behavior in between (see Figure 15-6). This condition is listed in DSM-III as a *bipolar disorder;* the individual goes from one pole of the affect continuum to the other.[2]

[2]A person who has recurring periods of severe depression is said to have a *unipolar disorder.* However, unipolar disorder is not a major DSM-III category.

Figure 15-5
Manic Reaction

Robert B., a 56-year-old dentist, had provided well for his wife and three daughters for most of his 25 years of dental practice. Mrs. B. reported that at times Robert had displayed behavior similar to the behavior that preceded his hospitalization, but that this was the worst he had ever been.

About two weeks prior to hospitalization, the patient awoke one morning with the idea that he was the most gifted dental surgeon in his tri-state area; his mission then was to provide services for as many persons as possible so that they could benefit from his talents. Consequently, he decided to enlarge his two-chair practice to a 20-chair one and planned to reconstruct his two dental offices into 20 booths so that he could simultaneously attend to as many patients. That very day he drew up the plans for this arrangement and telephoned a number of remodelers and invited them to submit bids for the work. He also ordered the additional necessary dental equipment.

Toward the end of that day, he became irritated with the "interminable delays" and, after he attended to his last patient, rolled up his sleeves and began to knock down the walls of his dental offices. When he discovered that he couldn't manage this chore with the sledge hammer he had purchased for this purpose earlier, he became frustrated and proceeded to smash his more destructible tools, washbasins, and X-ray equipment. He justified this behavior in his own mind by saying, "This junk is not suitable for the likes of me; it'll have to be replaced anyway."

He did not tell anyone in his family about these activities for a week, and his wife started to receive frantic telephone calls from patients whom he had turned away from his office. During this time, his wife realized something was "upsetting him" because he looked "haggard, wild-eyed, and run-down." He was in perpetual motion, and his speech was "overexcited." That evening, Robert's wife mentioned the phone calls and his condition, and she was subjected to a 15-minute tirade of "ranting and raving." She said later that the only reason he stopped shouting was because he became hoarse and barely audible.

After several more days of "mad goings-on," according to Mrs. B., she telephoned two of her married daughters for help and told them that their father was completely unreasonable and that he was beyond her ability to reach him. Her daughters, who lived within several minutes' drive, visited their parents one evening and brought along their husbands. The father, after bragging about his sexual prowess, made aggressive advances toward his daughters. When his sons-in-law attempted to curtail this behavior, Robert assaulted them with a chair and had to be physically subdued. The police were then called, and he was admitted to the hospital several hours later.

During the interview with Robert, it was apparent that he was hyperactive and overwrought. He could not sit in his chair; instead he paced the office floor like a caged animal. Throughout his pacing, he talked constantly about his frustrated plans and how his wife and two favorite daughters double-crossed him. It was also learned (both from Robert himself and subsequently from Mrs. B.) that this was not the first episode of this behavior; Robert had a history of three prior hospitalizations.

The patient responded well to lithium treatment and was discharged within several weeks of admission to the hospital (Kleinmuntz, 1974, p. 234).

Bipolar or *manic-depressive disorders* are relatively rare. Although about 20 percent of adult females and 10 percent of adult males in the United States have experienced a major depression at some time, only about 1 percent of the adult population has had a manic-depressive disorder, and the disorder appears to be equally common in men and women. Manic-depressive disorders differ from the other affective disorders in that they tend to occur at an earlier age, are more likely to run in families, respond to different therapeutic medications (as we will see later), and are apt to recur unless treated. These facts suggest that biological variables may play a more important role than psychological variables in bipolar disorders.

Understanding affective disorders

Depression is one of the most prevalent emotional disorders. Because depression is so common and can be so debilitating, much effort has been devoted to determining its causes. We will look briefly at several approaches to understanding affective disorders.

Depression Days 0–23	Looks sad, preoccupied, cries frequently. Expresses death wishes and suicidal thoughts. Isolated most of the time, indifferent to unit activities. Slow in speech and movements. Falls asleep at times in meetings.
Switch Day 24	Had a congenial, pleasant visit with family members; says she enjoyed herself. Does not appear depressed; talks easily with staff members.
Mania Days 25–31	This period characterized by two episodes of mania separated by a five-day interval during which she appeared calmer and normally engaged in ward activities. Exhibited pressure of speech and flight of ideas on the morning of day 25. Actively showed recent purchases to everyone. Great deal of talk about money matters and how much she spends. Less active in the evening. Days 26 to 30: Appeared in good spirits, was personable and talkative. Judged to be either euthymic or mildly hypomanic. Became hyperactive and combative on day 30 while on leave from the hospital. Returned early on day 31, apparently angry with her husband and staff members.
Depression Days 32–45	Looks sad, facial expression of pain and fear. Needs encouragement to initiate activities and to talk. Seclusive, indifferent to the environment.
Switch Day 46	Morning: Happy to see her family; had pleasent visit with them. Pleasant interactions with patients and staff. Evening: Calm, verbalized her good feelings for family visit. Regretted that she becomes manic but remarked that it helps pass the time and keeps her from being bored.
Mania Days 47–53	Day 47: Up all night, appeared in good spirits, superficial conversation. Dressed nicely for breakfast, talkative and seductive, moderately hyperactive. Less active in the evenings; appears happy. Needs close observation. Days 48, 49, and 50: Exhibits behavior similar to other manic episodes, such as riding up and down hall on wheel chair, fighting with staff, destroying valuable belongings. Escapes from unit, causing problems on other wards.

Figure 15-6
Mood Changes in a Manic-Depressive Disorder
Descriptions of the patient's behavior are excerpted from the notes of hospital staff members. (After Jones and others, 1973)

PSYCHOANALYTIC THEORIES In psychoanalytic theories, depression is interpreted as a *reaction to loss*. Whatever the nature of the loss (loss of a loved one, loss of status, loss of moral support provided by a group of friends), the depressed person reacts to it intensely because the current situation brings back all the fears and feelings of an earlier loss that occurred in childhood—the loss of parental affection. For some reason, the individual's needs for affection and care were not satisfied as a child. A loss in later life causes the individual to *regress* to his or her helpless, dependent state when the original loss occurred. Part of the depressed person's behavior therefore represents a cry for love—a display of helplessness and an appeal for affection and security (White and Watt, 1981).

Reaction to loss is complicated by angry feelings toward the deserting person. An underlying assumption of psychoanalytic theories is that people who are prone to depression have learned to repress their hostile feelings because they are afraid of alienating those on whom they depend for support. When things go wrong, they turn their anger inward and blame themselves. For example, a woman may feel extremely hostile toward the employer who

"You were manic yesterday? That's a riot—I was depressive."

fired her, but because her anger arouses anxiety, she uses the defense mechanism of projection to internalize her feelings. She is not angry; others are angry at her. She assumes the employer had a good reason for rejecting her: she is incompetent and worthless.

Psychoanalytic theories suggest that the depressed person's low self-esteem and feelings of worthlessness stem from a childlike need for parental approval. A small child's self-esteem depends on the approval and affection of the parents. But as a person matures, feelings of worth also should be derived from the individual's sense of his or her own accomplishments and effectiveness. The self-esteem of a person prone to depression depends primarily on external sources—the approval and support of others. When these supports fail, the individual may be thrown into a state of depression.

Psychoanalytic theories of depression therefore focus on loss, over-dependence on external approval, and internalization of anger. They seem to provide a reasonable explanation for some of the behaviors exhibited by depressed individuals, but they are difficult to prove or to refute. Some studies indicate that people who are prone to depression are more likely than the average person to have lost a parent in early life (Roy, 1981). But parental loss (through death or separation) is also found in the case histories of people who suffer from other types of mental disorders, and most people who suffer such a loss do not develop emotional problems in adulthood (Tennant and others, 1981).

LEARNING THEORIES   Learning theories of depression focus on what is going on *now* in the individual's life rather than on earlier experiences. Within the learning theory framework, there are two major approaches to the causes of depression. One emphasizes reinforcement; the other, cognitive factors.

The *reinforcement approach* is based on the assumption that people become depressed when their social environment provides little positive reinforcement (Lewinsohn and others, 1980). Many of the events that precipitate depression (such as the death of a loved one, failure in a job, and impaired health) involve a reduction in accustomed reinforcement.

Once people become depressed and inactive, their main source of reinforcement is the sympathy and attention they receive from relatives and friends. This attention may initially reinforce the very behaviors that are maladaptive (weeping, complaining, criticizing self, talking about suicide). But because it is tiresome to be around someone who refuses to cheer up, the depressed person's behavior eventually alienates even close associates, producing a further reduction in reinforcement and increasing the individual's social isolation and unhappiness.

A low rate of positive reinforcement still further reduces the individual's activities and the expression of behavior that might be rewarded. Both activities and rewards decrease in a vicious cycle. A schematic representation of the *reduced-reinforcement theory of depression,* showing how various contributing factors are interrelated, appears in Figure 15-7.

Cognitive approaches to depression focus not on what people *do* but on how they view themselves and the world. One cognitive theory suggests that individuals who are prone to depression have developed a general attitude of appraising events from a negative and self-critical viewpoint (Beck, 1976). They expect to fail rather than to succeed; and they tend to magnify failures and minimize successes in evaluating their performance. (For example, a student who receives a poor grade on only one examination out of many considers himself an academic misfit; a woman views herself as inadequate, despite a

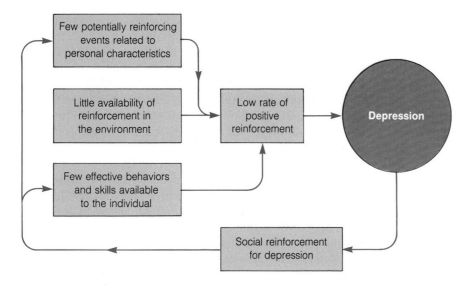

Figure 15-7
A Reduced-Reinforcement Model
of Depression
Feelings of depression may result when the individual's social environment provides little positive reinforcement or gratification. A low rate of reinforcement tends to reduce activity even more, thereby producing fewer reinforcements. The amount of potential reinforcement is a function of the individual's personal characteristics (such as age and physical attractiveness), living environment (for example, a home versus a prison cell), and repertoire of behavior for gaining reinforcement (special talents, vocational and social skills). Sympathy provided by concerned friends and relatives may reinforce depressive behavior. The model diagrams the interrelationships of these factors. (After Lewinsohn and others, 1980)

succession of praiseworthy achievements.) They also tend to blame themselves rather than the circumstances when things go wrong. (When rain dampens spirits at an outdoor buffet, the host blames himself rather than the weather.) According to this view, encouraging depressed people to become more socially active so that they can receive more positive reinforcement will not, in itself, be helpful; they will simply find new opportunities to criticize themselves.

Another cognitive approach to depression is based on the concept of *learned helplessness* discussed in Chapter 14. According to this theory, people become depressed when they *believe* that their actions make no difference in bringing about either pleasure or pain. Depression is the individual's belief in his or her own helplessness.

The concept of learned helplessness grew out of experiments with animals. As we noted in Chapter 14, animals that are subjected to traumatic conditions they are unable to avoid (electric shock or loud noise) develop signs of depression: apathy, decreased appetite, loss of sexual potency, and a lack of normal aggressiveness. These symptoms are *not* found in animals that are subjected to traumatic conditions they can avoid or terminate by an appropriate response (Seligman, 1975).

Seligman originally proposed that repeated experiences of being unable to change or influence important events in a person's life led to depression. But several factors prompted him to modify his theory. First, there is little evidence to support the idea that people who are chronically depressed have experienced such patterns of failure. Second, research suggests that a person's *appraisal* of a situation is often more important than the objective nature of the situation. When depressed individuals fail at a task, they are more likely than normal individuals to blame themselves (they were not skillful or did not try hard enough) rather than the circumstances. In contrast, when depressed individuals succeed, they are more likely to explain their success in terms of "luck" rather than their own ability (Rizley, 1978).

Seligman has subsequently revised his helplessness theory to include the subjective interpretation of situations over which the individual has no control (Seligman and others, 1979; Peterson, Schwartz, and Seligman, 1981). Not uncontrollable outcomes per se but the person's *causal explanations* for these outcomes determine the degree of depression. When an undesirable event occurs, the individual presumably reviews the facts of the current situation as well as what has happened in similar situations in the past and attempts to explain the events. If the explanation leads the individual to conclude that he or she cannot control the situation in the future, the symptoms of helplessness may follow.

Let us consider a simplified example. Three students fail a course that is required for graduation. One attributes the failure to external factors (the teacher did an inferior job of presenting the material and the final exam was unfair). The second ascribes her failure to inadequate effort (she did not spend enough time studying). The third student decides that he simply does not have the ability (he worked hard and his past performance in similar courses has been poor). According to Seligman's theory, all three students may feel depressed; but the third student should be most severely depressed and most reluctant to try again because he attributes his failure to something internal that is not likely to change in the future. Some evidence suggests that blaming a personal attribute as stable as "character" for bad events is associated with depression but that blaming "behavior" is not (Peterson and others, 1981).

Although negative expectations about oneself and the world seem to play an important role in depression, the extent to which such thoughts *precede* rather than *accompany* a depressed episode is not clear. Self-critical attitudes and feelings of helplessness may lead to depression. But it is also possible that being depressed causes the individual to think negatively (Lewinsohn and others, 1981).

BIOLOGICAL THEORIES   A tendency to develop affective disorders, particularly manic-depressive (bipolar) disorders, appears to be inherited. The evidence comes from twin studies. Identical or *monozygotic* twins develop from the same egg and share the same heredity; fraternal or *dizygotic* twins develop from different eggs and are no more alike genetically than ordinary siblings. If one monozygotic twin is diagnosed as manic-depressive, there is a 72 percent chance that the other twin will suffer from the same disorder; the corresponding figure for dizygotic twins is only 14 percent. These figures, called *concordance rates*, represent the likelihood that both twins will have a specific characteristic, given that one of the twins has the characteristic. The concordance rate for monozygotic twins suffering from depression (40 percent) also exceeds the rate for dizygotic twins (11 percent)—but the difference between these two rates is much less than the difference for manic depressives (Allen, 1976). The comparison of these differences indicates that manic-depressive disorders are more closely related than depressive disorders to genetic factors.

The specific role that genetic factors play in affective disorders is far from clear. However, it seems likely that some sort of biochemical abnormality is involved. Mounting evidence indicates that our moods are regulated by a group of chemicals called *neurotransmitters* that affect the transmission of nerve impulses across the synapse from one neuron to another (see page 34). A number of chemicals serve as neurotransmitters in different parts of the nervous system, and normal behavior requires a careful balance among them. Two neurotransmitters believed to play an important role in affective disorders are *norepinephrine* and *serotonin*. Both of these neurotransmitters are localized in areas of the brain involved in the regulation of emotional behavior—the limbic system and the hypothalamus. A widely accepted hypothesis is that depression is associated with a deficiency and that mania is associated with an excess of one or both of these neurotransmitters. However, the evidence is indirect, based largely on the effects that certain drugs have on behavior and on neurotransmitter activity. For example, the drug reserpine, which is used to treat high blood pressure, sometimes produces severe depression as a side effect; animal research has shown that the drug causes a decrease in the brain levels of serotonin and norepinephrine. In contrast, amphetamines (or "speed"), which produce an emotional "high," facilitate the release of both of these neurotransmitters.

Drugs that are effective in relieving depression increase the availability of both norepinephrine and serotonin in the nervous system. There are two major classes of antidepressant drugs, and they act in different ways to increase neurotransmitter levels. The *monoamine oxidase (MAO) inhibitors* block the activity of an enzyme that can destroy both norepinephrine and serotonin, thereby increasing the concentration of these two neurotransmitters in the brain. The *tricyclic antidepressants* prevent *reuptake* (the process by which neurotransmitters are sucked back into the nerve terminals from which they were released) of serotonin and norepinephrine, thereby prolonging the duration of their activity.

Since all of these drugs affect both serotonin and norepinephrine, it is difficult to distinguish between the roles of these two neurotransmitters in depressive disorders. Some studies indicate that serotonin plays the major role; others implicate norepinephrine (Snyder, 1980). It is possible that each neurotransmitter may be involved but in different subtypes of depression.

The fact that antidepressants sometimes cause bipolar patients who are in a depressed state to switch abruptly to a manic state supports the idea that mania is caused by an *excess* of serotonin and norepinephrine. However, one set of facts is difficult to explain. The chemical *lithium carbonate* has proved to be remarkably successful in calming the manic behavior of bipolar individuals and in preventing future manic episodes. One would assume that it somehow decreases the levels of serotonin and norepinephrine. However, given regularly, this chemical also prevents the recurrence of *depressive* episodes. In a sense, it "normalizes" the person.

Animal studies have shown that lithium does reduce the brain concentration of norepinephrine but that it *increases* serotonin levels. The crucial factor in maintaining moods within normal limits may therefore be the *balance* among serotonin, norepinephrine, and probably several other neurotransmitters yet to be identified. Serotonin may have nothing to do with mood states per se but may serve as a regulator, keeping norepinephrine fluctuations within certain boundaries at both ends of the mood scale (Kety, 1980).

It is also possible that the various affective disorders have different causes. Some depressions may be linked to low levels of norepinephrine and others to low levels of serotonin (Cobbin and others, 1979).

There is no doubt that affective disorders involve biochemical changes in the nervous system. The unresolved question is whether the physiological changes are the cause or the result of the psychological changes. For example, people who deliberately behave as if they were experiencing a manic episode exhibit changes in neurotransmitter levels similar to those found among actual manic patients (Post and others, 1973). It may be that the depletion of norepinephrine causes certain kinds of depression, but an earlier link in the causal chain leading to depression may be feelings of helplessness or loss of emotional support.

VULNERABILITY AND STRESS All of the theories we have discussed make important points about the nature of depression. Inherited physiological characteristics may predispose an individual to extreme mood changes. Early experiences (the loss of parental affection and/or the inability to gain gratification through the individual's own efforts) may also make a person *vulnerable* to depression in later life. The kinds of stressful events that depressed patients report precipitated their disorder are usually within the range of normal life experiences; they are experiences most people can handle without becoming abnormally depressed. Thus, the concept of vulnerability is helpful in understanding why some people develop depression but others do not when confronted with a particular stressful experience.

SCHIZOPHRENIA

Schizophrenia is the label applied to a group of disorders characterized by severe personality disorganization, distortion of reality, and an inability to function in daily life. *Schizophrenic disorders,* the category listed in DSM-III (see Table 15-1), is a more accurate term because most experts believe schizophrenia encompasses several disorders, each of which may have a different cause. However, "schizophrenia" is the historical term and the one still most commonly used.

Schizophrenia occurs in all cultures, even those that are remote from the stresses of modern civilization, and appears to have plagued humanity throughout history. In the United States, about 6 out of every 1,000 people are treated for schizophrenia in any given year. Because the disorder tends to reoccur and because some patients become chronically incapacitated, about 50 percent of all psychiatric hospital beds are occupied by patients diagnosed as schizophrenic.

Schizophrenia usually appears in young adulthood; the peak of incidence is between ages 25 and 35. Sometimes the disorder develops slowly as a gradual process of increasing seclusiveness and inappropriate behavior. Sometimes the onset of schizophrenia is sudden, marked by intense confusion and emotional turmoil; such cases are usually precipitated by a period of stress in individuals whose lives have tended toward isolation, self-preoccupation, and feelings of insecurity. The case described in Figure 15-8 seems to fall into the latter category, although it lacks the intensity of onset that sometimes occurs.

Characteristics of schizophrenia

Whether a schizophrenic disorder develops slowly or suddenly, the symptoms are many and varied. The primary characteristics of schizophrenia can be summarized under the following headings, although not every person diagnosed as schizophrenic will exhibit all of these symptoms.

DISTURBANCES OF THOUGHT AND ATTENTION   Whereas affective disorders are characterized by disturbances of mood, schizophrenia is characterized by disturbances of *thought*. The following excerpt from a patient's writings illustrates how difficult it is to understand schizophrenic thinking.

If things turn by rotation of agriculture or levels in regards and timed to everything; I am re-fering to a previous document when I made some remarks that were facts also tested and there is another that concerns my daughter she has a lobed bottom right ear, her name being Mary Lou. Much of abstraction has been left unsaid and undone in these productmilk syrup, and others, due to economics, differentials, subsidies, bankruptcy, tools, buildings, bonds,

Figure 15-8
Schizophrenic Disorder

W.G., a handsome, athletic-looking youth of 19, was admitted to the psychiatric service on the referral of his family physician. The boy's parents said, on his admission, that their son's behavior during the previous several months had changed drastically. He had been an adequate student in high school, but he had had to leave college recently because he was failing all his subjects. He had excelled in a variety of nonteam sports—swimming, weight-lifting, track—winning several letters, but now he did not exercise at all. Although he had always been careful about his health and had hardly ever mentioned any physical problems, within the past several weeks he had repeatedly expressed vague complaints about his head and chest, which, he said, indicated that he was "in very bad shape." During the past several days, the patient had spent most of his time sitting in his room, staring vacantly out of his window. He had become (quite uncharacteristically) careless about his personal appearance and habits.

Although there was no doubt that the patient had exhibited serious recent changes in behavior, further conversation with the parents indicated that the patient's childhood and adolescent adjustment had not been healthy. He had always been painfully shy, except in highly structured situations, and had spent much of his free time alone (often working out with weights). Despite his athletic achievements, he had no really close friends. . . .

The personnel of the psychiatric service found it difficult to converse with the patient; an ordinary diagnostic interview was impossible. For the most part, the boy volunteered no information. He would usually answer direct questions, but often in a flat, toneless way devoid of emotional coloring. Frequently, his answers . . . were not logically connected to the questions. Observers often found it taxing to record their conversations with the patient. After speaking to him for a while, they would find themselves wondering just what the conversation had been about.

At times, the disharmony between the content of the patient's words and his emotional expression was striking. For example, while speaking sympathetically of an acute illness that had rendered his mother bedridden during a portion of the previous fall, the boy giggled constantly.

At times, W.G. became agitated and spoke with a curious intensity. On one occasion, he spoke of "electrical sensations" and "an electrical current" in his brain. On another, he revealed that when lying awake at night, he often heard a voice repeating the command, "You'll have to do it." The patient felt that he was somehow being influenced by a force outside himself to commit an act of violence—as yet undefined—toward his parents (Hofling, 1975, pp. 372–73).

national stocks, foundation craps, weather, trades, government in levels of breakages and fuses in electronics too all formerly states not necessarily factuated. (Maher, 1966, p. 395)

By themselves, the words and phrases make sense, but they are meaningless in relation to each other. The juxtaposition of unrelated words and phrases and the idiosyncratic word associations (sometimes called a "word salad") are characteristic of schizophrenic writing and speech.

The thought disorder in schizophrenia appears to be a general difficulty in "filtering out" irrelevant stimuli. Most of us are able to focus our attention selectively. From a mass of incoming sensory information, we are able to select the stimuli that are relevant to the task at hand and to ignore the rest. A person who suffers from schizophrenia appears to be unable to screen out irrelevant stimuli or to distinguish relevant inputs. The individual is perceptually receptive to many stimuli at the same time and has trouble making sense out of the profusion of inputs, as the following statement by a schizophrenic patient illustrates.

I can't concentrate. It's diversion of attention that trouble me. I am picking up different conversations. It's like being a transmitter. The sounds are coming through to me, but I feel my mind cannot cope with everything. It's difficult to concentrate on any one sound. (McGhie and Chapman, 1961, p. 104)

The inability to "filter out" irrelevant stimuli is evident in many aspects of the schizophrenic person's thinking. The disjointed nature of schizophrenic speech reflects the intrusion of irrelevant associations. Often one word will set off a string of associations, as illustrated by the following sentence written by a schizophrenic patient.

> I may be a "Blue Baby" but "Social Baby" not, but yet a blue heart baby could be in the Blue Book published before the war.

This patient had suffered from heart trouble and may have started out to say "I was a blue baby." The association of "blue baby" with "blue blood" in the sense of social status prompted the interruption of "Social Baby not." The last phrase shows the interplay between the two meanings: "yet a blue baby could have been in the Society Blue Book" (Maher, 1966, p. 413).

DISTURBANCES OF PERCEPTION   During acute schizophrenic episodes, people often report that the world appears *different* to them (noises seem louder; colors, more intense). Their own bodies may no longer appear the same (their hands may seem to be too large or too small; their legs, overly extended; their eyes, dislocated in the face). Some patients fail to recognize themselves in a mirror or see their reflection as a triple image. During the acute stage of schizophrenia, many patients go through periods when they are unable to perceive wholes; for instance, they cannot see nurses or physicians as persons but can perceive them only in parts (a nose, the left eye, an arm, and so on). The drawing in Figure 15-9 shows a schizophrenic patient's fragmentation of the whole.

DISTURBANCES OF AFFECT   Schizophrenic individuals usually fail to exhibit "normal" or appropriate emotional responses. They often are withdrawn and unresponsive in situations that should make them sad or happy. For example, a man may show no emotional response when informed that his daughter has cancer. However, this blunting or flattening of emotional expression can conceal inner turmoil, and the person may erupt with angry outbursts.

Sometimes the schizophrenic individual expresses emotions that are inappropriately linked to the situation or to the thought being expressed. For example, a patient may smile while speaking of tragic events. Since our emotions are influenced by cognitive processes, it is not surprising that disorganized thoughts and perceptions are accompanied by changes in emotional responses.

> Half the time I am talking about one thing and thinking about half a dozen other things at the same time. It must look queer to people when I laugh about something that has got nothing to do with what I am talking about, but they don't know what's going on inside and how much of it is running around in my head. You see I might be talking about something quiet serious to you and other things come into my head at the same time that are funny and this makes me laugh. If I could only concentrate on one thing at the one time I wouldn't look half so silly. (McGhie and Chapman, 1961, p. 104.)

WITHDRAWAL FROM REALITY   During schizophrenic episodes, the individual tends to withdraw from interaction with others and become absorbed in his or her own inner thoughts and fantasies. This state of self-absorption is known as *autism* (from the Greek word *autos*, meaning "self"). As the preceding quotation suggests, inappropriate emotional behavior can sometimes be explained by the fact that the person may be reacting to what is going on in his or her private world rather than to external events. Self-absorption may be so intense that the person may not know the day or month or where he or she is.

Figure 15-9
Perceptual Fragmentation
This drawing by a schizophrenic woman shows the difficulty she has perceiving the face as a whole. (Arieti, 1974)

In acute cases of schizophrenia, withdrawal from reality is temporary. In chronic cases, withdrawal may become more enduring and progress to the point that the individual is completely unresponsive to external events, remains silent and immobile for days, and must be cared for like an infant.

DELUSIONS AND HALLUCINATIONS During the acute stage of schizophrenia, distorted thought processes and perceptions are accompanied by delusions. The most common delusions are beliefs that external forces are trying to control the individual's thought and actions. These *delusions of influence* include the belief that one's thoughts are being broadcast to the world so that others can hear them, that strange thoughts (not one's own) are being inserted into the individual's mind, or that feelings and actions are being imposed on the person by some external force. Also frequent are beliefs that certain people or groups are threatening or plotting against the individual (*delusions of persecution*). Less common are beliefs that the person is powerful and important (*delusions of grandeur*).

A person with persecutory delusions is called *paranoid*. He or she may become suspicious of friends and relatives, fear being poisoned, or complain of being watched, followed, and talked about. So-called "motiveless" crimes, when an individual attacks or kills someone for no apparent cause, are sometimes committed by people who are later diagnosed as suffering from paranoid schizophrenia.

Hallucinations may occur independently or as part of a delusional belief. Auditory hallucinations–usually voices telling the person what to do or commenting on his or her actions—are the most common. Visual hallucinations—for example, seeing strange creatures or heavenly beings—are somewhat less frequent. Other sensory hallucinations (a bad odor emanating from the individual's body, the taste of poison in food, the feeling of being touched or pricked by needles) occur infrequently. Mark Vonnegut, in writing about his own schizophrenic experience, describes his first visual hallucination.

Rigidly held position characteristic of some schizophrenic patients

And then one night, as I was trying to get to sleep, I started listening to and feeling my heart beat. Suddenly I became terribly frightened that it would stop. And from out of nowhere came an incredibly wrinkled, iridescent face. Starting as a small point infinitely distant, it rushed forward, becoming infinitely huge. I could see nothing else. My heart had stopped. The moment stretched forever. I tried to make the face go away, but it mocked me. I had somehow gained control over my heartbeat, but I didn't know how to use it. I was holding my life in my hands and was powerless to stop it from dripping through my fingers. I tried to look the face in the eyes and realized I had left all familiar ground.

He, she, or whatever seemed not to like me much. But the worst of it was it didn't stop coming. It had no respect for my personal space, no inclination to maintain a conversational distance. When I could easily make out all its features, when it and I were more or less on the same scale, when I thought there was maybe a foot or two between us, it had actually been hundreds of miles away, and it kept coming and coming till I was lost somewhere in some pore in its nose and it still kept coming.

There was nothing at all unreal about that face. Its concreteness made the Rock of Gibraltar look like so much cotton candy. I hoped I could get enough rest simply by lying motionless. In any event, the prospect of not sleeping frightened me far less than the possibility of losing contact with the world. (Vonnegut, 1975, pp. 96–98)

The signs of schizophrenia are many and varied. Trying to make sense out of the variety of symptoms is complicated by the fact that some may result directly from the disorder, while others may result from a reaction to the restrictive and often boring life in a mental hospital or from the effects of medication.

Understanding schizophrenia

More research has been devoted to trying to understand the nature of schizophrenia than to any other mental disorder. In an attempt to explain the disturbances in communication and perception that often characterize the schizophrenic state, some investigators have studied the cognitive functioning of people diagnosed as schizophrenic—the way they selectively attend to stimuli, store information in memory, and use language. Others have looked at the ways in which schizophrenic individuals differ biologically from other people in terms of their genetic inheritance, the functioning of their nervous system, and their brain biochemistry. Still others have examined the effects of such environmental factors as social class, family interaction, and stressful life events on schizophrenia. (For a review of the research, see Neale and Oltmanns, 1980.)

Despite a voluminous body of research, the causes of schizophrenia are still not well understood. Nevertheless, some areas of research are promising, and we will consider three of them here.

GENETIC FACTORS   We will discuss genetic factors first because it is becoming increasingly evident that there is a hereditary predisposition toward developing schizophrenia. Family studies show that relatives of schizophrenics are more likely to develop the disorder than people from families free of schizophrenia. And monozygotic (MZ) twins are *both* more apt to turn out to be schizophrenic than dizygotic (DZ) twins. As Table 15-3 indicates, the concordance rate is higher for MZ than for DZ twins.

Even if the MZ twin of a schizophrenic is not diagnosed as schizophrenic, there is a high probability that he or she will be abnormal in certain respects. A review of a number of studies suggests that only about 13 percent of the MZ twins of schizophrenics can be regarded as normal (Heston, 1970). The pres-

Table 15-3
Schizophrenia in Twins
The number of twin pairs varied from 19 MZ and 13 DZ in the Essen–Moller study to 174 MZ and 296 DZ in the Kallmann study. The concordance rate is the percentage of pairs in which both twins are diagnosed as schizophrenic. The later studies, reported in the lower half of the table, employed a more carefully controlled method of diagnosing schizophrenia, which probably accounts for their slightly lower rates for MZ twins. (After Gottesman and Shields, 1973, 1982)

INVESTIGATOR	COUNTRY	CONCORDANCE RATE	
		MZ TWINS	DZ TWINS (SAME SEX)
Early studies			
Luxenburger (1928)	Germany	58	0
Rosanoff and others (1934)	United States	61	13
Essen–Moller (1941)	Sweden	64	15
Kallmann (1946)	United States	69	11
Slater (1953)	United Kingdom	65	14
Inouye (1961)	Japan	59	15
Later studies			
Kringlen (1967)	Norway	45	15
Fischer and others (1969)	Denmark	56	27
Tienari (1971)	Finland	35	13
Pollin and others (1972)	United States	43	9
Gottesman and Shields (1972)	United Kingdom	58	12

RELATIONSHIP	SCHIZOPHRENIA	SCHIZOIDIA	TOTAL
Relatives of schizophrenics			
Children	16.4	32.6	49.0
Siblings	14.3	31.5	45.8
Parents	9.2	34.8	44.0
Both parents schizophrenic			
Children	33.9	32.2	66.1

Table 15-4
Relatives of Schizophrenics
Who Are Schizophrenic or Schizoid
The table shows the percentages of schizophrenia and schizophrenic-like traits among (1) relatives of schizophrenics and (2) children with two schizophrenic parents. (After Heston, 1970)

ence of schizophrenic-like disabilities among relatives of schizophrenics is so striking that the term *schizoid* has been coined to refer to individuals who exhibit many schizophrenic traits but whose symptoms are not severe enough to warrant the diagnosis of schizophrenia. When the presence of both schizophrenia and schizoidia in families is studied, the evidence of a genetic basis is even more striking, as shown in Table 15-4.

It can be argued, of course, that the clustering of schizophrenia and schizoidia in families may result solely from environmental factors. The schizophrenic parent may transmit the disorder to the offspring by means of faulty child-rearing practices rather than faulty genes. However, a study of children born to schizophrenic mothers but separated from their parents shortly after birth and raised in foster homes provides additional support for a genetic hypothesis. These individuals were assessed in adulthood and compared with a control group born to normal parents and reared in foster homes. The incidence of schizophrenia and schizoidia was much higher among those individuals whose biological mothers were schizophrenic (Heston, 1970). In the reverse situation, evidence indicates that the chances for developing schizophrenia do not increase when children born to normal parents are raised by a schizophrenic foster parent, although the number of such cases is fairly small (Wender and others, 1974).

Although the evidence favors a hereditary factor in the development of schizophrenia, we do not know how this susceptibility is transmitted. And it is clear that environmental factors play a significant role. If the disorder depended solely on heredity, MZ twins would exhibit a 100 percent concordance rate.

BIOCHEMICAL FACTORS The genetic component of schizophrenia may manifest itself through some sort of defect or imbalance in body chemistry. Investigators concerned with this possibility have searched for products in the blood or urine of people suffering from schizophrenia that distinguish them from normal individuals. A number of differences have been found, and each has been viewed as a possible "breakthrough" in understanding the cause of schizophrenia. Unfortunately, many of these discoveries have not been consistently replicated or have been found to be related to some condition of the schizophrenic individual other than his or her disorder. For example, one study found that schizophrenics had increased levels of a chemical called ceruloplasmin in their blood (Akerfeldt, 1957). But subsequent studies showed that this chemical imbalance was due to a deficiency of vitamin C—the result of poor appetite and/or poor hospital diet.

This example illustrates one of the major problems in the search for a causal explanation of schizophrenia. An abnormality found in schizophrenic patients but not in control subjects may be the *cause* of the disorder or the *result* of the disorder, or it may stem from some *aspect of treatment*. For example, a

"There are several reasons for your problem: environmental stress, early childhood experience, chemical imbalance, and, primarily, the fact that both of your parents are as cuckoo as a Bavarian clock."

schizophrenic's first admission to a hospital is often preceded by weeks of intense panic and agitation that undoubtedly produce a number of bodily changes. These changes—related to lack of sleep, inadequate diet, and general stress—cannot be considered the cause of the disorder. Other biochemical abnormalities may be related to treatment. Most schizophrenic patients take antipsychotic drugs, traces of which may remain in the blood for some time. Some of the conditions of prolonged hospitalization, such as a change in diet and inactivity, may also produce biochemical changes.

All of these factors compound the problem of finding differences between schizophrenic and control subjects that tell us something about the origin of schizophrenia. Despite such obstacles, there are several promising biochemical theories of schizophrenia, all related to an abnormality in the metabolism of neurotransmitters.

Biochemical theories of affective disorders have focused on norepinephrine and serotonin, but research on schizophrenia has centered on *dopamine*—a neurotransmitter active in an area of the brain believed to be involved in the regulation of emotion (the limbic system). A number of drugs developed in recent years have proved to be highly effective in relieving the symptoms of schizophrenia. These *antipsychotic* (or *neuroleptic*) *drugs* have been shown to block dopamine receptors in the brain, and the therapeutic effectiveness of a particular drug closely parallels its potency in blocking dopamine receptors (Creese, Burt, and Snyder, 1978). These facts suggest an abnormality in dopamine metabolism may be the underlying cause of schizophrenia. Further evidence is derived from observations of the effects of amphetamines, or "speed," which are known to increase the release of dopamine. Drug users who overdose on amphetamines exhibit psychotic behavior that closely resembles paranoid schizophrenia, and their symptoms can be relieved by the same antipsychotic drugs used to treat schizophrenia. When low doses of amphetamines are given to schizophrenic patients, their symptoms become much worse. In these cases, the drug does not produce a psychosis of its own; rather, it exacerbates whatever symptoms the patient may be experiencing (Snyder, 1980).

Thus, enhancing the actions of dopamine aggravates schizophrenic symptoms, and blocking dopamine receptors alleviates them. The exact way in which the dopamine metabolisms of schizophrenics and normal individuals differ is not known; several complex theories are currently being investigated. (For a review, see Neale and Oltmanns, 1980.)

A large number of chemicals serve as neurotransmitters, and schizophrenia is probably influenced by the complex interaction of several of them. We need to know more about how these neurotransmitters influence behavior, how they are affected by stress, and how they interact with each other before we will have a clear understanding of the biochemical nature of schizophrenia. However, even if an inherited predisposition to certain biochemical abnormalities can be demonstrated, psychological factors will probably determine whether the individual actually develops schizophrenia.

SOCIAL AND PSYCHOLOGICAL FACTORS   Numerous studies in the United States and other countries have revealed that the incidence of schizophrenia is significantly higher among the lower classes than among the middle and upper classes (see Dohrenwend, 1973; Strauss, 1982). No one knows why social class is related to schizophrenia, but several explanations have been suggested.

1   *Differential diagnosis.*   Therapists are reluctant to apply the label schizophrenia to higher-income patients because it could have a damaging effect on their clients' careers.

2   *Downward drift.*   Because their coping skills are poor, individuals who suffer
    from schizophrenia have difficulty completing their education and getting a
    decent job. They gradually drift downward in society and become part of the
    lower class.

3   *Increased stress.*   Living under conditions of poverty in areas with high crime
    rates, rundown housing, and inadequate schools creates enough additional
    stress to precipitate schizophrenic disorders, particularly in individuals who
    are genetically predisposed to schizophrenia.

There is evidence that all of these explanations, especially the last two, may be
true (Kosa and Zola, 1975; Brenner, 1982; Fried, 1982).

Research on the role of psychological factors in the origins of schizophrenia
has focused on parent-child relationships and patterns of communication
within the family. Studies of the families of schizophrenic patients have
identified two types of family relationships that seem to contribute to the
disorder. In one type, the parents are sharply divided and unwilling to cooperate in the pursuit of mutual goals; each devalues and tries to dominate the other
and competes for the children's loyalty. In the second type, there is no open
strife; the dominant parent shows serious psychopathology that the other parent passively accepts as normal (Lidz, 1973). Both family types include parents
who are peculiar, immature, and who use their children to fulfill their own
needs, and both are apt to produce children who feel confused, rejected, and
uncertain about people's true feelings. In a sense, the children grow up learning
to accept their parents' distortions of reality as normal.

Although it seems reasonable to assume that such unhealthy family relationships can produce schizophrenia, two questions still remain. Why don't
all of the children in such a family become schizophrenic? Might not families
without schizophrenic offspring also exhibit highly deviant characteristics if
they were studied closely?

Observations of interactions in schizophrenic families suggest that problems in communication constitute an important part of the parents' deviance.
They often seem unable to focus their attention and to communicate a coherent
message to their listener. Their conversation is therefore disjointed and confused, as the following example illustrates (Singer and Wynne, 1965).

DAUGHTER (the patient), *complainingly:* Nobody will listen to me. Everybody is
        trying to still me.
MOTHER: Nobody wants to kill you.
FATHER: If you're going to associate with intellectual people, you're going to
        have to remember that *still* is a noun and not a verb.

The members of this family are clearly not talking to each other in a meaningful
way; each is following his or her own idiosyncratic train of thought. After
several conversations like this, a normal person might end up with a thought
disorder!

Laboratory studies in which schizophrenic patients and their parents are
videotaped while they try to solve a problem together indicate that these families do have trouble focusing their attention, compared to other family groups
(Wild, Shapiro, and Goldenberg, 1975). However, it is possible that the communication difficulties do not originate with the parents but result from their
attempts to cope with a disturbed child. One study suggests that this may be
the case. The experimenter asked parents and sons, working separately, to
describe specific objects so that someone listening to their descriptions could
identify the objects without seeing them. The descriptions were tape-recorded
and played for others in the experiment, including normal and schizophrenic

sons and their normal parents. The investigator found that the parents of schizophrenic sons did not differ from the parents of normal sons in their ability to communicate ideas. The poorest communicators were the schizophrenic sons (Liem, 1974).

Despite the difficulties of establishing cause and effect, disturbed home life and early trauma are frequently found in the background of schizophrenics. The early death of one or both parents, the influence of emotionally disturbed parents whose behavior is irrational and inconsistent, and an atmosphere of discord and strife between parents are all factors found with much greater than average frequency in the backgrounds of people who develop schizophrenia.

Research efforts have failed to reveal any single pattern of family inter-action that leads to schizophrenia; stressful childhoods of various kinds may contribute to the disorder. In general, the more stressful the childhood, the more severe the schizophrenic disorder (Rosenthal and others, 1975).

INTERACTION AMONG FACTORS   Most individuals who live in poverty or who experience a disturbing and stressful childhood do *not* develop schizo-phrenia (although they may develop other psychological disorders). Some individuals who are eventually labeled "schizophrenic" may begin life with a hereditary predisposition to the disorder—probably in the form of a defect in the metabolism of certain neurotransmitters. But it seems unlikely that heredity alone can account for schizophrenia. Undoubtedly, genetic predisposition and environmental stress interact to produce the disorder. The situation may be similar to the development of allergies: there is an inherited predisposition to allergic sensitivities, but certain environmental events are necessary to trigger the reaction. The controversial issue is whether schizophrenia can result from a stressful childhood in the absence of an inherited predisposition for the disorder. Advocates of an extreme hereditary viewpoint maintain that all indi-viduals who have an inherited predisposition will eventually become schizo-phrenic, regardless of the nature of the early family environment. A stressful childhood will lead to an early and more severe illness. Children raised in a favorable family environment will not develop the disorder until they encoun-ter stress later in life; their illness will be less severe and more easily reversible.

Currently, a number of longitudinal studies are being conducted with children who have been identified as having a "high risk" of developing schizophrenia. The studies follow the children from their early years to adult-hood in an attempt to pinpoint some of the factors that determine whether or not the disorder will develop. In some of these studies, the children are consid-ered "high risk" because they have at least one schizophrenic parent (see Mednick and Schulsinger, 1968; Mednick, 1973). Other investigators have se-lected their "high risk" group on the basis of psychophysiological measures or behavioral characteristics they believe to be precursors of psychopathology (see Garmezy, 1974).

The high-risk subjects are usually matched with a control group of children who have no family background of mental illness and who show no early signs of psychopathology. The development of both groups is carefully monitored through periodic testing and interviews with parents, teachers, and peers. Once a high-risk subject has a schizophrenic breakdown, he or she is matched with a subject from the high-risk group who has remained well and with a well member of the control group.

Because most of these studies are still in progress, the data available at present consist mainly of comparisons between high-risk and low-risk groups. These data indicate that the high-risk child performs similarly to an adult schizophrenic in many ways. For example, high-risk children are rated low in social competence and tend to perform poorly on tasks that require sustained attention or abstract thinking.

Preliminary data on high-risk subjects who later developed schizophrenia indicate that they differ from the high-risk subjects who remained well in the following ways.

1 They were more apt to have experienced birth complications that may have affected the functioning of their nervous system.
2 They were separated from their mother at an earlier age (usually because the mother was hospitalized for schizophrenia).
3 Their fathers were more likely to have been hospitalized, with diagnoses ranging from alcoholism to schizophrenia.
4 Their teachers noted that they were more often disruptive in the classroom and took longer to recover from emotional upsets.

When more data from these ongoing high-risk studies become available, we should have a better understanding of how innate and environmental factors interact to produce schizophrenia.

PERSONALITY DISORDERS

Personality disorders are longstanding patterns of maladaptive behavior. In Chapter 13, we described *personality traits* as enduring ways of perceiving or relating to the environment or thinking about oneself. When personality traits become inflexible and maladaptive, so that they significantly impair the individual's ability to function, they are personality disorders. Personality disorders constitute immature and inappropriate ways of coping with stress or solving problems. They are usually evident by early adolescence and may continue throughout adult life.

Unlike people with affective or anxiety disorders, which also involve maladaptive behavior, people with personality disorders usually do not feel very upset or anxious and are not motivated to change their behavior. They do not lose contact with reality or display marked disorganization of behavior, unlike individuals with schizophrenic disorders.

DSM-III lists 12 personality disorders. For example, someone with a *narcissistic personality disorder* is described as having an inflated sense of self-importance, being preoccupied with fantasies of success, constantly seeking admiration and attention, and being insensitive to the needs of others and often exploiting them. *Dependent personality disorders* are characterized by a passive orientation to life, an inability to make decisions or accept responsibility, a tendency to be self-deprecating, and a need for continual support from others.

Most of the personality disorders listed in DSM-III have not been the subject of much research. Moreover, the characteristics of the various personality disorders overlap, so that agreement in classifying individuals is poor. The personality disorder that has been studied the most and is the most reliably diagnosed is the *antisocial personality*.

Antisocial personality

People with antisocial personalities (also called *psychopathic personalities*) seem to have little sense of responsibility, morality, or concern for others. Their behavior is determined almost entirely by their own needs. In other words, they lack a *conscience*. Whereas the average person realizes at an early age that some restrictions are placed on behavior and that pleasures must sometimes be postponed in consideration of the needs of others, people with antisocial personalities seldom consider any desires except their own. They behave impulsively, seek immediate gratification of their needs, and cannot tolerate frustration.

The term "antisocial personality" is somewhat misleading, because these characteristics do not describe most people who commit antisocial acts. Antisocial *behavior* results from a number of causes, including membership in a delinquent gang or a criminal subculture, the need for attention and status, loss of contact with reality, and an inability to control impulses. And most juvenile delinquents and adult criminals have some concern for others (for family or gang members) and some code of moral conduct (you don't squeal on a friend). In contrast, antisocial *personalities* have little feeling for anyone except themselves and seem to experience little guilt or remorse, no matter how much suffering their behavior may cause others.

Other characteristics of the antisocial personality include a great facility for lying, a need for thrills and excitement with little concern for possible injury, and an inability to alter behavior as a consequence of punishment. Such individuals are often attractive, intelligent, charming people who are quite facile in manipulating others—in other words, good "con artists." Their facade of competence and sincerity wins them promising jobs, but they have little staying power. Their restlessness and impulsivity soon lead them into an escapade that reveals their true nature; they accumulate debts, desert their families, squander company money, or commit crimes. When caught, their declarations of repentance are so convincing that they often escape punishment and are given another chance. But they seldom live up to such expectations; what they say has little relation to what they feel or do (see Figure 15-10).

The two most diagnostic characteristics of an antisocial personality disorder are considered to be "lovelessness" (the inability to feel any empathy for, or loyalty to, another person) and "guiltlessness" (the inability to feel any remorse for one's action, no matter how reprehensible it is).

Understanding antisocial personalities

What factors contribute to the development of the antisocial personality? We might expect individuals with such personalities to have been raised by parents who provided no discipline or moral training, but the answer is not that simple. Although some antisocial individuals come from environments in which antisocial behavior is reinforced and adult criminals serve as models for personality development, many more come from "good" homes and were raised by parents who are prominent and respected members of the community.

As yet, there is no well-supported theory to explain why antisocial personalities develop; many factors are probably involved and may vary from case to case. Current research focuses on biological determinants and on the quality of the parent-child relationship.

BIOLOGICAL FACTORS   The clinical impression that the antisocial individual experiences little anxiety about future discomforts or punishments has been supported by experimental studies. One study compared two groups of adolescent male delinquents selected from the detention unit of a juvenile court. One group had been diagnosed "antisocial personality disorders"; the other, "adjustment reactions of adolescence." The experimenters tested galvanic skin

Figure 15-10
Antisocial Personality

A 40-year-old man was convicted of check forgery and embezzlement. He was arrested with a young woman, age 18, whom he had married bigamously some months before. She was unaware of the existence of any previous marriage. The subject in this case had already been convicted for two previous bigamous marriages and for 40 other cases of passing fraudulent checks.

The circumstances of his arrest illustrate the impulsivity and lack of insight characteristic of many antisocial personalities. He had gotten a job managing a small restaurant; the absentee owner, who lived in a neighboring town, had arranged to stop by at the end of each week to check on progress and to collect the income. The subject was provided with living quarters over the restaurant, a small salary, and a percentage of the cash register receipts. At the end of the first week, the subject took all the money (he had failed to bank it nightly as he had been instructed) and departed shortly before the employer arrived; he left a series of vulgar messages scribbled on the walls saying he had taken the money because the salary was "too low." He found lodgings with "his wife" a few blocks from the restaurant and made no effort to escape detection. He was arrested a few days later.

During the inquiry, it emerged that the subject had spent the past few months cashing checks in department stores in various cities. He would make out the check and send his wife in to cash it; he commented that her genuine innocence of the fact that he had no bank account made her very effective in not arousing suspicion. He had not bothered to use a false name when he signed the checks or the bigamous marriage contract, but he seemed surprised that the police discovered him so quickly.

Inquiry into the subject's past history revealed that he had been educated (mostly in private schools) and that his parents were financially well to do. They had planned for him to go to college, but his academic record was not good enough (although on examination he proved to have superior intelligence). Failing to get into college, he started work as an insurance salesman trainee and did very well. He was a distinguished-looking young man and an exceptionally fluent speaker.

Just as it appeared that he could anticipate a successful career in the insurance business, he ran into trouble because he failed to turn in the checks that customers had given him to pay their initial premiums. He admitted to having cashed these checks and spending the money (mostly on clothes and liquor). It apparently did not occur to

him that the company's accounting system would quickly discern this type of embezzlement. In fact, he expressed amused indignation at the company's failure to realize that he intended to pay back the money from his salary. No legal action was taken, but he was requested to resign; his parents reimbursed the company for the missing money.

At this point, the subject enlisted in the Army and was sent to Officer Candidate School, from which he graduated as a second lieutenant. He was assigned to an infantry unit, where he soon got into trouble that progressed from minor infractions (drunk on duty, smuggling women into his quarters) to cashing fraudulent checks. He was court-martialed and given a dishonorable discharge. From then on, his life followed a pattern of finding a woman to support him (with or without marriage) and then running off with her money to the next woman when life became too tedious.

At his trial, where he was sentenced fo five years in prison, he gave a long and articulate speech, pleading clemency for the young woman who was being tried with him, expressing repentance for having ruined her life, and stating that he was glad to have the opportunity to repay society for his crimes. (Maher, 1966, pp. 214–15)

response (GSR, see page 197) under stress. Dummy electrodes were attached to each subject's leg, and he was told that in 10 minutes, he would be given a very strong but not harmful shock. (A large clock was visible so that the subject knew precisely when the shock was supposed to occur; no shock was actually administered.) The two groups showed no difference in GSR measures during periods of rest or in response to auditory or visual stimulation. However, during the 10 minutes of shock anticipation, the "maladjusted" group showed signficantly more tension than the antisocial group. At the moment when the clock indicated the shock was due, most of the maladjusted subjects exhibited an abrupt drop in skin resistance (indicating a sharp increase in anxiety); *none* of the antisocial subjects showed this reaction (Lippert and Senter, 1966).

Other studies in prisons have shown that compared to other prisoners, antisocial personalities do not learn to avoid shocks as quickly and do not exhibit as much autonomic nervous system activity under a variety of condi-

How should the law treat a mentally disturbed person who commits a criminal offense? Should individuals whose mental faculties are impaired be held responsible for their actions? These questions are of concern to social scientists, to members of the legal profession, and to individuals who work with criminal offenders.

Over the centuries, an important part of Western law has been the concept that a civilized society should not punish a person who is mentally incapable of controlling his or her conduct. In 1724, an English court maintained that a man was not responsible for an act if "he doth not know what he is doing, no more than . . . a wild beast." Modern standards of legal responsibility, however, have been based on the M'Naghten decision of 1843. M'Naghten, a Scotsman, suffered the paranoid delusion that he was being persecuted by the English prime minister, Sir Robert Peel. In an attempt to kill Peel, he mistakenly shot Peel's secretary. Everyone involved in the trial was convinced by M'Naghten's senseless ramblings that he was insane. He was judged not responsible by reason of insanity and sent to a mental hospital, where he remained until his death. But Queen Victoria was not pleased with the verdict—apparently she felt that political assassinations should not be taken lightly—and called on the House of Lords to review the decision. The deci-

sion was upheld, and rules for the legal definition of insanity were put into writing. The M'Naghten Rule states that a defendant may be found "not guilty by reason of insanity" only if he were so severely disturbed at the time of his act that he did not know what he was doing or if he did know what he was doing, did not know that it was wrong.

The M'Naghten Rule was adopted in the United States, and the distinction of knowing right from wrong remained the basis of most decisions of legal insanity for over a century. Some states added to their statutes the doctrine of "irresistible impulse," which recognizes that some mentally ill individuals may respond correctly when asked if a particular act is morally right or wrong but be unable to control their behavior.

During the 1970s, a number of state and federal courts adopted a broader legal definition of insanity proposed by the American Law Institute, which states: "A person is not responsible for criminal conduct if at the time of such conduct, as a result of mental disease or defect, he lacks substantial capacity either to appreciate the wrongfulness of his conduct or to conform his conduct to the requirements of the law." The word *substantial* suggests that "any" incapacity is not enough to avoid criminal responsibility but that "total" incapacity is not required either. The use of the word *appreciate* rather than *know* implies that intellectual awareness of right or wrong

is not enough; individuals must have some understanding of the moral or legal consequences of their behavior before they can be held criminally responsible.

The problem of legal responsibility in the case of mentally disordered individuals is currently a topic of intense debate, and a number of legal and mental health professionals have recommended abolishing the insanity plea as a defense. The reasons for this recommendation are varied. Many experts believe that the current courtroom procedures—in which psychiatrists and psychologists for the prosecution and the defense present contradictory evidence as to the defendant's mental state—is confusing to the jury and does little to help the cause of justice. Some also argue that the abuse of the insanity plea by clever lawyers has allowed too many criminals to escape conviction. Others claim that acquittal by reason of insanity often leads to a worse punishment (an *indeterminate* sentence to an institution for the criminally insane that may confine a person for life) than being convicted and sent to prison (with the possibility of parole in a few years).

One proposed change is to replace the verdict "not guilty by reason of insanity" with a new verdict "guilty but mentally ill." Several states have made this change. The person subjected to this verdict would be given psychotherapeutic treatment in jail or would be

tions (Lykken, 1957; Hare, 1970). These findings have led to the hypothesis that antisocial individuals may have been born with an *underreactive autonomic nervous system*; this deficiency would explain why they seem to require so much excitement and why they fail to respond normally to threats of danger that deter most people from antisocial acts. Interpretations must be made with caution, however. It is possible that antisocial personalities may view an experimental situation as a game and may try to play it "extra cool" by attempting to control their responses.

PARENTAL INFLUENCES According to psychoanalytic theory, the development of a conscience, or superego, depends on an affectionate relationship

Insanity as a Legal Defense

treated in a mental hospital and returned to jail when he or she was deemed mentally fit to complete the sentence. The problem remains as to whether treatment in either place would be sufficient to rehabilitate the individual.

Despite the current controversy, actual cases of acquittal by reason of insanity are quite rare. Jurors seem reluctant to believe that people are not morally responsible for their acts, and lawyers, knowing that an insanity plea is apt to fail, tend to use it only as a last resort. In California in 1980, only 259 defendants (out of approximately 52,000) were successful in pleading not guilty by reason of insanity.

The question of mental disorder exerts its greatest impact earlier in the legal process. Many people who are "mentally ill" never come to trial. In the United States, the law requires that the defendant be *competent to stand trial* (*Pate v. Robinson*, 1966). An individual is judged competent to stand trial if he or she is able (1) to understand the charges and (2) to cooperate with a lawyer in preparing a defense. The competency issue is basic to the American ideal of a fair trial and is quite separate from the question of whether the person was "insane" at the time the crime was committed. In a preliminary hearing, the judge receives evidence about the accused's mental competency. The judge may drop the charges and commit the individual to a psychiatric facility (if the crime is not serious) or commit the accused and file the charges until she or he is deemed competent to stand trial. Because court calendars are congested and trials are expensive, judges often prefer to deal with mentally disturbed defendants in this way, particularly if they believe that the psychiatric hospital will provide adequate treatment and secure confinement.

Many more persons are confined to mental institutions because they are found incompetent to stand trial than because they are found not guilty by reason of insanity. These people, many of whom are not dangerous, often are confined longer than they would have been if they had been convicted of the crime in question. Indeed, before the widespread use of antipsychotic drugs, individuals deemed incompetent to stand trial were often committed to mental institutions for life. However, in 1972, the Supreme Court ruled that defendants found incompetent to stand trial due to mental illness could not be held indefinitely. Judges now attempt to bring such individuals to trial or to release them within 18 months. In deciding on release, the seriousness of the crime and the potential for future dangerous behavior are important considerations. Unfortunately, at present, our data for predicting whether an individual is likely to commit a dangerous act are not very reliable. More research is needed in this area.

with an adult during early childhood. Normal children internalize their parents' values (which generally reflect the values of society) because they want to be like their parents and fear the loss of their love if they do not behave in accordance with these values. A child who receives no love from either parent does not fear its loss; he or she does not identify with the rejecting parents and does not internalize their rules. Reasonable as this theory seems, it does not conform to all of the data. Many rejected children do not develop antisocial personalities, and some people who do were indulged in childhood.

According to social learning theory, antisocial behavior is influenced by the kind of models the parents provide and the kind of behavior they reward. A child may develop an antisocial personality if she or he learns that punishment can be avoided by being charming, lovable, and repentant. A child who is consistently able to avoid punishment by claiming to be sorry and promising "never to do it again" may learn that it is not the deed that counts but charm and ability to act repentant. If the same child is indulged in other respects and never has to wait or work for a reward, he or she does not learn to tolerate frustration. Two characteristics of the antisocial personality are a lack of frustration tolerance and the conviction that being charming and appearing contrite excuses wrongdoing. In addition, a child who is always protected from frustration or distress may have no ability to empathize with the distress of others (Maher, 1966).

Undoubtedly, a number of family interaction patterns may foster the development of an antisocial personality. Another interaction pattern implicates parents who are inconsistent in supplying affection, rewards, and punishments; as a consequence, the child lacks clear guidelines for behavior as well as a reliable model on which to base his or her own identity (Buss, 1966).

ALCOHOLISM AND DRUG DEPENDENCE

The past two decades have been referred to as the "drug era." Drugs can prevent conception, calm us when we are nervous, excite us when we are bored, put us to sleep, wake us up, cure us when we are sick, and make us sick when we are well! Alcoholism and drug abuse are major medical and social problems in this country.

The effects of psychoactive drugs on consciousness were discussed in Chapter 6. The major psychoactive drugs that people use and abuse are listed in Table 15-5. With repeated use, an individual can become physically and/or psychologically dependent on any of these drugs. *Physical dependence*, formerly called "addiction," is characterized by *tolerance* (with continued use, the individual must take more and more of the drug to achieve the same effect) and *withdrawal* (if use is discontinued, the person experiences unpleasant physical symptoms). Alcohol, barbiturates, and narcotics can all produce physical dependence.

Psychological dependence refers to a need that develops through learning. People who habitually use a drug to relieve anxiety may become dependent on it, even though no physical need develops. For example, marijuana smokers do not appear to build up tolerance for the drug and experience minimal withdrawal symptoms. Nevertheless, a person who learns to use marijuana when faced with stressful situations will find the habit difficult to break. When some drugs such as alcohol are used, psychological dependence progresses to physical dependence as more and more of the substance is consumed.

Alcoholism

Despite public concern over the increasing use of marijuana and hard drugs, alcohol is still the most widely used and abused drug in this country. It is estimated that some 9 million people in the United States are alcoholics or problem drinkers, and alcohol consumption appears to be steadily increasing. The cost in terms of lost productivity and medical care for alcohol-related illnesses is staggering. Other social consequences include increased crime (homicides and child abuse are both related to alcohol use), family discord, deaths and injuries on the highway, and suicide.

Table 15-5
Psychoactive Drugs That Are Commonly Abused
Only a few examples of each class of drug are given. The generic name (for example, psilocybin) or the brand name (for example, Miltown—meprobramate; Seconal—secobarbital) is used, depending on which is more familiar. The antipsychotics and antidepressants used in the treatment of schizophrenia and affective disorders are not included because they are rarely abused. Also omitted are the volatile hydrocarbons (glue, paint thinner) and the fluorocarbons (aerosol sprays), which can be highly dangerous when sniffed for the psychoactive effects.

CLASSIFICATION	DRUGS	USAGE	TOLERANCE	PHYSICAL DEPENDENCE	PSYCHOLOGICAL DEPENDENCE
Sedatives	Alcohol (ethanol)	Reduce tension; release inhibitions	Yes	Yes	Yes
	Barbiturates Nembutal Seconal	Induce relaxation and sleep	Yes	Yes	Yes
	Mild tranquilizers Miltown Valium	Reduce anxiety and tension	Yes	Yes	Yes
Opiates/Narcotics	Opium and its derivatives Codeine Heroin Morphine	Alleviate physical pain; induce relaxation and pleasant reveries	Yes	Yes	Yes
	Methadone	Treatment of heroin dependence	Yes	Yes	Yes
Stimulants	Amphetamines Benzedrine Dexedrine Methedrine	Increase alertness; decrease fatigue	Yes	Yes—to the extent that withdrawal produces physical and psychological depression	Yes
	Cocaine	Increase alertness; decrease fatigue	Yes		Yes
	Nicotine	Increase alertness	Slight	Possibly	Yes
	Caffeine	Increase alertness	Slight	No	Yes
Hallucinogens	LSD*	"Expand the mind" and produce changes in perception, thought, and mood	Yes	No	Only for a minority of users
	Mescaline*		Yes	No	
	Psilocybin*		Yes	No	
	Phencyclidine (PCP)†		?	?	?
	Marijuana		No	No	Only for heavy users

*LSD, mescaline, and psilocybin all show "cross-tolerance"; for example, a person who takes LSD will develop an increased tolerance for mescaline; similarly, a user of psilocybin will require more mescaline or LSD to achieve the same effects.
†PCP is a synthetic drug that was used as a surgical anaesthetic until severe psychotic-like reactions were noted among a number of patients. In large doses, PCP can produce prolonged coma and sometimes death. What is sold on the streets as THC (the active ingredient in marijuana) is frequently PCP, and consequently is highly dangerous.

VARIETIES OF ALCOHOLISM The stereotype of an alcoholic—the skid-row drunk—constitutes only a small proportion of the individuals who have serious drinking problems. The depressed housewife who takes a few drinks to get through the day and a few more to gear up for a social evening, the businessman who needs a three-martini lunch to make it through the afternoon, the overworked physician who keeps a bottle in her desk drawer, and the high-school student who drinks more and more to gain acceptance from peers are all on their way to becoming alcoholics. There are various definitions of alcoholism, but almost all of them include the *inability to abstain* (the feeling that you cannot get through the day without a drink) and/or a *lack of control* (an

Figure 15-11
Signs of Alcoholism
Questions developed by the National Institute on Alcohol Abuse and Alcoholism to help people determine whether they have a drinking problem.

The sooner you recognize a drinking problem in yourself, the easier it is to get out from under it. Below are some questions that will help you learn how dependent you are on drinking. This is a time to be absolutely honest with yourself—only *you* can know how seriously you are being hurt by the role alcohol plays in your life.

1 Has someone close to you sometimes expressed concern about your drinking?
2 When faced with a problem, do you often turn to alcohol for relief?
3 Are you sometimes unable to meet home or work responsibilities because of drinking?
4 Have you ever required medical attention as a result of drinking?
5 Have you ever experienced a blackout—a total loss of memory while still awake—when drinking?
6 Have you ever come in conflict with the law in connection with your drinking?
7 Have you often failed to keep the promises you have made to yourself about controlling or cutting out your drinking?

If you have answered yes to any of the above questions, your drinking is probably affecting your life in some major ways and you should do something about it —before it gets worse.

inability to stop after one or two drinks). Figure 15-11 lists some questions formulated by the National Institute on Alcohol Abuse and Alcoholism to help people determine whether they may have a drinking problem.

An individual can progress from social drinking to alcoholism in many ways. One survey of alcoholics describes the following four stages.

1 *Prealcoholic stage.*   Individual drinks socially and on occasion heavily to relieve tension and forget about problems. Heavy drinking becomes more frequent, and in times of crisis, the person resorts more and more to the bolstering effects of alcohol.
2 *Prodromal stage.*   Drinking becomes furtive and may be accompanied by "blackouts," during which the person remains conscious and relatively coherent but later cannot recall events. The individual becomes preoccupied with drinking and feels guilty about it but worries about when and where she or he will have the next drink.
3 *Crucial stage.*   All control is lost; once the person starts drinking, he or she continues until sick or stuporous. Social adjustment deteriorates, and the drinking becomes evident to family, friends, and employers. The person starts drinking in the morning, neglects his or her diet, and may go on the first "bender"—several days of continuous drinking. Abstinence is still possible (the individual may go for several weeks or even months without drinking), but once he or she takes a drink, the whole pattern begins again. This is called the "crucial" stage because unless the individual seeks help, she or he is in danger of becoming a chronic alcoholic.
4 *Chronic stage.*   Drinking is continual; the individual lives only to drink. The body has become so accustomed to alcohol that the person may suffer withdrawal symptoms without it. Malnutrition and alcohol have produced numerous physiological disorders. The person has lost all concern for physical appearance, self-esteem, family, friends, and social status. This is the stage of the skid-row drunk.

Not all elements of these stages have been corroborated. Some alcoholics seldom get drunk but consume enough alcohol each day to maintain a certain level of relaxation, and some never experience blackouts. Nevertheless, the general progression from stage to stage is typical of many alcoholics (Jellinek, 1952).

THEORIES OF ALCOHOLISM   In view of the disastrous consequences, why do people continue to drink? Some evidence suggests a hereditary predisposition. If a monozygotic twin is alcoholic, there is a 60 percent chance that his or her twin will also be alcoholic; the concordance rate for dizygotic twins is only 20 percent (Kaij, 1960).

Further support for a genetic predisposition to alcoholism is derived from studies of children of alcoholic parents who were adopted in infancy and raised by nonalcoholic parents. By their late twenties, almost twice as many of these individuals had alcohol problems as did members of a control group of adopted children whose biological parents were not alcoholic (Goodwin and others, 1973).

Although there appears to be an inherited tendency toward alcoholism, the majority of children born to alcoholic parents do *not* become alcoholic. Until now, research has failed to find any physical basis for alcoholism—any differences between alcoholics and nonalcoholics in the rate at which alcohol is metabolized or in other body functions (except for alterations occurring as the *result* of prolonged alcohol consumption).

The common-sense view and the one initially proposed by learning theorists is that people drink to reduce anxiety. Alcohol is a powerful reinforcer in its ability to alleviate tension, and this immediate effect may outweigh the aversive effects that occur later. If you had a hangover 5 seconds after your first sip of an alcoholic beverage, would you continue drinking?

The theory that an alcoholic drinks to relieve tension is an incomplete explanation, however. It may be one reason why a person *begins* to drink, but it does not account for the continuation of long drinking periods. Careful observations of alcoholics in a specially designed hospital ward showed that anxiety decreases during the first 12- to 24-hour period of drinking but that

Social drinking

Solitary drinking

alcohol actually *increases* levels of tension and anxiety after that point (Nathan and O'Brien, 1971). It may be that due to memory "blackouts" in the chronic stage of alcoholism, the alcoholic forgets the increased anxiety that occurs later (Lisman, 1974).

Clearly, the motives for drinking are not simple, and, considered collectively, they must be strong or drinking would not occur so frequently in cultures that differ so markedly in other respects.

TREATMENT   Regardless of the reasons for starting to drink, once a person becomes psychologically dependent on alcohol, it is difficult to give up. The sooner the individual recognizes that alcohol is seriously interfering with his or her life, the easier it is to correct the problem before the body becomes physiologically dependent on alcohol. Alcoholics Anonymous, a worldwide organization of exalcoholics dedicated to helping others overcome drinking problems, has been helpful in many cases. Behavior-therapy techniques that attempt to change the individual's attitude toward alcohol and to substitute other ways of handling anxiety have also shown some success.

Drug dependence

People apparently use other psychoactive drugs for many of the same reasons that they use alcohol; individuals who use hard drugs also tend to drink heavily and to smoke cigarettes. A longitudinal study of high-school students in New York State indicates the following stages in the sequence of drug usage:

beer/wine → hard liquor → marijuana → other illegal drugs

This does not mean that the use of a particular drug invariably leads to the use of drugs further along in the sequence. Only about 27 percent of those students who drank hard liquor progressed to marijuana, and only 26 percent of the marijuana users went on to try such drugs as LSD, amphetamines, or heroin. The students stopped at different stages of usage, but none of them progressed directly from beer or wine to illegal drugs without drinking liquor first and very few students progressed from liquor to hard drugs without trying marijuana first (Kandel, 1975). Positive experiences with one drug may encourage experimentation with another drug.

This "stepping-stone" theory of drug usage has been criticized because the majority of young people who smoke marijuana do not go on to use other drugs. Nevertheless, heavy use of marijuana does appear to increase the likelihood of using other illegal drugs. A nationwide survey of men 20–30 years of age showed that of those who had smoked marijuana 1,000 times or more (roughly equivalent to daily usage for three years), 73 percent later tried cocaine and 35 percent tried heroin. In contrast, less than 1 percent of the nonsmokers surveyed used these harder drugs. Of those who had used marijuana fewer than 100 times, only 7 percent later tried cocaine and 4 percent tried heroin (O'Donnell and Clayton, 1982). Heavy marijuana smoking does increase the risk of becoming involved with more dangerous drugs.

WHY PEOPLE START USING DRUGS   Many studies have been conducted to determine what personality characteristics and social factors prompt people to use psychoactive drugs. Because some of these studies involved individuals who were already taking drugs, the results must be viewed with caution. For example, heroin addicts have been described as antisocial personalities who

Drug usage can be fatal.

have difficulty relating to other people and who seek to escape responsibility through drugs (Berzins and others, 1974). But we cannot be certain that these characteristics did not *result from* addiction rather than precede it. Nevertheless, the following factors seem important in determining whether a person will try illegal drugs.

1   *Parental influences.*   One finding is that young people who come from unhappy homes, where parents show little interest in their children and inflict harsh physical punishment, are more apt to use drugs than young people who come from happier home environments (Baer and Corrado, 1974). Parental values also play an important role in drug usage. Youths from conservative homes, where traditional social and religious values and the importance of long-range goals are emphasized, are *less* apt to become involved with drugs than youths from more permissive and liberal homes, where "doing your own thing" is encouraged (Blum and others, 1972). Perhaps the most powerful influence is the degree to which parents model drug use. The children of parents who use alcohol, tranquilizers, and other legal drugs freely are likely to sample drugs themselves (Smart and Fejer, 1972).

2   *Peer influences.*   Numerous studies have revealed that the greater variety of drugs a young person tries, the more likely his or her friends are to be users, and vice versa (see Sadave, 1973). This finding is subject to several interpretations, however. Drug-using friends may encourage the youth to experiment with drugs, or the youth may start using drugs and then select friends who are drug users (Johnson, 1973). Both explanations may be true.

3   *Personality factors.*   No single personality "type" is associated with drug use. People try drugs for a variety of reasons—curiosity or the desire to experience a new state of consciousness, escape from physical or mental pain, relief from boredom. However, the one personality trait that *is* predictive of drug usage is social conformity. People who score high on various tests of social conformity (who see themselves as conforming to the traditional values of American society) are less apt to use drugs than those who score low on such tests. The nonconformist may be a "loner" who feels no involvement with other people or a member of a subculture that encourages drug usage.

WHY PEOPLE CONTINUE TO USE DRUGS   These factors may influence initial drug use, but once an individual becomes physically dependent on drugs, the motivation changes radically. The person has acquired a new need that may be so powerful he or she ignores all other concerns and lives only for the next "fix."

Dependence on opiates (narcotics) can develop very quickly. For example, after a person has been smoking or "sniffing" (inhaling) heroin for a while, tolerance builds up and this method of ingestion no longer produces the desired effect. At this point, the individual may progress to "skin popping" (injecting under the skin) and then to "mainlining" (injecting into a vein). Once the user starts mainlining, stronger and stronger doses of heroin are required to produce a "high," and the physical discomforts of withdrawal from the drug become intense (chills and sweating, stomach cramps, vomiting, headaches). In an effort to gain relief, the individual may overdose and die.

Most heroin users who restricted themselves to smoking or "sniffing" are able to give up the habit. Only about 7 percent of all U.S. soldiers who sniffed heroin regularly in Vietnam (where the drug was easily available) continued to use the drug after they returned to this country (Robins, 1974). However, once larger amounts are absorbed into the body through injection, the majority of users become physically dependent, or addicted.

Treatment usually involves helping the individual through the withdrawal period, building up his or her physical condition, and teaching more effective ways of coping. Unfortunately, treatment often fails to relieve the craving for heroin, and many addicts must be maintained on *methadone* (a synthetic opiate that is addictive but produces less psychological impairment than heroin). The recent discovery that the brain has specific receptor sites for opiates may help us to discover how addiction actually occurs and how it may be treated effectively (see Chapter 2, pages 36–37).

Summary

1   The diagnosis of abnormal behavior is based on *statistical frequency, social norms, adaptiveness of behavior,* and *personal distress.* Characteristics indicative of good mental health include an *efficient perception of reality, self-knowledge, control of behavior, self-esteem,* an *ability to form affectionate relationships,* and *productivity.*

2   DSM-III classifies mental disorders according to specific behavioral symptoms. Such a classification system helps to communicate information and provides a basis for research. However, each case is unique, and diagnostic labels should not be used to pigeonhole individuals.

3   Anxiety disorders include *generalized anxiety* (constant worry and tension), *panic disorders* (sudden attacks of overwhelming apprehension), *phobias* (irrational fears of specific objects or situations), and *obsessive-compulsive disorders* (persistent unwanted thoughts, or *obsessions,* combined with urges, or *compulsions,* to perform certain acts). Psychoanalytic theory attributes anxiety disorders to unresolved, unconscious conflicts. Learning theories focus on learned fear responses and feelings of being unable to control life events.

4   *Affective disorders* are disturbances of mood: *depression, mania,* or a cyclical alternation between the two moods, referred to as a *manic-depressive disorder.* Psychoanalytic theories view depression as a *reactivation of the loss of parental affection* in a person who is *dependent on external approval* and tends to *turn anger inward.* Learning theories focus on *reduced positive reinforcement, self-critical attitudes,* and *learned helplessness.* Some affective disorders may be influenced by inherited abnormalities in the metabolism of certain *neurotransmitters* (such as *norepinephrine* and *serotonin*). Inherited predispositions and/or early experiences may make people *vulnerable* to depression when under stress.

5   *Schizophrenia* is primarily a thought disorder characterized by difficulty in "filtering out" irrelevant stimuli, disturbances in perception, inappropriate affect, delusions and hallucinations, and withdrawal. Research on the causes of schizophrenia has focused on evidence for a hereditary disposition to the disorder, possible defects in the metabolism of neurotransmitters (such as *dopamine*), social factors, and deviant family relationships.

6   *Personality disorders* are longstanding patterns of maladaptive behavior that constitute immature and inappropriate ways of coping with stress or solving problems. Individuals classified as having *antisocial personalities* are impulsive, show little guilt, are concerned only with their own needs, and are frequently in trouble with the law. An *underreactive nervous system* and *inconsistent parental rewards and punishments* are two possible explanations for the disorder.

7   The use of alcohol and other psychoactive drugs may lead to *psychological dependence* (compulsive use to reduce anxiety) and *physical dependence* (increased tolerance and withdrawal symptoms). *Alcohol* is the most widely used drug; the *inability to abstain* from drinking or to *stop* after one or two drinks classifies one as an *alcoholic.*

8   A number of factors may predispose people to drug usage, including an *unhappy home life*, parents who are *permissive* or who *model drug use*, *peer influences*, and a *lack of social conformity*. With continued use, *physical dependency* develops, creating a new need that must be satisfied.

General textbooks on abnormal psychology include Coleman, *Abnormal psychology and modern life* (6th ed., 1980); Sarason and Sarason, *Abnormal psychology* (3rd ed., 1980); White and Watt, *The abnormal personality* (5th ed., 1981); and Davison and Neale, *Abnormal psychology* (3rd ed., 1982).

See Tarter and Sugerman (eds.), *Alcoholism* (1976) for a wide range of papers on this topic; and Moore and Gerstein (eds.), *Alcohol and public policy* (1981) for a discussion of prevention. For more on drugs, see Ray, *Drugs, society, and human behavior* (2nd ed., 1978); and Julien, *A primer of drug action* (3rd ed., 1981).

The hereditary aspects of mental illness are reviewed in Plomin, DeFries, and McClearn, *Behavioral genetics: A primer* (1980); and Gottesman and Shields, *Schizophrenia: The epigenetic puzzle* (1982).

The world of psychosis from the patient's viewpoint is graphically described in Kesey, *One flew over the cuckoo's nest* (1962); Green, *I never promised you a rose garden* (1971), and Vonnegut, *The Eden express* (1975).

Further Reading

16
METHODS OF THERAPY

I n this chapter, we will look at methods for treating various types of abnormal behavior. Some of these methods focus on helping individuals gain an understanding of the causes of their problems, some attempt to modify behavior directly, some treat the body, and some specify ways in which the community can help.

The treatment of mental disorders is closely linked to theories about the causes of such disorders. A brief history of the treatment of the mentally ill will illustrate how methods change as theories about human nature and the causes of its disorders change.

HISTORICAL BACKGROUND

According to one of the earliest theories (espoused by the ancient Chinese, Egyptians, and Hebrews), a person with a mental disorder was possessed by evil spirits. These demons were exorcised by such techniques as prayer, incantation, magic, and the use of purgatives concocted from herbs. If these treatments were unsuccessful, more extreme measures were taken to ensure that the body would be an unpleasant dwelling place for the evil spirit. Flogging, starving, burning, and even stoning to death were not infrequent forms of "treatment." Although most cases of possession were considered to be caused by evil spirits, behavior of a mystical or religious nature was believed to result from possession by a good or holy spirit, and people who exhibited such behavior were respected and worshiped. During this period, the mentally ill were treated by priests, who had the power to perform exorcisms.

The first progress in understanding mental disorders was made by the Greek physician Hippocrates (circa 460–377 B.C.), who rejected demonology and maintained that mental disorders were the result of a disturbance in the balance of body fluids. Hippocrates, and the Greek and Roman physicians who followed him, argued for a more humane teatment of the mentally ill. They stressed the

As late as the early nineteenth century, English asylums used rotating devices of this nature, in which patients were whirled around at high speeds.

importance of pleasant surroundings, exercise, proper diet, massage, and soothing baths, as well as some less desirable treatments, such as bleeding, purging, and mechanical restraints. Although there were no institutions for the mentally ill during this period, many individuals were cared for with great kindness by physicians in temples dedicated to the Greek and Roman gods.

This progressive view of mental illness did not continue, however. Primitive superstitions and a belief in demonology were revived during the Middle Ages. The mentally ill were considered to be in league with Satan and to possess supernatural powers with which they could cause floods, pestilence, and injuries to others. Insane individuals were treated cruelly; people believed that by beating, starving, and torturing the mentally ill, they were punishing the devil. This type of cruelty culminated in the witchcraft trials that sentenced to death thousands of people (many of them mentally ill) during the fifteenth, sixteenth, and seventeenth centuries.

Early asylums

In the latter part of the Middle Ages, asylums were created to cope with the mentally ill. These asylums were not treatment centers but simply prisons; the inmates were chained in dark, filthy cells and treated more like animals than human beings. It was not until 1792, when Phillippe Pinel was placed in charge of an asylum in Paris, that some improvements were made in the treatment of these unfortunate people. As an experiment, Pinel was allowed to remove the chains that restrained the inmates. Much to the amazement of skeptics who thought Pinel was mad to unchain such "animals," the experiment was a success. When released from their restraints, placed in clean, sunny rooms, and treated kindly, many people who had been considered hopelessly mad for years improved enough to leave the asylum.

By the beginning of the twentieth century, great advances were being made in the fields of medicine and psychology. In 1905, a mental disorder known as *general paresis* was shown to have a physical cause—a syphilis infection acquired many years before the symptoms of the disorder appeared. General paresis is characterized by a gradual decline in mental and physical functions, marked personality changes, and delusions and hallucinations. Without treatment, death occurs within a few years. The syphilis spirochete remains in the body after the initial genital infection disappears and gradually destroys the nervous system. At one time, general paresis accounted for more

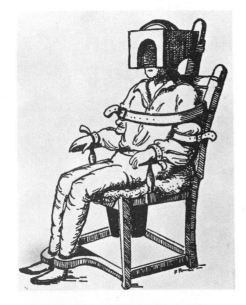

A "tranquilizing chair" used to restrain patients in a Pennsylvania hospital, circa 1800

The "crib"—a restraining device used in a New York mental institution in 1882

than 10 percent of all admissions to mental hospitals, but today few cases are reported due to the effectiveness of penicillin in treating syphilis (Dale, 1975).

The discovery that general paresis was the result of a disease encouraged those who believed that mental illness was biological in origin. At about the same time, Sigmund Freud and his followers laid the groundwork for understanding mental illness in terms of psychological factors, and Pavlov's laboratory experiments demonstrated that animals could become emotionally disturbed if forced to make decisions beyond their capacities.

Despite these scientific advances, the public in the early 1900s still did not understand mental illness and viewed mental hospitals and their inmates with fear and horror. Public education in mental health was begun by Clifford Beers. As a young man, Beers developed a manic-depressive disorder and was confined for three years in several private and state hospitals. Although chains and other methods of torture had been abandoned long before, the straitjacket was still widely used to restrain excited patients. Lack of funds made the average state mental hospital—with its overcrowded wards, poor food, and unsympathetic attendants—a far from pleasant place to live. After his recovery, Beers wrote about his experiences in the now-famous book *A Mind That Found Itself* (1908), which aroused considerable public interest. Beers worked ceaselessly to educate the public about mental illness and helped to organize the National Committee for Mental Hygiene. In 1950, this organization joined with two related groups to form the National Association for Mental Health. The mental hygiene movement played an invaluable role in stimulating the organization of child-guidance clinics and community mental health centers to aid in the prevention as well as the treatment of mental disorders.

Modern treatment facilities

Mental hospitals have been upgraded markedly since the time of Clifford Beers, but there is still much more room for improvement. Most people who require hospitalization for mental disorders are first admitted to the psychiatric ward of a general hospital, where their condition is evaluated. If more than a brief period of hospitalization is indicated, they may be transferred to a public or private mental hospital. The best of these hospitals are comfortable and well-kept places that provide a number of therapeutic activities: individual and group psychotherapy, recreational activities, occupational therapy (designed to teach skills as well as to provide relaxation), and educational courses to help patients prepare for a job on release from the hospital. The worst are primarily custodial institutions where inmates lead a boring existence in rundown, overcrowded wards and receive little treatment except for medication. Most mental hospitals fall somewhere in between these two extremes. Private hospitals, because they have more money, tend to be superior to public hospitals that are funded by the state or the federal government, but their cost is beyond the means of most people.

During the past 20 years, emphasis has shifted from treating mentally disturbed patients in hospitals to treating them within their home community whenever possible. No matter how good the facilities, hospitalization has inherent disadvantages. It cuts the patient off from family and friends, tends to make the individual feel "sick" and unable to cope with the outside world, encourages dependency, and may discourage active problem solving. The Community Mental Health Centers Act of 1963 made federal funds available for the establishment of community treatment centers. These centers provide a number of services, including treatment of emotionally disturbed individuals

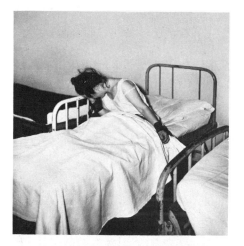

Conditions in a mental hospital in the 1950s

before their condition becomes serious, short-term hospitalization, and partial hospitalization. Partial hospitalization provides greater flexibility than traditional hospitalization; individuals may receive treatment at the center during the day and return home in the evening or may work during the day and spend nights at the center.

Although treating mentally ill people in their home communities is a worthwhile goal, the current trend toward short-term hospitalization has produced some unfortunate consequnces, largely because the facilities in most communities are still inadequate. About 50 percent of all patients who are discharged from state hospitals are readmitted within one year. Many individuals who improve with hospitalization are not adequately cared for after discharge in terms of follow-up therapy or help in finding friends, housing, and a job. Many older patients who are released after years of custodial care are unable to support themselves and live in dirty, overcrowded housing or roam the streets. The disheveled young man standing on the corner talking to himself and occasionally shouting gibberish to passers-by may be one victim of the move toward "deinstitutionalization." The middle-aged woman with all of her worldly possessions piled in a shopping bag, who spends one night in the doorway of an office building and the next in a subway station, may be another. Community mental health centers must have more funds and personnel if they are to care for individuals who suffer from a range of emotional disorders. And society must provide an "asylum" or refuge for those who are unable to care for themselves—be it a mental hospital, community home, or some other residential facility.

Professions involved in psychotherapy

Whether therapy takes place in a hospital, a community mental health center, a private clinic, or an office, several different types of professionals may be involved. A psychiatrist, clinical psychologist, and psychiatric social worker may work together, or independently, on a given case. A *psychiatrist* is a physician who specializes in the diagnosis and treatment of abnormal behavior. The psychiatrist assumes medical responsibility for the patient in addition to playing a psychotherapeutic role. A *psychoanalyst* is a specialist within psychiatry who uses methods and theories derived from Freud. Psychoanalysts have spent several years enrolled in a psychoanalytic institute learning the specific techniques of psychoanalysis and receiving in-depth psychoanalysis themselves. Although a psychoanalyst is usually a psychiatrist, most psychiatrists are not psychoanalysts.

A *clinical psychologist* has a Ph.D. in psychology and has served special internships in the fields of testing and diagnosis, psychotherapy, and research. The clinical psychologist administers and interprets psychological tests, conducts psychotherapy, and is also active in research.

A *counseling psychologist* has earned an M.A. or a Ph.D. and has had similar graduate training to that of the clinical psychologist but usually with less emphasis on research.

A *psychiatric social worker* usually has an M.A. or an M.S. from a graduate school of social work as well as special training in interviewing and in extending treatment procedures to the home and community. The social worker is often called on to collect information about the patient's home and to interview relatives, in addition to participating in therapeutic procedures with the patient.

In mental hospitals, a fourth professional is involved—the *psychiatric nurse.*

"Deinstitutionalization" has unfortunate consequences for individuals who are too mentally disturbed to function outside a protected environment.

Psychiatric nursing is a field within the nursing profession that requires special training in the understanding and treatment of mental disorders.

In our discussion of psychotherapeutic techniques, we will not specify the profession of the psychotherapists; we will assume that they are trained and competent members of any one of these professions.

TECHNIQUES OF PSYCHOTHERAPY

Psychotherapy refers to the treatment of mental disorders by *psychological* (rather than physical or biological) means. The term embraces a variety of techniques, all of which are intended to help emotionally disturbed individuals modify their behavior and feelings so that they can develop more useful ways of dealing with stress and with other people. Some psychotherapists believe that modification of behavior is dependent on the individual's understanding of his or her unconscious motives and conflicts; others feel that people can learn to cope with their problems without necessarily exploring the factors that have led to their development. Despite differences in techniques, most methods of psychotherapy have certain basic features in common. They involve communication between two individuals—the *client* (patient) and the *therapist*. The client is encouraged to express intimate fears, emotions, and experiences freely without fear of being judged or condemned by the therapist. The therapist, in turn offers sympathy and understanding and tries to help the client develop more effective ways of handling his or her problems.

Psychoanalysis

Psychoanalysis is a method of therapy based on Freudian concepts. We discussed Freud's theory of personality in Chapter 13 and the psychoanalytic concept of anxiety as a response to unconscious conflicts in Chapter 14. The goal of psychoanalysis is to make the individual aware of unconscious conflicts and of the defense mechanisms she or he has been using to control anxiety. Once unconscious motives and fears are acknowledged, they can be dealt with in a more rational and realistic way.

In its original form, psychoanalytic therapy was intensive and lengthy. Analyst and client usually met for 50-minute visits several times a week for periods ranging from one to several years. Psychoanalytically oriented therapists currently feel that it is advantageous to limit the length of therapy (giving both client and therapist a fixed time limit within which to work on problems and achieve certain goals) and to schedule sessions less frequently, usually once a week (giving the client time between sessions to think about what was discussed and to examine his or her daily interactions in light of the discussion).

FREE ASSOCIATION One of the main techniques psychoanalysts use to facilitate the recovery of unconscious conflicts is *free association:* the client is encouraged to give free rein to thoughts and feelings and to verbalize whatever comes to mind without editing or censoring. This is not easy to do, however; in conversation, we usually try to keep a connecting thread running through our remarks and exclude irrelevant ideas so that we do not wander too far from the point. In addition, most of us have spent a lifetime learning to be cautious and to think before speaking; passing thoughts that strike us as inappropriate, stupid, or shameful usually remain unspoken.

Caricature of Sigmund Freud using Freudian imagery to analyze a figure of himself lying on a couch

With practice, however, and encouragement from the analyst, free association becomes easier. But even individuals who conscientiously try to give free rein to their thoughts will occasionally find themselves blocked. When a client remains silent, abruptly changes the subject, or is unable to recall the details of an event, the analyst assumes that the person is resisting the recall of certain thoughts or feelings. Freud believed that blocking, or *resistance*, resulted from the individual's unconscious control over sensitive areas and that these were precisely the areas the analyst should explore.

INTERPRETATION The psychoanalyst attempts to overcome the client's resistance and to encourage fuller self-understanding through *interpretation*. The interpretation usually assumes one of two forms. First, the analyst calls attention to the individual's resistances. People often learn something about themselves simply by discovering when a train of associations is suddenly blocked, when they forget an appointment, when they want to change the subject, and so on. Second, the analyst may privately deduce the nature of what lies behind the client's statements and attempt to facilitate further associations. For example, a client may say something that he or she thinks is trivial and half apologize for its unimportance. At this point, the analyst may point out that what seems trivial may allude to something important. If the interpretation is appropriately timed, this hint may lead to significant new associations. It should be noted that the analyst is careful not to suggest *just what it is* that is important; the individual must discover this for himself or herself.

TRANSFERENCE In psychoanalysis, the client's attitudes toward the analyst are considered to be an important part of treatment. Sooner or later, the client develops strong emotional responses to the psychoanalyst. Sometimes the responses are positive and friendly; sometimes, negative and hostile. Often these reactions are inappropriate responses to what is taking place in the therapy sessions. The tendency for the client to make the therapist the object of emotional responses is known as *transference:* the client expresses attitudes toward the analyst that the client actually feels toward other people who are important in his or her life. Freud assumed that transference represented relics of childhood reactions to parents.

The following example illustrates transference. A young woman being treated by a woman psychoanalyst remarked one day as she entered the analyst's office, "I'm glad you're not wearing those lace collars you wore the last several times I was here. I don't like them on you." During the hour, the analyst pointed out that she had never worn a lace collar. Discussions during the preceding sessions had focused on some stressful childhood experiences, and the client, casting the analyst into the mother role, had falsely pictured the analyst as dressing the way her own mother had dressed. Although surprised by her misperception, the client accepted the interpretation, thereby gaining an understanding of transference.

Transference does not always involve false perceptions; often the patient simply expresses feelings toward the analyst that he or she had felt toward people who were important earlier in life. On the basis of these expressed feelings, the analyst is able to interpret the nature of the displaced impulses. For example, a man who has always admired an older brother detects something in the analyst's attitude that reminds him of the brother. An angry attack on the analyst may lead the client to uncover hostile feelings toward his brother that were never acknowledged before. By studying how their clients feel toward them, analysts help their patients achieve a better understanding of their conduct in relation to others.

"That's exactly what I mean. When you're late, *don't* bring me a note from your mother."

ABREACTION, INSIGHT, AND WORKING THROUGH The course of improvement during psychoanalytic therapy is commonly attributed to three main experiences: *abreaction*, gradual *insight* into one's difficulties, and a repeated *working through* of conflicts and one's reactions to them.

Abreaction is the release of suppressed emotion. Expressing intense emotions or reliving earlier emotional experiences in the safety of the therapy session often brings relief to the client. (The process is also called *catharsis*, as though it were a kind of emotional cleansing.) Abreaction does not eliminate the causes of conflict, but it may open the way for further exploration of repressed feelings and experiences.

A person achieves *insight* when he or she understands the roots of the conflict. Sometimes insight comes when the patient recovers the memory of a repressed experience, but the popular notion that most psychoanalytic cures result from the sudden recall of a single dramatic episode is untrue. The individual's troubles seldom stem from a single source, and insight is gained through a gradual increase in self-knowledge. Insight and abreaction must work together: patients must understand their feelings and feel what they understand. The reorientation is never simply an intellectual process.

As analysis progresses, the patient goes through a lengthy process of reeducation known as *working through*. By examining the same conflicts over and over as they have appeared in a variety of situations, the person learns to face rather than deny reality and to react in more mature and effective ways. By working through these conflicts during therapy, the person becomes strong enough to face the threat of the original conflict situation and to react to it without undue anxiety.

The result claimed for a successful psychoanalysis is a deep-seated modification of the individual's personality that allows her or him to cope with problems on a realistic basis.

Psychoanalysis is a lengthy and usually expensive process. It is most successful with individuals who are highly motivated to solve their problems, can verbalize their feelings with some ease, and can afford it.

Behavior therapies

The term *behavior therapy* includes a number of different therapeutic methods based on learning theory. Behavior therapists assume that maladaptive behaviors are learned ways of coping with stress and that some of the techniques developed in experimental work on learning can be used to substitute new and more appropriate responses for maladaptive ones. Whereas psychoanalysis is concerned with understanding how the individual's past conflicts influence behavior, behavior therapy focuses more directly on the behavior itself.

Behavior therapists point out that although the achievement of insight, or self-knowledge, is a worthwhile goal, it does not ensure behavior change. Often we understand why we behave the way we do in a certain situation but are not able to change our behavior. If you are unusually timid about speaking in class, you may be able to trace this fear to a number of past events (your father criticized your opinions whenever you expressed them; your mother made a point of correcting your grammar; you had little experience in public speaking during high school because you were afraid to compete with your older brother who was captain of the debate team). Understanding the reasons behind your fear probably will not make it easier for you to contribute to class discussions.

"Leave us alone! I am a behavior therapist! I am helping my patient overcome a fear of heights!"

Originally, behavior therapies emphasized the principles of classical and operant conditioning as they related to overt behavior (see Chapter 7). The behavior therapist tried to determine the stimuli that preceded the maladaptive response and the environmental conditions that reinforced or maintained the behavior (Ullmann and Krasner, 1969; Lazarus, 1971). More recently, behavior therapists have recognized the influence of cognitive variables on behavior (for example, the individual's thoughts about anxiety-producing situations or expectations about the consequences of certain actions) and have included attempts to modify such variables in combination with procedures directed specifically at the behavior (Bandura, 1982; Meichenbaum and Jaremko, 1982).

In contrast to psychoanalysis, which attempts to change the individual's personality, behavior therapies tend to focus on fairly circumscribed goals—the modification of maladaptive behaviors in specific situations. Behavior therapists are also more concerned than psychoanalysts with obtaining scientific validation of their techniques.

SYSTEMATIC DESENSITIZATION *Systematic desensitization* can be viewed as a "deconditioning" or "counter-conditioning" process. This procedure is highly effective in eliminating fears or phobias. The principle of the treatment is to weaken a maladaptive response by strengthening an incompatible or antagonistic response. For example, relaxation is antagonistic to anxiety; it is difficult to be both relaxed and anxious at the same time. One method of systematically desensitizing a person to a feared situation involves first training the individual to relax and then gradually exposing him or her to the feared situation, either in imagination or in reality. Through relaxation training, the individual learns to contract and relax various muscles, starting, for example, with the feet and ankles and proceeding up the body to face and neck muscles. The person learns what muscles feel like when they are truly relaxed (compared to tense) and how to discriminate among various degrees of tension. Sometimes drugs and hypnosis are used to help people who cannot relax otherwise.

While the individual is learning to relax, he or she works with the behavior therapist to construct an *anxiety hierarchy*—a list of situations or stimuli that make the person feel anxious; the situations are ranked in order from the one that produces the least anxiety to the most fearful. For example, a woman who suffers from agoraphobia (see page 458) and experiences intense anxiety whenever she leaves the security of her home might construct a hierarchy that begins with a walk to the corner mailbox. Somewhere around the middle of the list might be a drive to the supermarket, and at the top, a plane trip alone to a distant city. After the woman has learned to relax and the hierarchy has been constructed, desensitization begins. She sits with her eyes closed in a comfortable chair while the therapist describes the least anxiety-producing situation to her. If she can imagine herself in the situation without any increase in muscle tension, the therapist proceeds to the next item on the list. If the woman reports any anxiety while visualizing a scene, she concentrates on relaxing; the same scene is visualized until all anxiety is neutralized. This process continues through a series of sessions until the situation that originally provoked the most anxiety now elicits only relaxation. At this point, the woman has been systematically desensitized to anxiety-provoking situations through the strengthening of an antagonistic or incompatible response—relaxation.

Although desensitization through visually imagined scenes has been effective in reducing fears or phobias, it is less effective than desensitization through actual encounters with the feared stimuli, which is not surprising. The woman

A class meeting at LaGuardia Airport in New York City to overcome a fear of flying. The first stage—learning to relax in an airplane— is accomplished on the ground!

in our hypothetical case would probably lose her fears more rapidly and more permanently if she actually exposed herself to the anxiety-producing situations in a sequence of graduated steps and managed to remain calm (Sherman, 1972). Whenever possible, a behavior therapist tries to combine real-life with symbolic desensitization.

ASSERTIVE TRAINING   Another kind of response that is antagonistic to anxiety is an *approach* or *assertive response*. Some people feel anxious in social situations because they do not know how to "speak up" for what they feel is right or to "say no" when others take advantage of them. By practicing *assertive responses* (first in role playing with the therapist and then in real-life situations), the individual not only reduces anxiety but also develops more effective coping techniques. The therapist determines the kinds of situations in which the person is passive and then helps him or her think of and practice some assertive responses that might be effective in those situations. The following situations might be worked through during a sequence of therapy sessions:

- Someone steps in front of you in line.
- A friend asks you to do something you do not want to do.
- Your boss criticizes you unjustly.
- You return defective merchandise to a store.
- You are annoyed by the continual conversation of people behind you in the movies.
- The mechanic did an unsatisfactory job of repairing your car.

Most people do not enjoy dealing with such situations, but some individuals are so fearful of asserting themselves that they say nothing and build up feelings of resentment and inadequacy instead. In assertive training, the client rehearses effective responses that could be made in such situations with the therapist and gradually tries them in real life.

POSITIVE REINFORCEMENT AND EXTINCTION   When a timid person learns and practices assertive responses, she or he is likely to receive considerable *positive reinforcement* from the therapist who praises such new skills, from other people who are impressed by the change in behavior, and from the fact that actions produce worthwhile results. *Systematic reinforcement*, based on the principles of operant conditioning (see Chapter 7), has proved to be an effective method of modifying behavior.

The procedure can be illustrated by the case of a third-grade student who was inattentive in school, refused to complete assignments or participate in class, and spent most of her time daydreaming. In addition, her social skills were poor, and she had few friends. The behavior to be reinforced was defined as "on task" behavior, which included paying attention to schoolwork or instructions from the teacher, completing reading assignments, and taking part in any type of class participation. The reinforcement consisted of beans that were used as tokens to be exchanged for special privileges that the girl valued, such as standing first in line (3 beans) or being allowed to stay after school to help the teacher with special projects (9 beans). Any time the teacher observed the student performing on-task behaviors, she placed one bean in a jar. The beans were cashed in daily and not allowed to accumulate.

During the first three months of treatment, the girl completed 12 units of work in contrast to 0 units during the three months before the reinforcement

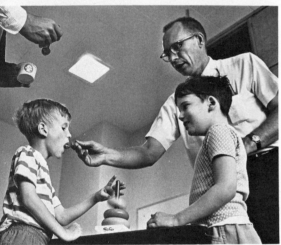

Figure 16-1
Behavior Reinforcement
These two autistic children were enrolled in an intensive behavior therapy program at the UCLA Neuropsychiatric Institute. Here they are shown receiving immediate reinforcement in the form of food for interacting with each other. Other techniques included punishment (electric shock) for self-destructive behavior or tantrums and modeling of the appropriate behavior. The boy on the right, mute and self-destructive when he entered the program, was able to return home in less than a year, and two years later was doing first-grade work in a special school.

regime started. During the last three months of treatment (which terminated with the close of school), she completed 36 units and was performing at the same level as the rest of the class. A follow-up the next year showed that the student's academic performance was maintained; in addition, she showed a marked improvement in social skills and in acceptance by the other children (Walker and others, 1981). This is a common finding; improving behavior in one area of life often produces added benefits.

Reinforcement of desirable responses can be accompanied by extinction of undesirable ones. For example, a young boy who habitually shouts to get his mother's attention could be ignored whenever he does so and reinforced by her attention only when he comes to where she is and speaks in a conversational tone.

Sometimes the behavior that the therapist wants to reinforce occurs infrequently or is totally absent, such as talking in a mute child or a schizophrenic. In this case, a technique similar to Skinner's *shaping* of behavior (see Chapter 7) is used: responses that approximate the desired behavior are reinforced, and the therapist gradually requires closer and closer approximations until the desired behavior occurs. For example, with one very withdrawn schizophrenic (who had remained mute for 19 years), chewing gum proved to be an effective reinforcement for shaping speech. At first, the therapist rewarded the patient with a stick of gum simply for looking at it when it was held in front of his face; then, for moving his lips; then, for making any verbalization, if only a croak; and then for saying the word "gum." All this took place over a period of weeks. Once the patient reached the point where he said "gum, please," he began to respond to questions by the therapist. The hospital personnel were then asked to respond to the patient's requests only if they were verbalized. If he brought his coat to the nurse to indicate that he wanted to go for a walk, she did not acquiesce unless he expressed his desire in speech. Other kinds of reinforcement gradually took the place of chewing gum, and the formerly mute schizophrenic became more and more verbal (Isaacs, Thomas, and Goldiamond, 1965).

Similar procedures have been effective in teaching seriously disturbed children to talk, to interact with other children, to sit quietly at a desk, and to respond appropriately to questions (see Figure 16-1). Instead of receiving regular breakfasts or lunches, these children were provided with bits of food when their responses approximated the desired behaviors. Although such procedures may seem cruel, they are an effective means of establishing normal behavior when all other attempts have failed. Once the child begins to respond to primary forms of reward (such as food), social rewards (praise, attention, and special privileges) become effective reinforcers.

A number of mental hospitals have instituted "token economies" on wards with very regressed, chronic patients to induce socially appropriate behavior. Tokens (which can later be exchanged for food and privileges such as watching television) are given for dressing properly, interacting with other patients, eliminating "psychotic talk," helping on the wards, and so on. Such programs have proved successful in improving both the patients' behavior and the general functioning of the ward.

MODELING   Another effective means of changing behavior is *modeling* (see page 325). Modeling and several other behavior modification techniques were used in a study designed to eliminate fear of snakes (Bandura, Blanchard, and Ritter, 1969). The subjects were young adults whose snake phobias were severe enough to restrict their activities in various ways (for example, some could not participate in gardening or hiking for fear of encountering snakes). After an

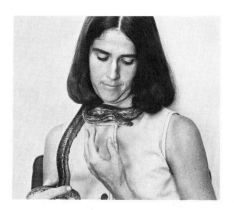

initial test to determine how closely they would approach a live but harmless king snake, the subjects were rated according to their degree of fearfulness and divided into four matched groups. One group watched a film in which child and adult models interacted with a large king snake. The models gave every indication of enjoying a series of interactions that most people would find progressively more frightening. The subjects in the group had been trained in relaxation and were instructed to stop the film whenever a particular scene provoked anxiety, to reverse the film to the beginning of the sequence that bothered them, and to reinduce relaxation. This procedure was termed "symbolic modeling." A second group imitated the behavior of a live model as the model performed progressively more fearful activities with the snake (see Figure 16-2). Gradually, the subjects were guided in such activities as touching the snake with a gloved hand, touching the snake with their bare hands, holding the snake, letting it coil around their arms, and finally letting the snake loose in the room, retrieving it, and letting it crawl over their bodies. The procedure was termed "live modeling with participation." Subjects assigned to the third group underwent the standard desensitization procedure described earlier, in which deep relaxation was successively paired with imagined scenes of snakes until the subject's anxiety disappeared. The fourth group served as a control group and received no special training.

Figure 16-3 indicates the number of snake-approach responses by the subjects before and after they received the different treatments. All three treatment groups showed improvement in comparison with the control group, but the group that combined live modeling with guided participation achieved the best results. Almost all the subjects in this group completely overcame their fear of snakes. Interestingly enough, the fears of these subjects in a variety of other situations were also reduced. A follow-up investigation indicated that the subjects' snake phobias did not recur.

Subsequent studies have shown that the most effective method of eliminating snake phobias is to start with participant modeling, during which the individual is guided in handling the snake, and then let the person proceed through various degrees of snake intimacy on his or her own (Bandura, Adams, and Beyer, 1976). In this way, the individual gains a sense of mastery over the situation—a feeling that effective performance is the result of his or her own actions (Bandura and others, 1980).

Modeling has been used successfully to overcome a variety of fears or avoidance behaviors and to teach new, more adaptive responses. Modeling is often combined with role playing, during which the therapist helps the individual rehearse or practice more adaptive behaviors. In the following excerpt, a

Figure 16-2
Modeling as a Treatment
for Snake Phobia
The photos show an individual modeling interactions with a live king snake. Modeling of this sort, combined with guided participation, in which the subject is helped to handle the snake, proves very effective in eliminating snake phobias.

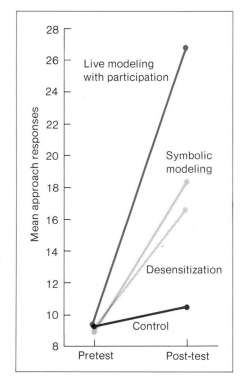

Figure 16-3
Treatment of Snake Phobia
The mean number of snake-approach responses by subjects before and after they received different behavior therapy treatments. (After Bandura, Blanchard, and Ritter, 1969)

therapist helps a young man overcome his anxieties about asking girls for dates. The young man has been pretending to talk to a girl over the phone and finishes by asking for a date.

CLIENT: By the way (pause), I don't suppose you want to go out Saturday night?

THERAPIST: Up to actually asking for the date, you were very good. However, if I were the girl, I think I might have been a bit offended when you said, "By the way." It's like asking her out is pretty casual. Also, the way you phrased the question, you are kind of suggesting to her that she doesn't want to go out with you. Pretend for the moment I'm you. Now, how does this sound: "There is a movie at the Varsity Theater this Saturday that I want to see. If you don't have other plans, I'd like very much to take you."

CLIENT: That sounded good. Like you were sure of yourself and liked the girl, too.

THERAPIST: Why don't you try it.

CLIENT: You know that movie at the Varsity? Well, I'd like to go, and I'd like to take you Saturday if you don't have anything better to do.

THERAPIST: Well, that certainly was better. Your tone of voice was especially good. But the last line "if you don't have anything better to do" sounds like you don't think you have too much to offer. Why not run through it one more time.

CLIENT: I'd like to see the show at the Varsity Saturday, and if you haven't made other plans, I'd like to take you.

THERAPIST: Much better. Excellent, in fact. You were confident, forceful, and sincere (Rimm and Masters, 1974, p. 94).

SELF-REGULATION   Because client and therapist seldom meet more than once a week, it is to the client's advantage to learn to control or regulate his or her own behavior so that progress can be made outside the therapy hour. Moreover, if people feel they are responsible for their own improvement, they are more likely to maintain such gains. Self-regulation involves monitoring, or observing, one's own behavior and using various techniques—*self-reinforcement, self-punishment, control of stimulus conditions, development of incompatible responses*—to change the maladaptive behavior. An individual monitors his or her behavior by keeping a careful record of the kinds of stimuli or situations that elicit the maladaptive behavior and the kinds of responses that are incompatible with it. A person concerned with alcohol dependency would note the kinds of situations in which she or he is most tempted to drink and try to control such situations or devise a response that is incompatible with drinking. A man who finds it hard not to join his co-workers in a noontime cocktail might plan to eat lunch at his desk, thereby avoiding the situation. If he is tempted to relax with a drink on arriving home from work, he might substitute a game of tennis or a jog around the block as a means of relieving tension. Both of these activities would be incompatible with drinking.

Self-reinforcement is rewarding yourself immediately for achieving a specific goal; the reward could be praising yourself, watching a favorite TV program, telephoning a friend, eating a favorite food. Self-punishment is arranging some aversive consequence for failing to achieve a goal, such as depriving yourself of something you enjoy (*not* watching a favorite TV program) or making yourself do some unpleasant task (cleaning your room). Depending on the kind of behavior the individual wants to change, various combinations of self-reinforcement, self-punishment, or control of stimuli and responses may be used. Table 16-1 outlines a program for the self-regulation of eating.

Table 16-1
Self-Regulation of Eating
The program illustrates the use of learning principles to help control food intake. (Based in part on Stuart and Davis, 1972; O'Leary and Wilson, 1975.)

SELF-MONITORING

Daily Log. Keep a detailed record of everything you eat. Note amount eaten, type of food and caloric value, time of day, and the circumstances of eating. This record will establish the caloric intake that is maintaining your present weight. It will also help to identify the stimuli that elicit and reinforce your eating behavior.

Weight Chart. Decide how much you want to lose and set a weekly goal for weight loss. Your weekly goal should be realistic (between 1 and 2 pounds). Record your weight each day on graph paper. In addition to showing how your weight varies with food intake, this visual record will reinforce your dieting efforts as you observe progress toward your goal.

CONTROLLING STIMULUS CONDITIONS

Use these procedures to narrow the range of stimuli associated with eating:

1. Eat only at predetermined times, at a specific table, using a special place mat, napkin, dishes, and so forth. Do *not* eat at other times or in other places (for example, while standing in the kitchen).
2. Do *not* combine eating with other activities, such as reading or watching television.
3. Keep in the house only those foods that are permitted on your diet.
4. Shop for food only after having had a full meal; buy only those items that are on a previously prepared list.

MODIFYING ACTUAL EATING BEHAVIOR

Use these procedures to break the chain of responses that make eating automatic:

1. Eat very slowly, paying close attention to the food.
2. Finish chewing and swallowing before putting more food on the fork.
3. Put your utensils down for periodic short breaks before continuing to eat.

DEVELOPING INCOMPATIBLE RESPONSES

When tempted to eat at times other than those specified, find a substitute activity that is incompatible with eating. For example, exercise to music, go for a walk, talk with a friend (preferably one who knows you are dieting), study your diet plan and weight graph, noting how much weight you have lost.

SELF-REINFORCEMENT

Arrange to reward yourself with an activity you enjoy (watching television, reading, planning a new wardrobe, visiting a friend) when you have maintained appropriate eating behavior for a day. Plan larger rewards (for example, buying something you want) for a specified amount of weight loss. Self-punishment (other than forgoing a reward) is probably less effective because dieting is a fairly depressing business anyway. But you might decrease the frequency of binge eating by immediately reciting to yourself the aversive consequences or by looking at an unattractive picture of yourself in a bathing suit.

COGNITIVE PROCESSES IN BEHAVIOR CHANGE   Although the procedures we have discussed thus far focus on behavior, it is clear that cognitive factors—the individual's thoughts and expectations—are important in determining behavior and in mediating behavior change. What we think about a situation clearly influences our emotional response to it. For example, two students are to present papers in an informal seminar. One says to herself, "This should be an interesting session; there are a lot of debatable points on this topic, and it should be fun to hear what the other students have to say about my ideas." The other speaker thinks, "I'm not sure I can present my ideas effectively; there are

CRITICAL DISCUSSION

"Mental Illness" Versus "Maladaptive Habits"

Whether an individual with an abnormal behavior (for example, a fear of crowds or compulsive hand-washing) is exhibiting a "maladaptive habit" or a "symptom of an underlying disorder" is an issue on which *behavior therapists* and *insight therapists* disagree. Behavior therapists feel that once the behavior has been changed, the disorder is cured. Psychoanalysts and other more traditional therapists maintain that maladaptive behavior is only a symptom of an underlying "disease." They view mental disorders as analogous to physical disorders and consider it futile to treat the symptoms without removing the underlying pathology. (The physician treating a case of syphilis does not simply apply an ointment to the rash but destroys the syphilis spirochete with antibiotics.) Insight therapists consider a phobia to be only the surface expression of more complex emotional difficulties; removal of the phobia without treatment of the underlying problem may result in *symptom substitution*. The patient can develop *new* symptoms (new defenses against the anxiety caused by internal conflict) if the therapist eliminates the original symptom without

curing the underlying conflict. Some traditional therapists criticize behavior therapy as a superficial method of treatment that removes the symptoms without dealing with the inner conflicts and leaves the patient vulnerable to symptom substitution.

Behavior therapists maintain that abnormal behavior often consists of maladaptive habits that have been learned and does not always indicate an underlying conflict. Once the habits (symptoms) are extinguished and replaced by more adaptive ones, the "illness is cured." The symptom *is* the problem, and eliminating the symptom eliminates the problem.

The debate is not an easy one to settle for a number of reasons, but the evidence suggests that symptom substitution does not occur very often. Several reviews of post-treatment evaluation studies found few instances of new symptoms up to two years after successful treatment by behavior modication methods (Grossberg, 1964; Paul and Bernstein, 1973). Instead, the removal of a disturbing "symptom" usually creates better emotional health; the person's self-esteem is increased by this accom-

plishment, and other people respond more favorably to the individual once his or her behavior has changed.

The broader issue of whether abnormal behavior should be viewed as "mental illness" or "maladaptive behavior" is more difficult to resolve. Biochemical abnormalities do appear to play an important role in schizophrenia and in some affective disorders (see Chapter 15). And biological differences in the sensitivity of the autonomic nervous system may predispose some people to develop anxiety disorders. Throughout the text, we have emphasized the complex interplay between physical and mental functioning. To view the more serious mental disorders (for example, schizophrenic and manic-depressive disorders) as solely a problem of relearning is a misleading oversimplification.

On the other hand, labeling emotionally disturbed people "ill" has several disadvantages. It tends to absolve them of responsibility for their own behavior. It may prompt them to act as if they were "sick" and helpless, thereby discouraging them from attempting to solve their problems.

---

a lot of bright students in the group, and I'm sure they're going to be evaluating me, pointing out any flaws in my presentation." Clearly, the second student is anxious about the seminar, and the more she thinks about being "on the spot" or being evaluated by others, the more anxious she becomes. Our thoughts influence our actions, and our actions influence our thoughts.

In discussing social learning theory (see pages 392–94), we noted that a person's behavior depends partly on his or her expectations of the *outcome* of the behavior ("What will be the result if I take this action?") and partly on his or her expectations of *personal effectiveness* ("Will I be able to perform the necessary actions?"). Sometimes our expectations of the outcome of a certain behavior may be irrational or unrealistic ("If I assert myself or stand up for my rights, other people won't like me"). More often, we may be fairly realistic about the outcome of certain behaviors but may have grave doubts about our ability to execute them successfully. Many of the procedures that are effective in changing behavior appear to increase the person's feelings of mastery, or *self-efficacy*.

For example, to reduce a fear of snakes, it is helpful to watch another person handle a snake without dire consequences or to imagine interacting with a boa constrictor while you are relaxed, but it is more effective to actually handle a snake. Actual performance increases feelings of self-mastery (Bandura, 1982).

Behavior therapists who use the cognitive approach attempt to help clients replace distorted expectations and beliefs with more realistic ones. For example, we noted in Chapter 15 that depressed individuals tend to appraise events from a negative and self-critical viewpoint. They expect to fail; when they do, they are apt to blame themselves rather than the circumstances. Cognitive therapy for depression encourages the individual to recognize the irrationality of his or her assumptions. The following dialogue illustrates how the therapist, by carefully directed questioning, makes a client aware of the unrealistic nature of her beliefs.

THERAPIST: Why do you want to end your life?

CLIENT: Without Raymond, I am nothing. . . . I can't be happy without Raymond. . . . But I can't save our marriage.

THERAPIST: What has your marriage been like?

CLIENT: It has been miserable from the very beginning. . . . Raymond has always been unfaithful. . . . I have hardly seen him in the past five years.

THERAPIST: You say that you can't be happy without Raymond. . . . Have you found yourself happy when you are with Raymond?

CLIENT: No, we fight all the time and I feel worse.

THERAPIST: You say you are nothing without Raymond. Before you met Raymond, did you feel you were nothing?

CLIENT: No, I felt I was somebody.

THERAPIST: If you were somebody before you knew Raymond, why do you need him to be somebody now?

CLIENT: (puzzled) Hmmm . . . .

THERAPIST: If you were free of the marriage, do you think that men might be interested in you—knowing that you were available?

CLIENT: I guess that maybe they would be.

THERAPIST: Is it possible that you might find a man who would be more constant than Raymond?

CLIENT: I don't know. . . . I guess it's possible . . . .

THERAPIST: Then what have you actually lost if you break up the marriage?

CLIENT: I don't know.

THERAPIST: Is it possible that you'll get along better if you end the marriage?

CLIENT: There is no guarantee of that.

THERAPIST: Do you have a *real marriage*?

CLIENT: I guess not.

THERAPIST: If you don't have a real marriage, what do you actually lose if you decide to end the marriage?

CLIENT: (long pause) Nothing, I guess. (Beck, 1976, pp. 289–91)

Some therapists, who call themselves *cognitive behavior therapists*, combine behavior modification techniques with specific instructions for handling negative thoughts. For example, a program to help someone overcome a fear of public speaking might include systematic desensitization (at first with imagery and later with practice in speaking situations of gradually increasing difficulty) along with training in "positive thinking." The therapist teaches the client to replace self-defeating internal dialogues ("I'm so nervous I'll forget what I'm going to say") with positive self-instructions ("Be calm; you know the material.

The audience is interested and sympathetic; even if you make an error, they won't think badly of you"). Adding the cognitive component appears to be more effective in treating such conditions as fear of public speaking and examination anxiety than systematic desensitization alone (Meichenbaum, 1972).

Behavior therapy and cognitive therapy have been used successfully in treating a variety of problems. Although some of the procedures may seem somewhat cold and unfeeling, in actual practice the therapist shows concern for the client's welfare and considerable warmth in the relationship. These qualities appear to be necessary in any type of therapy; when they are lacking, behavior modification techniques are not very successful.

Humanistic therapies

Practitioners of *humanistic therapy* are concerned with the uniqueness of the individual and focus on the person's natural tendency toward growth and self-actualization (see pages 401–402). The humanistic therapist does not interpret the person's behavior (as a psychoanalyst would) or try to modify it (as a behavior therapist would). The goal of the humanistic therapist is to facilitate exploration of the individual's own thoughts and feelings and to assist the individual in arriving at his or her own solutions. This approach will become clearer as we look at client-centered therapy—one of the most widely used humanistic therapies.

CLIENT-CENTERED THERAPY *Client-centered therapy*, developed by Carl Rogers, is based on the assumption that the client is the best expert on himself or herself and that people are capable of working out the solutions to their own problems. The task of the therapist is to facilitate this progress—not to ask probing questions, make interpretations, or suggest courses of action. In fact, Rogers prefers the term "facilitator" to therapist.

Client-centered therapy can be described rather simply, but in practice, it requires great skill and is much more subtle than it first appears. The therapist begins by explaining the nature of the interviews. The responsibility for working out problems is the client's; she or he is free to leave at any time and to choose whether to return. The relationship is private and confidential; the client is free to speak of intimate matters without fear of reproof or of the information being revealed to others. Once the situation is structured, the clients do most of the talking. Usually, they have much to "get off their chest." The therapist is a patient but alert listener. When the client stops, as though expecting the therapist so say something, the therapist usually acknowledges and accepts the feelings the client has expressed. For example, if a man has been talking about his nagging mother, the therapist may say, "You feel that your mother tries to control you." The object is to *clarify* the feelings the client has been expressing, not to judge them or to elaborate on them.

Generally, the clients begin therapy with rather low evaluations of themselves, but in the course of facing their problems and trying to arrive at solutions, they begin to view themselves more positively. For example, one case began with the following statements:

> Everything is wrong with me. I feel abnormal. I don't do even the ordinary things of life. I'm sure I will fail on anything I undertake. I'm inferior. When I try to imitate successful people, I'm only acting. I can't go on like this.

By the final interview, the client expressed attitudes that contrasted strikingly with the statements in the first interview:

Carl Rogers (top, center) "facilitating" discussion in a therapy group

I am taking a new course of my own choosing. I am really changing. I have always tried to live up to others' standards that were beyond my abilities. I've come to realize that I'm not so bright, but I can get along anyway. I no longer think so much about myself. I'm much more comfortable with people. I'm getting a feeling of success out of my job. I don't feel quite steady yet and would like to feel that I can come for more help if I need it. (Case reported by Snyder and others, 1947)

To determine whether this kind of progress is typical, experimenters have carefully analyzed recorded interviews. When clients' statements are classified and plotted, the course of therapy turns out to be fairly predictable. In the early inverviews, people spend a good deal of time talking about their problems and describing symptoms. During the course of therapy, they make more and more statements that indicate they are achieving an *understanding* of their particular problems. By classifying all clients' remarks as either "problem restatements" or "statements of understanding and insight," the progressive increase in insight as therapy proceeds becomes evident (see Figure 16-4).

What do client-centered therapists do to bring about these changes? Rogers believes that the most important qualities for a therapist are empathy, warmth, and genuineness. *Empathy* refers to the ability to understand the feelings the client is trying to express *and* the ability to communicate this understanding to the client. The therapist must adopt the client's frame of reference and strive to see the problems as the client sees them. By *warmth*, Rogers means a deep acceptance of the individual as he or she is, including the conviction that this person has the capacity to deal constructively with his or her problems. A therapist who is *genuine* is open and honest and does not play a role or operate behind a professional facade. People are reluctant to reveal themselves to those they perceive as "phony." Rogers believes that a therapist who possesses these attributes will facilitate growth and self-exploration on the part of the client (Rogers, 1970; Truax and Mitchell, 1971).

Much has been learned from client-centered therapy, but it is difficult to know with certainty what its range of usefulness and its limitations are. It does appear that this method—like psychoanalysis—is successful only with individuals who are fairly verbal and are motivated to discuss their problems. For people who do not voluntarily seek help or who are seriously disturbed and unable to discuss their feelings, more directive methods are usually necessary.

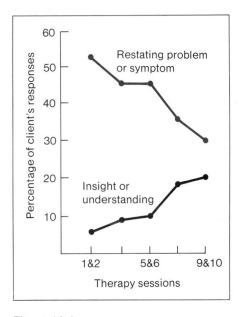

Figure 16-4
Changes During Client-Centered Therapy
Description and restatement of the problem on the part of the client gradually gives way during the course of therapy to increased frequency of statements indicating understanding. (After Seeman, 1949)

Group therapy

Many emotional problems involve an individual's difficulties in relating to others, including feelings of isolation, rejection, and loneliness and the inability to form meaningful relationships. Although the therapist can help the individual to work out some of these problems, the final test lies in how well the person can apply the attitudes and responses learned in therapy to relationships in everyday life. *Group therapy* permits clients to work out their problems in the presence of others, to observe how other people react to their behavior, and to try out new methods of responding when old ones prove unsatisfactory.

Therapists of various orientations (psychoanalytic, humanistic, and behaviorist) have modified their techniques to be applicable to therapy groups. Group therapy has been used in a variety of settings—in hospital wards and outpatient psychiatric clinics, with parents of disturbed children, and with teen-agers in correctional institutions, to name a few. Typically, the groups consist of a small number of individuals (6–12 is considered optimal) who have similar problems.

A therapy group at a drug rehabilitation center

The therapist generally remains in the background, allowing the members to exchange experiences, comment on one another's behavior, and discuss their own problems as well as those of the other members. Initially, the members tend to be defensive and uncomfortable when exposing their weaknesses, but they gradually become more objective about their own behavior and more aware of the effect their attitudes and behavior have on others. They gain an increased ability to identify and empathize with others in the group and a feeling of self-esteem when they are able to help another member by offering an understanding remark or a meaningful interpretation.

Group therapy has several advantages over individual therapy. It saves time because one therapist can help several people at once; people can derive comfort and support from observing that others have similar, perhaps more severe problems; people can learn vicariously by watching how others behave, and they can explore attitudes and reactions by interacting with a variety of people, not just with the therapist.

ENCOUNTER GROUPS   During the past 20 years, group therapy has expanded from a method for resolving emotional problems to a popular means of learning how to relate to others. *Encounter groups,* also known as *sensitivity training groups* (*T-groups,* for short), consist of 12 to 20 individuals who may meet for only one intensive weekend session or for sessions over a period of several months in an attempt to better understand how they behave in their interpersonal interactions. Members are urged to express attitudes and feelings not usually displayed in public. The group leader (or *facilitator,* as he or she is sometimes called, because the job is not really to lead) encourages participants to explore their feelings and motives as well as those of other group members. The objective is to stimulate an exchange that is not inhibited by defensiveness and that achieves a maximum of openness and honesty.

Carl Rogers, who has studied various types of encounter groups, describes a fairly consistent pattern of change as the sessions progress (Rogers, 1970). Initially, there tends to be confusion and some frustration when the facilitator makes it clear that he or she will not take the responsibility for directing the group. Members also resist expressing their feelings; if one member describes some personal feeling, other members may try to stop the person, questioning whether it is appropriate to express such feelings in the group. At the next stage, the participants gradually begin to talk about feeilngs and problems they have encountered outside the group. They then begin to discuss relationships within the group; often the first feeling expressed is a negative attitude toward oneself or toward another group member. When the individual finds that these feelings are accepted, a climate of trust begins to develop. By the final sessions, the group members have become impatient with defensiveness; they attempt to undercut facades, insisting that individuals be themselves. The tact and polite cover-up that are acceptable outside the group are not tolerated within it.

In theory, the feedback the individual receives about how his or her behavior affects others and feelings of acceptance by group members leads to increased self-awareness and to behavior change both within and outside the group. Studies of the effects of encounter-group participation, however, raise doubts about the extent of behavior change that actually occurs. One study of more than 200 college students who participated in encounter groups with well-trained leaders revealed that only one third of the students showed positive changes following their experience (based on self-reports and ratings by close friends). Another third of the students showed no change, and the remainder displayed negative changes—either dropping out of the group because they found it disturbing or feeling afterward that the experience aggravated personal problems without resolving them (Lieberman, Yalom, and Miles, 1973).

Although encounter groups provide an opportunity for psychologically healthy people to learn something about themselves from the honest reactions of others, they generally do not help individuals who have emotional problems. Encounter groups have proved to be less effective in producing behavior change than individual therapy or more traditional therapy groups, and the gains produced by encounter-group participation appear to be temporary (Bednar and Kaul, 1978). In more traditional groups, participants are carefully selected and meetings extend over a longer period so that interpersonal problems can be worked out. In addition, the emphasis on "the free expression of emotion" in encounter groups may prove harmful to individuals whose self-esteem is too tenuous to withstand group criticism and pressure (Kirsch and Glass, 1977).

FAMILY THERAPY *Family therapy* is a special form of group therapy. The group consists of a husband and a wife or parents and children who meet with one or two therapists (usually a male and a female). Based on the assumption that the individual's problems are indicative of a more general maladjustment within the family, the therapy is directed toward helping the family members clarify and express their feelings about one another, develop greater mutual understanding, and work out more effective ways of relating to one another and solving their common problems.

Sometimes videotape recordings are played back to make the family members aware of how they interact with each other. Or the therapist may visit the family in the home to observe conflicts and verbal exchanges as they occur in their natural setting. It often becomes apparent that problem behaviors are being reinforced by the responses of family members. For example, a young child's temper tantrums or a teen-ager's eating problems may be inadvertently reinforced by the attention they elicit from the parents. The therapist may teach the parents to monitor their own and their child's behavior, to determine how their reactions may be reinforcing the problem behavior, and then to alter the reinforcement contingencies.

An *eclectic approach*

There are many variations of psychotherapy in addition to the ones we have discussed here. Several other approaches to psychotherapy are listed in Table 16-2. However, most psychotherapists do not adhere strictly to any *one* particular method. Instead, they take an *eclectic approach,* selecting from the different techniques those they feel are most appropriate for the individual client. Although their theoretical orientation may be toward a particular method or "school" (for example, more psychoanalytic than behaviorist), they feel free to discard those concepts they view as not especially helpful and to select techniques from other schools. In short, they are flexible in their approach to therapy. In dealing with a very anxious individual, for instance, an eclectic psychotherapist might first prescribe tranquilizers and relaxation training to help reduce the person's level of anxiety. (Psychoanalysts would not, because they believe that anxiety is necessary to motivate the client to explore his or her conflicts.) To help the client understand the origins of his or her problems, the eclectic therapist might discuss certain aspects of the patient's history (a client-

A family therapy group

NAME	FOCUS	METHODS
Gestalt therapy	To become aware of the "whole" personality by working through unresolved conflicts and discovering those aspects of the individual's being that are blocked from awareness. Emphasis is on becoming intensely aware of how one is feeling and behaving at the moment.	Therapy in a group setting, but therapist works with one individual at a time. Acting out fantasies, dreams, or the two sides to a conflict are methods used to increase awareness. Combines psychoanalytic emphasis on resolving internal conflicts with behaviorist emphasis on awareness of one's behavior and humanistic concern for self-actualization.
Reality therapy	To clarify the individual's values and evaluate current behavior and future plans in relation to these values. To force the individual to accept responsibility.	Therapist helps the individual perceive the consequences of possible courses of action and decide on a realistic solution or goal. Once a plan of action is chosen, a "contract" may be signed in which the client agrees to follow through.
Rational-emotive therapy	To replace certain "irrational" ideas ("It is essential to be loved and admired by everyone all the time"; "I should be competent in all respects"; "People have little control over their sorrow and unhappiness") with more realistic ones. Assumes that cognitive change will produce emotional change.	Therapist attacks and contradicts the individual's ideas (sometimes subtly, sometimes directly) in an attempt to persuade her or him to take a more "rational" view of the situation.
Transactional analysis	To become aware of the intent behind the individual's communications; to eliminate subterfuge and deceit so that the individual can interpret his or her behavior accurately.	Therapy in a group setting. Communications between married couples or group members are analyzed in terms of the part of the personality that is speaking—"parent," "child," or "adult" (similar to Freud's superego, id, and ego)—and the intent of the message. Destructive social interactions or "games" are exposed for what they are.
Hypnotherapy	To relieve symptoms and strengthen ego processes by helping the individual set reality aside and make constructive use of imagery.	Therapist uses various hypnotic procedures, including self-hypnosis, in an attempt to reduce conflict and doubt by focusing the individual's attention, modify symptoms through direct suggestion or displacement, and strengthen the individual's ability to cope.

Table 16-2
Some Approaches to Psychotherapy

centered therapist does not delve into the past) but might feel it unnecessary to explore childhood experiences to the extent that a psychoanalyst would. The therapist might use educational techniques (provide information about sex and reproduction to help relieve the anxieties of an adolescent boy who has been misinformed and feels guilty about his sexual impulses, or explain the functioning of the autonomic nervous system to reassure an anxious woman that some of her symptoms, such as heart palpitations and hand tremors, are not indications of a disease).

Another psychotherapeutic technique is to change the patient's environment. The therapist might feel, for example, that a young man who has serious conflicts in his relationship with his parents can make little progress in overcoming his difficulties while remaining at home. In this instance, the therapist might recommend that the youth attend school away from home or seek employment in another community. Occasionally, with a younger child, the home environment may be so seriously detrimental to the child's mental health that the therapist, with the help of a welfare agency and the court, may have the child placed in a foster home.

EFFECTIVENESS OF PSYCHOTHERAPY

How effective is psychotherapy? Which methods work best? These questions are not easy to answer. Research into the effectiveness of psychotherapy is hampered by several major difficulties. How do we decide whether an individual has improved? How do we know which treatment variables were responsible? What about the "placebo effect"?

Defining success

How do we know that an individual has been helped by therapy? We cannot always rely on the individual's assessment. Some people report that they are feeling better simply to please the therapist or to convince themselves that their money was well spent. The *hello-goodbye effect* has long been recognized by therapists. When people say "hello" at the beginning of therapy, they tend to exaggerate their unhappiness and their problems to convince the therapist that they really need help. When they say "goodbye" at the end of therapy, they tend to exaggerate their well-being to express appreciation to the therapist for his or her efforts or to convince themselves that their time and money were not wasted. These phenomena must always be considered when evaluating the client's view of his or her progress.

The therapist's evaluation of the treatment as "successful" cannot always be considered an objective criterion either. The therapist has a vested interest in proclaiming that the client is better. And sometimes the changes that the client shows during the therapy session do not carry over into real-life situations.

Objective measures of improvement—performing more effectively on the job, getting along better with family and friends, drinking less, and so on—are more valid but are difficult to obtain in long-term studies of psychotherapeutic effectiveness.

Controlling extraneous variables

Even if we are convinced that an individual has improved following psychotherapy, how do we know what caused the change? Like the common cold, some mental disorders improve simply with the passage of time. This is particularly true of depression. The rate of *spontaneous recovery* (individuals who get better without treatment) must be used as a baseline in evaluating any type of psychotherapy.

To complicate matters still further, some people improve if they *think* they are receiving effective treatment, even if it is only a sugar pill. This is called the *placebo effect*. (A *placebo* is a biologically neutral substance given to a patient who believes the substance has curative powers.) Improvement with psychotherapy could be the result of placebo-like factors (including hope, expectation of a cure, attention received) rather than the result of the specific therapeutic method used. To demonstrate that psychotherapy works, studies must control for both spontaneous recovery and placebo effects.

Despite these difficulties, a number of controlled studies indicate that psychotherapy does help and that different therapeutic approaches do not differ greatly in effectiveness (Smith, Glass, and Miller, 1980; Landman and Dawes, 1982). We will describe one study as an example. At a unversity clinic, 90 outpatients were randomly assigned to one of three groups: behavior ther-

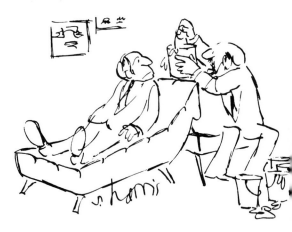

"Today we'll try aversion therapy. Every time you say something stupid, I'll spill a bucket of water on your head."

apy, short-term psychoanalytic therapy, and a wait-list (members of the wait-list group were interviewed to gather information but received no treatment). Both the behavior therapists and the analysts were well trained and experienced. The clients were evaluated before and after "treatment" on a number of measures—psychological tests, reports from people who knew them well, and ratings by the therapist, the client, and an independent assessor. In addition, tape recordings were made of every fifth therapy session so that the behavior of both the therapists and the clients could be evaluated. After four months of "treatment," all three groups showed significant improvement, but the two therapy groups had improved more markedly than the wait-list group. In overall outcome, for example, the independent assessor rated 80 percent of both therapy groups improved but only 48 percent of the wait-list group improved. Similar results were found with other measures, although there was a tendency for the behavior therapy group to show slightly more improvement than the psychoanalytic group (Sloane and others, 1975).

The question that concerns most current researchers is not which therapeutic approach is best but which method is most effective in solving a particular problem. The latter question is difficult to investigate because it requires finding a large number of people who have the same problem and assigning them to different treatment conditions; as we have seen, mental disorders differ markedly from one person to the next. Findings to date indicate that behavior therapy is more effective than psychoanalytic or client-centered therapy in treating specific anxieties and phobias (Kazdin and Wilson, 1978).

Common factors in psychotherapies

In general, experienced therapists with quite different orientations appear to be equally effective in helping their clients (Garfield and Bergin, 1978). These results suggest that factors common to the various psychotherapies we have been discussing may be more important in producing change than the specific procedures used by the therapist (Garfield, 1980). Let us consider what some of these factors might be.

AN INTERPERSONAL RELATIONSHIP OF WARMTH AND TRUST   Regardless of the type of therapy provided, in a "good" therapeutic relationship, client and therapist have a mutual respect and regard for one another. The client must believe that the therapist understands and is concerned with his or her problems. Although behavior therapy may sound like a rather impersonal procedure when it is described in a textbook, studies indicate that experienced behavior therapists show as much empathy and depth of interpersonal involvement as experienced psychoanalytically oriented therapists (Sloane and others, 1975).

REASSURANCE AND SUPPORT   Our problems often seem insurmountable and unique to us. Discussing them with an "expert" who accepts our problems as not unusual and indicates that they can be resolved is reassuring. Having someone to help us with problems we have not been able to solve alone also provides a sense of support and a feeling of hope.

DESENSITIZATION   We have already talked about systematic desensitization—the specific techniques of behavior therapy aimed at helping individuals lose their fear of certain objects or situations. But a broader kind of desensitization can occur in many types of psychotherapy. When we discuss events and problems that have been troubling us in the accepting atmosphere of a therapy session, they gradually lose their threatening quality. Problems that we brood about alone can become magnified beyond their seriousness; sharing problems with someone else often makes them seem less troublesome. Several other hypotheses can also explain how desensitization occurs in psychotherapy. For example, putting into words events that are disturbing may help us reappraise the situation in a more realistic and objective manner. From the viewpoint of learning theory, repeatedly discussing distressing experiences in the security of a therapeutic setting (where punishment is not forthcoming) may gradually extinguish the anxiety associated with them. Whatever the process, desensitization does appear to be a factor common to many kinds of psychotherapy.

UNDERSTANDING OR INSIGHT   All of the psychotherapies we have been discussing provide the client with some *explanation* of his or her difficulties—how they arose, why they persist, and how they can be changed. For the individual in psychoanalysis, this explanation may take the form of a gradual understanding of repressed childhood fears and the ways in which these unconscious feelings have contributed to current problems. A client seeing a rational-emotive therapist might be told that his or her difficulties stem from the irrational belief that one must be perfect or must be loved by everyone. A behavior therapist might inform the client that current fears are the result of previous conditioning and can be conquered by learning responses that are antagonistic to the current ones.

How can such different explanations all produce positive results? Perhaps the precise nature of the insights and understanding provided by the therapist is relatively unimportant. It may be more important to provide the client with an explanation for the behavior or feelings that the individual finds so distressing, along with a set of activities (such as free association or relaxation training) that both therapist and client believe will alleviate the distress. When someone is experiencing disturbing symptoms and is unsure of their cause or how serious they might be, it is reassuring to contact a professional who seems to know what the problem is and offers ways of relieving it. It gives the individual hope that change is possible, and hope is an important variable in facilitating change.

REINFORCEMENT OF ADAPTIVE RESPONSES   Behavior therapists use reinforcement as a technique to increase positive attitudes and actions. But any therapist in whom a client places trust and confidence functions as a reinforcing agent; that is, the therapist tends to express approval of those behaviors or attitudes deemed conducive to better adjustment and to ignore or express disapproval of maladaptive attitudes or responses. Which particular responses are reinforced depends on the therapist's orientation and therapeutic goals. The use of reinforcement may be intentional or unintentional; in some instances, the therapist may be unaware that she or he is reinforcing or failing to reinforce a particualr client behavior. For example, client-centered therapists believe in letting the client determine what is discussed during the therapy sessions and do not wish to influence the trend of the client's conversation. However, reinforcement can be subtle; a smile, nod of the head, or a simple "umhmm" following certain client statements may increase the likelihood of their recurrence. An analysis of a recording of one of Carl Rogers' cases showed that certain client responses were in fact reinforced by positive reactions from Rogers (Truax, 1966).

Since the goal of all psychotherapies is to bring about a change in the client's attitudes and behaviors, some type of learning must take place in therapy. The therapist should be aware of his or her role in influencing the client by means of reinforcement and should use this knowledge consciously to facilitate desired changes.

Despite apparent differences in the theories and methods of the various approaches to psychotherapy, a number of common factors appear to operate in most of them. And these factors may be the most influential in producing some of the positive changes that take place during psychotherapy.

BIOLOGICAL THERAPIES

Biological therapies for the treatment of abnormal behavior include the use of drugs, electroconvulsive shock, and surgical procedures. Several biological theories were mentioned in conjunction with the causes of affective disorders and schizophrenia discussed in Chapter 15. "Mind" and "body" share an intimate relationship; biological changes undoubtedly affect thoughts and behavior, and vice versa.

Electroconvulsive therapy and psychosurgery

In *electroconvulsive therapy* (ECT), also know as *electroshock therapy*, a mild electric current is applied to the brain to produce a seizure similar to an epileptic convulsion. ECT was a popular treatment from about 1940–1960, before antipsychotic and antidepressant drugs became readily available. Today, ECT is used only in cases of severe depression when patients fail to respond to drug therapy.

ECT has been the subject of much controversy and public apprehension for several reasons. At one time, it was used indiscriminately in mental hospitals to treat such disorders as alcoholism and schizophrenia, for which it produced no beneficial results. Before more refined procedures were developed, ECT was a frightening experience for the patient, who was often awake until the electric current triggered the seizure and produced momentary unconsciousness and who frequently suffered confusion and memory loss afterward. Occasionally, the intensity of the muscle spasms accompanying the brain seizure resulted in physical injuries.

Today, ECT involves little discomfort. The patient is given a short-acting anesthesia and then injected with a muscle relaxant. A brief, very weak electric current is delivered to the brain either across both temples or to the temple on the side of the nondominant cerebral hemisphere. The minimum current required to produce a brain seizure is administered, since the seizure itself is therapeutic—*not* the electricity. The muscle relaxant prevents the convulsive spasm of body muscles and possible injury. The patient awakens within a few minutes and remembers nothing about the treatment. Confusion and memory loss appear to be minimal, especially if the current is applied only to the nondominant hemisphere. Four to six treatments are usually administered over a period of two weeks.

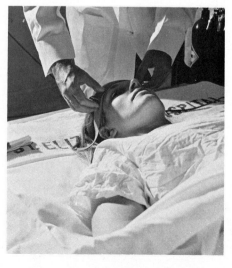

Electroshock therapy being administered to a patient

No one knows exactly how ECT works. Brain seizures do cause the massive release of a number of neurotransmitters, including norepinephrine and serotonin; deficiencies of these two neurotransmitters may be an important factor in some cases of depression (see page 468). However it works, ETC is very effective in bringing people out of a severe, immobilizing depression and does so faster than drug therapy.

In *psychosurgery*, selected areas of the brain are destroyed by cutting nerve fibers or by ultrasonic irradiation. Most often, the fibers that connect the frontal lobes with the limbic system or with certain regions of the hypothalamus are destroyed. (Both the limbic system and the hypothalamus are believed to play important roles in emotion.) Psychosurgery is a highly controversial procedure, and congressional committees have investigated whether it should be legally banned (National Commission for the Protection of Human Subjects of Biomedical and Behavioral Research, 1977). Some early surgical methods produced individuals who were relaxed and cheerful (no longer violent or suicidal) but whose brains were so impaired that they could not function efficiently. Newer techniques appear to cause minimal intellectual impairment, and the procedure may help severely depressed and suicidal patients or those who suffer from intractable pain when all other forms of treatment have failed to relieve distress (Valenstein, 1980). Psychosurgery has not proved effective in treating schizophrenia or obsessive-compulsive disorders.

Drug therapies

By far the most successful biological therapy is the use of drugs to modify mood and behavior. The discovery in the early 1950s of drugs that relieved some of the symptoms of schizophrenia represented a major breakthrough in the treatment of severely disturbed individuals. Intensely agitated patients no longer had to be physically restrained by straitjackets; patients who previously spent most of their time hallucinating and exhibiting bizarre behavior became more responsive and functional. As a result, psychiatric wards became more manageable and patients could be discharged more quickly. A few years later, the discovery of drugs that could relieve severe depression had a similar beneficial effect on hospital management and population. Figure 16-5 shows the reduction in the number of mental-hospital residents that occurred following the introduction of antipsychotic and antidepressant drugs. About the same time, a group of drugs were being developed to relieve anxiety.

ANTIANXIETY DRUGS   Drugs such as *diazepam* (trade name Valium), *meprobamate* (Miltown), and *chlordiazepoxide* (Librium)—commonly known as *tranquilizers*—reduce tension and cause drowsiness. Like alcohol and the barbiturates, these drugs depress the action of the central nervous system. Family physicians often prescribe tranquilizers to help people cope during difficult periods in their lives. They are also used to treat anxiety disorders, withdrawal from alcohol, and physical disorders related to stress. For example, antianxiety drugs may be combined with systematic desensitization in the treatment of a phobia to help the individual relax when confronting the feared situation.

Although tranquilizers may be useful on a short-term basis, the overall benefits are debatable, and such drugs clearly are overprescribed and misused. Until quite recently (before some of the dangers became apparent), Valium and Librium were the two most widely prescribed drugs in this country (Julien, 1981). The dangers of tranquilizer overuse are several. Depending on a pill to relieve anxiety may prevent the person from exploring the *cause* of the anxiety and from learning more effective ways of coping with tension. More importantly, long-term use of tranquilizers can lead to physical dependency, or addiction (see page 484). Although tranquilizers are not as addictive as barbi-

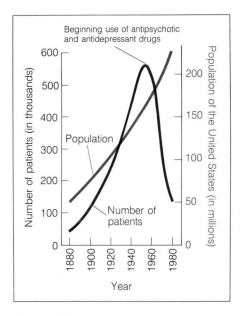

Figure 16-5
Patients in Public Mental Hospitals
The graph presents the number of residents in state and county mental hospitals from 1880 to 1980; also shown is the population of the United States during the same period. In the mid-1950s, the number of hospitalized patients began to decline dramatically, both in absolute numbers and as a proportion of the population. The most important factor contributing to this decline has been the widespread use of antipsychotic and antidepressant drugs. Other factors include more adequate outpatient clinics, day hospitals, and related community health facilities. (Data from the National Institute of Mental Health)

turates, tolerance does develop with repeated use and the individual experiences severe withdrawal symptoms if the drug is discontinued. In addition, tranquilizers impair concentration, including driving performance, and can cause death if combined with alcohol.

ANTIPSYCHOTIC DRUGS   *Antipsychotic drugs* that relieve the symptoms of schizophrenia include *chlorpromazine* (Thorazine) and *fluphenazine decanoate* (Prolixin), both belonging to the family of drugs called *phenothiazines, reserpine* (Serpasil), and *haloperidol* (Haldol). These drugs have been called "major tranquilizers," but the term is not really appropriate because they do not act on the nervous system in the same way as barbiturates or antianxiety drugs. They may cause some degree of drowsiness and lethargy, but they do not induce deep sleep even in massive doses (the person can be easily aroused). These drugs appear to produce an indifference to external stimuli. (We noted in Chapter 15 that people suffering from schizophrenia seem unable to filter out irrelevant stimuli.)

The differences in the behavioral effects of antipsychotic drugs and tranquilizers can be demonstrated by administering both types of drugs to animals trained to make a conditioned avoidance response. A rat is placed in a cage on a wire grid and is given a mild electric shock immediately after a buzzer sounds. The rat quickly climbs a pole to escape the shock. After a few trials, the animal learns to associate the buzzer with the shock and climbs the pole whenever it hears the buzzer (the conditioned avoidance response). After very small doses of chlorpromazine, the rat will ignore the buzzer but will still climb the pole to escape shock once the shock starts. In contrast, barbiturates and tranquilizers depress the animal's responses to both the buzzer *and* the shock (Julien, 1981).

The mechanisms that produce this behavior are not clearly understood, but evidence indicates that antipsychotic drugs act on a part of the brain stem—the *reticular system* (see page 39)—that controls the input of messages from the sense organs to the cerebral cortex. These drugs appear to reduce the sensory input to the reticular system, so that the information does not reach the cerebral cortex. Tranquilizers and barbiturates, on the other hand, act directly to depress the activity of neurons in the reticular system, thereby inducing sleep.

In Chapter 15, we discussed the theory that schizophrenia is caused by excessive activity of the neurotransmitter dopamine. (Neurons that use dopamine as a neurotransmitter are concentrated in the reticular formation, hypothalamus, and limbic system.) Because phenothiazine molecules are structurally similar to dopamine molecules, they could occupy the post-synaptic receptors of dopamine neurons and prevent the neurons from firing.

Independent of how they work, anti-psychotic drugs have proved effective in relieving the symptoms of schizophrenia, shortening the length of time patients must be hospitalized, and preventing relapse. For example, studies of schizophrenics living in the community find that the relapse rate for those taking Prolixin is typically less than half the relapse rate of those receiving a placebo (Hirsch and others, 1973; Hogarty and others, 1979). However, such drugs are not a cure-all. Most patients must continue to receive a maintenance dosage of medication to function outside the hopsital. And because the side effects can be unpleasant—dryness of the mouth, blurred vision, difficulty concentrating—many discontinue their medication. In addition, long-term use of the drugs can produce more serious side effects in some cases (for example, low blood pressure and a muscular disorder in which there are involuntary movements of the mouth and chin).

CRITICAL DISCUSSION

Evaluating the Effectiveness of a Drug

The initial enthusiam for a new treatment method is almost always dampened by evidence provided by more carefully controlled research. This has been particularly true in the area of drug therapy. The results of a drug study may be influenced by a number of variables other than the therapeutic properties of the drug itself.

One variable is the hope and confidence the patient places in the new treatment. In discussing research on the effectiveness of psychotherapy we noted the importance of the placebo effect. A sugar pill or injections of a harmless salt solution often can markedly improve a person's condition. Improvement in such cases stems from the patients' expectations that the treatment will make them feel better. Another variable is the confidence of the doctors and nurses in the new treatment method, which can inadvertently affect their judgment of the results. The extra attention focused on a patient who is the subject of a re-

search project can also produce beneficial effects. To control these variables, researchers employ a *double-blind procedure*. One half of the patients in the study receive a placebo; the others, the actual drug. Neither the patients nor the doctors and nurses who must judge the results of the treatment know which patients received the drug. Thus, in the ideally controlled study, both the patients and the judges are "blind"— hence, the term "double-blind."

The importance of a well-controlled research design has been demonstrated by a survey of a large number of studies dealing with the effect of chlorpromazine on hospitalized schizophrenics. Each study was classified according to the extent that awareness of medication was controlled: *double-blind*, in which neither patient nor judges were aware, or *single-blind*, in which only judges were aware. In double-blind studies, 37 percent of the patients were judged to be "improved"; in contrast,

the single-blind studies showed an improvement rate of 60 percent. More carefully controlled studies report considerably less improvement following treatment with chlorpromazine than less well-controlled studies (Glick and Margolis, 1962).

However, the situation is more complicated than it first appears. Although it seems probable that differences in adequacy of experimental control were partly responsible for differences in the results, the double-blind studies differed from the single-blind studies in another major respect. The average period of drug treatment was significantly longer for patients in the single-blind studies than for patients in the double-blind studies, which could account for the higher improvement rate among patients in the single-blind studies. The greater the degree of control required in a study, the more difficult it is to sustain the procedures for a long period of time.

ANTIDEPRESSANT DRUGS *Antidepressant drugs* help to elevate the mood of depressed individuals. These drugs energize rather than tranquilize, apparently by increasing the availability of two neurotransmitters (norepinephrine and serotonin) that are deficient in some cases of depression (see page 468). The two major classes of antidepressant drugs act in different ways to increase neurotransmitter levels. The *monoamine oxidase (MAO) inhibiters* (examples are Nardil and Parnate) block the activity of an enzyme that can destroy both norepinephrine and serotonin, thereby increasing the concentration of these two neurotransmitters in the brain. The *tricyclic antidepressants* (examples are Tofranil and Elavil) prevent the *reuptake* of serotonin and norepinephrine, thereby prolonging the duration of their action. (*Reuptake* is the process by which neurotransmitters are sucked back into the nerve terminals that released them.) Both classes of drugs have proved effective in relieving certain types of depression, presumably those caused more by biological than environmental factors (Raskin and others, 1970). However, like the antipsychotic drugs, the antidepressants can produce some undesirable side effects.

As we noted in Chapter 15, *lithium carbonate* has been used successfully in treating manic-depressive, or bipolar, disorders. This drug reduces extreme mood swings and returns the individual to a more normal state of emotional equilibrium.

Drug therapy has successfully reduced the severity of some types of mental disorders. Many individuals who otherwise would require hospitalization can function within the community with the help of these drugs. On the other hand, there are limitations to the application of drug therapy. All therapeutic drugs can produce undesirable side effects. In addition, many psychologists feel that these drugs alleviate symptoms without requiring the individual to face the personal problems that are contributing to the disorder. Biochemical abnormalities undoubtedly play a role in schizophrenia and in the more severe affective disorders, but psychological factors (for example, environmental stress and methods of coping with it) are equally important. Attitudes and methods of coping with problems that have developed gradually over a lifetime cannot be changed suddenly by the administration of a drug. When therapeutic drugs are prescribed, psychotherapeutic help is usually also required.

ENHANCING MENTAL HEALTH

The prevention and treatment of mental disorders is a problem of tremendous concern for both the nation and the community. Considerable progress has been made in this area within the past two decades. Early in this chapter, we noted that the Community Mental Health Centers Act, passed by Congress in 1963, provided funds for the establishment of community mental health centers where people could be treated close to family and friends rather than in a large state psychiatric hospital. These community centers provide short-term hospitalization, outpatient treatment, and a 24-hour emergency service. They are also concerned with *preventing* emotional problems through consultation with schools, juvenile courts, and other community agencies.

Community resources and the role of nonprofessionals

A variety of community resources have been developed in response to the psychological needs of different groups. During the 1960s, for example, a *free clinic* was established in the Haight-Ashbury district of San Francisco to meet the needs of young people who had drifted there to join the "hippie" movement. Many of these individuals developed serious physical and psychological problems (often associated with malnutrition and the use of drugs) but were reluctant to seek help from usual private or public resources because they were suspicious of the "establishment." The Haight-Ashbury Free Clinic—organized by volunteer physicians, psychiatrists, and psychologists—offered free treatment with no questions asked about drug usage, sexual behavior, or delinquency and gave no information to relatives or police. The success of this clinic prompted other communities to follow suit; free clinics have now been established in many areas and have expanded their services to meet the needs of individuals of all ages.

Another community resource is the *half-way house*, where patients who have been hospitalized can live while making the transition back to an independent life in the community. Residential centers are also available to people recovering from alcohol and drug problems, delinquent or runaway youths, and battered wives. *Rap centers*, where troubled teen-agers can discuss their problems with each other and with sympathetic counselors, play an important role in many communities; *youth centers* in poverty areas provide job counseling, remedial education, and help with family and personal problems.

Community centers provide help for a variety of physical and emotional problems.

CRISIS INTERVENTION A fairly recent development—*crisis intervention*— provides immediate help for individuals and families undergoing intense stress. During periods of acute emotional turmoil, people often feel overwhelmed and incapable of dealing with the situation; they may not be able to wait for a therapy appointment, or they may not know where to turn. One form of crisis intervention is provided by 24-hour, walk-in services, often in a Community Mental Health Center, where the individual receives immediate attention. There, a therapist helps to clarify the problem, provides reassurance, suggests a plan of action, and mobilizes the support of other agencies or family members. This kind of therapy is usually short-term (five or six sessions) and provides the support the person requires to handle the current crisis. Such short-term intervention often prevents the need for hospitalization.

Another form of crisis intervention is the *telephone hot line.* Telephone crisis centers are usually staffed by volunteers under the direction of mental health professionals. Some focus specifically on suicide prevention; others are more general and help distressed callers find the particular kind of assistance they need. The volunteers usually receive training that emphasizes listening with care, evaluating the potential for suicide, conveying empathy and understanding, providing information about community resources, giving hope and reassurance, and recording the caller's name and phone number before he or she hangs up so that a professional can follow up on the problem. Most major cities in the United States have developed some form of telephone hot line to help people who are undergoing periods of severe stress as well as specialized hot lines to deal with child abuse, rape victims, battered wives, and runaways. The phone numbers are widely publicized in the hope of reaching those who need help.

It is too early to conclude much about the effectiveness of telephone crisis centers. Several studies have revealed no difference in suicide rates for cities with and without hot line services (Weiner, 1969; Lester, 1974). Another study suggests that calling a friend or relative may be more beneficial to a person than calling a crisis center (Speer, 1972). But research on suicide prevention and the effectiveness of hot lines is difficult because there are so many uncontrolled variables. For people without friends, relatives, or other forms of emotional support, the hot line may provide a life-saving service.

NONPROFESSIONALS AS THERAPISTS Most of the community programs we have discussed could not function without the help of nonprofessionals. Because the need for psychological services has outstripped the supply of available therapists, concerned citizens can play a valuable role. People of all ages and backgrounds have been trained to work in the area of community mental health. College students have served as companions for hospitalized patients (Matarazzo, 1971); older women who have successfully raised families have been trained as "mental health counselors" to work with adolescents in community clinics, to counsel mothers of youngsters with behavior problems, and to work with schizophrenic children (Donahue, 1967; Rioch, 1967); former mental patients, drug addicts, and prison inmates have been trained to help those faced with problems similar to the ones they have experienced.

Many residential mental health programs are run by nonprofessionals in consultation with trained therapists. An outstanding example is Achievement Place—a home located in a middle-class community where a couple acts as surrogate parents for about a dozen boys referred by the courts because of their delinquent behavior (Phillips and others, 1972). Behavior therapy methods are used to extinguish aggressive behavior and to reward social skills (see Figure 16-6).

Nonprofessionals as therapists
College students and other volunteers can do much to augment therapeutic programs in hospitals and mental health centers, whether they are trained in special therapeutic techniques or they simply provide conversation and companionship. This young woman is working with a disturbed child.

Figure 16-6
Residential Program
for Delinquent Youths
A family conference at Achievement Place—a group home for boys with behavior problems who are referred by the courts. The boys and their professional teacher-parents meet daily to discuss rules of conduct, decide on consequences for violations of the rules, criticize aspects of the program, and evaluate a peer manager who oversees many of the boys' activities.

Promoting your own emotional well-being

The problems that people face vary greatly, and there are no universal guidelines for staying psychologically healthy. However, a few general suggestions have emerged from the experiences of therapists.

ACCEPT YOUR FEELINGS Strong emotions can produce anxiety. Anger, sorrow, fear, a feeling of having fallen short of ideals or goals are all unpleasant emotions, and we may try to escape anxiety by denying these feelings. Sometimes the desire to avoid anxiety by facing situations unemotionally leads to a false kind of detachment or "cool" that may be destructive. We may try to suppress all emotions, thereby losing the ability to accept as normal the joys and sorrows that are a part of our involvement with other people.

Unpleasant emotions are a normal reaction to many situations. There is no reason to be ashamed of feeling homesick, being afraid when learning to ski, or becoming angry at someone who has disappointed us. These emotions are natural, and it is better to recognize than to deny them. When emotions cannot be expressed directly (for example, it may not be wise to tell off your boss), it helps to find some kind of outlet for releasing tension. Taking a long walk, pounding a tennis ball, or discussing the situation with a sympathetic friend can help to dissipate anger. As long as you accept your right to feel emotion, you can express it in indirect or substitute ways when direct channels of expression are blocked.

KNOW YOUR VULNERABILITIES Discovering the kinds of situations that upset you or cause you to overreact may help to guard against stress. Perhaps certain people annoy you. You could avoid them, or you could try to understand just what it is about them that disturbs you; maybe they seem so poised and confident that they make you feel insecure. Trying to pinpoint the cause of your discomfort may help you to see the situation in a new light. Perhaps you become very anxious when you have to speak in class or present a paper. Again, you could try to avoid such situations, or you could gain confidence by taking a course in public speaking. (Many colleges offer courses specifically aimed at learning to control speech anxiety.) You could also reinterpret the situation. Instead of thinking "Everyone is waiting to criticize me as soon as I open my mouth," you could tell yourself "The class will be interested in what I have to say, and I'm not going to let it worry me if I make a few mistakes."

Many people feel especially anxious when they are under pressure. Careful planning and spacing of work can help you avoid feeling overwhelmed at the last minute. The strategy of purposely allowing more time than you think you need to get to classes or appointments can eliminate one source of stress.

DEVELOP YOUR TALENTS AND INTERESTS   People who are bored and unhappy seldom have many interests. Today's college and community programs offer almost unlimited opportunities for people of all ages to explore their talents in many areas, including sports and physical skills, academic interests, music, art, drama, and crafts. Often, the more you know about a subject, the more interesting it (and life) becomes. In addition, the feeling of competency gained from developing skills can do a great deal to bolster self-esteem. As we noted earlier, depression often results from a reduction in rewarding activities.

BECOME INVOLVED WITH OTHER PEOPLE   Feelings of isolation and loneliness form the core of most emotional disorders. We are "social beings," and we need the support, comfort, and reassurance provided by other people. Focusing all of your attention on your own problems can lead to an unhealthy preoccupation with yourself. Sharing your concerns with others often helps you to view your troubles in a clearer perspective. Also, becoming concerned with the welfare of other people—who may be troubled and lonely too—can reinforce your feelings of self-worth.

KNOW WHEN TO SEEK HELP   Although these suggestions can help to promote emotional well-being, there are limits to self-understanding and self-help. Some problems are difficult to solve alone. Our tendency toward self-deception makes it hard to view problems objectively, and we may not know all of the possible solutions. When you feel that you are making little headway in gaining control over a problem, it is time to seek professional help from a counseling or clinical psychologist, a psychiatrist, or some other trained therapist. The willingness to seek help is a sign of emotional maturity, not a sign of weakness; do not wait until you feel overwhelmed. You do not wait until your teeth are falling out before going to a dentist. Obtaining psychological help when it is needed should become as accepted a practice as going to a dentist.

Summary

1   Treatment of the mentally ill has progressed from the ancient notion that abnormal behavior resulted from the possession of evil spirits and should be punished, to custodial care in ill-kept and isolated asylums, to our modern mental hospitals and community mental health centers, which offer a variety of activities designed to help people understand and modify their behavior.

2   *Psychotherapy* is the treatment of mental disorders by psychological means. One type of psychotherapy is *psychoanalysis*, which is based on concepts developed by Freud. Through the method of *free association*, repressed thoughts and feelings are brought to the client's conscious awareness. By *interpreting* these associations, the analyst helps the individual understand the roots of his or her problems. *Transference*—the tendency to express feelings toward the analyst that the client has for important people in his or her

3   life—provides another source of interpretation. Through the processes of *abreaction, insight,* and *working through,* the individual becomes able to cope with problems more realistically.

3   Another psychotherapeutic approach is *behavior therapy,* which applies methods based on learning principles to *modify* the individual's behavior. These methods include *systematic desensitization* (the individual learns to relax in situations that previously produced anxiety), *assertive training, reinforcement* of adaptive behaviors and *extinction* of maladaptive ones, *modeling* of appropriate behavior, and techniques for *self-regulation* of behavior. *Cognitive therapy,* aimed at replacing distorted expectations and beliefs with more realistic ones, is often combined with behavior therapy.

4   *Humanistic therapies* help the individual to explore his or her own problems and solve them with a minimum of therapist intervention. Carl Rogers' *client-centered psychotherapy* maintains a *nondirective* approach, letting the client determine the topics to be discussed and the goals to be accomplished.

5   *Group therapy* provides an opportunity for the individual to explore his or her attitudes and behavior in interaction with others who have similar problems. *Encounter groups*—a popular offshoot of group therapy—may help psychologically healthy individuals learn something about themselves, but they do not appear to help individuals who have emotional problems. *Family therapy* is a special form of group therapy in which couples, or parents and children, can learn more effective ways of relating to one another.

6   The effectiveness of psychotherapy is difficult to evaluate due to problems in *defining a "successful" outcome* and *controlling for placebo effects* and *rates of spontaneous remission.* Research indicates that psychotherapy does help and that different approaches do not differ greatly in effectiveness. Factors common to the various psychotherapies—a *warm and trustful interpersonal relationship, reassurance and support, desensitization, insight,* and *reinforcement of adaptive responses*—may be more important in producing positive change than specific therapeutic methods.

7   *Biological therapies* include *electroconvulsive therapy* (ECT), *psychosurgery,* and the use of *drugs* to modify behavior. Of these three treatments, drug therapy has proved to be the most successful by far. *Antianxiety drugs* are used to reduce severe anxiety and to help individuals cope with life crises. *Antipsychotic drugs* have proved highly effective in the treatment of schizophrenia. *Antidepressants* help to elevate the mood of depressed patients, and *lithium carbonate* has been successful in treating manic-depressive disorders.

8   The *prevention* and *treatment* of mental disorders is of great concern in our society. Community resources that offer help include *free clinics, half-way houses, residential centers* for people with special problems, and various forms of *crisis intervention.* We can promote our own emotional health by accepting our feelings as natural, discovering our vulnerabilities, developing talents and interests, becoming involved with others, and recognizing when to seek professional help.

Further Reading

Interesting material on the historical treatment of the mentally ill may be found in Zilboorg and Henry, *A history of medical psychology* (1941); Veith, *Hysteria: The history of a disease* (1970); and Bell, *Treating the mentally ill: From colonial times to the present* (1980).

A review of the various methods of psychotherapy is provided by Martin, *Introduction to psychotherapy* (1971). The *Handbook of psychotherapy and behavior change: An empirical analysis* (1978), edited by Garfield and Bergin, discusses results of psychotherapeutic research and possible applications. *The handbook of research methods in clinical psychology* (1982), edited by Kendall and Butcher, includes a section on methods for evaluating the outcome of psychotherapy.

For an introduction to psychoanalytic methods, see Menninger and Holzman, *Theory of psychoanalytic technique* (2nd ed., 1973). On client-centered therapy, see Rogers, *On becoming a person: A therapist's view of psychotherapy* (1970); and *Carl Rogers on personal power* (1977). The principles of behavior therapy are presented in Craighead, Kazdin, and Mahoney, *Behavior modification: Principles, issues, and applications* (2nd ed., 1981); and Turner, Calhoun, and Adams (eds.), *The handbook of clinical behavior therapy* (1981).

An overview of group therapy is presented in Yalom, *The theory and practice of group psychotherapy* (2nd ed., 1975). On encounter groups, see Lieberman, Yalom, and Miles, *Encounter groups: First facts* (1973).

For ways to modify your own behavior, see Bower and Bower, *Asserting yourself* (1976); and Watson and Tharp, *Self-directed behavior: Self-modification for personal adjustment* (3rd ed., 1981).

Part eight
SOCIAL BEHAVIOR

17
INDIVIDUAL SOCIAL BEHAVIOR

Social psychology is the study of how we think, feel, and act in social environments and how, in turn, social environments influence our thoughts, feelings, and actions. How do we perceive and interpret the behaviors and motives of other people? How are our beliefs and attitudes shaped? What determines whom we like and dislike or love and hate?

Social psychology bases its approach to topics like these on two fundamental observations about human behavior. The first is that behavior is a function of both the person and the situation. As we all know, different people act differently in the same situation; each person's behavior reflects the unique constellation of attributes that he or she brings to the setting. Personality psychology specializes in the study of such individual differences. But we also know that the same person acts differently in different situations; each situation brings a unique set of forces to bear on the individual's behavior. Social psychology specializes in the study of situational influences.

The second observation underlying social psychology is that if persons define situations as real, they are real in their consequences (Thomas and Thomas, 1928). That is, people do not react simply to the objective features of a situation but to their own subjective interpretations of it. This is one reason different people behave differently in the same objective situation. The person who interprets a hurtful act as the product of malice reacts differently from the person who interprets that same act as the product of incompetence. For this reason, social psychology is concerned with the processes of social perception and interpretation—that is, with our strategies for processing social information and with the systematic biases those strategies may contain. As we will see, we can begin to understand social behavior through an understanding of social information processing.

Accordingly, this chapter on individual social behavior starts with a discussion of social information processing, in which the emphasis is on thinking and perceiving. An examination of beliefs, attitudes, and values follows, adding an affective dimension—feelings and emotions—to the discussion. The chapter ends with interpersonal attraction—liking and loving—in which feelings and emotions are the major focus. In Chapter 18, we discuss the social and environmental influences on human social behavior.

SOCIAL INFORMATION PROCESSING

Everyday social interaction typically presents us with two major information processing questions: What is this person like? And why is this person behaving in this way? The first question concerns *impression formation*. The second assigns us a *causal attribution* task: we must attribute the person's behavior to some mixture of causes. This section begins with the first question. How do we code and process information about the characteristics of other people?

Schematic processing and person perception

SCHEMATIC PROCESSING   In earlier chapters, we saw that our perceptions and memories of objects and events are not simply mirrored representations of the stimuli that impinge on us. Our memories of objects and events are often simplified but highly organized reconstructions of our original perceptions rather than photographic-like reproductions or exhaustive lists of specific detailed features. As noted in Chapter 8, such memory structures are often called *schemata*, and the process of searching for the schema in memory that is most consistent with incoming sensory information is called *schematic processing*. Schemata and schematic processing permit us to organize and process an enormous amount of information with great efficiency. Instead of having to perceive and remember all the details of each new object or event, we can simply note that it is like one of our pre-existing schemata and encode or remember only its most prominent features. Schematic processing typically occurs rapidly and automatically; usually, we are not even aware that any processing of information is taking place at all.

This view of perception is particularly applicable to social perception, where the stimuli are very complex and often susceptible to more than one possible interpretation. We have many different kinds of social schemata. For example, we have schemata for social events. When we are invited to a birthday party, we invoke a general birthday party schema, an abstract picture or cognitive structure in our minds that helps us anticipate the general outlines of what will take place. We also have schemata for kinds of people. When someone tells you that you are about to meet an extravert, you immediately retrieve your extravert schema in order to anticipate the coming encounter. The extravert schema consists of a set of interrelated traits such as sociability, warmth, and possibly loudness and impulsiveness. General person schemata like these are sometimes called *prototypes* (Cantor and Mischel, 1979) or *implicit personality theories* (Schneider, 1973).

As we get to know a person better, we replace such general and abstract schemata with a more specific schema for that person. Thus, we also have schemata for particular persons, such as the president, Jane Fonda, our mothers, even ourselves (Markus, 1977). When you see a job advertisement for a peer counselor, you can quickly and automatically evaluate the match between your schema for a counselor and your self-schema to decide if you should apply.

Research confirms that schemata help us process social information. For example, if people are explicitly instructed to remember as much information as they can about a stimulus person, they actually remember *less* than if they are simply told to try to form an impression of the person (Hamilton, 1979). The instruction to form an impression induces the subjects to search for various person-relevant schemata that help them organize and recall material better. Similarly, people can recall a list of traits better if they are told to think about each trait as it applies to them than if they just try to learn them in the abstract (Rogers, Kuiper, and Kirker, 1977). The self-schema provides a way of organizing the items to be memorized.

But because they constitute simplifications of reality, schemata and schematic processing have shortcomings that produce biases in our processing of social information. These shortcomings are evident in one of the basic tasks of social perception, forming an impression of someone we are meeting for the first time.

IMPRESSION FORMATION AND THE PRIMACY EFFECT   What kind of impression do you have of Jim from the following observations of his behavior?

> Jim left the house to get some stationery. He walked out into the sun-filled street with two of his friends, basking in the sun as he walked. Jim entered the stationery store, which was full of people. Jim talked with an acquaintance while he waited to catch the clerk's eye. On his way out, he stopped to chat with the school friend who was just coming into the store. Leaving the store, he walked toward the school. On his way, he met the girl to whom he had been introduced the night before. They talked for a short while, and then Jim left for school. After school, Jim left the classroom alone. Leaving the school, he started on his long walk home. The street was brilliantly filled with sunshine. Jim walked down the street on the shady side. Coming down the street toward him, he saw the pretty girl whom he had met on the previous evening. Jim crossed the street and entered a candy store. The store was crowded with students, and he noticed a few familiar faces. Jim waited quietly until he caught the counterman's eye and then gave his order. Taking his drink, he sat down at a side table. When he had finished his drink, he went home. (Luchins, 1957b, pp. 34–35)

What is Jim like? Do you think of him as a friendly, outgoing person, or do you have the impression that he is rather shy and introverted? If you think Jim is better described as friendly than unfriendly, you are in agreement with most people (78 percent) who read this description. But examine the description closely; it is actually composed of two very different portraits. Up to the sentence that begins "After school, Jim left . . . ," Jim is portrayed in several situations as a fairly friendly guy. After that point, however, a nearly identical set of situations shows him to be much more of a loner. In fact, 95 percent of the people who are shown only the first half of the description rate Jim as friendly, whereas only 3 percent who are shown only the second half do so. Thus, in the combined description that you read, Jim's friendliness seems to win over his unfriendliness. Why is this so? Is it something about the trait of friendliness, or is it that Jim is described as friendly first and unfriendly second? To find out, Luchins had individuals read the same description with the unfriendly half of the paragraph appearing first. As Table 17-1 shows, only 18 percent found Jim to be friendly under this condition; Jim's unfriendly behavior left the major impression. The first information we receive has the greater impact on our overall impressions. This is known as the *primacy effect*.

The primacy effect has been found repeatedly in several different kinds of impression formation studies, including studies using real rather than hypothetical persons. For example, subjects who watched a male student attempt to

CONDITIONS	PERCENTAGE RATING JIM AS FRIENDLY
Friendly description only	95
Friendly first—unfriendly last	78
Unfriendly first—friendly last	18
Unfriendly description only	3

Table 17-1
Primacy Effect in Impression Formation
What subjects thought of Jim depended on what they learned first. (After Luchins, 1957b)

solve a series of difficult multiple-choice problems were asked to assess his general ability. Although the student always solved exactly 15 of the 30 problems correctly, he was judged more capable if the successes came mostly at the beginning of the series than if they came near the end. Moreover, when asked to recall how many problems the student had solved, subjects who had seen the 15 successes bunched at the beginning estimated an average of 20.6, whereas subjects who had seen the successes at the end estimated an average of 12.5 (Jones and others, 1968).

Although several factors contribute to the primacy effect, it appears to be mainly a consequence of schematic processing. When we are first attempting to form our impressions of a person, we are actively searching for the person schema that seems to best match the person. At some point, we make a preliminary decision: this person is an extravert (or whatever). What we then appear to do is assimilate any further information into that schema and dismiss any discrepant information as not representative of the "real" person we have come to know. For example, when asked how they reconcile the apparent contradictions in Jim's behavior, subjects sometimes say that Jim is "really" friendly but was probably tired by the end of the day (Luchins, 1957b). Thus, one of the shortcomings of schematic processing is that our perceptions become "schema-driven" and hence resistant to change and relatively impervious to new data.

In Chapter 8, we described a study in which individuals reconstructed their memories about a woman's past life in ways that were consistent with new information they had just received about her, thus showing that schematic processing can affect our memories of the past (Snyder and Uranowitz, 1978). The primacy effect exemplifies the process in reverse by showing how schematic processing causes our past knowledge to affect our interpretation of the present.

It is possible to block the primacy effect by warning subjects about the dangers of making judgments on insufficient information or by inserting a time interval or some interfering task between the receipt of the two blocks of information (Luchins, 1957a). This latter procedure sometimes even produces a *recency effect*. The earlier information is forgotten and the second block of information replaces it, determining the final impression. In real life, we sometimes have the opportunity to correct erroneous first impressions and to revise our schema of a person. Friends and lovers enjoy remembering with amusement their disastrous first encounters and laughing about the warped first impressions they formed of each other. In general, however, the primacy effect holds sway, and it is probably fortunate that we remain ignorant of the many potential friendships and love affairs that never materialized because of disastrous first encounters. Such is one consequence of schematic processing.

STEREOTYPES As we noted in Chapter 8, schemata about identifiable groups (such as blacks, Orientals, women with blond hair, or short men) have traditionally been called *stereotypes*, and it is here that the biases of schematic processing are clearly evident and the negative consequences are of greatest concern. But even in this domain, it is important to recognize that the thinking process that gives rise to stereotypes—schematic processing of social information—is not itself evil or pathological. Since it is simply not possible to deal with every new person as unique, the use of schemata or "working stereotypes" is inevitable until further experiences either refine or discredit them. For example, some students from rural areas of the country who attend college in New York City spend their first few weeks of college thinking that all New Yorkers are Jews and all Jews are New Yorkers. There is not necessarily any malice or ill will behind such a stereotype; the new student has simply not yet seen enough Catholic New Yorkers or Texas Jews to sort the social environment into more accurate and finely differentiated categories or schemata. Many of our stereotypes are of this benign variety and are discarded as our experiences multiply.

As we saw in the case of the primacy effect, however, schematic processing produces perceptions that are resistant to change and relatively impervious to new data. Sometimes they are not so easily discarded even as experiences multiply. Moreover, our stereotypes can become both self-perpetuating and self-fulfilling by influencing our own behavior toward those we stereotype. This was dramatically shown in a study in which white college students played the role of job interviewers; they were assigned to interview both black and white job applicants, who were actually confederates of the experimenters. It was found that the subjects (the interviewers) were less friendly when interviewing black applicants than when interviewing white applicants, maintaining greater interpersonal distance, making more speech errors, and terminating the interview sooner.

But that was only the first part of the research study. The experimenters then trained white confederates to act as interviewers so that they would be able to reproduce both the friendly and the less friendly interviewing styles shown by the original subjects. New subjects—all white—were then recruited, this time to play the role of the job applicants. Some received the friendly interview treatment; others received the less friendly treatment. Videotapes of the subjects were made, and judges later rated the subjects' performance and composure during the interview. It was found that subjects who received the less positive pattern of nonverbal behavior from the interviewer (as had the black applicants in the first experiment) were rated significantly lower on both performance and demeanor than were those who had received the more positive pattern of nonverbal behavior (Word, Zanna, and Cooper, 1974). What this study indicates is that prejudiced individuals may interact in ways that actually create the stereotyped behavior that sustains their prejudice. We shall see further examples of self-fulfilling stereotypes later in this chapter when we discuss interpersonal attraction.

CHANGING STEREOTYPES   If stereotypes are a "natural" consequence of our normal ways of thinking and if their self-fulfilling and self-perpetuating features are similarly a consequence of "natural" biases built into our cognitive processes, attempting to change stereotypes simply by increasing the amount of contact that people have with one another would not seem very promising. Certainly some interracial contacts seem to increase prejudice rather than diminish it (for example, contacts between black ghetto residents and white police officers). Moreover, no two groups have more contact than men and women, and yet stereotypes about both are still commonplace. The question, then, is whether there are conditions under which stereotypes can be made to yield to new evidence.

Social psychologists have been seeking an answer to this question for many years, and tests of the "contact hypothesis" of prejudice reduction date to the 1930s. From all the studies—most of them concerned with white prejudice toward blacks—it is clear that simple contact by itself is not sufficient; rather, there appear to be five main conditions that need to be present before the participants begin to discard their prejudices (Cook, 1978).

The first is *equal status of the participants.* For schemata to change, they must be subjected to new kinds of data. This is unlikely to happen if the roles in

Some stereotypes are based on physical appearance. What personality traits and attitudes (friendly, conscientious, liberal) would you attribute to each of these students?

Stereotypes can be quite subtle, so much so that we can be unaware that we hold them. Thus, until the recent women's movement began to raise the issues of sexism, our schemata about women's "natural" abilities—or lack of them—remained hidden and unquestioned by many people of both sexes. For example, in a study conducted in 1968, somewhat before the women's movement had become prominent, female college students were asked to rate a number of professional articles from various fields. The articles were put into two equal sets of booklets, and the names of the authors were changed so that the identical article was attributed to a male author (for example, John T. McKay) in one booklet and to a female author (for example, Joan T. McKay) in the other booklet. Each student was asked to read the articles in her booklet and rate them for value, competence, persuasiveness, writing style, and so forth.

The investigator found that the identical article received significantly lower ratings when it was attributed to a female author than when it was attributed to a male author. This was true not only for articles from professional fields

generally considered the province of men, such as law, but for articles from the fields of dietetics and elementary-school education as well (Goldberg, 1968). In other words, these female students rated the male authors as better at everything, apparently agreeing with Aristotle that "we should regard the female nature as afflicted with a natural defectiveness." But Aristotle was at least aware of his belief in the inferiority of women; these students, like most Americans, were not.

More recent studies have not always yielded the same results. One study found that both men and women tended to rate male authors higher in male-dominated fields but female authors higher in female-dominated fields (Mischel, 1974). Another study found no effects at all (Levenson and others, 1975). The changing patterns of results in such studies probably reflect, in part, the fact that most Americans have become more aware of their own sex-role schemata in recent years and guard against expressing them.

As society's "consciousness is raised" about sexism and as more young women look forward to professional ca-

reers, many young couples are now challenging other hidden assumptions about men and women as well, such as the traditional division of labor within marriage. Many couples claim that they seek fully egalitarian (equal) relationships in which the older assumptions about men's and women's roles are discarded. They often cite examples:

Both my wife and I earned college degrees in our respective disciplines. I turned down a superior job offer in Oregon and accepted a slightly less desirable position in New York where my wife would have more opportunities for part-time work in her specialty. Although I would have preferred to live in a suburb, we purchased a home near my wife's job so that she could have an office at home where she would be when the children returned from school. Because my wife earns a good salary, she can easily afford to pay a housekeeper to do her major household chores. My wife and I share all the other tasks around the house equally. For example, she cooks the meals, but I

which people meet one another continue to reinforce the old stereotypes—for example, if the white professional continues to interact only with blacks in low-status occupational roles.

The second condition is the *potential for personal acquaintance*. It is possible to have daily contact with another person over several years without ever getting to know anything about him or her individually, and most interracial contacts have this characteristic. Research has shown that when black and white housewives who live in the same apartment building are brought together under circumstances in which they get to know each other as individuals, greater acceptance is the result (Deutsch and Collins, 1951); other studies reach similar conclusions (Hamilton and Bishop, 1976).

A third condition is for the prejudiced individual to receive *exposure to nonstereotypic individuals*. Even when we do not get to know people from another group on a personal basis, we may revise our schemata if we begin to meet individuals who violate our stereotypes—particularly if the individuals seem to be similar to ourselves. The white worker who realizes that black

The Subtle Schemata of Sexism

do the laundry for her and help her with many of her other household tasks.

Without questioning the happiness of such a marriage or its appropriateness for many couples, we can still legitimately ask if the marriage is, in fact, egalitarian. Have the hidden assumptions about the woman's "natural" role really been eliminated? There is a very simple test. If the marriage is truly egalitarian, its description should retain the same flavor and tone even if the roles of the husband and wife are reversed:

Both my husband and I earned college degrees in our respective disciplines. I turned down a superior job offer in Oregon and accepted a slightly less desirable position in New York where my husband would have more opportunities for part-time work in his specialty. Although I would have preferred to live in a suburb, we purchased a home near my husband's job so that he could have an office at home where he would be when the children returned from school. Because my husband earns a good sal-

ary, he can easily afford to pay a housekeeper to do his major household chores. My husband and I share all other tasks around the house equally. For example, he cooks the meals, but I do the laundry for him and help him with many of his other household tasks. (Bem and Bem, 1977)

Somehow the marriage sounds different, and yet only the pronouns have been changed. Certainly, no one would ever mistake the marriage just described as egalitarian, and it thus becomes apparent that the ideology about woman's "natural" place unconsciously persists even in the thinking of people who believe that they have rejected it. It is true that a wife gains some measure of equality when she can have a career of sufficient importance to influence where the couple lives. But why is it the wife who automatically seeks the part-time position? Why is it *her* housekeeper rather than *theirs*? Why *her* household tasks? Such is the subtlety of the schemata about the woman's role. If you failed to spot the inequity in the first description, you too still have some consciousness-raising ahead of you.

co-workers share many of his or her aspirations, grievances, and attitudes toward the company begins to discard stereotyped images of blacks (Blanchard, Weigel, and Cook, 1975). (The same holds true of black workers' stereotypes of whites, of course.) With the increased willingness of homosexual men and women to let their sexual orientation be known, many people are also learning that very few homosexual individuals conform to the traditional stereotypes. Recent movies and television dramas are beginning to present nonstereotypic images of gay men and women as well.

All three of these conditions operate by repeatedly forcing new and disconfirming data on the schema over extended periods. Repeated experiences are needed to overcome our natural tendency to dismiss new data or reinterpret new data to fit our pre-existing schema. The remaining two conditions focus less on cognitive schemata and more on social factors that can diminish prejudice.

The fourth condition requires *social support for the intergroup contact*. Group contact is more likely to reduce prejudice if the surrounding social environment

"Remember when you went back to work and I decided to stay home and take care of the house, how we thought it wouldn't work out?"

Encounters with individuals in occupational roles that do not fit one's stereotype may reduce prejudice.

favors equality, fair treatment, and intergroup contact. The teacher in a newly desegregated school who conveys to the students that working together is a necessary evil being forced on them is creating a social environment that works against favorable attitude change. Similarly, contact between two individuals from different groups has more potential for reducing prejudice between them if there is support for the encounter among their respective friends and families. This condition emphasizes the role of social norms in changing attitudes, a theme to which we will return in Chapter 18.

The fifth condition is *cooperative effort.* One of the most potent factors in reducing prejudice is a situation in which two individuals or two groups must cooperate with one another in order to attain some mutually desired goal. This was shown in a classic field study conducted at a summer camp for 11- and 12-year-old boys (Sherif, 1966). The camp was first divided into two groups, and in-group loyalties were allowed to develop naturally. When the groups were placed in competition for rewards, members of the opposing groups began to call each other names, pick fights, and generally treat each other badly. The resulting intergroup hostility could not be reduced simply by having the boys go to the movies or engage in activities together. Such occasions simply provided additional opportunities to fight. Only by introducing goals important to both groups that required joint cooperation could intergroup harmony be brought about. Hostility diminished as the groups had to fix a breakdown in the water supply, pool money to rent a movie, and use a rope to start the food supply truck. By the end of the camp session, the two groups of boys were friends.

Creating situations in which all five conditions are satisfied can lead to impressive prejudice reduction even among quite racially prejudiced individuals (Cook, 1970, 1978). In addition to reducing prejudice by changing the stereotypes that the groups hold about one another, several of these conditions foster interaction that is rewarding in itself, motivating the participants to interact in the future. It is possible that the boys at the camp would not have become friends so quickly if the group interaction had not been rewarded—if, for example, they had been unable to fix the waterline or start the food supply truck despite their joint efforts.

Explaining the behavior of others: Causal attribution

Forming impressions of other people is one of the major tasks of social interaction. A second major task is understanding the meanings and causes of their behavior. Such meanings and causes are often ambiguous. Suppose, for example, a famous athlete endorses a breakfast cereal on television. Why does she do it? Does she really like the cereal? Or is she doing it for the money? A man kisses his female companion at the end of an evening out. Is this just a social norm, or is he really fond of her? Perhaps this particular man kisses everyone. Or perhaps everyone would kiss this particular woman. You give a five-dollar donation to UNICEF. Why? You are altruistic? You were being pressured? You need a tax writeoff? You believe in the work of UNICEF?

Each of these cases creates an attribution problem. We see some behavior—perhaps even our own—and must decide to which of many possible causes the action should be attributed. This is, of course, what psychologists try to do in a formal way; thus, in everyday social interaction, we all play the role of amateur, or intuitive, psychologist. The study of the attribution process has become a central concern in social psychology; the goal is to discover the rules we use and the errors we make when we attempt to interpret behavior (Heider, 1958; Kelley, 1967).

Cooperative effort reduces prejudice.

THE COVARIANCE RULE   Suppose that you wake up one morning with a runny nose. You see that the azaleas in your yard have just bloomed and hypothesize that they are causing your sniffles. Note how you test this hypothesis. You look to see if your symptoms come and go as you enter and leave areas containing azaleas. That is, you run an experiment to see if your symptoms and azaleas *covary* (vary together). Does the effect come and go with the suspected cause? If it does, azaleas are convicted. But if your sniffles remain constant, there is nothing distinctive about azaleas, and you conclude that they are not the cause. Thus, you use the *distinctiveness* of your reactions to the suspected stimulus as one criterion for deciding if it caused the problem.

Another criterion is *consistency*. If you had the same symptoms the last three years when the azaleas bloomed, you are fairly certain that they are the culprit. But if this is the first time the symptoms have occurred (if this is not a consistent event), you might not be so certain.

Finally, you call your doctor, who says that yours is the sixteenth such complaint of the day and that "this always happens when the azaleas bloom." In other words, you are not unique; others share the same reaction to the same stimulus. This is the criterion of *consensus*.

Your detective work to determine the cause of your allergy is simply an informal version of the scientific method. Using three criteria, you apply the covariance rule: Do the effect and suspected cause covary? You ask if the effect varies only with the suspected cause (distinctiveness), if it does so every time the experiment is conducted (consistency), and if other people get the same result (consensus).

We use the same processes of inference in interpreting other people's behavior (Kelley, 1973). Suppose that Julia raves about a recent meal at a local Chinese restaurant. In very general terms, there are three potential "causes" of her praise. The first is the stimulus object itself: maybe the food really was terrific. The second possible source of the praise is something about the person: Julia is a real Chinese-food nut. The third possibility is the particular situation: it was her birthday and anything would have seemed great to her. To choose among these three classes of causes, you again invoke the three criteria of distinctiveness, consistency, and consensus. If she praises no restaurants but this one (distinctiveness) and does so every time she eats there (consistency) and so does everyone else (consensus), the restaurant must be terrific. But if Julia praises all Chinese restaurants all of the time—but nobody else does—we are probably learning more about Julia than about the restaurant. And, finally, if she has never praised any restaurant before—including this one—and nobody else in Julia's party liked it much, we can probably conclude that something about this particular situation (like her birthday) is coloring her perceptions of the meal. Research confirms that people do, in fact, utilize these criteria in this way (McArthur, 1972).

THE DISCOUNTING RULE   Both natural phenomena and human behavior often have multiple causes. Julia could easily have enjoyed her meal for more than one reason, and as intuitive psychologists we are aware of this possibility. When we see an athlete endorsing a breakfast cereal on television, we know that she is being paid, and thus we partially discount her true attitudes as a reason for her endorsement. If we are really cynical, we conclude that we know nothing at all about her real feelings about the cereal and attribute her behavior entirely to the money. This general strategy has been called the *discounting rule* or principle: "The role of a given cause in producing a given effect is discounted if other plausible causes are also present" (Kelley, 1972, p. 8).

The covariance and discounting rules describe how individuals should

"Folks, I endorse Scrunchies because I *eat* Scrunchies. As God is my witness, I don't just *say* I eat them, I really and truly *do* eat them. In fact, folks, I never eat anything but. And if you don't believe me, I can supply documentation from my personal physician."

Drawing by Ross; © 1976 *The New Yorker Magazine*, Inc.

solve attribution problems if they really proceeded according to the logic of scientific investigation. And although these examples illustrate that we do seem to make use of these rules, research has now revealed that we are far from perfect information processors. We frequently fail to apply these prescriptive rules correctly or sufficiently (Nisbett and Ross, 1980). For example, there is some evidence that we fail to utilize the consensus criterion as fully as we should. But as we will now see, it is the discounting rule that we most often fail to follow.

THE DISPOSITIONAL BIAS IN ATTRIBUTIONS   As the above examples illustrate, one of the major attribution tasks we face daily is deciding whether an observed behavior reflects something unique about the person (his or her attitudes, personality characteristics, and so forth) or something about the situation in which we observe the person. If we infer that something about the person is primarily responsible for the behavior—the athlete really loves the cereal—our inference is called an *internal* or *dispositional attribution* (so named because a person's beliefs, attitudes, and personality characteristics are called his or her dispositions). If, however, we conclude that some external cause is primarily responsible for the behavior (for example, money, strong social norms, threats), it is called an *external* or *situational attribution*.

The founder of modern attribution theory, Fritz Heider, noted that an individual's behavior is so compelling to observers that they take it at face value and give insufficient weight to the circumstances surrounding it (Heider, 1958). Recent research has confirmed Heider's speculation. We underestimate the situational causes of behavior, jumping too easily to conclusions about the dispositions of the person. One psychologist has termed this bias toward dispositional rather than situational attributions the *fundamental attribution error* (Ross, 1977).

In one of the first studies to reveal this bias, subjects were asked to listen to an individual giving a speech either favoring or opposing racial segregation. The subjects were explicitly informed that the individual was participating in an experiment and had been told which side of the issue to argue; the speaker had no choice. Despite this knowledge, when asked to estimate the individual's actual attitude toward racial segregation, subjects inferred that the individual held a position close to the one argued in the speech. In other words, the subjects made a dispositional attribution, even though situational forces were fully sufficient to account for the behavior (Jones and Harris, 1967). They failed to apply the discounting rule sufficiently. This effect is quite powerful. Even if the presentations are deliberately designed to be drab and unenthusiastic and even if the speaker simply reads a transcribed version of the talk, speaking in a monotone and using no gestures, observers are still willing to attribute the attitudes expressed to the speaker (Schneider and Miller, 1975).

Self-perception and attribution

Many of the principles of schematic processing and attribution that we have discussed so far apply not only to judgments about others but also to judgments about ourselves. Thus, we appear to have self-schemata (knowledge structures about our own personalities) that help us process self-relevant information quickly and efficiently. One investigator has suggested that we probably have a self-schema in memory for any trait that both describes us and is important to our self-concept. For example, people for whom the trait of independence is both pertinent and important are very fast and very confident when asked to determine whether traits related to independence (for example, assertiveness, unconventionality) apply to themselves. Moreover, they are able to supply many more examples of independent behaviors than are people for whom the trait is less pertinent or less important (Markus, 1977). The collections of traits called "femininity" and "masculinity" may also be more important to some people than to others, with similar results (see the following Critical Discussion).

SELF-ATTRIBUTION AND INSUFFICIENT JUSTIFICATION   Just as we try to evaluate the surrounding situational forces to decide if the athlete on television really loves the cereal she endorses, so, too, we sometimes look at our own behavior and its surrounding circumstances to decide what we feel or believe. This may sound odd because we generally assume that we have direct knowledge of our feelings and beliefs. Not always. Consider the common remark, "This is my second sandwich; I guess I was hungrier than I thought." Clearly, this person originally misjudged an internal state and has now decided on the basis of observing his or her behavior that he or she was wrong. This suggests that whenever internal feelings are not very strong, an individual is actually forced into the role of an outside observer to make the correct attributions. Thus, the self-observation "I've been biting my nails all day; something must be bugging me" is based on the same kind of evidence as a friend's observation, "You've been biting your nails all day; something must be bugging you." Both the self and the external observer make use of the same evidence—the nail-biter's overt behavior.

Self-perception theory suggests that we must often decide whether to attribute our own behavior to our dispositions or to situational forces, just as we must make this decision when trying to interpret the behavior of others (D. Bem, 1972). Consider the following experiment. College students were brought one at a time to a small room to work for an hour on dull, repetitive tasks (stacking spools and turning pegs). After completing the tasks, some were offered $1 to tell the next subjects that the tasks had been fun and interesting; others were offered $20 to say the same. Later, all the students were asked how interesting the tasks really were. As shown in Figure 17-1, the results were that the students who had been paid only $1 stated that they had, in fact, enjoyed the tasks. But the students who had been paid $20 did not; they found them dull, as did a control group of subjects who were not asked to talk to the next subjects (Festinger and Carlsmith, 1959). This phenomenon has been termed the *insufficient justification effect* because it is when the subjects receive insufficient justification for their behavior—the $1 payoff—that the attitude change is observed.

This experiment was actually conducted to test Festinger's theory of cognitive dissonance, which is discussed later in this chapter. For now, let us look at these results from the perspective of self-perception theory. Why might insufficient justification, the small sum of money but not the large sum, lead individuals to believe what they had heard themselves say?

Self-perception theory assumes that the subjects looked at their behavior (saying that the tasks were fun and interesting) and had to solve the attribution problem, "Why did I say this?" It further assumes that they solved the problem the same way an outside observer would, using the discounting rule. Such a hypothetical observer hears the individual say the tasks were fun and must decide whether to make a dispositional attribution (the individual did it because she or he believes it) or a situational attribution (the individual did it for the money). When the individual is paid $20, the observer is most likely to make a situational attribution: "Anyone would have done it for that sum." On the other hand, if the individual is paid only $1, the observer is more likely to

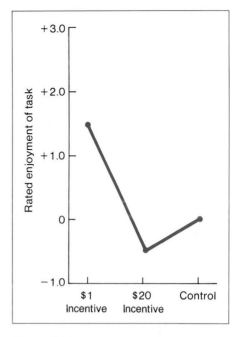

Figure 17-1
Attitude Change and Incentive
The smaller the incentive for complying with the experimenter's request, the greater the attitude change. (After Festinger and Carlsmith, 1959)

The distinction between male and female serves as a basic organizing principle for every human culture. Not only are young boys and girls expected to acquire sex-specific skills and behaviors, but they are also expected to have or to acquire sex-specific self-concepts and personality attributes, to be masculine or feminine as defined by that particular culture. As we saw in Chapter 3, the process by which a society teaches children to conform to such expectations is called *sex typing*.

Psychologist Sandra Bem (1981) has suggested that besides learning the specific concepts and behaviors that the culture happens to associate with sex, the child may also be learning to process many diverse kinds of information in terms of a *gender schema*—that is, learning to organize the world on the basis of the distinction between male and female. According to this gender schema theory, sex-typed individuals differ from non-sex-typed individuals not primarily in terms of how much masculinity or femininity they possess, but in terms of how likely they are to use a gender schema to organize their perceptions and memories.

To test this hypothesis, Bem first selected sex-typed and non-sex-typed individuals for study on the basis of their responses on the Bem Sex Role Inventory, a list of traits that permits individuals to be identified as masculine, feminine, or androgynous. Androgynous individuals possess both so-called masculine and feminine attributes; for example, in a series of studies, androgynous individuals displayed both "masculine" independence and "feminine" nurturance, whereas sex-typed individuals tended to display only the sex-appropriate behavior. (S. L. Bem, 1975; S. L. Bem, Martyna, and Watson, 1976.)

In one study, the subjects were shown a list of words and later asked to recall as many of the words as they could in any order. The list of words included proper names, animal names, verbs, and articles of clothing. Half of the proper names were male and half were female, and one third of the items within each of the other categories had been rated by judges as masculine (for example, *gorilla, hurling, trousers*), one third as feminine (for example, *butterfly, blushing, bikini*), and one third as neutral (for example, *ant, stepping, sweater*). As explained in Chapter 8, research in memory has shown that if an individual has encoded a number of words in terms of an underlying schema or network of associations, thinking of one schema-related item enhances the probability of thinking of another. Accordingly, the sequence of recall should reveal runs or clusters of items that are linked in memory by the schema. For example, if a subject thinks of an animal word, she or he is likely to think next of one of the other animal words. Note that in this experiment subjects could cluster words either according to semantic category (proper names, animals, verbs, clothing) or according to gender.

It was found that sex-typed individuals showed significantly more gender clustering than did non-sex-typed individuals. For example, if a sex-typed person happened to recall the "feminine" animal butterfly, he or she was more likely to follow with another "fem-

make a dispositional attribution: "He or she wouldn't be willing to say it for only $1 and so must believe it." If we assume that the individual follows the same discounting rule as the outside observer, the subjects who received $20 attribute their behavior to situational factors and decide they did not really find the tasks interesting. But subjects paid $1 make a dispositional attribution: "I must think the tasks are interesting; otherwise, I would not have said so."

There is a subtle point about these findings. The subjects are committing the fundamental attribution error about their own behavior, making a dispositional attribution when they should be making a situational attribution. In fact, the $1 incentive *was* sufficient to get all subjects to comply with the experimenter's request to say that the tasks were fun. When the $1 subjects conclude that they must think the tasks are interesting because they would not have said so otherwise, they are wrong. They should be concluding that they did it because they were paid $1. In short, the insufficient justification *is* sufficient, but the subjects do not recognize that fact.

THE OVERJUSTIFICATION EFFECT   As we have just seen, one can lead individuals to commit the fundamental attribution error about their own behavior by giving them insufficient justification for performing acts that they would not

Processing Information by Gender

inine" word such as *bikini*, whereas a non-sex-typed individual would be more likely to follow the word *butterfly* with another animal name or an unrelated word such as *stepping*. In other words, the sex-typed subjects were more likely to link words in memory on the basis of gender. Their gender schemata were more cognitively available for processing information, as gender schema theory predicts.

Sex-typed individuals also seem to process information about the self in terms of the gender schema. In a study investigating self-schemata, sex-typed individuals were much faster at deciding that gender-congruent traits apply to themselves and that gender-incongruent traits do not than they were at making similar decisions about sex-neutral traits. For example, a masculine male can quickly decide that *assertive* applies to him and that *loves children* does not because both his self-concept and the personality trait terms are already encoded in memory according to a gender schema; all he has to do is "look up" the trait in his schema to

see if it is there. Because non-sex-typed individuals have neither their self-concepts nor personality traits encoded according to the gender schema, they were no faster on sex-relevant traits than they were on sex-neutral traits (Girvin, 1978; reported in S. L. Bem, 1981). Later studies on the self-schemata of sex-typed individuals have had similar results (Markus and others, 1982).

The lesson to be learned from gender schema theory is *not* that every individual ought to be androgynous, to be both masculine and feminine; that prescription constrains the person from being a unique individual just as much as the traditional prescription that men must be masculine and women must be feminine. Rather, the moral is that society's gender schema ought to become more limited in scope, that human behaviors and personality attributes should cease to have gender, and that society should stop projecting gender into situations irrelevant to genitalia (S. L. Bem, 1981). In short, the individual should not have to be androgynous; the society should be aschematic.

have performed otherwise. It is also possible to produce the opposite attribution error—to cause individuals to make a situational attribution about their own behavior when they should be making a dispositional attribution. This is accomplished by giving them external or situational *overjustification* for activities that they would have done simply for intrinsic reasons.

We saw an example of this in a study, described in Chapter 7 (page 206), in which children who had been offered a reward for drawing with felt pens later showed a decreased interest in that activity (Lepper, Greene, and Nisbett, 1973). We can interpret this effect by assuming that the children see themselves drawing with the pens after being offered the reward and conclude that they must be drawing *because* of the reward and not because they simply enjoy the activity. They thus mistakenly attribute their behavior to external or situational causes rather than to dispositional causes, the reverse of the fundamental attribution error. Later, when no reward is offered, they have come to believe that they are not intrinsically interested in the activity and do not choose to engage in it.

ACTORS VERSUS OBSERVERS Up to this point, we have emphasized the similarity between the observer and the self (the actor) in making attributions.

But there are differences as well. In particular, it has been suggested that we are more likely to make the fundamental attribution error when judging the behavior of others than when judging our own behavior; to put this in slightly different terms, observers may emphasize dispositional causes in circumstances in which the actors emphasize situational ones.

In an early test of this, male students were asked to write a paragraph on why they liked the woman they dated most, and another paragraph on why they had chosen their major. They were then asked to write similar paragraphs for their best friend; that is, to play the role of the friend as he would answer questions about his dates and major. These paragraphs were analyzed to determine the extent to which the behavior was attributed to the actor's dispositions (for example, "I need someone I can talk to about personal things" and "I want to get a good-paying job after college") or externally to the object of choice (for example, "She is a terrific tennis player" and "Chemistry has the best professors"). It was found that external reasons were given for one's own choices much more than for the best friend's choices (Nisbett and others, 1973).

Some of the reasons for the differences between attributions of actors and observers are obvious. Actors have access to both internal and historical information about themselves that the observer does not share. For example, actors are better situated to know their own intentions, attitudes, and emotions—although we have seen some limitations on such knowledge. Similarly, actors are in a better position to assess the consistency and distinctiveness of their behavior in different situations. A more intriguing difference between actors and observers is the difference in perceptual orientation: the observer is naturally focused on the actor, and this special salience of the actor may lead the observer to explain the actor's behavior by referring to internal dispositions. But the actor is looking out at the situation; from this perspective, the actor's own behavior may be less salient than aspects of the setting (Jones and Nisbett, 1971).

This possibility was tested by setting up a get-acquainted meeting between two strangers, who were the actors in the study. At the other end of the table were two observers. Each observer was instructed to focus his or her attention on one of the two actors. When actors and observers were later asked to interpret the conversation, the usual actor-observer difference was noted. The observers made more dispositional attributions than the actors did.

When the investigator played a videotape showing one of the actors, he found that the videotaped actor became more dispositionally oriented toward his or her own behavior. In addition, the observer who had originally focused on the other actor became more situationally oriented in his remarks about that actor because the videotape focused on the situation to which that actor had been responding (Storms, 1973). Other studies have shown that observers' attributions become more situational if they are explicitly instructed to empathize with the person they are observing, imagining how the person feels as he or she engages in the conversation (Regan and Totten, 1975). Finally, actors become more dispositional about their own behavior after a lapse of three weeks (Moore and others, 1979). With the passage of time, individuals may have difficulty recalling the situation and hence place more emphasis on their own stable traits.

SELF-SERVING BIASES   All of the information processing biases we have discussed so far are rooted in cognitive or perceptual factors. But when we are talking about an individual's interpretation of his or her behavior, we must also consider the possibility of motivationally produced distortions, distortions that serve to enhance one's self-esteem or defend one's self-image. A commonplace example comes from a study of college students' explanations for the grades they received in three examinations. Students attributed "A" and "B" grades to personal internal factors such as ability and effort, whereas they attributed "C," "D," and "F" grades to external factors such as test difficulty and bad luck (Bernstein, Stephan, and Davis, 1979). In one study, subjects played a competitive game that was rigged so that winners and losers were randomly determined. It was found that winners attributed their wins to skill and effort, whereas losers blamed their losses on luck (Snyder, Stephan, and Rosenfeld, 1976).

But it is necessary to be cautious before concluding that the explanations of these attributions are necessarily motivational. Because we usually try to succeed and rarely try to fail, it makes some sense to attribute our successes to internal factors and failures to external factors. We fail *despite* our abilities and efforts, not because of them. And if we have a history of success, it is certainly rational to attribute the unexpected failure to external rather than to enduring internal causes. On the other hand, one well-designed study controlled for the subjects' expectancies of success and failure and still found self-serving bias (Ross and Sicoly, 1979). There is still active debate among researchers over the degree to which attributional biases can be explained in purely cognitive terms or require motivational explanations (Nisbett and Ross, 1980).

ATTITUDES

Except for the brief consideration of possible motivational biases in self-attributions, our discussion of social information processing has focused exclusively on cognitive functioning, the processes of perceiving and thinking. With the concept of *attitude,* social psychology's most central concept, we can begin to incorporate affective functioning—emotions and feelings—into our portrait of the person as a processor of social information.

Attitudes are likes and dislikes; affinities for and aversions to situations, objects, persons, groups; and any other identifiable aspect of the environment, including abstract ideas and social policies. We often express our attitudes in opinion statements: "I love oranges"; "I can't abide Republicans." But even though they express feelings, attitudes are still closely linked to cognitions—specifically, to beliefs about the attitude objects (oranges contain many vitamins; Republicans are bad for the economy). Moreover, attitudes are also linked to actions we take with respect to the attitude objects (I eat an orange every morning; I always vote for Democrats). Accordingly, social psychologists have typically studied attitudes as one component of a three-part system. The beliefs constitute the *cognitive* component; the attitude is the *affective* component; and the actions constitute the *behavioral* component. Research on attitudes has been directed to two major questions. The first concerns the degree of consistency among a person's beliefs, attitudes, and behaviors, and the second concerns the ways in which attitudes are developed and changed. We will consider the topic of attitude change in Chapter 18 when we discuss social influence. Here we take up the consistency question.

Cognitive consistency .

Certain opinions seem to go together. For example, people who support affirmative action often seem to be the same people who support gun control laws, oppose book censorship, and are most concerned about nuclear disarmament. On the surface, these diverse attitudes do not seem to follow logically from one another, and yet knowing that the person holds one of the attitudes often permits us to guess the others with fair accuracy. And there does seem to be a kind of logic involved. The attitudes all appear to follow more or less from a common set of underlying values that we might label as "liberal."

The same kind of logic can be discerned among "conservative" attitudes. Many people who oppose laws outlawing racial discrimination or laws regulating the possession of firearms cite their belief in the value of individual freedom as the basis for their opinions. Even those who disagree with such opinions can appreciate the logic involved. However, many such freedom-loving individuals also feel that women belong in the home, that penalties for the use of marijuana should be stiffer, and that homosexual behavior among consenting adults should be illegal. Here the logic is less than clear, yet these opinions too seem strangely predictable.

In short, attitudes do seem to be coherently organized, but the basis of that organization is not always a strict kind of formal logic. Instead, it is a kind of psycho-logic, and it is this psycho-logic that social psychologists have studied under the label of *cognitive consistency*. The basic premise of cognitive consistency theories is that we all strive to be consistent in our beliefs, attitudes, and behaviors and that inconsistency acts as an irritant or stimulus that motivates us to modify or change them until they form a coherent if not logical package. Researchers in this area have explored the consistency among beliefs, among attitudes, between beliefs and attitudes, and between attitudes and behaviors. We shall look at each of these in turn.

CONSISTENCY AMONG BELIEFS One of the earliest studies of cognitive consistency assessed the degree to which sets of beliefs did, in fact, follow the rules of formal logic. Subjects in the study were given a questionnaire containing 48 propositions that had been taken from 16 logical syllogisms. A logical syllogism contains three propositions—two premises and a conclusion drawn from those premises. For example, three of the propositons on the questionnaire were drawn from the syllogism:

> Any form of recreation that constitutes a serious health menace will be outlawed by the City Health Authority.
>
> The increasing water pollution in this area will make swimming a serious health menace.
>
> Swimming at the local beaches will be outlawed by the City Health Authority.

On the questionnaire, the propositions did not appear in syllogistic form but were dispersed among propositions from other syllogisms and filler items.

High-school students filled out the questionnaire by indicating their belief in the truth of each proposition on a numerical scale. About a week later, these students received persuasive messages arguing for the truth of the first premise in each syllogism; the messages did not mention the second premises or the conclusions. Immediately after receiving the messages and also one week later, the students again indicated their beliefs on each of the 48 propositions.

Immediately after the persuasion, there was not only a significant change toward a greater belief in the proposition explicitly mentioned in the persuasive messages, as might be expected, but also a significant though smaller change toward a greater belief in the unmentioned conclusions—as a cognitive consis-

"And don't waste your time canvassing the whole building, young man. We all think alike."

	PARTICIPATED	SYMPATHETIC	UNSYMPATHETIC
Freedom	1	1	2
Equality	3	6	11

Table 17-2
Freedom and Equality in
Relation to Civil Rights Attitudes
Three groups of individuals, with different attitudes toward civil rights, ranked *freedom* **and** *equality* **among a list of 12 values. Although all subjects ranked the value of** *freedom* **high, only those who were favorable toward civil rights demonstrations also ranked** *equality* **high. (After Rokeach, 1968)**

tency hypothesis would predict. One week later, the effects of the persuasion on the propositions discussed in the messages had diminished, but most of the stronger belief in the conclusions had been retained. The investigator suggests that this shows a kind of mental inertia; the change originally induced in belief in the premises continued to "filter down" to the conclusions during the intervening week, partly overcoming the fading of the more direct effects of the persuasion (McGuire, 1960). A later study showed that persuasion itself is not always necessary. Merely having subjects fill out the questionnaire causes them to adjust their beliefs so that one week later there is somewhat greater consistency between their belief in the premises and their belief in the conclusions.

CONSISTENCY AMONG ATTITUDES The observation that attitudes seem to cohere because they derive from a core set of values has been elaborated most explicitly by Milton Rokeach (1968, 1973). Rokeach defines a *value* as a basic attitude toward certain broad modes of conduct (such as courage, honesty, friendship) or certain end-states of existence (such as equality, salvation, freedom, self-fulfillment). Values are thus a kind of attitude, but they refer to ends, not means. Thus, a woman who has a positive attitude toward money might explain it by saying that money would allow her to retire; retirement would permit her to take music lessons; and music lessons would help her attain self-fulfillment. Money, retirement, and music lessons do not qualify as values under Rokeach's definition because they are all seen as means not ends, means toward the value of self-fulfillment. Such labels as "liberal" and "conservative" enable us to predict many of an individual's attitudes because these two terms refer to broad underlying values that are shared by large segments of the population. In fact, most Americans, liberals and conservatives alike, share many values, and our differences of opinion stem from the relative importance we assign to them. This is nicely illustrated in one of Rokeach's early studies of values.

Rokeach asked a number of individuals to rank 12 values in order of the values' importance to them. He was particularly interested in the importance individuals would attach to the values *freedom* and *equality*. For example, he tallied these rankings separately for individuals who had participated in civil rights demonstrations during the 1960s, for individuals who had not participated but who were sympathetic to them, and for individuals who were unsympathetic to them. Table 17-2 shows how each of these groups ranked the two values *freedom* and *equality* in the list of 12. As the table shows, *freedom* ranked high for all groups, but *equality* was considered relatively unimportant (next to last among the 12 values) for those unsympathetic to civil rights demonstrations.

Rokeach then conducted a study similar to McGuire's study of belief consistency. After obtaining students' value rankings and their attitudes toward civil rights demonstrations, he discussed with them the low ranking given to *equality* by those unsympathetic to civil rights demonstrations and speculated aloud that maybe such individuals cared a great deal about their own freedom but were indifferent to other people's freedom. Students were invited to ponder their own values and attitudes in this light. Three weeks later and then again three to five months later, they were asked to rank their values and state their attitudes once more.

This study, like the syllogism study, found that inconsistency produced attitude change. In particular, students who had ranked *equality* high but who were initially against civil rights demonstrations became more pro-civil rights while retaining the importance of *equality* in their value rankings. Moreover, there was a delay effect similar to the one reported in the syllogism study: the change in civil rights attitudes was greater after three to five months than it was only three weeks after the experiment. Again, the changes apparently needed time to filter through the belief system. Finally, students who had initially ranked *equality* low but were pro-civil rights raised the importance of *equality* in their value rankings and retained their pro-civil rights attitudes (Rokeach, 1968).

Although these results provide support for the premise that people strive for consistency between their attitudes and their values, they do not directly confirm Rokeach's causal hypothesis that the attitudes derive from the values. It is possible, for example, that people arrive at their abstract value rankings by taking an inventory of their more concrete attitudes.

CONSISTENCY BETWEEN BELIEFS AND ATTITUDES   Consistency between our beliefs and our attitudes is a common occurrence in daily life. If we come to believe that a certain automobile is highly reliable, gives a comfortable ride, and has good gas mileage, we are likely to have a favorable attitude toward it. In such cases, our attitude seems to arise naturally and inevitably from the supporting beliefs. A number of researchers over the years have shown that it is even possible to make quantitative predictions of people's attitudes by using numerical scales and algebraic formulas to combine the relevant underlying beliefs and values (see Rosenberg, 1956; Fishbein, 1963). This kind of consistency closely follows the rules of formal logic demonstrated in McGuire's study of syllogisms.

But even that study found a kind of consistency between beliefs and attitudes that formal logic does not anticipate. When McGuire asked his subjects to rate their *attitudes* toward each of the 48 propositions on his questionnaire, he found a high correlation between these attitude ratings and the degree to which the subjects believed the propositions to be true. That is, the more the subjects believed something to be true, on the average, the more they thought it to be desirable. Furthermore, when the degree of belief in a proposition changed as a result of persuasion, the desirability of the proposition also changed. This kind of consistency is often called "rationalization." If we come to believe that something is true, we persuade ourselves that it is desirable as well. The reverse sequence of reasoning may also take place: because we believe something to be desirable, we persuade ourselves that it is true. We usually call this "wishful thinking." Both rationalization and wishful thinking could account for the correlation between belief ratings and attitude ratings observed prior to the persuasion. Both produce a consistency not of logic, but of psycho-logic.

The ability of attitudes to alter beliefs was shown even more strikingly in a study of racial attitudes. After obtaining beliefs about and attitudes toward blacks and racial integration from a group of white subjects, the investigator hypnotized them and gave them a post-hypnotic suggestion that their attitude toward blacks moving into their community would be the opposite of what it had previously been. This suggestion worked. For example, a subject who had previously been strongly against integrated housing became in favor of it after the hypnotic suggestion. Note that this change occurred even though the subjects were given no arguments for such a change; that is, only the affective component was changed through hypnotic induction, not the cognitive component. After awakening from the hypnosis, subjects were questioned about their current attitudes and beliefs about blacks and integration. The striking finding was that the subjects now expressed different *beliefs,* beliefs that were consistent with their new attitudes. Thus, subjects who had changed to favorable attitudes toward integrated housing now expressed beliefs that housing integration was necessary for racial harmony, that it was the only fair thing to do, and so forth (Rosenberg, 1960).

These studies illustrate one way in which affective functioning can influence cognitive functioning. They also illustrate that our attitudes and feelings are often based on many factors besides "rational" beliefs. For example, individuals who hold positive attitudes toward cigarette smoking find little cognitive support these days, and the inconsistency or disharmony between their feelings and their beliefs can be a cause of discomfort. Smokers can, of course, hold a number of positive beliefs about smoking (for example, it is relaxing; it prevents undesirable weight gain) that simply override the negative beliefs and hence can reduce the inconsistencies between beliefs and attitudes. But perhaps most common of all are smokers who are consistent in holding both negative beliefs about and negative attitudes toward smoking but who still continue to smoke. And this raises the most important consistency question of all: What is the degree of correspondence between attitudes and behavior?

CONSISTENCY BETWEEN ATTITUDES AND BEHAVIOR   A major reason for studying attitudes is the expectation that they enable us to predict behavior. A political candidate is interested in a survey of voter attitudes only if the attitudes expressed relate to voting behavior. The assumption that a person's attitudes determine his or her behavior is deeply ingrained in Western thinking, and in many instances the assumption holds. For example, a survey of presidential campaigns from 1952 to 1964 reveals that 85 percent of the voters surveyed showed a correspondence between their attitudes two months before the election and their actual vote in the election (Kelley and Mirer, 1974).

But in other cases, the assumption of attitude-behavior consistency appears to be violated. In a classic study conducted during the 1930s, a white professor traveled across the United States with a young Chinese couple. At that time, there was quite strong prejudice against Orientals and no laws against racial discrimination in public accommodations. The three travelers stopped at over 200 hotels, motels, and restaurants and were served at all the restaurants and all but one of the hotels and motels without problem. Later, a letter was sent to all of the establishments visited asking them whether they would accept a Chinese couple as guests. Of the 128 replies received, 92 percent said they would not. In other words, these proprietors expressed attitudes that were much more prejudiced than their behavior (LaPiere, 1934).

Clearly, behavior is determined by many factors of which our attitude is but one, and these other factors affect attitude-behavior consistency. One obvious factor is the degree of constraint in the situation; we must often act in ways that are not consonant with what we feel or believe. As children, we ate asparagus that we detested, and as adults, we attend lectures and dinner parties that we would compare unfavorably to asparagus. In the racial discrimination study, the prejudiced proprietors may have found it difficult to act on their prejudices when actually faced with an Oriental couple seeking service.

Public accommodation laws against discrimination now make it even more difficult than it was in 1934. Peer pressure can exert similar influences on behavior. For example, a teen-ager's attitude toward marijuana is correlated about .50 with his or her actual marijuana use, but the number of marijuana-using friends the teen-ager has is an even better predictor (Andrews and Kandel, 1979).

The strength and consistency of a person's attitudes also determine how well they will predict behavior. Thus, in the presidential voting surveys cited above, most of the attitude-vote inconsistencies came from voters with weak or ambivalent attitudes to begin with. Many such voters experience ambivalence because they are "cross-pressured" by friends and associates who do not agree with one another. For example, the Jewish businessperson belongs to an ethnic group that generally holds liberal political positions, but she or he also belongs to a business community that frequently holds conservative political positions, particularly on economic issues. When it comes time to vote, such a person is subjected to conflicting pressures. Such ambivalence and conflict can arise from within the person as well. It has been found that when the cognitive and affective components (the beliefs and the attitude, respectively) are not consistent with one another, the attitude is not a reliable predictor of behavior (Norman, 1975).

Attitude-behavior consistency may also fail to show up if the attitude assessed is related generally but not specifically to the behavior. For example, general environmental attitudes in one study were not related to a willingness to take action on behalf of the Sierra Club, but attitudes specifically toward the Sierra Club were strongly related (Weigel, Vernon, and Tognacci, 1974). Attitudes toward birth control correlated only .08 with a woman's use of oral contraceptives, but attitudes toward "the pill" in particular correlated .7 with that behavior (Davidson and Jaccard, 1979).

Many of the factors that enable us to predict behaviors from attitudes have been put into a single theoretical framework (Fishbein, 1972; Fishbein and Ajzen, 1975). Using quantitative measures of attitudes, expectations, and social pressure, the theory has successfully predicted which university students would engage in premarital sex (Fishbein, 1966), women's use of oral contraceptives (Werner and Middlestadt, 1979), reactions to nuclear energy proposals (Bowman and Fishbein, 1978), and church attendance (Brinberg, 1979).

From behavior to attitudes: Cognitive dissonance theory

Our discussion of the consistency between attitudes and behavior has covered only half of the topic so far. We have examined how attitudes might lead to behavior, but it is also possible for behavior to lead to attitudes. The most influential theory of this sequence of events has been Leon Festinger's theory of cognitive dissonance. Like cognitive consistency theories in general, cognitive dissonance theory assumes that there is a drive toward cognitive consistency; two cognitions that are inconsistent with one another will produce discomfort that motivates the person to remove the inconsistency and bring the cognitions into harmony. Such inconsistency is called *cognitive dissonance* (Festinger, 1957).

Although cognitive dissonance theory speaks generally about many kinds of dissonance, it has been the most provocative in predicting one type: engaging in behavior that is counter to one's attitudes creates pressure to reduce the dissonance by changing one's attitudes so they are consistent with the behavior. The theory further states that engaging in counter-attitudinal behavior produces the most dissonance, and hence the most attitude change, when there are no other "consonant" reasons for engaging in the behavior. This was illustrated in an ingenious experiment that we have already described, the Festinger–Carlsmith study of insufficient justification.

It will be recalled that in that study, subjects were induced to tell a waiting subject that a series of dull tasks had been fun and interesting. Subjects who had been paid $20 to say this did not change their attitudes, but subjects who had been paid only $1 came to believe that the tasks had, in fact, been fun and interesting. According to cognitive dissonance theory, being paid $20 provides a very consonant reason for engaging in the behavior, and hence the person experiences little or no dissonance. The inconsistency between the person's behavior and his or her attitude toward the tasks is swamped by the far greater consistency between the behavior and the incentive for engaging in it. Accordingly, the subjects who were paid $20 did not change their attitudes; the subjects who were paid $1, however, had no consonant reason for engaging in the behavior. Accordingly, they experienced dissonance, which they reduced by coming to believe that they really did enjoy the tasks. The general conclusion is that dissonance-causing behavior will lead to attitude change when the behavior can be induced with a *minimum* amount of pressure, whether the inducement is in the form of a reward or a punishment.

Experiments with children have confirmed the prediction about minimal punishment. If children obey a very mild request not to play with an attractive toy, they come to believe that the toy is not as attractive as they first thought— a belief that is consistent with their observation that they are not playing with it. But if the children refrain from playing with the toy under a strong threat of punishment, they do not change their liking for the toy (Aronson and Carlsmith, 1963; Freedman, 1965).

Cognitive dissonance theory successfully predicts a number of other attitude-change phenomena as well, and it has inspired much debate and research.

Dissonance theory versus self-perception theory

Dissonance theory and self-perception theory both claim to explain the results of studies showing that a person's behavior influences his or her attitudes, but they offer different explanations. Dissonance theory is a motivational theory in that the inconsistency between the behavior and the person's initial attitude is assumed to motivate him or her to change that attitude. In contrast, self-perception theory implies that the person's initial attitude is irrelevant and there is no discomfort produced by the behavior. People are seen not as *changing* their attitudes but as *inferring* what their attitudes must be by observing their behavior. There is no drive or motivational process involved.

A number of investigators have attempted to decide between the two theories, with mixed results. After a series of studies, one group of researchers concluded that dissonance theory is probably the better theory when the behavior is sharply inconsistent with the person's initial attitudes, but self-perception theory is the better theory when the behavior is broadly within the person's acceptable range of behaviors—even if not exactly what the person's attitudes would imply (Fazio, Zanna, and Cooper, 1977). In general, cognitive dissonance theory was most useful to social psychologists during the 1960s when they were most interested in attitude-change phenomena; self-perception theory seemed to provide a more congenial set of concepts when attention shifted during the 1970s to problems of attribution.

The case for nonconsistency

Although the evidence for consistency among beliefs, attitudes, and behaviors seems impressive, many psychologists and political scientists who have analyzed the public mind outside the social psychology laboratory are more impressed with the evidence for nonconsistency. As one student of public opinion put it:

> As intellectuals and students of politics we are disposed by training and sensibility to take political ideas seriously. . . . We are therefore prone to forget that most people take them less seriously than we do, that they pay little attention to issues, rarely worry about the consistency of their opinions, and spend little or no time thinking about the values, presuppositions and implications that distinguish one political orientation from another (McClosky, quoted in Abelson, 1968).

An example of such nonconsistency was revealed in a national survey taken by *The New York Times* and CBS News in the late 1970s. The survey showed that a majority of Americans disapprove of "most government-sponsored welfare programs." Yet 81 percent said they approve of the government's "program providing financial assistance for children raised in low-income homes where one parent is missing" (Aid to Families with Dependent Children, a major welfare program). Similarly, 81 percent endorsed the government's "helping poor people buy food for their families at cheaper prices" (the essence of the federal food-stamp program) and 82 percent approved of paying for health care for poor people (the Medicaid program). This pattern of support was similar among almost all types of people—rich and poor, liberal and conservative, Democrat and Republican.

An earlier national survey, designed specifically to probe this kind of inconsistency, found a similar contradiction between an *ideological* conservatism and an *operational* liberalism in attitudes toward welfare. One out of four Americans was classified as conservative on questions concerning the general concept of welfare but simultaneously classified as liberal on questions concerning specific welfare programs (Free and Cantril, 1967).

Findings like these have led one investigator to propose that many of our opinions are not part of a consistent belief system—as the consistency theories postulate—but exist as isolated "opinion molecules." Each molecule is made up of (1) a belief, (2) an attitude, and (3) a perception of social support for the opinion. In other words, each opinion molecule contains a fact, a feeling, and a following (Abelson, 1968). For example: "It's a fact that when my Uncle Charlie had back trouble, he was cured by a chiropractor [*fact*]. You know, I feel that chiropractors have been sneered at too much [*feeling*], and I'm not ashamed to say so because I know a lot of people who feel the same way [*following*]." Or "Americans don't really want the Equal Rights Amendment [*following*], and neither do I [*feeling*]. It would lead to unisex bathrooms [*fact*]."

Opinion molecules function as conversational units; they give us something coherent to say when a particular topic comes up in conversation. Accordingly, they do not need to have logical connections between them, and they are fairly invulnerable to argument because they serve primarily to rationalize our unexamined agreement with friends and neighbors on most issues. This is probably how many beliefs and attitudes are organized in everyday life, when we are not being interrogated by a researcher who is asking us to think hard about what we believe.

INTERPERSONAL ATTRACTION

Of all our attitudes, the most important are probably our attitudes toward other people. The questions that often concern us most when we meet new people are will they like us and will we like them. And beyond the initial encounter, our concerns often center on how to nurture and guide the relationship from an initial liking or attraction to a deeper friendship or possibly even to intimacy and love. It is probably not an exaggeration to say that fostering personal relationships is a top priority for most people much of the time. Accordingly, social psychologists have long been interested in the factors that promote liking or interpersonal attraction, and they have more recently and belatedly shown a willingness to enter the thickets of love and intimacy as well. Some of the findings have confirmed commonly held notions about liking and loving, but others have produced surprises. We begin with liking—namely, friendship and the early stages of more intimate love relationships.

Determinants of liking

After years of speculation and gossip, England's Prince Charles finally married. To social psychologists, the least surprising aspect of his choice was that he married "the girl next door"—a woman whom he had known for many years and who shared many of his social background characteristics, attitudes, and interests. And as many proud British were quick to point out, she was as pretty as he was handsome. As we shall see, these are precisely the determinants of interpersonal attraction: proximity, familiarity, and similarity. It also helps, alas, to be beautiful.

PROXIMITY An examination of 5,000 marriage license applications in Philadelphia in the 1930s found that one third of the couples lived within five blocks of each other (Rubin, 1973). Research shows that the best single predictor of whether two people are friends is how far apart they live. In a study of friendship patterns in apartment houses, residents were asked to name the three people they saw socially most often (Festinger, Schachter, and Back, 1950). It was found that residents mentioned 41 percent of neighbors who lived in the apartment next door, 22 percent of those who lived two doors away (about 30 feet), and only 10 percent of those who lived at the other end of the hall.

Studies of college dormitories show the same effect. After a full academic year, roommates were twice as likely as floormates to be friends, and floormates were more than twice as likely as dormitory residents in general to be friends (Priest and Sawyer, 1967).

There are, of course, cases in which neighbors and roommates hate one another, and the major exception to the friendship-promoting effect of proximity seems to occur when there are initial antagonisms. In a test of this, a subject waited in a laboratory with a female confederate who acted in either a pleasant or an unpleasant way toward the subject. When she acted pleasantly, the closer she sat to the subject the better she was liked; when she acted unpleasantly, the closer she sat to the subject, the less she was liked. Proximity simply increased the intensity of the initial reaction (Schiffenbauer and Schiavo, 1976). But since most initial encounters probably range from neutral to pleasant, the most frequent result of sustained proximity is friendship.

Proximity is an important determinant of liking.

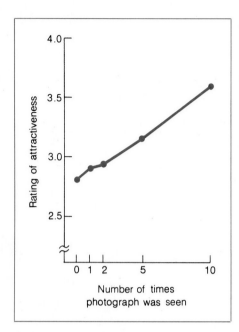

Figure 17-2
Familiarity Breeds Liking
Subjects were asked to rate photographs of unknown faces according to how much they thought they would like the person. The lowest ratings of attractiveness were made by subjects who had never seen the photograph before; the highest ratings of attractiveness were made by subjects who had seen the photograph most often. (After Zajonc, 1968)

Those who believe in miracles when it comes to matters of the heart may believe that there is a perfect mate chosen for each of us waiting to be discovered somewhere in the world. But if this is true, the far greater miracle is the frequency with which the fates conspire to place this person within walking distance.

FAMILIARITY   One of the major reasons that proximity creates liking is that it increases familiarity, and there is now abundant research that familiarity all by itself—sheer exposure—increases liking (Zajonc, 1968). This is a quite general phenomenon. For example, rats repeatedly exposed to either the music of Mozart or Schoenberg come to prefer the composer they have heard, and humans repeatedly exposed to selected nonsense syllables or Chinese characters come to prefer those they have seen most often. Perhaps more germane to the present discussion is a study in which subjects were exposed to pictures of faces and then asked how much they thought they would like the person pictured. The more frequently a particular face had been seen, the more they said they liked it and thought they would like the person (see Figure 17-2).

In one of the cleverest demonstrations of the "familiarity-breeds-liking" effect, the investigators took photographs of college women and then prepared prints of both the original face and its mirror image. These prints were then shown to the women themselves, their women friends, and their lovers. The women themselves preferred the mirror image prints by a margin of 68 percent to 32 percent, but the friends and lovers preferred the nonreversed prints by a margin of 61 percent to 39 percent (Mita, Dermer, and Knight, 1977). Can you guess why?

The familiarity-breeds-liking effect is quite robust. It has been found in studies that use actual interaction, not just photographs, and also in studies in which the person remains unaware of the stimulus (Moreland and Zajonc, 1979; Wilson, 1979). The effect is observed even when the surrounding situation is unpleasant (Saegert, Swap, and Zajonc, 1973) and when the target stimuli themselves are neutral or moderately negative to begin with. Only when the stimuli are quite negative does the effect fail to occur (Perlman and Oskamp, 1971). There is a possibility, too, that extreme levels of repetition may induce boredom and limit the effect.

The moral is clear. If you find your admiration of someone unreciprocated, be persistent and hang around. Proximity and familiarity are your most powerful weapons.

SIMILARITY   There is an old saying that opposites attract, and lovers are fond of recounting how different they are from each other: "I love boating, but she prefers mountain climbing"; "I'm in engineering, but he's a history major." What such lovers overlook is that they both like outdoor activities; they are both pre-professionals; they are both Democrats; they are both the same nationality, the same religion, the same social class, the same educational level, and they are probably within three years of each other in age and within 2 IQ points of each other in intelligence. In short, the old saying is mostly false.

Research all the way back to 1870 supports this conclusion. Over 99 percent of the married couples in the United States are of the same race; 94 percent are of the same religion. Moreover, statistical surveys show that husbands and wives are significantly similar to each other not only on sociological characteristics such as age, race, religion, education, and socioeconomic class but also with respect to physical characteristics such as height and eye color and psychological characteristics such as intelligence (Rubin, 1973).

In one ambitious study of similarity and friendship, male students received free room for the year in a large house at the University of Michigan in exchange for their participation. On the basis of information from tests and questionnaires, some men were assigned roommates who were quite similar to them and others were assigned roommates who were quite dissimilar. Then the investigator observed the friendship patterns that developed over the course of the year, obtaining more questionnaire and attitude data from the participants at regular intervals. In all other respects, the men lived as they would in any dormitory.

Roommates who were initially similar generally liked each other and ended up as better friends than those who were dissimilar. When the study was repeated with a new group of men the next year, however, the familiarity-breeds-liking effect turned out to be even more powerful than similarity. Regardless of whether low or high similarity had been the basis for room assignments, roommates came to like each other (Newcomb, 1961).

One reason that similarity produces liking is probably that people value their own opinions and preferences and enjoy being with others who validate their choices, possibly boosting their self-esteem in the process. But perhaps the major reason that similarity produces liking is just a repeat of factors we have seen before, proximity and familiarity. Both social norms and situational circumstances throw us together with people who are like us. Most religious groups prefer or insist that their members date and mate within the religion, and cultural norms regulate what is considered "acceptable" in terms of race and age matches—an older woman and a younger man is still viewed as inappropriate. Situational circumstances also play an important role. Many couples meet in college or graduate school, thus assuring that they will be similar in educational level, general intelligence, professional aspirations, and probably in age and socioeconomic status. Moreover, tennis players will have met on the tennis courts, political liberals at the anti-apartheid rally, and gay people at a meeting of the Gay People's Union.

Despite all this, the saying that "opposites attract" may still apply to certain complementary personality traits (Winch, Ktsanes, and Ktsanes, 1954). To take the most obvious example, one partner may be quite dominant and thus require someone who is relatively more submissive. A person with strong preferences may do best with someone who is very flexible or even "wishy-washy." This has been called the *need-complementarity hypothesis*. But even in the case of complementary traits, an underlying similarity of attitudes can often be discerned. For example, the marital relationship in which the husband is dominant and the wife is submissive will be smooth only if both agree on the desirability of these traditional sex roles. Even successful complementarity requires a basic similarity of attitudes favoring the dissimilarity.

But the major problem with the need-complementarity hypothesis is that there is not much evidence for it (Levinger, Senn, and Jorgensen, 1970). In one study, marital adjustment among couples married for up to five years was found to depend more on similarity than on complementarity (Meyer and Pepper, 1977). And attempts to identify the pairs of personality traits that bring about complementarity have not been very successful. When all is said and done, it is similarity that wins the day.

PHYSICAL ATTRACTIVENESS   To most of us, there is something mildly un-democratic about the possibility that a person's physical appearance is a deter-minant of how well others like him or her. Unlike character, niceness, and other personal attributes, physical appearance is a factor over which we have little control, and hence it seems unfair to use it as a criterion for liking someone. And, in fact, surveys taken over a span of several decades have shown that people do not rank physical attractiveness as very important in their liking of other people (Perrin, 1921; Tesser and Brodie, 1971).

But research on actual behavior shows otherwise. For example, a group of psychologists set up a "computer dance" in which each person was randomly paired with a partner. At intermission, each person filled out an anonymous questionnaire evaluating his or her date. In addition, the experimenters obtained several personality test scores for each person as well as an independent estimate of his or her physical attractiveness. The results showed that only physical attractiveness played a role in how much each person was liked by his or her partner. None of the measures of intelligence, social skills, or personality were related to the partners' liking for one another (Walster and others, 1966). Moreover, the importance of physical attractiveness continues to operate on later dates (Mathes, 1975). Physical attractiveness does appear to decline in importance, however, when a marriage partner is being chosen (Stroebe and others, 1971).

The importance of physical attractiveness is not confined to dating and mating patterns. For example, physically attractive boys and girls (5 and 6 years of age) are more popular with their peers than are less attractive children (Dion and Berscheid, 1972). Even adults are affected by a child's physical attractiveness. One investigator had women read a description of an aggressive act committed by a 7-year-old child. The description was accompanied by a photograph of either an attractive or an unattractive child. The women believed that attractive children were less likely than unattractive children to commit a similar aggressive act in the future (Dion, 1972).

Why is physical attractiveness so important? Part of the reason is that people hold a stereotype or schema about the physically attractive person, believing that she or he has a cluster of other desirable characteristics. For example, in one study male and female subjects were presented with photographs of men and women from a college yearbook and asked to rate the pictured individuals on a number of traits. The photographs had been previously rated as very attractive, average, or unattractive. Compared to the unattractive individuals, the attractive individuals were rated as being more sensitive, kind, interesting, strong, poised, sociable, outgoing, exciting, and sexually warm and responsive. They were also rated as having higher status and as being more likely to get married, to have a successful marriage, and to be happy. The only exception to this rosy portrait was that the more attractive individuals were rated as being slightly, but not significantly, less likely to be good parents than neutral or unattractive individuals (Dion, Berscheid, and Walster, 1972).

This stereotype or schema operates in the reverse direction, too. Male and female subjects were shown photographs and personality descriptions of college women and asked to rate the women in the photographs for physical attractiveness. Favorable personality descriptions produced higher ratings of physical attractiveness than did unfavorable personality descriptions, despite the fact that the photographs and descriptions had been paired at random (Gross and Crofton, 1977). Other studies show that essays are rated as higher in quality when they are supposedly written by more attractive women (Landy and Sigall, 1974), and an unattractive defendant was sentenced to more years in prison by a mock jury than an attractive defendant who was described as committing the same crime (Landy and Aronson, 1969). These same investigators found that killing an attractive victim brought a longer sentence than killing an unattractive victim.

There are some limits to this stereotype, however. In a study using actual interaction rather than photographs, subjects liked a female confederate better when she was made attractive by makeup and clothing than when she was made unattractive, but the subjects did not attribute more socially desirable personality traits to her. Also, a more attractive defendant received a harsher sentence than an unattractive one when she used her attractiveness to swindle someone (Sigall and Ostrove, 1975). But, in general, people tend to believe that what is beautiful is good and what is good is beautiful.

Interestingly, this stereotype of the physically attractive person may have a grain of truth. In one study, male students spoke on the phone with female students for about 5 minutes and then rated them for social skills. Independent observers rated the physical attractiveness of the women. The more attractive the women, the greater the social skills they were viewed as having by their phone partners (Goldman and Lewis, 1977). Note that the social skill ratings were made by individuals who had never seen the women or their photographs; they had only talked to them by phone. Other studies have shown that physical attractiveness is correlated with a positive self-concept (Lerner and Karabenick, 1974), mental health (Adams, 1981), assertiveness and self-confidence (Dion and Stein, 1978), and a variety of other positive attributes.

Why should this all be so? The most likely explanation is that the stereotype is self-fulfilling in the way we discussed earlier when we were considering stereotypes in general. People may treat physically attractive individuals in ways that lead them to have more self-esteem and self-confidence and greater social skills. They may, in fact, be promoted faster, go further occupationally, and so on. This possibility has been cleverly demonstrated. Male students engaged in a 10-minute telephone conversation with a female student whom they believed to be either physically attractive or unattractive. Again, of course, these assignments were made at random and bore no relationship to the actual attractiveness of the woman on the other end of the conversation. Analyses of these conversations showed that males who believed they were interacting with an attractive female were friendlier, more outgoing, and more sociable, and they took the initiative in the conversation more often than did men who believed that they were talking to a less attractive woman (Snyder, Tanke, and Berscheid, 1977).

But the powerful finding in this study was that judges who listened *only to the women's half of the conversation and did not know the partners' beliefs about their attractiveness* rated the women who conversed with men who believed they were attractive as more sociable, poised, and humorous than women who conversed with men who believed they were unattractive. The conversational style of the men who believed they were talking to attractive or unattractive women produced a self-fulfilling stereotype in a 10-minute phone conversation! Is there hope for the unbeautiful among us? As we shall now see, the answer is yes.

THE MATCHING HYPOTHESIS   As noted above, physical attractiveness plays a less important role when people seek marriage partners. In pairing off, people tend to end up with partners who closely match them in appearance (Berscheid and Walster, 1974). In one study, judges rated photographs of each partner of 99 couples for physical attractiveness without knowing who was paired with whom. The physical attractiveness ratings of the couples matched

People tend to choose partners who closely match them in physical attractiveness.

each other significantly more closely than did the ratings of photographs that were randomly paired into "couples" (Murstein, 1972). Similar results were obtained in a real-life field study in which separate observers rated the physical attractiveness of members of couples in bars and theater lobbies and at social events (Silverman, 1971).

The matching phenomenon is usually explained in terms of the *expectancy-value theory* of decision making. This approach argues that people try to maximize the product obtained by multiplying the value of a physically attractive partner by their expectancy of obtaining one. In other words, we try to obtain the most attractive person we realistically believe might want us. This analysis suggests that less attractive people seek less attractive people because they expect to be rejected if they aim too high. The overall result of this chilling marketplace process is attractiveness matching: Most of us end up with partners who are about as attractive as we are.

Love

The process by which relationships move from liking toward greater closeness and intimacy has been called *social penetration* (Altman and Taylor, 1973). Social penetration has both breadth and depth. Breadth refers to the number of different areas of the partners' lives and personalities that are involved in the relationship, and depth refers to the degree to which the pair know and share things that are close to the cores of their personalities—fears, anxieties, uncertainties, hopes, and so forth.

The key to social penetration is reciprocal self-disclosure; the partners must gradually reveal themselves to each other, and this can be a very delicate process. At the beginning of a relationship, there is a strong *norm of reciprocity;* as one person begins to disclose things about himself or herself, the other person must also be willing to do so. In this way, trust builds and intimacy increases. Research shows that the pace of self-disclosure is very important. If one of the partners discloses too much too soon, it can cause the other person to pull back (Rubin, 1975).

In romantic relationships these days, self-disclosure takes place rather early. In one recent study, most of the couples who had been going together an average of eight months had engaged in full and equal disclosure about very personal and private areas of their lives (Rubin and others, 1980). About three fourths of the women and men said they had fully revealed their feelings about their sexual relationship; almost half had fully disclosed their thoughts about the future of the relationship; and over half had provided full information about their previous sexual experiences. A third of each sex had revealed fully those things about themselves that they were most ashamed of.

Such rapid and full self-disclosure has not always been the norm. In one study, both college students and senior citizens were asked to describe relationships characteristic of 22-year-olds of their own generations. It was found that today's young people expect pairs to disclose both positive and negative feelings more openly and freely than previous generations (Rands and Levinger, 1979). Up through the 1950s, the middle-class norm emphasized much more self-restraint and self-protectiveness. The sexual revolution of the 1960s changed not only sexual behavior but also social norms concerning self-disclosure (Altman and Taylor, 1973). This was the era of the encounter group and instant intimacy. Although much of the popularity of encounter groups has declined, the new norms of self-disclosure have been sustained in romantic relationships.

The concept of romantic love is an old one, but the belief that it has much to do with marriage is more recent and far from universal. In some non-Western cultures, marriage is still considered to be a contractual or financial arrangement that has nothing whatever to do with love. In our own society, the link between love and marriage has actually become stronger in the past 15 years. In 1967, about two thirds of college men but only about one fourth of college women stated that they would not marry a person they did not love even if the person had all the other qualities they desired (Kephart, 1967). Perhaps the women at that time had to be more practical about their financial security. But in a 1976 replication of the study, it was found that a full 86 percent of the men and 80 percent of the women would now refuse to marry without being in love. In fact, these researchers report that many young men and women believe that if romantic love disappears from the relationship, that is sufficient reason to end it (Campbell and Berscheid, 1976).

A study of long-term marriages in the United States and Japan suggests that these romantic views may change with time. The American marriages started out with a higher level of love than did the Japanese arranged marriages, as measured by expressions of affection, sexual interest, and marital satisfaction. Love decreased in both groups, and after 10 years, there were no differences (Blood, 1967). As the sixteenth-century writer Giraldi put it: "The history of a love affair is in some sense the drama of its fight against time."

This does not imply, however, that all the marriages were failures: some couples had gratifying marriages, and others experienced failure. The successful marriages were characterized by communication between the partners, an equitable division of labor, and equality of decision-making power. Romantic love is terrific for starters, but the sustaining forces of a good long-term relationship are less exciting, undoubtedly require more work, and have more to do with equality than with passion. A disappointment for romantics, perhaps, but heartening news and powerful propaganda for advocates of sexual equality.

Summary

1 *Social psychology* is the study of how we think, feel, and act in social environments, and of how social environments influence our thoughts, feelings, and actions. Social psychology emphasizes that human behavior is a function of both the person and the situation.

2 *Schematic processing* is the perceiving and interpreting of incoming information in terms of simplified memory structures called *schemata*. These structures allow us to process social information efficiently so that we encode and remember only the unique or most prominent features of a new object or event.

3 Because schemata constitute simplifications of reality, schematic processing produces biases and errors in our processing of social information. In forming impressions of other people, for example, we are prone to the *primacy effect;* the first information we receive about an individual is more powerful in determining our impression than later information. In general, schematic processing produces perceptions that are resistant to change and relatively impervious to new data.

4 Schemata about identifiable groups are called *stereotypes*. Like other schemata, they are resistant to change. Moreover, they can be self-perpetuating and self-fulfilling because they influence those who hold them to behave in ways that actually create the stereotyped behavior in others.

5   Changing negative racial stereotypes through interracial contacts works best when five conditions are met: (1) participants have equal status; (2) contact has potential for personal acquaintance; (3) contact exposes the prejudiced person to nonstereotypic individuals from the stereotyped group; (4) contact has social support; and (5) cooperative effort is made toward a mutually desired goal.

6   *Attribution* is the process by which we attempt to interpret and explain the behavior of other people—that is, to discern the causes of their actions. One major attribution task is to decide whether someone's action should be attributed to *dispositional causes* (the person's personality or attitudes) or to *situational causes* (social forces or other external circumstances).

7   People seem to follow rules when making attributions. The *covariance rule* states that behavior is attributed to the variable with which it appears to covary, according to the criteria of distinctiveness, consistency, and consensus. According to the *discounting rule,* we tend to discount the role of any particular cause when other plausible causes seem to be present. We use these rules imperfectly, however. In particular, we tend to give too much weight to dispositional factors and too little to situational factors. This bias has been called the *fundamental attribution error.*

8   Many principles of schematic processing and attribution apply to the process of *self-perception.* For example, individuals sometimes commit the fundamental attribution error about their own behavior, although dispositional bias appears to be stronger when judging the behavior of others.

9   *Attitudes* are likes and dislikes for identifiable aspects of the environment—persons, things, events, or ideas. Attitudes are the *affective* component in a three-part system that also includes beliefs (the *cognitive* component) and actions (the *behavioral* component). A major question in attitude research is the degree of consistency among these components, particularly between attitudes and behavior.

10 *Cognitive dissonance theory* proposes that when a person's actions are inconsistent with his or her attitudes, the discomfort produced by this dissonance leads the person to bring the attitudes into line with the actions. *Self-perception theory* offers an alternative interpretation for studies in which behavior seems to determine attitudes; individuals observe their own actions and infer that they must hold the attitude implied by those actions.

11 Political surveys and other observations of real life suggest that people are often not very concerned about consistency. We seem inclined to develop "opinion molecules" that remain isolated from each other instead of becoming part of a rational, coherent system of beliefs.

12 Many factors influence whether we will be attracted to someone. The most important are *proximity, familiarity, similarity,* and *physical attractiveness.* Physical attractiveness is more important than is generally acknowledged, although people tend to end up with partners who match their own attractiveness.

13 The process by which relationships move from liking toward greater intimacy has been called *social penetration.* The key to social penetration is reciprocal self-disclosure. Early and full self-disclosure among couples is much commoner now than it was in earlier years.

14 Cross-cultural observations suggest that the sustaining forces of a good long-term relationship have less to do with the intensity of romantic love than with communication between the partners, an equitable division of labor, and equality of decision making.

Further Reading

A number of books deal in more depth with the topics discussed in this chapter. Recommended are Bem, *Beliefs, attitudes, and human affairs* (1970); Shaver, *An introduction to attribution processes* (1975); Aronson, *The social animal* (3rd ed., 1980); and Offir, *Human sexuality* (1982). More technical but well worth the effort is Nisbett and Ross, *Human inference: Strategies and shortcomings of social judgment* (1980).

Two comprehensive textbooks in this area are Freedman, Sears, and Carlsmith, *Social psychology* (4th ed., 1981); and Gergen and Gergen, *Social psychology* (1981).

18
SOCIAL INFLUENCE

We noted in Chapter 17 that social psychology is the study of how we think, feel, and act in social environments and how, in turn, social environments influence our thoughts, feelings, and actions. In that chapter, we focused on the first part of this definition, individual social behavior. In this chapter, we turn our attention to the process of social and environmental influence.

To most of us, the term *social influence* connotes a deliberate attempt by some person or group to change our opinions or alter our behavior. Examples range from the attempts of TV commercials to influence our buying decisions to the more dramatic efforts of religious cults to persuade young people to abandon school and family and devote full loyalty to a "higher" mission. Such forms of persuasion are overt and obvious, even if the psychological principles by which they operate are not.

But there are other influences on our attitudes and behaviors that we are less likely to recognize. A few of these effects can even be observed in infra-human species and appear to stem from the mere physical presence of other members of the same species. Most are due to social norms: implicit rules and expectations about what we should think and how we should behave. These, too, range from the trivial to the profound. Social norms tell us to face forward when riding in an elevator and not to sit next to a stranger on an uncrowded bus or train; social norms also create and maintain an entire ideology of racism or sexism in a society. As we will see in this chapter, even overt forms of influence often rest on subtle social norms to which we give allegiance without realizing it.

We begin this chapter by examining the effects produced by the mere physical presence of others and then consider forms of influence that rest increasingly on social norms and expectations. We end the chapter with a discussion of a fairly new subfield of social psychology, the study of environmental influences such as noise and crowding on human behavior.

While reading this chapter, it is important to keep in mind that social influence is central to human interaction and communal life. Cooperation, community, altruism, and love all involve social influences. But we tend to take these phenomena for granted and to focus our concern on the influences that cause us grief. And for sociohistorical reasons, psychologists, too, have been pressed to investigate first those social influences that cause the society grief. Accordingly, just as the chapter on abnormal psychology focuses on what can go wrong with an individual's behavior, so, too, this chapter dwells at some length on what can go wrong with social interaction. Some of the findings are disturbing, even grim and depressing. But just as the study of psychopathology has led to effective therapies, so, too, the study of problematic social influences has led to more effective ways of dealing with the pathologies of social interaction. Moreover, we shall see that the principles of social influence that can produce evil consequences are the same principles that can produce concerned and effective citizens.

PRESENCE OF OTHERS

Social facilitation

In 1898, a psychologist named Triplett was examining the speed records of bicycle racers when he noticed that better speeds were obtained when cyclists raced against each other than when they raced against the clock. This led him to perform social psychology's first controlled laboratory experiment. He instructed children to turn a fishing reel as fast as possible for a fixed period of time. Sometimes two children worked at the same time in the same room, each with his or her own reel; at other times, they worked alone. The results confirmed the effect he sought: children worked faster in *coaction*—that is, when another child doing the same task was present—than when they worked alone.

Since this first experiment, many studies have demonstrated the facilitating effects of coaction with both human and infrahuman subjects. For example, chickens, puppies, rats, rhesus monkeys, armadillos, and opossums will all eat more if other members of their species are present (Harlow, 1932; James, 1953; Platt and James, 1966; Platt, Yaksh, and Darby, 1967; Stamm, 1961; Tolman, 1969); worker ants will dig more than three times as much sand per ant when working in groups than when working alone (Chen, 1937); and college students will complete more multiplication problems in coaction than when alone (Allport, 1920, 1924).

Soon after Triplett's experiment on coaction, it was discovered that the mere presence of a passive spectator—an audience rather than a coactor—was sufficient to facilitate performance. For example, the presence of an audience had the same facilitating effect on students' multiplication performance as did coactors in the earlier study (Dashiell, 1930). Together, these coaction and audience effects have been termed *social facilitation*.

But even in this simplest case of social influence, things began to get complicated. For example, it was found that more errors on the multiplication problems were made in coaction or with an audience than when subjects performed alone (Dashiell, 1930). In other words, the quality of performance declined even though quantity increased. But in other studies, the quality of performance improved with coactors or audiences present (see Dashiell, 1935; Cottrell, 1972). How can these contradictions be reconciled?

A close examination of the results of these studies indicates that behaviors showing improved performance in the presence of coactors or audiences usually involve highly practiced responses, or instinctive responses such as eating. When performing such behaviors, the most likely or most dominant response is the correct one. Behaviors showing impaired performance are those in which the most likely or most dominant response could be wrong. On a multiplication problem, for example, there are many wrong responses but only one correct one. This pattern of findings could result from the operation of a well-known principle of motivation: a high level of drive or arousal tends to energize the dominant responses of an organism. If the mere presence of another member of the species raises the general arousal or drive level of an organism, this would predict that simple or well-learned behaviors should show social facilitation, since these behaviors would be the dominant response. More complex behavior or behavior just being learned, in which the dominant response is apt to be incorrect, would be impaired (Zajonc, 1965, 1980).

This theory of social facilitation was tested in a number of ingenious experiments with both human and infrahuman subjects. In one particularly clever study, cockroaches were able to run down a straight runway into a darkened goal box to escape a bright floodlight. It was found that the roaches got to the goal box faster if they ran in pairs than if they ran alone. But when the escape response was made more complicated by requiring the roaches to make a right-angle turn to find the goal box, it took pairs of roaches longer to get there than single roaches. In other words, the presence of coactors facilitated performance in the simple runway but impaired performance in the complex runway (Zajonc, Heingartner, and Herman, 1969). This experiment was repeated by having all of the roaches run alone but with an "audience" of four roaches who watched from small plexiglass boxes set alongside the runways. Again, it was found that the presence of other roaches—even if they were just spectators—facilitated performance when the dominant response (running down the straight runway) was correct and impaired performance when the dominant response was incorrect.

Human studies have also confirmed Zajonc's theory of social facilitation. One such study was a direct analogue of the cockroach study, showing that human subjects learn a simple maze faster but a complex maze more slowly when an audience is present than when it is not (Hunt and Hillery, 1973). Human subjects also memorize easy word lists faster but difficult word lists more slowly in the presence of an audience than when alone (Cottrell, Rittle, and Wack, 1967).

Because social facilitation effects occur in infrahuman species, they may seem unrelated to complex cognitive processes. Nevertheless, it has been suggested that in humans the effects are not due to the mere presence of others but to feelings of competition or to concerns about being evaluated that raise the drive level. Thus, even the early studies of coaction found that if all elements of rivalry and competition were removed, social facilitation effects were reduced or eliminated (Dashiell, 1930). Other studies show that audience effects vary depending on how much the person feels that he or she is being evaluated. For example, audience effects are enhanced if it is an "expert" who is watching but diminished if the audience consists only of "undergraduates who want to watch a psychology experiment" (Henchy and Glass, 1968; Paulus and Murdock, 1971). When an audience wears blindfolds and hence cannot

Social facilitation—the presence of an audience can facilitate performance.

watch or evaluate an individual's performance, no audience effects at all are produced (Cottrell and others, 1968).

These studies leave open the question of whether social facilitation effects in humans ever arise only from the presence of other persons. One recent study designed specifically to answer this question suggests that they can. Each subject was asked to put on and take off shoes and other articles of outer clothing; some of these belonged to the subject, and some did not. The subjects were told only that they should eventually end up in their own clothes and were not aware that the speed with which they changed clothes was being unobtrusively timed by a hidden experimenter. (Note that the subject was never in a state of undress, since only shoes and other outer garments were involved.) The object was to compare the speed of performing a well-learned task—putting on and taking off one's own clothes—with the speed of performing an unfamiliar task—putting on and taking off someone else's clothes. Some subjects did this alone; other subjects did this with someone watching them; and still others did this with someone else in the room but not watching them (Markus, 1978).

The investigator found that the presence of the other person facilitated performance of the well-learned task but slowed the performance of the unfamiliar task. Because these effects occurred even when the other person was not watching and hence could not have been evaluating the subject, the experimenter interpreted her results as demonstrating that the mere presence of another person can cause social facilitation effects and therefore that the effects do not necessarily depend on competition or concern about evaluation.

Deindividuation and crowd behavior

At about the same time that Triplett was performing social psychology's first laboratory experiment on social facilitation, another observer of human behavior, the Frenchman Gustave LeBon, was taking a less dispassionate view of group coaction. In his book *The Crowd* (1895), he complained that "the crowd is always intellectually inferior to the isolated individual. . . . The mob man is fickle, credulous, and intolerant, showing the violence and ferocity of primitive beings, . . . women, children, savages, and lower classes . . . operating under the influence of the spinal cord." LeBon believed that the aggressive and immoral behaviors shown by lynch mobs (and, in his view, by the underclasses during the French Revolution) spread by "contagion" through a mob or crowd, breaking down the moral sense and self-control of men—if not of women, children, or savages. This caused crowds to commit destructive acts that no lone individual would commit.

Despite his obvious prejudices, LeBon's observations did seem to have some validity. The modern counterpart to his theory is built on the concept of *deindividuation,* an idea first proposed by Festinger, Pepitone, and Newcomb (1952) and extended by Zimbardo (1970) and Diener (1979, 1980). Their theories propose that certain conditions often present in groups can lead individuals to experience a psychological state of *deindividuation,* a feeling that they have lost their personal identities and merged anonymously into the group. This produces diminished restraints against impulsive behavior and other cognitive and emotional conditions associated with unruly mob behavior. The several antecedents and consequents of deindividuation are illustrated in Figure 18-1. Note that the antecedent conditions lead to deindividuation by producing a state of reduced self-awareness in the individual.

People in large crowds, as at this rock festival, are more likely to violate social norms.

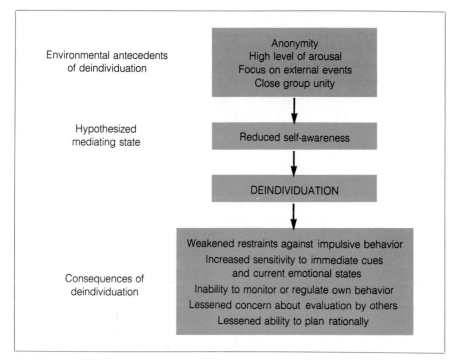

Figure 18-1
Antecedents and Consequences
of Deindividuation
**One explanation of crowd behavior traces it to
a loss of personal identity in certain group
situations. (After Diener, 1979)**

Most studies on deindividuation have explored the antecedent variable of
anonymity. In one study, college women, participating in groups of four, were
required to deliver electric shocks to another woman who was supposedly in
a learning experiment. Half of the women were deindividuated by making
them feel anonymous. They were dressed in bulky laboratory coats and hoods
that hid their faces, and the experimenter spoke to them only as a group, never
referring to any of them by name. The remaining women were individuated by
having them remain in their own clothes and wear large identification tags. In
addition, they were introduced to each other by name. During the experiment,
each woman had a shock button in front of her that she was to push when the
learner made an error. The results showed that the deindividuated women
delivered twice as much shock to the learner as did the individuated groups.
Moreover, deindividuated women gave as much shock to a learner they believed to be honest, sincere, and warm as they did to a learner they believed
to be conceited and critical, whereas individuated women gave less shock to
the nicer learner (Zimbardo, 1970).

A very clever demonstration of deindividuation took advantage of the
Halloween custom of trick-or-treating in identity-hiding costumes. Children
out trick-or-treating were greeted at the door by an adult who asked that each
child take only one piece of candy. The adult then disappeared into the house
briefly, giving the children the opportunity to take more candy. Some of the
children had been asked their names; others remained anonymous. It was
found that children who came in groups or who remained anonymous stole
more candy than did children who came alone or who had given their names
to the adult (Diener and others, 1976).

These experiments are not definitive, however. For instance, the laboratory coats and hoods worn in the first study carried negative connotations (they
resembled Ku Klux Klan outfits), and it may be that the roles suggested by the
outfits rather than anonymity produced the behavior. To test this possibility,

Mass suicide at Jonestown, Guyana
More than 900 followers of religious-cult leader Jim Jones obeyed his orders and committed suicide by poison. Shared beliefs and identification with a charismatic leader can exert a powerful influence on people's actions.

the shock experiment was repeated, except that the subjects wore either Ku Klux Klan-type costumes, nurses' uniforms, or their own clothes. The strong results found with the hooded outfits in the original study were not replicated; wearing Ku Klux Klan-type costumes had only a small effect on the level of shock the subjects administered. But more significantly, those wearing the nurses' uniforms actually gave fewer shocks than did the control group who wore their own clothes, suggesting that a uniform encourages the person to play the kind of role it connotes. Anonymity may increase aggression, but this study shows that such results are not inevitable (Johnson and Downing, 1979). On the other hand, this study can be interpreted as showing that anonymity did increase sensitivity to immediate cues—the uniforms—as the theory suggests. Moreover, as Figure 18-1 shows, the theory does not necessarily predict aggression as the inevitable outcome of deindividuation; other behaviors can result.

Unfortunately, deindividuation studies have proved to be more complicated than originally thought. It is now apparent that the experiments confound a number of different variables (for example, the effects of anonymity with the effects of being part of a group). Nevertheless, several studies show that the factors hypothesized to increase deindividuation, as outlined in Figure 18-1, do produce the results predicted (Diener, 1979; Prentice-Dunn and Rogers, 1980). The theory of deindividuation appears to have some validity for explaining the phenomena that so discomforted LeBon. However, other factors are also clearly at work. Some collective behaviors such as revolutions or the mass suicides that occurred within a religious cult at Jonestown, Guyana, in 1978 stem from shared and strongly held beliefs among group members coupled with the charisma of a group leader. It is also undoubtedly true that people in a mob may behave irresponsibly because they know they are less likely to be caught and punished than if they committed the same acts alone.

Bystander intervention

In earlier chapters, we noted that people do not react simply to the objective features of a situation but to their own subjective interpretations of it. In this chapter, we have seen that even social facilitation (which is a primitive kind of social influence) depends in part on the individual's interpretation of what others are doing or thinking. But as we will now see, the process of defining or interpreting the situation is often the very mechanism through which individuals influence one another.

In 1964, a young woman, Kitty Genovese, was murdered outside her home in New York City late at night. Because she resisted, the murder took over half an hour. Some 40 neighbors heard her screams for help, but no one came to her aid. No one even called the police (Rosenthal, 1964).

The American public was horrified by this incident, and social psychologists began to investigate the causes of what at first was termed "bystander apathy." Their work showed that "apathy," however, was not a very accurate term. It is not simple indifference that prevents bystanders from intervening in emergencies. First, there are realistic deterrents such as physical danger. Second, "getting involved" may mean lengthy court appearances or other entanglements. Third, emergencies are unpredictable and require quick unplanned action; few of us are prepared for them. Finally, one risks making a fool of oneself by misinterpreting a situation as an emergency when it is not. In summary, "the bystander to an emergency situation is in an unenviable position. It is perhaps surprising that anyone should intervene at all" (Latané and Darley, 1970, p. 247).

Although we might suppose that the presence of other bystanders would embolden an individual to act despite the risks, research demonstrates the reverse. Often it is the very presence of other people that prevents us from intervening. Specifically, the presence of others serves to (1) define the situation as a *non*emergency and (2) diffuse the responsibility for acting.

DEFINING THE SITUATION Most emergencies begin ambiguously. Is the man who is staggering about ill or simply drunk? Is the woman's life really being threatened, or is it just a family quarrel? Is that smoke or steam pouring out the window? One common way to deal with such dilemmas is to postpone action, act as if nothing is wrong, and look around to see how others are reacting. What are you likely to see? Other people who—for the same reasons—are also acting as if nothing is wrong. A state of *pluralistic ignorance* develops; that is, everybody in the group misleads everybody else by defining the situation as a nonemergency. We have all heard about crowds panicking because each person leads everybody else to overreact. The reverse, in which a crowd lulls its members into inaction, may be even more common. Several ingenious experiments demonstrate this effect.

In one, male college students were invited to an interview. As they sat in a small waiting room, a stream of smoke began to pour through a wall vent. Some subjects were alone in the waiting room when this occurred; others were in groups of three. The experimenters observed them through a one-way window and waited 6 minutes. Of the subjects tested alone, 75 percent reported the smoke within about 2 minutes. In contrast, fewer than 13 percent of the people tested in groups reported the smoke within the entire 6-minute period, even though the room was completely smoke-filled. Those who did not report the smoke had decided that it must have been steam, air conditioning vapors, smog, or practically anything but a real fire or emergency. This experiment thus showed that bystanders can define situations as nonemergencies for one another (Latané and Darley, 1968).

But perhaps these subjects were simply afraid to appear "cowardly." In a similar study, the "emergency" did not involve personal danger. Subjects in the testing room heard a female experimenter in the next office climb on a chair to reach a bookcase, fall to the floor, and yell "Oh, my God—my foot . . . I . . . can't move it. Oh . . . my ankle . . . I can't get this thing off me." She continued to moan for about a minute longer. The entire incident lasted about 2 minutes. Only a curtain separated the woman's office from the testing room where subjects waited, alone or in pairs. The results confirmed the findings of the smoke study. Of the subjects who were alone, 70 percent came to the woman's aid, whereas only 40 percent of those in two-person groups offered help. Again, those who had not intervened claimed later that they were unsure what had happened but had decided that it was not too serious (Latané and Rodin, 1969). The presence of others in these experiments produced pluralistic ignorance. Each person, observing the calmness of the others, resolved the ambiguity of the situation by deciding there was no emergency.

DIFFUSION OF RESPONSIBILITY Pluralistic ignorance can lead individuals to define a situation as a nonemergency, but this process does not explain incidents like the Genovese murder, in which the emergency is abundantly clear. Moreover, Kitty Genovese's neighbors could not observe one another behind their curtained windows and hence could not tell whether others were calm or panicked. The crucial process here was *diffusion of responsibility*. When each individual knows that many others are present, the burden of responsibility does not fall solely on him or her. Each can think, "certainly someone else must have done something by now; someone else will intervene."

Although each of these passers-by has undoubtedly noticed the man lying on the sidewalk, no one has stopped to help—to find out if he is asleep, sick, drunk, or dead. If others were not present, someone would be more likely to come to his aid.

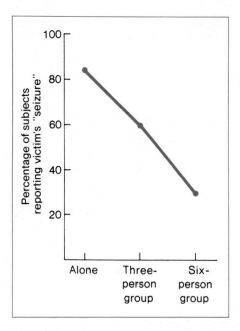

Figure 18-2
Diffusion of Responsibility
Percentage of subjects who reported a victim's apparent seizure declined as the number of other people the subject believed were in his or her discussion group increased. (After Darley and Latané, 1968)

To test this hypothesis, an experiment was conducted in which each subject was placed in an individual booth and told that she or he would participate in a group discussion about personal problems faced by college students. To avoid embarrassment, the discussion would be held through an intercom. Each person would speak for 2 minutes. The microphone would be turned on only in the booth of the person speaking, and the experimenter would not be listening. Actually, the voices of all participants except the subject's were tape recordings. On the first round, one of the taped participants mentioned that he had problems with seizures; on the second round, this individual sounded as if he were actually starting to have a seizure and begged for help. The experimenters waited to see if the subject would leave the booth to report the emergency and how long it would take. Note that (1) the emergency was not at all ambiguous, (2) the subject could not tell how the "bystanders" in the other booths were reacting, and (3) the subject knew the experimenter could not hear the emergency. Some subjects were led to believe that the discussion group consisted only of themselves and the seizure victim. Others were told it was a three-person group; and others, a six-person group.

Of the subjects who believed that they alone knew of the victim's seizure, 85 percent reported it; of those who thought they were in a three-person group, 62 percent reported the seizure; and only 31 percent of those who thought five other bystanders were present did so (see Figure 18-2). Interviews showed that all the subjects perceived the situation to be a real emergency. Most were very emotional about the conflict between letting the victim suffer and rushing, perhaps foolishly and unnecessarily, for help. In fact, subjects who did not report the seizure seemed far more upset than those who did. Clearly, we cannot interpret their nonintervention as apathy or indifference. Instead, the presence of others diffused the responsibility for acting.

If pluralistic ignorance and diffusion of responsibility are minimized, will people help one another? Three psychologists used the New York City subway system as their laboratory (Piliavin, Rodin, and Piliavin, 1969). Two male and two female experimenters boarded a subway train separately; the female experimenters took seats and recorded the results, while the two men remained standing. As the train moved along, one of the men staggered forward and collapsed, remaining prone and staring at the ceiling until he received help. If no help came, the other man finally helped him to his feet. Several variations of the study were tried: the victim either carried a cane (so he would appear ill) or smelled of alcohol (so he would appear drunk). Sometimes the victim was white; other times, black. There should be no ambiguity; clearly help is needed. Diffusion of responsibility should be minimized because each person cannot continue to assume that someone else will intervene if, in fact, nobody does. People should help.

The results supported this optimistic expectation. The victim with the cane received spontaneous help on over 95 percent of the trials, within an average of 5 seconds. Even the "drunk" victim received help in half of the trials, on the average within 109 seconds. Both black and white "cane" victims were aided by black and white bystanders. There was no relationship between the number of bystanders and the speed of help, suggesting that diffusion of responsibility had indeed been minimized. And all of this on the New York City subway system! This not only tends to support the proposed explanations of bystander nonintervention but should help us revise our stereotypes about New York City subway riders.

ROLE OF "HELPING" MODELS   In the subway study, as soon as one person moved to help, many others followed. This suggests that just as individuals use other people as models to define a situation as a nonemergency (pluralistic ignorance), they also use other people as models to indicate when to be helpful. This possibility was examined in a study by counting the number of drivers who stopped to help a woman whose car had a flat tire (the "test" car). During some test periods, another car with a flat tire (the "model" car) was parked alongside the highway one-quarter of a mile before the test car. The model car was raised on a jack and a woman was watching a man change the flat tire. Of 4,000 passing cars, 93 stopped to help the woman alone in the test car: 35 stopped when there was no model car and 58 when there was—a statistically significant difference. This experiment indicates that others not only help us decide when *not* to act in an emergency but also serve as models to show us how and when to be good Samaritans (Bryan and Test, 1967).

ROLE OF INFORMATION   Would you be more likely to intervene in an emergency now that you have read this section? An experiment at the University of Montana suggests that you would. Undergraduates were either given a lecture or shown a film about bystander intervention based on the material discussed in this section. Two weeks later, each undergraduate was confronted with a simulated emergency while walking with one other person (a confederate of the experimenters). A male "victim" was sprawled on the floor of a hallway. The confederate did not react as if the situation were an emergency. Of those who had heard the lecture or seen the film, 43 percent offered help, compared with only 25 percent of those who had not—a statistically significant difference (Beaman and others, 1978). For society's sake, perhaps you should reread this section!

When one person stops to help, others often follow suit. These bystanders not only notified the police but remained to give information after their arrival.

CONFORMITY AND OBEDIENCE

Norm formation in an ambiguous situation

The studies of bystander intervention indicate that people rely on one another when defining and interpreting ambiguous situations. This is the process that underlies the formation of *social norms* in a society—consensual agreements about the appropriate ways to behave in particular situations. People usually conform to such norms with little or no awareness of any external pressure to do so; in fact, we remain unaware of most social norms until someone happens to violate them. Many of the bizarre behaviors seen in psychiatric hospitals, for example, are nothing more than minor infractions of norms (Goffman, 1963). We suddenly become aware of social norms when we encounter people who look at the ceiling when they talk to us or people who pick their noses without hiding their behavior discreetly behind a handkerchief. The couple in a public park who go beyond simple handholding and cuddling to more involved forms of lovemaking alert us to the social norms that divide acceptable from unacceptable public behavior.

We are probably most aware of social norms when we visit another country—perhaps a country where picking one's nose is quite acceptable but holding hands is not. Here, too, we can observe ourselves carefully consulting the behavior of others to guide us lest we inadvertently make an embarrassing mistake. It is not irrelevant that one of the first psychologists to study social norms, Muzafir Sherif, was an immigrant from a foreign country. As a graduate student, Sherif was struck by the differences in norms between America and his native Turkey, and his dissertation at Columbia University became a book entitled *The Psychology of Social Norms* (1936).

Sherif was interested in studying the process of norm formation. He de-

Figure 18-3
Development of Group Norms
Using the Autokinetic Effect
When subjects were tested alone, their estimates of how much the light moved varied greatly. When tested in groups, the subjects' estimates became increasingly similar, and this group norm persisted when subjects were again tested alone. (After Sherif, 1936)

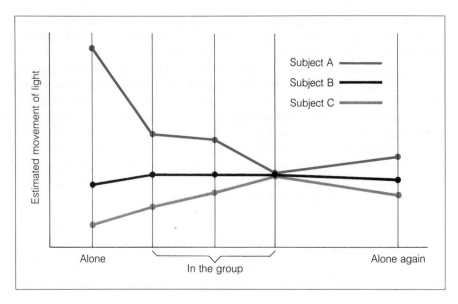

cided that he could only tackle such an enormous problem by constructing a simplified laboratory analogue, a situation in which the appropriate response was completely ambiguous and initially undefined. He chose a perceptual phenomenon known as the *autokinetic effect,* an effect in which a stationary pinpoint of light in a completely dark room appears to move about. This apparent movement occurs only in a visually impoverished environment, where there is no frame of reference to determine that the light is stationary. Sherif brought subjects into the darkened room and asked them to make judgments about how far and in what direction the light was moving. Such judgments are quite diverse, with some people perceiving movement of only a few inches and others perceiving movement of several feet. He then brought several subjects together in small groups and asked them to repeat the task. As shown in Figure 18-3, their judgments began to converge, and the group norm persisted when Sherif retested the subjects alone after the group session. Other research has shown that the group norm can persist for as long as a year (Rohrer and others, 1954) and that when subjects are moved to other groups they may try to influence the new group to accept the judgment norm of the original group (Jacobs and Campbell, 1961).

Conformity to peer pressure

Many people interpreted the Sherif studies as showing that humans are a blindly conforming species, a charge that troubled another social psychologist at the time, Solomon Asch. Asch reasoned that strong conformity was shown in the Sherif studies only because there was complete ambiguity about the correct response. In such a situation, using other people as a frame of reference seems only reasonable. Accordingly, Asch set up a series of studies calling for perceptual judgments that were not ambiguous.

In any kind of group, we may find ourselves in the minority on some issue. This is a fact of communal life to which most of us have become accustomed. If we decide that the majority is a more valid source of information than our own experience, we may change our minds and conform to the majority opinion. But imagine yourself in a situation in which you are sure your own opinion is correct and the group is wrong. Would you yield to social pressure under these circumstances? This is the kind of conformity that Asch decided to investigate (Asch, 1952, 1955).

In his standard procedure, the subject was seated at a table with a group of seven to nine others (actually confederates of the experimenter). The group was shown a display with three vertical lines of different lengths, and members of the group were asked to judge which line was the same length as a standard drawn on another display (see Figure 18-4). Each individual announced his or her decision in turn, and the actual subject sat in the next to last seat. The correct judgments were obvious, and everyone gave the same response on most trials. But on some trials, the confederates had been secretly instructed to give the wrong answer. Asch then observed the amount of conformity this procedure would elicit from his subjects.

The results were quite striking—and an unpleasant surprise for Asch. Even though the correct answer was always obvious, about 74 percent of the subjects conformed to the incorrect majority judgment at least once. On the average, subjects conformed on about 32 percent of the critical trials. Moreover, the group did not have to be large to obtain such conformity. When Asch varied the size of the group from two to 16, he found that a group of three or four confederates was just as effective at producing conformity as larger groups (Asch, 1958).

Why didn't the obviousness of the correct answer provide support for the individual's independence from the majority? Why isn't a person's confidence in his or her ability to make simple sensory judgments a strong force against conformity?

According to one line of argument, it is precisely the obviousness of the correct answer in the Asch experiment that produces the strong forces *toward* conformity (Ross, Bierbrauer, and Hoffman, 1976). Disagreements in real life typically involve difficult or subjective judgments such as which economic policy will best reduce inflation or which of two paintings is more aesthetically pleasing. In these cases, we expect to disagree with others occasionally; we even know that being a minority of one in an otherwise unanimous group is a plausible, if uncomfortable, possibility.

The Asch situation is much more extreme. Here the individual is confronted with unanimous disagreement about a simple physical fact, a bizarre and unprecedented occurrence that appears to have no rational explanation. Subjects are clearly puzzled and tense. They rub their eyes in disbelief and jump up to look more closely at the lines. They squirm, mumble, giggle in embarrassment, and look searchingly at others in the group for some clue to the mystery. After the experiment, they offer half-hearted hypotheses about optical illusions (Asch, 1952) or suggest—quite aptly—that perhaps the first person occasionally made mistakes and each successive person followed suit because of conformity pressures.

Consider what it means to dissent from the majority under these circumstances. Just as the judgments of the group seem incomprehensible to the subject, so, too, the subject believes that his or her dissent will be incomprehensible to the group. They will surely judge him or her to be incompetent, even out of touch with reality. Similarly, if the subject dissents repeatedly, this will seem to constitute a direct challenge to the group's competence—a challenge that requires enormous courage when one's own perceptual abilities are suddenly and inexplicably called into question. This fear of "what will they think of me and what will they think I think of them" inhibits dissent and generates the strong pressures to conform in the Asch situation.

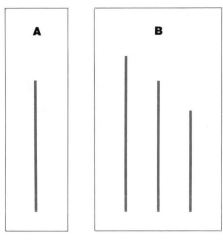

Figure 18-4
Representative Stimulus in Asch's Study
After viewing display A, the subjects were told to pick the matching line from display B. The displays shown here are typical in that the correct decision is obvious. (After Asch, 1958)

"Well, heck! If all you smart cookies agree, who am I to dissent?"

Drawing by Handelsman; copyright © 1972 *The New Yorker Magazine*, Inc.

A

B

C

Resistance to majority opinion

A. All of the group members except the man sixth from left are confederates previously instructed to give uniformly wrong answers on 12 of the 18 trials; number 6, who has been told he is participating in an experiment in visual judgment, therefore finds himself a lone dissenter when he gives the correct answers.

B. The subject, showing the strain of repeated disagreement with the majority, leans forward anxiously to look at the pair of cards.

C. This particular subject persists in his opinion, saying that "he has to call them as he sees them."

Conformity pressures are far less strong when the group is not unanimous. If even one confederate breaks with the majority, the amount of conformity drops from 32 percent of the trials to about 6 percent. In fact, a group of eight containing only one dissenter produces less conformity than a unanimous majority of three (Asch, 1958). Surprisingly, the dissenter does not even have to give the correct answer. Even when the dissenter's answers are *more* incorrect than the majority's, the spell is broken, and subjects are more inclined to give their own, correct judgments (Allen and Levine, 1969; Asch, 1955). Nor does it matter who the dissenter is. A black dissenter reduces the conformity rate among racially prejudiced white subjects just as effectively as a white dissenter (Malof and Lott, 1962). In a variation that approaches the absurd, conformity was significantly reduced even though the subjects thought the dissenter was so visually handicapped that he could not see the stimuli (Allen and Levine, 1971). It seems clear that the presence of but one other deviant to share the potential disapproval or ridicule of the group permits the subject to dissent without feeling totally isolated.

The original Asch situation is so unlike situations in real life that we may wonder why Asch used a task where the correct answer was obvious? The reason is that he wanted to study pure public conformity, uncontaminated by the possibility that subjects were actually changing their minds about the correct answers. The variations that introduce difficult or subjective judgments—or complete ambiguity as in the Sherif studies on the autokinetic phenomenon—are actually creating an unknown mixture of public conformity and private opinion change. Although this may more faithfully reflect real life, it does not permit us to assess the effects of pure pressure to comply with a majority judgment when we are certain that our own minority judgment is correct. This critical difference between the original Asch situation and later variations of it that use more difficult, subjective, or ambiguous tasks is almost never recognized (Ross, Bierbrauer, and Hoffman, 1976).

Obedience to authority

In Nazi Germany from 1933 to 1945, millions of innocent people were systematically put to death in concentration camps. The mastermind of this horror, Adolph Hitler, may well have been a psychopathic monster. But he could not have done it alone. What about all those who ran the day-to-day operation, who built the ovens and gas chambers, filled them with human beings, counted bodies, and did the necessary paper work? Were they all monsters?

Not according to Hannah Arendt (1963), who covered the trial of Nazi war criminal Adolph Eichmann. She found him a dull, uninspired, unaggressive bureaucrat who saw himself as a little cog in the machine. She subtitled her book about Eichmann *A Report on the Banality of Evil* and concluded that most of the "evil men" of the Third Reich were just ordinary people following orders from superiors. This is not an easy conclusion to accept because it suggests that each of us might be capable of such evil and that Nazi Germany was an event less wildly alien from the normal human condition than we might like to think. In fact, our emotional attachment to the "monster" explanation of great evil was vividly shown by the intensity of the attacks on Arendt and her conclusions. Can obedience to authority really be that powerful and pervasive among ordinary citizens?

This chilling possibility was explored in a series of important and controversial studies conducted by Stanley Milgram (1963, 1974). Ordinary men and women were recruited through a newspaper ad that offered $4 for one hour's participation in a "study of memory." On arriving at the laboratory, the subject was told that he or she would be playing the role of teacher in the study. The subject was to read a series of word pairs to another subject and then test the "learner's" memory by reading the first word of each pair and asking him to select the correct second word from four alternatives. Every time the learner made an error, the subject was to press a lever that delivered an electric shock to him.

The subject watched while the learner was strapped into an electrically wired chair and an electrode attached to his wrist. The subject was then seated in an adjoining room in front of a shock generator whose front panel contained 30 lever switches set in a horizontal line. Each switch was labeled with a voltage rating, ranging in sequence from 15 to 450 volts; groups of adjacent switches were labeled descriptively, ranging from "Slight Shock" up to "Danger: Severe Shock." When a switch was depressed, an electric buzz sounded, lights flashed, and the needle on a voltage meter deflected to the right. To illustrate how it worked, the subject was given a sample shock of 45 volts from the generator. As the procedure began, the experimenter instructed the subject to move one level higher on the shock generator after each successive error (see Figure 18-5).

The learner did not, of course, actually receive any shocks. He was a 47-year-old, mild-mannered accountant who had been specially trained for his

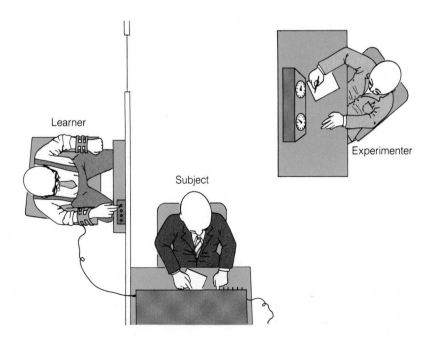

Learner

Subject

Experimenter

Figure 18-5
Milgram Obedience Experiment
The subject was told to give the "learner" a more intense shock after each error. If he or she objected, the experimenter insisted it was necessary to go on. (After Milgram, 1974)

Milgram experiment

(top left) The "shock generator" used in Milgram's experiment on obedience. (top right) The victim is strapped into the "electric chair." (bottom left) A subject receives the sample shock before starting the "teaching session." (bottom right) A subject refuses to go on with the experiment. Most subjects became deeply disturbed by the role they were being asked to play, whether they continued in the experiment to the end or refused at some point to go on any longer. (From the film *Obedience,* distributed by New York University Film Library; copyright © 1965, by Stanley Milgram)

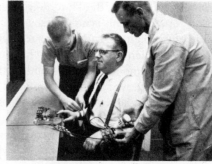

role. As he began to make errors and the shock levels escalated, he could be heard protesting through the adjoining wall. As they got stronger, he began to shout and curse. At 300 volts he began to kick the wall, and at the next shock level (marked "extreme intensity shock") he no longer answered the questions or made any noise. As you might expect, many subjects began to object to this excruciating procedure, pleading with the experimenter to call a halt. But the experimenter responded with a sequence of "prods," using as many as necessary to get the subject to go on: "Please continue"; "The experiment requires that you continue"; "It is absolutely essential that you continue"; and "You have no other choice—you *must* go on." Obedience to authority was measured by the maximum amount of shock the subject would administer before refusing to continue.

Milgram found that 65 percent of the subjects continued to obey throughout, going all the way to the end of the shock series (450 volts). Not one subject stopped prior to administering 300 volts—the point at which the learner began to kick the wall (see Figure 18-6). What produces such conformity?

Milgram suggests that the potential for obedience to authority is such a necessary requirement for communal life that it has probably been built into our species by evolution. The division of labor in a society requires that individuals have the capacity to subordinate and coordinate their own independent actions in the service of the goals and purposes of the larger social organization. Parents, school systems, and work organizations all nurture this capacity further by teaching the developing individual the importance of following the directives of others who "know the larger picture." To understand obedience in a particular situation, then, we need to understand the factors that persuade individuals to relinquish their autonomy and become voluntary agents for the system. Five such factors play important roles in the Milgram experiment.

THE SEQUENCE OF ENTRAPMENT   The Milgram experiment starts rather innocently as an experiment in memory and then gradually escalates. By the time the subjects want to quit, they are trapped. Once they begin to give shocks and to escalate the shock levels, there is no longer a natural stopping point. The experimenter makes no new demands, only that they continue to do what they are already doing. In order to break off, they must face the idea that they were wrong to begin at all; further, the longer they put off quitting, the harder it is to admit their misjudgment in going as far as they have. It is easier to continue. Imagine how much less obedience there would be if subjects had to begin by giving the strongest shock first.

THE ETIQUETTE OF THE SITUATION   Subjects have also been trapped earlier in the sequence by replying to the ad and agreeing to be in the study. Their assent establishes an implicit contract to cooperate with the experimenter, to follow the directions of the person in charge, and to see the job through to completion. We tend to underestimate how difficult it is to break such an agreement and go back on our implied word to cooperate. In addition, the potential quitter faced a dilemma similar to the one confronting a subject in the Asch studies. Dissenting in that case implied that the subject thought the group was incompetent. Dissenting in the Milgram situation is equivalent to accusing the experimenter himself of being incompetent, evil, or cruel—an even more compelling force toward staying in line.

There are other parallels. In the Asch situation, the presence of one other dissenter was sufficient to break the spell and prompt the subject to reassert his or her independence. A similar thing happens in the Milgram situation. In one variation of the procedure, two additional confederates were employed. They were introduced as subjects who would also play teacher roles. Teacher 1 would read the list of word pairs; teacher 2 would tell the learner if he was right or wrong; and teacher 3 (the real subject) would deliver the shocks. The confederates complied with the instructions through the 150 volt shock, at which point teacher 1 informed the experimenter that he was quitting. Despite the experimenter's insistence that he continue, teacher 1 left his chair and sat in another part of the room. After the 210 volt shock, teacher 2 also quit. The experimenter then turned to the subject and ordered him to continue by himself. Only 10 percent of the subjects were willing to complete the series in this situation (Milgram, 1974, pp. 116–21). In a second variation, there were two experimenters rather than two additional teachers. After a few shocks, they began to argue—one of them saying that they should stop the experiment, the other saying they should continue. Under these circumstances, not a single subject would continue despite the orders to do so by the second experimenter (Milgram, 1974, 105–107). The planted dissenters in these variations not only shoulder most of the responsibility for disobedience but serve as models for the subject.

BUFFERS   Milgram's subjects believed that they were committing acts of violence, but there were several buffers that obscured this fact or diluted the immediacy of the experience. For example, the learner was in the next room, out of sight and unable to communicate by using his own voice. Milgram reports that obedience drops from 65 percent to 40 percent if the learner is in the same room as the subject. If the subject must personally ensure that the learner holds his hand on the shock plate, obedience declines to 30 percent. The more direct the person's experience with the victim—the fewer buffers between the person and the consequences of his or her act—the less the obedience.

The most common buffer found in warlike situations is the remoteness of the person from the final act of violence. Thus, Adolph Eichmann argued that he was not directly responsible for killing Jews; he merely arranged for their

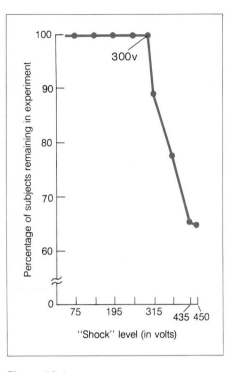

Figure 18-6
Obedience to Authority
The percentage of subjects willing to administer a punishing shock did not begin to decline until the intensity level of the shock reached 300 volts. (After Milgram, 1963)

"Oh, dear. I was trying to get you, Miss Kearney, but I think I pushed World War III by mistake."

In 1969, a group of American soldiers serving in Vietnam killed a number of civilians in the community of My Lai. This became one of the scandals of the Vietnam War and again brought into public consciousness the conflict between personal moral conscience and obedience to authority. The following is an account of the incident by one of the participants who was interviewed by Mike Wallace of CBS News.

Q. How many men aboard each chopper?
A. Five of us. And we landed next to the village, and we all got on line, and we started walking toward the village. And there was one man, one gook in the shelter, and he was all huddled up down in there, and the man called out and said there's a gook over there.
Q. How old a man was this? I mean was this a fighting man or an older man?
A. An older man. And the man hauled out and said that there's a gook over here, and then Sergeant Mitchell hollered back and said shoot him.
Q. Sergeant Mitchell was in charge of the twenty of you?
A. He was in charge of the whole squad. And so then, the man shot him. So, we moved into the village, and we started searching up the village and gathering people and running through the center of the village.
Q. How many people did you round up?
A. Well, there was about forty, fifty people that we gathered in the center of the village. And we placed them in there,

and it was like a little island, right there in the center of the village, I'd say. . . . And . . . .
Q. What kind of people—men, women, children?
A. Men, women, children.
Q. Babies?
A. Babies. And we huddled them up. We made them squat down, and Lieutenant Calley came over and said, "You know what to do with them, don't you?" And I said yes. So, I took it for granted that he just wanted us to watch them. And he left and came back about ten or fifteen minutes later and said, "How come you ain't killed them yet?" And I told him that I didn't think you wanted us to kill them, that you just wanted us to guard them. He said, "No. I want them dead." So—
Q. He told this to all of you or to you particularly?
A. Well, I was facing him. So, but the other three, four guys heard it, and so he stepped back about ten, fifteen feet, and he started shooting them. And he told me to start shooting. So, I started shooting; I poured about four clips into the group.
Q. You fired four clips from your . . .
A. M-16.
Q. And that's about how many clips—I mean, how many—
A. I carried seventeen rounds to each clip.
Q. So you fired something like sixty-seven shots?
A. Right.
Q. And you killed how many? At that time?
A. Well, I fired them automatic, so you can't—You just spray the area on them and so you can't know how many you

killed 'cause they were going fast. So, I might have killed ten or fifteen of them.
Q. Men, women, and children?
A. Men, women, and children.
Q. And babies?
A. And babies.
Q. Okay. Then what?
A. So we started to gather them up, more people, and we had about seven or eight people, that we was gonna put into the hootch, and we dropped a hand grenade in there with them.
Q. Now, you're rounding up more?
A. We're rounding up more, and we had about seven or eight people. And we was going to throw them in the hootch, and well, we put them in the hootch, and then we dropped a hand grenade down there with them. And somebody holed up in the ravine and told us to bring them over to the ravine, so we took them back out and led them over to—and by that time, we already had them over there, and they had about seventy, seventy-five people all gathered up. So, we threw ours in with them, and Lieutenant Calley told me, he said, "Soldier, we got another job to do." And so, he walked over to the people, and he started pushing them off and started shooting. . . .
Q. Started pushing them off into the ravine?
A. Off into the ravine. It was a ditch. And so, we started pushing them off, and we started shooting them, so all together we just pushed them all off, and just started using automatics on them. And then . . .
Q. Again—men, women, and children?
A. Men, women, and children.
Q. And babies?

deaths indirectly. Milgram conducted an analogue to this "link-in-the-chain" situation by requiring a subject only to pull a switch that enabled another teacher (a confederate) to deliver the shocks to the learner. Under these conditions, obedience soared: a full 93 percent of the subjects continued to the end of the shock series. In this situation, the subject can shift the blame to the person who actually delivers the shock. Note, too, that again the subject is provided with a model, but in this case the model's behavior implies that nothing is amiss.

    The shock generator itself served as a final buffer—an impersonal mechanical "agent" that actually delivered the shock. Imagine how obedience would have declined if subjects were required to hit the learner with their fists.

Just Following Orders in Vietnam

A. And babies. And so, we started shooting them and somebody told us to switch off to single shot so that we could save ammo. So, we switched off to single shot and shot a few more rounds. . . .

Q. Why did you do it?

A. Why did I do it? Because I felt like I was ordered to do it, and it seemed like that at the time I felt like I was doing the right thing because, like I said, I lost buddies. I lost a damn good buddy, Bobby Wilson, and it was on my conscience. So, after I done it, I felt good, but later on that day, it was getting to me.

Q. You're married?

A. Right.

Q. Children?

A. Two.

Q. How old?

A. The boy is two and a half, and the little girl is a year and a half.

Q. Obviously, the question comes to my mind . . . the father of two little kids like that . . . how can he shoot babies?

A. I didn't have the little girl. I just had the little boy at the time.

Q. Uh-huh. . . . How do you shoot babies?

A. I don't know. It's just one of these things.

Q. How many people would you imagine were killed that day?

A. I'd say about three hundred and seventy.

Q. How do you arrive at that figure?

A. Just looking.

Q. You say you think that many people, and you yourself were responsible for how many?

A. I couldn't say.

Q. Twenty-five? Fifty?

A. I couldn't say. Just too many.

Q. And how many men did the actual shooting?

A. Well, I really couldn't say that either. There was other . . . there was another platoon in there, and . . . but I just couldn't say how many.

Q. But these civilians were lined up and shot? They weren't killed by crossfire?

A. They weren't lined up. . . . They [were] just pushed in a ravine, or just sitting, squatting . . . and shot.

Q. What did these civilians—particularly the women and children, the old men—what did they do? What did they say to you?

A. They weren't much saying to them. They [were] just being pushed, and they were doing what they was told to do.

Q. They weren't begging, or saying, "No . . . no," or . . .

A. Right. They were begging and saying, "No, no." And the mothers was hugging their children, and . . . but they kept right on firing. Well, we kept right on firing. They was waving their arms and begging. . . .

(*The New York Times*, November 25, 1969)

Now that you have read this interview, perhaps you can appreciate more fully Hannah Arendt's view of Adolph Eichmann and his fellow Nazi war criminals. We are not dealing here with evil personalities, but with ordinary people striving to fulfill their duties as agents for the system. Perhaps the most striking characteristic of evil is its banality.

Ethologists have shown that several species of animals have built-in inhibitors of deadly aggression. For example, if two animals from the same species are fighting, either of them will halt the attack if the other "surrenders" by displaying a submissive gesture. Our species has developed a technology that permits us to destroy distant fellow humans by remote control, thereby removing us from any inhibiting signals sent by the victims and rendering these built-in safeguards to self-destruction ineffective (Lorenz, 1966). Although we can probably all agree that it is worse to kill thousands of people by pushing a button that releases a guided missile than it is to beat one individual to death with a rock, Milgram's findings suggest that it is still psychologically easier to push the button. Such are the effects of buffers.

SURVEILLANCE   An obvious factor in the Milgram experiment is the constant presence or surveillance of the experimenter. When the experimenter left the room and issued his orders by telephone, obedience dropped from the standard 65 percent to 21 percent (Milgram, 1974, pp. 58–62). Moreover, several of the subjects who continued under these conditions "cheated" by administering shocks of lower intensity than they were supposed to without telling the experimenter.

AUTHORITY AND THE OVERARCHING IDEOLOGY   The most important factor producing the kind of voluntary obedience we have been discussing is the individual's acceptance of an overarching ideology that legitimizes the authority of the person in charge and justifies following his or her directives. Officials like Eichmann, who followed orders in Nazi Germany, believed in the primacy of the German state and hence in the legitimacy of orders issued in the name of that cause. Similarly, the American soldiers who followed orders to shoot enemy civilians in Vietnam had committed themselves earlier to the idea that national security requires strict obedience to military commands.

In the Milgram experiments, "science" provides the overarching ideology that legitimizes even quite extraordinary demands. Some critics of the Milgram experiments have argued that the prestige of a scientific experiment led people to obey when they would not otherwise have done so. Indeed, when Milgram repeated his experiments in a rundown set of offices and removed any association with Yale University from the setting, obedience dropped from 65 percent to 48 percent (Milgram, 1974, pp. 66–70). But this criticism misses the major point. The prestige of science is not an irrelevant artificiality but an integral part of Milgram's demonstration. Science serves precisely the same legitimizing role in the Milgram situation that national security serves in wartime killing or that the German state served in Nazi Germany. It was the overarching ideology that prompted an individual to leave autonomy behind, voluntarily subordinating his or her own independence to goals and purposes of the larger social organization.

Remoteness from the final act of violence: (left) aerial view of the Pentagon; (right) the War Room of the Pentagon

Obedience to authority in everyday life

Because the Miligram experiments have been criticized for being artificial (see Orne and Holland, 1968), it is instructive to look at an example of obedience to authority under more ordinary conditions. Five researchers—two psychiatrists and three nurses—investigated whether nurses in 22 different wards of both a public and private hospital would obey an order that violated hospital rules and professional practice (Hofling and others, 1966). While on regular duty, the subject (a nurse) received a phone call from a doctor she knew to be on the staff but had not met: "This is Dr. Smith from Psychiatry calling. I was asked to see Mr. Jones this morning, and I'm going to have to see him again tonight. I'd like him to have had some medication by the time I get to the ward. Will you please check your medicine cabinet and see if you have some Astroten? That's ASTROTEN." When the nurse checked the medicine cabinet, she saw a pillbox labeled:

ASTROTEN
5 mg. capsules
Usual dose: 5 mg.
Maximum daily dose: 10 mg.

After she reported that she had found it, the doctor continued, "Now will you please give Mr. Jones a dose of 20 milligrams of Astroten. I'll be up within 10 minutes; I'll sign the order then, but I'd like the drug to have started taking effect." A staff psychiatrist, posted unobtrusively nearby, terminated each trial by disclosing its true nature when the nurse either poured the medication (actually a harmless placebo), refused to accept the order, or tried to contact another professional.

This order violated several rules. The dose was clearly excessive. Medication orders are not permitted to be given by telephone. The medication was "unauthorized"; that is, it was not on the ward stock list clearing it for use. Finally, the order was given by an unfamiliar person. Despite all of this, 95 percent of the nurses started to give the medication. Moreover, the telephone calls were brief, with little or no delay or resistance. None of the nurses insisted on a written order, although several sought reassurance that the doctor would arrive promptly. In interviews after the experiment, all the nurses stated that such orders had been received in the past and that doctors became annoyed if the nurses balked.

Power of situational influences

In the discussion of attribution theory in Chapter 17, we saw that people typically underestimate the degree to which external forces control behavior. The studies on conformity and obedience illustrate this point dramatically—not through their results but through our surprise at their results. In his social psychology class every year, one psychologist asks students to predict whether they would continue to administer the shocks in the Milgram situation after the "learner" begins to pound on the wall. About 99 percent of the students say they would not (Aronson, 1980). Milgram himself surveyed psychiatrists at a leading medical school; they predicted that most subjects would refuse to go on after reaching 150 volts, that only about 4 percent would go beyond 300 volts, and that fewer than 1 percent would go all the way to 450 volts. And in

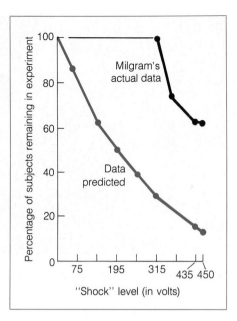

Figure 18-7
Predicted and Actual Compliance
The upper curve presents the Milgram data and shows the percentage of subjects who remained obedient in the situation, continuing to administer shocks as the voltage increased. The lower curve is from a study where observers witnessed a reenactment of the Milgram experiment and attempted to predict what percentage of the subjects would continue to be obedient as shock increased. The observers vastly underestimated the magnitude of the situational forces and the likelihood of obedience in the Milgram situation. (After Bierbrauer, 1973)

one study, subjects were asked to "walk through" the entire Milgram procedure complete with shock apparatus and a tape recording of the protesting "learner." Whether they role-played the part of the subject or the part of an observer, all subjects continued to vastly underestimate the compliance rates actually obtained by Milgram, as shown in Figure 18-7 (Bierbrauer, 1973). The nursing study yields comparable findings. When nurses who had not been subjects were given a complete description of the situation and asked how they themselves would respond, 85 percent reported that they would not have given the medication, and most of them thought a majority of nurses would also refuse. Of 21 nursing students asked the same question, all of them reported that they would not have given the medication as ordered.

The obedience experiments thus illustrate as dramatically as possible a major lesson of social psychology: we seriously underestimate the extent and power of social and/or situational forces on human behavior.

PERSUASION

Just as the practices of Nazi Germany under Hitler provoked social psychologists to be interested in obedience to authority, propaganda efforts on both sides in World War II led social psychologists to study persuasion and attitude change. The most intensive work began during the 1950s at Yale University, where attention was directed to the three components of persuasion: the communicator, the communication, and the target individual. Studies were conducted to determine the characteristics of the successful communicator or persuader, the characteristics of an effective communication (for example, the most effective order in which to present the arguments), and whether certain personality types are more easily persuaded than others (Hovland, Janis, and Kelley, 1953). The results of these studies were quite complex and are not easily summarized. Here we will focus on the characteristics of the effective communicator, for as we will see, this topic has wide-ranging implications for everyday social influence.

Communicator credibility and attractiveness

One of the most straightforward findings from the research on persuasion is that the higher a person's evaluation of the communicator, the more she or he is likely to be persuaded by the communication. This is a result that can be predicted from the theories of attitude consistency we discussed in Chapter 17. If someone you evaluate highly puts forth an argument or position that is at variance with your current attitudes, an inconsistency (or dissonance) is set up that can be reduced or eliminated either by changing your evaluation of the communicator or by changing your attitudes. Research has shown that changes of both kinds do occur in ways that such a theory predicts (Osgood and Tannenbaum, 1955). The two major elements in the target individual's evaluation of a communicator are the communicator's *credibility* and his or her *attractiveness* to the target individual.

CREDIBILITY   A communicator's credibility, the degree to which he or she can be believed, depends on how much expertise the communicator appears to have on the topic under discussion and whether he or she appears trustworthy and unbiased. Politicians and advertisers spend at least as much effort trying to persuade us that they are credible as they spend on the substance of the message itself.

One way of appearing credible is to argue for a position that appears to be against your own best interest. For example, one study presented arguments by a convicted criminal and a prosecutor. The criminal produced significantly more attitude change when he argued for more powerful courts than when he advocated less powerful courts. When the same arguments were presented by a prosecutor, the trend of the results went in the opposite direction (Walster, Aronson, and Abrahams, 1966).

It might also seem that a communicator's credibility would be damaged if it is known that she or he is trying to persuade us since we might then be suspicious that the communication is biased or even dishonest. And it has been shown that people are more persuaded by a communication if they happen to overhear it "accidentally" than if it is explicitly directed at them (Walster and Festinger, 1962). But what is surprising is that there is not in fact very strong evidence that knowledge of a communicator's intent to persuade reduces his or her persuasiveness (McGuire, 1969). Certainly everyone knows that the major aspirin companies are trying to persuade us to buy their brands in their TV commercials, and yet people are still willing to pay up to seven times as much for the heavily advertised brands as for equally effective but lesser known brands (Bem, 1970; Consumers Union, 1980).

Attractiveness is an important attribute for political leaders.

ATTRACTIVENESS The second major factor in a target's evaluation of a communicator is the communicator's attractiveness—the degree to which he or she is liked by the target. All of the factors discussed in Chapter 17 that enhance liking or interpersonal attraction also contribute to the liked individual's persuasiveness—even physical attractiveness. Credibility and attractiveness operate somewhat differently, however. Credibility produces attitude change because people take the arguments of a credible source more seriously than they take the arguments of a noncredible source. Attractiveness, however, seems to operate through the mechanism of *identification* (Kelman, 1961). People often seek to identify with or be like people whom they like and admire, which leads them to adopt the liked person's beliefs and attitudes. This implies that having sound, persuasive arguments is more important for a neutral or unattractive communicator than for a liked or attractive communicator. This prediction was tested in a study that used a physically unattractive expert and a physically attractive nonexpert to deliver persuasive communications. It was found that good arguments enhanced the persuasiveness of the expert but did not have much effect on the amount of attitude change obtained by the attractive nonexpert (Norman, 1976).

Identification as a mechanism of attitude changes has much deeper and more far-ranging implications than such laboratory studies would imply. In fact, it is probably the source of our most deeply held beliefs and attitudes, as we shall now see.

Reference groups and attitude change

Nearly every group to which we belong, from our family to society as a whole, has an implicit or explicit set of beliefs, attitudes, and behaviors that are considered "correct." Any member of the group who strays from those norms risks isolation and social disapproval. Thus, groups regulate their members through the use of social reward and punishment. More importantly, groups provide us with a frame of reference, a ready-made interpretation of events and social issues. They provide the glasses through which we look at the world. Any group that exercises either of these two kinds of influence—regulation or interpretation—is one of our *reference groups*. We "refer" to such groups in

Individuals belong to a number of reference groups. This young woman's attitudes and behavior may be influenced by her fellow cheerleaders, but she probably also identifies with other reference groups which may emphasize similar or different values.

order to evaluate and decide on our beliefs, attitudes, and behaviors. As we noted above, if we seek to be like them, we are said to "identify" with them.

The subtle influence of reference groups was illustrated in a study in which students at a progressive teachers' college listened to a recorded speech that called for a return to traditional classroom methods. The speech was interrupted several times by applause. Half the students had been told that the audience in the recording was composed of students from their own college; the other half, that it was composed of local townspeople. Members of the first group changed their opinions about progressive education in the direction advocated in the speech more than did the students who believed the applause came from "outsiders (Kelley and Woodruff, 1956).

Individuals do not necessarily belong to all their reference groups. For example, lower-middle-class individuals often use the middle-class as a reference group. A young, aspiring athlete may use professional athletes as a reference group, adopting their views and otherwise trying to model himself or herself after them.

Life would be simple if each of us identified with only one reference group. But most of us identify with several reference groups, which often leads to conflicting pressures on our beliefs, attitudes, and behaviors. In Chapter 17, for example, we noted the cross pressures that might be experienced by the Jewish businessperson because his or her ethnic reference group usually holds more liberal political positions than does his or her business reference group. But perhaps the most enduring example of competing reference groups is the conflict that many young people experience between their family reference group and their college or peer reference group, a conflict repeated in every generation. The most extensive investigation of this conflict is Theodore Newcomb's classic Bennington study—an examination of the political attitudes of the entire population of Bennington College, a small, politically liberal college in Vermont. The dates of the study (1935–1939) are a useful reminder to those who are just now discovering the generation gap for themselves. It is not a new phenomenon.

Today, Bennington College tends to attract liberal students, but in 1935, most students came from wealthy, conservative families. (It is also coed today; in 1935, it was a women's college.) Over two thirds of the parents of Bennington students were affiliated with the Republican party. The Bennington College community was liberal during the 1930s, but this was not why most of the women selected the college.

Newcomb's main finding was that with each year at Bennington, students moved further away from their parents' attitudes and closer to the attitudes of the college community. For example, in the 1936 presidential campaign, about 66 percent of parents favored the Republican candidate, Landon, over the Democratic candidate, Roosevelt. Landon was supported by 62 percent of the Bennington freshmen, 43 percent of the sophomores, and only 15 percent of the juniors and seniors.

Increasing liberalism reflected a deliberate choice between the two competing reference groups for most women. Two women discuss how they made this choice:

All my life, I've resented the protection of governesses and parents. At college, I got away from that, or rather, I guess I should say, I changed it to wanting the intellectual approval of teachers and more advanced students. Then I found that you can't be reactionary and be intellectually respectable.

Becoming radical meant thinking for myself and, figuratively, thumbing my nose at my family. It also meant intellectual identification with the faculty and students that I most wanted to be like. (Newcomb, 1943, pp. 134, 131)

Note that the second woman uses the term "identification" in the sense that we have been using it. Note, too, how the women describe a mixture of attitude change produced by social rewards and punishments and attitude change produced by identification—an attraction to an admired group whom they strive to emulate. But as mentioned earlier, reference groups also serve as "frame-of-reference" groups by providing their members with new perspectives on the world. The Bennington community, particularly the faculty, gave students a perspective on the Depression and the threat of world war that their wealthy and conservative home environments had not, and it would be a mistake to conclude that Bennington students adopted and maintained their liberalism simply as a means for gaining acceptance or for revolting against their parents. More "intellectually respectable" influences also played an important role:

Reference groups provide their members with a ready-made viewpoint on social issues.

It didn't take me long to see that liberal attitudes had prestige value. . . . I became liberal at first because of its prestige value; I remain so because the problems around which my liberalism centers are important. What I want now is to be effective in solving problems.

Prestige and recognition have always meant everything to me. . . . But I've sweat blood in trying to be honest with myself, and the result is that I really know what I want my attitudes to be, and I see what their consequences will be in my own life. (Newcomb, 1943, pp. 136–137)

This last woman's comment raises the most important question of all: does identification-induced attitude change sustain itself? Was the college-induced liberalism maintained when the students returned to the "real world"? A follow-up study of the Bennington women 25 years later found they had remained liberal. For example, in the 1960 presidential election, 60 percent of Bennington alumnae preferred the Democrat Kennedy over the Republican Nixon, compared to fewer than 30 percent of women from a similar socioeconomic class and geographical location and with a similar educational level. Moreover, about 60 percent of Bennington alumnae were politically active, most (66 percent) within the Democratic party (Newcomb and others, 1967).

But we never outgrow our need for identification with supporting reference groups. Thus, the political attitudes of Bennington women remained stable, in part, because they selected new reference groups—friends and husbands—after college who supported the attitudes they developed in college. As Newcomb noted, we often select our reference groups because they share our attitudes, and then our reference groups, in turn, help develop and sustain our attitudes. The relationship is circular.

The results of the Bennington study are hardly unique. A move toward political liberalism and away from parental conservatism in college is a common phenomenon. Surveys from 1961 to 1963 and again from 1969 to 1970 conducted by a politically conservative magazine showed this trend at a diverse array of colleges and universities (*National Review*, 1963, 1971). About 77 percent of the students in the 1970 survey said their political attitudes had moved toward the left since they entered college, whereas only 9 percent had moved toward the right. And although political radicalism on the college campuses quieted after the Vietnam War, surveys continue to show college students moving from parental attitudes toward more liberal positions. This is particularly true on social issues such as marijuana smoking, acceptance of homosexuality, and so forth (Yankelovich, 1974, 1981).

ENVIRONMENTAL PSYCHOLOGY

As we have seen, people influence one another in many ways. But the physical environment also influences us, and a branch of psychology called *environmental psychology* has been developed by those who study these influences. One of environmental psychology's main concerns has been the psychological effects of living in noisy and crowded urban environments; accordingly, we will look at the effects of both noise and crowding on our psychological functioning.

Effects of noise

In general, it is plausible to suppose that we should prefer peace and quiet to noise. And yet most of us have had the experience of having to adjust to sleeping in the mountains or the countryside because it was initially "too quiet," an experience that suggests that humans are capable of adapting to a wide range of noise levels. Research supports this view. For example, Glass and Singer (1972) exposed people to short bursts of very loud noise and then measured their ability to work problems and their physiological reactions to the noise. The noise was quite disruptive at first, but after about 4 minutes, the subjects were doing just as well on their tasks as control subjects who were not exposed to noise. Their physiological arousal also declined quickly to the same levels as those of the control subjects.

But there are limits to adaptation, and loud noise becomes more troublesome if the person is required to concentrate on more than one task. For example, high noise levels interfered with the performance of subjects who were required to monitor three dials at a time—a task not unlike that of an airplane pilot or an air-traffic controller (Broadbent, 1957). Similarly, noise did not affect a subject's ability to track a moving line with a steering wheel, but it did interfere with the subject's ability to repeat numbers while tracking (Finkelman and Glass, 1970).

Probably the most significant finding from research on noise is that its predictability is more important than how loud it is. We are much more able to "tune out" chronic background noise, even if it is quite loud, than to work under circumstances with unexpected intrusions of noise. In the Glass and Singer study in which subjects were exposed to bursts of noise as they worked on a task, some subjects heard loud bursts and others heard soft bursts. For some subjects, the bursts were spaced exactly 1 minute apart (predictable noise); others heard the same amount of noise overall, but the bursts occurred at random intervals (unpredictable noise). Subjects reported finding the predictable and unpredictable noise equally annoying, and all subjects performed at about the same level during the noise portion of the experiment. But the different noise conditions had quite different aftereffects when the subjects were required to proofread written material under conditions of no noise. As shown in Table 18-1, the unpredictable noise produced more errors in the later proofreading task than predictable noise; and soft, unpredictable noise actually produced slightly more errors on this task than the loud, predictable noise.

	UNPREDICTABLE NOISE	PREDICTABLE NOISE	MEAN
Loud noise	40.1	31.8	35.9
Soft noise	36.7	27.4	32.1
Mean	38.4	29.6	

Table 18-1
Proofreading Errors and Noise
The table presents the number of proof-reading errors made under conditions of no noise by four groups of subjects who previously had been exposed to either loud or soft, unpredictable or predictable noise. Predictability of noise was a greater determinant of number of errors made than intensity of noise. (After Glass and Singer, 1972)

Apparently, unpredictable noise produces more fatigue than predictable noise, but it takes a while for this fatigue to take its toll on performance.

Predictability is not the only variable that reduces or eliminates the negative effects of noise. Another is control. If the individual knows that she or he can control the noise, this seems to eliminate both its negative effects at the time and its aftereffects. This is true even if the individual never actually exercises his or her option to turn the noise off (Glass and Singer, 1972). Just the *knowledge* that one has control is sufficient. The variable of perceived personal control is of major importance in several areas of psychology. In Chapter 14, we noted its influence on the way people react to stress, and we will encounter it again when we discuss crowding.

The studies discussed so far exposed people to noise for only short periods, and only transient effects were studied. But the major worry about noisy environments is that living day after day with chronic noise may produce serious, lasting effects. One study, suggesting that this worry is a realistic one, compared elementary-school pupils who attended schools near Los Angeles' busiest airport with students who attended schools in quiet neighborhoods (Cohen and others, 1980). It was found that children from the noisy schools had higher blood pressure and were more easily distracted than those who attended the quiet schools. Moreover, there was no evidence of adaptability to the noise. In fact, the longer the children had attended the noisy schools, the more distractible they became. The effects also seem to be long-lasting. A follow-up study showed that children who were moved to less noisy classrooms still showed greater distractibility one year later than students who had always been in the quiet schools (Cohen and others, 1981.) It should be noted that the two groups of children had been carefully matched by the investigators so that they were comparable in age, ethnicity, race, and social class.

Effects of crowding

Crowding, like noise, is associated with urban living. Among animals, crowded conditions are known to lead to increased aggression, abnormal behavior, physical disorders, infant neglect, and high mortality (Freedman, 1975). Autopsies of animals that have died after living in crowded conditions reveal signs of prolonged stress (Calhoun, 1962). Early correlational studies seemed to support the possibility that crowded conditions might have similar effects on humans; they showed that *population density* (the number of persons per unit of space) was positively related to mental illness (see Hollingshead and Redlich, 1958) and to crime rates (see Lottier, 1938).

But correlation does not establish a cause-and-effect relationship. It seems quite possible that the real causes might be the poverty and lower socioeconomic level often associated with high-density living. Accordingly, more recent studies have attempted to control for these factors (Schmitt, 1966; Win-

Crowding is a fact of life in most large cities.

sborough, 1965; Galle, Gove, and McPherson, 1972; Freedman, Heshka, and Levy, 1975). Although these studies—conducted in Honolulu, Chicago, and New York City—have found an overall positive relationship between density and juvenile delinquency, mental illness, and other pathologies, the correlations tend to disappear when socioeconomic variables are controlled. This finding suggests that density per se is not the cause of the pathologies.

Another problem in drawing firm conclusions about the effects of crowding stems from differences in definition. The term "crowding" usually refers to the individual's subjective feeling that too many people are packed too closely. Most studies of crowding, however, actually measure density—the number of people in a given unit of space. Whether a person feels crowded is only partly a function of density. Other determinants include the person's accustomed level of density, the temperature, the noise level, the person's cultural background, whether the other people are strangers or acquaintances, and many other variables. Moreover, some investigators have found it useful to distinguish two kinds of density: outside density (the number of persons per square mile) and inside density (the number of persons with a residence) (Zlutnick and Altman, 1972). In most research, outside density by itself seems to have little effect. Compared with smaller communities, large cities with a high outside density do not have higher incidences of mental illness (Srole, 1972) or suicide (Gibbs, 1971). People who live in large cities report being just as happy as people who live in suburbs, small towns, and rural areas (Shaver and Freedman, 1976). The city of Tokyo, Japan, is often cited in this connection. Tokyo has more than 20,000 people per square mile—more than 10 times the average density of cities in North America; yet crime rates are remarkably low.

Inside density, on the other hand, has been found in some studies to be associated with indices of social pathology. A study in Chicago that controlled for socioeconomic status and ethnicity found that the number of persons per room within dwellings was significantly correlated with higher death rates and higher rates of juvenile delinquency (Galle, Gove, and McPherson, 1972). A study of census data from 65 nations found a significant relationship between inside density and homicide rates after controlling for socioeconomic status (Booth and Welch, 1973). And, finally, a study of inside density and crime rates in the United States used data from 656 cities with populations over 25,000 and controlled for race, education, and income. It was found that within the larger cities a higher number of persons per room was associated with slightly higher rates of murder, assault, and rape. The investigators suggest that crowded conditions within the home may lead to greater frustration as one's daily routines are constantly thwarted and that this frustration leads to greater aggression (Booth and Welch, 1974). It may be, however, that the people who live in crowded conditions are not the same ones who commit the crimes; the crowding-frustration-aggression theory remains to be tested adequately (Wrightsman, 1977).

But even the conclusion that inside density produces social pathology needs to be qualified. It may be true only for certain cultures, despite the positive evidence from the cross-national study cited previously (Booth and Welch, 1973). Such studies look only at aggregate data (census data across nations); data are not collected from separate homes within each culture. One ambitious investigator did visit individual homes in the city of Hong Kong— one of the most crowded communities in the world. He measured the exact size of each family's living space and took several measures of stress and strain among the family members. He found no strong relationships between density and pathology (Mitchell, 1971). Clearly, cultural factors play a role in deter-mining when and whether density becomes a negative environmental factor.

LABORATORY STUDIES OF CROWDING   All the studies discussed above are correlational; they look at the world to see whether density and pathology tend to increase and decrease together after taking socioeconomic class, race, and other variables into account. Psychologists have also attempted to find cause-and-effect relationships between crowding and distress by conducting labora-tory experiments.

The usual procedure is to place randomly selected subjects into a crowded or an uncrowded situation and then take a number of measures of task per-formance, physiological arousal, liking for the situation, decision making, aggression, friendliness, and so forth. The results from these studies are com-plicated and mixed (see Freedman, 1975, for a review). For example, sex differ-ences show up in most of the studies. Generally, all-female groups tend to react positively to others when room density is high, whereas all-male groups react negatively (see Ross and others, 1973). But at least one study shows the reverse (Loo, 1972). The effects of crowding are complex and depend on the particular characteristics of the subjects and the exact circumstances under which the experiment is conducted.

COMBINATION LABORATORY AND FIELD STUDIES   Like laboratory studies of noise, laboratory studies of crowding are not completely satisfactory because the subjects are placed in crowded circumstances for only a brief time. But as we have seen, the long-term effects of real-life crowding are hard to establish through data gathered from surveys, census tracts, and crime statistics. This has led some investigators to try a combination of the two approaches, study-ing individuals in the laboratory who actually live in different kinds of situ-ations. (An example of this approach is the study in which children from noisy and quiet school environments were tested for distractibility.) In contrast to the laboratory studies, in which the high-density situation is brief, the combination studies tend to show that the physical setting of the day-to-day living situation does, in fact, influence one's social behavior.

College dormitories have provided the testing laboratory in several such studies because on many campuses one can find both long-corridor living arrangements shared by large numbers of residents and smaller suites of rooms with shared common rooms for small groups of people. Surveys have shown that residents of long-corridor dormitories are less satisfied with their living arrangements than residents of short-corridor dormitories. They report that they feel more crowded and complain that the quality of social interaction seems to become more negative over time.

When observed in laboratory situations, long-corridor residents report more pessimism about being able to make changes in their living situations than short-corridor residents. They also appear to withdraw from the situation more, not asking as many questions about an experiment, sitting farther from a fellow student in the waiting room, and spending less time looking at and talking to him or her. When asked to play a game as part of an experiment, long-corridor residents were less cooperative than short-corridor residents, either acting more competitive or withdrawing from the game if given the option (Baum and Valins, 1977).

Findings like these support the hypothesis that the major frustration of living in either long-corridor dormitories or high-density situations is the inabil-ity to regulate or control the number, timing, and nature of one's social encounters. This hypothesis is patterned after the theory of learned helplessness (Chapters 14 and 15), which states that lack of control over one's environment leads to a feeling of helplessness, which, in turn, leads one to withdraw and give up trying even when placed in other situations (Seligman, 1975). It has been found that rats reared under conditions of high density not only show poorer performance on complex tasks but sometimes even fail to make any response at all when under stress (Goeckner, Greenough, and Mead, 1973).

In an attempt to test the learned helplessness hypothesis more directly, junior high-school students were given an unsolvable problem, followed by a solvable one. Students from high-density homes did worse on the solvable problem than did students from lower-density homes (Rodin, 1976). After failing to solve the first problem, these students apparently lapsed into a feeling of greater helplessness.

The negative effects of living in high-density environments may flow from a feeling of helplessness, a feeling that one lacks control over one's social interactions and cannot regulate the intrusions of other people into one's private space. This could explain why people in cultures with highly developed norms of etiquette—for example, in Hong Kong and in Tokyo—manage to live so gracefully with both high outside and high inside density (Schmitt, 1963; Mitchell, 1971). In these societies, high density may not lead to a feeling of lack of control over the social environment.

These conclusions parallel the findings on the effects of noise, discussed earlier. In both cases, it is not the physical variables themselves that are crucial; high noise levels and high population densities do not necessarily have negative effects. More relevant is the real or perceived lack of personal control. It is the unpredictable noise and the uncontrollable social intrusions that produce social pathology. And, in the cross-cultural data on crowding, we see once again the powerful and pervasive effects of social norms. Even the influences of the physical environment turn out to be social influences.

Summary

1 Both humans and infrahumans perform responses more quickly when in the presence of other members of their species. This effect, called *social facilitation*, occurs whether the others are performing the same task (coactors) or are simply watching (an audience). The presence of others appears to raise the organism's drive level; for humans, cognitive factors such as a concern with competition or evaluation also play a role.

2 The uninhibited aggressive behavior sometimes shown by mobs and crowds may be the result of a state of *deindividuation*, in which individuals experience a feeling that they have lost their personal identities and merged into the group. Anonymity and close group unity seem to reduce self-awareness and contribute to deindividuation. Some of the consequences of deindividuation are weakened restraints against impulsive behavior, increased sensitivity to immediate cues and current emotional states, and a lessened concern about the evaluation by others.

3 Bystanders to emergencies are more likely to fail to intervene if in a group than when alone. By attempting to appear calm, group members may define the situation as a nonemergency for each other (*pluralistic ignorance*). The presence of other people also *diffuses responsibility*, so that no one person feels the necessity to act. Bystanders are more likely to intervene when these factors are

minimized, particularly if at least one person displays helping behavior.

4   *Social norms* are consensual agreements about the appropriate ways to behave in particular situations. People usually conform to social norms with little awareness of external pressure to do so and often without awareness of the norm's existence. Laboratory studies, using an ambiguous perceptual task, have shown that group judgments, or norms, can have a strong and long-lasting effect on the individual's judgment.

5   Asch studied conformity to social pressure by using a simple perceptual task with an obvious correct answer. He found that incorrect responses by the group placed strong pressure on the individual to agree with the group's decision. Pressures to conform appear to arise from the message that dissenting would communicate to the group—namely, that they are incompetent or that the individual is out of touch with reality. Much less conformity is observed if the group is not unanimous.

6   A dramatic and controversial set of studies by Milgram demonstrated that people would obey an experimenter's order to deliver strong electric shocks to an innocent victim. Factors conspiring to produce the high obedience rates include the escalating sequence of demands by the experimenter, the implied contract to continue the experiment until completed, features of the setting that distance the person from the consequences of his or her acts (buffers), surveillance by the experimenter, and the legitimizing role of science, which leads people to abandon their autonomy to the experimenter.

7   Most people vastly underestimate compliance and obedience rates in such experiments and are surprised by the results, illustrating that we tend to underestimate the degree to which external forces influence behavior.

8   Studies of *persuasion* find that the higher a person's evaluation of a communicator, the more likely he or she is to be persuaded by the communication. The two major elements in the evaluation are the communicator's *credibility* and *attractiveness* to the target individual.

9   A *reference group* regulates the attitudes and behavior of individuals by administering social rewards and punishments and by providing them with ready-made interpretations of events and social issues. An individual may *identify with* reference groups without necessarily belonging to them.

10 Most of us identify with more than one reference group, which can lead to conflicting pressures. College students frequently move from the views of their family reference group toward those of the college reference group, which tends to be more liberal.

11 Two of *environmental psychology's* main concerns are the effects of noise and crowding on human behavior. Research on noise shows that loudness is less important than *predictability*. Unpredictable noise is much more disruptive than predictable noise, although chronic noise in the environment has been found to affect children's blood pressure and distractibility. Knowing that one can *control* noise diminishes its negative effects on performance.

12 Crowding refers to the subjective feeling that too many people are packed too closely together. Crowding is only partly a function of *density*, which refers to the number of people in a given area. Outside density (the number of persons per square mile) appears to have few negative effects by itself. Inside density (the number of persons within a residence) has been found to be associated with social pathology in some survey studies, but these effects do not appear in all cultures.

13 Laboratory studies that create crowded conditions fail to show consistent effects. Studies of individuals who live in high- and low-density situations,

however, do reveal negative effects of high-density living. The important variables again appear to be *predictability* and *control*. High-density living seems likeliest to cause problems when it leads to feelings of helplessness in controlling the number and quality of social interactions.

Further Reading

Many of the topics in this chapter are covered in paperback books written for a general audience, often by the original investigators. LeBon's classic book *The Crowd* (1895) is available in several editions. Latané and Darley, *The unresponsive bystander: Why doesn't he help?* (1970) is a report by two of the original researchers in that area. Milgram, *Obedience to Authority* (1974) is well worth reading, especially before forming an opinion about this controversial series of studies.

The Yale studies of persuasion are summarized by three of the original investigators in Hovland, Janis, and Kelley, *Communication and persuasion* (1953). The Bennington study and its follow-up of both the original women and Bennington College itself are reported in Newcomb, *Personality and social change* (1943); and in Newcomb and others, *Persistence and change: Bennington College and its students after twenty-five years* (1967).

Environmental psychology is described in the textbook by Bell, Fisher, and Loomis, *Environmental psychology* (1978). Noise and crowding, respectively, are considered in detail by Glass and Singer, *Urban stress* (1972); and by Freedman, *Crowding and behavior* (1975).

Freedman, Sears, and Carlsmith, *Social psychology* (4th ed., 1981); and Gergen and Gergen, *Social psychology* (1981) are general social psychology textbooks that cover the topics discussed in this chapter.

APPENDICES

I
BRIEF HISTORY OF PSYCHOLOGY

Although psychology is a young science, people throughout history have been concerned with psychological issues. Books on the history of psychology discuss the views of early Greek philosophers, especially those of Plato and Aristotle. After the Greeks, Saint Augustine (A.D. 354–430) is considered the next great precursor of modern psychology because of his interest in introspection and his curiosity about psychological phenomena, including the behavior of young infants and of crowds at chariot races. Descartes (1596–1650) left his mark on psychology by theorizing that animals are machines that can be studied much as other machines are studied. He also introduced the concept of reflex action, which has occupied a significant place in psychology. Many prominent philosophers of the seventeenth and eighteenth centuries—Leibnitz, Hobbes, Locke, Kant, and Hume, to name five—grappled with psychological questions.

ROOTS OF CONTEMPORARY PSYCHOLOGY

Two early approaches

In the nineteenth century, two theories of the mind competed for support. One, known as *faculty psychology,* was a doctrine of inherited mental powers. According to this theory, the mind had a few distinct and independent "faculties" or mental agencies—such as thinking, feeling, and willing—that accounted for its activities. These faculties were further broken into subfaculties: we remembered through the subfaculty of memory, imagined through the subfaculty of imagination, and so on. Faculty psychology encouraged early nineteenth-century *phrenologists,* such as Gall, to try to localize special faculties in different parts of the brain.

The *association psychologists* held an opposing view. They denied inborn faculties of the mind; instead, they limited the mind's content to ideas that entered by way of the senses and then became associated through such principles as similarity, contrast, and contiguity. They explained all mental activity through the *association of ideas*—a concept principally developed by British philosphers.

Both faculty psychology and association psychology have present-day counterparts. The search for mental abilities as factors in psychological tests is related to faculty psychology. Current research on memory and learning is related to earlier association theory. Faculty psychology took note of the inherited aspects of behavior, whereas associationism emphasized the environment as the determiner of behavior. The environment versus heredity issue runs throughout the history of psychology.

Wundt's laboratory

Wilhelm Wundt is given credit for founding psychology as an academic discipline. The founding date is usually cited as 1879, the year that Wundt established the first formal psychological laboratory at the University of Leipzig in Germany. Wundt's research was primarily concerned with the senses, especially vision; but he and his co-workers also studied attention, emotion, and associative processes in memory.

Wilhelm Wundt

Wundt's psychology relied on *introspection* as a method of studying mental processes. The introspective method was inherited from philosophy, but Wundt added a new dimension to the concept. Pure self-observation was not sufficient; it had to be supplemented by experiments. His experiments systematically varied some physical dimension of a stimulus, and the introspective method was used to determine how these physical changes modified consciousness.

Wundt's approach to research can be illustrated by one of his experiments on *reaction time*. In this experiment, the subject was required to press a key as quickly as possible after the onset of a light, and the subject's reaction time was carefully measured. Wundt found that when a subject paid careful attention to detecting the onset of the light, it took longer to respond than when the subject's attention was directed to making a quick finger movement when pressing the key. The subject reacted very quickly in both cases, but there was a difference in reaction time of about .1 second. To explain this strange finding, Wundt distinguished between *perception* and *apperception*. When attention was focused on the finger movement, simple perception occurred and the light triggered the response promptly. But when attention was focused on the stimulus, an additional activity of apperception occurred, which involved a "richer" perception of the light. Wundt decided that this apperception required about .1 second. His interpretation is no longer accepted, for we now know that the processes intervening between stimulus and response are organized in more complex ways; but such studies helped to launch psychology as an experimental science.

Until his death in 1920, Wundt's personal influence on psychology was singularly important. Many pioneers in American psychology were trained in Wundt's laboratory. The first formal psychology laboratory in the United States was established in 1883 at Johns Hopkins University by G. Stanley Hall (who had studied with Wundt), although William James had set up a small demonstration laboratory at Harvard by 1875. The first person to be called "professor of psychology" in the United States was J. McKeen Cattell, another Wundt student, who acquired that title at the University of Pennsylvania in 1888. Before the end of the 1890s, Wundt's students were to be found in a large number of American universities.

Other roots of contemporary psychology

Although the impetus for establishing psychological laboratories came largely from Germany, there were other influences. In England, Sir Francis Galton was a pioneer in the study of individual differences and also exerted an important influence on the development of intelligence tests. Galton invented the statistical technique of correlation and developed the index that later became known as the *coefficient of correlation.*

The influence of the theory of evolution through natural selection, propounded by Charles Darwin, also came from England. Darwin's theory established the continuity between animal and human being and thus led to comparative studies in psychology.

Another area of influence on psychology came from medicine, especially from the treatment of the mentally ill. Hypnotism, for example, has a long history as a form of therapy, dating from the work of Anton Mesmer in the late 1700s. Another Viennese physician, Sigmund Freud, founded psychoanalysis early in the present century.

Sir Francis Galton

SCHOOLS OF PSYCHOLOGY

Structuralism and functionalism

When scientific psychology emerged in the latter part of the nineteenth century, enormous advancements in chemistry and physics were being made in analyzing complex compounds (molecules) into their elements (atoms). These successes encouraged psychologists to look for the mental elements of which more complex experiences were composed. If the chemist made headway by analyzing water into hydrogen and oxygen, perhaps the psychologist could make progress by considering the taste of lemonade (perception) as a molecule of conscious experience to be analyzed into elements (sensations)—such as sweet, bitter, cold, and whatever—that could be identified by introspection. This was the approach taken by Wundt and his students; its major proponent in the United States was E.B. Titchener, a Wundt-trained psychologist at Cornell University. Since the goal was to specify mental structures, Titchener introduced the term *structuralism* to describe this brand of psychology.

But there was vigorous opposition to the purely analytical character of structuralism. William James—a distinguished Harvard University psychologist—was impatient with the restrictions on psychology as it was developing under the structuralists. James felt that less emphasis should be placed on analyzing the elements of consciousness and more emphasis should be placed on understanding its fluid, streaming, personal character. His principal interest was in studying how the mind worked so that an organism could adapt to its environment. Because James asked how consciousness functions (particularly in the adaptive process), his approach to psychology was named *functionalism.* James' writing on *habits* as a mode of adaptation helped set the stage for a psychology that included the learning process as a central topic of study.

Interest in adaptation was influenced by Darwin's theory of natural selec-

William James

Important Dates in the History
of Psychology

B.C.	400	Hippocrates relates personality characteristics to body types and proposes a physiological (as opposed to demonological) theory of mental illness.
B.C.	350	Aristotle stresses the objective observation of man's behavior and proposes three principles to account for the association of ideas.
A.D.	400	Saint Augustine, influenced by Platonic ideas, makes careful introspections in his *Confessions*.
	1650	René Descartes characterizes the mind–body relationship as one of interaction.
	1651	Thomas Hobbes foreshadows associationism by declaring that all ideas come from sensory experience.
	1690	John Locke carries Hobbes' notion a step further by declaring that the mind at birth is a blank slate (*tabula rasa*).
	1749	David Hartley formalizes a doctrine of associationism and suggests a neurological basis for memory.
	1781	Immanuel Kant's *Critique of Pure Reason* attacks associationism and the nativistic approach; it strongly influences later philosophers and psychologists.
	1809	Franz Gall and Johann Spurzheim give prominence through phrenology to the study of mental faculties and brain function.
	1821	Pierre Flourens performs the first significant experiments in localization of brain functions.
	1822	Friedrich Bessel measures individual differences in reaction time for astronomical observations.
	1838	Johannes Müller formulates the doctrine of specific nerve energies.
	1846	Ernst Weber derives the first quantitative law in psychology.
	1850	Hermann von Helmholtz measures the rates of conduction of nerve impulses.
	1859	Charles Darwin publishes *The Origin of Species*, propounding the theory of evolution through natural selection.
	1860	Gustav Fechner publishes *Elements of Psychophysics*, in which he presents various methods for measuring the relationship between physical stimuli and sensations.
	1869	Sir Francis Galton studies individual differences and applies Darwin's concept of selective adaptation to the evolution of races.
	1879	Wilhelm Wundt opens the first formal psychological laboratory at the University of Leipzig.
	1883	G. Stanley Hall establishes the first psychological laboratory in America at Johns Hopkins University.

1885 Hermann Ebbinghaus publishes the first experimental studies of memory.

1890 William James' *Principles of Psychology* is published in the United States.

1892 Edward Titchener at Cornell University establishes "structuralism" as a major influence in American psychology.

1898 Edward Thorndike performs some of the first controlled experiments on animal learning.

1900 Sigmund Freud publishes *The Interpretation of Dreams,* which presents many of his ideas on psychoanalysis.

1905 In France, Alfred Binet and Theodore Simon devise the first intelligence test.

1906 In Russia, Ivan Pavlov publishes the results of his studies on classical conditioning.

1908 William McDougall's publication of *An Introduction to Social Psychology* marks the formal inauguration of the field of social psychology.

1912 Max Wertheimer publishes the first formulation of Gestalt psychology.

1913 John Watson exerts a major impact on the course of psychology with his behaviorist manifesto.

1917 Wolfgang Köhler publishes the results of his studies on problem solving in primates.

1922 Edward Tolman presents his initial ideas on purposive behaviorism.

1929 Karl Lashley publishes *Brain Mechanisms and Intelligence.*

1935 Louis Thurstone develops factor analysis.

1938 B.F. Skinner publishes *The Behavior of Organisms,* which summarizes early research on operant conditioning.

1949 Donald Hebb, in *Organization of Behavior,* presents a theory that bridges the gap between neurophysiology and psychology.

1950 William Estes lays the foundation for a mathematical approach to theories of learning.

1954 The Swiss psychologist Jean Piaget publishes *The Construction of Reality in the Child,* a book that focuses attention on cognitive development.

1957 Noam Chomsky publishes *Syntactic Structures,* a book that presents a cognitive approach to language behavior.

1958 Herbert Simon and colleagues publish *Elements of a Theory of Human Problem Solving,* which reformulates classical psychological problems in terms of computer analogies.

Events since 1960 are not listed because not enough time has elapsed to judge their long-term impact on the field.

tion. Consciousness evolved, so the argument ran, only because it served some purpose in guiding the activities of the individual. With this emphasis on the functional role of consciousness came a recognition that the introspective method of structuralism was too restrictive. To find out how the organism adapts to its environment, the functionalists argued that data derived from introspection had to be supplemented by observations of actual behavior, including the study of animal behavior and the development of behavior (developmental psychology). Thus, functionalism broadened the scope of psychology to include behavior as a dependent variable. But along with the structuralists, functionalists still regarded psychology as the science of conscious experience and the principal investigative method as introspection.

Structuralism and functionalism played important roles in the early development of psychology. Because each viewpoint provided a systematic approach to the field, the two were considered competing *schools of psychology*. As psychology developed, other schools evolved and vied for leadership. By 1920, structuralism and functionalism were being displaced by three newer schools: behaviorism, Gestalt psychology, and psychoanalysis.

Behaviorism

Of the three, behaviorism had the greatest influence on scientific psychology. Its founder, John B. Watson, reacted against the tradition of his time—that conscious experience was the province of psychology—and boldly proclaimed a psychology *without* introspection. Watson made no assertions about consciousness when he studied the behavior of animals and infants. He decided not only that the results of animal psychology and child psychology could stand on their own as a science but also that they set a pattern that adult psychology might well follow.

In order to make psychology a science, Watson said, psychological data must be open to public inspection like the data of any other science. Behavior is public; consciousness is private. Science should deal with public facts. Because psychologists were growing impatient with introspection, the new behaviorism caught on rapidly, particularly in the 1920s; for a time, most of the younger psychologists in the United States called themselves "behaviorists." In Russia, the work of Ivan Pavlov on the conditioned response was regarded as an important area of research by the behaviorists. The conditioned response was being investigated in the United States in a limited way before the advent of behaviorism, but Watson was responsible for its subsequent widespread influence on psychology.

Behaviorists found it congenial to discuss psychological phenomena as beginning with a stimulus and ending with a response—giving rise to the term *stimulus-response (S-R) psychology*. S-R psychology, as it evolved from behaviorism, went beyond the earlier behaviorists in its willingness to infer hypothetical processes between the stimulus input and the response output, processes that were called *intervening variables*.

If broad definitions are used, so that "stimulus" refers to a whole class of antecedent conditions and "response" refers to a whole class of outcomes (actual behavior and products of behavior), S-R psychology becomes merely a psychology of independent and dependent variables. Viewed in this way, S-R psychology is not a particular theory but a *language* that can be used to make psychological information explicit and communicable. As such, the S-R outlook is widely prevalent in psychology today.

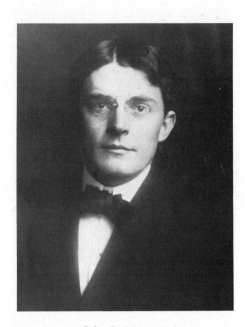

John B. Watson

Gestalt psychology

At about the same time that Watson announced behaviorism in America, Gestalt psychology was appearing in Germany. The word *Gestalt* translates from the German as "form" or "configuration," and the psychology announced by Max Wertheimer in 1912 was a psychology concerned with the organization of mental processes. The position came to be identified most closely with Wertheimer and his colleagues Kurt Koffka and Wolfgang Köhler, all of whom migrated to the United States.

The earliest Gestalt experiments dealt with perceived motion, particularly the *phi phenomenon*. When two separated lights are flashed in succession (provided the timing and spatial locations are proper), the subject sees a single light moving from the position of the first light to that of the second. The phenomenon of apparent motion was familiar, but the Gestalt psychologists sensed the theoretical importance of the patterning of stimuli in producing the effect. Our experiences depend on the *patterns* formed by stimuli and on the *organization* of experience, they decided. What we see is relative to background, to other aspects of the whole. The whole is different from the sum of its parts; the whole consists of parts in relationship.

Although the Gestalt psychologists did not subscribe to the introspective psychology of their day any more than Watson did, they were vigorous opponents of behaviorism. They did not want to give up a kind of free introspection that goes by the name of *phenomenology*. They wanted to be able to ask a person what something looked like, what it meant. They were interested in observed movement, in judged sizes, in the appearance of colors under changes in illumination.

The importance of perception in all psychological events has led those influenced by Gestalt psychology to a number of perception-centered interpretations of learning, memory, and problem solving. These interpretations, spoken of as forms of cognitive theory, were instrumental in laying the groundwork for current developments in cognitive psychology.

Wolfgang Köhler

Psychoanalysis

Sigmund Freud introduced psychoanalytic psychology to the United States in a series of lectures given at Clark University in 1909 on the invitation of psychologist G. Stanley Hall. Thus, the first scholarly recognition of Freud's work in the United States came from psychologists. Freud's influence became so pervasive that those who know nothing else about psychology have at least a nodding acquaintance with psychoanalysis.

If one of Freud's theories is to be singled out for consideration along with behaviorism and Gestalt psychology, it is his interpretation of the *unconscious*. Basic to Freud's theory of the unconscious is the conception that the unacceptable (forbidden, punished) wishes of childhood are driven out of awareness and become part of the unconscious, where (while out of awareness) they remain influential. The unconscious presses to find expression, which it does in numerous ways, including dreams, slips of speech, and unconscious mannerisms. The method of psychoanalysis—free association under the guidance of the analyst—is itself a way of helping unconscious wishes find verbal expression. In classical Freudian theory, these unconscious wishes were almost exclusively sexual. This emphasis on childhood sexuality was one of the barriers to the acceptance of Freud's theories when they were first announced.

Sigmund Freud

RECENT DEVELOPMENTS

Despite the important contribution of Gestalt psychology and psychoanalysis, psychology was dominated by behaviorism until World War II, particularly in the United States. With the end of the war, interest in psychology increased and many people were attracted to careers in the field. Sophisticated instruments and electronic equipment became available, and a wider range of problems could be examined. This expanded program of research made it evident that earlier theoretical approaches were too restrictive.

This viewpoint was strengthened by the development of high-speed computers in the 1950s. Computers, properly programmed, were able to perform tasks—like playing chess and proving mathematical theorems—that previously could only be done by human beings. It became apparent that the computer offered psychologists a powerful tool with which to theorize about psychological processes. A series of brilliant papers, published in the late 1950s by Herbert Simon (later awarded the Nobel prize) and his colleagues, indicated how psychological phenomena could be *simulated* using the computer. Many old psychological issues were recast in terms of *information processing systems.* The human being could now be viewed as a processor of information. The senses provide an input channel for information; mental operations are applied to the input; the transformed input creates a mental structure that is stored in memory; that structure interacts with others in memory to generate a response. The power of the computer permitted psychologists to theorize about complex mental processes and then to investigate the implications of the theory by simulating it on a computer. If the response (output) stage of the simulation agreed with the observed behavior, the psychologist could have some confidence in the theory.

The information processing approach provided a richer and more dynamic approach to psychology than S-R theory with its intervening variables. Similarly, the information processing approach permitted some of the speculations of Gestalt psychology and psychoanalysis to be formulated in a precise fashion as programs in a computer; in this way, earlier ideas about the nature of the mind could be made concrete and checked against actual data.

Another factor that led to a changing viewpoint in psychology in the 1950s was the development of modern linguistics. Prior to that time, linguists were primarily concerned with a description of a language; now they began to theorize about the mental structures required to comprehend and speak a language. Work in this area was pioneered by Noam Chomsky, whose book *Syntactic Structures*, published in 1957, provided the basis for an active collaboration betwen psychologists and linguists. A rapid development of the field of *psycholinguistics* followed, providing the first significant psychological analyses of language.

At the same time, important advances were occurring in neuropsychology. A number of discoveries about the brain and the nervous system established clear relationships between neurobiological events and mental processes. It became increasingly difficult to assert, as some of the early behaviorists had, that a science of psychology could be established without links to neurophysiology.

The development of information processing models, psycholinguistics, and neuropsychology has produced a psychology that is highly cognitive in orientation. There is no agreed definition of *cognitive psychology*, but its principal concern is the scientific analysis of mental processes and mental struc-

Herbert Simon

tures. Thus, within a period of 50 years, the focus of psychology has come full circle. After rejecting conscious experience as ill-suited to scientific investigation and turning to the study of behavior, psychologists are once again theorizing about the mind, but this time with new and more powerful tools. The gain from behaviorism has been an emphasis on the objectivity and reproducibility of findings—an emphasis that has found a place in cognitive psychology.

From a historical perspective, it is too early to judge the long-term significance of recent developments in psychology. What is evident, however, is that there is great excitement in the field today, and many psychologists believe that it is in a period of revolutionary change and progress. Understanding how the mind works is a worthy challenge that deserves the best intellectual effort we can put forth.

Further Reading

For a general survey of the history of psychology, see Watson, *The great psychologists: From Aristotle to Freud* (1978); Wertheimer, *A brief history of psychology* (1979); and Schultz, *A history of modern psychology* (3rd ed., 1981). See also Boring, *A history of experimental psychology* (rev. ed., 1949); and Herrnstein and Boring, *A sourcebook in the history of psychology* (1965).

II
STATISTICAL METHODS AND MEASUREMENT

Much of the work of psychologists, like work of other scientists, calls for making measurements—either in the laboratory or under field conditions. This work may involve measuring the eye movements of infants when first exposed to a novel stimulus, recording the galvanic skin response of people under stress, counting the number of trials required to condition a monkey with a prefrontal lobotomy, determining achievement test scores for students using computer-assisted learning, or counting the number of patients who show improvement following a particular type of psychotherapy. In all these examples, the *measurement operation* yields numbers; the psychologist's problem is to interpret them and arrive at some general conclusions. Basic to this task is *statistics*—the discipline that deals with collecting and handling numerical data and with making inferences from such data. The purpose of this appendix is to review certain statistical methods that play an important role in psychology.

The appendix is written on the assumption that the problems students have with statistics are essentially problems of clear thinking about data. An introductory acquaintance with statistics is *not* beyond the scope of anyone who understands enough algebra to use plus and minus signs and to substitute numbers for letters in equations.

Even an introductory acquaintance with statistics, however, requires practice in applying what has been learned. The treatment that follows states the essential relationships—first in words and then with simple numerical examples that require little computation.

DESCRIPTIVE STATISTICS

Statistics serves, first of all, to provide a shorthand description of large amounts of data. Suppose that we want to study the college entrance examination scores of 5,000 students recorded on cards in the registrar's office. These scores are the raw data. Thumbing through the cards will give us some impressions of the students' scores, but it will be impossible for us to keep all of them in mind. So we make some kind of summary of the data, possibly averaging all the scores or finding the highest and lowest scores. These statistical summaries make it easier to remember and to think about the data. Such summarizing statements are called *descriptive statistics*.

Frequency distributions

Items of raw data become comprehensible when they are grouped in a *frequency distribution*. To group data, we must first divide the scale along which they are measured into intervals and then count the number of items that fall into each interval. An interval in which scores are grouped is called a *class interval*. The decision of how many class intervals the data are to be grouped into is not fixed by any rules but is based on the judgment of the investigator.

Table 1 provides a sample of raw data representing college entrance examination scores for 15 students. The scores are listed in the order in which the students were tested (the first student tested had a score of 84; the second, 61; and so on). Table 2 shows these data arranged in a frequency distribution for which the class interval has been set at 10. One score falls in the interval from 50–59, three scores fall in the interval from 60–69, and so on. Note that most scores fall in the interval from 70–79 and that no scores fall below the 50–59 interval or above the 90–99 interval.

A frequency distribution is often easier to understand if it is presented graphically. The most widely used graph form is the *frequency histogram*; an example is shown in the top panel of Figure 1. Histograms are constructed by drawing bars, the bases of which are given by the class intervals and the heights of which are determined by the corresponding class frequencies. An alternative way of presenting frequency distributions in graph form is to use a *frequency polygon*, an example of which is shown in the bottom panel of Figure 1. Frequency polygons are constructed by plotting the class frequencies at the center of the class interval and connecting the points obtained by straight lines. To complete the picture, one extra class is added at each end of the distribution; since these classes have zero frequencies, both ends of the figure will touch the horizontal axis. The frequency polygon gives the same information as the frequency histrogram but by means of lines rather than bars.

In practice, we would obtain a much greater number of items than those plotted in Figure 1, but a minimum amount of data is shown in all of the illustrations in this appendix so that you can easily check the steps in tabulating and plotting.

Measures of central tendency

A *measure of central tendency* is simply some representative point on our scale—a central point with scores scattered on either side. Three such measures are commonly used: the *mean*, the *median*, and the *mode*.

The *mean* is the familiar arithmetic average obtained by adding the scores and dividing by the number of scores. The sum of the raw scores in Table 1 is 1125. If we divide this by 15 (the number of students' scores), the mean turns out to be 75.

84	75	91
61	75	67
72	87	79
75	79	83
77	51	69

Table 1
Raw Scores
College entrance examination scores for 15 students, listed in the order in which they were tested.

CLASS INTERVAL	NUMBER OF PERSONS IN CLASS
50–59	1
60–69	3
70–79	7
80–89	3
90–99	1

Table 2
Frequency Distribution
Scores from Table 1 accumulated with class intervals of 10

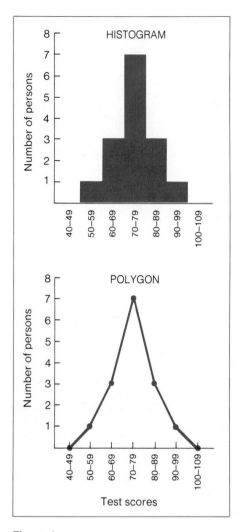

Figure I
Frequency Diagrams
The data from Table 2 are plotted here. A frequency histogram is on the top; a frequency polygon, on the bottom.

The *median* is the score of the middle item, which is obtained by arranging the scores in order and then counting into the middle from either end. When the 15 scores in Table 1 are placed in order from highest to lowest, the eighth score from either end turns out to be 75. If the number of cases is even, we simply average the two cases on either side of the middle. For instance, the median of 10 items is the arithmetic average of the fifth and sixth cases.

The *mode* is the most frequent score in a given distribution. In Table 1, the most frequent score is 75; hence, the mode of the distribution is 75.

In a *symmetrical distribution*, in which the scores are distributed evenly on either side of the middle (as in Figure 1), the mean, median, and mode all fall together. This is not true for distributions that are *skewed*, or unbalanced. Suppose we want to analyze the departure times of a morning train. The train usually leaves on time; occasionally it leaves late, but it never leaves early. For a train with a scheduled departure time of 8:00 A.M., one week's record might be:

M	8:00	Mean = 8:07
Tu	8:04	Median = 8:02
W	8:02	Mode = 8:00
Th	8:19	
F	8:22	
Sat	8:00	
Sun	8:00	

The distribution of departure times in this example is skewed because of the two late departures; they raise the mean departure time but do not have much effect on the median or the mode.

Skewness is important because unless it is understood, the differences between the median and the mean may sometimes be misleading (see Figure 2). If, for example, two political parties are arguing about the prosperity of the country, it is possible for the mean and median incomes to move in opposite directions. Suppose that a round of wage increases has been combined with a reduction in extremely high incomes. The median income might have gone up while the mean went down. The party wanting to show that incomes were getting higher would choose the median; the party wishing to show that incomes were getting lower would choose the mean.

The mean is the most widely used measure of central tendency, but there are times when the mode or the median is a more appropriate measure.

Measures of variation

Usually more information is needed about a distribution than can be obtained from a measure of central tendency. For example, we need a measure to tell us whether scores cluster closely around their average or whether they scatter widely. A measure of the spread of scores around the average is called a *measure of variation*.

Measures of variation are useful in at least two ways. First, they tell us how representative the average is. If the variation is small, we know that individual scores are close to it. If the variation is large, we cannot use the mean as a representative value with as much assurance. Suppose that clothing is being designed for a group of people without the benefit of precise measurements.

Knowing their average size would be helpful, but it also would be important to know the spread of sizes. The second measure provides a "yardstick" that we can use to measure the amount of variability among the sizes.

To illustrate, consider the data in Figure 3, which show frequency distributions of entrance examination scores for two classes of 30 students. Both classes have the same mean of 75 but they exhibit clearly different degrees of variation. The scores of all the students in Class I are clustered close to the mean, whereas the scores of the students in Class II are spread over a wide range. Some measure is required to specify more exactly how these two distributions differ. Two measures of variation frequently used by psychologists are the *range* and the *standard deviation*.

To simplify arithmetic computation, we will suppose that five students from each class seek entrance to college and that their entrance examination scores are as follows:

Student scores from Class I:
73, 74, 75, 76, 77 (mean = 75)

Student scores from Class II:
60, 65, 75, 85, 90 (mean = 75)

We will now compute the measures of variation for these two samples.

The *range* is the spread between the highest score and the lowest score. The range of scores for the five students from Class I is 4 (from 73 to 77); the range of scores from Class II is 30 (from 60 to 90).

The range is easy to compute, but the *standard deviation* is more frequently used because it has certain properties that make it the preferred measure. One such property is that it is an extremely sensitive measure of variation because it accounts for every score, not just extreme values as the range does. The standard deviation, denoted by the lower-case Greek letter *sigma* (σ), measures how far the scores making up a distribution depart from that distribution's mean. The deviation d of each score from the mean is computed and squared;

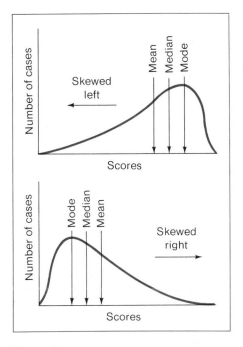

Figure 2
Skewed Distribution Curves
Note that skewed distributions are designated by the direction in which the tail falls. Also note that the mean, median, and mode are not identical for a skewed distribution; the median commonly falls between the mode and the mean.

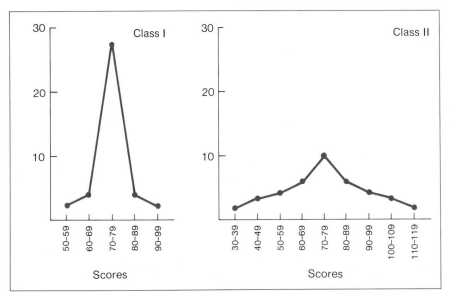

Figure 3
Distributions Differing in Variation
It is easy to see that the scores for Class I cluster closer to the mean than the scores for Class II, even though the means of the two classes are identical (75). For Class I, all the scores fall between 60 and 89, with most of the scores falling in the interval from 70 through 79. For Class II, the scores are distributed fairly uniformly over a wide range from 40 through 109. This difference in variability between the two distributions can be measured using the standard deviation, which is smaller for Class I than it is for Class II.

CLASS I SCORES (MEAN = 75)		
	d	d^2
77 − 75 =	2	4
76 − 75 =	1	1
75 − 75 =	0	0
74 − 75 =	−1	1
73 − 75 =	−2	4
		10

Sum of $d^2 = 10$
Mean of $d^2 = \frac{10}{5} = 2.0$
Standard deviation $(\sigma) = \sqrt{2.0} = 1.4$

CLASS II SCORES (MEAN = 75)		
	d	d^2
90 − 75 =	15	225
85 − 75 =	10	100
75 − 75 =	0	0
65 − 75 =	−10	100
60 − 75 =	−15	225
		650

Sum of $d^2 = 650$
Mean of $d^2 = \frac{650}{5} = 130$
Standard deviation $(\sigma) = \sqrt{130} = 11.4$

Table 3
Computation of the Standard Deviation

then the average of these squared values is obtained. The standard deviation is the square root of this avarage.[1] Written as a formula

$$\sigma = \sqrt{\frac{\text{sum of } d^2}{N}}$$

Specimen computation of the standard deviation. The scores for the samples from the two classes are arranged in Table 3 for computation of the standard deviation. The first step involves subtracting the mean from each score (the mean is 75 for both classes). This operation yields positive *d* values for scores above the mean and negative *d* values for scores below the mean. The minus signs disappear when the *d* values are squared in the next column. The squared deviations are added and then divided by *N*, the number of cases in the sample; in our example, $N = 5$. Taking the square root yields the standard deviation. In this example, the two standard deviations give us much the same information as the ranges.

STATISTICAL INFERENCE

Now that we have become familiar with statistics as ways of describing data, we are ready to turn to the processes of interpretation—to the making of inferences from data.

Populations and samples

First, it is necessary to distinguish between a *population* and a *sample* drawn from that population. The United States Census Bureau attempts to describe the whole population by obtaining descriptive material on age, marital status, and so on from everyone in the country. The word *population* is appropriate to the Census because it represents *all* the people living in the United States.

In statistics, the word "population" is not limited to people or animals or things. The population may be all of the temperatures registered on a thermometer during the last decade, all of the words in the English language, or all of any other specified supply of data. Often we do not have access to the total population, and so we try to represent it by a sample drawn in a *random* (unbiased) fashion. We may ask some questions of a random fraction of the people, as the United States Census Bureau has done as part of recent censuses; we may derive average temperatures by reading the thermometer at specified times, without taking a continuous record; we may estimate the words in the encyclopedia by counting the words on a random number of pages. These illustrations all involve the selection of a *sample* from a population. If any of these processes are repeated, we will obtain slightly different results due to the fact that a sample does not fully represent the whole population and therefore contains *errors of sampling*. This is where statistical inference enters.

A sample of data is collected from a population in order to make inferences

---

[1]For this introductory treatment, we will use *sigma* (σ) throughout. However, in scientific literature, the lower-case letter *s* is used to denote the standard deviation of a *sample* and σ is used to denote the standard deviation of the *population*. Moreover, in computing the standard deviation of a sample *s*, the sum of d^2 is divided by $N − 1$ rather than by N. For reasonably large samples, however, the actual value of the standard deviation is only slightly affected whether we divide by $N − 1$ or N. To simplify this presentation, we will not distinguish between the standard deviation of a sample and that of a population; instead, we will use the same formula to compute both. For a discussion of this point, see Phillips (1982).

about that population. A sample of census data may be examined to see whether the population is getting older or whether the trend of migration to the suburbs is continuing. Similarly, experimental results are studied to determine what effects experimental manipulations have had on behavior—whether the threshold for pitch is affected by loudness, whether child-rearing practices have detectable effects later in life. To make *statistical inferences*, we have to evaluate the relationships revealed by the sample data. These inferences are always made under some degree of uncertainty due to sampling errors. If the statistical tests indicate that the magnitude of the effect found in the sample is fairly large (relative to the estimate of the sampling error), then we can be confident that the effect observed in the sample holds for the population at large.

Thus, statistical inference deals with the problem of making an inference or judgment about some feature of a population based solely on information obtained from a sample of that population. As an introduction to statistical inference, we will consider the normal distribution and its use in interpreting standard deviations.

Normal distribution

When large amounts of data are collected, tabulated, and plotted on a graph, they often fall into a roughly bell-shaped symmetrical distribution known as the *normal distribution* and plotted as the *normal curve*. Most items fall near the mean (the high point of the bell), and the bell tapers off sharply at very high and very low scores. This form of curve is of special interest because it also arises when the outcome of a process is based on a large number of *chance* events all occurring independently. The demonstration device displayed in Figure 4 illustrates how a sequence of chance events gives rise to a normal distribution. The chance factor of whether a steel ball will fall to the left or right each time it encounters a point where the channel branches results in a symmetrical distribution; more balls fall straight down the middle, but occasionally one reaches one of the end compartments. This is a useful way of visualizing what is meant by a chance distribution closely approximating the normal curve.

The normal curve (Figure 5) is the mathematical representation of the idealized distribution approximated by the device shown in Figure 4. The normal curve represents the likelihood that items within a normally distributed population will depart from the mean by any stated amount. The percentages shown in Figure 5 represent the *percentage of the area* lying under the curve between the indicated scale values; the total area under the curve represents the whole population. Roughly two thirds of the cases (68 percent) will tend to fall between plus and minus one standard deviation from the mean ($\pm 1\sigma$); 95 percent of the cases within $\pm 2\sigma$; and virtually all cases (99.7 percent) within $\pm 3\sigma$. A more detailed listing of areas under portions of the normal curve is given in Table 4.

Using Table 4, let us trace how the 68-percent and 95-percent values in Figure 5 are derived. We find from column 3 of Table 4 that between -1σ and the mean lies .341 of the total area and between $+1\sigma$ and the mean also lies .341 of the area. Adding these values gives us .682, which is expressed in Figure 5 as 68 percent. Similarly, the area between -2σ and $+2\sigma$ is $2 \times .477 = .954$, which is expressed as 95 percent.

These percentages have several uses. One is in connection with the interpretation of standard scores, to which we will turn next. Another is in connection with tests of significance.

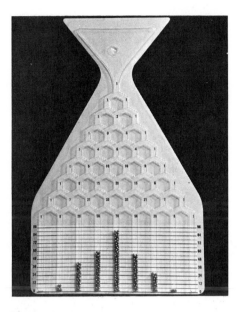

Figure 4
Device to Demonstrate
a Chance Distribution
To observe chance factors at work, the board is held upside down until all the steel balls fall into the reservoir. Then the board is turned over and held vertically until the balls fall into the nine columns at the bottom (as shown in the figure). The precise number of balls falling into each column will vary from one demonstration to the next. On the average, however, the heights of the columns of balls will approximate a normal distribution, with the greatest height in the center column and gradually decreasing heights in the outer columns. (Hexstat Probability Demonstrator, Harcourt Brace Jovanovich, Inc.)

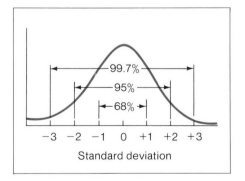

Figure 5
Normal Curve
The normal distribution curve can be constructed provided the mean and the standard deviation are known. The area under the curve below -3σ and above $+3\sigma$ is negligible.

STANDARD DEVIATION	(1) AREA TO THE LEFT OF THIS VALUE	(2) AREA TO THE RIGHT OF THIS VALUE	(3) AREA BETWEEN THIS VALUE AND MEAN
-3.0σ	.001	.999	.499
-2.5σ	.006	.994	.494
-2.0σ	.023	.977	.477
-1.5σ	.067	.933	.433
-1.0σ	.159	.841	.341
-0.5σ	.309	.691	.191
0.0σ	.500	.500	.000
$+0.5\sigma$	.691	.309	.191
$+1.0\sigma$	.841	.159	.341
$+1.5\sigma$	.933	.067	.433
$+2.0\sigma$	.977	.023	.477
$+2.5\sigma$	.994	.006	.494
$+3.0\sigma$	.999	.001	.499

Table 4
Area Under Normal Curve
as Proportion of Total Area

Scaling of data

In order to interpret a score, we often need to know whether it is high or low in relation to other scores. If a person taking a driver's test requires .500 seconds to brake after a danger signal, how can we tell whether the performance is fast or slow? Does a student who scores 60 on a physics examination pass the course? To answer questions of this kind, we have to derive some sort of *scale* against which the scores can be compared.

RANKED DATA   By placing scores in rank order from high to low, we derive one kind of scale. An individual score is interpreted on the basis of where it ranks among the group of scores. For example, the graduates of West Point know where they stand in their class—perhaps 35th or 125th among a class of 400.

STANDARD SCORES   The standard deviation is a convenient unit to use in scaling because we can interpret how far away 1σ or 2σ is from the mean (see Table 4). A score based on some multiple of the standard deviation is known as a *standard score*. Many scales used in psychological measurement are based on the principle of standard scores, with modifications often being made to eliminate negative signs and decimals. Some scales derived from standard scores are given in Table 5.

Specific computations of standard scores and transformation to arbitrary scales. Table 1 presented college entrance scores for 15 students. Without more information, we do not know whether these scores are representative of the population of all college applicants. On this examination, however, we will assume that the population mean is 75 and the standard deviation is 10.

Then what is the *standard score* for a student who had 90 on the examination? We must express how far this score lies above the mean in multiples of the standard deviation.

Standard score for grade of 90:

$$= \frac{90 - 75}{10}$$

$$= \frac{15}{10} = 1.5\sigma$$

As a second example, consider a student with a score of 53.

Standard score for grade of 53:

$$= \frac{53 - 75}{10}$$

$$= \frac{-22}{10}$$

$$= -2.2\sigma$$

In this case, the minus sign tells us that the student's score is below the mean by 2.2 standard deviations. Thus, the sign of the standard score (+ or −) indicates whether the score is above or below the mean, and its value indicates how far from the mean the score lies in standard deviations.

Suppose we wish to compare the first standard score computed above to a score on the scale used in the Navy General Classification Test, as shown in Table 5. This scale has a mean of 50 and a standard deviation of 10. Therefore, the standard score of 1.5σ becomes $50 + (10 \times 1.5) = 50 + 15 = 65$.

Using column 1 of Table 4, we find beside the value for a standard score of $+1.5\sigma$ the number .933. This means that 93 percent of the scores of a normal distribution will lie *below* a standard score of $+1.5\sigma$. Thus, a score of 65 on the Navy General Classification Test, or 650 on a Graduate Record Examination, or 8 on the Air Force Stanine (all equivalent standard scores) is above the scores achieved by 93 percent of the students on whom the test was calibrated. Scores representing any other multiple of the standard deviation can be similarly interpreted.

How representative is a mean?

How useful is the mean of a sample in estimating the population mean? If we measure the height of a random sample of 100 college students, how well does the sample mean predict the true population mean (that is, the mean height of *all* college students)? These questions raise the issue of making an *inference* about a population based on information from a sample.

The accuracy of such inferences depends on *errors of sampling*. Suppose we were to select two random samples from the same population, make the necessary measurements, and compute the mean for each sample. What differences between the first and the second mean could be expected to occur by chance?

Successive random samples drawn from the same population will have different means, forming a distribution of *sample means* around the *true mean* of the population. These sample means are themselves numbers for which the standard deviation can be computed. We call this standard deviation the *standard error of the mean*, or σ_M, and can estimate it on the basis of the following formula:

$$\sigma_M = \frac{\sigma}{\sqrt{N}}$$

where σ is the standard deviation of the sample and N is the number of cases from which each sample mean is computed.

Table 5
Some Representative Scales Derived from Standard Scores

	STANDARD SCORE	GRADUATE RECORD EXAMINATION	ARMY GENERAL CLASSIFICATION TEST	NAVY GENERAL CLASSIFICATION TEST	AIR FORCE STANINE*
	-3σ	200	40	20	—
	-2σ	300	60	30	1
	-1σ	400	80	40	3
	0σ	500	100	50	5
	$+1\sigma$	600	120	60	7
	$+2\sigma$	700	140	70	9
	$+3\sigma$	800	160	80	—
Mean	0	500	100	50	5
Standard deviation	1	100	20	10	2

*The word *stanine* was coined by the Air Force to refer to a scale with scores ranging from 1 to 9, known originally as "standard nine" (a type of standard score with a mean of 5 and a standard deviation of 2).

According to the formula, the size of the standard error of the mean decreases as the sample size increases; thus, a mean based on a large sample is more trustworthy (more likely to be close to the actual population mean) than a mean based on a smaller sample. Common sense would lead us to expect this. Computations of the standard error of the mean permit us to make clear assertions about the degree of uncertainty in our computed mean. The more cases in the sample, the more uncertainty has been reduced.

Specimen computation of the standard error of the mean. In order to estimate the standard error of the mean, we need to know the number of cases in the sample and the standard deviation of the sample. Suppose we take the mean and the standard deviation computed in Table 3 for Class II but assume that the sample is larger. The sample mean is 75, and the standard deviation is 11.4. Let us assume sample sizes of 25, 100, and 900 cases; the respective standard errors of the mean would be

$$N = 25: \quad \sigma_M = \frac{11.4}{\sqrt{25}} = 2.28$$

$$N = 100: \quad \sigma_M = \frac{11.4}{\sqrt{100}} = 1.14$$

$$N = 900: \quad \sigma_M = \frac{11.4}{\sqrt{900}} = .38$$

Now we may ask how much variation can be expected among means if we draw samples of 25, 100, and 900? We know from Table 4 that 68 percent of the cases in a normal distribution lie between -1σ and $+1\sigma$ from the mean. The sample mean of 75 is the best estimate of the population mean. We know the size of σ_M, so we may infer that the probability is .68 that the population mean lies between the following limits:

$$N = 25: \quad 75 \pm 2.88, \text{ or between } 72.72 \text{ and } 77.28$$

$$N = 100: \quad 75 \pm 1.14, \text{ or between } 73.86 \text{ and } 76.14$$

$$N = 900: \quad 75 \pm .38, \text{ or between } 74.62 \text{ and } 75.38$$

Thus, on the basis of sample data, it is possible to specify the probability that the mean for the entire population will lie in a certain interval. Note that the estimated interval decreases as the size of the sample increases. The larger the sample, the more precise the estimate of the true population mean.

Significance of a difference

In many psychological experiments, data are collected on two groups of subjects; one group is exposed to certain specified experimental conditions, and the other serves as a control group. The question is whether there is a difference in the mean performance of the two groups, and if such a difference is observed, whether it holds for the population from which these groups of subjects have been sampled. Basically, we are asking whether a difference between two sample means reflects a true difference or whether this difference is simply the result of sampling error.

As an example, we will compare the scores on a reading test for a sample of first-grade boys with the scores for a sample of first-grade girls. The boys score lower than the girls as far as mean performances are concerned, but there is a great deal of overlap; some boys do extremely well, and some girls do very poorly. Thus, we cannot accept the obtained difference in means without making a test of its *statistical significance*. Only then can we decide whether the observed differences in sample means reflect true differences in the population or are due to sampling error. If some of the brighter girls and some of the duller boys are sampled by sheer luck, the difference could be due to sampling error.

As another example, suppose that we have set up an experiment to compare the grip strength of right-handed and left-handed men. The top panel of Table 6 presents hypothetical data from such an experiment. A sample of five right-handed men averaged 8 kilograms stronger than a sample of five left-handed men. In general, what can we infer from these data about left-handed and right-handed men? Can we argue from the sample data that right-handed men are stronger than left-handed men? Obviously not, because the averages derived from most of the right-handed men would not differ from the averages derived from the left-handed men; the one markedly deviant score of 100 tells us we are dealing with an uncertain situation.

Now suppose that the results of the experiment were those shown in the bottom panel of Table 6. Again, we find the same mean difference of 8 kilograms, but we are now inclined to have greater confidence in the results because the left-handed men scored consistently lower than the right-handed men. Statistics provides a precise way of taking into account the reliability of the mean differences so that we do not have to depend solely on intuition to determine that one difference is more reliable than another.

These examples suggest that the significance of a difference will depend on both the size of the obtained difference and the variability of the means being compared. From the standard error of the means, we can compute the *standard error of the difference between two means* σ_{D_M}. We can then evaluate the obtained difference by using a *critical ratio*—the ratio of the obtained difference between the means D_M to the standard error of the difference between the means:

$$\text{Critical ratio} = \frac{D_M}{\sigma_{D_M}}$$

This ratio helps us to evaluate the significance of the difference between the two means. As a rule of thumb, a critical ratio should be 2.0 or larger for the difference between means to be accepted as significant. Throughout this book, statements that the difference between means is "statistically significant" indicate that the critical ratio is at least that large.

Why is a critical ratio of 2.0 selected as statistically significant? Simply because a value this large or larger can occur by chance only 5 out of 100 times. Where do we get the 5 out of 100? We can treat the critical ratio as a standard score because it is merely the difference between two means, expressed as a multiple of its standard error. Referring to column 2 in Table 4, we note that the likelihood is .023 that a standard deviation as high as or higher than $+2.0$ will occur by chance. Because the chance of deviating in the opposite direction is also .023, the total probability is .046. This means that 46 times out of 1,000, or about 5 times out of 100, a critical ratio as large as 2.0 would be found by chance if the population means were identical.

The rule of thumb that says a critical ratio should be at least 2.0 is just that—an arbitrary but convenient rule that defines the "5-percent level of significance." Following this rule, we will make less than 5 errors in 100 decisions by concluding on the basis of sample data that a difference in means exists when in fact there is none. The 5-percent level need not always be used;

STRENGTH OF GRIP IN KILOGRAMS, RIGHT-HANDED MEN	STRENGTH OF GRIP IN KILOGRAMS, LEFT-HANDED MEN
40	40
45	45
50	50
55	55
100	60
Sum 290	Sum 250
Mean 58	Mean 50

STRENGTH OF GRIP IN KILOGRAMS, RIGHT-HANDED MEN	STRENGTH OF GRIP IN KILOGRAMS, LEFT-HANDED MEN
56	48
57	49
58	50
59	51
60	52
Sum 290	Sum 250
Mean 58	Mean 50

Table 6
Significance of a Difference
Two examples that compare the difference between means are shown above. The difference between means is the same (8 kilograms) in both the top and the bottom panel. However, the data in the bottom panel indicate a more reliable difference between means than do the data in the top panel.

a higher or lower level of significance may be appropriate in certain experiments, depending on how willing we are to make an occasional error in inference.

Specimen computation of the critical ratio. The computation of the critical ratio calls for finding the *standard error of the difference between two means,* which is given by the following formula:

$$\sigma_{D_M} = \sqrt{(\sigma_{M_1})^2 + (\sigma_{M_2})^2}$$

In this formula, σ_{M_1} and σ_{M_2} are the standard errors of the two means being compared.

As an illustration, suppose we wanted to compare reading achievement tests scores for first-grade boys and girls in the United States. A random sample of boys and girls would be identified and given the test. We will assume that the mean score for the boys was 70 with a standard error of .40 and that the mean score for the girls was 72 with a standard error of .30. On the basis of these samples, we want to decide whether there is a real difference between the reading achievement of boys and girls in the population as a whole. The sample data suggest that girls do achieve better reading scores than boys, but can we infer that this would have been the case if we had tested all the girls and all the boys in the United States? The critical ratio helps us make this decision.

$$\sigma_{D_M} = \sqrt{(\sigma_{M_1})^2 + (\sigma_{M_2})^2}$$
$$= \sqrt{.16 + .09} = \sqrt{.25}$$
$$= .5$$

$$\text{Critical ratio} = \frac{D_M}{\sigma_{D_M}} = \frac{72 - 70}{.5} = \frac{2.0}{.5} = 4.0$$

Because the critical ratio is well above 2.0, we may assert that the observed mean difference is statistically significant at the 5-percent level. Thus, we can conclude that there is a reliable difference in performance on the reading test between boys and girls. Note that the sign of the critical ratio could be positive or negative, depending on which mean is subtracted from which; when the critical ratio is interpreted, only its magnitude (not its sign) is considered.

COEFFICIENT OF CORRELATION

Correlation refers to the concomitant variation of paired measures. Suppose that a test is designed to predict success in college. If it is a good test, high scores on it will be related to high performance in college and low scores will be related to poor performance. The *coefficient of correlation* gives us a way of stating the degree of relationship more precisely.[2]

Product-moment correlation

The most frequently used method of determining the coefficient of correlation is the *product-moment method,* which yields the index conventionally designated

[2]This topic was discussed on pages 23–25. The reader may find it helpful to review that material.

r. The product-moment coefficient *r* varies between perfect positive correlation ($r = +1.00$) and perfect negative correlation ($r = -1.00$). Lack of relationship is designated $r = .00$.

The formula for computing the product-moment correlation is

$$r = \frac{\text{Sum }(dx)(dy)}{N\sigma_x\sigma_y}$$

Here, one of the paired measures has been labeled the *x*-score; the other, the *y*-score. The *dx* and *dy* refer to the deviations of each score from its mean, *N* is the number of paired measures, and σ_x and σ_y are the standard deviations of the *x*-scores and the *y*-scores.

The computation of the coefficient of correlation requires the determination of the sum of the $(dx)(dy)$ products. This sum, in addition to the computed standard deviations for the *x*-scores and *y*-scores, can then be entered into the formula.

Specimen computation of product-movement correlation. Suppose that we have collected the data shown in Table 7. For each subject, we have obtained two scores—the first being a score on a college entrance test (to be labeled arbitrarily the *x*-score) and the second being freshman grades (the *y*-score).

Figure 6 is a *scatter diagram* of these data. Each point simultaneously represents the *x*-score and *y*-score for a given subject; for example, the uppermost right-hand point is for Adam (labeled A). Looking at these data, we can easily detect that there is some positive correlation between the *x*-scores and the *y*-scores. Adam attained the highest score on the entrance test and also earned the highest freshman grades; Edward received the lowest scores on both. The other students' test scores and grades are a little irregular, so we know that the correlation is not perfect; hence, *r* is less than 1.00.

We will compute the correlation to illustrate the method, although no researcher would consent, in practice, to determining a correlation for so few cases. The details are given in Table 7. Following the procedure outlined in Table 3, we compute the standard deviation of the *x*-scores and then the standard deviation of the *y*-scores. Next, we compute the $(dx)(dy)$ products for each subject and total the five cases. Entering these results in our equation yields an *r* of $+.85$.

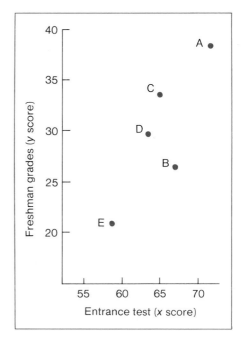

Figure 6
Scatter Diagram
Each point represents the *x*- and *y*-scores for a particular student. The letters next to the points identify the students in the data table (A = Adam, B = Bill, and so on).

STUDENT	ENTRANCE TEST (x-score)	FRESHMAN GRADES (y-score)	(dx)	(dy)	(dx)(dy)
Adam	71	39	6	9	+54
Bill	67	27	2	-3	-6
Charles	65	33	0	3	0
David	63	30	-2	0	0
Edward	59	21	-6	-9	+54
Sum	325	150	0	0	+102
Mean	65	30			

$$\sigma_x = 4 \qquad r = \frac{\text{Sum }(dx)(dy)}{N\sigma_x\sigma_y} = \frac{+102}{5 \times 4 \times 6} = +.85$$
$$\sigma_y = 6$$

Table 7
Computation of a Product-Moment Correlation

Interpreting a correlation coefficient

We can use correlations in making predictions. For example, if we know from past experience that a certain entrance test correlates with freshman grades, we can predict the freshman grades for beginning college students who have taken the test. If the correlation were perfect, we could predict their grades without error. But r is usually less than 1.00, and some errors in prediction will be made; the closer r is to 0, the greater the sizes of the errors in prediction.

Although we cannot go into the technical problems of predicting freshman grades from entrance examinations or of making other similar predictions, we can consider the meanings of correlation coefficients of different sizes. It is evident that with a correlation of 0 between x and y, knowledge of x will not help to predict y. If weight is unrelated to intelligence, it does us no good to know a subject's weight when we are trying to predict his or her intelligence. At the other extreme, a perfect correlation would mean 100 percent predictive efficiency—knowing x, we can predict y. What about intermediate values of r? Some appreciation of the meaning of correlations of intermediate sizes can be gained by examining the scatter diagrams in Figure 7.

In the preceding discussion, we did not emphasize the sign of the correlation coefficient, since this has no bearing on the strength of a relationship.

Figure 7
Scatter Diagrams Illustrating
Correlations of Various Sizes

Each dot represents one individual's score on two tests, x and y. In A, all cases fall on the diagonal and the correlation is perfect ($r = +1.00$); if we know a subject's score on x, we know that it will be the same on y. In B, the correlation is 0; knowing a subject's score on x, we cannot predict whether it will be at, above, or below the mean on y. For example, of the four subjects who score at the mean of x ($dx = 0$), one makes a very high score on y ($dy = +2$), one a very low score ($dy = -2$), and two remain average. In both C and D, there is a diagonal trend to the scores, so that a high score on x is associated with a high score on y and a low score on x with a low score on y, but the relationship is imperfect. It is possible to check the value of the correlations by using the formulas given in the text for the coefficient of correlation. The computation has been greatly simplified by presenting the scores in the deviation form that permits entering them directly into the formulas. The fact that the axes do not have conventional scales does not change the interpretation. For example, if we assigned the values 1 through 5 to the x and y coordinates and then computed r for these new values, the correlation coefficients would be the same.

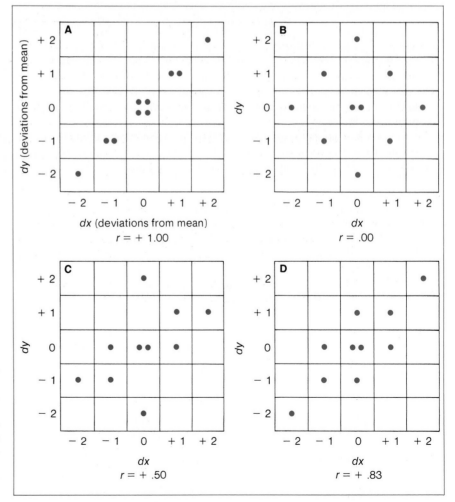

The only distinction between a correlation of $r = +.70$ and $r = -.70$ is that increases in x are accompanied by increases in y for the former, and increases in x are accompanied by decreases in y for the latter.

Although the correlation coefficient is one of the most widely used statistics in psychology, it is also one of the most widely misused procedures. First, those who use it sometimes overlook the fact that r measures only the strength of a *linear* (straight-line) relationship between x and y. Second, they often fail to recognize that r does not imply a cause-and-effect relationship between x and y.

CORRELATION MEASURES LINEAR RELATIONSHIPS   If r is calculated for the data plotted in Figure 8, a value close to 0 will be obtained, but this does not mean that the two variables are not related. The curve in Figure 8 provides an excellent fit, even though a straight line would not; knowing the value of x, we could predict very precisely what y would be by plotting it on the curve. Let us therefore emphasize that the correlation coefficient measures only the strength of a linear (straight-line) relationship. If there is reason to believe that a *nonlinear* relationship holds, other statistical procedures need to be used.

CORRELATION DOES NOT YIELD CAUSE   When two sets of scores are correlated, we may suspect that they have some causal factors in common, but we cannot conclude that one of them causes the other (see pages 23–25).

Correlations sometimes appear paradoxical. For example, the correlation between study time and college grades has been found to be slightly negative (about $-.10$). If a causal interpretation were assumed, we might conclude that the best way to raise grades would be to stop studying. The negative correlation arises because some students have advantages over others in grade making (possibly due to better college preparation), so that often those who study the hardest are those who have difficulty earning the best grades.

This example provides sufficient warning against assigning a causal interpretation to a coefficient of correlation. It is possible, however, that when two variables are correlated, one may be the cause of the other. The search for causes is a logical one, and correlations can help us by providing leads to experiments that can verify cause-and-effect relationships.

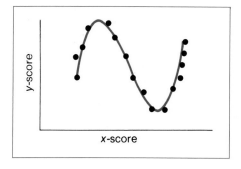

Figure 8
Hypothetical Scatter Diagram
Here, data would be poorly accounted for by a straight line but are well accounted for by the s-shaped curve. Application of the correlation coefficient to these data would be inappropriate.

Further Reading

There are a number of textbooks on statistics written from the viewpoint of psychological research. Excellent examples are Loftus and Loftus, *Essence of statistics* (1982); Minium and Clarke, *Elements of statistical reasoning* (1982); and Phillips, *Statistical thinking* (2nd ed., 1982).

The role of statistics in the design of psychological experiments is discussed in Keppel and Saufley, *Introduction to design and analysis* (1980).

III
PSYCHOLOGY JOURNALS

Listed alphabetically are some of the major journals of psychology and a description of the types of articles they publish. These journals are available in most college and university libraries; current issues of the journals usually can be found on racks in an open area of the library. An excellent introduction to psychology can be gained by spending some time perusing recent issues of these journals.

American Psychologist: Official papers of the American Psychological Association; articles on psychology; comments, announcements, and lists of regional, national, and international conventions.

Animal Learning and Behavior: Studies of animal learning, motivation, emotion, and comparative animal behavior.

Behavioral Neuroscience: Original research papers concerned with the biological bases of psychological phenomena; studies cover the entire range of relevant biological and neural sciences.

Cognitive Psychology: Theory and research in the area of cognitive processes and related fields of psychology.

Contemporary Psychology: Critical reviews of recent books, films, and other media; brief notes on new texts; previews of textbooks in psychology.

Developmental Psychology: Studies of the variables influencing growth, development, and aging.

Journal of Abnormal Psychology: Basic research and theory in the field of abnormal behavior, its determinants, and its correlates.

Journal of Applied Psychology: Theoretical and research contributions in applied fields such as business and industry; government, urban, and consumer affairs; legal, health, transportation, defense, and educational systems; and space and other new environments.

Journal of Comparative Psychology: Research reports in comparative psychology; publishes laboratory and field studies of the behavioral patterns of various species as they relate to such factors as evolution, development, ecology, and functional significance.

Journal of Consulting and Clinical Psychology: Research and theory concerning clinical psychology, including psychological diagnoses, psychotherapy, personality, and psychopathology.

Journal of Counseling Psychology: Theory, research, and practice concerning counseling and related activities of counselors and personnel workers.

Journal of Educational Psychology: Studies of learning and teaching, including measurement of psychological development, methods of instruction, and school adjustment.

Journal of Experimental Psychology—Animal Behavior Processes: Studies of the basic mechanisms of perception, learning, motivation, and performance, especially with infrahuman animals.

Journal of Experimental Psychology—General: Long, integrative reports leading to an advance in knowledge of interest to all experimental psychologists.

Journal of Experimental Psychology—Human Learning and Memory: Studies of human acquisition, retention, and transfer processes.

Journal of Experimental Psychology—Human Perception and Performance: Studies of information-processing operations as they relate to experience and performance.

Journal of Mathematical Psychology: Theoretical contributions in all fields of psychology, in which the work involves theories or models employing mathematical methods, formal logic, or computer simulation.

Journal of Personality and Social Psychology: Research on personality dynamics, group processes, and the psychological aspects of social structure.

Journal of Phenomenological Psychology: Theoretical and empirical contributions to psychology that emphasize a humanistic/phenomenological approach.

Memory and Cognition: Studies of human memory and learning, conceptual processes, psycholinguistics, problem solving, thinking, decision making, and skilled performance.

Perception and Psychophysics: Studies that deal with sensory processes, perception, and psychophysics.

Physiological Psychology: Basic studies in structural, chemical, and electrical aspects of brain organization and functions that have implications for behavior.

Psychological Abstracts: Noncritical abstracts of the world's literature in psychology and related subjects.

Psychological Bulletin: Evaluative reviews of research literature and discussions of research methodology in psychology.

Psychological Review: Theoretical contributions attempting to integrate and discuss a broad range of psychological phenomena.

Psychometrika: Articles on the development of quantitative models for psychological phenomena, including new mathematical and statistical techniques for the evaluation of psychological data.

GLOSSARY

The glossary defines the technical words that appear in the text and some common words that have special meanings when they are used in psychology. No attempt is made to give the range of meanings beyond those used in the text. For fuller definitions and other shades of meaning, consult any standard dictionary of psychology.

A

ability. Demonstrable knowledge or skill. Ability includes aptitude and achievement. See also **achievement, aptitude.**

abreaction. In psychoanalysis, the process of reducing emotional tension by reliving (in speech or action or both) the experience that caused the tension.

absolute threshold. The intensity or infrequency at which a stimulus becomes effective or ceases to become effective, as measured under experimental conditions. See also **difference threshold, threshold.**

accommodation. The process by which the lens of the eye varies its focus.

achievement. Acquired ability, such as school attainment in spelling. See also **aptitude.**

achievement motive. The social motive to accomplish something of value or importance, to meet standards of excellence in what one does.

achromatic colors. Black, white, and gray. See also **chromatic colors.**

acquisition. The stage during which a new response is learned and gradually strengthened. See also **classical conditioning.**

action potential. Synonymous with *nerve impulse.* The wave of electrical activity that is transmitted down the axon of the neuron when the cell membrane becomes depolarized. See also **depolar-** ization, graded potential, resting potential.

additive mixture. The mixture of colored lights; two spotlights of different colors focused on the same spot yield an additive color mixture. See also **subtractive mixture.**

ADH. See **antidiuretic hormone.**

adipocytes. Special fat cells in the body. Obese individuals have many more of them and thus, perhaps, a higher body fat base line.

adolescence. In human beings, the period from puberty to maturity, roughly the early teens to the early twenties. See also **puberty.**

adrenal gland. One of a pair of endocrine glands located above the kidneys. The medulla of the gland secretes the hormones epinephrine and norepinephrine. The cortex of the gland secretes a number of hormones, collectively called the *adrenocortical hormones,* which include cortisone. See also **endocrine gland.**

adrenalin. See **epinephrine.**

affective disorder. A mental disorder characterized by disturbances of mood, or affect. Mania (exaggerated excitement), depression, and a cyclical manic-depression are examples. See also **bipolar disorder, manic-depressive disorder.**

affective experience. An emotional experience, whether pleasant or unpleas- ant, mild or intense. See also **emotion.**

afferent neuron. See **sensory neuron.**

afterimage. The sensory experience that remains when a stimulus is withdrawn. Usually refers to visual experience—for example, the negative afterimage of a picture or the train of colored images that results after staring at the sun.

age regression. In hypnosis, the reliving through fantasy of experiences that are based on early memories or appropriate to a younger age. See also **hypnosis.**

aggression. Behavior intended to harm another person. See also **hostile aggression, instrumental aggression.**

agoraphobia. Fear of being alone or being in a public place where escape might be difficult or help unavailable should the individual be incapacitated by a panic attack. See also **panic disorder, phobia.**

all-or-none principle. The rule that the nerve impulse in a single neuron is independent of the strength of stimulation; the neuron either responds completely (fires its action potential) or not at all.

alpha waves. See **electroencephalogram.**

ambivalence. Simultaneous liking and disliking of an object or person; the conflict caused by an incentive that is at once positive and negative. See also **conflict.**

amnesia. The partial or total loss of memory for past experiences. The memories lost in amnesia have not been completely destroyed, for the forgotten events may again be remembered when the person recovers from the amnesia. See also **repression.**

amphetamines. Central nervous system stimulants that produce restlessness, irritability, anxiety, and rapid heart rate. Dexedrine sulfate ("speed") and methamphetamine ("meth") are two types of amphetamines. See also **depressants, stimulants.**

anal stage. The second stage according to the psychoanalytic theory of psychosexual development, following the oral stage. The sources of gratification and conflict have to do with the expulsion and retention of feces. See also **psychosexual development.**

analysis-by-synthesis. A theory of perception assuming that the perceiver analyzes a stimulus into features and then uses the features to synthesize, or construct, a percept that best fits all of the information.

androgens. The collective name for male sex hormones, of which testosterone, secreted by the testes, is best known. See also **gonads.**

anterograde amnesia. The inability to learn, or retain, new information; presumably because new information is not encoded into long-term memory. See also **retrograde amnesia.**

anthropology. The science that studies chiefly preliterate ("primitive") societies. Its main divisions are archaeology (the study of the physical monuments and remains from earlier civilizations), physical anthropology (concerned with the anatomical differences among men and their evolutionary origins), linguistic anthropology, and social anthropology (concerned with social institutions and behavior). See also **behavioral sciences.**

antianxiety drug. Central nervous system depressant that reduces tension. Causes some drowsiness but less than barbiturates. Examples are Valium and Librium (syn. *tranquilizer*).

antidepressant. Drug used to elevate the mood of depressed individuals, presumably by increasing the availability of the neurotransmitters norepinephrine and/or serotonin. Examples are imipramine (Tofranil), isocarboxazid

(Marplan), and tranylcypromine (Parnate).

antidiuretic hormone (ADH). Hormone secreted by the pituitary gland that signals the kidney to reabsorb water into the bloodstream instead of excreting it as urine.

antipsychotic drug. A drug that reduces psychotic symptoms, used most frequently in the treatment of schizophrenia. Chlorpromazine and reserpine are examples (syn. *neuroleptic drug*). See also **psychotic behavior.**

antisocial personality. A type of personality disorder marked by impulsivity, inability to abide by the customs and laws of society, and lack of anxiety or guilt regarding behavior (syn. *psychopathic personality*).

anxiety. A state of apprehension or uneasiness, related to fear. The object of anxiety (such as vague danger or foreboding) is ordinarily less specific than the object of fear (such as a vicious animal).

anxiety disorders. A group of mental disorders characterized by intense anxiety or by maladaptive behavior designed to relieve anxiety. Includes generalized anxiety and panic disorders, phobic and obsessive-compulsive disorders. Major category of DSM-III covering most of the disorders formerly called neuroses. See also **generalized anxiety disorders, neurosis, obsessive-compulsive disorder, panic disorder, phobic disorder.**

anxiety hierarchy. A list of situations or stimuli to which a person responds with anxiety ranked in order from the least anxiety-producing to the most fearful. Used by behavior therapists in systematically desensitizing patients to feared stimuli by associating deep relaxation with the situations rather than anxiety. See also **behavior therapy, systematic desensitization.**

apathy. Listlessness, indifference; one of the consequences of frustration. See also **frustration.**

aphagia. Inability to eat. See also **hyperphagia.**

aphasia. Impairment or loss of ability to articulate words or comprehend speech.

apnea. A sleep disturbance characterized by inhibited breathing during sleep.

apparent motion. See **autokinetic effect, phi phenomenon, stroboscopic motion.**

appetitive behavior. Seeking behavior. See also **aversive behavior.**

aptitude. The capacity to learn—for instance, a person's typing aptitude prior to practice on a typewriter. Aptitude tests are designed to predict the outcome of training, hence to predict future ability on the basis of present ability. See also **achievement.**

archetypes. In the psychology of Carl Jung, a basic idea, such as "God" or "mother," said to characterize a universal unconscious.

artificial intelligence. The performance by a computer of tasks that have hitherto required the application of human intelligence.

assertive training. A form of counter-conditioning in which assertive or approach responses are reinforced in an attempt to extinguish passivity or anxiety in certain situations. See also **behavior therapy, counter-conditioning.**

association areas. Areas of the cerebral cortex that are not directly concerned with sensory or motor processes; they integrate inputs from various sensory channels and presumably function in learning, memory, and thinking.

associative learning. Learning that certain contingencies (or relations) exist between events; learning that one event is associated with another.

attachment. The tendency of the young organism to seek closeness to particular individuals and to feel more secure in their presence.

attention. The focusing of perception leading to heightened awareness of a limited range of stimuli.

attribution. The process by which we attempt to explain the behavior of other people. Attribution theory deals with the rules people use to infer the causes of observed behavior. See also **dispositional attribution, situational attribution.**

autism. Absorption in fantasy to the exclusion of interest in reality; a symptom of schizophrenia. See also **schizophrenia.**

autistic thinking. A form of associative thinking, controlled more by the thinker's needs or desires than by reality; wishful thinking. See also **day-**

dreaming, rationalization.

automatic writing. Writing that the writer is unaware of (does not know that he or she is producing); familiar in hypnosis. See also **hypnosis.**

autonomic nervous system. The division of the peripheral nervous system that regulates smooth muscle (organ and glandular activities). It is divided into the sympathetic and parasympathetic divisions. See also **parasympathetic division, peripheral nervous system, sympathetic division.**

average. See **measure of central tendency.**

aversive behavior. Avoidance behavior. See also **appetitive behavior.**

aversive conditioning. A form of conditioning in which an undesirable response is extinguished through association with punishment; has been used in behavior therapy to treat alcoholism, smoking, and sexual problems. See also **behavior therapy, counter-conditioning.**

axon. That portion of a neuron that transmits impulses to other neurons. See also **dendrite, neuron.**

B

Barnum effect. Refers to the readiness of people to believe that general descriptions, as given in astrological characterizations, refer to them personally.

basal mental age. In individual tests of the Binet type, the highest age level at which, and below which, all tests are passed. See also **mental age.**

basilar membrane. A membrane of the ear within the coils of the cochlea supporting the organ of Corti. Movements of the basilar membrane stimulate the hair cells of the organ of Corti, producing the neural effects of auditory stimulation. See also **cochlea, organ of Corti.**

behavior. Those activities of an organism that can be observed by another organism or by an experimenter's instruments. Included within behavior are verbal reports made about subjective, conscious experiences. See also **conscious processes.**

behavior genetics. The study of the inheritance of behavioral characteristics.

behavior modification. See **behavior therapy.**

behavior therapy. A method of psychotherapy based on learning principles. It uses such techniques as counter-conditioning, reinforcement, and shaping to modify behavior (syn. *behavior modification*). See also **cognitive behavior therapy.**

behavioral sciences. The sciences concerned in one way or another with the behavior of humans and lower organisms—especially social anthropology, psychology, and sociology but including some aspects of biology, economics, political science, history, philosophy, and other fields of study.

behaviorism. A school or system of psychology associated with the name of John B. Watson; it defined psychology as the study of behavior and limited the data of psychology to observable activities. In its classical form it was more restrictive than the contemporary behavioral viewpoint in psychology.

binocular cues. See **distance cues.**

binocular disparity. The fact that an object projects slightly different images on the two retinas due to the different positions of the right and left eyes.

biofeedback. A procedure that permits individuals to monitor their own physiological processes (such as heart rate, blood pressure), which they are normally unaware of, to learn to control them.

biological therapy. Treatment of personality maladjustment or mental illness by drugs, electric shock, or other methods directly affecting bodily processes. See also **psychotherapy.**

bipolar disorder. An affective disorder in which people experience episodes of both mania and depression or of mania alone. The term in DSM-III for manic-depressive disorder. See also **affective disorder, manic-depressive disorder.**

blind spot. An insensitive area of the retina where the nerve fibers from the ganglion cells join to form the optic nerve.

blood pressure. The pressure of the blood against the walls of the blood vessels. Changes in blood pressure following stimulation serve as one indicator of emotion.

brain stem. The structures lying near the core of the brain; essentially all of the brain with the exception of the cere-brum and the cerebellum and their dependent parts.

brainwashing. See **coercive persuasion.**

brightness. The dimension of color that describes its nearness in brilliance to white (as contrasted to black). A bright color reflects more light than a dark one. See also **hue, saturation.**

Broca's area. A portion of the left cerebral hemisphere involved in the control of speech. Individuals with damage in this area have difficulty enunciating words correctly and speak in a slow and labored way; their speech often makes sense, but it includes only key words.

C

CAL. A common abbreviation for computer-assisted learning; in other words, instruction carried out under computer control.

Cannon–Bard theory. A classical theory of emotion proposed by Cannon and Bard. The theory states that an emotion-producing stimulus activates the cortex and bodily responses at the same time; bodily changes and the experience of emotion occur simultaneously. See also **cognitive-physiological theory, James–Lange theory.**

cardiac muscle. A special kind of muscle found only in the heart. See also **smooth muscle, striate muscle.**

case history. A biography obtained for scientific purposes; the material is sometimes supplied by interview, sometimes collected over the years. See also **longitudinal study.**

castration. Surgical removal of the gonads; in the male, removal of the testes; in the female, removal of the ovaries.

catharsis. Reduction of an impulse or emotion through direct or indirect expression, particularly verbal and fantasy expression.

central core. The most central and the evolutionarily oldest portion of the brain. It includes structures that regulate basic life processes, including most of the brain stem. See also **brain stem, cerebellum, hypothalamus, reticular system.**

central fissure. A fissure of each cerebral hemisphere that separates the frontal and parietal lobes (syn. *fissure of Rolando*).

central nervous system. In vertebrates, the brain and spinal cord, as distinct from the nerve trunks and their peripheral connections. See also **autonomic nervous system, peripheral nervous system.**

cerebellum. Lobed structure attached to the rear of the brain stem that regulates muscle tone and coordination of intricate movements.

cerebral cortex. The surface layer of the cerebral hemispheres in higher animals, including humans. It is commonly called gray matter because its many cell bodies give it a gray appearance in cross section, in contrast with the myelinated nerve fibers that make up the white matter in the center.

cerebral hemispheres. Two large masses of nerve cells and fibers constituting the bulk of the brain in humans and other higher animals. The hemispheres are separated by a deep fissure, but connected by a broad band of fibers, the corpus callosum (syn. *cerebrum*). See also **cerebral cortex, left hemisphere, right hemisphere, split-brain subject.**

cerebrum. See **cerebral hemispheres.**

chlorpromazine. See **antipsychotic drug.**

chromatic colors. All colors other than black, white, and gray; for instance, red, yellow, blue. See also **achromatic colors.**

chromosome. Rodlike structures found in pairs in all the cells of the body, carrying the genetic determiners (genes) that are transmitted from parent to offspring. A human cell has 46 chromosomes, arranged in 23 pairs, one member of each pair deriving from the mother, one from the father. See also **gene.**

chronological age (CA). Age from birth; calendar age. See also **mental age.**

chunk. The largest meaningful unit of information that can be stored in short-term memory; short-term memory holds 7 ± 2 chunks. See also **short-term memory.**

circadian rhythm. A cycle or rhythm that is roughly 24 hours long. Sleep-wakefulness, body temperature, and water excretion follow a circadian rhythm, as do a number of behavioral and physiological variables.

clairvoyance. A form of extrasensory perception in which the perceiver is said to identify a stimulus that is influencing neither his or her own sense organs nor those of another person. See also **extrasensory perception, precognition, psychokinesis, telepathy.**

classical concept. A concept where every instance must have every property mentioned in the concept. An example is the concept of *bachelor*; every instance must have the properties of being adult, male, and unmarried.

classical conditioning. Conditioned-response experiments conforming to the pattern of Pavlov's experiment. The main feature is that the originally neutral conditioned stimulus, through repeated pairing with the unconditioned one, acquires the response originally given to the unconditioned stimulus. See also **operant conditioning.**

claustrophobia. Fear of closed places. See also **phobia.**

client-centered therapy. A method of psychotherapy designed to let clients learn to take responsibility for their actions and to use their resourcefulness in solving their problems (syn. *nondirective counseling*).

clinical psychologist. A psychologist, usually with a Ph.D. degree, trained in the diagnosis and treatment of emotional or behavioral problems and mental disorders. See also **counseling psychologist, psychiatrist.**

cocaine. A central nervous system stimulant derived from leaves of the coca plant. Increases energy, produces euphoria, and in large doses causes paranoia.

cochlea. The portion of the inner ear containing the receptors for hearing. See also **basilar membrane, organ of Corti.**

coding. See **encoding.**

coefficient of correlation. A numerical index used to indicate the degree of correspondence between two sets of paired measurements. The most common kind is the product-moment coefficient designated by r.

cognition. An individual's thoughts, knowledge, interpretations, understandings, or ideas. See also **cognitive processes.**

cognitive behavior therapy. A psychotherapeutic approach that emphasizes the influence of a person's beliefs, thoughts, and self-statements on behavior. Combines behavior therapy methods with techniques designed to change the way the individual thinks about self and events. See also **behavior therapy.**

cognitive dissonance. The condition in which one has beliefs or knowledge that disagree with each other or with behavioral tendencies; when such cognitive dissonance arises, the subject is motivated to reduce the dissonance through changes in behavior or cognition.

cognitive map. A hypothetical structure in memory that preserves and organizes information about the various events that occur in a learning situation; a mental picture of the learning situation. See also **schema.**

cognitive-physiological theory. A theory of emotion: emotion is bodily arousal in interaction with cognitive processes. Emotion is determined by the label a person gives to his or her state of bodily arousal. See also **Cannon–Bard theory, James–Lange theory.**

cognitive processes. Mental processes of perception, memory, and information processing by which the individual acquires information, makes plans, and solves problems.

cognitive psychology. A point of view that stresses the dynamic role of cognitive processes. An emphasis on "knowing" and "perceiving" as contrasted with associative learning.

color blindness. Defective discrimination of chromatic colors. See also **dichromatism, monochromatism, red-green color blindness, trichromatism.**

color circle. An arrangement of chromatic colors on the circumference of a circle in the order in which they appear in the spectrum but with the addition of nonspectral reds and purples. The colors are so arranged that those opposite each other are complementaries in additive mixture. See also **color solid.**

color constancy. The tendency to see a familiar object as of the same color, regardless of changes in illumination on it that alter its stimulus properties. See also **object constancy**.

color solid. A three-dimensional representation of the psychological dimensions of color, with hue around the circumference, saturation along each radius, and brightness from top to bottom. See also **color circle**.

complementary colors. Two colors that in additive mixture yield either a gray or an unsaturated color of the hue of the stronger component.

complex cell. A cell in the visual cortex that responds to a bar of light or straight edge of a particular orientation located anywhere in the visual field. See also **simple cell**.

compliance. A form of social influence in which an individual conforms outwardly (to obtain a reward or avoid punishment) but does not necessarily believe in the opinions expressed or the behavior displayed.

compulsion. A repetitive action that a person feels driven to make and is unable to resist; ritualistic behavior. See also **obsession, obsessive-compulsive disorder**.

computer program. See **program**.

computer simulation. See **simulation**.

concept. The properties or relationships common to a class of objects or ideas. Concepts may be of concrete things (such as the concept *poodle* referring to a given variety of dog) or of abstract ideas (such as *equality, justice, number*), implying relationships common to many different kinds of objects or ideas. See also **classical concept, probabilistic concept**.

concrete operational stage. Piaget's third stage of cognitive development (ages 7–12 years) during which a child becomes capable of logical thought and achieves conservation concepts. See also **conservation**.

conditioned emotion. An emotional response acquired by conditioning: one aroused by a stimulus that did not originally evoke it. See also **conditioning**.

conditioned reinforcer. A stimulus that has become reinforcing through prior association with a reinforcing stimulus (syn. *secondary reinforcer*). See also **reinforcing stimulus**.

conditioned response (CR). In classical conditioning, the learned or acquired response to a conditioned stimulus; i.e., to a stimulus that did not evoke the response originally. See also **conditioned stimulus, unconditioned response, unconditioned stimulus**.

conditioned stimulus (CS). In classical conditioning, a stimulus previously neutral that comes to elicit a conditioned response through association with an unconditioned stimulus. See also **conditioned response, unconditioned response, unconditioned stimulus**.

conditioning. The process by which conditioned responses are learned. See also **classical conditioning, operant conditioning**.

cone. In the eye, a specialized cell of the retina found predominantly in the fovea and more sparsely throughout the retina. The cones mediate both chromatic and achromatic sensations. See also **fovea, retina, rod**.

conflict. The simultaneous presence of opposing or mutually exclusive impulses, desires, or tendencies. See also **ambivalence**.

connotative meaning. The suggestive and emotional meanings of a word or symbol, beyond its denotative meaning. Thus, *naked* and *nude* both refer to an unclothed body (denotative meaning), but they have somewhat different connotations. See also **denotative meaning**.

conscience. An internal recognition of standards of right and wrong by which the individual judges his or her conduct. See also **superego**.

conscious processes. Events such as perceptions, afterimages, private thoughts, and dreams, of which only the person is aware. They are accessible to others through verbal report or by way of inference from other behavior (syn. *experience, awareness*).

conservation. Piaget's term for the ability of the child to recognize that certain properties of objects (such as mass, volume, number) do not change despite transformations in the appearance of the objects. See also **preoperational stage**.

constructive memory. Using general knowledge stored in memory to construct and elaborate a more complete and detailed account of some events.

control group. In an experimental design contrasting two groups, that group not given the treatment whose effect is under study. See also **experimental group**.

control processes. Regulatory processes that serve to establish equilibrium or monitor goal-directed activities. See also **homeostasis**.

convergent thinking. In tests of intellect, producing a specified "correct" response in accordance with truth and fact. See also **divergent thinking**.

corpus callosum. A large band of nerve fibers connecting the two cerebral hemispheres.

correlation. See **coefficient of correlation**.

counseling psychologist. A trained psychologist, usually with a Ph.D. or Ed.D. degree, who deals with personal problems not classified as illness, such as academic, social, or vocational problems of students. He or she has skills similar to those of the clinical psychologist but usually works in a nonmedical setting. See also **clinical psychologist, psychiatrist**.

counter-conditioning. In behavior therapy, the replacement of a particular response to a stimulus by the establishment of another (usually incompatible) response. See also **assertive training**.

criterion. (1) A set of scores or other records against which the success of a predictive test is verified. (2) A standard selected as the goal to be achieved in a learning task; for example, the number of runs through a maze to be made without error as an indication that the maze has been mastered.

critical period. A stage in development during which the organism is optimally ready to learn certain response patterns. There is some evidence for a critical period in language learning; a child not exposed to language prior to adolescence has great difficulty acquiring language thereafter.

cues to distance. See **distance cues**.

culture-fair test. A type of intelligence test that has been constructed to minimize bias due to the differing experiences of children raised in a rural rather than an urban culture or in a lower-class rather than in a middle-class or upper-class culture (syn. *culture-free test*).

cumulative curve. A graphic record of the responses emitted during an operant conditioning session. The slope of the cumulative curve indicates the rate of response.

D

dark adaptation. The increased sensitivity to light when the subject has been continuously in the dark or under conditions of reduced illumination. See also light adaptation.

daydreaming. Reverie; free play of thought or imagination. Because of self-reference, usually a form of autistic thinking. See also autistic thinking.

db. See decibel.

decibel (db). A unit for measuring sound intensity.

defense mechanism. An adjustment made, often unconsciously, either through action or the avoidance of action to keep from recognizing personal qualities or motives that might lower self-esteem or heighten anxiety. Denial and projection are two examples.

deindividuation. A psychological state in which persons feel that they have lost their personal identities and have merged anonymously into a group. Hypothesized to be the basis for the impulsive, aggressive behaviors sometimes shown by mobs and crowds.

delayed conditioning. A classical conditioning procedure in which the CS begins several seconds or more before the onset of the US and continues with it until the response occurs. See also simultaneous conditioning, trace conditioning.

delta waves. See electroencephalogram.

delusion. False beliefs characteristic of some forms of psychotic disorder. They often take the form of delusions of grandeur or delusions of persecution. See also hallucination, illusion, paranoid schizophrenia.

dendrite. The specialized portion of the neuron that (together with the cell body) receives impulses from other neurons. See also axon, neuron.

denial. A defense mechanism by which unacceptable impulses or ideas are not perceived or allowed into full awareness. See also defense mechanism.

denotative meaning. The primary meaning of a symbol, something specific to which the symbol refers or points (for example, my street address is denotative; whether I live in a desirable neighborhood is a connotative meaning secondary to the address itself). See also connotative meaning.

deoxyribonucleic acid (DNA). The basic hereditary material of all organisms; a nucleic acid polymer incorporating the sugar deoxyribose. In higher organisms, the great bulk of DNA is located within the chromosomes.

dependent variable. The variable whose measured changes are attributed to (or correspond to) changes in the independent variable. In psychological experiments, the dependent variable is often a response to a measured stimulus. See also independent variable.

depolarization. Change in the resting potential of the nerve cell membrane in the direction of the action potential; the inside of the membrane becomes more positive. See also action potential, resting potential.

depressants. Psychoactive drugs that tend to reduce arousal. Alcohol, barbiturates, and opiates are examples.

depth perception. The perception of the distance of an object from the observer or the distance from front to back of a solid object. See also distance cues.

developmental psychologist. A psychologist whose research interest lies in studying the changes that occur as a function of the growth and development of the organism, in particular the relationship between early and later behavior.

deviation IQ. An intelligence quotient (IQ) computed as a standard score with a mean of 100 and a standard deviation of 15 (Wechsler) or 16 (Stanford–Binet), to correspond approximately to traditional intelligence quotient. See also intelligence quotient.

dichromatism. Color blindness in which either the red-green or the blue-yellow system is lacking. The red-green form is relatively common; the blue-yellow form is the rarest of all forms of color blindness. See also monochromatism, red-green color blindness, trichromatism.

difference threshold. The minimum difference between a pair of stimuli that can be perceived under experimental conditions. See also absolute threshold, just noticeable difference, threshold, Weber's law.

diffusion of responsibility. The tendency for persons in a group situation to fail to take action (as in an emergency) because others are present, thus diffusing the responsibility for acting. A major factor in inhibiting bystanders from intervening in emergencies.

discrimination. (1) In perception, the detection of differences between two stimuli. (2) In conditioning, the differential response to the positive (reinforced) stimulus and to the negative (nonreinforced) stimulus. See also generalization. (3) In social psychology, prejudicial treatment, as in racial discrimination.

discriminative stimulus. A stimulus that becomes an occasion for an operant response; for example, a knock that leads one to open the door. The stimulus does not elicit the operant response in the same sense that a stimulus elicits respondent behavior. See also operant behavior.

displaced aggression. Aggression against a person or object other than that that was (or is) the source of frustration. See also scapegoat.

displacement. (1) A defense mechanism whereby a motive that may not be directly expressed (such as sex or aggression) appears in a more acceptable form. See also defense mechanism. (2) The principle of loss of items from short-term memory as too many new items are added. See also chunk, short-term memory.

dispositional attribution. Attributing a person's actions to internal dispositions (attitudes, traits, motives), as opposed to situational factors. See also situational attribution.

dissociation. The process whereby some ideas, feelings, or activities lose relationship to other aspects of consciousness and personality and operate automatically or independently

dissonance. (1) In music, an inharmonious combination of sounds; contrasted with consonance. (2) In social psychology, Festinger's term for a perceived inconsistency between one's attitudes and one's behavior. See also **cognitive dissonance.**

distance cues. (1) In vision, the monocular cues according to which the distance of objects is perceived—such as superposition of objects, perspective, light and shadow, and relative movement—and the binocular cues used in stereoscopic vision. See also **stereoscopic vision.** (2) In audition, the corresponding cues governing perception of distance and direction, such as intensity and time differences of sound reaching the two ears.

divergent thinking. In tests of intellect (or creativity), producing one or more "possible" answers rather than a single "correct" one. See also **convergent thinking.**

dizygotic (DZ) twins. Twins developed from separate eggs. They are no more alike genetically than ordinary brothers and sisters and can be of the same or different sexes (syn. *fraternal twins*). See also **monozygotic twins.**

DNA. See **deoxyribonucleic acid.**

dominance. The higher status position when social rank is organized according to a dominance-submission hierarchy; commonly found in human societies and in certain animal groups.

dominant gene. A member of a gene pair, which, if present, determines that the individual will show the trait controlled by the gene, regardless of whether the other member of the pair is the same or different (that is, recessive). See also **recessive gene.**

dopamine. A neurotransmitter of the central nervous system believed to play a role in schizophrenia. It is synthesized from an amino acid by the action of certain body enzymes and, in turn, is converted into norepinephrine. See also **neurotransmitter, norepinephrine.**

dopamine hypothesis. The hypothesis that schizophrenia is related to an excess of the neurotransmitter dopamine; either schizophrenics produce too much dopamine or are deficient in the enzyme that converts dopamine to norepinephrine. See also **dopamine, norepinehprine, schizophrenia.**

double blind. An experimental design, often used in drug research, in which neither the investigator nor the patients know which subjects are in the treatment and which in the nontreatment condition until the experiment has been completed.

Down's syndrome. A form of mental deficiency produced by a genetic abnormality (an extra chromosome on pair 21). Characteristics include a thick tongue, extra eyelid folds, and short, stubby fingers (also known as **mongolism**).

drive. (1) An aroused condition of the organism based on deprivation or noxious stimulation, including tissue needs, drug or hormonal conditions, and specified internal or external stimuli, as in pain. (2) Loosely, any motive. See also **motive, need.**

drive-reduction theory. The theory that a motivated sequence of behavior can be best explained as moving from an aversive state of heightened tension (or drive) to a goal state in which the drive is reduced. The goal of the sequence, in other words, is drive reduction. See also **drive, incentive theory, motive, need.**

DSM-III. The third edition of the *Diagnostic and Statistical Manual of the American Psychiatric Association.*

dual-memory theory. A theory that distinguishes between a short-term memory of limited capacity and a virtually unlimited long-term memory. Information can only be encoded into long-term memory via short-term memory. See also **long-term memory, short-term memory.**

DZ twins. See **dizygotic twins.**

E

eardrum. The membrane at the inner end of the auditory canal, leading to the middle ear. See also **middle ear.**

ectomorph. The third of the three types of physique in Sheldon's type theory. It comprises delicacy of skin, fine hair, and ultrasensitive nervous system. See also **endomorph, mesomorph, type theory.**

educational psychologist. A psychologist whose research interest lies in the application of psychological principles to the education of children and adults in schools. See also **school psychologist.**

EEG. See **electroencephalogram.**

efferent neuron. See **motor neuron.**

ego. In Freud's tripartite division of the personality, that part corresponding most nearly to the perceived self, the controlling self that holds back the impulsiveness of the id in the effort to delay gratification until it can be found in socially approved ways. See also **id, superego.**

eidetic imagery. The ability to retain visual images of pictures that are almost photographic in clarity. Such images can be described in far greater detail than would be possible from memory alone. See also **mental imagery.**

elaboration. A memory process wherein one expands verbal material so as to increase the number of ways to retrieve the material.

electroconvulsive therapy (ECT). A treatment for severe depression in which a mild electric current is applied to the brain, producing a seizure similar to an epileptic convulsion. Also known as **electroshock therapy.**

electroencephalogram (EEG). A record obtained by attaching electrodes to the scalp (or occasionally to the exposed brain) and amplifying the spontaneous electrical activity of the brain. Familiar aspects of the EEG are alpha waves (8–13 Hz) and delta waves of slower frequency.

electroshock therapy. See **electroconvulsive shock.**

emotion. The condition of the organism during affectively toned experience, whether mild or intense. See also **affective experience.**

empiricism. The view that behavior is learned as a result of experience. See also **nativism.**

encoding. Transforming a sensory input into a form (code) that can be processed by the memory system.

encounter group. A general term for various types of groups in which people meet to learn more about themselves in relation to other people (syn. *sensitivity group, T group*).

endocrine gland. A ductless gland, or gland of internal secretion, that discharges its products directly into the bloodstream. The hormones secreted by the endocrine glands are important chemical integrators of bodily activity. See also **hormones.**

endomorph. The first of three types of physique in Sheldon's type theory. It comprises prominence of intestines and other visceral organs, including a prominent abdomen, as in the obese individual. See also **ectomorph, mesomorph, type theory.**

endorphins. A group of chemical substances found naturally in the brain that act like opiates; believed to be neurotransmitters released by neurons in response to stress. Appear to play an important role in emotion, pain reduction, and the process by which the body builds up tolerance to opiates and is distressed by their withdrawal. See also **neurotransmitter.**

engineering psychologist. A psychologist who specializes in the relationship between people and machines, seeking, for example, to design machines that minimize human error.

epinephrine. One of the hormones secreted by the adrenal medulla, active in emotional excitement (syn. *adrenalin*). See also **adrenal gland, norepinephrine.**

equilibratory senses. The senses that give discrimination of the position of the body in space and of the movement of the body as a whole. See also **kinesthesis, semicircular canals, vestibular sacs.**

ESP. See **extrasensory perception.**

estrogen. A female sex hormone manufactured and secreted by the ovaries; it is partially responsible for the growth of the female secondary sex characteristics and influences the sex drive. See also **androgens.**

estrous. The sexually receptive state in female mammals. It is a cyclical state, related to menstruation in the primates and humans (syn. *heat*). See also **menstruation.**

ethologist. Zoologists and naturalists particularly interested in kinds of behavior that are specific to a species. More of their work has been on insects, birds, and fishes than on mammals. See also **imprinting, instinct.**

evoked potential. An electrical discharge in some part of the nervous system produced by stimulation elsewhere. The measured potential is commonly based on response averaging by a computer.

excitatory synapse. A synapse at which the neurotransmitter changes the membrane permeability of the receiving cell in the direction of depolarization. See also **depolarization, inhibitory synapse, synapse.**

expectation. An anticipation or prediction of future events based on past experience and present stimuli.

experimental design. A plan for collecting and treating the data of a proposed experiment. The design is evolved after preliminary exploration, with the aims of economy, precision, and control, so that appropriate inferences and decisions can be made from the data.

experimental group. In an experimental design contrasting two groups, that group of subjects given the treatment whose effect is under investigation. See also **control group.**

experimental method. The method of investigation of natural events that seeks to control the variables involved so as to more precisely define cause-and-effect relationships. Most frequently done in a laboratory, but need not be. See also **observational method, variable.**

experimental psychologist. A psychologist whose research interest is in the laboratory study of general psychological principles as revealed in the behavior of lower organisms and human beings.

extinction. (1) The experimental procedure, following classical or operant conditioning, of presenting the conditioned stimulus without the usual reinforcement. (2) The reduction in response that results from this procedure. See also **reinforcement.**

extrasensory perception (ESP). A controversial category of experience consisting of perception not mediated by sense-organ stimulation. See also **clairvoyance, parapsychology, precognition, psychokinesis, telepathy.**

extravert. One of the psychological types proposed by Jung. The extravert is more preoccupied with social life and the external world than with his or her inward experience. See also **introvert.**

F

factor analysis. A statistical method used in test construction and in interpreting scores from batteries of tests. The method enables the investigator to compute the minimum number of determiners (factors) required to account for the intercorrelations among the scores on the tests making up the battery. See also **general factor, special factor.**

family therapy. Psychotherapy with the family members as a group rather than treatment of the patient alone. See also **group therapy.**

fantasy. Daydreaming, "woolgathering" imagination; sometimes a consequence of frustration. It is used as a personality indicator in projective tests. See also **projective tests.**

Fechner's law. The assertion that the perceived magnitude of a stimulus increases in proportion to the logarithm of its physical intensity.

figure-ground perception. Perceiving a pattern as foreground against a background. Patterns are commonly perceived this way even when the stimuli are ambiguous and the foreground-background relationships are reversible.

fixation. In psychoanalysis, arrested development through failure to pass beyond one of the earlier stages of psychosexual development or to change the objects of attachment (such as fixated at the oral stage or fixated on the mother).

flow chart. A diagramatic representation of the sequence of choices and actions in an activity.

formal operational stage. Piaget's fourth stage of cognitive development (age 12 and up) in which the child becomes able to use abstract rules.

fovea. In the eye, a small area in the central part of the retina, packed with cones; in daylight, the most sensitive part of the retina for detail vision and color vision. See also **cone, retina.**

fraternal twins. See **dizygotic twins.**

free association. (1) The form of word-association experiment in which the subject gives any word he or she thinks of in response to the stimulus word. (2) In psychoanalysis, the effort to report without modification everything that comes into awareness.

free recall. A memory task in which a subject is given a list of items (usually one at a time) and is later asked to recall them in any order.

frequency theory. A theory of hearing that assumes that neural impulses arising in the organ of Corti are activated by the basilar membrane of the ear in accordance with the frequency of its vibration rather than with the place of movement. See also **place theory, volley principle.**

frontal lobe. A portion of each cerebral hemisphere, in front of the central fissure. See also **occipital lobe, parietal lobe, temporal lobe.**

frustration. (1) As an event, the thwarting circumstances that block or interfere with goal-directed activity. (2) As a state, the annoyance, confusion, or anger engendered by being thwarted, disappointed, defeated.

frustration-aggression hypothesis. The hypothesis that frustration (thwarting a person's goal-directed efforts) induces an aggressive drive, which, in turn, motivates aggressive behavior.

fundamental attribution error. The tendency to underestimate situational influences on behavior and assume that some personal characteristic of the individual is responsible; the bias toward dispositional rather than situational attributions. See also **attribution, dispositional attribution, situational attribution.**

G

galvanic skin response (GSR). Changes in electrical conductivity of, or activity in, the skin, detected by a sensitive galvanometer. The reactions are commonly used as an emotional indicator.

ganglia (sing. *ganglion*). A collection of nerve cell bodies and synapses, constituting a center lying outside the brain and spinal cord, as in the sympathetic ganglia. See also **nuclei.**

gastrointestinal motility. Movements of parts of the digestive tract caused by contraction of smooth muscle; one form of emotional indicator.

gene. The basic unit of hereditary transmission, localized within the chromosomes. Each chromosome contains many genes. Genes are typically in pairs, one member of the pair being found in the chromosome from the father, the other in the corresponding chromosome from the mother. See also **chromosome, dominant gene, recessive gene.**

general factor (g). (1) A general ability underlying test scores, especially in tests of intelligence, as distinct from special abilities unique to each test. (2) A general ability with which each of the primary factors correlates. See also **factor analysis, special factor.**

General Problem Solver (GPS). A computer program to simulate human problem solving by setting up subgoals and reducing the discrepancies to each subsequent subgoal. See also **simulation.**

generalization. (1) In concept formation, problem solving, and transfer of learning, the detection by the learner of a characteristic or principle common to a class of objects, events, or problems. (2) In conditioning, the principle that once a conditioned response has been established to a given stimulus, similar stimuli will also evoke that response. See also **discrimination.**

generalized anxiety disorder. An anxiety disorder characterized by persistent tension and apprehension. May be accompanied by such physical symptoms as rapid heart rate, fatigue, disturbed sleep, and dizziness. See also **anxiety disorder.**

genetics. That branch of biology concerned with heredity and the means by which hereditary characteristics are transmitted.

genital stage. In classical psychoanalysis, the final stage of psychosexual development, culminating in sexual union with a member of the opposite sex. See also **psychosexual development.**

genotype. In genetics, the characteristics that an individual has inherited and will transmit to his or her descendants, whether or not the individual manifests these characteristics. See also **phenotype.**

Gestalt psychology. A system of psychological theory concerned primarily with perception that emphasizes pattern, organization, wholes, and field properties.

glia cells. Supporting cells (not neurons) composing a substantial portion of brain tissue; recent speculation suggests that they may play a role in neural conduction.

gonads. Testes in the male, ovaries in the female. As duct glands, the sex glands are active in mating behavior, but as endocrine glands their hormones affect secondary sex characteristics as well as maintaining functional sexual activity. The male hormones are known as androgens, the female hormones as estrogen (syn. *sex glands*). See also **androgens, endocrine gland, estrogen.**

graded potentials. Potential changes of varying size induced in a neuron's dendrites or cell body by stimulation from synapses from other neurons. When the graded potentials reach a threshold of depolarization, an action potential occurs. See also **action potential, depolarization.**

gradient of texture. If a surface is perceived visually as having substantial texture (hard, soft, smooth, rough, etc.) and if the texture has a noticeable grain, it becomes fine as the surface recedes from the viewing person, producing a gradient of texture that is important in judgments of slant and of distance. See also **distance cues.**

group test. A test administered to several people at once by a single tester. A college exam is usually a group test.

group therapy. A group discussion or other group activity with a therapeutic purpose participated in by more than one client or patient at a time. See also **psychotherapy.**

GSR. See **galvanic skin response.**

H

habit. A learned stimulus-response sequence. See also **conditioned response.**

hallucination. A sense experience in the absence of appropriate external stimuli;

a misinterpretation of imaginary experiences as actual perceptions. See also **delusion, illusion, schizophrenia.**

hallucinogens. Drugs whose main effect is to change perceptual experience and "expand consciousness." LSD and marijuana are examples (syn. *psychedelic drugs*).

halo effect. The tendency to bias our perception of another person in the direction of one particular characteristic that we like or dislike.

hedonism. The theory that human beings seek pleasure and avoid pain; an extreme form of the theory (in philosophy) is that pleasure or happiness is the highest good.

heritability. The proportion of the total variability of a trait in a given population that is attributable to genetic differences among individuals within that population.

hermaphrodite. An individual born with genitals that are ambiguous in appearance or that are in conflict with the internal sex glands. See also **transsexual.**

heroin. An extremely addictive central nervous system depressant derived from opium. See also **opiates.**

hertz (Hz). The wave frequency of a sound source, or other cyclical phenomena, measured in cycles per second.

heterosexuality. Interest in or attachment to a member of the opposite sex; the usual adult outcome of psychosexual development.

heuristic. In problem solving, a strategy that can be applied to a variety of problems and that usually, but not always, yields a correct solution.

hidden observer. A metaphor to describe the concealed consciousness in hypnosis, inferred to have experiences differing from, but parallel to, the hypnotic consciousness.

hierarchies of concepts. The relationships among individual concepts. See also **concept.**

hierarchy of motives. Maslow's way of classifying motives, ascending from basic biological motives to a peak of self-actualization, supposedly the highest human motive.

home sign. A system of gestures used by deaf children that initially functions as a kind of simple pantomime but eventually takes on the properties of a language.

homeostasis. An optimal level of organic function, maintained by regulatory mechanisms known as homeostatic mechanisms; for example, the mechanisms maintaining a uniform body temperature.

homosexual. A person who prefers to have sexual relations with others of the same sex. Can be male or female, but female homosexuals are often termed *lesbians. Not* to be confused with transsexual. See also **transsexual.**

hormones. The internal secretions of the endocrine glands that are distributed via the bloodstream and affect behavior. See also **endocrine gland.**

hostile aggression. Aggression whose primary aim is to inflict injury. See also **instrumental aggression.**

hue. The dimension of color from which the major color names are derived (red, yellow, green, etc.), corresponding to wavelength of light. See also **brightness, saturation.**

humanistic psychology. A psychological approach that emphasizes the uniqueness of human beings; it is concerned with subjective experience and human values. Often referred to as a third force in psychology in contrast to behaviorism and psychoanalysis. See also **phenomenology.**

hunger drive. A drive based on food deprivation. See also **drive, specific hunger.**

hyperphagia. Pathological overeating. See also **aphagia.**

hypnosis. The responsive state achieved following a typical hypnotic induction or its equivalent.

hypnotic induction. The procedure used in establishing hypnosis in a responsive person. It usually involves relaxation and stimulated imagination. See also **hypnosis.**

hypnotic trance. The dreamlike state of heightened suggestibility induced in a subject by a hypnotist. See also **posthypnotic suggestion.**

hypothalamus. A small but very important structure located just above the brain stem and just below the thalamus. Considered a part of the central core of the brain, it includes centers that govern motivated behavior such as eating, drinking, sex, and emotions; it also regulates endocrine activity and maintains body homeostasis. See also **lateral hypothalamus, ventromedial hypothalamus.**

hypothesis testing. Gathering information and testing alternative explanations of some phenomenon.

hypothetical construct. One form of inferred intermediate mechanism. The construct is conceived of as having properties of its own, other than those specifically required for the explanation; for example, drive that is inferred from the behavior of a deprived organism and is used in the explanation of later behavior.

Hz. See **hertz.**

_____

I

_____

id. In Freud's tripartite division of the personality, that part reflecting unorganized, instinctual impulses. If unbridled, it seeks immediate gratification of primitive needs. See also **ego, superego.**

identical twins. See **monozygotic twins.**

identification. (1) The normal process of acquiring appropriate social roles in childhood through copying, in part unconsciously, the behavior of significant adults; for example, the child's identification with his or her like-sexed parent. See also **imitation.** (2) Close affiliation with others of like interest, such as identifying with a group.

identification figures. Adult models (especially parents) copied, partly unconsciously, by the child. See also **identification.**

identity formation. The process of achieving adult personality integration, as an outgrowth of earlier identifications and other influences. See also **identification, role confusion.**

illusion. In perception, a misinterpretation of the relationships among presented stimuli so that what is perceived does not correspond to physical reality, especially, but not exclusively, an optical or visual illusion. See also **delusion, hallucination.**

imitation. Behavior that is modeled on or

copies that of another. See also **identification.**

imprinting. A term used by ethologists for a species-specific type of learning that occurs within a limited period early in the life of the organism and is relatively unmodifiable thereafter, such as young ducklings learning to follow one adult female (usually the mother) within 11–18 hours after birth. But whatever object they are given to follow at this time, they will thereafter continue to follow. See also **ethologist.**

incentive. (1) A tangible goal object that provides the stimuli that lead to goal activity. (2) Loosely, any goal. See also **negative incentive, positive incentive.**

incentive theory. A theory of motivation that emphasizes the importance of negative and positive incentives in determining behavior; internal drives are not the sole instigators of activity. See also **drive-reduction theory.**

independent variable. The variable under experimental control with which the changes studied in the experiment are correlated. In psychological experiments, the independent variable is often a stimulus, responses to which are the dependent variables under investigation. See also **dependent variable.**

individual differences. Relatively persistent dissimilarities in structure or behavior among persons or members of the same species.

infancy. The period of helplessness and dependency in humans and other organisms; in humans, roughly the first two years.

information-processing model. A model based on assumptions regarding the flow of information through a system; usually best realized by a computer program.

inhibitory synapse. A synapse at which the neurotransmitter changes the membrane permeability of the receiving cell in the direction of the resting potential; i.e., keeps it from firing. See also **excitatory synapse, synapse.**

inner ear. The internal portion of the ear containing, in addition to the cochlea, the vestibular sacs and the semicircular canals. See also **cochlea, semicircular canals, vestibular sacs.**

insight. (1) In problem-solving experiments, the perception of relationships leading to solution. Such a solution can be repeated promptly when the problem is again confronted. (2) In psychotherapy, the discovery by the individuals of dynamic connections between earlier and later events so that they come to recognize the roots of their conflicts.

instinct. The name given to unlearned, patterned, goal-directed behavior, which is species-specific, as illustrated by nest-building in birds or by the migration of salmon (syn. *species-specific behavior*). See also **ethologist.**

instrumental aggression. Aggression aimed at obtaining rewards other than the victim's suffering. See also **hostile aggression.**

insulin. The hormone secreted by the pancreas. See also **hormones.**

intellectualization. A defense mechanism whereby a person tries to gain detachment from an emotionally threatening situation by dealing with it in abstract, intellectual terms. See also **defense mechanism.**

intelligence. (1) That which a properly standardized intelligence test measures. (2) The ability to learn from experience, think in abstract terms, and deal effectively with one's environment. See also **intelligence quotient, mental age.**

intelligence quotient (IQ). A scale unit used in reporting intelligence test scores, based on the ratio between mental age and chronological age. The decimal point is omitted so that the average IQ for children of any one chronological age is set at 100. See also **chronological age, deviation IQ, mental age.**

intermittent reinforcement. See **partial reinforcement.**

internalization. The incorporation of someone else's opinions or behaviors into one's own value system.

interneurons. Neurons in the central nervous system that receive messages from sensory neurons and send them to other interneurons or to motor neurons. See also **sensory neuron, motor neuron.**

interpretation. In psychoanalysis, the analyst's calling attention to the patient's resistances in order to facilitate the flow of associations; also the explanation of symbols, as in dream interpretation. See also **resistance.**

intervening variable. A process inferred to occur between stimulus and response, thus accounting for one response rather than another to the same stimulus. The intervening variable may be inferred without further specification, or it may be given concrete properties and become an object of investigation.

interview. A conversation between an investigator (the interviewer) and a subject (the respondent) used for gathering pertinent data for the subject's benefit (as in the psychotherapeutic interview) or for information-gathering (as in a sample survey).

introspection. (1) A specified form of introspection (trained introspection) describing mental content only, without the intrusion of meanings or interpretations. (2) Any form of reporting on subjective (conscious) events or experiences. See also **phenomenology.**

introvert. One of the psychological types proposed by Jung, referring to the individual who, especially in time of emotional stress, tends to withdraw into himself or herself and to avoid other people. See also **extravert.**

J

James–Lange theory. A classical theory of emotion, named for the two men who independently proposed it. The theory states that the stimulus first leads to bodily responses, and then the awareness of these responses constitutes the experience of emotion. See also **Cannon–Bard theory, cognitive-physiological theory.**

jnd. See **just noticeable difference.**

just noticeable difference (*jnd*). A barely perceptible physical change in a stimulus; a measure of the difference threshold. The term is used also as a unit for scaling the steps of sensation corresponding to increase in the magnitude of stimulation. See also **difference threshold, Weber's law.**

K

key-word method. A technique for learning vocabulary of a foreign language via an intermediate key word related to the sound of the foreign word and the meaning of the English equivalent. See also **mnemonics.**

kinesthesis. The muscle, tendon, and joint senses, yielding discrimination of position and movement of parts of the body. See also **equilibratory senses.**

Klinefelter's syndrome. An abnormal condition of the sex chromosomes (XXY instead of XX or XY); the individual is physically a male with penis and testicles but has marked feminine characteristics.

L

latency. (1) A temporal measure of response, referring to the time delay between the occurrence of the stimulus and the onset of the response. (2) In psychoanalysis, a period in middle childhood, roughly the years from 6–12, when both sexual and aggressive impulses are said to be in a somewhat subdued state, so that the child's attention is directed outward, and curiosity about the environment makes him or her ready to learn. See also **psychosexual development.**

latent content. The underlying significance of a dream (such as the motives or wishes being expressed by it) as interpreted from the manifest content. See also **interpretation, manifest content.**

latent learning. Learning that is not demonstrated by behavior at the time of learning but can be shown to have occurred by increasing the reinforcement for such behavior.

lateral fissure. A deep fissure at the side of each cerebral hemisphere, below which lies the temporal lobe (syn. *fissure of Sylvius*).

lateral hypothalamus (LH). Area of the hypothalamus important to the regulation of food intake. Electrical stimulation of this area will make an experimental animal start to eat; destruction of brain tissue here causes an animal to stop eating. See also **hypothalamus, ventromedial hypothalamus.**

learned helplessness. A condition of apathy or helplessness created experimentally by subjecting an organism to unavoidable trauma (such as shock, heat, or cold). Being unable to avoid or escape an aversive situation produces a feeling of helplessness that generalizes to subsequent situations.

learning. A relatively permanent change in behavior that occurs as the result of practice. Behavior changes due to maturation or temporary conditions of the organism (such as fatigue, the influence of drugs, adaptation) are not included.

learning curve. A graph plotting the course of learning, in which the vertical axis (ordinate) plots a measure of proficiency (amount per unit time, time per unit amount, errors made, etc.), while the horizontal axis (abscissa) represents some measure of practice (trials, time, etc.)

left hemisphere. The left cerebral hemisphere. Controls the right side of the body and, for most people, speech and other logical, sequential activities (syn. *major hemisphere*). See also **cerebral hemisphere, corpus callosum, right hemisphere, split-brain subject.**

lesbian. See **homosexual.**

LH. See **lateral hypothalamus.**

libido. In psychoanalysis, the energy of the sexual instinct, which throughout life becomes attached to new objects and is expressed through various types of motivated behavior.

lie detector. See **polygraph, voice stress analyzer.**

light adaptation. The decreased sensitivity of the eye to light when the subject has been continuously exposed to high levels of illumination. See also **dark adaptation.**

lightness constancy. The tendency to see a familiar object as of the same brightness, regardless of light and shadow that change its stimulus properties. See also **color constancy, object constancy.**

limbic system. A set of structures in and around the midbrain, forming a functional unit regulating motivational-emotional types of behavior, such as waking and sleeping, excitement and quiescence, feeding, and mating.

linguistic relativity hypothesis. The proposition that one's thought processes, the way one perceives the world, are related to one's language.

lithium carbonate. A compound based on lithium, an element related to sodium. Has been successful in treating manic-depressive disorders.

localized functions. Behavior controlled by known areas of the brain; for example, vision is localized in the occipital lobes. See also **projection area.**

location constancy. The tendency to perceive the place at which a resting object is located as remaining the same even though the relationship to the observer has changed. See also **object constancy.**

longitudinal study. A research method that studies an individual through time, taking measurements at periodic intervals. See also **case history.**

long-term memory (LTM). The relatively permanent component of the memory system, as opposed to short-term memory. See also **short-term memory.**

loudness. An intensity dimension of hearing correlated with the amplitude of the sound waves that constitute the stimulus. Greater amplitudes yield greater loudnesses. See also **pitch, timbre.**

LSD. See **lysergic acid derivatives.**

lysergic acid derivatives. Chemical substances derived from lysergic acid, the most important of which is LSD. When taken by a normal person, it produces symptoms similar in some respects to those of schizophrenia. See also **schizophrenia.**

M

major hemisphere. See **left hemisphere.**

manic-depressive disorder. An affective disorder characterized by alternating moods of excitement and elation (manic phase) and despondency and sadness (depressive phase), often with periods of normal mood in between. Some individuals experience only the manic phase. Alternations between normal mood and periods of depression are *not* diagnosed manic–depressive disorder. See also **affective disorder, bipolar disorder.**

manifest content. The remembered content of a dream, the characters, and their actions, as distinguished from the inferred latent content. See also **latent content.**

mantra. See **Transcendental Meditation.**

marijuana. The dried leaves of the hemp plant; also known as hashish, "pot," or "grass." Hashish is actually an extract of the plant material and, hence, is usually stronger than marijuana. Intake may enhance sensory experiences and produce a state of euphoria.

masochism. A pathological desire to inflict pain on oneself or to suffer pain at the hands of others. See also **sadism.**

maternal drive. The drive, particularly in animals, induced in the female through bearing and nursing young, leading to nest-building, retrieving, and other forms of care. See also **drive.**

maturation. Growth processes in the individual that result in orderly changes in behavior, whose timing and patterning are relatively independent of exercise or experience though they may require a normal environment.

maze. A device used in the study of animal and human learning, consisting of a correct path and blind alleys.

mean. The arithmetical average; the sum of all scores divided by their number. See also **measure of central tendency.**

measure of central tendency. A value representative of a frequency distribution, around which other values are dispersed; for example, the mean, median, or mode of a distribution of scores. See also **mean, median, mode.**

measure of variation. A measure of the dispersion or spread of scores in a frequency distribution, such as the range or the standard deviation. See also **standard deviation.**

median. The score of the middle case when cases are arranged in order of size of score. See also **measure of central tendency.**

memory span. The number of items (digits, letters, words) that can be reproduced in order after a single presentation; usually 7 ± 2. See also **chunk, short-term memory.**

memory trace. The inferred change in the nervous system that persists between the time something is learned and the time it is recalled.

menarche. The first menstrual period, indicative of sexual maturation in a girl. See also **menstruation.**

menstruation. The approximately monthly discharge from the uterus. See also **menarche.**

mental age (MA). A scale unit proposed by Binet for use in intelligence testing. If an intelligence test is properly standardized, a representative group of children of age 6 should earn an average mental age of 6, those of age 7, a mental age of 7, etc. A child whose MA is above his or her chronological age (CA) is advanced; one whose MA lags behind is retarded. See also **chronological age, intelligence quotient.**

mental imagery. Mental pictures used as an aid to memory. *Not* the same as eidetic imagery. See also **eidetic imagery.**

mental retardation. Subnormal intellectual functioning with impairment in social adjustment.

mental rotation. The notion that a mental image of an object can be rotated in the mind in a fashion analogous to rotating the real object.

mesomorph. The second of three types of physique in Sheldon's type theory. Refers to the prominence of bone and muscle, as in the typical athlete. See also **ectomorph, endomorph, type theory.**

method of loci. An aid to serial memory. Verbal material is transformed into mental images, which are then located at successive positions along a visualized route, such as an imaged walk through the house or down a familiar street.

middle ear. The portion of the ear containing the hammer, anvil, and stirrup bones, which connect the eardrum to the oval window of the inner ear.

minor hemisphere. See **right hemisphere.**

mnemonics. A system for improving memory often involving a set of symbols that can substitute for the material to be remembered; for example, in attempting to remember a number sequence, one may translate the sequence into letters of the alphabet that in turn approximate words that are easily remembered.

mode. The most frequent score in a distribution, or the class interval in which the greatest number of cases fall. See also **measure of central tendency.**

model. (1) Miniature systems are often constructed according to a logical, mathematical, or physical model. That is, the principles according to which data are organized and made understandable parallel those of the model; for instance, the piano keyboard is a model for understanding the basilar membrane; the thermostat is a model for the feedback principle of homeostasis. (2) In behavior therapy, one who *models* or performs behaviors that the therapist wishes the patient to imitate.

modeling. In social learning theory, the process by which a child learns social and cognitive behaviors by observing and imitating others. See also **identification.**

mongolism. See **Down's syndrome.**

monochromatism. Total color blindness, the visual system being achromatic. A rare disorder. See also **dichromatism, trichromatism.**

monocular cues. See **distance cues.**

monozygotic (MZ) twins. Twins developed from a single egg. They are always of the same sex and commonly much alike in appearance, although some characteristics may be in mirror image; for example one right-handed, the other left-handed (syn. *identical twins*). See also **dizygotic twins.**

morpheme. The smallest meaningful unit in the structure of a language, whether a word, base, or affix; such as, *man, strange, ing, pro.* See also **phoneme.**

motivation. A general term referring to the regulation of need-satisfying and goal-seeking behavior. See also **motive.**

motive. Any condition of the organism that affects its readiness to start on or continue in a sequence of behavior.

motor area. A projection area in the brain lying in front of the central fissure. Electrical stimulation commonly results in movement, or motor, responses. See also **somatosensory area.**

motor neuron. A neuron, or nerve cell, that conveys messages from the brain or spinal cord to the muscles and glands (syn. *efferent neuron*). See also **sensory neuron.**

myelin sheath. The fatty sheath surrounding certain nerve fibers known as myelinated fibers. Impulses travel faster and with less energy expenditure in myelinated fibers than in unmyelinated fibers.

MZ twins. See **monozygotic twins**.

N

nanometer (nm). A billionth of a meter. Wavelength of light is measured in nanometers.

narcissism. Self-love; in psychoanalytic theory, the normal expression of pregenital development.

narcolepsy. A sleep disturbance characterized by an uncontrollable tendency to fall asleep for brief periods at inopportune times.

narcotics. See **opiates**.

nativism. The view that behavior is innately determined. See also **empiricism**.

nature-nurture issue. The problem of determining the relative importance of heredity (nature) and the result of upbringing in the particular environment (nurture) on mature ability.

need. A physical state involving any lack or deficit within the organism. See also **drive, motive**.

negative incentive. An object or circumstance away from which behavior is directed when the object or circumstance is perceived or anticipated. See also **positive incentive**.

negative reinforcement. Reinforcing a response by the removal of an aversive stimulus. See also **negative reinforcer**.

negative reinforcer. Any stimulus that, when removed following a response, increases the probability of the response. Loud noise, electric shock, and extreme heat or cold classify as negative reinforcers. See also **punishment**.

nerve. A bundle of elongated axons belonging to hundreds or thousands of neurons, possibly both afferent and efferent neurons. Connects portions of the nervous system to other portions and to receptors and effectors. See also **axon, neuron**.

nerve cell. See **neuron**.

neuron. The nerve cell; the unit of a synaptic nervous system.

neurosis (pl. *neuroses*). A mental disorder in which the individual is unable to cope with anxieties and conflicts and develops symptons that he or she finds distressing, such as obsessions, compulsions, phobias, or anxiety attacks. In psychoanalytic theory, neurosis results from the use of defense mechanisms to ward off anxiety caused by unconscious conflicts. No longer a diagnostic category of DSM-III. See also **anxiety disorder, obsessive-compulsive disorder, phobias**.

neurotransmitter. A chemical involved in the transmission of nerve impulses across the synapse from one neuron to another. Usually released from small vesicles in the terminal button of the axon in response to the action potential; diffuses across synapse to influence electrical activity in another neuron. See also **dopamine, epinephrine, norepinephrine, serotonin**.

noncontingent reinforcement. Reinforcement not contingent on a specific response.

noradrenalin. See **norepinephrine**.

norepinephrine. One of the hormones secreted by the adrenal medulla. Its action is in some, but not all, respects similar to that of epinephrine (syn. *noradrenalin*). See also **adrenal gland, epinephrine**.

norm. An average, common, or standard performance under specified conditions; for example, the average achievement test score of 9-year-old children or the average birth weight of male children. See also **social norm, test standardization**.

normal curve. The plotted form of the normal distribution.

normal distribution. The standard symmetrical bell-shaped frequency distribution, whose properties are commonly used in making statistical inferences from measures derived from samples. See also **normal curve**.

nuclei (sing. *nucleus*). A collection of nerve cell bodies grouped in the brain or spinal cord. See also **ganglia**.

null hypothesis. A statistical hypothesis that any difference observed among treatment conditions occurs by chance and does not reflect a true difference. Rejection of the null hypothesis means that we believe the treatment conditions are actually having an effect.

O

object constancy. The tendency to see objects as relatively unchanged under widely altered conditions of illumination, distance, and position. See also **color constancy, lightness constancy, location constancy, shape constancy, size constancy**.

object permanence. A term used by Piaget to refer to the child's realization that an object continues to exist even though it is hidden from view. See also **sensorimotor stage**.

object size. The size of an object as determined from measurement at its surface. When size constancy holds, the observer perceives a distant object as being near its object size. See also **retinal size**.

observational method. Studying events as they occur in nature, without experimental control of variables; for instance, studying the nest-building of birds or observing children's behavior in a play situation. See also **experimental method**.

obsession. A persistent, unwelcome, intrusive thought, often suggesting an aggressive or sexual act. See also **compulsion, obsessive-compulsive disorder**.

obsessive-compulsive disorder. An anxiety disorder taking one of three forms: (1) recurrent thoughts, often disturbing and unwelcome (obsessions); (2) irresistible urges to repeat stereotyped or ritualistic acts (compulsions); (3) both of these in combination. See also **anxiety disorder**.

occipital lobe. A portion of the cerebral hemisphere, behind the parietal and temporal lobes. See also **frontal lobe, parietal lobe, temporal lobe**.

Oedipal stage. In psychoanalysis, an alternative designation of the phallic stage of psychosexual development, because it is at this stage that the Oedipus complex arises. See also **Oedipus complex, psychosexual development**.

Oedipus complex. In psychoanalytic theory, sexual attachment to the parent of the opposite sex, originating as the normal culmination of the infantile period of development.

olfactory epithelium. The portion of specialized skin within the nasal cavity that contains the receptors for the sense of smell.

operant behavior. Behavior defined by the stimulus to which it leads rather than by the stimulus that elicits it; such as behavior leading to reward (syn. *instrumental behavior*). See also *respondent behavior*.

operant conditioning. The strengthening of an operant response by presenting a reinforcing stimulus if, and only if, the response occurs (syn. *instrumental conditioning, reward learning*). See also **classical conditioning.**

opiates. Opium or one or its chemical derivatives: codeine, morphine, or heroin. Central nervous system depressants that relieve pain and produce euphoria, all highly addictive (syn. *narcotics*). See also **heroin.**

opponent-process theory. (1) In perception, the theory that human color vision depends on three pairs of opposing processes: white-black, yellow-blue, and red-green. (2) In emotion, the theory that assumes the brain is organized to oppose or suppress emotional responses, whether they are pleasurable or aversive.

oral behavior. Behavior deriving from the infant's need to suck or, more generally, to be fed through the mouth.

oral stage. In psychoanalysis, the first stage of psychosexual development, in which pleasure is derived from the lips and mouth, as in sucking at the mother's breast. See also **psychosexual development.**

organ of Corti. In the ear, the actual receptor for hearing, lying on the basilar membrane in the cochlea and containing the hair cells where the fibers of the auditory nerve originate. See also **basilar membrane, cochlea.**

orienting reflex. (1) A nonspecific response to change in stimulation involving depression of cortical alpha rhythm, galvanic skin response, pupillary dilation, and complex vasomotor responses (a term introduced by Russian psychologists). (2) Head or body movements that orient the organism's receptors to those parts of the environment in which stimulus changes are occurring.

osmoreceptors. Hypothesized cells in the hypothalamus that respond to dehydration by stimulating the release of ADH by the pituitary gland, which, in turn, signals the kidneys to reabsorb water into the bloodstream. See also **antidiuretic hormone, volumetric receptors.**

otoliths. "Ear stones." See also **vestibular sacs.**

ovarian hormones. See **estrogen.**

overextension. The tendency of a child, in learning a language, to apply a new word too widely; for example, to call all animals "doggie."

overtone. A higher frequency tone, a multiple of the fundamental frequency, that occurs when a tone is sounded by a musical instrument. See also **timbre.**

P

paired-associate learning. The learning of stimulus-response pairs, as in the acquisition of a foreign language vocabulary. When the first member of a pair (the stimulus) is presented, the subject's task is to give the second member (the response).

pancreas. A bodily organ situated near the stomach. As a duct gland, it secretes pancreatic juice into the intestines, but some specialized cells function as an endocrine gland, secreting the hormone insulin into the bloodstream. See also **endocrine gland.**

panic disorder. An anxiety disorder in which the individual has sudden and inexplicable episodes of terror and feelings of impending doom accompanied by physiological symptoms of fear (such as heart palpitations, shortness of breath, muscle tremors, faintness). See also **anxiety, anxiety disorder.**

parallel processing. A theoretical interpretation of information processing in which several sources of information are all processed simultaneously. See also **serial processing.**

paranoid schizophrenia. A schizophrenic reaction in which the patient has delusions of persecution. See also **schizophrenia.**

parapsychology. A subfield of psychology that studies such paranormal phenomena as extrasensory perception and psychokinesis. See also **clairvoyance, extrasensory perception, precognition, psychokinesis, telepathy.**

parasympathetic division. A division of the autonomic nervous system, the nerve fibers of which originate in the cranial and sacral portions of the spinal cord. Active in relaxed or quiescent states of the body and to some extent antagonistic to the sympathetic division. See also **sympathetic division.**

parathyroid glands. Endocrine glands adjacent to the thyroid gland in the neck, whose hormones regulate calcium metabolism, thus maintaining the normal excitability of the nervous system. Parathyroid inadequacy leads to tetany. See also **endocrine gland.**

parietal lobe. A portion of the cerebral hemisphere, behind the central fissure and between the frontal and occipital lobes. See also **frontal lobe, occipital lobe, temporal lobe.**

partial reinforcement. Reinforcing a given response only some proportion of the times it occurs (syn. *intermittent reinforcement*). See also **reinforcement, reinforcement schedule.**

percept. The result of the perceptual process; that which the individual perceives.

perception. The process of becoming aware of objects, qualities, or relations by way of the sense organs. Although sensory content is always present in perception, what is perceived is influenced by set and prior experience so that perception is more than a passive registration of stimuli impinging on the sense organs. See also **subliminal perception.**

perceptual patterning. The tendency to perceive stimuli according to principles such as proximity, similarity, continuity, and closure. Emphasized by Gestalt psychologists. See also **figure-ground perception, Gestalt psychology.**

performance. Overt behavior, as distinguished from knowledge or information not translated into action. The distinction is important in theories of learning.

peripheral nervous system. That part of the nervous system outside the brain and spinal cord; it includes the autonomic nervous system and the somatic nervous system. See also **autonomic nervous system, somatic nervous system.**

personality. The individual characteristics and ways of behaving that in their organization or patterning, account for an individual's unique adjustments to his or her total environment (syn. *individuality*).

personality assessment. (1) Generally, the appraisal of personality by any method. (2) More specifically, personality appraisal through complex observations and judgments, usually based in part on behavior in contrived social situations.

personality disorders. Ingrained, habitual, and rigid patterns of behavior or character that severely limit the individual's adaptive potential; often society sees the behavior as maladaptive whereas the individual does not.

personality dynamics. Theories of personality that stress personality dynamics are concerned with the interactive aspects of behavior (as in conflict resolution), with value hierarchies, with the permeability of boundaries between differentiated aspects of personality, etc. Contrasted with developmental theories, though not incompatible with them.

personality inventory. An inventory for self-appraisal, consisting of many statements or questions about personal characteristics and behavior that the person judges to apply or not to apply to him or her. See also **projective test.**

personality psychologist. A psychologist whose area of interest focuses on classifying individuals and studying the differences between them. This specialty overlaps both developmental and social psychologists to some extent. See also **developmental psychologist, social psychologist.**

phallic stage. In psychoanalysis, that stage of psychosexual development in which gratification is associated with stimulation of the sex organs and the sexual attachment is to the parent of the opposite sex. See also **Oedipal stage, psychosexual development.**

phenomenology. The study of an individual's subjective experience or unique perception of the world. Em-

phasis is on understanding events from the subject's point of view rather than focusing on behavior. See also **humanistic psychology, introspection.**

phenotype. In genetics, the characteristics that are displayed by the individual organism—such as eye color or intelligence—as distinct from those traits that one may carry genetically but not display. See also **genotype.**

pheromones. Special chemicals secreted by many animals that float through the air to attract other members of the same species. They represent a primitive form of communication.

phi phenomenon. Stroboscopic motion in its simpler form. Commonly produced by successively turning on and off two separated stationary light sources; as the first is turned off and the second turned on, the subject perceives a spot of light moving from the position of the first to that of the second. See also **stroboscopic motion.**

phobia. Excessive fear in the absence of real danger. See also **agoraphobia, claustrophobia.**

phobic disorder. An anxiety disorder in which phobias are severe or pervasive enough to interfere seriously with the individual's daily life. See also **anxiety disorder, phobia.**

phoneme. The smallest unit in the sound system of a language; it serves to distinguish utterances from one another. See also **morpheme.**

physiological motive. A motive based on an evident bodily need, such as the need for food or water.

physiological psychologist. A psychologist concerned with the relationship between physiological functions and behavior.

physiology. That branch of biology concerned primarily with the functioning of organ systems within the body.

pitch. A qualitative dimension of hearing correlated with the frequency of the sound waves that constitute the stimulus. Higher frequencies yield higher pitches. See also **loudness, timbre.**

pituitary gland. An endocrine gland joined to the brain just below the hypothalamus. It consists of two parts, the anterior pituitary and the posterior pituitary. The anterior pituitary is the

more important part because of its regulation of growth and of other endocrine glands (syn. *hypophysis*). See also **endocrine gland.**

place theory. A theory of hearing that associates pitch with the place on the basilar membrane where activation occurs. See also **frequency theory, volley principle.**

placebo. An inert substance used in place of an active drug; given to the control group in an experimental test.

pluralistic ignorance. The tendency for persons in a group to mislead each other about a situation; e.g., to define an emergency as a nonemergency because others are remaining calm and are not taking action.

polygenic traits. Characteristics—intelligence, height, emotional stability—determined by many sets of genes.

polygraph. A device that measures simultaneously several physiological responses that accompany emotion; for instance, heart and respiration rate, blood pressure, and GSR. Commonly known as a "lie detector" because of its use in determining the guilt of a subject through responses while he or she answers questions. See also **voice stress analyzer.**

population. The total universe of all possible cases from which a sample is selected. The usual statistical formulas for making inferences from samples apply when the population is appreciably larger than the sample—for instance, 5 to 10 times larger than the sample. See also **sample.**

positive incentive. An object or circumstance toward which behavior is directed when the object or circumstance is perceived or anticipated. See also **negative incentive.**

positive reinforcement. Reinforcing a response by the presentation of a positive stimulus. See also **positive reinforcer.**

positive reinforcer. Any stimulus that, when applied following a response, increases the probability of the response (syn. *reward*). See also **negative reinforcer.**

post-hypnotic amnesia. A particular form of post-hypnotic suggestion in which the hypnotized person forgets what has happened during the hypnosis until signaled to remember. See also **post-hypnotic suggestion.**

post-hypnotic suggestion. A suggestion made to a hypnotized person that she or he will perform in a prescribed way (commonly to a prearranged signal) when no longer hypnotized. The activity is usually carried out without the subject's awareness of its origin. See also **hypnosis.**

precognition. A claimed form of extrasensory perception in which a future event is perceived. See also **clairvoyance, extrasensory perception, telepathy.**

prejudice. A prejudgment that something or someone is good or bad on the basis of little or no evidence; an attitude that is firmly fixed, not open to free and rational discussion, and resistant to change.

preoperational stage. Piaget's second stage of cognitive development (ages 2–7 years). The child can think in terms of symbols but does not yet comprehend certain rules or operations, such as the principle of conservation. See also **conservation.**

preparatory set. See **set.**

primacy effect. (1) In memory experiments, the tendency for initial words in a list to be recalled more readily than later words. (2) In studies of impression formation or attitude change, the tendency for initial information to carry more weight than information received later. See also **recency effect.**

primary abilities. The abilities, discovered by factor analysis, that underlie intelligence test performance. See also **factor analysis.**

primary sex characteristics. The structural or physiological characteristics that make possible sexual union and reproduction. See also **secondary sex characteristics.**

proactive interference. The interference of earlier learning with the learning and recall of new material. See also **retroactive interference.**

probabilistic concept. A concept where every instance need not have every property mentioned in the concept. An example is the concept of *bird*; although many instances will have the

property of flying, some will not (for instance, ostriches).

probe. In studies of memory, a digit or other item from a list to be remembered that is presented as a cue to the subject; for example, the subject could be asked to give the next digit in the list.

product-moment correlation. See **coefficient of correlation.**

progesterone. A female sex hormone produced by the ovaries; it helps prepare the uterus for pregnancy and the breasts for lactation.

program. (1) A plan for the solution of a problem; often used interchangeably with "routine" to specify the precise sequence of instructions enabling a computer to solve a problem. (2) In connection with teaching, a set of materials arranged so as to maximize the learning process.

projection. A defense mechanism by which people protect themselves from awareness of their own undesirable traits by attributing those traits excessively to others. See also **defense mechanism.**

projective test. A personality test in which subjects reveal ("project") themselves through imaginative productions. The projective test gives much freer possibilities of response than the fixed-alternative personality inventory. Examples of projective tests are the Rorschach Test (ink blots to be interpreted) and the Thematic Apperception Test (pictures that elicit stories). See also **personality inventory.**

prolactin. A pituitary hormone associated with the secretion of milk. See also **hormones.**

proposition. A sentence or component of a sentence that asserts something, the predicate, about somebody (or something), the subject. All sentences can be broken into propositions.

PS4R method. A technique for improving memory for a reading assignment. The technique involves six stages: (1) *Preview* the material; (2) Make up *Questions* about the material; (3) *Read* the material; (4) *Reflect* while reading; (5) *Recite* the main points of each section after you read it; and (6) *Review* the main points of the entire assignment.

psi. The special ability said to be pos-

sessed by the subject who performs successfully in experiments on extrasensory perception and psychokinesis. See also **extrasensory perception, psychokinesis.**

psychedelic drugs. See **hallucinogens.**

psychiatric nurse. A nurse specially trained to deal with patients suffering from mental disorders. See also **psychiatrist.**

psychiatric social worker. A social worker trained to work with patients and their families on problems of mental health and illness, usually in close relationship with psychiatrists and clinical psychologists. See also **clinical psychologist, psychiatrist.**

psychiatrist. A medical doctor specializing in the treatment and prevention of mental disorders both mild and severe. See also **clinical psychologist, psychoanalyst.**

psychiatry. A branch of medicine concerned with mental health and mental illness. See also **psychiatrist, psychoanalyst.**

psychoactive drugs. Drugs that affect one's behavior and thought processes. See also **depressants, hallucinogens, stimulants.**

psychoanalysis. (1) The method developed by Freud and extended by his followers for treating neuroses. (2) The system of psychological theory growing out of experiences with the psychoanalytic method.

psychoanalyst. A psychotherapist, usually trained as a psychiatrist, who uses methods related to those originally proposed by Freud for treating neuroses and other mental disorders. See also **clinical psychologist, psychiatrist.**

psychodrama. A form of spontaneous play acting used in psychotherapy.

psychogenic. Caused by psychological factors (such as emotional conflict or faulty habits) rather than by disease, injury, or other somatic cause; functional rather than organic.

psychograph. See **trait profile.**

psychokinesis (PK). A claimed form of mental operation said to affect a material body or an energy system without any evidence of more usual contact or energy transfer; for example, affecting the number that comes up in the throw of dice by a machine through wishing for that number. See also **extrasensory perception.**

psycholinguistics. The study of the psychological aspects of language and its acquisition.

psychological motive. A motive that is primarily learned rather than based on biological needs.

psychology. The science that studies behavior and mental processes.

psychometric function. A curve plotting the percentage of times the subject reports detecting a stimulus against a measure of the physical energy of the stimulus.

psychopathic personality. See **antisocial personality.**

psychopharmacology. The study of the effects of drugs on behavior.

psychophysics. A name used by Fechner for the science of the relationship between mental processes and the physical world. Now usually restricted to the study of the sensory consequences of controlled physical stimulation.

psychosexual development. In psychoanalysis, the theory that development takes place through stages (oral, anal, phallic, latent, genital), each stage characterized by a zone of pleasurable stimulation and appropriate objects of sexual attachment, culminating in normal heterosexual mating. See also **anal stage, genital stage, latency stage, oral stage, phallic stage, psychosocial stages.**

psychosis (pl. *psychoses*). A severe mental disorder in which thinking and emotion are so impaired that the individual is seriously out of contact with reality. No longer a major diagnostic category in DSM-III. See also **psychotic behavior.**

psychosocial stages. A modification by Erikson of the psychoanalytic theory of psychosexual development, giving more attention to the social and environmental problems associated with the various stages of development and adding some adult stages beyond genital maturing. See also **psychosexual development.**

psychosomatic illness. Physical illness that has psychological causes (syn. *psycho-physiological disorder*).

psychosurgery. A form of biological therapy for abnormal behavior. Involves destroying selected areas of the brain, most often the nerve fibers connecting the frontal lobes to the limbic system and/or the hypothalamus.

psychotherapy. Treatment of personality maladjustment or mental illness by psychological means, usually, but not exclusively, through personal consultation. See also **biological therapy.**

psychotic behavior. Behavior indicating gross impairment in reality contact as evidenced by delusions and/or hallucinations. May result from damage to the brain or from a mental disorder such as schizophrenia or a manic-depressive disorder. See also **psychosis.**

puberty. The climax of pubescence, marked by menstruation in girls and the appearance of live sperm cells in the urine of boys. See also **adolescence.**

punishment. A procedure used to decrease the strength of a response by presenting an aversive stimulus whenever the response occurs. Note that such a stimulus when applied would be a punisher; when removed, it would act as a negative reinforcer, reinforcing whatever led to its removal. See also **negative reinforcer.**

R

rapid eye movements (REMs). Eye movements that usually occur during dreaming and that can be measured by attaching small electrodes laterally to and above the subject's eye. These register changes in electrical activity associated with movements of the eyeball in its socket.

rapport. (1) A comfortable relationship between the subject and the tester, ensuring cooperation in replying to test questions. (2) A similar relationship between therapist and patient. (3) A special relationship of hypnotic subject to hypnotist.

rating scale. A device by which raters can record their judgments of others (or of themselves) on the traits defined by the scale.

rationalization. A defense mechanism in which self-esteem is maintained by assigning plausible and acceptable reasons for conduct entered on impulsively or for less acceptable reasons. See also **defense mechanism.**

reaction formation. A defense mechanism in which a person denies a disapproved motive through giving strong expression to its opposite. See also **defense mechanism.**

reaction range. The range of potential intellectual ability specified by a person's genes. According to this concept, the effects of an enriched, average, or a deprived enrivonment will be to change the person's IQ but only within his or her genetically specified reaction range.

reaction time. The time between the presentation of a stimulus and the occurrence of a response. See also **latency.**

receiver-operating-characteristic curve (ROC curve). The function relating the probability of hits and false alarms for a fixed signal level in a detection task. Factors influencing response bias may cause hits and false alarms to vary, but their variation is constrained to the ROC curve. See also **signal detection task.**

recency effect. (1) In memory experiments, the tendency for the last words in a list to be recalled more readily than other list words. (2) In studies of impression formation or attitude change, the tendency for later information to carry more weight than earlier information. See also **primacy effect.**

receptor. A specialized portion of the body sensitive to particular kinds of stimuli and connected to nerves composed of afferent neurons (such as the retina of the eye). Used more loosely, the organ containing these sensitive portions (such as the eye or the ear). See also **afferent neuron, effector.**

recessive gene. A member of a gene pair that determines the characteristic trait or appearance of the individual only if the other member of the pair is recessive. If the other member of the pair is dominant, the effect of the recessive gene is masked. See also **dominant gene.**

recoding. A process for improving short-term memory by grouping items into a familiar unit or chunk.

recurrent inhibition. A process whereby some receptors in the visual system when stimulated by nerve impulses inhibit the firing of other visual receptors, thus making the visual system responsive to changes in illumination.

red-green color blindness. The commonest form of color blindness, a variety of dichromatism. In the two subvarieties, red-blindness and green-blindness, both red and green vision are lacking, but achromatic bands are seen at different parts of the spectrum. See also **color blindness, dichromatism.**

reference group. Any group to which an individual refers for comparing, judging, and deciding on his or her opinions, and behaviors.

refractory phase. The period of temporary inactivity in a neuron after it has fired once.

registration. A term to describe receptive processing in which information is processed but not perceived. See also **perception, subliminal perception.**

regression. A return to the more primitive or infantile modes of response.

rehearsal. The conscious repetition of information in short-term memory, usually involving speech. The process facilitates the short-term recall of information and its transfer to long-term memory. See also **dual-memory theory.**

reincarnation. The belief in rebirth; i.e., that a person has lived before.

reinforcement. (1) In classical conditioning, the experimental procedure of following the conditioned stimulus by the unconditioned stimulus. (2) In operant conditioning, the analogous procedure of following the occurrence of the operant response by the reinforcing stimulus. (3) The process that increases the strength of conditioning as a result of these arrangements. See also **negative reinforcement, partial reinforcement, positive reinforcement.**

reinforcement schedule. A well-defined procedure for reinforcing a given response only some proportion of the time it occurs. See also **partial reinforcement.**

reinforcing stimulus. (1) In classical conditioning, the unconditioned stimulus. (2) In operant conditioning, the stimulus that reinforces the operant (typically, a reward) (syn. *reinforcer*). See also **negative reinforcer, positive reinforcer.**

releaser. A term used by ethologists for a stimulus that sets off a cycle of instinctive behavior. See also **ethologist, instinct.**

reliability. The self-consistency of a test as a measuring instrument. Reliability is measured by a coefficient of correlation between scores on two halves of a test, alternate forms of the test, or retests with the same test; a high correlation signifies high consistency of scores for the population tested. See also **validity.**

REMs. See **rapid eye movements.**

repression. (1) A defense mechanism in which an impulse or memory that might provoke feelings of guilt is denied by its disappearance from awareness. See also **defense mechanism, suppression.** (2) A theory of forgetting.

reserpine. See **antipsychotic drugs.**

resistance. In psychoanalysis, a blocking of free association; a psychological barrier against bringing unconscious impulses to the level of awareness. Resistance is part of the process of maintaining repression. See also **interpretation, repression.**

respondent behavior. A type of behavior corresponding to reflex action, in that it is largely under the control of and predictable from the stimulus (syn. *elicited behavior*). See also **operant behavior.**

response. (1) The behavioral result of stimulation in the form of a movement or glandular secretion. (2) Sometimes, any activity of the organism, including central responses (such as an image or fantasy) regardless of whether the stimulus is identified and whether identifiable movements occur. (3) Products of the organism's activity, such as words typed per minute.

resting potential. The electrical potential across the nerve cell membrane when it is in its resting state (i.e., not responding to other neurons); the inside of the cell membrane is slightly more negative than the outside. See also **action potential.**

reticular system. A system of ill-defined nerve paths and connections within the brain stem, lying outside the well-defined nerve pathways, and important as an arousal mechanism.

retina. The portion of the eye sensitive to light, containing the rods and the cones. See also **cone, rod.**

retinal image. The image projected onto the retina by an object in the visual field.

retinal size. The size of the retinal image of an object; retinal size decreases in direct proportion to the object's distance. See also **object size.**

retrieval. Locating information in memory.

retroactive interference. The interference in recall of something earlier learned by something subsequently learned. See also **proactive interference.**

retrograde amnesia. The inability to recall events that occurred during a time immediately prior to a shock or functional disturbance, although the memory for earlier events remains relatively unimpaired. See also **anterograde amnesia.**

reward. A synonym for *positive reinforcement.* See also **positive reinforcement.**

right hemisphere. The right cerebral hemisphere. Controls the left side of the body and, for most people, spatial and patterned activities (syn. *minor hemisphere*). See also **cerebral hemispheres, corpus callosum, left hemisphere, split-brain subject.**

ROC curve. See **receiver-operating-characteristic curve.**

rod. In the eye, an element of the retina mediating achromatic sensation only; particularly important in peripheral vision and night vision. See also **cone, retina.**

role confusion. A stage of development said by Erikson to characterize many adolescents (and others) in which various identifications have not been harmonized and integrated. See also **identification, identity formation.**

role playing. A method for teaching attitudes and behaviors important to interpersonal relations by having the subject assume a part in a spontaneous play, whether in psychotherapy or in leadership training. See also **psychodrama.**

S

saccade. The quick, almost instantaneous movement of the eyes between eye fixations.

sadism. A pathological motive that leads to inflicting pain on another person. See also **masochism.**

sample. A selection of scores from a total set of scores known as the "population." If selection is random, an unbiased sample results; if selection is nonrandom, the sample is biased and unrepresentative. See also **population.**

saturation. The dimension of color that describes its purity; if highly saturated, it appears to be pure hue and free of gray, but if of low saturation, it appears to have a great deal of gray mixed with it. See also **brightness, hue.**

scaling. Converting raw data into types of scores more readily interpreted, such as ranks, centiles, standard scores.

scapegoat. A form of displaced aggression in which an innocent but helpless victim is blamed or punished as the source of the scapegoater's frustration. See also **displaced aggression.**

schema (pl. *schemata*). Some psychologists use the term to designate specific theoretical ideas about mental events; others use it in a very broad and vaguely defined sense. However used, the term refers to cognitive structures stored in memory that are abstract representations of events, objects, and relationships in the real world. It is a key ingredient of cognitive theories of psychological phenomena. See also **cognitive map.**

schizoid. Having some characteristics that resemble schizophrenia but are less severe. Occurs with higher frequency in families of schizophrenics and thus tends to support a genetic basis for schizophrenia. See also **schizophrenia.**

schizophrenia. A group of mental disorders characterized by major disturbances in thought, perception, emotion, and behavior. Thinking is illogical and usually includes delusional beliefs; distorted perceptions may take the form of hallucinations; emotions are flat or inappropriate; bizarre behavior includes unusual postures, stereotyped movements, and "crazy talk." The individual withdraws from other people and from reality. Inherited biochemical abnormalities are implicated in some cases.

school psychologist. A professional psychologist employed by a school or school system, with responsibility for testing, guidance, research, etc. See also **educational psychologist.**

secondary sex characteristics. The physical features distinguishing the mature male from the mature female, apart from the reproductive organs. In humans, the deeper voice of the male and the growth of the beard are illustrative. See also **primary sex characteristics.**

selective breeding. A method of studying genetic influences by mating animals that display certain traits and selecting for breeding from among their offspring those that express the trait. If the trait is primarily determined by heredity, continued selection for a number of generations will produce a strain that breeds true for that trait.

self-actualization. A person's fundamental tendency toward maximal realization of his or her potentials; a basic concept in humanistic theories of personality such as those developed by Maslow and Rogers.

self-concept. The composite of ideas, feelings, and attitudes people have about themselves.

self-consciousness. A form of heightened self-awareness when an individual is especially concerned about reactions of others to him or her.

self-perception. The individual's awareness of himself or herself; differs from self-consciousness because it may take the form of objective self-appraisal. See also **self-consciousness.**

self-perception theory. The theory that attitudes and beliefs are influenced by observations of one's own behavior; sometimes we judge how we feel by observing how we act (Bem).

self-persuasion. The process by which individuals' opinions change so that they are consistent with their behavior.

self-regulation. In behavior therapy, monitoring one's own behavior and using techniques such as self-reinforcement or controlling stimulus conditions to modify maladaptive behavior. See also **behavior therapy.**

semantic conditioning. A form of classical conditioning in which semantic concepts are used as the conditioned stimuli and generalization occurs through semantic similarities.

semicircular canals. Three curved tubular canals, in three planes, which form part of the labyrinth of the inner ear and are concerned with equilibrium and motion. See also **equilibratory senses.**

sensation. The conscious experience associated with a very simple stimulus like the onset of a tone or light. At one time, the distinction between sensation and perception had great theoretical importance with perception viewed as a combination of sensations. Today, the dividing line between sensation and perception is much less clear, and it seems best to view such experiences as lying along a continuum.

sensorimotor stage. Piaget's first stage of cognitive development (birth–2 years) during which the infant discovers relationships between sensations and motor behavior. See also **object permanence.**

sensory adaptation. The reduction in sensitivity that occurs with prolonged stimulation and the increase in sensitivity that occurs with lack of stimulation; most noted in vision, smell, taste, and temperature sensitivity. See also **dark adaptation, light adaptation.**

sensory neuron. A neuron, or nerve cell, that conveys messages to the brain or spinal cord from the sense receptors informing the organism about events in the environment or within the body (syn. *afferent neuron*). See also **motor neuron, receptor.**

septal area. A portion of the brain deep in the central part, between the lateral ventricles, that appears to yield a state akin to pleasure when stimulated electrically (in a rat, at least).

serial memory search. Comparing a test

stimulus in sequence to each item in short-term memory. See also **short-term memory.**

serial processing. A theoretical interpretation of information processing in which several sources of information are processed in a serial order; only one source being attended to at a time. See also **parallel processing.**

serotonin. A neurotransmitter found in the midbrain and believed to play a role in mental illness, particularly in depression. See also **neurotransmitter.**

sex-linked trait. A trait determined by a gene transmitted on the same chromosomes that determine sex, such as red-green color blindness. See also **X, Y chromosome.**

sex-role standards. Behavior that a society considers appropriate for the individual because of his or her sex.

shape constancy. The tendency to see a familiar object as of the same shape regardless of the viewing angle. See also **object constancy.**

shaping of behavior. Modifying operant behavior by reinforcing only those variations in response that deviate in the direction desired by the experimenter.

shock therapy. See **electroconvulsive therapy.**

short-term memory (STM). The assumption that certain components of the memory system have limited capacity and will maintain information for only a brief time. The definition varies somewhat from theory to theory. See also **long-term memory.**

sibling. A brother or a sister.

sibling rivalry. Jealousy between siblings, often based on their competition for parental affection.

signal detectability theory. A theory of the sensory and decision processes involved in psychophysical judgments, with special reference to the problem of detecting weak signals in noise. See also **signal detection task.**

signal detection task. A procedure whereby the subject must judge on each trial whether a weak signal was embedded in a noise background. Saying "yes" when the signal was presented is called a *hit* and saying "yes" when the signal was not presented is called a *false alarm*. See also **receiver-operating-characteristic curve.**

simple cell. A cell in the visual cortex that responds to a bar of light or straight edge of a particular orientation and location in the visual field. See also **complex cell.**

simulation. The representation of the essential elements of some phenomenon, system, or environment to facilitate its study (often by or involving a computer).

simultaneous conditioning. A classical conditioning procedure in which the CS begins a fraction of a second before the onset of the US and continues with it until the response occurs. See also **delayed conditioning, trace conditioning.**

sine wave. A cyclical wave that when plotted corresponds to the plot of the trigonometric sine function. The sound waves of pure tones yield this function when plotted.

situational attribution. Attributing a person's actions to factors in the situation or environment, as opposed to internal attitudes and motives. See also **dispositional attribution.**

size constancy. The tendency to see a familiar object as of its actual size regardless of its distance. See also **object constancy.**

smooth muscle. The type of muscle found in the digestive organs, blood vessels, and other internal organs. Controlled via the autonomic nervous system. See also **cardiac muscle, striate muscle.**

social learning theory. The application of learning theory to the problems of personal and social behavior (syn. *social behavior theory*).

social norms. A group or community's unwritten rules that govern its members' behavior, attitudes, and beliefs.

social psychologist. A psychologist who studies social interaction and the ways in which individuals influence one another.

socialization. The shaping of individual characteristics and behavior through the training that the social environment provides.

sociology. The science dealing with group life and social organization in literate societies. See also **behavioral sciences.**

somatic nervous system. A division of

the peripheral nervous system consisting of nerves that connect the brain and spinal cord with the sense receptors, muscles, and body surface. See also **autonomic nervous system, peripheral nervous system.**

somatosensory area. Area in the parietal lobe of the brain that registers sensory experiences, such as heat, cold, touch, and pain. Also called *body-sense area*. See also **motor area.**

special factor (s). A specialized ability underlying test scores, especially in tests of intelligence; for example, a special ability in mathematics, as distinct from general intelligence. See also **factor analysis, general factor.**

species-specific behavior. See instinct.

specific hunger. Hunger for a specific food incentive, such as a craving for sweets. See also **hunger drive.**

spindle. An EEG characteristic of stage-2 sleep, consisting of short bursts of rhythmical responses of 13–16 Hz; slightly higher than alpha. See also **electroencephalogram.**

split-brain subject. A person who has had an operation that severed the corpus callosum, thus separating the functions of the two cerebral hemispheres. See also **cerebral hemispheres, corpus callosum.**

spontaneous recovery. Recovery from an illness or improvement without treatment.

S-R psychology. See **stimulus-response psychology.**

stabilized retinal image. The image of an object on the retina when special techniques are used to counteract the minute movements of the eyeball that occur in normal vision. When an image is thus stabilized it quickly disappears, suggesting that the changes in stimulation of retinal cells provided by the eye movements are necessary for vision.

stages of development. Developmental periods, usually following a progressive sequence, that appear to represent qualitative changes in either the structure or the function of the organism (such as Freud's psychosexual stages, Piaget's cognitive stages).

standard deviation. The square root of the mean of the squares of the amount by which each case departs from the mean of all the cases (syn. *root mean square deviation*).

state-dependent learning. Learning that occurs during a particular biological state—such as when drugged—so that it can only be demonstrated or is most effective when the person is put in the same state again.

statistical significance. The trustworthiness of an obtained statisical measure as a statement about reality; for example, the probability that the population mean falls within the limits determined from a sample. The expression refers to the reliability of the statistical finding and not to its importance.

stereoscopic vision. (1) The binocular perception of depth and distance of an object owing to the overlapping fields of the two eyes. (2) The equivalent effect when slightly unlike pictures are presented individually to each eye in a stereoscope. See also **distance cues.**

stereotype. An overgeneralized, often false, belief about a group of people that lets one assume that every member of the group possesses a particular trait; for instance, the false stereotyped belief that all male homosexuals are effeminate.

steroids. Complex chemical substances, some of which are prominent in the secretions of the adrenal cortex and may be related to some forms of mental illness. See also **adrenal gland.**

stimulants. Psychoactive drugs that increase arousal. Amphetamines, cocaine, and caffeine are examples.

stimulus (pl. *stimuli*). (1) Some specific physical energy impinging on a receptor sensitive to that kind of energy. (2) Any objectively describable situation or event (whether outside or inside the organism) that is the occasion for an organisms' response. See also **response.**

stimulus-response (S-R) psychology. A psychological view that all behavior is in response to stimuli and that the appropriate tasks of psychological science are those identifying stimuli, the responses correlated with them, and the processes intervening between stimulus and response.

STM. See **short-term memory.**

striate muscle. Striped muscle; the characteristic muscles controlling the skele-

ton, as in the arms and legs. Activated by the somatic, as opposed to the autonomic, nervous system. See also **cardiac muscle, smooth muscle.**

stroboscopic motion. An illusion of motion resulting from the successive presentation of discrete stimulus patterns arranged in a progression corresponding to movement; such as motion pictures. See also **phi phenomenon.**

subtractive mixture. Color mixture in which absorption occurs so that results differ from additive mixture obtained by mixing projected lights. Subtractive mixture occurs when transparent colored filters are placed one in front of the other and when pigments are mixed. See also **additive mixture.**

superego. In Freud's tripartite division of the personality, that part corresponding most nearly to conscience, controlling through moral scruples rather than by way of social expediency. The superego is said to be an uncompromising and punishing conscience. See also **conscience, ego, id.**

suppression. A process of self-control in which impulses, tendencies to action, and wishes to perform disapproved acts are in awareness but not overtly revealed. See also **repression.**

survey method. A method of obtaining information by questioning a large sample of people.

symbol. Anything that stands for or refers to something other than itself.

sympathetic division. A division of the autonomic nervous system, characterized by a chain of ganglia on either side of the spinal cord, with nerve fibers originating in the thoracic and lumbar portions of the spinal cord. Active in emotional excitement and to some extent antagonistic to the parasympathetic division. See also **parasympathetic division.**

synapse. The close functional connection between the axon of one neuron and the dendrites or cell body of another neuron. See also **excitatory synapse, inhibitory synapse.**

systematic desensitization. A behavior therapy technique in which hierarchies of anxiety-producing situations are imagined (or sometimes confronted in reality) while the person is in a state of

deep relaxation. Gradually the situations become dissociated from the anxiety response. See also **behavior therapy, counter-conditioning.**

T

tachistoscope. An instrument for the brief exposure of words, symbols, pictures, or other visually presented material; sometimes called a T-scope.

telegraphic speech. A stage in the development of speech where the child preserves only the most meaningful and perceptually salient elements of adult speech. The child tends to omit prepositions, articles, prefixes, suffixes, and auxiliary words.

telepathy. The claimed form of extrasensory perception in which what is perceived depends on thought transference from one person to another. See also **clairvoyance, extrasensory perception, precognition.**

temperament. That aspect of personality revealed in the tendency to experience moods or mood changes in characteristic ways; general level of reactivity and energy.

temporal lobe. A portion of the cerebral hemisphere, at the side below the lateral fissure and in front of the occipital lobe. See also **frontal lobe, occipital lobe, parietal lobe.**

terminal button. A specialized knob at the end of the axon that releases a chemical into the synapse to continue transmission of the nerve impulse. See also **neurotransmitter.**

test battery. A collection of tests whose composite scores are used to appraise individiual differences.

test method. A method of psychological investigation. Its advantages are that it allows the psychologist to collect large quantities of useful data from many people, with a minimum of disturbance of their routines of existence and with a minimum of laboratory equipment.

test profile. A chart plotting scores from a number of tests given to the same individual (or group of individuals) in parallel rows on a common scale, with the scores connected by lines, so that high and low scores can be readily perceived. See also **trait profile.**

test standardization. The establishment of norms for interpreting scores by giving a test to a representative population and by making appropriate studies of its reliability and validity. See also **norm, reliability, validity.**

testosterone. The primary male sex hormone produced by the testes; it is important for the growth of the male sex organs and the development of the secondary male sex characteristics. It influences the sex drive. See also **androgens, secondary sex characteristics.**

thalamus. Two groups of nerve cell nuclei located just above the brain stem and inside the cerebral hemispheres. Considered a part of the central core of the brain. One area acts as a sensory relay station, the other plays a role in sleep and waking; this portion is considered part of the limbic system. See also **hypothalamus.**

theory. A set of assumptions (axioms) advanced to explain existing data and predict new events; usually applicable to a wide array of phenomena.

thinking. The ability to imagine or represent objects or events in memory and to operate on these representations. Ideational problem solving as distinguished from solution through overt manipulation.

threshold. The transitional point at which an increasing stimulus or an increasing difference not previously perceived becomes perceptible (or at which a decreasing stimulus or previously perceived difference becomes imperceptible). The value obtained depends in part on the methods used in determining it. See also **absolute threshold, difference threshold.**

thyroid gland. An endocrine gland located in the neck, whose hormone thyroxin is important in determining metabolic rate. See also **endocrine gland.**

timbre. The quality distinguishing a tone of a given pitch sounded by one instrument from that sounded by another. The differences are due to overtones and other impurities. See also **overtone.**

tip-of-the-tongue phenomenon. The experience of failing to recall a word or name when we are quite certain we know it.

T-maze. An apparatus in which an animal is presented with two alternative paths, one of which leads to a goal box. It is usually used with rats and lower organisms. See also **maze.**

tolerance. The need to take more and more of a drug to achieve the same effect. An important factor in physical dependency on drugs.

trace conditioning. A classical conditioning procedure in which the CS terminates before the onset of the US. See also **delayed conditioning, simultaneous conditioning.**

trait. A persisting characteristic or dimension of personality according to which individuals can be rated or measured. See also **trait profile.**

trait profile. A chart plotting the ratings of a number of traits of the same individual on a common scale in parallel rows so that the pattern of traits can be visually perceived (syn. *psychograph*). See also **test profile, trait.**

trait theory. The theory that human personality is most profitably characterized by the scores that an individual makes on a number of scales, each of which represents a trait or dimension of his or her personality.

Transcendental Meditation (TM). A form of meditation practiced by some who follow Hindu yoga. The meditative state is induced by repeating a particular sound or phrase, called a *mantra*, over and over. Each individual has his or her own mantra selected as most appropriate.

transducer. A device such as an electrode or gauge that, in psychophysiology, converts physiological indicators into other forms of energy that can be recorded and measured.

tranquilizer. A drug that reduces anxiety and agitation, such as *Valium*.

transference. In psychoanalysis, the patient's unconsciously making the therapist the object of emotional response, transferring to the therapist responses appropriate to other persons important in the patient's life history.

transsexual. An individual who is physically one sex but psychologically the other. Transsexuals sometimes resort to surgery and hormonal treatment to change their physical gender. They do not, however, consider themselves to be homosexual. See also **homosexual.**

trichromatism. Normal color vision, based on the classification of color vision according to three color systems: black-white, blue-yellow, and red-green. The normal eye sees all three; the colorblind eye is defective in one or two of the three systems. See also **dichromatism, monochromatism.**

Turner's syndrome. An abnormal condition of the sex chromosomes in which a female is born with one X chromosome instead of the usual XX. See also **X chromosome.**

type A and type B. Two contrasting behavior patterns found in studies of coronary heart disease. Type A people are rushed, competitive, aggressive, and overcommitted to achieving; type Bs are more relaxed and feel less pressure. Type As are at risk for heart disease.

type theory. The theory that human subjects can profitably be classified into a small number of classes or types, each class or type having characteristics in common that set its members apart from other classes or types. See also **trait theory.**

U

unconditioned response (UR). In classical conditioning, the response given originally to the unconditioned stimulus used as the basis for establishing a conditioned response to a previously neutral stimulus. See also **conditioned response, conditioned stimulus, unconditioned stimulus.**

unconditioned stimulus (US). In classical conditioning, a stimulus that automatically elicits a response, typically via a reflex, without prior conditioning. See also **conditioned response, conditioned stimulus, unconditioned response.**

unconscious motive. A motive of which the subject is unaware or aware of in distorted form. Because there is no sharp dividing line between conscious and unconscious, many motives have both conscious and unconscious aspects.

unconscious processes. (1) Processes, such as wishes or fears, that might be conscious but of which the subject is unaware. (2) Less commonly, physiological processes of the body (circulation, metabolism, etc.) that go on outside of awareness, preferably called *nonconscious*.

V

validity. The predictive significance of a test for its intended purposes. Validity can be measured by a coefficient of correlation between scores on the test and the scores that the test seeks to predict; i.e., scores on some criterion. See also **criterion, reliability.**

variable. One of the conditions measured or controlled in an experiment. See also **dependent variable, independent variable.**

variance. The square of a standard deviation.

ventromedial hypothalamus (VMH). Area of the hypothalamus important to the regulation of food intake. Electrical stimulation of this area will make an experimental animal stop eating; destruction of brain tissue here produces voracious eating, eventually leading to obesity. See also **hypothalamus, lateral hypothalamus.**

vestibular sacs. Two sacs in the labyrinth of the inner ear, called the *saccule* and *utricle*, which contain the otoliths ("ear stones"). Pressure of the otoliths on the hair cells in the gelatinous material of the utricle and saccule gives us the sense of upright position or departure from it. See also **equilibratory senses.**

vicarious learning. Learning by observing the behavior of others and noting the consequences of that behavior (syn. *observational learning*).

visual area. A projection area lying in the occipital lobe. In humans, damage to this area produces blindness in portions of the visual field corresponding to the amount and location of the damage.

visual cliff. An experimental apparatus with glass over a patterned surface, one half of which is just below the glass and the other half, several feet below. Used to test the depth perception of animals and human infants.

visual field. The total visual array acting on the eye when it is directed toward a fixation point.

VMH. See **ventromedial hypothalamus.**

voice stress analyzer. A device that graphically represents changes in a person's voice associated with emotion. Used in lie detection. See also **polygraph.**

volley principle. A necessary part of the frequency theory of learning; the principle suggests that frequencies above the maximum rate at which a neuron can fire are coded by groups of neurons firing in sequence to give a net rate higher than any single group. See also **frequency theory, place theory.**

volumetric receptors. Hypothesized receptors that regulate water intake by responding to the volume of blood and body fluids. Renin, a substance secreted by the kidneys into the bloodstream, may be one volumetric receptor; it constricts the blood vessels and stimulates the release of the hormone, angiotensin, which acts on cells in the hypothalamus to produce thirst. See also **osmoreceptors.**

voluntary processes. Activities selected by choice and controlled or monitored according to intention or plan. See also **control processes.**

W

Weber's law. A law stating that the difference threshold is proportional to the stimulus magnitude at which it is measured. The law is not accurate over the full stimulus range. See also **difference threshold.**

Wernicke's area. A portion of the left cerebral hemisphere involved in language understanding. Individuals with damage in this area are not able to comprehend words; they can hear words, but they do not know their meanings.

working through. In psychoanalytic therapy, the process of reeducation by having patients face the same conflicts over and over in the consultation room, until they can independently face and master the conflicts in ordinary life.

X

X chromosome. A chromosome that, if paired with another X chromosome, determines that the individual will be a female. If it is combined with a Y chromosome, the individual will be a male. The X chromosome transmits sex-linked traits. See also **chromosome, sex-linked trait, Y chromosome.**

XYY syndrome. An abnormal condition in which a male has an extra Y sex chromosome; reputedly associated with unusual aggressiveness, although the evidence is not conclusive. See also **Y chromosome.**

Y

Y chromosome. The chromosome that, combined with an X chromosome, determines maleness. See also **chromosome, sex-linked trait, X chromosome.**

Young–Helmholtz theory. A theory of color perception that postulates three basic color receptors, a "red" receptor, a "green" receptor, and a "blue" receptor. See also **opponent-process theory.**

Z

zygote. A fertilized ovum or egg. See also **dizygotic twins, monozygotic twins.**

REFERENCES AND INDEX TO AUTHORS OF WORKS CITED

The numbers in boldface following each reference give the text pages on which the paper or book is cited. Citations in the text are made by author and date of publication.

A

ABELSON, R.P. (1968) Computers, polls, and public opinion—some puzzles and paradoxes. *Transaction*, 5:20–27. **550**

ABERNATHY, E.M. (1940) The effect of changed environmental conditions upon the results of college examinations. *Journal of Psychology*, 10:293–301. **240**

ABRAHAMS, D., see WALSTER, ARONSON, and ABRAHAMS (1966).

ABRAHAMS, D., see WALSTER, ARONSON, ABRAHAMS, and ROTTMAN (1966).

ABRAMSON, L.V., see SELIGMAN, ABRAMSON, SEMMEL, and VON BAEYER (1979).

ADAMS, G.R. (1981) The effects of physical attractiveness on the socialization process. In Lucher, G.W., Ribbens, K.A., and McNamara, J.A., Jr. (eds.) *Psychological aspects of facial form*. Craniofacial growth series. Ann Arbor: Univ. of Michigan. **555**

ADAMS, H.E., see TURNER, CALHOUN, and ADAMS (eds.) (1981).

ADAMS, J., see COEHLO, HAMBURG, and ADAMS (1974).

ADAMS, J.L. (1974) *Conceptual blockbusting*. Stanford, Calif.: Stanford Alumni Association. **276**

ADAMS, M., and COLLINS, A. (1979) A schema-theoretic view of reading. In Freedle, R.O. (ed.) *New directions discourse processing*, Vol. 12. Norwood, N.J.: Ablex. **265**

ADAMS, N.E., see BANDURA, ADAMS, HARDY, and HOWELLS (1980).

ADAMS, N.E., see BANDURA, ADAMS, and BEYER (1976).

ADAMS, N., see SMITH, ADAMS, and SCHORR (1978).

ADAMS, R. MCC., SMELSER, N.J., and TREIMAN, D.J. (eds.) (1982) *Behavioral and social science research: A national resource*. Washington, D.C.: National Academy Press. **27**

ADESSO, V.J., see BOONE and ADESSO (1974).

AGNEW, J.W., Jr., see WEBB, AGNEW, and WILLIAMS (1971).

AGRAS, W.S., SYLVESTER, D., and OLIVEAU, D. (1969) The epidemiology of common fears and phobia. *Comprehensive Psychiatry*, 10:151–56. **459**

AGRAS, W.S. (1975) Fears and phobias. *The Stanford Magazine*, 3:59–62. **458, 459**

AINSWORTH, M.D.S. (1979) Infant-mother attachment. *American Psychologist*, 34:932–37. **76**

AINSWORTH, M.D.S., BLEHAR, M.C., WALTERS, E., and WALL, S. (1978) *Patterns of attachment: A psychological study of the strange situation*. Hillsdale, N.J.: Erlbaum. **75**

AJZEN, I., see FISHBEIN and AJZEN (1975).

AKERFELDT, S. (1957) Oxidation of N, N-dimethyl-p-phenylenediamine by serum from patients with mental disease. *Science*, 125:117–19. **475**

ALLEN, A., see BEM and ALLEN (1974).

ALLEN, M.G. (1976) Twin studies of affective illness. *Archives of General Psychiatry*, 35:1476–78. **468**

ALLEN, V.L., and LEVINE, J.M. (1969) Consensus and conformity. *Journal of Experimental and Social Psychology*, 5(4):389. **572**

ALLEN, V.L., and LEVINE, J.M. (1971) Social support and conformity: The role of independent assessment of reality. *Journal of Experimental Social Psychology*, 7:48–58. **572**

ALLPORT, F.H. (1920) The influence of the group upon association and thought. *Journal of Experimental Psychology*, 3:159–82. **562**

ALLPORT, F.H. (1924) *Social psychology*. Boston: Riverside Editions, Houghton Mifflin. **562**

ALTMAN, I., and TAYLOR, D.A. (1973) *Social penetration: The development of interpersonal relationships*. New York: Holt, Rinehart and Winston. **556**

ALTMAN, I., see ZLUTNICK and ALTMAN (1972).

ALTUS, W.C. (1966) Birth order and its sequelae. *Science*, 151:44–49. **92**

AMERICAN PSYCHIATRIC ASSOCIATION (1980) *Diagnostic and statistical manual of mental disorders* (3rd ed.). Washington, D.C.: American Psychiatric Association. **456**

ANAND, B.K., SHARMA, K.W., and DUA, S. (1964) Activity of single neurons in the hypothalamic feeding centers: Effect of glucose. *American Journal of Physiology,* 207:1146–54. **290**

ANASTASI, A. (1982) *Psychological testing* (5th ed.). New York: Macmillan. **381**

ANCOLI-ISRAEL, S. (1981) Sleep apnea and nocturnal myocolonus in a senior population. *Sleep,* 4:349–58. **171**

ANDERSON, J.R. (1976) *Language, memory, and thought.* Hillsdale, N.J.: Erlbaum. **251, 279**

ANDERSON, J.R. (1980) *Cognitive psychology and its implications.* San Francisco: Freeman. **9, 163, 232, 236, 251**

ANDERSON, J.R., and BOWER, G.H. (1973) *Human associative memory.* Washington, D.C.: Winston. **251, 260**

ANDERSON, J.R., and REDER, L.M. (1979) An elaborative processing explanation of depth of processing. In Cermak, L.S., and Craik, F.I.M. (eds.) *Levels of processing in human memory.* Hillsdale, N.J.: Erlbaum. **231**

ANDERSON, N.H., and BUTZIN, C.A. (1978) Integration theory applied to children's judgments of equity. *Developmental Psychology,* 14:593–606. **83**

ANDERSON, R.C., and PICHERT, J.W. (1978) Recall of previously unrecallable information following a shift in perspective. *Journal of Verbal Learning and Verbal Behavior,* 17:1–12. **250**

ANDRES, D., see GOLD, ANDRES, and GLORIEUX (1979). **78**

ANDREWS, K.H., and KANDEL, D.B. (1979) Attitude and behavior. *American Sociological Review,* 44:298–310. **548**

ANDRYSIAK, T., see SCHAEFFER, ANDRYSIAK, and UNGERLEIDER (1981). **180**

ANNIS, R.C., and FROST, B. (1973) Human visual ecology and orientation antistropies in acuity. *Science,* 182:729–31. **157**

ANTONOVSKY, A. (1979) *Health, stress and coping.* San Francisco: Jossey-Bass. **445, 449**

ANTROBUS, J.S., GREENBERG, S., and SINGER, J.L. (1966) Studies in the stream of consciousness: Experi-

mental enhancement and suppression of spontaneous cognitive processes. *Perceptual and Motor Skills,* 23:399–417. **168**

ANTROBUS, J.S., see ARKIN and ANTROBUS (1978). **172**

ANTROBUS, J.S., see ARKIN, ANTROBUS, and ELLMAN (eds.) (1978). **189**

APPLEFIELD, J.M., see STEUER, APPLEFIELD, and SMITH (1971). **328**

ARAKAKI, K., see KOBASIGAWA, ARAKAKI, and AWIGUNI (1966). **88**

AREND, R.A., see MATAS, AREND, and SROUFE (1978). **77**

ARENDT, H. (1963) *Eichmann in Jerusalem: A report on the banality of evil.* New York: Viking Press. **572**

ARIETI, S. (1974) *Interpretation of schizophrenia* (2nd ed.). New York: Basic Books. **472**

ARKIN, A.M., and ANTROBUS, J.S. (1978) The effects of external stimuli applied prior to and during sleep on the sleep experience. In Arkin, A.M., Antrobus, J.S., and Ellman, S.J. (eds.) *The mind in sleep.* Hillsdale, N.J.: Erlbaum. **172**

ARKIN, A.M., ANTROBUS, J.S., and ELLMAN, S.J. (eds.) (1978) *The mind in sleep.* Hillsdale, N.J.: Erlbaum. **189**

ARKIN, A.M., TOTH, M.F., BAKER, J., and HASTEY, J.M. (1970) The frequency of sleep talking in the laboratory among chronic sleep talkers and good dream recallers. *Journal of Nervous and Mental Disease,* 151:369–74. **173**

ARONSON, E. (1980) *The social animal* (3rd ed.). San Francisco: Freeman. **559, 579**

ARONSON, E., and CARLSMITH, J.M. (1963) The effect of the severity of threat on the devaluation of forbidden behavior. *Journal of Abnormal and Social Psychology,* 66:584–88. **549**

ARONSON, E., see LANDY and ARONSON (1969). **554**

ARONSON, E., see WALSTER, ARONSON, and ABRAHAMS (1966). **581**

ARONSON, E., see WALSTER, ARONSON, ABRAHAMS, and ROTTMAN (1966). **554**

ASCH, S.E. (1952) *Social psychology.* Englewood Cliffs, N.J.: Prentice-Hall. **571**

ASCH, S.E. (1955) Opinions and social pressures. *Scientific American,* 193:31–35. **571, 572**

ASCH, S.E. (1958) Effects of group pres-

sure upon modification and distortion of judgments. In Maccoby, E.E., Newcomb, T.M., and Hartley, E.L. (eds.) *Readings in social psychology* (3rd ed.). New York: Holt, Rinehart and Winston. **571, 572**

ASCHOFF, J. (1965) Circadian rhythm of a Russian vocabulary. *Journal of Experimental Psychology: Human Learning and Memory,* 104:126–33. **169**

ATKINSON, J.W., and BIRCH, D. (1978) *An introduction to motivation.* New York: Van Nostrand. **315**

ATKINSON, R.C. (1975) Mnemotechnics in second-language learning. *American Psychologist,* 30:821–28. **239**

ATKINSON, R.C. (1976) Teaching children to read using a computer. *American Psychologist,* 29:169–78. **23, 216**

ATKINSON, R.C., and SHIFFRIN, R.M. (1971) The control of short-term memory. *Scientific American,* 224:82–90. **244**

ATKINSON, R.C., and SHIFFRIN, R.M. (1977) Human memory: A proposed system and its control processes. In Bower, G.H. (ed.) *Human memory: Basic processes.* New York: Academic Press. **244**

ATKINSON, R.C., see DARLEY, TINKLENBERG, ROTH, HOLLISTER, and ATKINSON (1973). **19**

AWIGUNI, A., see KOBASIGAWA, ARAKAKI, and AWIGUNI (1966). **88**

B

BACK, K., see FESTINGER, SCHACHTER, AND BACK (1950).

BADDELEY, A.D., and HITCH, G. (1974) Working memory. In Bower, G.H. (ed.) *The psychology of learning and motivation,* Vol. 8. New York: Academic Press. **228**

BADIA P., CULBERTSON, S., and HARSH, J. (1973) Choice of longer or stronger signalled shock over shorter or weaker unsignalled shock. *Journal of the Experimental Analysis of Behavior,* 19:25–33. **444**

BAER, D., see ROSENFELD and BAER (1969).

BAER, D.J., and CORRADO, J.J. (1974) Heroin addict relationships with parents during childhood and early adolescent years. *Journal of Genetic Psychology,* 124:99–103. **489**

BAER, P.E., and FUHRER, M.J. (1968) Cognitive processes during differential trace and delayed conditioning of the G.S.R. *Journal of Experimental Psychology*, 78:81–88. **200**

BAGCHI, B., see WENGER and BAGCHI (1961).

BAIRD, R.A., see LEWIS, BAIRD, LEVERENZ, and KOYAMA (1982).

BAKER, J., see ARKIN, TOTH, BAKER, and HASTEY (1970).

BALL, T.M., see KOSSLYN, BALL, and REISER (1978).

BANDUCCI, R. (1967) The effect of mother's employment on the achievement, aspirations, and expectations of the child. *Personnel and Guidance Journal*, 46:263–67. **78**

BANDURA, A. (1973) *Aggression: A social learning analysis*. Englewood Cliffs, N.J.: Prentice-Hall. **325, 345**

BANDURA, A. (1977) *Social learning theory*. Englewood Cliffs, N.J.: Prentice-Hall. **324, 345, 394, 418**

BANDURA, A. (1982) The self and mechanisms of agency. In Suls, J. (ed.) *Psychological perspectives on the self*. Hillsdale, N.J.: Erlbaum. **500, 507**

BANDURA, A., ADAMS, N.E., and BEYER, J. (1976) Cognitive processes mediating behavioral change. *Journal of Personality and Social Psychology*, 35:125–39. **503**

BANDURA, A., ADAMS, N.E., HARDY, A.B., and HOWELLS, G.N. (1980) Tests of the generality of self-efficacy theory. *Cognitive Therapy and Research*, 4:39–66. **503**

BANDURA, A., BLANCHARD, E.B., and RITTER, B. (1969) The relative efficacy of desensitization and modeling approaches for inducing behavioral, affective, and attitudinal changes. *Journal of Personality and Social Psychology*, 13:173–99. **502, 503**

BANDURA, A., and MCDONALD, F.J. (1963) Influence of social reinforcement and the behavior of models in shaping children's moral judgments. *Journal of Abnormal and Social Psychology*, 67:274–81. **83**

BANET, B., see HOHMANN, BANET, and WEIKART (1979).

BANYAI, E.I., and HILGARD, E.R. (1976) A comparison of active-alert hypnotic induction with traditional relaxation induction. *Journal of Abnormal Psychology*, 85:218–24. **181**

BARBER, T.X., and WILSON, S.C. (1977) Hypnosis, suggestions, and altered states of consciousness: Experimental evaluation of a new cognitive-behavioral theory and the traditional trance-state therapy of "hypnosis." *Annals of the New York Academy of Sciences*, 296:34–47. **186**

BARBER, T.X., see SPANOS and BARBER (1974).

BARCLAY, J.R., see BRANSFORD, BARCLAY, and FRANKS (1972).

BARD, P. (1934) The neurohumoral basis of emotional reactions. In Murchison, C.A. (ed.) *Handbook of general experimental psychology*. Worcester, Mass.: Clark Univ. Press. **338**

BARKER, R.G., DEMBO, T., and LEWIN, K. (1941) Frustration and regression: An experiment with young children, *University of Iowa Studies in Child Welfare*, 18, No.386. **426**

BARKER, W.B., see SCARR, PAKSTIS, KATZ, and BARKER (1977).

BARNES, P.J., see BEAMAN, BARNES, KLENTZ, and MCQUIRK (1978).

BARON, R.A., and LAWTON, S.F. (1972) Environmental influences on aggression: The facilitation of modeling effects by high ambient temperatures. *Psychonomic Science*, 26:80–82. **324**

BARON, S.H., see ROHRER, BARON, HOFFMAN, and SWANDER (1954).

BARR, A., and FEIGENBAUM, E.A. (1981) *The handbook of artificial intelligence*. Los Altos, Calif.: William Kaufman. **279**

BARTLETT, F.C. (1932) *Remembering: A study in experimental and social psychology*. Cambridge, England: Cambridge Univ. Press. **249**

BARTON, R., see LEWINSOHN, MISCHEL, CHAPLIN, and BARTON (1980).

BATEMAN, F., see SOAL and BATEMAN (1954).

BAUM, A., and VALINS, S. (1977) *Architecture and social behavior: Psychological studies of social density*. Hillsdale, N.J.: Erlbaum. **587**

BAUMRIND, D. (1967) Child care practices anteceding three patterns of preschool behavior. *Genetic Psychology Monographs*, 75:43–88. **86**

BAUMRIND, D. (1972) Socialization and instrumental competence in young children. In Hartup, W.W. (ed.) *The young child: Reviews of research*, Vol. 2. Washington, D.C.: National Association for the Education of Young Children, pp. 202–24. **86**

BAYLEY, N. (1970) Development of mental abilities. In Mussen, P. (ed.) *Carmichael's manual of child psychology*. New York: Wiley, 1:1163–1209. **375**

BEAMAN, A.L., BARNES, P.J., KLENTZ, B., and MCQUIRK, B. (1978). Increasing helping rates through information dissemination: Teaching pays. *Personality and Social Psychology Bulletin*, 4:406–11. **569**

BEAMAN, A.L., see DIENER, FRASER, BEAMAN, and KELEM (1976).

BEBBINGTON, P., see TENNANT, SMITH, BEBBINGTON, and HURRY (1981).

BECK, A.T. (1976) *Cognitive therapy and the emotional disorders*. New York: International Universities Press. **466, 507**

BECK, R.C. (1978) *Motivation: Theories and principles*. Englewood Cliffs, N.J.: Prentice-Hall. **315**

BEDNAR, R.L., and KAUL, T.J. (1978) Experiential group research: Current perspectives. In Garfield, S.L., and Bergin, A.E. (eds.) *Handbook of psychotherapy and behavior change* (2nd ed.). New York: Wiley. **511**

BEE, H.L., see MACCOBY and BEE (1965).

BEERS, C.W. (1908) *A mind that found itself*. New York: Doubleday.

BELL, A.P., WEINBERG, M.S., and HAMMERSMITH, S.K. (1981) *Sexual preference: Its development in men and women*. Bloomington, Ind.: Indiana Univ. Press. **306**

BELL, L.V. (1980) *Treating the mentally ill: From colonial times to the present*. New York: Praeger. **524**

BELL, P.A., FISHER, J.D., and LOOMIS, R.J. (1978) *Environmental psychology*. Philadelphia: W.B. Saunders. **590**

BELLEZZA, F.S., and BOWER, G.H. (1981) Person stereotypes and memory for people. *Journal of Personality and Social Psychology*, 41(5):856–65. **248**

BELLUGI, U., see BROWN, CAZDEN, and BELLUGI (1969).

BEM, D.J. (1970) *Beliefs, attitudes and human affairs*. Belmont, Calif.: Brooks/Cole. **559, 581**

BEM, D.J. (1972) Self-perception theory. *Advances in experimental social psychology*. New York: Academic Press, 6:1–62, **539**

BEM, D.J., and ALLEN, A. (1974) On predicting some of the people some of the time: The search for cross-situational consistencies in behavior. *Psychological Review*, 81:506–20. **415**

BEM, D.J., see BEM and BEM (1977). **535**

BEM, S.L. (1975) Sex-role adaptability: One consequence of psychological androgyny. *Journal of Personality and Social Psychology*, 31:634–43. **541**

BEM, S.L. (1981) Gender schema theory: A cognitive account of sex typing. *Psychological Review*, 88:354–64. **540, 541**

BEM, S.L., and BEM, D.J. (1977) Homogenizing the American woman: The power of an unconscious ideology. In Zimbardo, P., and Maslach, C. (eds.) *Psychology for our times* (2nd ed.). Glenview, Ill: Scott, Foresman. **535**

BEM, S.L., MARTYNA, W., and WATSON, C. (1976) Sex typing and androgyny: Further explorations of the expressive domain. *Journal of Personality and Social Psychology*, 34:1016–23. **540**

BENBOW, C.P., and STANLEY, J.C. (1980) Sex differences in mathematical ability: Fact or artifact? *Science*, 210:1262–64. **364**

BENJAMIN, B., see PARKES, BENJAMIN, and FITZGERALD (1969).

BENSON, H. (1975) *The relaxation response*. New York: Morrow. **189**

BENSON, H., KOTCH, J.B., CRASSWELLER, K.D., and GREENWOOD, M.M. (1977) Historical and clinical considerations of the relaxation response. *American Scientist*, 65:441–43. **175–76**

BERGIN, A.E., see GARFIELD and BERGIN (1978).

BERLIN, B., and KAY, P. (1969) *Basic color terms: Their universality and evolution*. Berkeley and Los Angeles: Univ. of California Press. **259**

BERMAN, L., see YUSSEN and BERMAN (1981).

BERNSTEIN, D.R., see PAUL and BERNSTEIN (1973).

BERNSTEIN, M. (1956) *The search for Bridey Murphy*. New York: Doubleday. **187**

BERNSTEIN, S., see MARKUS, CRANE, BERNSTEIN, and SILADI (1982).

BERNSTEIN, W.M., STEPHAN, W.G., and DAVIS, M.H. (1979) Explaining attributions for achievement: A path analytic approach. *Journal of Personality and Social Psychology*, 37:1810–21. **543**

BERSCHEID, E., and WALSTER, E. (1974) Physical attractiveness. In Berkowitz, L. (ed.) *Advances in experimental social psychology*. New York: Academic Press. **555**

BERSCHEID, E., see CAMPBELL and BERSCHEID (1976). **557**

BERSCHEID, E., see DION and BERSCHEID (1972). **554**

BERSCHEID, E., see DION, BERSCHEID, and WALSTER (1972). **554**

BERSCHEID, E., see SNYDER, TANKE, and BERSCHEID (1977). **555**

BERZINS, J.I., ROSS, W.F., ENGLISH, G.E., and HALEY, J.V. (1974) Subgroups among opiate addicts: A typological investigation. *Journal of Abnormal and Social Psychology*, 83:65–73. **489**

BEVER, T.G., see FODOR, BEVER, and GARRETT (1974).

BEVER, T.G., see TERRACE, PETITTO, SANDERS, and BEVER (1979).

BEYER, J., see BANDURA, ADAMS, and BEYER (1976).

BIEHLER, R.F. (1976) *Child development: An introduction*. Boston: Houghton Mifflin. **101**

BIERBRAUER, G., see ROSS, BIERBRAUER, and HOFFMAN (1976).

BIERBRAUER, G.A. (1973) *Attribution and perspective: Effects of time, set, and role on interpersonal inference*. Unpublished doctoral dissertation, Stanford University. **580**

BINET, A., and SIMON, T. (1905) New methods for the diagnosis of the intellectual level of subnormals. *Annals of Psychology*, 11:191. **366**

BIRCH, D., see ATKINSON and BIRCH (1978).

BIRDSALL, T.G., see GREEN and BIRDSALL (1978).

BIRNBAUM, J.A. (1975) Life patterns and self-esteem in gifted family oriented and career committed women. In Mednick, M.S., Tangri, S.S., and Hoffman, L.W. (eds.) *Women and achievement*, 396–419. Washington: Hemisphere Publisher. **78**

BISHOP, G.D., see HAMILTON and BISHOP (1976).

BJORK, R.A., and WHITTEN, W.B. (1974) Recency-sensitive retrieval in long-term free recall. *Cognitive Psychology*, 6:173–89. **245**

BLACK, J.B., see BOWER, BLACK, and TURNER (1979).

BLAKEMORE, C., and COOPER, G.F. (1970) Development of the brain depends on the visual environment. *Nature*, 228:477–78. **156**

BLANCHARD, E.B., see BANDURA, BLANCHARD, and RITTER (1969).

BLANCHARD, F.A., WEIGEL, R.H., and COOK, S.W. (1975) The effect of relative competence of group members upon interpersonal attraction in cooperating interracial groups. *Journal of Personality and Social Psychology*, 32:519–30. **535**

BLEHAR, M.C., see AINSWORTH, BLEHAR, WALTERS, and WALL (1979).

BLOCK, J. (1971) *Lives through time*. Berkeley, Calif.: Bancroft Books. **411, 412**

BLOCK, J. (1977) Recognizing the coherence of personality. In Magnusson, D., and Endler, N.S. (eds.) *Interactional psychology: Current issues and future prospects*. New York: LEA/Wiley. **412**

BLOCK, J. (1981) Some enduring and consequential structures of personality. In Rabin, A.I., Aronoff, J., Barclay, A.M., and Zucker, R.A. (eds.) *Further explorations in personality*. New York: Wiley-Interscience. **411**

BLOCK, J., BUSS, D.M., BLOCK, J.H., and GJERDE, P.F. (1981) The cognitive style of breadth of categorization: Longitudinal consistency of personality correlates. *Journal of Personality and Social Psychology*, 40:770–79. **417**

BLOCK, J.H. (1980) Another look at sex differentiation in the socialization behavior of mothers and fathers. In Denmark, F., and Sherman, J. (eds.) *Psychology of women: Future directions of research*. New York: Psychological Dimensions. **88**

BLOCK, J.H., see BLOCK, BUSS, BLOCK, and GJERDE (1981).

BLOOD, R.O. (1967) *Love match and arranged marriage*. New York: Free Press. **557**

BLOOM, L.M., HOOD, L., and LIGHTBOWN, P. (1974) Imitation in language development: If, when and why. *Cognitive Psychology*, 6:380–420. **268**

BLUM, R., and ASSOCIATES (1972) *Horatio Alger's children*. San Francisco: Jossey-Bass. **489**

BOCK, R.D., and MOORE, E. (1982) *Advantage and disadvantage: Vocational pros-*

pects of American young people. Techincal Report, National Opinion Research Center, University of Chicago, Chicago, Ill. **364**

BODEN, M. (1977) *Artificial intelligence and natural man.* New York: Basic Books. **163, 279**

BOLLES, R.C. (1975) *Theory of motivation* (2nd ed.). New York: Harper and Row. **283, 315, 345**

BONNO, B., see LEVENSON, BURFORD, BONNO, and LOREN (1975).

BONSALL, R.W., see MICHAEL, BONSALL, and WARNER (1974).

BOONE, J.A., and ADESSO, V.J. (1974) Racial differences on a black intelligence test. *Journal of Negro Education,* 43:429–536. **362**

BOOTH, A., and WELCH, S. (1974) *Crowding and urban crime rates.* Paper presented at the meeting of the Midwest Sociological Association, Omaha, Neb. **586**

BOOTH, A., and WELCH, S. (1973) *The effects of crowding: A cross-national study.* Unpublished manuscript, Ministry of State of Urban Affairs, Ottawa, Canada. **586**

BOOTHE, J., see RASKIN, SCHULTERBRANDT, BOOTHE, REATIG, and MCKEON (1970).

BOUCHARD, T.J. (1976) Genetic factors in intelligence. In Kaplan, A.R. (ed.) *Human behavior genetics.* Springfield, Ill.: Charles Thomas, 164–95. **374**

BOUCHARD, T.J., HESTON, L., ECKERT, E., KEYES, M., and RESNICK, S. (1981) The Minnesota study of twins reared apart: Project description and sample results in the developmental domain. *Twin Research 3: Intelligence, Personality, and Development:* 227–33. New York: Alan R. Liss. **389**

BOUCHARD, T.J., JR., and MCGUE, M. (1981) Familial studies of intelligence: A review. *Science,* 212:1055–59. **373**

BOURNE, L.E., DOMINOWSKY, R.L., and LOFTUS, E.F. (1979) *Cognitive processes.* Englewood Cliffs, N.J.: Prentice-Hall. **257**

BOWE-ANDERS, C., see ROFFWARG, HERMAN, BOWE-ANDERS, and TAUBER (1978).

BOWER, G.H. (1972) Mental imagery and associative learning. In Gregg, L.W. (ed.) *Cognition in learning and memory.* New York: Wiley. **230**

BOWER, G.H. (1981) Mood and memory. *American Psychologist,* 36:129–48. **237**

BOWER, G.H., BLACK, J.B., and TURNER, T.R. (1979) Scripts in memory for text. *Cognitive Psychology,* 11:177–220. **249**

BOWER, G.H., CLARK, M., WINZENZ, D., and LESGOLD, A. (1969) Hierarchical retrieval schemes in recall of categorized word lists. *Journal of Verbal Learning and Verbal Behavior,* 8:323–43. **234**

BOWER, G.H., and CLARK, M.C. (1969) Narrative stories as mediators for serial learning. *Psychonomic Science,* 14:181–82. **241**

BOWER, G.H., and HILGARD, E.R. (1981) Theories of learning (5th ed.). Englewood Cliffs, N.J.: Prentice-Hall. **27, 219, 251**

BOWER, G.H., and SPRINGSTON, F. (1970) Pauses as recoding points in letter series. *Journal of Experimental Psychology,* 83:421–30. **229**

BOWER, G.H., see ANDERSON and BOWER (1973).

BOWER, G.H., see BELLEZZA and BOWER (1981).

BOWER, G.H., see BOWER and BOWER (1976).

BOWER, S.A., and BOWER, G.H. (1976) *Asserting yourself.* Reading, Mass.: Addison-Wesley. **525**

BOWER, T.G.R. (1981) *Development in infancy* (2nd ed.). San Francisco: Freeman. **101, 158**

BOWLBY, J. (1973) Separation. *Attachment and loss,* Vol. 2. New York: Basic Books. **73, 75**

BOWMAN, C.H., and FISHBEIN, M. (1978) Understanding public reaction to energy proposals: An application of the Fishbein model. *Journal of Applied Social Psychology,* 8:319–40. **548**

BRAINE, M.D.S. (1976) Children's first word combinations. *Monographs of the Society for Research in Child Development,* 41 (Serial No. 164). **266**

BRAND, R.J., see ROSENMAN, BRAND, JENKINS, FRIEDMAN, STRAUS, and WRUM (1975).

BRANDT, U., see EYFERTH, BRANDT, and WOLFGANG (1960).

BRANSFORD, J.D., BARCLAY, J.R., and FRANKS, J.J. (1972) Sentence memory: A constructive versus interpretive approach. *Cognitive Psychology,* 3:193–209. **246**

BRANSFORD, J.D., and JOHNSON, M.K. (1973) Considerations of some problems of comprehension. In Chase,

W.G. (ed.) *Visual information processing.* New York: Academic Press. **249**

BRELAND, K., and BRELAND, M. (1966) *Animal behavior.* New York: Macmillan. **205**

BRELAND, M., see BRELAND and BRELAND (1966).

BRENNER, M.H. (1982) Mental illness and the economy. In Parron, D.L., Solomon, F., and Jenkins, C.D., (eds.) *Behavior, health risks, and social disadvantage.* Washington, D.C.: National Academy Press.

BRICKER, W.A., see PATTERSON, LITTMAN, and BRICKER (1967).

BRIGGS, J.L. (1970) *Never in anger.* Cambridge, Mass.: Harvard Univ. Press. **62**

BRINBERG, D. (1979) An examination of the determinants of intention and behavior: A comparison of two models. *Journal of Applied Social Psychology,* 9:560–75. **548**

BROADBENT, D.E. (1957) Effects of noise on behavior. In Harris, C.M. (ed.) *Handbook of noise control.* New York: McGraw-Hill. **584**

BRODIE, M., see TESSER and BRODIE (1971).

BRONSON, G.W. (1972) Infants' reactions to unfamiliar persons and novel objects. *Monographs of the Society for Research in Child Development,* 37:(3, Serial No. 148). **74**

BROOK, D.W., see JERSILD, BROOK, and BROOK (1978).

BROOK, J.S., see JERSILD, BROOK, and BROOK (1978).

BROTZMAN, E., see HOFLING, BROTZMAN, DALRYMPLE, GRAVES, and PIERCE (1966).

BROWN, A.E. (1936) Dreams in which the dreamer knows he is asleep. *Journal of Abnormal Psychology,* 31:59–66. **172**

BROWN, D.P. (1977) A model for the levels of concentrative meditation. *International Journal of Clinical and Experimental Hypnosis,* 25:236–73. **175**

BROWN, J.S., see SLEEMAN and BROWN (eds.) (1982).

BROWN, P.L., and JENKINS, H.M. (1968) Autoshaping of the pigeon's key-peck. *Journal of the Experimental Analysis of Behavior,* 11:1–8. **206**

BROWN, R. (1973) *A first language: The early stages.* Cambridge, Mass.: Harvard Univ. Press. **267**

BROWN, R., CAZDEN, C.B., and BELLUGI, U. (1969) The child's grammar from I to III. In Hill, J.P. (ed.) *Minnesota symposium on child psychology*, Vol. 2. Minneapolis: Univ. of Minnesota Press. **268**

BROWN, R., see SACHS, BROWN, and SALERNO (1976).

BROWN, R.W., and MCNEILL, D. (1966) The "tip-of-the-tongue" phenomenon. *Journal of Verbal Learning and Verbal Behavior*, 5:325–37. **232**

BROWN, S.W. (1970) *A comparative study of maternal employment and nonemployment*. Unpublished doctoral dissertation. University Microfilms, 70-8610. Mississippi State University. **78**

BROWN, T.S., and WALLACE, P.M. (1980) *Physiological psychology*. New York: Academic Press. **59**

BRUCKEN, L., see KUHN, NASH, and BRUCKEN (1978).

BRYAN, J.H., and TEST, M.A. (1967) Models and helping: Naturalistic studies in aiding behavior. *Journal of Personality and Social Psychology*, 6:400–707. **569**

BUCK, R. (1976) *Human motivation and emotion*. New York: Wiley. **345**

BUGELSKI, R., see MILLER and BUGELSKI (1948).

BURFORD, B., see LEVENSON, BURFORD, BONNO, and LOREN (1975).

BURT, D.R., see CREESE, BURT, and SNYDER (1978).

BUSCHKE, H., see KINTSCH and BUSCHKE (1969).

BUSS, A.H. (1966) *Psychopathology*. New York: Wiley. **484**

BUSS, A.H., and PLOMIN, R. (1975) *A temperament theory of personality development*. New York: Wiley. **385**

BUSS, D.M., see BLOCK, BUSS, BLOCK, and GJERDE (1981).

BUTCHER, J.N., see KENDALL and BUTCHER (1982).

BUTZIN, C.A., see ANDERSON and BUTZIN (1978).

BYCK, R. (ed.) (1974) *Cocaine papers*. New York: Stonehill. **189**

C

CAGGIULA, A.R. (1967) Specificity of copulation reward systems in the posterior hypothalamus. *Proceedings of the 75th Convention, American Psychological Association*, 125–26. **301**

CAGGIULA, A.R., and HOEBEL, B.G. (1966) A "copulation-reward site" in the posterior hypothalamus. *Science*, 153: 1284–85. **301**

CALHOUN, J.B. (1962) Population density and social pathology. *Scientific American*, 206:139–48. **585**

CALHOUN, K.S., see TURNER, CALHOUN, and ADAMS (1981).

CALVIN, W.H., and OJEMANN, G.A. (1980) *Inside the brain*. New York: New American Library. **49**

CAMPBELL, B., and BERSCHEID, E. (1976) The perceived importance of romantic love as a determinant of marital choice: Kephart revisited ten years later. Unpublished manuscript. **557**

CAMPBELL, D.T., see JACOBS and CAMPBELL (1961).

CAMPBELL, E.Q., see COLEMAN, CAMPBELL, HOBSON, MCPARTLAND, MOODY, WEINFELD, and YORK (1966).

CAMPBELL, H.J. (1973) *The pleasure areas*. London: Eyre Methuen. **211**

CANNON, W.B. (1927) The James–Lange theory of emotions: A critical examination and an alternative theory. *American Journal of Psychology*, 39:106–24. **338**

CANTOR, N., and MISCHEL, W. (1979) Prototypes in person perception. In Berkowitz, L. (ed.) *Advances in experimental social psychology*, Vol. 12. New York: Academic Press. **530**

CANTRIL, H., see FREE and CANTRIL (1967).

CAPUTO, C., see NISBETT, CAPUTO, LEGANT, and MARACEK (1973).

CARLSMITH, J.M., DORNBUSCH, S.M., and GROSS, R.T. (1983) Paper in preparation. Stanford University. **90**

CARLSMITH, J.M., see ARONSON and CARLSMITH (1963).

CARLSMITH, J.M., see FESTINGER and CARLSMITH (1959).

CARLSMITH, J.M., see FREEDMAN, SEARS, and CARLSMITH (1981).

CARLSON, N.R. (1981) *Physiology of behavior* (2nd ed.). Boston: Allyn and Bacon. **59**

CARLSON, R. (1971) Where is the person in personality research? *Psychological Bulletin*, 75:203–19. **394**

CARPENTER, G.C. (1973) Differential response to mother and stranger within the first month of life. *Bulletin of the British Psychological Society*, 16:138. **66**

CARPENTER, P.A., see DANEMAN and CARPENTER (1981).

CARPENTER, P.A., see JUST and CARPENTER (1980).

CARR, K.D., and COONS, E.E. (1982) Rats self-administered nonrewarding brain stimulation to ameliorate aversion. *Science*, 215:1516–17. **211**

CARROL, E.N., ZUCKERMAN, M., and VOGEL, W.H. (1982) A test of the optimal level of arousal theory of sensation seeking. *Journal of Personality and Social Psychology*, 42:572–75. **312**

CARSKADON, M.A., MITLER, M.M., and DEMENT, W.C. (1974) A comparison of insomniacs and normals: Total sleep time and sleep latency. *Sleep Research*, 3:130. **170**

CARTERETTE, E.C., and FRIEDMAN, M.P. (eds.) (1975) *Historical and philosophical roots of perception*. Handbook of perception series, Vol. 1. New York: Academic Press. **131**

CARTERETTE, E.C., and FRIEDMAN, M.P. (eds.) (1975) *Psychophysical judgment and measurement*. Handbook of perception series, Vol. 2. New York: Academic Press. **131**

CARTERETTE, E.C., and FRIEDMAN, M.P. (eds.) (1975) *Biology of perceptual systems*. Handbook of perception series, Vol. 3. New York: Academic Press. **131**

CARTERETTE, E.C., and FRIEDMAN, M.P. (eds.) (1977) *Seeing*. Handbook of perception series, Vol. 5. New York: Academic Press. **131**

CARTERETTE, E.C., and FRIEDMAN, M.P. (eds.) (1977) *Language and speech*. Handbook of perception series, Vol. 7. New York: Academic Press. **131**

CARTERETTE, E.C., and FRIEDMAN, M.P. (eds.) (1978) *Hearing*. Handbook of perception series, Vol. 4. New York: Academic Press. **131**

CARTERETTE, E.C., and FRIEDMAN, M.P. (eds.) (1978) *Tasting and smelling*. Handbook of perception series, Vol. 6a. New York: Academic Press. **131**

CARTERETTE, E.C., and FRIEDMAN, M.P. (eds.) (1978) *Space and object perception*. Handbook of perception series, Vol. 8. New York: Academic Press. **131**

CARTERETTE, E.C., and FRIEDMAN, M.P. (eds.) (1978) *Perceptual processing*. Handbook of perception series, Vol. 9. New York: Academic Press. **131**

CARTERETTE, E.C., and FRIEDMAN, M.P. (eds.) (1978) *Perceptual ecology*. Handbook of perception series, Vol. 10. New York: Academic Press. **131**

CARTERETTE, E.C., and FRIEDMAN, M.P. (eds.) (1979) *Feeling and hurting.* Handbook of perception series, Vol. 6b. New York: Academic Press. **131**

CARTWRIGHT, R.D. (1974) The influence of a conscious wish on dreams: A methodological study of dream meaning and function. *Journal of Abnormal Psychology*, 83:387–93. **173**

CARTWRIGHT, R.D. (1978) *A primer on sleep and dreaming.* Reading, Mass.: Addison-Wesley. **172, 189**

CARVER, R.P. (1981) *Reading comprehension and reading theory.* Springfield, Ill.: Charles C. Thomas. **154**

CASE, R. (1982) *Intellectual development: A systematic reinterpretation,* in press. **73**

CASSEM, N.H., see HACKETT and CASSEM (1970).

CATTELL, R.B. (1973) Personality pinned down. *Psychology Today*, 7:40–46. **391**

CAZDEN, C.B., see BROWN, CAZDEN, and BELLUGI (1969).

CHANCE, J.E., see ROTTER, CHANCE, and PHARES (1972).

CHAPLIN, W., see LEWINSOHN, MISCHEL, CHAPLIN, and BARTON (1980).

CHAPMAN, J., see MCGHIE and CHAPMAN (1961).

CHASE, W.G., and SIMON, H.A. (1973) The mind's eye in chess. In Chase, W.G. (ed.) *Visual information processing.* New York: Academic Press. **277**

CHASE, W.G., see ERICSSON, CHASE, and FALOON (1980).

CHAUDURI, H. (1965) *Philosophy of meditation.* New York: Philosophical Library. **175**

CHEIN, I., GERARD, D.L., LEE, R.S., and ROSENFELD, E. (1964) *The road to H.* New York: Basic Books. **177**

CHEN, S.C. (1937) Social modification of the activity of ants in nest-building. *Physiological Zoology*, 10:420–36. **562**

CHESS, S., see THOMAS and CHESS (1977).

CHIPMAN, S., see SHEPARD and CHIPMAN (1970).

CHODOROW, N. (1978) *The reproduction of mothering.* Berkeley and Los Angeles: Univ. of California Press. **398**

CHOMSKY, N. (1957) *Syntatic structures.* The Hague: Mouton. **597**

CHOMSKY, N. (1965) *Aspects of the theory of syntax.* Cambridge, Mass.: M.I.T. Press. **264**

CHOMSKY, N. (1972) *Language and mind*

(2nd ed.). New York: Harcourt Brace Jovanovich. **270, 279**

CHUTE, D., see HO, CHUTE, and RICHARDS (1977).

CLARK, E.V. (1973b) Non-linguistic strategies and the acquisition of word meaning. *Cognition*, 2:161–82. **266**

CLARK, E.V. (1973a) What's in a word? On the child's acquisition of semantics in his first language. In Moore, T.E. (ed.) *Cognitive development and the acquisition of language.* New York: Academic Press. **266**

CLARK, E.V., see CLARK and CLARK (1977).

CLARK, H.H. (1971) More about "adjectives, comparatives, and syllogisms": A reply to Huttenlocher and Higgins. *Psychological Review*, 78:505–14. **276**

CLARK, H.H., and CLARK, E.V. (1977) *Psychology and language: An introduction to psycholinguistics.* New York: Harcourt Brace Jovanovich. **258, 260, 279**

CLARK, M., see BOWER, CLARK, WINZENZ, and LESGOLD (1969).

CLARK, M.C., see BOWER and CLARK (1969).

CLARKE, R.W., see MINIUM and CLARKE (1982).

CLARKE-STEWART, A.K. (1973) Interactions between mothers and their young children: Characteristics and consequences. *Monographs of the Society for Research in Child Development*, 38. **77**

CLAYTON, K.N. (1964) T-maze choice-learning as a joint function of the reward magnitudes of the alternatives. *Journal of Comparative and Physiological Psychology*, 58:333–38. **210**

CLAYTON, R.R., see O'DONNELL and CLAYTON (1982).

CLEMENT, P.W., see WALKER, HEDBERG, CLEMENT, and WRIGHT (1981).

CLINE, V.B., CROFT, R.C., and COURRIER, S. (1973) The desensitization of children to television violence. *Journal of Personality and Social Psychology*, 27:360–65. **330**

COATES, B., see HARTUP and COATES (1967).

COBB, S. (1976) Social support as a moderator of life stress. *Psychosomatic Medicine*, 38:300–14. **445**

COBBIN, D.M., REQUIN-BLOW, B., WILLIAMS, L.R., and WILLIAMS, W.O. (1979) Urinary MHPG levels and tricyclic antidepressant drug selection. *Archives of General Psychiatry*, 36:1111–15. **469**

COE, W.C., and SARBIN, T.R. (1977) Hypnosis from the standpoint of a contextualist. *Annals of the New York Academy of Sciences*, 296:2–13. **186**

COEHLO, G., HAMBURG, D., and ADAMS, J. (eds.) (1974) *Coping and adaptation.* New York: Basic Books. **449**

COHEN, H.D., see EVANS, COOK, COHEN, ORNE, and ORNE (1977).

COHEN, S., EVANS, G.W., KRANTZ, D.S., and STOKOLS, D. (1980) Physiological, motivational, and cognitive effects of aircraft noise on children: Moving from the laboratory to the field. *American Psychologist*, 35:231–43. **585**

COHEN, S., EVANS, G.W., KRANTZ, D.S., STOKOLS, D., and KELLY, S. (1981) Aircraft noise and children: Longitudinal and cross-sectional evidence on adaptation to noise and the effectiveness of noise abatement. *Journal of Personality and Social Psychology*, 40:331–45. **585**

COLE, M. (1981) Mind as a cultural achievement: Implications for IQ testing. *Annual Report, 1979–1980: Research and Clinical Center for Child Development.* Faculty of Education, Hokkaido University, Sapporo, Japan. **363**

COLEMAN, J. (1980) *Abnormal psychology and modern life* (6th ed.). New York: Scott, Foresman. **449, 491**

COLEMAN, J.S., CAMPBELL, E.Q., HOBSON, C.J., MCPARTLAND, J., MOODY, A.M., WEINFELD, F.D., and YORK, R.L. (1966) *Equality of Educational Opportunity,* Supplemental Appendix 9.10. Washington, D.C.: U.S. Office of Department of Health, Education, and Welfare. **364**

COLLEGE ENTRANCE EXAMINATION BOARD (1978) *Taking the SAT.* Educational Testing Service, Princeton, N.J. **351**

COLLINS, A., see ADAMS and COLLINS (1979).

COLLINS, A.M., and QUILLIAN, M.R. (1969) Retrieval time from semantic memory. *Journal of Verbal Learning and Verbal Behavior*, 8:240–48. **255**

COLLINS, M.E., see DEUTSCH and COLLINS (1951).

CONDRY, J., and CONDRY, S. (1976) Sex differences: A study in the eye of the beholder. *Child Development*, 47:812–19. **88**

CONDRY, S., see CONDRY and CONDRY (1976).

CONGER, J.J. (1977) *Adolescence and youth: Psychological development in a changing world* (2nd ed.). New York: Harper and Row. **101**

CONGER, J.J., see MUSSEN, CONGER, and KAGAN (1982).

CONGER, J.J., see SAWREY, CONGER, and TURRELL (1956).

CONRAD, R. (1964) Acoustic confusions in immediate memory. *British Journal of Psychology*, 55:75–84. **223**

CONSUMERS UNION (1980) *The medicine show* (5th ed.). Mount Vernon, N.Y.: Consumers Union of U.S., Inc. **581**

COOK, M.R., see EVANS, COOK, COHEN, ORNE, and ORNE (1977).

COOK, S.W. (1970) Motives in a conceptual analysis of attitude-related behavior. In Arnold, W.J., and Levine, D. (eds.) *Nebraska symposium on motivation, 1969.* Lincoln: Univ. of Nebraska Press. **536**

COOK, S.W. (1978) Interpersonal and attitudinal outcomes in cooperating interracial groups. *Journal of Research and Development in Education*, 12. **533, 536**

COOK, S.W., see BLANCHARD, WEIGEL, and COOK (1975).

COONS, E.E., see CARR and COONS (1982).

COOPER, F., see LIBERMAN, COOPER, SHANKWEILER, and STUDDERT-KENNEDY (1967).

COOPER, G.F., see BLAKEMORE and COOPER (1970).

COOPER, J., see FAZIO, ZANNA, and COOPER (1977).

COOPER, J., see WORD, ZANNA, and COOPER (1974).

COOPER, L.A., and SHEPARD, R.N. (1973) Chronometric studies of the rotation of mental images. In Chase, W.G. (ed.) *Visual information processing.* New York: Academic Press. **274, 275**

COOPER, L.A., see SHEPARD and COOPER (1982).

COOPER, L.M. (1979) Hypnotic amnesia. In Fromm, E., and Shor, R.E. *Hypnosis: Developments in research and new perspectives* (rev. ed.). New York: Aldine. **183**

CORBIT, J.D., see SOLOMON and CORBIT (1974).

CORDUA, G.D., MCGRAW, K.O., and DRABMAN, R.S. (1979) Doctor or nurse: Children's perception of sex-typed occupations. *Child Development,* 50:590–93. **89**

COREN, S., PORAC, C., and WARD, L.M. (1978) *Sensation and perception.* New York: Academic Press. **131, 163**

CORNSWEET, T.N. (1970) *Visual perception.* New York: Academic Press. **117, 118**

CORRADO, J.J., see BAER and CORRADO (1974).

COSTA, P., see MADDI and COSTA (1972).

COTMAN, C.W., and MCGAUGH, J.L. (1980) *Behavioral neuroscience: An introduction.* New York: Academic Press. **59, 243**

COTTRELL, N.B. (1972) Social facilitation. In McClintock, C.G. (ed.), *Experimental social psychology.* New York: Holt, Rinehart and Winston. **563**

COTTRELL, N.B., RITTLE, R.H., and WACK, D.L. (1967) Presence of an audience and list type (competitional or noncompetitional) as joint determinants of performance in paired-associates learning. *Journal of Personality,* 35:425–34. **563**

COTTRELL, N.B., WACK, D.L., SEKERAK, G.J., and RITTLE, R.H. (1968) Social facilitation of dominant responses by the presence of an audience and the mere presence of others. *Journal of Personality and Social Psychology,* 9:245–50. **564**

COURRIER, S., see CLINE, CROFT, and COURRIER (1973).

CRAIGHEAD, L.W., STUNKARD, A.J., and O'BRIEN, R.M. (1981) Behavior therapy and pharmacotherapy for obesity. *Archives of General Psychiatry,* 38:763–68. **298**

CRAIGHEAD, W.E., KAZDIN, A.E., and MAHONEY, M.J. (1981) *Behavior modification: Principles, issues, and applications* (2nd ed.). Boston: Houghton Mifflin. **525**

CRAIK, F.I.M. (1977) Depth of processing in recall and recognition. In Dornic, S. (ed.) *Attention and performance VI.* Hillsdale, N.J.: Erlbaum. **231**

CRAIK, F.I.M. (1979) Human memory. *Annual Review of Psychology,* 30:63–102. **246**

CRAIK, F.I.M., and LOCKHART, R.S. (1972) Levels of processing: A framework for memory research. *Journal of Verbal Learning and Verbal Behavior,* 11:671–84. **246**

CRAIK, F.I.M., and WATKINS, M.J. (1973) The role of rehearsal in short-term memory. *Journal of Verbal Learning and Verbal Behavior,* 12:599–607. **246**

CRAIK, K. (1943) The nature of explanation. New York: Cambridge Univ. Press. **9**

CRANE, M., see MARKUS, CRANE, BERNSTEIN, and SILADI (1982).

CRASSWELLER, K.D., see BENSON, KOTCH, CRASSWELLER, and GREENWOOD (1977).

CREESE, I., BURT, D.R., and SNYDER, S.H. (1978) Biochemical actions of neuroleptic drugs. In Iversen, L.L., Iversen, S.D., and Snyder, S.H. (eds.) *Handbook of psychopharmacology,* Vol. 10. New York: Plenum Press. **476**

CRISTOL, A.H., see SLOANE, STAPLES, CRISTOL, YORKSTON, and WHIPPLE (1975).

CROCKENBURG, S.B. (1972) Creativity tests: A boon or boondoggle for education? *Review of Educational Research,* 42:27–45. **372**

CROFT, R.C. see CLINE, CROFT, and COURRIER (1973).

CROFTON, C., see GROSS AND CROFTON (1977).

CRONBACH, L.J. (1970) *Essentials of psychological testing* (3rd. ed.). New York: Harper and Row. **419**

CRUTCHFIELD, L., see KNOX, CRUTCHFIELD, and HILGARD (1975).

CULBERTSON, S., see BADIA, CULBERTSON, and HARSH (1973).

CURETON, K.J., see THOMPSON, JARVIE, LAKEY, and CURETON (1982).

CURTISS, S., see FROMKIN, KRASHEN, CURTISS, RIGLER, and RIGLER (1974).

D

D'ANDRADE, R.G. (1967) *Report on some testing and training procedures at Bassawa Primary School, Zaria, Nigeria.* Unpublished manuscript. **363**

DALE, A.J.D. (1975) Organic brain syndromes associated with infections. In Freedman, A.M., Kaplan, H.I., and Sadock, B.J. (eds.) *Comprehensive textbook of psychiatry-II,* 1:1121–30. Baltimore, Md.: Williams and Wilkins. **525**

DALE, L.A., see WOLMAN, DALE, SCHMEIDLER, and ULLMAN (1977).

DALRYMPLE, S., see HOFLING, BROTZMAN, DALRYMPLE, GRAVES, and PIERCE (1966).

DAMON, W. (1977) *The social world of the child.* San Francisco: Jossey-Bass. **84**

DANEMAN, M., and CARPENTER, P.A. (1981) Individual differences in working memory and reading. *Journal of Verbal Learning and Verbal Behavior*, 19:450–66. **228**

DANKS, J.H., see GLUCKSBERG and DANKS (1975).

DARBY, C.L., see PLATT, YAKSH, and DARBY (1967).

DARLEY, C.F., TINKLENBERG, J.R., ROTH, W.T., HOLLISTER, L.E., and ATKINSON, R.C. (1973) Influence of marijuana on storage and retrieval processes in memory. *Memory and Cognition*, 1:196–200. **19**

DARLEY, J.M., and LATANÉ, B. (1968) Bystander intervention in emergencies: Diffusion of responsibility. *Journal of Personality and Social Psychology* 8:377–83. **568**

DARLEY, J.M., see LATANÉ and DARLEY (1968).

DARLEY, I.M., see LATANÉ and DARLEY (1970).

DARWIN, C. (1872) *The expression of emotions in man and animals*. New York: Philosophical Library. **336**

DASHIELL, J.F. (1930) An experimental analysis of some group effects. *Journal of Abnormal and Social Psychology*, 25:190–99. **562, 563**

DASHIELL, J.F. (1935) Experimental studies of the influence of social situations on the behavior of individual human adults. In Murchison, C. (ed.) *Handbook of social psychology*. Worcester, Mass.: Clark University. **563**

DAVIDSON, A.R., and JACCARD, J.J. (1979) Variables that moderate the attitude-behavior relations: Results of a longitudinal survey. *Journal of Personality and Social Psychology*, 37:1364–76. **548**

DAVIDSON, E.S., YASUNA, A., and TOWER, A. (1979) The effects of television cartoons on sex-role strereotyping in young girls. *Child Development*, 50:597–600. **89**

DAVIS, A., see EELLS, DAVIS, HAVIGHURST, HERRICK, and TYLER (1951).

DAVIS, B. see STUART and DAVIS (1972).

DAVIS, K. L., and MOHS, R.C. (1982) Multiple dose intravenous physostigmine in Alzheimer's disease: Enhancement of memory processes. *American Journal of Psychiatry*, in press. **37**

DAVIS, M.H., see BERNSTEIN, STEPHAN, and DAVIS (1979).

DAVISON, G.C., and NEALE, J.M. (1982) *Abnormal psychology* (3rd ed.). New York: Wiley. **491**

DAWES, R.M., see LANDMAN and DAWES (1982).

DE BACA, P.C., see HOMME, DE BACA, DEVINE, STEINHORST, and RICKERT (1963).

DE LUCIA, L.A. (1963) The toy preference test: A measure of sex-role identification. *Child Development*, 34:107–17. **89**

DEFRIES, J.C., see PLOMIN, DEFRIES, and MCCLEARN (1980)

DEIKMAN, A.J. (1963) Experimental meditation. *Journal of Nervous and Mental Disease*, 136:329–73. **175**

DEIKMAN, A.J. (1971) Bimodal consciousness. *Archives of General Psychiatry*, 25:481–89. **166**

DEKIRMENJIAN, H., see JONES, MAAS, DEKIRMENJIAN, and FAWCETT (1973).

DELANEY, H.D., see PRESSLEY, LEVIN, and DELANEY (1982).

DEMBO, T., see BARKER, DEMBO, and LEWIN (1941).

DEMBROSKI, T.M., MACDOUGALL, J.M., HERD, J.A., and SHIELDS, J.L. (1981) The type A coronary-prone behavior pattern: A review. *Circulation*, 63:1199–1215. **440**

DEMENT, W.C. (1960) The effect of dream deprivation. *Science*, 131:1705–1707. **171**

DEMENT, W.C. (1976) *Some must watch while some must sleep*. New York: Simon and Schuster. **171**

DEMENT, W.C., and KLEITMAN, N. (1957) The relation of eye movements during sleep to dream activity: An objective method for the study of dreaming. *Journal of Experimental Psychology*, 53:339–46. **169**

DEMENT, W.C., and WOLPERT, E. (1958) The relation of eye movements, bodily motility, and external stimuli to dream content. *Journal of Experimental Psychology*, 55:543–53. **172**

DEMENT, W.C., see CARSKADON, MITLER, and DEMENT (1974).

DEMENT, W.C., see GULEVICH, DEMENT, and JOHNSON (1966).

DENNIS, W. (1960) Causes of retardation among institutional children: Iran. *Journal of Genetic Psychology*, 96:47–59. **66**

DENNIS, W. (1973) *Children of the creche*. Englewood Cliffs, N.J.: Prentice-Hall. **67**

DERMAN, D., see EKSTROM, FRENCH, HARMAN, and DERMAN (1976).

DERMER, M., see MITA, DERMER, and KNIGHT (1977).

DESILVA, R.A., see REICH, DESILVA, LOWN, and MURAWSKI (1981).

DETHIER, V.G. (1978) Other tastes, other worlds. *Science*, 201:224–28. **128**

DEUTSCH, G., see SPRINGER and DEUTSCH (1981).

DEUTSCH, J.A., YOUNG, W.G., and KALOGERIS, T.J. (1978) The stomach signals satiety. *Science*, 201:165–67. **291**

DEUTSCH, M., and COLLINS, M.E. (1951) *Interracial housing: A psychological evaluation of a social experiment*. Minneapolis: Univ. of Minnesota Press. **534**

DEVALOIS, K.K., see DEVALOIS and DEVALOIS (1980).

DEVALOIS, R.L., and DEVALOIS, K.K. (1980) Spatial vision. In *Annual Review of Psychology*, 31:309–41. **120**

DEVINE, J.V., see HOMME, DE BACA, DEVINE, STEINHORST, and RICKERT (1963).

DIACONIS, P. (1978) Statistical problems in ESP research. *Science*, 201:131–36. **161**

DICARA, L., and MILLER, W.E. (1968) Instrumental learning of systolic blood pressure responses by curarized rats. *Psychosomatic Medicine*, 30:489–94. **442**

DICK, L., see TART and DICK (1970).

DIENER, E. (1976) Effects of prior destructive behavior, anonymity, and group presence on deindividuation and aggression. *Journal of Personality and Social Psychology*, 33:497–507. **330**

DIENER, E. (1979) Deindividuation, self-awareness, and disinhibition. *Journal of Personality and Social Psychology*, 37:1160–71. **564, 565, 566**

DIENER, E. (1980) Deindividuation: The absence of self-awareness and self-regulation in group members. In Paulus, P.B. (ed.) *The psychology of group influence*. Hillsdale, N.J.: Erlbaum. **564**

DIENER, E., FRASER, S.C., BEAMAN, A.L., and KELEM, R.T. (1976) Effects of deindividuation variables on stealing among Halloween trick-or-treaters. *Journal of Personality and Social Psychology*, 33:178–83. **565**

DION, K., BERSCHEID, E., and WALSTER, E. (1972) What is beautiful is good. *Jour-*

nal of Personality and Social Psychology, 24:285–90. **554**

DION, K.K. (1972) Physical attractiveness and evaluations of children's transgressions. *Journal of Personality and Social Psychology*, 24:207–13. **554**

DION, K.K., and BERSCHEID, E. (1972) Physical attractiveness and social perception of peers in preschool children. Unpublished manuscript, Univ. of Minnesota, Minneapolis. **554**

DION, K.K., and STEIN, S. (1978) Physical attractiveness and interpersonal influence. *Journal of Experimental Social Psychology*, 14:97–108. **555**

DIPIETRO, J.A. (1981) Rough and tumble play: A function of gender. *Developmental Psychology*, 17:50–58. **91**

DOANE, B.K., see HERON, DOANE, and SCOTT (1956).

DOBELLE, W.H., MLADEJOVSKY, M.G., EVANS, J.R., ROBERTS, T.S., and GIRVIN, J.P. (1976) ''Braille'' reading by a blind volunteer by visual cortex stimulation. *Nature*, 259:111–12. **43**

DODDS, J.B., see FRANKENBURG and DODDS (1967).

DOHRENWEND, B.S. (1973) Social status and stressful life events. *Journal of Personality and Social Psychology*, 28:225–35. **476**

DOLLARD, J., DOOB, L.W., MILLER, N.E., MOWRER, O.H., and SEARS, R.R. (1939) *Frustration and aggression.* New Haven, Conn.: Yale Univ. Press. **322**

DOMINO, G. (1971) Interactive effects of achievement orientation and teaching style of academic achievement. *Journal of Educational Psychology*, 62:427–31. **407**

DOMINOWSKY, R.L., see BOURNE, DOMINOWSKY, and LOFTUS (1979).

DONAHUE, G. (1967) A school district program for schizophrenic children. In Cowen, E., and Zax, M. (eds.) *Emergent approaches to mental health problems.* New York: Appleton-Century-Crofts. **521**

DOOB. A.N., and WOOD, L.E. (1972) Catharsis and aggression: Effects of annoyance and retaliation on aggressive behavior. *Journal of Personality and Social Psychology*, 22:156–62. **330**

DOOB, L.W., see DOLLARD, DOOB, MILLER, MOWRER, and SEARS (1939).

DORNBUSCH, S.M., see CARLSMITH, DORNBUSCH, and GROSS (1983).

DOWNING, L.L., see JOHNSON and DOWNING (1979).

DOWNS, A.C., see LANGLOIS and DOWNS (1980).

DRABMAN, R.S., see CORDUA, MCGRAW, and DRABMAN (1979).

DRABMAN, R.S., see THOMAS, HORTON, LIPPINCOTT, and DRABMAN (1977).

DRUCKER-COLIN, R., SHKUROVICH, M., and STERMAN, M.B. (eds.) (1979) *The functions of sleep.* New York: Academic Press. **189**

DUA, S., see ANAND, SHARMA, and DUA (1964).

DUNKEL-SCHETTER, C., see RUBIN, HILL, PEPLAU, and DUNKEL-SCHETTER (1980).

DYE, H.B., see SKEELS and DYE (1939).

E

EAGLESTON, J.R., see THORESEN, TELCH, and EAGLESTON (1981).

ECKERT, E., see BOUCHARD, HESTON, ECKERT, KEYES, and RESNICK (1981).

EDMONSTON, W.E., JR. (1981) *Hypnosis and relaxation.* New York: Wiley. **186**

EELLS, K., DAVIS, A., HAVIGHURST, R.J., HERRICK, V.E., and TYLER, R.W. (1951) *Intelligence and cultural differences.* Chicago: Univ. of Chicago Press. **363**

EIBL-EIBESFELDT, I. (1970) *Ethology: The biology of behavior* (E. Klinghammer, trans.). New York: Holt, Rinehart and Winston. **73, 326**

EICH, J., WEINGARTNER, H., STILLMAN, R.C., and GILLIAN, J.C. (1975) State-dependent accessibility of retrieval cues in the retention of a categorized list. *Journal of Verbal Learning and Verbal Behavior*, 14:408–17. **235**

EIMAS, P.D., SIQUELAND, E.R., JUSCZYK, P., and VIGORITO, J. (1971) Speech perception in infants. *Science*, 171:303–306. **263**

EISDORFER, C., see ELLIOTT and EISDORFER (eds.) (1982).

EISENBERG, J.G., see LANGNER, GERSTEN, and EISENBERG (1977).

EKMAN, P. (1982) *Emotion in the human face* (2nd ed.). New York: Cambridge Univ. Press. **336, 345**

EKSTROM, R.B., FRENCH, J.W., HARMAN, H.H., and DERMAN, D. (1976) *Manual for kit of factor-referenced cognitive tests, 1976.* Princeton, N.J.: Educational Testing Service. **369**

ELKIND, D., and WEINER, I.B. (1978) *Development of the child.* New York: Wiley. **101**

ELLINWOOD, E.H., Jr., and KILBEY, M.M. (eds.) (1977) *Cocaine and other stimulants.* New York: Plenum Press. **189**

ELLIOTT, G.R., and EISDORFER, C. (eds.) (1982) *Stress and human health: Analysis and implications of research.* New York: Springer-Verlag. **449**

ELLIOTT, G.R., see HAMBURG, ELLIOTT, and PARRON (1982).

ELLMAN, S.J., see ARKIN, ANTROBUS, and ELLMAN (eds.) (1978).

ELLMAN, S.J., see HERMAN, ELLMAN, and ROFFWARG (1978).

EMMERT, E. (1881) Grössenverhaltnisse der Nachbilder. *Klin. Monatsbl. d. Augenheilk.*, 19:443–50. **144**

ENDLER, N.S. (1977) The role of person-by-situation interactions in personality theory. In Magnusson, D., and Endler, N.S. (eds.) *Personality at the crossroads: Current issues in interactional psychology.* New York: Halsted Press. **416**

ENDLER, N.S., and OKADA, M. (1974) An S-R inventory of general trait anxiousness. *Department of Psychology Reports* (No.1). Toronto: York Univ. **416**

ENDLER, N.S., see MAGNUSSON and ENDLER (1977).

ENDSLEY, R.C., see OSBORN and ENDSLEY (1971).

ENGLISH, G.E., see BERZINS, ROSS, ENGLISH, and HALEY (1974).

EPSTEIN, R. (1981) On pigeons and people: A preliminary look at the Columban Simulation Project. *The Behavior Analyst*, 4:43–55. **213**

EPSTEIN, S. (1967) Toward a unified theory of anxiety. In Maher, B.A. (ed.) *Progress in experimental personality research*, Vol. 4. New York: Academic Press. **340**

EPSTEIN, S. (1977) Traits are alive and well. In Magnusson, D., and Endler, N.S. (eds.) *Personality at the crossroads: Current issues in interactional psychology.* Erlbaum **414**

EPSTEIN, S. (1979) The stability of behavior: I. On predicting most of the people much of the time. *Journal of Personality and Social Psychology*, 37:1097–1126. **414**

EPSTEIN, S., and FENZ, W.D. (1965) Steepness of approach and avoidance gradients in humans as a function of experience. *Journal of Experimental Psychology*, 70:1–12. **425**

ERICKSON, B., see ROSS, LAYTON, ERICKSON, and SCHOPLER (1973).

ERICSSON, K.A., CHASE, W.G., and FALOON, S. (1980) Acquisition of a memory skill. *Science*, 208:1181–82. **238, 239**

ERIKSON, E.H. (1963) *Childhood and society* (2nd ed.). New York: Norton. **73, 97**

ERIKSON, E.H. (1976) *Toys and reasons.* New York: Norton. **73**

ERON, L.D., HUESMANN, L.R., LEFKOWITZ, M.M., and WALDER, L.O. (1972) Does television violence cause aggression? *American Psychologist*, 27:253–63. **329**

ERVIN-TRIPP, S. (1964) Imitation and structural change in children's language. In Lenneberg, E.H. (ed.) *New directions in the study of language.* Cambridge, Mass.: M.I.T. Press. **268**

ESTES, W.K. (1972) An associative basis for coding and organization in memory. In Melton, A.W., and Martin, E. (eds.) *Coding processes in human memory.* Washington, D.C.: Winston. **234**

ESTES, W.K. (ed.) (1975) *Introduction to concepts and issues.* Handbook of learning and cognitive processes, Vol. 1. Hillsdale, N.J.: Erlbaum. **219, 251**

ESTES, W.K. (ed.) (1976) *Conditioning and behavior theory.* Handbook of learning and cognitive processes series, Vol. 2. Hillsdale, N.J.: Erlbaum. **219, 251**

ESTES, W.K. (ed.) (1976) *Attention and memory.* Handbook of learning and cognitive processes series, Vol. 4. Hillsdale, N.J.: Erlbaum. **219, 251**

ESTES, W.K. (ed.) (1978) *Approaches to human learning and motivation.* Handbook of learning and cognitive processes series, Vol. 3. Hillsdale, N.J.: Erlbaum. **219, 251**

ESTES, W.K. (ed.) (1978) *Human information processing.* Handbook of learning and cognitive processes series, Vol. 5. Hillsdale, N.J.: Erlbaum. **219, 251**

ESTES, W.K. (ed.) (1979) *Human information processing.* Handbook of learning and cognitive processes series, Vol. 6. Hillsdale, N.J.: Erlbaum. **219, 251**

EVANS, F.J., COOK, M.R., COHEN, H.D., ORNE, E.C., and ORNE, M.T. (1977) Appetitive and replacement naps: EEG and behavior. *Science*, 197:687–89. **170**

EVANS, F.J., see KIHLSTROM and EVANS (1979).

EVANS, G.W., see COHEN, EVANS, KRANTZ, and STOKOLS (1980).

EVANS, G.W., see COHEN, EVANS, KRANTZ, STOKOLS, and KELLY (1981).

EVANS, J.R., see DOBELLE, MLADEJOVSKY, EVANS, ROBERTS, and GIRVIN (1976).

EYFERTH, K., BRANDT, U., and WOLFGANG, H. (1960) *Farbige Kinder in Deutschland.* Munich: Juventa. **377**

F

FALOON, S., see ERICSSON, CHASE, and FALOON (1980).

FANTINO, E. (1977) Conditioned reinforcement: Choice and information. In Honig, W.K., and Staddon, J.E.R. (eds.) *Handbook of operant behavior.* Englewood Cliffs, N.J.: Prentice-Hall. **204**

FANTINO, E., and LOGAN, C.A. (1979) *The experimental analysis of behavior: A biological perspective.* San Francisco: Freeman. **199, 203, 219**

FANTINO, E., see ROSE and FANTINO (1978).

FANTZ, R.L., ORDY, J.M., and UDELF, M.S. (1962) Maturation of pattern vision in infants during the first six months. *Journal of Comparative and Physiological Psychology*, 55:907–17. **157**

FAWCETT, J.A., see JONES, MAAS, DEKIRMENJIAN, and FAWCETT (1973).

FAZIO, R.H., ZANNA, M.P., and COOPER, J. (1977) Dissonance and self-perception: An integrative view of each theory's proper domain of application. *Journal of Experimental Social Psychology*, 13:464–79. **549**

FECHNER, G. (1860) *Elements of psychophysics* (H.E. Adler, trans.). New York: Holt, Rinehart and Winston, 1966. **108**

FEIGENBAUM, E.A., see BARR and FEIGENBAUM (1981).

FEINLEIB, M., see HAYNES, FEINLEIB, and KANNEL (1980).

FEJER, D., see SMART and FEJER (1972).

FELDMAN, H., GOLDIN-MEADOW, S., and GLEITMAN, L.R. (1978) Beyond Herodotus: The creation of language by linguistically deprived children. In Lock, A. (ed.) *Action, gesture, and symbol: The emergence of language.* London: Academic Press. **270**

FELDMAN, S.S., see MACCOBY and FELDMAN (1972).

FENZ, W.D., see EPSTEIN and FENZ (1965).

FERRO, P., see HOGARTY, SCHOOLER, ULRICH, MUSSARE, FERRO, and HERRON (1979).

FESHBACH, N., see FESHBACH and FESHBACH (1973).

FESHBACH, S., and FESHBACH, N. (1973) The young aggressors. *Psychology Today*, 6:90–95. **91**

FESTINGER, L. (1957) *A theory of cognitive dissonance.* Stanford, Calif.: Stanford Univ. Press. **548**

FESTINGER, L., and CARLSMITH, J.M. (1959) Cognitive consequences of forced compliance. *Journal of Abnormal and Social Psychology*, 58:203–10. **539**

FESTINGER, L., PEPITONE, A., and NEWCOMB, T.M. (1952) Some consequences of deindividuation in a group. *Journal of Abnormal and Social Psychology*, 47:383–89. **564**

FESTINGER, L., SCHACHTER, S., and BACK, K. (1950) *Social pressures in informal groups: A study of human factors in housing.* New York: Harper and Row. **551**

FESTINGER, L., see WALSTER and FESTINGER (1962).

FINKELMAN, J.M., and GLASS, D.C. (1970) Reappraisal of the relationship between noise and human performance by means of a subsidiary task measure. *Journal of Applied Psychology*, 54:211–13. **584**

FISHBEIN, M. (1963) An investigation of the relationships between beliefs about an object and the attitude toward that object. *Human Relations*, 16:233–40. **546**

FISHBEIN, M. (1972) Toward an understanding of family planning behaviors. *Journal of Applied Social Psychology*, 2:214–27. **548**

FISHBEIN, M., and AJZEN, I. (1975) *Belief, attitude, intention, and behavior: An introduction to theory and research.* Reading, Mass.: Addison-Wesley. **548**

FISHBEIN, M., see BOWMAN and FISHBEIN (1978).

FISHER, I.V., ZUCKERMAN, M., and NEEB, M. (1981) Marital compatibility in sensation seeking trait as a factor in marital adjustment. *Journal of Sex and Marital Therapy*, 7:60–69. **313**

FISHER, J.D., see BELL, FISHER, and LOOMIS (1978).

FISHER, S., and GREENBERG, R.P. (1977) *The scientific credibility of Freud's theories and therapy.* New York: Basic Books. **399**

FITZGERALD, R.G., see PARKES, BENJAMIN, and FITZGERALD (1969).

FIXSEN, D.L., see PHILLIPS, PHILLIPS, FIXSEN, and WOLF (1972).

FLACKS, R., see NEWCOMB, KOENIG, FLACKS, and WARWICK (1967).

FLANAGAN, J.C. (1963) The definition and measurement of ingenuity. In Taylor, C.W., and Barron, F. (eds.) *Scientific creativity: Its recognition and development.* New York: Wiley. **372**

FLAVELL, J.H. (1977) *Cognitive development.* Englewood Cliffs, N.J.: Prentice-Hall. **101**

FOBES, J.L., see OLDS and FOBES (1981).

FODOR, J.A., BEVER, T.G., and GARRETT, M.F. (1974) *The psychology of language: An introduction to psycholinguistics and generative grammar.* New York: McGraw-Hill. **269, 279**

FOLEY, J.M. (1978) Primary distance perception. In Held, R., Leibowitz, H. W., and Teuber, H.L. (eds.) *Handbook of sensory physiology*, Vol. 8. Berlin: Springer-Verlag. **136**

FOREM, J. (1973) *Transcendental meditation: Maharishi Mahesh Yogi and the science of creative intelligence.* New York: Dutton. **175**

FORER, B.R. (1949) The fallacy of personality validation: A classroom demonstration of gullibility. *Journal of Abnormal and Social Psychology*, 44:118–23. **411**

FOSS, D.J., and HAKES, D.T. (1978) *Psycholinguistics: An introduction to the psychology of language.* Englewood Cliffs, N.J.: Prentice-Hall. **279**

FOULKES, D. (1978) *A grammar of dreams.* New York: Basic Books. **174**

FOX, N.A. (1975) *Developmental and birth-order determinants of separation protest: A cross-cultural study of infants on the Israeli kibbutz.* Doctoral dissertation, Harvard Graduate School of Education. **79**

FRANKEN, R.E. (1982) *Human motivation.* Monterey, Calif.: Brooks/Cole. **345**

FRANKENBURG, W.K., and DODDS, J.B. (1967) The Denver developmental screening test. *Journal of Pediatrics*, 71:181–91. **64**

FRANKIE, G., see HETHERINGTON and FRANKIE (1967).

FRANKLIN, J., see LEWINSOHN, STEINMETZ, LARSON, and FRANKLIN (1981).

FRANKLIN, R.M., see STANTON, MINTZ, and FRANKLIN (1976).

FRANKS, J.J., see BRANSFORD, BARCLAY, and FRANKS (1972).

FRASE, L.T. (1975) Prose processing. In Bower, G.H. (ed.) *The psychology of learning and motivation*, Vol. 9. New York: Academic Press. **232**

FRASER, S.C., see DIENER, FRASER, BEAMAN, and KELEM (1976).

FREE, L.A., and CANTRIL, H. (1967) *The political beliefs of Americans.* New Brunswick, N.J.: Rutgers Univ. Press. **550**

FREEDMAN, J.L. (1965) Long-term behavioral effects of cognitive dissonance. *Journal of Experimental Social Psychology*, 1:145–55. **549**

FREEDMAN, J.L. (1975) *Crowding and behavior.* New York: Viking. **585, 587, 590**

FREEDMAN, J.L., HESHKA, S., and LEVY, A. (1975) Population density and pathology: Is there a relationship? *Journal of Experimental Social Psychology*, 11:539–52. **586**

FREEDMAN, J.L., SEARS, D.O., and CARLSMITH, J.M. (1981) *Social psychology* (4th ed.). Englewood Cliffs, N.J.: Prentice-Hall. **559, 590**

FREEDMAN, J.L., see SHAVER and FREEDMAN (1976).

FRENCH, G.M., and HARLOW, H.F. (1962) Variability of delayed-reaction performance in normal and brain-damaged rhesus monkeys. *Journal of Neurophysiology*, 25:585–99. **44**

FRENCH, J.W., see EKSTROM, FRENCH, HARMAN, and DERMAN (1976).

FRENCH, T.M., and FROMM, E. (1963) *Dream interpretation: A new approach.* New York: Basic Books. **174**

FREUD, A. (1967) *The ego and the mechanisms of defense* (2nd ed.). London: Hogarth Press. **449**

FREUD, S. (1885) *Ueber Coca.* Vienna: Moritz Perles. (Translation in Freud, 1974). **178**

FREUD, S. (1900) *The interpretation of dreams*, Vols. 4, 5. London: Hogarth Press. (Stand. ed., 1953). **173, 319**

FREUD, S. (1920) *Beyond the pleasure principle.* 1975 edition. New York: Norton. **345**

FREUD, S. (1933) *New introductory lectures on psychoanalysis.* New York: Norton. 1965 edition. **345, 419**

FREUD, S. (1933) Revision of the theory of dreams. Lecture 29, in *New intro-ductory lectures on psychoanalysis*, Vol. 22 (Stand. ed.) 1964. London: Hogarth Press. **173**

FREUD, S. (1963) Why war? In Reiff, P. (ed.) *Freud: Character and culture.* New York: Collier Books. **322**

FREUD, S. (1974) *Cocaine papers.* Edited and introduction by R. Byck; notes by A. Freud. New York: Stonehill. **178, 189**

FRICKE, B.G. (1975) *Report to the faculty.* Ann Arbor: Evaluation and Examinations Office, Univ. of Michigan. **363**

FRIED, M. (1982) Disadvantage, vulnerability, and mental illness. In Parron, D.L., Solomon, F., and Jenkins, C.D. (eds.). *Behavior, health risks, and social disadvantage*, pp. 113–24. Washington, D.C.: National Academy Press. **477**

FRIEDMAN, M., and ROSENMAN, R.H. (1974) *Type A behavior and your heart.* New York: Knopf. **440, 441**

FRIEDMAN, M., THORESEN, C.E., and GILL, J.J. (1981) Type A behavior: Its possible role, detection, and alteration in patients with ischemic heart disease. In Hurst, J. Willis (ed.) *Heart Update V.* New York: McGraw-Hill. **440**

FRIEDMAN, M., see ROSENMAN, BRAND, JENKINS, FRIEDMAN, STRAUS, and WRUM (1975).

FRIEDMAN, M.P., see CARTERETTE and FRIEDMAN (1975–1979).

FROMKIN, V., KRASHEN, S., CURTISS, S., RIGLER, D., and RIGLER, M. (1974) The development of language in Genie: A case of language acquisition beyond the "critical period." *Brain and Language*, 1:81–107. **270**

FROMM, E. (1970) Age regression with unexpected reappearance of a repressed childhood language. *International Journal of Clinical and Experimental Hypnosis*, 18:79–88. **184**

FROMM, E., and SHOR, R.E. (eds.) (1979) *Hypnosis: Developments in research and new perspectives* (2nd. ed.). Chicago: Aldine. **189**

FROMM, E., see FRENCH and FROMM (1963).

FROST, B., see ANNIS and FROST (1973).

FUHRER, M.J., see BAER and FUHRER (1968).

FULCHER, R., see STAPP and FULCHER (1981).

FULLER, J.L., and THOMPSON, W.R. (1978) *Foundations of behavior genetics*. St. Louis: Mosby. **59**

G

GAIND, R., see HIRSCH, GAIND, ROHDE, STEVENS, and WING (1973).

GALANTER, E. (1962) Contemporary psychophysics. In Brown, R., and others (eds.) *New directions in psychology I*. New York: Holt, Rinehart and Winston. **106**

GALLE, O.R., GOVE, W.R., and MCPHERSON, J.M. (1972) Population density and pathology: What are the relations for man? *Science*, 176:23–30. **585, 586**

GALLISTEL, C.R., see GELMAN and GALLISTEL (1978).

GAMZU, E., see SCHWARTZ and GAMZU (1977).

GARCIA, J., MCGOWAN, B.K., and GREEN, K.F. (1972) Biological constraints on conditioning. In Black, A.H., and Prokasy, W.F. (eds.) *Classical conditioning II: Current theory and research*. New York: Appleton-Century-Crofts. **197**

GARDNER, B.T., and GARDNER, R.A. (1972) Two-way communication with an infant chimpanzee. In Schrier, A.M., and Stollnitz, F. (eds.) *Behavior of nonhuman primates*, Vol. 4. New York: Academic Press. **197, 270, 272**

GARDNER, H. (1978) *Developmental Psychology: An introduction*. Boston: Little, Brown. **101**

GARDNER, M. (1975) *Fads and fallacies in the name of science*. New York: Dover. **187**

GARDNER, M. (1981) *Science: Good, bad and bogus*. New York: Prometheus. **189**

GARDNER, R.A., see GARDNER and GARDNER (1972).

GARFIELD, S.L. (1980) *Psychotherapy: An eclectic approach*. New York: Wiley-Interscience. **514**

GARFIELD, S.L., and BERGIN, A.E. (eds.) (1978) *Handbook of psychotherapy and behavior change: An empirical analysis*. New York: Wiley. **514, 525**

GARMEZY, N. (1974) Children at risk: The search for the antecedents of schizophrenia: II. Ongoing research programs, issues and intervention. *Schizophrenia Bulletin*, 1(9):55–125. **478**

GARNER, W.R., see WIGDOR and GARNER (eds.) (1982)

GARRETT, M.F. (1975) The analysis of sentence production. In Bower, G.H. (ed.) *The psychology of learning and motivation*, Vol. 9. New York: Academic Press. **264**

GARRETT, M.F., see FODOR, BEVER, and GARRETT (1974).

GARROW, J. (1978) The regulation of energy expenditure. In Bray, G.A. (ed.) *Recent advances in obesity research*, Vol. 2. London: Newman. **295**

GATES, A.I. (1917) Recitation as a factor in memorizing. *Archives of Psychology*, No. 40. **242**

GAZZANIGA, M.S. (1970) *The bisected brain*. New York: Appleton-Century-Crofts. **50**

GEBHARD, P.H., see KINSEY, POMEROY, MARTIN, and GEBHARD (1953).

GEEN, R.G. (1976) *Personality: The skein of behavior*. St. Louis: Mosby. **418**

GEEN, R.G., and QUANTY, M.B. (1977) The catharsis of aggression. In Berkowitz, L. (ed.) *Advances in experimental social psychology*, Vol. 10. New York: Academic Press. **328**

GEER, J., and MAISEL, E. (1972) Evaluating the effects of the prediction-control confound. *Journal of Personality and Social Psychology*, 23:314–19. **444**

GELMAN, R., and GALLISTEL, C.R. (1978) *The young child's understanding of number: A window on early cognitive development*. Cambridge, Mass.: Harvard Univ. Press. **72**

GERARD, D.L., see CHEIN, GERARD, LEE, and ROSENFELD (1964).

GERGEN, K.J., and GERGEN, M. M. (1981) *Social psychology*. New York: Harcourt Brace Jovanovich. **559, 590**

GERGEN, M.M., see GERGEN and GERGEN (1981).

GERSTEIN, D.R., see MOORE and GERSTEIN (1981)

GERSTEN, J.C., see LANGNER, GERSTEN, and EISENBERG (1977).

GESCHWIND, N. (1979) Specializations of the human brain. *Scientific American*, 241:180–99. **49**

GETZELS, J.W., and JACKSON, P.W. (1962) *Creativity and intelligence: Explorations with gifted students*. New York: Wiley. **372**

GIBBS, J.P. (1971) Suicide. In Merton, R.K., and Nisbet, R.A. (eds.) *Contemporary social problems* (3rd ed.). New York: Harcourt Brace Jovanovich. **586**

GIBSON, E.J., and WALK, R.D. (1960) The "visual cliff." *Scientific American*, 202:64–71. **157**

GIBSON, J.J. (1968) What gives rise to the perception of motion? *Psychological Review*, 75:335–46. **136**

GILL, J.J., see FRIEDMAN, THORESEN, and GILL (1981).

GILL, M.M. (1972) Hypnosis as an altered and regressed state. *International Journal of Clinical and Experimental Hypnosis*, 20:224–337. **186**

GILLIAN, J.C., see EICH, WEINGARTNER, STILLMAN, and GILLIAN (1975).

GIRVIN, B. (1978) *The nature of being schematic: Sex-role, self-schemas and differential processing of masculine and feminine information*. Unpublished doctoral dissertation, Stanford University. **541**

GIRVIN, J.P., see DOBELLE, MLADEJOVSKY, EVANS, ROBERTS, and GIRVIN (1976).

GJERDE, P.F., see BLOCK, BUSS, BLOCK, and GJERDE (1981).

GLANZER, M. (1972) Storage mechanisms in recall. In Bower, G.H., and Spence, J.T. (eds.) *The psychology of learning and motivation*, Vol. 5. New York: Academic Press. **245**

GLASS, A.L., HOLYOAK, K.J., and SANTA, J.L. (1979) *Cognition*. Reading, Mass.: Addison-Wesley. **251**

GLASS, D.C., and SINGER, J.E. (1972) *Urban stress: Experiments on noise and social stressors*. New York: Academic Press. **444, 584, 585, 590**

GLASS, D.C., see FINKELMAN and GLASS (1970).

GLASS, D.C., see HENCHY and GLASS (1968).

GLASS, G.V., see SMITH, GLASS, and MILLER (1980).

GLASS, L.L., see KIRSCH and GLASS (1977).

GLEITMAN, H., see GLEITMAN and GLEITMAN (1981).

GLEITMAN, L.R. (1981) Maturational determinants of language growth. *Cognition*, 10:103–14. **265, 269**

GLEITMAN, L.R., and GLEITMAN, H. (1981) Language. In Gleitman, H. (ed.) *Psychology*. New York: Norton. **270**

GLEITMAN, L.R., see FELDMAN, GOLDIN-MEADOW, and GLEITMAN (1978).

GLEITMAN, L.R., see WANNER and GLEITMAN (eds.) (1982).

GLICK, B.S., and MARGOLIS, R. (1962) A study on the influence of experimental design on clinical outcome in drug research. *American Journal of Psychiatry*, 118:1087–96. **519**

GLORIEUX, J., see GOLD, ANDRES, and GLORIEUX (1979).

GLUCKSBERG, S., and DANKS, J.H. (1975) *Experimental psycholinguistics.* New York: Halsted Press. **279**

GOBLE, F. (1970) *The third force: The psychology of Abraham Maslow.* New York: Pocket Books. **419**

GOECKNER, D., GREENOUGH, W., and MEAD, W. (1973) Deficits in learning tasks following chronic overcrowding in rats. *Journal of Personality and Social Psychology*, 28:256–61. **588**

GOETHALS, G.R., see JONES, ROCK, SHAVER, GOETHALS, and WARD (1968).

GOFFMAN, E. (1963) *Behavior in public places.* New York: Free Press. **569**

GOLD, D., ANDRES, D., and GLORIEUX, J. (1979) The development of Francophone nursery-school children with employed and nonemployed mothers. *Canadian Journal of Behavioral Science*, 11:169–73. **78**

GOLDBERG, P. (1968) Are women prejudiced against women? *Transaction*, 5:28–30. **534**

GOLDBERG, R. J., (1978) Development in the family and school context: Who is responsible for the education of young children in America? Paper presented at the National Association for the Education of Young Children Annual Conference, New York, N.Y. **79**

GOLDENBERG, L., see WILD, SHAPIRO, and GOLDENBERG (1975).

GOLDIAMOND, I., see ISAACS, THOMAS, and GOLDIAMOND (1965).

GOLDIN-MEADOW, S., see FELDMAN, GOLDIN-MEADOW, and GLEITMAN (1978).

GOLDMAN, W., and LEWIS, P. (1977) Beautiful is good: Evidence that the physically attractive are more socially skillful. *Journal of Experimental Social Psychology*, 13:125–30. **555**

GOLDSTEIN, E.B. (1980) *Sensation and perception.* Belmont, Calif.: Wadsworth. **131**

GOLEMAN, D.J. (1977) *The varieties of meditative experience.* New York: Dutton. **189**

GOODALL, J. (1978) Chimp killings: Is it the man in them? *Science News*, 113:276. **327**

GOODENOUGH, D.R., SHAPIRO, A., HOLDEN, M., and STEINSCHRIBER, L. (1959) A comparison of dreamers and non-dreamers: Eye movements, electroencephalograms and the recall of dreams. *Journal of Abnormal and Social Psychology*, 59:295–302. **172**

GOODENOUGH, D.R., see KOULACK and GOODENOUGH (1976).

GOODENOUGH, D.R., see LEWIS, GOODENOUGH, SHAPIRO, and SLESER (1966).

GOODWIN, D.W., SCHULSINGER, F., HERMANSEN, L., GUZE, S.B., and WINOKUR, G. (1973) Alcohol problems in adoptees raised apart from alcoholic biological parents. *Archives of General Psychiatry*, 28:238–43. **487**

GOODWIN, F. K., see POST, KOTIN, GOODWIN, and GORDON (1973).

GORDON, E. (1967) *A three-year longitudinal predictive validity study of the Musical Aptitude Profile.* Studies in the Psychology of Music, Vol. 5. Iowa City: Univ. of Iowa Press. **350**

GORDON, E., see POST, KOTIN, GOODWIN, and GORDON (1973).

GOTTESMAN, I.I. (1963) Genetic aspects of intelligent behavior. In Ellis, N. (ed.) *Handbook of mental deficiency: Psychological theory and research.* New York: McGraw-Hill. **375**

GOTTESMAN, I.I. and SHIELDS, J. (1973) *Schizophrenia and genetics: A twin study vantage point.* New York: Academic Press. **474**

GOTTESMAN, I.I., and SHIELDS, J. (1982) *Schizophrenia: The epigenetic puzzle.* Cambridge, England: Cambridge Univ. Press. **474, 491**

GOULD, A. (1977) Discarnate survival. In Wolman, B.B. (ed.) *Handbook of parapsychology.* New York: Van Nostrand Reinhold. **187**

GOVE, W.R., see GALLE, GOVE, and MCPHERSON (1972).

GRAVES, N., see HOFLING, BROTZMAN, DALRYMPLE, GRAVES, and PIERCE (1966).

GRAYSON, R. (1972) Air controllers syndrome: Peptic ulcers in air traffic controllers. *Illinois Medical Journal* (August). **440**

GREEN, D.M. (1976) An introduction to hearing. Hillsdale, N.J.: Erlbaum. **126**

GREEN, D.M., and BIRDSALL, T.G. (1978) Detection and recognition. *Psychological Review*, 85:192–206. **109**

GREEN, H. (1971) *I never promised you a rose garden.* New York: New American Library. **491**

GREEN, K.F., see GARCIA, MCGOWAN, and GREEN (1972).

GREENBERG, R.P., see FISHER and GREENBERG (1977).

GREENBERG, S., see ANTROBUS, GREENBERG, and SINGER (1966).

GREENE, D., see LEPPER, GREENE, and NISBETT (1973).

GREENOUGH, W., see GOECKNER, GREENOUGH, and MEAD (1973).

GREENWOOD, M.M., see BENSON, KOTCH, CRASSWELLER, and GREENWOOD (1977).

GREGORY, R.L. (1970) *The intelligent eye.* New York: McGraw-Hill. **146**

GREGORY, R.L. (1977) *Eye and brain* (3rd ed.). New York: McGraw-Hill. **155**

GREGORY, R.L. (1981) *Mind in science.* New York: Cambridge Univ. Press. **146**

GROSS, A.E., and CROFTON, C. (1977) What is good is beautiful. *Sociometry*, 40:85–90. **554**

GROSS, R.T., see CARLSMITH, DORNBUSCH, and GROSS (1983).

GROSSBERG, J.M. (1964) Behavior therapy: A review. *Psychological Bulletin*, 62:73–85. **506**

GROSSEN, N.E., see MEYERS and GROSSEN (1978).

GROVES, P.M., and SCHLESINGER, K. (1982) *Introduction to biological psychology* (2nd ed.). Dubuque, Iowa: Wm. C. Brown Co. **59**

GUILFORD, J.P. (1954) A factor analytic study across the domains of reasoning, creativity, and evaluation I: Hypothesis and description of tests. *Reports from the psychology laboratory.* Los Angeles: Univ. of Southern California Press. **372**

GUILFORD, J.P. (1967) *The nature of human intelligence.* New York: McGraw-Hill. **369**

GUILFORD, J.P., and HOEPFNER, R. (1971) *The analysis of intelligence.* New York: McGraw-Hill. **371**

GULEVICH, G., DEMENT, W., and JOHNSON, L. (1966) Psychiatric and EEG observations on a case of prolonged wakefulness. *Archives of General Psychiatry*, 15:29–35. **171**

GUZE, S.B., see GOODWIN, SCHULSINGER, HERMANSEN, GUZE, and WINOKUR (1973).

H

HABER, R.N. (1969) Eidetic images. *Scientific American*, 220:36–55. **224**

HACKETT, T.P., and CASSEM, N.H. (1970) Psychological reactions to life-threatening illness: Acute myocardial infarction. In Abram, H.S. (ed.) *Psychological aspects of stress*. Springfield, Ill.: Thomas. **434**

HAKES, D.T., see FOSS and HAKES (1978).

HALEY, J.V., see BERZINS, ROSS, ENGLISH, and HALEY (1974).

HALL, C.S. (1966) *The meaning of dreams*. New York: McGraw-Hill. **174**

HALL, C.S., and LINDZEY, G. (1978) *Theories of personality* (3rd ed.) New York: Wiley. **418**

HALPERN, J. (1977) Projection: A test of the psychoanalytic hypothesis. *Journal of Abnormal Psychology*, 86:536–42. **437**

HAMBURG, D., and TRUDEAU, M.B. (eds.) (1981) *Biobehavioral aspects of aggression*. New York: Alan Liss, Inc. **345**

HAMBURG, D., see COEHLO, HAMBURG, and ADAMS (1974).

HAMBURG, D.A., ELLIOTT, G.R., and PARRON, D.L. (eds.) (1982) *Health and behavior: Frontiers of research in the biobehavioral sciences*. Washington, D.C.: National Academy Press. **449**

HAMILTON, D.L. (1979) A cognitive-attributional analysis of stereotyping. In Berkowitz, L. (ed.) *Advances in experimental social psychology*, Vol. 12. New York: Academic Press. **531**

HAMILTON, D.L., and BISHOP, G.D. (1976) Attitudinal and behavioral effects of initial integration of white suburban neighborhoods. *Journal of Social Issues*, 32:47–68. **534**

HAMMER, A.G., see NACE, ORNE, and HAMMER (1974).

HAMMERSMITH, S.K., see BELL, WEINBERG, and HAMMERSMITH (1981).

HAMPSON, J.L., see HUNT and HAMPSON (1980).

HANSEL, C.E.M. (1980) *ESP and parapsychology: A critical reevaluation*. Buffalo, N.Y.: Prometheus Books. **160**

HARDY, A.B., see BANDURA, ADAMS, HARDY, and HOWELLS (1980).

HARE, R.D. (1970) *Psychopathy: Theory and research*. New York: Wiley. **482**

HARITON, E.B. (1973) The sexual fantasies of women. *Psychology Today*, 6(10):39–44. **303**

HARLOW, H.F. (1932) Social facilitation of feeding in the albino rat. *Journal of Genetic Psychology*, 41:211–21. **562**

HARLOW, H.F. (1971) *Learning to love*. San Francisco: Albion. **301**

HARLOW, H.F., HARLOW, M.K., and MEYER, D.R. (1950) Learning motivated by a manipulation drive. *Journal of Experimental Psychology*, 40:228–34. **311**

HARLOW, H.F., see FRENCH and HARLOW (1962).

HARLOW, M.K., see HARLOW, HARLOW, and MEYER (1950).

HARMAN, H.H., see EKSTROM, FRENCH, HARMAN, and DERMAN (1976).

HARRIS, V.A., see JONES and HARRIS (1967).

HARSH, J., see BADIA, CULBERTSON, and HARSH (1973).

HARTUP, W.W., and COATES, B. (1967) Imitation of a peer as a function of reinforcement from the peer group and rewardingness of the model. *Child Development*, 38:1003–16. **81**

HARTUP, W.W., and MOORE, S.G. (1963) Avoidance of inappropriate sex-typing by young children. *Journal of Consulting Psychology*, 27:467–73. **88**

HARVEY, E.N., see LOOMIS, HARVEY, and HOBART (1937).

HASTEY, J.M., see ARKIN, TOTH, BAKER, and HASTEY (1970).

HATFIELD, E., see TRAUPMANN and HATFIELD (1981).

HAURI, P. (1976) A case series analysis of 141 consecutive insomniacs evaluated at the Dartmouth Sleep Lab. In Chase, M.H., Mitler, M.M., and Walters, P.L. (eds.) *Sleep Research*, Vol. 5. Los Angeles: Brain Research Institute. **170**

HAVIGHURST, R.J., see EELLS, DAVIS, HAVIGHURST, HERRICK, and TYLER (1951).

HAYNES, S.G., FEINLEIB, M., and KANNEL, W.B. (1980) The relationship of psychosocial factors to coronary heart disease in the Framingham Study,

III. Eight-year incidence of coronary heart disease. *American Journal of Epidemiology*, 111(1):37–58. **440**

HEARST, E. (1975) The classical-instrumental distinction: Reflexes, voluntary behavior, and categories of associative learning. In Estes, W.K. (ed.) *Handbook of learning and cognition: Conditioning and behavior theory*, Vol. 2. Hillsdale, N.J.: Erlbaum. **207**

HEBB, D.O. (1972) *Textbook of psychology* (3rd ed.). Philadelphia: Saunders. **343**

HEBB, D.O. (1982) Understanding psychological man: A state-of-the-science report. *Psychology Today*, 16:52–53. **185**

HEDBERG, A., see WALKER, HEDBERG, CLEMENT, and WRIGHT (1981).

HEIDER, F. (1958) *The psychology of interpersonal relations*. New York: Wiley. **536, 538**

HEINGARTNER, A., see ZAJONC, HEINGARTNER, and HERMAN (1969).

HENCHY, T., and GLASS, D.C. (1968) Evaluation apprehension and social facilitation of dominant and subordinate responses. *Journal of Personality and Social Psychology*, 10:446–54. **563**

HENDRICK, G. (1977) When television is a school for criminals. *TV Guide* (January 29): 4–10. **329**

HENRY, G.W., see ZILBOORG and HENRY (1941).

HERD, J.A., see DEMBROSKI, MACDOUGALL, HERD, and SHIELDS (1981).

HERMAN, C.P., and MACK, D. (1975) Restrained and unrestrained eating. *Journal of Personality*, 43:647–60. **295**

HERMAN, C.P., and POLIVY, J. (1980) Restrained eating. In Stunkard, A.J. (ed.) *Obesity*, pp. 298–25. Philadelphia: Saunders. **294, 295**

HERMAN, C.P., see HIBSCHER and HERMAN (1977).

HERMAN, C.P., see POLIVY and HERMAN (1976).

HERMAN, E.M., see ZAJONC, HEINGARTNER, and HERMAN (1969).

HERMAN, J.H., ELLMAN, S.J., and ROFFWARG, H.P. (1978) The problem of NREM dream recall re-examined. In Arkin, A.M., Antrobus, J.S., and Ellman, S.J. (eds.) *The mind in sleep*. Hillsdale, N.J.: Erlbaum. **173**

HERMAN, J.H., see ROFFWARG, HERMAN, BOWE-ANDERS, and TAUBER (1978).

HERMANSEN, L., see GOODWIN, SCHUL-SINGER, HERMANSEN, GUZE, and WINOKUR (1973).

HERON, W., DOANE, B.K., and SCOTT, T.H. (1956) Visual disturbances after prolonged perceptual isolation. *Canadian Journal of Psychology*, 10:13–16. **311**

HERRICK, V.E., see EELLS, DAVIS, HAVIGHURST, HERRICK, and TYLER (1951).

HERRON, E., see HOGARTY, SCHOOLER, ULRICH, MUSSARE, FERRO, and HERRON (1979).

HERRON, E.W., see HOLTZMAN, THORPE, SWARTZ, and HERRON (1961).

HESHKA, S., see FREEDMAN, HESHKA, and LEVY (1975).

HESS, E.H. (1958) ''Imprinting'' in animals. *Scientific American*, 198:81–90. **286**

HESS, E.H. (1972) ''Imprinting'' in a natural laboratory. *Scientific American*, 227:24–31. **287**

HESSELLUND, H. (1976) Masturbation and sexual fantasies in married couples. *Archives of Sexual Behavior*, 5:133–47. **303**

HESTON, L. (1970) The genetics of schizophrenia and schizoid disease. *Science*, 167:249–56. **474, 475**

HESTON, L., see BOUCHARD, HESTON, ECKERT, KEYES, and RESNICK (1981).

HETHERINGTON, E.M., and FRANKIE, G. (1967) Effects of parental dominance, warmth, and conflict on imitation in children. *Journal of Personality and Social Psychology*, 6:119–25. **91**

HEWITT, E.C., see SPANOS and HEWITT (1980).

HEWITT, P., and MASSEY, J.O. (1969) *Clinical clues from the WISC*. Palo Alto, Calif.: Consulting Psychologists Press. **362**

HIBSCHER, J.A., and HERMAN, C.P. (1977) Obesity, dieting, and the expression of ''obese'' characteristics. *Journal of Comparative and Physiological Psychology*, 91:374–80. **295**

HIGGINS, E.T., see HUTTENLOCHER and HIGGINS (1971).

HILGARD, E.R. (1961) Hypnosis and experimental psychodynamics. In Brosen, H. (ed.) *Lectures on experimental psychiatry*. Pittsburgh: Pittsburgh Univ. Press. **24**

HILGARD, E.R. (1965) *Hypnotic susceptibility*. New York: Harcourt Brace Jovanovich, **182, 436**

HILGARD, E.R. (1968) *The experience of hypnosis*. New York: Harcourt Brace Jovanovich. **189**

HILGARD, E.R. (1973) The domain of hypnosis, with some comments on alternative paradigms. *American Psychologist*, 28:972–82. **186**

HILGARD, E.R. (1977) *Divided consciousness: Multiple controls in human thought and action*. New York: Wiley-Interscience. **185, 186, 189**

HILGARD, E.R., and HILGARD, J.R. (1975) *Hypnosis in the relief of pain*. Los Altos, Calif.: William Kaufmann. **184**

HILGARD, E.R., HILGARD, J.R., MACDONALD, H., MORGAN, A.H., and JOHNSON, L.S. (1978) Covert pain in hypnotic analgesia: Its reality as tested by the real-simulator design. *Journal of Abnormal Psychology*, 87:655–63. **185**

HILGARD, E.R., see BANYAI and HILGARD (1976).

HILGARD, E.R., see BOWER and HILGARD (1981).

HILGARD, E.R., see KNOX, CRUTCHFIELD, and HILGARD (1975).

HILGARD, E.R., see MORGAN, JOHNSON, and HILGARD (1974).

HILGARD, E.R., see RUCH, MORGAN, and HILGARD (1973).

HILGARD, J.R. (1970) *Personality and hypnosis: A study of imaginative involvement*. Chicago: Univ. of Chicago Press. **89**

HILGARD, J.R. (1979) *Personality and hypnosis: A study of imaginative involvement* (2nd ed.). Chicago: Univ. of Chicago Press. **182, 189**

HILGARD, J.R., see HILGARD and HILGARD (1975).

HILGARD, J.R., see HILGARD, HILGARD, MACDONALD, MORGAN, and JOHNSON (1978).

HILL, C.T., see RUBIN, HILL, PEPLAU, and DUNKEL-SCHETTER (1980).

HILLERY, J.M., see HUNT and HILLERY (1973).

HINTZMAN, D.L. (1978) *The psychology of learning and memory*. San Francisco: Freeman. **219**

HIROTO, D.S., and SELIGMAN, M.E.P. (1975) Generality of learned helplessness in man. *Journal of Personality and Social Psychology*, 31:311–27. **430**

HIRSCH, J., see KNITTLE and HIRSCH (1968).

HIRSCH, S., GAIND, R., ROHDE, L.D., STEVENS, B.C., and WING, J.K. (1973) Outpatient maintenance of chronic schizophrenics with fluphenazine decanoate injections: A double-blind placebo trial. *British Medical Journal*, 1:633 ff. **518**

HITCH, G., see BADDELEY and HITCH (1974).

HJELLE, L.A., and ZIEGLER, D.J., (1981) Personality theories: Basic assumptions, research, and applications (2nd ed.). New York: McGraw-Hill. **418**

HO, B., CHUTE, D., RICHARDS, D. (eds.) (1977) *Drug discrimination and state dependent learning*. New York: Academic Press. **177**

HO, E., see WATKINS, HO, and TULVING (1976).

HOBART, G.A., see LOOMIS, HARVEY, and HOBART (1937).

HOBSON, C.J., see COLEMAN, CAMPBELL, HOBSON, MCPARTLAND, MOODY, WEINFELD, and YORK (1966).

HOBSON, J.A., and MCCARLEY, R.W. (1977) The brain as a dream state generator: An activation-synthesis hypothesis of the dream process. *American Journal of Psychiatry*, 134:1335–48. **174**

HOCHBERG, J. (1978) *Perception* (2nd ed.). Englewood Cliffs, N.J.: Prentice-Hall. **163**

HOEBEL, B.G., and TEITELBAUM, P. (1966) Effects of force-feeding and starvation on food intake and body weight on a rat with ventromedial hypothalamic lesions. *Journal of Comparative and Physiological Psychology*, 61:189–93. **292**

HOEBEL, B.G., see CAGGIULA and HOEBEL (1966).

HOEBEL, B.G., see SMITH, KING, and HOEBEL (1970).

HOEPFNER, R., see GUILFORD and HOEPFNER (1971).

HOFFMAN, E., see MCCARLEY and HOFFMAN (1981).

HOFFMAN, E.L., see ROHRER, BARON, HOFFMAN, and SWANDER (1954).

HOFFMAN, L.W. (1980) The effects of maternal employment on the academic attitudes and performance of school-aged children. *School Psychology Review*, 9:319–35. **78**

HOFFMAN, S., see ROSS, BIERBRAUER, and HOFFMAN (1976).

HOFLING, C.K. (1975) *Textbook of psychiatry for medical practice* (3rd ed.). Philadelphia: Lippincott. **471**

HOFLING, C.K., BROTZMAN, E., DALRYMPLE, S., GRAVES, N., and PIERCE, C.M. (1966)

An experimental study in nurse-physician relationships. *Journal of Nervous and Mental Disease*, 143:171–80. **579**

HOGARTY, G.E., SCHOOLER, N.R., ULRICH, R., MUSSARE, F., FERRO, P., and HERRON, E. (1979) Fluphenazine and social therapy in the after care of schizophrenic patients. *Archives of General Psychiatry*, 36:1283–94. **518**

HOHMANN, G.W. (1962) Some effects of spinal cord lesions on experienced emotional feelings. *Psychophysiology*, 3:143–56. **333**

HOHMANN, M., BANET, B., and WEIKART, D. (1979) *Young children in action*. Ypsilanti, Mich.: High/Scope Press. **378**

HOLDEN, C. (1975) Lie detectors: PSE gains audience despite critic's doubt. *Science*, 190:359–62. **335, 378**

HOLDEN, M., see GOODENOUGH, SHAPIRO, HOLDEN, and STEINSCHRIBER (1959).

HOLLAN, J.D., see WILLIAMS and HOLLAN (1981).

HOLLAND, C.C., see ORNE and HOLLAND (1968).

HOLLINGSHEAD, A.B., and REDLICH, F.C. (1958) *Social class and mental illness*. New York: Wiley. **585**

HOLLISTER, L.E., see DARLEY, TINKLENBERG, ROTH, HOLLISTER, and ATKINSON (1973).

HOLMES, D.S. (1974) Investigations of repression: Differential recall of material experimentally or naturally associated with ego threat. *Psychological Bulletin*, 81:632–53. **237, 435**

HOLMES, T.H., and RAHE, R.H. (1967) The social readjustment rating scale. *Journal of Psychosomatic Research*, 11:213–18. **446**

HOLTZMAN, W.H., THORPE, J.S., SWARTZ, J.D., and HERRON, E.W. (1961) *Inkblot perception and personality*. Austin: Univ. of Texas Press. **410**

HOLYOAK, K.J., see GLASS, HOLYOAK, and SANTA (1979).

HOLZMAN, P.S. (1970) *Psychoanalysis and psychopathology*. New York: McGraw-Hill. **419**

HOLZMAN, P.S., see MENNINGER and HOLZMAN (1973).

HOMME, L.E., DE BACA, P.C., DEVINE, J.V., STEINHORST, R., and RICKERT, E.J. (1963) Use of the Premack principle in controlling the behavior of nursery school children. *Journal of the Experimental Analysis of Behavior*, 6:544. **209**

HONIG, W.K., and STADDON, J.E.R. (eds). (1977) *Handbook of operant behavior*. Englewood Cliffs, N.J.: Prentice-Hall. **219**

HONZIK, C.H., see TOLMAN and HONZIK (1930).

HOOD, L., see BLOOM, HOOD, and LIGHTBOWN (1974).

HOOK, E.B. (1973) Behavioral implications of the human XYY genotype. *Science*, 179:139–50. **55**

HORTON, R.W., see THOMAS, HORTON. LIPPINCOTT, and DRABMAN (1977).

HOUSTON, J.P. (1981) *Fundamentals of learning and memory* (2nd ed.). New York: Academic Press. **203, 219**

HOVLAND, C. (1937) The generalization of conditioned responses: I. The sensory generalization of conditioned responses with varying frequencies of tone. *Journal of General Psychology*, 17:125–48. **197**

HOVLAND, C., JANIS, I., and KELLEY, H.H. (1953) *Communication and persuasion*. New Haven: Yale Univ. Press. **580, 590**

HOWELLS, G.N., see BANDURA, ADAMS, HARDY, and HOWELLS (1980).

HUBEL, D.H., and WIESEL, T.N. (1962) Perceptive fields, binocular interaction and functional architecture in the cat's visual cortex. *Journal of Physiology* (London). **156**

HUBEL, D.H., and WIESEL, T.N. (1968) Receptive fields and functional architecture of monkey striate cortex. *Journal of Physiology* (London), 195:215–43. **119, 120**

HUESMANN, L.R., see ERON, HUESMANN, LEFKOWITZ, and WALDER (1972).

HUNT, B.M., see KLEIN, WEGMANN, and HUNT (1972).

HUNT, D.D., and HAMPSON, J.L. (1980) Follow up of 17 biologic male transsexuals after sex reassignment surgery. *American Journal of Psychiatry*, 137:432–38. **307**

HUNT, M. (1974) *Sexual behavior in the 1970's*. Chicago: Playboy Press. **299, 303, 304**

HUNT, P.J., and HILLERY, J.M. (1973) *Social facilitation at different stages in learning*. Paper presented at the Midwestern Psychological Association Meetings, Cleveland, Ohio. **563**

HUNTER, I.M.L. (1974) *Memory*. Baltimore: Penguin. **248**

HURRY, J., see TENNANT, SMITH, BEBBINGTON, and HURRY (1981).

HUSTON, T.L., and KORTE, C. (1976) The responsive bystander. In Lickona, T. (ed.) *Moral development and behavior*. New York: Holt, Rinehart and Winston. **84**

HUTTENLOCHER, J., and HIGGINS, E.T. (1971) Adjectives, comparatives, and syllogisms. *Psychological Review*, 78:487–504. **276**

HYDE, J.S. (1979) *Understanding human sexuality*. New York: McGraw-Hill. **315**

HYDE, J.S. (1981) How large are cognitive gender differences? *American Psychologist*, 36:892–901. **90**

HYMAN, R. (1977) The case against parapsychology. *The Humanist*, 37:47–49. **161**

I

INSKO, C.A., see STROEBE, INSKO, THOMPSON, and LAYTON (1971).

ISAACS, W., THOMAS, J., and GOLDIAMOND, I. (1965) Application of operant conditioning to reinstate verbal behavior in psychotics. In Ullmann, L.P., and Krasner, L. (eds.) *Case studies in behavior modification*. New York: Holt, Rinehart and Winston. **502**

IZARD, C.E. (ed.) (1979) *Emotion in personality and psychopathology*. New York: Plenum Press. **345**

IZARD, C.E. (1977) *Human emotions*. New York: Plenum Press. **336**

J

JACCARD, J.J., see DAVIDSON AND JACCARD (1979).

JACKLIN, C.N., see MACCOBY and JACKLIN (1974).

JACKSON, P.W., see GETZELS and JACKSON (1962).

JACOBS, P.D., see THORNTON and JACOBS (1971).

JACOBS, R.C., and CAMPBELL, D.T. (1961) The perpetuation of an arbitrary tradition through several generations of a laboratory microculture. *Journal of Abnormal and Social Psychology*, 62:649–58. **570**

JACOBSON, A., and KALES, A. (1967) Somnambulism: All-night EEG and related studies. In Kety, S.S., Evarts, E.V., and Williams, H.L. (eds.) *Sleep and altered states of consciousness*. Baltimore: Williams and Wilkins. **173**

JAMES, W. (1890) *The principles of psychology*. New York: Holt, Rinehart and Winston. **232**

JAMES, W.T. (1953) Social facilitation of eating behavior in puppies after satiation. *Journal of Comparative and Physiological Psychology*, 46:427–28. **562**

JAMES, W.T., see PLATT and JAMES (1966).

JANIS, I., see HOVLAND, JANIS, and KELLEY (1953).

JAREMKO, M., see MEICHENBAUM and JAREMKO (1982).

JARVIE, G.J., see THOMPSON, JARVIE, LAKEY, and CURETON (1982).

JELLINEK, E.M. (1952) Phases of alcohol addiction. *Quarterly Journal of Studies on Alcohol*, 13:673–84. **487**

JENKINS, C.D., see ROSENMAN, BRAND, JENKINS, FRIEDMAN, STRAUS, and WRUM (1975).

JENKINS, H.M., and MOORE, B.R. (1973) The form of the autoshaped response with food or water reinforcers. *Journal of the Experimental Analysis of Behavior*, 20:163–81. **206**

JENKINS, H.M., see BROWN and JENKINS (1968).

JENSEN, A.R. (1980) *Bias in mental testing*. New York: The Free Press. **360, 362, 374, 376**

JENSEN, R.A., see MCGAUGH, JENSEN, and MARTINEZ (1979).

JERSILD, A.T., BROOK, J.S., and BROOK, D.W. (1978) *The psychology of adolescence* (3rd ed.). New York: Macmillan. **101**

JOHNSON, B.D. (1973) *Marijuana users and drug subcultures*. New York: Wiley. **489**

JOHNSON, D.L., see MORGAN, JOHNSON, and HILGARD (1974).

JOHNSON, H.H., and SOLSO, R.L. (1978) *An introduction to experimental design in psychology: A case approach* (2nd ed.). New York: Harper and Row. **27**

JOHNSON, J.I., see WELKER, JOHNSON, and PUBOLS (1964).

JOHNSON, L., see GULEVICH, DEMENT, and JOHNSON (1966).

JOHNSON, L.S., see HILGARD, HILGARD, MACDONALD, MORGAN, and JOHNSON (1978).

JOHNSON, M.K., see BRANSFORD and JOHNSON (1973).

JOHNSON, R.D., and DOWNING, L.L. (1979) Deindividuation and valence of cues: Effects on prosocial and antisocial behavior. *Journal of Personality and Social Psychology*, 37:1532–38. **566**

JOHNSON, R.N. (1972) *Aggression in man and animals*. Philadelphia: Saunders. **345**

JOHNSON, V.E., see MASTERS and JOHNSON (1966).

JOHNSON-LAIRD, P.N., see MILLER and JOHNSON-LAIRD (1976).

JOHNSON-LAIRD, P.N., see WASON and JOHNSON-LAIRD (1972).

JONES, E.E., and HARRIS, V.A. (1967) The attribution of attitudes. *Journal of Experimental Social Psychology*, 3:1–24. **538**

JONES, E.E., and NISBETT, R.E. (1971) The actor and the observer: Divergent perceptions of the causes of behavior. *Attribution: Perceiving the causes of behavior*. Morristown, N.J.: Silver Burdett/General Learning Press. **542**

JONES, E.E., ROCK, L., SHAVER, K.G., GOETHALS, G.R., and WARD, L.M. (1968) Pattern of performance and ability attribution: An unexpected primacy effect. *Journal of Personality and Social Psychology*, 9:317–40. **532**

JONES, F.D., MAAS, J.W., DEKIRMENJIAN, H., and FAWCETT, J.A. (1973) Urinary catecholamine metabolites during behavioral changes in a patient with manic-depressive cycles. *Science*, 179:300–302. **465**

JONES, J.S., and OSWALD, I. (1968) Two cases of healthy insomnia. *EEG and Clinical Neurology*, 24:378–80. **169**

JONES, M.C., see MUSSEN and JONES (1958).

JORGENSON, B.W., see LEVINGER, SENN, and JORGENSEN (1970).

JULIEN, R.M. (1981) *A primer of drug action* (3rd ed.). San Francisco: Freeman. **491, 517, 518**

JUNGEBLUT, A., see MESSICK and JUNGEBLUT (1981).

JUSCZYK, P., see EIMAS, SIQUELAND, JUSCZYK, and VIGORITO (1971).

JUST, M.A., and CARPENTER, P.A. (1980) A theory of reading: From eye fixations to comprehension. *Psychological Review*, 87:329–54. **151, 153**

K

KAGAN, J. (1979) Overview: Perspectives on human infancy. In Osofsky, J.D. (ed.) *Handbook of infant development*, 1–25. New York: Wiley-Interscience. **63, 74**

KAGAN, J., KEARSLEY, R., and ZELAGO, P.R. (1978) *Infancy: Its place in human development*. Cambridge, Mass.: Harvard Univ. Press. **79**

KAGAN, J., and KLEIN, R.E. (1973) Cross-cultural perspectives on early development. *American Psychologist*, 28:947–61. **67**

KAGAN, J., see MUSSEN, CONGER, and KAGAN (1982).

KAHN, S., see KOBASA, MADDI, and KAHN (1982).

KAHNEMAN, D., SLOVIC, P., and TVERSKY, A. (eds.) (1982) *Judgment under uncertainty*. New York: Cambridge Univ. Press. **255**

KAIJ, L. (1960) *Alcoholism in twins: Studies on the etiology and sequels of abuse of alcohol*. Stockholm: Alcuquist and Wiksell. **487**

KALES, A., see JACOBSON and KALES (1967).

KALOGERIS, T.J., see DEUTSCH, YOUNG, and KALOGERIS (1978).

KAMIN, L.J. (1976) Heredity, intelligence, politics, and psychology. In Block, N.J., and Dworkin, G. (eds.) *The IQ controversy*. New York: Pantheon. **374, 376**

KAMMANN, R., see MARKS and KAMMANN (1980).

KAMMANN, R., see MARKS and KAMMANN (1977).

KANDEL, D. (1975) Stages in adolescent involvement in drug use. *Science*, 190:912–14. **488**

KANDEL, D.B., see ANDREWS AND KANDEL (1979).

KANNEL, W.B., see HAYNES, FEINLEIB, and KANNEL (1980).

KANTER, J.F., see ZELNIK and KANTER (1977).

KARABENICK, S.A., see LERNER and KARABENICK (1974).

KATCHER, A.H., see ZILLMANN, KATCHER, and MILAVSKY (1972).

KATZ, S.H., see SCARR, PAKSTIS, KATZ, and BARKER (1977).

KAUFMAN, L. (1979) *Perception: The world transformed*. New York and Toronto: Oxford Univ. Press. **131, 163**

KAUL, T.J., see BEDNAR and KAUL (1978).

KAY, P. see BERLIN and KAY (1969).

KAZDIN, A.E., and WILSON, G.T. (1978) Evaluation of behavior therapy: *Issues, evidence, and research strategies*. Cambridge, Mass.: Ballenger. **514**

KAZDIN, A.E., see CRAIGHEAD, KAZDIN, and MAHONEY (1981).

KEARSLEY, R., see KAGAN, KEARSLEY, and ZELAGO (1978).

KEELE, S.W., see POSNER and KEELE (1967).

KEEN, E. 1977 *A primer in phenomenological psychology*. New York: Holt, Rinehart and Winston. **418**

KEESEY, R.E., and POWLEY, T.L. (1975) Hypothalamic regulation of body weight. *American Scientist*, 63:558–65. **292**

KEESEY, R.E., see MITCHEL and KEESEY (1974).

KEESEY, R.E., see POWLEY and KEESEY (1970).

KELEM, R.T., see DIENER, FRASER, BEAMAN, and KELEM (1976).

KELLERMAN, H., see PLUTCHIK and KELLERMAN (eds.) (1980).

KELLEY, H.H. (1967) Attribution theory in social psychology. In Levine, D. (ed.) *Nebraska Symposium on Motivation*, Vol. 15. Lincoln: Univ. of Nebraska Press. **536**

KELLEY, H.H. (1972) Causal schemata and the attribution process. In Jones, E.E., Kanouse, D.E., Kelley, H.H., Nisbett, R.E., Valins, S., and Weiner, B. (eds.) *Attribution: Perceiving the causes of behavior*. Morristown, N.J.: General Learning Press. **537**

KELLEY, H.H. (1973) The processes of causal attribution. *American Psychologist*, 28:107–28. **537**

KELLEY, H.H., and WOODRUFF, C.L. (1956) Members' reactions to apparent group approval of a counternorm communication. *Journal of Abnormal and Social Psychology*, 52:67–74. **582**

KELLEY, H.H., see HOVLAND, JANIS, and KELLEY (1953).

KELLEY, S., JR., and MIRER, T.W. (1974) The simple act of voting. *American Political Science Review*, 68:572–91. **547**

KELLOGG, R.T. (1982) When can we introspect accurately about mental processes? *Memory and Cognition*, 10:141–44. **215**

KELLY, S., see COHEN, EVANS, KRANTZ, STOKOLS, and KELLY (1981).

KELMAN, H.C. (1961) Processes of opinion change. *Public Opinion Quarterly*, 25:57–78. **581**

KENDALL, P.C., and BUTCHER, J.N. (eds.) (1982) *Handbook of research methods in clinical psychology*. New York: Wiley. **525**

KENNEDY, C.E. (1978) *Human development: The adult years and aging*. New York: Macmillan. **101**

KENNEDY, R.A., see WILKES and KENNEDY (1969).

KEPHART, W.M. (1967) Some correlates of romantic love. *Journal of Marriage and the Family*, 29:470–74. **557**

KEPPEL, G., and SAUFLEY, W.H., JR. (1980) *Introduction to design and analysis*. San Francisco: Freeman. **615**

KERSEY, J., see WEBB and KERSEY (1967).

KESEY, K. (1962) *One flew over the cuckoo's nest*. New York: Viking. **491**

KESSEN, W., see NOWLIS and KESSEN (1976).

KESTENBAUM, R.S., see RESNICK, KESTENBAUM, and SCHWARTZ (1977).

KETY, S.S. (1980) Quoted in Scarf, M. *Unfinished business: Pressure points in the lives of women*. p. 240. New York: Doubleday. **469**

KETY, S.S., see ROSENTHAL, WENDER, KETY, SCHULSINGER, WELNER, and RIEDER (1975).

KETY, S.S., see WENDER, ROSENTHAL, KETY, SCHULSINGER, and WELNER (1974).

KEYES, M., see BOUCHARD, HESTON, ECKERT, KEYES, and RESNICK (1981).

KIHLSTROM, J.F. (1980) Posthypnotic amnesia for recently learned material: Interactions with "episodic" and "semantic" memory. *Cognitive Psychology*, 12:227–51. **183**

KIHLSTROM, J.F., and EVANS, F.J. (1979) Memory retrieval processes during posthypnotic amnesia. In Kihlstrom, J.F., and Evans, F.G. (eds.) *Functional disorders of memory*. Hillsdale, N.J.: Erlbaum. **183**

KILBEY, M.M., see ELLINWOOD and KILBEY (1977).

KIMMEL, H.D. (1974) Instrumental conditioning of automatically mediated responses in human beings. *American Psychologist*, 29:325–35. **207**

KING, M., see SMITH, KING, and HOEBEL (1970).

KINSEY, A.C., POMEROY, W.B., and MARTIN, C.E. (1948) *Sexual behavior in the human male*. Philadelphia: Saunders. **21, 304**

KINSEY, A.C., POMEROY, W.B., MARTIN, C.E., and GEBHARD, P.H. (1953) *Sexual behavior in the human female*. Philadelphia: Saunders. **21, 303, 304**

KINTSCH, W. (1974) *The representation of meaning in memory*. Hillsdale, N.J.: Erlbaum. **251, 260, 263**

KINTSCH, W., and BUSCHKE, H. (1969) Homophones and synonyms in short-term memory. *Journal of Experimental Psychology*. 80:403–407. **230**

KINTSCH, W., see MILLER and KINTSCH (1980).

KIRKER, W.S., see ROGERS, KUIPER, and KIRKER (1977).

KIRSCH, M.A., and GLASS, L.L. (1977) Psychiatric disturbances associated with Erhard Seminars Training: II. Additional cases and theoretical considerations. *American Journal of Psychiatry*, 134:1254–58. **511**

KLATZKY, R.L. (1980) *Human memory: Structures and processes* (2nd ed.). San Francisco: Freeman. **251**

KLEIN, K.E., WEGMANN, H.M., and HUNT, B.M. (1972) Desynchronization of body temperature and performance circadian rhythm as a result of outgoing and home-going transmeridian flights. *Aerospace Medicine*, 43:119–32. **169**

KLEIN, R.E., see KAGAN and KLEIN (1973).

KLEINMUNTZ, B. (1974) *Essentials of abnormal psychology*. New York: Harper and Row. **460, 464**

KLEITMAN, N., see DEMENT and KLEITMAN (1957).

KLENTZ, B., see BEAMAN, BARNES, KLENTZ, and MCQUIRK (1978).

KLINEBERG, O. (1938) Emotional expression in Chinese literature. *Journal of Abnormal and Social Psychology*, 33:517–20. **337**

KLING, J.W., and RIGGS, L.A. (1971) *Experimental psychology* (3rd ed.). New York: Holt, Rinehart and Winston. **131**

KNIGHT, J., see MITA, DERMER, and KNIGHT (1977).

KNITTLE, J.L. (1975) Early influences on development of adipose tissue. In Bray, G.A. (ed.) *Obesity in perspective*. Washington, D.C.: U.S. Government Printing Office. **297**

KNITTLE, J.L., and HIRSCH, J. (1968) Effect of early nutrition on the development of rat epididymal fat pads: Cellularity and metabolism. *Journal of Clinical Investigation*, 47:2091. **297**

KNOX, V.J., CRUTCHFIELD, L., and HILGARD, E.R. (1975) The nature of task interference in hypnotic dissociation: An investigation of hypnotic behavior. *International Journal of Clinical and Experimental Hypnosis*, 23:305–23. **185**

KOBASA, S.C. (1979) Stressful life events, personality, and health: An inquiry into hardiness. *Journal of Personality and Social Psychology*, 37:1–11. **447**

KOBASA, S.C., MADDI, S.R., and KAHN, S. (1982) Hardiness and health: A prospective study. *Journal of Personality and Social Psychology*, 42:168–77. **447**

KOBASIGAWA, A., ARAKAKI, K., and AWIGUNI, A. (1966) Avoidance of feminine toys by kindergarten boys: The effects of adult presence or absence, and an adult's attitudes toward sex-typing. *Japanese Journal of Psychology*, 37:96–103. **88**

KOENIG, K.E., see NEWCOMB, KOENIG, FLACKS, and WARWICK (1967).

KOGAN, N., and PANKOVE, E. (1974) Long-term predictive validity of divergent-thinking tests: Some negative evidence. *Journal of Educational Psychology*, 66:802–10. **373**

KOGAN, N., see WALLACH and KOGAN (1965).

KOHEN-RAZ, R. (1968) Mental and motor development of kibbutz, institutionalized, and home-reared infants in Israel. *Child Development*, 39:489–504. **79**

KOHLBERG, L. (1969) Stage and sequence: The cognitive-developmental approach to socialization. In Goslin, D.A. (ed.) *Handbook of socialization theory and research*. Chicago: Rand McNally. **81, 82, 83**

KOHLBERG, L. (1973) Implications of developmental psychology for education: Examples from moral development. *Educational Psychologist*, 10:2–14. **81, 83**

KOHLER, W. (1925) *The mentality of apes*. New York: Harcourt Brace Jovanovich. **212, 219**

KOLB, B., and WHISHAW, I.Q. (1980) *Fundamentals of human neuropsychology*. San Francisco: Freeman. **37**

KORTE, C., see HUSTON and KORTE (1976).

KOSA, J., and ZOLA, I.K. (eds.) (1975) *Poverty and health: A sociological analysis*. Cambridge, Mass.: Harvard Univ. Press. **477**

KOSSLYN, S.M. (1980) *Image and mind*. Cambridge, Mass.: Harvard Univ. Press. **260, 274, 279**

KOSSLYN, S.M., BALL, T.M., and REISER, B.J. (1978) Visual images preserve metric spatial information: Evidence from studies of image scanning. *Journal of Experimental Psychology: Human Perception and Performance*, 4:47–60. **275**

KOTCH, J.B., see BENSON, KOTCH, CRASS-WELLER, and GREENWOOD (1977).

KOTELCHUK, M. (1976) The infant's relationship to the father: Experimental evidence. In Lamb, M. (ed.) *The role of the father in child development*. New York: Wiley. **77, 80**

KOTIN, J., see POST, KOTIN, GOODWIN, and GORDON (1973).

KOULACK, D., and GOODENOUGH, D.R. (1976) Dream recall and dream recall failure: An arousal-retrieval model. *Psychological Bulletin*, 83:975–84. **172**

KOVACH, J., see MURPHY and KOVACH (1972).

KOYAMA, H., see LEWIS, BAIRD, LEVERENZ, and KOYAMA (1982).

KRANTZ, D.S., see COHEN, EVANS, KRANTZ, and STOKOLS (1980).

KRANTZ, D.S., see COHEN, EVANS, KRANTZ, STOKOLS, and KELLY (1981).

KRASHEN, S., see FROMKIN, KRASHEN, CURTISS, RIGLER, and RIGLER (1974).

KRASNER, L., see ULLMANN and KRASNER (1969).

KRETSCHMER, E. (1925) *Physique and character*. London: Kegan Paul. **385**

KRIPKE, D.F., and SIMONS, R.N. (1976) Average sleep, insomnia, and sleeping pill use. *Sleep Research*, 5:110. **170**

KTSANES, T., see WINCH, KTSANES, and KTSANES (1954).

KTSANES, V., see WINCH, KTSANES, and KTSANES (1954).

KUBIS, J.F. (1962). Cited in Smith, B.M., The polygraph. In Atkinson, R.C. (ed.) *Contemporary psychology*. San Francisco: Freeman. **335**

KUHN, D., NASH, S.C., and BRUCKEN, L. (1978) Sex role concepts of two- and three-year-olds. *Child Development*, 49:445–51. **88**

KUIPER, N.A., see ROGERS, KUIPER, and KIRKER (1977).

L

LABRUZZA, A.L. (1978) Activation-synthesis hypothesis of dreams. Theoretical note. *American Journal of Psychiatry*, 35:1537–38. **174**

LAIRD, J.D. (1974) Self-attribution of emotion: The effects of expressive behavior on the quality of emotional experience. *Journal of Personality and Social Psychology*, 29:475–86. **336**

LAKEY, B.B., see THOMPSON, JARVIE, LAKEY, and CURETON (1982).

LANDMAN, J.T., and DAWES, R.M. (1982) Psychotherapy outcome. *American Psychologist*, 37:504–16. **513**

LANDY, D., and ARONSON, E. (1969) The influence of the character of the criminal and his victim on the decisions of simulated jurors. *Journal of Experimental Social Psychology*, 5:141–52. **554**

LANDY, D., and SIGALL, H. (1974) Beauty is talent: Task evaluation as a function of the performer's physical attractiveness. *Journal of Personality and Social Psychology*, 29:299–304. **554**

LANGACKER, R.W. (1973) *Language and its structure* (2nd ed.). New York: Harcourt Brace Jovanovich. **272**

LANGFORD, G., see MEDDIS, PEARSON, and LANGFORD (1973).

LANGLOIS, J.H., and DOWNS, A.C. (1980) Mothers, fathers, and peers as socialization agents of sex-typed play behaviors in young children. *Child Development*, 51:1237–47. **89**

LANGNER, T.S., GERSTEN, J.C., and EISENBERG, J.G. (1977) *Family research project*. Paper presented at the meeting of the Kittay Scientific Foundation, New York, N.Y. **62**

LAPIERE, R. (1934) Attitudes versus actions. *Social Forces*, 13:230–37. **547**

LARKIN, J.H., MCDERMOTT, J., SIMON, D.P. and SIMON, H.A. (1980) Expert and novice performance in solving physics problems. *Science*, 208:1335–42. **277**

LARSON, D.W., see LEWINSOHN, STEINMETZ, LARSON, and FRANKLIN (1981).

LATANÉ, B., and DARLEY, J.M. (1968) Group inhibition of bystander intervention in emergencies. *Journal of Personality and Social Psychology*, 10:215–21. **567**

LATANÉ, B., and DARLEY, J.M. (1970) *The unresponsive bystander: Why doesn't he help?* New York: Appleton-Century-Crofts. **566, 590**

LATANÉ, B., and RODIN, J. (1969) A lady in distress: Inhibiting effects of friends and strangers on bystander intervention. *Journal of Experimental and Social Psychology*, 5:189–202. **567**

LATANÉ, B., see DARLEY and LATANE (1968).

LATIES, V.G., see WEISS and LATIES (1962).

LAUGHLIN, H.P. (1967) *The neuroses*. Washington, D.C.: Butterworths. **461**

LAURENCE, J.R. (1980) *Duality and dissociation in hypnosis.* Unpublished M.A. thesis, Concordia University, Montreal. **185**

LAWTON, S.F., see BARON and LAWTON (1972).

LAYTON, B., see ROSS, LAYTON, ERICKSON, and SCHOPLER (1973).

LAYTON, B.D., see STROEBE, INSKO, THOMPSON, and LAYTON (1971).

LAZAR, I. (1977) *Longitudinal data in child development programs (I).* Paper presented at the Office of Child Development (OHD, HEW) Conference: Parents, Children, Continuity, El Paso, Tex. (May 1977). **378**

LAZARUS, A.A. (1971) *Behavior therapy and beyond.* New York: McGraw-Hill. **500**

LEBON, G. (1895) *The crowd.* London: Ernest Benn. **564, 590**

LEE, R.S., see CHEIN, GERARD, LEE, and ROSENFELD (1964).

LEFKOWITZ, M.M., see ERON, HUESMANN, LEFKOWITZ, and WALDER (1972).

LEGANT, P., see NISBETT, CAPUTO, LEGANT, and MARACEK (1973).

LEHMKUHLE, S.W., see SPOEHR and LEHMKUHLE (1982).

LEHRMAN, D.S. (1964) Control of behavior cycles in reproduction. In Etkin, W. (ed.) *Social behavior and organization among vertebrates.* Chicago: Univ. of Chicago Press. **287**

LEIBOWITZ, H., see ZEIGLER and LEIBOWITZ (1957).

LEIBOWITZ, H.W., see PARRISH, LUNDY, and LEIBOWITZ (1968).

LEIMAN, A.L., see ROSENZWEIG and LEIMAN (1982).

LENNEBERG, E.H. (1967) *Biological foundations of language.* New York: Wiley. **270**

LEON, M. (1977) *Coordination of intent and consequence information in children's moral judgments.* (Tech. Rep. CHIP 72.) La Jolla, Calif.: University of California, San Diego, Center for Human Information Processing. **83, 414**

LEPPER, M.R., GREENE, D., and NISBETT, R.E. (1973) Undermining children's intrinsic interest with extrinsic reward: A test of the "overjustification" hypothesis. *Journal of Personality and Social Psychology,* 28:129–37. **206, 541**

LERNER, R.M., and KARABENICK, S.A. (1974) Physical attractiveness, body atti-tudes, and self-concept in late adolescents. *Journal of Youth and Adolescence,* 3:307–16. **555**

LESGOLD, A., see BOWER, CLARK, WINZENZ, and LESGOLD (1969).

LESTER, D. (1974) Effect of suicide prevention centers on suicide rates in the United States. *Public Health Reports,* 89:37–39. **521**

LEVENSON, H., BURFORD, B., BONNO, B., and LOREN, D. (1975) Are women still prejudiced against women? A replication and extension of Goldberg's study. *Journal of Psychology,* 89:67–71. **534**

LEVERENZ, E.L., see LEWIS, BAIRD, LEVERENZ, and KOYAMA (1982).

LEVIN, J.R., see PRESSLEY, LEVIN, and DELANEY (1982).

LEVINE, J.M., see ALLEN and LEVINE (1969).

LEVINE, J.M., see ALLEN and LEVINE (1971).

LEVINGER, G., SENN, D.J., and JORGENSEN, B.W. (1970) Progress toward permanence in courtship: A test of the Kerckhoff-Davis hypotheses. *Sociometry,* 33:427–43. **553**

LEVINGER, G., see RANDS and LEVINGER (1979).

LEVY, A., see FREEDMAN, HESHKA, and LEVY (1975).

LEWIN, K., see BARKER, DEMBO, and LEWIN (1941).

LEWINSOHN, P.M., MISCHEL, W., CHAPLIN, W., and BARTON, R. (1980) Social competence and depression: The role of illusory self-perceptions. *Journal of Abnormal Psychology,* 89:203–12. **466**

LEWINSOHN, P.M., STEINMETZ, J.L., LARSON, D.W., and FRANKLIN, J. (1981) Depression-related cognitions: Antecedent or consequence? *Journal of Abnormal Psychology,* 90:213–19. **467, 468**

LEWIS, E.R., BAIRD, R.A., LEVERENZ, E.L., and KOYAMA, H. (1982) Inner ear: Dye injection reveals peripheral origins of specific sensitivities. *Science,* 215:1641–43. **126**

LEWIS, H.B., GOODENOUGH, D.R., SHAPIRO, A., and SLESER, I. (1966) Individual differences in dream recall. *Journal of Abnormal Psychology,* 71:52–59. **172**

LEWIS, P., see GOLDMAN and LEWIS (1977).

LEWIS, S. (1934) *Work of art.* Garden City, N.Y.: Doubleday. **388**

LIBERMAN, A.M., COOPER, F., SHANKWEILER, D., and STUDDERT-KENNEDY, M. (1967) Perception of the speech code. *Psychological Review,* 74:431–59. **262**

LIDZ, T. (1973) *The origin and treatment of schizophrenic disorders.* New York: Basic Books. **477**

LIEBERMAN, M.A., YALOM, I.D., and MILES, M.B. (1973) *Encounter groups: First facts.* New York: Basic Books. **511, 525**

LIEM, J.H. (1974) Effect of verbal communications of parents and children: A comparison of normal and schizophrenic families. *Journal of Consulting and Clinical Psychology,* 42:438–50. **478**

LIGHTBOWN, P., see BLOOM, HOOD, and LIGHTBOWN (1974).

LINDSAY, P.H., and NORMAN, D.A. (1977) *Human information processing* (2nd ed.). New York: Academic Press. **131, 279**

LINDZEY, G., see HALL and LINDZEY (1978).

LINDZEY, G., see LOEHLIN, LINDZEY, and SPUHLER (1975).

LINN, R.L. (1982) Ability testing: Individual differences, prediction, and differential prediction. In Wigdor, A., and Gardner, W. (eds.) *Ability testing: Uses, consequences, and controversies.* Washington, D.C.: National Academy Press. **362, 364, 366**

LIPPERT, W.W., and SENTER, R.J. (1966) Electrodermal responses in the sociopath. *Psychonomic Science,* 4:25–26. **481**

LIPPINCOTT, E.C., see THOMAS, HORTON, LIPPINCOTT, and DRABMAN (1977).

LISMAN, S.A. (1974) Alcoholic "blackout": State-dependent learning? *Archives of General Psychiatry,* 30:46–53. **488**

LITTMAN, R.A., see PATTERSON, LITTMAN, and BRICKER (1967).

LIU, T.J., see MOORE, SHERROD, LIU, and UNDERWOOD (1979).

LOCKHART, R.S., see CRAIK and LOCKHART (1972).

LOEHLIN, J.C., LINDZEY, G., and SPUHLER, J.N. (1975) *Race differences in intelligence.* San Francisco: Freeman. **376**

LOEHLIN, J.C., and NICHOLS, R.C. (1976) *Heredity, environment, and personality: A study of 850 twin sets.* Austin: Univ. of Texas Press. **385**

LOFTUS, E.F. (1980) *Memory.* Reading, Mass.: Addison-Wesley. **247, 251**

LOFTUS, E.F., see BOURNE, DOMINOWSKY, and LOFTUS (1979).

LOFTUS, E.F., see LOFTUS and LOFTUS (1975).

LOFTUS, E.F., see LOFTUS and LOFTUS (1982).

LOFTUS, G.R., and LOFTUS, E.F. (1975) *Human memory: The processing of information.* New York: Halsted Press. **247**

LOFTUS, G.R., and LOFTUS, E.F. (1982) *Essence of statistics.* Monterey, Calif.: Brooks/Cole. **615**

LOGAN, C.A., see FANTINO and LOGAN (1979).

LOO, C.M. (1972) The effects of spatial density on the social behavior of children. *Journal of Applied Social Psychology,* 2:372, 381. **587**

LOOMIS, A.L., HARVEY, E.N., and HOBART, G.A. (1937) Cerebral states during sleep as studied by human potentials. *Journal of Experimental Psychology,* 21:127–44. **169**

LOOMIS, R.J., see BELL, FISHER, and LOOMIS (1978).

LOREN, D., see LEVENSON, BURFORD, BONNO, and LOREN (1975).

LORENZ, K., (1966) *On aggression.* New York: Harcourt Brace Jovanovich. **326, 577**

LORENZ, K. (1981) *The foundation of ethology.* New York: Springer-Verlag. **286, 315, 326**

LOTT, A.J., see MALOF and LOTT (1962).

LOTTIER, S. (1938) Distribution of criminal offenses in metropolitan regions. *Journal of Criminal Law and Criminology,* 29:39–45. **585**

LOWN, B., see REICH, DESILVA, LOWN, and MURAWSKI (1981).

LUBORSKY, L., and SPENCE, D.P. (1978) Quantitative research on psychoanalytic therapy. In Garfield, S.L., and Bergin, A.E. (eds.) *Handbook of psychotherapy and behavior change: An empirical analysis* (2nd ed.). New York: Wiley. **435**

LUCE, R.D., see KRANTZ, LUCE, SUPPES, and TVERSKY (1971).

LUCHINS, A. (1957a) Experimental attempts to minimize the impact of first impressions. In Hovland, C.I. (ed.) *The order of presentation in persuasion.* New Haven, Conn.: Yale Univ. Press. **532**

LUCHINS, A. (1957b) Primacy-recency in impression formation. In Hovland, C.I. (ed.) *The order of presentation in persuasion.* New Haven, Conn.: Yale Univ. Press. **531, 532**

LUNDY, R.M., see PARRISH, LUNDY, and LEIBOWITZ (1968).

LURIA, Z., and RUBIN, J.Z. (1974) The eye of the beholder: Parents' views on sex of newborns. *American Journal of Orthopsychiatry,* 44:512–19. **88**

LYKKEN, D.T. (1982) Research with twins: The concept of emergencies. *The Society for Psychophysiological Research,* 19:361–73. **389**

LYKKEN, D.T. (1957) A study of anxiety in the sociopathic personality. *Journal of Abnormal and Social Psychology,* 55:6–10. **482**

LYKKEN, D.T. (1981) *A tremor in the blood: Uses and abuses of the lie detector.* New York: McGraw-Hill. **334, 335, 345**

LYNN, R. (1982) IQ in Japan and the United States shows a disparity. *Nature,* 297:222–23. **377**

M

MAAS, J.W., see JONES, MAAS, DEKIRMENJIAN, and FAWCETT (1973).

MACCOBY, E.E., and BEE, H.L. (1965) Some speculations concerning the lag between perceiving and performing. *Child Development,* 36:367–77. **264**

MACCOBY, E.E., and FELDMAN, S.S. (1972) Mother attachment and stranger reactions in the third year of life. *Monograph of the Society for Research in Child Development,* No. 1, 37:1–86. **79**

MACCOBY, E.E., and JACKLIN, C.N. (1974) *The psychology of sex differences.* Stanford, Calif.: Stanford Univ. Press. **90**

MACDONALD, H., see HILGARD, HILGARD, MACDONALD, MORGAN, and JOHNSON (1978).

MACDOUGALL, J.M., see DEMBROSKI, MACDOUGALL, HERD, and SHIELDS (1981).

MACFARLANE, J.A. (1977) *The psychology of childbirth.* Cambridge, Mass.: Harvard Univ. Press. **65**

MACK, D., see HERMAN and MACK (1975).

MACKAY, D.G. (1966) To end ambiguous sentences. *Perception and Psychophysics,* 1:426–36. **262**

MACKINTOSH, N.J. (1983) *Conditioning and associative learning.* New York, N.Y.: Oxford Univ. Press. **219**

MADDI, S., and COSTA, P. (1972) *Humanism in personology.* Chicago: Aldine. **419**

MADDI, S.R., see KOBASA, MADDI, and KAHN (1982).

MAGNUSSON, D., and ENDLER, N.S. (eds.) (1977) *Personality at the crossroads: Current issues in interactional psy-chology.* New York: Halsted Press. **418**

MAHER, B.A. (1966) *Principles of psychotherapy: An experimental approach.* New York: McGraw-Hill. **471, 472, 481, 484**

MAHONEY, K., see MAHONEY and MAHONEY (1976).

MAHONEY, M.H., and MAHONEY, K. (1976) *Permanent weight control.* New York: W.W. Norton. **315**

MAHONEY, M.J., see CRAIGHEAD, KAZDIN, and MAHONEY (1981).

MAISEL, E., see GEER and MAISEL (1972).

MALOF, M., and LOTT, A.J. (1962) Ethnocentrism and the acceptance of Negro support in a group pressure situation. *Journal of Abnormal and Social Psychology,* 65:254–58. **572**

MANDLER, G. (1980) "The generation of emotion: A psychological theory." In Plutchik, R., and Kellerman, H. (eds.) *Theories of emotion.* New York: Academic Press. **343**

MANKIEWICZ, F., and SWERDLOW, J. (1977) *Remote control.* New York: Quadrangle. **330**

MANN, L., see KILHAM and MANN (1974).

MARACEK, J., see NISBETT, CAPUTO, LEGANT, and MARACEK (1973).

MARGOLIS, R., see GLICK and MARGOLIS (1962).

MARGULIS, S., see YERKES and MARGULIS (1909).

MARKS, D., and KAMMANN, R. (1977) The nonpsychic powers of Uri Geller. *The Zetetic,* 1:9–17. **187**

MARKS, D., and KAMMANN, R. (1980) *The psychology of the psychic.* Buffalo, N.Y.: Prometheus Books. **160, 163**

MARKUS, H. (1977) Self-schemata and processing information about the self. *Journal of Personality and Social Psychology,* 35:63–78. **530, 539**

MARKUS, H. (1978) The effect of mere presence on social facilitation: An unobtrusive test. *Journal of Experimental Social Psychology,* 14:389–97. **564**

MARKUS, H., CRANE, M., BERNSTEIN, S., and SILADI, M. (1982) Self-schemas and gender. *Journal of Personality and Social Psychology,* 42:38–50. **541**

MARRON, J.E. (1965) *Special test preparation, its effects on College Board scores and the relationship of effected scores to subsequent college performance.* Office of the Director of Admissions and

Registrar. U.S. Military Academy, West Point, N.Y. **365**

MARSHALL, G. (1976) *The affective consequences of "inadequately explained" physiological arousal.* Unpublished doctoral dissertation, Stanford University. **342**

MARTIN, C.E., see KINSEY, POMEROY, and MARTIN (1948).

MARTIN, C.E., see KINSEY, POMEROY, MARTIN, and GEBHARD (1953).

MARTIN, D.G. (1971) *Introduction to psychotherapy.* Monterey, Calif.: Brooks/Cole. **524**

MARTINEZ, J.L., JR., see MCGAUGH, JENSEN, and MARTINEZ (1979).

MARTYNA, W., see BEM, MARTYNA, and WATSON (1976).

MASLACH, C. (1979) The emotional consequences of arousal without reason. In Izard, C.E. (ed.) *Emotion in personality and psychopathology.* New York: Plenum Press. **342**

MASLOW, A.H. (1954) *Motivation and personality.* New York: Harper and Row. **318**

MASLOW, A.H. (1967) Self-actualization and beyond. In Bugental, J.F.T. (ed.) *Challenges of humanistic psychology.* New York: McGraw-Hill. **402**

MASLOW, A.H. (1970) *Motivation and personality* (2nd ed.). New York: Harper and Row. **401**

MASSERMAN, J.H. (1961) *Principles of dynamic psychiatry* (2nd ed.). Philadelphia: Saunders. **430**

MASSEY, J.O., see HEWITT and MASSEY (1969).

MASTERS, J.C., see RIMM and MASTERS, 1974.

MASTERS, W.H., and JOHNSON, V.E. (1966) *Human sexual response.* Boston: Little, Brown. **20**

MATARAZZO, J.D. (1971) Some national developments in the utilization of nontraditional mental health manpower. *American Psychologist,* 26: 363–72. **521**

MATARAZZO, J.D., and WIENS, A.W. (1972) *The interview: Research on its anatomy and structure.* Chicago: Aldine-Atherton. **404**

MATARAZZO, J.D., and WIENS, A.W. (1977) Black Intelligence Test of Cultural Homogeneity and Wechsler Adult Intelligence Scale scores of black and white police applicants. *Journal of Applied Psychology,* 62:57–63. **362**

MATAS, L., AREND, R.A., and SROUFE, L.A. (1978) Continuity of adaption in the second year: The relationship between quality of attachment and later competence. *Child Development,* 49:547–56. **77**

MATHES, E.W. (1975) The effects of physical attractiveness and anxiety on heterosexual attraction over a series of five encounters. *Journal of Marriage and the Family,* 37:769–73. **554**

MAYER, R.E. (1981) *The promise of cognitive psychology.* San Francisco: Freeman. **27**

MCALLISTER, B.H., see NILSON, NILSON, OLSON, and MCALLISTER (1981).

MCARTHUR, L.A. (1972) The how and what of why: Some determinants and consequences of causal attribution. *Journal of Personality and Social Psychology,* 22:171–93. **537**

MCCARLEY, R.W., and HOFFMAN, E. (1981) REM sleep dreams and the activation-synthesis hypothesis. *American Journal of Psychiatry,* 138:904–12. **174**

MCCARLEY, R.W., see HOBSON and MCCARLEY (1977).

MCCLEARN, G.E., see PLOMIN, DEFRIES, and MCCLEARN (1980).

MCDERMOTT, J., see LARKIN, MCDERMOTT, SIMON, and SIMON (1980).

MCDONALD, F.J., see BANDURA and MCDONALD (1963).

MCDOUGALL, W. (1908) *Social psychology.* New York: G.P. Putnam's Sons. **284**

MCGAUGH, J.L., JENSEN, R.A., and MARTINEZ, J.L., JR. (1979) Sleep, brain state, and memory. In Drucker-Colin, R., Shkurovich, M., and Sterman, M.B. (eds.) *The functions of sleep.* New York: Academic Press. **171**

MCGAUGH, J.L., see COTMAN and MCGAUGH (1980).

MCGAUGH, J.L., see HUDSPETH, MCGAUGH, and THOMPSON (1964).

MCGHIE, A., and CHAPMAN, J. (1961) Disorders of attention and perception in early schizophrenia. *British Journal of Medical Psychology,* 34:103–16. **471, 472**

MCGOWAN, B.K., see GARCIA, MCGOWAN, and GREEN (1972).

MCGRAW, K.O., see CORDUA, MCGRAW, and DRABMAN (1979).

MCGUE, M., see BOUCHARD and MCGUE (1981).

MCGUIRE, W.J. (1960) A syllogistic analysis of cognitive relationships. In Hovland, C.I., and Rosenberg, M.J. (eds.), *Attitude organization and change,* pp. 65–111. New Haven, Conn.: Yale Univ. Press. **545**

MCGUIRE, W.J. (1969) The nature of attitudes and attitude change. In Lindzey, G., and Aronson, E. (eds.), *The handbook of social psychology* (2nd ed.) 3:136–314. Reading, Mass.: Addison-Wesley. **581**

MCKENNA, R.J. (1972) Some effects of anxiety level and food cues on the eating behavior of obese and normal subjects. *Journal of Personality and Social Psychology,* 22:311–19. **294**

MCKEON, J., see RASKIN, SCHULTERBRANDT, BOOTHE, REATIG, and MCKEON (1970).

MCNEILL, D. (1966) Developmental psycholinguistics. In Smith, F., and Miller, G.A. (eds.) *The genesis of language: A psycholinguistic approach.* Cambridge, Mass.: M.I.T. Press. **268**

MCNEILL, D., see BROWN and MCNEILL (1966).

MCPARTLAND, J., see COLEMAN, CAMPBELL, HOBSON, MCPARTLAND, MOODY, WEINFELD, and YORK (1966).

MCPHERSON, J.M., see GALLE, GOVE, and MCPHERSON (1972).

MCQUIRK, B., see BEAMAN, BARNES, KLENTZ, and MCQUIRK (1978).

MEAD, W., see GOECKNER, GREENOUGH, and MEAD (1973).

MECHANIC, D. (1962) *Students under stress.* New York: Free Press. **445**

MECHANIC, D. (1975) Sociocultural and social-psychological factors affecting personal responses to psychological disorder. *Journal of Health and Social Behavior,* 16:393–404. **447**

MEDDIS, R., PEARSON, A.J.D., and LANGFORD, G. (1973) An extreme case of healthy insomnia. *EEG and Clinical Neurology,* 35:213–14. **169**

MEDIN, D.L., see SMITH and MEDIN (1981).

MEDNICK, B.K. (1973) Breakdown in high-risk subjects: Familial and early environmental factors. *Journal of Abnormal Psychology,* 82:469–75. **478**

MEDNICK, S.A. (1962) The associative basis of the creative process. *Psychological Review,* 69:220–32. **372**

MEDNICK, S.A., and SCHULSINGER, F. (1968) Some premorbid characteristics related to the breakdown of children with schizophrenic mothers. In

Rosenthal, D., and Kety, S.S. (eds.) *The transmission of schizophrenia.* New York: Pergamon. **478**

MEICHENBAUM, D.H. (1972) Cognitive modification of test-anxious college students. *Journal of Consulting and Clinical Psychology,* 39:370–80. **508**

MEICHENBAUM, D.H., and JAREMKO, M. (1982) *Stress prevention and management.* New York: Plenum Press. **500**

MELVILLE, J. (1977) *Phobias and obsessions.* New York: Coward, McCann, and Geoghegan. **458**

MENNINGER, K., and HOLZMAN, P.S. (1973) *Theory of psychoanalytic technique* (2nd ed.). New York: Basic Books. **525**

MENZIES, R. (1937) Conditioned vasomotor responses in human subjects. *Journal of Psychology,* 4:75–120. **196**

MERRILL, M.A., see TERMAN and MERRILL (1937).

MERVIS, C.B., and PANI, J.R. (1981) Acquisition of basic object categories. *Cognitive Psychology,* 12:496–522. **258**

MERVIS, C.B., and ROSCH, E. (1981) Categorization of natural objects. In Rosenzweig, M.R., and Porter, L.W. (eds.) *Annual Review of Psychology,* Vol. 21. **256**

MERVIS, C.B., see ROSCH and MERVIS (1975).

MESSER, S. (1967) Implicit phonology in children. *Journal of Verbal Learning and Verbal Behavior,* 6:609–13. **264**

MESSICK, S., and JUNGEBLUT, A. (1981) Time and method in coaching for the SAT, *Psychological Bulletin,* 89:191–216. **365**

MEYER, D.R., see HARLOW, HARLOW, and MEYER (1950).

MEYER, J.P., and PEPPER, S. (1977) Need compatibility and marital adjustment in young married couples. *Journal of Personality and Social Psychology,* 35:331–42. **553**

MEYERS, L.S., and GROSSEN, N.E. (1978) *Behavioral research: Theory, procedure, and design* (2nd ed.). San Francisco: Freeman. **27**

MICHAEL, R.P., BONSALL, R.W. and WARNER, P. (1974) Human vaginal secretions: Volatile fatty acid content. *Science,* 186:1217–19. **127**

MIDDLESTADT, S.E., see WERNER and MIDDLESTADT (1979).

MILAVSKY, B., see ZILLMANN, KATCHER, and MILAVSKY (1972).

MILES, L.E., RAYNAL, D.M., and WILSON, M.A. (1977) Blind man living in normal society has circadian rhythm of 24.9 hours. *Science,* 198:421–23. **169**

MILES, M.B., see LIEBERMAN, YALOM, and MILES (1973).

MILGRAM, S. (1963) Behavioral study of obedience. *Journal of Abnormal and Social Psychology,* 67:371–78. **573, 575**

MILGRAM, S. (1974) *Obedience to authority: An experimental view.* New York: Harper and Row. **573, 575, 578, 590**

MILLER, G.A. (1956) The magical number seven plus or minus two: Some limits on our capacity for processing information. *Psychological Review,* 63:81–97. **224, 229**

MILLER, G.A. (1981) *Language and speech.* San Francisco: Freeman. **279**

MILLER, G.A., and JOHNSON-LAIRD, P.N. (1976) *Language and perception.* Cambridge, Mass.: Harvard Univ. Press. **265**

MILLER, J.R., and KINTSCH, W. (1980) Readability and recall of short prose passages: A theoretical analysis. *Journal of Experimental Psychology: Human Learning and Memory,* 6:335–54. **228**

MILLER, N.E. (1974) Introduction: Current issues and key problems. In Miller, N.E., Barber, T.X., DiCara, L., Kamiya, J., Shapiro, D., and Stoyva, J. (eds.) *Biofeedback and self-control.* Chicago: Aldine. **207**

MILLER, N.E., and BUGELSKI, R. (1948) Minor studies of aggression: II. The influence of frustrations imposed by the in-group on attitudes expressed toward out-groups. *The Journal of Psychology,* 25:437–42. **428**

MILLER, N.E., see DOLLARD, DOOB, MILLER, MOWRER, and SEARS (1939).

MILLER, R.S., see SCHNEIDER AND MILLER (1975).

MILLER, T.I., see SMITH, GLASS, and MILLER (1980).

MILLER, W.E., see DICARA and MILLER (1968).

MILNER, P.M. (1966) *Physiological psychology.* New York: Holt, Rinehart and Winston. **244**

MILSTEIN, R.M. (1980) Responsiveness in newborn infants of overweight and normal weight parents. *Appetite,* 1:65–74. **294**

MINIUM, E.W., and CLARKE, R.W. (1982) *Elements of statistical reasoning.* New York: Wiley. **615**

MINTZ, J., see STANTON, MINTZ, and FRANKLIN (1976).

MIRER, T.W., see KELLEY and MIRER (1974).

MISCHEL, H. (1974) Sex bias in the evaluation of professional achievements. *Journal of Educational Psychology,* 66:157–66. **534**

MISCHEL, H., see MISCHEL and MISCHEL (1976).

MISCHEL, W. (1968) *Personality and assessment.* New York: Wiley. **229**

MISCHEL, W. (1976) *Introduction to personality* (2nd. ed.). New York: Holt, Rinehart and Winston. **413**

MISCHEL, W. (1981) *Introduction to personality* (3rd ed.). New York: Holt, Rinehart and Winston. **394, 418**

MISCHEL, W., and MISCHEL, H. (1976) A cognitive social learning approach to morality and self regulation. In Lickona, T. (ed.) *Moral development and behavior.* New York: Holt, Rinehart and Winston. **84**

MISCHEL, W., see CANTOR and MISCHEL (1979).

MISCHEL, W., see LEWINSOHN, MISCHEL, CHAPLIN, and BARTON (1980).

MITA, T.H., DERMER, M., and KNIGHT, J. (1977) Reversed facial images and the mere-exposure hypothesis. *Journal of Personality and Social Psychology,* 35:597–601. **552**

MITCHEL, J.S., and KEESEY, R.E. (1974) The effects of lateral hypothalamic lesions and castration upon the body weight of male rats. *Behavioral Biology,* 11:69–82. **291**

MITCHELL, K.M., see TRUAX and MITCHELL (1971).

MITCHELL, R.E. (1971) Some social implications of high density housing. *American Sociological Review,* 36:18–29. **587, 588**

MITLER, M.M., see CARSKADON, MITLER, and DEMENT (1974).

MLADEJOVSKY, M.G., see DOBELLE, MLADEJOVSKY, EVANS, ROBERTS, and GIRVIN (1976).

MOHS, R.C., see DAVIS AND MOHS (1982).

MONEY, J. (1980) Endocrine influences and psychosexual status spanning the life cycle. In Van Praag, H.M. (ed.) *Handbook of biological psychiatry* (Part III). New York: Marcel Dekker. **300, 308**

MONEY, J., and MUSAPH, H. (eds.) (1977) *Handbook of sexology.* Amsterdam:

Elsevier/North Holland Biomedical Press. **315**

MONTAGU, A. (ed.) (1978) *Learning non-aggression: The experience of non-literate societies.* New York: Oxford Univ. Press. **345**

MOODY, A.M., see COLEMAN, CAMPBELL, HOBSON, MCPARTLAND, MOODY, WEINFELD, and YORK (1966).

MOORE, B.R., see JENKINS and MOORE (1973).

MOORE, B.S., SHERROD, D.R., LIU, T.J., and UNDERWOOD, B. (1979) The dispositional shift in attribution over time. *Journal of Experimental Social Psychology*, 15:553–69. **542**

MOORE, B.S., see UNDERWOOD and MOORE (1981).

MOORE, R.D., see BOCK and MOORE (1982).

MOORE, M.H., and GERSTEIN, D.R., (eds.) (1981) *Alcohol and public policy.* Washington, D.C.: National Academy Press. **491**

MOORE, S.G., see HARTUP and MOORE (1963).

MORELAND, R.L., and ZAJONC, R.B. (1979) Exposure effects may not depend on stimulus recognition. *Journal of Personality and Social Psychology*, 37:1085–89. **552**

MORGAN, A.H. (1973) The heritability of hypnotic susceptibility in twins. *Journal of Abnormal Psychology*, 82:55–61. **182**

MORGAN, A.H., JOHNSON, D.L., and HILGARD, E.R. (1974) The stability of hypnotic susceptibility: A longitudinal study. *International Journal of Clinical and Experimental Hypnosis*, 22:249–57. **182**

MORGAN, A.H., see HILGARD, HILGARD, MACDONALD, MORGAN, and JOHNSON (1978).

MORGAN, A.H., see RUCH, MORGAN, and HILGARD (1973).

MOS, L.P., see ROYCE and MOS (eds.) (1981).

MOWRER, O.H., see DOLLARD, DOOB, MILLER, MOWRER, and SEARS (1939).

MURAWSKI, B.J., see REICH, DESILVA, LOWN, and MURAWSKI (1981).

MURDOCK, B.B., Jr. (1962) The serial position effect in free recall. *Journal of Experimental Psychology*, 64:482–88. **245**

MURDOCK, P., see PAULUS and MURDOCK (1971).

MURPHY, G., and KOVACH, J. (1972) *Historical introduction to modern psychology* (3rd ed.). New York: Harcourt Brace Jovanovich. **27**

MURSTEIN, B.I. (1972) Physical attractiveness and marital choice. *Journal of Personality and Social Psychology*, 22:8–12. **556**

MUSAPH, H., see MONEY and MUSAPH (1977).

MUSSARE, F., see HOGARTY, SCHOOLER, URLICH, MUSSARE, FERRO, and HERRON (1979).

MUSSEN, P.H. (ed.) (1983) *Manual of child psychology* (4th ed.). New York: Wiley. **101**

MUSSEN, P.H., CONGER, J.J., and KAGAN, J. (1982) *Child development and personality* (5th ed.). New York: Harper and Row. **101**

MUSSEN, P.H., and JONES, M.C. (1958) The behavior-inferred motivations of late- and early-maturing boys. *Child Development*, 29:61–67. **94**

MUSSEN, P., and RUTHERFORD, E. (1963) Parent-child relations and parental personality in relation to young children's sex-role preferences. *Child Development*, 34:589–607. **90**

N

NACE, E.P., ORNE, M.T., and HAMMER, A.G. (1974) Posthypnotic amnesia as an active psychic process: The reversibility of amnesia. *Archives of General Psychiatry*, 31:257–60. **183**

NAHIR, H.Y., and YUSSEN, S.R. (1977) Performance of kibbutz- and city-reared Israeli children on two role-taking tasks. *Developmental Psychology*, 13:450–55. **79**

NARANJO, C., and ORNSTEIN, R.E. (1977) *On the psychology of meditation.* New York: Penguin. **175, 189**

NASH, S.C., see KUHN, NASH, and BRUCKEN (1978).

NATHAN, P.E., and O'BRIEN, J.S. (1971) An experimental analysis of the behavior of alcoholics and nonalcoholics during prolonged experimental drinking: A necessary precursor of behavior therapy? *Behavior Therapy*, 2:455–76. **488**

NATIONAL COMMISSION FOR THE PROTECTION OF HUMAN SUBJECTS OF BIOMEDICAL AND BEHAVIOR RESEARCH (1977) *Report and recommendations:* *Psychosurgery.* Department of Health, Education, and Welfare, Pub. No. [OS]77-0002, U.S. Government Printing Office. **517**

NATIONAL INSTITUTE OF MENTAL HEALTH REPORT (1982) *Television and behavior: Ten years of scientific progress and implications for the eighties*, Vol. 1. Summary Report. U.S. Department of Health and Human Services Publication Number (ADM)82-1195. **329, 451**

NATIONAL REVIEW (October 8, 1963) A survey of the political and religious attitudes of American college students, pp. 279–302. **583**

NATIONAL REVIEW (June 15, 1971) Opinion on the campus, pp. 635–50. **583**

NEALE, J.M., and OLTMANNS, T.F. (1980) *Schizophrenia.* New York: Wiley. **474, 476**

NEALE, J.M., see DAVISON and NEALE (1982).

NEBES, R.D., and SPERRY, R.W. (1971) Cerebral dominance in perception. *Neuropsychologia*, 9:247. **47**

NEEB, M., see FISHER, ZUCKERMAN, and NEEB (1981).

NEEB, M., see ZUCKERMAN and NEEB (1980).

NEELY, J.E., see THOMPSON and NEELY (1970).

NEISSER, U. (1976) *Cognition and reality: Principles and implications of cognitive psychology.* San Francisco: Freeman. **147**

NEISSER, U., see SELFRIDGE and NEISSER (1960).

NELSON, T.O. (1977) Repetition and depth of processing. *Journal of Verbal Learning and Verbal Behavior*, 16:152–71. **246**

NEUGARTEN, B. (1971) Grow old with me, the best is yet to be. *Psychology Today*, 5:45–49. **99**

NEWCOMB, T.M., see FESTINGER, PEPITONE, and NEWCOMB (1952).

NEWCOMB, T.M. (1943) *Personality and social change.* New York: Dryden Press. **583, 590**

NEWCOMB, T.M. (1961) *The acquaintance process.* New York: Holt, Rinehart and Winston. **553**

NEWCOMB, T.M., KOENING, K.E., FLACKS, R., and WARWICK, D.P. (1967) *Persistence and change: Bennington College and its students after twenty-five years.* New York: Wiley. **583, 590**

NEWELL, A., and SIMON, H.A. (1972) *Human problem solving.* Englewood Cliffs, N.J.: Prentice-Hall. **277, 279**

NEW YORK TIMES, November 25, 1969. **577**

NICHOLS, R.C. (1968) Nature and nurture in adolescence. In Adams, J.F. (ed.) *Understanding adolescence.* Boston: Allyn and Bacon. **92**

NICHOLS, R.C., see LOEHLIN and NICHOLS (1976).

NILSON, D.C., NILSON, L.B., OLSON, R.S., and MCALLISTER, B.H. (1981) *The planning environment report for the Southern California Earthquake Safety Advisory Board.* Redlands, Calif.: The Social Research Advisory and the Policy Research Center. **445**

NILSON, L.B., see NILSON, NILSON, OLSON, and MCALLISTER (1981).

NISBETT, R.E. (1968a) Birth order and participation in dangerous sports. *Journal of Personality and Social Psychology,* 8:351–53. **92**

NISBETT, R.E. (1968b) Taste, deprivation, and weight determinants of eating behavior. *Journal of Personality and Social Psychology,* 10:107–16. **293**

NISBETT, R.E. (1972) Hunger, obesity, and the ventromedial hypothalamus. *Psychological Review,* 79:433–53. **297**

NISBETT, R.E., CAPUTO, C., LEGANT, P., and MARACEK, J. (1973) Behavior as seen by the observer. *Journal of Personality and Social Psychology,* 27:154–64. **542**

NISBETT, R.E., and ROSS, L. (1980) *Human inference: Strategies and short-comings of social judgment.* Englewood Cliffs, N.J.: Prentice-Hall. **538, 543, 559**

NISBETT, R.E., see JONES AND NISBETT (1971).

NISBETT, R.E., see LEPPER, GREENE, and NISBETT (1973).

NOLEN, W.A. (1974) *Healing: A doctor in search of a miracle.* New York: Random House. **187**

NORMAN, D.A. (1976) *Memory and attention: An introduction to human information processing* (2nd ed.). New York: Wiley. **149, 163, 240, 581**

NORMAN, D.A. (1982) *Learning and memory.* San Francisco: Freeman. **219, 251**

NORMAN, D.A., see LINDSAY and NORMAN (1977).

NORMAN, D.A., see WAUGH and NORMAN (1965).

NORMAN, R. (1975) Affective-cognitive consistency, attitudes, conformity, and behavior. *Journal of Personality and Social Psychology,* 32:83–91. **548**

NORMAN, W.T. (1963) Toward an adequate taxonomy of personality attributes: Replicated factor structure in peer nomination personality ratings. *Journal of Abnormal and Social Psychology,* 66:574–83. **390**

NOWLIS, G.H., and KESSEN, W. (1976) Human newborns differentiate differing concentrations of sucrose and glucose. *Science,* 191:865–66. **65**

O

O'BRIEN, J.S., see NATHAN and O'BRIEN (1971).

O'BRIEN, R.M., see CRAIGHEAD, STUNKARD, and O'BRIEN (1981).

O'DONNELL, J.A., and CLAYTON, R.R. (1982) The stepping stone hypothesis—Marijuana, heroin, and causality. *Chemical Dependencies,* Vol 4: No. 3 **488**

O'LEARY, K.D., and WILSON, G.T. (1975) *Behavior therapy: Application and outcome.* Englewood Cliffs, N.J.: Prentice-Hall. **505**

OFFIR, C. (1982) *Human sexuality.* New York: Harcourt Brace Jovanovich. **303, 315, 559**

OFFIR, C., see TAVRIS and OFFIR (1977).

OJEMANN, G.A., see CALVIN and OJEMANN (1980).

OKADA, M., see ENDLER and OKADA (1974).

OLDS, M.E., and FOBES, J.L. (1981) The central basis of motivation: Intracranial self-stimulation studies. *Annual Review of Psychology,* 32:523–74. Palo Alto, Calif.: Annual Reviews, Inc. **211**

OLIVEAU, D., see AGRAS, SYLVESTER, and OLIVEAU (1969).

OLSON, R.S., see NILSON, NILSON, OLSON, and MCALLISTER (1981).

OLTMANNS, T.F., see NEALE and OLTMANNS (1980).

OLWEUS, D. (1969) *Prediction of aggression.* Scandinavian Test Corporation. **410**

OLWEUS, D. (1979) Stability of aggressive reaction patterns in males: A review. *Psychological Bulletin,* 86:852–75. **415**

OOMURA, Y. (1975) Effects of glucose and free fatty acid in chemosensitive neurons in the rat hypothalamus. In Novin, D., Wyrwicka, W., and Bray, G.A. (eds.) *Hunger: Basic mechanisms and clinical implications.* New York: Raven Press. **290**

ORDY, J.M., see FANTZ, ORDY, and UDELF (1962).

ORNE, E.C., see EVANS, COOK, COHEN, ORNE, and ORNE (1977).

ORNE, M.T., and HOLLAND, C.C. (1968) On the ecological validity of laboratory deceptions. *International Journal of Psychiatry,* 6:282–93. **579**

ORNE, M.T., see EVANS, COOK, COHEN, ORNE, and ORNE (1977).

ORNE, M.T., see NACE, ORNE, and HAMMER (1974).

ORNSTEIN, R.E. (1977) *The psychology of consciousness* (2nd ed.). New York: Harcourt Brace Jovanovich. **49, 186, 189**

ORNSTEIN, R.E., see NARANJO and ORNSTEIN (1977).

OSBORN, D.K., and ENDSLEY, R.C. (1971) Emotional reactions of young children to TV violence. *Child Development,* 42:321–31. **330**

OSGOOD, C.E., and TANNENBAUM, P.H. (1955) The principle of congruity in the prediction of attitude change. *Psychological Review,* 62:42–55. **580**

OSKAMP, S., see PERLMAN AND OSKAMP (1971).

OSTROVE, N., see SIGALL and OSTROVE (1975).

OSWALD, I., see JONES and OSWALD (1968).

OVERTON, D.A. (1972) State-dependent learning produced by alcohol and its relevance to alcoholism. In Kissin, B., and Begleiter, H. (eds.) *Physiology and behavior: The biology of alcoholism,* Vol. 2. New York: Plenum Press. **177**

OWEN, D.R. (1972) The 47, XYY male: A review. *Psychological Review,* 78:209–33. **55**

P

PACKARD, V. (1970) *The sexual wilderness: The contemporary upheaval in male-female relationships.* New York: Pocket Books. **304**

PAKSTIS, A.J., see SCARR, PAKSTIS, KATZ, and BARKER (1977).

PALLONE, N.J. (1961) Effects of short- and long-term developmental reading courses upon SAT verbal scores. *Personnel and Guidance Journal,* 39:654–57. **365**

PALMER, F.H. (1976) *The effects of minimal*

early intervention on subsequent IQ scores and reading achievement (Final report to the Education Commission of the States, Contract 13-76-06846). Stony Brook, N.Y.: State Univ. of New York. **378**

PANATI, C. (ed.) (1976) *The Geller papers: Scientific observations on the paranormal powers of Uri Geller.* Boston: Houghton Mifflin. **187**

PANI, J.R., see MERVIS and PANI (1981).

PANKOVE, E., see KOGAN and PANKOVE (1974).

PARKES, M.C., BENJAMIN, B., and FITZGERALD, R.G. (1969) Broken heart: A statistical study of increased mortality among widowers. *British Medical Journal*, 1:740–43. **446**

PARRISH, M., LUNDY, R.M., and LEIBOWITZ, H.W. (1968) Hypnotic age-regression and magnitudes of the Ponzo and Poggendorff illusions. *Science*, 159: 1375–76. **146**

PARRON, D., see HAMBURG, ELLIOTT, and PARRON (1982).

PATTERSON, F.G. (1978) The gestures of a gorilla: Language acquisition in another pongid. *Brain and Language*, 5:72–97. **271**

PATTERSON, G.R., LITTMAN, R.A., and BRICKER, W.A. (1967) Assertive behavior in children: A step toward a theory of aggression. *Monographs of the Society for Research in Child Development*, Serial No. 113, 32:5. **327**

PAUL, G.L., and BERNSTEIN, D.R. (1973) *Anxiety and clinical problems: Systematic desensitization and related techniques.* Morristown, N.J.: General Learning Press. **506**

PAULUS, P.B., and MURDOCK, P. (1971) Anticipated evaluation and audience presence in the enhancement of dominant responses. *Journal of Experimental Social Psychology*, 7:280–91. **563**

PAVLOV, I.P. (1927) *Conditioned reflexes.* New York: Oxford Univ. Press. **196, 219**

PEARLSTONE, Z., see TULVING and PEARLSTONE (1966).

PEARSON, A.J.D., see MEDDIS, PEARSON, and LANGFORD (1973).

PEPITONE, A., see FESTINGER, PEPITONE, and NEWCOMB (1952).

PEPLAU, L.A., see RUBIN, HILL, PEPLAU, and DUNKEL-SCHETTER (1980).

PEPPER, S., see MEYER and PEPPER (1977).

PERLMAN, D., and OSKAMP, S. (1971) The effects of picture content and exposure frequency on evaluations of negroes and whites. *Journal of Experimental Social Psychology*, 7:503–14. **552**

PERRIN, F.A.C. (1921) Physical attractiveness and repulsiveness. *Journal of Experimental Psychology*, 4:203–17. **554**

PERRY, C.W., see SHEEHAN and PERRY (1976).

PETERSON, C., SCHWARTZ, S.M., and SELIGMAN, M.E.P. (1981) Self-blame and depressive symptoms. *Journal of Abnormal and Social Psychology*, 41:253–59. **467, 468**

PETERSON, R.C., and STILLMAN, R.C. (eds.) (1977) *Cocaine: 1977* (NIDA Monograph No. 13). Washington, D.C.: U.S. Government Printing Office. **189**

PETITTO, L.A., see SEIDENBERG and PETITTO (1979).

PETITTO, L.A., see TERRACE, PETITTO, SANDERS, and BEVER (1979).

PETRI, H.L. (1981) *Motivation: Theory and research.* Belmont, Calif.: Wadsworth. **315, 345**

PHARES, E.J., see ROTTER, CHANCE, and PHARES (1972).

PHILLIPS, E.A., see PHILLIPS, PHILLIPS, FIXSEN, and WOLF, 1972.

PHILLIPS, E.L., PHILLIPS, E.A., FIXSEN, D.L., and WOLF, M.M. (1972) *The teaching-family handbook.* Lawrence, Kans.: Kansas Printing Service. **521**

PHILLIPS, J.L., JR. (1981) *Piaget's theory: A primer.* San Francisco: Freeman. **101**

PHILLIPS, J.L., JR. (1982) *Statistical thinking: A structural approach* (2nd ed.). San Francisco: Freeman. **27, 606**

PIAGET, J. (1932, 1965) *The moral judgment of the child.* New York: Free Press. **81, 83**

PIAGET, J. (1952) *The origins of intelligence in children.* New York: International Universities Press. **311**

PICHERT, J.W., see ANDERSON and PICHERT (1978).

PIERCE, C.M., see HOFLING, BROTZMAN, DALRYMPLE, GRAVES, and PIERCE (1966).

PILIAVIN, I.M., RODIN, J., and PILIAVIN, J.A. (1969) Good Samaritanism: An underground phenomenon? *Journal of Personality and Social Psychology*, 13:289–99. **568**

PILIAVIN, J.A., see PILIAVIN, RODIN, and PILIAVIN (1969).

PLATT, J.J., and JAMES, W.T. (1966) Social facilitation of eating behavior in young opossums. I. Group vs. solitary feeding. *Psychonomic Science*, 6:421–22. **562**

PLATT, J.J., YAKSH, T., and DARBY, C.L. (1967) Social facilitation of eating behavior in armadillos. *Psychological Reports*, 20:1136. **562**

PLOMIN, R., DEFRIES, J.C., and MCCLEARN, G.E. (1980) *Behavioral genetics: A primer.* San Francisco: Freeman. **59, 381, 491**

PLOMIN, R., see BUSS and PLOMIN (1975).

PLUTCHIK, R. (1980) *Emotion: A psychoevolutionary synthesis.* New York: Harper and Row. **345**

PLUTCHIK, R., and KELLERMAN, H. (eds.) (1980) *Theories of emotion.* New York: Academic Press. **345**

POLIVY, J., and HERMAN, C.P. (1976) Effects of alcohol on eating behavior: Influence of mood and perceived intoxication. *Journal of Abnormal Psychology*, 85:601–606. **295**

POLIVY, J., see HERMAN and POLIVY (1980).

POLT, J.M., see HESS and POLT (1960).

POMEROY, A.C., see KINSEY, POMEROY, and MARTIN (1948).

POMEROY, W.B., see KINSEY, POMEROY, MARTIN, and GEBHARD (1953).

POON, L.W. (ed.) (1980) *Aging in the 1980s.* Washington, D.C.: American Psychological Association. **101**

POPE, K.S., and SINGER, J.L. (eds.) (1978) *The stream of consciousness.* New York: Plenum Press. **189**

PORAC, C., see COREN, PORAC, and WARD (1978).

POSNER, M.I., and KEELE, S.W. (1967) Decay of visual information from a single letter. *Science*, 158:137–39. **223**

POST, R.M., KOTIN, J., GOODWIN, F.K., and GORDON, E. (1973) Psychomotor activity and cerebrospinal fluid amine metabolites in affective illness. *American Journal of Psychiatry*, 130:67–72. **469**

POWLEY, T.L., and KEESEY, R.E. (1970) Relationship of body weight to the lateral hypothalamic feeding syndrome. *Journal of Comparative and Physiological Psychology*, 70:25–36. **292**

POWLEY, T.L., see KEESEY and POWLEY (1975).

PREMACK, D. (1959) Toward empirical behavior laws: I. Positive reinforcement. *Psychological Review*, 66: 219–33. **208**

PREMACK, D. (1962) Reversibility of the reinforcement relation. *Science*, 136: 255–57. **209**

PREMACK, D. (1971) Language in chimpanzees? *Science*, 172:808–22. **271**

PRENTICE-DUNN, S., and ROGERS, R.W. (1980) Effects of deindividuating situational cues and aggressive models on subjective deindividuation and aggression. *Journal of Personality and Social Psychology*, 39:104–13. **566**

PRESSLEY, M., LEVIN, J.R., and DELANEY, H.D. (1982) The mnemonic keyword method. *Review of Educational Research* 52:61–91. **239**

PRIEST, R.F., and SAWYER, J. (1967) Proximity and peership: Bases of balance in interpersonal attraction. *American Journal of Sociology*. 72:633–49. **551**

PUBOLS, B.H., see WELKER, JOHNSON, and PUBOLS (1964).

Q

QUANTY, M.B., see GEEN and QUANTY (1977).

QUILLIAN, M.R., see COLLINS and QUILLIAN (1969).

R

RAAIJMAKERS, J.G., and SHIFFRIN, R.M. (1981) Search of associative memory. *Psychological Review*, 88:93–134. **234**

RABKIN, K., see RABKIN and RABKIN (1969).

RABKIN, Y., and RABKIN, K. (1969) Children of the kibbutz. *Psychology Today*, 3:40–46. **79**

RACHMAN, S.J. (1978) *Fear and courage.* San Francisco: Freeman. **449**

RAHE, R.H., see HOLMES and RAHE (1967).

RANDI, J. (1978) The psychology of conjuring. *Technology Review*, 80:56–63. **161**

RANDS, M., and LEVINGER, G. (1979) Implicit theories of relationship: An intergenerational study. *Journal of Personality and Social Psychology*, 37:645–61. **556**

RAPAPORT, D. (1942) *Emotions and memory.* Baltimore: Williams and Wilkins. **237**

RASKIN, A., SCHULTERBRANDT, J., BOOTHE, J., REATIG, N., and MCKEON, J. (1970) Treatment, social and psychiatric variables related to symptom reduction in hospitalized depressives. In Wittenborn, J.R., Goldberg, S., and May, P. (eds.) *Psychopharmacology and the individual patient.* New York: Raven Press. **519**

RAVIZZA, R., see RAY and RAVIZZA (1981).

RAY, O.S. (1978) *Drugs, society, and human behavior* (2nd ed.). St. Louis: Mosby. **491**

RAY, W.J., and RAVIZZA, R. (1981) *Methods toward a science of behavior and experience.* Belmont, Calif.: Wadsworth. **27**

RAYNAL, D.M., see MILES, RAYNAL, and WILSON (1977).

REATIG, N., see RASKIN, SCHULTERBRANDT, BOOTHE, REATIG, and MCKEON (1970).

REDER, L.M., see ANDERSON and REDER (1979).

REDLICH, F.C., see HOLLINGSHEAD and REDLICH (1958).

REGAN, D.T., and TOTTEN, J. (1975) Empathy and attribution: Turning observers into actors. *Journal of Personality and Social Psychology*, 32:850–56. **542**

REISER, B.J., see KOSSLYN, BALL, and REISER (1978).

REITMAN, J.S. (1974) Without surreptitious rehearsal, information in short-term memory decays. *Journal of Verbal Learning and Verbal Behavior*, 13:365–77. **226**

REQUIN-BLOW, B., see COBBIN, REQUIN-BLOW, WILLIAMS, and WILLIAMS (1979).

RESCORLA, R.A. (1968) Probability of shock in the presence and absence of CS in fear conditioning. *Journal of Comparative and Physiological Psychology*, 66:1–5. **198**

RESCORLA, R.A. (1972) Informational variables in Pavlovian conditioning. In Bower, G.H. (ed.) *Psychology of learning and motivation*, Vol. 6. New York: Academic Press. **199**

RESNICK, R.B., KESTENBAUM, R.S., and SCHWARTZ, L.K. (1977) Acute systemic effects of cocaine in man: A controlled study of intranasal and intravenous routes of administration. In Ellinwood, E.H., Jr., and Kilbey, M.M. (eds.) *Cocaine and other stimulants.* New York: Plenum Press. **179**

RESNICK, S., see BOUCHARD, HESTON, ECKERT, KEYES, and RESNICK (1981).

RHINE, J.B. (1942) Evidence of precognition in the covariation of salience ratios. *Journal of Parapsychology*, 6:111–43. **159**

RICE, B. (1978) The new truth machine. *Psychology Today*, 12:61–78. **335**

RICHARDS, D., see HO, CHUTE, and RICHARDS (1977).

RICHLIN, M. (1977) Positive and negative residuals of prolonged stress. Paper presented at Military Family Research Conference, San Diego, California, September 3, 1977. **429**

RICKERT, E.J., see HOMME, DE BACA, DEVINE, STEINHORST, and RICKERT (1963).

RIEDER, R.O., see ROSENTHAL, WENDER, KETY, SCHULSINGER, WELNER, and RIEDER (1975).

RIESEN, A.H. (1965) Effects of early deprivation of photic stimulation. In Osler, S., and Cooke, R. (eds.) *The biosocial basis of mental retardation.* Baltimore: Johns Hopkins Univ. Press. **156**

RIGGS, L.A., see KLING and RIGGS (1971).

RIGLER, D., see FROMKIN, KRASHEN, CURTISS, RIGLER, and RIGLER (1974).

RIGLER, M., see FROMKIN, KRASHEN, CURTISS, RIGLER, and RIGLER (1974).

RILEY, V. (1981) Psychoneuroendocrine influence on immunocompetence and neoplasia. *Science*, 212:1100–09. **446**

RIMM, D.C., and MASTERS, J.C. (1974) *Behavior therapy: Techniques and empirical findings.* New York: Academic Press. **504**

RIOCH, M.J. (1967) Pilot projects in training mental health counselors. In Cowen, E.L., Gardner, E.A., and Zax, M. (eds.) *Emergent approaches to mental health problems.* New York: Appleton-Century-Crofts. **521**

RITTER, B., see BANDURA, BLANCHARD, and RITTER (1969).

RITTLE, R.H., see COTTRELL, RITTLE, and WACK (1967).

RITTLE, R.H., see COTTRELL, WACK, SEKERAK, and RITTLE (1968).

RIZLEY, R. (1978) Depression and distortion in the attribution of causality. *Journal of Abnormal Psychology*, 87:32–48. **467**

ROBERTS, T.S., see DOBELLE, MLADEJOVSKY, EVANS, ROBERTS, and GIRVIN (1976).

ROBINS, L. (1974) *The Viet Nam drug abuser returns.* New York: McGraw-Hill. **489**

ROBINSON, D.L., and WURTZ, R. (1976) Use of an extra-retinal signal by monkey superior colliculus neurons to distinguish real from self-induced stimulus movement. *Journal of Neurophysiology*, 39:852–70. **145**

ROBINSON, H.A., see THOMAS and ROBINSON (1972).

ROCK, I. (1975) *An introduction to perception*. New York: Macmillan. **131**

ROCK, J., see VIERLING and ROCK (1967).

ROCK, L., see JONES, ROCK, SHAVER, GOETHALS, and WARD (1968).

RODIN, J. (1976) Crowding, perceived choice, and response to controllable and uncontrollable outcomes. *Journal of Experimental Social Psychology*, 12:564–78. **588**

RODIN, J. (1981) Current status of the internal-external hypothesis of obesity: What went wrong? *American Psychologist*, 36:361–72. **293, 294, 297**

RODIN, J., see LATANE and RODIN (1969).

RODIN, J., see PILIAVIN, RODIN, and PILIAVIN (1969).

ROEDERER, J.G. (1975) Introduction to the physics and psychophysics of music. Berlin: Springer-Verlag. **125**

ROFFWARG, H.P., HERMAN, J.H., BOWE-ANDERS, C., and TAUBER, E.S. (1978) The effects of sustained alterations of waking visual input on dream content. In Arkin, A.M., Antrobus, J.S., and Ellman, S.J. (eds.) *The mind in sleep*. Hillsdale, N.J.: Erlbaum. **173**

ROFFWARG, H.P., see HERMAN, ELLMAN, and ROFFWARG (1978).

ROGERS, C.R. (1951) *Client-centered therapy*. Boston: Houghton Mifflin. **399, 525**

ROGERS, C.R. (1970) *On becoming a person: A therapist's view of psychotherapy*. Boston: Houghton Mifflin. **510, 525**

ROGERS, C.R. (1977) *Carl Rogers on personal power*. New York: Delacorte Press. **399, 419**

ROGERS, C.R., and STEVENS, B. (1967) *Person to person: The problem of being human*. New York: Pocket Books. **419**

ROGERS, R.W., see PRENTICE-DUNN and ROGERS (1980).

ROGERS, T.B., KUIPER, N.A., and KIRKER, W.S. (1977) Self-reference and the encoding of personal information. *Journal of Personality and Social Psychology*, 35:677–88. **531**

ROHDE, L.D., see HIRSCH, GAIND, ROHDE, STEVENS, and WING (1973).

ROHRER, J.H., BARON, S.H., HOFFMAN, E.L., and SWANDER, D.V. (1954) The stability of autokinetic judgments. *Journal of Abnormal and Social Psychology*, 49:595–97. **570**

ROKEACH, M. (1968) *Beliefs, attitudes, and values*. San Francisco: Jossey-Bass. **545, 546**

ROKEACH, M. (1973) *The nature of human values*. New York: The Free Press. **545**

ROLLS, B.J., and ROLLS, E.T. (1982) *Thirst*. New York: Cambridge Univ. Press. **309**

ROLLS, E.T., see ROLLS and ROLLS (1982).

ROSCH, E. (1974) Linguistic relativity. In Silverstein, A. (ed.) *Human communication: Theoretical perspectives*. New York: Halsted Press. **259**

ROSCH, E. (1978) Principles of categorization. In Rosch, E., and Lloyd, B.L. (eds.) *Cognition and categorization*. Hillsdale, N.J.: Erlbaum. **255**

ROSCH, E., see MERVIS and ROSCH (1981).

ROSE, J.E., and FANTINO, E. (1978) Conditioned reinforcement and discrimination in second-order schedules. *Journal of the Experimental Analysis of Behavior*, 29:393–418. **204**

ROSENBERG, M.J. (1956) Cognitive structure and attitudinal affect. *Journal of Abnormal and Social Psychology*, 53:367–72. **546**

ROSENBERG, M.J. (1960) An analysis of affective-cognitive consistency. In Hovland, C. I., and Rosenberg, M.J. (eds.), *Attitude organization and change*, pp. 15–64. New Haven, Conn.: Yale Univ., Press. **547**

ROSENBLATT, J.S., see TERKEL and ROSENBLATT (1972).

ROSENFELD, D., see SNYDER, STEPHAN, and ROSENFELD (1976).

ROSENFELD, E., see CHEIN, GERARD, LEE, and ROSENFELD (1964).

ROSENFELD, H., and BAER, D. (1969) Unnoticed verbal conditioning of an aware experimenter by a more aware subject: The double-agent effect. *Psychological Review*, 76:425–32. **206**

ROSENMAN, R.H., BRAND, R.J., JENKINS, C.D., FRIEDMAN, M., STRAUS, R., and WRUM, M. (1975) Coronary heart disease in the Western Collaborative Group Study. Final follow-up experience of $8\frac{1}{2}$ years. *JAMA*, 233:872–77. **440**

ROSENMAN, R.H., see FRIEDMAN and ROSENMAN (1974).

ROSENTHAL, D., WENDER, P.H., KETY, S.S., SCHULSINGER, F., WELNER, J., and RIEDER, R.O. (1975) Parent-child relationships and psychopathological disorder in the child. *Archives of General Psychiatry*, 32:466–76. **478**

ROSENTHAL, D., see WENDER, ROSENTHAL, KETY, SCHULSINGER, and WELNER (1974).

ROSENTHAL, R. (1964) Experimental outcome-orientation and the results of the psychological experiment. *Psychological Bulletin*, 61:405–12. **566**

ROSENZWEIG, M.R., and LEIMAN, A.L. (1982) *Physiological psychology*. Lexington, Mass.: D.C. Heath. **59**

ROSS, L. (1974) Obesity and externality. In Schachter, S., and Rodin, J. (eds.) *Obese humans and rats*. Potomac, Md.: Erlbaum. **293**

ROSS, L. (1977) The intuitive psychologist and his shortcomings: Distortions in the attribution process. In Berkowitz, L. (ed.) *Advances in experimental social psychology*, Vol. 10. New York: Academic Press. **538**

ROSS, L., see NISBETT and ROSS (1980).

ROSS, M., LAYTON, B., ERICKSON, B., and SCHOPLER, J. (1973) Affect, facial regard, and reactions to crowding. *Journal of Personality and Social Psychology*, 28:69–76. **587**

ROSS, M., and SICOLY, F. (1979) Egocentric biases in availability and attribution. *Journal of Personality and Social Psychology*, 37:322–36. **543**

ROSS, R., BIERBRAUER, G., and HOFFMAN, S. (1976) The role of attribution processes in conformity and dissent: Revisiting the Asch Situation. *American Psychologist*, 31:148–57. **571, 572**

ROSS, W.F., see BERZINS, ROSS, ENGLISH, and HALEY (1974).

ROTH, W.T., see DARLEY, TINKLENBERG, ROTH, HOLLISTER, and ATKINSON (1973).

ROTTER, J.B., CHANCE, J.E., and PHARES, E.J. (1972) *Applications of a social learning theory of personality*. New York: Holt, Rinehart and Winston. **418**

ROTTMANN, L., see WALSTER, ARONSON, ABRAHAMS, and ROTTMANN (1966).

ROY, A. (1981) Role of past loss in depression. *Archives of General Psychiatry*, 38(3):301–302. **466**

ROYCE, J.R., and MOS, L.P. (eds.) (1981) *Humanistic psychology: Concepts and criticisms.* New York: Plenum Press. **11, 27**

RUBIN, J.Z., see LURIA and RUBIN (1974).

RUBIN, Z. (1973) *Liking and loving.* New York: Holt, Rinehart and Winston. **97, 551, 552**

RUBIN, Z. (1975) Disclosing oneself to a stranger: Reciprocity and its limits. *Journal of Experimental Social Psychology,* 11:233–60. **556**

RUBIN, Z., HILL, C.T., PEPLAU, L.A., and DUNKEL-SCHETTER, C. (1980) Self-disclosure in dating couples: Sex roles and ethic of openness. *Journal of Marriage and the Family,* 42:305–17. **556**

RUCH, J.C. (1975) Self-hypnosis: The result of heterohypnosis or vice versa? *International Journal of Clinical and Experimental Hypnosis,* 23:282–304. **182**

RUCH, J.C., MORGAN, A.H., and HILGARD, E.R. (1973) Behavioral predictions from hypnotic responsiveness scores when obtained with and without prior induction procedures. *Journal of Abnormal Psychology,* 82:543–46. **182**

RUMBAUGH, D.M. (ed.) (1977) *Language learning by a chimpanzee: The Lana project.* New York: Academic Press. **271**

RUMELHART, D.E. (1977) *An introduction to human information processing.* New York: Wiley. **279**

RUNCK, B. (1980) *Biofeedback—Issues in treatment assessment.* National Institute of Mental Health Science Reports. **443**

RUTHERFORD, E., see MUSSEN and RUTHERFORD (1963).

S

SACHS, J.D.S. (1967) Recognition memory for syntactic and semantic aspects of connected discourse. *Perception and Psychophysics,* 2:437–42. **230**

SACHS, J.S., BROWN, R., and SALERNO, R.A. (1976) Adults' speech to children. In Van Raffler Engel, W., and LeBrun, Y. (eds.) *Baby talk and infant speech* (Neurolinguists 5). Amsterdam: Swets and Zeitlinger. **269**

SADAVE, S.W. (1973) Patterns of college student drug use: A longitudinal social learning study. *Psychological Reports,* 33:75–86. **489**

SAEGERT, S., SWAP, W., and ZAJONC, R.B. (1973) Exposure, context, and interpersonal attraction. *Journal of Personality and Social Psychology,* 25:234–42. **552**

SALAMY, J. (1970) Instrumental responding to internal cues associated with REM sleep. *Psychonomic Science,* 18:342–43. **172**

SALERNO, R.A., see SACHS, BROWN, and SALERNO (1976).

SANDERS, D.J., see TERRACE, PETITTO, SANDERS, and BEVER (1979).

SANTA, J.L., see GLASS, HOLYOAK, and SANTA (1979).

SAPOLSKY, B.S., see ZILLMANN and SAPOLSKY (1977).

SARASON, B.R., see SARASON and SARASON (1980).

SARASON, I.G., and SARASON, B.R. (1980) *Abnormal psychology: The problem of maladaptive behavior.* (3rd ed.). Englewood Cliffs, N.J.: Prentice-Hall. **458, 459, 491**

SARBIN, T.R., see COE AND SARBIN (1977).

SAUFLEY, W.H., JR., see KEPPEL and SAUFLEY (1980).

SAWREY, W.L., CONGER, J.J., and TURRELL, E.S. (1956) An experimental investigation of the role of psychological factors in the production of gastric ulcers of rats. *Journal of Comparative and Physiological Psychology,* 49:457–61. **195**

SAWYER, J., see PRIEST and SAWYER (1967).

SCARR, S. (1981) *Race, social class, and individual differences in IQ.* Hillsdale, N.J.: Erlbaum. **381**

SCARR, S., PAKSTIS, A.J., KATZ, S.H., and BARKER, W.B. (1977) The absence of a relationship between degree of white ancestry and intellectual skills within a black population. *Human Genetics,* 857:1–18. **376**

SCARR, S., and WEINBERG, R.A. (1976) IQ test performance of black children adopted by white families. *American Psychologist,* 31:726–39. **373, 377**

SCARR-SALAPATEK, S. (1971) Race, social class, and IQ. *Science,* 174:1285. **375**

SCHACHTER, S. (1971) *Emotion, obesity, and crime.* New York: Academic Press. **333, 339**

SCHACHTER, S., and SINGER, J.E. (1962) Cognitive, social, and physiological determinants of emotional state. *Psychological Review,* 69:379–99. **342**

SCHACHTER, S., see FESTINGER, SCHACHTER, and BACK (1950).

SCHAEFFER, J., ANDRYSIAK, T., and UNGERLEIDER, J.T. (1981) Cognition and long-term use of ganja (cannabis). *Science,* 213:456–66. **180**

SCHANK, R.C. (1982) *Dynamic memory.* New York: Cambridge Univ. Press. **265, 279**

SCHEIN, E.H., see STRASSMAN, THALER, and SCHEIN (1956).

SCHIAVO, R.S., see SCHIFFENBAUER AND SCHIAVO (1976).

SCHIFFENBAUER, A., and SCHIAVO, R.S. (1976) Physical distance and attraction: An intensification effect. *Journal of Experimental Social Psychology,* 12:274–82. **551**

SCHIFFMAN, H.R. (1982) *Sensation and perception. An integrated approach* (2nd ed.). New York: Wiley. **131, 163**

SCHLESINGER, K., see GROVES and SCHLESINGER (1982).

SCHMEIDLER, G.R., see WOLMAN, DALE, SCHMEIDLER, and ULLMAN (1977).

SCHMITT, R.C. (1963) Implications of density in Hong Kong. *American Institute of Planners Journal,* 29:210–17. **588**

SCHMITT, R.C. (1966) Density, health and social disorganization. *Journal of American Institute of Planners,* 32:38–40. **585**

SCHNEIDER, D.J. (1973) Implicit personality theory: A review. *Psychological Bulletin,* 79:294–309. **530**

SCHNEIDER, D.J., and MILLER, R.S. (1975) The effects of enthusiasm and quality of arguments on attitude attribution. *Journal of Personality,* 43:693–708. **538**

SCHOOLER, N.R., see HOGARTY, SCHOOLER, ULRICH, MUSSARE, FERRO, and HERRON (1979).

SCHOPLER, J., see ROSS, LAYTON, ERICKSON, and SCHOPLER (1973).

SCHORR, D., see SMITH, ADAMS, and SCHORR (1978).

SCHRADER, W.B. (1971) The predictive validity of College Board Admissions tests. In Angoff, W.H. (ed.) *The College Board Admissions Testing Program: A technical report on research and development activities relating to the Scholastic Aptitude Test and Achievement Tests.* New York: College Entrance Examination Board. **363**

SCHRADER, W.B. (1965) A taxonomy of expectancy tables. *Journal of Educational Measurement*, 2:29–35. **344**

SCHULSINGER, F., see GOODWIN, SCHULSINGER, HERMANSEN, GUZE, and WINOKUR (1973).

SCHULSINGER, F., see MEDNICK and SCHULSINGER (1968).

SCHULSINGER, F., see ROSENTHAL, WENDER, KETY, SCHULSINGER, WELNER, and RIEDER (1975).

SCHULSINGER, F., see WENDER, ROSENTHAL, KETY, SCHULSINGER, and WELNER (1974).

SCHULTERBRANDT, J., see RASKIN, SCHULTERBRANDT, BOOTHE, REATIG, and MCKEON (1970).

SCHULTZ, D. (1981) *A history of modern psychology* (3rd ed.). New York: Academic Press. **27**

SCHWARTZ, B., and GAMZU, E. (1977) Pavlovian control of operant behavior. In Honig. W.K., and Staddon, J.E.R. (eds.) *Handbook of operant behavior*. Englewood Cliffs, N.J.: Prentice-Hall. **206**

SCHWARTZ, G.E. (1975) Biofeedback, self-regulation, and the patterning of physiological processes. *American Scientist*, 63:314–24. **443**

SCHWARTZ, L.K., see RESNICK, KESTENBAUM, and SCHWARTZ (1977).

SCHWARTZ, S.M., see PETERSON, SCHWARTZ, and SELIGMAN (1981).

SCOTT, J.P. (1968) *Early experience and the organization of behavior*. Belmont, Calif.: Brooks/Cole. **309**

SCOTT, T.H., see HERON, DOANE, and SCOTT (1956).

SEARS, D.O., see FREEDMAN, SEARS, and CARLSMITH (1981).

SEARS, R.R. (1936) Experimental studies of projection: I. Attribution of traits. *Journal of Social Psychology*, 7:151–63. **437**

SEARS, R.R., see DOLLARD, DOOB, MILLER, MOWRER, and SEARS (1939).

SEEMAN, J. (1949) A study of the process of nondirective therapy. *Journal of Consulting Psychology*, 13:157–68. **509**

SEIDENBERG, M.S., and PETITTO, L.A. (1979) Signing behavior in apes. *Cognition*, 7:177–215. **273**

SEKERAK, G.J., see COTTRELL, WACK, SEKERAK, and RITTLE (1968).

SELFRIDGE, O., and NEISSER, U. (1960) Pattern recognition by machine. *Scientific American*, 203:60–80. **120**

SELIGMAN, M.E.P. (1975) *Helplessness*. San Francisco: Freeman. **428, 467, 588**

SELIGMAN, M.E.P., ABRAMSON, L.V., SEMMEL, A., and VON BAEYER, C. (1979) Depressive attributional style. *Journal of Abnormal Psychology*, 88:242–47. **467**

SELIGMAN, M.E.P., see HIROTO and SELIGMAN (1975).

SELIGMAN, M.E.P., see PETERSON, SCHWARTZ, and SELIGMAN (1981).

SEMMEL, A., see SELIGMAN, ABRAMSON, SEMMEL, and VON BAEYER (1979).

SENDEN, M.V. (1960) *Space and sight* (P. Heath, trans.). New York: Free Press. **155**

SENN, D.J., see LEVINGER, SENN, and JORGENSEN (1970).

SENTER, R.J., see LIPPERT and SENTER (1966).

SERBIN, L.A., see STERNGLANZ and SERBIN (1974).

SHAFFER, L.F. (1947) Fear and courage in aerial combat. *Journal of Consulting Psychology*, 11:137–43. **332**

SHANKWEILER, D., see LIBERMAN, COOPER, SHANKWEILER, and STUDDERT-KENNEDY (1967).

SHAPIRO, A., see GOODENOUGH, SHAPIRO, HOLDEN, and STEINSCHRIBER (1959).

SHAPIRO, A., see LEWIS, GOODENOUGH, SHAPIRO, and SLESER (1966).

SHAPIRO, L.N., see WILD, SHAPIRO, and GOLDENBERG (1975).

SHARMA, K.W., see ANAND, SHARMA, and DUA (1964).

SHAVER, K.G. (1975) *An introduction to attribution processes*. Cambridge, Mass.: Winthrop. **559**

SHAVER, K.G., see JONES, ROCK, SHAVER, GOETHALS, and WARD (1968).

SHAVER, P., and FREEDMAN, J.L. (1976) Your pursuit of happiness. *Psychology Today*, 10:26–32, 75. **586**

SHEEHAN, P.W., and PERRY, C.W. (1976) *Methodologies of hypnosis: A critical appraisal of contemporary paradigms of hypnosis*. Hillsdale, N.J.: Erlbaum. **186**

SHELDON, W.H. (1954) *Atlas of men: A guide for somatotyping the adult male at all ages*. New York: Harper and Row. **385**

SHEPARD, R.N. (1978) The mental image. *American Psychologist*, 33:125–37. **275**

SHEPARD, R.N., and CHIPMAN, S. (1970) Second-order isomorphism of internal representations: Shapes of states. *Cognitive Psychology*, 1:1–17. **276**

SHEPARD, R.N., and COOPER, L.A. (1982) *Mental images and their transformations*. Cambridge, Mass.: Bedford Books/MIT Press. **274**

SHEPARD, R.N., see COOPER and SHEPARD (1973).

SHERIF, M. (1936) *The psychology of social norms*. New York: Harper and Row (Harper Torchbooks, 1966). **569, 570**

SHERIF, M. (1966) *In common predicament: Social psychology of intergroup conflict and cooperation*. Boston: Houghton Mifflin. **536**

SHERMAN, A.R. (1972) Real-life exposure as a primary therapeutic factor in the desensitization treatment of fear. *Journal of Abnormal Psychology*, 79:19–28. **501**

SHERROD, D.R., see MOORE, SHERROD, LIU, and UNDERWOOD (1979).

SHIELDS, J., see GOTTESMAN and SHIELDS (1982).

SHIELDS, J.L., see DEMBROSKI, MACDOUGALL, HERD, and SHIELDS (1981).

SHIFFRIN, R.M., see ATKINSON and SHIFFRIN (1971).

SHIFFRIN, R.M., see ATKINSON and SHIFFRIN (1977).

SHIFFRIN, R.M., see RAAIJMAKERS and SHIFFRIN (1981).

SHKUROVICH, M., see DRUCKER-COLIN, SHKUROVICH, and STERMAN (eds.) (1979).

SHOR, R.E., see FROMM and SHOR (1979).

SICOLY, F., see ROSS and SICOLY (1979).

SIEGEL, R.K., and WEST, L.J. (eds.) (1975) *Hallucinations: Behavior, experience, and theory*. New York: Wiley. **189**

SIGALL, H., and OSTROVE, N. (1975) Beautiful but dangerous: Effects of offender attractiveness and nature of the crime on juridic judgment. *Journal of Personality and Social Psychology*, 31:410–14. **555**

SIGALL, H., see LANDY AND SIGALL (1974).

SILADI, M., see MARKUS, CRANE, BERNSTEIN, and SILADI (1982).

SILVERMAN, I. (1971) Physical attractiveness and courtship. *Sexual Behavior*, 1:22–25. **556**

SILVERMAN, L.H. (1976) Psychoanalytic theory: The reports of my death are greatly exaggerated. *American Psychologist*, 31:621–37. **399**

SIMMONS, J.V. (1981) Project sea hunt: A report on prototype development and tests, Technical report 746, Naval Ocean Systems Center, San Diego, Calif. **205**

SIMON, D.P., see LARKIN, MCDERMOTT, SIMON, and SIMON (1980).

SIMON, H.A., see CHASE and SIMON (1973).

SIMON, H.A., see LARKIN, MCDERMOTT, SIMON, and SIMON (1980).

SIMON, H.A., see NEWELL and SIMON (1972).

SIMON, T., see BINET and SIMON (1905).

SIMONS, R.N., see KRIPKE and SIMONS (1976).

SINGER, D.G., see SINGER and SINGER (1981).

SINGER, J.E., see GLASS and SINGER (1972).

SINGER, J.E., see SCHACHTER and SINGER (1962).

SINGER, J.L. (1975) *The inner world of daydreaming.* New York: Harper and Row. **168**

SINGER, J.L. (1983) *The human personality: An introductory textbook.* New York: Harcourt Brace Jovanovich. In preparation. **418**

SINGER, J.L., and SINGER, D.G. (1981) *Television, imagination and aggression.* Hillsdale, N.J.: Erlbaum. **329, 330**

SINGER, J.L., see ANTROBUS, GREENBERG, and SINGER (1966).

SINGER, J.L., see POPE and SINGER (1978).

SINGER, M.T., and WYNNE. L.C. (1965) Thought disorder and family relations of schizophrenics: IV. Results and implications. *Archives of General Psychiatry,* 12:201–12. **477**

SIQUELAND, E.R., see EIMAS, SIQUELAND, JUSCZYK, and VIGORITO (1971).

SKEELS, H.M. (1966) Adult status of children with contrasting early life experiences: A follow-up study. *Monographs of the Society for Research in Child Development,* 31, Serial No. 105. **68**

SKEELS, H.M., and DYE, H.B. (1939) A study of the effects of differential stimulation on mentally retarded children. *Proceedings of the American Association for Mental Deficiency,* 44:114–36. **68**

SKINNER, B.F. (1938) *The behavior of organisms.* New York: Appleton-Century-Crofts. **219**

SKINNER, B.F. (1981) Selection by consequences. *Science,* 213:501–504. **8**

SLEEMAN, D., and BROWN, J.S. (eds.) (1982) *Intelligent tutoring systems.* New York: Academic Press. **217**

SLESER, I., see LEWIS, GOODENOUGH, SHAPIRO, and SLESER (1966).

SLOANE, R.B., STAPLES, F.R., CRISTOL, A.H., YORKSTON, N.J., and WHIPPLE, K. (1975) *Psychotherapy vs. behavior therapy.* Cambridge, Mass.: Harvard Univ. Press. **514**

SLOBIN, D.I. (1971) Cognitive prerequisites for the acquisition of grammar. In Ferguson, C.A., and Slobin, D.I. (eds.) *Studies of child language development.* New York: Holt, Rinehart and Winston. **267, 269**

SLOBIN, D.I. (1979) *Psycholinguistics* (2nd. ed.). Glenville, Ill.: Scott, Foresman. **258, 271, 279**

SLOVIC, P., see KAHNEMAN, SLOVIC, and TVERSKY (eds.) (1982).

SMART, R.G., and FEJER, D. (1972) Drug use among adolescents and their parents: Closing the generation gap in mood modification. *Journal of Abnormal Psychology,* 79:153–60. **489**

SMELSER, N.J., see ADAMS, SMELSER, and TREIMAN (eds.) (1982).

SMILANSKY, B. (1974) Paper presented at the meeting of the American Educational Research Association, Chicago, Ill. **378**

SMITH, A., see TENNANT, SMITH, BEBBINGTON, and HURRY (1981).

SMITH, D., KING, M., and HOEBEL, B.G. (1970) Lateral hypothalamic control of killing: Evidence for a cholinoceptive mechanism. *Science,* 167:900–901. **323**

SMITH, E.E., ADAMS, N., and SCHORR, D. (1978) Fact retrieval and the paradox of interference. *Cognitive Psychology,* 10:438–64. **236**

SMITH, E.E., and MEDIN, D.L. (1981) *Categories and concepts.* Cambridge, Mass.: Harvard Univ. Press **254**

SMITH, M.B. (1973) Is psychology relevant to new priorities? *American Psychologist,* 6:463–71. **11**

SMITH, M.L., GLASS, G.V., and MILLER, T.I. (1980) *The benefits of psychotherapy.* Baltimore, Md.: Johns Hopkins Univ. Press. **513**

SMITH, R., see STEUER, APPLEFIELD, and SMITH (1971).

SNYDER, C.R. (1974) Acceptance of personality interpretations as a function of assessment procedures. *Journal of Consulting Psychology,* 42:150. **411**

SNYDER, M., and SWANN, W.B., Jr. (1978) Hypothesis-testing processes in social interaction. *Journal of Personality and Social Psychology,* 36:1202–12. **257**

SNYDER, M., and URANOWITZ, S.W. (1978) Reconstructing the past: Some cognitive consequences of person perception. *Journal of Personality and Social Psychology,* 36:941–50. **248, 532**

SNYDER, M.L., STEPHAN, W.G., and ROSENFELD, D. (1976) Egotism and attribution. *Journal of Personality and Social Psychology,* 33:435–41. **543**

SNYDER, M.L., TANKE, E. D., and BERSCHEID, E. (1977) Social perception and interpersonal behavior: On the self-fulfilling nature of social stereotypes. *Journal of Personality and Social Psychology,* 35:656–66. **555**

SNYDER, S.H. (1973) Amphetamine psychosis: A "model" schizophrenia mediated by catecholamines. *American Journal of Psychiatry,* 130:61–67. **178**

SNYDER, S.H. (1980) *Biological aspects of mental disorder.* New York: Oxford Univ. Press. **469, 476**

SNYDER, S.H., see CREESE, BURT, and SNYDER (1978).

SNYDER, W.U., and OTHERS (1947) *Casebook of nondirective counseling.* Boston: Houghton Mifflin. **509**

SOAL, S.G., and BATEMAN, F. (1954) *Modern experiments in telepathy.* New Haven, Conn.: Yale Univ. Press. **159, 161**

SOKOLOV, E.N. (1976) Learning and memory: Habituation as negative learning. In Rosenzweig, M.R., and Bennett, E.L. (eds.) *Neural mechanisms of learning and memory.* Cambridge, Mass.: MIT Press. **150**

SOLOMON, R.L. (1980) The opponent-process theory of acquired motivation. *American Psychologist,* 35:691–712. **340, 341**

SOLOMON, R.L., and CORBIT, J.D. (1974) An opponent-process theory of motivation: I. Temporal dynamics of affect. *Psychological Review,* 81:119–45. **340**

SOLSO, R.L. (1979) *Cognitive psychology.* New York: Harcourt Brace Jovanovich. **251**

SOLSO, R.L., see JOHNSON and SOLSO (1978).

SORENSEN, R.C. (1973) *Adolescent sexuality in contemporary America.* New York: World Publishing. **94**

SPANOS, N.P., and BARBER, T.X. (1974) Toward a convergence in hypnosis research. *American Psychologist,* 29:500–11. **186**

SPANOS, N.P., and HEWITT, E.C. (1980) The hidden observer in hypnotic analgesia: Discovery or experimental creation? *Journal of Personality and Social Psychology*, 39:1201–14. **185**

SPEATH, J.L. (1976) Characteristics of the work setting and the job as determinants of income. In Sewell, W.H., Hauser, R.M., and Featherman, D.L. (eds.) *Schooling and achievement in American society*. New York: Academic Press. **364**

SPEER, D.C. (1972) An evaluation of a telephone crisis service. Paper presented at the meeting of the Midwestern Psychological Association, Cleveland, 1972. **521**

SPENCE, D.P., see LUBORSKY and SPENCE (1978).

SPERRY, R. (1982) Some effects of disconnecting the cerebral hemispheres. *Science*, 217:1223–26. **50**

SPERRY, R.W. (1970) Perception in the absence of neocortical commissures. In *Perception and Its Disorders* (Res. Publ. A.R.N.M.D., Vol. 48). New York: The Association for Research in Nervous and Mental Disease. **47**

SPERRY, R.W., see NEBES and SPERRY (1971).

SPIELBERGER, C.D. (ed.) (1972) *Anxiety: Current trends in theory and research*. New York: Academic Press. **445**

SPOEHR, K.T., and LEHMKUHLE, S.W. (1982) *Visual information processing*. San Francisco: Freeman. **163**

SPRINGER, S.P., and DEUTSCH, G. (1981) *Left brain, right brain*. San Francisco: Freeman. **59**

SPRINGSTON, F., see BOWER and SPRINGSTON (1970).

SPUHLER, J.N., see LOEHLIN, LINDZEY, and SPUHLER (1975).

SROLE, L. (1972) Urbanization and mental health: Some reformulations. *American Scientist*, 60:576–83. **586**

SROUFE, L.A., see MATAS, AREND, and SROUFE (1978).

SROUFE, L.A., see WATERS, WIPPMAN, and SROUFE (1979).

STADDON, J.E.R., see HONIG and STADDON (eds.) (1977).

STAMM, J.S. (1961) Social facilitation in monkeys. *Psychological Reports*, 8:479–84. **562**

STANLEY, J.C., see BENBOW aznd STANLEY (1980).

STANTON, M., MINTZ, J., and FRANKLIN, R.M. (1976) Drug flashbacks. *International Journal of Addictions*, 11:53–59. **179**

STAPLES, F.R., see SLOANE, STAPLES, CRISTOL, YORKSTON, and WHIPPLE (1975).

STAPP, J., and FULCHER, R. (1981) The employment of APA members. *American Psychologist*, 36:1263–1314. **15**

STAYTON, D.J. (1973) *Infant responses to brief everyday separations: Distress, following, and greeting*. Paper presented at the meeting of the Society for Research in Child Development, March 1973. **76**

STEIN, S., see DION and STEIN (1978).

STEINER, J.A. (1972) A questionnaire study of risk taking in psychiatric patients. *British Journal of Medical Psychology*, 45:365–74. **462**

STEINHORST, R., see HOMME, DE BACA, DEVINE, STEINHORST, and RICKERT (1963).

STEINMETZ, J.L., see LEWINSOHN, STEINMETZ, LARSON, and FRANKLIN (1981).

STEINSCHRIBER, L., see GOODENOUGH, SHAPIRO, HOLDEN, and STEINSCHRIBER (1959).

STEPHAN, W.G., see BERNSTEIN, STEPHAN, and DAVIS (1979).

STEPHAN, W.G., see SNYDER, STEPHAN, and ROSENFELD (1976).

STERMAN, M.B., see DRUCKER-COLIN, SHKUROVICH, and STERMAN (eds.) (1979).

STERNBERG, R.J. (1981) Testing and cognitive psychology. *American Psychologist*, 36:1181–89. **309**

STERNBERG, R.J. (ed.) (1982) *Handbook of human intelligence*. New York: Cambridge Univ. Press. **381**

STERNBERG, R.J. (1982) Reasoning, problem solving, and intelligence. In Sternberg, R.J. (ed.) *Handbook of human intelligence*. New York: Cambridge Univ. Press. **369**

STERNBERG, S. (1966) High-speed scanning in human memory. *Science*, 153:652–54. **226, 227, 228**

STERNBERG, S. (1969) Memory-scanning: Mental processes revealed by reaction-time experiments. *American Scientist*, 57:421–57. **227**

STERNGLANZ, S.H., and SERBIN, L.A. (1974) Sex-role stereotyping in children's television programs. *Developmental Psychology*, 10:710–15. **89**

STEUER, F.B., APPLEFIELD, J.M., and SMITH, R. (1971) Televised aggression and the interpersonal aggression of preschool children. *Journal of Experimental Child Psychology*, 11:422–47. **328**

STEVENS, A.G. (1971) Attachment behavior, separation anxiety, and stranger anxiety in polymatrically reared infants. In Schaffer, H.R. (ed.) *The Origins of Human Social Relations*. New York: Academic Press. **74**

STEVENS, B., see ROGERS and STEVENS (1967).

STEVENS, B.C., see HIRSCH, GAIND, ROHDE, STEVENS, and WING (1973).

STEVENSON, I. (1977) Reincarnation: Field studies and theoretical issues. In Wolman, B.B. (ed.) *Handbook of parapsychology*. New York: Van Nostrand Reinhold. **187**

STILLMAN, R.C., see EICH, WEINGARTNER, STILLMAN, and GILLIAN (1975).

STILLMAN, R.C., see PETERSON and STILLMAN (1977).

STOKOLS, D., see COHEN, EVANS, KRANTZ, and STOKOLS (1980).

STOKOLS, D., see COHEN, EVANS, KRANTZ, STOKOLS, and KELLY (1981).

STORMS, M.D. (1973) Videotape and the attribution process: Reversing actors' and observers' points of view. *Journal of Personality and Social Psychology*, 27:165–75. **542**

STORMS, M.D. (1981) A theory of erotic orientation development. *Psychological Review*, 88:340–53. **303, 307**

STRASSMAN, H.D., THALER, M.B., and SCHEIN, E.H. (1956) A prisoner of war syndrome: Apathy as a reaction to severe stress. *American Journal of Psychiatry*, 112:998–1003. **429**

STRATTON, G.M. (1897) Vision without inversion of the retinal image. *Psychological Review*, 4:341–60. **142**

STRAUS, R., see ROSENMAN, BRAND, JENKINS, FRIEDMAN, STRAUS, and WRUM (1975).

STRAUSS, J.S. (1982) Behavioral aspects of being disadvantaged and risk for schizophrenia. In Parron, D.L., Solomon, F., and Jenkins, C.D. (eds.). *Behavior, health risks, and social disadvantage*, pp. 63–73. Washington, D.C.: National Academy Press. **476**

STROEBE, W., INSKO, C.A., THOMPSON, V.D., and LAYTON, B.D. (1971) Effects of physical attractiveness, attitude similarity and sex on various aspects of interpersonal attraction. *Journal of Personality and Social Psychology*, 18:79–91. **554**

STRONGMAN, K.T. (1978) *The psychology of emotion* (2nd ed.). New York: Wiley. **345**

STUART, R.B., and DAVIS, B. (1972) *Slim chance in a fat world*. Champaign, Ill.: Research Press. **505**

STUDDERT-KENNEDY, M., see LIBERMAN, COOPER, SHANKWEILER, and STUDDERT-KENNEDY (1967).

STUNKARD, A.J. (ed.) (1980. *Obesity*. Philadelphia: Saunders. **315**

STUNKARD, A.J. (1982) Obesity. In Hersen, M., Bellack, A., Kazdin, A. (eds.). *International handbook of behavior modification and therapy*. New York: Plenum Press. **297**

STUNKARD, A.J., see CRAIGHEAD, STUNKARD, and O'BRIEN (1981).

SUE, D. (1979) Erotic fantasies of college students during coitus. *Journal of Sex Research*, 15:299–305. **303**

SUGERMAN, A.A., see TARTER and SUGERMAN (1976).

SUNDBERG, N. (1977) *The assessment of persons*. Englewood Cliffs, N.J.: Prentice-Hall. **419**

SUOMI, S.J. (1977) Peers, play, and primary prevention in primates. In *Proceedings of the Third Vermont Conference on the Primary Prevention of Psychopathology: Promoting Social Competence and Coping in Children*. Hanover, N.H.: Univ. Press of New England. **80**

SUPPES, P. (ed.) (1981) *University-level computer-assisted instruction at Stanford: 1968–1980*. Stanford, Calif.: Institute for Mathematical Studies in the Social Sciences, Stanford University. **217**

SUPPES, P., see KRANTZ, LUCE, SUPPES, and TVERSKY (1971).

SURBER, C.F. (1977) Developmental processes in social inference: Averaging of intentions and consequences in moral judgment. *Developmental Psychology*, 13:654–65. **83**

SWANDER, D.V., see ROHRER, BARON, HOFFMAN, and SWANDER (1954).

SWANN, W.B., Jr., see SNYDER and SWANN (1978).

SWAP, W., see SAEGERT, SWAP, and ZAJONC (1973).

SWARTZ, J.D., see HOLTZMANN, THORPE, SWARTZ, and HERRON (1961).

SWERDLOW, J., see MANKIEWICZ and SWERDLOW (1977).

SYLVESTER, D., see AGRAS, SYLVESTER, and OLIVEAU (1969).

T

TAKAISHI, M., see TANNER, WHITEHOUSE, and TAKAISHI (1966).

TANKE, E.D., see SNYDER, TANKE, and BERSCHEID (1977).

TANNENBAUM, P.H., see OSGOOD and TANNENBAUM (1955).

TANNER, J.M., WHITEHOUSE, R.H., and TAKAISHI, M. (1966) Standards from birth to maturity for height, weight, height velocity and weight velocity: British children 1965. *Archives of Diseases of Childhood*, 41:613–35. **93**

TARLER-BENLOLO, L. (1978) The role of relaxation in biofeedback training. *Psychological Bulletin*, 85:727–55. **208, 442, 443**

TART, C.T. (1971) *On being stoned: A psychological study of marijuana intoxication*. Palo Alto, Calif.: Science and Behavior Books. **180, 181**

TART, C.T. (ed.) (1975) *States of consciousness*. New York: Dutton. **165, 186, 189**

TART, C.T. (1979) Measuring the depth of an altered state of consciousness, with particular reference to self-report scales of hypnotic depth. In Fromm, E., and Shor, R.E. *Hypnosis: Developments in research and new perspectives* (2nd ed.). New York: Aldine. **182**

TART, C., and DICK, L. (1970) Conscious control of dreaming: I. The posthypnotic dream. *Journal of Abnormal Psychology*, 76:304–15. **173**

TARTER, R.E., and SUGERMAN, A.A. (eds.) (1976) *Alcoholism*. Reading, Mass.: Addison-Wesley. **491**

TAUBER, E.S., see ROFFWARG, HERMAN, BOWE-ANDERS, and TAUBER (1978).

TAVRIS, C., and OFFIR, C. (1977) *The longest war: Sex differences in perspective*. New York: Harcourt Brace Jovanovich. **305**

TAYLOR, D.A., see ALTMAN and TAYLOR (1973).

TEITELBAUM, P., see HOEBEL and TEITELBAUM (1966).

TELCH, M.J., see THORESEN, TELCH, and EAGLESTON (1981).

TENNANT, C., SMITH, A., BEBBINGTON, P., and HURRY, J. (1981) Parental loss in childhood: Relationship to adult

psychiatric impairment and contact with psychiatric services. *Archives of General Psychiatry*, 38:309–14. **466**

TERKEL, J., and ROSENBLATT, J.S. (1972) Humoral factors underlying maternal behavior at parturition: Cross transfusion between freely moving rats. *Journal of Comparative and Physiological Psychology*, 80:365–71. **309**

TERMAN, L.M., and MERRILL, M.A. (1937) *Measuring intelligence*. Boston: Houghton Mifflin. **358**

TERRACE, H.S., PETITTO, L.A., SANDERS, D.J., and BEVER, T.G. (1979) Can an ape create a sentence? *Science*, 206:891–902. **274**

TESSER, A., and BRODIE, M. (1971) A note on the evaluation of a "computer date." *Psychonomic Science*, 23:300. **554**

TEST, M.A., see BRYAN and TEST (1967).

THALER, M.B., see STRASSMAN, THALER, and SCHEIN (1956).

THARP, R.G., see WATSON and THARP (1981).

THOMAS, A., and CHESS, S. (1977) *Temperament and development*. New York: Brunner/Mazel. **384**

THOMAS, D.S., see THOMAS and THOMAS (1928).

THOMAS, E.L., and ROBINSON, H.A. (1972) *Improving reading in every class: A sourcebook for teachers*. Boston: Allyn and Bacon. **242**

THOMAS, J., see ISAACS, THOMAS, and GOLDIAMOND (1965).

THOMAS, M.H., HORTON, R.W., LIPPINCOTT, E.C., and DRABMAN, R.S. (1977) Desensitization to portrayals of real-life aggression as a function of exposure to television violence. *Journal of Personality and Social Psychology*, 35:450–58. **330**

THOMAS, W.I., and THOMAS, D.S. (1928) *The child in America*. New York: Knopf. **529**

THOMPSON, C.W., see HUDSPETH, MCGAUGH, and THOMPSON (1964).

THOMPSON, J.K., JARVIE, G.J., LAKEY, B.B., and CURETON, K.J. (1982) Exercise and obesity: Etiology, physiology, and intervention. *Psychological Bulletin*, 91:55–79. **295**

THOMPSON, V.D., see STROEBE, INSKO, THOMPSON, and LAYTON (1971).

THOMPSON, W.R. (1954) The inheritance and development of intelligence. *Proceedings of the Association for Research on Nervous and Mental Disease*, 33:209–31. **57**

THOMPSON, W.R., see FULLER and THOMPSON (1978).

THORESEN, C.E., TELCH, M.J., and EAGLESTON, J.R. (1981) Altering type A behavior. *Psychosomatics*, 8:472–82. **440**

THORESEN, C.E., see FRIEDMAN, THORESEN, and GILL (1981).

THORNTON, J.W., and JACOBS, P.D. (1971) Learned helplessness in human subjects. *Journal of Experimental Psychology*, 87:369–72. **428**

THORPE, J.S., see HOLTZMAN, THORPE, SWARTZ, and HERRON (1961).

THURBER, J. (1942) The secret life of Walter Mitty. *My world and welcome to it*, pp. 72–81. New York: Harcourt Brace Jovanovich. **168**

THURSTONE, L.L. (1938) Primary mental abilities. *Psychometric Monographs*, No. 1. Chicago: Univ. of Chicago Press. **367**

THURSTONE, L.L., and THURSTONE, T.G. (1963) *SRA primary abilities*. Chicago: Science Research Associates. **369**

THURSTONE, T.G., see THURSTONE and THURSTONE (1963).

TINKLENBERG, J.R. (1972) A current view of the amphetamines. In Blachy, P.H. (ed.) *Progress in drug abuse*. Springfield, Ill.: Thomas. **178**

TINKLENBERG, J.R., see DARLEY, TINKLENBERG, ROTH, HOLLISTER, and ATKINSON (1973).

TITLEY, R.W., and VINEY, W. (1969) Expression of aggression toward the physically handicapped. *Perceptual and Motor Skills*, 29:51–56. **91**

TOGNACCI, L.N., see WEIGEL, VERNON, and TOGNACCI (1974).

TOLMAN, C.W. (1969) Social feeding in domestic chicks: Effects of food deprivation of non-feeding companions. *Psychonomic Science*, 15:234. **562**

TOLMAN, E.C. (1932) *Purposive behavior in animals and men*. New York: Appleton-Century-Crofts. **213, 219**

TOLMAN, E.C., and HONZIK, C.H. (1930) Introduction and removal of reward, and maze performance in rats. *University of California Publications in Psychology*, 4:257–75. **214**

TOMKINS, S. (1981) The quest for primary motives. *Journal of Personality and Social Psychology*, 41:306–29. **342**

TORRANCE, E.P. (1966) *Torrance Tests of Creative Thinking, Verbal Forms A and B*. Princeton, N.J.: Personnel Press. **372**

TOTH, M.F., see ARKIN, TOTH, BAKER, and HASTEY (1970).

TOTTEN, J., see REGAN AND TOTTEN (1975).

TOWER, A., see DAVIDSON, YASUNA, and TOWER (1979).

TOWNSEND, J.T. (1971) A note on the identifiability of parallel and serial processes. *Perception and Psychophysics*, 10:161–63. **228**

TRAUPMANN, J., and HATFIELD, E. (1981) Love and its effects on mental and physical health. In Fogel, R.W., Hatfield, E., Kiesler, S.B., and Shanas, E. (eds.) *Aging: Stability and change in the family*. New York: Academic Press. **97**

TREIMAN, D.J., see ADAMS, SMELSER, and TREIMAN (eds.) (1982)

TRUAX, C.B. (1966) Reinforcement and nonreinforcement in Rogerian psychotherapy. *Journal of Abnormal Psychology*, 71:1–9. **515**

TRUAX, C.B., and MITCHELL, K.M. (1971) Research on certain therapist interpersonal skills in relation to process and outcome. In Bergin, A.E., and Garfield, S.L. (eds.) *Handbook of psychotherapy and behavior change: An emperical analysis*. New York: Wiley. **509**

TRUDEAU, M.B., see HAMBURG and TRUDEAU (eds.) (1981).

TULVING, E. (1974) Cue-dependent forgetting. *American Scientist*, 62:74–82. **232**

TULVING, E., and PEARLSTONE, Z. (1966) Availability versus accessibility of information in memory for words. *Journal of Verbal Learning and Verbal Behavior*, 5:381–91. **233**

TULVING, E., see WATKINS, HO, and TULVING (1976).

TURNBULL, C.M. (1961) Some observations regarding the experiences and behavior of the Ba Mbuti Pygmies. *American Journal of Psychology*, 74:304–308. **142**

TURNER, S.M., CALHOUN, K.S., and ADAMS, H.E. (eds.) (1981) *Handbook of clinical behavior therapy*. New York: Wiley. **525**

TURNER, T.R., see BOWER, BLACK, and TURNER (1979).

TURRELL, E.S., see SAWREY, CONGER, and TURRELL (1956).

TVERSKY, A., see KAHNEMAN, SLOVIC, and TVERSKY (eds.) (1982).

TVERSKY, A., see KRANTZ, LUCE, SUPPES, and TVERSKY (1971).

TYHURST, J.S. (1951) Individual reactions to community disaster. *American Journal of Psychiatry*, 10:746–69. **344**

TYLER, R.W., see EELLS, DAVIS, HAVIGHURST, HERRICK, and TYLER (1951).

U

UDELF, M.S., see FANTZ, ORDY, and UDELF (1962).

ULLMAN, M., see WOLMAN, DALE, SCHMEIDLER, and ULLMAN (1977).

ULLMANN, L.P., and KRASNER, L. (1969) psychological approach to abnormal behavior. Englewood Cliffs, N.J.: Prentice-Hall. **500**

ULRICH, R., see HOGARTY, SCHOOLER, ULRICH, MUSSARE, FERRO, and HERRON (1979).

UNDERWOOD, B., and MOORE, B.S. (1981) Sources of behavioral consistency. *Journal of Personality and Social Psychology*, 40:780–85. **415**

UNDERWOOD, B., see MOORE, SHERROD, LIU, and UNDERWOOD (1979).

UNGERLEIDER, J.T., see SCHAEFFER, ANDRYSIAK, and UNGERLEIDER (1981).

URANOWITZ, S.W., see SNYDER and URANOWITZ (1978).

V

VALENSTEIN, E.S. (1980) A prospective study of cingulatomy. In Valenstein, E.S. (ed.) *The psychosurgery debate: Scientific, legal, and ethical perspectives*. San Francisco: Freeman. **517**

VALINS, S., see BAUM and VALINS (1977).

VAN DER LOOS, H., and WOOLSEY, T.A. (1973) Somatosensory cortex: Structural alterations following early injury to sense organs. *Science*, 179:395–98. **43**

VAN EEDEN, F. (1913) A study of dreams. *Proceedings of the Society for Psychical Research*, 26:431–61. **172**

VEITH, I. (1970) *Hysteria: The history of a disease*. Chicago: Univ. of Chicago Press. **524**

VERNON, D.T.A., see WEIGEL, VERNON, and TOGNACCI (1974).

VERNON, P.E. (1979) *Intelligence: Heredity and environment*. San Francisco: Freeman. **381**

VERPLANCK, W.S. (1955) The control of the content of conversation: Reinforcement of statements of opinion. *Journal of Abnormal and Social Psychology*, 51:668–76. **206**

VIERLING, J.S., and ROCK, J. (1967) Variations in olfactory sensitivity to Exaltolide during the menstrual cycle. *Journal of Applied Physiology*, 22:311–15. **127**

VIGORITO, J., see EIMAS, SIQUELAND, JUSCZYK, and VIGORITO (1971).

VINEY, W., see TITLEY and VINEY (1969).

VOGEL, G.W. (1978) Alternative view of neurobiology of dreaming. *American Journal of Psychiatry*, 135:1531–35. **174**

VOGEL, W.H., see CARROL, ZUCKERMAN, and VOGEL (1982).

VOLKOVA, V.D. (1953) On certain characteristics of conditioned reflexes to speech stimuli in children. *Fiziologicheskii Zhurnal SSSR*, 39:540–48. **197**

VON BAEYER, C., see SELIGMAN, ABRAMSON, SEMMEL, and VON BAEYER (1979).

VON FRISCH, K. (1974) Decoding the language of the bee. *Science*, 185:663–68. **272, 273**

VONNEGUT, M. (1975) *The Eden express*. New York: Bantam. **473, 491**

W

WABER, D.P. (1977) Sex differences in mental abilities, hemispheric lateralization, and rate of physical growth at adolescence. *Developmental Psychology*, 13:29–38. **90**

WACK, D.L., see COTTRELL, RITTLE, and WACK (1967).

WACK, D.L., see COTTRELL, WACK, SEKERAK, and RITTLE (1968).

WALDER, L.O., see ERON, HUESMANN, LEFKOWITZ, and WALDER (1972).

WALK, R.D., see GIBSON and WALK (1960).

WALKER, C.E., HEDBERG, A., CLEMENT, P.W., and WRIGHT, L. (1981) *Clinical procedures for behavior therapy*. Englewood Cliffs, N.J.: Prentice-Hall. **502**

WALKER, J. (1977) Drops of water dance on a hot skillet and the experimenter walks on hot coals. *Scientific American*, 237:126–31. **187**

WALL, S., see AINSWORTH, BLEHAR, WALTERS, and WALL (1979).

WALLACE, P.M., see BROWN and WALLACE (1980).

WALLACH, M.A., and KOGAN, N. (1965) *Modes of thinking in young children*. New York: Holt, Rinehart and Winston. **372**

WALSTER, E., ARONSON, E., and ABRAHAMS, D. (1966) On increasing the persuasiveness of a low prestige communicator. *Journal of Experimental Social Psychology*, 2:325–42. **581**

WALSTER, E., ARONSON, V., ABRAHAMS, D., and ROTTMANN, L. (1966) Importance of physical attractiveness in dating behavior. *Journal of Personality and Social Psychology*, 4:508–16. **554**

WALSTER, E., and FESTINGER, L. (1962) The effectiveness of "overheard" persuasive communications. *Journal of Abnormal and Social Psychology*, 65:395–402. **581**

WALTERS, E., see AINSWORTH, BLEHAR, WALTERS, and WALL (1979).

WALSTER, E., see BERSCHEID and WALSTER (1974).

WALSTER, E., see DION, BERSCHEID, and WALSTER (1972).

WANNER, E., and GLEITMAN, L.R. (eds.) (1982) *Language acquisition: The state of the art*. New York: Cambridge Univ. Press. **279**

WARD, L.M., see COREN, PORAC, and WARD (1978).

WARD, L.M., see JONES, ROCK, SHAVER, GOETHALS, and WARD (1968).

WARNER, P., see MICHAEL, BONSALL, and WARNER (1974).

WARWICK, D.P., see NEWCOMB, KOENIG, FLACKS, and WARWICK (1967).

WASON, P.C., and JOHNSON-LAIRD, P.N. (1972) *Psychology of reasoning: Structure and content*. London: Batsford. **257**

WATERMAN, A.S., and WATERMAN, C.K. (1974) A longitudinal study of changes in ego identity status during the freshman to the senior year in college. *Developmental Psychology*, 10:387–92. **96**

WATERMAN, C.K., see WATERMAN and WATERMAN (1974).

WATERS, E., WIPPMAN, J., and SROUFE, L.A. (1979) Attachment, positive affect, and competence in the peer group: Two studies in construct validation. *Child Development*, 50:821–29. **77**

WATKINS, M.J., HO, E., and TULVING, E. (1976) Context effects in recognition memory for faces. *Journal of Verbal Learning and Verbal Behavior*, 15:505–18. **235**

WATKINS, M.J., see CRAIK and WATKINS (1973).

WATSON, C., see BEM, MARTYNA, and WATSON (1976).

WATSON, D.L., and THARP, R.G. (1981) Self-directed behavior: Self-modification for personal adjustment (3rd ed.). Belmont, Calif.: Wadsworth. **525**

WATSON, J.B. (1928) *Psychological care of infant and child*. New York: W.W. Norton. **85**

WATSON, R.I. (1978) *The great psychologists: From Aristotle to Freud*. Philadelphia: Lippincott. **27**

WATT, N.F., see WHITE and WATT (1981).

WAUGH, N.C., and NORMAN, D.A. (1965) Primary memory. *Psychological Review*, 72:89–104. **226**

WEATHERLY, D. (1964) Self-perceived rate of physical maturation and personality in late adolescence. *Child Development*, 35:1197–1210. **94**

WEBB, W.B. (1975) *Sleep the gentle tyrant*. Englewood Cliffs, N.J.: Prentice-Hall. **169, 171, 189**

WEBB, W.B., AGNEW, J.W., Jr., and WILLIAMS, R.L. (1971) Effect on sleep of a sleep period time displacement. *Aerospace Medicine*, 42:152–55. **169**

WEBB, W.B., and KERSEY, J. (1967) Recall of dreams and the probability of Stage 1-REM sleep. *Perceptual and Motor Skills*, 24:627–30. **172**

WECHSLER, D. (1958) *The measurement and appraisal of adult intelligence*. Baltimore: Williams. **367**

WEGMANN, H.M., see KLEIN, WEGMANN, and HUNT (1972).

WEIGEL, R.H., VERNON, D.T.A., and TOGNACCI, L.N. (1974) Specificity of the attitude as a determinant of attitude-behavior congruence. *Journal of Personality and Social Psychology*, 30:724–28. **548**

WEIGEL, R.H., see BLANCHARD, WEIGEL, and COOK (1975).

WEIKART, D., see HOHMANN, BANET, and WEIKART (1979).

WEINBERG, M.S., see BELL, WEINBERG, and HAMMERSMITH (1981).

WEINBERG, R.A., see SCARR and WEINBERG (1976).

WEINER, I.B. (1976) *Clinical methods in psychology*. New York: Wiley. **419**

WEINER, I.B., see ELKIND and WEINER (1978).

WEINER, I.W. (1969) The effectiveness of a suicide prevention program. *Mental Hygiene*, 53:357–73. **521**

WEINFELD, F.D., see COLEMAN, CAMPBELL,

HOBSON, MCPARTLAND, MOODY, WEIN-FELD, and YORK (1966).

WEINGARTNER, H., see EICH, WEIN-GARTNER, STILLMAN, and GILLIAN (1975).

WEISMAN, S. (1966) Environmental and innate factors and educational attainment. In Meade, J.E., and Parkes, A.S. (eds.) *Genetic and environmental factors in human ability.* London: Oliver and Boyd. **375**

WEISS, B., and LATIES, V.G. (1962) Enhancement of human performance by caffeine and amphetamines. *Pharmacological Review,* 14:1–27. **178**

WEISS, J.M. (1972) Psychological factors in stress and disease. *Scientific American,* 226:106. **439, 440**

WELCH, R.B. (1978) *Perceptual modification.* New York: Academic Press. **143**

WELCH, S., see BOOTH and WELCH (1973).

WELCH, S., see BOOTH and WELCH (1974).

WELKER, W.L., JOHNSON, J.I., and PUBOLS, B.H. (1964) Some morphological and physiological characteristics of the somatic sensory system in raccoons. *American Zoologist,* 4:75–94. **43**

WELNER, J., see ROSENTHAL, WENDER, KETY, SCHULSINGER, WELNER, and RIEDER (1975).

WELNER, J., see WENDER, ROSENTHAL, KETY, SCHULSINGER, and WELNER (1974).

WENDER, P.H., ROSENTHAL, D., KETY, S.S., SCHULSINGER, F., and WELNER, J. (1974) Crossfostering: A research strategy for clarifying the role of genetic and experiential factors in the etiology of schizophrenia. *Archives of General Psychiatry,* 30:121–28. **475**

WENDER, P.H., see ROSENTHAL, WENDER, KETY, SCHULSINGER, WELNER, and RIEDER (1975).

WENGER, M., and BAGCHI, B. (1961) Studies of autonomic function in practitioners of yoga in India. *Behavioral Science,* 6:312–23. **186**

WERNER, P.D., and MIDDLESTADT, S.E. (1979) Factors in the use of oral contraceptives by young women. *Journal of Applied Social Psychology,* 9:537–47. **548**

WERTHEIMER, M. (1979) *A brief history of psychology* (2nd ed.). New York: Holt, Rinehart and Winston. **27**

WEST, L.J., see SIEGEL and WEST (1975).

WHIPPLE, K., see SLOANE, STAPLES, CRISTOL, YORKSTON, and WHIPPLE (1975).

WHISHAW, I.Q., see KOLB and WHISHAW (1980).

WHITE, C. (1977) Unpublished doctoral dissertation. Catholic University, Washington, D.C. **294**

WHITE, P.L. (1971) *Human infants: Experience and psychological development.* Englewood Cliffs, N.J.: Prentice-Hall. **67**

WHITE, R.W., and WATT, N.F. (1981) *The abnormal personality* (5th ed.). New York: Wiley. **465, 491**

WHITEHOUSE, R.H., see TANNER, WHITEHOUSE, and TAKAISHI (1966).

WHITTEN, W.B., see BJORK and WHITTEN (1974).

WHORF, B.L. (1956) Science and linguistics. In Carroll, J.B. (ed.) *Language, thought and reality: Selected writings of Benjamin Lee Whorf.* Cambridge, Mass.: M.I.T. Press. **258**

WICKELGREN, W.A. (1979) *Cognitive psychology.* Englewood Cliffs, N.J.: Prentice-Hall. **163**

WIENS, A.W., see MATARAZZO and WIENS (1977).

WIENS, A.W., and MATARAZZO and WIENS (1972).

WIESEL, T.N., see HUBEL and WIESEL (1962).

WIESEL, T.N., see HUBEL and WIESEL (1968).

WIGDOR, A.K., and GARNER, W.R. (eds.) (1982) *Ability testing: Uses, consequences, and controversies.* Washington, D.C.: National Academy Press. **378, 381**

WIGGINS, J.S. (1973) *Personality and prediction: Principles of personality assessment.* Reading, Mass.: Addison-Wesley. **419**

WIGGINS, J.S., see WINDER and WIGGINS (1964).

WILD, C.M., SHAPIRO, L.N., and GOLDENBERG, L. (1975) Transactional communication disturbances in families of male schizophrenics. *Family Process,* 14:131–60. **477**

WILKES, A.L., and KENNEDY, R.A. (1969) Relationship between pausing and retrieval latency in sentences of varying grammatical form. *Journal of Experimental Psychology,* 79:241–45. **262**

WILLERMAN, L. (1979) *The psychology of individual differences.* San Francisco: Freeman. **385**

WILLIAMS, L.R., see COBBIN, REQUIN-BLOW, WILLIAMS, and WILLIAMS (1979).

WILLIAMS, M.D., and HOLLAN, J.D. (1981) The process of retrieval from very long-term memory. *Cognitive Science,* 5:87–119. **240**

WILLIAMS, R.L. (1972) The BITCH Test (Black Intelligence Test of Cultural Homogeneity). St. Louis, Mo.: Black Studies Program, Washington University. **362**

WILLIAMS, R.L., see WEBB, AGNEW, and WILLIAMS (1971).

WILLIAMS, W.O., see COBBIN, REQUIN-BLOW, WILLIAMS, and WILLIAMS, (1979).

WILSON, G.T., see KAZDIN and WILSON (1978).

WILSON, G.T., see O'LEARY and WILSON (1975).

WILSON, I. (1982) *All in the mind: Reincarnation, stigmata, multiple personality and other little-understood powers of the mind.* Garden City, N.Y.: Doubleday. **187, 189**

WILSON, M.A., see MILES, RAYNAL, and WILSON (1977).

WILSON, S.C., see BARBER and WILSON (1977).

WILSON, W.R. (1979) Feeling more than we can know: Exposure effects without learning. *Journal of Personality and Social Psychology,* 37:811–21. **552**

WINCH, R.F., KTSANES, T., and KTSANES, V. (1954) The theory of complementary needs in mate selection: An analytic and descriptive study. *American Sociological Review,* 29:241–49. **553**

WINDER, C.L., and WIGGINS, J.S. (1964) Social reputation and social behavior: A further validation of the peer nomination inventory. *Journal of Abnormal and Social Psychology,* 68:681–85. **404**

WING, J.K., see HIRSCH, GAIND, ROHDE, STEVENS, and WING (1973).

WINOKUR, G., see GOODWIN, SCHULSINGER, HERMANSEN, GUZE, and WINOKUR (1973).

WINSBOROUGH, H. (1965) The social consequences of high population density. *Law and Contemporary Problems,* 30:120–26. **585**

WINZENZ, D., see BOWER, CLARK, WINZENZ, and LESGOLD (1969).

WIPPMAN, J., see WATERS, WIPPMAN, and SROUFE (1979).

WITELSON, S.F. (1976) Sex and the single hemisphere: Right hemisphere specialization for spatial processing. *Science,* 193:425–27. **91**

WOLF, M.M., see PHILLIPS, PHILLIPS, FIXSEN, and WOLF, 1972.

WOLFGANG, H., see EYFERTH, BRANDT, and WOLFGANG (1960).

WOLMAN, B.B. (ed.) (1982) *The handbook of developmental psychology.* Englewood Cliffs, N.J.: Prentice-Hall. **101**

WOLMAN, B.B., DALE, L.A., SCHMEIDLER, G.R., and ULLMAN, M. (eds.) (1977) *Handbook of parapsychology.* New York: Van Nostrand Reinhold. **160, 163, 189**

WOLPERT, E., see DEMENT and WOLPERT (1958).

WOOD, G. (1977) *Fundamentals of psychological research* (2nd ed.). Boston: Little, Brown. **27**

WOOD, L.E., see DOOB and WOOD (1972).

WOODRUFF, C.L., see KELLEY and WOODRUFF (1956).

WOOLSEY, T.A., see VAN DER LOOS and WOOLSEY (1973).

WORD, C.O., ZANNA, M.P., and COOPER, J. (1974) The nonverbal mediation of self-fulfilling prophecies in interracial interaction. *Journal of Experimental Social Psychology,* 10:109–20. **533**

WRIGHT, L., see WALKER, HEDBERG, CLEMENT, and WRIGHT (1981).

WRIGHTSMAN, L.S. (1977) *Social psychology* (2nd ed.). Monterey, Calif.: Brooks/Cole. **586**

WRUM, M., see ROSENMAN, BRAND, JENKINS, FRIEDMAN, STRAUS, and WRUM (1975).

WURTZ, R., see ROBINSON and WURTZ (1976).

WYLIE, R.C. (1974) *The self-concept: A review of methodological considerations and measuring instruments.* Lincoln: Univ. of Nebraska Press. **403**

WYNNE, L.C., see SINGER and WYNNE (1965).

Y

YAKSH, T., see PLATT, YAKSH, and DARBY (1967).

YALOM, I.D. (1975) *The theory and practice of group psychotherapy* (2nd ed.). New York: Basic Books. **525**

YALOM, I.D., see LIEBERMAN, YALOM, and MILES (1973).

YANKELOVICH, D. (1974) *The new morality: A profile of American youth in the seventies.* New York: McGraw-Hill. **584**

YANKELOVICH, D. (1981) *New rules: Searching for self-fulfillment in a world turned upside down.* New York: Random House. **584**

YARBUS, D.L. (1967) *Eye movements and vision.* New York: Plenum Press. **150**

YASUNA, A., see DAVIDSON, YASUNA, and TOWER, (1979).

YERKES, R.M., and MARGULIS, S. (1909) The method of Pavlov in animal psychology. *Psychological Bulletin,* 6:257–73. **194**

YORK, R.L., see COLEMAN, CAMPBELL, HOBSON, MCPARTLAND, MOODY, WEINFELD, and YORK (1966).

YORKSTON, N.J., see SLOANE, STAPLES, CRISTOL, YORKSTON, and WHIPPLE (1975).

YOUNG, W.G., see DEUTSCH, YOUNG, and KALOGERIS (1978).

YUSSEN, S.R., and BERMAN, L. (1981) Memory predictions for recall and recognition in first-, third-, and fifth-grade children. *Developmental Psychology,* 17:224–29. **73**

YUSSEN, S.R., see NAHIR and YUSSEN (1977).

Z

ZAJONC, R.B. (1965) Social facilitation. *Science,* 149:269–74. **563**

ZAJONC, R.B. (1968) Attitudinal effects of mere exposure. *Journal of Personality and Social Psychology,* Monograph Supplement, 9(2):1–29. **552**

ZAJONC, R.B. (1980) Compresence. In Paulus, P.B. (ed.), *Psychology of group influence.* Hillsdale, N.J.: Erlbaum. **563**

ZAJONC, R.B., HEINGARTNER, A., and HERMAN, E.M. (1969) Social enhancement and impairment of performance in the cockroach. *Journal of Personality and Social Psychology,* 13:83–92. **563**

ZAJONC, R.B., see MORELAND AND ZAJONC (1979).

ZAJONC, R.B., see SAEGERT, SWAP, AND ZAJONC (1973).

ZANNA, M.P., see FAZIO, ZANNA, and COOPER (1977).

ZANNA, M.P., see WORD, ZANNA, and COOPER (1974).

ZEIGLER, H.P., and LEIBOWITZ, H. (1957) Apparent visual size as a function of distance for children and adults. *American Journal of Psychology,* 70:106–109. **142**

ZELAGO, P.R., see KAGAN, KEARSLEY, and ZELAGO (1978).

ZELNIK, M., and KANTER, J.F. (1977) Sexual and contraceptive experience of young unmarried women in the United States, 1976 and 1971. *Family Planning Perspectives,* 9:55–71. **94**

ZIEGLER, D.J., see HJELLE and ZIEGLER (1981).

ZIKMUND, V. (1972) Physiological correlates of visual imagery. In Sheehan, P.W. (ed.) *The function and nature of imagery.* New York: Academic Press. **177**

ZILBOORG, G., and HENRY, G.W. (1941) *A history of medical psychology.* New York: W.W. Norton. **524**

ZILLMANN, D., KATCHER, A.H., and MILAVSKY, B. (1972) Excitation transfer from physical exercise to subsequent aggressive behavior. *Journal of Experimental Social Psychology,* 8:247–59. **324**

ZILLMANN, D., and SAPOLSKY, B.S. (1977) What mediates the effect of mild erotica on annoyance and hostile behavior in males? *Journal of Personality and Social Psychology,* 35:587–96. **324**

ZIMBARDO, P.G. (1970) The human choice: Individuation, reason and order versus deindividuation, impulse and chaos. In Arnold, W.J., and Levine, D. (eds.), *Nebraska symposium on motivation, 1969,* Vol. 16. Lincoln: Univ. of Nebraska Press. **564, 565**

ZLUTNICK, S., and ALTMAN, I. (1972) Crowding and human behavior. In Wohlwill, J., and Carson, D. (eds.) *Environment and the social sciences.* Washington, D.C.: American Psychological Association. **586**

ZOLA, I.K., see KOSA and ZOLA (eds.) (1975).

ZUBEK, J.P. (1969) *Sensory deprivation: Fifteen years of research.* New York: Appleton-Century-Crofts. **312**

ZUBIN, J. (1972) Discussion of symposium on newer approaches to personality assessment. *Journal of Personality Assessment,* 36:427–34. **410**

ZUCKERMAN, M. (1979) *Sensation seeking: Beyond the optimal level of arousal.* Hillsdale, N.J.: Erlbaum. **312, 386**

ZUCKERMAN, M., and NEEB, M. (1980) Demographic influences in sensation seeking and expressions of sensation seeking in religion, smoking and driving habits. *Personality and Individual Differences,* 1(3):197–206. **313**

ZUCKERMAN, M., see CARROL, ZUCKERMAN, and VOGEL (1982).

ZUCKERMAN, M., see FISHER, ZUCKERMAN, and NEEB (1981).

ZWISLOCKI, J.J. (1981) Sound analysis in the ear: A history of discoveries. *American Scientist,* 69:184–92. **126**

ACKNOWLEDGMENTS AND COPYRIGHTS

FIGURES

Chapter 1

1-3 Darley, C.F., Tinklenberg, J.R., Roth, W.T., Hollister, L.E., and Atkinson, R.C., "Influence of marijuana on storage and retrieval processes in memory," *Memory and cognition* 1 (1973): 196–200. **1-5** Atkinson, R.C., "Teaching children to read using a computer," *American psychologist* 29 (1976): 169–78. Copyright 1976 by the American Psychological Association. Reprinted by permission. **1-6** Hilgard, E.R., "Hypnosis and experimental psychodynamics," reprinted from H.W. Brosin, *Lectures on experimental psychiatry*, by permission of the University of Pittsburgh Press. © 1961 by the University of Pittsburgh Press.

Chapter 2

2-11 Sperry, R.W., "Perception in the absence of neocortical commissures," in *Perception and its disorders*, Res. Publ. A.R.N.M.D., Vol. 48, The Association for Research in Nervous and Mental Disease; Nebes, R.D., and Sperry, R.W., "Cerebral dominance in perception," *Neuropsychologia* 9 (1971):247. Reprinted with permission from Pergamon Press, Ltd. **2-12** Same as Figure 2-11. **2-13** Gazzaniga, M.S., "The bisected brain." New York: Plenum Publishing Co., 1970, p. 99. **2-18** Thompson, W.R., "The inheritance and development of intelligence," *Proceedings of the association for research in nervous and mental*

disease 33 (1954):209–31. Reprinted with permission from Pergamon Press, Ltd.

Chapter 3

3-1 Frankenburg, W.K., and Dodds, J.B., "The Denver developmental screening test," *Journal of Pediatrics* 71 (1967):181–91. **3-7** M. Lamb, (ed.) *The role of the father in child development* (after Kotelchuk). New York: John Wiley & Sons, 1976. **3-8** Baumrind, D., "Child care practices anteceding three patterns of preschool behavior," *Genetic psychology monographs* 75 (1967):43–88. **3-9** Delucia, L.A., "The toy preference test: A measure of sex-role identification," *Child development* 34 (1963):107–17. Copyright 1964 by The Society for Research in Child Development. **3-10** Ellis, W.D. (ed.), *A source book of Gestalt psychology*. Atlantic Highlands, N.J.: Humanities Press, Inc.; London: Routledge & Kegan Paul, Ltd. **3-11** Nisbett, R.E., "Birth order and participation in dangerous sports," *Journal of personality and social psychology* 8 (1968):351–53. Copyright 1968 by the American Psychological Association. Reprinted by permission. **3-12** Tanner, J.M., Whitehouse, R.H., and Takaishi, M., "Standards from birth to maturity for height, weight, height velocity, and weight velocity," *Archives of diseases of childhood* 41 (1966):467.

Chapter 4

4-16 Cornsweet, T.N., *Visual perception*, New York: Academic Press, Inc., 1970. **4-19** Cornsweet, T.N., *Stanford Research Institute*

Journal. January 5, 1969. Reprinted with permission from SRI International.

Chapter 5

5-20 Carpenter, P.A., and Just, M., (eds.), "A theory of reading: From eye fixations to comprehension," *Cognitive Processes in Comprehension*, Carnegie Mellon University Cognition series, 1977. **5-21** Same as Figure 5-20. **5-22** Blakemore, C., and Cooper, "Controlled visual environment," *Nature*, Vol. 228, (October 31, 1970):478.

Chapter 6

6-1 Klein, K.E., Wegmann, H.M., and Hunt, B.M., "Desynchronization of body temperature and performance circadian rhythm as a result of outgoing and homegoing transmeridian flights," *Aerospace medicine* 43 (1972):119–32. **6-2** Adapted from M'Guinness, J., for W.C. Dement, *Some must watch while some must sleep*, New York: W.W. Norton & Company, Inc. 1978. Copyright © 1972, 1974, 1976 by William C. Dement. **6-4** Cartwright, R.D., *A primer of sleep and dreaming*. Reading, MA: Addison-Wesley, 1978. Reprinted with permission. **6-5** Benson, H., Kotch, J.B., Crassweller, K.D., and Greenwood, M.M., "Historical and clinical considerations of the relaxation response," *American scientist* 65 (1977): 441–45. Reprinted by permission of *American Scientist*, *Journal of Sigma Xi*, The Scientific Research Society of North America. **6-7** Cooper, L.M. "Hypnotic amnesia," in E. Fromm and R.E. Shor

681

after Hogarth. The Metropolitan Museum of Art, Gift of Sarah Lazarus, 1891; (right) M.C. Escher, *Waterfall*, 1961. Escher Foundation, Haags Gemeentemuseum, The Hague. **137** NASA. **138** Georges Seurat, *Invitation to the Side-Show (La Parade)*. The Metropolitan Museum of Art, Bequest of Stephen C. Clark. **140** Salvador Dali, *The Slave Market with Disappearing Bust of Voltaire*, The Salvador Dali Foundation. **143** Harvey Stein. **149** Peter Vilms, Jeroboam. **150** A.L. Yarbus. **155** © Sidney Harris. **157** The American Museum of Natural History. **158** (both) William Vandivert. **160** © King Features Syndicate, Inc., 1971. **166** (top) Laurie Cameron, Jeroboam; (bottom) Emilio A. Mercado, Jeroboam. **170** Michal Heron © 1980, Woodfin Camp & Assoc. **173** Reprinted by permission of Tribune Company Syndicate, Inc. **174** J. Daniels, Rapho/Photo Researchers, Inc. **175** © 1975 Jules Feiffer. **179** Charles Gatewood, Stock, Boston. **180** Paul S. Conklin, Monkmeyer Press Photo. **181** Mimi Forsyth, Monkmeyer Press Photo. **184** Photo by Erik Arneson, courtesy Human Nature Magazine. **187** Philip Daly. **190** © M.E. Warren, 1972, Photo Researchers, Inc. **194** Bettmann Archive. **197** Lewis Lipsitt, Brown University, Courtesy Arlene H. Little. **198** © 1979 Sidney Harris. **201** (left) Sibyl Shelton, Monkmeyer Press Photo; (right) Gerbands Co. **204** Courtesy Sea World. **205** Courtesy James Simmons, Naval Ocean Systems Center, Hawaii. **206** Photo courtesy of Bruce Moore from H.M. Jenkins and B.R. Moore, Journal of Experimental Analysis of Behavior, 1973, *20*. p. 175. **207** Both Yerkes Regional Primate Research Center, Emory University, Atlanta. **210** Sepp Seitz, Woodfin Camp & Assoc. **212** Yerkes Regional Primate Research Center, Emory University, Atlanta. **213** Lilo Hess, Three Lions. **214** © Sidney Harris. **215** Will Rapport. **216** HBJ Photo. **224** From Carroll, L., *Alice in Wonderland*, illustrated by M. Torrey. Copyright © 1955 by Random House, Inc. Reprinted by permission of the publisher. **232** Bettmann Archive. **230, 240, 243** © Sidney Harris. **265** © Michal Heron 1980, Woodfin Camp & Assoc. **266** (top) © Joan Menschenfreund, Taurus Photos; (bottom) William Hamilton. **270** © Sidney Harris. **271** (both) Courtesy of R.A. and B.T. Gardner. **280** Carl Purcell from National Education Assoc. **287** Thomas McAvoy, Life Magazine © 1955 Time, Inc. **288** Rene Burri, Magnum Photos, Inc. **289** Cary Walinsky, Stock, Boston. **290** Courtesy of Neal E. Miller. **291** David Attie. **294** Hank Morgan. **296** © Don Ivers, Jeroboam, Inc. **302** Harry F. Harlow, University of Wisconsin Primate Laboratory. **305** Bettye Lane. **310**

Harry F. Harlow, University of Wisconsin Primate Laboratory. **311** (top) Suzanne Szasz; (bottom) A.T.& T. Bell Systems Science Service Film, *Gateways of the Mind*. **320** Wayne Miller, Magnum Photos, Inc. **321** Bruce Roberts, Rapho/Photo Researchers, Inc. **322, 323** Professor José M.R. Delgado. **325** Management Safeguard, Inc. **326** Richard D. Estes. **327** S. Nagendra, Photo Researchers, Inc. **328** George Roos, Peter Arnold, Inc. **330** © John Garrett 1978, Woodfin Camp & Assoc. **336** (top) De Sazo, Rapho © 1982 Photo Researchers, Inc.; (center) Michael D. Sullivan; (bottom) Peter Southwick, Stock, Boston. **346** Mimi Forsyth, Monkmeyer Press Photo. **354** © Van Bucher, Photo Researchers, Inc. **356** Courtesy of Georgette and Geraldine Binet. **366** Hugh Rogers, Monkmeyer Press Photo. **374** Shirley Zeiberg, Taurus. **374** Jeff Albertson, Stock, Boston. **378** Marion Bernstein. **384** Pinney, Monkmeyer Press Photo. **386** (top) Owen Franken, Stock, Boston; (bottom) © Peter Menzel, Stock, Boston. **387** United Press International. **393** Elizabeth Crews. **394** © Michal Heron 1981, Woodfin Camp & Assoc. **395** © Sidney Harris. **397** Erika Stone © Peter Arnold, Inc. **399** Photo courtesy Dr. Carl Rogers. **400** Shirley Zeiberg. **401** (both) Bettmann Archive. **408** © Sidney Harris. **409** Sepp Seitz, Woodfin Camp & Assoc. **420** Joel Gordon. **423** United Press International. **425** Jerry Irwin, Black Star. **426** © Frostie 1982, Woodfin Camp & Assoc. **427** © Suzanne Szasz, 1981, Photo Researchers, Inc. **427** Reprinted by permission of Medical Tribune and Joseph Farris. **428** Margaret Bourke-White, Life Magazine © 1945 Time, Inc. **430** Masser-man, J.H., *Principles of Dynamic Psychiatry*, 2nd ed., Philadelphia: W.B. Saunders & Co. 1961. **432** © Erika Stone 1981, Photo Researchers. **435** Cartoon by Charles Schultz, courtesy United Features Syndicate. **438** Arthur Tress, © 1981, Photo Researchers. **440** Ken Karp. **442** Sibyl Shelton, Monkmeyer Press Photo. **445** Jack Corn, Image, Inc. **454** (top) Detail from Edvard Munch, *Evening (Melancholia: On the Beach)*, woodcut colored by hand. Cleveland Museum of Art, Gift of Mrs. Clive Runnells in memory of Leonard C. Hanna, Jr.; (bottom) Vincent van Gogh, *Sorrow* (1882), photograph by Soichi Sunami, The Museum of Modern Art, New York. **461** © Sidney Harris. **463** © Joel Gordon 1978. **465** © Sidney Harris. **473** Bill Bridges, Globe Photos. **475** © Sidney Harris. **487** (left) © Bill Owens, Jeroboam, Inc.; (right) © Jock Pottle 1980. **488** © Joel Gordon. **494** All Bettmann Archive. **495** Both Jerry Cooke, Photo Researchers, Inc. **496** Allan Mercer, Stock, Boston. **497** Bett-

mann Archive. **498** © Sidney Harris. **499** © Sidney Harris. **500** Owen Franken, Stock, Boston. **502** Allan Grant. **503** J. Olin Campbell. **508** Ted Lane Photography. **510** © Joel Gordon, 1981. **511** Linda Rogers, Woodfin Camp & Assoc. **513** © Sidney Harris. **516** NIMH. **520** Marion Bernstein. **521** St. Louis Post Dispatch, Black Star. **522** Boys Town. **526** Ken Karp. **533** Both Hugh Rogers, Monkmeyer Press Photo. **535** © Sidney Harris. **536** (top) Burk Uzzle, Magnum; (bottom) Ken Karp. **551** Frank Lateman, Stock, Boston. **555** (top) K. Ruohomoa, Black Star; (center) Charles Horbatt/Archive Pictures, Inc.; (bottom) Barbara Pfeffer. **556** (top) Ginger Chih; (center and bottom) Arthur Grace, Stock, Boston. **563** Michael Rothstein, Jeroboam. **564** Burk Uzzle, Magnum. **566** United Press International. **567** Beryl Goldberg. **569** Georg Gerster, Rapho/Photo Researchers, Inc. **572** William Vandivert. **574** © 1965 by Stanley Milgram. **575** © 1979, Henry R. Martin. **578** Both Roger Malloch, Magnum. **581** Michael Evans, Sygma. **582** Bob S. Smith, Rapho/Photo Researchers, Inc. **583** © Volker Corell, 1980, Black Star. **586** HBJ Photo. **594, 595, 599** (bottom) Brown Brothers. **598** Culver Pictures. **599** (top) Archives of the History of American Psychology, University of Akron, Akron, Ohio. **600** Courtesy Carnegie Mellon University.

Color Section

4-10 Fritz Goro, Life Magazine, 1944, Time, Inc. **4-11** Inmont Corp. **4-12** Purkinjie Shift courtesy Academic Press, Inc., and Inmont Corp. **4-13** American Optical Corp. Jasper Johns, *Targets*, 1967–1968. Original lithograph. Published by Universal Limited Art Editions.

TEXT

pages 175–176 Benson, H., Kotch, J.B., Crasweller, K.D., and Greenwood, M.M., ''Historical and clinical considerations of the relaxation response,'' *American scientist* 65 (July 1977): 441–43.

page 212 Köhler, W., *The mentality of apes*. New York: Harcourt Brace Jovanovich Inc., 1925, pp. 174–75. Reprinted by permission of Routledge & Kegan Paul, Ltd.

pages 304–305 From Tavris, C., and Offir, C., *The longest war: Sex differences in perspective*. ©

TABLES

Chapter 1

Chapter 2

Chapter 3

Chapter 4

Chapter 5

Chapter 6

Chapter 8

Chapter 9

Chapter 10

Chapter 12

INDEX

Page numbers in *italics* refer to figures and tables.

negative reinforcement, 208
Pupil, of eye, 110, *110*
Pure tone, 123, *123*

R

Race and intelligence, 376–77
Range, as measure of variation, 605
Ranked data, 608
Rap centers, as resource for mental health community, 520
Rapid eye movements. *See* REM sleep
Rate of response, as measure of operant strength, 201
Rating scales, and personality assessment, 404, *405*
Rationalism, 284
Rationalization, as defense mechanism, 435–36
Reaction formation, as defense mechanism, 398, 436
Reaction range, 375
Reaction to loss, depression as, 465–66
Reading: and eye movements, 150–54, *151*; theories of, 152–53, *153*
Real motion, 137–38
Reality: and normality, 453; withdrawal from, 472–73
Reality principle, 395
Recall. *See* Free recall
Receiver–operating–characteristic. *See* ROC curve
Recency effect, 532
Receptive field, of cells, 119
Receptor molecules, 36
Receptors: in anabolic phase, 114; in catabolic phase, 114; for skin sensations, 128; in taste, 128
Recessiveness, in genes, 54
Reciprocal self-disclosure. *See* Intimacy
Reference groups, and persuasion, 581–84
Reflex arc, three-neuron, *38*
Refractory phase, in synaptic transmission, 34
Regression: age, and hypnosis, 183–84; and depression, 465; and frustration, 430–31, *430*
Rehearsal: and dual-memory theory, 244, *244*; in short-term memory, 223
Reincarnation, 187
Reinforcement: of aggression, 325–27; amount and delay of, 209–10, *209*; and brain stimulation, 211, *211*; in classical conditioning, 195; defined,

208; in learning and performance, 208–12; in operant conditioning, 202–204, *202*; and personality development, 392–93
Reinforcement approach, to depression, 466, *467*
Reinforcement schedules, in operant conditioning, 203
Relaxation: meditation for, 175–76, *176*; and hypnosis, 186
Relaxation training, and biofeedback, 442–43, *443*
Releaser, in species-specific behavior, 287
Reliability, of tests, 354–55
Reliability coefficient, 354
REM sleep, deprivation of, 171
Renin, 309
Repression, as defense mechanism, 434–35; in memory and emotion, 167–68, 237–38; and motivation, 319; vs. suppression, 434
Rescorla, R.A., and classical conditioning, 198–99, *199*
Research: basic and applied, 105; case histories as, 21; evaluation, 17–18; experimental method of, 18–20; observational method of, 20, *20*; survey method of, 21; test method of, 21
Reserpine, 518
Respondent behavior, 200
Responsibility, diffusion of, and bystander intervention, 566–69
Resting potential, 33
Reticular system, 39–40, 518
Retina, of eye, 110, *111*
Retrieval: and context, in memory, *235*, 240; and hierarchical organization, *234*, 238–39, *238*; in long-term memory, 232–33, *233*; and organization, in memory, 233–35, *234, 238*, 241; practicing, 242, *242*; in short-term memory, 226–27, *227*; as stage, in memory, 221
Retrieval cue, 232
Retrograde amnesia, 243
Reuptake, 519
Reward, and reinforcement, 208
Right hemisphere, of cerebral cortex, as minor (nondominant) hemisphere, 50
Rituals, compulsive, *462*
ROC curve, 108–109, *109*
Rod–cone break, *112*
Rods and cones, of eye, 111–12

Rogers, Carl: and client-centered therapy, 508–509; and self theory, 399–400
Role confusion, in adolescence, 95
Romantic love, 557
Rorschach Test, 408–409, *408*

S

Saccades, and eye movements and reading, 150–51
Salt, as taste quality, 128
Sample, in statistics, 606–607
Sample means, 609
Saturation, of color, 115
Scaling, of data, 608–609
Scapegoat, and displaced aggression, 428
Scatter diagram, of correlation, *24*, 613, *613, 614*
Schachter, Stanley, and cognitive–physiological theory of emotion, 399–40
Schemata: and analysis-by-synthesis, 147; and cognitive maps, 213–14; and constructive memory, 249–50; and feature lists, 121; gender, 540; and mental images, 74; processing, 530–31, *532*; and prototypes, 530
Schizoidia, 475, *475*
Schizophrenia. *See* Schizophrenic disorders
Schizophrenic disorders, 57, 470–79, *471*; biochemical factors in, 36, 475–76; disturbances of thought and attention in, 470; genetic factors in, 474–75; social and psychological factors in, 476–78; in twins, 57, *474*
Scholastic Aptitude Test (SAT), 351, *351, 352*
School psychology, 17
Secondary sex characteristics, 93
Secure attachment, 76
Selective attention, 148–49
Selective breeding, 56, *57*
Selective rearing, 155–57, *156*
Self, development of, 400–401
Self-actualization, 11, 318, 399, 401, *402*; and normality, 453
Self-concept, 400
Self-deception, and defense mechanisms, 433
Self-esteem, and normality, 453
Self-generated environments, 394
Self-knowledge, and normality, 453
Self-perception: and attribution,